Encyclopedia of

THE MEDIEVAL WORLD

VOLUME II

(M TO Z)

Edward D. English

☑®

Facts On File, Inc.

Encyclopedia of the Medieval World

Copyright © 2005 Edward D. English

Facts On File, Inc.
132 West 31st Street
New York NY 10001

Library of Congress Cataloging-in-Publication Data

English, Edward D.
Encyclopedia of the medieval world / Edward D. English.
p. cm.
Includes bibliographical references and index.
ISBN 0-8160-4690-5 (set) (alk. paper)
ISBN 0-8160-4688-3 (vol. 1)—ISBN 0-8160-4689-1 (vol. 2)
1. Middle ages—History—Encyclopedias. 2. Civilization, Medieval—Encyclopedias.
I. Title.
D114.E55 2004
940.1'03— dc22   2003027825

Facts On File books are available at special discounts when purchased in bulk quantities for businesses, associations, institutions, or sales promotions. Please call our
Special Sales Department in New York at (212) 967-8800 or (800) 322-8755.

You can find Facts On File on the World Wide Web at http://www.factsonfile.com

Text design by Joan Toro
Cover design by Cathy Rincon
Line art by Richard Garratt and Facts On File

Printed in the United States of America

VB FOF 10 9 8 7 6 5 4 3 2

This book is printed on acid-free paper.

CONTENTS

ENTRIES M TO Z

Mabinogi (*Mabinogion*)   This was an important collection of medieval Welsh folk tales, legends, and ROMANCES. The name of the work was applied by a 19th century translator, Charlotte Guest. The collection consisted of 11 units, divided into three groups. The first four related stories were tales of Pwyll, the prince of Dyfed, Branwen, the daughter of Llŷr; Manawydan, the son of Llŷr; and Math, the son of Mathonwy. These are followed by four other tales and by three romances, that are similar to stories in CHRETIEN DE TROYES, *Geraint Son of Erbin, The Lady of the Fountain,* and *Peredur Son of Efrawg.* Composed in their present form between about 1050 and 1120, probably by a cleric in south WALES, they were based on an oral tradition that had its origins in Celtic mythology and reflected the craft of a Welsh teller of tales. The chief characters were based on Celtic gods and goddesses, transferred to contemporary aristocratic environment. It has survived in two late 14th-century manuscripts, but the earliest stories may go to the 11th century.

The three romances have features that suggest a bilingual environment in southeastern Wales open to ANGLO-NORMAN and French influences. Probably the work of more than one author, these romances were part of an Arthurian cycle. The earliest VERNACULAR Arthurian narrative, they reflected the aristocratic and chivalric culture of their time.

See also ARTHUR, KING, AND ARTHURIAN LITERATURE.

Further reading: Jeffrey Gantz, trans., *The Mabinogion* (New York: Penguin Books, 1976); A. O. H. Jarman and Gwilym Rees Hughes, eds., *A Guide to Welsh Literature,* Vol. 1 (Swansea: C. Davies, 1976), 189–202, 203–243.

MacAlpin, Kenneth I (Cináed mac Allpín) (r. ca. 834–858) *traditional founder of the kingdom of Scotland*
In the face of attacks from the Britons, the VIKINGS, and the people of neighboring Lothian, Kenneth tried to unite the people of the future kingdom of SCOTLAND, the PICTS and the Dalriadan Scots. As king of Dalriada, he transported the RELICS of Saint Columba from Iona to Dunkeld to protect them and establish a religious center. The new kingdom was called Alba or Albany. After founding a permanent patrilineal dynasty, he died in 858.

Further reading: Alan Orr Anderson, *Early Sources of Scottish History,* A.D. *500 to 1286* (Edinburgh: Oliver and Boyd, 1922); Archibald A. M. Duncan, *Scotland, the Making of the Kingdom* (Edinburgh: Oliver and Boyd, 1975).

Macbeth (r. 1040–1057) *king of Scots*
The grandson of King Kenneth II (r. 971–995). Macbeth was a member of the northern Cenél Loairn branch of the Dalriadan royal house. In 1031 he inherited the earldom of Murray or Moray in northern Scotland from his father. In 1040 he revolted against his cousin, King Duncan I (r. 1034–40), and killed him. He married the daughter of Kenneth III (r. 997–1005), Gruoch (fl. 1040–57) and took the kingship for himself. He actually only was able to attain the throne after four years of civil war. Even so the rest of reign was marked by periodic civil war and dynastic conflict. It was peaceful enough, however, to allow Macbeth to make a pilgrimage to ROME, where he acquired renown through his generosity to the poor. Supported by the ANGLO-SAXONS, the future king, Malcolm III (r. 1058–93), laid a legitimate claim to the throne. In 1057 Macbeth was killed by Malcolm's troops. Macbeth

became the subject of the classic tragedy by William Shakespeare.

Further reading: Archibald A. M. Duncan, *Scotland, the Making of the Kingdom* (Edinburgh: Oliver and Boyd, 1975); Peter Berresford Ellis, *MacBeth: High King of Scotland, 1040–57 AD* (London: F. Muller, 1980); William E. Kapelle, *The Norman Conquest of the North: The Region and Its Transformation, 1000–1135* (Chapel Hill: University of North Carolina Press, 1979).

Macedonia   This was a province, now a country, on the Balkan Peninsula. After the BARBARIAN incursions in the early fifth century, the Byzantines retook control and Macedonia became a province with Greek as its spoken language. In the second half of the sixth century, SLAV tribes entered, augmenting and changing the area's population and ethnicity. The northern parts essentially lost a Greek character, but THESSALONIKI, the provincial capital, and the south remained Greek.

In the ninth century, Bulgarians settled in the southern Balkans and created an empire, conquering and annexing the Slavic half of Macedonia. In the ninth century, CYRIL AND METHODIOS began to convert the Slav population to Orthodox Christianity with an ecclesiastical center at OCHRIDA in the northwest. In 971, after a defeat of Bulgaria, the Bulgarian prince SAMUEL proclaimed himself czar of the Bulgarians at Ochrida, making it the center of his new Bulgarian state. After his first destructive campaign in 1004, the Byzantine emperor, BASIL II, returned in 1014 to destroy that state and annex it as a province of the empire. The new Byzantine government promoted the immigration of Greeks and other groups back to Macedonia to merge with the local population.

In 1204, after the destruction of the BYZANTINE EMPIRE by crusaders, the province was divided. Thessaloniki was taken by the crusaders, who established the Latin kingdom of Salonica there; the rest of the province was taken over by Bulgarians. After an era of domination by the despots of EPIROS, Thessaloniki was reconquered by the revived Byzantine Empire of Nicaea in 1246. The northern part of the region was contested by Bulgarians and Serbs. SERBIA conquered it in 1345 and established a new capital at Skopje, but its dominance was short lived. The OTTOMAN TURKS subsequently invaded and conquered much of the Balkans; by 1371, only Thessaloniki remained part of a much-shrunken Byzantine Empire. In 1423 the Turks overwhelmed the remaining areas and absorbed Macedonia into the Ottoman Empire.

See also BULGARIA AND THE BULGARIANS.

Further reading: Blaga Aleksova, *Loca Sanctorum Macedoniae: The Cult of Martyrs in Macedonia from the Fourth to the Ninth Centuries,* trans. Ana Lazarevska (Prilep: Institute for Old Slav Culture, Skopje, 1997); Elizabeth Barker, *Macedonia and Its Place in Balkan Power Politics* (1950; reprint, Westport, Conn.: Greenwood Press, 1980); Djurdje Boskovic, *Medieval Art in Serbia and Macedonia: Church Architecture and Sculpture* (Belgrade: Jugoslovenska Knjiga, 1936?); Stoyan Pribichevich, *Macedonia, Its People and History* (University Park: Pennsylvania State University Press, 1982); M. B. Sakellariou, ed., *Macedonia, 4000 Years of Greek History and Civilization* (1983; reprint, Athens: Ekdotike Athenon, 1995): Apostolos E. Vakalopoulos, *History of Macedonia, 1354–1833,* trans. Peter Megann (Thessaloniki: Institute for Balkan Studies, 1973).

Macedonian dynasty   The Macedonian dynasty (867–1056) ruled during the most successful period of the medieval BYZANTINE Empire. Its founder, BASIL I (812–886), was a peasant born in Macedonia of Armenian descent. He owed his fortune to Emperor Michael III (r. 838–867). Basil amazingly so charmed him by his ability to train HORSES that Michael made him coemperor. Having probably assassinated his benefactor, he pursued throughout his reign aggressive politics. His successors, Leo VI (r. 886–912), CONSTANTINE VII PORPHYROGENITOS, and Romanos II (r. 959–963), remained in the imperial palace, but their generals retook much of the East from the Muslims. Leo VI proclaimed the last great Byzantine legislative code, the *Basilica,* and his intellectual son, Constantine, was responsible for encyclopedic works on ceremonies and the imperial administration.

During the minorities of the emperors Constantine VII, then BASIL II (r. 976–1025) and his brother, Constantine VIII (r. 1025–28), dynastic legitimacy was so accepted that the coemperors, imposed by regents, such as the successful generals Romanos I Lekapenos (r. 920–944), Nikephoros Phokas (r. 963–969), and John I Tzimiskes (r. 969–976), did not try to seize the throne for themselves. Nikephoros Phokas recaptured CRETE. As an emperor appointed by a regency council, he crossed the Taurus Mountains, recovered Cilicia in southeastern ANATOLIA and northern SYRIA, and reestablished the patriarchate at ANTIOCH. John Tzimiskes drove off a KIEVAN RUS attack in the Balkans and further consolidated the Byzantine frontiers in eastern Anatolia. He led his army into PALESTINE, up to JERUSALEM. Basil II, overcame the rebellious aristocracy of Anatolia, and conducted a successful elimination of the Bulgarian state. In 1018 he began the work of reestablishing a frontier on the Danube, which required a quarter of a century of almost uninterrupted warfare. It earned him the title of Bulgar Slayer. Basil II's nieces married men who became emperors, Michael IV (r. 1034–41) and Constantine Monomachos (r. 1042–55). On the death of Basil's niece, Theodora (r. 1056–57), who also reigned, a competition for the Crown began; it ended with the accession of ALEXIOS I KOMNENOS in 1081 (r. 1081–1118).

See also PSELLOS, MICHAEL.

Further reading: Michael Psellus, *Fourteen Byzantine Rulers: The Chronographia of Michael Psellus,* trans. E. R. A. Sewter (1953; reprint, Harmondsworth: Penguin Books, 1966); Theodora Antonopoulou, *The Homilies of the Emperor Leo VI* (Leiden: Brill, 1997); J. B. Bury, *A History of the Later Roman Empire: A Supplement Containing the Emperors from Basil II to Isaac Komnenos (A.D. 976–1057), and Other Essays on Byzantine History* (Chicago: Ares, 1974); Romilly Jenkins, *Byzantium: The Imperial Centuries, A.D. 610–1071* (New York: Random House, 1966); Shaun Tougher, *The Reign of Leo VI (886–912): Politics and People* (Leiden: E. J. Brill, 1997).

Machaut, Guillaume de (William, Machault) (ca. 1300–1377) *French musician, poet*
Machaut was born to a noble family about 1300 in Champagne. In about 1323 he took orders and entered the service of John of Luxembourg (r. 1310–46), the king of BOHEMIA, as a secretary and canon of RHEIMS cathedral. He traveled to POLAND, LITHUANIA, and ITALY before settling at Rheims. When John of Luxembourg was killed in battle in 1346, Machaut went into services of John's daughter, then that of Charles II the Bad (r. 1349–87), the king of NAVARRE, and subsequently CHARLES V (r. 1364–80), the king of FRANCE. Much in demand, he also had as patrons such princes as JOHN, DUKE OF BERRY, and Amadeus VI, the Green Count of Savoy (r. 1343–83) and held canonries at Rheims, Verdun, and Arras. He died in 1377 at Rheims.

We possess more works by him than by any other 14th-century composer. His literary inspiration was in the tradition of COURTLY LOVE. In music, he wrote in both religious and secular pieces. He developed new procedures for musical composition, known as the *Ars nova,* as distinct from the ARS ANTIQUA. A master of versification, he wrote didactic and allegorical poems, lays and virelays, rondeaux, ballads, secular polyphonic songs, music for masses, and 24 MOTETS for three or four voices. His poetry influenced CHAUCER.

Further reading: Guillaume, de Machaut, *The Works of Guillaume de Machaut,* ed. Leo Schrade, 2 vols. (Monaco: Editions de l'Oiseau-Lyre, 1956); Lawrence Marshburn Earp, *Guillaume de Machaut: A Guide to Research* (New York: Garland, 1995); Gilbert Reaney, *Guillaume de Machaut* (London: Oxford University Press, 1971).

al-Madina al-Zahira It was a 10th-century palace city, now in ruins, eight miles (13 kilometers) outside CÓRDOBA in AL-ANDALUS. It was founded by Abd al-Rahman III (r. 891–961), CALIPH and the emir of Córdoba, and finished by his son, al-Hakim II (r. 961–976). Named after Abd al-Rahman's favorite wife, Zahra, the complex was located near springs at the foot of the Sierra Morena. It was founded as a palatial residence and administrative center away from crowded Córdoba. The staff included 20,000 guards, officials, and their families, who lived in this palace city. Al-Madina al-Zahira was destroyed by fire in 1010 by rebellious Berber soldiers, who resented the lavishness of the caliph's personal residence. Material from the palace was later redeployed by Pedro the Cruel (r. 1350–69) for his palace in SEVILLE.

DETAILS

Al Madina al-Zahira was built on three terraces with abundant gardens, pools, and water channels. On the lowest terrace was a pavilion built for Abd al-Rahman as a formal ceremonial center. This pavilion had intricate decoration in stone, like the stucco work of the Great MOSQUE in Córdoba. Across a bridge from the pavilion was the main mosque, with an arcaded courtyard leading to a sanctuary. Beside the mosque were the military headquarters, a basilicalike hall with triple-arched arcades and a ramp leading out to the parade ground. The upper part was the caliph's personal residence, which included several apartments around courtyards enclosing a central hall. In the art and architecture of al Madina al-Zahira, the Spanish UMAYYADS were clearly influenced by the legacy of their ancestors in SYRIA and Mesopotamia or IRAQ.

Further reading: Markus Hattstein and Peter Delius, eds., *Islam: Art and Architecture,* trans. George Ansell et al. (Cologne: Könemann, 2000), 229–233; Robert Hillenbrand, *Islamic Art and Architecture* (New York: Thames and Hudson, 1999); D. Fairchild Ruggles, *Gardens, Landscape, and Vision in the Palaces of Islamic Spain* (University Park: Pennsylvania State University Press, 2000), especially 53–85.

madrasa (theological college, place of study) A *madrasa* is a place of study or residential college for the teaching of Islamic law and other religious disciplines or sciences, usually associated with a MOSQUE. *Madrasah* were also residences for subsidized students. The curriculum of study was based on the QURAN and the HADITH, the latter complemented by the study of Islamic law and jurisprudence. *Madrasah* owe their beginnings to a SELJUK vizier, who created the first great Sunni *madrasah* at BAGHDAD in 1067 and in several other great cities. In 1184, the Andalusian traveler Ibn Jubayr (d. 1217) remarked on some 30 *madrasah* in Baghdad alone. By the 12th century there were such schools in SYRIA, at DAMASCUS from 1121 and at ALEPPO from 1123.

Madrasah functioned under the patronage of a local ruler, who remunerated the professors and ensured the upkeep of the students. But they were basically private institutions, usually endowed by their founder. They were designed primarily to combat heresies or other points of view, initially Shiite tendencies, and to develop a strict orthodoxy by training an intellectual SUNNI elite. The extent to which they influenced the organization of universities in Europe is not clear. Their building styles reflect important aspects of Islamic architecture.

See also ART AND ARCHITECTURE, ISLAMIC.

Further reading: Michael Chamberlain, *Knowledge and Social Practice in Medieval Damascus, 1190–1350* (Cambridge: Cambridge University Press, 1994); Robert Hillenbrand, Islamic Architecture: Form, Function and Meaning (New York: Columbus University Press, 1994), 173–251; George Makdisi, *The Rise of Colleges: Institutions of Learning in Islam and the West* (Edinburgh: Edinburgh University Press, 1981); George Makdisi, *The Rise of Humanism in Classical Islam and the Christian West: With Special Reference to Scholasticism* (Edinburgh: Edinburgh University Press, 1990); J. Pederson, George Makdisi, and Robert Hillenbrand, "Madrasa," *Encyclopedia of Islam* 5.1,123–1,154; Ahmad Shalabi, *History of Muslim Education* (Karachi: Indus, 1979).

al-Maghrib (Maghreb, the West) Al-Maghrib has its origins in an Arabic word meaning "sunset." Al-Maghrib was considered the furthest western part of the Muslim world, but its regions have varied. One tradition was in the 14th century IBN KHALDUN made al-Maghrib coincide with BERBER areas from before the ARAB conquest, from the Atlantic coast and along the Mediterranean to the edge of the Sahara. Al-Maghrib can be divided into four parts, the modern states of Libya (Tripolitania), Tunisia (Ifriqiya), Algeria, and MOROCCO (the far Maghrib). Its history began with Islamization in the seventh century, with the invasion of nomadic Arab armies, then the Berber empires of the 11th and 12th centuries, first the ALMORAVIDS and then the ALMOHADS.

LONG SERIES OF INVASIONS

Muslim armies began to raid al-Maghrib in 643, 647, and 665. Byzantine armies were defeated by them at Sufetula in Tunisia and at Hadrumetum, but the Muslims only withdrew with their booty. A permanent conquest began in 670, when a military camp was founded at AL-QAYRAWAN. The capture of Carthage in 698 ended most Berber resistance. Many of the BERBERS converted to ISLAM and enrolled in Muslim armies in search of further conquest. The Arabs, few in number, occupied the fortresses and certain parts of the lower elevations of the country. The Berbers sometimes resisted Arab dominance by welcoming heterodox sects banished by the UMAYYADS, especially the KHARIJITES. In 742, they defeated a caliphal army, and they massacred the population of al-Qayrawan in 758. In 777 Kharijite principalities grew up at Tahert, at Sijilmassa, and at Tlemcen. The whole Saharan border of al-Maghrib was in the hands of the Kharijites.

RULING DYNASTIES

The IDRISIDS, opponents of the caliph in BAGHDAD, introduced Arab culture to the far Maghrib, founding the town of FEZ. The other point of resistance to Kharijism was in Tunisia an Ifriqiya, where the AGHLABIDS became the dominant dynasty between 800 and 909. The FATIMIDS, displaced the Aghlabids and other dynasties, and spent more than half a century there without having much of an impact on the region before departing for EGYPT, allowing the ZIRIDS to govern.

CRIPPLING DISUNITY

In the mid-11th century, two events changed the political and social landscape of al-Maghrib: the invasion of the nomadic Banu Hilal Arabs and the establishment of the Almoravid Empire. Political unity in al-Maghrib decreased steadily thereafter. Various other dynasties took control over the next few centuries, sometimes seizing wider areas of the Maghrib but often confined to smaller regions. The MERINIDS, who conquered the far Maghrib and ruled from the 13th to the 15th century, tried to unify the entire region. But after a short occupation of Tlemcen and TUNIS, they retreated to Morocco, where, in the 14th century, they developed a brilliant society and culture, attracting European scholars and merchants. By the later Middle Ages, when the Europeans began attacks along the coasts, the response of the various kingdoms of the Maghrib was only partially effective because of their lack of unity.

See also AL-ANDALUS; ATLAS MOUNTAINS; HAFSIDS; HAMDANIDS; PORTUGAL; RECONQUEST.

Further reading: Michael Brett, "The Maghrib," in *The New Cambridge Medieval History.* Vol. 5, *c. 1198–c. 1300,* ed. David Abulafia (Cambridge: Cambridge University Press, 1999), 622–635; Michael Brett, *The Moors: Islam in the West* (London: Orbis, 1980); Michael Brett, *Ibn Khaldun and the Medieval Maghrib* (Aldershot: Ashgate Variorum, 1999); Clifford Edmund Bosworth, *The New Islamic Dynasties: A Chronological and Genealogical Manual* (Edinburgh: Edinburgh University Press, 1996); G. S. Colin, G. Yver, and E. Levi-Provençal, "Al-Maghrib" and "Al-Maghrib, al-Mamlaka, al-Maghribiyya, Morocco," *Encyclopedia of Islam* 5.1,183–1,209; H. T. Norris, *The Arab Conquest of the Western Sahara: Studies of the Historical Events, Religious Beliefs and Social Customs Which Made the Remotest Sahara a Part of the Arab World* (Burnt Mill, England: Longman, 1986).

magic and folklore Magic in the Middle Ages was a central but alternate mode of rationality, almost always portrayed as deviant because it varied from elite and official religious and scientific practices and ideas. It ranged from occult practices such as ASTROLOGY and ALCHEMY, to the use of CHARMS and amulets, to sorcery and necromancy, all based on the principle that the natural world contained hidden powers that human beings through various practices and activities can use for good or evil.

The activities and ideas surrounding these beliefs varied in terms of acceptability and approval throughout the

Middle Ages. The practices could encompass simple magic tricks, quack healing, incantations, occult games, fortune telling, witchcraft, and divination, all aiming to harness supernatural forces for the benefit of individuals or groups. The church believed that all of these ideas were at least pagan, possibly originating in satanic powers, and therefore condemned them. However, Christianity's own practices and ideas, including reverence for RELICS and appeals to saints, had some similarities to the kind of reasoning and supplication for intervention in the world the practices employed. Christianity often tolerated the more learned or scientific aspects of magic, studies that allegedly aimed for a better understanding of the natural world. Modern students of folklore, consider magic to be an important and traditional form of popular culture. The ideas and practices are studied for their relationship to mainstream aspects of the history of culture.

See also FICINO, MARSILIO; MIRANDOLA, PICO DELLA; WITCHCRAFT.

Further reading: Ioan P. Culianu, *Eros and Magic in the Renaissance,* trans. Margaret Cook (Chicago: University of Chicago Press, 1987); Claire Fanger, ed., *Conjuring Spirits: Texts and Traditions of Medieval Ritual Magic* (University Park: Pennsylvania State University Press, 1998); Valerie I. J. Flint, *The Rise of Magic in Early Medieval Europe* (Princeton, N.J.: Princeton University Press, 1991); Richard Kieckhefer, *Forbidden Rites: A Necromancer's Manual of the Fifteenth Century* (University Park: Pennsylvania State University Press, 1997); Richard Kieckhefer, *Magic in the Middle Ages* (Cambridge: Cambridge University Press, 1990).

Magna Carta (Great Charter, Charta libertatum, Charta Garonum)   The loss of NORMANDY led King JOHN LACKLAND to intensify exploitation of feudal and royal rights. In 1213 he imposed a new tax on knights. The barons of the north reacted negatively and rebellion developed rapidly thereafter. John was defeated at the Battle of BOUVINES in 1214 and forced to acknowledge that he was a vassal of the pope. He then had to concede to the assembled barons at Runnymede near Windsor, on June 15, 1215, the Great Charter, or Magna Carta. It was rapidly later annulled by the king and Pope INNOCENT III on August 24, 1215. But one clause among its initial 63, "No free man will be arrested, deprived of his goods, put outside the law, or exiled . . . unless by the judgment of his peers or by the law of the land," became an important part of the foundation of the English "Constitution."

The Magna Carta was a unilateral concession by a king, a contract between the king and the barons of mutual rights and obligations. Its original recipients were not the people or a person, but John's vassals and barons. It was solemnly reissued by the new child king, HENRY III, several times and was sanctioned in 1258 by the rebellious Great Council, called a PARLIAMENT. The charter was a landmark in the struggle to secure government without oppression and tyranny. Many of its clauses were designed to control the arbitrary or tyrannical behavior of a king and his officials. Others were concerned with the proper administration of justice and relations with WALES, SCOTLAND, and the city of LONDON.

See also JURY TRIAL.

Further reading: Harry Rothwell, ed., *English Historical Documents.* Vol. 3, *1189–1327* (New York: reprint, 1996; 1979; reprint, Oxford University Press, 1996), 310–349; James C. Holt, *Magna Carta,* 2d ed. (Cambridge: Cambridge University Press, 1992); Claire Breay, *Magna Carta: Manuscripts and Myths* (London: British Library, 2002); Faith Thompson, *Magna Carta: Its Role in the Making of the English Constitution, 1300–1629* (Minneapolis: University of Minnesota Press, 1948); A. E. D. Howard, *Magna Carta: Text and Commentary* (Charlottesville: University Press of Virginia, 1998).

magnetic compass   *See* COMPASS, MAGNETIC.

Magyars   *See* HUNGARY.

Maimonides, Moses (Moses ben Maimon, Rambam) (1135–1204) *Jewish philosopher, Talmudist, physician*
Moses Maimonides, called Rambam, was born at CÓRDOBA IN 1135. Because of ALMOHAD persecution, he left first for FEZ in 1060, then for PALESTINE before finally settling more permanently in EGYPT in 1165. He was renowned for introducing philosophical ideas into JUDAISM. After moving to Egypt, he became an influential member of the Jewish community there and a highly respected physician. He died in 1204. His two great works were a code called the *Mishnah Torah* and *The Guide for the Perplexed.*

OPUS

In his work on the *halakhic,* or legal code, completed by Maimonides over 10 years, he specified that, seeing a need, he was undertaking a second Torah (*Mishnah Torah,* mighty hand), which would contain all the commandments and all the laws of Judaism surpassing all other books on this subject. This encyclopedic and comprehensive code did not just deal only with contemporary laws, but also those linked to the Temple of Jerusalem, sacrificial rites, wars, and biblical kings. The work had an original and unprecedented organization. It was divided into 14 books, each focused on specific laws, and further subdivided into 1,000 chapters. These chapters contained nearly 15,000 articles. The code was written in a clear and precise Hebrew, of impressive clarity and style. Even today Maimonides' influence remains important in rabbinic law.

Besides the code, *The Guide for the Perplexed* was composed in his old age in 1190. Written in Arabic but

Moses Maimonides *(Courtesy Library of Congress)*

subsequently translated into Hebrew and LATIN, it was a philosophical Aristotelian meditation on the fundamentals of literalist religion. It was written for cases where religious practice and biblical and Talmudic culture were in conflict with contemporary philosophical reasoning and knowledge. It specifically addressed those who were perplexed but had a solid acquaintance with Judaic knowledge and theology. Reconciling faith and reason, they could become true philosophers capable of understanding metaphysical realities and gaining a true knowledge of God for themselves. Some found this synthesis of faith and reason too heterodox and controversial and condemned the guide. Christian scholars such as Thomas AQUINAS read this guide with much interest.

Further reading: Moses Maimonides, *The Guide of the Perplexed,* 2 vols., trans. Shlomo Pines (Chicago: University of Chicago Press, 1963); Moses Maimonides, *Letters of Maimonides,* ed. Leon D. Suslin (New York: Yeshiva University Press, 1977); Raymond L. Weiss and Charles Butterworth, eds., *Ethical Writings of Maimonides* (New York: New York University Press, 1975); Gil Anidjar, *"Our Place in al-Andalus": Kabbalah, Philosophy, Literature in Arab Jewish Letters* (Stanford, Calif.: Stanford University Press, 2002); Idit Dobbs-Weinstein, *Maimonides and St. Thomas on the Limits of Reason* (Albany: State University of New York Press, 1995); Isidore Epstein, ed., *Moses Maimonides, 1135–1204: Anglo-Jewish Papers in Connection with the Eighth Centenary of His Birth* (London: Soncino Press, 1935); Howard T. Kreisel, *Maimonides'*

Political Thought: Studies in Ethnics, Law, and the Human Ideal (Albany: State University of New York Press, 1999); Harry A. Wolfson, *The Kalam Arguments for Creation in Saadia, Averroës, Maimonides and St. Thomas* (New York: Reprinted from the Saadia Anniversary Volume of the American Academy for Jewish Research, 1943), 197–245.

Majorca Majorca is the largest island of the BALEARIC ISLANDS, an archipelago in the western Mediterranean, off the Spanish coast. Conquered by the VANDALS in the fifth century, it became part of the Visigothic kingdom in the seventh century. In 713 it was conquered by the ARABS. In 1229 King JAMES I conquered and annexed it to ARAGON, when it became a province. Before his death in 1276, James divided his realm and ceded Majorca and its royal title, to his younger son, James II (r. 1264–1327), who was also lord of areas in southern France, Roussillon, Cerdagne, and MONTPELLIER. The independent existence of this set of holdings was always challenged by the elder branch of the Aragonese ruling dynasty. In 1344, during one of these dynastic battles, King James III (r. 1324–49) of Majorca was defeated and killed by King Peter IV (r. 1336–87) of Aragon. Majorca and the counties of Roussillon and Cerdagne were then annexed to the Crown of Aragon, while Montpellier was sold to FRANCE. Majorca then became again a prosperous province of Aragon and an important cultural center with strong commercial links with BARCELONA.

Further reading: David Abulafia, *A Mediterranean Emporium: The Catalan Kingdom of Majorca* (Cambridge: Cambridge University Press, 1994); J. N. Hillgarth, *Readers and Books in Majorca, 1229–1550,* 2 vols. (Paris: Centre national de la recherche scientifique, 1991).

Maldon, Battle of   This battle inspired a vivid poem in Old English by an unknown author not long after it occurred in 991. According to the ANGLO-SAXON CHRONICLES, Danish or Norwegian raiders descended on the southeastern coast of ENGLAND during the reign of ÆTHELRED II the Unready, defeated and killed the local lord in Essex, and extracted huge sums of money as tribute. This chronicle included some facts, but few about the battle itself and the English leader killed in battle, Bryhtnoth or Byrhtnoth. Humiliation was emphasized. Despite King ALFRED's earlier victories in the ninth century, Scandinavian raiders kept returning to attack and plunder a pathetically divided England. Incompetence, bad judgment, and treachery marked the Anglo-Saxon responses. The poet, may have intended his poem as encouragement to his contemporaries to resist better such incursions. He celebrated a noble Christian earl's fruitless, heroic courage against pagan raiders and showed contempt for the cowardice and treachery of many of the other Anglo-Saxon lords.

The poem survived in a much later transcription from a partially destroyed manuscript. It was a presentation of the warrior ethos of a Germanic people. This included acceptance by the lesser nobility of an obligation to serve lords during periods of war and peace. The lords were in turn obligated to provide protection if necessary, equipment for combat; clothing, ornaments, property; and entertainment and hospitality.

Further reading: Bill Griffiths, trans., *The Battle of Maldon: Text and Translation* (Pinner, England: Anglo-Saxon Books, 1991); Donald Scragg, ed., *The Battle of Maldon, A.D. 991* (Oxford: B. Blackwell, 1991).

Mali (a place of the king)   The African empire of Mali was documented from the 13th until the 17th century. It was concentrated around the banks of the Niger River and developed from a confederation of the Malinke people. In 1230 they were united by Sundiata Keita and the Mandinka, who established a strong government and was supported by the GOLD TRADE. By the time of his death in 1255, he had converted to ISLAM, conquered neighboring peoples, especially those in GHANA, and had begun to expand north into the Sahara Desert. This project continued under his descendants, and by the 14th century a major part of western Africa, together with the countries of the Gambian Valley, was part of the empire of Mali. Muslim missionaries in the meantime had spread Islam.

During the reign of Mansa Musa I (r. ca. 1307–37), the greatest ruler of Mali, the empire reached its greatest power, prestige, and prosperity, especially from dominating all the routes of the gold trade between black AFRICA and the Mediterranean. Mansa Musa's visit, with perhaps as many as 100,000 people accompanying him, to CAIRO in 1324, on a pilgrimage to MECCA, marked the height of his and the kingdom's prestige, legitimizing Mali as an Islamic country for the Muslim world. Mansa based his government on the royal Malinke clan, served by slaves in the bureaucracy and army. His kingdom was rich, well administered, and safe for foreign merchants. His capital was at Niani and included TIMBUKTU where he built palaces and established schools. His successors lacked sufficient power to maintain unity. At the beginning of the 15th century, internal struggles and constant rebellions weakened the state. The revolt of two of its main cities, Gao in 1400 and Timbuktu, in 1431, was followed by a general revolt of northern tribes and the establishment of the SONGHAI. This led to the disintegration of what was left of the Mali state.

Further reading: Daniel Chu and Elliott Skinner, *A Glorious Age in Africa: The Story of Three Great African Empires* (Trenton, N.J.: Africa World Press, 1990); Pat McKissack, *The Royal Kingdoms of Ghana, Mali, and Songhay: Life in Medieval Africa* (New York: H. Holt, 1994).

malnutrition   *See* FAMINE.

Malory, Thomas (1414/1418–1471) *author of* Le Morte d'Arthur
Little is known about Thomas Malory, except his famous work itself. There have been nine possible candidates for this figure. The author was called Sir Thomas Malory or Maleore; he completed the book in prison in the ninth year of the reign of King EDWARD IV, between March 1469 and March 1470. He was probably Sir Thomas Malory of Newbold Revel in Warwickshire. He was born into a family of gentry about 1415 and seemed to have had estates in Warwickshire and Northamptonshire. He might have served as a member of PARLIAMENT. From 1450 he was either in prison or on the run from justice. Among a long list of charges against him were wounding, robbing, imprisoning, ambush with intent to murder, cattle raiding, extortion, breaking into an abbey, assaulting the abbot and stealing its property, forcible entry into houses, rape, and escaping from custody. This Malory received a pardon in 1455 but was soon back in prison. During the WARS OF THE ROSES, he fought first for the Yorkists, later for the Lancastrians. This Malory seemed to have been unscrupulous and rash, barely escaping execution. He may have died in prison between March 12 and 14, 1471, having not been included in the general pardons of 1468 and 1470.

The only extant manuscript on this "matter of Britain" was discovered in Winchester in 1934. The sole available version before that was edited and printed in 1485 by William CAXTON, who called it "The Book of King Arthur and of his noble knights of the Round Table" and "this noble and joyous book entitled Le Morte Darthur." This chronological narrative recounted the whole of Arthur's life, as well as his death. It was the fullest, and perhaps the best, telling of the Arthurian legend in English. It used contemporary common language and has been described as fluent, self-confident in language and style, and sensitive. It emphasized the brotherhood of the knights and downplayed ideas of COURTLY LOVE.

See also ARTHUR, KING, AND ARTHURIAN LITERATURE; ROUND TABLE.

Further reading: Sir Thomas Malory, *Works,* ed. Eugène Vinaver, 2d ed. (Oxford: Oxford University Press, 1971); Elizabeth Archibald and A. S. G. Edwards, eds., *A Companion to Malory,* Arthurian Studies, 37 (Cambridge: Cambridge University Press, 1996); Larry D. Benson, *Malory's Morte Darthur* (Cambridge, Mass.: Harvard University Press, 1976); P. J. C. Field, *The Life and Times of Sir Thomas Malory* (Cambridge: Cambridge University Press, 1993).

Malta Malta is an island and part of an archipelago near SICILY but outside the main navigation routes. The VANDALS held it from 435 to 533. It was taken from the Byzantine by the AGHLABIDS in 870 was left a populated colony until Malta repelled an attempted Byzantine reconquest in 1053–54. In 1090, there was a brief occupation of the island by the Normans of Sicily under Count ROGER I, but the island remained Muslim. A second conquest in 1127 led to the establishment of a basically Christian political and religious government. Immigration from Sicily began a slow process of Christianization. Two communities, Christian and Muslim, were tolerated by the Sicilian court at PALERMO, until an expulsion of the Muslims in 1249. The archipelago remained an Arabic-speaking province of the kingdom of Sicily. The Aragonese gained control of it in the late 13th century.

The maritime republics of GENOA, PISA, and VENICE and various great lords tried to take the archipelago from the Aragonese kingdom of Sicily. From 1360, the rise of the pirates produced HAFSID retaliations from AFRICA. The cost of guarding the islands led the Aragonese monarchy, who had held it since 1282, to try to shift the burden onto the MILITARY ORDERS. After the fall of RHODES in 1522, the HOSPITALLERS obtained possession of Malta and Gozo in 1530.

See also NORMANS IN ITALY; SICILIAN VESPERS.

Further reading: Anthony Luttrell, ed., *Medieval Malta: Studies on Malta before the Knights* (London:

British School at Rome, 1975); Anthony Luttrell, *The Making of Christian Malta: From the Early Middle Ages to 1530* (Aldershot: Ashgate, 2002).

Mamluks (Mamelukes) The Arabic word *mamlak* as a past participle meant "to be possessed." Before becoming a Turkish military aristocracy, the Mamluks started as slaves abducted in infancy to make them servile and professional military horsemen. They should not be confused with black slaves, who remain so and had been kidnapped as children or adults. It was a common practice in Islam to make up part or all of an army with military slaves. In EGYPT, the AYYUBIDS, between 1171 and 1250, added to units composed of free Kurds, bought Turkish slaves to fill out the ranks of their army. These men received military instruction and accepted Muslim religious teaching. When the Ayyubid dynasty failed to defend Islam against the crusaders and then the MONGOLS, these Mamluk soldiers took power and held on to it for the next three centuries. They even tried to legitimize their rule by moving an ABBASID prince from BAGHDAD, who had been captured by the Mongols in 1258, to CAIRO and calling him the CALIPH. Their empire soon extended over Egypt, SYRIA, and the holy cities of the Hejaz, MECCA and MEDINA.

RISE, DECLINE, AND FALL

The Mamluks were not really a dynasty, since a sultan's son did not necessarily succeed him. It was assumed that another former ambitious, ruthless, and competent slave after defeating all rivals would become the new sultan. The Mamluk hierarchy was organized from the top with the 100 emirs commanding 1,000 Mamluks, then emirs commanding 40 Mamluks, and finally emirs in charge of 10. Each was supported and rewarded by revenue from land, that corresponded to his rank as an administrator or soldier. These posts and incomes could pass to descendants but were not inheritable FIEFS as such. They had a strong military force based on CAVALRY and a fleet that unsuccessfully attack CYPRUS on several occasions.

Their court protocol, diplomacy, and administration required numerous well-trained personnel, and certain families, often Christian, occupied these positions and ultimately formed dynasties of secretaries or bureaucrats. The pious Mamluks supported large numbers of charitable foundations, especially in Cairo. As were the Ayyubids, the Mamluks were strictly orthodox SUNNI in religion.

In 1260 they defeated the MONGOLS at the Battle of AYN-JALUT in PALESTINE. The Mamluk sultan, BAYBARS I, captured most of the Christian-held territory in Palestine and Syria between 1263 and 1268, including ANTIOCH, and made himself sultan of a united kingdom of Syria and Egypt, which he ruled until his death in 1277. This state was to exist for more than two centuries. In 1291 the Mamluk sultan al-Ashraf Khalil (r. 1290–93) won back ACRE and the last of the coastal towns held by the crusaders. However, neglect of economic institutions, the epidemics of the 14th century and changes in the trade routes to the east undermined Mamluk political and economic power. The Mamluks were later defeated by the OTTOMANS, losing Syria in 1516, then Egypt and the rest of their empire by 1517.

Further reading: Reuven Amitai-Preiss, *Mongols and Mamluks: The Mamluk–Ilkhanid War, 1260–1281* (Cambridge: Cambridge University Press, 1995); David Ayalon, *The Mamluk Military Society* (London: Variorum, 1979); Shai Har-El, ed., *Struggle for Domination in the Middle East: The Ottoman–Mamluk War, 1485–91* (Leiden: E. J. Brill, 1995); David Ayalon, "Mamluk" and "Mamluks," *Encyclopedia of Islam*, 6.314–321, 6.321–331; Robert Irwin, *The Middle East in the Middle Ages: The Early Mamluk Sultanate, 1250–1382* (Carbondale: Southern Illinois University Press, 1986); Carl F. Petry, ed., *The Cambridge History of Egypt.* Vol. 1, *Islamic Egypt, 640–1517* (Cambridge: Cambridge University Press, 1998); Daniel Pipes, *Slave Soldiers and Islam: The Genesis of a Military System* (New Haven, Conn.: Yale University Press, 1981).

al-Mamun, Abu l-Abbas Abd Allah bin Harun al Rasd (786–833) *seventh Abbasid caliph*
Al-Mamun was the son of the caliph HARUN AL-RASHID. In 813 he headed a conspiracy against his brother, al-Amin (r. 809–813); took BAGHDAD; and was proclaimed caliph. He attempted to rule by reconciling different Muslim factions. His ideas of rationalist faith were opposed by the factions. That motivated him to support an academy of Baghdad. It became one of world's most important centers of any kind of learning. He invited the important philosophers and scientists from all over the Muslim world and hired them to translate Greek and Indian works. He established this center for scholarship at the House of Knowledge or Wisdom (Bayt al-Hikmah), which was a library, an academy, and a center for the acquisition, translation, and study of ancient Greek manuscripts about science and philosophy. The works of Galen, Hippocrates, Euclid, Ptolemy, Archimedes, PLATO, and ARISTOTLE were studied. He died suddenly in 833.

Further reading: Paul M. Cobb, *White Banners: Contention in Abbasid Syria, 750–880* (Albany: State University of New York Press, 2001); Elton L. Daniel, *The Political and Social History of Khurasan under Abbasid Rule, 747–820* (Minneapolis: Bibliotheca Islamica, 1979); Hugh Kennedy, *The Early Abbasid Caliphate: A Political History* (London: Croom Helm, 1981); Jacob Lassner, *The Shaping of Abbasid Rule* (Princeton, N.J.: Princeton University Press, 1980); George Sawa, *Music Performance Practice in the Early Abbasid Era 132–320 AH/750–932 AD* (Toronto: Pontifical Institute of Mediaeval Studies, 1989).

Mandeville, John (d. ca. 1372), **and** *Mandeville's Travels author*
Mandeville's precise identity has remained unclear. In one well-attested tradition he wrote his book at Liège and died there in 1372. An epitaph on a tomb, visible until 1798 in a church near there, related that he, the presumed occupant, had traveled the whole world. This has been disproved by 19th- and 20th-century scholarship. In his book about his travels he claimed to be an adventurous knight born at Saint Albans in ENGLAND, who traveled to the Middle East before retiring and doing good works in Liège. References in his book suggest that he was a layman, had an extensive education, was able to read LATIN, and had access to a good library.

Mandeville's Travels was widely read from its first appearance. It was probably written in French about 1360. More than 300 manuscripts in 10 languages survived. It was one of the first books to be printed, in German, and other languages. The book presented an itinerary to the Holy Land, from England to CONSTANTINOPLE and then via the Mediterranean islands to JERUSALEM. The author described Christian sites in PALESTINE and took an interest in ISLAM and MUHAMMAD. He told of his visits to lands, countries, and islands beyond ABYSSINIA, India, China, a Mongol domain, and the islands in the Indian Ocean that were filled with fabulous and monstrous peoples and animals. He mentioned the realm of PRESTER JOHN. He affirmed the roundness of the Earth and the possibility of circumnavigating it and finding inhabited countries everywhere. His tolerance to non-Christians and JEWS varied according to the translations. For example the Latin version, likely for a learned and clerical audience, was very intolerant and blatantly anti-Jewish. He supposedly quit traveling in 1356/57 because of gout and died about 1372.

See also ANTIPODES.

Further reading: John Mandeville, *Mandeville's Travels*, ed. M. C. Seymour (Oxford: Clarendon Press, 1967); J. W. Bennett, *The Rediscovery of Sir John Mandeville* (New York: Modern Language Association of America, 1954); Iain Macleod Higgins, *Writing East: The "Travels of Sir John Mandeville"* (Philadelphia: University of Pennsylvania Press, 1997); Giles Milton, *The Riddle and the Knight: In Search of Sir John Mandeville, the World's Greatest Traveller* (New York: Farrar, Straus, & Giroux, 2001); M. C. Seymour, *Sir John Mandeville* (Aldershot: Ashgate, 1993).

Manfred of Hohenstaufen (1232–1266) *illegitimate son of Frederick II, king of Sicily*
Manfred was the natural son of the emperor FREDERICK II of HOHENSTAUFEN and Bianca Lancia. He may have studied at PARIS and BOLOGNA. He was legitimized by his father, who intended him to rule the kingdom of Arles in

southern FRANCE and married him to Beatrice of SAVOY. Manfred inherited from Frederick an interest in culture. Active in Frederick's courtly culture, he sponsored translators of Greek and Arabic and supposedly knew LATIN, Arabic, and Hebrew.

POLITICAL VICISSITUDES

In his father's will of 1250, he received the government of the kingdom of SICILY as temporary regent until the arrival of his older brother, the king of GERMANY and emperor, Conrad IV (r. 1250–54). He also received the principality of Taranto, and the honor of Monte Sant' Angelo on the Gargano peninsula in APULIA. He crushed a rebellion of several Italian cities with the help of his mother's relatives. Conrad arrived in 1252, but his death in 1254 led to a general conflict over who would rule. Pope INNOCENT IV excommunicated' Manfred and proclaimed the church's control over the kingdom. Manfred acted quickly and managed to seize the imperial treasure, and to remove a regent, who had taken power in the name of Conradin or Conrad V (r. 1254–68), the duke of SWABIA and the young son of Conrad IV. Manfred outmaneuvered the papal legate and took Messina and PALERMO. Recognized as regent in 1256 by a parliament at Barletta, he spread a rumor of Conradin's death and had himself crowned king of Sicily at Palermo in 1258. Trying to win over the GUELF party, he vainly sought an agreement with the PAPACY; he was refused and was forced to depend on a network of Ghibelline alliances.

He subsequently neglected his Italian power base and allies for a failed eastern adventure in ALBANIA and CONSTANTINOPLE. Instead of exploiting the Ghibelline victory at Montaperti in 1260 near SIENA, he failed to block the routes through Piedmont and LOMBARDY, so when Pope Urban IV (r. 1261–64) invested CHARLES I OF ANJOU with the kingdom of SICILY, Charles easily entered Italy. Manfred failed to exploit his alliances with the Lombard barons related to him and could not maintain his fragile family-based political network in central and southern Italy. Manfred was defeated and killed at Benevento, on February 22, 1266, by the Guelf and papal forces of Charles of Anjou. He was survived by his daughter, Constance, who married King Peter III of ARAGON (r. 1276–85).

Further reading: Henri Bresc, "Manfred (1232–1266)," *EMA*, 2.900; John Larner, *Italy in the Age of Dante and Petrarch, 1216–1380* (London: Longman, 1980); Steven Runciman, *The Sicilian Vespers: A History of the Mediterranean World in the Later Thirteenth Century* (Cambridge: Cambridge University Press, 1958).

Manichaeism and Mani   Manichaeism was based on the vision of the founder of the sect, Mani or Manes (216–276 C.E.), and was brought to the west by his evangelistic disciples. Mani was a member of a Jewish-Christian baptizing sect in southern Babylonia. Sponsored by the emperor Shapur I (r. 241–273), his teachings spread both in the Sassanian Empire, the frontier regions of the Roman Empire, and central Asia. Nonetheless, Mani was killed for his beliefs in 276. By the end of the third century, the sect had spread around the Mediterranean, assisted by TRADE connections between ROME and Sassanian IRAN and by the conversion of the empire to Christianity, which helped missionary possibilities for a sect copying Christianity's organization and claiming to be a better form of Christianity. Mani proclaimed himself an apostle of Jesus Christ and the promised paraclete or holy spirit. He wrote mostly lost doctrinal, liturgical, and homiletic texts supposedly beautifully written in decorated manuscripts.

THEOLOGY AND PERSECUTION

From fragmentary documentation, Manichaeism seemed to be based on a radical DUALISM rooted in an extreme dichotomy between the material and the spiritual. There were two principles, one light and one darkness, originally separate and distinct. A penetration of a Kingdom of Light by the forces of the Prince of Darkness in a middle epoch caused the necessary sending of a redeeming primal individual, who was to repel this malignant invasion. A complicated battle ensued that involved drugging, a divine reviving, cannibalism, and INCEST. Eventually the human SOUL, regarded as an element of divine nature, was left captive in the flesh. They would become separate again after a purifying conflagration. The elect in this system were forbidden to have sex, marry, eat meat, or prepare food. The daily needs of the elect had to be tended to by "hearers," who were permitted to live a normal life with the promise of reincarnation as one of the elect. All of this held a certain attraction to people in the late Roman Empire. One temporary adherent was AUGUSTINE, who eventually found it a collection of myths unable to help with any intellectual understanding of the world.

The Manichaean religion, viewed as a threat from Persia, was heavily persecuted by the Christian Roman state from the emperor Theodosios I (r. 379–395) onward and was the target of vehement polemics by orthodox churchmen. Their polemical writings were our main source for the history and beliefs of the sect until the beginning of the 20th century. The writings were also used regularly by the Eastern and Western Churches in the Middle Ages as weapons against "Neo-Manichaean" sects, such as the Paulicians, BOGOMILS, and CATHARS. The Manichaeans were also persecuted by Muslims as nonbelievers considered evil and immoral, but not necessarily pagan.

See also GNOSTICISM.

Further reading: Francis C. Burkitt, *The Religion of the Manichees* (New York: AMS Press, 1978); Hans-Joachim Klimkeit, *Gnosis on the Silk Road* (New York: HarperCollins, 1993); Samuel N. C. Lieu, *Manichaeism in the Later Roman Empire and Medieval China: A Historical*

Survey 2d ed. (Tübingen: Mohr, 1992); Paul Mirecki and Jason BeDuhn, ends., *Emerging from Darkness: Studies in the Recovery of Manichaean Sources* (Leiden: Brill, 1997); L. J. R. Ort, *Mani: A Religio-Historical Description of His Personality* (Leiden: E. J. Brill, 1967).

manors and manorial lordship   Over the course of the early Middle Ages, and especially by the 10th century, villages or estates owned by nobles evolved into manors (mansi) with certain reciprocal obligations on the laboring PEASANTRY and on the lord. Both sides had to meet the terms of tenure and protection. These manors had a lord, who held it as a vassal and as a tenant of his own lord. The system can be theoretically viewed as a pyramid with the king or prince at the top. These relations were distinct from those of FEUDALISM but mirrored some of its terms and conditions. A lord exercised legal jurisdiction over petty vassals and peasants, who were compelled to yield labor and meet obligations to him.

PHYSICAL FEATURES AND DETAILS OF THE SYSTEM

A classic manorial estate was divided into a lord's section, the demesne. This property might contain a CASTLE or house for the lord, land cultivated by SERFS as part of their duties, and areas left to nature or waste such as lakes or forests. Some of these were for common use or set aside for certain activities. There were often MILLS and bakeries owned by the lord. Manorial courts regularly met and were presided over by the lord or his representative, to ensure compliance with manorial rules. The peasants, when they acted together, might be able to protect themselves against excessive seigniorial oppression.

In an agricultural revolution around the 11th century, heavy ploughs were introduced, that permitted a more intensive cultivation. They became part of the manorial inventory of tools and were lent to peasants in exchange for fees or additional services. Peasants' lands and fields might be arranged in long strips, to accommodate a plough team made up of six to eight oxen. Peasants often had to give lords a fairly high portion of his produce, pay certain taxes, and supply work services. The amounts for all were set in the peasantry's terms of tenure, which were heavily influenced by labor supply.

COMMERCIALIZATION, MOBILITY, REPRESSION

From the 12th century there was a revival of commerce and a growth in towns. Some of these old obligations were commuted to monetary payments, which eventually led to a more commercial agrarian economy. Members of peasant communities, especially when they were unified, became more autonomous or at least could try to limit burdens placed on them. Many peasants improved their situation and bought freedom from the more servile exactions. New colonization or clearing of waste by churches or lords offered opportunities for better tenure and conditions to peasants, since the lords needed to attract colonists. Landless peasants were recruited for eastern Germany from the overpopulated areas of the Rhineland and the Low Countries. Their new lords organized them and established new villages on the newly cleared land. This happened in Western Europe, too, as more and more land was cleared and put into production. Labor shortages and a more monetized economy led to the employment of hired peasants to work on the manorial demesne. The great PLAGUES and crises of the 14th century inevitably affected agriculture. As a result of the ensuing extreme shortage of laborers, lords demanded the restoration of work services, taxes, and the closing of common areas. This led to peasant revolts that met with harsh reprisals. This model of the manorial system is a theoretical and basic construct. Many aspects of the manorial system were dependent on farming techniques and the labor supply.

See also AGRICULTURE; HORSES; JACQUÉRIE; LABOR; PEASANT REBELLIONS; SOCIAL STATUS AND STRUCTURE; VILLAGE COMMUNITIES AND SETTLEMENTS; VILLEIN AND VILLEINAGE.

Further reading: L. R. Poos and Lloyd Bonfield, eds., *Select Cases in Manorial Courts, 1250–1550: Property and Family Law* (London: Selden Society, 1998); P. D. A. Harvey, *Manorial Records* (London: British Records Association, 1984); George C. Homans, *English Villagers of the Thirteenth Century* (Cambridge, Mass.: Harvard University Press, 1941); J. Ambrose Raftis, *Peasant Economic Development within the English Manorial System* (Montreal: McGill-Queen's University Press, 1996).

al-Mansur, Muhammad ibn Abu Amr (Almanzor, the Victorious) (938–1002) *victorious general in Islamic Spain*
From a distinguished Arab line, al-Mansur in 967 entered the court of the caliphate of CÓRDOBA. There he was placed in charge of the administration of caliphal estates. He soon also proved himself a victorious general and became one of the regents during the minority of Caliph Hisham II (ca. 964–1013). In 977 he led a successful military expedition against the Christians in northern SPAIN. On his return, he seized power over the state and kept the caliph a prisoner in his own palace.

With a mercenary army of BERBERS and Christians, al-Mansur made himself the sole ruler of AL-ANDALUS. He called for a holy war or JIHAD against the Christians, and in 985 he captured BARCELONA and in 987, even SANTIAGO DE COMPOSTELA in northern Spain. Instead of permanently occupying them, al-Mansur gave them to Christian princes, who were compelled to pay tribute. Al-Mansur, ostentatiously pious, imposed strict Muslim practices on his state, built several MOSQUES, and enlarged the great mosque of Córdoba. He burned secular books that seemed unacceptable to him from the famous caliphal library. Al-Mansur had to engage in continuous military campaigns to pay his soldiers and he accomplish his building schemes, including the great mosque at Córdoba and his palace, AL-MADINA AL-ZAHIRA. He died in 1002 on his way back from a campaign against the Christians, who rejoiced greatly at his death.

Further reading: Titus Burckhardt, *Moorish Culture in Spain,* trans. Alisa Jaffa (London: Allen and Unwin, 1972); Richard Fletcher, *Moorish Spain* (Berkeley: University of California Press, 1992); Jan Read, *The Moors in Spain and Portugal* (London: Faber, 1974).

Mantegna, Andrea (1430/31–1506) *Italian court painter, engraver*
He was born to a humble family in Vicenza about 1431 and was educated at Padua by his teacher, Francesco Squarcione. His first major work was the FRESCO cycle of the *Life of Saint James and Saint Christopher* in the Ovetari Chapel of the church of the Eremitani in Padua. It was completed in 1459 but was destroyed by a bomb in 1944. His style was influenced by the sculpture of DONATELLO and the painting of Paolo UCCELLO, Jacopo Bellini, and Filippo LIPPI.

His most important surviving religious works are the *Madonna and Saints* from about 1456 at VERONA in San Zeno and images of the *Martyrdom of Saint Sebastian* and a *Madonna of Victory* from about 1495 now at PARIS in the Louvre Museum. He became the Gonzaga family's court painter in 1460. For them he painted the copula of the Camera degli Sposi or "Bridal Chamber" in their palace at Mantua in 1474. He died on September 13, 1506, in Mantua.

See also BELLINI FAMILY; PAINTING.

Further reading: Nike Bätzner, *Andrea Mantegna: 1430/31–1506,* trans. Phyll Greenhead (Cologne: Könemann, 1998); Dawson W. Carr, *Andrea Mantegna: The Adoration of the Magi* (Los Angeles: J. Paul Getty Museum, 1997); Jack M. Greenstein, *Mantegna and Painting as Historical Narrative* (Chicago: University of Chicago Press, 1992); Paul Kristeller, *Andrea Mantegna,* ed. S. Arthur Strong (London: Longmans, Green and Co., 1901); Andrew Martindale, *The Triumphs of Caesar by Andrea Mantegna in the Collection of Her Majesty the Queen at Hampton Court* (London: Harvey Miller, 1979); Jane Martineau, *Andrea Mantegna* (Milan: Electa, 1992).

manuscript illumination *See* ILLUMINATION.

manuscripts *See* ARCHIVES AND ARCHIVAL INSTITUTIONS; CODICOLOGY; ILLUMINATION; PALEOGRAPHY.

Manzikert, Battle of (Malazgird) This was a battle in August 1071 in eastern ANATOLIA near Lake Van between the SELJUK TURKS, led by ALP ARSLAN, and the Byzantines, led by Romanos IV Diogenes (r. 1067–72). The emperor was betrayed by a general and his Turkish mercenaries. Forced to fight, he lost and was captured. The defeat left all of Anatolia open to the advancing Seljuks. The office of emperor was disputed and Romanos, though quickly released by Alp Arslan, was deposed. Arslan repudiated the treaty he had made with Romanos and moved en masse into the rest of Anatolia, which was quickly and permanently lost to the Greeks.

See also ALEXIOS I KOMNENOS.

Further reading: Michael Ango Angold, *The Byzantine Empire, 1025–1204: A Political History,* 2d ed. (New York: Longman, 1997); Alfred Friendly, *The Dreadful Day: The Battle of Manzikert, 1071* (London: Hutchinson, 1981); Speros Vryonis, *The Decline of Medieval Hellenism in Asia Minor and the Process of Islamization from the Eleventh through the Fifteenth Century* (Berkeley: University of California Press, 1971).

maps Drawn in manuscripts on a range of topics and places, medieval maps were numerous, at least 500 even before 1200. Inhabited lands in them were represented in schema that showed Asia, Europe, and AFRICA. The notion of the roundness of the Earth was never contested in the Middle Ages. Diagrams often depicted the Earth as a globe divided into five zones. They were frequently done as T-O maps, a circle divided into three parts divided by rivers forming a T inside the circle.

The term *mappa mundi* or map of the world generally meant a more detailed image of the inhabited Earth, with names of places and labels. Larger-scale regional maps, some painted on walls, appeared in the 13th century and plans of towns or lands were drawn when they were involved in litigation. There were rough nautical maps or charts of the Mediterranean and Atlantic coasts, which illustrated ideas about the Earth, located place-names mentioned by classical authors, aided teaching, and even gave viewers an idea of their location with regard to JERUSALEM, the traditional center of the Earth. Maps were also intended for contemplation of God's plan and of humankind's place in the world. They could symbolize the pretense to learning and prestige of a ruler. In the 15th century, Ptolemy's *Geography* was published. With the opening of a wider world, the contents of maps evolved as knowledge of the world grew.

See also ANTIPODES; GEOGRAPHY AND CARTOGRAPHY; AL-IDRISI; NAVIGATION; PORTOLAN CHARTS.

Further reading: Evelyn Edson, *Mapping Time and Space: How Medieval Mapmakers Viewed Their World* (London: British Library, 1999); P. D. A. Harvey, *Medieval Maps* (Toronto: University of Toronto Press, 1991); J. B. Harley and David Woodward, eds., *The History of Cartography,* 2 vols. (Chicago: University of Chicago Press, 1987–1994); R. A. Skelton and P. D. A. Harvey, eds., *Local Maps and Plans from Medieval England* (Oxford: Clarendon Press, 1986); Donald Wigal, *Historic Maritime Maps*

Used for Historic Exploration, 1290–1699 (New York: Parkstone Press, 2000).

Marco Polo (Marcus Paulus) (1254–1324) *famous traveler*

The son of a merchant, Marco Polo was born in VENICE in 1254. Very little is known about him except what is in his account of his travels to the court of the great khan in China. According to Polo's account, his uncle, Matteo, and his father, Niccolò, set out from Soldaia on the BLACK SEA, and arrived by a long and difficult journey on the Silk Road at the residence of KUBLAI KHAN. After returning to ITALY, Matteo and Niccolò set off again in 1271, furnished with letters from the pope and accompanied by the young Marco. They arrived at the MONGOL court in 1275. According to Marco's account, the khan, was impressed by Marco's knowledge of languages and took him into his service, entrusting him with important missions in the Mongol Empire and India. The khan eventually asked that the pope send him 100 men instructed in the Christian religion and oil from a lamp in front of the Holy Sepulchre at JERUSALEM. At the end of 16 years, in 1291, the Polos left to return home by sea, while escorting a Mongol princess intended for a royal marriage in Persia. They reached Venice between 1295 and 1297.

HIS BOOK OF MARVELS

In 1298 Marco was captured during a naval battle between Venice and GENOA and imprisoned, probably until May 1299. There Marco Polo was supposed to have dictated the account of his adventures to a fellow captive, who happened to be a successful writer of romances. It is not clear whether he actually wrote or dictated the book in prison. Nor is it even clear that it was first written in the Venetian dialect. In tradition he then ended his life in peace, heaped with honors by the republic of Venice. He was well off but not rich and had three daughters. There is a document recording that he granted freedom to a Mongol slave. A will suggested that he died on January 8, 1324. There are still disputes about which route he used and whether he actually arrived.

THE BOOK

The *Book of Marvels* or *Il Milione* still commands great success. It described the countries of Central Asia and the khan's empire, almost in the form of an itinerary, with directions and the number of days' travel required to each place. Polo was interested in the number of inhabitants, their religion, their customs, the resources of each region, towns, and monuments. Marco admired the khan and the competence of his government. He might have done service in the government of the khan, but certain aspects and details of the book demonstrated a strange lack of knowledge and were simply erroneous. The book was not initially very popular but became so soon after his death. It was a chief source for information on Asia for Europeans and was influential in COLUMBUS's plan to sail west to reach the East.

See also JOHN OF PLANO CARPINI.

Marco Polo and Kublai Khan, *Livre des Merveilles* (ca. 1413), Ms. 2810, fol. 3v., Bibliothèque Nationale, Paris *(Art Resource)*

Further reading: Marco Polo, *The Travels of Marco Polo*, trans. Ronald Latham (New York: Penguin Books, 1958); John Larner, *Marco Polo and the Discovery of the World* (New Haven, Conn.: Yale University Press, 1999); J. R. S. Phillips, *The Medieval Expansion of Europe*, 2d ed. (1988; reprint, Oxford: Oxford University Press, 1998); Frances Wood, *Did Marco Polo Go to China?* (Boulder, Colo.: Westview Press, 1996).

Margaret of Denmark, Norway, and Sweden (Margrethe) (1353–1412) *Scandinavian ruler*

Daughter of King Waldemar IV (r. 1340–75) of DENMARK, Margaret inherited the kingdoms of Denmark, NORWAY, and SWEDEN in 1387 and ruled them as regent for her nephew, ERIC of Pomerania (d. 1442). Her husband, Haakon VI (r. 1350–80) of Norway, died in 1380, and her son, Olaf (r. 1380–87) died in 1387. Accepted as ruler, she defeated and captured in battle in 1389 her rival, Albert of Mecklenburg (r. 1364–89), the king of Sweden. She added GOTLAND and Schleswig to her Crown. Her belief in Scandinavian unity was furthered by the Union of Kalmar in 1397, which joined the three Crowns but left each country under its own government. Margaret was esteemed for her statesmanship, though opposition and problems were developing when she died on October 27, 1412.

Further reading: Brigit Sawyer and Peter Sawyer, *Medieval Scandinavia: From Conversion to Reformation, circa 800–1500* (Minneapolis: University of Minnesota Press, 1993).

Margery Kempe, The Book of   The Book of Margery Kempe was preserved in a single manuscript not found until 1934. An autobiography, it provided remarkable documentation of a Christian woman in 15th-century English society. She was born to an upper-middle-class family in King's Lynn in Norfolk, that of John Burnham (d. 1413); married John Kempe (d. ca. 1431), a burgess of Lynn; and became the mother of 14 children. She and her husband took vows of CHASTITY in 1413. She experienced a spiritual conversion in 1413 and modeled herself on BIRGITTA OF SWEDEN, loudly denouncing all pleasure. In her book she described speaking with Christ. She made PILGRIMAGES and harangued crowds, a dangerous practice during a period when LOLLARD heretics were persecuted for such activities. Her public devotions and actions prompted accusations of exhibitionism. Her public and mystical experience did not resemble that of the contemporary English mystics, but her biography has been viewed as a source of great psychological and sociological importance. She died about 1439.

See also MYSTICISM, CHRISTIAN.

Further reading: Margery Kempe, *The Book of Margery Kempe,* trans. B. A. Windeatt (New York: Pen-

guin, 1985); Clarissa W. Atkinson, *Mystic and Pilgrim: The Book and the World of Margery Kempe* (Ithaca, N.Y.: Cornell University Press, 1983); Anthony Goodman, *Margery Kempe and Her World* (London: Longman, 2002); Karma Lochrie, *Margery Kempe and Translations of the Flesh* (Philadelphia: University of Pennsylvania Press, 1991); *Margery Kempe: A Book of Essays,* ed. Sandra J. McEntire (New York: Garland, 1992); Lynn Staley, *Margery Kempe's Dissenting Fictions* (University Park: The Pennsylvania State University Press, 1994).

Marie de Champagne (1145–1198) *patron of poets*

Marie de Champagne was born in 1145, the eldest daughter of King Louis VII (ca. 1120–80) and ELEANOR OF AQUITAINE. Betrothed very young to Henry I the Liberal of Champagne (r. 1152–81), son of Thibaut II of Blois (r. 1125–52), she married him in 1159. His brother, Thibaut IV (r. 1197–1201), married Marie's sister. Marie went on to host a brilliant court and center of patronage that had great influence on the development of literature in the last part of the 12th century.

Marie was widowed when her husband died on return from a PILGRIMAGE to JERUSALEM in 1181. Marie served as regent of Champagne three times: until the majority of her son, Henry II (r. 1181–97), in 1187; when Henry left on the Third CRUSADE, where he died at ACRE in 1197; and during the minority of her second son, Thibaut IV (r. 1201–53). Contemporary chroniclers extolled her political acumen.

As was her mother, Eleanor, Marie patronized and was interested in literature. She could read and write. Her name was linked especially to those of CHRÉTIEN DE TROYES, Gautier d'Arras (d. 1185), Andreas Capellanus, Gace Brulé, and Conon of Béthune. She and her circle explored the romantic themes of the TROUBADOURS and the traditions of ROMANCE. Opinions attributed to her were part of literary convention allowing the expression of thoughts on MARRIAGE and sex. She died in 1198.

Further reading: John C. Moore, *Love in Twelfth Century France* (Philadelphia: University of Pennsylvania Press, 1972); Lynette R. Muir, *Literature and Society in Medieval France: The Mirror and the Image, 1100–1500* (London: Macmillan, 1985).

Marie de France (fl. late 12th century) *earliest known French woman poet*

Marie lived in the middle of the 12th century, but almost nothing is known about her life. She lived for some years, and probably wrote, at the court in ENGLAND of King HENRY II, where she composed a poem that began, "My name is Marie, and I am of France." Marie wrote verse narrative and lyrical poems in French in praise of LOVE and composed lays inspired by the Breton tradition. She also wrote FABLES.

Further reading: Marie de France, *The Lais of Marie de France*, trans. Robert Hanning and Joan Ferrante (New York: Dutton, 1978); Glyn S. Burgess and Keith Busby, trans., *The Lais of Marie de France* (London: Penguin, 1986); Emanuel J. Mickel Jr., *Marie de France* (New York: Twayne Publishers, 1974); Judith Rice Rothschild, *Narrative Technique in the Lais of Marie de France: Themes and Variations* (Chapel Hill: University of North Carolina, Department of Romance Languages, 1974).

Marie of Oignies (1177–1213) *mystic*

Marie was born at Nivelles, in the diocese of Liège. JAMES OF VITRY wrote about Marie's life soon after her death. He became her confessor late in her life. In his writing she was a model for emulation by women. Married by her parents when she was 14, Marie persuaded her husband to accept a chaste marriage and service at a leper hospital. She aspired to more solitude and so got permission from her husband and her confessor to retire alone to Oignies-sur-Sambre. Marie was soon joined by other women, who wished, as she did, to live a life of penintential practice in a community. James paid little attention to this idea of lay and female community and instead described in detail her religious experiences; her devotion to Christ, to the Cross, to the Passion; her revelations and mystical ecstasies; her fasts, her vigils, and her ascetic practices, even self-mutilation. She did not provide rules for the religious life or take any explicit vows. James intended her as an example for a saintly and orthodox Christian lifestyle in opposition to contemporary CATHAR heretics. However, her beguinal life made her suspect because of its minimal links to male clerics. Her other admirable religious practices as described by James included frequent attendance at SERMONS, frequent CONFESSION, and desire to receive the Eucharist, all of these practices could be considered a way the church could exercise control over the BEGUINES. Her biography itself was a common source for exemplary sermon material. She died in 1213 but was never canonized.

Further reading: James of Vitry, *The Life of Marie d'Oignies*, trans. Margot H. King (Saskatoon: Peregrina, 1986).

Maritime Republics *See* GENOA; PISA; VENICE.

markets *See* FAIRS AND MARKETS.

Marrakech (Marakesh, Marrakesh) Marrakech is located on a wide plain about 25 miles (or 40 kilometers) from the ATLAS MOUNTAINS in southern MOROCCO. It was founded by the ALMORAVID ruler Yusf ibn Tashfin (r. 1060–1106), founder of the Almoravid dynasty, in 1062.

Remains from the ALMOHAD period from the 12th to the 13th century include the Kutubiya MOSQUE from 1147, the Kasba Mosque, and the Bab Agnau. The city had three *madrasah*. The oldest is the Bin Yusuf Madrasa, originally built as a mosque in the 12th century. The town also contains the tombs of various Moroccan rulers, including that of Yusuf ibn Tashfin as well as the tomb of the seven local saints, still the object of annual PILGRIMAGES. There are several medieval palaces within the city, the oldest of which is the Dar al Makhzan, built by the Almohads. The city also contains historic gardens.

See also BERBERS; AL-MAGHRIB.

Further reading: Leo Africanus, *The History and Description of Africa and of the Notable Things Therein Contained*, 3 vols. (1986; reprint, New York: B. Franklin, 1963); Thomas Kerlin Park, *Historical Dictionary of Morocco* (Lanham, Md.: Scarecrow Press, 1996); Maya Shatzmiller, *The Berbers and the Islamic State: The Marinid Experience in Pre-Protectorate Morocco* (Princeton, N.J.: Markus Wiener, 2000); Henri Terrasse, *History of Morroco*, trans. Hilary Tee (Casablanca: Éditions Atlantides, 1952).

Marranos (conversos, swine, *muharran* [forbidden])

The word *marrano* originally designated a pig, or an unclean creature. From the second half of the 14th century, *marrano* was used essentially to designate converted JEWS, whose numbers grew after the huge pogroms of 1391, when perhaps 50,000 Jews were killed. Although there was some effort to ban the term, it became common and generic in the second half of the 15th century, especially after the expulsion in 1492. Ideas about these people of every social class were tied to an obsession with purity, both purity of FAITH and purity of blood. Not even baptism could wash away the sin of the Jews, who some considered guilty of killing Christ. Sincerity or length of conversion was ignored. From the 1480s, the INQUISITION and statutes defining purity of blood were established. One theological current defended the Marranos, or conversos, who often had attained more social integration, prestige, and wealth; but it had little effect.

See also ANTI-JUDAISM AND ANTI-SEMITISM.

Further reading: Haim Beinart, *Conversos on Trial: The Inquisition in Ciudad Real*, trans. Yael Guiladi. (Jerusalem: Magnes Press, Hebrew University, 1981); Renée Levine Melammed, *Heretics of Daughters of Israel?: The Crypto-Jewish Women of Castile* (New York: Oxford University Press, 1999); Benzion Netanyahu, *The Marranos of Spain: From the Late 14th to the Early 16th Century, According to Contemporary Hebrew Sources*, 3d ed. (Ithaca, N.Y.: Cornell University Press, 1999); Cecil Roth, *A History of the Marranos*, 2d ed. (1932; reprint, Philadelphia: Jewish Publication Society of America, 1959).

marriage   In the Middle Ages Christian theologians saw in marriage what Saint Paul had called a sacrament involving both Christ and the church. So over the centuries it became a matter of integrating into this evolving concept of marriage as a sacrament the ideas of a mutual contract, a carnal union that was its consummation, and the pleasure involved. Conjugal pleasure was sometimes even deemed acceptable, and much of the thought about marriage was even cast in terms of classical ideas about friendship. Peter DAMIAN suggested that the aim of marriage was an opportunity for the practice of mutual charity between the spouses. It was more than a functional union, but one oriented toward the transmission of life. The theologian IVO of Chartres insisted on mutual love; so without love, there was no marriage. However, virginity was always considered better. The failings of human nature resulting form original sin, however, created a need for marriage to prevent fornication.

DEVELOPMENT OF
MARITAL CONCEPTS IN THE WEST

In wider social terms, marriage was considered a union between a man and a woman, enforced by a set of rules that defined the status of the partners, gave them specific rights and duties, and recognized any children as legitimate. Marriage and even its preceding engagement or betrothal created bonds between the two individuals directly involved and, for the upper class, their respective kinship groups. The church tried to control secular ideas and doctrines about marriage, but they were always linked with the needs, whether perceived or not, of society. The church recognized marriage of everyone regardless of personal status, so including that of slaves or those of a servile status. All bonds were to be monogamous and were not dissolvable except under strict conditions that in any case would have rendered the marriage invalid from the beginning, such as a kin relationship within prohibited degrees. God had created these unions through the mutual consent of the partners and human beings could not break it. There was no divorce, but annulments could be obtained. The church set rules for consanguinity that prohibited marriages between people related by blood within certain degrees and also those related by marital unions. Its ecclesiastical courts handled legal questions about marriage itself, since it became considered a sacrament in which the consent was recognized by God. A priest did not have to be present at the exchange of vows, which had to be made between the

A celebration of a marriage, 15th-century fresco from the school of Domenico Ghirlandaio in San Martino dei Buonomini, Florence, Italy *(Scala / Art Resource)*

contracting partners and were increasingly expected to occur in a public ritual. Clandestine marriages were unacceptable, but if they occurred, they were valid, if there had been mutual consent and especially if there had been a physical consummation. Always at the core of ideas and doctrines about marriage was its absolute link with procreation and mutual consent.

EASTERN ORTHODOX CONCEPTS AND PRACTICES

Following more closely the traditions of Roman law, marriage was considered by the EASTERN Orthodox Church to be a lifelong union between man and woman instituted and recognized by divine and human law. Marriage was regulated and fostered by ecclesiastical law and by imperial legislation. Divorce was possible, but remarriage, even after the death of a partner, was strongly discouraged. The Orthodox Church worked more closely and explicitly with the imperial law than did Western Christianity to regulate aspects of marriage such as contractual obligations, dowry, and public ritual. JUSTINIAN's legal collection, the CORPUS IURIS CIVILIS, emphasized consent as the principal quality of a licit and valid marriage.

ISLAM

In ISLAM the HADITH or traditional thought of Muhammad forbade CELIBACY and even self-denial. Temporary marriages were controversial. They were permissible in the thought of some, especially in the Shia tradition, but not in others. There were rules on the number of wives one could have, consanguity, affinity, religion, and social status and rank. One could not marry an unbeliever, though males were able to marry non-Muslim women. The husband had complete sexual rights over the wife and the wife had the right to financial support. Divorce or *talaq* was permissible when done with the correct rituals. Muhammad's own marital life was the basis for much of this.

JUDAISM

Marriage was considered a social institution integral to the divine plan and was viewed as a command, a sacred bond, and even a means of personal fulfillment. It was to be the norm and was considered the ideal way of life. Besides being viewed as a contract between two parties, it was deemed a sacrament. There were strict rules about remarrying and divorce was possible. In the Middle Ages it could be performed anywhere, but was usually done in the courtyard of a SYNAGOGUE. From the 15th century, a rabbi was usually present to witness and bless the vows. There were various prenuptial financial agreements and arrangements.

See also CONTRACEPTION AND ABORTION; FAMILY AND KINSHIP; LOVE; SEXUALITY AND SEXUAL ATTITUDES.

Further reading: Christopher N. L. Brooke, *The Medieval Idea of Marriage* (Oxford: Clarendon Press,

1994); Neil Cartlidge, *Medieval Marriage: Literary Approaches, 1100–1300* (Cambridge: D. S. Brewer, 1997); Georges Duby, *Medieval Marriage: Two Models from Twelfth-Century France,* trans. Elborg Forster (Baltimore: Johns Hopkins University Press, 1978); R. H. Helmholz, *Marriage Litigation in Medieval England* (London: Cambridge University Press, 1974); Ahmad ibn Hanbal, *Chapters on Marriage and Divorce: Responses of Ibn Hanbal and Ibn Rahwayh,* trans. Susan Spectorsky (Austin: University of Texas Press, 1993); P. L. Reynolds, *Marriage in the Western Church: The Christianization of Marriage during the Patristic and Early Medieval Periods* (Leiden: E. J. Brill, 1994); Julius Kirshner, *Pursuing Honor While Avoiding Sin: The Monte delle Doti of Florence* (Milan: A. Giuffrè, 1978); Anthony Molho, *Marriage Alliance in Late Medieval Florence* (Cambridge, Mass.: Harvard University Press, 1994).

Marshal, William   *See* WILLIAM THE MARSHAL.

Marsilius of Padua (Marsiglio da Padova, Marsilio, Marsilius de Mainardino) (1275/80–1343) *Italian antipapal political theorist*
The son of a notary of the University of PADUA, Marsilius belonged to a circle of magistrates who played an important role in the city of Padua in the late 13th and early 14th centuries. A member of the GHIBELLINE faction, he joined the emperor's faction and service. In 1313, he was master of arts and rector of the University of PARIS and practiced MEDICINE there from 1320. In Paris he became friendly with John of Jandun (1286–1328), a master of arts, already notorious for ideas described as heterodox Aristotelianism.

Marsilius fled to the court of the emperor Louis of Bavaria (r. 1328–47) after the publication of his *Defender of Peace* in 1324 and was excommunicated by Pope JOHN XXII. At the imperial court in Munich, he met WILLIAM OF OCKHAM and a group of SPIRITUAL FRANCISCANS who had fled there because of a dispute over mendicant poverty. His books *Defender of Peace,* and *Defensor minor,* and other tracts revealed him to be devoted to the imperial cause and a convinced opponent of the papal pretensions to secular power. Marsilius wanted to restore the autonomy and independence of the HOLY ROMAN EMPIRE as in the best interests of society and CHRISTENDOM.

IDEAS AND BELIEFS

Inspired by the ideas of Aristotle's *Politics,* Marsilius defined a civil community as a perfect form of political organization. The totality of citizens accepted legislative authority by its preponderant or majority part expressed by means of a vote. Such an assembly of the people, as in some of the Italian cities, ratified laws and conferred on them their coercive force.

As an elective monarchy, his reasoning continued, the imperial regime corresponded to this theoretical model. The prince or emperor was alone qualified to hold coercive authority at a more general level. Priestly authority was limited to that of advice and exhortation. The church was defined as all the faithful, both CLERGY and LAITY. Only a general council representing all the faithful had authority in matters of FAITH. Composed of priests and laity, the council represented the universal church as headed by the emperor. The Christian prince held his power directly from GOD, with no need for papal mediation. Priests were to live in poverty and humility, in the image of apostolic times. These assertions were all condemned by the church. Marsilius was dead by April 1343.

See also ARISTOTLE AND ARISTOTELIANISM IN THE MIDDLE AGES; POLITICAL THEORY AND TREATISES.

Further reading: Marsilius of Padua, *Marsilius of Padua: The Defender of Peace, the "Defensor pacis,"* Vol. 2, trans. Alan Gewirth (New York: Columbia University Press, 1956); Marsilius of Padua, *Marsiglio of Padua: Writings on the Empire,* trans. Cary J. Nederman (Cambridge: Cambridge University Press, 1993); Alan Gewirth, *Marsilius of Padua: The Defender of Peace, the "Defensor pacis,"* Vol. 1, *Marsilius of Padua and Medieval Political Philosophy* (New York: Columbia University Press, 1951).

Martianus Capella (Martianus Minneus Felix Capella) (fl. after 410) *writer*
Martianus was perhaps a lawyer who lived under the VANDALS in the later fifth century at Carthage. Between 410 and 439 he wrote an allegorical encyclopedia known as *On the Marriage of Mercury and Philology*, but he called the *Philologia*. The *Philologia* was an original Neoplatonic myth in prose and verse describing the ascent to heaven of Philology, her apotheosis, and her wedding to Mercury. At this wedding her seven bridesmaids, the personified SEVEN LIBERAL ARTS, each presented and explained her discipline to the assembled gods. The *Philologia* had an immediate influence on BOETHIUS's *Consolation of Philosophy* and was known in Merovingian Gaul by the time of GREGORY OF TOURS. As a model for allegories and cosmographical information it was popular during the Carolingian period and the 12th century renaissance and Platonic revival, and used as a textbook, literary source, and compendium of the liberal arts.

See also CAROLINGIAN RENAISSANCE; CASSIODORUS.

Further reading: William Harris Stahl, *Martianus Capella and the Seven Liberal Arts.* Vol. 2, *The Marriage of Philology and Mercury* (New York: Columbia University Press, 1977); William Harris Stahl, *Martianus Capella and the Seven Liberal Arts: The Quadrivium of Martianus Capella, Latin Traditions in the Mathematical Sciences, 50 B.C.–A.D. 1250* (1971; reprint, New York: Columbia University Press, 1991); Bernard Silvestris, *The Commentary*

on *Martianus Capella's De nuptiis Philologiae et Mercurii Attributed to Bernardus Silvestris,* ed. Haijo Jan Westra (Toronto: Pontifical Institute of Mediaeval Studies, 1986); Danuta Shanzer, *A Philosophical and Literary Commentary on Martianus Capella's De nuptiis Philologiae et Mercurii* (Berkeley: University of California Press, 1986).

Martin of Tours, Saint (ca. 315–397) *bishop of Tours*
Martin was a former soldier from PANNONIA, expelled from the army for something like conscientious objection. He became the founder of the monastery of Ligugé, then the bishop of Tours in 371. Until his death, in 397, however, he basically led a monastic life at Marmoutier, the first monastery in Gaul. As part of effort to convert people in the countryside, he was also famous as a wonder worker. In the *Life of Martin*, Sulpicius Severus (ca. 360–ca. 420), a friend, exalted him as a model of sanctity and as a charitable monk-bishop. He died in November of 397, and was buried in Tours.

LATER CULT

In the midfifth century, the bishops of Tours strongly promoted the cult of Saint Martin as effective protector against the evils of war and against ARIANISM. A basilica was then built and pilgrimages organized twice a year, on November 11, his feast, and on July 4. In a conflict with

Saint Martin of Tours dividing his cloak to share it with a beggar, from a fresco by Simone Martini in the Lower Church of San Francesco in Assisi, Italy *(Scala / Art Resource)*

the VISIGOTHS, the bishops of Gaul directed miraculously by Martin, sided with CLOVIS, the king of the FRANKS, who was ultimately victorious in 507. Clovis gave thanks to Martin by making him a patron of the kingdom of the Franks. Devotion to Martin grew in several stages, reaching a peak in the sixth century with revivals in the eighth and ninth centuries. He remained one of the most popular saints of the Middle Ages and a very common image in art.

Further reading: Christopher Donaldson, *Martin of Tours: Parish Priest, Mystic and Exorcist* (London: Routledge and Kegan Paul, 1980); Sharon Framer, *Communities of Saint Martin: Legend and Ritual in Medieval Tours* (Ithaca, N.Y.: Cornell University Press, 1991); Clare Stancliffe, *St. Martin and His Hagiographer: History and Miracle in Sulpicius Severus* (Oxford: Clarendon Press, 1991).

Martini, Simone (ca. 1284–1344) *Gothic artist*
Simone was employed on prestigious commissions and worked for eminent patrons. We are fairly well informed about his career and the date of several of his signed works. However, the dating, and the authenticity of key works have remained controversial. He was born about 1284, probably in SIENA, and was a pupil of DUCCIO and learned FRESCO techniques through working at ASSISI.

Martini was now particularly admired for his use of line and color in his narrative painting. He introduced several innovative altarpiece designs and devised methods of stamping a surface and overlaying gold leaf to create elaborate surface textures. To fresco painting, he introduced new decorative techniques and the three-dimensional representation through the use of recession and light.

For much of his life Simone was based in Siena. His earliest known work, probably completed in 1315, was the fresco of the *Virgin and Child Enthroned with Saints and Angels* in the main council chamber in Siena. He continued to function as almost the official painter of the Sienese commune until about 1333. He also worked at Assisi, decorating the Saint Martin chapel in the Lower Church of San Francesco, and in NAPLES, where he painted a panel of Saint Louis of Toulouse crowning Robert of

Simone Martini's *Annunciation,* Uffizi, Florence, Italy *(Alinari / Art Resource)*

Anjou. He painted altarpieces in San Gimignano, PISA, and Orvieto. The end of his career, from 1340 onward, was spent at the papal court in AVIGNON, where he met PETRARCH. He died in 1344.

See also GOTHIC ART AND ARCHITECTURE; PAINTING.

Further reading: Cecilia Jannell, *Simone Martini,* trans. Lisa Pelletti (Florence: Scala, 1989); Andrew Martindale, *Simone Martini: Complete Edition* (Oxford: Phaidon, 1988); Gordon Moran and Michael Mallory, *Guido Riccio: A Guide to the Controversy for Tourists, Scholars, Students, Art Librarians* (Florence: Edizioni Notizie d'Arte, 2000).

Mary, cult of (the Blessed Virgin) The cult devoted to the Virgin Mary, called the cult of *hyperdulia* in the Middle Ages, was based on the important role played by Mary in carrying out the incarnation enabling the redemption of humanity by Jesus Christ. She was frequently present in scenes and representations involving Christ and his divine and human characteristics. The Virgin became a narrative element leading to the central image of Christ. Mary was particularly honored above the saints. Her cult grew to consist of liturgical celebrations; feast days; manifestations of collective piety in her honor such as PILGRIMAGES and CONFRATERNITIES; and private invocation and homage personal and devotion. Ideas and doctrines about her perpetual VIRGINITY, her own immaculate conception free of original SIN, and the ASSUMPTION of her body into HEAVEN were discussed in the Middle Ages but only partially accepted. The ANNUNCIATION of her miraculous pregnancy with the future Christ was a common theme in medieval art. She was the great maternal mediator, intercessor, or advocate who could obtain answers to prayers from GOD. This was a much-promoted advocate and theme in liturgical activities, artistic representation, and pastoral care.

Further reading: Hilda C. Graef, *Mary: A History of Doctrine and Devotion* (New York: Sheed & Ward, 1964); Jaroslav Jan Pelikan, *Mary through the Centuries: Her Place in the History of Culture* (New Haven, Conn.: Yale University Press, 1996); George H. Tavard, *The Thousand Faces of the Virgin Mary* (Collegeville, Minn.: Liturgical Press, 1996).

Masaccio, Tomasso di Giovanni di Simone Cassai (Slovenly, Awkward, Bad-Tempered Tom) (1401–ca. 1428) *Florentine painter*
Tomasso was born at Castel San Giovanni near Arezzo on December 21, 1401. He moved to FLORENCE, where he was exposed to the art of BRUNELLESCHI and DONATELLO. Documented there from 1418 he entered the painters' guild on January 7, 1422. Masaccio's new poeticism was clear in one of his first works, a triptych with *Madonna and Saints* in the church of San Giovenale at Cascia in 1423. In 1424 he began working with Masolino (1383–ca. 1440) on their first collaborative effort, *Saint*

Masaccio's *Trinity with the Virgin, Saint John, and Two Donors* with a skeleton on tomb below, a fresco (1425), Santa Maria Novella, Florence, Italy *(Scala / Art Resource)*

Anne with Madonna and Child, now in the Uffizi Gallery in Florence. Between 1425 and 1427, Masaccio collaborated with Masolino on the decorations of the Brancacci Chapel in the church of the Carmine at Florence. Also from these years was the *Trinity* in the church of Santa Maria Novella at Florence. The latter image was inserted into an architectonic framework and with daring system of perspective in relation to a spectator whose eye was set at the height of the shelf on which knelt the two donors. Soon after completing this, he moved to ROME, where he died in 1428 at age 27, perhaps poisoned.

Further reading: James Beck, *Masaccio, the Documents* (Locust Valley, N.Y.: J. J. Augustin, 1978); Bruce Cole, *Masaccio and the Art of Early Renaissance Florence* (Bloomington: Indiana University Press, 1980); Paul Joannides, *Masaccio and Masolino: A Complete Catalogue* (London: Phaidon, 1993).

masons and masonry   Masons did the stonework or brickwork on building projects throughout the Middle Ages and some may have functioned as architects. Masons employed several types of instruments and tools. With a compass with mobile legs, they designed plans but also traced patterns for executing detailed designs on stone and drawing surfaces. Using such a simple device, they could measure, divide, and reproduce lengths and trace curves. A square was also used in tracing designs, as well as laying cut stones. Ropes were used for laying foundations, for verifying distances, for tracing curves and straight lines. Weighted cords served as plumb lines for verifying the directions and angles of elements along with levels. As stonecutters they used hammers and chisels of different types.

Masons also had measuring rods and wooden or metal templates corresponding to stone faces and moldings. For transporting materials, the workers had hand barrows and wheelbarrows from the 14th century. Shovels and trowels were used to mix and spread mortar, which was composed of lime and sand and transported in wooden buckets or troughs.

Further reading: Nicola Coldstream, *Masons and Sculptors* (Toronto: University of Toronto Press, 1991); John Harvey, *English Mediaeval Architects. A Biographical Dictionary Down to 1550: Including Master Masons, Carpenters, Carvers, Building Contractors and Others Responsible for Design* (Gloucester: A. Sutton, 1987); Douglas Knoop, *The Mediœval Mason: An Economic History of English Stone Building in the Later Middle Ages and Early*

Masons at work from *The Story of Alexander the Great,* by Quintus Curtius Rufus, illumination by Liedet, Loyset, or Louis (15th century), Bibliothèque Nationale, Paris *(Snark / Art Resource)*

Modern Times (Manchester: Manchester University Press, 1949).

Mass, liturgy of

Mass, liturgy of   Mass was the name used to designate the celebration of the Eucharist beginning in the fourth century and became usual in the fifth. It designated the recital of prayers, sending to GOD the prayers that the priest said at the ALTAR while celebrating the sacrament of the Eucharist. It was the central liturgical practice of Christianity during the Middle Ages. Pope GREGORY I THE GREAT established Mass in its later usual form; later changes related merely to details. He set the prayers to be offered, the doctrines to be promoted, and the music to accompany the commemoration of and actual reenactment of the Last Supper, when Christ turned the bread and wine into his body and blood. It was also a commemoration of Christ's sacrifice on the cross to redeem and make HEAVEN attainable for humankind.

The ritual had to convey this in a way comprehensible to the average Christian. It had to include gestures and activities to accomplish this, thus the paraphernalia and the impressive but distancing ceremony. It was usually conducted publicly or before an audience. Private masses by individual PRIESTS became common over the course of the Middle Ages, especially after the evolution of the idea of PURGATORY and hired intercession for the DEAD. The content of masses were linked with particular devotions and the liturgical year. Rules were established to encourage attendance and participation. Artistic representations concentrated on the role of the priest in bringing all this about. Only the priest could officiate and carry out Mass. He was necessary for the sacrament of the Eucharist and for effecting the real presence of Christ.

See also GREGORIAN CHANT; HYMNS, HYMNALS, AND HYMNOLOGY; LITURGICAL BOOKS; MISSAL; SEVEN SACRAMENTS; UTRAQUISTS.

Further reading: Adrian Fortescue, *The Mass: A Study of the Roman Liturgy* (London: Longmans, Green, 1917); Josef A. Jungmann, *The Mass: An Historical, Theological, and Pastoral Survey,* trans. Julian Fernandes and ed. Mary Ellen Evans (Collegeville, Minn.: Liturgical Press, 1976); Hans Lietzmann, *Mass and Lord's Supper: A Study in the History of the Liturgy,* trans. Dorothea H. G. Reeve (Leiden: E. J. Brill, 1979); Richard W. Pfaff, *Medieval Latin Liturgy: A Select Bibliography* (Toronto: University of Toronto Press, 1982), 18–25.

al-Masudi, Abul-Hasan Ali

al-Masudi, Abul-Hasan Ali (ca. 896–956) *historian, polymath*
Al-Masudi was born in BAGHDAD about 896, moved to SYRIA, and died in Egypt in 956. A SHIITE, he traveled extensively and wrote *The Meadows of Gold,* an important and famous topical history of early medieval ISLAM and the non-Islamic world. He was a good storyteller and included much useful knowledge for modern scholars.

Further reading: al-Masudi, *The Meadows of Gold: The Abbasids,* trans. and ed. Paul Lunde and Caroline Stone (London: Kegan Paul, 1989); Tarif Khalidi, *Islamic Historiography: The Histories of Masudi* (Albany: State University of New York Press, 1975); C. Pellat, "Al-Masudi, Abul-Hasan Ali b. al-Husayn," *Encyclopedia of Islam* 6.784–789; Ahmad M. H. Shboul, *Al-Masudi and His World: A Muslim Humanist and His Interest in Non-Muslims* (London: Ithaca Press, 1979).

matrimony

matrimony   *See* FAMILY AND KINSHIP; MARRIAGE.

Matthew Paris

Matthew Paris (ca. 1200–1259) *English Benedictine monk, chronicler*
Born about 1200, Matthew became a monk in 1217 at the BENEDICTINE abbey of Saint Alban's, among the most important in ENGLAND. Though a monk, he had access to information since Saint Alban's was an important center on the road north from LONDON. He was also personally present at several events, such as the marriage in 1236 of King HENRY III and Eleanor of Provence (1223–91) and a feast of Saint EDWARD THE CONFESSOR in 1247 at the palace near the Abbey of WESTMINSTER. In 1247 or 1248 Pope INNOCENT IV sent him to NORWAY to reform a monastery. He became the annalist for Saint Alban's in 1236.

His immense works survived in a fairly complete state. His *Chronica majora,* a universal chronicle begun in about 1240, was a revised continuation of a chronicle of one of his predecessors at Saint Alban's, Roger of Wendover (d. 1236). His historical work included a history of ENGLAND from 1066 to 1253 and two abridged histories. He also wrote a history of the abbots of Saint Alban's from 793 to 1255, a history of the founders of the monastery, and several saints' lives. Matthew was critical of his sources, a good storyteller with a taste for gossip and a strong conservative bent. Some of his colorful anecdotes, especially those about King JOHN, should not be taken too seriously. He was critical of the king and of taxation on the church and was jealous of the MENDICANT friars. He drew many interesting and enlightening heraldric devices, illustrations, and maps for these manuscripts. He died in 1259.

Further reading: Richard Vaughan, ed. and trans., *Chronicles of Matthew Paris: Monastic Life in the Thirteenth Century* (Gloucester: A. Sutton, 1984); Suzanne Lewis, *The Art of Matthew Paris in the Chronica Majora* (Berkeley: University of California Press, 1987); Richard Vaughan, *Matthew Paris* (Cambridge: Cambridge University Press, 1958).

Mecca (Makka)

Mecca (Makka)   Mecca is a pilgrimage city in the Hejaz in the western part of the Arabian Peninsula, which became the holiest site for Muslims. It was an important commercial and religious town even before the time of

MUHAMMAD because of its shrine of the KABA. That occupied an enclosed space or basin which rain-fed torrents often submerged. Not based on an oasis, it occupied an important spot halfway because of its reliable wells on the caravan routes between the Syrian and Palestinian north and the Yemeni south. It was central to the rise of ISLAM, the place where Muhammad began his preaching. Muslims are supposed to make a PILGRIMAGE there at least once during their life. A HAJJ was to take place during the second week of the last month of the Muslim year.

See also ISLAMIC CONQUESTS AND EARLY EMPIRE; MEDINA.

Further reading: Emel Esin, *Mecca, the Blessed; Madinah, the Radiant* (London: Elek Books, 1963); F. E. Peters, *Mecca* (Princeton, N.J.: Princeton University Press, 1994); W. Montgomery Watt, *Muhammad at Mecca* (Oxford: Clarendon Press, 1953); W. Montgomery Watt, A. J. Wensinck, C. E. Bosworth, and R. B. Winder, "Makka" in *Encyclopedia of Islam* 6:144–187.

Mechthild von Magdeburg (ca. 1207–ca. 1282/1301)
German Beguine

There are only bits of biographical information in Mechthild's book, *The Flowing Light of the Godhead*. Probably of noble origin, she was born about 1207 in a family in the diocese of Magdeburg, as was apparent in her style and local vocabulary. She seemed to have had a secular education marked by CHIVALRY and court life. She claimed that she was challenged at 12 years of age by VISIONS that changed her life. From then on she took little joy of things of this world, sensual pleasure, or mundane honors. In about 1230, she left her family and friends and moved to Magdeburg to lead a life of poverty and penitence. At the encouragement of her DOMINICAN confessor, she recorded her spiritual experiences in the VERNACULAR in six books. In 1260, at an advanced age, she moved in with the CISTERCIAN NUNS of Helfta and devoted herself to a spiritual life and study. She died at Helfta after 1282, much venerated. Mechthild was an exceptional figure among women mystics of the Middle Ages because of her independence as well as the beauty and vigor of her writing in German.

See also BEGUINES AND BEGHARDS; MYSTICISM, CHRISTIAN.

Further reading: Mechthild of Magdeburg, *Flowing Light of the Divinity,* trans. Christiane Mesch Galvani and ed. Susan Clark (New York: Garland, 1991); Frank Tobin, *Mechthild von Magdeburg: A Medieval Mystic in Modern Eyes* (Columbia, S.C.: Camden House, 1995); James C. Franklin, *Mystical Transformations: The Imagery of Liquids in the Work of Mechthild von Magdeburg* (Rutherford, N.J.: Fairleigh Dickinson University Press, 1978); Amy M. Hollywood, *The Soul as Virgin Wife: Mechthild of Magdeburg, Marguerite Porete, and Meister Eckhart* (Notre Dame, Ind.: University of Notre Dame Press, 1995); Bernard McGinn, ed., *Meister Eckhart and the Beguine Mystics:*

Hadewijch of Brabant, Mechthild of Magdeburg, and Marguerite Porete (New York: Continuum, 1994); Ulrike Wiethaus, *Ecstatic Transformation: Transpersonal Psychology in the Work of Mechthild of Magdeburg* (Syracuse, N.Y.: Syracuse University Press, 1996).

Medici family
The Medici family, resident in FLORENCE from 1216, was originally from the Mugello, an area north of the city of Florence. At the end of the 14th century, with the success of the banker Giovanni de Bicci (1360–1429), the Medici were among the richest Florentine families. Cosimo the Elder (1389–1464); his son, Piero (1416–69); and his grandson, Lorenzo the Magnificent (1449–92), consolidated the Medicis' supremacy in Florence. The Medici ruled the city in a precarious balance of power with the other families of the Florentine patriciate. They were chosen by Pope Martin V (r. 1417–31) as treasures of the papal treasury, a lucrative office that provided access to a wider political and diplomatic role.

POLITICS AND CULTURE

The cultural life of 15th-century Florence was shaped by the political power of the Medici and their court. Lorenzo the Magnificent was one of the foremost patrons of literature and culture, having perceived the importance of both as instruments of political propaganda. The Medici dominated Florence from the 1430s to the 1490s through a skillful manipulation of political traditions and office-holding. There was opposition to their domination, but their wealth and shrewd politics kept them in charge.

See also BANKS AND BANKING; TRADE AND COMMERCE.

Further reading: John Hale, *Florence and the Medici: The Pattern of Control* (London: Thames and Hudson, 1977); Dale Kent, *The Rise of the Medici: Faction in Florence, 1426–1434* (Oxford: Oxford University Press, 1978); Dale Kent, *Cosimo de' Medici and the Florentine Renaissance* (New Haven, Conn.: Yale University Press, 2000); Raymond de Roover, *The Rise and Decline of the Medici Bank, 1397–1494* (Cambridge, Mass.: Harvard University Press, 1963); Nicolai Rubinstein, *The Government of Florence under the Medici (1434 to 1494)* (Oxford: Clarendon Press, 1966).

medicine
Though the Middle Ages did not make and leave behind spectacular discoveries in medicine, important advances were made in the intellectual history of the discipline and in terms of professionalization and institutionalization. Arabic practices and ideas were an important influence and precedent.

The study of medicine in the Middle Ages was an extension of developments begun in classical times. In the West medical traditions, such as they were, were first based on the encyclopedic works of ISIDORE OF SEVILLE. In ISLAM the writings of Greek physicians, such as Hippocrates, were translated into Arabic. Greek, Arabic,

Persian, Indian, and Jewish sources on anatomy and diseases formed the basis of the study and development of the medieval medical sciences in Islam. In the 10th century Arabic physicians such as IBN SINA (Avicenna) and AL-RAZI synthesized the classical heritage with their own experience in their writings. By the 11th century these theoretical and practical achievements were known to the West, especially in southern ITALY.

VARIOUS ADVANCES

The practice of medicine, was a basic part of the daily activity in Western monasteries, involving simple surgical treatment and the healing of wounds. With the establishment of the medical school at Salerno, just south of NAPLES, in about 1030, medical science became a systematic field of study in the West. Treatises written in Arabic were translated into LATIN. Jewish physicians living in the West and trained in the study of anatomy contributed to medical knowledge in the 12th century. In the 13th century, medicine became part of the university curriculum in the West. After that, new trends of study based on an emphasis on experimentation over mere theory developed. Dissections on animals and human beings, though considered morally dubious, increased real knowledge of the human body. By the 14th century, dissections were part of the study program at medical schools in Italy and especially at MONTPELLIER. Developments in chemistry and other natural sciences advanced pharmaceutical remedies and prompted systematic research on the healing properties of plants and chemicals. A more popular, magical, and traditional medicine was practiced by HERMITS and village women. At the end of the Middle Ages, the church began to persecute those woman as witches.

According to the theories prevalent at that time, the human body was composed of the humors fire, earth, air, and water or hot, cold, dry, and wet. The doctor's role was to maintain or restore a balance among these primary qualities in the bones, nerves, flesh, vessels, membranes, and organs and the four liquid substances or humors in blood such as phlegm and bile. The preservation of health and the treatment of sickness relied on three types of therapy: dietetics, pharmacology, and surgery. Medieval medicine created and organized the medical profession. Charlatans and quacks were persecuted, although defining what might be inappropriate about their treatments was not always clear beyond their lack of university training.

See also ANATOMY; BOTANY; CONSTANTINE THE AFRICAN; GERARD OF CREMONA; HOSPITALS; PLAGUE; TROTA.

Further reading: Edward Kealey, *Medieval medicus: A Social History of Anglo-Norman Medicine* (Baltimore: Johns Hopkins University Press, 1981); Katharine Park, *Doctors and Medicine in Early Renaissance Florence* (Princeton, N.J.: Princeton University Press, 1985); Nancy Siraisi, *Avicenna in Renaissance Italy: The Canon and Medical Teaching in Italian Universities after 1500* (Princeton, N.J.: Princeton University Press, 1987); Nancy G. Siraisi, *Medieval and Early Renaissance Medicine: An Introduction to Knowledge and Practice* (Chicago: University of Chicago Press, 1990).

Medina (Medina al-Monawwara, Madinat al-Nabi, City of the Prophet)   One of the two most important cites for ISLAM, "Medina" means "the town." It had its origins in the ancient oasis of Yathrib. After the Hegira in 622 until his death in 632, MUHAMMAD found refuge in the town with a related clan after he had fled his hometown of MECCA, which had rejected his message. His partisans, called the "émigrés" or *al-muhajiran,* followed him. He achieved political recognition through his successful raids against the caravans of his old Meccan tribe. An intertribal confederation, the *umma* or "the rightly-guided group," took Mecca in 630, then controlled all western Arabia. After Muhammad's death, the town became the center of the first Muslim caliphate, which carried out great conquests before being swamped in intertribal war. It lost the position of Islamic capital to DAMASCUS, then al-Kufa, in the 660s.

See also ABU BAKR.

Further reading: W. Montgomery Watt, *Muhammad at Medina* (Oxford: Clarendon Press, 1956); W. Montgomery Watt and R. B. Winder, "Al-Medina" in *Encyclopedia of Islam* 5:994–1,007; Michael Lecker, *Muslims, Jews, and Pagans: Studies on Early Islamic Medina* (Leiden: E. J. Brill, 1995).

Mehmed II (Mehmet, Muhammad, the Conqueror) (r. 1444–1446, 1451–1481) *founder of the Ottoman Empire* Mehmed was the sultan between 1444 and 1446 and from 1451 to 1481. Born on March 30, 1432, at ADRIANOPLE, he was the fourth son of MURAD II and took the throne when his father abdicated in 1446. His first sultanate ended in chaos, and his father had to return to power. On his father's death in 1451, he had another chance and was one of the most successful Ottoman rulers. He carefully prepared for the capture of CONSTANTINOPLE, providing large cannons for military operations. The ensuing siege lasted from April 6 to May 29, 1453. After sacking the city, he declared HAGIA SOPHIA a MOSQUE. He extended the OTTOMAN EMPIRE into ANATOLIA, the Balkans, WALLACHIA, MOLDAVIA, and the Crimea. Tolerant of minorities, he encouraged learning, inviting Christians to his rebuilt capital, Constantinople. He also codified Ottoman law. He died, possibly poisoned, on May 3, 1481.

Further reading: Kritovoulos, *History of Mehmed the Conqueror,* trans. Charles T. Riggs (1954; reprint, Westport, Conn.: Greenwood Press, 1970); Franz Babinger, *Mehmed the Conqueror and His Time,* trans. Ralph Manheim (Princeton, N.J.: Princeton University Press, 1978); Halil Inalcik, *The Ottoman Empire: The Classical Age,*

Mehmed II the Conqueror, the sultan responsible for the conquest of Constantinople in 1453, Gentile Bellini (1429–1507), Oil on wood, National Gallery, London *(Erich Lessing / Art Resource)*

1300–1600, trans. Norman Itzkowitz and Colin Imber (London: Weidenfeld and Nicolson, 1973); Steven Runciman, *The Fall of Contantinople, 1453* (Cambridge: Cambridge University Press, 1965).

Meister Eckhart   *See* ECKHART, MEISTER.

Melfi, Constitutions of   *See* FREDERICK II; SICILY.

Memling, Hans (Memline) (ca. 1433/40–1494) *Flemish painter*

Hans Memling was born probably at Seligenstadt near Frankfurt between 1430 and 1440. After studying in COLOGNE, he worked in Roger van der WEYDEN's workshop in 1459 and 1460. On January 30, 1465, he acquired citizen's rights at BRUGES, where he was to pay some of the highest levels of taxes in the city and worked until his death on August 11, 1494. He worked mostly for wealthy merchants. Some of his early work was done for Italian patrons, including a *Last Judgment* for Angelo

at Trani in Sicily and a *Passion* for Tommaso Portinari. He made a number of fine portraits of burghers from Bruges. His art was eclectic, combining ideas and forms from different masters, and was known for its fine drawing and elegance of forms.

See also EYCK, HUBERT VAN, AND EYCK, JAN VAN.

Further reading: K. B. McFarlane, *Hans Memling,* ed. Edgar Wind (Oxford: Clarendon Press, 1971); Dirk de Vos, *Hans Memling: The Complete Works* (New York: Harry N. Abrams, 1994); Maximilian P. J. Martens, *Bruges and the Renaissance: Memling to Pourbus* (New York: Harry N. Abrams, 1998).

mendicant orders   A number of medieval religious orders formed in the 13th century were mendicant, that is, made up of monks who practiced a form of poverty that involved a whole community. In contrast to the old, rich, and stable monastic tradition, the mendicants initially renounced landed property and rents, to live only by the alms of the faithful and payments for pastoral care. Their role was primarily to preach to the LAITY and combat HERESY. They promoted devotion to MARY, the Blessed Virgin; the cult of the saints; a higher standard of clerical education; and sacramental participation by the laity. Their legal definition, long contested by the traditionalists, had to wait until 1274 and the Second Council of Lyon, which also forbade the formation of any new religious orders devoted to mendicancy.

Their rise was linked to the development and proliferation of urban life and a more elaborate money economy. They had to be able to beg among concentrations of people who had liquid wealth. The appearance of the mendicant orders was also a response to criticism leveled at the church for its excessive accumulation of wealth in the 12th century. Their ideas about the imitation of Christ or the apostolic life were based on a perceived Christian indifference to the material world. They were very popular with the laity who gave them large quantities of money to build churches in cities. The other CLERGY did not welcome their draining income from the parish and secular clergy. This rivalry extended to universities and Scholastic thought.

These orders all went through various reform movements throughout the later Middle Ages. The PAPACY tended to favor mendicants, since they were supposed to be independent of the diocesan system and the episcopacy and more likely to further the interests of a pope and to enforce orthodoxy against heretical ideas. On occasion, however, the mendicant ideals of clerical poverty clashed with papal ambitions.

See also AUGUSTINIAN (AUSTIN) FRIARS OR HERMITS; CARMELITES; DOMINICAN ORDER; FRANCIS OF ASSISI, SAINT; FRANCISCAN ORDER; MONASTICISM; SPIRITUAL FRANCISCANS.

Further reading: Louis Duval-Arnould. "Mendicants and Seculars, Quarrel of," *EMA,* 2.939; Richard Emery,

The Friars in Medieval France: A Catalogue of French Mendicant Convents, 1200–1550 (New York: Columbia University Press, 1962); Herbert Grundmann, *Religious Movements in the Middle Ages: The Historical Links between Heresy, the Mendicant Orders, and the Women's Religious Movement in the Twelfth and Thirteenth Century, with the Historical Foundations of German Mysticism,* trans. Steven Rowan (Notre Dame, Ind.: University of Notre Dame Press, 1995); C. H. Lawrence, *The Friars: The Impact of the Early Mendicant Movement on Western Society* (London: Longman, 1994).

menorah   The menorah is a seven-branched candelabrum, the most common symbol of JUDAISM. It was the ancestor of the sanctuary light used by Christianity to indicate the presence of Christ in the tabernacle. It was based on the seven-branched candlestick or lamp described in the Old Testament or Hebrew BIBLE in Exodus 25:31–38.

See also JEWS AND JUDAISM.

Further reading: Joseph Gutmann, *Jewish Ceremonial Art* (New York: T. Yoseloff, 1964); Joseph Gutmann, *Hebrew Manuscript Painting* (London: Chatto and Windus, 1979).

mercenaries   *See* CONDOTTIERI, COMPANIES, AND MERCENARIES.

merchants   Merchants, those in the business of buying and selling, in the Middle Ages were considered a suspicious group who engaged in questionable activities. Canonical legislation forbade USURY. Profiting from any kind of monetary transaction was also suspicious. Only a just price for a service or commodity was licit. Despite this, commercial activities did not stop during the Middle Ages. Theologians rationalized ways of making such activities less sinful by not questioning the creative commercial techniques employed by merchants to cover their collection of interest. It should be remembered that many practices in the late medieval church were also illicit but widespread, such as SIMONY and the promotion of clerics based on their kinship ties (nepotism).

COMMERCIAL REVOLUTION

There was a veritable commercial revolution in the 12th and 13th centuries. Merchants became ubiquitous in medieval society, especially in the cities, doing business at the local as well as international level. Alongside these merchants was the great merchant, who controlled capital and was often the confidential agent of kings, popes, or princes. The popes especially needed BANKS and merchants to assist them in moving the greatly expanding income of the Holy See in the 13th century.

COMPANIES

Powerful companies arose. Their capital was based on family assets and the deposits of clients in search of lucrative profits, especially at the inland Italian cities of Piacenza, SIENA, LUCCA, and FLORENCE. Merchant bankers circulated money and merchandise. They established branches with representatives in all the great commercial localities of the time. They often combined commercial traffic, banking activities, and industrial enterprise, especially in wool and cloth. The earlier companies all failed around 1300. New ones arose that managed risk better by avoiding loans to monarchs and investing in a wider variety of activities. They also improved their accounting methods, in particular double-entry, which made easily accessible the statistics on exactly where and how their business was going. These newer techniques decreased their required mobility while maintaining their knowledge and control. As a group, merchants often left the profession to return to the land and marry into more noble social classes.

See also BANKS AND BANKING; BRUGES; COEUR, JACQUES; DATINI, FRANCESCO; ECONOMIC THOUGHT AND JUSTICE; HANSEATIC LEAGUE; MEDICI FAMILY; NOBILITY AND NOBLES; SOCIAL STATUS AND STRUCTURE.

Further reading: Robert S. Lopez and Irving W. Raymond, eds., *Medieval Trade in the Mediterranean World: Illustrative Documents with Introductions and Notes* (New York: Columbia University Press, 1955); James Masschaele, *Peasants, Merchants, and Markets: Inland Trade in Medieval England, 1150–1350* (New York: St. Martin's Press, 1997); Timothy O'Neill, *Merchants and Mariners in Medieval Ireland* (Dublin: Irish Academic Press, 1987); Armando Sapori, *The Italian Merchant in the Middle Ages,* trans. Patricia Ann Kennen (New York: W. W. Norton, 1970); Peter Spufford, *Power and Profit: The Merchant in Medieval Europe* (London: Thames & Hudson, 2002).

Merinids (Marinids, Banu Marin)   The Merinids were a BERBER dynasty who reigned over the far al-MAGHRIB or MOROCCO from the mid-13th to the mid-15th century, having divided up the territory of the ALMOHADS with the HAFSIDS of Tunisia. The Merinid state pursued an ambition to unify al-Maghrib and for a while subjugated the sultanate of Tlemcen and the Hafsid sultanate of TUNIS. They dreamed of taking back the lands that the Muslims had earlier lost in SPAIN but were defeated in a battle in 1340 and never again tried to interfere in Iberia again. Instead, they settled at FEZ, built a new town (Fas al-Jadid), and made it the capital of a kingdom that became prosperous through their partial control of the Sudanese gold route.

From the late 14th century, however their difficulties increased. Their dynastic instability was exploited by ambitions court officials, leading to internal civil wars. The Portuguese captured the town of Ceuta in 1415 and sought possession of the trade in Sudanese gold. A branch of the dynasty, the Wattasids, attempted to restore the dynasty's fortunes, but they were only partially successful. The last Merinid was removed in 1465 in a popular revolt, with branches emerging into the 16th century.

See also IDRISIDS; MALI; MARRAKECH.

Further reading: Clifford Edmund Bosworth, *The Islamic Dynasties* (Edinburgh: Edinburgh University Press, 1967), 32–34; Michael Brett and Werner Forman, *The Moors: Islam in the West* (London: Orbis, 1980); Jamil Abun-Nasr, *A History of the Maghrib in the Islamic Period* (Cambridge: Cambridge University Press, 1987).

Merovingian dynasty   With the accession of CLOVIS in 481 or 482, the Merovingian dynasty took control of Francia or Gaul, ruling there until 751, when the last king of the dynasty, Childeric II (r. 743–751), was deposed by PÉPIN III THE SHORT with the help of the PAPACY.

Clovis became king at age 15 in succession to his father, Childeric I (d. 481/482), the son of the almost legendary Merovech (r. 448–457), the source for the name Merovingians. Childeric and his FRANKS settled between the Somme and the Scheldt, cultivating their ties with ROME. In his reign of 30 years, Clovis conquered the greater part of Gaul, from FRISIA to the Pyrenees mountains in the south, from the Atlantic to the Rhine River in the east. He defeated the Alamanni in 496 near COLOGNE and the VISIGOTHS in 506. He made PARIS his capital; converted to Catholicism, the religion of his wife, Clotilda (ca. 470–545); and made an alliance of the Franks with the papacy.

The history of the Merovingians was frequently determined by the legal necessity to divide succession among whatever numbers of sons were produced. The unity of the kingdom was rarely maintained, under Clotaire I from 558 to 561 and, more lastingly, from 613 to 639 under Clothar II (r. 613–629) and his son, Dagobert I (r. 629–639). The mayors of the PALACE held real power. By 662, the Pepinids occupied the mayoralty of the palace in Austrasia and later NEUSTRIA.

These Frankish leaders were and had to be war leaders; and a taste for conquest never disappeared. The Merovingians were the almost magical "long-haired kings," the purveyors of lands and the guarantors of peace. They had to vanquish the enemy and procure good harvests. If they failed, they were deposed. Their conversion under Clovis to Christianity was helpful to them, in that they acquired the support of the church, which they generally respected and enriched. With PRAYERS and episcopal advisers, the church called down divine favors on the dynasty. Other forms of power rested on interpersonal relations. Lords swore an oath to the king and pledged to support him, and thus this warrior people was directly and personally linked to a leader.

See also CAROLINGIAN DYNASTY; GREGORY OF TOURS.

Further reading: Gregory of Tours, *History of the Franks,* trans. Ernest Brehaut (1916; reprint, New York,

Octagon Books, 1965); Peter Lasko, *Ars Sacra, 800–1200,* 2nd ed. (New Haven, Conn.: Yale University Press, 1994); J. M. Wallace-Hadrill, *Merovingian Military Organization, 481–751* (Minneapolis, University of Minnesota Press, 1972); Paul Fouracre and Richard A. Gerberding, trans. and eds., *Late Merovingian France: History and Hagiography, 640–720* (Manchester: Manchester University Press, 1996); Yitzhak Hen, *Culture and Religion in Merovingian Gaul,* A.D. *481–751* (Leiden: E. J. Brill, 1995); Ian N. Wood, *The Merovingian Kingdoms, 450–751* (London: Longman, 1994).

metalsmiths and metal work, metallurgy   Medieval metalsmiths worked with several metals, including iron, gold, and silver. At that time, western Europe did not possess the same mineral resources as had the Roman Empire as a whole. It was rich in iron, particularly in the regions of central and northern Europe. But it had lost ready access to the important mineral deposits of the Muslim-controlled Iberian Peninsula. Metals from elsewhere also were controlled by Muslims and were not easily obtained.

Iron was widely used in daily life and was diffused throughout continental Europe in the early Middle Ages. It was less frequent in the south or Mediterranean world, where nonferrous metals such as copper, tin, and their alloys remained common in daily life until the mid-14th century. Iron was commonly used and part of a considerable TRADE from the regions of production such as the BASQUE provinces in northern Iberia and LOMBARDY in northern Italy. The mining of iron did not require great investment, and its production was common. Abundance

A bellows for metalworking at the abbey of Fontenay in Burgundy *(Courtesy Edward English)*

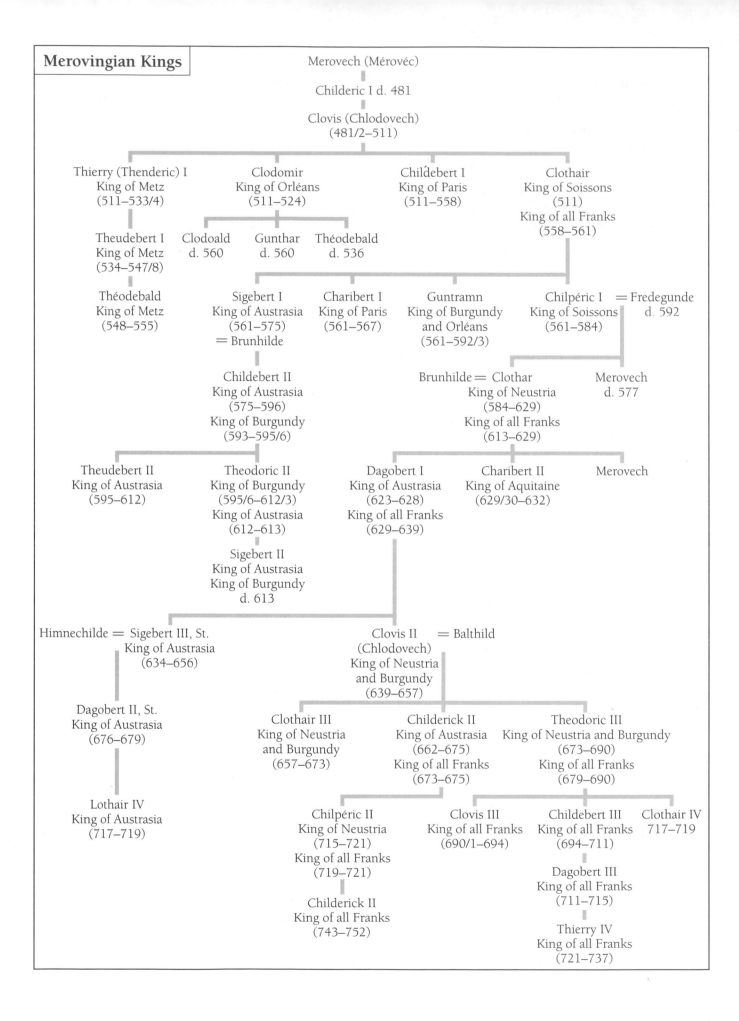

Merovingian Kings

Merovech (Mérovéc)

Childeric I d. 481

Clovis (Chlodovech)
(481/2–511)

Thierry (Thenderic) I
King of Metz
(511–533/4)

Clodomir
King of Orléans
(511–524)

Childebert I
King of Paris
(511–558)

Clothair
King of Soissons
(511)
King of all Franks
(558–561)

Theudebert I
King of Metz
(534–547/8)

Clodoald
d. 560

Gunthar
d. 560

Théodebald
d. 536

Théodebald
King of Metz
(548–555)

Sigebert I
King of Austrasia
(561–575)
= Brunhilde

Charibert I
King of Paris
(561–567)

Guntramn
King of Burgundy
and Orléans
(561–592/3)

Chilpéric I = Fredegunde
King of Soissons   d. 592
(561–584)

Childebert II
King of Austrasia
(575–596)
King of Burgundy
(593–595/6)

Brunhilde = Clothar
King of Neustria
(584–629)
King of all Franks
(613–629)

Merovech
d. 577

Theudebert II
King of Austrasia
(595–612)

Theodoric II
King of Burgundy
(595/6–612/3)
King of Austrasia
(612–613)

Dagobert I
King of Austrasia
(623–628)
King of all Franks
(629–639)

Charibert II
King of Aquitaine
(629/30–632)

Merovech

Sigebert II
King of Austrasia
King of Burgundy
d. 613

Himnechilde = Sigebert III, St.
King of Austrasia
(634–656)

Clovis II = Balthild
(Chlodovech)
King of Neustria
and Burgundy
(639–657)

Dagobert II, St.
King of Austrasia
(676–679)

Clothair III
King of Neustria
and Burgundy
(657–673)

Childerick II
King of Austrasia
(662–675)
King of all Franks
(673–675)

Theodoric III
King of Neustria and Burgundy
(673–690)
King of all Franks
(679–690)

Lothair IV
King of Austrasia
(717–719)

Chilpéric II
King of Neustria
(715–721)
King of all Franks
(719–721)

Clovis III
King of all Franks
(690/1–694)

Childebert III
King of all Franks
(694–711)

Clothair IV
717–719

Childerick II
King of all Franks
(743–752)

Dagobert III
King of all Franks
(711–715)

Thierry IV
King of all Franks
(721–737)

of fuel or proximity of water transport played an essential role in promoting sites of production. By the 14th century, the quality of steel was much improved.

The need for silver was particularly pressing at a time when the European continent had to secure the greater part of its supplies of this monetary metal internally. There was early development of innovative techniques at these metal production sites, not only for the technical aspects of operation but also for the legal and economic management of the works. There were silver mining operations at Trent, LANGUEDOC, Massa Marittima in TUSCANY, and Iglau in BOHEMIA. Essential for the production of sound coinage, these sites attracted enormous investments that generated considerable fortunes. There was a mining boom in the 15th century, particularly in central Europe, and hardly any continental country remained uninvolved. The boom was favored by a series of technical innovations and encouraged by the demand for metal for coinage.

See also COINAGE AND CURRENCY; GOLD TRADE AND GOLD WORKING; WEAPONS AND WEAPONRY.

Further reading: Theophilius, *The Various Arts, De diversis artibus,* ed. and trans. C. R. Dodwell (Oxford: Clarendon Press, 1986); Leslie Aitchison, *A History of Metals* (New York: Interscience, 1960); Janet Backhouse and Leslie Webster, eds., *The Making of England: Anglo-Saxon Art and Culture,* A.D. *600–900* (Toronto: University of Toronto Press, 1991).

Methodios *See* CYRIL AND METHODIOS.

Michael Scot (before 1200–d. ca. 1253) *astrologer, translator*
Born in SCOTLAND in the late 12th century, Michael was educated in ENGLAND and SPAIN, where he studied Arabic. There he became acquainted with the Aristotelian treatises on astronomy. In 1223 he traveled to ITALY and served in the papal court. There he won the favor of Pope GREGORY IX, who recommended him unsuccessfully for the archbishopric of CANTERBURY. Moving to PISA, he became interested in mathematics. Michael eventually joined the court of the emperor FREDERICK II and was appointed, according to a tradition, as the emperor's astrologer. Besides translating from Arabic and Hebrew, Michael did a study of volcanic activity on the Lipari Islands. Roger BACON and ALBERTUS MAGNUS regarded him as a charlatan. He died about 1253.

See also ASTROLOGY.

Further reading: J. Ward Brown, *An Enquiry into the Life and Legend of Michael Scot* (Edinburgh: D. Douglas, 1897); Charles Homer Haskins, *The Renaissance of the Twelfth Century* (1927; reprint, New York: Meridian, 1957); Lynn Thorndike, *History of Magic and Experimental Science.* Vol. 2, *The First Thirteen Centuries of Our Era* (New York: Columbia University Press, 1925), 2.307–337; Lynn Thorndike, *Michael Scot* (London: Nelson, 1965).

Middle Ages, concept of The expression "Middle Ages" was based on the belittling concept of a middle age between the glories of antiquity and modern times, or initially the late 14th and early 15th centuries. It acquired this name among Italian humanists, such as PETRARCH, who sought to rediscover classical antiquity in all its purity and authenticity and to eliminate the later GOTHIC frivolous elaborations. Later scholars from the 17th century onward readily adopted this terminology and concept. In the early 19th century, the romantic movement formed a more positive conception of the Middle Ages, emphasizing genuine cultural innovations and accomplishments, and perpetuated the idea, adding to this the concept of the rebirth of culture in a RENAISSANCE of the 15th and 16th centuries. *Middle Ages* was also a judgmental term that was widely adopted because of a need to break up the past into comprehensible chronological periods.

Further reading: David C. Douglas, *English Scholars, 1600–1730,* 2d ed. (London: Eyre and Spottiswoode, 1951); Wallace K. Ferguson, *The Renaissance in Historical Thought: Five Centuries of Interpretation* (Boston: Houghton Mifflin, 1948); Barbara G. Keller, *The Middle Ages Reconsidered: Attitudes in France from the Eighteenth Century through the Romantic Movement* (New York: P. Lang, 1994); Donald R. Kelley, *History and the Disciplines: The Reclassification of Knowledge in Early Modern Europe* (Rochester, N.Y.: University of Rochester Press, 1997); Donald R. Kelley, ed., *Versions of History from Antiquity to the Enlightenment* (New Haven, Conn.: Yale University Press, 1991).

Midrash *See* BIBLE; JEWS AND JUDAISM.

Milan (Milano) Milan is a city in the Po Valley in northern Italy in LOMBARDY whose position made it the natural center of a network of communication routes by land, lake, and river between the Adriatic and Tyrrhenian Seas and between the Po Valley and the transalpine provinces. From 290 to 291, after the reorganization of the empire under DIOCLETIAN, Milan, along with its status as the seat of a vicariate, became the center of the government of the West and the site where the edict of toleration of Christianity was issued by CONSTANTINE and Licinius (ca. 250–324) in 313. Milan further became a religious capital, especially during the episcopate of AMBROSE, who firmly opposed any secular political interference in the religious sphere and exercised undisputed preeminence over nearly all the other churches of northern ITALY.

CRISIS AND DECLINE

In 402, after an incursion of ALARIC'S VISIGOTHS into Italy, the seat of the imperial court was moved to the more easily defendable RAVENNA. This led to a period of

Milan Cathedral (Duomo), began 1380 *(Courtesy Library of Congress)*

decline. A recovery, already evident by the end of the LOMBARD kingdom in the social and economic sphere, became more evident in the eighth century. This revival was especially tied to the activity of the bishops, who were among the most powerful in Italy, gaining political power to add to the economic power derived from their vast temporal possessions.

The archbishop's long dominance of the life of the city suffered a crisis in 1057, when political and religious struggle caused by the powerful Patarine dissent movement. The movement was opposed to SIMONY, the lack of clerical discipline, and to church and papal reform that originated in ROME, the later GREGORIAN REFORM.

THE LOMBARD LEAGUE; FAMILY RULE

In the first half of the 12th century, a COMMUNE assumed responsibility for government and the economic and political interests of the urban community. In the mid-12th century, this led some cities of northern Italy to ask the emperor FREDERICK I BARBAROSSA for help against expansionist Milan. In the ensuing wars, Milan was nearly permanently destroyed. In 1167 the city became part of the LOMBARD LEAGUE, a close alliance of Lombard communes. It gained increasing prominence within the league, especially after its victory at the Battle of LEGNANO in 1176 and the peace of Constance in 1183. Milan then acquired a dominant position in Lombardy.

Internal conflicts continued, in particular resulting from the wars against the emperor FREDERICK II and his allies. The struggle was at first between a popular party, under the leadership of the Della Torre family and the nobles. Later it was between the VISCONTI and Torriani families. The Visconti finally won and consolidated government in Milan and around their family. Giangaleazzo Visconti (r. 1378–1402), who obtained the title of duke in 1395, tried to expand his power well beyond northern Italy but died suddenly in 1402 on campaign on the verge of success over FLORENCE.

The death of Filippo Maria Visconti (r. 1412–47) in 1447 without male heirs opened another dynastic crisis. After a short-lived republic (1447–50), Francesco SFORZA (1401–66), the son-in-law of the deceased duke, took power and obtained recognition of his ducal title. The Sforza produced a period of peace and prosperity in most of the last half of the 15th century. Sforza rule ended in the last years of the 15th century, as Milan fell under French influence in the 1490s.

Further reading: C. M. Ady, *A History of Milan under the Sforza* (London: Methuen, 1907); Annamaria Ambrosioni, "Milan," *EMA* 2.950–952; E. R. Chamberlin, *The Count of Virtue: Giangaleazzo Visconti, Duke of Milan* (1965; reprint, New York: Scribner, 1966); Richard Krautheimer, *Three Christian Capitals: Topography and Politics* (Berkeley: University of California Press, 1983); Gary Ianziti, *Humanistic Historiography under the Sforzas: Politics and Propaganda in Fifteenth-Century Milan* (Oxford: Clarendon Press, 1988); Gregory Lubkin, *A Renaissance Court: Milan under Galeazzo Maria Sforza* (Berkeley: University of California Press, 1994); Evelyn S. Welch, *Art and Authority in Renaissance Milan* (New Haven, Conn.: Yale University Press, 1995).

military orders The principal military and religious orders were the HOSPITALLERS and TEMPLARS. The movements of the PEACE AND TRUCE OF GOD had striven to restrain and channel the violence of KNIGHTS. When at CLERMONT in 1095 Pope URBAN II preached the First Crusade to deliver JERUSALEM, he assigned value to the function of the warrior class. The success of the First Crusade created a need to defend the conquests made in PALESTINE and SYRIA. The military orders were then founded in the 12th century, as a regular force of knights stationed there to defend the Latin Kingdom of Jerusalem and the other new states. The Templars and the Hospitallers were the principal orders in the Levant or eastern Mediterranean. Others would follow in Iberia and in northern Europe.

In an attempt to reconcile military life with religious life, the rulers of the new orders were inspired by the Rule of Saint BENEDICT, which they adapted, but also by that of AUGUSTINE. Independent of the local bishops and other authorities, they became almost states within states and subject only to the PAPACY. They accepted free adults, who were required to take the three vows, of obedience, CHASTITY, and POVERTY. In continental Europe, the orders created incomes to pay for the brothers' great expenses in the East.

In the Holy Land the orders soon provided more than half the manpower of the Latin armies, and in the 13th century they held most of the fortresses. They bore a great deal of the blame for the ultimate collapse of the Christian states. The orders were more successful in the reconquest in SPAIN and along the Baltic Sea. They mostly disappeared in the 16th century, except the Hospitallers, who remained in the Mediterranean far longer. Successor orders are tied to the papacy to this day.

See also ALCÁNTARA, ORDER OF; CALATRAVA, ORDER OF; CRUSADES; JAMES OF MILAN; PHILIP IV THE FAIR, KING OF FRANCE; TEUTONIC KNIGHTS, ORDER OF.

Further reading: Malcolm Barber, ed., *The Military Orders: Fighting for the Faith and Caring for the Sick* (Aldershot: Variorum, 1994); Alan Forey, *The Military Orders from the Twelfth to the Early Fourteenth Centuries* (Toronto: University of Toronto Press, 1992); Alan Forey, *Military Orders and Crusades* (Brookfield: Variorum, 1993); Helen Nicholson, *Templars, Hospitallers, and Teutonic Knights: Images of the Military Orders, 1128–1291* (Leicester: Leicester University Press, 1993); Helen Nicholson, *Love, War and the Grail* (Leiden: Brill, 2001).

millenarianism, Christian There has always been an idea in Christianity that the end of the world was near and people should prepare for it, if not hasten it. The just would receive their rewards and the evil, their punishments.

In his *City of God,* AUGUSTINE of Hippo rejected the expectation of an imminent end of the world based on the text of the biblical book of the Apocalypse. According to Augustine, Christ's final kingdom coincided with the history of the church. Influential Western authors, such as ISIDORE OF SEVILLE, BEDE, RUPERT OF DEUTZ, OTTO OF FREISING, and HILDEGARD OF BINGEN, followed Augustine's line of thought. In the Eastern Orthodox Empire, the prophet Daniel's vision of four successive kingdoms assisted the spread of millenarian expectations tied to succession to the imperial throne.

There was some concept of the end of the world around the year 1000, but few really expected it. It was always a good preaching and pastoral strategy to imply that it could happen any time. The good Christian should always be ready. At the turn of the 12th century, the Calabrian theologian JOACHIM OF FIORE formulated an original theology of historical development, in which the whole history of humankind was subdivided into three stages, each related to a person of the Trinity. The third and last, the reign of the Holy Spirit, was to begin in the 13th century. However, such millenarianism was strongly rejected by Thomas AQUINAS, who linked it to HERESY. These expectations remained present within dissident fringes and heterodox groups such as the SPIRITUAL FRANCISCANS and the Hussite movement in BOHEMIA, some of whom even announced the end of the world for February 10–14, 1420.

Throughout the later Middle Ages, many dissident groups expected the end of the world and looked for judgments by God on their religious and social oppressors.

See also ANTICHRIST; HUS, JOHN; TABORITES.

Further reading: Bernard McGinn, ed., *Visions of the End: Apocalyptic Traditions in the Middle Ages* (1979;

reprint, New York: Columbia University Press, 1998); Paul J. Alexander, *The Byzantine Apocalyptic Tradition* (Berkeley: University of California Press, 1985); Norman Cohn, *The Pursuit of the Millennium: Revolutionary Millenarians and Mystical Anarchists of the Middle Ages* (New York: Oxford University Press, 1970).

Further reading: Richard Holt, *The Mills of Medieval England* (Oxford: B. Blackwell, 1988); Edward J. Kealey, *Harvesting the Air: Windmill Pioneers in Twelfth-Century England* (Berkeley: University of California Press, 1987); Lynn White, Jr., *Medieval Technology and Social Change* (Oxford: Clarendon Press, 1962).

mills, wind and water The first machines, mills and presses, were built to mill grain and to press olives and grapes. They were common in the ancient world and became more so with the decline of slavery. They used human, water, wind, and animal power. Because they were expensive to build and maintain, peasants often had to depend on and pay their lords for access to these necessary agricultural machines. Lords soon sought to reserve for themselves monopolies for access to these indispensable tools, charging customary taxes or labor dues. Over the Middle Ages, mills grew in complexity and efficiency. Some were used in industrial activities, for manufacturing cloth or metal products. Windmills were limited to the grinding of cereals and were wide spread from the 13th century.

See also BAN; MANORS AND MANORIAL LORDSHIP.

minaret The minaret is a towerlike structure that is a recognizable sign of a Muslim presence in terms of MOSQUES for PRAYER. Introduced by the ABBASIDS to signify their power, they did not take on a monumental aspect before the ninth century, when the Great Mosque of AL-QAYRAWAN was built. Never universal, the form varied throughout the Islamic world. Some dynasties did not build them. The immense minaret with spiral ramp at Samarra in IRAQ was built some years later in 848. In Western ISLAM, the minarets of SEVILLE, the Giralda, and at MARRAKECH, the Kutubiya, had square bases and graceful proportions. As well, these examples had decorative panels covered with tracery, sometimes set off by squares of colors. In the Middle East and Asia, several great minarets with circular or star-shaped plans were remarkable for their monumental appearance, outstanding

The remains of a Muslim watermill on the Guadalquivir River in Córdoba in Spain *(Courtesy Edward English)*

The minaret of the Holy Mosque of Medina, built in 1483, beside the green cupola over the Prophet's grave, built in 1840 *(Courtesy Library of Congress)*

among them the minaret at BUKHARA from 1127, and that of Jam in Afghanistan from about 1180.

See also ART AND ARCHITECTURE, ISLAMIC; ISLAM; MINBAR; MOSQUE.

Further reading: Jonathan Bloom, *Minaret, Symbol of Islam* (Oxford: Board of the Faculty of Oriental Studies, University of Oxford, 1989); Robert Hillenbrand, *Islamic Architecture: Form, Function, and Meaning* (New York: Columbia University Press, 1994), 129–171.

minbar (mimbar) The minbar was a type of pulpit usually found in MOSQUES from which PRAYERS, speeches, and religious guidance were given. The minbar was situated to the right of the mihrab, the niche indicating the correct direction for prayer, and consisted of a raised platform reached by a set of steps, often a door at the entrance to the steps, and a dome or canopy above the platform.

The minbar was one of the earliest architectural features identified with Islamic architecture for mosques. In 629 MUHAMMAD supposedly used a minbar from which he preached. At that time the minbar consisted of two steps and a seat resembling a throne. After the death of the Prophet, the minbar was used by caliphs and governors as a symbol of authority. In 750 all the mosques of EGYPT were to be provided with minbars. This process was repeated in other Islamic lands so that by the beginning of the Abbasid period its function as a pulpit was universally established.

Most minbars were made of wood and highly decorated; those made of stone or brick tended to be simpler and were often a bare platform reached by three to five steps. In the FATIMID period minbars were built with a door at the entrance to the stairway and a domed canopy above the platform. The Friday sermon was delivered from them.

See also ART AND ARCHITECTURE, ISLAMIC; FRIDAY PRAYER.

Further reading: Robert Hillenbrand, *Islamic Art and Architecture* (New York: Thames and Hudson, 1999); Robert Irwin, *Islamic Art in Context: Art, Architecture, and the Literary World* (New York: Harry N. Abrams, 1997).

mines and mining *See* METALSMITHS AND METAL WORK, METALLURGY.

ministerials Ministerials were persons who exercised a function, an office, or a TRADE. They made up the household that surrounded a ruler or an important institution, especially in the area of the HOLY ROMAN EMPIRE in the central Middle Ages. These individuals were needed to exercise control. They usually emerged from a servile class and gained status and opportunity because of their capacity to fill an office. They were ultimately distinguished from the usual servants of the Crown and called *ministeriales*. Indispensable for government, they soon extracted the right to transmit inheritances and marry at their own discretion. They demanded more freedoms and did not hesitate to rebel to get them. They took places in a feudal system, received FIEFS, became lords, had KNIGHTS under their orders, and held CASTLES. They then took on the status of nobles in the thirteenth century. By the end of the Middle Ages, the ministeriality had formed a social group of knights.

See also NOBILITY AND NOBLES; SOCIAL STATUS AND STRUCTURE.

Further reading: John B. Freed, *The Counts of Falkenstein: Noble Self-Consciousness in Twelfth-Century Germany* (Philadelphia: American Philosophical Society, 1984); John B. Freed, *Noble Bondsmen: Ministerial Marriages in the Archdiocese of Salzburg, 1100–1343* (Ithaca, N.Y.: Cornell University Press, 1995); Timothy Reuter, ed., *The Medieval Nobility: Studies on the Ruling Classes of*

France and Germany from the Sixth to the Twelfth Century (Amsterdam: North-Holland, 1979).

mints *See* MONEY AND MINTS.

miracle plays *See* MYSTERY AND MIRACLE PLAYS.

miracles and collections of miracles Miracles were believed to be of divine origin and contrary to the laws of nature. Jesus Christ himself worked many miracles. Faced with the difficulties of life in the Middle Ages, people often invoked divine aid through the intermediary of the saints, in their roles as intercessors between human beings and GOD. Certain living holy men, and to a far lesser extent holy women, were held to be endowed with magical or miraculous powers, including the gift of healing, clairvoyance, and ensuring protection.

It was mainly after DEATH, through the intermediary of their RELICS, that the saints worked miracles. Healings were the most frequent miracles, but miracles involving the deliverance of prisoners, preservations from various dangers, and other favorable interventions such as recovery of lost objects or multiplication of food or drink were considered common enough. Some saints were much more effective in these events and their cult grew accordingly. Miracles of a more negative or revenging nature could also occur when God or his saints were insulted or not respected adequately. The saints could even play jokes of a cautionary or warning kind. The lives of saints and hagiographical traditions demanded and emphasized miracles as proof of holiness. Saints had to be careful, however, in dispensing the miraculous. God was considered their actual source. Saints were not empowered to perform MAGIC. There was also the possibility that the DEVIL or Satan might act in the world and perform miracles for his own nefarious ends.

For the Orthodox Church, every sign of God's direct or indirect intervention was considered a miracle. Unusual events could be logical responses of God to the impiety or the credulous faith of the believer. The miraculous is nothing but a revelation of the supernatural always present to those who deserve it. For the Orthodox, the miracle was a sign of sanctity, a mark of a divine choice rather than divine intervention.

See also HAGIOGRAPHY.

Further reading: Benedicta Ward, *Miracles and the Medieval Mind: Theory, Record, and Event, 1000–1215* (Philadelphia: University of Pennsylvania Press, 1982); Carolyn L. Connor, *Art and Miracles in Medieval Byzantium: The Crypt at Hosios Loukas and Its Frescoes* (Princeton, N.J.: Princeton University Press, 1991); Ronald F. Finucane, *Miracles and Pilgrims: Popular Beliefs in Medieval England* (London: J. M. Dent, 1977); William D. McCready, *Signs of Sanctity: Miracles in the Thought of Gregory the Great* (Toronto: Pontifical Institute of Mediaeval Studies, 1989); Raymond Van Dam, *Saints and Their Miracles in Late Antique Gaul* (Princeton, N.J.: Princeton University Press, 1993).

Mirandola, Giovanni Pico della (1463–1494) *Italian Neoplatonic philosopher*
Pico was born in 1463, the son of the prince of Mirandola, near FERRARA. Unlike other Florentine Platonists he was primarily interested in a synthesis of Christian THEOLOGY and diverse philosophies, including Jewish Kabbalism and the Arabic doctrines of IBN RUSHD or Averroës. He was a friend of Marsilio FICINO. In 1486, he defended the conclusions of certain suspect philosophers; but some of these theses were later condemned by the PAPACY and he had to flee to FRANCE. His interest in the Jewish KABBALA was deemed highly suspicious by Pope Innocent VIII (r. 1484–92). At the intervention of Lorenzo de' MEDICI (1449–92), he was allowed to return and remained in FLORENCE until his early death. His *Oration of the Dignity of Man* exalted human dignity and the freedom of the individual to influence his or her own spiritual development. He died quite young in 1494.

Further reading: Giovanni Pico della Mirandola, *On the Dignity of Man,* trans. Charles Glenn Wallis (Indianapolis: Bobbs-Merrill, 1965); Giovanni Pico della Mirandola, *Commentary on a Poem of Platonic Love,* trans. Douglas Carmichael (Lanham, Md.: University Press of America, 1986); William G. Craven, *Giovanni Pico della Mirandola: Symbol of His Age, Modern Interpretations of a Renaissance Philosopher* (Geneva: Librairie Droz, 1981); Charles B. Schmitt, *Gianfrancesco Pico della Mirandola (1469–1533) and His Critique of Aristotle* (The Hague: Martinus Nijhoff, 1967).

Mirror of Princes Mirrors of Princes were didactic works intended for kings or future kings. They sought to teach morality and the art of governing. Oriented toward theory, they presented a conventional model for a perfect prince. They listed the virtues a ruler should cultivate and possess to rule a kingdom justly.

Their origins can be found in the manuals on government produced in Greek and Roman antiquity. From the fourth century C.E., they became Christian and were usually written by clerics. AUGUSTINE's *City of God* can be seen to offer an early portrait of the ideal Christian prince. By the Carolingian period, they were common and explicitly moral in intent. In the 12th century JOHN OF SALISBURY's *Policraticus* (1159) was a true political treatise. Giles of Rome's (d. 1316) *De regimine principum* from 1285 was intended for King PHILIP IV THE FAIR of France. It was influenced by Aristotelian theoretical political ideas and was translated many times. Such works of the later Middle Ages became more intended for a broader audience. They transcended the perspective of the prince and were for directed to anyone or any group seeking to build a well-governed state or lead an ethical life in government.

See also POLITICAL THEORY AND TREATISES.

Further reading: Christine de Pisan, *The Book of the Body Politic,* ed. and trans. Kate Langdon Forhan (Cambridge: Cambridge University Press, 1994); Gervase of Tilbury, Otia imperialia: *Recreation for an Emperor,* ed. and trans. S. E. Banks and J. W. Binns (Oxford: Clarendon Press, 2002); Charles F. Briggs, *Giles of Rome's* De regimine principum: *Reading and Writing Politics at Court and University, c. 1275–c. 1525* (Cambridge: Cambridge University Press, 1999); Judith Ferster, *Fictions of Advice: The Literature and Politics of Counsel in Late Medieval England* (Philadelphia: University of Pennsylvania Press, 1996).

missal   The missal was the main liturgical book for the celebration of the MASS. From the 11th century the missal progressively replaced the SACRAMENTARY, which had been the essential book for the celebration of the Eucharist. The missal was created to make all the texts available in one book. The liturgy had concentrated liturgical action in the hands of a clerical celebrant. Such a celebrant was to recite all the words of Mass, even if they were also being performed by others in attendance. The sacramentary, the antiphonary of the mass lectionary or readings, were collected to form a single book for the celebration of the Mass. It contained all the texts for feasts, PRAYERS, readings, and the beginnings or *incipits* of the sung sections. In other words the missal included all the material necessary for the celebration of the Eucharist, so that priests could celebrate the Mass alone and correctly.

See also LITURGICAL BOOKS.

Further reading: Éric Palazzo, "Missal," *EMA,* 2.961; Richard W. Pfaff, *Medieval Latin Liturgy: A Select Bibliography* (Toronto: University of Toronto Press, 1982), 18–25.

missi dominici   These were agents charged with controlling officials in a local administration and were first used by MEROVINGIANS. The kings delegated these temporary controllers with defined political or legal missions. The practice was not permanent and did not apply to the whole kingdom. The CAROLINGIAN monarchs rediscovered the *missi dominici* and again made them part of their much more efficient system of government.

CHARLEMAGNE in the late eighth century, along with an imposition of a general OATH of loyalty, made these envoys a regular and permanent means of his control. In 789 a CAPITULARY charged the *missi* or envoys for AQUITAINE with obtaining an oath of loyalty to the king and his successors. They were, moreover, to find out whether the capitularies or laws were being applied by asking a particular set of questions. Those sent on such missions were to number at least two, sometimes four or five. They would include a bishop or abbot, a layman,

and always a high noble, with their powers temporary for a defined region. They were sent outside their home areas of authority and filed reports when they returned. In the ninth century they became even more fundamental to Carolingian government.

See also CHARLES I THE BALD; LOUIS I THE PIOUS.

Further reading: H. R. Loyn and John Percival, *The Reign of Charlemagne* (London: Edward Arnold, 1975); Heinrich Fichtenau, *The Carolingian Empire: The Age of Charlemagne,* trans. Peter Munz (1957; reprint, New York: Harper & Row, 1964); Rosamond McKitterick, *The Frankish Kingdoms under the Carolingians, 751–987* (London: Longman, 1983); James Westfall Thompson, *The Decline of the "Missi Dominici" in Frankish Gaul* (Chicago: University of Chicago Press, 1903).

missions and missionaries, Christian   Propagating faith to call all humankind to attain heaven through belief was a fundamental notion of Christianity and ISLAM during the Middle Ages. Muslims were much less aggressive in trying to convince people to convert, allowing the virtues and qualities of Islam to speak for themselves. Judaism was not interested in missionizing. However, Christianity sent out emissaries to convert the heathen, · Muslims, and Jews.

Christianity, soon after it became a state church, started the spread of the gospel among pagans at the periphery of the Christianized world. This became an object of a conscious policy of the church. The first successful mission was that organized by Pope GREGORY I the Great at the end of the sixth century to convert the peoples of Anglo-Saxon England and was led by AUGUSTINE of Canterbury. CHARLEMAGNE pursued a similar policy to convert his pagan Germanic neighbors, but he did not hesitate to impose baptism by force on the conquered SAXONS between 770 and 800.

From the 10th to the 12th century, missionary efforts were directed to the SLAVS, Hungarians, and Scandinavians. The BYZANTINE EMPIRE pushed the spread of Christianity with diplomatic pressures on the Slavic peoples of eastern and central Europe. By such efforts, it drew the BULGARS, Ruś, and SERBS into the Orthodox world.

In the 13th century, missionary activity, both warlike and peaceful, occurred in the Baltic countries of LIVONIA, PRUSSIA, and FINLAND. The last pagans in the region, the LITHUANIANS, were only converted in the late 14th century as part of a political marriage and agreement with POLAND. Moreover, in the 13th century the new MENDICANT ORDERS tried to spread the Christian faith among the Muslims and peoples of Central Asia. The friars studied Arabic and the ideas of Islam and tried in vain to make headway against Islam. The overthrow of the Mongol dynasty and the establishment of the Ottomans in Anatolia made missionary activity to the east more difficult during the final centuries of the Middle Ages. By the end of the Middle Ages the church had developed a strong missionary program that it was to put to use ardently during European expansion after 1500.

See also BONIFACE, SAINT; COLUMBA, SAINT; COLUMBAN, SAINT; CYRIL, SAINT, AND METHODIOS, SAINT, APOSTLES OF THE SLAVS; JOHN OF PLANO CARPINI; LULL, RAMÓN, AND LULLISM; PATRICK, SAINT; TEUTONIC KNIGHTS, ORDER OF; WILLIAM OF RUBRUCK.

Further reading: J. N. Hillgarth, ed., *Christianity and Paganism, 350–750: The Conversion of Western Europe*, rev. ed. (1969; reprint, Philadelphia: University of Pennsylvania Press, 1986); Eric Christiansen, *The Northern Crusades: The Baltic and the Catholic Frontier, 1100–1525* (1980; reprint, New York: Penguin Books, 1997); Richard Fletcher, *The Barbarian Conversion from Paganism to Christianity* (New York: Henry Holt, 1997).

Mistra (Misithra, Mystras) Not far from Sparta in the Peloponnese, medieval Mistra was perched on a hill. It initially was clustered around a fortress built in 1249 by William II de Villehardouin (d. 1278) that was lost by the Franks to the Greeks in 1262. After that it became an important Byzantine town and later the capital of the Despotate of the MOREA from 1348 to 1460. After the fall of CONSTANTINOPLE, it became one of the last strongholds of the Byzantines against the Ottomans. It was one of the last centers of Byzantine culture, under the rule of the Cantacuzeni family and then the PALAIOLOGOS dynasty. As well as texts, painting, inscriptions, and remains of palaces and houses, there are churches at the site. It was captured by the Ottomans in 1460 and began a long period of decline.

See also ART AND ARCHITECTURE, BYZANTINE; LATIN STATES IN GREECE.

Further reading: Rodoniki Etseoglu, *Mistras: A Byzantine Capital*, 2d ed. (Athens: Apollo Editions, 1977); Steven Runciman, *Mistra: Byzantine Capital of the Peloponnese* (London: Thames and Hudson, 1980).

Moldavia Medieval Moldavia was a region named after the Moldava River, lying between the eastern Carpathian Mountains, the river Dniestr, and the BLACK SEA. It is presently divided, part in Romania, part in the republic of Moldava, and part in Ukraine.

The arrival of SLAVS in the sixth and seventh centuries changed the native Roman-Dacian culture into the Dridu culture of the eighth and ninth centuries. The Slavs developed fortified sites in northern and central Moldavia and tried to defend themselves against the attacks of Hungarians, Petchenegs, and CUMANS. In 1241–42, the territory of Moldavia was subjected to the MONGOLS of the Golden Horde. In the 13th and 14th centuries, Moldavia became a land open to the immigration of the Romanian, Hungarian, and German populations of TRANSYLVANIA and for Asiatic peoples, the Cumans, Mongols, ALANS, and Armenians.

In 1344–45, a Hungarian-Polish-Lithuanian attitude on the Golden Horde freed Moldavia. Two states appeared, one in the north and one in the south. There was widespread conversion to Catholicism about 1400. After a revolution against the Hungarians in 1360, Peter I (r. ca. 1371–91) was the first Moldavian prince to swear in 1387 an oath of vassalage to the king of POLAND. In 1391–92, the northern principality of Moldavia conquered the southern. During the long reign of Alexander the Good (r. 1400–32), Moldavia, a tolerant Orthodox country, welcomed persecuted people from ARMENIA and Hussites from Hungary and BOHEMIA. The Ottomans eventually imposed an annual tribute in 1454–56. Nonetheless, between 1457 and 1504 Moldavia reached great prosperity and size under the reign of Stephen or Stefan the Great (r. 1457–1504), who promoted a flourishing economy and maintained a powerful army. These factors allowed it to play important, albeit temporary, political and economic roles in eastern Europe. The Ottoman occupation of its ports in 1484 was a serious blow that ended its access to the Black Sea and began a decline of the country's fortunes that resulted in further territorial losses to the Ottomans in the 16th century.

See also VLACHS.

Further reading: Nicolae Iorga, *Byzantium after Byzantium*, trans. Laura Treptow (Portland, Oreg.: Center for Romanian Studies, 2000); Serban Papacostea, *Stephen the Great: Prince of Moldavia, 1457–1504*, trans. Sergiu Celac (Bucharest: Editura Enciclopedica, 1996); Victor Spinei, *Moldavia in the Eleventh–Fourteenth Centuries*, trans. Liliana Teodoreanu and Ioana Sturza (Bucharest: Editura Academiei Republicii Socialiste România, 1986).

monarchy *See* KINGS AND KINGSHIP, RITUALS AND THEORIES OF.

monasticism Christian monasticism had it origins in EGYPT at the end of the third century. In coenobitic monasticism pious men devoted themselves to the practice of retiring to the desert to the worship GOD and withdrawing from secular matters. They did this primarily as individuals. There was no work involved in their activities. These monastic groups soon became organized into communities, sometimes under the particular influence of one person. Eremitic communities studied THEOLOGY and other subjects and sometimes worked in the service of the church as missionaries, theologians, and manpower for rioting crowds in cities. They retained close ties with the LAITY and entered towns frequently. Strict CELIBACY was expected of them, although no such obligation was as yet imposed on the rest of the CLERGY.

WESTERN MONASTICISM

In the West, with the establishment of the monasteries of Subiaco and MONTE CASSINO by Saint BENEDICT OF

NURSIA, the aims of Western monasticism were defined by the BENEDICTINE Rule. It was based on a desire to lead a life of perfection and sanctification. This necessitated poverty, withdrawal from family life and society, physical work, intellectual activity or study, and obedience to the abbot. With the foundation of CLUNY in 910, this type of reformed Benedictine monasticism spread throughout Christian Europe. PRAYER and living according to the monastic rule produced SALVATION, not only to the individual monk, but also to all of Christian society. Cluniac monks did no work and left that to a lesser group of worker monks known as *conversi*.

At the end of the 11th century, other reform movements came into being. The CISTERCIANS, CARTHUSIANS, and other minor orders put a renewed stress on ASCETICISM and simplicity of worship. Cistercians such as BERNARD OF CLAIRVAUX remained active and influential in worldly affairs. In the 13th century the MENDICANT orders, especially the FRANCISCANS and the DOMINICANS, were founded to be involved in daily social and religious life, especially in the cities and universities. They had their own rules and lived inside or near the new cities.

Monasticism continued throughout the rest of the Middle Ages. The image of the monk suffered, however, as many monasteries grew rich and compliance with the rigors expected of the monastic life was less frequently observed. REFORM movements only partially corrected these perceived abuses, and heretics such as the followers of John HUS and the LOLLARDS were strongly opposed to such rich religious institutions.

BYZANTINE MONASTICISM

Monasticism occupied an important place in the Byzantine religious and sometimes political world. Orders of monks such as those in the West did not exist. In the Greek Orthodox and Eastern Churches, Byzantine monasticism stressed the place of the individual within the monastic community. The collective was less important. With a few exceptions, such as the monasteries at Mount Athos, Byzantine monks did not withdraw from earthly affairs, and abbots or monks frequently and explicitly served in secular and political life. They often clashed with the emperor and were ardent in their opposition to union or compliance with the Western Church and the PAPACY.

The rise of monasticism was one of the most important and most characteristic phenomena of medieval society. Monasteries were endowed with lands, lordships, and rents. They were economic units and sources of revenues, besides being centers of religious life.

See also ANCHORITES AND ANCHORESSES; BASIL OF CAESAREA; BONIFACE, SAINT; BRUNO THE CARTHUSIAN, SAINT; CAROLINGIAN RENAISSANCE; CELESTINE V, POPE, AND THE CELESTINE ORDER; COLUMBIA, SAINT; COLUMBAN,

The 12th-century Benedictine abbey of Sant'Antimo, south of Siena in Tuscany in Italy, supposedly founded by Charlemagne *(Courtesy Edward English)*

SAINT; HERMITS AND EREMITISM; ICONOCLASM AND ICONO-
CLASTIC CONTROVERSY; MILITARY ORDERS; NORBERT OF
XANTEN, SAINT; NUNS AND NUNNERIES; ODILO OF CLUNY;
ROBERT OF ARBISSEL.

Further reading: Derwas Chitty, *The Desert a City*
(London: Mowbrays, 1966); Giles Constable, *Medieval
Monasticism: A Select Bibliography* (Toronto: University of
Toronto Press, 1976); David Knowles, *Christian Monasti-
cism* (New York: McGraw-Hill, 1969); C. H. Lawrence,
*Medieval Monasticism: Forms of Religious Life in Western
Europe in the Middle Ages* (New York: Longman, 1989);
Henrietta Leyser, *Hermits and the New Monasticism: A
Study of Religious Communities in Western Europe,
1000–1150* (London: Macmillan, 1984).

money and mints   The vast majority of the coinage
that was struck and circulated in the Middle Ages was
made from silver in the form of the penny piece or *denar-
ius* and its multiples or submultiples. After the barbarian
invasions, the new Frankish, Visigothic, and Ostrogothic
rulers struck gold coins in the Roman manner. They usually bore the effigy of an emperor at CONSTANTINOPLE.
After the death of CLOVIS in 511, barbarian rulers began
to introduce their own monograms.

The Roman emperors reserved a monopoly on coining money in their own mints, but the barbarian rulers
could not maintain such a monopoly. Bishops, great
landed owners, and towns started to coin money. Only
the Lombard kings in Italy were able to maintain, for
their profit, a monopoly on striking coins. They punished
false coiners by cutting off their hands. Coinage in gold
was not maintained because supplies of gold bullion
dried up in the West.

CHARLEMAGNE began a return to the control of
coining. The dissolution of public authority under his
successors prevented this policy from continued imple-
mentation. Again bishops, counts, abbots, and territorial
princes by royal concession and by usurpation issued
coins, often of suspect value. Though a silver monomet-
allism was imposed in the West, mints continued to mul-
tiply, causing difficulties of exchange and reliability and
hampering the spread of international commerce. When
the economic expansion of Western Europe began in the
central Middle Ages, the need for greater quantities of
precious metals and the minting and circulation of
denominations of coins of higher value than the penny
grew. Coins and monies of account in large denominations soon entered use. Rulers and princes tried for at
least their own benefit to put pieces of good reputation
and sound quality into circulation for international trade.

During the second half of the 13th century, more
gold bullion appeared in the West by way of the sub-
Saharan trade. The Florentine florin minted first in 1253
had rapid success and numerous imitators. The resumption of the striking of gold coins by several cities and

governments meant a return to bimetallism, but variations in the values of bullion content caused constant
problems in exchange and pricing. Manipulations in the
content of precious metals in coins by rulers done for
their own benefit also complicated the money market.

According to Scholastic theologians, money was the
measure of the value of goods, as expressed clearly by
Thomas AQUINAS. The popes maintained this position,
recommending that rulers resort to changes in exceptional circumstances. The frequency of variations in the
real values of money led Nicholas ORESME to expound
the ideas of Gresham's later law: bad money drove out the
good, which was hoarded, used for international payments, or even melted down by private individuals at the
mint to exchange for many more pieces of "bad" money.
All this hurt the possibilities of economic investment and
growth. The later Middle Ages saw the increased use of
fiduciary money, rather like checks, and additional efforts
to increase the supply of gold from Africa.

See also COINAGE AND CURRENCY; ECONOMIC THOUGHT
AND JUSTICE; JUSTICE; TRADE AND COMMERCE.

Further reading: S. M. H. Bozorgnia, *The Role of Pre-
cious Metals in European Economic Development: From
Roman Times to the Eve of the Industrial Revolution* (West-
port, Conn.: Greenwood Press, 1998); N. J. Mayhew and
Peter Spufford, eds., "Later Medieval Mints: Organisa-
tion, Administration and Techniques" (The Eighth
Oxford Symposium on Coinage and Monetary History)
(Oxford: B. A. R., 1988); Peter Spufford, *Handbook of
Medieval Exchange* (London: Offices of the Royal Histori-
cal Society, 1986); Peter Spufford, *Money and Its Use in
Medieval Europe* (Cambridge: Cambridge University
Press, 1988).

Mongols and the Mongol Empire   The Mongols
were originally nomads living in the upper Orkhon Valley
by the Amur River. They achieved unity under JENGHIZ
Khan and absorbed other peoples, one of whom, the
TATARS, gave their name a group of Mongols known by
that name in China and the West. Jenghiz Khan campaigned throughout central Asia and into IRAN and northern China. His son, Ogodai (r. 1229–41), completed that
conquest, overran the CUMANS and RUŚ, and sent west an
army that devastated much of POLAND and HUNGARY.
Guyuk (r. 1246–48) invaded ANATOLIA and Georgia.
Mongke (r. 1249–59) began the conquest of southern
China, to be completed later by KUBLAI KHAN. Their
brother, HULEGU, destroyed the caliphate of BAGHDAD and
devastated much of SYRIA. The disputed succession to
Mongke led to warfare that fractured the empire. In 1260
Mongols suffered a rare defeat at the Battle of AYN JALUT.
They continued their raids, even to JERUSALEM, but were
not able to expand into EGYPT. From 1335, Persia freed
itself from the Mongols. In 1368 China drove the Mongols back onto the steppe.

Around 1390 TAMERLANE, an adventurer, attached himself to another Mongol dynasty in Turkestan by marriage and reorganized an empire around his capital, at SAMARKAND. His conquests did not survive him. Other Mongols recovered Turkestan. Tamerlane's descendants went on to found a "Mogul" empire in India.

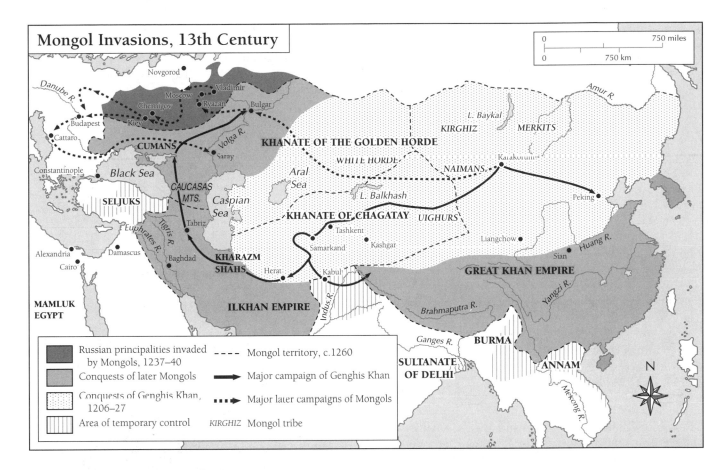

Mongol Invasions, 13th Century

| | 0 | | 750 miles |
| | 0 | | 750 km |

Legend:
- Russian principalities invaded by Mongols, 1237–40
- Conquests of later Mongols
- Conquests of Genghis Khan, 1206–27
- Area of temporary control
- - - - Mongol territory, c.1260
- → Major campaign of Genghis Khan
- ••••► Major later campaigns of Mongols
- *KIRGHIZ* Mongol tribe

Jenghiz Khan and his sons by Rashid al-Din (d. 1318), Persian manuscript, Ms. 19157, Sup Pers 113, fol. 44, Bibliothèque Nationale, Paris *(Art Resource)*

LIFE UNDER THE MONGOLS

After the massacres and destruction that generally accompanied these conquests, the Mongol Empire, though often divided against itself, had a basic structure that provided considerable security in the Mongol peace. MERCHANTS and missionaries from the West as well as Muslims used the routes protected by the Mongols to travel to India and China. The initial toleration of the first Mongols was favorable to the Christians. The khans of Persia converted to Islam in 1295, and in the 14th century those of the Golden Horde and Jagatai did likewise. The Mongol Empire facilitated contacts among civilizations, and travelers were able to gather geographical facts that had great influence on later European expansions.

See also BUKHARA; MARCO POLO; IL-KHANS; JOHN OF PLANO CARPINI; MISSIONS AND MISSIONARIES, CHRISTIAN; SELJUK TURKS OF RUM; WILLIAM OF RUBRUCK.

Further reading: Ala al-Din Ata Malek Joveyni, 1226–1283, The History of the World-Conqueror, 2 vols., trans. John Andrew Boyle (Cambridge, Mass.: Harvard University Press, 1958); Arthur Waley, The Secret History of the Mongols and Other Pieces (London: Allen & Unwin, 1963); Reuven Amitai-Preiss and David O. Morgan, eds., The Mongol Empire and Its Legacy (Leiden: E. J. Brill, 1999); Robert Marshall, Storm from the East: From Ghengis Khan to Khubilai Khan (Berkeley: University of California Press, 1993); David Morgan, The Mongols (Cambridge, Mass.: Blackwell, 1986).

Monophysitism   Monophysitism was the doctrine on the one and single nature of Christ. Somewhat prompted by politics, it was part of the theological problem of expressing in linguistic terms the mystery of the unity of divinity and humanity in Christ. It stated that Christ had but one nature.

The Monophysites were those who opposed the terminological teachings of the Council of CHALCEDON in 451 of two natures and held an old formula of CYRIL OF ALEXANDRIA and were called Monophysites only in the seventh century. The monophysite understanding of Christ was that the divinity of Christ was the principle of this union and the humanity of Christ was absorbed into it. Cyril had used texts that circulated under the names of Athanasius and the popes Julius and Felix and believed that the Incarnation was not merely an apparent unity of divinity and humanity but a real and ontological, physical, or hypostatic union. The Byzantine emperors and the patriarchies of ROME, CONSTANTINOPLE, and ANTIOCH all took part in the disputes that lasted for a century or more. After 518, under the emperors Justin (r. 518–527) and JUSTINIAN, a reaffirmation of the Chalcedonian ideas took place, and opponents of that council's definition were persecuted.

See also CHRISTOLOGY AND CHRISTOLOGICAL CONTROVERSY; COPTS AND COPTIC ART.

Further reading: R. C. Chestnut, Three Monophysite Christologies (Oxford: Oxford University Press, 1976); William H. C. Frend, The Rise of the Monophysite Movement (Cambridge: Cambridge University Press, 1972); Robert V. Sellers, Two Ancient Christologies: A Study in the Christological Thought of the Schools of Alexandria and Antioch in the Early History of Christian Doctrine (London: Society for Promoting Christian Knowledge, 1954); William A. Wigram, The Separation of the Monophysites (New York: AMS Press, 1978).

Monreale (royal mountain)   The BENEDICTINE monastery of Monreale was founded in 1174 by King WILLIAM II of SICILY, inspired by a dream, to be the burial church of the Hauteville family. Monreale is situated a few kilometers or miles from PALERMO, at the end of a valley called the Conca d'Oro. Its function was political. Its foundation allowed the prince to escape the domain of the bishop of

The Romanesque and ornamental bronze "Door of Paradise" by Bonanno Pisano in 1186 from the Cathedral of Monreale near Palermo in Sicily (Courtesy Edward English)

Palermo. The king supported his foundation by the incomes from the fortified mountains towns of Lato, Calatrasi, and Corleone, overwhelmingly populated with Muslims after the anti-Muslim pogroms of 1160–61. FREDERICK II quelled rebellions there between 1222 and 1224, and these Muslims were deported to Lucera in APULIA. The lands of this bishopric then had to be repopulated.

Although the monastery of Monreale was no longer connected with the ruling dynasty after the mid-13th century, it remained one of the richest dioceses in southern ITALY. Built within a few years and completed in 1189, the church was framed by towers and fortifications, entered by impressive doors, with a marvelous CLOISTER with cosmatesque columns and sculpted capitals. A palace was directly connected to the apse. The church was built on the plan of a basilica reproducing aspects of the royal Palatine chapel in Palermo. It had tall columns and arches supporting a roof, with marble plaques and MOSAICS in the BYZANTINE style. A costly endeavor, Monreale was a church founded to be directly subject to the will of a monarchy.

Further reading: Ernst Kitzinger, *Mosaics of Monreale* (Palermo: S. F. Flaccovio, 1960); Wolfgang Krönig, *The Cathedral of Monreale and Norman Architecture in Sicily* (Palermo: S. F. Flaccovio, 1965); Roberto Salvini, *The Cloister of Monreale and Romanesque Sculpture in Sicily*, trans. Laura Valdes and Rose George (1962; reprint, Palermo: S. F. Flaccovio, 1964).

Monte Cassino, Monastery of

According to the hagiographical account in GREGORY I THE GREAT's *Dialogues*, Saint BENEDICT left Subiaco and settled in the 520s on this mountaintop between ROME and NAPLES once occupied by a pagan temple. He wrote his rule for this monastery. The first establishment was destroyed by the LOMBARDS in about 570. Around 718, at the request of Pope Gregory II (r. 715–731), the monastery was refounded by the duke of Benevento. In the eighth and ninth centuries, the abbey received numerous properties in southern ITALY. The Carolingians imposed their rule on the empire and granted the monastery properties in Frankish Italy. The monastery remained subject only to the pope.

In 883, Muslim raiders burned the monastery, which was then abandoned again for more than half a century. In 949, Abbot Baldwin, a disciple of Odo of Cluny (ca. 879–942), restored the old abbey. Monte Cassino then concentrated on building a compact lordship around the monastery.

Monte Cassino's golden age was the late 11th and early 12th centuries as the mother church of the BENEDICTINE ORDER. The abbey provided three popes, Stephen IX (r. 1057–58), Victor III (r. 1087), and Gelasius II (r. 1118–19), as well as cardinals and bishops. Abbot DESIDERIUS totally rebuilt the abbey, and Abbot Oderisius (1087–1105) made it a great intellectual center with a famous library and SCRIPTORIUM. In 1239, FREDERICK II installed a garrison there. The abbots Bernard Ayglier (1263–82) and Thomas (1285–88) were able to revive the prosperity of the temporal properties. In 1322, JOHN XXII elevated the monastery to a bishopric, but it was destroyed by an earthquake in 1349. In 1369, Pope Urban V (r. 1362–70) asked all Benedictine monasteries for contributions to help rebuild Monte Cassino and invited monks from all over Europe to move there. It has survived today.

See also CONSTANTINE THE AFRICAN.

Further reading: Herbert Bloch, *Monte Cassino in the Middle Ages*, 3 vols. (Cambridge, Mass.: Harvard University Press, 1981); H. E. J. Cowdrey, *The Age of Abbot Desiderius: Montecassino, the Papacy, and the Normans in the Eleventh and Early Twelfth Centuries* (Oxford: Clarendon Press, 1983); G. A. Loud, *Montecassino and Benevento in the Middle Ages: Essays in South Italian Church History* (Aldershot: Ashgate/Variorum, 2000).

Montefeltro, Federico da

See FEDERICO DA MONTEFELTRO.

Montpellier

The town of Montpellier appeared first in an act of donation in 985, but it was probably not much of an urban center then. By the late 11th century, it was a town under the seigniorial family of Guilhem. In December 1090 he submitted to the bishop and became the lord of Montpellier.

In the first half of the 12th century, a town wall was built, followed in the late 12th and early 13th centuries by another. In 1180 a certain Guy de Montpellier founded the Hospitallers of the Holy Spirit. The Guilhem family now had to govern with an urban class of lawyers, notaries, and members of 72 guilds.

An Aragonese phase of Montpellier's history began with the marriage of Marie, daughter of Guilhem VIII, to King Peter II (r. 1196–1213) of ARAGON. This produced a written constitution of the customs of Montpellier. King JAMES I of Aragon, having weakened the influence of the bishop of Maguelone, here established a joint rule with the town that was mutually profitable. The period ended in 1349 with the sale of Montpellier for 120,000 crowns to the French king, Philip VI (r. 1328–50). It had 30,000 to 40,000 inhabitants in about 1340 before the Black Death. Its merchants worked all over the Mediterranean and at the Champagne FAIRS. It also possessed a university that was famous for its law and medical schools.

By then the capital of the kingdom of Majorca, Montpellier did not escape the demographic and economic calamities of the 14th century. During the crisis and despite the decline in its population, the town maintained considerable prosperity until the 16th century.

This was due to a TEXTILE industry, banking, commerce, and the important presence of Italian, Catalan, and German MERCHANTS.

See also CATHARS; LANGUEDOC; PROVENCE.

Further reading: Jean-Claude Hélas, "Montpellier," *EMA* 2.981–982; Kathryn Reyerson, *Business, Banking, and Finance in Medieval Montpellier* (Toronto: Pontifical Institute of Mediaeval Studies, 1985); Kathryn Reyerson, *The Art of the Deal: Intermediaries of Trade in Medieval Montpellier* (Leiden: E. J. Brill, 2002).

Mont Saint-Michel The famous Norman monastery of Mont Saint-Michel is at the summit of a granite mountainous island cut off from the main land by tides. The site is 3,000 feet around and 260 feet high. In 708, after a revelation to him by the archangel Michael, the bishop of Avranches founded an oratory on it with RELICS taken from Monte Sant' Angelo in Italy. In 966 the canons originally controlling the site were replaced by BENEDICTINE monks. From this period only a church of Notre Dame-sous-Terre has survived. It became subterranean when it was incorporated into the lower infrastructure of the later ROMANESQUE churches.

Abbot Hildebert began to build a new abbey church in 1023. This building required the creation of the upper platform with chapels on the sides and a CRYPT. On the north aisle of the church were added an almonry, a monks' walk, a refectory, and a kitchen with an infirmary, the usual components of a Benedictine monastery. In 1103 the north side of the nave collapsed. Lightning caused a new disaster in 1112. All that remained of this early building campaign were the southern bays of the nave built between about 1060 and 1080. A miniature illumination in 15th-century *Très riches heures du duc de Berry* showed a church with a rounded choir surrounded by an ambulatory with one axial chapel. The central tower was rebuilt several times; the present spire is from the modern period. A few monastic buildings from the Romanesque period have survived.

In 1204 a fire started in the town below by Bretons reached the abbey and destroyed several structures. Another rebuilding program in the Gothic style was begun and was finished by 1228. New walls were added during the 15th century for protection during the HUNDRED YEARS' WAR. It was later a prison in the 19th century and massively restored between 1872 and 1922.

Further reading: Henry Adams, *Mont-Saint-Michel and Chartres* (Boston: Houghton Mifflin, 1962); J. J. G. Alexander, *Norman Illumination at Mont St. Michel, 966–1100* (Oxford: Clarendon Press, 1970); Edward Francis Hunt, *The Architecture of Mont-St-Michel (1203–1228)* (Washington, D.C.: The Catholic University of America Press, 1928); Jacques Thiébaut "Mont Saint Michel," *EMA,* 2.982–984.

morality plays Most of the surviving medieval drama in English and French consists of MYSTERY PLAYS. There is also a small group of anonymous allegorical dramas, from the 15th and early 16th centuries, that were known collectively as moralities. Some of these, such as mummings and the later interludes, were apparently intended for outdoor performance, in the great hall of a palace, CASTLE, mansion, inn yard, religious house, or institution such as a college. Among the plays in English were *The King of Life (Pride of Life)*; *The Castle of Perseverance* (ca. 1425), for which there survived, uniquely, a 15th-century staging plan, indicating an outdoor performance; *Mankind*; *Wisdom*; EVERYMAN; *Mundus and Infans*; *Hickscorner*; and *Youth*.

While mystery plays treated human life in terms of a Christian scheme of SALVATION, from Creation to the LAST JUDGMENT, morality plays were single compositions, dramatizing the psychological combat between good and evil for mastery over a soul. They dealt with humanity and the passage from innocence through experience to Redemption by GRACE. Free will and a fallen appetite led to SIN, from which only repentance could give relief.

Such plays can be seen as "popular" manifestations promoting the sacrament of penance. Some were written by members of the CLERGY deploying the theological knowledge and confessional experience of their fellows. These plays had close links with SERMONS. With their emphasis on the need for confession, they had strong affinities with the message and activities of the friars.

Further reading: Peter Happé, ed., *Four Morality Plays* (New York: Penguin Books, 1979); Dorothy H. Brown, *Christian Humanism in the Late English Morality Plays* (Gainesville: University Press of Florida, 1999); Clifford Davidson, *Visualizing the Moral Life: Medieval Iconography and the Macro Morality Plays* (New York: AMS Press, 1989); Robert A. Potter, *The English Morality Play: Origins, History, and Influence of a Dramatic Tradition* (London: Routledge and K. Paul, 1975).

Moravia (Morava) The eastern province of the present Czech Republic, Moravia was named after the river Morava, a tributary of the Danube. Often tied to BOHEMIA, Moravia has its own history. A SLAV population lived on the territory of Moravia from the mid-sixth century. From the ninth century, Moravian was linked with BOHEMIA to its west. Among local princes, Mojmír I (r. 830–846) won control of western Slovakia, creating a Great Moravia. A successor, Rostislav (r. 846–870), beat back the assaults of the Carolingians. Christianity first arrived in Moravia in the early ninth century through BAVARIA, but, wary of the FRANKS, Rostislav preferred to ask the BYZANTINES to send missionaries. CYRIL and Methodios arrived in Moravia about 863.

GREAT MORAVIA AND BOHEMIA

Great Moravia reached its high point of power and influence under Borivoj, or Svatopluk (870–894), who ruled Bohemia, parts of POLAND, Silesia, PANNONIA, and part of Saxony. The decline of this state began at the end of the ninth century with discord among his successors and tensions between the adherents of the liturgy in Slavonic and those in favor of the Latin rite. In 906, the army of Moravia was defeated by the Magyars and the state collapsed.

Around 955, the Bohemian Boleslav I annexed Moravia but it was conquered again in 1003 by BOLESLAV THE GREAT (r. 992–1025) of Poland, was only taken by Bohemia in 1019–20. Bretislav I (r. 1034–55) strengthened Moravia's ties with Bohemia, built royal strongholds, and created a centralized administration. The knights who had come to Moravia with Bretislav acquired official positions and supported themselves by property holdings there, forming a new Moravian nobility.

THE PREMYSL DYNASTY AND SOCIETY

In the 12th century, a series of conflicts broke out between the royal court at PRAGUE and the Moravian Premyslids. Two Moravian Premysls gained power at Bohemia, Svatopluk (r. 1107–09) and Conrad II Otto (r. 1189–91). A title, margrave of Moravia, was created at the end of the 12th century. By about 1200, the Moravian Premysls had died out. From the time of Premysl Ottokar II (1253–78), the king of Bohemia was also the margrave of Moravia.

In the 13th century the Moravian barons controlled the local administration and soon claimed more political power. From the 1220s, through the rest of century, towns were founded by the king. German immigrants colonized the countryside and populated new remote areas at higher altitudes. Apart from frequent skirmishing on the frontiers with AUSTRIA and HUNGARY, the only serious warfare occurred during the invasion of the MONGOLS in 1241 and during the years of dynastic conflict after the death of Premysl Ottokar II in 1278.

When the Premysl dynasty died out in 1306, the throne of Bohemia and margravate of Moravia passed to John of Luxembourg (r. 1310–46), son of the German Holy Roman Emperor, Henry VII (r. 1313). In 1334, John gave the margravete to his son, the future king of Bohemia and Holy Roman Emperor CHARLES IV. In an act as the Holy Roman Emperor on April 7, 1348, Charles made Moravia part of the kingdom of Bohemia and part of the lands of its Crown.

LATER MEDIEVAL CONFLICTS

By 1349, Charles IV was heavily involved in trying to govern the empire, so he delegated Moravia to a younger brother, John Henry (d. 1375). The region's political and economic life deteriorated under his successor, Jošt (d. 1411), as part of the conflict with Wenceslas IV, king of Bohemia (1378–1419), and his younger brother, Sigismund of Luxembourg (1387–1432), king of Hungary. Rival factions of the nobility threatened to take over Moravia and internal social and religious conflicts increased.

Ideas for the reform of the church were expressed in Bohemia from the early 15th, centered on John HUS. His ideas reached Moravia, but the populace remained faithful to Sigismund and the church, as a result of the decisive stance of the great royal towns dominated by Germans. Moravia was soon transformed into an imperial military staging area for attacks against Hussite Bohemia. The Bohemian king, George of Podebrady (r. 1458–71), tried to keep Moravia linked to Bohemia. Another crusade against "heretical" Bohemia and the ensuing war with Hungary made this difficult. Matthias CORVINUS, the king of Hungary (1458–90), occupied a large part of Moravia in 1469 and was elected king of Bohemia by the nobility. After this Moravia remained detached from Bohemia until the 16th century when it became linked with the Austrians HABSBURGS.

Further reading: Francis Dvornik, *The Making of Central and Eastern Europe,* 2d ed. (Gulf Breeze, Fla.: Academic International Press, 1974); Imre Boba, *Moravia's History Reconsidered: A Reinterpretation of Medieval Sources* (The Hague: Nijhoff, 1971); Ján Dekan, *Moravia Magna: The Great Moravian Empire, Its Art and Times,* trans. Heather Trebatická (Bratislava: Tatran, 1980); Josef Žemlička, "Moravia," *EMA* 2.985–986.

Morea, Chronicle of, and despot of   The four versions of the *Chronicle of Morea* are the most important sources for the history of the principalities of Achaia and Morea between 1204 and 1430. The despotate of Morea was a Frankish and later a Byzantine principality in the Peloponnese in Greece. It was conquered by the Frankish crusaders in 1204/05. Geoffroi of VILLEHARDOUIN took over the province and established a princely dynasty based on feudal ties bolstered with Western concepts of nobility and CHIVALRY, but all supported by a traditional Byzantine system of landholding. In the mid-13th century a restored Byzantine Empire attacked the principality and forced it to surrender the castle of MISTRA and parts of the Peloponnese. Much of the rest of the Morea fell under the influence of CHARLES I OF ANJOU, king of SICILY. Soon marriages between the last of the Villehardouin line and the Angevins of NAPLES led to the establishment of a Neapolitan colony. In the 14th century VENICE acquired large parts of the Morea and became the dominant power in the principality. However, companies of Catalan mercenary soldiers conquered other portions of the province in 1383. So at the beginning of the 15th century, the Morea was divided into Neapolitan, Venetian, and Catalan Company states or colonies. In 1430 the Byzantine governors of MISTRA managed to conquer all of the Morea; but in 1460 it fell to the Ottomans.

Further reading: Harold E. Lurier, ed. and trans., *crusaders as Conquerors: The Chronicle of Morea* (New York: Columbia University Press, 1964); Donald M. Nicol, *The Last Centuries of Byzantium, 1261–1453* (London: Rupert Hart-Davis, 1972); James R. R. Rennell, *The Princes of Achaia and the Chronicles of Morea, A Study of Greece in the Middle Ages* (London: E. Arnold, 1907).

Moriscos   *See* FERDINAND II (V); GRANADA; ISABEL I.

Morocco (Maghreb, the west)   Morocco, also referred to as the far Maghrib or al-Maghrib, was a region and is a country in northwestern Africa. Under the Romans Morocco was part of the province of Mauritania. Roman culture and influence were superficial only affecting the Mediterranean coast. The interior of the country was inhabited by BERBER tribes who did not recognize any authority. The VANDAL conquest of 429 did not affect this situation, which persisted during the Byzantine reconquest between 534 and 680. The ARAB conquest, begun in 680 but completed only in 790 because of the fierce resistance from the Berbers, caused real changes in local societies and political structures. Berber revolts continued to be frequent and the UMAYYADS found the complete Islamization of the region a difficult undertaking.

BERBERS, FEZ, ISLAMIZATION

A local revolt in 740 became a general uprising against the distant caliphate. A caliphal army sent to destroy the rebels was defeated in 742. Berber religious feelings found expression among KHARIJITES, Islamic dissidents. A Berber principality was established by the Banu-Madrar family between 771 and 958 and was based on those doctrines. Orthodox Islam gained ground under the leadership of the IDRISID dynasty (789–985). About 790 Idris I (r. 789–793) founded his capital the city of FEZ and accepted the distant sovereignty of the ABBASID caliphs at BAGHDAD. They enjoyed considerable independence. A more complete Islamization was achieved in the 10th century and the region enjoyed economic prosperity from the GOLD trade passing from the south to Europe.

DYNASTIC FLUCTUATION

During the 10th century the Spanish Umayyads and the FATIMIDS fought for control, creating chaos by 985. The ultimate victors were the ALMORAVIDS, who conquered Morocco at the end of the 10th century. Berbers were pushed back into the mountains and urban dwellers accepted the orthodox Islamic beliefs of the Almoravids.

Fez and MARRAKECH became regional places of worship and centers of learning characterized by impressive architecture.

In 1243 the Almoravids were defeated by a rival dynasty, the ALMOHADS, whose empire was centered in Algeria. But by the end of the 13th century the Almohads had shifted their center to Morocco. The later Marinid line of the Almohads was defeated in Tunisia in 1348 and lost power to the Wattasids, though they retained the royal title until 1415. The Wattasids, the last Moroccan dynasty of the Middle Ages, ruled the region from 1472; but with the rising power of PORTUGAL and SPAIN along the coasts, the Wattasids were driven into the interior.

Further reading: G. S. Colin, G. Yver, and E. Levi-Provençal, "Al-Maghrib" and "Al-Maghrib, al-Mamlaka, al-Maghribiyya, Morocco," *Encyclopedia of Islam* 5.1,183–1,209; Said Ennahid, *Political Economy and Settlement Systems of Medieval Northern Morocco: An Archaeological–Historical Approach* (Oxford: Archaeopress, 2002); Thomas Kerlin Park, *Historical Dictionary of Morocco* (Lanham, Md.: Scarecrow Press, 1996); Maya Shatzmiller, *The Berbers and the Islamic State: The Marinid Experience in Pre-Protectorate Morocco* (Princeton, N.J.: Markus Wiener Publishers, 2000); Henri Terrasse, *History of Morocco,* trans. Hilary Tee (Casablanca: Éditions Atlantides, 1952).

mortmain (dead hand)   Mortmain was for SERFS the incapacity to perform any legal act. It also referred to the properties that had passed into the hands of the church and were henceforth inalienable. In other words, such property fell under the dead hand of the church. The term was based on the Latin words *manus* or "possession of power" and *mortua* in the sense of "rigid and death-like stiffness."

Those burdened by the status of serfdom initially could not dispose of any patrimony they might acquire or earn. They could neither pledge themselves personally nor buy property or movable goods. These handicaps of tenure or serfdom changed over the course of the Middle Ages as the terms of servitude began to be negotiated more often in the favor of agricultural workers because of a tighter labor supply or more general economic conditions unfavorable to the exploitative powers of landlords.

In terms of the property of the church, any rights or properties acquired became problematic for the state in terms of taxation and the collection of other kinds of obligations tied to them. Secular powers tried over the course of the Middle Ages to reduce these limitations as more and more properties fell into the hands of the church and out of the fiscal control of the Crown and the LAITY.

See also MANORS AND MANORIAL LORDSHIP; PEASANTRY; SOCIAL STATUS AND STRUCTURE; TAXATION, TAXES, AND TRIBUTE.

Further reading: Ernst H. Kantorowicz, *The King's Two Bodies: A Study in Mediaeval Political Theology* (Princeton, N.J.: Princeton University Press, 1957), 164–192; Sandra Raban, *Mortmain Legislation and the English Church, 1279–1500* (Cambridge: Cambridge University Press, 1982).

mosaic The art of mosaic began as the laying of luxurious pavements made of pebbles. It can be made of tiles or tesserae of stone, terra-cotta or glass set in a bed of lime or gypsum. This was soon transferred to wall and ceiling decoration. On walls there were two layers, one attached to the walls and one on which artists laid out their designs. Because the use of mosaic was slow and expensive, it became a luxury and was gradually restricted to places of worship and particularly to privileged and prominent areas such as choirs, transepts, or CRYPTS. During the ROMANESQUE period glazed tiles, pieces of marble, and ALABASTER came into use as mosaic media. The best examples of mosaic work can be found in Italy at RAVENNA, VENICE, PALERMO, and ROME and in the BYZANTINE EMPIRE.

See also ART AND ARCHITECTURE, BYZANTINE.

Further reading: Hans Belting, *The Mosaics and Frescoes of St. Mary Pammakaristos (Fethiye Camii) at Istanbul* (Locust Valley, N.Y.: J. J. Augustin, 1978); Eve Borsook, Fiorella Gioffredi Superbi, and Giovanni Pagliarulo, eds., *Medieval Mosaics: Light, Color, Materials* (Milan: Silvana Editoriale, 2000); Otto Demus, *The Mosaics of Norman Sicily* (London: Routledge and K. Paul, 1949); Otto Demus, *The Mosaic Decoration of San Marco, Venice,* ed. Herbert L. Kessler (Chicago: University of Chicago Press, 1988).

Moscow (Moskva) Moscow got its name from the river along whose banks it evolved, the Moskova, a tributary of the Oka, that linked the town to the Volga River basin. Occupied from the seventh century, it is mentioned in sources from 1147 onward. A long-time stronghold of the princes of Rostov and then of Vladimir, in 1263 it became the capital of a growing principality, when Alexander NEVSKY left it to his younger son, Daniel (d. 1304). Daniel's sons began a struggle for power in northeast Russia and benefited from the support of the Golden Horde, the MONGOLS and the Orthodox Church. Peter, the metropolitan, established his residence to Moscow in 1326, but only under IVAN III (1462–1505) that Moscow became the capital of a Russian state.

The core of the city was the fortress or the KREMLIN situated in a triangle of land formed by the Moscova and Neglinnaya Rivers. Around the kremlin, villages and suburbs developed, along with small CASTLES, and monasteries. The first cathedral of the Assumption (1326–27) and a second that collapsed in 1472–74 were replaced by the present church in 1475. A palace was built between 1487 and 1491, and the area was enclosed by walls between 1385 and 1516. To these buildings were added the church of the Deposition of the Virgin's Robe (1484–86), a private chapel for the metropolitans, the collegiate church of the Annunciation (1484–89), and a prince's chapel.

See also DIMITRI OF THE DON, GRAND DUKE.

Further reading: Robert O. Crummey, *The Formation of Muscovy, 1304–1613* (New York: Longman, 1987); J. H. Hamilton, *The Art and Architecture of Russia* (Harmondsworth: Penguin, 1983); John L. I. Fennell, *The Emergence of Moscow, 1304–1359* (Berkeley: University of California Press, 1968); Nancy Shields Kollmann, *Kinship and Politics: The Making of the Muscovite Political System, 1345–1547* (Stanford, Calif.: Stanford University Press, 1987); Arthur Voyce, *The Art and Architecture of Medieval Russia* (Norman: University of Oklahoma Press, 1967).

mosque (*masdjid*, **place where one prostrates oneself in worship**) The term, as used in the QURAN, referred to the pre-Islamic places of prayer or sanctuaries at MECCA, the KABA, or at JERUSALEM. After his flight to MEDINA in 622, Muhammad built a wall of bricks around a rectangular court that was open to the sky. It was flanked by apartments for the Prophet's wives. So the first mosque was a home, a political and military headquarters of the Prophet, and a place of worship for Muslims.

Muslims built or expropriated a building for a great mosque in each town they took during the early conquests. There were to be a great Friday mosque, one per town, and more scattered and lesser ones for daily PRAYER. These great mosques were central to a Muslim town and were close to the seat of local government. Soon funerary mosques were added, containing the TOMB of a member of the Prophet's family, or a companion, or a saint, near the Friday mosques.

The mosque in medieval Islam usually had a MINARET, a mihrab or niche designating the direction of MECCA for prayer, a MINBAR or pulpit for Friday preaching, and a central court surrounded by rooms for teaching, administration of justice, accommodation for travelers, and places for worship, daily life, and study. The later rooms became the meeting places for Sufi CONFRATERNITIES.

GREAT MOSQUES

The great mosques of medieval Islam were, under the UMAYYADS, the Great Mosque of DAMASCUS and, under the ABBASIDS, the ninth-century mosque of Samarra,

Mosque of Sultan Darkhour, Cairo, 1860–90 *(Courtesy Library of Congress)*

near BAGHDAD, which has a spiral minaret and a capacity of 100,000 faithful. In the 10th and 11th centuries, the FATIMIDS introduced corner domes of the *qibla* hall into mosques in EGYPT, while farther east the GHAZNAWIDS built brick minarets decorated with KUFIC letters. In AL-ANDALUS, the Great Mosque of CÓRDOBA was begun in 786. This Iberian style was repeated under the ALMOHADS in the Kutubiya mosque at MARRAKECH in the 12th century. The SELJUKS in ANATOLIA added domes and vaulted halls with an open side. The architectural details of mosques in different areas of ISLAM were often dependent on local building traditions and available materials.

See also ART AND ARCHITECTURE, ISLAMIC.

Further reading: Martin Frishman and Hasan-Uddin Khan, eds., *The Mosque: History, Architectural Development and Regional Diversity* (London: Thames and Hudson, 1994); Robert Hillenbrand, *Islamic Architecture: Form, Function and Meaning* (New York: Columbia University Press, 1994), 31–128; R. Nath, *Mosque Architecture: From Medina to Hindustan, 622–1654* A.D. (Jaipur: Historical Research Documentation Programme, 1994); Johannes Pedersen, "Masdjid," *Encyclopedia of Islam* (1930), 3.314–376.

Mosul (al-Mawsil)   Mosul is a city in northern IRAQ founded by the Persian Sassanians on a bank of the upper Tigris River, avoiding the Syrian desert and controlling the principal commercial route between IRAN and SYRIA. By the Arab conquest in 641, it had become one of the most important Christian and Byzantine strongholds in this frontier region. After the conquest, many Arabs and their families settled in this strategic and commercial center. In the eighth century the city became important town for TEXTILE production, especially for its famous muslin cloth, much sought after throughout the caliphate and western Europe. In the 10th century local dynasties ruled Mosul under the authority of the ABBASID caliphs in BAGHDAD. In 1095 the SELJUK TURKS conquered the city. Zangi (r. 1127–46) proclaimed his independence in Mosul from the Seljuks in 1127. He established a Turkish principality that became one of the launching places for attacks against the crusader states. When it was part of the Zangid and then the AYYUBID states, Mosul prospered in the 12th and 13th centuries until it was destroyed by the MONGOLS under HULEGU in 1258. Although rebuilt, it remained a poor and struggling provincial town in the 14th and 15th centuries and remain initially so under the OTTOMAN TURKS.

See also ALEPPO; ANTIOCH.

Further reading: Douglas Patton, *Badr al-Din Lulu: Atabeg of Mosul, 1211–1259* (Seattle: Distributed by the University of Washington Press, 1991); Chase F. Robinson, *Empire and Elites after the Muslim conquest: The Transformation of Northern Mesopotamia* (Cambridge: Cambridge University Press, 2000).

motet Popular from the mid-13th century, a motet was a piece of unaccompanied polyphonic MUSIC sung to a Latin liturgical text. For two voices with both sung in a Gregorian melody, the motet included a second voice singing a slightly different parallel text in the same melody than that sung by the first voice. The words of the texts were of primary importance.

Motets rapidly grew more complicated with the addition of voices and texts. Some became linguistically mixed. In most a bass sang the text in Latin, while other voices sang in the vernacular. By the 15th century, the motet had become polyphonic, but the words were either exclusively Latin or exclusively vernacular. Authors composed motets for the Mass and were mainly concerned with introducing into choral music feelings and ideas expressed by words and images. In the MASS, motets were sung at the offertory and after the singing of an ANTIPHON. In about 1320 Philip of Vitry (1290–1361) wrote the *Art of Composing of Motets* that influenced their composition for centuries. The Renaissance style of motet of Josquin des Prez (ca. 1440–1521) prevailed between 1480 and 1520.

See also MACHAUT, GUILLAUME DE.

Further reading: Mark Everist, *French Motets in the Thirteenth Century: Music, Poetry, and Genre* (Cambridge: Cambridge University Press, 1994); Sylvia Huot, *Allegorical Play in the Old French Motet: The Sacred and the Profane in Thirteenth-Century Polyphony* (Stanford, Calif.: Stanford University Press, 1997); Daniel Leech-Wilkinson, *Compositional Techniques in the Four-Part Isorhythmic Motets of Philippe de Vitry and His Contemporaries,* 2 vols. (New York: Garland, 1989); Robyn E. Smith, *French Double and Triple Motets in the Montpellier Manuscript: Textual Edition, Translation, and Commentary* (Ottawa: Institute of Mediæval Music, 1997).

Mozarabs Mozarabs were Christians who remained in the territories of the Iberian Peninsula that fell to ISLAM after the conquest of 711. By the 12th century and with the recapture of TOLEDO, Castilian royal authorities applied this term to their Christian minority. It is not clear how well they had been absorbed into tolerant Islamic states or their reactions to the northern Christian RECONQUEST.

The rapid conquest and the occupation of the peninsula had introduced no more than 100,000 Arab or Berber migrants, who were greatly outnumbered by several million Christian inhabitants. The conquered Christians enjoyed the rights that Islam accorded to people of the Book as DHIMMI. This meant freedom of worship in exchange for a tribute from which Muslims were exempt. They had their own count, and officials who regulated the community's internal conflicts, maintained order, and raised taxes for the Muslim rulers. The Mozarabic Christian Church continued to exist and had a functioning episcopal hierarchy under Islam.

In the midninth century, some 50 fanatical monks and nuns provocatively requested martyrdom by publicly asserting their apostatizing from Islam; the Muslims reluctantly martyred them. During this period of decreasing toleration there was a large migration toward the Christian areas in the north and rebellions by those desiring to return to their Christian identity. After these revolts were put down, Islamization progressed rapidly, and many Mozarabs served Muslim princes as mercenary soldiers and tax collectors.

In the course of the Reconquest in the 11th century, the victorious Christian princes moved populations around while the ALMOHADS expelled all infidels from their territories. The Mozarabs were progressively integrated back into Christian society as the Reconquest moved slowly southward to its ultimate success at the capture of GRANADA in 1492.

Further reading: Thomas E. Burman, *Religious Polemic and the Intellectual History of the Mozarabs, ca. 1050–1200* (Leiden: E. J. Brill, 1994); W. C. Bishop, *The Mozarabic and Ambrosian Rites: Four Essays in Comparative Liturgiology* (Milwaukee: Morehouse, 1924); Mireille Mentré, *Illuminated Manuscripts of Medieval Spain* (New York: Thames and Hudson, 1996).

Mudejar The Spanish term *mudéjar* and in the plural *mudéjares* designated the Muslims of the Iberian Peninsula who remained in territory retaken by the advancing Christians. The word was only adopted in Castilian immediately before and during the war of GRANADA around 1492. Before that, the Mudejares were called Moors and SARACENS. After 1520 the Muslims who chose to remain, or had no choice but to remain, on the Iberian Peninsula had to accept baptism and were no longer called Mudejares but Moriscos. The Christian majority ceased to recognize the

Mudejares' right to toleration or even existence. This was enforced by the Spanish Inquisition.

Further reading: L. P. Harvey, *Islamic Spain, 1250 to 1500* (Chicago: University of Chicago Press, 1990); Georgiana Goddard King, *Mudéjar* (London: Longmans, Green, 1927); François-Auguste de Montêquin, *Compendium of Hispano-Islamic Art and Architecture* (Saint Paul: Minn.: Hamline University, 1976).

Muhammad ibn Abdullah ibn Abd al-Muttalib (Mohammad) (571–632) *founder of Islam, prophet*

Muhammad was the son of Abd Allah, son of Abd al-Muttalib of the Hashemite clan. He was a member of the Quraysh tribe, who controlled the town of MECCA in the

Muhammad, on his camel, bidding farewell to his fiancée. Persian miniature, Bibliothèque Nationale, Paris *(Snark / Art Resource)*

early 7th century. They had settled there about 150 years before. Most of what we know of Muhammad is from a sacred tradition whose oldest writings belong to the period of the ABBASID Caliphate of BAGHDAD. Some Quranic passages relate to him and even name him during his prophetic period at Mecca and MEDINA.

EXTANT BIOGRAPHY

A biography of his whole life is not really possible. According to tradition as a young man he had the traits of an ideal prophetic figure as awaited prophet, such as a quasi-miraculous birth, a purification by angels during childhood, and as a boy recognition as a prophet by a Christian monk. Muhammad was said to have been an orphan from birth. He belonged to a clan who had fallen on hard times and were living off the exploitation of seasonal pagan pilgrims. More powerful rival clans were engaged in the trans-Arabian caravan trade. The poor future Prophet first married a wealthy patroness, Khadija, a widow much older than he, in 595. He would also be a man without a surviving son.

REVELATION

A divine revelation took him by surprise around 610. He received his message on Mount Hira from the angel Gabriel and later recorded and compiled it into the QURAN. He always placed himself in the tradition of early prophets such as Abraham, Moses, and Jesus. However, he had explicitly received what was to be the final and comprehensive message from GOD, or Allah. This message was to be the culmination of all previous revelations, and his teachings were the final message. Among the earliest aspects of this revelation, there was an appeal to reform and to return to the traditional values of tribal society. It also, and most importantly, involved an absolute belief in a single god. Muhammad was rejected and rebuked by his own tribe as it violently refused to believe the message of the inspired Muhammad. Accused of betraying the ancestors of the tribe, he was expelled it around 619.

HEJIRA

In 622 he fled to Medina with his followers, to a clan to whom he was related: This flight is AL-HIJR (the hejira). He then entered politics. Over the next 10 years, Muhammad received recognition for his message because of successful raids, seemingly divinely favored, against Meccan caravans, nomads, and those of other hostile cities. The city of Mecca finally surrendered to him and his message, almost without a fight, in 630. He won a battle that same year at Hunayn against the great nomad tribes of western Arabia. He then imposed conversion to ISLAM as a condition for any alliance with Medina. PAGANISM was banned and new laws reflecting his message were established. He also stressed that humanity was one family under God. This emphasis a strong exerted check on the earlier and common tribal rivalries and WARFARE. Before that, political goals seemed always to have preceded religious motives. Just before his death in 632, Muhammad attempted to launch raids on the Byzantines to the north. His successors continued this policy and made great conquests.

Further reading: Abd al-Malik Ibn Hisham, *The Life of Muhammad,* trans. Alfred Guillaume (Lahore: Oxford University Press, 1955); Karen Armstrong, *Muhammad: A Biography of the Prophet* (San Francisco: Harper San Francisco, 1992); F. E. Peters, *Mecca: A Literary History of the Muslim Holy Land* (Princeton, N.J.: Princeton University Press, 1994); Maxime Rodinson, *Muhammad,* trans. Anne Carter, 2d ed. (London: Penguin Books, 1996); W. Montgomery Watt, *Muhammad: Prophet and Statesman* (London: Oxford University Press, 1964).

Murad I (Muhammad I) (1319–1389) *Ottoman sultan*

Murad I began the OTTOMAN expansion in the Balkan Peninsula, achieving spectacular results. In 1360 or 1362 he invaded Thrace and conquered ADRIANOPLE, making it the Ottoman capital. The Byzantine emperor, John V Palaeologos (1332–91), was compelled to pay him tribute, which Murad used to expand his army. In 1371, Murad continued his advance into the Balkans and defeated a coalition of forces from SERBIA and BULGARIA. In 1385 he conquered SOFIA and forced the Bulgarians into vassalage. As the Ottoman advance into the Balkans slowed, Murad turned back to ANATOLIA, where he attacked the SELJUK principalities in central Anatolia. In 1388 he returned to Europe and defeated another Serbian coalition at KOSOVO on June 15, 1389. He was assassinated by a Serb eight days later or was killed on the battlefield.

Further reading: Halil Inalcik, *The Ottoman Empire: The Classical Age, 1300–1600* (1973; reprint, London: Phoenix Press, 1988); Halil Inalcik, *The Middle East and the Balkans under the Ottoman Empire: Essays on Economy and Society* (Bloomington: Indiana University Turkish Studies, 1993).

Murad II (r. 1421–1444, 1446–1451) *successful soldier, Ottoman sultan*

He succeeded his father, Mehmed I (r. 1413–21), as sultan of the OTTOMAN TURKS in 1421. By 1425 he had forced CONSTANTINOPLE to return to paying an annual tribute again. In 1430 as part of a campaign in the Balkans he seized THESSALONIKI, which the Byzantines had sold to VENICE in 1423. Three years after this triumph Murad married a Serbian princess to consolidate his European conquests. The progress into the Balkans was halted in 1443 by a Hungarian counteroffensive led by John HUNYADI. Murad, however, stopped this Christian advance with a crushing victory at Varna in 1444. He retired and temporarily left political affairs to his son, MEHMED II, whose first sultanate between 1444 and 1446 ended in chaos; Murad resumed control. When the Hungarians under Hunyadi launched a new offensive, he inflicted an overwhelming defeat on them at the second Battle of KOSOVO in October 1448. Murad died on February 3, 1451, at ADRIANOPLE. His victories laid the basis for future Ottoman conquest, especially the capture of Constantinople in 1453 by his son, Mehmed II.

Further reading: John W. Barker, *Manuel II Palaeologus 1391–1425): A Study in Late Byzantine Statesmanship* (New Brunswick, N.J.: Rutgers University Press, 1969); Halil Inalcik, *The Ottoman Empire: The Classical Age, 1300–1600* (1973; reprint, London: Phoenix Press, 1988).

music (*musiki, musika*)

In the Middle Ages, as in antiquity, music was oral and a metrical SCIENCE of numbers concerned with the proportions that regulate sounds among themselves. Its growth in sophistication was heavily tied to the liturgical needs and development of the church, both Western and Eastern. Among the SEVEN LIBERAL ARTS taught first in monasteries and then at universities, it belonged to the *quadrivium,* a group also comprising arithmetic, geometry, and astronomy, not to the *trivium* (grammar, RHETORIC, and dialectic). Within the *quadrivium,* music was preceded by arithmetic, which made music comprehensible. This correlation continued well into the 18th century.

In the early Middle Ages, secular and religious music was monophonic and oral. The earliest surviving manuscripts with musical notes date from the second half of the ninth century. During the CAROLINGIAN RENAISSANCE, a need to unify diverse peoples with diverse religious practices was recognized. They sought to impose a more standardized or the Roman rite on liturgical music. Monks needed clues to learn melodies, so notation was added above the text as an aid to memory. These systems of notation indicated pitch and rhythm and further evolved by the 11th century.

For the liturgy of the OFFICE and the MASS, the musical script was that of plainchant. This was a melody that followed the rhythm of the liturgical text and did not use proportional division of lengths, a genre that appeared in the 13th century. Two new kinds of music appeared in the ninth century, both magnifying and elaborating plainchant: polyphony and tropes. Polyphony added to the melodic line one or more extra voices that formed consonances or dissonances with a principal voice. Tropes added text under words, forming a sort of commentary or gloss. Throughout the church consistently placed the greatest emphasis on the text, not on the way it was performed. Music was meant to witness and emphasize the word of GOD. There is little surviving evidence of secular music, which was clearly very commonly sung and enjoyed.

See also ANTIPHONS; ARS ANTIQUA AND ARS NOVA; GOLIARDIC POETS; GREGORIAN CHANT; HYMNS, HYMNALS, AND HYMNOLOGY; MACHAUT, GUILLAUME DE; MOTETS; POLYPHONY; TROUBADOURS.

Further reading: See the numerous detailed articles on "Music" "Musical Notation," and "Musical Treatises" in the *DMA* 8.550–649 and several others in *Encyclopedia of the Renaissance,* ed. Paul F. Grendler (New York: Charles Scribner's Sons, 1999) 4.200–268; Richard Crocker and David Hiley, eds., *The Early Middle Ages to 1300,* 2d ed. (Oxford: Oxford University Press, 1990); Gareth Curtis, "Music," in *The New Cambridge Medieval History,* Vol. 7, *c. 1415–c. 1500,* ed. Christopher Allmand (Cambridge: Cambridge University Press, 1998), 319–333; Tess Knighton and David Fallows, eds., *Companion to Medieval and Renaissance Music* (London: Dent, 1992); James McKinnon, *Music in Early Christian Literature* (Cambridge: Cambridge University Press, 1987); Gustave Reese, *Music in the Middle Ages, with an Introduction on the Music of Ancient Times* (New York: W. W. Norton, 1940); M. L. Switten, *Music and Poetry in the Middle Ages: A Guide to Research on French and Occitan Song, 1100–1400* (New York: Garland, 1995).

mystery and miracle plays   Mystery and miracle plays were the common form of religious drama during the Middle Ages. Usually performed in front of churches, they were dramatic presentations of stories from the New Testament or were tied to specific liturgical feasts. The English VERNACULAR mystery or Corpus Christi plays were relatively late developments in the Middle Ages, belonging to the 15th century. More than 100 English cities and towns staged single pageants or consecutive cycles of five to 48 separate pageants. There are four major English cycles, those from YORK, Chester, Wakefield (Towneley), and the N-Town which was not tied to a particular town. Some cycles are closely related through parallel pageants, and borrowing seems to have taken place also.

STAGING

The staging of the civic cycles was in the hands of the GUILDS of MERCHANTS and craftsmen. These associations or CONFRATERNITIES of LAITY were known as mysteries, thence the name *mystery play.* The guilds took responsibility for the preparations for and entire staging of the plays, sometimes placing chief responsibility in the hands of one person. Each guild chose a subject that fitted its craft or calling and may sometimes have even commissioned a new composition. The various roles were regularly played in successive years by the same actors, sometimes from other towns. The written texts were sometimes checked against performance, revised, or even reassigned to different guilds. The cycles were played in the open, at set points in the city, either on pageants (*pagine*), consisting of roofed stages on wheels moved from point to point, or on fixed stages. Stage machinery was used and costumes were worn, including masks, wigs, robes, crowns, a rib for the creation of Eve, skin-tight white leather suits for the naked Adam and Eve, and a close-fitting skin for the serpent in Eden.

THEMES

Presenting stories of the Old Testament and a culmination in the New, these plays usually emphasized the devil's temptations of Adam and Eve prefiguring his temptations of Christ, Noah's saving beings from the flood suggesting Christ as savior of humankind, and Abraham's sacrifice of his son, Isaac, foreshadowing the Crucifixion. Often stories from the recognized BIBLE were supplemented by others from familiar apocryphal New Testament books. The actors were usually male. The plays were written in rhymed verse reinforced by alliteration.

Further reading: Peter Happé. ed. and trans., *English Mystery Plays: A Selection* (Baltimore: Penguin Books, 1975); Rosemary Woolf, *The English Mystery Plays* (Berkeley: University of California Press, 1972); Richard P. Axton, *Medieval French Plays,* trans. Richard Axton and John Stevens (Oxford: B. Blackwell, 1971).

mysticism, Christian   In the Early Middle Ages *mysticism* vaguely designated contemplation on the mysteries of the faith. In the late Middle Ages, the term much more specifically meant direct union and knowledge of God through personal religious experiences. By the first half of the 12th century, BERNARD of Clairvaux and William of Saint-Thierry (d. 1148/49) saw the spiritual life as a search based on love for union with God.

WESTERN CHRISTIANITY

By the end of the 12th century, some clerics, and numerous laymen and laywomen, claimed to have had mystical experiences. These were prompted by intense meditation on the sufferings of Christ and ascetic exercises promoting detachment from earthly goods. These practices led to an interiorization of religious feeling, an ardent desire for God, and an intense devotion to the Eucharist. All this promoted a loving fusion or mystical union with God. Such mysticism was an individual experience, knowable only through the voice of the person feeling and experiencing it. Since priestly intermediation was not necessary, the church was suspicious of it and its practitioners. Clerical confessors tried to tame or control it. However, some of those claiming it or promoting its practice, such as Margaret PORETTE, were executed for heresy. In intellectual terms, it was not compatible with the rationalist efforts of SCHOLASTICISM to reconcile faith and reason.

EASTERN ORTHODOX

Byzantine mysticism was rooted in the ideas of ORIGEN and the experience of the early desert fathers and mothers, hermits following the models of John the Baptist and

Christ, who had abandoned civilization to contemplate God and salvation in the wilderness. ORIGEN and GREGORY of Nyssa encouraged meditation on the Scriptures. Its spiritual themes were about the earthly life as a passage from the visible to the invisible world, a passage on a ladder ascending to heaven during which God slowly revealed himself. Byzantine mysticism was in part related to spiritual combat against demons for knowledge and control of the human heart.

See also ANGELA OF FOLIGNO; BIRGITTA OF SWEDEN, SAINT; CATHERINE OF SIENA, SAINT; ECKHART, MEISTER; HADEWIJCH OF ANTWERP; HENRY SUSO; JOHN TAULER; KABBALA; MECHTHILD VON MAGDEBURG; RUYSBROECK, JAN VAN; SUFISM

Further reading: Ray C. Petry, *Late Medieval Mysticism* (Philadelphia: Westminster Press, 1957); Bernard McGinn, *The Flowering of Mysticism: Men and Women in the New Mysticism (1200–1350)* (New York: Crossroad, 1998); Elizabeth Petroff, *Body and Soul: Essays on Medieval Women and Mysticism* (New York: Oxford University Press, 1994).

mysticism, Islamic *See* RUMI; SUFISM.

mysticism, Jewish *See* KABBALA; NACHMANIDES, MOSES.

N

Nachmanides, Moses (Nahmanides, Moshe ben Nachman, Ramban, Bonastrug da Porta) (ca. 1194–ca. 1270)
scholar, philosopher, exegete
Ramban (an acronym of the name Rabbi Moses ben Nahman) was a member of a family of rabbis and scholars. Little is known of his early life except that he was born about 1194 and went to school in Gerona in CATALONIA. He was initiated into the KABBALA; studied Christian THEOLOGY, the sciences, and MEDICINE; and was an opponent of MAIMONIDES and the rationalist integration and reconciliation of PHILOSOPHY into theological thought.

In July 1263, given full freedom of speech, he defended JUDAISM at BARCELONA before King JAMES I of Aragon in a disputation on the validity of Judaism against a converted Jew. Well respected at the court and by the Jewish community in Catalonia, he later refuted the convert's arguments and his understanding of the rabbinical tradition on the coming of the Messiah in his *Book of the Debate*. In 1265, the DOMINICANS accused him of committing BLASPHEMY and of insulting Christianity. Pope Clement IV (r. 1265–68) granted their petition for pursuing him in 1267. At the age of 70 or older, he had to leave for PALESTINE, where he reorganized a Jerusalem community disrupted by the MONGOL invasion of 1267 and the occupation by the crusaders.

A prolific author, Nachmanides also wrote biblical and Talmudic commentaries, treatises on rabbinic custom, and homilies or SERMONS. His commentary on the PENTATEUCH rejected Maimonides' allegorical interpretations. His commentary on Job solved the problem of a just sufferer and a sinner by means of the concept of a transmigration of SOULS. He benefited while he was in Palestine from access to the Babylonian and Jerusalem Talmuds. His few kabbalistic treatises were a commentary on the first chapter of the Book of Creation and the section entitled "Portico of Retribution." His disciples claimed to find his kabbalistic ideas scattered throughout his commentary on the Pentateuch. It was of the most important kabbalistic books until the appearance of the *Zohar* in about 1325. He died at ACRE or Erets in about 1270 and is buried at the foot of Mount Carmel.

See also HALAKAH; TALMUD.

Further reading: Charles Ber Chavel, *Ramban: His Life and Teachings* (New York: P. Feldheim, 1960); Robert Chazan, *Daggers of the Faith: Thirteenth-Century Christian Missionizing and Jewish Response* (Berkeley: University of California Press, 1989); Robert Chazan, *Barcelona and Beyond: The Disputation of 1263 and Its Aftermath* (Berkeley: University of California Press, 1992); Jeremy Cohen, *The Friars and the Jews: The Evolution of Medieval Anti-Judaism* (Ithaca, N.Y.: Cornell University Press, 1982); David Novak, *The Theology of Nahmanides Systematically Presented* (Atlanta: Scholar Press, 1992); Isadore Twersky, ed., *Rabbi Moses Nahmanides (Ramban): Explorations in His Religious and Literary Virtuosity* (Cambridge, Mass.: Harvard University Press, 1983).

Naples and Kingdom of Naples An important city under the Roman Empire, Naples was conquered by the OSTROGOTHS in 493 and then twice more by the BYZANTINES under BELISARIUS in 536 and 553. Naples remained under Constantinople's theoretical authority from 544 to 1137 but gained essential independence in 763, resisting later attacks by the LOMBARDS, Byzantines, and NORMANS in Italy. Arab raiders did heavy damage to its harbor in the ninth century. Naples was a port for coastal traffic but was less active than nearby AMALFI. It profited from the fertility of the surrounding countryside. Naples passed under the rule of the NORMAN king of SICILY, ROGER II, in 1137. Its privileges were then limited by its integration into the centralized, competent, but exploitative feudal state of the Norman monarchy. It used local nobles as civil servants to manage the town.

After the Norman dynasty died out in 1194, it was replaced by the HOHENSTAUFEN and the emperor

Fifteenth-century view of Naples, Francesco Pagano, Tavola Strozzi, Museo Nazionale di Capodimonte, Naples, Italy *(Alinari / Art Resource)*

FREDERICK II. He encouraged economic development by fostering maritime commerce and the textile industry. In 1224 Frederick founded a university in the town. It was intended to train jurists for the imperial administration, replacing the older and the more GUELF or anti-imperial one at BOLOGNA.

A CULTURAL CENTER

In 1267 CHARLES I OF ANJOU, brother of King LOUIS IX, defeated and replaced the Hohenstaufen dynasty, and became the king of Sicily. He made Naples his capital especially after the SICILIAN VESPERS of 1282. He introduced a court full of French nobles and the Tuscan MERCHANTS who had financed his conquest. Local crafts developed to provide luxury products for the court; shipyards grew to maintain a much larger navy. A building boom occurred and the population rose to perhaps as many as 60,000 inhabitants in the 14th century, making Naples one of the largest cities in Europe. The royal patronage of his successors made the court an intellectual center, as famous writers such as BOCCACCIO and PETRARCH gained royal patronage. Artists from TUSCANY and northern Italy produced PAINTING and sculpture in the kingdom.

The economic and demographic catastrophes of the second half of the 14th century and the incompetence and wars of its Angevin rulers opened possibilities for at least temporary municipal independence. Several rebellions against the Crown, never gained more than a temporary release from Angevin exploitation and dominance. In 1442 ALFONSO V OF ARAGON captured the city after a devastating siege and sack. Under this new administration the local artisans and merchants lost control over the economy as Tuscan merchants once again took over and were needed to pay for the wars and policies of Alfonso. However, there was a cultural revival and some of the great artists and authors of the 15th century worked in Naples. This prosperity and peace continued under the competent king Ferrante I (r. 1458–94). The city was still a great enough prize that it became the goal of the devastating French invasions of the last decade of the 15th century.

Further reading: Cecil Headlam, *The Story of Naples* (London: J. M. Dent, 1927); Jerry H. Bentley, *Politics and Culture in Renaissance Naples* (Princeton, N.J.: Princeton University Press, 1987); Benedetto Croce, *History of the Kingdom of Naples,* ed. H. Stuart Hughes and trans. Frances Frenaye (Chicago: University of Chicago Press, 1970); Alan Ryder, *The Kingdom of Naples under Alfonso the Magnanimous: The Making of a Modern State* (Oxford: Clarendon Press, 1976); Alan Ryder, *Alfonso the Magnanimous: King of Aragon, Naples, and Sicily, 1396–1458* (Oxford: Clarendon Press, 1990).

narthex The term *narthex,* meaning "box" or "casket" in Greek, designated the vestibule, just inside the door to the interior, opening onto the NAVE, and situated at the entrance to a ROMANESQUE church. It was supposed to be a place of purification. In Byzantine churches, it usually had an opening or staircase to the galleries above. In the early church, catechumens, candidates for baptism, and penitents were allowed to be present only at the first part of the MASS and had to stay in the narthex. A narthex should not be confused with a porch, which was open to the outside. The narthex was used for the formation of processions.

Further reading: Richard Krautheimer, *Early Christian and Byzantine Architecture,* 3d ed. (Harmondsworth: Penguin Books, 1979); Thomas F. Mathews, *Byzantium: From Antiquity to the Renaissance* (New York: Abrams, 1998).

Nasrids (Banu Nasr) They were the last Muslim dynasty in SPAIN. They ruled in GRANADA from 1238 to 1492, gaining power after the defeat of the ALMOHADS at the Battle of Las Navas de Tolosa in 1212. Muhammad I al-Ghalib, also called Ibn al-Ahmav (r. 1232–72), was its founder and was from Málaga. He managed to retain the easily defendable mountainous district in the south of Spain around the city of Granada. His relations with CASTILE were generally peaceful, although he was forced to recognize Castilian supremacy as a more-or-less client ruler. He also initiated the Nasrid practice of accepting Muslim refugees from the rest of the reconquered peninsula and began construction of a remarkable Islamic monument, the palace of the ALHAMBRA. The Nasrids tried to strike a balance between the Marinids of FEZ and the kings of Castile.

Under the reserved and timid Yusuf I (r. 1333–54), an alliance of Nasrids with the Marinids proved catastrophic when they were defeated by King Alfonso XI of Castile (r. 1312–50) in 1340 at the Rio Salado. Despite being racked by internal conflict throughout the 15th century, the kingdom survived, still a client state to Christians but remaining a center of Muslim culture. Nasrid rule ended in 1492 with a long campaign and the capture of the city of Granada by FERDINAND and ISABEL I. The last Nasrid ruler was Muhammad XI (r. 1482–92) or Bobadilla, who had rashly refused to pay the annual tribute. He fled to MOROCCO.

See also ART AND ARCHITECTURE; GARDENS.

Further reading: David Abulafia, "The Nasrid Kingdom of Granada," in *The New Cambridge Medieval History.* Vol. 5 *c. 1198–c. 1300,* ed. David Abulafia (Cambridge: Cambridge University Press, 1999), 636–643; Clifford Edmund Bosworth, *The Islamic Dynasties* (Edinburgh: Edinburgh University Press, 1967), 18–19; John Edwards, *The Spain of the Catholic Monarchs, 1474–1520* (Oxford: Blackwell, 2000); L. P. Harvey, *Islamic Spain, 1250–1500* (Chicago: University of Chicago Press, 1990); Markus Hattstein and Peter Delius, eds., *Islam: Art and Architecture,* trans. George Ansell et al.

(Cologne: Könemann, 2000), 272–297; Hugh Kennedy, *Muslim Spain and Portugal: A Political History of al-Andalus* (New York: Longman, 1996).

nature, idea of   The word *nature* was derived from the Latin *natura*, suggesting birth. In the Christian Middle Ages, nature was viewed as the created work of GOD according to the account in the biblical book of Genesis. For BOETHIUS, nature was the inner principle of all movement, common to every individual. The term could be used in the sense of the nature of an action or power.

There was also divine nature. For AUGUSTINE nature was the universal whole that included God as well as his creatures. All created nature was the work of God. From the 13th century, the ideas of ARISTOTLE were added to the concept, providing further scientific visions of the cosmos, making possible a PHILOSOPHY of nature. Nature played an important role in the division of the sciences. Natural philosophy was distinguished from ethics, it comprised the knowledge of things or creatures. The only necessity characterizing this kind of nature was participation in the necessary being of God. Nature equaled necessity, but this necessity did not exclude change decreed freely by God.

Christian nature also implied further perfection by GRACE and Redemption. This term designated the "nature" of God, becoming synonymous with *essence* or *substance*. In terms of the Trinity, the term *natura* designated the unity of God and the term *persona* or persons designated the three individual components of the Trinity.

See also ANIMALS AND ANIMAL HUSBANDRY; MIRACLES; PHILOSOPHY AND THEOLOGY; SCIENCE.

Further reading: A. C. Crombie, *Science, Art, and Nature in Medieval and Modern Thought* (London: Hambledon Press, 1996); William Eamon, *Science and the Secrets of Nature: Books of Secrets in Medieval and Early Modern Culture* (Princeton, N.J.: Princeton University Press, 1994); Patricia May Gathercole, *The Landscape of Nature in Medieval French Manuscript Illumination* (Lewiston, N.Y.: Edwin Mellen Press, 1997); Chumaru Koyama, ed., *Nature in Medieval Thought: Some Approaches East and West* (Leiden: Brill, 2000); Lawrence D. Roberts, ed., *Approaches to Nature in the Middle Ages: Papers of the Tenth Annual Conference of the Center for Medieval and Early Renaissance Studies, State University of New York at Binghamton, 1976* (Binghamton, N.Y.: Medieval and Renaissance Texts and Studies, Center for Medieval and Early Renaissance Studies, 1983); Joyce E. Salisbury, ed., *The Medieval World of Nature: A Book of Essays* (New York: Garland, 1993); William J. Short, *Saints in the World of Nature: The Animal Story as Spiritual Parable in Medieval Hagiography (900–1200)* (Rome: Pontificia Universitas Gregoriana, Facultas Theologiæ, Institutum Spiritualitatis, 1983); Hugh White, *Nature, Sex, and Goodness in a Medieval Literary Tradition* (Oxford: Oxford University Press, 2000).

Navarre, kingdom of   A kingdom of Navarre was created, when CHARLEMAGNE conquered the western Pyrenees around Pamplona, its main city, and made it part of his kingdom of AQUITAINE. It, however, kept its own rulers as the kings of Pamplona until the 10th century. Later its king, King Sancho III the Great (r. 1000–35) of Navarre, was one of its most accomplished and important rulers, ruling a group of counties from the Aran Valley to the borders of LEÓN, and the northern slopes of the Pyrenees. He died in 1035 and his realm was shared among his sons; García (r. 1035–54), the eldest received Navarre; Ferdinand I (r. 1038–65) received CASTILE; and Ramiro I (r. 1035–63) was bequeathed ARAGON. This arrangement lasted from 1035 to 1134, when Navarre was disputed between the kings of Castile and Aragon at the death of Alfonso I the Battler (r. 1104–34), the king of Aragon and Pamplona. From 1200 to 1205 the kingdom of Navarre was a little more than 10,000 square kilometers (6,000 square miles), a small, but strategic, state on the Iberian Peninsula. It was overtaken and limited to the far north of Spain by the territorial expansion and consolidation of Castile and Aragon.

THE RECONQUEST

Despite its small size, the kings of Navarre participated in the CRUSADE against the Muslims of AL-ANDALUS. In 1212, at the victorious Battle of Las Navas de Tolosa, the king of Navarre, Sancho VII the Strong (r. 1194–1234), was one of the leaders of the Christian forces. Navarre's main objectives were the conquest and re-Christianization of the Ebro Valley. The kings of Navarre called in colonists to repopulate towns and villages. In the course of this Reconquista, the kings permitted Muslim minorities and Jewish communities to remain in most of the towns and villages of the kingdom. The king of Navarre also took charge of the lucrative task of accommodating the large number of pilgrims to SANTIAGO DE COMPOSTELA.

On the death of Sancho VII the Strong (r. 1194–1234) in 1234, the king's legitimate heir was a nephew, Count Thibaut IV of Champagne, who was crowned at Pamplona as Thibaut I of Navarre (r. 1234–53). These French rulers with ties to Champagne ruled until 1274. They were followed by the kings of France from 1274 to 1328 and from then by the counts of Évreux until 1425. The kingdom of Navarre was weakened in the 15th century by its involvement in French dynastic struggles and wars. The marriage of a daughter of King Charles III the Noble (r. 1387–1425) led to a union of Navarre and Aragon between 1425 and 1479. After a temporary French rule, FERDINAND II completed the union with

Aragon by occupying the Spanish part of the kingdom in 1512.

See also ASTURIAS-LEÓN, KINGDOM OF; BASQUES.

Further reading: Béatrice Leroy, "Navarre," *EMA,* 2.1,006–1,007; Angus MacKay, *Spain in the Middle Ages: From Frontier to Empire, 1000–1500* (New York: St. Martin's Press, 1977); Joseph O'Callaghan, *A History of Medieval Spain* (Ithaca, N.Y.: Cornell University Press, 1975).

nave The nave was the central part of a church between the main entrance or west portal and the chancel and choir. It was often flanked by aisles. It was assigned to the LAITY or the congregation and was separated from the sanctuary by a screen and from the aisles by columns or pillars. It was based on the LATIN word for "ship," *navis,* since it resembled an upside-down ship or in another way the ark of SALVATION. In Byzantine churches the laity were sometimes even removed from it and herded into the aisles. Aisles were often added to the nave for chapels and side altars.

Further reading: Nicola Coldstream, *Medieval Architecture* (Oxford: Oxford University Press, 2002); Roger Stalley, *Early Medieval Architecture* (Oxford: Oxford University Press, 1999); Rolf Toman, ed., *Romanesque: Architecture, Sculpture, Painting* (Cologne: Könemann, 1997); Rolf Toman, ed., *The Art of the Gothic: Architecture, Sculpture, Painting* (Cologne: Könemann, 1998).

navies   *See* SHIPS AND SHIPBUILDING.

navigation (*Milāha*) Medieval navigation involved several geographic areas: the Atlantic Ocean, the Red Sea, the Indian Ocean, and the Mediterranean Sea. During the Middle Ages the magnetic COMPASS began to be used in the West, and shipbuilding technology progressed. The Irish and the VIKINGS or Scandinavians had pioneered open ocean navigation from the fifth century. The development of the ASTROLABE, mathematically based charts, the expansion of commerce, the reprovisioning needs of the CRUSADES, and the rediscovery of the ideas of the classical geographers all contributed to the advancement of navigation during the Middle Ages. The great voyages of the 15th century and beyond became possible as a result of these discoveries and additional tools.

See also BRENDAN, SAINT; GEOGRAPHY AND CARTOGRAPHY; HENRY "THE NAVIGATOR"; MAPS; PORTOLAN CHARTS; SHIPS AND SHIPBUILDING.

Further reading: George Fletcher Bass, ed., *A History of Seafaring: Based on Underwater Archaeology* (New York: Walker, 1972); J. A. Bennett, *The Divided Circle: A History of Instruments for Astronomy, Navigation, and Surveying* (Oxford: Phaidon, Christie's, 1987); W. E. May, *A History of Marine Navigation* (New York: Norton, 1973); J. E. D. Williams, *From Sails to Satellites: The Origin and Development of Navigational Science* (Oxford: Oxford University Press, 1992); W. G. L. Randles, *Geography, Cartography and Nautical Science in the Renaissance: The Impact of the Great Discoveries* (Aldershot: Ashgate/Variorum, 2000).

Neoplatonism and Platonism in the Middle Ages Medieval Platonism, with its modern name Neoplatonism, was not based on the direct study of the works of Plato. Instead it was based on a movement from the early Christian era, a school of thought of ALEXANDRIA and linked to PLOTINUS. In western Europe, direct knowledge of Plato's work was limited to a translated part of the *Timaeus.* Nonetheless a lack of translations and texts did not prevent this form of Platonism from exercising influence on Christian metaphysics through intermediaries. Numerous Christian authors, such as AUGUSTINE OF HIPPO, integrated the ideas of such Platonism into their thought; other commonly read authors sympathized with and drew on Platonism, such as Cicero or BOETHIUS; and the secondhand Platonic materials that entered the Latin world through Arabic or Jewish intermediaries.

The pagan Neoplatonic philosophy of the third century of PLOTINUS and Porphyry (ca. 232–ca. 305) influenced Christian thought in terms of the concepts of the hierarchy of spiritual beings, the spiritual name of reality, the return of the soul to the One the unknowable source from which all exists and emanates, through contemplation, and the essential goodness and fullness of being itself. On the other hand, Neoplatonism denied God's voluntary creation. Its triad or hypostases of the One, the Intelligence or intuitive knowledge, and the Soul, the realm of discursive thought and activity was completely unlike the Christian Trinity. The One's omnipresence suggested pantheism.

More direct knowledge of explicit Neoplatonism was not really accessible until the ideas of the Muslims AL-FARABI, AL-GHAZALI, and IBN SINA (Avicenna) and those of the Jewish scholar Avicebron or Ibn Gabirol (1021–ca. 1058) reached Latin Europe in the late 12th century. Their thought combined the physical ideas of Aristotle and the spiritual ideas of a Neoplatonic system to explain a universe. Later translations of Proclus (ca. 411–485), for example, provided by WILLIAM of Moerbeke (1215–86) went further, allowing a possible disentangling of Neoplatonism and Aristotelianism. The availability of these translations led to a disenchantment with the ideas of Aristotle and certain aspects of SCHOLASTIC thought. In the 15th century a complete translation of the dialogues of Plato was made by Marsilio FICINO. This allowed scholars and humanists to discover the authentic thought of Plato and to cultivate his philosophy as an alternative to ARISTOTELIAN AND SCHOLASTIC philosophies.

See also ABÉLARD PETER; DIONYSIUS THE AREOPAGITE; JOHN SCOTTUS ERIUGENA; MIRANDOLA, PICO DELLA; PLATO AND PLATONISM.

Further reading: Stephen Gersh, *Middle Platonism and Neoplatonism: The Latin Tradition,* 2 vols. (Notre Dame, Ind.: University of Notre Dame Press, 1986); Raymond Klibansky, *The Continuity of the Platonic Tradition during the Middle Ages: With a New Preface and Four Supplementary Chapters, Together with Plato's Parmenides in the Middle Ages and the Renaissance* (Munich: Kraus International Publications, 1981); Haijo Jan Westra, ed., *From Athens to Chartres, Neoplatonism and Medieval Thought: Studies in Honour of Edouard Jeauneau* (Leiden: E. J. Brill, 1992).

Nestorianism (the Church of the East) This was a Christian HERESY that arose in the BYZANTINE EMPIRE from the ideas of Nestorius (ca. 381–ca. 452), the Syrian patriarch of CONSTANTINOPLE (428–431). According to its doctrine, there were two separate natures and persons in the incarnate Christ, one fully divine and one fully human. This perspective was opposed to the Orthodox and Monophysite views that, Nestorius feared, destroyed the full humanity of Jesus and detracted from the dignity of GOD. The emperor summoned a general council of bishops to adjudicate the matter at the Council of EPHESUS in 431. CYRIL the bishop of Alexandria, himself vehemently opposed to Nestorianism, convened the council and swiftly accomplished the condemnation of Nestorius before Eastern bishops friendly to the latter had arrived. After these irregular proceedings, Nestorius resigned voluntarily. Under government pressure in 433, however, Cyril made surprising concessions, reconciling with the more moderate of Nestorius's allies through the Formulary of Reunion. Nestorius was condemned again at the COUNCIL OF EPHESUS in 431 and died in exile in EGYPT.

Syriac-speaking Bishops in SYRIA, IRAQ, and Persia (IRAN) refused to accept this condemnation and founded their own church, which flourished and expanded, surviving periodic persecutions by the Muslims and MONGOLS. Through theologically static, they sent missionaries to China and the Mongols with some success. Some Mongols did convert, but when the majority of them embraced ISLAM in Iran, the sect was destined to remain small and marginal. The Byzantines persecuted them. Many were killed and their centers destroyed in the invasions of TAMERLANE around 1395. In the 15th century some of them returned to communion with the PAPACY, but others did not and survive to this day.

See also CHRISTOLOGY AND CHRISTOLOGICAL CONTROVERSY.

Further reading: Nestorius, *The Bazaar of Heracleides,* trans. G. R. Driver and Leonard Hodgson (New York: AMS Press, 1978; Luise Abramowski and Alan E. Goodman, eds. and trans., *A Nestorian Collection of Christological Texts, Cambridge University Library Ms. Oriental 1319* (Cambridge: Cambridge University Press, 1972); James F. Bethune-Baker, *Nestorius and His Teaching: A Fresh Examination of the Evidence* (Cambridge: Cambridge University Press, 1908); Friedrich Loofs, *Nestorius and His Place in the History of Christian Doctrine* (1914; reprint, New York: B. Franklin, 1975).

Nestorius *See* NESTORIANISM.

Netherlands In the Middle Ages the Low Countries or Netherlands comprised the regions around the Rhine, Meuse, and Scheldt River estuaries. This included present-day HOLLAND, BELGIUM, LUXEMBOURG, and parts of GERMANY and FRANCE, which had been divided into several counties, duchies, and principalities with a prosperous and widespread urban life during the Middle Ages.

From the late fifth century, the region of the Netherlands was under the century of the FRANKS. A linguistic frontier between Romance-speaking and Germanic-speaking regions was established during this period. Christianization, which had begun under the Romans, was slowed by the Frankish invasions, but was completed during the seventh century.

A FLOURISHING AGE

In the eighth century, the Carolingians ushered in a period of prosperity. CHARLEMAGNE subdued the Frisians and SAXONS and divided the area into counties, where a count represented the ruler as a judge and a military commander. After the TREATY OF VERDUN in 843, all the territories on the left bank of the Scheldt were attached to West Francia, the future France, and all the territories on the right bank slowly became part of the German Empire. On both sides of the Scheldt, the old administrative districts evolved into principalities, where counts remained marginally attached by feudal ties to the rulers of France and Germany, respectively. The later success of the towns of this region created an abundant source of artistic patronage and expanded horizons for various dynastic families throughout the rest of the Middle Ages. From the 11th century, its history must be followed through that of its cities, counties, and rulers.

See also BALDWIN I OF FLANDERS; BELGIUM; BRABANT, DUCHY OF; BRUGES; BURGUNDY; EYCK, HUBERT VAN, AND EYCK, JAN VAN; FLANDERS AND THE LOW COUNTRIES; FRISIA; GHENT; PHILIP THE GOOD; WEYDEN, ROGIER VAN DER.

Further reading: Willem Pieter Blockmans and Walter Prevenier, *The Promised Lands: The Low Countries under Burgundian Rule, 1369–1530,* trans. Elizabeth Fackelman (Philadelphia: University of Pennsylvania Press, 1999); H. A. Heidinga and H. H. van Regteren Altena, eds., *Medemblik and Monnickendam: Aspects of Medieval Urbanization in Northern Holland* (Amsterdam: Universiteit van Amsterdam, Albert Egges van Giffen Institut voor Prae-uen Protohistorie, 1989); Walter Prevenier, *The Burgundian Netherlands* (Cambridge: Cambridge University Press, 1986).

Neustria   The word Neustria, or "new land," entered use around 642 to refer to the land of the FRANKS, who usually called it Francia. It was applied to the western part of three regions that made up Gaul in the sixth century after partitions of the Merovingian kingdom and a decentralization of power. Its capital was Soissons. Neustria consisted of the lands bordered by the Loire, BRITTANY, the English Channel, and the Meuse, the northwestern area of the Frankish kingdom. In reality it was the heart of CLOVIS's great kingdom. It encompassed the prestigious cultural centers of SAINT-DENIS near Paris, Saint-Martin at Tours, Saint-Médard at Soissons, and the towns of ROUEN and PARIS. A more clear regional consciousness developed later when the Neustrians considered themselves to be the true Franks.

The Merovingian kings Clotar II (r. 613–629) and Dagobert I (r. 629–639) reunified the Merovingian kingdom from 613 to 639. Paris became its capital, and the basilica of Saint-Denis became a necropolis for the Frankish Merovingian family. From about 640, however, power was exercised by a mayor of the palace. Austrasia, the other part of the Frankish realm, eventually dominated its western neighbor, especially after Pépin II of Heristal (d. 714) defeated the Neustrians at the Battle of Tetry in 687. PÉPIN III THE SHORT formally united the two regions in his consecration at Saint-Denis in 754. The CAROLINGIANS stayed in the region when not on campaign, choosing AACHEN as their capital. The area between the Seine and the Rhine became a new royal area, Francia, or FRANCE. Much of its territory was eventually taken over by the Normans when they settled in NORMANDY.

Further reading: Edward James, *The Franks* (Oxford: Basil Blackwell, 1988); Felice Lifshitz, *The Norman Conquest of Pious Neustria: Historiographic Discourse and Saintly Relics, 684–1090* (Toronto: Pontifical Institute of Mediaeval Studies, 1995); J. M. Wallace-Hadrill, *The Long-Haired Kings and Other Studies in Frankish History* (London: Methuen, 1962).

Nevsky, Alexander, Saint (Alexandr Yaroslavich) (1220–1263) *grand prince of Vladimir, Kiev, and Novgorod* Born on May 30, 1220, the son of Grand Prince Yaroslav II of Vladimir (r. 1238–46), Alexander was elected prince of NOVGOROD in 1236 and defeated the Swedes at the Battle of Neva in 1240. He took the name Nevsky from the site of that battle on the banks of the Neva River. The Swedes had invaded the region to punish Novgorod for its attacks on their territory. In 1242 he achieved his greatest success by destroying the Livonian TEUTONIC KNIGHTS in the Battle on the Ice, fought on Lakes Peypus and Pskov. These victories preserved Orthodox RUSSIA. Alexander foresaw the futility of opposing the MONGOLS, who had just captured KIEV, and rendered them allegiance and tribute.

After the death of his father in 1246, Alexander was appointed prince of Kiev, while his brother was named grand prince of Vladimir by the Mongols. In 1252 he replaced his brother as grand prince and appointed his own son, Vasily, as the prince of Novgorod. As a vassal and appeaser of the Mongols or TATARS of the Golden Horde, Alexander assisted them in conducting their tax census and in furthering their supremacy in northern Russia. Since the church was left out of his revised tax system, it ardently supported Alexander and later made him a saint for that reason and for protecting orthodoxy. He built extensive fortifications and enacted numerous laws. After a period of illness and taking of monastic tonsure, he died on November 14/15, 1263. His reign marked the end of resistance to the Mongols for a long time and was followed by conflict over succession.

See also RUSSIA AND RUS.

Further reading: S. A. Zenkovsky, ed., *The Nikonian Chronicle.* Vol. 3, *From the Year 1241 to the Year 1381* (Princeton, N.J.: Kingston Press, 1986); John Fennell, *The Crisis of Medieval Russia, 1200–1304* (New York: Longman, 1983); Charles J. Halperin, *Russia and the Golden Horde: The Mongol Impact on Medieval Russian History* (Bloomington: Indiana University Press, 1985); Nicholas Riasanovsky, *A History of Russia*, 3d ed. (New York: Oxford University Press, 1977); George Vernadsky, *The Mongols and Russia* (New Haven, Conn.: Yale University Press, 1953).

Nibelungenlied **(the Song of the Nibelungs, sons of the mist)**   An anonymous German popular epic set in Austro-Bavarian in several versions composed about 1200, it was one of the great and best known works of medieval German literature. This poem had a strong influence on subsequent literature and music.

In German mythology, the Nibelungen were the sons of the mist and a race of dwarfs who inhabited the underground world. They held a treasure that symbolized power. The hero of this epic, Siegfried, stole their treasure and become king of the Rhine. At the court at Worms of the weak king of the BURGUNDIANS, Siegfried asked for the hand of the king's sister, Kriemhild. The story told of Siegfried's assistance to Gunther to win the hand of Brunhilde, his own marriage to Kriemhild, his murder by Hagen, the disposal of the treasure in the Rhine, Kriemhild's marriage to ATTILA THE HUN (Etzel), and an avenging slaughter at a meeting between the Burgundians and HUNS. It was based on popular legends dating back to the time of the invasions, when the Burgundians were defeated by the Huns near Worms in 436. It was about ideas of power, domination, heroic virtues, ambition, honor, and vengeance—all issues in the feudal Germany of the early 13th century.

See also ICELAND AND ICELANDIC LITERATURE.

Further reading: Arthur T. Hatto, trans., *The Nibelungenlied* (New York: Penguin, 1969); Michael S. Batts, "The *Nibelungenlied*," in *European Writers: The Middle Ages and the Renaissance*. Vol. 1, *Prudentius to Medieval Drama*, ed. William T. H. Jackson and George Stade (New York: Charles Scribner's Sons, 1983), 211–236; Hugo Bekker, *The Nibelungenlied: A Literary Analysis* (Toronto: University of Toronto Press, 1971); Winder McConnell, ed., *A Companion to the Nibelungenlied* (Columbia, S.C.: Camden House, 1998); David G. Mowatt and Hugh Sacker, *The Nibelungenlied: An Interpretative Commentary* (Toronto: University of Toronto Press, 1967).

Nicaea, Councils of   There were two important ecumenical councils at Nicaea (present-day Iznik, Turkey), a town in Bithynia in the northwestern part of ANATOLIA not far from CONSTANTINOPLE. The first in May and June of 325 dealt with the problem of ARIANISM. The second in September and October of 787 was about ICONOCLASM and the cult of icons.

COUNCIL OF 325

After CONSTANTINE's victory over Licinius (ca. 250–324) in 324, Christianity in the Roman Empire was divided over the teaching of Arius or Arianism. Arius was a priest from ALEXANDRIA who taught that the Christ was not coeternal with the supreme Father. He was at best an adopted son of God and did not have a human soul. The emperor convoked a general synod or council at Nicaea in 325; wanting to impose unity on his church, he opened the council himself. It was presided over by a small papal delegation and was attended by perhaps as many as 300 bishops, but only a few from the West. In acrimonious and long debates, an Arian formula of FAITH was proposed and overwhelmingly rejected. EUSEBIOS OF CAESAREA's creed was introduced and given general approval. The ideas of Arianism continued to exist. The council also decided the date of the celebration of EASTER. It was to be held on the first Sunday after the first full moon after the vernal equinox.

COUNCIL OF 787

The second Council of Nicaea was convened in 787 by the emperors IRENE and Constantine VI (r. 780–797) and Patriarch Tarasios (r. 784–806) of Constantinople, to abolish the decisions of the council of Hiereia in 754 and to restore the cult of ICONS. It was the last ecumenical council recognized by both the Orthodox and the Roman Church. Initially meeting in 786 at Constantinople, it had been broken up by soldiers allied to bishops faithful to Iconoclasm. Representatives of Pope Adrian I (772–795), of the Oriental patriarchates, the patriarch of Constantinople, perhaps 365 bishops, and more than 130 monks were present. At the council notorious Iconoclast bishops were allowed back to their sees despite the objections of monks after the prelates publicly accepted the cult of icons. The council compiled texts to support the use of icons and refuted the acts of the Council of Hiereia. It further rejected the accusation of idolatry in the cult of icons. The marks of respect and veneration, such as prostration and kissing, paid to icons and other sacred objects did not constitute adoration, which was due to God alone. The council justified devotion to icons, as had been accepted by the church from the earliest times. The council ended by restoring icons in all public and private places and imposed correct gestures of veneration toward them. The decisions of Nicaea II were accepted with hesitation and difficulty in the West. The CAROLINGIANS rejected them at the Council of Frankfurt and presented their rejection in the *LIBRI CAROLINI*. The popes did not officially accept them until the ninth century.

Further reading: Norman P. Tanner, ed., *Decrees of the Ecumenical Councils*, 2 vols. (London: Sheed and Ward, 1990), 1.1–19, 1.131–156; Marvin M. Arnold, *Nicaea and the Nicene Council of AD 325* (Washington, Mich.: Arno, 1987); Robert Grant, *Religion and Politics at the Council of Nicaea* (Chicago: University of Chicago Press, 1973); Colm Luibhéid, *The Council of Nicaea* (Galway, Ireland: Galway University Press, 1982); D. J. Sahas, *Icon and Logos: Sources in Eighth-Century Iconoclasm* (Toronto: Pontifical Institute of Mediaeval Studies, 1986).

Nicaea, Empire of   This was the temporary Byzantine state established by refugees from CONSTANTINOPLE during the capture and sack of the city by the crusaders of the Fourth CRUSADE. Just before the sack of Constantinople in 1204, Theodore I Laskaris (r. 1205–21), the son-in-law of the emperor Alexios III Angelos (r. 1195–1203), left the city to cross to ANATOLIA, because of dynastic conflicts over the Byzantine throne and with the crusaders. He was not initially well received in the nearby town of Nicaea, but after a year of fighting and the sacking of the capital by the crusaders, he was finally recognized as the new emperor. He soon restored the Orthodox Church, now to be centered in Nicaea. He was crowned in 1208 by its first patriarch, Michael IV Autoreianos (r. 1208–14). Though not recognized as emperor in the West or by the Frankish rulers of Constantinople, he survived due to a military victory in 1211 at ANTIOCH over the SELJUK Turks and by the signing of a peace treaty in 1214 and proposing marriage alliances with the Latin emperor in Constantinople, Henry of Hainault (r. 1206–16).

His son-in-law and successor, John III Vatatzes (r. 1222–54), considered a saint after his death, moved the seat of government near Smyrna and began the full reconstruction of a new Byzantine state. To restore its economic life, John III Vatatzes promoted agriculture and the development of land, especially on his exemplary personal and imperial estates. Trying to promote economic growth, he forbade his subjects to buy luxury products to limit such wasteful losses of wealth. He even tried to make money by selling the Seljuks food. With this newfound regional prosperity, he rebuilt the Byzantine army and began the reconquest of the former Byzantine territories then held by the Latins. He drove them completely out of Anatolia and in 1234 crossed to Europe, Thrace, taking advantage of the defeat of a Latin-supported rival by the Bulgarians. In the meantime the Seljuk Turks were crushed by the Mongols in 1243 and from then on ceased to pose a threat to his rear approaches in Anatolia. John continued his campaigns in Europe, taking THESSALONIKI in 1246. To weaken further the position of the Latin Empire, he opened negotiations with the papacy with a view to uniting the two churches. This amounted to nothing. In fact, Pope GREGORY IX blocked any kind of deal and was hostile that eventually he was excommunicated by the patriarch at Nicaea. On John's death, his son, Theodore II (r. 1254–58), continued this slow rebuilding process. It was Michael VIII Palaeologos (r. 1261–82), who finally recovered Constantinople from the Westerners on July 25, 1261. He and his dynasty founded a new, but traditional, Byzantine state and ended this imperial power provincially based at Nicaea.

See also EPIROS AND DESPOTATE OF; PALAIOLOGOS, IMPERIAL DYNASTY.

Further reading: Michael J. Angold, *A Byzantine Government in Exile: Government and Society under the Laskarids of Nicaea, 1204–1261* (Oxford: Oxford University Press, 1975); John Mauropus, Metropolitan of Euchaita, *The Letters of Ioannes Mauropous Metropolitan of Euchata*, ed. Apostolos Karpozilos (Thessalonike: Association for Byzantine Research, 1990).

Nicholas II, Pope (Gerard of Florence) (ca. 980–1061) *reforming pope at the beginning of the Gregorian reform movement*

Little is known beyond that Gerard was born about 980 in BURGUNDY. He grew up and became a cleric in the ecclesiastical reforming circles of Lorraine and Burgundy and probably accompanied Pope Leo IX (r. 1049–54) to ROME. He does not seem to have been a CLUNIAC monk but was a canon of Liège. By 1045 he was the bishop of the see of FLORENCE.

ELECTION AS POPE

In 1058, after the death of Stephen IX (r. 1057–58), the Roman aristocracy engineered the election of John of Velletri as pope. He took the name Benedict X (r. 1058–59). The reform-minded clerics around Hildebrand (the later Pope GREGORY VII) and Peter DAMIAN were not yet present and were not involved in Benedict's election. With the support of the duke of Lorraine, and German court, the reformers and most of the College of Cardinals fled from Rome and elected the Frenchman Gerard of Florence, then in SIENA, as pope. He took the name Nicholas II. The antipope Benedict X was banished by the synod of Sutri in January 1059 and Nicholas was then able to battle his way into Rome to be enthroned enthusiastically as pope at Old Saint Peter's on January 24, 1059.

REFORMING DECREES

His pontificate opened with a decree on papal elections at the Lateran synod of April 1059. This decree gave the preponderant role to the College of CARDINALS in the election of the pope, as the cardinal-bishops took precedent over the other cardinals, over the other clergy, and over the people and nobility of Rome. In this new procedure the cardinal-bishops were to choose a person to elect, the cardinal-priests were to give their approval, and then the rest of the clergy and the people of Rome were reduced merely to acclaiming a new pope. Papal elections did not have to take place in Rome. Nicholas also issued other important decrees. One banned lay investiture for clerical offices. Another stated that a pope might concede to the emperor some rights over clerical elections, if they were deemed acceptable at the time by the pontiff.

ALLIANCE WITH THE NORMANS

The Holy See then struck an agreement with the Norman princes in southern Italy, Robert GUISCARD and Richard, the count of Aversa (1047–78). In August 1059, at the council of Melfi, the NORMANS IN ITALY swore an oath of support for the Holy See in return for recognition of their titles to the lands they had recently conquered. This alliance was intended to give the papacy some protection from German imperial power. There were also decrees against SIMONY or the selling of ecclesiastical offices, and others demanding clerical CELIBACY. A German synod of bishops in 1061 condemned Nicholas for the alliance with the Normans against the emperor in Italy and annulled the new rules on papal elections. This foreshadowed the later conflictions of the investiture struggles. Nicholas II died in Florence on July 27, 1061. Another schism soon arose over succession to the Holy See.

See also BERENGAR OF TOURS.

Further reading: Uta-Renate Blumenthal, *The Investiture Controversy: Church and Monarchy from the Ninth to the Twelfth Century* (Philadelphia: University of Pennsylvania Press, 1988); Gerd Tellenbach, *Church, State and Christian Society at the Time of the Investiture Contest*, trans. R. F. Bennett (New York: Harper & Row, 1959).

Nicholas Breakspear *See* ADRIAN IV, POPE.

Nicholas of Autrécourt (ca. 1300–after 1350) *a problematic natural philosopher, civil lawyer, theologian*

Born in Lorraine around 1300 and educated at the University of Paris, Nicholas was at AVIGNON, where his trial took place at some point between 1341 and 1347. He had been condemned for a confused group of anti-Aristotelian theses and banned from teaching in faculties of THEOLOGY. He retracted his controversial ideas at Avignon and at Paris, where he burned his own manuscripts. From 1348, he lived at Metz as canon and dean of the cathedral chapter. He had alternative ideas about the creation of the universe, the study of being, and epistemology. He also wrote about OPTICS. There also exist his *Theological Question* concerning medieval optics, and some valuable letters about a theory of demonstration. He died after 1350, perhaps as late as 1369.

See also NOMINALISM.

Further reading: Nicholas of Autrecourt, *The Universal Treatise of Nicholas of Autrecourt,* trans. Leonard A. Kennedy (Milwaukee: Marquette University Press, 1971); Nicholas of Autrecourt, *Nicholas of Autrecourt: His Correspondence with Master Giles and Bernard of Arezzo, A Critical Edition from the Two Parisian Manuscripts with an Introduction, English Translation, Explanatory Notes, and Indexes* (Leiden: E. J. Brill, 1994); Julius R. Weinberg, *Nicolaus of Autrecourt: A Study in Fourteenth Century Thought* (1948; reprint, New York: Greenwood Press, 1969).

Nicholas of Cusa (Nicholas of Krebs, Nicholas Kryfts) (1401–1464) *humanist, theologian, jurist, canonist, cardinal, papal legate*

Nicholas Krebs received his name Nicholas of Cusa from the German village of Kues near Trier, where he was born in 1401. His library is still preserved there. He studied with the BRETHREN OF THE COMMON LIFE at Deventer and attended the universities of Heidelberg in 1416, where the ideas of WILLIAM of Ockham were taught; the university of PADUA in 1417, where he had contact with Italian humanist thought; and the university of COLOGNE in 1425. He was ordained in 1430, having also earned a doctorate in canon law.

In 1448, he was made titular CARDINAL of San Pietro in Vincoli. He was already famous as a learned mathematician, physician, astronomer, and cosmographer. A collector of manuscripts, he was interested in geographical discoveries. Nicholas rejected the hypothesis of concentric spheres bounding the universe and affirmed that the Earth was in movement. He believed that the Earth revolved around the Sun.

According to his mystical vision of the world and humankind, the human mind was not able to grasp reality, which is the object of metaphysics and THEOLOGY. Knowledge was therefore just "learned ignorance." This idea and that of the "coincidence of contraries" were foundational assumptions in all of his work. Truth was an absolute, he maintained. However, knowledge was necessarily relative, complex, finite, and comparative. To seek truth, one must rise above reason and appeal to one's

intuition and thereby attain such a simplicity of thought that contradictions would coincide. Besides pursuing his intellectual work, Nicholas was active especially at the Council of BASEL (1431–49), in which he presented his famous treatise on reform of church and state, *De concordantia catholica,* in 1433. He was also dispatched on numerous diplomatic missions, such as his great legation to CONSTANTINOPLE of 1451–52. Initially a partisan of conciliarism, he shifted to support the maintenance of papal power. He also worked in favor of toleration and reconciliation with the followers of John HUS. Nicholas of Cusa died at Todi in Umbria on August 11, 1464, on his way to Ancona, where his friend Pope PIUS II had summoned him to help send off a CRUSADE.

Further reading: Nicholas, of Cusa, Cardinal, *Nicholas of Cusa "On Learned Ignorance": A Translation and an Appraisal* of De Docta Ignorantia (Minneapolis: A. J. Benning Press, 1981); Nicholas of Cusa, *Unity and Reform: Selected Writings of Nicholas de Cusa,* ed. John P. Dolan (Notre Dame, Ind.: University of Notre Dame Press, 1962); F. Edward Cranz, *Nicholas of Cusa and the Renaissance,* ed. Thomas M. Izbicki and Gerald Christianson (Aldershot: Ashgate, 2000); Jasper Hopkins, *A Concise Introduction to the Philosophy of Nicholas of Cusa* (Minneapolis: University of Minnesota Press, 1978); Paul E. Sigmund, *Nicholas of Cusa and Medieval Political Thought* (Cambridge, Mass.: Harvard University Press, 1963).

Nicholas of Myra, Bishop (fifth century) *one of the most renowned and legendary saints*

Little is actually known about the life of Nicholas of Myra. He was bishop of Myra in Lycia in ANATOLIA in the fifth century. His cult was established from the sixth century at CONSTANTINOPLE. His reputation was built around some famous episodes, saving young girls from prostitution, saving three officials condemned to DEATH, restoring life to three children cut up by a butcher, and calming a storm threatening sailors. He had saintly patronage over young girls, boys, pawnbrokers, apothecaries, perfume makers, students, sailors, and MERCHANTS. He was also the patron saint of RUSSIA. When Myra fell to ISLAM or when some Italian merchants simply stole his RELICS, they were taken to BARI and his cult quickly spread throughout the West. He was a favorite subject in the art and drama of the East and the West. As the patron of and bearer of gifts for children, he easily became the basis for the modern Santa Claus or Father Christmas. His feast day is December 6.

Further reading: Edward G. Clare, *St. Nicholas: His Legends and Iconography* (Florence: L. S. Olschki, 1985); Charles Jones, *Saint Nicholas of Myra, Bari, and Manhattan: Biography of a Legend* (Chicago: University of Chicago Press, 1978).

Nicolaism *See* NICOLAITISM.

Nicolaitism (Nicolaism) The name and concept of Nicolaitism refer to Nicolaus of ANTIOCH, one of the seven deacons mentioned in the New Testament. His principal HERESY or SIN was the idea that priests can marry, a practice that was considered a return to PAGANISM or GNOSTICISM. There seems to have been a sect, the Nicolaitans, advocating this in the first century or two of Christianity. They were also accused of eating meat offered to the gods and of practicing sexual immorality. Clerical CELIBACY was promoted in the church from the fourth century, especially after the rise of MONASTICISM.

During the Middle Ages, as the popes condemned the practice, clerical marriage became a heresy for its obdurate disobedience to the authority of the Holy See. There was always some tolerance for priests who were unable to leave their concubines. Their sin was categorized with SIMONY and the passage of ecclesiastical property to the families of priests. It was, and remained, an issue in the reconciliation of the Catholic and Orthodox Churches.

See also DAMIAN, PETER; NICHOLAS II, POPE.

Further reading: James A. Brundage, *Law, Sex and Christian Society in Medieval Europe* (Chicago: University of Chicago Press, 1987); Michael Frassetto, ed., *Medieval Purity and Piety: Essays on Medieval Clerical Celibacy and Religious Reform* (New York: Garland, 1998), especially Uta-Renate Blumenthal, "Pope Gregory VII and the Prohibition of Nicolaitism," 239–267.

Nicopolis, Crusade and Battle of (Nikopolis) The town was founded by the Roman emperor Trajan (r. 98–117) on the Danube in BULGARIA. By the late 14th century, it had become an Ottoman fortress, near which an important defeat of a Western Christian army by the OTTOMAN TURKS took place on September 25, 1396. After the defeat of the Balkan princes by the armies of MURAD I at KOSOVO Polje on June 15, 1389, SIGISMUND OF HUNGARY (r. 1387–1437) mounted a CRUSADE against the Ottomans. Sigismund appealed to the West. An army composed mostly of Burgundian knights under the command of several important French nobles, Jean de Nevers, Jean Boucicaut, Philippe d' Artois, Jacques de Bourbon, and Enguerrand de Coucy, joined the Hungarian armies at BUDA at the end of July.

Rather than await an attack from the Ottomans now under the sultan BAYAZID I, the Western KNIGHTS drove into Bulgaria and laid siege to the Ottoman fortress at Nicopolis. The two armies, each of about 20,000 men, met on September 25, 1396. The Western knights exhausted themselves against Turkish infantry and were then massacred by the Turkish cavalry, while the VLACH and Transylvanian auxiliaries of the king of Hungary deserted. The principal crusader leaders were taken prisoner, and only Sigismund escaped. The Turks demanded the payment of heavy ransoms and the kings from FRANCE and ENGLAND became even more reluctant to go on crusade. The Ottomans were enabled to continue their advance into the Balkans.

See also FROISSART, JEAN.

Further reading: Aziz Suryal Atiya, *The Crusade of Nicopolis* (London: Methuen, 1934); Norman Housley, *The Later Crusades, from Lyons to Alcazar 1274–1580* (Oxford: Oxford University Press, 1992), 73–79.

Nika revolt *See* JUSTINIAN I.

Nile River *See* EGYPT.

Nithard (790/800–844) *Charlemagne's illegitimate grandson or nephew, soldier, court official, historian*
Nithard was born about 790, the son of Charlemagne's daughter, Bertha, and a member of his household, Angilbert. He was raised in the northern abbey of Saint Riquier and at the court. He was an adviser and soldier for CHARLES THE BALD, the future emperor. He wrote an almost unique four-volume history or chronicle of the struggles among the sons of LOUIS I THE PIOUS to succeed to the Crown. He admired CHARLEMAGNE, who Nithard believed knew how to tame both the FRANKS and the BARBARIANS. As court historian Nithard especially approved of Charlemagne's success in compelling the unruly Frankish aristocracy to participate in his government. After being appointed, as his father had been, a lay abbot of Saint Requier in Picard in 843, Nithard probably died in the battle of Angoumois against Pépin II of AQUITAINE on June 14, 844.

See also FONTENAY, BATTLE OF.

Further reading: Bernhard Scholz, trans., *Carolingian Chronicles: Royal Frankish Annals and Nithard's Histories* (Ann Arbor: University of Michigan Press, 1970); Janet L. Nelson, *Charles the Bald* (New York: Longman, 1992).

nobility and nobles Medieval societies tended to be aristocratic societies in which wealth, power, and prestige belonged to a nobility. This was a small group that tried to reproduce itself from generation to generation. Sometimes these people were called nobles and possessed great landed wealth and some variety of legal status. A common feature of the nobility, however, were their military, legal, and administrative duties; they usually owned or were given land to support these functions. If these privileges were not initially inheritable, they tended to become so.

These aristocrats usually depended on a prince or ruler, and their membership could be open to new blood on the basis of wealth or talent. Access to their ranks varied over the course of the Middle Ages but tended to become more restricted. Considerable tension, however, was provoked, along with opposition, when newcomers rose to the rank of noble, while various statuses became more elaborate and closely defined. But still a ruler could elevate a commoner to the rank of noble. In the BYZANTINE EMPIRE, the nobility was tied tightly to the emperor.

QUALIFICATIONS AND TRAPPINGS

To be considered noble, one had to live nobly, participating in such activities as HUNTING, WARFARE, and court life and having the leisure to do so. A noble was to live off an income based on land supplemented by activities, such as war plunder and lucrative service to a lord. The nobility was often exempt from taxes but had to respond to a lordly call to armed service. It was fundamental that one be recognized as noble by fellow nobles and reciprocate with solidarity. Succession was usually along the lines of primogeniture, with adequate and strategic provision for women but little for sons other than the eldest. The illegitimate offspring of the male nobility were usually considered noble, regardless of the status of their mother. By the end of the Middle Ages and for far longer, a male noble was required to act honorably and loyally, with magnanimity or generosity, courage, courtesy, and respect for the values of Christianity and the church. Female nobles were expected to act the same way, in addition to remaining chaste to keep succession pure and protect the honor of their husband. The nobility also tried to maintain a number of outward signs of its status to receive respectful treatment and command appropriate deference.

ARAB-MUSLIM ARISTOCRACY

From the founding of ARAB caliphate, the old tribal aristocracy and military command of the seventh century long made up a nobility or elite. From the eighth century, non-Arabs, state officials, and wealthy land owner joined this class. Military revolts, dynastic changes, and political removals or assassinations contributed to a great deal of mobility within this upper class, but its qualities were much less specifically defined than in Christendom.

See also BARTOLO DA SASSOFERRATO; CASTLES AND FORTIFICATIONS; FEUDALISM; HERALDRY AND HERALDS; KNIGHTS AND KNIGHTHOOD; MINISTERIALS; SOCIAL STATUS AND STRUCTURE.

Further reading: Simon R. Doubleday, *The Lara Family: Crown and Nobility in Medieval Spain* (Cambridge: Harvard University Press, 2001); Anne J. Duggan, ed., *Nobles and Nobility in Medieval Europe: Concepts, Origins, Transformations* (Woodbridge: Boydell Press, 2000); Timothy Reuter, ed., *The Medieval Nobility: Studies on the Ruling Classes of France and Germany from the Sixth to the Twelfth Century* (Amsterdam: North-Holland, 1979); Joel T. Rosenthal, *Nobles and the Noble life, 1295–1500* (London: George Allen and Unwin, 1976); K. B. McFarlane, *The Nobility of Later Medieval England: The Ford Lectures for 1953 and Related Studies* (Oxford: Clarendon Press, 1973).

nominalism   Nominalism was one possible solution to the medieval philosophical problem of universals. This problem, in LOGIC and dialectic studies, was, When we attribute to a subject a universal predicate, genus, or species, such as animal or man, does this make a thing, the animalness, present in each individual subject? Or was this simply a word, a name, a mental construct formed by experience of various singular individuals? For nominalists the coincidence of individual traits permitted us to posit a universal concept. The first solution was realist and the second, nominalist. The term *nominalist* was applied to various philosophical or theological positions referring to the primacy of the individual, the rejection of the reification of forms of relationship between substances. It emphasized instead the sense of the contingence of the singular, and the constructed nature of signs.

Peter ABÉLARD tried to refute realism. He accepted an idea that singular individuals, instead belonging to a one real essence, participated in a common nature. WILLIAM of Ockham started from the epistemological presuppositions similar to those of Abélard but extended them to natural PHILOSOPHY, metaphysics, THEOLOGY, and ideas about the nature of the church. His resulting idea of the absolute power of GOD led him to deny that theology could be a SCIENCE and that a hierarchical church was anything like a perfect institution. The opponents of traditional Aristotelianism and Thomism rallied to Ockham and his *via moderna*.

See also BIEL, GABRIEL; BURIDAN, JOHN; IBN RUSHD; UNIVERSALS.

Further reading: John L. Farthing, *Thomas Aquinas and Gabriel Biel: Interpretations of St. Thomas Aquinas in German Nominalism on the Eve of the Reformation* (Durham, N.C.: Duke University Press, 1988); Heiko A. Oberman, *The Harvest of Medieval Theology: Gabriel Biel and Late Medieval Nominalism* (Cambridge, Mass.: Harvard University Press, 1963).

Norbert of Xanten, Saint (ca. 1080–1134) *archbishop of Magdeburg, founder of the Premonstratensian order of canons*
Norbert was born at Gennep in what is now HOLLAND, between 1080 and 1085. His noble parents pledged him as a boy to an ecclesiastical life in the comfortable chapter of canons of Xanten. He accompanied as a chaplain the emperor Henry V (r. 1105–25) to ROME in 1110. The emperor's attitude toward the pope in the INVESTITURE CONTROVERSY distressed him. In 1115 Norbert underwent a sudden conversion, returned home, and tried to reform his fellow corrupt and wealthy canons. He gave up and became an itinerant preacher. By 1118, he was deemed suspicious because he was not a priest, nor even a cleric of any kind. He also preached without any clerical permission. He obtained that from Pope Gelasius

II (r. 1118–19), but the pope died soon after at CLUNY and with him Norbert's license to preach.

Norbert then went to RHEIMS in October 1119 to ask Gelasius's successor, Calixtus II (r. 1119–24), to renew his license. The pope passed him to a bishop of LAON, to employ in his diocese as the provost of the chapter of Saint-Martin at Laon. The canons there readily refused to accept any strict conditions. The bishop then sent him to the solitude of the valley of Prémontré, between Laon and Soissons. By the end of 1120, disciples, at least 40 clerics and LAITY, joined him. These clerics chose for their rule the Rule of Saint AUGUSTINE and made their somewhat irregular professions of the religious life on Christmas night 1121. The Order of Canons Regular of Prémontré (Premonstratensians) was born. The foundation spread in northern FRANCE, BELGIUM, and GERMANY. On February 16, 1126, Pope Honorius II (r. 1124–30) recognized the group's canonical status according to traditional forms once established by Augustine.

AS ARCHBISHOP AND CHANCELLOR

In 1126 Norbert was elected archbishop of Magdeburg and chancellor of the empire. As an ardent opponent of the alienation of church property and a strong supporter of clerical CELIBACY, he reformed the clergy of this diocese, preached, and began the conversion of the WENDS, a pagan tribe beyond the Elbe. He took a stand against investiture, and in the schism that followed the death of Pope Honorius II, he pushed the emperor Lothair III (1075–1137) into supporting Pope Innocent II (r. 1130–43) against a rival antipope, Anacletus II (r. 1130–38), who was supported by the NORMANS in ITALY. Both had been elected irregularly on the same day. On May 30, 1133, Norbert's pope, Innocent II, entered Rome and crowned the emperor. Now ill, Norbert returned to Germany and died a year later at Magdeburg on June 6, 1134; he was buried in the church of the Premonstratensians there.

Further reading: Cornelius James Kirkfleet, *History of Saint Norbert: Founder of the Norbertine (Premonstratensian) Order, Apostle of the Blessed Sacrament, Archbishop of Magdeburg* (London: B. Herder, 1916).

Normandy and the Normans Normandy has been defined since the 10th century as the region conceded by Charles the Simple (879–929) in 911. By the treaty of Saint-Clair-sur-Epte, the VIKINGS, or Northmen, settled at ROUEN under the command of ROLLO. By the mid-11th century, the principality coincided with the ecclesiastical province of Rouen or roughly the old MEROVINGIAN kingdom of NEUSTRIA. With the consolidation of such principality, Normandy acquired a distinct identity separate from that of the neighboring principalities of BRITTANY, the Capetian kingdom in PARIS, and the county of FLANDERS.

The dukes of Normandy and their allied aristocracy kept their Viking traditions alive, and chronicles even called them the "pirate princes." Christianized by the mid-10th century, these Scandinavian invaders, now settlers, were strong supporters of the GREGORIAN REFORM. The dukes William Longsword (r. 932–943), Richard II (r. 996–1026), and WILLIAM THE CONQUEROR (r. 1035–87) and his wife, Matilda, were moreover ardent supporters of the monastic life and made numerous rich foundations.

GROWTH, WAR, LOYALTY, AND TRADITION

Church reform formed only part of the agenda for constructing an extraordinarily stable and expansionist feudal state, even after William's conquest of ENGLAND in 1066. At the same time there was almost constant war with all of the country's neighbors, especially under angevin king and duke HENRY II. Norman nobles were not docile subjects, so each ducal succession became a catalyst for their demands. Many nobles and young men left for the wars in England, SPAIN, southern ITALY, and the CRUSADES. Their ambitions were too confined within the frontiers of the province, where the power of the dukes and the resistance of a peasant population aggressive in defense of their rights hindered any expansion of local seigniorial power.

The county was also rich and economically developed. Annexed by conquest to Capetian France in 1204 by PHILIP II AUGUSTUS, the duchy was soon the Crown's greatest source of revenue. It continued to have strong and prosperous peasant communities, very ready to defend their rights against seigniorial and royal exactions. This was due to a strong attachment to customary rights, a principle of identity in Norman society, which did survive absorption into the centralized French Crown. The later Middle Ages saw the long HUNDRED YEARS' WAR between France and England, in which Normandy suffered frequently from the consequences of the fighting but never wavered from its loyalty to the French Crown.

See also ANJOU; HENRY I, KING OF ENGLAND; JOHN LACKLAND, KING OF ENGLAND; NORMANS IN ITALY; ORDERIS VITALIS.

Further reading: Dudo of St. Quentin, *History of the Normans,* trans. Eric Christianson (Woodbridge: Boydell Press, 1998); David Bates, *Normandy before 1066* (New York: Longman, 1982); Marjorie Chibnall, *The Normans* (Oxford: Blackwell, 2000); R. H. C. Davis, *The Normans and Their Myth* (London: Thames and Hudson, 1976).

Normans in Italy During the 11th and 12th centuries, southern ITALY was militarily, administratively, and politically conquered and organized under a NORMAN dynasty. First APULIA and Calabria, then SICILY, came under a single lordship.

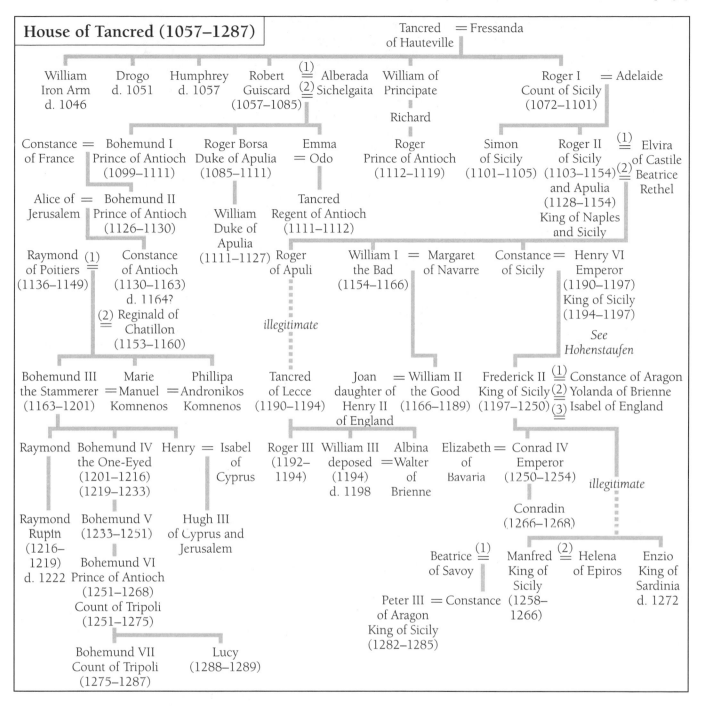

House of Tancred (1057–1287)

In 1035 William "Iron Arm" of Hauteville (d. 1046) began with his brothers the military conquest of Apulia and Calabria. The Norman entrance into Italy was tied to several events and causes, including LOMBARD weakness from dynastic struggles in the duchy of Benevento, possibilities and consequences of the secession of the rich principality of Salerno and the county of Capua from BYZANTINE and Lombard control, and an anti-Byzantine revolt in Bari. These struggles and problems were a real attraction for these ambitious adventurers and skilled warriors. Further incentives were the endless struggles over land among the younger sons of Normandy's feudal aristocracy, whom primogeniture had deprived of the right to inherit much at all.

ESTABLISHMENT AND FURTHER CONQUEST

The Normans ultimately constructed their own territorial lordships, oriented around the family of Hauteville. Their military and administrative experience served them well. Pope Leo IX (r. 1049–54) had already been allied with the Lombards of Benevento and directed a defense against the growing power of these immigrants, but was defeated at the Battle of Civitate in 1053 and even taken prisoner. After a papal ransom and an agreement between Robert GUISCARD, who had succeeded his brother, William, in 1046, and the new pope, NICHOLAS II, in 1059, Robert was recognized as the legitimate duke of Apulia, Calabria, and Sicily; the latter two were still under Muslim control, however. The conquest of that island began in 1061 led by Guiscard and his brother, ROGER I, the future "great count" of Sicily. It was completed officially only in 1130, when ROGER II was recognized as king of Sicily, after oaths of loyalty to the church of Rome, first to an antipope, Anacletus II, and then, after the end of a schism, to Innocent II (r. 1130–43).

The very large city of PALERMO then became the capital of the whole of southern Italy. The new kingdom was helped by older Muslim administrative efficiency, and a tolerant culture. The Hautevilles recognized local autonomies and legal and administrative customs. They used Muslim officials, who were allowed to keep their Arab and Greek titles as well as assume new Norman ones. The new kingdom had a sound fiscal and administrative efficiency, a shrewd control of the ecclesiastical machinery, and a balanced feudal monarchy, based on feudal institutions with a network of military loyalties built on local seigniorial rights. The success of this system probably depended on the skills of the Normans in general and the Hautevilles in particular. Peace and prosperity started to unravel, though, with the death of King WILLIAM II the Good in 1189 after 57 years of internal harmony and peace with the church. The HOHENSTAUFEN dynasty took control in 1194 through a marriage of William's daughter, CONSTANCE, to Henry VI (r. 1194–97).

See also FREDERICK II; MONREALE; NORMANS AND NORMANDY; SICILY.

Further reading: Edmund Curtis, *Roger of Sicily and the Normans in Lower Italy, 1016–1154* (New York: G. P. Putnam's Sons, 1912); David C. Douglas, *The Norman Achievement, 1050–1110* (Berkeley: University of California Press, 1969); Barbara M. Kreutz, *Before the Normans: Southern Italy in the Ninth and Tenth Centuries* (Philadelphia: University of Pennsylvania Press, 1991); G. A. Loud, *The Age of Robert Guiscard: Southern Italy and the Norman Conquest* (New York: Longman, 2000); David Matthew, *The Norman Kingdom of Sicily* (Cambridge: Cambridge University Press, 1992); John Julius Norwich, *The Other Conquest* (New York: Harper & Row, 1967); Kenneth Baxter Wolf, *Making History: The Normans and Their Historians in Eleventh-Century Italy* (Philadelphia: University of Pennsylvania Press, 1995).

North Africa *See* AFRICA; IFRIQIYA; AL-MAGHRIB; MOROCCO.

Norway   The history of medieval Norway was bound up with its colonizing and trading activities around Britain, in the Atlantic, and in relation to DENMARK and SWEDEN.

Harald I Fairhair (d. 932) at the Battle of Hafrsfjord in about 890 acquired supremacy over a number of local chiefs that led a century later to a unified Norway. The two converting kings, Olaf I Tryggvason (r. 995–1000) and then Olaf II Haraldsson (r. 1015–30) or Saint Olaf, continued Harald's efforts with greater success, basing their state-building efforts on what they had seen of the effects of Christianity farther south in Europe. Conversion to Christianity was one means they pursued and applied it in ways both brutal and peaceful. At the same time this society of peasant–fisherman and free independent proprietors consciously opposed losing their independence to a central authority.

Both kings were killed in battle. Saint Olaf was defeated by CANUTE II, but his political and religious structures survived. The bishopric of Trondheim became the ecclesiastical center of northern Europe. Canute tried to incorporate Norway into his empire and temporarily succeeded, but a series of able rulers—Magnus I the Good (r. 1035–46), Harald III Hardraade (r. 1046–66), and Olaf III the Peaceful or Gentle (1066–93)—maintained the countries' independence. The 12th century saw considerable conflict over the church, succession to the throne, and control of the country.

A SHORT-LIVED "GOLDEN AGE"

Haakon the Old (r. 1217–63) was one of the great kings of Norway, firmly established hereditary kingship, and laid permanent foundations for a kingdom. He also annexed ICELAND and GREENLAND and developed a literary and artistic policy more influenced by Europe to the south. In the meantime the HANSEATIC LEAGUE had introduced all over the Baltic and North Sea area a trading network that included Bergen in Norway. This economic union worked to the detriment of royal political and his economic power. From 1300 a period of political and economic decline began, aggravated by the Black Death between 1349 and 1351. By 1385 Norway had passed definitively under the control of the Danish Crown that lasted until the early 19th century.

See also MARGARET OF DENMARK, NORWAY, AND SWEDEN.

Further reading: Svend Gissel, *Desertion and Land Colonization in the Nordic Countries c. 1300–1600: Comparative Report from the Scandinavian Research Project on Deserted Farms and Villages* (Stockholm: Almqvist and Wiksell International, 1981); Kurt Helle, "Norway in the High Middle Ages: Recent Views on the Structure of Society," *Scandinavian Journal of History* 6 (1981); 161–189; Kurt Helle, "Norway," *DMA* 9.179–186; P. Urbanczyk, *Medieval Arctic Norway* (Warsaw: Semper, 1992); Rolf Danielsen, ed., *Norway: A History from the Vikings to Our Own Times,* trans. Michael Drake (Oslo: Scandinavian

University Press, 1995); T. K. Derry, *A History of Norway* (London: Allen and Unwin, 1957).

notaries and the notariate   Medieval and Renaissance notaries wrote acts or contracts and guaranteed their authenticity and validity. In the countries of customary law on northern Europe, scribes or notaries wrote acts that were given reliability by the seals of participants or by an enclosed guarantee from public authorities. In countries of Roman LAW, from the 12th century, the notary documented acts and, acting like a public official, had the power to authenticate them himself by his signature and his device or sign. A more elaborate notariate developed in ITALY, in the 12th century, with the revival and elaboration of Roman law at BOLOGNA, and rapidly thereafter developed in the legal systems of southern FRANCE and the Iberian Peninsula.

THE PROCESS

Writing and devising contracts had several steps for notaries. The first was the minute, brief, or *imbreviatura,* in which the notary recorded in simple language what his clients wanted accomplished in a more formal document. He wrote next the original formal instrument, complete with the required legal clauses and particular details of the transaction or agreement. The notary handed over this instrument copied on parchment to his client. He had written the minute in his register, minute

book, or protocol, which he kept, authenticated, and then usually passed on to his successor or to a depository run by local public authorities. This had the same authenticity and legal status as the original instrument. These compilations and documents involved all kinds of acts including sales, rentals, dowry agreements, peace accords, receipts, and WILLS or last testaments. They still exist in huge numbers in Italy, southern France, and SPAIN.

THE PROFILE

Notaries received their office as public officials, akin to judges, from public authorities after an examination demonstrated their knowledge of law, legal formulary or verbiage, and LATIN. In Italian cities they sometimes gained considerable political power because the developing COMMUNES needed bureaucracies and literate people knowledgeable in the law. Notaries both created and administered those bureaucracies. They had important roles in Latin and VERNACULAR culture and education. They served all aspects of society that could afford to pay them for proper documentation.

See also ARCHIVES AND ARCHIVAL INSTITUTIONS; COMMUNE.

Further reading: Geoffrey Barraclough, *Public Notaries and the Papal Curia: A Calendar and a Study of a Formularium Notariorum Curie from the Early Years of the Fourteenth Century* (London: Macmillan, 1934); C. R. Cheney, *Notaries Public in England in the Thirteenth and Fourteenth Centuries* (Oxford: Clarendon Press, 1972).

A procession of the guild of the notaries of Perugia, Bibliotheca Augusta, Ms. 973, Perugia, Italy *(Alinari / Art Resource)*

Notker the Stammerer, Saint (Notker Balbulus) (ca. 840–912) *German monk, scholar*
Notker entered the Monastery of Saint Gall as a very young man. A chronicler described him as "weak of body, sickly, stammering, and shy." Nonetheless, he became the monastery's librarian and was for 40 years a remarkable teacher. Among his disciples were a bishop of Constance and a bishop of Freising. After the emperor Charles III the Fat (r. 881–887) heaped praise on him in 883, he responded by writing for him the *Gesta Karoli Magni* (Deeds of Charles the Great), a contrived, moralizing, more or less legendary history of CHARLEMAGNE.

Notker was best known for his *Book of Sequences* or tropes and other liturgical writings. Learning from a monk of Jumièges, he devised a mnemonic method for remembering the long vocalizations for the singing of the *Kyrie* and the *Alleluia.* Not the inventor of tropes, he greatly contributed to the development of Carolingian liturgy, HYMNS, and music. He died in 912.

See also CAROLINGIAN RENAISSANCE.

Further reading: Lewis G. M. Thorpe, trans., *Two Lives of Charlemagne* (Harmondsworth: Penguin, 1969); Albert L. Lloyd, *The Manuscripts and Fragments of Notker's Psalter* (Giessen: W. Schmitz, 1958).

Notre-Dame of Paris, Cathedral of   This was the CATHEDRAL for the city of PARIS. Situated on the picturesque Île de la Cité, it was and remained among the most famous, almost a prototype for, GOTHIC cathedrals in the world. It was begun on a site previously occupied by a pagan temple and then two earlier churches. During the bishopric of Maurice de Sully in the early 12th century, construction began. Its foundation was blessed by Pope ALEXANDER III in 1163. Completed in about 1230, it was best known for its flying buttresses, mathematically derived west façade, the statue of Our Lady of Paris, and its STAINED GLASS, especially in its ROSE WINDOWS.

> **Further reading:** Yves Bottineau, *Notre-Dame de Paris and the Sainte-Chapelle,* trans. Lovett F. Edwards (London: Allen, 1967); Alain Erlande-Brandenburg, *Notre-Dame de Paris,* trans. John Goodman (New York: Harry N. Abrams, 1998); Allan Temko, *Notre-Dame of Paris* (London: Secker and Warburg, 1956).

Novels of Justinian   *See* CORPUS IURIS CIVILIS.

Novgorod (**Novyi Gorod, New Town**)   Novgorod was a town on the banks of the upper Volkhov River near Lake Ilmen and the capital of a medieval Ruś state that once ran from the Gulf of FINLAND to the Ural Mountains. Founded by Scandinavian merchants in the ninth century, it linked the Scandinavian north with the Muslim south for TRADE. It was first mentioned in chronicles in 862, when King RURIK made it the center of his new kingdom of Ruś. When his successor, Oleg (d. ca. 912), captured KIEV in 882, the center of the kingdom gravitated to the south. The city accepted Kievan princes and became more Slavic in population, language, and institutional life. Its economic prosperity and social development continued and nurtured an active urban population.

In 1136 the system of appointment of a prince by the "eldest" prince of Kiev was rejected as the method of selecting its rulers. A local uprising installed a municipal almost republican government, whose officials were elected by an assembly of the landed aristocracy. The city grew richer and extended its control over much of the surrounding country side. It became a prominent member of the HANSEATIC LEAGUE, trading in FURS, amber, wax, honey, and slaves. The Rurikid princes tried to retake control of the town but were limited to mere participation in the assembly. Alexander NEVSKY, its prince, defeated the Swedes and the TEUTONIC KNIGHTS and started his career in Novgorod before becoming prince of Suzdal and Vladimir in 1252. Helped by its geographical situation in the north, Novgorod kept much of its independence from the MONGOLS in return for payments of tribute. In 1416 the local aristocracy or BOYARS seized control of the governing council. This event in combination with the rise of MOSCOW contributed to the town's decline in the 15th century. IVAN III defeated its army in

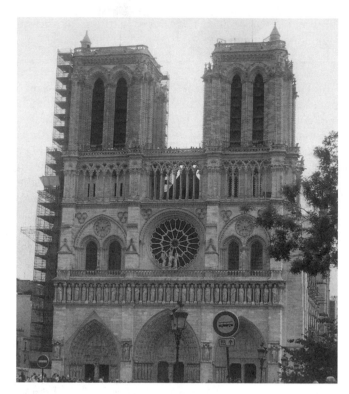

The Gothic western façade of the Cathedral of Notre-Dame in Paris, from about 1250 *(Courtesy Edward English)*

battle in 1471 and won recognition of Muscovite sovereignty over it in 1478.

See also FURS AND FUR TRADE.

> **Further reading:** Robert Michell and Nevill Forbes, trans., *The Chronicle of Novgorod, 1016–1471* (London: Offices of the Society, 1914); Henrik Birnbaum, *Lord Novgorod the Great: Essays in the History and Culture of a Medieval City-State* (Columbus, Ohio: Slavica, 1981); Mark A. Brisbane, ed., *The Archaeology of Novgorod, Russia: Recent Results from the Town and Its Hinterland* (Lincoln, Nebr.: Society for Medieval Archaeology, 1992); M. W. Thompson, *Novgorod the Great: Excavations at the Medieval City Directed by A. V. Artsikhovsky and B. A. Kolchin* (New York: Praeger, 1967).

novice and novitiate   A novice in the Middle Ages was a person undergoing a period of probation in a religious house before pronouncing his or her permanent vows. At the end of the novitiate, a postulant could choose to return to the lay world or make his or her profession before the community. The religious institution was free to accept or reject the postulant. The Rule of Saint BENEDICT in chapter 58 defined this process and the status of the novice.

Before the late 11th century monastic sources rarely mentioned novices. Until then the novitiate, even when practiced, was probably of very short duration. The community used isolation, fear, and stern disciple to judge a postulant's vocation or desire for the monastic life. Benedictine orders, such as the CISTERCIANS, paid especially close attention to the novitiate as an important evaluative process. The MENDICANT ORDERS such as the FRANCISCANS and DOMINICANS initially considered it an optional state. Not until the late 16th century did the novitiate become standard for all orders of monks, NUNS, and friars.

Further reading: Benedict, *The Rule of St. Benedict in English*, ed. Timothy Fry (New York: Vintage Books, 1998); Isabelle Cochelin, "Novice," *EMA*, 2.1,032–1,033); Giles Constable, *Medieval Monasticism: A Select Bibliography* (Toronto: University of Toronto Press, 1976); David Knowles, *Christian Monasticism* (New York: McGraw-Hill, 1969); C. H. Lawrence, *Medieval Monasticism: Forms of Religious Life in Western Europe in the Middle Ages* (New York: Longman, 1989).

Nubia (Nuba)

Medieval Nubia was a Christian kingdom in northeastern AFRICA up the Nile River from EGYPT. Now partially covered by the blocked water of the Aswan Dam, Nubia once extended from Aswan south to Khartoum. Called the "Land of Kush," with its capital at Meroë. It had strongly influenced Egypt from the time of the pharaohs. Conquered in the fourth century C.E. by an Ethiopian king, it became part of the empire of AXUM and Christianized by the sixth century by Melkite missionaries and MONOPHYSITES.

Nubia soon possessed churches in the BYZANTINE style, wonderfully decorated and still extant. Its church was dependent on the patriarchate of ALEXANDRIA, but the Nubians always used Greek and never switched to COPTIC for the liturgy. The two kingdoms of the region, Nobatia and Makuria, merged in the early eighth century into one Christian kingdom with a capital at Dongola. It had signed peace treaty with the ARABS immediately before that union. The agreement allowed the Nubians to retain their independence for the next seven centuries and to prosper from commercial ties with Egypt and the East. The MAMLUKS' control of Egypt in the mid-13th century resulted in Bedouin migration that led to an Islamization of Nubia. The last king of Dongola was deposed in the early 14th century. Its last Christian communities disappeared around 1500.

See also COPTS AND COPTIC ART.

Further reading: W. Y. Adams, *Nubia: Corridor to Africa* (Princeton, N.J.: Princeton University Press, 1977); S. Burstein, ed., *Ancient African Civilizations: Kush and Axum* (Princeton, N.J.: M. Wiener, 1998); W. B. Emery, *Lost Land Emerging* (New York: Scribner, 1967); Yvan G. Lepage, "Nubia," *EMA* 2.1,034; P. L. Shinnie, *Medieval Nubia* (Khartoum: Sudan Antiquities Service, 1954); D. A. Welsby, *The Medieval Kingdoms of Nubia: Pagans, Christians and Muslims on the Middle Nile* (London: British Museum, 2002).

numbers

In the Middle Ages, the exegesis or interpretation of numbers in the BIBLE was based on the Pythagorean, Platonic, and Jewish traditions, combining a certain mysticism with arithmetic. Numbers were see to represent ideas and even the fundamental principles of all things. Each number possessed a hidden meaning corresponding to an intrinsic quality of the number itself or to the nature of what it was linked. For example, 1 designated GOD, FAITH, and baptism; 2 meant division and opposition, but also unification, as in the two natures in the one Christ; 3 was linked with the Trinity. AUGUSTINE in his philosophy of numbers and interpretation of biblical numbers by arithmetic laid the basis for numerological reflection and speculation throughout the Middle Ages.

CASSIODORUS, ISIDORE of Seveille, BEDE, ALCUIN, RABANUS Maurus, JOHN SCOTUS ERIUGENA, and HINCMAR of Rheims all used and speculated on numbers in their works. In the 12th century, theologians such as RUPERT OF DEUTZ, THIERRY OF CHARTRES, and HUGH OF SAINT-VICTOR all worked out allegorical and exegetical systems using arithmetic, geometry, the numerical value of letters, and the figures of numbers. These ideas were perpetuated and elaborated upon in the 13th century by John Peckham (1225–92), in the 14th century by Nicholas ORESME, and in the 15th century by NICHOLAS of Cusa and Marsilio FICINO.

Further reading: Michael J. B. Allen, *Nuptial Arithmetic: Marsilio Ficino's Commentary on the Fatal Number in Book VIII of Plato's Republic* (Berkeley: University of California Press, 1994); Vincent Foster Hopper, *Medieval Number Symbolism: Its Sources, Meaning, and Influence on Thought and Expression* (New York: Cooper Square Publishers, 1969); Hanne Lange, "Numbers, Numerology," *EMA*, 2.1,034; Karl Menninger, *Number Words and Number Symbols: A Cultural History of Numbers*, trans. Paul Broneer (Cambridge, Mass.: M.I.T. Press, 1969); Robert L. Surles, ed., *Medieval Numerology: A Book of Essays* (New York: Garland, 1993).

numismatics

See MONEY AND MINTS.

nuns and nunneries

The word *nun* was based on the LATIN term *nonnus*, which meant a monk. It was used for any female religious devotée, whatever the order to which she belonged or rule she followed as a canoness, enclosed nun, or sister. In the late antique world and sometimes later, nuns were called "virile women" and more frequently later "the brides of Christ." A member of a religious community, the nun was subject to the rule that governed for her house. She publicly received a veil from a bishop and usually took vows of POVERTY and obedience. Her life could be devoted to secluded contemplation or charitable activities in the world. She was expected to carry out the daily recital of the OFFICE or canonical hours as well as participate in MASS with her community.

Nuns played important roles in medieval society and culture as scholars, mystics, artists, political activists, nurses, and teachers. Entrance into a convent was an important and vital option for many women in the Middle Ages, though sometimes they actually had little choice in this matter. Economic and familial realities could close off the option to marry and limit women in their choices about what order or convent they could enter or what tasks they would undertake in monastic life. There was always a great concern among the male clergy to control and oversee the activity of these women. Resistance to such patriarchal intervention was frequent.

See also MONASTICISM; WOMEN, STATUS OF.

Further reading: Rebecca Krawiec, *Shenoute and the Women of the White Monastery: Egyptian Monasticism in Late Antiquity* (Oxford: Oxford University Press, 2002); Jo Ann Kay McNamara, *Sisters in Arms: Catholic Nuns through Two Millenia* (Cambridge, Mass.: Harvard University Press, 1996); Eileen Power, *Medieval English Nunneries c. 1275 to 1535* (Cambridge: Cambridge University Press, 1922); Sally Thompson, *Women Religious: The Founding of English Nunneries after the Norman Conquest* (Oxford: Clarendon Press, 1991); Ann K. Warren, *Anchorites and Their Patrons in Medieval England* (Berkeley: University of California Press, 1985).

Nur al-Din Muhammad ibn Zangi (Light of the Faith) (r. 1146–1171) *ruler of Syria*

Nur al-Din succeeded his father, Zangi (d. 1127), first of the Zengid line, in 1146 as *atabeg* or ruler of Halab or ALEPPO. He gave his oath of loyalty to the ABBASID caliphs but then forged an extensive empire. He promoted a form of JIHAD, or holy war, to expel the crusaders. To accomplish this he also needed and desired Islamic unity. Successfully forging a jihad, his armies conquered DAMASCUS, EDESSA, and TRIPOLI. In 1163, Nur al-Din attacked the castle KRAK DES CHEVALIERS but was routed by its defenders. Between 1169 and 1171 he annexed EGYPT. As the founder of the Zengid dynasty, by the time he died, SYRIA, Egypt, and parts of IRAQ and ANATOLIA were all under his control. Much of this was accomplished at the expense of the Shiites as he laid the foundation for a strong and unified SUNNI state. He sponsored the foundation of numerous Islamic schools and MADRASAS and laid the groundwork for the achievements of his successor, SALADIN. Nur al-Din was honored for his piety, and his use of captured treasure to build these establishments, MOSQUES, HOSPITALS, and schools. He died in 1171 as he was planning to limit the power of one of his Kurdish officers, Saladin.

Further reading: H. A. R. Gibb, "The Career of Nūr-ad-Dīn," *A History of the Crusades*, Vol. 1, ed. Kenneth M. Setton (Philadelphia: University of Pennsylvania Press, 1955), 513–527; Carole Hillenbrand, *The Crusades: Islamic Perspectives* (New York: Routledge, 1999); P. M. Holt, *The Age of the Crusades: The Near East from the Eleventh Century to 1517* (New York: Longman, 1986), 38–52.

Nuremberg (Nürnberg)

Nuremberg became an important town in northern BAVARIA in late medieval GERMANY. It had its origins around a CASTLE from the eleventh century. It soon developed a prosperous FAIR. The emperor FREDERICK I BARBAROSSA granted it the status of an imperial city and appointed a governor. A member of the HOHENZOLLERN FAMILY AND DYNASTY held this position until 1427.

In 1219 Nuremberg obtained a CHARTER of liberties from the emperor FREDRICK II. It joined the confederation of the cities of the Rhine in 1256 and remained a member until the end of the Middle Ages. It was very prosperous in the 14th and 15th centuries as a center of AGRICULTURE, industry, especially metallurgy and TEXTILES, and commerce, since it was at the heart of the HOLY ROMAN EMPIRE on the transit routes to the south.

In 1356, the emperor CHARLES IV proclaimed the GOLDEN BULL at a diet there. The crown jewels of the Holy Roman Empire were moved there in 1424. It was at the same time a rich cultural and artistic center, dominated by a closed mercantile and patrician clique that held power throughout the Middle Ages.

Further reading: Cecil Headlam, *The Story of Nuremberg* (London: J. M. Dent, 1901); Jeffrey Chipps Smith, *Nuremberg: A Renaissance City, 1500–1618* (Austin: University of Texas Press, 1983); *Gothic and Renaissance Art in Nuremberg, 1300–1550* (New York: Metropolitan Museum of Art, 1986).

oath In the Middle Ages the oath or solemn pledge invoking a divine name to witness the truth of a statement was an essential social and legal act reflecting the value placed on a person's word. Fundamentally a verbal statement, with a physical gesture, as important as the words said, the oath was formally recorded. It was sworn on a symbolic object. In the early Middle Ages, this was usually on arms, as the guarantee of an oath. With the progress of Christianization, oaths were taken on RELICS or on the BIBLE. Special oaths were devised for JEWS, the *inramentum judaeorum.*

The CAROLINGIANS imposed oaths of allegiance to the emperor on all the men of the empire to try form a bond to uniting all subjects. From 1000, the PEACE AND TRUCE OF GOD movements attempted to unite Christian, feudal, and knightly society around an oath of peace that was publicly sworn on relics. In the early medieval administration of JUSTICE, because of distrust of written proofs or documents, an oath by the accused and by his guarantors sufficed for purposes of exoneration in many cases. The declarations of a witness were likewise tied to oaths and could free a defendant.

A PERMANENT INSTITUTION

These concepts endured throughout the Middle Ages. Oaths among the seigniorial or noble classes reflected social status and established relations with themselves and others. Interpersonal relations were often based on oaths promising and guaranteeing reciprocity. The vassal's swore homage to lords. The dubbing or making of a KNIGHT, the consecration of bishops, and the coronations of a king involved all oaths that entailed rituals. Soon written CHARTERS listed witnesses and guarantors.

PERJURY AND OTHER PITFALLS

The frequency of oaths and the play of multiple loyalties made preventing perjury difficult. Judicial oaths in some instances displaced probatory oaths. There was some concern to confine the use of sworn pledges to the nobility, so peasants or townspeople were forbidden to bind themselves by oath in many matters. Groups based on mutual oaths—peace movements, leagues, commercial agreements, GUILDS, or COMMUNES—antagonized the nobility and the church. For the nobility such groups could only subvert lordly status and privileges. According to some, the dependent status of peasants and workers entailed an inability to keep their word if it was contrary to the bond owed to their lords. To permit them to swear oaths was to increase the probability that they would sin by breaking oaths they should never have presumed to make. Compounding this ethical difficulty was the church's tendency to avoid involvement with group oaths or their verbal administration. The increasing sophistication of the legal structures of the later Middle Ages gradually marginalized the judicial oath, which nonetheless persisted as an indispensable portion of legal processes and the discernment of justice.

See also ORDEALS.

Further reading: Frederick Pollock and Frederic William Maitland, *The History of English Law before the Time of Edward I,* 2d ed. (1895; reprint, Cambridge: Cambridge University Press, 1968); J. E. Tyler, *Oaths: Their Origin, Nature, and History,* 2d ed. (London: John W. Parker, 1835).

oblates Oblates were children who had not yet reached the age of puberty, that is, barely beyond the age of reason, who were offered to a monastery by parents to become monks or nuns for life. This offering was a commending of the child to a sacred patron for his or her benefit. It was in reality perhaps a parental sacrifice or an abandonment, according to circumstances. The practice was not often questioned between the sixth and 11th centuries, since oblates formed an essential part of monastic recruitment. These children were customarily accompanied by a gift to the monastery. The gifts could determine their status within the monastic family.

The children so oblated were removed from the MARRIAGE plans and strategies of families. Oblation became an economic and familial practice to position and support second sons and daughters. The gifts were usually smaller than the marriage expenses would be. For the poor, oblation fed another mouth the family was unable to feed. From the mid-11th century, certain religious orders complained that the children being offered were family rejects, whom new orders usually refused to admit. During the later Middle Ages, the oblation of male children gradually disappeared. The term *oblate* was increasingly used only for adults who had attached themselves to a religious house.

Further reading: Mayke De Jong, *In Samuel's Image: Child Oblation in the Early Medieval West* (Leiden: E. J. Brill, 1996).

Ochrida (Orchrid, Ohrid, Achrida)

Ochrida (Achrida, ancient Lychnidos), a religious center and city in medieval MACEDONIA, was on a terraced site beside a lake of the same name. It had a Christian culture from the fourth and fifth centuries that survived ravages in the sixth- and seventh-century invasions by various peoples. Conversion to Christianity in 865 by the Bulgar king BORIS I, then also the ruler of Macedonia, led to King SIMEON I to set up a Byzantine and Slavic school at Ochrida in the 10th century. Threatened by BYZANTINE armies, SAMUEL II, retreated to Ochrida. The victories of BASIL II, THE BULGAR SLAYER, crushed the Bulgar army in 1014 and Basil made an entry into Ochrida in 1018.

INCURSIONS AND CHANGES

Despite SLAV, VLACH, NORMAN, and Venetian interventions and attacks on the town, the BYZANTINE Empire maintained control at least until 1187. The religious center of Macedonia remained Ochrida, although the bishop usually spent his time in the imperial court in CONSTANTINOPLE. In 1259 Ochrida supported the armies of Michael Palaiologos from the Empire of NICAEA.

From the late 13th century, SERBIA began to intervene in Macedonia. STEPHEN DUŠAN took power over Ochrida in 1334, but the Serbs were unable to save the region and Ochrida from the OTTOMAN advance. After the Ottomans annihilated Serbian troops on the Maritsa, Macedonia, Ochrida lost its independence before an occupation in 1385.

REMAINS

Ruins from the medieval town survive. Excavations have revealed the remains of a building from the fourth century, a baptistery and a chapel near a NARTHEX. From the older Bulgar kingdoms, all that remains are traces of the CATHEDRAL of Saint Sophia, a basilica from the late 10th or early 11th century, with FRESCOES from the mid-eleventh century. Dating from early 14th century, the church of Saint Nicholas at Bolnitsa has preserved frescoes from 1330 and 1345.

See also BULGARIA AND THE BULGARS.

Further reading: Kosta Balabanov, *Ohrid: Cultural–Historical and Natural Region in the Catalogue of the World's Heritage,* trans. Tom Petsinis (Skopje: Misla, 1987); Suzy Dufrenne, "Ohrid," *EMA* 2.1,044–1,045; Vojislav J. Duric, *The Church of St. Sophia in Ohrid,* trans. Sonja Bicanic (Belgrade: Jugoslavija, 1963).

Ockham, William of   *See* WILLIAM OF OCKHAM.

Odilo of Cluny, Saint (961/962–1049) *abbot of Cluny*

Odilo was born in 961 or 962 in an aristocratic family and started his career as a canon of Saint-Julien de Brioude. From there he moved to CLUNY to be with the abbot, Saint Maiolus (ca. 909–994). Maiolus chose his loyal disciple, Odilo, as replacement in 993 and in 994 as the fifth abbot of Cluny. It was under his government that Cluny acquired from Popes Gregory V (r. 996–999) in 998 and John XIX (r. 1024–32) in 1024 its unique independence with immunity and a full exemption from other monastic establishments and ecclesiastical authorities. All except the pope. Odilo provided the community with the rules and liturgical practices reflecting this spiritual freedom and independence from lords. Odilo devised a network of establishments dependent on a mother house personified by the abbot of Cluny. Odilo linked by the memorial function for a "Cluniac Church" to celebrate the Feast of All Souls on November 2. This feast for the souls of the departed spread throughout Christendom, as it grew from concern for dead monks to concern for all of the clerical and lay DEAD. He was active in the PEACE AND TRUCE OF GOD movement and in adjudicating secular disputes. The Cluniac grew from 37 houses to 65 under Odilo.

Under Odilo's abbacy, there was a major building program for the church at Cluny and the monastery's *scriptorium* was very productive. Odilo was an ardent commissioner of the copying and illuminating of texts and manuscripts. He also wrote HYMNS, and SERMONS demonstrating his devotion to the Incarnation of Christ, the Eucharist, and MARY. He wrote hagiographical biographies for Maiolus and the empress ADELAIDE. Having became famous for his generosity to those in need, he died at Souvigny at age 87 and was soon canonized in 1063.

Further reading: Giles Constable, *Cluny from the Tenth to the Twelfth Centuries: Further Studies* (Aldershot: Ashgate, 2000); Joan Evans, *Monastic Life at Cluny, 910–1157* (Hamden, Conn.: Archon Books, 1968); Barbara H. Rosenwein, *Rhinoceros Bound: Cluny in the Tenth Century* (Philadelphia: University of Pennsylvania Press, 1982); Barbara H. Rosenwein, *To Be the Neighbor of Saint Peter: The Social Meaning of Cluny's Property, 909–1049* (Ithaca, N.Y.: Cornell University Press, 1989)

Odo (Eudes) (ca. 1030–1097) *dissolute bishop of Bayeaux, half brother of William the Conqueror*
Odo or (Eudes) was the son of Arlette or Herleva, a former concubine of Duke Robert of NORMANDY, and Erluin of Conteville. Aged about 20, he received the see of Bayeaux from Duke WILLIAM, the future Conqueror, in 1049–50. He took part in the conquest of ENGLAND in 1066, when he became infamous for carrying a studded club instead of a sword, since metal weapons were forbidden to the CLERGY. He was rewarded by being made the earl of Kent, the greatest landowner in the country. He held a prominent place in the government of England under William. It was probably Odo's idea to help justify William's accession to the throne by creating the BAYEUX TAPESTRY, which showed HAROLD II Godewineson breaking his oath to William.

Odo's illegal raising of troops for a campaign in ITALY disgraced him in 1082; he was to be imprisoned for life. Odo seems to have had strong ambitions, including even the PAPACY. He was freed from prison at ROUEN on William's death in 1087 by WILLIAM II RUFUS, the Conqueror's successor. He tried to continue to play a role in a failed conspiracy of Robert Curthose (ca. 1054–1134) against William Rufus, but primarily he concerned himself as a patron of religion with building his cathedral church and administering his diocese. He tried to take part in the First CRUSADE with Robert Curthose but died at PALERMO in 1097.

Further reading: Joannes, Monk of Cluny, fl. 945, *St. Odo of Cluny: Being the Life of St. Odo of Cluny,* trans. and ed. Gerard Sitwell (New York: Sheed & Ward, 1958); David Bates, *Normandy before 1066* (New York: Longman, 1982); Sarell Everett Gleason, *An Ecclesiastical Barony of the Middle Ages: The Bishopric of Bayeux, 1066–1204* (Cambridge, Mass.: Harvard University Press, 1936).

Odoacer (Odovacar) (ca. 433–493) *Germanic king, ally of Rome*
Odoacer was a German chieftain of the Scirian tribe allied for a time with the HUNS, who entered ITALY in 470 and became king of the Heruli. As other German chieftains did, he joined the Roman army, but he revolted against his general and defeated him in battle in 476. After this victory, he entered ROME and on August 28, 476 deposed the last Roman emperor of the West, Romulus Augustulus (r. 475–476). He acknowledged the overlordship of the Eastern emperor Zeno (r. 474–491) at CONSTANTINOPLE, but he soon proclaimed himself the Arian ruler of Italy. Never to gain recognition in CONSTANTINOPLE, he opposed any attempts by the Byzantine emperors to interfere in Italy and, to assure his independence, invaded the Balkans. He failed to prevent the Byzantine-sponsored OSTROGOTHIC invasion of Italy in 493 and tried to reach an understanding with their king, THEODORIC. He was murdered and his followers were massacred during a reception at Ravenna in March of 493.

See also BARBARIANS AND BARBARIAN MIGRATIONS.

Further reading: Lucien Musset, *The Germanic Invasions: The Making of Europe, AD 400–600,* trans. Edward and Columba James (1969; reprint, University Park: Pennsylvania State University Press, 1975); E. A. Thompson, *Romans and Barbarians: The Decline of the Western Empire* (Madison: University of Wisconsin Press, 1982); J. M. Wallace-Hadrill, *The Barbarian West, 400–1000,* rev. ed. (Oxford: B. Blackwell, 1996).

offertory *See* MASS.

offices, monastic and canonical The divine office is the most important element, in length and frequency, of the rites and PRAYERS of the Catholic liturgy. It could be celebrated privately or publicly: in a monastic setting or in a church more open to the LAITY. Its aim was to sanctify time weekly according to the hours of the day. Its transition from private to public prayer came about in the fourth century and arose from a growing ascetic and elitist movement in the church. Monks and even HERMITS, though living in community, solemnized the hours of the day by prayer and by common celebration of these prayers, the divine office proper. Most lay Christians attended prayer meetings on certain occasions, such as on Sundays and feast days, either for vigils or for the evening office along with the MASS.

Monks followed a system of hours, vigils, lauds, prime, terce, sext, none, vespers, and compline. They also established the essential content of the hours of the office, including the introduction of the psalms as Christian prayer, through a continuous oral reading in common of the PSALTER. In the eighth century, the secular clerical office and the monastic office began to differ in terms of the number and distribution of the psalms in the course of each office; otherwise, the office was celebrated identically by the secular clerics and the monks. The laity participated or at least listened to these offices in churches or monasteries, especially at evening vespers.

The rhythm and ordering of the office were devised on what might be possible for a community to carry out. Any decision on that was ultimately a bishop's. The whole office did not have to be celebrated. Carolingian reforms made the office of clerics and monks exactly the same in frequency and solemnity. They also insisted on the obligation of each cleric to take part in any office celebrated in his church. As the public recitation of the office became too long to be practical, clerics were allowed to recite it privately. For monks, the divine office had been the most important aspects of the prayer life as far back as the time of Saint BENEDICT in the sixth century. It was done to promote contemplation and a life of continual prayer.

See also LITURGICAL BOOKS.

Further reading: Andrew Hughes, *Medieval Manuscripts for Mass and Office: A Guide to Their Organization and Terminology* (Toronto: University of Toronto Press, 1982); Sally Elizabeth Roper, *Medieval English Benedictine Liturgy: Studies in the Formation, Structure, and Content of the Monastic Votive Office, c. 950–1540* (New York: Garland, 1993); Robert F. Taft, *The Liturgy of the Hours in East and West: The Origins of the Divine Office and Its Meaning for Today* (Collegeville, Minn.: Liturgical Press, 1986).

Olaf I Trygvesson (Óláfr) (ca. 968–1000) *king of Norway*
Olaf was born after the murder of his father, Trygve in about 968. Legend has it that he grew up among the Ruś and became a mercenary. In 991 he entered the service of the Danish king, Svein I Forkbeard (r. 986–1014), and participated in attacks on ENGLAND. After returning to NORWAY, he took the throne on the death of Haakon the Great (r. 968–995) and reigned from 995 to 1000. He was one of the great Christianizers of Norway and western Scandinavia, including ICELAND, the Orkney Islands, and GREENLAND. In hagiographical traditions, he was the model VIKING. As king (r. 1015–30), he tried to unite his kingdom through a common religion. His mysterious origins and his odd disappearance during a battle increased the legendary aspects of his life. A biographer, the Icelander SNORRI STURLUSON, was well aware of its mythological aspect in 1220. He died in battle on September 9, 1000.

Further reading: *The Saga of King Olaf Tryggwason Who Reigned over Norway* A.D. *995 to* A.D. *1000* (London: D. Nutt, 1895); Gwyn Jones, *The Legendary History of Olaf Tryggvason: The Twenty-Second W. P. Ker Memorial Lecture, Delivered in the University of Glasgow, 6th March 1968* (Glasgow: Jackson, 1968).

Old English   *See* ANGLO-SAXONS.

Oleg (Helgi) (r. ca. 879–913) *legendary Viking prince of Kiev*
Oleg followed his probable kinsman, the Scandinavian chieftain RURIK, to NOVGOROD, where Rurik took power. At Rurik's death, he took over Novgorod, but in 882 he left and conquered Smolensk and KIEV. He then established a new capital at Kiev. Oleg united the SLAV tribes of the Dnieper Valley and after a number of victories over the KHAZARS founded an important Russian principality, which stretched from Kiev to Novgorod. In 907, he led an expedition against CONSTANTINOPLE. He failed to capture the city but forced the BYZANTINES to sign a favorable treaty on commerce. He died about 912 or 913, from the bite of a snake, according to a legend.

Further reading: Samuel H. Cross, ed. and trans., *The Russian Primary Chronicle: Laurentian Text* (Cambridge, Mass.: Mediaeval Academy of America, 1953); Simon Franklin and Jonathan Shepard, *The Emergence of Ruś, 750–1200* (New York: Longman, 1996).

olives   *See* AGRICULTURE; FOOD, DRINK, AND NUTRITION.

Olivi, Peter John (1247/1248–1298) *leader of the Spiritual Franciscans*
Peter John Olivi was born in southern France near Béziers and entered the FRANCISCAN ORDER at age 12. He studied THEOLOGY at PARIS, and perhaps at OXFORD, and was a pupil of BONAVENTURE, who greatly influenced him. He never obtained the title of master. He taught theology in several Provençal schools of the Franciscans. He especially defended what he considered absolutely essential to the Franciscan vocation, the strict observance of fully voluntary POVERTY. In 1279 he was consulted on the drafting of a papal bull in which Pope Nicholas III (r. 1277–80) granted the order new privileges and confirmed the evangelical character of the Franciscan Rule, recognizing moderation in its contact with the material world for the Franciscans and only for the necessities of life.

In 1282 some Parisian masters of theology condemned propositions in his commentary on the SENTENCES of PETER LOMBARD. The next year Olivi agreed to retract them. From 1287 to 1289 he taught theology at the convent of Santa Croce in FLORENCE with DANTE in the audience. Returning to PROVENCE and continuing work as theologian and preacher, he exercised a growing influence on his order, and among a LAITY becoming more receptive to his ideas about the necessity of clerical poverty.

IDEAS AND WORKS

He wrote numerous small treatises about attaining a perfect love of GOD. This could only be achieved by living in absolute poverty and detachment from the goods of this world. Peter saw in a revived Franciscan order the most complete fulfillment of an ideal of life involving action and contemplation. In later life he wrote an interpretation of human history divided into seven ages and envisioned as a ceaseless combat between good and evil. It dealt with the ideas of JOACHIM OF FIORE and the coming of the ANTICHRIST. Always loyal to the church, he even promoted a radical ideal of papal infallibility, especially on certain questions of importance to the Franciscans. He vigorously denounced corruption and made a comparison of the church "of this world" to the biblical Babylon. After his death in 1298, some of his ideas were condemned at the Council of VIENNA in 1311 and more at Bern in 1326. His tomb, long a place of PILGRIMAGE, was destroyed and his remains scattered. His ideas on poverty continued to be influential within the Franciscan order long after his death.

See also BIBLE; CLEMENT V, POPE; JOHN XXII, POPE; SPIRITUAL FRANCISCANS.

Further reading: David Burr, *Olivi and Franciscan Poverty: The Origins of the Usus Pauper Controversy* (Philadelphia: University of Pennsylvania Press, 1989); David Burr, *Olivi's Peaceable Kingdom: A Reading of the Apocalypse Commentary* (Philadelphia: University of Pennsylvania Press, 1993); Decima L. Douie, *The Nature and the Effect of the Heresy of the Fraticelli* (Manchester: Manchester University Press, 1932).

Omar, Mosque of (Umar) *See* DOME OF THE ROCK.

Omar I, Abu Hafsa ibn al-Khattab *See* UMAR IBN AL-KHATTAD.

Omar Khayyam (Ghiyath al-Din Abul-Fath Umar ibn Ibrahim al-Khayyami, Umar-I Khayyam, Omar the Tentmaker) (ca. 1048–1131/32) *Persian astronomer, mathematician, poet*
Omar Khayyam was probably born at Nishapur in IRAN in about 1048. He was well educated there and later at SAMARKAND. He won wide recognition for treatises on algebra and astronomy. The SELJUK ruler of Persia, Malik Shah (r. 1055–92), was so impressed by his knowledge that he called him to his palace and commissioned him to reform the CALENDAR using astronomical observations. He finished that in 1079 and then constructed an observatory at Isfahan.

In 1092, after the death of Malik Shah, Omar went on pilgrimage to MECCA. When he returned home to Nishapur, he lived a reclusive life, and wrote his poetic masterpiece the *Rubaiyat* (Quatrains). These poems were only gradually collected and his status as a great poet only gradually evolved. Ultimately he became recognized as one of the greatest poets of the Middle Ages. He left retirement only to do some weather forecasting for a sultan worried about prospects for hunting activities. Throughout his life he was said to prefer reason to revelation. He died in 1131/32 and was buried at Isfahan, where his tomb became a symbol of Persian identity. His calendar, the *Maliki* or *Jalali,* of 1079 was considered among the most accurate of the Middle Ages, and may be more precise than the Gregorian calendar developed 500 years later.

Further reading: Omar Khayyam, *The Rubiyat of Omar Khayyam,* trans. Peter Avery and John Heath-Stubbs (New York: Penguin Books, 1979); Ali Dashti, *In Search of Omar Khayyam,* trans. L. P. Elwell-Sutton (London: G. Allen and Unwin, 1971); John Andrew Boyle, "Umar Khayyam: Astronomer, Mathematician and Poet," in *The Cambridge History of Iran.* Vol. 4. *The Period from the Arab Invasion to the Saljuks,* ed. R. N. Frye (Cambridge: Cambridge University Press, 1975), 658–664; Otto Rothfield, *Umar Khayyam and His Age* (Bombay: D.B. Taraporevala, 1922); Rushdi Rashid, *Omar Khayyam, the Mathematician* (New York: Bibliotheca Persica Press, 2000).

optics The theories of PLATO were fundamental in medieval optics until the 11th century. According to Plato, a ray was sent out uninterruptedly by the eye. It originated in a human inner fire. Called the theory of emission, it was accepted first by AUGUSTINE and then over the course of the Middle Ages by William of Conches (ca. 1100–54), ADELARD OF BATH, and Robert GROSSETESTE. However, when the anatomy of the eye became known, it brought this into question. At the same time, the work of ARISTOTLE and his Arabic commentators, such as IBN SINA (Avicenna) and IBN RUSHD (Averroës), led to a better understanding of optics. According to Avicenna *lux* was the quality of bodies that emitted light and *lumen* was the optical effect this provoked. After the ancient works of Euclid and Ptolemy on optics became available in the Latin West from the mid-12th century, Optics began to be studied from the point of view of geometry. Authors concentrated their attention on the path followed by a ray of vision explaining it by the laws of perspective, reflection, and refraction. This thought produced a science of perspective in the 13th century. The works of such scholars as Roger BACON, John Peckham (1225–92), Witelo (ca. 1230–78), and Henry of Langenstein (d. 1397) were essentially based on the ideas of the Arab scholar IBN AL-HAYTHAM (Alhazen).

There remained the problem of color. After Roger Bacon, Witelo, and John Peckham, a DOMINICAN, Theodoric of Freiberg, in 1304, proposed a theory drawing together the laws of the reflection and refraction of rays as seen in a rainbow. To understand colors, he constructed six-angled prisms. The existence of such knowledge that permitted the making of lenses from about 1280 to improve vision. Optics remained primarily a theoretical discipline.

See also AL-KINDI, ABU YUSUF YAQUB IBN ISHAQ AL-SABBAH; LENSES AND EYEGLASSES.

Further reading: John Peckham, *John Pecham and the Science of Optics: Perspectiva communis,* ed. and trans. David C. Lindberg (Madison: University of Wisconsin Press, 1970); David C. Lindberg, *Studies in the History of Medieval Optics* (London: Variorum Reprints, 1983).

Orcagna, Andrea di Cione Arcagnolo (ca. 1308/15–ca. 1368) *Florentine painter, sculptor, architect*

Andrea studied in FLORENCE and was first mentioned in 1343, when he was admitted to the guild of PAINTERS. He was admitted to the guild of the stonemasons in 1352. Having won fame for his work at the Strozzi Chapel (1354–57), in Santa Maria Novella in Florence where he painted an altarpiece, he was commissioned in 1357 as the architect of the Cathedral of Florence, where he worked until 1367. His principal accomplishment was a tabernacle with a relief of the DEATH and ASSUMPTION of the Virgin MARY in Orsanmichele in Florence. In the meantime, he also planned the rebuilding of the Orvieto Cathedral. His brothers, Nardo (active 1343–66) and Jacopo (active 1365–98), were among the most influential painters in Florence in the second half of the 14th century. Andrea died about 1368.

See also FRESCO PAINTING; PAINTING.

Further reading: Gert Kreytenberg, *Orcagna's Tabernacle in Orsanmichele, Florence* (New York: H. N. Abrams, 1994); Millard Meiss, *Painting in Florence and Siena after the Black Death: The Arts, Religion and Society in the Mid-Fourteenth Century* (1951; reprint, New York: Harper & Row, 1964).

ordeals

Ordeals were supposed to be judgments of GOD that allowed judges to decide the guilt or innocence of an accused according to the person's physical behavior. They were thought to give judicial proof. This often meant holding in hand or walking over fire or plunging a hand into boiling water or cold water. It was not rational, in our terms, but could make sense to minds expecting GOD to be active in this world. Of Frankish origin and mentioned in the first Salic law, the ordeal was widely deployed from the sixth century in Gaul and was gradually adopted throughout much of Europe.

This irrational procedure has long been unfavorably compared with the rational spirit of Roman LAW. It was applied most often in murky and undecided cases, crimes without witnesses or with conflicting evidence, or cases recognizably susceptible to supernatural or divine intervention. It was a dramatized way to address the uncertainty of judges. Religious rituals and FASTING preceded its application, giving those involved time to weigh the possible results of such a procedure and to move to conclude an agreement to preclude it, which was always preferable to a condemnation. Because interpreting the results was not necessarily easy, a majority of those tried were acquitted. After growing opposition to the ordeal, there was a general suppression after the Fourth Lateran Council of 1215.

An offer to submit to an ordeal allowed an accused to demonstrate good faith. In reality there was little need to push the procedure further. It was used in 1083 by Pope GREGORY VII in his conflict with the emperor Henry IV (r. 1050–1106). In that case the result did not favor the PAPACY, and Gregory had to resort to other means to try to win the INVESTITURE CONTROVERSY. Legal progress and the rediscovery of Roman law prompted the suppression of the ordeal in the first half of the 13th century.

See also HENRY II, KING OF ENGLAND; HUGUCCIO; OATHS.

Further reading: Robert Bartlett, *Trial by Fire and Water: The Medieval Judicial Ordeal* (Oxford: Oxford University Press, 1986); Ralph J. Hexter, *Equivocal Oaths and Ordeals in Medieval Literature* (Cambridge, Mass.: Harvard University Press, 1975).

Orderic Vitalis (Odericus) (1075–ca. 1142) *Benedictine monk, historian*

Orderic was born on February 16, 1075 at Atcham in Shropshire in England and educated at Shrewsbury. His father, Ordelerius, was a priest from Orléans who had followed a Norman knight with WILLIAM I the CONQUEROR to ENGLAND at the time of the Norman Conquest in 1066. Though a cleric, he had three sons by an anonymous Englishwoman.

Orderic, after receiving some rudiments of Old English, was sent by his father in 1085 to the Norman monastery of Saint-Évroult in the diocese of Lisieux. He became a monk there and copied manuscripts from which he learned some history. He received the name Vitalis and studied LATIN and grammar. He probably took his monastic vows in 1090; he became subdeacon in 1091, deacon in 1093, and priest in 1108. He journeyed to NORMANDY, England, FRANCE, the abbey of CLUNY, and Cambrai. There he gathered all kinds of information from the LAITY and the CLERGY. This information formed the basis of his writing.

WORKS

From 1114 at the latest and at the request of an abbot, Orderic started to write his *Ecclesiastical History,* which he finished in 1141 near his DEATH. The history was organized into 13 books. Books I and II were a chronological history from the birth of Christ. Books III, IV, V, and VI were a history of the monastery of Saint-Évroult; the others cover the deeds of the Normans to 1083. His history was a lively and detailed picture of the Anglo-Norman world of the second half of the 11th century and the first third of the 12th. Using dramatic dialogues, he presented individual portraits of members of lay and ecclesiastical aristocracy, to describe knightly life and the monastic world. It is the main and most reliable source for English, French, and Norman history for the period 1082 to 1141.

See also NORMANDY AND THE NORMANS.

Further reading: Orderic Vitalis, *The Ecclesiastical History of Orderic Vitalis,* ed. and trans. Marjorie Chibnall, 6 vols. (Oxford: Clarendon Press, 1969–1980); Marjorie Chibnall, *The World of Orderic Vitalis* (Oxford: Clarendon Press, 1984).

Order of Preachers *See* DOMINICAN ORDER.

ordination, clerical *See* SEVEN SACRAMENTS.

Oresme, Nicholas (ca. 1320–1382) *French scholar, translator*
Oresme was born in about 1320 near Bayeaux in NORMANDY. He later became the grand master (1356–61) of the Collège de Navarre in PARIS. He attended the lectures of John BURIDAN, and earned a license in the arts and later a doctorate of THEOLOGY. He was a canon of NOTRE-DAME in Paris, dean of the CATHEDRAL chapter of ROUEN, and finally in 1377 bishop of Lisieux. Requested by King CHARLES V, he translated and commented in French on Aristotle's principal works, the *Ethics,* the *Politics,* the *Economics,* and the *On Heaven and Earth.* He was a strong supporter of the use of the VERNACULAR.

Nicholas also wrote original works in LATIN and in French on mathematics, MUSIC, physics, astronomy, cosmology, and economics. He understood the utility of coordinates for the graphic representation of things subject to quantitative variations and took an interest in the acceleration of falling bodies. He believed that the Earth moved and was not the center of all movement. He undertook a vigorous denunciation of ASTROLOGY, divination, and all forms of MAGIC. In his treatise *On Money* from 1360, he protested against the harmful devaluation of COINAGE. He maintained that MONEY belonged to the community as a whole and not to the issuing ruler, even if it was struck with his effigy on it. He died at Rouen in 1382.

Further reading: Oresme, Nicole, *The De moneta of Nicholas Oresme, and English Mint Documents,* trans. Charles Johnson (London: Nelson, 1956); Nicole Oresme, *Nicole Oresme and the Marvels of Nature: A Study of His "De causis mirabilium" with Critical Edition, Translation, and Commentary* (Toronto: Pontifical Institute of Mediaeval Studies, 1985); Nicole Oresme, *De proportionibus proportionum, and Ad pauca respicientes,* ed. Edward Grant (Madison: University of Wisconsin Press, 1966); G. W. Coopland, *Nicole Oresme and the Astrologers: A Study of His "Livre de divinacions"* (Liverpool: University Liverpool Press, 1952).

Orientalism Orientalism is the defining of people outside one's group or personal experience in a certain way, usually disparagingly. Latin Christians in the Middle Ages constructed an image of Muslims and all people outside Western Europe as different and inferior to themselves in many ways. This categorizing or stereotyping was soon applied to Slavic Eastern Europeans and even to Orthodox Greek Christians. Their ways of life and culture were seen to be enticing, appalling, or both at the same time, but always different from, and probably inferior to, those of Western Europe. Often these medieval stereotypical ideas were further developed in the 18th and 19th centuries and extended to devolve contemporary "backward" peoples within or near a progressive and modern northern Europe. Cultural exchange was, and could only be, one way—diffused from the West to the rest of the world.

In the 10th and 11th centuries, as Roman Catholicism and Eastern Orthodox Christianity found themselves increasingly at odds over theological, political, and cultural matters, Byzantium became more and more a land of strange and irrational people. The perception of attributing inferiority to outsiders was, of course, not limited to the Latin West, as in the writings describing NORMANS by Anna KOMNENE and other Byzantines demonstrate. Such "Otherness" might be a product of doctrinal differences, denied desires, political and cultural conflict, and interior feelings or fears of a perceived inferiority.

ISLAM AND FARTHER EAST

Farther east, the exotic world of the SARACENS was seen as both more dangerous and even more attractive than that of the scheming and dishonest Byzantines. Literature and crusade chronicles ignorantly portrayed the Muslims as pagans who worshiped golden idols of MUHAMMAD, one of which was even found by the crusader TANCRED in a temple at JERUSALEM in 1099 and destroyed. In other 12th-century descriptions, Muslims were said to originate in strange places where no wheat grew, people had skin of iron, and demons commonly dwelled. At the same time there were enticing and fantastic tales of sexual liaisons between Christian men and Muslim princesses. The great and successful enemy of the crusaders, SALADIN, even oddly acquired a reputation for the utmost chivalric conduct.

The mythical world beyond Islam was the domain of strange creatures and strange customs, such as men's sharing their wives and daughters with guests and people's washing themselves in their own urine. Dog-headed people, cyclopses, and cannibals abounded as the world grew stranger the farther east one went. Modern scholars have suggested that on these other peoples and cultures, it was easier to project, often polemically, fears and fantasies tied more to defensiveness about European problems and life than to perceive any genuine reality or positive qualities.

See also ANTI-JUDAISM AND ANTI-SEMITISM; ANTIPODES; CRUSADES; GOG AND MAGOG; JEWS AND JUDAISM; MANDEVILLE, JOHN, AND *MANDEVILLE'S TRAVELS*; MAPS; PRESTER JOHN.

Further reading: Maxime Rodinson, *Europe and the Mystique of Islam,* trans. T. Veinus (Seattle: University of Washington Press, 1987); Edward Said, *Orientalism* (New York: Vintage, 1978); John V. Tolan, ed., *Medieval Christian Perceptions of Islam: A Book of Essays* (New York: Garland, 1995).

Origen (ca. 185–ca. 251/254) *biblical exegete, theologian*
He was probably born at ALEXANDRIA, the son of a Christian martyr, who was killed in 202. He barely missed martyrdom himself. While he was still young, the bishop of Alexandria put him in charge of his catechetical school. There he taught PHILOSOPHY, THEOLOGY, and biblical exegesis. He led an ascetic life of FASTING, vigils, and VOLUNTARY POVERTY. Taking the text of the GOSPEL, literally, he even mutilated his genitals. To escape from the massacres of the emperor Caracalla (r. 211–217), he fled to Caesarea in PALESTINE where he got in trouble for preaching. Recalled he returned to Alexandria. In 230, on a voyage to GREECE, he was illicitly ordained a priest. The bishop of Alexandria threw him out his diocese because of this questionable ordination and probably also because of his preaching heterodox ideas as a layman. Origen then settled permanently at Caesarea, where he founded a school, and remained there until the mid-third century. In Decian persecutions of 250, he was imprisoned and tortured at Caesarea. He died sometime after June 251 at Tyre as a result of his torture.

OPUS

Origen's learned and celebrated work, the *Hexapla*, established parallel texts of the Septuagint. It had many clarifications of difficult passages or terms. He also wrote homilies or commentaries that we possess only in fragments. He composed an apologia for Christianity, *Against Celsus*. Another treatise, *On First Principles*, was a dogmatic synthesis of the Christian faith interwoven with NEOPLATONISM. It covered the doctrine of the Trinity, ANGELS and their fall, the creation of the world, humankind as having fallen SOULS enclosed in a body, REDEMPTION by Jesus Christ, ESCHATOLOGY or the end of the world, principles of moral THEOLOGY, problems of free will, SIN, the Holy Scripture as source of FAITH, and the three interpretive senses for Scripture, the literal, moral, allegorical. He also suggested that all creatures, even the DEVIL, would eventually be saved. These were to become some of the main preoccupations of subsequent theological thought.

Some of his doctrines or Origenism, or the eternity of Creation, the preexistence of souls, and his allegorical interpretation of biblical accounts, led to controversies in the fourth and sixth centuries and as part of the "Origenist controversy." They were condemned by regional synods and in 553 at the second Council of Constantinople. Origen probably did not intend to promote unorthodox ideas, but they were discerned in his elusive, audacious, and creative thought.

Further reading: Origen, *Contra Celsum*, trans. Henry Chadwick (Cambridge: Cambridge University Press, 1965); Henry Chadwick, *Early Christian Thought and the Classical Tradition: Studies in Justin, Clement, and Origen* (New York: Oxford University Press, 1966); Elizabeth A. Clark, *The Origenist Controversy: The Cultural Construction of an Early Christian Debate* (Princeton, N.J.: Princeton University Press, 1992); Charles Kannengiesser and William L. Petersen, eds., *Origen of Alexandria: His World and His Legacy* (Notre Dame, Ind.: University of Notre Dame Press, 1988); Joseph W. Trigg, *Origen* (London: Routledge, 1998).

Orosius, Paulus (fl. early fifth century) *Spanish historian*
Paulus was a Spanish priest from Braga in modern PORTUGAL who fled to Hippo in North Africa in 414 to evade the invasion by Goths. Working as a pupil with AUGUSTINE, he wrote several works in defense of orthodoxy. The first was on the origin of the human SOUL. He was sent in 415 to debate with PELAGIUS in PALESTINE. The outcome was inconclusive. An episcopal report sent to ROME questioned his orthodoxy. Augustine then asked him to produce a historical supplement to his *City of God*. After finishing it in 418, he began to oppose a popular contemporary argument that Rome's fall was directly caused by mass conversion to Christianity. The resulting *History against the Pagans in Seven Books* was dominated by the themes of providential history and beleaguered but triumphant Christianity. Completed in 418, the book was well received and widely read. Nothing is known about him after its appearance.

See also CHRONICLES AND ANNALS.

Further reading: Paulus Orosius, *Seven Books of History against the Pagans: The Apology of Paulus Orosius,* trans. Irving Woodworth Raymond (New York: Columbia University Press, 1936); Paulus Orosius, *The Seven Books of History against the Pagans,* trans. Roy J. Deferrari (Washington, D.C.: Catholic University of America Press, 1964).

Oseberg find or ship This discovery comprised a VIKING ship and the skeletons of two women found in 1903 at Oseberg, west of the Oslofjord in NORWAY. They are now in the Viking Ship Museum in Oslo, along with a host of well-preserved wooden objects. The ship is about 65 feet long, with 15 pairs of oars, and was built of oak in about the year 820. It was not designed for making long voyages, but for show and hugging coasts. The find included grave goods, FURNITURE, sledges, farm tools, and a wagon. There are also fine animal carvings, such as the serpent's head at the prow. The skeletal remains of two women were found in the boat, once believed to be Queen Asa, grandmother of King Harald I Fairhair (r. 880–930), and her maidservant. However, the ship is too old for that. The Oseberg find and ship are sometimes called the grandmother of the Norwegian nation.

See also GOKSTAD SHIP; SHIPS AND SHIPBUILDING; SUTTON HOO.

Further reading: Anton W. Brögger and Haakon Shetelig, *The Viking Ships: Their Ancestry and Evolution,* trans. Katherine John (1953; reprint, London: C. Hurst, 1971); Else Roesdahl, *The Vikings,* 2d ed., trans. Susan M. Margeson and Kirsten Williams (1987; reprint, London: Penguin Books, 1998).

Osman I (Uthman, Othman, Osman Gazi) (ca. 1254– ca. 1326) *Ottoman sultan, considered the founder of the Turkish state*

Osman I was a Turkish chieftain, born in ANATOLIA as the son of a certain Ertugrul or Ertoghrïl. He inherited a small principality founded by the SELJUK sultans of Konya in Anatolia. Osman was a member of the Gazis, frontier Turkish fighters. One of their duties was to ravage countries of the infidels who resisted them. After succeeding his father about 1283 as emir, he built a powerful army and consolidated his principality during the disintegration of the Seljuk power in Anatolia. He attacked his Byzantine neighbors, gradually extending his control over several CASTLES in the area. In 1290 he started calling himself sultan of the TURKS. In 1304 he attempted to conquer Gallipoli but was decisively defeated by the Catalan Company.

Back in Anatolia and avoiding battle, he continued to increase his territories at the expense of the BYZANTINE EMPIRE. The strategic city of Bursa was captured around the time of his death in 1326. It became the stepping stone for the OTTOMANS' crossing into Europe. His successes drew more Turkish immigrants to his territory. The Turkish state, adopting his name, became known as the Osman or Ottoman realm.

Further reading: Halil Inalcik, *An Economic and Social History of the Ottoman Empire, 1300–1914* (Cambridge: Cambridge University Press, 1994); Norman Itzkowitz, *Ottoman Empire and Islamic Tradition* (1972; reprint, Chicago: University of Chicago Press, 1980); Rudi Paul Lindner, *Nomads and Ottomans in Medieval Anatolia* (Bloomington: Research Institute for Inner Asian Studies, Indiana University, Bloomington, 1983); Paul Wittek, *The Rise of the Ottoman Empire* (1938; reprint, New York: Burt Franklin, 1971).

Ostrogoths (East Goth, Goths of the rising sun, Greutungs)

In the third and the fourth centuries, the Ostrogoths, the eastern branch of the GOTHS, seemed to have detach themselves from the VISIGOTHS. As a confederation they lived in the region between the Don and Dneister Rivers along the BLACK SEA. They were a people well experienced in arms and in combat on horseback. The HUNS subjugated them in 375–376 and forced them to accompany their raids as far west as Gaul. On the death of ATTILA in 451 the Ostrogoths were settled by the Romans as federates or allies in PANNONIA and Noricum, just north of the Balkans.

After 473, they moved south into the Balkans, and under the leadership of THEODORIC they settled in Moesia. The Byzantine emperor Zeno (r. 474–491) adopted Theodoric and appointed him military commander for ITALY. He was supposed to destroy the power of ODOACER. Between 489 and 493, Theodoric conquered Italy and killed Odoacer. His Ostrogoths settled and helped themselves to a third of Italian lands and the agrarian yields. The main cities of their kingdom were RAVENNA, Pavia, and VERONA. The basis of Theodoric's state was full Ostrogoth jurisdiction over their subjects and full responsibility for their defense. The Romans or Italians maintained the civil administration and its structures. There was a difference in religion: The Ostrogoths were Arians but were initially tolerant of religious difference. There was a considerable growth in tension near the end of the reign of Theodoric, mostly due to Byzantine intrigue.

On Theodoric's death in 526, the emperor JUSTINIAN decided to restore Byzantine control. This led to the long and devastating Gothic Wars between 535 and 553. The Ostrogoths, despite their strong resistance, especially under TOTILA, were ultimately completely defeated. Under Ostrogoth rule, Italy had enjoyed a period of peace and prosperity despite religious and political tensions between the Ostrogoths and their Roman subjects. It had a sound COINAGE and was well administered and blessed with impressive building projects.

See also ARIANISM; BELISARIUS; BOETHIUS, ANICIUS MANLIS TORQUATUS SEVERINUS; CASSIODORUS, SENATOR; CLOVIS; PROCOPIUS OF CAESAREA; TOTILA, KING OF THE OSTROGOTHS.

Further reading: Cassiodorus, *The Variae of Magnus Aurelius Cassiodorus Senator,* trans. S. J. B. Barnish (Liverpool: Liverpool University Press, 1992); Jordanes, *The Gothic History of Jordanes,* ed. Charles Christopher Mierow (Cambridge: Speculum Historiale, 1960); Peter Amory, *People and Identity in Ostrogothic Italy, 489–554* (Cambridge: Cambridge University Press, 1997); Thomas S. Burns, *A History of the Ostrogoths* (Bloomington: Indiana University Press, 1984); Walter A. Goffart, *Barbarians and Romans,* A.D. *418–584: The Techniques of Accommodation* (Princeton, N.J.: Princeton University Press, 1980).

Othman Ibn Affan   *See* UTHMAN IBN AFFAN.

Otto I the Great (912–973) *founder of the first Reich and the kingdom of Germany*

Born November 23, 912, Otto was the eldest son of the duke of SAXONY and future emperor, Henry I the

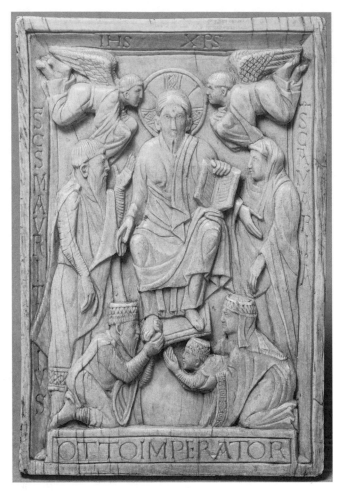

Christ enthroned with the family of Emperor Otto I at his feet, Ottonian ivory plaque from a Lombard workshop (10th century), Castello Sforzesco, Milan, Italy *(Scala / Art Resource)*

Fowler (r. 919–936) and of Saint Matilda (d. 968). Otto married in 929 an Anglo-Saxon princess named Edith (d. 936) and was chosen by his father to be his sole heir. That choice went against the custom of dividing the kingdom among all the surviving legitimate sons.

In 936 Otto was crowned at AACHEN. He sought a more centralized government than that of his father, one closer to that of the Carolingians. To accomplish that, he had to tame the rulers of the great territorial states of Germany. He succeeded in taking over the administration of FRANCONIA and Saxony and appointed princes of his royal house in SWABIA, BAVARIA, and Lotharingia, but restricted their prerogatives to imperial representation. Otto overcame several revolts by his relatives, including his half brother in 938, his brother in 939 and 941, his son-in-law, and his eldest son in 952–954.

RELATIONS WITH THE CHURCH

He developed a close association with the church during these crises. As a consecrated king, he made the church an organ of his government. He further made massive gifts of property and public rights to bishops and abbots. He also protected them against the encroachments of the LAITY. He kept close control over appointments to ecclesiastical posts and used his royal chapel as a nursery for loyal and competent clerical administrators. It was started and run by his younger brother, BRUNO, who later became the archbishop of COLOGNE in 955, the duke of Lotharingia, and a saint.

CONQUESTS AND EMPIRE

Outside Germany, Otto acquired a protectorate over the kingdom of BURGUNDY in 937. In western Francia, he arbitrated between the rival lines of Carolingians and Robertians or CAPETIANS, to whom he had links through marriage. He managed the conquest of ITALY in 951 and married ADELAIDE, a descendant of CHARLEMAGNE and the widow of King Lothair of Italy (r. 947–50). In 955 he won a great victory at LECHFELD over the MAGYARS or HUNGARIANS, who then had to end their raids into central Europe.

Otto was essentially proclaimed emperor anew by the army after that victory. In a second Italian expedition in 961, he completed the annexation of the peninsula and went to ROME, where he was consecrated as emperor on February 2, 962, by the notoriously degenerate Pope John XII (r. 955–964). The pope promptly changed his support as soon as he could to Otto's great rival in Italy, King Berengar II (r. 950–963). Otto deposed the pope and forced Berengar into exile. He negotiated successfully with the Byzantines, who were unhappy with his activities in Italy and his consecration as emperor. He was able to negotiate the marriage of his son and successor, Otto II (r. 973–983), to the Greek princess THEOPHANO. Near the end of his reign, he established the archdiocese of Magdeburg in 968 as a province and frontier region bordering the lands of the SLAVS. He had ambitions for further conquest to the east, into what became POLAND and RUSSIA. But these plans came to little at the time. Otto died on May 7, 973, and was buried at Magdeburg. Much admired and feared, he was the first great German imperial ruler and has been called the true creator of the German HOLY ROMAN EMPIRE. He was also a great patron of the arts, creator of what has been called the Ottonian Renaissance.

See also LIUTPRAND OF CREMONA; OTTONIAN ART.

Further reading: Thietmar of Mersburg, *Ottonian Germany: The Chronicle of Thietmar of Mersburg,* trans. David A. Warner (Manchester: Manchester University Press, 2001); Boyd H. Hill, *The Rise of the First Reich: Germany in the Tenth Century* (New York: Wiley, 1969); Karl J. Leyser, *Rule and Conflict in an Early Medieval Society: Ottonian Saxony* (London: Edward Arnold, 1979), 9–47, 143–156; Eckhard Müller-Mertens, "The Ottonians as Kings and Emperors," in *The New Cambridge Medieval History,* Vol. 3. *c. 900–c. 1024,* ed. Timothy Reuter (Cambridge: Cambridge University Press, 1999), 233–266.

Otto III (980–1002) *king of Germany, Holy Roman Emperor*

Otto III was crowned king in December 983 at the age of three, on the death of his father, Otto II (r. 973–983). Henry the Quarrelsome, once a duke of BAVARIA (r. 955–976, 985–995), acted as regent but was soon replaced by Otto's Byzantine mother, THEOPHANO, until her death in 991. After another regency by his grandmother, ADELAIDE, Otto himself directed the empire from 994.

The main concern of Otto's government was ITALY. He went there in May 996 to receive imperial consecration from his cousin, the first German pope, Gregory V (r. 996–999), whom Otto had just appointed. At ROME he met Adalbert (ca. 956–997), the exiled bishop of PRAGUE, and the famous intellectual Gerbert of Aurillac, the future Pope SYLVESTER II. He returned to Germany but in 998 had to go back to Rome, where the noble Crescenti family had taken power and placed an antipope (John XVI [r. 997–998]) on the papal throne. Otto defeated the Crescenti and executed the antipope, who also happened to have been his old teacher, while putting the unpopular foreigner, Gregory, back on the papal throne.

THE IMPERIAL COURT

Otto III then stayed at Rome on the Palatine Hill, and there he formed an imperial court on the model of Byzantium. Under the influence of Gerbert, whom he appointed pope as Sylvester II, he tried to establish a new, universal conception of empire, a federation of kingdoms and local ecclesiastical institutions under the joint authority of the emperor and his client, the pope. Otto went on pilgrimage to Gniezno in February 1000, to the tomb of Adalbert, who had been martyred in 997; he made Duke BOLESLAV of POLAND the king and gave him control of the church in his country. He then participated in crowning STEPHEN I of Hungary and honored bishop of Gran by giving him control over the Magyar church. These were not acceptable to the powerful German bishops, who had ambitions for a widespread German domination of Eastern Europe.

Otto returned to Rome but was forced to leave the city by an uprising in January 1001. While waiting for reinforcements to return to Rome, he died January 24, 1002, at the age of 21 and was buried near his imperial role model CHARLEMAGNE at AACHEN. His successors were not able to continue his ambitious imperial plans.

See also HOLY ROMAN EMPIRE; OTTONIAN ART.

Further reading: Thietmar of Mersburg, *Ottonian Germany: The Chronicle of Thietmar of Mersburg,* trans. David A. Warner (Manchester: Manchester University Press, 2001); Robert Folz, *the Concept of Empire in Western Europe from the Fifth to the Fourteenth Century,* trans. Sheila Ann Ogilvie (New York: Harper & Row, 1969).

Ottoman Turks and Empire The Ottomans were a dynasty of Oghuz Turks founded by a chief named OSMAN I, the son of Ertoghrul. He founded an emirate in ANATOLIA. As other Turkoman chiefs did in the late 13th and early 14th centuries, he profited from the weakening of SELJUK, MONGOL, and BYZANTINE power. His emirate was the base of the future Ottoman domination of the Balkans and eventually of nearly all of ISLAM.

These beginnings were modest. From Bithynia, they expanded by attacks and raids at the expense of the last Byzantine strongholds in Anatolia, including the important capture of Bursa in 1326 and the occupation of the southern side of the Dardanelles in 1345. The Ottoman sultanate, as did the other small Turkish states of Anatolia, maintained a seminomadic pastoral life that only gradually promoted Islamization of formerly Byzantine territories.

In 1354, after an opportune earthquake, the Ottomans captured Gallipoli on the European coast of the Dardanelles. Now in Europe, they began the conquest of the Balkans. They were successful because of sound military organization, the formation of the elite JANISSARY Corps and the zeal of their warriors. These were the foundations of the great conquests of MURAD I between 1362 and 1389 and of BAYAZID I "the Thunderbolt" between 1389 and 1402. Over some 40 years, they conquered most of the southeastern Balkans, including Thrace, MACEDONIA, BULGARIA, and southern SERBIA. They encircled CONSTANTINOPLE, crushed the Serbs at KOSOVO Polje in 1389, and destroyed Western crusaders at the Battle of NICOPOLIS in 1396.

In the meantime in Anatolia, the Ottomans occupied most of the rival Turkish emirates of western and central Anatolia. Even the death of Bayazid I, defeated in battle by TAMERLANE at Ankara in 1402, slowed this march of conquest by only 20 years. From 1421, Ottoman expansion recommenced under MURAD II between 1421 and 1451 and MEHMED II between 1451 and 1481. Murad continued the conquest of GREECE and ALBANIA, crossed the Danube, attacked HUNGARY, crushed Serbia, and routed another great coalition of Western crusaders at the Battle of Varna in 1444. Sultan Mehmed II captured Constantinople on May 29, 1453, and continued on to attack the colonies of VENICE along the Adriatic, ALBANIA, and the VLACHS. He created an imperial state, combining both the Seljuk and Byzantine legacies. By the 16th century, the Ottomans controlled EGYPT, SYRIA, and IRAQ.

See ART AND ARCHITECTURE, ISLAMIC; ILLUMINATION.

Further reading: Jason Goodwin, *Lords of the Horizons: A History of the Ottoman Empire* (New York: H. Holt, 1999); Colin Imber, *The Ottoman Empire, 1300–1481* (Istanbul: Isis Press, 1990); I. Metin Kunt, "The Rise of the Ottomans," in *The New Cambridge Medieval History,* Vol. 6, *c. 1300–c. 1415,* ed. Michael Jones (Cambridge: Cambridge University Press, 2000), 839–63; Stanford J.

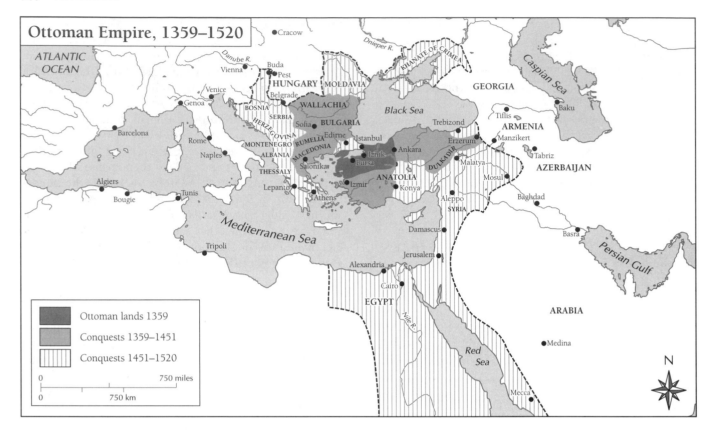

Ottoman Empire, 1359–1520

ATLANTIC OCEAN

Legend:
- Ottoman lands 1359
- Conquests 1359–1451
- Conquests 1451–1520

0 — 750 miles
0 — 750 km

N

Shaw, *History of the Ottoman Empire and Modern Turkey*, 2 vols. (Cambridge: Cambridge University Press, 1976–1977); Elizabeth Zachariadou, "The Ottoman World," in *The New Cambridge Medieval History*, Vol. 7, *c. 1415–c. 1500*, ed. Christopher Allmand (Cambridge: Cambridge University Press, 1998), 812–30.

Ottonian art   This was a distinctive style of art, especially manuscript ILLUMINATION, and architecture carried out under the reigns of the emperors OTTO I THE GREAT, Otto II (r. 973–983), and OTTO III in the 10th century and into the first half of the 11th century. Carolingian artistic forms and practices were revived along with an expansion of monastic foundations. It was a court art tied to the patronage of rulers and high officials, especially bishops. It was not as concentrated in one center or around one person as had been the case in the Carolingian era. There was a great increase in the production of deluxe manuscripts with sophisticated and beautiful illumination and in GOLD and IVORY work for book covers. There were numerous women patrons, especially the Byzantine empress and wife of Otto II, THEOPHANO.

In architecture, important and influential buildings linked to this style were erected at Hildesheim, Gernrode, and Reichenau. Ottonian architects were innovative in their design of transepts and CRYPTS. Besides monastic architecture, there were important civil buildings and palaces for the emperors, even though they were often on the move from place to place. Manuscript painting was much influenced by the Byzantine style and primarily involved books of GOSPELS and liturgical books for ceremonial use. These images consisted primarily of narrative cycles of scenes from the life of Christ.

Further reading: C. R. Dodwell, *The Pictorial Arts of the West, 800–1200* (New Haven, Conn.: Yale University Press, 1993); Peter Lasko, *Ars Sacra, 800–1200*, 2d ed. (New Haven, Conn.: Yale University Press, 1994); Henry Mayr-Harting, *Ottonian Book Illumination: An Historical Study* 2d ed., 2 vol. (1991; reprint, London, Harvey Miller, 1999).

Otto of Freising (ca. 1112/15–1158) *bishop of Freising, margrave of Austria, Cistercian monk, crusader, historian*
The son of margrave Leopold III (1096–1136) of AUSTRIA, Otto of Freising was a witness to and participant in many important events of the early 12th century. He was born into the high aristocracy of the empire, as the half brother of Conrad III (r. 1138–52), the king of GERMANY, and the uncle of FREDERICK I BARBAROSSA. Otto took the CISTERCIAN habit at the Cistercian monastery of Morimond in Champagne in 1132 or 1133, at the end of his studies at PARIS. As bishop of Freising from 1138, he introduced reformed MONASTICISM to his diocese and went on the Second CRUSADE in 1148.

As a famous and important historian, he wrote his *The Two Cities* between 1143 and 1145; it ended with the near contemporary and controversial INVESTITURE CONTROVERSY. Starting from the ideas about history provided by AUGUSTINE and OROSIUS, he interpreted secular history as a conflict between this world and the next, the kingdom of GOD. Both were to be united through the church. He then wrote a history of the activities of Frederick I Barbarossa near the end of his own life. There was a strong theme of peace in his work on Frederick, much of the conflict between church and state seemed to be in the past. His pupil Rahewin (d. 1165) wrote the second half of this work, advancing it to the time of some of Frederick's failures and disasters in Italy. Otto died in 1158.

Further reading: Otto I, Bishop of Freising, *The Deeds of Frederick Barbarossa,* trans. Charles Christopher Mierow and Richard Emery (1953; reprint, Toronto: University of Toronto Press, 1994); Otto I, Bishop of Freising, *The Two Cities: A Chronicle of Universal History to the Year 1146 A.D.,* trans. and ed. Charles Christopher Mierow, Austin P. Evans, and Charles Knapp (New York: Columbia University Press, 1928).

outlawry This was a legal status primarily in ENGLAND but also, in a slightly different form, on the Continent. It was applied to those cited but not cooperating in a legal process. Outlawry involved those captured or cited for crimes of all sorts. It was both a coercive measure and a punishment. If an accused failed to appear in a court to answer charges brought against him or her, a sentence could not be pronounced in absentia. So instead, the process of outlawry was invoked. A writ ordering the sheriff or another official to confirm that the prospective outlaw had been advised of his or her citation was issued. If on the third summons he or she still could not be found, then a formal demand compelled the subject to attend a trial or hearing. At the first stage, he or she forfeited goods and chattels to the king. After the last stage, the person was outlawed and placed outside the protection of the law.

These rulings applied in only one jurisdiction or county in England. One could flee to another county to escape. Early in the Middle Ages, outlaws for serious crimes could be killed with impunity. In practice this severity was mitigated. Outlaws were numerous, for example, in medieval England. For every person actually convicted by the courts, another 10 were outlawed. Some outlaws, such as the legendary ROBIN HOOD or real people such as William WALLACE, took on the status of popular heroes because of the perceived unfairness and corruption of the government and the legal system.

See also CRIME, PUNISHMENT, AND THE COURTS; IMPEACHMENT AND ATTAINDER; JURY TRIAL.

Further reading: Henry de Bracton, *On the Laws and Customs of England,* trans. Samuel E. Thorne (Cambridge: Selden Society, 1968); R. F. Hunnisett, *The Medieval Coroner* (Cambridge: Cambridge University Press, 1961); Maurice Keen, *The Outlaws of Medieval Legend* (1961; reprint, London: Routledge, 2000); Ralph Bernard Pugh, *Imprisonment in Medieval England* (Cambridge: Cambridge University Press, 1968); Ralph Bernard Pugh, *Some Reflections of a Medieval Criminologist* (London: Oxford University Press, 1973).

Owain Gwynedd *See* GLYN DWR, OWIAN.

Owen Glendower *See* GLYN DWR, OWIAN.

Oxford and Oxford University Medieval Oxford was a town in the upper Thames River basin in ENGLAND, which was the site of one of the great European universities. The town first appeared in the seventh century as a cattle market. In the eighth century it became a PILGRIMAGE site and location of a FAIR. Although Oxford itself was a secondary town, its schools in the 12th century grew out of monastic and collegiate churches, especially those for the SEVEN LIBERAL ARTS and THEOLOGY. King HENRY II aided English education in 1167 by prohibiting English students to study in PARIS. The Oxford schools were transformed into a university around 1200. In 1209 occurred the first of many bloody brawls between scholars and townspeople, which led to the departure of many scholars and students to CAMBRIDGE, where they created a second university. Most of them returned in 1214.

Between 1214 and 1233, papal and royal privileges further organized the university, basing its institutions and teaching system on the model of Paris. In contrast to that of Paris, however, the head of the university was a chancellor elected from among the doctors of THEOLOGY or canon LAW and confirmed by the bishop of Lincoln. The Parisian head was a rector chosen from among the faculty of arts. The chancellor of Oxford shared power with an assembly of masters, especially those from the arts. The course of study favored the *quadrivium*. The university's reputation was based on theology, PHILOSOPHY, LOGIC, mathematics, and SCIENCE. The faculties of arts and theology seem to have been much more important than those of law or MEDICINE.

In the 13th century the first colleges of the university, Balliol and Merton, were founded, and the new MENDICANT ORDERS arrived to study and set up schools. The university became a hotbed of heterodox ideas, such as those of John WYCLIFFE, in the late 14th and early 15th centuries. Most students were from England. They generally lived in boarding houses or in the convents of the friars, not in the colleges, which had few facilities as yet.

By 1500 there were some 10 secular colleges with some 200 students with the religious colleges involving about the same numbers.

See also BACON, ROGER; GROSSETESTE, ROBERT; DUNS SCOTUS, JOHN; LOLLARDS; WILLIAM OF OCKHAM.

Further reading: J. I. Catto, ed., *The History of the University of Oxford.* Vol. 1, *The Early Oxford Schools* (Oxford: Oxford University Press, 1984); J. I. Catto and Ralph Evans, eds., *The History of the University of Oxford.* Vol. 2, *Late Medieval Oxford* (Oxford: Clarendon Press, 1992); Alan B. Cobban, *English University Life in the Middle Ages* (London: UCL Press, 1999); Alfred Brotherston Emden, *A Biographical Register of the University of Oxford to A.D. 1500* (Oxford: Clarendon Press, 1957); Alfred Brotherston Emden, *An Oxford Hall in Medieval Times, Being the Early History of St. Edmund Hall* (Oxford: Clarendon Press, 1968); Gordon Leff, *Paris and Oxford Universities in the Thirteenth and Fourteenth Centuries: An Institutional and Intellectual History* (New York: Wiley, 1968).

P

Pachomius (ca. 292–346) *traditional founder of coenobitic monasticism*

Pachomius was born about 292 in southern EGYPT. He was converted at about age 20 while serving in a Roman army, when he experienced Christian CHARITY. Released at the end of the war, he returned to the village of Chenoboskion in Upper Egypt to be baptized. He took up an ascetic life as a hermit and practicing forms of penance under a spiritual father and fellow anchorite.

In 323, while gathering wood in an abandoned village, Tabennesi, he had a VISION that instructed him to build a monastery there for the good of himself and others. Previously, early MONASTICISM had been dominated by hermit monks, such as Anthony (ca. 251–356). He and others had withdrawn from the world in solitude as ANCHORITES. Pachomius's new experiment grew so that within six years, the number of monks had increased, requiring the establishment of a second monastery nearby. Pachomius also devised the first monastic rule for efficiently governing monks as they live in a common economic and spiritual life of shared meals, work, and PRAYER with a walled complex.

When Pachomius died in 346 of a PLAGUE that swept his communities, as many as nine monasteries and two affiliated nunneries were under his control. They varied in size and structure, all to the central house in a loose federation. By about 420, supposedly some 3,000 monks belonged to this movement. The community continued to grow after Pachomius's death. They built a five-aisle basilica, the largest in Egypt, at the main house at Pbow in the fifth century. The Pachomian movement, however, disappeared in the latter part of the fifth century, probably a casualty of the CHRISTOLOGICAL CONTROVERSIES at the Council of CHALCEDON in 451.

See also ASCETICISM; HERMITS AND HERMETICISM.

Further reading: Pachomius, *Instructions, Letters, and Other Writings of Saint Pachomius and His Disciples,* trans. Armand Veilleux (Kalamazoo, Mich.: Cistercian, 1982); Armand Veilleux, trans., *The Life of Saint Pachomius and His Disciples* (Kalamazoo, Mich.: Cistercian, 1980); Philip Rousseau, *Pachomius. The Making of a Community in Fourth-Century Egypt* (Berkeley: University of California Press, 1985); Susanna Elm, *"Virgins of God": The Making of Asceticism in Late Antiquity* (Oxford: Clarendon Press, 1994).

Padua (**Patavium, Padoua**) Medieval Padua, the Roman Patavium, was a town 22 miles from VENICE in northeastern ITALY. It had a bishop by 350. Although captured by the OSTROGOTHS in 493 and the BYZANTINES in 540, it escaped conquest by the LOMBARDS in 568. The town reverted to Byzantine control until 602, when the LOMBARD king, Agilulf (r. 590–615), captured it and erased what was left of its Roman past. Its territory was then dismembered between the neighboring cities of Treviso and Vicenza. CHARLEMAGNE made it a seat for one of his counties in 774, after he conquered the Lombard Kingdom.

From the 11th century, Padua revived and grew. The INVESTITURE struggles weakened the once-dominant episcopal power, so Padua's first colleges of consuls appeared in 1138, forming a COMMUNE, which tended to be dominated by the GUELF faction. The 13th century included cultural and religious change marked by the birth in 1226 of the university. The DOMINICANS settled at Padua in about 1226 and the Portuguese FRANCISCAN preacher ANTHONY was enthusiastically received until his death in

1231. A major basilica built in his honor drew a large number of pilgrims.

In the 12th century Padua was part of the LOMBARD LEAGUE and became an important member of the Guelf party aligned against the emperor FREDERICK II. In 1237, without outside Guelf help, however, it had to surrender to the head of the imperial party, the Ghibelline feudal lord Ezzelino da Romano (1194–1259), who set up an authoritarian regime in Padua, VERONA, and Vicenza. At first the town's economy derived some benefit as part of this territorial unity, especially for a regional textile industry. But in 1256 Ezzelino was expelled. This led to a new communal regime between 1256 and 1318. During this period MERCHANTS, such as the Scrovegni family, for whom GIOTTO painted in the ARENA CHAPEL, flourished. As a prosperous town it had perhaps 30,000 inhabitants on the eve of the PLAGUE of 1348. Internal division, however, led to a lordship by the Carrara family (1337–1405), clients of the powerful Della Scala in nearby Verona. The Carrara were patrons of humanists such as PETRARCH and the university. The history of medieval Padua ended with the brutal Venetian conquest in 1405. From then on it was part of the Venetian territorial state.

See also MARSILIUS OF PADUA.

Further reading: J. K. Hyde, *Padua in the Age of Dante: A Social History of an Italian City-State* (Manchester: Manchester University Press, 1966); Benjamin G. Kohl, *Padua under the Carrara, 1318–1405* (Baltimore: Johns Hopkins University Press, 1998); Diana Norman, ed., *Siena, Florence, and Padua: Art, Society, and Religion 1280–1400* (New Haven, Conn.: Yale University Press in association with the Open University, 1995); Nancy G. Siraisi, *Arts and Sciences at Padua: The Studium of Padua before 1350* (Toronto, Pontifical Institute of Mediaeval Studies, 1973).

paganism and Christianization   As with any of a number of polytheistic religions, medieval and late antique paganism involved the ritualistic worship of more than one god, unlike monotheistic Christianity, Judaism, and ISLAM.

In Christian antiquity the term *pagan* usually designated those who lived in the countryside and had resisted conversion to Christianity. In the early Middle Ages such pagans venerated ancient or traditional gods associated with the forces of nature. In the Roman Empire there had been an official cult of the emperor to whom sacrifices had to be made. This was used as a test to expose Christians who sometimes succumbed to martyrdom rather than offer a sacrifice to the emperor. In the third century Egyptian, eastern, and Persian cults of Isis, Cybele, and Mithras became popular. In northern Europe some of the gods of the Germans and Scandinavians were Wotan and Thor. For the Celts, there were Taranis, Nerthus, and a group of female deities. These northern pagans apparently met around sacred springs and trees to indulge in sacrifices and ritualistic drinking. To use these natural forces for human benefit or harm, the Celts and Germans practiced MAGIC in various forms, including incantations and rituals for the healing of beasts, the fertility of the fields, and military victory. People wore CHARMS and perhaps used secret formulaic writing such as RUNES or ogham. The Celts believed in the immortality of the soul; the Germanic tradition believed in VALHALLA where honorable dead warriors went after death. Many of these practices and beliefs were, however, susceptible to assimilation into orthodox Christianity.

Even after Christianization, prayer to such deities for intervention in worldly matters remained popular at springs, certain trees, rocks, and sacred caves, especially during agrarian festivals at the June and December solstices. Funerals and BURIAL continued to include banquets and "diabolical" chants that had little relation to Christianity. Pagan or superstitious practices clearly continued, even designating certain days as preferable for certain activities, such as Fridays or Venus's day for weddings. To these social practices were added divination to foretell the future and magical acts to guarantee protection against the forces of evil or to harm others. Incantations promoted feelings of love between people, and there were formulas for healing the sick. Others were employed for casting evil spells.

PUNISHMENT AND REPRESSION

The emperor Theodosios I (r. 379–395) in the late fourth century had banned classical and Oriental paganism. He particularly targeted sacrificial rituals, the funding of civic rituals, and the financial support of temples. However, many aspects of these religions lingered on in local forms and cults. The arrival of barbarians introduced a new form of paganism. In the sixth century the sermons of Saint Caesarius of Arles (ca. 470–542), a work entitled *The Correction of Rustics* by Martin of Braga (d. 580), several letters of Pope GREGORY I the Great, and the canons of councils demonstrated a strong concern that paganism was not being eliminated. Slightly later seventh-century PENITENTIALS defined and discussed penalties for such SIN. Around 1000, in his canonistic writings BURCHARD of Worms expressed a clear pastoral interest in the necessity for the suppression of pagan rituals and beliefs.

Much of these pagan practices or beliefs, well recognized as contrary to Christian belief, were punishable by death. At times they were suppressed by force. Numerous kings and rulers destroyed sanctuaries and forbade idolatrous cults and magic. Despite this violent suppression, there were other clerics, and even a few rulers, who fostered more gentle attempts to convert people from such beliefs and practices by assimilation, persuasion, and example.

See also AUGUSTINE OF CANTERBURY, SAINT; BONI-
FACE, SAINT; MISSIONS AND MISSIONARIES; PREACHING AND
PREACHERS.

Further reading: J. N. Hillgarth, ed., *Christianity and
Paganism, 350–750: The Conversion of Western Europe,* rev.
ed. (1969; reprint, Philadelphia: University of Pennsylva-
nia Press, 1986); Pierre Chuvin, *A Chronicle of the Last
Pagans,* trans. B. A. Archer (Cambridge, Mass.: Harvard
University Press, 1990); John R. Curran, *Pagan City and
Christian Capital: Rome in the Fourth Century* (Oxford:
Oxford University Press, 1999); H. R. Ellis Davidson,
Gods and Myths of Northern Europe (Baltimore: Penguin
Books, 1964); Jean Seznec, *The Survival of the Pagan
Gods: The Mythological Tradition and Its Place in Renais-
sance Humanism and Art,* trans. Barbara F. Sessions (1940;
reprint, New York: Pantheon Books, 1953); Ronald Sheri-
dan and Anne Ross, *Gargoyles and Grotesques: Paganism
in the Medieval Church* (Boston: New York Graphic Society, 1975).

painting In the Middle Ages and RENAISSANCE, painting employed several media, including various forms of
FRESCO on walls, on PARCHMENT in manuscripts, and from
easels onto wooden panels and ALTARPIECES. These formats survived from late antiquity to continue in the Middle Ages. The overwhelming majority of painting was
religious, but by the 14th and 15th centuries there was a
considerable increase in secular and civic art in palaces
and in public buildings. With the revival of classical
learning and education in the 15th century, pagan and
classical themes appeared, especially in the painting produced for the LAITY. From the mid-14th century, true portraits of individuals and saints appeared on smaller
panels, wooden containers, or disks.

Techniques changed, especially from egg tempera to
oil bases. Painting on stretched canvas also become more
common from the 15th century. Besides being ornamental and complementary to architecture, the iconography
of religious painting was used to instruct Christians in
their faith and to illustrate liturgical rites. There are
numerous examples of preaches' using images in just that
way in the later Middle Ages. Secular themes reminded
viewers of the power of the patron, whether an individual
or a corporate body such as a town. Although little of
that has survived from the Carolingian period, there
still exist excellent examples in the town hall of SIENA,
the ducal fortress in Mantua, and the Papal Palace in
AVIGNON, as well as fragments in the imperial palaces of
CONSTANTINOPLE.

BYZANTINE AND ISLAMIC
Painting decorated the apses, ceilings, and naves of Orthodox churches, wherever they might be, to complement the
complex liturgy and to display iconic representations of
Christ, the Blessed Virgin MARY, and the saints. The early

CALIPHS of ISLAM also decorated their palaces and hunting
lodges with secular paintings, including human and animal figures. MOSQUES tended to be very simply decorated.
Islamic manuscripts were illuminated with complex patterns and quotations from the QURAN for the edification of
the reader and as mnemonic aids.

See also individual artists; ALTARS AND ALTARPIECES; ART
AND ARCHITECTURE, BYZANTINE; ART AND ARCHITECTURE,
ISLAMIC; ART AND ARCHITECTURE, JEWISH; FRESCO; GOTHIC
ART AND ARCHITECTURE; ICONOCLASM AND ICONOCLASTIC
CONTROVERSY; ICONS, HISTORY AND THEOLOGY OF; ILLUMI-
NATION; OTTONIAN ART; RENAISSANCE AND REVIVALS IN ART;
ROMANESQUE ART AND ARCHITECTURE.

Further reading: Cennino Cennini, *The Book of the
Art of Cennino Cennini: A Contemporary Practical Treatise
on Quattrocento Painting,* trans. Christiana J. Herringham
(London: G. Allen and Unwin, 1922); Ferdinando
Bologna, *Early Italian Painting: Romanesque and Early
Medieval Art* (Princeton, N.J.: Van Nostrand, 1964);
Bruce Cole, *Italian Art, 1250–1550: The Relation of
Renaissance Art to Life and Society* (New York: Harper &
Row, 1987); Richard Fremantle, *Florentine Gothic
Painters from Giotto to Masaccio: A Guide to Painting in
and Near Florence, 1300 to 1450* (London: Secker and
Warburg, 1975); André Grabar, *Early Medieval Painting
from the Fourth to the Eleventh Century: Mosaics and
Mutual Painting,* trans. Stuart Gilbert (New York: Skira,
1957); Robert Hillenbrand, *Islamic Art and Architecture*
(London: Thames and Hudson, 1999); Andrew Martin
dale, *Painting the Palace: Studies in the History of Medieval
Secular Painting* (London: Pindar Press, 1995); Thomas
F. Mathews, *Byzantium: From Antiquity to the Renaissance*
(New York: Harry N. Abrams, 1998); John White, *The
Birth and Rebirth of Pictorial Space* (New York: Harper &
Row, 1967).

Palaiologos imperial dynasty The Palaiologoi were
the BYZANTINE family dynasty who recaptured CON-
STANTINOPLE from the Latins, provided the last Byzantine
emperors, and held the throne between 1261 and 1453.

MICHAEL VIII
At the death of Emperor Theodore II Laskaris (r.
1254–58) of NICAEA in 1258, Michael Palaiologos VIII
(r. 1261–82), a general, had himself proclaimed
emperor. Three years later, he retook Constantinople
from the Latins and restored the empire. To help the
Greeks resist the aggression of Western princes, he
sought help from the PAPACY. In 1274, he concluded a
union of the Byzantine and Roman churches at the first
Council of LYON. Such a union alienated the Greek
CLERGY and monks, despite the pleas of the patriarch,
John XI Bekkos (r. 1275–82). On March 30, 1282, the
SICILIAN VESPERS, a massacre of the French subjects and
soldiers by the population of PALERMO, diverted a

planned Western expedition by CHARLES I OF ANJOU against him. He also died in 1282.

ANDRONIKOS II AND ANDRONIKOS III

Michael's Son, Andronikos II (r. 1282–1328), succeeded him as emperor and ruled from 1282 to 1328, a long and unsuccessful reign. He was an intellectual who patronized intellectual and artistic endeavors. He also ended the union of churches that had been worked out at Lyon. Combined attacks by Westerners, SERBS, mercenary Catalans, and TURKS produced an influx of refugees into Constantinople. In 1320 civil war broke out between Andronikos II and his grandson, Andronikos III (r. 1328–41). Andronikos III took power in 1328 after overthrowing his grandfather. Andronikos III battled ethical problems such as government corruption and usury and the external threats of the Serbs and the OTTOMAN TURKS. ANATOLIA was lost to the Turks in 1330s. His reign saw the inception of a serious ecclesiastical controversy between Barlaam the Calabrian (d. 1350) and Gregory PALAMAS over monastic practices concerning bodily function.

JOHN V

The death of Andronikos III in 1341 led to a confrontation between the supporters of the young John VI Kantakouzenos (r. 1347–54) and those of the regent, the grand domestic John Kantakouzenos. The regent upheld the supporters of Palamas and sought a religious settlement with the West. In 1354, after three years of civil war, John V Palaiologos took back the throne, which he periodically held with difficulty from 1341 to 1354, from 1355 to 1376, and from 1379 to 1391. Faced with the progress of the Turkish conquest and outbreaks of the PLAGUE, he desperately sought a Western alliance. He even became a Roman Catholic himself in 1369. Despite these efforts, in 1373 he became a vassal of Sultan MURAD I. The Ottomans profited from the rebellion of his son, Andronikos IV (r. 1376–79), between 1376 to 1379, by consolidating their conquests around Constantinople.

MANUEL II, JOHN VIII, CONSTANTINE XI DRAGASES

Manuel II (r. 1391–1425) became emperor in 1391. He followed his father's accommodating Western policy. For four years, he left the government the empire to his nephew, John VII (1399–1408), the son of Andronikos IV. He traveled throughout Europe, vainly seeking alliances against the Ottomans. The defeat of BAYAZID I IN 1402 by TAMERLANE provided the empire more time. During the rule of John VIII (r. 1425–48), Byzantium had no alternative to defeat than a Western political and religious alliance. In 1438 the emperor and many of his clergy attended the Council of FLORENCE, where this ecumenical council proclaimed a union of the two

churches with a vague promise of military assistance. This union was disavowed by the Byzantine Church back in Constantinople. A crusading army assembled to save Byzantium was annihilated by the Ottomans at the Battle of Varna in 1444. Constantine XI Dragases (r. 1448–53), the despot of MOREA, succeeded his brother in 1449. He assumed the throne at Constantinople in time to fall in the final siege of the town by the Ottomans. He died fighting in 1453.

Further reading: Manuel II Palaeologus (1350–1425), *The Letters of Manuel II Palaeologus: Text, Translation, and Notes,* ed. George T. Dennis (Washington, D.C.: Dumbarton Oaks Center for Byzantine Studies, 1977); John W. Barker, *Manuel II Palaeologus (1391–1425): A Study in Late Byzantine Statesmanship* (New Brunswick, N.J.: Rutgers University Press, 1969); Deno John Geanakoplos, *Emperor Michael Palaeologus and the West, 1258–1282* (Cambridge, Mass.: Harvard University Press, 1959); Donald M. Nicol, *The Last Centuries of Byzantium, 1261–1453,* 2d ed. (Cambridge: Cambridge University Press, 1993); Donald M. Nicol, *The Immortal Emperor: The Life and Legend of Constantine Palaiologos, Last Emperor of the Romans* (Cambridge: Cambridge University Press, 1992); John Julius Norwich, *Byzantium: The Decline and Fall* (New York: Knopf, 1996).

Palamas, Gregory, Saint (ca. 1296–1359) *Byzantine monk, theologian*
Born in CONSTANTINOPLE of a noble Anatolian family, Gregory Palamas became a monk at Mount ATHOS in about 1314 and was ordained a priest in about 1326 at THESSALONIKI, where he had fled to escape the Ottomans. He lived as a HERMIT for a while and then returned in 1331 to Mount Athos, where he became familiar with the Hesychast tradition of mystical prayer. He persuaded his brothers, sisters, and mother to enter the religious life. Between 1335 and 1341 he engaged in a polemical debate with Barlaam the Calabrian (d. 1350). During this Palamas wrote his first major work, the *Triads in Defense of the Holy Hesychasts.* He defended Christianity as a true experience of GOD. The doctrine developed by Palamas in these debates became known as Palamism. A council at Constantinople in 1341 condemned Barlaam.

SECOND CONTROVERSY

This debate was followed by a second period of controversy over divine substance and uncreated energies. Palamas was subjected to a period of EXCOMMUNICATION, condemnation, and imprisonment between 1342 and 1347. Councils in 1347 and 1351 then confirmed his doctrines. From 1347 to his death, he was metropolitan of Thessaloniki. Captured by the Turks in 1354, he remained imprisoned for more than a year. During the calm of the intervening years between 1349 and 1350, Palamas wrote a summary of his theological teaching in *The One Hundred and Fifty Chapters*. In 1351, a third synod was summoned, which affirmed the theological themes and ideas proposed by Palamas as the official teaching of Orthodoxy. These involved a doctrine of creation of the natural world and of the human person, specific discussions of natural human faculties, spiritual knowledge, rational nature, the divine nature, and its image in the human person.

THIRD CONTROVERSY

A third period of controversy on creation and the human person occupied the years 1351–58. Palamas was canonized and given the title doctor of the church by the Greek Orthodox Church in 1368 after his death in 1359. His feast day in the Eastern Church is celebrated November 14 and the second Sunday of Lent.

Further reading: Gregory Palamas, *The One Hundred and Fifty Chapters,* ed. and trans. Robert E. Sinkewicz (Toronto: Pontifical Institute of Mediaeval Studies, 1988); John Meyendorff, *A Study of Gregory Palamas,* trans. George Lawrence, 2d ed. (London: Faith Press, 1974); George C. Papademetriou, *Maimonides and Palamas on God* (Brookline, Mass.: Holy Cross Orthodox Press, 1994).

paleography (palaeography) For the study of the Middle Ages and the Renaissance, paleography, a word coined in the 18th century, in the strict sense is the study and deciphering of old handwriting on manuscripts. In more general terms it can amount to a study of the institutions and culture that produced this written material. Paleography had its modern roots in the 17th century, long after the invention of printing, in the works of monks editing, criticizing, and evaluating written documents involving their own contemporary disputes over the accuracy and authenticity of medieval monastic charters or deeds.

As a discipline in the 19th century, it embraced the study of writing and its media and instruments, such as ink, PAPYRUS, PARCHMENT, and PAPER. Founded to study the documents of the Western Middle Ages, it now forms the basis for the study of the manuscripts and manuscript cultures of all medieval peoples who wrote. According to the modern understanding of the value of the discipline of paleography, medieval texts, either in print or in manuscript, have to be interpreted within the context of the ways in which they were produced and the needs of the institutions and ideologies that produced them. Modern paleographers have extended paleography to include all the aspects of a written monument or artifact, both internal and external material qualities and the cultural and social implications affecting writing and the people who produced it.

MEDIEVAL HANDWRITING

Paleography was practiced in the Middle Ages and the Renaissance. It had to be done for readers then to be able to read, understand, and interpret handwritten sources of knowledge or information. Then as now, in a more informal way than in the past, scripts were classified and evaluated by the forms of their letters. To combat medieval FORGERY, there was to be some attempt to date handwriting by recognizing changes in the writing itself and in textual and literary styles. Charters had to be evaluated as forgeries or as genuine transactions. The accuracy of transcriptions of sacred texts was important for all the religious of the medieval word, such as Christianity, JUDAISM, and ISLAM. Skillful and accurate scribes were fundamental to these religious cultures.

Handwriting forms used for clarity, beauty, or utility evolved over the course of the Middle Ages as the needs and goals of society changed, especially in terms of bureaucracy, education, law, and commerce. In the 15th century, there was a strong movement for the reform of Western European writing to increase clarity and ease of reading. Crabbed gothic hands, common in the elite and specialized university and Scholastic systems, were to be replaced by a humanist script based on the writing reforms of the CAROLINGIAN RENAISSANCE. These letter forms and styles were much more clear and words were less abbreviated, so readers and writers could more accurately comprehend and reproduce the classical texts being rediscovered and deemed so important for the betterment of society and a proper education. These reforms laid the basis for the movable type and textual forms used in the PRINTING revolution of the 15th century.

See also ARCHIVES AND ARCHIVAL INSTITUTIONS; CODICOLOGY; NOTARIES AND THE NOTARIATE; PUNCTUATION; SCRIPTORIUM; SCRIPTS.

Further reading: Michelle P. Brown, *A Guide to Western Historical Scripts from Antiquity to 1600* (Toronto: University of Toronto Press, 1990); Leonard E. Boyle, *Medieval Latin Paleography: A Bibliographical Introduction* (Toronto: University of Toronto Press, 1984); Bernhard Bischoff, *Latin Paleography: Antiquity and the Middle Ages,* trans. Dáibhí óCróinín and David Ganz (Cambridge: Cambridge University Press, 1990); Jacqueline Brown and William P. Stoneman, eds., *A Distinct Voice: Medieval Studies in Honor of Leonard E. Boyle, O.P.* (Notre Dame, Ind.: University of Notre Dame Press, 1997); Hubert Hall, *A Formula Book of English Official Historical Documents,* 2 vols. (Cambridge: Cambridge University Press, 1908–1909); Walther Björkman, "Diplomatic," *Encyclopedia of Islam,* 2.301–316.

Palermo Palermo was founded by the Phoenicians, was the Roman Panormus, and became the capital of SICILY under the Muslims. By the 10th century it was one of the major metropolises of the Mediterranean. Its population was at least as large as it was to be in the 18th century. It consisted of the old Roman and Punic or Carthaginian city and the newer Arabic quarters. It was also a garrison town with some of the fortress and military aspects of DAMASCUS and AL-QAYRAWAN. It had been taken by the VANDALS in 440 and then by the forces of the German chieftain ODOACER and the Ostrogoth THEODORIC. The BYZANTINES controlled the city from 535 to 831.

ARRIVAL OF THE NORMANS

The Norman conquest in the 12th century did not change the town significantly. Byzantine, Arabic, and Latin culture coexisted. The new Norman conquerors had a palace and a group of towers, as in Muslim architecture, on the highest point of the old town. These were surrounded by a town enclosed with walls and gates, including a cathedral,the palaces of the feudal aristocracy, and numerous churches. Its population became even more a mixture of Muslims, Arab and Greek Christians, Arabic-speaking JEWS, and Latin immigrants. There was an outlying quarter of gardens around reservoirs of water for suburban palaces in an area called the Conca d'Oro or Horn of Plenty.

This changed in 1161. The Muslims were transported into a northern quarter, and many others deported. The HOHENSTAUFEN dynasty took over in 1194 with the coronation of the emperor HENRY VI. His son, the emperor FREDRICK II, deported more Muslims, causing harm to trade and economic activity. Some quarters were abandoned to gardens, and by 1277 the population had shrunk to no more than 50,000. Palermo became more culturally unified as the Muslims left and more Christians immigrated from ITALY. CHARLES I OF ANJOU took control of the city and the island by defeating the Hohenstaufen in the 1260s. In 1282, as a consequence of the SICILIAN VESPERS, the occupying French were driven out. This led to a long series of wars over Sicily and Palermo between the Aragonese and the Angevins.

Slowly, under the victorious Aragonese, Palermo in the early 14th century recovered its place as a political capital and became a main trading market and clearing house between the island and PISA, GENOA, and BARCELONA. However, the government, from Aragon and Barcelona, preferred to live elsewhere. From 1348 to 1392 Palermo was governed by the vice royal counts of Chiaramonte. After 1412 the union between Sicily and Aragon endured beyond the Middle Ages, until the 17th century.

See also MONREALE; NORMANS IN ITALY; ROGER I; ROGER II; WILLIAM I THE BAD OF SICILY.

Further reading: Ahmad Aziz, *A History of Islamic Sicily* (Edinburgh: Edinburgh University Press, 1975); Giuseppe Bellafiore, *The Cathedral of Palermo* (Palermo: S. F. Flaccovio, 1976); William Tronzo, *The Cultures of His Kingdom: Roger II and the Cappella Palatina in Palermo* (Princeton, N.J.: Princeton University Press, 1997).

Palestine The Roman province of Palestine was divided about 400 into three administrative districts. One, centered at Caesarea, included Judea, Samaria, and the coastal regions. The second, with its capital at Scythopolis, was composed of Galilee, Golan, and part of the Decapolis, an older area that included five major towns. The third district encompassed southern Palestine with its metropolis at PETRA. These Byzantine administrative divisions lasted until 638 after the Persian invasions (614) and the subsequent Arabs takeover. There was also one of the main patriarchates at JERUSALEM.

This region was never totally Christianized. There were JEWS, the only dissident group who still preserved their freedom of worship in the BYZANTINE EMPIRE. They may have formed a majority of the population in some areas such as Galilee, but had been forbidden to live in Jerusalem from the time of the Roman emperor Hadrian (r. 117–38) in the second century. The Byzantine emperor HERAKLEIOS in 634 ordered that they be baptized under pain of death. For this reason, the Arab conquest a few years later offered them some hope of freedom to practice their religion. Other peoples such as the Samaritans were also considered unauthorized dissidents or heretics. They rose up in revolt in 484 and in 529 and maintained a persistent hostility to Byzantine power.

PILGRIMAGE SITES

Despite the presence of a hostile locals, Palestine became one of the goals of Christian PILGRIMAGE. From the early fourth century, Christians traveled to Palestine to view and worship at the sites of the New Testament and of the Old Testament, also considered part of the history of salvation. These sites were listed, enriched with sanctuaries and churches, and, loaded with RELICS. They were more and more often visited by pilgrims. Jerusalem was the most important site, but others such as Bethlehem with the basilica of the Nativity, Hebron, where the tomb of the patriarchs was venerated, the Jordan Valley, site of Christ's baptism, temptation, and miracles, the DEAD SEA with the salt statue of Lot's wife, and Samaria, with Jacob's well and the tombs of the patriarch Joseph, John the Baptist, and Eliza. In the north in Galilee were the places significant in the life of Christ, including Cana, Tabor, Nazareth, the mount of the Beatitudes, and Capernaum. In the region south west of Jerusalem were tombs of Old Testament prophets and martyrs of the Roman persecutions. Finally there was a pilgrimage circuit south in the Sinai Peninsula. The emperors CONSTANTINE and JUSTINIAN in particular oversaw the construction of numerous churches and sanctuaries. In the fourth and fifth centuries coenobitic and anchorite monasteries were founded.

ISLAMIC CONQUEST

After 638, when the Arabs took possession of the whole country, and its non-Muslim inhabitants were subjected to taxes on persons and on land. The laws of the UMAYYADS, and ABBASIDS, were fairly tolerant. Christians were able to buy back their churches, but monasteries were pillaged, and taxes were periodically raised. Many Christians converted to ISLAM whether out of convenience or belief. Pilgrimage continued after the Islamic conquest, although pilgrims, too, were periodically harassed and taxed.

THE CHRISTIAN PRESENCE AND CONFLICT

By the time of CHARLEMAGNE, tensions had eased. In 801, the emperor, whom the patriarch of Jerusalem had asked to defend the Christians of Palestine, sent an embassy. The Abassid caliph, HARUN AL-RASHID, granted Charlemagne ownership of the Latin establishments and a right of protection over the holy places. Charlemagne sent numerous subsidies and built monasteries. All this produced an atmosphere considerably more favorable to pilgrimage and local Christianity. Something like a Frankish protectorate lasted until the 10th century. In 974, the Byzantines under the emperor John I Tzimiskes (r. 969–976) seized Tiberias, Nazareth, ACRE, and Caesarea; the conquest led to a Byzantine protectorate over Palestine. In the 11th century SELJUK TURKS took possession of it and were less accommodating of Christians. This new perceived abuse combined with the collapse of Byzantine power in ANATOLIA and SYRIA, were two factors that led to the CRUSADES.

In 1099, the crusaders took Jerusalem and created the Latin Kingdom of Jerusalem. The next 200 years was occupied with the building of Christian fortresses, churches, monasteries, and charitable establishments. At the same time hostilities between the Latins and the Byzantines, and the Christians and the Muslims, increased. In 1187, SALADIN won an overwhelming victory over the Latin forces at the battle of HATTIN and retook Jerusalem. In 1192 RICHARD I LIONHEART negotiated a treaty that protected the remaining possessions of the Latins, a small band of territory between Jaffa and Tyre. The emperor FREDERICK II obtained, via the treaty of Jaffa in 1229, safe access for pilgrims to Jerusalem, Bethlehem, Nazareth, and the roads along the way. In 1244 access to Jerusalem was reduced. Nazareth was taken in 1264, and then in 1291, Acre, the last possession of the Latins in Palestine, fell.

INTEGRATION AND THE MAMLUKS

The 13th century saw a great migration of Jews back to Palestine from Western Europe. In the 14th and 15th centuries, Palestine was under the rule of the MAMLUKS of Egypt. They treated Palestine merely as a corridor between their main interests, Egypt and Syria, and devastated the regions along the coast to prevent the return of the crusaders. Jerusalem was once again the main city of the region and numerous Arab families moved there. Jewish and Islamic schools were founded in the city. In the later Middle Ages, pilgrimages from outside became much less common, although many Eastern and Orthodox Christians moved into Jerusalem. The OTTOMAN TURKS controlled the region from 1516.

Further reading: Michael Avi-Yonah, *A History of the Holy Land,* trans. Charles Weiss and Pamela Fitton (New York: Macmillan, 1969); Alex Carmel, Peter Schäfer, and Yossi Ben-Artzi, eds., *The Jewish Settlement in Palestine, 634–1881* (Wiesbaden: L. Reichert, 1990); Moshe Gil, *A History of Palestine, 634–1099,* trans. Ethel Broido (Cambridge: Cambridge University Press, 1992); Joshua Prawer, *The crusaders' Kingdom: European Colonialism in the Middle Ages* (New York: Praeger, 1972); Robert Schick, *The Christian Communities of Palestine from Byzantine to Islamic Rule: A Historical and Archaeological Study* (Princeton, N.J.: Darwin Press, 1995); Robert L. Wilken, *The Land Called Holy: Palestine in Christian History and Thought* (New Haven, Conn.: Yale University Press, 1992).

pallium The pallium, a papal and imperial insignia known from the late fifth century, was a long scarf of white wool, draped around the shoulders, whose two extremities fell, in front and behind the wearer. The popes conceded the right to wear the prestigious pallium to only certain bishops to signify their jurisdictional authority over other bishops. It appeared in MOSAICS in ROME and in RAVENNA in the fifth and sixth centuries. By the eighth century, it had evolved into a large ring of cloth around the neck of the wearer with two vertical bands. It was requested by secular rulers for prominent ecclesiastical dignitaries of interest to them to signify a special relationship with the papacy. It was reserved for special occasions except for the pope, who wore it daily, in his case to signify the plenitude of papal power and the union and allegiance of the Roman Church with its head, the pope. The pope required an oath of loyalty and a fee for the right of another to wear it. It went out of use during the 16th century.

See also INVESTITURE CONTROVERSY OR DISPUTES; PAPACY.

Further reading: John Albert Eidenschink, *The Election of Bishops in the Letters of Gregory the Great: With an Appendix on the Pallium . . .* (Washington, D.C.: Catholic University of America Press, 1945); Janet Mayo, *A History of Ecclesiastical Dress* (New York: Holmes & Meier, 1984); Herbert Norris, *Church Vestments, Their Origin and Development* (New York: Dutton, 1950).

Palm Sunday In the medieval Roman liturgy, Palm Sunday occurred on the Sunday before EASTER. It marked the beginning of Christ's Passion when he entered Jerusalem on the back of a donkey and was greeted with joy by the inhabitants who saluted him with palms. It was commemorated by a procession into a church and the blessing of palms. The Passion according to the gospel of Saint Matthew was read at MASS on that day. The blessed palms were kept in houses after the ceremony to commemorate the passion.

See also HOLY WEEK.

Further reading: Thomas J. Talley, *The Origins of the Liturgical Year* (New York: Pueblo, 1986).

Palmyra (Tadmor) This ruined city was at an oasis in the Syrian desert, northeast of DAMASCUS. It contained monumental ruins of a great city and was one of the most important cultural centers of the ancient world. It united the art and architecture of GREECE and ROME with that of Persia or IRAN.

During the third century, wars between Rome and Persia intensified. In 260 the emperor Valerian (r. 253–260) himself was captured by a SASSANIAN king. Palmyra was caught in between, as an import stop on the TRADE routes between the two great empires. It tried to be independent of both, changing for this purpose from a MERCHANT republic into a kingdom under Odenathus (d. 267), who allied with Rome and had considerable military success against the Persians by 267. But at the end of 267, Odenathus and his heir to the throne, were mysteriously assassinated. Zenobia (d. ca. 275), the king's second wife and mother of a very young son, was probably involved in the murder.

Zenobia quickly showed herself to be an able monarch, who was boundlessly ambitious for herself, for her son, and for her people. Within six years she had affected the whole life of Palmyra. In 270, claiming descent from Cleopatra, she took possession of SYRIA and Lower EGYPT, even sending her armies into ANATOLIA. All this was in defiance of Rome and the emperor Aurelian (r. 270–275), who left the northern front, raised a new army, crossed Anatolia, and captured Palmyra after a short siege. Zenobia fled east to seek help from the Sassanians. However, Romans recaptured her as she was crossing the Euphrates in 272 and took her back to Rome, where she was forced to ride in Aurelian's triumph in 274. She died soon afterward in comfortable exile at Tivoli.

The once splendid and wealthy city was pillaged and destroyed in 273. The emperor DIOCLETIAN established a military camp to the west of the city. Palmyra never recovered its position, now replaced in trading networks by ALEPPO and Damascus. The temples of Palmyra were converted first into churches and then into MOSQUES after the ARAB conquest, with the ruins of the city sheltering only a few peasants. It was rediscovered by Western adventurers in the 18th century.

Further reading: Malcolm A. R. Colledge, *The Art of Palmyra* (London: Thames and Hudson, 1976); Robert G. Hoyland, *Arabia and the Arabs: From the Bronze Age to the Coming of Islam* (New York: Routledge, 2001).

panel painting See PAINTING.

Pannonia From the second century to its occupation by the Magyars in 895, the name Pannonia was applied to a region in the Carpathian basin on the north bank of the Danube in central Europe, now modern HUNGARY. Many migrating peoples passed through it on their way into the Roman Empire. It was ideal for nomadic steppe peoples with its large grassy plains.

Its initial native population was made up of Thracians, Illyrians, and Celts. From the midsecond century, Christianity entered southern Pannonia. From the first barbarian incursions of the late third century, the VANDALS, the Sarmatians, the GOTHS, the ALANS, and the HUNS all moved in it. In 433, it passed officially to the rule of the Huns. These events led to a depopulation of the region, as insecurity and chaotic changes in political control prevailed.

The OSTROGOTHS profited from the collapse of the Hunnic federation after ATTILA's death in 453. They occupied Pannonia until the early 470s, when they moved into ITALY. The LOMBARDS followed them into Pannonia and then into Italy between 527 and 568. The AVARS then extended their rule over the whole of the Carpathian basin, intermingling with SLAVS who had recently arrived in the region. CHARLEMAGNE conquered the Avars in 791 and 797, and Frankish and German colonists were settled among the Avar and Slav populations. The internal disputes of the CAROLINGIAN FAMILY led them to appeal for aid from the Magyars in the second half of the ninth century. In 894 the chief of these Hungarian tribes, ÁRPÁD, attacked Carolingian Pannonia, beginning the Magyar conquest of the Carpathian basin. The region then became the medieval kingdom of HUNGARY.

Further reading: A. Lengyel and G. T. B. Radan, eds., *The Archaeology of Roman Pannonia* (Lexington: University Press of Kentucky, 1980); Jeno Fitz, *The Great Age of Pannonia: (A.D. 193–284),* trans. Ildikó Varga (Budapest: Corvina, 1982); András Mócsy, *Pannonia and Upper Moesia: A History of the Middle Danube Provinces of the Roman Empire,* trans. and ed. Sheppard Frere (London: Routledge and K. Paul, 1974).

papacy The medieval pope was the bishop of ROME and patriarch of the West. He claimed succession from Saint Peter, whom Christ named as head of the apostles. During the Middle Ages, the separate evolution of the Western and Eastern Churches, doctrinal and political differences, and the efforts of the popes themselves to give their primacy a practical reality divided the Byzantine, or Greek Orthodox, Church and the Latin Church. Mutual EXCOMMUNICATION and anathema occurred in 1054. The papally launched CRUSADE of 1204 that sacked CONSTANTINOPLE soured relations even more. Unsuccessful attempts at reconciliation followed at the councils of LYON in 1274 and FLORENCE in 1439. The supreme authority of the medieval popes rarely extended beyond the limits of western and central Europe and was often contested there.

PAPAL POLITICS

Until the mid-11th century, the ambitions and actions of the popes were primarily confined to ITALY, where they had to maneuver among the LOMBARDS, the Muslims, the Byzantines, and the noble families of ROME. They had the prestige of the apostolic see, but effective legal and political interventions were difficult and not always successful. They supported MISSIONS to ENGLAND under GREGORY I THE GREAT, to GERMANY in the eighth century, and to central Europe in the ninth. In the eighth century, they formed an alliance with the FRANKS, which accentuated a split with a rival imperial government and the Byzantine Church but permitted a temporal papal state in central Italy, creatively legitimized by the false *DONATION OF CONSTANTINE*. The papal coronation of CHARLEMAGNE as emperor by LEO III in 800 drew the pope even closer to the secular powers. The spiritual and temporal powers of both were accepted as legitimate but were never easy to keep separate or even complementary.

PAPAL REFORMS

From the mid-11th century, in the papacy of GREGORY VII, the GREGORIAN REFORM began the gradual establishment of a true papal monarchy. As part of the papal plan to control more closely the institutions of the church, this reform attacked what it perceived to be abuses: the purchase of clerical office, the appointment to ecclesiastical office by the LAITY, and the CELIBACY of the priesthood. Over time the papacy accomplished a great deal in all of these matters, but at the cost of sometimes open warfare with secular rulers. To accomplish these aims, the papacy recognized the need for and completed the establishment of a papal state in central Italy. It devised a system of election to the see of Saint Peter through the College of CARDINALS, promoted the growth of a legal system that had the pope as its authority (canon law), and embarked on a large increase in all taxation paid to the Holy See. These were in effect the organs of government that any secular ruler would need to carry out his aims. In the 13th and 14th centuries, the pope developed the Apostolic Camera to collect and account for its growing tax or fiscal system and a chancery and system of legates to facilitate communication and convey papal intentions to the rest of the church and to the secular powers. It established the Penitentiary and the INQUISITION to control the ecclesiastical legal system and promoted new orders, such as the MENDICANTS, who were responsible only to the Holy See, not to the local bishops.

ASPIRATIONS AND SCHISMS

The popes raised armies and made and funded crusading alliances with princes to carry out their objectives. In the 13th century between the reigns of Pope INNOCENT III and BONIFACE VIII, the popes tried to exercise a full plenitude of powers, acting as monarch in spiritual and temporal affairs. Papal iconography associated the popes with imperial themes to demonstrate and assert apostolic and imperial traditions, power, origins, and glory. Papal tombs became much more pretentious. Various popes did succeed in destroying the German emperors but were unable to cow the kings of FRANCE. When they were forced to leave Rome and move to AVIGNON in the early 14th century, they fell much more under the influence of the French monarchy. During the Great SCHISM (1378–1417), when there were two, and then three, popes with competing claims and allegiances, the prestige of the popes fell, too disgraced to compete with the growing power of the developing state systems of Western Europe. This did not slow an ambitious building program in Avignon or the development of papal institutions and bureaucracies, especially those to gather taxes and keep the pope at the center of the pastoral activities of the church.

In the 15th century after much squabbling, the schism ended. In 1417 the papacy was reunified, and in 1420 it returned to Rome under Pope Martin V (r. 1417–31), who sought to restore papal power. The papacy then, had to face CONCILIARISM and the conciliar movement, which sought to center authority in the church in a conciliar system of government. Councils met at PISA, CONSTANCE, BASEL, and Florence. But in the end the papacy managed to avoid conceding much authority, and the councils were unable to carry out the reform deemed necessary by many of the clergy and laity alike.

CONCORDATS; FUND-RAISING

The 15th century also saw the appearance of concordats between the Holy See and secular governments. These recognized considerably more influence by kings and princes in their regional or national churches. The popes sought the least unfavorable terms for the Holy See in these agreements. The popes of the 15th century were as incapable of effecting church reform as the councils and they became even more involved in affairs in Italy in their attempt to protect their temporal power in the PAPAL STATES. To finance their ambitions of maintaining control of this region in Italy, the popes had to resort to more and more taxation, even to sanctioning more jubilees to draw more pilgrims to Rome to be taxed and to granting INDULGENCES for payments of money.

See also ALEXANDER III, POPE; ALEXANDER VI, POPE; CELESTINE V, POPE AND THE CELESTINES; CHARLES I OF ANJOU; CHURCH, EASTERN ORTHODOX; EUGENUIS IV, POPE; FREDERICK I BARBAROSSA HOHENSTAUFEN, HOLY ROMAN EMPEROR; FREDERICK II, EMPEROR AND KING OF SICILY; GREGORY IX, POPE; HOLY YEAR; INNOCENT IV, POPE; LAW CANON AND ECCLESIASTICAL; LEO I, THE GREAT, POPE; LEO III, POPE; MISSIONS AND MISSIONARIES, CHRISTIAN; NICOLAITISM; PAPAL STATES; PASCHAL II, POPE;

PHILIP IV THE FAIR; PIUS II, POPE; SYLVESTER II, POPE; URBAN II, POPE; URBAN VI, POPE.

Further reading: J. T. Shotwell and Louise Ropes Loomis, *The See of Peter* (New York: Columbia University Press, 1927); Geoffrey Barraclough, *The Medieval Papacy* (London: Thames and Hudson, 1968); Eamon Duffy, *Saints and Sinners: A History of the Popes* (New Haven, Conn.: Yale University Press, 1997); J. N. D. Kelly, *The Oxford Dictionary of Popes* (Oxford: Oxford University Press, 1986); Walter Ullman, *A Short History of the Papacy in the Middle Ages* (London: Methuen, 1972).

Papal States (Patrimonium Sancti Petri, Patrimony of Saint Peter) These were the provinces over which the popes claimed rights in ITALY that belonged to the PAPACY as its domain and were under its temporal sovereignty. They had their origins in the donations of several popes, in the fifth and sixth centuries, of their personal possessions and family properties in and near ROME. Until the end of the sixth century, these estates were considered the private possessions of the popes and were therefore exempt from taxes by imperial privileges.

CAROLINGIAN INTERVENTION

During a LOMBARD attack on ROME in 590 when the BYZANTINE governor in RAVENNA was unable to defend the city, Pope GREGORY I THE GREAT put the Sign of Saint Peter on the walls of the city transferring sovereignty, giving the Holy See or himself public authority over the region and the city. The Byzantine duchy of Rome was abolished in the seventh century, and its functions were assumed by the papacy. The popes then became the sovereign possessors of the surrounding province of Latium (Lazio). They clashed with the Lombards in the seventh and eighth centuries, because of the latter's efforts to take over Italy, including Rome. The popes then appealed to the FRANKS. For confirmation of his title, PÉPIN III THE SHORT confirmed in 754 papal claims in Italy, including Rome, the Byzantine lands around RAVENNA, and the Lombard lands between the city of Rome and the Po River. This area corresponded with a traditional patrimony that lasted through the rest of the Middle Ages. Parts of it remained in papal hands until the 19th century.

In 774 CHARLEMAGNE confirmed this but undertook to incorporate this state into his empire. With the collapse of the Carolingian Empire, the patrimony theoretically returned to the papacy, but only Latium was under real papal rule. Control of the rest was divided among local rulers.

THE PATRIMONY AND RETURN TO ROME

From the 10th century the feudal aristocracy sought to impose its authority over the various FIEFS of the patrimony and even over the popes themselves. In the second half of the 13th century, the popes recovered much of their sovereignty by obtaining the allegiance of several of GUELF leaders in Ravenna and BOLOGNA. After the settlement of the papacy at AVIGNON in 1305, local lords and tyrants gained an effective autonomy. Even a republic took over temporarily in Rome. The papacy did gain sovereignty over the area around Avignon itself. In 1350 Pope Clement VI (r. 1342–52) dispatched the Spanish cardinal ALBORNOZ to Rome to restore papal authority in the city and over the Patrimony of Saint Peter. Albornoz restored papal authority in most of the patrimony, defeating many local tyrants and communes. After the end of the GREAT SCHISM, the return of the papacy to Rome in 1417, and the conciliar conflicts of the first half of the 15th century, the popes continued to try to maintain their authority over the Papal States, employing many mercenaries and fighting many wars to do so. They succeeded in maintaining control over Latium, Umbria, Ancona, Ravenna, and Bologna.

See also ALEXANDER VI, POPE; CHARLES I OF ANJOU; DONATION OF CONSTANTINE; FREDERICK II; LAW, CANON AND ECCLESIASTICAL; PASCHAL II, POPE; ROME.

Further reading: Thomas F. X. Noble, *The Republic of St. Peter: The Birth of the Papal State, 680–825* (Philadelphia: University of Pennsylvania Press, 1984); Peter Partner, *The Lands of St. Peter: The Papal State in the Middle Ages and the Early Renaissance* (London: Eyre Methuen, 1972); Walter Ullman, *The Growth of Papal Government in the Middle Ages: A Study in the Ideological Relation of Clerical to Lay Power* (New York: Barnes and Noble, 1955); Daniel P. Waley, *The Papal State in the Thirteenth Century* (London: Macmillan, 1961).

paper, introduction of Paper was supposedly discovered in the year 105 C.E. by an official at the court of the Han emperor in China. It was made from pieces of hemp and cloth. In the eighth century the ARABS acquired the technique from two Chinese prisoners. They created a factory at SAMARKAND. From there paper spread west and south to the Mediterranean, SYRIA, EGYPT, the Byzantine world, North AFRICA, and SPAIN by the 11th century. In the 13th century its manufacture and use spread through Spain at VALENCIA, ITALY at Fabriano, FRANCE in PROVENCE, and northern Europe in FLANDERS and GERMANY by 1390.

THE PROCESS

Medieval paper manufacturing began by mixing cloth rags or hemp cut into pieces. This was then washed with water and soaked in lime and afterward placed in troughs and beaten into pulp. This pulp was heated in a vat, and hung on a wooden frame fitted with a lattice. At the center of this lattice was usually a metal wire forming a letter or figure, the watermark, which showed the source for the paper and was transparently visible.

After the stretched form was drained, it was placed between layers of felt and pressed to remove the water. The resulting sheets were hung from lines for drying. With one side smooth and the other rougher, the sheets were then polished to produce a smooth surface and seal the pores of the paper, making it more receptive to ink.

PROLIFERATION OF USE

Paper was cheaper than PARCHMENT to produce and therefore, in the 13th century, quickly supplanted it for administrative and legal documents. Such a light and cheap material led to the increase in archival and bureaucratic collections from the 14th century. It thus made the work of bureaucracies easier and capable of utilizing past documents and precedents. It made books marginally less expensive to produce, initially and especially after when printing was developed in the 15th century. The more deluxe manuscripts continued to be written on parchment.

See also ARCHIVES AND ARCHIVAL INSTITUTIONS; CODICOLOGY; PRINTING, ORIGINS OF.

Further reading: Jonathan M. Bloom, *Paper before Print: The History and Impact of Paper in the Islamic World* (New Haven, Conn.: Yale University Press, 2002); I. P. Leif, *An International Sourcebook of Paper History* (Hamden, Conn.: Archon, 1978); E. J. Labarre, *Dictionary and Encyclopedia of Paper and Paper-Making: With Equivalents of the Technical Terms in French, German, Dutch, Italian, Spanish & Swedish* (Amsterdam: Swets and Zeitlinger, 1967).

papyrus and papyrology Papyrus as a writing material was made from *Cyperus papyrus,* a plant that grew in the lower region of Mesopotamia, in SYRIA, in eastern SICILY, and especially in the Nile delta of EGYPT. Papyrus was the medium for written documents in the ancient world. Because of its fragility, only a handful of rolls survived from the many produced. Smaller pieces exist in the thousands. Most of them were preserved in the warm and dry climate of Egypt. For manuscript books, parchment in the form of codices, shaped as our books are, replaced papyrus as early as the fourth century.

MANUFACTURE AND LATER USE

The manufacture of papyrus involved cutting the pith of the plant stem into ribbons, which were impregnated with water on a table. A first layer was set vertically and a second one horizontally. They were stuck together with a paste made of millet and water. This sheet was pressed, lightly beaten, and rinsed to eliminate surplus paste. It was then dried in the sun and its surface was polished.

The resulting sheets were square and limited to 10 inches in width and 11 inches in height. They were joined by a border to one another to form a roll made up of 20 or so of them, measuring 20 to 40 meters long (or 70 to 100 feet). Writing was usually done only on one side, the inner face of the roll, but could also be on the reverse side. Papyrus continued to be used for documents in western Europe even after the banning of the export of papyrus from Egypt by the ARABS in 692. The papal chancellery used it until the 11th century. By the 14th century, except in the case of formal and ornamental documents, paper largely replaced papyrus as a medium for transmitting the written word.

See also CODICOLOGY; PALEOGRAPHY; PARLIAMENT.

Further reading: Nabia Abbott, *Studies in Arabic Literary Papyri,* 3 vols. (Chicago: University of Chicago Press, 1957–1972); Roger S. Bagnall, *Reading Papyri, Writing Ancient History* (London: Routledge, 1995); Naphtali Lewis, *Papyrus in Classical Antiquity* (Oxford: Claredon Press, 1974); R. B. Parkinson, *Papyrus* (Austin: University of Texas Press, 1995); E. G. Turner, *The Typology of the Early Codex* (Philadelphia: University of Pennsylvania Press, 1977).

Paradise The word *paradise* was of Persian origin (*pairidaeza*). It became the Hebrew word for an "orchard, a park, or an enclosed garden," rather close to the Sumerian concept and word, *eden.* In the LATIN of the VULGATE version of the BIBLE, it was called *Paradisus.* This became the Garden of Eden of Adam and Eve, with rich vegetation, watered by four rivers, reflecting the presence of GOD, and human mastery over animals. DEATH was not present.

FURTHER MEANINGS OF PARADISE

Another paradise was eschatological, or a place or state where the SOULS of the just enjoyed eternal happiness with GOD, possibly in the Garden of Eden. There the just would receive the reward promised them and enjoy eternal happiness while contemplating God. There were many disputes and discussions about this Paradise during the Middle Ages. Questions were asked about the nature of Paradise, whether material or spiritual, and its location. Another was about whether souls separated from bodies had access to the BEATIFIC VISION until the end of time. Theologians at the University of PARIS decided that the blessed see the divine essence immediately. This idea was reaffirmed in the 14th century.

Another Paradise was perhaps on earth, even the church on earth. For monks, it might mean the CLOISTER, an anticipation of the heavenly life. There was also a belief in an earthly location for the Garden of Eden somewhere. Such a concept appeared in the writings of MARCO POLO, John MANDEVILLE, and Christopher COLUMBUS.

THE MUSLIM CONCEPTION

Paradise, or *al-Jannah* (Arabic) or *firdaws* (Persian) for Muslims, was the place or garden of reward for dead Muslims. It included enjoyable food, drink, and companionship. Located under the throne of God, it was different

The Archangel Michael expels Adam and Eve from Paradise from a bas-relief from the façade of the cathedral of Orvieto, ascribed to Lorenzo Maitani and made about 1325 *(Courtesy Edward English)*

from the Garden of Eden. There were specific rewards for specific actions. There was no agreement among all Muslims as to whether it was a literal or physical place or an allegorical one. However, belief in reward or punishment for actions has always been fundamental in ISLAM. One was to do good, avoid evil, exhibit true repentance, and believe in the QURAN. It was a state that had not been seen or heard by humankind. MUHAMMAD believed that women would be a minority in heaven and no nonbelievers would be present.

See also ESCHATOLOGY; HARROWING OF HELL; HEAVEN; HELL; LAST JUDGMENT; LIMBO; PURGATORY; REDEMPTION.

Further reading: Jean Delumeau, *History of Paradise: The Garden of Eden in Myth and Tradition,* trans. Matthew O'Connell (New York: Continuum, 1995); Eileen Gardiner, *Medieval Visions of Heaven and Hell: A Sourcebook* (New York: Garland, 1993); Colleen McDannell and Bernhard Lang, *Heaven: A History* (New Haven, Conn.: Yale University Press, 1988); Alister McGrath, *A Brief History of Heaven* (Oxford: Blackwell, 2003); Howard Rollin Patch, *The Other World, According to Descriptions in Medieval Literature* (Cambridge, Mass.: Harvard University Press, 1950); Jeffrey Burton Russell, *A History of Heaven: The Singing Silence* (Princeton, N.J.: Princeton University Press, 1997).

parasites   In the Middle Ages as now parasites were usually living organisms that existed temporarily or permanently within or upon a body of another organism, the host. They derived nourishment from the host but did nor provide any benefits. They could damage bodily functions and cause death. Parasitism could occur among all kinds of agents such as fungi, worms, bacteria, viruses, arthropods, protozoa, and worms (helminths). They could cause disease in humans and nonhumans. Humans often contracted parasitic diseases from animals.

VARIETIES AND ENVIRONMENTS

Worms were the most common internal parasite or endoparasite, including: flukes, spread through water; tapeworms, transmitted through fur or contaminated food and water from dogs and cats; and thorny-headed worms and roundworms, transmitted by mosquitoes. Head and body lice, fleas, bedbugs, mosquitoes, mites, and ticks could transmit parasitic infection. Protozoa, or unicellular animals, could also cause a variety of conditions ranging from toxoplasmosis, a common parasite of birds and mammals and contracted by humans from raw or undercooked meat, to leishmaniasis, a skin disease transmitted to humans by sand flies. Most parasitic diseases did not cause bone or skeletal damage; they were limited to soft tissue.

Evidence for the parasites in historical contexts has been found primarily in coprolites from dry environments, intestinal contents of bodies preserved, deposits from latrines and cesspools, and remnants on hair and combs. Preservation depended on the condition of the containing deposits.

Further reading: R. J. Donaldson, ed., *Parasites and Western Man* (Lancaster: MTP Press, 1979); K. F. Kiple, ed., *Plague, Pox and Pestilence* (London: Weidenfeld and Nicolson, 1997).

parchment   Parchment was the most widely used writing material in the medieval world. It was made from animal skins. The technique for turning skins into parchment was developed first, according to legend, in Pergamum in ANATOLIA. The Hellenistic king of EGYPT was jealous of the establishment of a library by his rival, King Eumenes II (197–158 B.C.E.). So he forbade the export of PAPYRUS. Parchment as a writing medium was favored by disruption in the Mediterranean Sea of the Muslim invasion and conquest of AFRICA. Parchment, complex and expensive to produce, worked well enough as the use of writing declined.

In the Middle Ages there were numerous recipes and techniques for the preparation of a skin, be it goat, calf, or sheep. In the basic procedure, skins were first soaked in water for a day and then, washed, to remove oils. They were smeared with a layer of acid lime on the flesh side and folded with the flesh side always facing a flesh side. Lime was to loosen any hair and open pores. Left to stand for 10 days in that state, they were stretched, rewashed in water, and any remaining hair removed. They were scraped again to get rid of any residue, hung on wooden frames, smeared with a chalky powder, and polished with a pumice stone.

USES

The parchment for charters and official documents was usually of high quality. For everyday material the use of leaves of different formats, full of nodules, holes, and faults, was common. For important books the practice from late antiquity was to use parchment dyed purple with silver or gold ink. This method or style continued, though in frequently, until the 12th century.

Parchment was made in monastic workshops following various local recipes. With the great increase commercial activity and the number of schools, students, and universities, the manufacture of parchment, as did the work of copying, became commercialized, industrialized, and organized. Monastic communities continued to manufacture parchment. From the 13th century, PAPER gradually replaced parchment for more mundane uses. Parchment continued to be used for manuscripts, as well as for deluxe books throughout the 15th century. PRINTING did not lead to the disappearance of parchment, which continued to be produced for works for princes or kings. Parchment was even used in printing, for luxurious books.

Further reading: Ronald Reed, *Ancient Skins, Parchments and Leathers* (London: Seminar Press, 1972); Ronald Reed, *The Nature and Making of Parchment* (Leeds: Elmete, 1975); Herbert Fahey, *Parchment and Vellum* (San Francisco: Fahey, 1940).

Paris, Matthew   *See* MATTHEW PARIS.

Paris and the University of Paris   Paris is in the middle of a well-populated region in FRANCE agriculturally rich in gain, vines, and forests and favorable for TRADE and communication. It began on an island, the Île de la Cité, on the Seine River. It was the Gallo-Roman town of Lutetia Parisiorum. The Roman governor's palace was in the west and the temple of Jupiter on the eastern end of the island. The island remained the center for government and for religion for the city. The town was heavily damaged by BARBARIAN raids in the third century and contracted for a time to the island.

EARLY HISTORY

CLOVIS and the Merovingians made it a Christian town. Clovis died at the age of 45 in a royal villa there in 511. He founded a monastery dedicated to Saint Geneviève and other monasteries and abbeys in the town such as Saint-Germain-des-Prés, Saint-Victor, Saint-Martin-des-Champs, the royal abbey of Saint Denis outside the town, and Saint-Maur-des-Fossés. Robert the Strong (d. 866) was elected king after he defended the town against VIKINGS in the mid-ninth century. Paris became the principal town of the Capetians. It grew quickly after that, with the right or north bank forming the center of population around the church of Saint-Germain-l'Auxerrois; along certain roads, the Rue Saint-Martin and the Rue Saint Denis; and at the outlets of bridges or gates. The WINE trade grew and there were

FAIRS from the early 12th century on the road to the monastery of Saint Denis.

On the left bank, schools were established among vineyards. On the Île de la Cité, the building of the new cathedral of NOTRE-DAME began in 1163. Around 1200, its bishop, Maurice de Sully (ca. 1120–96), set an urban parochial organization and King PHILIP II AUGUSTUS expanded his administration and lived in the city. His palace of the Cité and royal residence became the center of his realm with archives, the royal chapel, administrative offices, and the royal courts. He kept his treasury and prisons in the city at the church of the Temple and in the fortress of the Louvre. In 1190 he started building a wall and towers around the new sections of the city. He promoted commerce and protected it on the Seine, so MERCHANTS gave Philip II Augustus their support by lending him money and managing his finances.

AN EDUCATIONAL CENTER AND THE UNIVERSITY

From the 12th century, Paris became an important educational center, with schools at Notre-Dame and the abbeys of Saint-Victor and Sainte-Geneviève. Scholars traveled from all over CHRISTENDOM for the teaching of famous masters such as Peter ABÉLARD. They were initially under the authority of the chancellor of the school at Notre-Dame, but with the royal support, they had organized themselves into an autonomous community. It was powerful and privileged by 1200, with the university, exempt from secular justice and royal taxation. These privileges made 13th-century Paris the intellectual capital of Christendom with teachers such as ALBERTUS Magnus and Thomas AQUINAS.

UNIVERSITY CURRICULUM AND ORGANIZATION

In the 13th century the MENDICANT ORDERS established convents on the Left Bank, and colleges were created for the students, such as the Sorbonne in 1257. The disciplines taught in the new university were THEOLOGY, especially at Notre-Dame; the SEVEN LIBERAL ARTS; and above all dialectic, which became the great specialty of the university. Schools of LAW and MEDICINE appeared slightly later. The first object of these communities was to organize mutual aid among members, who were often subjected to the hostility of the population and the local authorities. They obtained, with the support of popes, the statutes and privileges of 1215 and numerous fiscal and legal exemptions, gaining a great deal of autonomy. The university organized the internal discipline of the schools and fixed programs. Teaching masters accepted whom they wished and a license to teach was granted by the chancellor after examination by a jury of masters. By 1260 there appeared the *nations* of France, Picardy, NORMANDY, and ENGLAND, into which students were divided by geographical origin; the office of rector; the head of the university; and finally the four faculties of arts, theology, canon law, and medicine, each run by a dean. This system became a model imitated all over northern Europe. Popes tried to make the new university doctrinal auxiliaries of their own authority, the Roman *magisterium*. They watched over the orthodoxy of teachings and promoted their agents from the new mendicant orders into the system.

To the end of the Middle Ages, the University of Paris remained the largest in the Europe. Around 1400, it had some 4,000 masters and students, 3,000 of them in the faculty of arts. There were also numerous supporting occupations, such as copyists and booksellers. By 1500 there were about 60 colleges. Famous and influential masters continued to teach at Paris in the 14th century, and later, including John BURIDAN, Nicholas ORESME, Pierre d'AILLY, John GERSON, and WILLIAM OF OCKHAM. In the 15th century, the university did not participate in the new humanist learning. During the GREAT SCHISM, the university unsuccessfully tried to play a decisive role. As a result, those who disagreed with its stance on the legitimate pope began to foster their own universities, especially in GERMANY and eastern Europe. The student and teaching bodies changed as a result, more often from northern France, subjects of the French crown. From the mid-15th century and after the revival of royal power at the end of the HUNDRED YEARS' WAR, the centralizing French kings imposed much more control over university affairs.

LATER MIDDLE AGES: POLITICS AND THE CROWN

In the meantime, Paris became even more of a political center for the French monarchy, with a population around estimated at 200,000. More building for administrative offices and the court occurred on the island. LOUIS IX built the SAINTE CHAPEL there to house his RELIC collection. In 1299 King PHILIP IV began the reconstruction of the old royal palace and built the great hall of PARLEMENT. He lived nearby with a large household, a garden, and docks for boats on the river. King CHARLES V abandoned the palace to legal and administrative offices and moved to the Hôtel Saint-Pol on the Right Bank.

The city itself was kept under close royal control and not allowed to form a COMMUNE or have a city council. Several revolts and numerous riots in the city resulted, such as those of Étienne Marcel (1356–58), the Maillotins (1382–83), and the Cabochiens in 1413 and when the Burgundians took control of the city in 1418. Paris fell to the English in 1420, and the English king, Henry VI (1422–61), was crowned king of France there in 1431. In 1436 the French recaptured the city, which had not prospered under the Anglo-Burgundian administration. The king himself did not live there most of the time, but the royal administration in the city slowly revived over the course of the 15th century. Paris did, however, regain much of its prosperity and commercial vitality and some of its population in the second half of the 15th century.

See also ARISTOTLE AND ARISTOTELIANISM IN THE MIDDLE AGES; PETER LOMBARD; PHILOSOPHY AND THEOLOGY; UNIVERSITIES AND SCHOOLS; SCHOLASTICISM AND SCHOLASTIC METHOD.

Further reading: Pierre Couperie, *Paris Through the Ages* (New York: Braziller, 1968); William J. Courtenay, *Teaching Careers at the University of Paris in the Thirteenth and Fourteenth Centuries* (Notre Dame, Ind.: University of Notre Dame, 1988); Virginia W. Egbert, *On the Bridges of Medieval Paris* (Princeton: N.J.: Princeton University Press, 1974); Stephen C. Ferruolo, *The Origins of the University: The Schools of Paris and Their Critics, 1100–1215* (Stanford, Calif.: Stanford University Press, 1985); Mary Martin McLaughlin, *Intellectual Freedom and Its Limitations in the University of Paris in the Thirteenth and Fourteenth Centuries* (New York: Arno Press, 1977); Guy Llewelyn Thompson, *Paris and Its People under English Rule: The Anglo-Burgundian Regime, 1420–1436* (Oxford: Clarendon Press, 1991); Craig Wright, *Music and Ceremony at Notre Dame of Paris, 500–1550* (Cambridge: Cambridge University Press, 1989).

parish The medieval parish was a local and defined area that included a church building under the spiritual care of a particular priest. The priest was paid out of the income attached to the parish. There was conflict during the Middle Ages over the right to nominate a cleric to this position. In the mid-13th century, the canonist and Cardinal Henry of Susa or HOSTIENSIS devised the first definition of the parish. The church was the place of worship where most of the SEVEN SACRAMENTS and other ceremonies were celebrated for the faithful under the authority of a priest. The priest sometimes levied fees or dues connected with the administration, a practice, previously imprecise that evolved in the ninth century.

ORIGINS AND CHRISTIANIZATION

In Christian antiquity, there was only one ecclesiastical region, that of the urban cathedral church, which was the only church for baptism and the residence of the head, or the bishop, of the diocese. There were local chapels for elite families. Parish churches date from the conversion of the countryside. They became places of worship and reproduced the structure and functions of the old cathedral church. The bishop was entitled to confer orders on priests and to grant local churches some autonomy. To this network of rural churches were added chapels on rural estates and attached to monasteries that sometimes performed religious services for the public. There was tension about any income of these churches and who had the right of appointment to them. Some became in effect the FIEFS of their owner. The number of churches built to serve a growing urban population also of necessity increased.

DEFINITIONS AND LATER HISTORY

The COUNCIL of CLERMONT in 1095 tried to establish a strict separation of the temporal and spiritual aspects of parish. The financial endowments remained the property of the lord, either lay or ecclesiastical, who disposed of the right of PATRONAGE or the presentation of the clerical incumbent. The priest received the cure of SOULS from the bishop and was subject to the control of the diocesan hierarchy. The appointment to a church was no longer defined as a FIEF, but as a BENEFICE. This has remained the basic definition of parish administration. In the later Middle Ages, the LAITY or parishioners acquired more responsibility and control over the fabric of the church.

In the later Middle Ages, decades of war and insecurity destabilized many parishes and ruined their temporal incomes. A number of churches lost an incumbent or priest. At the same time, the beneficial system became rife with nonresidence and pluralism, leading to a decline in the quality of pastoral care. However, the movement that grew up in response to improve the local priesthood increased literacy and improved training in pastoral care activities. CONFRATERNITIES of laity attached to parishes in the later Middle Ages also became more numerous.

See also CLERGY AND CLERICAL ORDERS; GREGORIAN REFORM; INVESTITURE CONTROVERSY OR DISPUTES; SIMONY.

Further reading: George W. O. Addleshaw, *The Development of the Parochial System from Charlemagne (768–814) to Urban II (1088–1099)* (London: St. Anthony's Press, 1954); Joseph Avril, "Parish." *EMA* 2.1,084–1,086; Peter Heath, *The English Parish Clergy on the Eve of the Reformation* (Toronto: University of Toronto Press, 1969); John R. H. Moorman, *Church Life in England in the Thirteenth Century* (Cambridge: University Press, 1955); Colin Platt, *The Parish Churches of Medieval England* (London: Secker and Warburg, 1981); Norman J. G. Pounds, *A History of the English Parish: The Culture of Religion from Augustine to Victoria* (Cambridge: Cambridge University Press, 2000); A. Hamilton Thompson, *The English Clergy and Their Organization in the Later Middle Ages* (Oxford: Clarendon Press, 1966).

Parlement of Paris or France

The Parlement was the supreme court of JUSTICE of the kingdom of FRANCE from 1250 until the French Revolution in 1790. It was established to fulfill the prime duty of the king to provide justice. The publication and registration of royal ordinances were performed at this court. It had its seat in the royal palace on the Île de la Cité at PARIS from the time of King LOUIS IX's reforms of 1258 and 1260 forbidding trial by battle and judicial duel in the royal domain. Louis also made possible a general appeal to the king's court for justice. Appeals then flew in from the whole kingdom to the king's court. Its judicial session became an institution, the Parlement. From then it acquired a name, a fixed seat, and an archive of judgments to use as reference.

An ordinance of 1345 specified the personnel of the Parlement, whose members were now a set number of professional counselors. The king appointed and paid them, and divided them into three chambers: The Great Chamber or Chamber of Pleas heard pleas spoken in French by advocates before a "bar" in front of the judges. It gave a judgment or final legal decree in LATIN and oversaw the other two chambers. The Chamber of Inquiries was charged with making preliminary investigations of cases and determining the appropriateness of petitions to the upper chamber. If it granted a petition to cite an adversary before the court, letters were issued to that effect and a commissioner was sent to investigate the local particulars of the case. The Chamber of Petitions further examined the admissibility of the case and its documentation. From there the case was sent back to the Great Chamber for judgment.

The personnel of Parlement numbered about 100, including presidents, counselors, king's procurator and advocate, clerks, and ushers. Some of these offices became hereditary and some of these families eventually joined the nobility. The whole system had a reputation for slow action, if not sloth, in the later Middle Ages. Its functioning also suffered from the political and military setbacks of the monarchy in the HUNDRED YEARS' WAR in the early 15th century. After an attempt at reform in 1436, provincial parliaments were established in TOULOUSE in 1443, Grenoble in 1453, Bordeaux in 1463, and Dijon in 1477.

Further reading: J. H. Shennan, *The Parlement of Paris*, 2d. ed. (Phoenix: Sutton, 1998).

Parliament, English

Starting in the 1230s certain assemblies were called *parliaments,* which meant "meetings or councils between the king, his ministers, and the magnates and prelates or high ecclesiastical officials of the kingdom to discuss the judicial, political, and fiscal matters of state and to present petitions." Parliament was an instrument of the king, who called it, dissolved it, and set its agenda. During the reign of EDWARD III it was to evolve into two bodies, the House of Lords and the House of Commons. Its essential and initial function revolved around the dispensing of JUSTICE guided by the king. In the mid-13th century representatives of the shires and boroughs, administrative districts of the kingdom, were summoned. From 1327 and the important deposition of King EDWARD II, such representatives were regularly summoned and so constituted.

DEFINITION AND GROWTH OF JURISDICTION

In about the 1320s a document called *The Way of Holding Parliament* was written. Later in the century there were conflicts in 1341 involving the composition of the peerage and the House of Lords. At the end of the century, the deposition of RICHARD II and accession of Henry IV involved the institution of Parliament more in the functioning of the succession according to the constitution.

When Parliament became enlarged by the attendance of the commons, those representatives of the shires and the boroughs, a distinction was drawn between them and the magnates and prelates, and the term *peers* came into use for the latter two groups. The commons presented petitions to the king and the peers as judges.

In the reign of Edward III a noble group of about 50 became accepted and in 1387 hereditary baronies were created by royal letters that required attendance at Parliament. They were joined by a clerical element consisting of bishops and certain important abbots and priors of religious houses. These bishops were often employed as the principal ministers in the royal civil service. The clergy in this part of Parliament also controlled the taxation of the church in England.

BUSINESS: ISSUES AND AGENDAS

The business of Parliament became a discussion of affairs of state, more especially of foreign affairs, legislation, taxation, petitions, judicial business involving criminal and civil clauses, difficult administrative matters, and feudal questions on such procedures as homage. WESTMINSTER palace and abbey became the usual meeting place. Sessions opened with the monarch's receiving petitions, a statement of agenda or questions, and the fiscal needs of the Crown. The two houses, lords and commons, then met separately to discuss these questions. The lords expressed their opinion individually, but the commons had to present corporate opinions. The commons would provide answers to the king by a committee or by 1276 through a speaker. The lords were all summoned as individuals and represented nobody but themselves.

During the HUNDRED YEARS' WAR, taxation, either direct or indirect, dominated Parliament, which levied indirect taxes or duties on imports or exports. It could agree to impose quotas for payment on every shire or direct taxation. Parliament tried to maintain control over such matters and had to be consulted regularly for permission for these taxes. The commons were endowed with full power to give legal consent to taxation.

Petitions of two kinds, singular and common, could be presented to and discussed in Parliament. Singular petitions were for one person or subject, not necessarily a member, who wished to make a request to the king. They were passed to persons named to act and dispose of the petitions as seemed appropriate. Common petitions were put forward in the name of the commons attending the Parliament. They were supposed to concern grievances from the common people. These petitions always went to the king and his council. Answers were given by the king with the advice and consent of the lords and eventually with the assent of the commons.

In 1404 the commons claimed by ancient custom certain privileges such as freedom from arrest for debt, trespass, or contract and in 1429 exemption from arrest for all offenses except treason and serious crimes or felonies. Genuine liberty of speech was not allowed to members in the Middle Ages. The member clergy, in the event of legal issues, could be tried solely in church courts. The lay magnates claimed the privilege of trial by peers and demanded that freedom from arrest extend to their servants.

By the 15th century Parliament had become a national assembly whose statutes prevailed over common law and whose approval was required before TAXES could be levied.

See also CORTES; PARLEMENT OF PARIS OR FRANCE.

Further reading: R. G. Davies and J. H. Denton, eds., *The English Parliament in the Middle Ages* (Manchester: Manchester University Press, 1981); Nicholas Pronay and John Taylor, *Parliamentary Texts of the Later Middle Ages* (Oxford: Clarendon Press, 1980); H. G. Richardson, *The Irish Parliament in the Middle Ages* (Philadelphia: University of Pennsylvania Press, 1952); J. S. Roskell, *Parliament and Politics in Late Medieval England,* 3 vols. (London: Hambledon Press, 1981–1983); G. O. Sayles, *The King's Parliament of England* (New York: Norton, 1974).

Parzival   *See* WOLFRAM VON ESCHENBACH.

Paschal II, Pope **(Raniero or Ranerius of San Lorenzo)** **(ca. 1058–1118)** *Italian pope, Cluniac monk*
Raniero was born in RAVENNA or near Faenza in central Italy about 1058. His first mission to ROME at about age 20 in 1080 demonstrated his early involvement with religion and recognition of this ability. He soon became abbot of the monastery of San Lorenzo or St. Paul's Outside the Walls. Pope GREGORY VII employed him in his household and raised him to the status of CARDINAL. After Urban's death in 1099, the cardinals chose him to be pope, on August 13, 1099. He inherited major problems in carrying out the reform program of his predecessors. He had to confront a schism, pressures from the emperor on investiture, and troubled relations with the Greek Orthodox Church and the Byzantine government. There were four different antipopes raised against him during his reign. The imperial party promoted conflict in the city of Rome and in Latium or Lazio, the surrounding region. More than once Paschal had to leave the city and take up arms to defend the Patrimony of Saint Peter or the PAPAL STATES.

INVESTITURE DISPUTES

Paschal tried to stand firmly against the attempts of the emperor Henry IV (1050–1106) to eliminate papal investiture of bishops in Germany. Henry's second son, the emperor Henry V (1086–1125), reached an agreement with Paschal when he needed papal help to replace his father in 1105–6. But Paschal, a weak and timid man, reneged on his promises. He went to FRANCE and reached a peaceful agreement on the INVESTITURE CONTROVERSY somewhat favorable to the PAPACY with the royal governments of FRANCE and ENGLAND. The kings agreed to renounce rights of investiture but retained the right to receive homage or oaths of loyalty from bishops before their investiture. In the discussions at Sutri near Rome before Henry's coronation in 1111, Henry V reciprocally reneged on his promises. Paschal proposed as a solution that the papacy renounce rights on the royal temporalities or regalia in exchange for a renunciation by the emperor of his rights of investiture of bishops and abbots, or much control over the succession to ecclesiastical office. German churches could still levy tithes and receive private donations. The German episcopate quickly refused to cooperate and broke up a coronation ceremony on February 12, 1111. Henry then had the pope arrested and tried to oblige Paschal to invest him with the imperial staff and ring and crown him at Old Saint Peter's in Rome. The pope refused and was imprisoned; eventually he abjectly agreed to crown him on April 13, 1111, only to revoke this agreement, the Privilege of Mammolo, when he was released from prison. A council in 1116 confirmed Paschal's revocation in 1116 and an imperial army marched on Rome in 1117. Paschal fled into exile in Benevento during the ensuing riots.

Paschal sponsored a CRUSADE that attacked the Byzantines rather than the Muslims in 1105. Despite the considerable recrimination that resulted, the Byzantine emperor, ALEXIOS I, proposed a union of the two churches in 1112. It floundered on Paschal's strong demand for recognition of papal supremacy. Paschal returned to Rome in disappointment in 1118 and died a few days later, on January 21. He was buried secretly in Castel Sant' Angelo with Rome under the control of the emperor.

See also GREGORIAN REFORM; INVESTITURE CONTROVERSY OR DISPUTES.

Further reading: Uta-Renate Blumenthal, *The Early Councils of Pope Paschal II, 1100–1110* (Toronto: Pontifical Institute of Mediaeval Studies, 1978); I. S. Robinson, *Authority and Resistance in the Investiture Contest: The Polemical Literature of the Late Eleventh Century* (Manchester: Manchester University Press, 1978.)

Passover (Pesah) Passover during the Middle Ages was the Jewish festival observed every spring to celebrate the liberation of the Children of Israel from Egyptian bondage, as related in Exodus 12. According to the ancient prescription, a lamb was to be slain in each Hebrew household and its blood sprinkled on lintel and doorposts to commemorate the initial act, which spared firstborn Hebrew males from death. Instead, the Bible related that the firstborn sons of the Egyptians were slain. This Tenth Plague imposed on the Egyptians by the Hebrew God compelled the pharaoh to free the Israelite slaves from bondage. The Lord "passed over" the Hebrew houses marked by the blood of the sacrificed lamb. According to Deuteronomy 16, after the initial event, the sacrifice was performed at the Temple. The eating of this Paschal lamb was associated with the ancient sacrifice.

There have been theories about the festival's origins in nomadic practices or agricultural rites for beginning a harvest or simply a holiday to celebrate the arrival of spring. Passover became the principal Jewish festival of the year, celebrated for eight days from the night of 14/15 Nisan. After the destruction of the Temple in 70 C.E., the Jews continued to observe the feast, omitting the sacrifice of a lamb, using only a bone in its place. The later details of the observance were recorded in the Mishnah tractate *Pesahim*.

GOOD FRIDAY

The Last Supper of Christ with his apostles on the night before he was crucified was probably a Passover meal. The Eucharist was instituted at Passover time, and Christian writers stressed that the death of Christ was the fulfillment of the sacrifice foreshadowed by Passover. It is likely that the earliest celebrations of the Christian Easter and the Paschal Vigil Service developed from the Jewish Passover rite. The account of the events in Exodus has traditionally been read at the services.

Further reading: Baruch M. Bokser, *The Origins of the Seder: The Passover Rite and Early Rabbinic Judaism* (Berkeley: University of California Press, 1984); Paul F. Bradshaw and Lawrence A. Hoffman, eds. *Passover and Easter: Origin and History to Modern Times* (Notre Dame, Ind.: University of Notre Dame Press, 1999); Theodor Herzl Gaster, *Passover, Its History and Traditions* (1949; reprint, Westport, Conn.: Greenwood Press, 1984).

pastoral care *See* MENDICANT ORDERS; MISSIONS AND MISSIONARIES; CHRISTIAN; PAGANISM AND CHRISTIANIZATION; PREACHING AND PREACHERS.

pasture and rights of pasture *See* AGRICULTURE; PEASANTRY.

Patrick, Saint (ca. 389–ca. 461) *fifth-century legendary apostle of Ireland*
Patrick was the only Romano-British citizen who left a significant account of his life. His *Confessio* and *Letter to the Soldiers of Coroticus,* both in LATIN, were among the earliest documents known to have been written in IRELAND. Yet little is reliably known of Patrick's life, and information must be gleaned from his own writings, though these were overwhelmingly self-reflectively hagiographical in nature. These events were later elaborated in

about 690 by the saint's biographers, Muirchú and Tírechán, among others.

EARLY LIFE

Patrick grew up on a small estate, a *villula,* near the villa of Bannavem Taberniae, whose location is unclear. He was the son of a certain Calpurnius, deacon of the church, and the grandson of the priest Potitus. Patrick's Christianity was not a driving force in his youth. At the age of 16, he was kidnapped by Irish raiders or pirates and subsequently sold as a slave in Ireland. He spent six years tending sheep, a period when his religious faith greatly increased. He escaped to Britain, a years later had a VISION in which a messenger of the Irish, called upon him to return to the land of his captivity. Patrick decided at once and contrary to the wishes of his religious superiors in Britain, to devote his life to preaching the gospel in Ireland. Patrick's ecclesiastical education and organizational preference are not clear. He may have had religious instruction in Britain, Ireland, or Auxerre in France.

PATRICK'S MISSION

Patrick focused on converting and baptizing new Christians, consecrating deacons, and consolidating the FAITH of those who had already become Christians after the episcopate of Palladius (ca. 364–430) in earlier in the fifth century. He was concerned with abolishing pagan practices, idolatry, and Sun worship. It is almost certain that Patrick's mission began in the middle of the fifth century, perhaps between 431/432 and 461, but the dates are problematic and could even be between 456 and 490. He began his mission in Leinster and established his see at Armagh.

He may have visited ROME in 442 to explain his activities and been consecrated bishop of Ireland. He introduced to Irish Christians the forms of English church, especially episcopal government. He encouraged the study of Latin and introduced MONASTICISM into Ireland, although most of his foundations were soon taken over by other religious houses. He died, according to various traditions, between 460 and even 490. The place of his death and burial are not known. His feast day is March 17.

Further reading: Patrick, *St. Patrick, His Writings and Life,* ed. J. D. White. (New York: Macmillan, 1920); David N. Dumville, with Lesley Abrams, *Saint Patrick, A.D. 493–1993* (Woodbridge: Boydell Press, 1993); Richard P. C. Hanson, *Saint Patrick, His Origins and Career* (New York, Oxford University Press, 1968); E. A. Thompson, *Who Was Saint Patrick?* (Rochester: Boydell Press, 1999).

Patrimony of Saint Peter   *See* DONATION OF CONSTANTINE; PAPACY; PAPAL STATES.

patronage   Patronage was a medieval and early RENAISSANCE institution and practice, a relationship between a more powerful person and someone dependent on him or her for assistance. The arrangement could be almost contractual, an obligation of reciprocal support, which could be legal, economic, social, or political. Patronage could bind two people or a community and an individual. Ecclesiastical and lay institutions were often part of these social networks. Patronage could be formally recognized or much more informal and personal, at all levels of society up to a prince or king. Patronage could parallel feudal relationships or be integral to them. The roles of protector or protected could be temporary or close to permanent, constantly contested or mutually comfortable. Given all these conditions, patronage was fundamental and nearly all-pervasive in medieval society and persisted in the modern era in some societies.

ARTISTIC PATRONAGE

Artistic patronage could involve individual projects or long-term work on more than one endeavor. Groups of artists sometime formed stables of workers for projects from the building of a CATHEDRAL to the decoration of a chapel. Artists' workshops constituted patronage of younger artists as apprentices of a client, the master or patron. In the later Middle Ages and Renaissance, the artist gained more status than a mere artisan hired for a job, enhancing the terms of patronage. Famous artists and those in demand had more control over the style and content of their works for individual patrons, besides receiving superior pay and protection. However, it is usually unclear who during this era was actually responsible for the style and content. Contacts survived in far greater numbers for the later Middle Ages, and some of them, reflecting a market, showed what was expected and how the artist could be creative and innovative within guidelines set by the patron. Royal and princely courts were centers of patronage that could deeply influence style and content of all artistic objects.

See also BENEFICE; CRIME, PUNISHMENT, AND THE COURTS; ELECTIONS; FEUDALISM AND FEUDAL SYSTEM; FIEF; GREGORIAN REFORM; MANORS AND MANORIAL LORDSHIP; POLITICAL THEORY AND TREATISES.

Further reading: Iain Fenlon, ed., *Music in Medieval and Early Modern Europe: Patronage, Sources, and Texts* (Cambridge: Cambridge University Press, 1981); Richard Firth Green, *Poets and Princepleasers: Literature and the English Court in the Late Middle Ages* (Toronto: University of Toronto Press, 1980); Mary Hollingsworth, *Patronage in Renaissance Italy: From 1400 to the Early Sixteenth Century* (London: John Murray, 1994); Karl J. Holzknecht, *Literary Patronage in the Middle Ages* (1923; reprint, New York: Octagon Books, 1966); Bram Kempers, *Painting, Power, and Patronage: The Rise of the Professional Artist in the Italian Renaissance,* trans. Beverley Jackson (London: Penguin Books, 1994); F. William Kent and Patricia

Simons, eds., *Patronage, Art, and Society in Renaissance Italy* (New York: Oxford University Press, 1987); June Hall McCash, *The Cultural Patronage of Medieval Women* (Athens: University of Georgia Press, 1996).

Paul the Deacon (Paulus Levita, Warnefrid) (ca. 720–ca. 800) *historian, grammarian, poet, deacon, monk at Monte Cassino*

Paul was a member of one of the oldest LOMBARD families long settled in Friuli by King ALBOIN, the first king of the Lombards in Italy. At Pavia, he was educated in the court of the Lombard king Ratchis (r. 744–749). He was instructed in letters, and learned LATIN. He also received some education in Greek. At Ratchis's court, he heard about the old exploits of the Lombards, which he recorded at the end of his life in his best known work, the *History of the Lombards*. He became a deacon, of the Church of Aquileia and perhaps a notary and adviser of the Lombard king Desiderius (r. 757–774). He taught the royal children.

After 774, when CHARLEMAGNE conquered the Lombards, Paul became a monk at MONTE CASSINO. In 776, his brother participated in a revolt against the FRANKS, for which he was despoiled of his patrimony and banished to Francia. In about 782, Paul visited Charlemagne's court at AACHEN, likely brought there by the grammarian Peter of Pisa (d. ca. 800). While there between 782 and 786, Paul tried to help his brother and worked among the Frankish and other clerics working on a reform education. Back at Benevento again in 786–787 and after the death of the duke of Benevento, Paul returned to Monte Cassino, where he died about 800.

LITERARY ACCOMPLISHMENTS

In a clear and cultivated Latin, he composed a commentary on Donatus (fl. fourth century), a summary of Festus's (fl. ca. 200) dictionary, a homiliary composed at Charlemagne's request, a commentary on the Benedictine Rule, a Roman history, a history of the bishops of Metz, and a hagiographical life of Pope GREGORY I. He is best known for his epic history of the Lombards from their origins in 586 to the death of King LIUTPRAND in 744, written while he was at Monte Cassino. In it he emphasized the triumph of Christianity over Lombard PAGANISM.

Further reading: Paul, the Deacon, *History of the Langobards*, trans. William Dudley Foulke (Philadelphia: University of Pennsylvania, 1907); Walter A. Goffart, *The Narrators of Barbarian History (A.D. 550–800): Jordanes, Gregory of Tours, Bede, and Paul the Deacon* (Princeton, N.J.: Princeton University Press, 1988).

Peace and Truce of God   The Peace of God, or in Latin *Pax Dei,* was a movement with a moral vision and concern for community that began in southern FRANCE in the late 10th century and spread to most of CHRISTENDOM. Its influence was apparent until at least the 13th century. Its ideals involved lay and ecclesiastical legislation that regulated WARFARE and tried to establish a social and political peace under the influence of Christianity.

The Peace and Truce of God was a popular religious movement, coinciding with the collapse of the government of the CAROLINGIAN FAMILY AND DYNASTY and the violence of the rise of the CAPETIAN DYNASTY in the 10th century, events that generated violence at the local level because of the absence of effective central government. Church councils or meetings of bishops and other clerics with some powerful LAITY were called to stem the rising level of disorder from which all of society was suffering. The resulting synodal legislation in France was designed to protect unarmed civilians, such as churchmen, peasants, MERCHANTS, and pilgrims; and to control the behavior of warriors, who were henceforth obliged to swear an OATH on RELICS in the presence of others. The new controls relied on noncoercive spiritual sanctions such as EXCOMMUNICATION, the INTERDICT, and the anathema rather than any royal administration of justice. The success of these measures depended on the combined force of a perceived divine will and popular pressure expressed sometimes in miraculous events. In the 11th century, princes and kings joined the Peace and Truce of God. It was especially effective in 1033, the supposed anniversary of Christ's passion and DEATH. Peace leagues grew up. Peasants and lower-level clerics joined nobility in this effort to maintain peace.

TREUGA DEI

By the 1040s the Truce of God (*Treuga Dei*) continued to be a center of legislative efforts at control. Aimed at the nobility, involved a voluntary relinquishing of arms at certain times, seeking to limit feuds and private warfare, forming a temporary link between the earlier peace movements and the development of public institutions that could effectively control violence. These truces specified collective peace at specific times: every week from Wednesday evening to Monday and on numerous other Christian feast days the rest of the time. It was sometimes effective. There were attempts to follow its guidelines even during civil wars in ENGLAND and the HOLY ROMAN EMPIRE. Monarchs resorted to such truces to control unruly nobles in the 12th century. Canonists, such as IVO OF CHARTRES, and popes, such as ALEXANDER III, tried to promote it and give it some kind of canonical underpinning, but popular enthusiasm for it began to wane as the strength and coercive power of central governments and other institutions increased.

In the 12th and 13th centuries, ambitious and violent nobles found alternatives for their bellicose energies—they could go off on Crusade and "ethically" combat Muslims or only too often whomever they encountered, including JEWS and other Christians. Even the religiously inspired peasants, once attracted to oppose these local marauders, joined their Crusades outside Western Europe. Little was heard about the Peace and Truce of God in the later Middle Ages.

See also COMMUNE.

Further reading: Thomas Head and Richard Landes, eds., *The Peace of God: Social Violence and Religious Response in France around the Year 1000* (Ithaca, N.Y.: Cornell University Press, 1992); Robert I. Moore, *The Formation of a Persecuting Society: Power and Deviance in Western Europe, 950–1250* (New York: Basil Blackwell, 1987); Robert I. Moore, *The First European Revolution, c. 970–1215* (Oxford: Blackwell, 2000).

peasant rebellions There were numerous peasant rebellions during the Middle Ages in Western Europe; the best known and most important ones occurred in the 14th and 15th centuries. Documentation of others in Eastern Europe, in the BYZANTINE EMPIRE, and among Muslims is much less extant, if it exists at all. The earlier European revolts were more local than later efforts.

There were common points of conflict in all of the medieval peasant rebellions: the concept of free status, labor service due the lord, rents, taxes, access to vital common rights such as pasture, administration of JUSTICE in the lords' courts, and other particulars of the relationship between the community of peasants and its lord. The success of these movements varied, but they served as reminders of the scope of aristocratic power: there was a limit to what the peasantry would tolerate. The revolts also reflected economic change in labor markets, the rural economy, and agricultural organization. In the 14th century the revolts became more violent, frequent, and ambitious, especially after the PLAGUE of the late 1340s. Major conflicts exploded in FLANDERS between 1323 and 1328 and in FRANCE in the JACQUÉRIE in 1358. The Tuchin movement in central France in the 1360s that lasted until the end of the century. Other uprisings included the English peasant rebellion of 1381 and peasant wars in Catalonia from 1460 into the 1480s. At the same time growing urban labor populations, many of whom were recent transplants from the countryside, caused disorder and conflict over industrial labor conditions in the towns.

THE REVOLT IN ENGLAND

The most important and widespread insurrection in English history was the revolt of English peasants during the months of May and June in 1381; it was also the popular rebellion with the best remaining documentation anywhere in medieval Europe. Several causes have been suggested, including a Marxist crisis of FEUDALISM, a dispute over customary relationships, and a violent and unpremeditated reaction of the peasantry to misadministration in government and justice and excessive war taxation—in particular, three oppressive poll taxes between 1377 and 1381.

The uprising was first documented in southern Essex toward the end of May 1381; then, early in June, the commons of Kent forcibly entered the towns of Rochester on June 6 and CANTERBURY on June 10. They chose an obscure but charismatic leader, Wat Tyler. They marched to Blackheath, near LONDON, intending to present grievances to the 14-year-old king, RICHARD II. After the rebels of Essex and Kent broke through the defenses of London, Richard agreed to meet them on Friday, June 14, promising a general emancipation of English tenants from VILLEIN status, the most oppressive form of peasant status.

In the meantime the insurgents were joined by disaffected urban artisans and craftsmen. They sacked the luxurious palace of the Savoy owned by JOHN OF GAUNT and had Archbishop Simon Sudbury (d. 1381) and Treasurer Robert Hales (d. 1381), the most infamous of the king's ministers, executed in the Tower of London. At the meeting between Richard and Wat Tyler, a mêlée ensued in which Tyler was killed, perhaps foiled in an assassination attempt on the king. Thereupon the crowd dispersed and Richard claimed some kind of victory. The rebellion fell apart after that, especially after the city of London did not rise up in support. The king quickly reneged on his promises and his government brutally quelled any further resistance.

Executions of the perceived ringleaders, including the priest John BALL, followed over the next summer. The new poll and ecclesiastical taxes however, were not levied again. Later rebellions involving rural unrest followed, including one led by Jack CADE in 1451. This rebellion had an afterlife in English history for its egalitarian aspirations and for its dream of applying Christian justice to all of society. Conditions of rural work and servitude did not immediately improve, but in the longer run, at least because of change in the rural labor market, genuine serfdom became unprofitable for lords.

See also AGRICULTURE; CIOMPI REVOLT; FOOD, DRINK, AND NUTRITION; MANORS AND MANORIAL LORDSHIP; PEASANTRY; SERFS AND SERFDOM; VILLEINS AND VILLEINAGE.

Further reading: Richard B. Dobson, ed., *The Peasants' Revolt of 1381* (New York: St. Martin's Press, 1970); Rodney H. Hilton, *Bond Men Made Free: Medieval Peasant Movements and the English Rising of 1381* (London: Temple Smith, 1973); Steven Justice, *Writing and Rebellion: England in 1381* (Berkeley: University of California Press, 1994); Michael Mollat and Philippe Wolff, *The Popular Revolutions of the Late Middle Ages*, trans. A. L. Lytton-Sells (London: Allen and Unwin, 1973); William H. TeBrake, *A Plague of Insurrection: Popular Politics and Peasant Revolt in Flanders, 1323–1328* (Philadelphia: University of Pennsylvania Press, 1993).

peasantry In the medieval world, peasants represented perhaps 80 to 85 percent of the European population.

The conditions for these peasants varied according to a number of factors, including the topography of land on which they had to work, the labor market, the production for the demands of towns and urban populations, the solidarity of their own community, the needs and powers of lords, the type of farming, and the crops and animals involved in production.

In the late antique world and the early Middle Ages, peasants' holdings were not closely tied to particular pieces of land, lords, or institutions. In the 10th century, fixed villages came into being and family houses replaced more collective dwellings. From those evolved much more precise sets of relationships with lords. The legal status of peasants then became more or less free or obligated to certain services and taxes. True slavery had become very rare for production from the land in Europe. The lord had responsibilities to his peasantry, but these were limited. There were also small landholders or tenant farmers, independent of any lord except in certain legal ties to the manorial court system. True serfs, who were not technically slaves but were essentially owned by their master, constituted another element of the peasantry. Their proportion of the rural population varied from region to region, sometimes as high as 35 percent, though in many regions they were completely absent.

THE BYZANTINE PEASANTRY

Byzantine peasants played an important role in the empire. They were for several centuries one of the principal supports of the realm. In the early days of BYZANTIUM, the plight of the peasants improved because of a chronic shortage of labor, though the number of agricultural slaves was always low. Small proprietors always existed, with monopolies in a significant number of villages, usually reinforced by the presence of hereditary leaseholders. The fiscal administration had to abandon taxing cities and found taxpayers in rural areas. Peasants also constituted a portion of the support for the Byzantine military districts or themes, which they helped to finance for defense against foreign invasions, especially those of the ARABS.

See also AGRICULTURE; BAN; FOOD, DRINK, AND NUTRITION; MANORS AND MANORIAL LORDSHIP; PEASANT REBELLIONS; SERFS AND SERFDOM; VILLEINS, AND VILLEINAGE.

Further reading: Robert Fossier, *Peasant Life in the Medieval West*, trans. Juliet Vale (Oxford: B. Blackwell, 1988); Paul H. Freedman, *Images of the Medieval Peasant* (Stanford, Calif.: Stanford University Press, 1999); Angeliki E. Laiou, *Peasant Society in the Late Byzantine Empire: A Social and Demographic Study* (Princeton, N.J.: Princeton University Press, 1977); Emmanuel Le Roy Ladurie, *The Peasants of Languedoc*, trans. John Day (1966; reprint, Urbana: University of Illinois Press, 1974); Werner Rösener, *The Peasantry of Europe*, trans. Thomas M. Barker (Oxford: Blackwell, 1994).

Peć (Péc, Pečūy) Péc was one of two monastic sites that alternated as residences of the archbishop of the Serbs, who became a patriarch in 1346. At the heart of the town were three churches built and decorated within a century of one another. The oldest of this group was the church of the Holy Apostles; its date is not fixed with certainty, perhaps the 1230s. It has FRESCOES from the 1260s. Two 14th-century churches surround the Holy Apostles. To the north is Saint Demetrius (1316–24), and to the south is the Theotokos Hodeghetria, built about 1330. Both are decorated with frescoes from the 14th century.

See also SERBIA AND SERBS; STEPHEN DUŠAN.

Further reading: Suzy Dufrenne, "Peć," *EMA* 2.1,107; John V. A. Fine, *The Late Medieval Balkans: A Critical Survey from the Late Twelfth Century to the Ottoman Conquest* (Ann Arbor: University of Michigan Press, 1994); Radivoje Ljubinkovic, *The Church of the Apostles in the Patriarchate of Pec*, trans. Veselin Kostic (Belgrade: Jugoslavija, 1964).

pecia The Latin word *pecia* designated "a piece." In the book production industry and trade, it designated a partial stage in the copying procedure of a manuscript text that permitted a more rapid circulation and publication of works for scholars. Students and teachers needed manuscript copies of works, producing which was not a simple or cheap process. To avoid the necessity of reproducing a whole manuscript, at once which could tie up the best model text for a long time and yet only obtain a single copy, a scribe was lent an *exemplar* compiled in numbered sections. These were called *pecie* in the plural. The scribe used the "pieces" one after the other, so the other sections might be available for other copies. Several copyists worked on the same text at the same time, so a greater number of full copies of a single work to be rapidly produced. The model text made up of all of the pieces was called an *exemplar*. This was done by booksellers called stationers.

This system arose toward the end of the 12th century at BOLOGNA and spread in the 13th century to PARIS and elsewhere, becoming a commercial enterprise. The university authorities regulated this business strictly. The price for producing each piece was taxed, and each *exemplar* was subjected to checks, and proofreading, even by the authors involved. All this aimed toward ensuring the integrity of the texts. The quality of the texts, nonetheless, transmitted by exemplars was variable. It could be excellent when the stationer had a clear autograph, sometimes even checked by the author, or a very good model. But it could be mediocre. There are numerous examples of corrupted texts. Any modern or scientific editing of these complex philosophical, theological, and legal texts had to confront issues of fragmentation, accuracy, and problematic descent.

See also PHILOSOPHY AND THEOLOGY; SCHOLASTICISM AND SCHOLASTIC METHOD; UNIVERSITIES AND SCHOOLS.

Further reading: Leonard E. Boyle, *Medieval Latin Paleography: A Bibliographical Introduction* (Toronto: University of Toronto Press, 1984), 267–269, 312–313.

Pelagianism Pelagianism was a fourth- and fifth-century Christian HERESY, according to which humankind won SALVATION through its own efforts, without the help of divine GRACE. One could win grace by one's efforts. It took its name from PELAGIUS, a British scholar who settled in ROME in the 380s. The doctrine was attacked by the church, which perceived such ideas as dangerous to its role in the administration of sacraments as instruments of divine grace. Such ideas eliminated the need for assistance by the clergy as mediators in Christian FAITH and practice. This heresy's chief adversary was AUGUSTINE of Hippo, who, among several others, brought about its condemnation in 415. Prosper of Aquitaine (ca. 390–after 455) tried to defend Pelagian ideas, which initially were influential in the East. But they were condemned again by Pope Innocent I (r. 401–417) in 417. Many believers in Pelagianism retired to SPAIN, where they enjoyed a certain degree of liberty under the VISIGOTHS. The movement itself disappeared in the sixth century, but the ideas continued to be discussed.

Further reading: Augustine, *Four Anti-Pelagian Writings*, trans. John A. Mourant and William J. Collinge (Washington, D.C.: Catholic University of America Press, 1992); Gerald Bonner, *Church and Faith in the Patristic Tradition: Augustine, Pelagianism, and Early Christian Northumbria* (Brookfield: Variorum, 1996).

Pelagius (ca. 357–ca. 418) *monk, theologian*
Probably of British origin, Pelagius arrived in about 380 in ROME, where he began to teach. By 410 he had moved to AFRICA, where his views were opposed by AUGUSTINE in 411. According to Pelagius, the human will was completely free, capable of good or evil. Divine GRACE was externally given according to one's earned merits, its purpose merely to facilitate what the will could do by itself. Adam's SIN, or original sin, was purely personal and had no effect on the rest of humanity. All humanity did not bear the guilt of original sin. DEATH was not a punishment for sin but a necessary aspect of human nature.

Pelagius created a THEOLOGY vindicating Christian ASCETICISM against the charge of MANICHAEISM by emphasizing human freedom to choose good. Since all were born without original sin, there was no need for infant baptism. PRAYER for the conversion of others was hopeless since it could not help them. REDEMPTION carried out by Christ had no effect except as an example. This became a widespread movement, not especially tied to Pelagius himself.

OPPOSITION

All these ideas produced a torrent of orthodox opposition and the promotion of Roman hegemony. Augustine in 412, OROSIUS in 415, and JEROME in 415 all attempted refutations. A conference of African bishops persuaded Pope Innocent I (r. 401–417) in 417 to excommunicate Pelagius and denounce his views. However, later that year the Greek pope and saint Zosimus I (r. 417–418) reopened the case and accepted him back into the church. The emperor Honorius (r. 395–423), with papal support, exiled Pelagius from Rome on April 30, 418, because of his renewed heretical teaching. At the Sixteenth Council of Carthage, more than 200 African bishops condemned his teaching. A council of ANTIOCH expelled him from PALESTINE, where he had taken refuge, the following year. Pelagius himself did not try to defend these ideas much himself. He disappeared from history and probably died, perhaps in EGYPT, soon after the condemnations of 418. Others did try to defend these ideas on free will for the next few decades, especially in Britain. Such ideas continued to surface throughout the Middle Ages and returned to full bloom in the reforming movements of the 16th century.

See also GRACE; PREDESTINATION.

Further reading: Pelagius, *The Letters of Pelagius and His Followers*, ed. and trans. B. R. Rees (Woodbridge: Boydell Press, 1991); John Ferguson, *Pelagius: A Historical and Theological Study* (New York: AMS Press, 1978); B. R. Rees, *Pelagius: Life and Letters* (Rochester, N.Y.: Boydell Press, 1998).

Peloponnese *See* MOREA, CHRONICLE OF, AND DESPOT OF.

penance *See* SEVEN SACRAMENTS.

Penitentials Penitentials, or *Libri paenitentiales*, were texts containing lists of sins. For each sin, moreover, there were corresponding penances to be assigned to truly penitent sinners who had to perform them voluntarily. Compiled for the use of confessors in private penance, they were particularly popular in the Celtic church, whose penitential tradition sought correction and improvement, not simple punishment. Most of these texts in manuscripts circulated anonymously or were linked with famous and reputable authors. The earliest examples appeared in IRELAND and WALES in the sixth century. COLUMBAN introduced these ideas and lists to the Continent and Anglo-Saxon England in the first half of the seventh century. By the eighth century, Irish MISSIONS and missionaries had further spread the use of Penitentials.

The concept of establishing specific expiating penalties for specific sins was probably based on such practices in barbarian law codes. The principal act of penance advised in these Penitentials was the FAST, which could vary in severity and length by a set number of days, weeks, months, or years, depending on the sin and the social and religious status of the penitent. These periods of fasting could usually be replaced by other kinds of penitential activities, including huge quantities of genuflections, numerous recitations of psalms, difficult and dangerous pilgrimages, long vigils, hefty payments for masses, charitable gifts to ecclesiastical institutions, and straightforward monetary payments. Soon even third parties could be employed to carry out penances for wealthy penitents. However, at the councils of Châlon in 813 and Paris in 829, it was decided that bishops were to find any Penitentials in their dioceses and destroy them. They were not canonically or officially approved.

ORTHODOX CHURCH

In the Orthodox Church, Penitentials were collected into manuals for categories of sins and were intended to provide confessors with a list of penances specified by the decisions of church councils, or as prescribed by the early fathers, or as explicitly stated in rituals for administering the sacrament of penance. They were usually attributed in manuscripts to the patriarch John the Faster (582–595). In the application of this pastoral system, the confessor was to help the penitent improve his or her life by taking account of the age, the social rank, the state of life, and the circumstances of the sin, all done benevolently to inspire a more confident attitude in the penitent that he or she might be able to reform and avoid further sin. These kinds of *Penitentials* had a wider and longer deployment in the Eastern Church.

Further reading: Ludwig Bieler, *The Irish Penitentials* (Dublin: Dublin Institute for Advanced Studies, 1963); John T. McNeil and Helena M. Gamer, trans., *Medieval Handbooks of Penance: A Translation of the Principal "Libri poenitentiales" and Selections from Related Documents* (1938; reprint, New York: Columbia University Press, 1990); Pierre J. Payer, *Sex and the Penitentials: The Development of a Sexual Code, 550–1150* (Toronto: University of Toronto Press, 1984); Julie Ann Smith, *Ordering Women's Lives: Penitentials and Nunnery Rules in the Early Medieval West* (Aldershot: Ashgate, 2001).

Pentateuch The five books of Moses or Genesis, Exodus, Leviticus, Numbers, and Deuteronomy, were considered by Jewish and Christian exegetes to constitute a coherent unit. Called Torah by the Jews, they were supposed to have been written by Moses to represent the essence of the "old law" and were sometimes contrasted with the four GOSPELS. Both had normative elements supplemented by doctrinal considerations; both contained many narrative elements, and the Pentateuch had traditionally been included among the historical books of the BIBLE. The Pentateuch provided the stories of creation, Adam and Eve, Cain and Abel, the patriarchs, Joseph,

Moses, and much more. These characters became the basis of allegorical and typological interpretations. Historical aspects of the narratives such as chronological, geographical, and archaeological details were studied from the 12th century onward by both Christians and Jews.

For the JEWS, the Torah was the basis of the social and religious legislation known as the *HALAKAH*. It was believed to be decreed by GOD. Its rules and commandments had a permanent value and were the basis of the organization of Jewish religious and community life. The main groups concerned alimentary laws; observance of the sabbath and other festivals, some nostagically relating to Israel; sacrifices; and numerous social laws that applied to the family, hospitality to strangers, assistance to the needy, and even slavery. Christianity inherited this system, but after Christ, the Old Testament practices and social laws were deemed obsolete. Canon law, however, was inspired by ideas and rules from the Pentateuch.

In the doctrinal sphere, the Pentateuch did not have the importance for Christian thought of John's gospel and the Pauline epistles. However, some fundamental aspects of Christian doctrine were set out in Genesis and Deuteronomy. Christian thought followed the idea, the absolute oneness of God, while understanding other passages as clear indications of the Trinity and the creation of the universe by God from nothing.

See also GLOSSA ORDINARIA; HRABANUS MAURUS; JEROME, SAINT; RUPERT OF DEUTZ; STEPHEN LANGTON.

Further reading: Joseph Blenkinsopp, *The Pentateuch: An Introduction to the First Five Books of the Bible* (New York: Doubleday, 1992); Suzanne Boorer, *The Promise of the Land as Oath: A Key to the Formation of the Pentateuch* (Berlin: W. de Gruyter, 1992); Martin Noth, *A History of Pentateuchal Traditions*, trans. Bernhard W. Anderson (Englewood Cliffs, N.J.: Prentice-Hall, 1972); M. H. Segal, *The Pentateuch: Its Composition and Its Authorship and Other Biblical Studies* (Jerusalem: Magnes Press, Hebrew University, 1967).

Pentecost (Whitsunday) Pentecost was the Greek name for the feast of weeks on the 50th day after Passover or EASTER. The HOLY SPIRIT, the third person of the Trinity, descended on the apostles on this feast to enable them to speak all the languages necessary for their preaching among the Gentiles. As an artistic presentation, it took its source from the description in the Acts of the Apostles. Pentecost was considered the collective feast of the apostles and was celebrated as an institution of the church.

Further reading: A. A. McArthur, *The Evolution of the Christian Year* (London: SCM Press, 1955); John Gunstone, *The Feast of Pentecost: The Great Fifty Days in the Liturgy* (London: Faith Press, 1967); Valentine Zander, *Pentecost in the Orthodox Church* (Wirral, England: Anargyroi Press for the Monastery of Saint Seraphim of Sarov, 1994).

people of the Book   *See* DHIMMI.

Pépin III the Short (Pippin) (ca. 714/715–768) *mayor of the palace for the last of the Merovingians, king of the Franks*

Born about 714/715 at Jupille, Pépin was the son of CHARLES MARTEL and Rothrude and became the father of CHARLEMAGNE. From 741 to 751, he held the office of mayor of the palace and the chief official for the Merovingian king. From 751 to 768, he was king himself after his accession to the Crown. He had spent his youth with the monks of Saint Denis near PARIS. In 735 he was sent to the court of Liutprand (r. 713–744), the king of the LOMBARDS, where he saw a sound administration of government. On his father's death, he inherited control of BURGUNDY, NEUSTRIA, PROVENCE, and the cities of Metz and Trier. His brother, Carloman (d. 754), held the rest of the Frankish kingdom and the mayoralty of Austrasia. In 743 the princes decided to reproclaim and restore the pretense of

the rule of the Merovingian dynasty, interrupted since 737, to satisfy some of objections the Frankish aristocracy.

Pépin and Carloman reformed the Frankish church with the advice of Saint BONIFACE, a representative of the pope. In 744 Pépin assembled Frankish bishops for a council at Soissons, where the resulting legislation or canons obliged clerics to lead a more appropriate life, no longer bear arms, and wear clothing similar to that of monks. Pépin would not restore church property that had been confiscated by Charles Martel, since it was in the hands of his important supporters.

PÉPIN AS KING

After Carloman's abdication in 747, Pépin united the two mayorships and began to drive back the SAXONS from the left bank of the Rhine and impose his lordship over BAVARIA. Having received support from the pope, he had himself elected king at Soissons in November of 751. The last Merovingian king, Chilperic III (r. 742–752); entered a monastery. Pépin was then consecrated by the

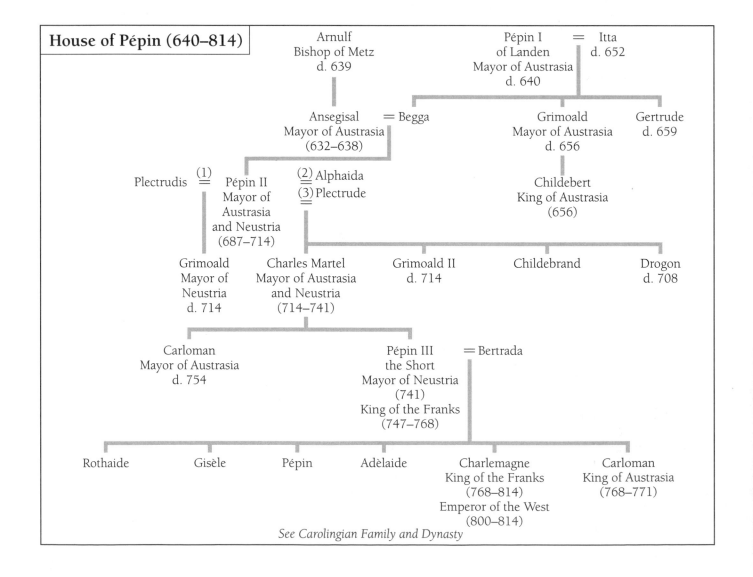

See Carolingian Family and Dynasty

Frankish bishops. Threatened by the LOMBARDS, Pope Stephen II (752–757) appealed to Pépin. The pope traveled to Gaul to meet the new king in January of 754. He obtained a promise from Pépin to intervene in Italy and consecrated and anointed Pépin and his sons as the ruling family, addressing them as "patricians of the Romans." The Franks were in theory to choose their king solely from Pépin's descendants from then on. Pépin then led two successful expeditions to ITALY, in 754 and 756. He restored to the pope the lands confiscated by the Lombards, or the Patrimony of Saint Peter, the basis for the PAPAL STATES. His prestige as the first Carolingian king grew, and he managed to subject AQUITAINE, to defeat the Frisians and the Saxons, and to expel the ARABS from western Provence. He reorganized his court and government by entrusting administrative posts to educated clerics and monks. He resumed a monopoly on coining money and struck a silver penny. He had a new basilica built at SAINT-DENIS, where he died on September 24, 768.

Further reading: J. M. Wallace-Hadrill, *The Long-Haired Kings and Other Studies in Frankish History* (London: Methuen, 1962); Rosamund McKitterick, *The Frankish Kingdoms under the Carolingians, 751–987* (London: Longman, 1983); Ian Wood, *The Merovingian Kingdoms, 450–751* (New York: Longman, 1994).

Perceval (Parsifal) *literary character, hero of several Arthurian romances*
CHRÉTIEN DE TROYES first wrote Perceval's history in his *Conte du Graal* from about 1182, but perhaps as late as 1191. Supposedly from a rustic background, he was raised apart from knightly life but did have knightly training and then went to the court of ARTHUR where he has several outrageous experiences. There he learned that CHIVALRY did not just consist in bearing arms, but in committing one's strength and courage to a mission conducted under a precise code, such as the search for the GRAIL. He learned to love from afar. He became aware of his election for a task and need to take responsibility for and purify his past. When he failed on his first visit to the Grail castle, the cause was a SIN committed earlier. He was obliged to evaluate this act and its consequences and free himself by a penance. His faults or those of others and his possible redemption confronted each other inside him. In WOLFRAM VON ESCHENBACH's *Parzival* (ca. 1210), the stain was a sin of the flesh. This fault and its redemption remained aspects of Perceval's later existence as a hero in literature, but eventually as the genre reduced to Galahad's, his son, companion on the quest for the Holy Grail.

Further reading: D. H. Green, *The Art of Recognition in Wolfram's Parzival* (Cambridge: Cambridge University Press, 1982); Arthur Groos and Norris J. Lacy, eds., *Perceval-Parzival: A Casebook* (New York: Routledge, 2002); Will Hasty, ed., *A Companion to Wolfram's Parzival* (Columbia, S.C.: Camden House, 1999).

person The medieval philosophical notion of a person had its roots in the definition of BOETHIUS, who explained it as an individual substance with a rational nature. In THEOLOGY it was applied to GOD as a Trinity of persons with Christ as a divine person. Medieval thinkers insisted on individuation or singularity, a fundamental concept that was used in theological and philosophical speculation on God, TRINITARIAN doctrine, the SOUL, substance, NATURE, the nature of humans, ethics, and many other topics.

See also AQUINAS, THOMAS, SAINT; IBN RUSHD; PHILOSOPHY AND THEOLOGY.

Further reading: Étienne Gilson, *History of Christian Philosophy in the Middle Ages* (New York: Random House, 1955); Norman Kretzmann, Anthony Kenny, Jan Pinborg, and Eleonore Stump, eds., *The Cambridge History of Later Medieval Philosophy: From the Rediscovery of Aristotle to the Disintegration of Scholasticism, 1100–1600* (Cambridge: Cambridge University Press, 1982); Quentin Skinner and Eckhard Kessler, eds., *The Cambridge History of Renaissance Philosophy* (Cambridge: Cambridge University Press, 1989).

Pest *See* BUDA AND PEST.

Peter I (d. 969) *king of the Bulgarians*
Peter I was the son of SIMON I, whom he succeeded in 927. Soon after that, he led a raid near CONSTANTINOPLE to demonstrate his power and then negotiated a favorable treaty with the BYZANTINE EMPIRE that lasted until 965. He married a Byzantine princess. His kingdom was prosperous despite Magyar raids and internal unrest, often linked to his own family. Constantinople even recognized his title as a czar, though inferior to the emperor. When the Byzantine emperor refused to pay tribute in 965, war began. The Russians of KIEV attacked BULGARIA as an ally of the Byzantines. Peter grew sick and in 967 had to abdicate and retire to a monastery, where he died in 969.

Further reading: John V. A. Fine Jr., *The Early Medieval Balkans: A Critical Survey from the Sixth to the Late Twelfth Century* (Ann Arbor: University of Michigan Press, 1991).

Peter Damien *See* DAMIAN, PETER.

Peter Lombard (ca. 1095–1160) *bishop of Paris, theologian, biblical exegete*
Peter Lombard was born near Novara in northern ITALY about 1095. Trained first in the law schools of northern Italy, he then attended the CATHEDRAL school at RHEIMS.

There he studied the glosses of ANSELM OF LAON and GILBERT OF POITIERS on the Psalms. He eventually opposed the teaching of Gilbert at the Council of Rheims in 1148. He was accepted at the monastery Saint-Victor in PARIS on the recommendation of BERNARD OF CLAIRVAUX; there he studied with HUGH OF SAINT-VICTOR. By 1145–47, he had received as a BENEFICE a canonry at NOTRE-DAME in Paris. He was ordained subdeacon in 1147, deacon in 1152, and priest and archdeacon in 1156 or 1157. From 1143 or 1144, he taught at the cathedral school of Notre-Dame, until he was elected to the office of bishop of Paris in 1159, but he died the following year, on May 3, 1160, and was buried in the church of Saint-Marcel.

WORKS: GLOSSES, A TEXTBOOK, AND SERMONS

Peter Lombard left several collections of glosses on Scripture, 33 SERMONS, and a set of questions on the Trinity, the incarnation, and SINS against the HOLY SPIRIT. His most famous and important work was the *Sententiae in IV libris distinctae* (Four Books of Sentences). Peter Lombard asserted that he felt a need for a new organization of theological teaching. In the prologue to his work (1155–58), he stated that he wished to collect together the sentences or opinions of the FATHERS OF THE CHURCH, with supporting texts and new sources, for the masters and students in the universities. The *Sentences* were divided into books, distinctions, chapters, and articles by the Franciscan Alexander of Hales (ca. 1185–1245), who in 1223–27 was the first Parisian master to use Lombard's work as a basic teaching text. It remained the basic text and reference source for theological studies until the 16th century; nearly every theologian had to write a commentary as a basic part of an advanced theological education.

Lombard's *Sententiae* set the basic framework for systematic theological study and laid the basis and was a model for a synthesis of conflicting opinion. A Scholastic treatise, it dealt with TRINITARIAN DOCTRINE, creation, the Incarnation, REDEMPTION, the VIRTUES, SIN, ANGELS, DEMONS, the gifts of the Holy Spirit, the commandments, DEATH, HEAVEN, HELL, the LAST JUDGMENT, and the SEVEN SACRAMENTS. Lombard sought to bring the heritage of the learning of the past to bear on contemporary doctrinal questions.

See also GLOSSA ORDINARIA; SENTENCES.

Further reading: Marcia L. Colish, *Peter Lombard* (Leiden: E. J. Brill, 1994); G. R. Evans, ed., *Mediaeval Commentaries on the Sentences of Peter Lombard: Current Research* (Leiden: Brill, 2002); Michael P. Malloy, *Civil Authority in Medieval Philosophy: Lombard, Aquinas, and Bonaventure* (Lanham, Md.: University Press of America, 1985); Elizabeth Frances Rogers, *Peter Lombard and the Sacramental System* (Merrick, N.Y.: Richwood, 1976).

Peter the Hermit (ca. 1050–1115) *French preacher*
Peter the Hermit was a native of the Amiens region who left his hermitage and began in 1096 to preach charismatically in Berry for the First CRUSADE. In April, he set out from COLOGNE for JERUSALEM with perhaps 20,000 ill-trained and inadequately equipped companions. They attacked numerous Jewish communities on the way. He was well received at CONSTANTINOPLE by the emperor, ALEXIOS I. The troops with him, however, pillaged the city. They were then transferred to ANATOLIA but largely annihilated in a battle by the SELJUK TURKS near NICAEA; survivors joined the main crusading army.

Peter was not with them. His role after that became secondary. His prestige decreased sharply after his ignominious attempt to desert during the siege of ANTIOCH in 1097–98. After the capture of Jerusalem, he returned to Europe and became prior at Saint Augustine at Neufmontier in BELGIUM. He died there in 1115.

Further reading: Robert Chazan, *European Jewry and the First Crusade* (Berkeley: University of California Press, 1987); Robert Chazan, *In the Year 1096: The First Crusade and the Jews* (Philadelphia: Jewish Publication Society, 1996); John France, *Victory in the East: A Military History of the First Crusade* (Cambridge: Cambridge University Press, 1994); Jonathan Riley-Smith, *The First crusaders, 1095–1131* (Cambridge: Cambridge University Press, 1997); Steven Runciman, *A History of the Crusades*. Vol. 1, *The First Crusade and the Foundation of the Kingdom of Jerusalem* (Cambridge: Cambridge University Press, 1951).

Peter the Venerable (ca. 1092–1156) *abbot of Cluny*
Born about 1092 in central FRANCE, Peter was the son of the noble Maurice II of Montboissier and his wife, Raingarde. Peter was first a BENEDICTINE oblate at Sauxillanges, but in 1109 he was professed as a monk at CLUNY. He was instituted "doctor of the elders and guardian of the order" at VÉZELAY, where he was prior between 1116 and 1120.

On August 22–23, 1122, Peter was elected abbot of Cluny. With the monastery in disorder, he immediately began a program of reform. In spring 1130, on his first journey to ENGLAND, he took back gifts from King HENRY I that gave him the resources to finish the construction of the great church of Cluny. It was consecrated by Pope Innocent II (r. 1130–43) on December 25, 1130. In September 1130, Peter took a stand against the antipope, Anacletus II (d. 1138). Until 1138 he made several journeys to AQUITAINE to try to end this schism. In 1132 he convened at Cluny the first general chapter of the congregation, which ratified his proposals for reform and austerity. These were confirmed by additional statutes of 1146–47 that reduced luxuries in food, dress, and display within the order.

WORKS AND INFLUENCE

In 1130s and early 1140s, Peter wrote a life of the monk Gerard, attended the council of PISA, a life of Saint Matthew, a treatise on MIRACLES, and a treatise against the heretic Peter of Bruys (d. ca. 1139), which he finished in 1144. In June 1140, after the condemnation of his former teacher, ABÉLARD, Peter kindly allowed him to stay at Cluny and effected the reconciliation of Abélard with BERNARD OF CLAIRVAUX. After Abélard's death on April 21, 1142, Peter had his body taken to the monastery of the Paraclete, where HÉLOÏSE was abbess.

From March to October 1142, Peter went to SPAIN to meet King Alfonso VII (r. 1126–57) of León and Castile. On the way he commissioned a translation of the QURAN and several other polemical works on ISLAM, yet hoped for fruitful dialogue with and conversion of the Muslims. He also promoted an alliance against the BYZANTINE EMPIRE. In June or July 1143, he wrote a very negative treatise against the JEWS. In mid-March 1147, Peter took part in a diet of Frankfurt-am-Main in preparation for the Second CRUSADE. After the failure of this Crusade, with Bernard and SUGER OF Saint DENIS, he again promoted a new expedition but was unable to attend a council on the matter at CHARTRES in May 1150. He was honored by his contemporaries for his holiness and gentleness and even then called the Venerable. Peter died at Cluny on Christmas in 1156. His feast was May 11.

See also ANTI-JUDAISM and ANTI-SEMITISM.

Further reading: Peter, the Venerable, *The Letters of Peter the Venerable,* ed. Giles Constable (Cambridge, Mass.: Harvard University Press, 1967); Gillian R. Knight, *The Correspondence between Peter the Venerable and Bernard of Clairvaux: A Semantic and Structural Analysis* (Aldershot: Ashgate, 2002); James Kritzeck, *Peter the Venerable and Islam* (Princeton, N.J.: Princeton University Press, 1964).

Petra   Petra and its basin, where the ancient city rests, were a stronghold, and probably the capital city, of the biblical Edomites. The Greek name Petra simply means "rock." After the Roman occupation of the city in 106 C.E., Petra acquired other names as well, such as Petra Hadriana, from 131. Petra was the major city of a little-known people, the Aramaic-speaking Nabataeans, who were famous for their ceramics and had unique MOSAICS, architecture, religion, and hydraulic technology. The form of their writing was an ancestor of Arabic. It was an important stop and commercial center on the TRADE routes from the western Arabian Peninsula, carrying spices, frankincense, myrrh, gems, balsam, bitumen, and even SILK from China.

Petra and the Nabataeans were not integrated into the Roman Empire until the second century C.E. It prospered after the Roman takeover, until trade routes shifted. There were vineyards, gardens, orchards, and cultivated fields within the confines of the city. It was also a natural fortress and not at all easy to access.

LATER FRAGMENTED HISTORY

By the early 12th century, the site had acquired the name "The Valley of Moses," as Christian religious zeal extended Mosaic relationships to all parts of Petra. Its urban fabric suffered major destruction from earthquakes and was gradually hidden by sand. Thirty-nine levels of culture were identified between an earthquake of 363 and the modern era. There were five occupations between 363 and another earthquake in 551, followed by six temporary occupations between 551 and the present. It was first abandoned in the seventh century but was known and occupied during the CRUSADES, forgotten until the early 19th century, and rarely visited until after the World War I. It contained numerous famous buildings carved into the rose-red rock in the sides of the hills producing its dispersed city center. The supposed tomb of Aaron, long venerated by Muslims, was nearby.

Further reading: Christian Augé and Jean-Marie Dentzer, *Petra: Lost City of the Ancient World,* trans. Laurel Hirsch and David Baker (1999; reprint, New York: H. N. Abrams, 2000); Robert G. Hoyland, *Arabia and the Arabs: From the Bronze Age to the Coming of Islam* (New York: Routledge, 2001); Alexander B. W. Kennedy, *Petra: Its History and Monuments* (London: Country Life, 1925).

Petrarch, Francesco (Petrarca) (1304–1374) *Italian poet, humanist*
A child of Pietro di Parenzo and Eletta Canisiani of Florence, exiled to Arezzo in 1302, Francesco Petrarch spent his childhood in TUSCANY. In 1311, he moved with his family to Carpentras, near AVIGNON, where his father, a notary, worked at the papal court of CLEMENT V. Following his father's wish that he become a lawyer, he studied LAW at MONTPELLIER in 1319 and 1320 and at BOLOGNA between 1323 and 1325.

He returned to Avignon on his father's death in 1326 and abandoned law for letters to enter the service of the Colonna family. With their PATRONAGE he undertook numerous missions that led to important discoveries of manuscripts and texts for the field of classical philology in Europe and especially ITALY, such as the later discovery at VERONA of Cicero's more personal letters in 1345. On Good Friday, April 6, 1327, he met and immediately fell in love with Laura, the personification of his ideas of truth and beauty and the inspiration for much of his work. In 1341 he was crowned in Rome as a poet laureate in the classical tradition. He made trips back to Italy for the HOLY YEAR of 1350 but quarreled with other potential clerical patrons. He had come to loath the corruption of the papal court at Avignon, although he did scruple to minor orders in return for financial support. He had two illegitimate children. In 1353, he moved back permanently to Italy, first to MILAN under the patronage of the VISCONTI family, then to VENICE, and to PADUA under Francesco il Vecchio da Carrara (r. 1350–88). He was criticized by his republican friends for accepting the patronage of such princes and tyrants. He died at Arquà, near Padua, perhaps on July 18, 1374. He was discovered then with his head resting on a manuscript of Virgil.

OPUS

Petrarch did most of his work in LATIN. Often focusing on himself and his own situation, he wrote a huge number of letters, which he carefully collected, and several invectives in response to criticism. His major work, unfinished, was the *Africa* (1338–39), a Latin work telling in Virgilian hexameters the story of the second Punic War. In it he exalted the figure of Scipio Africanus. He also emphasized, in his more intimate and personal writings, the value of the withdrawn solitary life. In the *Secretum*, a dialogue with AUGUSTINE, he proposed remedies for the consequences and results of both good and ill fortune and more or less publicly confessed his faults and weaknesses. He created a series of biographies of famous classical characters over the course of his life and an edition of Livy when he was still in his 20s. He developed a close friendship and mutually supportive relationship with BOCCACCIO.

Two of his works in the VERNACULAR were of major importance. The first was a collection of poems consisting of sonnets, songs, sestinas, ballades, and madrigals, about his love for Laura and his inner crisis at Laura's death on April 6 in the PLAGUE of 1348. The second was the *Triumphs*, an allegorical poem combining a vision of a SOUL with a classical triumph heading toward fulfillment with GOD.

See also AVIGNON AND THE AVIGNONESE PAPACY.

Further reading: Julia Conaway Bondanella and Mark Musa, "Petrarch," in *European Writers: The Middle Ages and the Renaissance.* Vol. 1, *Petrarch to Renaissance Short Fiction,* ed. William T. H. Jackson and George Stade (New York: Charles Scribner's Sons, 1983), 475–507, especially the list of translations of works by Petrarch up to 1983 on 505–506; William J. Kennedy, *Authorizing Petrarch* (Ithaca, N.Y.: Cornell University Press, 1994); Nicholas Mann, *Petrarch* (Oxford: Oxford University Press, 1984); Giuseppe Mazzotta, *The Worlds of Petrarch* (Durham, N.C.: Duke University Press, 1993); E. H. Wilkins, *Life of Petrarch* (Chicago: University of Chicago Press, 1961).

Philip II Augustus (1165–1223) *king of France*
Born in 1165, Philip was the son of Louis VII (1137–80) and his third wife, Adèle of Champagne (d. 1206); he succeeded his father on September 19, 1180. He was surnamed Augustus because he enhanced his royal domain as the Roman emperor Augustus had. He freed himself of the influence of his advisers from about 1190, the time of the Third CRUSADE, in which he took part with the king of England, RICHARD I LIONHEART. Quarreling with Richard, on his return he started to move against the English PLANTAGENET family empire on the Continent. He had earlier stirred up rivalries among King HENRY II and his sons, allying with them against him in a humiliating scenario that led to Henry's death. Philip was later less successful against King Richard in occupying NORMANDY and suffered a defeat at Fréteval in 1194. With Richard's death in 1199 and the failures and problems of his successor, King JOHN Lackland, Philip took control of NORMANDY, Maine, ANJOU, Touraine, Berry, and Poitou between 1203 and 1205. He won a great victory at the Battle of BOUVINES, July 27, 1214, against a coalition of King John, the emperor Otto IV (d. 1218), and the count of FLANDERS, which further secured his earlier conquests. Philip more peacefully gained control of other regions, including the Valois, Amiénois, Vermandois, Alençon, and Clermont-en-Beauvaisis, all not far from PARIS, his capital. He was now in charge of the strongest kingdom in western Europe.

ACCOMPLISHMENTS

For Philip's government to enhance its effectiveness to rule over his expanded domain, it had to develop new methods of administration between 1190 and 1200. While centralizing authority, Philip created a circle linked to himself, including the great barons and educated clerics. Philip then devised specialized judicial sessions in feudal courts to insist on royal rights, an archive to document his rule and his rights, as well as a new bureau of accounts to control the financial resources of his domain. His conquest of Normandy in 1204 confirmed and refined these innovations. His regime enlarged the social and political connections and basis of the Crown, introducing into government the urban middle classes and the CLERGY. He embarked on the great building projects in Paris at NOTRE-DAME, the palace or fortress of the Louvre, and a food market. Philip promoted the development of the city's commercial activities, and the growth of the university, making it the capital of his newly enlarged realm.

A wily diplomat and fine administrator, Philip also promoted a royal ideology and the notions of royal blood and consecration. In France, he carefully cultivated the church, which gave him a great deal of support, especially after he supported the Crusade against the ALBIGENSIANS in the south. He died at Mantes enroute to an ecclesiastical convocation in Paris on July 14, 1223.

Further reading: John W. Baldwin, *The Government of Philip Augustus: Foundations of French Royal Power in the Middle Ages* (Berkeley: University of California Press, 1986); Jim Bradbury, *Philip Augustus: King of France, 1180–1223* (New York: Longman, 1998); Elizabeth Hallam, and Judith Everard, *Capetian France, 987–1328,* 2d ed. (New York: Longman, 2001).

Philip IV the Fair (1268–1314) *king of France*
Born between April and June in 1268, Philip was the grandson of LOUIS IX and the second son of King Philip III the Bold (1245–85) and Isabella of ARAGON (d. 1271). In 1285 he succeeded his father, who had died on a failed Crusade against Aragon in support of his brother CHARLES I OF ANJOU. Philip IV soon restored peaceful relations with the Aragonese. Promoting the reputation of his ancestor Louis IX, he obtained his canonization in 1297. Conventionally pious and voicing moral imperatives, he maintained a realistic political program to enforce, consolidate, and expand royal authority and sovereignty. He sought to reduce the power of the great FIEFS or counties of his realm such as FLANDERS, waging a long war but suffering a serious defeat at the Battle of COURTRAI in 1302.

MAJOR CONFLICTS WITH THE PAPACY

He then confronted the pretensions of papal theocratic power over his kingdom by prosecuting clerics for crimes, refusing to permit papal taxation, and imposing emergency royal taxation on the church. These acts led to a confrontation with Pope BONIFACE VIII who was assaulted by one of his ministers in 1303, Philip was the antagonist against whom the papal bull *Unam Sanctam* was issued. He dismantled the rich crusader order of the TEMPLARS. Papal prestige suffered a precipitous decline because of its failures in this confrontation. He relied on advisers trained in the newly evolving system of Roman LAW that promoted secular central authority and independence from ecclesiastical control. The French Estates General, representing all ranks of society, convened for the first time in 1302 to discuss these controversies with the papacy.

FINANCIAL DIFFICULTIES UNRESOLVED

Differing from the policies followed by Louis IX and Philip III, Philip IV the Fair concentrated his political efforts on internally strengthening royal control of his own kingdom. He let his brother, Charles of Valois (1270–1325), pursue ambitions outside the kingdom. Philip often discussed crusading but never actually crusaded. He had major problems in financing his wars against EDWARD I and Flanders. He expanded taxation as much as he was able, debased the COINAGE, and defaulted on and attacked the resources of his Italian bankers. In 1306 he expelled the JEWS from his kingdom and confiscated their property. But none of these measures solved his fiscal difficulties, and the manipulation of the coinage caused considerable harm to the economy. Philip tried to use the marriage connections of his children for allies with limited success. There was a strong reaction against his ambitions and unscrupulous policies on his death. His successor, Louis X the Quarrelsome (r. 1314–16), had to make numerous concessions in royal prerogatives. At age 46, Philip died on November 29, 1314.

See also AVIGNON AND THE AVIGNONESE PAPACY; CLEMENT V, POPE; PARIS AND THE UNIVERSITY OF PARIS.

Further reading: Franklin J. Pegues, *The Lawyers of the Last Capetians* (Princeton, N.J.: Princeton University Press, 1962); Joseph R Strayer, *The Reign of Philip the Fair* (Princeton, N.J.: Princeton University Press, 1980); Elizabeth A. R. Brown, *Customary Aids and Royal Finance in Capetian France: The Marriage Aid of Philip the Fair* (Cambridge, Mass.: Mediaeval Academy of America, 1992); Charles T. Wood, ed., *Philip the Fair and Boniface VIII: State vs. Papacy* (New York: Holt, Rinehart, 1967).

Philip the Good (1396–1467) *duke of Burgundy*
Born on July 31, 1396, Philip was the son and successor of John the Fearless (r. 1404–19), the duke of BURGUNDY and count of FLANDERS. When his father was assassinated in 1419, he became duke of many of the wealthiest regions of FRANCE and the Low Countries. He blamed the assassination of his father on King CHARLES VII of FRANCE. He reigned for 47 years and conferred prosperity, prestige, and territorial expansion on his lands because he was an astute diplomat and judicious warrior. Philip tried to pursue an independent role among ENGLAND, France, and the empire. In the Treaty of Troyes in 1420, he allied with HENRY V of England, in an arrangement that enabled him to augment his control of his French holdings and solidify his possessions in the Low Countries. He expanded his domain by a second agreement in 1422 and a third treaty in 1430. His conquests of HOLLAND between 1425 and 1433 and of Luxembourg in 1443 and peaceful acquisitions of Namur in 1420 and BRABANT in 1430 greatly increased his territories. Philip, however, failed in 1447 to acquire the Crown of a restored kingdom of Lotharingia around the Rhine from the emperor Frederick III (r. 1452–93).

Within France, Philip offered little support to the government of Henry VI (r. 1422–61, 1470–71) of England. He later even aligned himself with his old enemy, Charles VII, in 1435 in the Treaty of Arras. Wary of a revived French monarchy, Philip sat out the last campaigns of the HUNDRED YEARS' WAR but gave shelter to the fugitive dauphin, the future LOUIS XI, in 1456. Despite this, his duchy was threatened again with war by the French Crown at the end of his reign.

HISTORICAL HINDSIGHT

Philip made much of ideas of CHIVALRY to strengthen the cohesiveness of his duchy, founding the Order of the Golden Fleece to link the nobility of his territories and to define a relationship with princes outside it. His court was famous for its spectacle, ritual, and festivals, all confirming his wealth and prestige. On the personal level, he played the role of handsome, courageous, pious, self-indulgent, and extravagant model chivalric KNIGHT and king.

He associated himself frequently with a proposed CRUSADE but never made any real efforts either to undertake one personally or support those who did. He supported some outstanding artists and writers of his time, such as Jan Van EYCK, his court painter. A great patron of the arts, he collected and commissioned illuminated manuscripts, tapestries, and PAINTINGS. He died on June 15, 1467.

Further reading: Joseph Calmette, *The Golden Age of Burgundy: The Magnificent Dukes and Their Courts,* trans. Doreen Weightman (1962; reprint New York: W. W. Norton, 1963); Otto Cartellieri, *The Court of Burgundy: Studies in the History of Civilization* (London: Kegan Paul, 1929); William R. Tyler, *Dijon and the Valois Dukes of Burgundy* (Norman: University of Oklahoma Press, 1971); Richard Vaughan, *Philip the Good: The Apogee of Burgundy* (New York: Barnes & Noble, 1970); Richard Vaughan, *Valois Burgundy* (Hamden, Conn.: Archon Books, 1975).

philosophy and theology   The reconciliation of philosophy, a love of and search for wisdom, and theology, true doctrine seeking GOD, was always a main concern for the exclusive, monotheistic religions of Christianity, ISLAM, and JUDAISM. Philosophers and theologians often had to reconcile reason or rational speculation, FAITH, and revelation. This difficulty became even more acute as the ideas and culture of the classical pagans, especially the Greeks, became more accessible.

FINER POINTS OF COMPARISON AND RECONCILIATION

There always had to be a theological aspect and development of medieval speculation. Orthodoxy was always to be maintained and defended. Philosophy itself had three aspects, all with theological implications: Moral philosophy dealt with action; natural philosophy was reserved for theory; rational philosophy distinguished the true from the false. Despite a great diversity of approaches and conceptions, medieval philosophy was a specific form of knowledge that was distinguished by its method and unique foundation. It was a work of reason, and its universal application was rarely questioned in the Middle Ages.

When these methods were applied to theological questions there were, however, always concerns about reconciling reason with faith. At the same time there were interaction and exchange among the philosophers and theologians of all three of these religions, particularly when they shared accurate texts and debated one another. In the later Middle Ages and RENAISSANCE, more new texts entered Europe with the increased interest in classical writers and cultures.

THE ISLAMIC PERSPECTIVE

These problems were of less importance in Islam, in which philosophy was more marginalized and called *Falsafa.* This concept tended to oppose KALAM, which served the purposes of the revealed law. *Falsafa* was interested in apologetic theology, methodology of LAW, mystical speculation, ethics, reflection on language, and the lessons of history. It never had official sanction and was often even linked with HERESY and heterodoxy. Greek philosophers were well known, especially ARISTOTLE and the NEOPLATONISTS. The SUNNA linked it with SHIA and speculation, and thus found it antithetical to Islam.

See also AQUINAS, THOMAS, SAINT; ARISTOTLE AND ARISTOTELIANISM IN THE MIDDLE AGES; AUGUSTINE OF HIPPO, SAINT; BOETHIUS; BONAVENTURE, SAINT; AL-GHAZALI; IBN RUSHD; ISLAM; JEWS AND JUDAISM; JUDAH BEN SAMUEL HALEVI; MAIMONIDES, MOSES; NOMINALISM; PLATO AND PLATONISM; REALISM; SCHOLASTICISM AND SCHOLASTIC METHOD; UNIVERSITIES AND SCHOOLS.

Further reading: Brian P. Copenhaver and Charles B. Schmitt, *Renaissance Philosophy* (Oxford: Oxford University Press, 1992); Henry Corbin, *History of Islamic Philosophy,* trans. Liadain Sherrard (1964; reprint, London: Kegan Paul International, 1993); Étienne Gilson, *Reason and Revelation in the Middle Ages* (New York: Charles Scribners's Sons, 1938); Étienne Gilson, *History of Christian Philosophy in the Middle Ages* (New York: Random House, 1955); Isaac Husik, *A History of Jewish Philosophy* (1941; reprint, Mineola, N.Y.: Dover Publications, 2002); Norman Kretzmann, Anthony Kenny, Jan Pinborg, and Eleonore Stump, eds., *The Cambridge History of Later Medieval Philosophy: From the Rediscovery of Aristotle to the Disintegration of Scholasticism, 1100–1600* (Cambridge: Cambridge University Press, 1982); Seyyed Hossein Nasr and Oliver Leaman, eds., *History of Islamic Philosophy,* 2 vols. (New York: Routledge, 1996).

Photian Schism   *See* PHOTIOS I THE GREAT, SAINT.

Photios I the Great, Saint (Photius) (ca. 810–ca. 893) *patriarch of Constantinople*
Photios was born in CONSTANTINOPLE about 810 of a noble family, the nephew of Patriarch Tarasios (r. 784–806). After the restoration of Orthodoxy during the Iconoclastic controversy and following a career, he was in charge of the imperial chancery. When the patriarch Ignatios (r. 847–858) was banished, the emperor Michael III the Drunkard (r. 842–867) replaced him with Photios. After successfully becoming a cleric in three days, he was consecrated patriarch on Christmas of 858. He soon held a synod, in early 859, that confirmed the deposition of Ignatios and the exile of his supporters. This was not an end of this problem which troubled the Byzantine Church until the end of the ninth century.

In 867, the new emperor, BASIL I, restored Ignatios, called a council at Constantinople (869–870) to approve

Ignatios (second tenure, 867–877), and deposed and sent Photios to a monastery. In 873, however, Basil I allowed Photios to be in charge of the education of his children. An agreement was reached between Ignatios and Photios. On Ignatios's death in 877 Photios became patriarch again. With the approval of Pope John VIII (r. 872–882), a new council at Constantinople in 879–880 canceled the decisions taken against Photios a decade before. On the death of Basil I in 886, Leo VI the Wise (r. 886–912) deposed Photios and replaced him with his own brother, Stephen I (r. 886–893). Banished once again to a monastery, this time to Armeniaki, he died there about 893.

FURTHER CONFLICT AND SOME SUCCESS

Photios's patriarchate was the occasion for successful Christianizing missions to the BULGARS and for conflict with the PAPACY. The unbending personality of Pope Nicholas I (r. 858–867) and the Bulgarian conversions to Orthodoxy aggravated the developing schism between ROME and Constantinople. The pope held a synod in March 862 and annulled the decisions taken against Ignatios and another Roman council in April 863 condemned Photios. King BORIS I, KHAN of BULGARIA, was baptized in about 860 and sought the creation of a patriarchate for Bulgaria. When Photios declined to give his permission, Boris applied to Rome. The Byzantine clergy was expelled and replaced by Latin clerics. Photios in 867 denounced Rome for its conduct in Bulgaria, some of its practices such as Saturday FASTS, priestly CELIBACY, and certain dogmatic innovations such as the addition of the *FILIOQUE* CLAUSE to the Creed. He next called a council at Constantinople that anathematized Pope Nicholas. In autumn 867, the uncompromising Nicholas I was replaced by Adrian II (r. 867–972). A council in Rome in June 869 condemned the Photian council of 867 and anathematized Photios. It further called for a great council, which met in Constantinople in 869–870 and ratified the Roman positions and condemned Photios. The Bulgarian czar, Boris I, became dissatisfied with the pope and turned to Constantinople for support. Yet another council at Constantinople in 879–880 rehabilitated Photios and annulled the decisions of 869–870.

WORKS AND LEGACY

Photios left letters, HOMILIES, and dogmatic works against the *Filioque* clause. He was a major figure in a ninth-century Byzantine renaissance with his encyclopedic work called *Bibliotheca* (Library). It showed the culture of a learned man and constituted a monument of early Byzantine HUMANISM. His *Treatise on the Holy Spirit* formed the basis for later Byzantine objections to Western ideas on dogma. The Photian schism about the nature of Christ and Papal authority was an important step in dividing the Eastern and Western Churches.

Further reading: Photios I, *The Homilies of Photius, Patriarch of Constantinople*, trans. Cyril Mango (Cambridge, Mass.: Harvard University Press, 1958); Francis Dvornik, *The Photian Schism, History and Legend* (1948; reprint, Cambridge: Cambridge University Press, 1970); Richard S. Haugh, *Photius and the Carolingians: The Trinitarian Controversy* (Belmont, Mass.: Nordland, 1975); Joan M. Hussey, *The Orthodox Church in the Byzantine Empire* (Oxford: Oxford University Press, 1986); Liliana Simeonova, *Diplomacy of the Letter and the Cross: Photios, Bulgaria and the Papacy, 860s–880s* (Amsterdam: A. M. Hakkert, 1998); Warren T. Treadgold, *The Nature of the Bibliotheca of Photius* (Washington, D.C.: Dumbarton Oaks Center for Byzantine Studies, 1980); N. G. Wilson, *Scholars of Byzantium* (Baltimore: Johns Hopkins University Press, 1983).

Piast dynasty   The Piasts were the reigning dynasty of the state of POLAND from its beginnings to 1370. Piast, a farmer, was the legendary founder of the Kingdom of Poland, according to the early 12th-century chronicle by the "Gallus Anonymous." He united Slavic tribes between the Oder and Vistula Rivers. This legend probably related some of the events that transpired in the ninth century. The first member of the family to be documented was Mieszko I (r. 963–992). He was the creator of a Polish state whose center was at Gniezno. Mieszko I and his son, BOLESLAV I THE GREAT or Brave became rulers in popular memory and legend over a "Golden Age." Mieszko II Lambert (r. 1025–34) had a good education and married a granddaughter of the emperor Otto II (r. 973–983), but under his reign the state lost several territories to BOHEMIA and the HOLY ROMAN EMPIRE. His son, Casimir I the Restorer (r. 1034–58), led at the cost of a long effort a reconstruction of the Polish state, whose center moved to CRACOW. Casimir's son, Boleslav II, the Bold (r. 1058–79), was crowned king in 1076. He lost wars to the Bohemians and became very dependent on the clergy for support.

The murder of Bishop Stanislas of Cracow in 1079, perhaps by the king's order, led to a revolt and flight of the king to HUNGARY, where he died in 1082. He was succeeded by his brother, Ladislas I Herman (r. 1079– 1102), who was a weak and incompetent ruler. Boleslav III Wrymouth (r. 1102–38) led several successful wars early in his reign and became the real founder of the kingdom. He ruthlessly put down a Pomeranian revolt, but the wars of his later years against the Bohemians and Hungarians were fruitless. When he died, he divided the kingdom into duchies for each of already quarreling sons. After this the family disintegrated into a series of lines linked to particular provinces. The princes of Cracow were supposed to exercise supreme government over the others, but there were repeated challenges to the unity of the state and internecine conflicts during the 13th century. Prince Ladislas (r. 1314–33) the Short had himself crowned king of Poland at Cracow in 1320 with the

Polish Rulers: Piast Dynasty

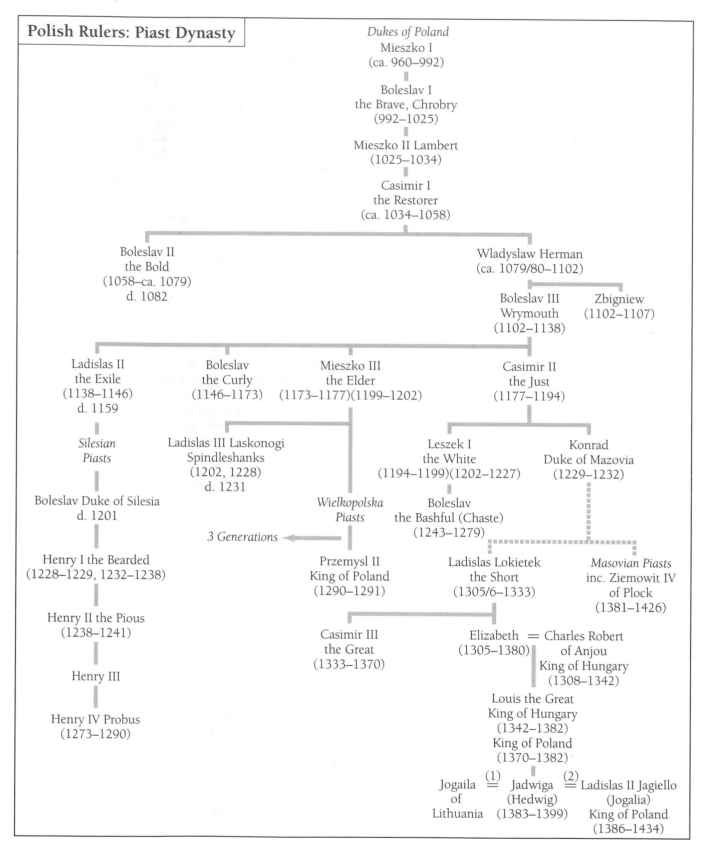

Dukes of Poland
Mieszko I
(ca. 960–992)

Boleslav I
the Brave, Chrobry
(992–1025)

Mieszko II Lambert
(1025–1034)

Casimir I
the Restorer
(ca. 1034–1058)

Boleslav II
the Bold
(1058–ca. 1079)
d. 1082

Wladyslaw Herman
(ca. 1079/80–1102)

Boleslav III   Zbigniew
Wrymouth   (1102–1107)
(1102–1138)

Ladislas II   Boleslav   Mieszko III   Casimir II
the Exile   the Curly   the Elder   the Just
(1138–1146)   (1146–1173)   (1173–1177)(1199–1202)   (1177–1194)
d. 1159

Silesian   Ladislas III Laskonogi   Leszek I   Konrad
Piast   Spindleshanks   the White   Duke of Mazovia
          (1202, 1228)   (1194–1199)(1202–1227)   (1229–1232)
          d. 1231

Boleslav Duke of Silesia   *Wielkopolska*   Boleslav
d. 1201   *Piast*   the Bashful (Chaste)
          (1243–1279)

Henry I the Bearded   *3 Generations* ←   Przemysl II   Ladislas Lokietek   *Masovian Piast*
(1228–1229, 1232–1238)   King of Poland   the Short   inc. Ziemowit IV
          (1290–1291)   (1305/6–1333)   of Plock
          (1381–1426)

Henry II the Pious
(1238–1241)   Casimir III   Elizabeth = Charles Robert
          the Great   (1305–1380)   of Anjou
          (1333–1370)   King of Hungary
Henry III   (1308–1342)

          Louis the Great
Henry IV Probus   King of Hungary
(1273–1290)   (1342–1382)
          King of Poland
          (1370–1382)

          Jogaila ═⁽¹⁾ Jadwiga ═⁽²⁾ Ladislas II Jagiello
          of   (Hedwig)   (Jogalia)
          Lithuania   (1383–1399)   King of Poland
          (1386–1434)

support of the pope and the Angevin rulers of Hungary. His son, Casimir III the Great (r. 1333–70), ensured peace and internal prosperity with success in diplomacy and in war against the Tatars. Ending the dynasty and dying without issue, he left the throne to his nephew, Louis the Great of Anjou, king of Hungary in 1370. He died in 1382. Other Piast princes ruled Silesia and Mozovia longer but were never kings of a united Poland.

Further reading: Norman Davies, *God's Playground: A History of Poland,* Vol. 1 (New York: Columbia University Press, 1984); Paul Knoll, *The Rise of the Polish Monarchy: Piast Poland in East-Central Europe, 1320–1370* (Chicago: University of Chicago Press, 1972).

Piccolomini, Aeneas Sylvius *See* PIUS II, POPE.

Pico della Mirandola, Giovanni *See* MIRANDOLA, GIOVANNI PICO DELLA.

Picts The Picts were a Celtic tribe in SCOTLAND who were never conquered by the Romans. Their society was based on clans led by military chieftains, who frequently attacked Roman Britain in the fourth and fifth centuries. By the end of the fifth century, they were ruled by kings; in the sixth century Irish monks arrived to spread Christianity. About the same time Scottish tribes from IRELAND penetrated the southwestern part of the kingdom, and by the eighth century the Picts had been absorbed by the Scots, forming a newly united kingdom.

The Picts in the south spoke a Celtic language, related to Welsh, but the language of those in the north has remained unclear. Until the settlement of Scandinavians in the north and on the islands, during the ninth and 10th centuries, the Picts along with the Scots probably controlled all of Scotland north of the Forth and Clyde. Their new royal family followed the principle of matrilineal succession: That is, the kings were selected according to the royal status of their mother rather than their father. Thus a king's nephew or brother, rather than his son, would succeed him.

See also MACALPIN, KENNETH.

Further reading: J. M. P. Calise, ed., *Pictish Sourcebook: Documents of Medieval Legend and Dark Age History* (Westport, Conn.: Greenwood Press, 2002); Sally M. Foster, *Picts, Gaels, and Scots: Early Historic Scotland* (London: B.T. Batsford/Historic Scotland, 1996); Isabel Henderson, *The Picts* (New York: Praeger, 1967); Lloyd Robert Laing, *The Picts and the Scots* (Wolfeboro Falls, N.H.: Alan Sutton, 1993); A. F. T. Wainwright, ed., *The Problem of the Picts* (1956; reprint, Westport, Conn.: Greenwood Press, 1970).

Piero della Francesca (de' Franceschi) (1410/1420–1492) *painter*
Piero was born at Borgo San Sepolcro in Umbria between 1410 and 1420, the son of Benedetto dei Franceschi and Romana Pierino da Monterchi. Little is known of his artistic training and formation. He seemed to have been impressed by the work of Paolo UCCELLO, for his geometrical formalism, and by the paintings of Fra ANGELICO. In 1439 historical records trace him to FLORENCE, where he worked with Domenico Veneziano (ca. 1400–61) and Alessio Baldovinetti (1426–99) on a cycle of paintings now lost. In 1445, his first known work was commissioned, the *Misericordia Polyptych,* clearly influenced by MASACCIO. From 1450 his painting the *Baptism of Christ* has survived in the National Gallery in London. In the same year, Piero was at the ESTE court at FERRARA, where he painted more FRESCOES that are now lost to us. In 1451, he was working for Sigismondo Pandolfo Malatesta (1417–68), the lord of Rimini. He painted an idealized and flattering version of his patron and Peter, his namesake saint, in an architectural space suggested by the style of Leon Battista ALBERTI. Between 1450 and 1455 he painted the pregnant Madonna for a chapel at Monterchi near Arezzo, where his mother was probably buried.

In the later 1450s he traveled to ROME to decorate the Vatican rooms later covered over by Raphael's frescoes. From around this time were the famous *Flagellation of Christ* in Urbino, and the cycle of the *History of Discovery of the Holy Cross* from 1466 for the choir of the

Piero della Francesca, portrait of Federico da Montefeltro, duke of Urbino, Uffizi, Florence, Italy *(Scala / Art Resource)*

church of San Francesco at Arezzo. It was inspired by the frescoes of Agnolo Gaddi (d. 1369) and by JAMES OF VORAGINE's GOLDEN LEGEND. In these paintings and frescoes, he showed the influence of Flemish art, combining geometrical styles and perspectives with light and naturalism. In 1465 he was at the court of FEDERICO DA MONTEFELTRO, the lord of Urbino, for whom he painted portraits of Federico and his wife, Battista Sforza. Between 1472 and 1474, he created the Brera altarpiece in MILAN, depicting the Virgin gazing at the sleeping Christ Child. Piero wrote treatises on geometry, perspective, and PAINTING. He stopped painting in the early 1470s; however, there is a reference to yet another lost fresco in 1478. Although Vasari reported that his sight might have failed, he probably devoted his attention to writing until he died in 1492.

Further reading: Perry Brooks, *Piero della Francesca: The Arezzo Frescoes* (New York: Rizzoli, 1992); Kenneth Clark, *Piero della Francesca,* 2d ed. (1969; reprint, Ithaca, N.Y.: Cornell University Press, 1981); Carlo Ginzburg, *The Enigma of Piero: Piero della Francesca,* trans. Martin Ryle and Kate Soper (London: Verso, 2000); Anna Maria Maetzke and Carlo Bertelli, eds., *Piero della Francesca: The Legend of the True Cross in the Church of San Francesco, Arezzo* (New York: St. Martin's Press, 2001); Jeryldene M. Wood, ed., *The Cambridge Companion to Piero della Francesca* (Cambridge: Cambridge University Press, 2002).

Pierre d'Ailly   *See* AILLY, PIERRE D'.

Piers Plowman   The allegorical work called *The Visions of Will Concerning Piers Plowman* existed in many manuscripts from the 14th and 15th centuries and in several printed versions from the 16th century. They were linked with an author named William LANGLAND, who referred to himself as Will several times in the manuscripts. There were three versions, known as A, B, and C, all said to have been composed between about 1360 and 1395. They were allegorical accounts of the corruption of society and an attempt to purify it through a certain Piers the Plowman, the personification of the ordinary man. He sought goodness through humility, honest endeavor, and obedience to the law of GOD. This didactic, somewhat satirical, and alliterative poem could be read in several ways. There have been numerous disputes about the relationships of the different versions and whether they were written by one person.

Piers Plowman was a long dream allegory describing aspects of social and religious conditions in ENGLAND that needed reform. The author used the techniques of the dream and allegory for a moral and religious purpose, to examine the natures of heavenly love and virtue, at both the literal and figurative levels. This view of the world left little room for sympathy for conditions as they were. The world had been corrupted by love of money and by vice pretending to be virtue, especially among the CLERGY. Its concern for the poor, the oppressed, and the wretched was obvious and credible. *Piers Plowman* was contemporary with the Peasant Rebellion of 1381, built on popular religious ideas, anticlericalism, and contemporary exemplars or didactic stories common in sermons.

See also JUSTICE; SOCIAL STATUS AND STRUCTURE VISIONS AND DREAMS.

Further reading: William Langland, *Piers the Plowman,* trans. J. F. Goodridge (Harmondsworth: Penguin Classics, 1959); David Aers, *Chaucer, Langland, and the Creative Imagination* (London: Routledge and Kegan Paul, 1980); John A. Alford, ed., *A Companion to Piers Plowman* (Berkeley: University of California Press, 1988); Morton W. Bloomfield, *Piers Plowman as a Fourteenth-Century Apocalypse* (New Brunswick, N.J.: Rutgers University Press, 1962); Charlotte Brewer, *Editing Piers Plowman: The Evolution of the Text* (Cambridge: Cambridge University Press, 1996); Derek Pearsall, *An Annotated Critical Bibliography of Langland* (Ann Arbor: University of Michigan Press, 1990).

Pietro of Morrone   *See* CELESTINE V, POPE AND THE CELESTINE ORDER.

pilgrimage and pilgrimage sites   In Christianity, JUDAISM, and ISLAM, a *pilgrimage* could be defined as "a journey to a holy place done out of religious piety." The pilgrimage was supposed to be a manifestation of piety and was one of the five pillars of Islam. The HAJJ to MECCA was required sometime during the life of every Muslim. The pilgrim was one who devotedly, perhaps penitentially, certainly voluntarily, exiled him or herself to break with the world, purifying his or her souls by the very fact of departure. Some Christian pilgrims even wandered perpetually, seeking pardon for their sins. Pilgrims were directed to the temple in the Jewish BIBLE then to the holy places that had been sanctified by the passage of Christ or the presence of RELICS. There were two main sites for medieval Christianity: Christ's tomb at JERUSALEM and the tombs of Saints Peter and Paul at ROME. In the ninth century another was added, the tomb wrongly considered to be that of Saint James the Great at Compostela in SPAIN. Eventually it became possible to hire another to perform a meritorious pilgrimage.

The number of local places of pilgrimage grew as a result of intense popular piety and the realization by the CLERGY that such visits could produce considerable revenues while helping people save their SOUL. The relics at these locations could supposedly produce the MIRACLES that seekers hoped for, so sanctuaries abounded all over Europe, especially as more relics and saints' bodies were found or discerned. Papal jubilees or HOLY YEARS in

Pilgrimage Routes and Places

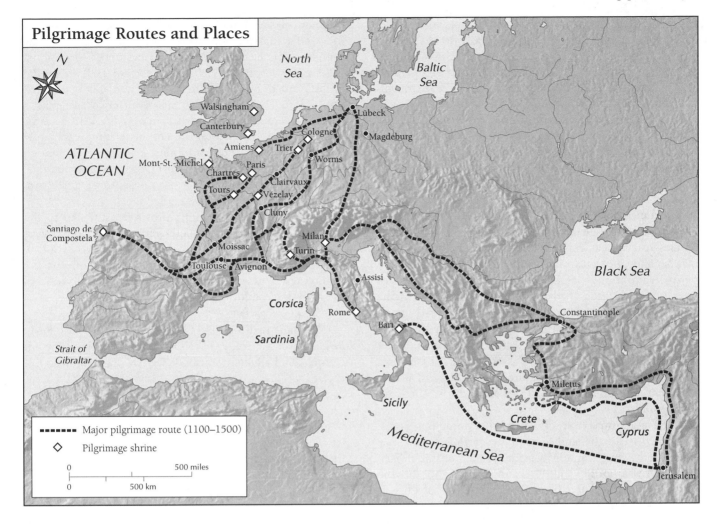

Rome produced revenue for the people of Rome and prestige for the Holy See. The rituals of pilgrimage became more elaborate over the course of the Middle Ages, and the status and legal rights of pilgrims became more defined and protected in canon LAW and practice.

The CRUSADES were seen as a form of pilgrimage. They could also be an interesting, albeit somewhat dangerous, form of recreational travel. In the later Middle Ages, the more mystically minded clergy and LAITY set about on interior pilgrimages of the mind and soul to GOD. As pious works designed to gain merit and GRACE, they became a primary target of many of the Protestant reformers of the 16th century.

See also BONIFACE VIII, POPE; INDULGENCES; PALESTINE.

Further reading: Richard W. Barber, *Pilgrimages* (Woodbridge, England: Boydell Press, 1991); Linda Kay Davidson, *Pilgrimage in the Middle Ages: A Research Guide* (New York: Garland, 1993); R. C. Finucane, *Miracles and Pilgrims: Popular Beliefs in Medieval England* (Totowa, N.J.: Rowman & Littlefield, 1977); Donald R. Howard, *Writers and Pilgrims: Medieval Pilgrimage Narratives and Their Posterity* (Berkeley: University of California Press, 1980); George Majeska, *Russian Travelers to Constantinople*

in the Fourteenth and Fifteenth Centuries (Washington, D.C.: Dumbarton Oaks Research Library and Collection, 1984); Jonathan Sumption, *Pilgrimage: An Image of Mediaeval Religion* (London: Faber and Faber, 1975); Gary Vikan, *Byzantine Pilgrimage Art* (Washington, D.C.: Dumbarton Oaks Center for Byzantine Studies, 1982); Diana Webb, *Medieval European Pilgrimage, c. 700–c. 1500* (New York: Palgrave, 2002).

pipe rolls The pipe rolls contained the financial accounts of the COURT OF EXCHEQUER in ENGLAND. Many of them have been preserved and have been used as important sources for the economic and administrative history of medieval England.

Further reading: Richard Fitzneale, *Dialogus de Scaccario—The Course of the Exchequer,* ed. and trans. Charles Johnson, with corrections by F. E. L. Carter and D. E. Greenway (Oxford: Clarendon Press, 1983); Pipe Roll Society, London, *Introduction to the Study of the Pipe Rolls* (1884; reprint, Vaduz: Kraus Reprint, 1966); Reginald Lane Poole, *The Exchequer in the Twelfth Century* (Oxford: Clarendon Press, 1912).

Pisa Medieval Pisa was an Italian city in TUSCANY on an alluvial plain formed by the Arno, a short distance, 6 miles, from the Tyrrhenian or Mediterranean coast. Its original position, at the intersection of the rivers Arno and Serchio and connected with main roads, was strategically protected and important in the city's development.

At the end of the Roman Empire, the fortunes of Pisa declined, while the buildings and architecture were oriented toward defensive requirements, mainly fortified buildings. During the rule of the FRANKS, from the eighth century, churches were added to the urban landscape. Its commercial exchanges and links with the eastern Mediterranean were never interrupted and enabled the city to have an appearance and culture of its own, based on classical models enriched with Byzantine or Arab elements. The CRUSADES produced added commercial prosperity from the 11th century, as did the conquest of SARDINIA in 1163, as had that of CORSICA earlier in the 10th century. A cloth and SILK industry evolved in the 13th century. However, Pisa suffered a devastating defeat by its great rival GENOA at the Battle of Meloria in 1284 and lost most of its colonial possessions in the eastern Mediterranean. It never reacquired its prestige or power after that, and the PLAGUE of 1348 might have killed half of its population.

These traumas were followed by numerous social conflicts in the city and control by various tyrants. By 1406, after a long war, Pisa was under the control of FLORENCE. An important church council called to end the GREAT SCHISM met there from March to August of 1409. It tried to end the Great Schism by deposing the two pretenders but failed and merely elected yet a third pope. It remained an important port until silt deposited by the Arno blocked navigation up the river to the city by the mid-15th century.

ROMANESQUE PISA; THE CATHEDRAL

From the 11th century, Pisan architecture saw its greatest accomplishment in the complex or building in the Piazza dei Miracoli. There the bell tower, CATHEDRAL, Camposanto or graveyard, and baptistery were built. The occasion traditionally given for transforming the old, simple complex was an important military victory in 1063/64, when off PALERMO a small Pisan fleet defeated a powerful Arab one and sacked the city. The planning of the area and a new group of buildings were entrusted to Maestro Buscheto. Buscheto tried to build a sacred complex reflecting the civil and urban-political ideals of Pisa. The works proceeded comparatively rapidly, especially from 1189, so that in 1116, 50 years after its beginning, a cathedral was completed; it was consecrated two years later.

A decision to enlarge the cathedral was made soon after 1116 and construction was then directed by Rainaldo, Buscheto's collaborator from 1110. Between 1115 and 1130 he furnished the façade with an extensive program of sculpture. The largely unknown Guglielmo followed Rainaldo, who with workshop worked on the sculptures of the lower façade and the upper levels, during the 1160s and 1170s. An important and influential pulpit carved by Giovanni PISANO was not completed until 1310. The small octagonal baptistery was replaced by the present cylindrical structure over the 12th century. In 1170 or shortly before, the famous leaning campanile or bell tower was added and almost immediately started to lean perhaps because of poorly designed foundations. By 1278 a final element, the Camposanto or graveyard, was completed.

The city's great economic prosperity attained in the 12th century was accompanied by a large increase in population, and suburbs had to be added, encircled by a new set of walls. In the 14th century the city suffered the beginnings of a severe economic depression and a long-suspension of building activities.

See also ROMANESQUE ART.

Further reading: David Herlihy, *Pisa in the Early Renaissance: A Study of Urban Growth* (New Haven, Conn.: Yale University Press, 1958); William Heywood, *A History of Pisa, Eleventh and Twelfth Centuries* (Cambridge: Cambridge University Press, 1921); Janet Ross, *The Story of Pisa* (London: J. M. Dent, 1909).

Pisan, Christine de (Pizan, of Pisa) (1364–ca. 1430) *French poet, author*
Christine's life can be reconstructed from her literary works, which are highly revealing about her and her ideas about writing. She was born in ITALY, probably in VENICE, in 1364 and moved to FRANCE in 1368 with her father, a certain Tommaso Pizzano, a Bolognese doctor and astrologist. She looked back on her childhood as a golden age. She much admired the French King, CHARLES V THE WISE. In 1389, at age 25, she became the widow of Étienne du Castel, her husband and a notary in the royal household, by whom she had had three children. After the end of this happy marriage, she had to face and surmount many financial difficulties. From 1400 on, she had to live by her writing, viewing it as "becoming a man." As a writer she first wrote love poetry and then participated in the debate over the satirical ideas about women in the ROMAN DE LA ROSE. She defended the honor and position of women. Much admired by her contemporaries, she also wrote lyrical and didactic poems, ballads, a biography of Charles V, and a manual for the education of women.

She knew well the from classical antiquity, in French or in LATIN. She adapted these pagan ideas to Christian morality and created distillations touching on nearly every intellectual field, including chivalry and the art of war. She gained the patronage of the dukes of Orléans, BURGUNDY, and Berry. Christine wished, moreover, to be a critical and constructive political adviser. She had little success in coping with the madness of Charles VI (r. 1380–1422), the king of France, and in resolving a civil war between Burgundy and the rest of France. Frustrated, she retired probably to Poissy, reappearing only to celebrate JOAN of Arc in a poem in 1429. Her writing tells us much about court life around 1400 and contemporary ideas and reactions to female authors. She died in 1430 or as late as 1434.

Further reading: Christine de Pisan, *The Treasure of the City of Ladies* (Harmondsworth: Penguin Books, 1985); Christine de Pizan, *The Book of the Body Politic*, ed. Kate Langdon Forhan (Cambridge: Cambridge University Press, 1994); Christine de Pisan, *Christine de Pizan's Letter of Othea to Hector*, ed. Jane Chance (Newburyport, Mass.: Focus Information Group, 1997); Angus Kennedy, *Christine de Pizan: A Bibliographical Guide* (London: Grant and Cutler, 1994); Charity Cannon Willard, *Christine de Piza: Her Life and Works* (New York: Persea Books, 1984).

Pisanello (Antonio Pisano, Il Pisanello) (1395–ca. 1450/55) *court painter*

Antonio Pisano, called Pisanello, was a maker of medals and a painter, who worked at the most impressive Italian courts of his time, the VISCONTI and the SFORZA at MILAN, the Gonzaga at Mantua, the ESTE at FERRARA, the Malatesta at Rimini, the Aragonese kings at NAPLES, and Pope EUGENIUS IV at ROME.

Born at PISA in about 1395, he grew up in VERONA. He had many contacts with the artists of the time and especially with GENTILE DA FABRIANO. Before that he had studied at Verona and painted FRESCOES now lost in the Doge's Palace in VENICE in 1415–22. Others are lost, such as those in the castle of Mantua, and those at Saint John Lateran in Rome. All done between 1422 and 1426. Later, in 1441, he did a portrait of Lionello D'Este (1407–50), part of a competition with Jacopo BELLINI, another portrait of a princess of the house of Este, the *Vision of Saint Eustace;* and the *Madonna with Saints Anthony Abbot and George.*

Famous for his metals and as draftsman, Pisanello's international GOTHIC painting style included sharp forms, naturalistic detail, as well as color. In his drawings, in the Vallardi Codex, and in his medals, there are a clear lines, such as in his images of the Byzantine emperor JOHN VIII PALAIOLOGOS; Filippo Maria Visconti (1392–1447); Cecilia, Gianfrancesco (1466–1519), and Ludovico (1412–78) Gonzaga; Francesco I Sforza (1401–66); Lionello d'Este; ALFONSO V of ARAGON; and many other court and literary personalities of the time. He died about 1455.

Further reading: Jakob Rosenberg, *Great Draughtsmen from Pisanello to Picasso* (Cambridge, Mass.: Harvard University Press, 1959); Luke Syson and Dillian Gordon, *Pisanello: Painter to the Renaissance Court* (London: Yale University Press, 2001); Johanna Woods-Marsden, *The Gonzaga of Mantua and Pisanello's Arthurian Frescoes* (Princeton, N.J.: Princeton University Press, 1988).

Pisano, Andrea (Andrea di Ugolino di Nino da Pontedera) (ca. 1290–ca. 1348/49) *goldsmith, sculptor*

Andrea da Pontedera, was trained in PISA as a goldsmith, before winning fame for the bronze south doors of the baptistery in FLORENCE done between 1330 and 1336. These doors were innovative in their assimilation of French styles in an Italian context. On GIOTTO's death, Andrea was called upon in 1337 to continue Giotto's work on the bell tower of Santa Maria del Fiore, the CATHEDRAL of Florence. He later appeared in documents at Pisa and then at Orvieto, where he was in charge of the works for the cathedral. He died at Orvieto in 1348.

See also GOTHIC ART AND ARCHITECTURE.

Further reading: Charles Avery, *Florentine Renaissance Sculpture* (London: J. Murray, 1970); G. H. Crichton and E. R. Cichton, *Nicola Pisano and the Revival of Sculpture in Italy* (Cambridge: Cambridge University Press, 1938); Anita Fiderer Moskowitz, *Nicola Pisano's Arca di San Domenico and Its Legacy* (University Park: Published for College Art Association by the Pennsylvania State University Press, 1994); Anita Fiderer Moskowitz, *Italian Gothic Sculpture, c. 1250–c. 1400* (Cambridge: Cambridge University Press, 2001).

Pisano, Giovanni (ca. 1245/50–ca. 1314/18) *pioneer in the development of modern sculpture*

The son of Niccolò PISANO, Giovanni was trained in his father's studio, collaborating with him and his assistants on the pulpit of the CATHEDRAL between 1265 and 1268 at SIENA and on the large fountain, finished in 1278, at Perugia. Between 1284 and 1299 he lived in Siena, as the master builder of the cathedral. From 1295 he moved to PISA, where again he was in charge of the works on the cathedral between 1299 and 1308. He created a pulpit for that cathedral between 1302 and 1310. At about the same time, he worked in other cities doing a pulpit of Sant' Andrea in Pistoia in 1301 and the tomb of Margaret, the wife of the emperor Henry VII of Luxembourg (r. 1308–13), in GENOA. Besides assisting in the design of the façade of the cathedral of Massa Marittima in TUSCANY, he began the façade of the Cathedral of Siena.

Giovanni followed his father's forms in his earliest works but soon grew to express his own sensibility. He was much more intensely interested than his father in French GOTHIC art. He may have traveled to FRANCE between 1270 and 1275, perhaps to RHEIMS and PARIS. He, too, drew on French sculpture, inspired by the ivory carvings circulating widely at Pisa. Giovanni was also interested in the forms of classical art, but from it he sought ideas and models different from those of his father. He died probably at Siena between 1314 and 1318.

See also GOTHIC ART AND ARCHITECTURE.

Further reading: Michael Ayrton, *Giovanni Pisano, Sculptor* (New York: Weybright & Talley, 1969); John Pope-Hennessy, *Italian Gothic Sculpture,* Vol. 1, 4th ed. (London: Phaidon Press, 1996); Adolfo Venturi, *Giovanni Pisano: His Life and Work* (Paris: Pegasus Press, 1928); John White, *Art and Architecture in Italy, 1250–1400,* 2d ed. (1967; reprint, New York: Viking Penguin, 1987).

Pisano, Niccolò (Nicola) (ca. 1220–1280/84) *regarded by some as the founder of modern sculpture, Italian artist*
Niccolò was probably a native of Apulia in southern Italy. He was probably trained in LOMBARDY and in the workshops of the emperor FREDERICK II, in the revived classical style. He knew French and GOTHIC sculpture mainly through ivory and bronze works and studied the works of antiquity, as preserved in ancient sarcophagi or caskets in the graveyard at PISA.

His most famous work was a pulpit in the Pisan baptistery. It was a hexagonal construction, remarkable for its monumental conception as well as its adaptation of the iconographical program to the style of the surrounding architecture. Its panels illustrated the narrative of Christ's infancy and Crucifixion and the LAST JUDGMENT. In 1264 he carved with other artists the shrine for Saint DOMINIC in San Domenico in BOLOGNA and a deposition from the Cross in the CATHEDRAL in LUCCA. From 1260 to 1268 he worked on the pulpit in the cathedral of SIENA. Its structure was also octagonal, with the iconography again centered on Christ. Much more innovation was his bas-relief done for the lower basin of a major fountain at Perugia made between 1277 and 1278. Much of this was done with his son, Giovanni PISANO, who worked in his workshop for years. Niccolò was celebrated by Vasari in connection with the architecture of the church of Santa Trinità in FLORENCE. He died in Pisa between 1280 and 1284.

See also GOTHIC ART AND ARCHITECTURE.

Further reading: G. H. Crichton, *Nicola Pisano and the Revival of Sculpture in Italy* (Cambridge: Cambridge University Press, 1938); Barbara W. Dodsworth, *The Arca di San Domenico* (New York: P. Lang, 1995); Anita Fiderer Moskowitz, *Nicola Pisano's Arca di San Domenico and Its Legacy* (University Park: Published for College Art Association by the Pennsylvania State University Press, 1994).

Pius II, Pope (Aeneas Silvius Piccolomini, Enea Silvio) (1405–1464) *Italian humanist*
Born in Corsignano near SIENA in 1405, Aeneas Silvius Piccolomini was a member of an impoverished branch of that noble family. Despite preferring humanist studies, he

first became a doctor of LAW. From 1432 he was a household familiar of cardinals and bishops, whom he accompanied on their missions in ITALY and elsewhere. In 1436 attended the COUNCIL OF BASEL where he supported conciliar ideas as secretary to the antipope Felix V (Amadeus VIII of Savoy, 1383–1451).

He joined the imperial chancery of the emperor Frederick III (r. 1440–93), who crowned him poet laureate in 1442 and in 1450 appointed him a councilor of the empire. In 1446 he went to ROME as an ambassador. After making amends to Pope EUGENIUS IV for his past indiscretions in supporting conciliarism, having several illegitimate children, and writing erotic stories, he was ordained a priest in 1446. Pope Nicholas V (r. 1447–55) appointed him bishop of Trieste in 1447, then of SIENA in 1449. In 1456 Pope Calixtus III (r. 1455–58) made him cardinal of Santa Sabina. After 1455 he lived in Rome and was elected pope on August 19, 1458, and crowned on September 3 at age 53, though already in failing health. He took the name Pius after Virgil's Pius Aeneas in the *Aeneid.* According to his own account, he was chosen over the French candidate, Guillaume d'Estouteville (1403–83), because of the support of the duke of MILAN, King Ferdinand I (r. 1458–94) of NAPLES, and the cardinals Borgia, Colonna, and Barbo.

ATTEMPT AT CRUSADE

His main preoccupation during his reign was the CRUSADE against the OTTOMAN TURKS because of the catastrophic defeat at the Battle of Varna in 1444 and the fall of CONSTANTINOPLE in 1453. Pius II issued the bull *Vocavit nos* in October 1458 and summoned all princes to a congress at Mantua in 1459. There was little

The late 15th-century palace and loggia of the Piccolomini family in Siena, made possible by the benefits derived from the papacy of Pius II *(Courtesy Edward English)*

The architectural remains for a massive expansion of the cathedral of Siena that had to be abandoned because of financial difficulties resulting from the plague of 1347, among other causes *(Courtesy Edward English)*

response. Realizing that peace within Europe was necessary before rulers would contemplate a crusade, Pius II sought to mediate among the Italian states and the northern European states. He recognized Ferdinand I of Aragon as the king of NAPLES. He further persuaded King LOUIS XI of France to agree to minor changes in the PRAGMATIC SANCTION OF BOURGES in 1461 limiting the control of the French Crown over the French church. He was unable to prevent the wars in GERMANY and obliged to excommunicate the lord of the Tyrol for an attack on NICHOLAS OF CUSA, Pius's friend, and the archbishop of Mainz.

The pope also had to deal with conflict in BOHEMIA caused by George Poděbrady, the king of Bohemia, and the hostility of the heretical UTRAQUISTS. When Pius II revived the idea of a Crusade in 1462–63, Venice, George SKANDERBEG OF ALBANIA, and MATTHIAS I CORVINUS OF HUNGARY promised their support. The discovery of alum at Tolfa near ROME provided a new source of papal income that could be used toward the expenses of a crusade. Despite ill health, Pius II tried to travel to Ancona on the Adriatic Sea, where he was supposed to embark as a leader. Disappointed again, he found only a few Venetian galleys and few crusaders there. He died there on August 15, 1464. His heart was buried in Ancona and his body was taken to Rome.

OTHER ISSUES OF THE PAPACY

Pius II as pope abandoned any pretense of support for CONCILIARISM and published a bull on January 18, 1460, in which he forbade the submission of any papal acts to any scrutiny by a council. He spent most of his reign in or near Siena, sometimes conducting papal business under a tree in the open. He also badgered that city to readmit his family, who had earlier made attempts to establish a lordship over the city and been banished for their schemes and uprisings, into its politics. By threatening to move the bishopric of Siena to Florence and by promising to canonize CATHERINE OF SIENA, he persuaded the COMMUNE to permit the Piccolomini to reenter its political circle. He also had the village of his birth, Corsignano, reconstructed into a model of Renaissance architecture, renamed Pienza. As soon as Pius died, the Sienese political rights of the Piccolomini were revoked; Catherine of Siena had already been canonized.

He tried to defend the JEWS and to reform the morals and quality of the CLERGY, with little success. Before his conversion to a more moral life, he had written a number of works that gained him wide attention as a humanist and author. These included erotic poetry, historical and geographical texts, an autobiography, hundreds of letters, commentaries on his times, and a proposal for educational reform using classical models. He sponsored other building projects in Rome and in Siena.

Further reading: Pius II, *Memoirs of a Renaissance Pope: The Commentaries of Pius II, an Abridgement,* trans. Florence A. Gragg (London: Allen and Unwin, 1959); C. M. Ady, *Pius II (Æneas Silvius Piccolomini) the Humanist Pope* (London: Methuen, 1913); R. J. Mitchell, *The Laurels and the Tiara: Pope Pius II, 1458–1464* (London: Harvill Press, 1962).

plague There were major pandemics of disease in the sixth century and in the 14th century. Plagues disappeared in the West by 750 but returned before 1350 and persisted until after 1650. The earlier pandemic spread from ABYSSINIA or Ethiopia, traveled through Byzantium, then under the rule of JUSTINIAN; and eventually reached the British Isles between 541 and 546. There were other outbreaks in about 542, about 558, about 572, about 581, about 590, and about 600. By the seventh century urban centers, such as CONSTANTINOPLE and ANTIOCH, had been greatly depopulated. In the seventh century and after the Arab conquests, the situation stabilized in the east. The ARABS initially left the cities during the summers and their armies moved into the desert or the mountains, thus escaping the worst of the plagues season. However, episodes of plague did catch up to them, especially in the second half of the seventh century. In the first half of the eighth century, plagues afflicted the eastern Mediterranean but were generally absent from northern Europe.

It is not clear which diseases were actually involved, but the mortality rate seemed to have been high and

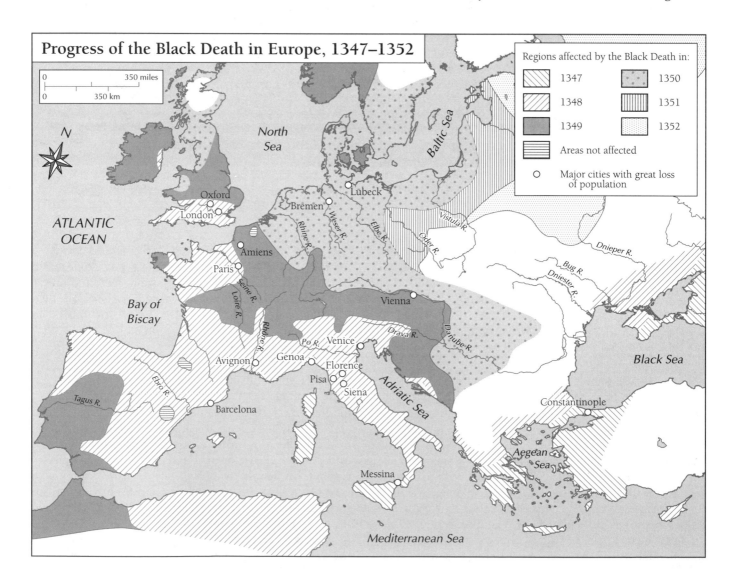

Progress of the Black Death in Europe, 1347–1352

Regions affected by the Black Death in:

1347	1350
1348	1351
1349	1352

Areas not affected

○ Major cities with great loss of population

varied according to locale and age group, a characteristic of plagues in general. Some areas escaped one outbreak only to be devastated in the next. Any devastation was horrific and perceived as arbitrary; repetitions compounded insecurity and a sense of helplessness in that no controls or cures were available. All of this took place in an environment of other endemics unfortunately more familiar such as smallpox. It has remained unclear whether these earlier plagues were bubonic or even a form of influenza.

BLACK DEATH

In the 1340s a new plague, usually associated with the Yersin bacillus, spread again, this time from central Asia, as tracked by mortality rates on dated central Asia and Nestorian gravestones from 1339. The weather had been abnormally dry, forcing rodents and their disease-bearing fleas into greater contact with human beings. In 1346 the plague appeared at Caffa in the Crimea, a colony of GENOA on the BLACK SEA. From there it spread by sea and land to most part of Europe and throughout the Middle East. By 1348 it had reached Constantinople, ITALY, and FRANCE. ENGLAND was affected in the winter of 1348–49, and by 1350 plague had swept across GERMANY, POLAND, and Scandinavia. This pandemic was later called the Black Death. It was again followed by successive waves of great severity all over the west and the Mediterranean, in 1348, 1362, 1374, 1383, 1389, and 1400. After that the outbreaks became less frequent and slightly less intense, taking on marginally different forms and probably involving different and evolving communicable diseases.

CAUSES AND CONSEQUENCES

The disease generally called the plague last appeared in England as the Great Plague of 1665. Symptoms changed over time as the microbes evolved and resistance in human beings increased. It is reasonable to believe that a third of the population of Europe died in the first visitation of 1348 and that the plague was a definite factor in the great demographic collapse of the late 14th century. Populations in most places did not reattain earlier levels until well after 1500, and some not until the 19th century.

The FAMINES of the early 14th century continued in some areas, creating a population of undernourished and permanently stunted or weakened people who were even more vulnerable to the plague. The weather might have also contributed to its severity as it also promoted famine. There was no effective treatment except avoidance of those suffering it and their dwelling places. It seemed to be transmitted by fleas, contact with fluids, and even sometimes droplets in the air as in pneumonic plague, this concept was not clearly understood in the 14th century. The agent for this disease was probably a bacillus called *Pasteurella pestis,* a form of which still exists all over the world. It is unclear whether the plague that regularly but occasionally has appeared in modern times was quite like the 14th-century one, in which some have suggested a form of anthrax may have been combined with pneumonia. The symptoms and conditions of transmission were not consistently described in the 14th century. Its behavior did not neatly match that of the modern version.

The 14th-century plagues had many consequences. JEWS were blamed for transmission of the disease and were persecuted and massacred. Fear of Black Death also led to the growth of fanatical religious groups. The effect of the plague on the agrarian economy and society was complex, leading at least initially to attempts to impose and restore more oppressive feudal rights and services. This in turn led to outbreaks of violence such as the risings of the JACQUÉRIE in France in 1358 and the Peasants' Revolt in England in 1381; but in the longer run it altered the landlord and peasant tenant relationship, because of the reduced labor supply. This plague also may have influenced the development of more labor-saving devices, as well as promoting a changed and more open environment in the universities and art world as whole generations of scholars and artists were devastated. The same kind of devastating consequences also occurred in the Islamic world, especially in great cities such as CAIRO.

See also BOCCACCIO, GIOVANNI; DANCE OF DEATH; FLAGELLANTS; PEASANT REBELLIONS.

Further reading: Rosemary Horrox, ed. and trans., *The Black Death* (Manchester: Manchester University Press, 1994); John Aberth, *From the Brink of the Apocalypse: Confronting War Famine, War, Plague, and Death in the Later Middle Ages* (New York: Routledge, 2000); Norman F. Cantor, *In the Wake of the Plague: The Black Death and the World It Made* (New York: Free Press, 2001); Samuel K. Cohn Jr., *The Black Death Transformed: Disease and Culture in Early Renaissance Europe* (London: Hodder, 2002); Michael W. Dols, *The Black Death in the Middle East* (Princeton, N.J.: Princeton University Press, 1977); John Hatcher, *Plague Population and the English Economy, 1348–1530* (London: Macmillan, 1977); David Herlihy, *The Black Death and the Transformation of the West,* ed. Samuel K. Cohn Jr. (Cambridge, Mass.: Harvard University Press, 1997); William H. McNeil, *Plagues and Peoples* (Garden City, N.Y.: Anchor Books, 1977).

Plantagenets The name Plantagenet has sometimes been given to the dynasty who ruled ENGLAND from 1154 to 1485. None of the Plantagenets actually bore this surname, which was derived from Geoffrey IV (r. 1129–51), the count of ANJOU-Maine-Touraine, and the father of the future king HENRY II. Geoffrey had married the daughter of King Henry I, Matilda (1102–67), in 1128. The name was applied by historians to the dynasty after Henry II succeeded King Stephen (r. 1135–54), after a civil war between Stephen and Matilda. It was taken up again by the Yorkists in the WARS OF THE ROSES in the 15th century. On the death of RICHARD III in 1485, the line became extinct.

See also ANJOU; AQUITAINE; EDWARD I, KING OF ENGLAND; EDWARD II, KING OF ENGLAND; EDWARD III, KING OF ENGLAND; EDWARD IV, KING OF ENGLAND; HENRY III, KING OF ENGLAND; HENRY V, KING OF ENGLAND: JOHN LACKLAND, KING OF ENGLAND; RICHARD I LIONHEART; RICHARD II.

Further reading: Jean-Marc Bienvenu, "Plantagenets," *EMA* 2.1,149–52; Paul Binski, *Westminster Abbey and the Plantagenets: Kingship and the Representation of Power, 1200–1400* (New Haven, Conn.: Yale University Press, 1995); Elizabeth Hallam, ed., *Four Gothic Kings: Henry III, Edward I, Edward II, Edward II—Seen through the Eyes of Their Contemporaries* (New York: Weidenfeld & Nicolson, 1987); Frederick Hepburn, *Portraits of the Latter Plantagenets* (Woodbridge: Boydell Press, 1986).

Plato and Platonism   The thought of Plato itself and its later form in NEOPLATONISM were a philosophical system, which evolved through time. Initially it was based on the works of Plato of Athens and was developed after Plato's lifetime at Hellenistic academies at Athens and ALEXANDRIA. Two FATHERS OF THE CHURCH, Clement of Alexandria (ca. 160–215) and ORIGEN, were deeply influenced by it in the second and third centuries and tried to Christianize it. AUGUSTINE referred to its ideas in his work and made it an acceptable philosophical tool and method. Platonism was practically the only method of learning in early medieval Christian society and until the works of ARISTOTLE reappeared in the 12th and 13th centuries through Muslim intermediaries. Even after the reappearance of Aristotelian thought in UNIVERSITIES AND SCHOOLS, Platonism continued to be influential. As part of a humanist movement in the 15th century, interest in Plato himself and his ideas revived as new translations became available and Platonic academies became fashionable.

See also ADELARD OF BATH; BACON, ROGER; BOETHIUS; DIONYSIUS THE AREOPAGITE FICINO, MARSILIO; GROSSETESTE, ROBERT; JOHN SCOTTUS ERIUGENA; JOHN TAULER; MIRANDOLA, PICO DELLA NEOPLATONISM; NICHOLAS OF CUSA; PLOTINUS IN THE MIDDLE AGES.

Further reading: A. H. Armstrong, ed., *The Cambridge History of Later Greek and Early Medieval Philosophy* (Cambridge: Cambridge University Press, 1970); Peter Dronke, *Fabula: Explorations into the Uses of Myth in Medieval Platonism* (Leiden: E. J. Brill, 1974), Stephen Gersh, *Concord in Discourse: Harmonics and Semiotics in Late Classical and Early Medieval Platonism* (Berlin: Mouton de Gruyter, 1996); James Hankins, *Plato in the Italian Renaissance,* 2 vols. (Leiden: E. J. Brill, 1990); Raymond Klibansky, *The Continuity of the Platonic Tradition during the Middle Ages with a New Preface and Four Supplementary Chapters; Together with*

Plato's Parmenides in the Middle Ages and the Renaissance, with a New Introductory Preface (Munich: Kraus International Publications, 1981); Dominic J. O'Meara, *The Structure of Being and the Search for the Good: Essays on Ancient and Early Medieval Platonism* (Aldershot: Ashgate/Variorum, 1998).

Platonism, medieval   *See* NEOPLATONISM AND PLATONISM IN THE MIDDLE AGES; PLATO AND PLATONISM.

Plotinus in the Middle Ages   (ca. 204–270) *founder of the Neoplatonic system*
Plotinus was born in Lycopolis in Upper EGYPT to an upper-class Greek family in about 204. He moved to ALEXANDRIA in 232 and settled in ROME in 244, after narrowly escaping death on a failed Roman expedition to the East led by the emperor Gordian III (r. 238–244). He had gone on this campaign to learn about Indian and Persian philosophy. His biographer and pupil, Porphyry (ca. 232–ca. 305), also edited his lectures.

In his most famous work, the *Enneads*, Plotinus synthesized the PHILOSOPHY of PLATO with other philosophies. He never aspired to be more than an interpreter of Plato, while combining Aristotelian and Stoic ideas with those of Plato. His main concern was spiritual progress toward the "One" or the "Good." He also saw reality at several ascending levels. Matter was only the projection of forms. The THEOLOGY of Plotinus was distinctly Hellenistic and its mystical monotheism influenced Christian ideas, especially about the Trinity. Plotinus was only known indirectly in the Middle Ages through his influence on AUGUSTINE, BASIL, BOETHIUS, and PSEUDO-DIONYSUS. In 1492 Marsilio FICINO translated into Latin the Greek *Enneads*, which became a fundamental contribution to Renaissance NEOPLATONISM.

See also PHOTIOS I, THE GREAT, PATRIARCH OF CONSTANTINOPLE; PLATO AND PLATONISM.

Further reading: Plotinus, *Plotinus,* trans. A. H. Armstrong. 7 vols. (London: Harvard University Press, 1966–1988); A. H. Armstrong, *The Architecture and the Intelligible Universe in the Philosophy of Plotinus: An Analytical and Historical Study* (Amsterdam: A. M. Hakkert, 1967); Lloyd P. Gerson, ed., *The Cambridge Companion to Plotinus* (Cambridge: Cambridge University Press, 1996); Thomas Whittaker, *The Neo-Platonists: A Study in the History of Hellenism,* 4th ed. (Hildesheim: G. Olms Verlagsbuchhandlung, 1961).

podestà (podesta)   The *podestà* was one of the supreme magistrates of Italian cities governed by COMMUNES. The powers and characteristic of the office varied over time and place. The *podestà* had the greatest power and institutional significance in the first half of the 13th century. In later and broader-based regimes, the *podestà* lost some of its primacy, regressing into a bureaucratic and jurisdictional position.

In the 13th century, he was chosen annually or semiannually from qualified candidates from other cities and thus theoretically outside local politics and interests. As the government's chief executive officer and head judge, he was hired and paid by the commune and was accompanied by a "family" of professional officials, including judges, notaries, and soldiers who sometimes served as his police force. He represented the commune, personifying its prestige and power and protecting rights fundamental to its autonomy. After swearing to uphold the town's statutes or legal system, he convened and presided over various councils. Besides that he led the army, ensured public order, administered criminal justice, oversaw the collection of taxes and public works, and protected the road system and commerce. At the end of his tenure, he was audited and held accountable. These duties accumulated from the beginnings of the communes in the late 12th century as they tried to govern themselves.

Over the 13th and 14th centuries, the *podestà* lost many of his administrative roles to other magistrates, to assure fair treatment to other, new elements of the commune, that is, the new social classes that demanded other officials to protect them and their interests from the old elite. Podestas were now regarded as the promoters and agents of the old original communal elites. The office further evolved in the Renaissance. It became the office maintained by cities over subject towns as part of an evolving city-state system. The podestas became the officials of an external, sometimes oppressive, regime either princely or republican. The office still kept order but now explicitly represented the interests of a ruler or other town.

See also FREDERICK I BARBAROSSA; CRIME, PUNISHMENT, AND THE COURTS; FLORENCE; ITALY; MILAN; POLITICAL THEORY AND TREATISES; SIENA.

Further reading: David Chambers and Trevor Dean, *Clean Hands and Rough Justice: An Investigating Magistrate in Renaissance Italy* (Ann Arbor: University of Michigan Press, 1997); Laura Ilkins Stern, *The Criminal Law System of Medieval and Renaissance Florence* (Baltimore: Johns Hopkins University Press, 1994); Daniel Waley, *The Italian City-Republics,* 3d ed. (London: Longman, 1988).

Poggio Bracciolini *See* BRACCIOLINI, POGGIO.

Poitiers, Battles of There were two battles of Poitiers. On October 25, 732, CHARLES MARTEL and the FRANKS defeated an Arab and Muslim raiding party from the Iberian Peninsula. The defeat has long been regarded as the turning point in the first Islamic assault on Europe, and the farthest point of Muslim penetration into northern Europe. Charles has traditionally received credit for halting the advance of Muslim progress into Europe. The second Battle of Poitiers took place on September 19,

1356, during the HUNDRED YEARS' WAR between ENGLAND and FRANCE. The Anglo-Gascon forces were led by EDWARD THE BLACK PRINCE. At least 2,000 nobles on the French side were killed or captured, including King John II of France (r. 1350–64) and his son, Philip the Bold (1342–1404). King John remained a prisoner of the English until he agreed to major and humiliating concessions of territory and a three-million-gold-crown ransom. This also forced the 18-year-old dauphin, CHARLES V, to assume temporary control of the French government. This loss was a serious blow to the French crown, a disaster not overcome for years.

Further reading: Bernard S. Bachrach, *Early Carolingian Warfare: Prelude to Empire* (Philadelphia. University of Pennsylvania Press, 2001); Philippe Contamine, *War in the Middle Ages,* trans. Michael Jones (1980; reprint, Oxford: Basil Blackwell, 1984); Jonathan Sumption, *The Hundred Years' War.* Vol. 2, *Trial by Fire* (Philadelphia: University of Pennsylvania Press, 1999), 195–249.

Poland Medieval Poland was a Slavic kingdom situated on the eastern territories of Western Christendom, north of the Carpathian Mountains and south of the Baltic Sea. It took definitive form in the reigns of Duke Mieszko I (r. ca. 960–992) and BOLESLAV I THE BRAVE, both of the PIAST dynasty. Mieszko was baptized in 966 into the Western Church; in return he received a bishopric directly dependent on Rome in 968 and finally an archbishopric at Gniezno in 999/1000. Boleslav's victorious war against the emperor Henry II (r. 1002–24) and his conquest of KIEV in 1018 confirmed the strength of the new state. Boleslav was crowned king of Poland in 1025. His realm at the end of his reign consisted of five provinces: Great Poland, Little Poland, Silesia, Mazovia, and part of Pomerania.

After a crisis of state and church in the 1030s, Boleslav II the Bold (1058–79) was crowned king in 1076. However, he was forced to leave the country after his murder of Bishop Saint Stanislas in 1079. From the middle of the 11th century, the capital of the country was CRACOW. King Boleslav III Wrymouth (r. 1102–38) conquered and Christianized Pomerania, on the shores of the Baltic. The position of the church was strengthened and Gregorian ideas of reform were put into practice. The religious orders, both monastic and MENDICANT, then flooded into the country.

After the death of Boleslav III in 1138 the realm was divided into smaller states or duchies and this period was marked by the Tatar invasions, the expansion of Brandenburg, and the creation of the state of the TEUTONIC KNIGHTS to the north. There was a widespread colonization of the countryside by Germans, particularly in Silesia and on the Baltic. Large villages and towns appeared, provided with considerable autonomy based on the Magdeburg Charter of Urban Liberties. Alongside the Germans, present in strength particularly in the

Poland and Lithuania, 1386–1470

ESTONIA
LIVONIA
Novgorod
SWEDEN
GOTLAND
Baltic
Sea
TEUTONIC
KNIGHTS
Riga
Pskov
RUSSIAN PRINCIPALITIES
Volga R.
Königsberg
Danzig
PRUSSIA
Vilna
MOSCOVY
Moscow
Oka R.
POMERANIA
Tannenberg
Minsk
Smolensk
GREAT POLAND
Vistula R.
MAZOVIA
BELLORUSSIA
Don R.
Warsaw
POLAND-LITHUANIA
Oder R.
LITTLE
POLAND
HOLY
ROMAN
EMPIRE
Cracow
UKRAINE
Kursk
Kiev
Dnieper R.
CRIMEAN
KHANATE
Donets R.
Dneister R.
Bug R.
HUNGARY

MOLDAVIA

OTTOMAN
EMPIRE
Black Sea

- - - Poland in 1386, at time of union with Lithuania
-·-·- Lithuania in 1386, at time of union with Poland
Territorial gains by 1470, on the eve of Poland-Lithuania's gradual reduction in the east by an expansionist Principality of Moscow

0   120 miles
0   120 km

larger towns and in certain regions, Jewish communities appeared in Silesia, emphasizing still more the diversity of a commercial middle class.

CASIMIR THE GREAT AND LATER HISTORY

At the time he was crowned king in 1320, Ladislas or Wladyslaw the Short (r. 1305/06–1333), held only two provinces, Great Poland and Little Poland. The Teutonic Knights had occupied East Pomerania and the town of Gdańsk or Danzig, while the Bohemians had taken possession of the rich province, of Silesia. The reign of CASIMIR the Great (r. 1333–70) produced stability. He

profited from the his successes against the Tatars and annexed Red Ruthenia or GALICIA, the western part of Ukraine, into Poland after 1340. The old province of Mazovia became a FIEF of the Crown. Founded by Casimir in 1364, the University of CRACOW grew and trained jurists for royal service. Casimir's nephew, Louis of Anjou, king of HUNGARY (r. 1370–82), united Poland and Hungary. Louis's daughter, Hedwig or Jadwiga (ca. 1383–99) was queen of Poland between 1384 and 1399. She married in 1386 the pagan Jagiello, or Jagailo, the grand duke of LITHUANIA, who took the name Ladislas, or Wladyslav, II at his baptism on February 15, 1386. At the same time he became king of Poland (r. 1386–1433). This Polish Lithuanian Union of 1385 lasted for centuries, despite differences between the Catholic kingdom of Poland and the pagan and Orthodox Lithuanian-Ruthenian grand duchy. The Lithuanian nobility, however, converted to Roman Catholicism. A Polish victory over the Teutonic Knights at the Battle of Grunwald or Tannenberg on July 15, 1410; gravely weakened the Teutonic Knights, who later piecemeal joined themselves to Poland in the 1460s. The Jagiellonian dynasty made several attempts to take over BOHEMIA and Hungary, winning battles but ultimately failing. At the same time the realm suffered territorial losses in the northeast as a result of the expansion of MOSCOW.

PROSPERITY AND NOBLE POLITICAL INSTITUTIONS

This period of rule by Casimir and the later Jagiellonians was marked by peace, cultural development, and economic prosperity. The nobility gained a series of privileges and followed the principle of equality of rights for all its members, regardless of their real social and economic position in a hierarchy. In the 15th century, a "little diet" of nobles became an important organ of territorial autonomy. In the late 15th century, the nobles of the little diets even created a body called the "chamber of deputies." The old royal council was transformed into a senate of high dignitaries and bishops. The later Polish parliament has its origins in these diets and councils. These bodies were primarily representative of the nobility, and limited the rights and opportunities of an urban middle class and the PEASANTRY. There were a few major towns such as Gdańsk, Cracow, Toruri, and Elblag or Elbing.

CULTURE AND TOLERANCE

GOTHIC architecture was important in the towns, especially Cracow. The University of Cracow had great prestige in Eastern Europe, and in fact all Europe. By 1500 there were small SCHOOLS in nearly every parish, town, and village. The rate of literacy was high and literature in the Polish language grew. From the 14th century, the Catholic Church coexisted well with the Orthodox Church. Jewish communities grew and enjoyed wide autonomy, as the Jagiellonians, including Gediminas (r. 1316–42), in Lithuania, Ladislas II Jagiello, and Casimir IV (1440–92) in Poland, favored religious toleration.

Further reading: Aleksander Gieysztor, "The Kingdom of Poland and the Grand Duchy of Lithuania," in *The New Cambridge Medieval History.* Vol. 7, *c. 1415–c. 1500,* ed. Christopher Allmand (Cambridge: Cambridge University Press, 1998), 727–747; Paul W. Knoll, *The Rise of the Polish Monarchy: Piast Poland in East Central Europe, 1320–1370* (Chicago: University of Chicago Press, 1972); Jacob Litman, *The Economic Role of Jews in Medieval Poland: The Contribution of Yitzhak Schipper* (Lanham, Md.: University Press of America, 1984); Tadeusz Manteuffel, *The Formation of the Polish State: The Period of Ducal Rule, 963–1194,* trans. Andrew Gorski (Detroit: Wayne State University Press, 1982); Michael J. Mikos, trans., *Medieval Literature of Poland: An Anthology* (New York: Garland, 1992); W. F. Reddaway, ed. *The Cambridge History of Poland* (Cambridge: Cambridge University Press, 1941); H. B. Segel, *Renaissance Culture in Poland: The Rise of Humanism, 1470–1543* (Ithaca, N.Y.: Cornell University Press, 1989).

political structure *See* CALIPHATE AND CALIPH; KINGS AND KINGSHIP, RITUALS AND THEORIES OF; LAW, CANON AND ECCLESIASTICAL; PAPACY; *PODESTÀ*; POLITICAL THEORY AND TREATISES; SOCIAL STATUS AND STRUCTURE.

political theory and treatises For medieval authors, politics was an important aspect of theological and philosophical reflection. The nature of society and of the practice of public affairs were two of the essential ethical dimensions of a person. The political community and the religious community were not thought of as separate or opposed. There was, however, throughout most of the Middle Ages and early RENAISSANCE, much conflict over the relationship between the power of the church and the power of temporal or secular realms or states. GOD delegated power on earth to Christ, who according to the church delegated it to the pope, who delegated it to bishops and lay rulers, according to the idea of the Two Swords, one held by the church and the other held by the state. Yet all was to be controlled by the pope in the minds of some. The question was whether God intended the emperor, or a monarch, or the state to wield the temporal sword, independent of the pope but as part of a rightly ordered Christian society.

Politics and political power existed to protect order and virtue from the consequences of the naturally sinful human condition. The introduction of Roman LAW and Aristotelian thought in the *Ethics* and *Politics* complicated these matters in the 12th and 13th centuries. The later development of NOMINALISM encouraged the idea that only the individual was fundamental and the state existed for the protection of individual liberty. This was countered by the early development of the idea of absolutism of either a monarch or a pope. The addition of such new entities as the city-states of ITALY complicated the issues of this scheme. The new cities, much influenced by Ciceronian republicanism at least in theory, wanted to pay as little attention to an emperor as possible. From the political thought and practice of the Middle Ages and Renaissance, historians have discerned, perhaps to an exaggerated degree, the beginnings of the modern ideas of the separation of church and state, representative government, the popular roots of political power and government, the evolution of authority and justice, the function of the law, and justification of property rights.

ISLAMIC THOUGHT AND COMPARISONS TO CHRISTIANITY

Medieval Islamic political thought was based on the QURAN and the HADITH, in other words, the ideas of MUHAMMAD as a prophet or messenger inspired by God. These encompassed religion, law, ethics, PHILOSOPHY, and statecraft. During the Middle Ages Muslim writers produced systematic treatises, occasional writings, official rhetorical statements, and popular slogans all based primarily on them.

Just as in Christianity, Islamic political thought was a religious ideology active in society. Both the religious and the secular communities were the products of the legacy of Abraham and the classical world. Their medieval traditions and cultures were monotheistic, believed in a final revelation by God to humanity in particular texts, and were strongly influenced by the ideas and systems of classical antiquity.

See also ALIGHIERI, DANTE; AUGUSTINE OF HIPPO, SAINT; CALIPHATE AND CALIPH; FORTESCUE, JOHN; GREGORIAN REFORM; ISLAM; IBN KHALDUN, WALI AL-DIN ABD AL-RAHMAN IBN MUHAMMAD; JOHN OF PARIS; JOHN OF SALISBURY; LAW, CANON AND ECCLESIASTICAL; MARSILIUS OF PADUA; MIRROR OF PRINCES; PAPACY; WILLIAM OF OCKHAM; WYCLIFFE, JOHN.

Further reading: Ralph Lerner and Muhsin Mahdi, eds., *Medieval Political Philosophy* (Ithaca, N.Y.: Cornell University Press, 1963); Cary J. Nederman and Kate Langdon Forhan, eds., *Medieval Political Theory—a Reader: The Quest for the Body Politic, 1100–1400* (New York: Routledge, 1993); Hans Baron, *In Search of Florentine Civic Humanism: Essays on the Transition from Medieval to Modern Thought,* 2 vols. (Princeton, N.J.: Princeton University Press, 1988); Antony J. Black, *Political Thought in Europe, 1250–1450* (Cambridge: Cambridge University Press, 1992); Antony Black, *The History of Islamic Political Thought: From the Prophet to the Present* (New York: Routledge, 2001); J. H. Burns, ed., *The Cambridge History of Medieval Political Thought c. 350–c. 1450* (Cambridge: Cambridge University Press, 1988); Joseph Canning, *A History of Medieval Political Thought, 300–1450* (New York, Routledge, 1996); Quentin Skinner, *The Foundations of Modern Political Thought,* 2 vols. (Cambridge: Cambridge University Press, 1978).

poll tax   *See* PEASANT REBELLIONS.

Polo, Marco   *See* MARCO POLO.

polyphony   Medieval polyphony was a method of writing music in which several voices were superimposed on each other while harmonizing with melodies not parallel to each other. It appeared in the ninth century in the West. Several kinds of polyphonic musical forms succeeded each other or coexisted in the Middle Ages.

The *conductus* was a polyphonic piece in which a low or tenor voice followed a more or less spontaneous melody. Thus polyphony was no longer just an ornament of GREGORIAN CHANT, but a new and autonomous way of writing music. *Conductus* often accompanied the liturgy as processional chants. In the 13th century, the principal polyphonic musical form was the MOTET. In the 14th century, rhythmic relations between voices characterized a new style, the *ars nova,* in contrast to the ARS ANTIQUA cultivated earlier in the 13th century. The most celebrated musician of the *Ars nova* was Guillaume de MACHAUT. From the late 14th century, polyphonic composition began to be simplified in the Franco-Flemish school best represented by Guillaume Dufay (ca. 1400– 74). Secular polyphonic song also developed, but composing for the MASS remained the most complex genre.

Further reading: David Fallows, *Dufay* (London: J. M. Dent and Sons, 1982); Anselm Hughes, *Medieval Polyphony in the Bodleian Library* (Oxford: Bodleian Library, 1951); Heinrich Husmann, *Medieval Polyphony,* trans. Robert Kolben (Cologne: Arno Volk, 1962); Ernest Helmut Sanders, *Medieval English Polyphony and Its Significance for the Continent* (New York: Sanders, 1968). There are available numerous sound recordings and musical scores.

polyptych   In the Middle Ages, the word *polyptych* and its derivatives designated land registers. Polyptychs, especially in the ninth century, recorded lands, tenants, and the services they owed to the lord of the estate. Some 30 CAROLINGIAN polyptychs have survived. They were drawn up on land between the Loire and the Rhine; on the estates of Saint-Germain-dès-Prés, Saint-Remi at RHEIMS, and at Prüm; but also in other regions of the Frankish Empire such as northern ITALY at Bobbio. Most were compiled from great monasteries and demonstrated the great expansion of cultivation taking place during that era.

HISTORICAL VALUE

Polyptychs were also intended to assist in the management of royal FIEFS and ecclesiastical properties. They were used by a few lay lords. Studied by modern scholars as sources for social and economic history, they recorded transport services and monetary payments. By listing various members of peasant households they provided a snapshot for the history of the family. They contained place- and human names useful to philologists. They were, however, limited in scope and in time to only the particular property and people inventoried, with little on anything outside the estate. They recorded what the lord thought he should be able to collect from his estate and his tenants, not what he actually collected. The polyptych was particular to the Carolingian period, but other kinds of similar surveys and inventories existed for later estates, especially for taxation purposes in ENGLAND.

See also AGRICULTURE; *DOMESDAY BOOK;* MANORS AND MANORIAL LORDSHIP; PEASANTRY.

Further reading: Georges Duby, *Rural Economy and Country Life in the Medieval West,* trans. Cynthia Postan (1962; reprint, Columbia: University of South Carolina Press, 1968), especially 366–371; Adriaan Verhulst, *The Carolingian Economy* (Cambridge: Cambridge University Press, 2002).

poor   *See* CHARITY AND POVERTY.

Poor Clares   *See* CLARE OF ASSISI, SAINT.

pope(s)   *See individual popes;* PAPACY.

popular art and religion   Medieval popular religion was made up of the practices, images, behavior, beliefs, representations, and ideas of the majority of the population of CHRISTENDOM, ISLAM, or JUDAISM. It could also include the artistic output, both secular and religious, designed to teach people or to convey their beliefs and images. Such a concept is vague but can form a useful starting point for studying and understanding popular and marginal culture in the Middle Ages and RENAISSANCE.

Some historians had called it folk religion. It has been studied primarily in terms of its relationship and interaction with what is called learned or institutional religion or that of the clergy or specialists in religious matters, those who teach and formulate its norms. It has been a way to transcend mere religious doctrine and theological disputes to analyze religions and cultures as they functioned in society and were understood by the unlettered but not necessarily passive. It can also indicate how the literate and pastoral class saw their flocks and tried to influence them. This relationship worked both ways: doctrines and pastoral care could be influenced by popular ideas and expectations. It has been a tool to study influenced by methods and focuses of anthropologists and folklorists, who compare the "rational" with the "irrational" or the "written" with the "oral" in a society or culture. It can discern the real issues or needs of the mass of religious believers or unbelievers. The study of popular art and religion reminds us that both popular and learned religion existed together. Neither concept or classification reflects by itself the reality of any religious community.

See also BEGUINES AND BEGHARDS; DEVIL; FEASTS AND FESTIVALS; GHOSTS; HAGIOGRAPHY; HERESY AND HERESIES; INDULGENCES; LAITY; MAGIC AND FOLKLORE; MARY, CULT OF; MASS, LITURGY OF; MISSIONS OF MISSIONARIES, CHRISTIAN; PILGRIMAGE AND PILGRIMAGE SITES; PREACHING AND PREACHERS; PURGATORY; WITCHCRAFT.

Further reading: John Shinners, ed., *Medieval Popular Religion, 1000–1500: A Reader* (Peterborough, Canada: Broadview Press, 1997); Rosalind B. Brooke and Christopher N. L. Brooke, *Popular Religion in the Middle Ages: Western Europe, 1000–1300* (London: Thames and Hudson 1984); Andrew D. Brown, *Popular Piety in Late Medieval England: The Diocese of Salisbury, 1250–1550* (Oxford: Clarendon Press, 1995), Gábor Klaniczay, *The Uses of Supernatural Power: The Transformation of Popular Religion in Medieval and Early-Modern Europe,* trans. Susan Singerman and ed. Karen Margolis (Princeton, N.J.: Princeton University Press, 1990).

Porette, Margaret (Marguerite Porete) (d. 1310) *member of the heresy of the Free Spirit*
Margaret was probably a BEGUINE and a native of Hainault in FRANCE. As a visionary and adherent of the sect of the Brethren of the FREE SPIRIT, she was burned at the stake in PARIS on June 1, 1310, for continuing to circulate copies of her book, *The Mirror of Simple Souls,* written sometime between 1296 and 1310. It can be seen as a NEOPLATONIC dialogue among allegorical figures about the nature of the relationship between the individual SOUL and GOD. It had been explicitly condemned as heretical. Known as an executed heretic, she became better understood when her authorship of that work was discovered in the 20th century. The work itself was long considered to be anonymous. It had circulated in Latin, English, and Italian translations.

Her *The Mirror of Simple* was a rare and important witness to the beliefs and ideas of adherents of what has been called the HERESY of the Free Spirit, whose beliefs were only really known from the records of their trials and references to their ideas by their persecutors. The major threat they posed for Christianity was their suspicion of the necessity of clerical intermediation between the Christian and God. To suggest and circulate such ideas usually led to a death sentence.

See also VISIONS AND DREAMS.

Further reading: Marguerite Porete, *The Mirror of Simple Souls,* trans. Edmund Colledge, J. C. Marler, and Judith Grant (Notre Dame, Ind.: University of Notre Dame Press, 1999); Peter Dronke, *Women Writers of the Middle Ages: A Critical Study of Texts from Perpetua (d. 203) to Marguerite Porete (d. 1310)* (Cambridge: Cambridge University Press, 1984); Amy M. Hollywood, *The Soul as Virgin Wife: Mechthild of Magdeburg, Marguerite Porete, and Meister Eckhart* (Notre Dame, Ind.: University of Notre Dame Press, 1995); Joanne Maguire Robinson,

Nobility and Annihilation in Marguerite Porete's Mirror of Simple Souls (Albany: State University of New York Press, 2001); Bernard McGinn, ed., *Meister Eckhart and the Beguine Mystics: Hadewijch of Brabant, Mechthild of Magdeburg, and Marguerite Porete* (New York: Continuum, 1994).

pork *See* AGRICULTURE; ANIMALS AND ANIMAL HUSBANDRY; FOOD, DRINK AND NUTRITION; FORESTS AND FOREST LAW.

portolan charts (*portulan*) In modern usage, the term *portolan chart* means "a nautical map or chart"; in the Middle Ages and RENAISSANCE the *portolanus* was a text listing distances and directions between places on a coast. It also contained the conditions and dangers of navigation. The most common charts depicted the Mediterranean, BLACK SEA, and Atlantic coasts from MOROCCO to the Baltic. They used conventional signs for directions, coasts, and places.

The surviving examples date from 1296 and number more than 100, preserved separately or within atlases. They had earliest origins among Italians and Majorcans, who employed then for information on the Mediterranean Sea. Using them skillfully and in combination with a magnetic COMPASS, one could follow known routes and perhaps even navigate to destinations. There is some question, however, about how much they were actually used aboard ships. They might have been employed more by MERCHANTS planning trading voyages than by practicing mariners.

See also NAVIGATION.

Further reading: Leo Bagrow, *History of Cartography,* trans. D. L. Paisey (Cambridge, Mass.: Harvard University Press, 1966); Jonathan T. Lanman, *On the Origin of Portolan Charts* (Chicago: Newberry Library, 1987); Raleigh A. Skelton, *Explorers' Maps: Chapters in the Cartographic Record of Geographical Discovery* (New York: Praeger, 1958); Ronald V. Tooley, *Maps and Map-Makers* (London: Batsford, 1949); John Noble Wilford, *The Mapmakers* (New York: Knopf, 1981).

Portugal Medieval Portugal was a country in the western part of the Iberian Peninsula. Its name developed from its first capital city, Porto. In the fifth century the region, the Roman-dominated province of Lusitania, was conquered by the Suevi, BARBARIANS who conquered its northern area; the VISIGOTHS, who took the center; and the VANDALS, who settled in the southernmost region. In the sixth century the Visigoths annexed all of the future Portugal to their kingdom. In 711–714 Portugal was overrun by the ARABS and incorporated into the UMAYYAD CALIPHATE of CÓRDOBA. After the caliphate's fall in the 11th century, it was subject to the Muslim kings of SEVILLE. In 1097 King Alfonso VI (r. 1065–1109), the king of CASTILE, conquered its northern section and made it a Castilian county, giving it to his son-in-law, Henry of BURGUNDY (r. 1097–1112), who was married to his illegitimate daughter Teresa.

A SEPARATE KINGDOM

Portugal became independent in 1109 and started pursuing wars of reconquest against the Muslims. In 1139, Henry's son, Afonso I (r. 1112–85), was proclaimed king and established the new state of Portugal. In 1148, he conquered LISBON, with the help of English and Scandinavian crusaders. This established his realm's southern border on the Tagus River. In the second half of the 12th and beginning of the 13th century, under the rule of Sancho I (r. 1185–1211) and Afonso III (r. 1248–79), there was continued southward expansion at the expense of the Muslims. This culminated in the conquest of the Algarve, the southernmost region of Portugal.

In the 13th century the kings dedicated their efforts to organizing the kingdom and imposing royal authority on the church and the nobility. The kings worked with the commoners, who were admitted in 1254 to the CORTES or representative assembly, to help balance and check the nobility. In 1280, a university was founded at Lisbon and later transferred to Coimbra, the capital before Lisbon. In the 14th century, Portugal became involved in the political affairs and dynastic conflicts of Castile. The Crown and the Cortes, however, strongly resisted extensive Castilian influence, though there were intermarriages between members of the ruling dynasties of both realms. During the 14th century also, the Portuguese people became aware of an identity. A linguistic unification of the country occurred on the basis of a synthesis between the Galician-Portuguese of the north and the Arabic-tinged dialects of the south, particularly in the reign of Denis (Dinis) I (r. 1279–1325). King John (João) I (r. 1385–1433) defeated the Castilians at the Battle of Aljubarrota in August 1385 and preserved Portugal's independence.

THE AGE OF EXPLORATION

The great age of Portuguese expansion and search for GOLD, and eventually African slaves, began in the late 14th century and was carried forward by Prince HENRY, called the Navigator. Henry and King John I took advantage of the anarchy in North AFRICA to capture towns in MOROCCO such as Ceuta in 1415. Maritime expeditions followed along the African coast from 1415. The CANARY ISLANDS in the 14th century, Madeira in about 1419, and the AZORES in about 1427 were discovered and colonized. Cape BOJADOR, once considered impassable, was rounded in 1434. Factories or trading posts were established all along the African coast. King John II (r. 1481–95) continued Henry's maritime exploration and sought to find PRESTER JOHN in the East. Bartholomew DIAZ rounded the Cape of Good Hope in southern Africa in 1488, and Vasco da GAMA reached India and returned in 1497. The Treaty of Tordesillas in 1494 divided the "new" discoveries

Portugal: Burgundian House (1112–1325)

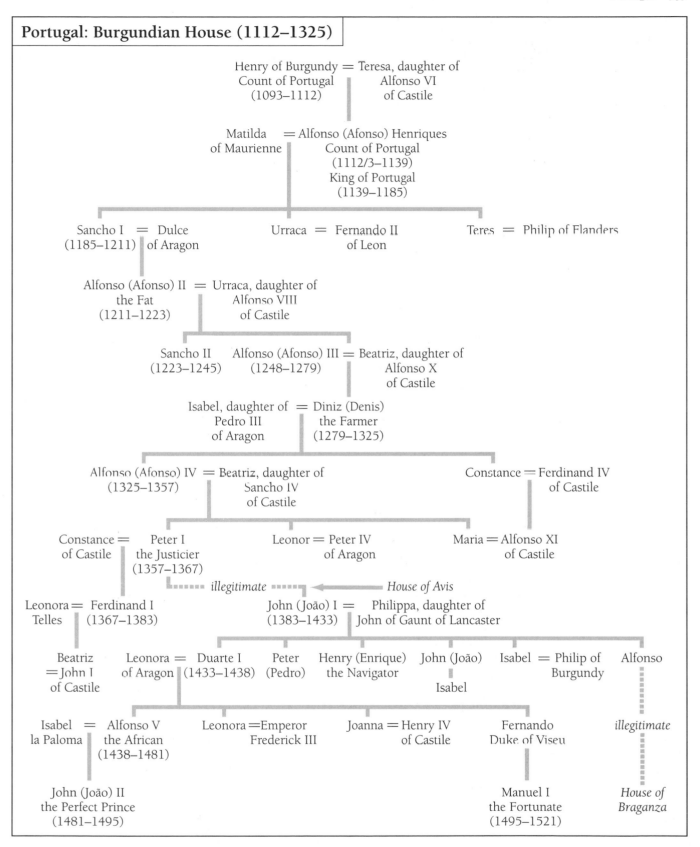

between SPAIN and Portugal in 1494. All these events led to Portugal's vast colonial empire in Africa, Brazil, southern Asia, and the Far East.

See also GALICIA; SLAVE TRADE AND SLAVERY.

Further reading: Charles Wendell David, trans., *De expugnatione Lyxbonensi: The Conquest of Lisbon* (1936;

reprint, New York: Columbia University Press, 2001); Peter Linehan, "Castile, Portugal and Navarre," in *The New Cambridge Medieval History. Vol. 5, c. 1198–c. 1300*, ed. David Abulafia (Cambridge: Cambridge University Press, 1999), 668–699; Bailey W. Diffie and George D. Winius, *Foundations of the Portuguese Empire, 1415–1580* (Minneapolis: University of Minnesota Press, 1977); C. R. Boxer, *The Portuguese Seaborne Empire* (London: Hutchinson, 1969); A. J. R. Russell-Wood, *A World on the Move: The Portuguese in Africa, Asia and America, 1415–1808* (Manchester: Carcanet, 1992).

Portuguese expansion and trade   *See* PORTUGAL.

poverty   *See* CHARITY AND POVERTY; POVERTY, VOLUNTARY.

poverty, voluntary   Voluntary poverty, traditionally one of the three vows of religious life, had various forms before 1500. Voluntary or spiritual poverty was based on the GOSPEL inviting Christians to follow the example of Jesus and renounce material goods. They impeded the gaining of salvation and lessened trust in the good providence of GOD. BENEDICTINE MONASTICISM made poverty obligatory on the individual monk but authorized the ownership of goods by the monastic community.

With the new prosperity arising from agrarian and commercial revolutions between 1000 and 1300, spiritual poverty became a new fundamental and external way of life through the MENDICANT ORDERS. There were attacks on clerical wealth throughout the 12th and 13th centuries, both by orthodox reformers and by heretics. Voluntary poverty was one of the main aspects of the mendicant idea as founded by FRANCIS of Assisi. The quick relaxation of his original austere practices created divisions within the Order of Friars Minor, especially among the SPIRITUAL FRANCISCANS. Pope JOHN XXII condemned their doctrine of Christ's poverty in 1323.

Further reading: David Burr, *Olivi and Franciscan Poverty: The Origins of the Usus Pauper Controversy* (Philadelphia: University of Pennsylvania Press, 1989); Jan G. J. van den Eijnden, *Poverty on the Way to God: Thomas Aquinas on Evangelical Poverty* (Louvain: Peeters, 1994); David Flood, ed., *Poverty in the Middle Ages* (Werl: D. Coelde, 1975); Lester K. Little, *Religious Poverty and the Profit Economy in Medieval Europe* (Ithaca, N.Y.: Cornell University Press, 1978); Michel Mollat, *The Poor in the Middle Ages: An Essay in Social History*, trans. Arthur Goldhammer (New Haven, Conn.: Yale University Press, 1986).

Praemunire   The Statutes of Praemunire were issued by English kings to protect their rights from encroachment by the PAPACY and as an effort to assert royal sovereignty over the church in ENGLAND. The first such statutes were issued in 1353, 1365, and 1393. That of 1353 forbade appeal to the papal court of cases usually and traditionally kept within the purview of the king's courts. That of 1393 forbade EXCOMMUNICATION of a person or issuance of a papal bull without royal assent.

See also PROVISIONS, ECCLESIASTICAL.

Further reading: May McKisack, *The Fourteenth Century, 1307–1399* (Oxford: Clarendon Press, 1959); W. A. Pantin, *The English Church in the Fourteenth Century* (1955; reprint, Notre Dame: University of Notre Dame Press, 1963).

Pragmatic Sanction of Bourges   The Pragmatic Sanction was promulgated as a royal decree by King CHARLES VII in 1438 at Bourges, to regulate relationships among the Crown, the French church, and the PAPACY. There had been much conflict between Pope EUGENIUS IV and the COUNCIL of BASEL. The king of France tried to follow a policy of neutrality. Largely influenced by Gallican bishops and the traditional antipathy to papal pretensions from at least the reign of PHILIP IV THE FAIR, Charles called an assembly of the clergy at Bourges. There most of the conciliar decrees of Basel were adopted, including the council's superiority to the pope, the suppression of certain taxes, annates, and limits on appeals to the court of ROME and on papal influence on and control of the distribution of clerical BENEFICES. To these were added a series of prescriptions on the sacraments and a long treatise on the necessity of reform of the church. These ideas were not all acceptable to the clergy of France and naturally aroused strong opposition from the Holy See. King LOUIS XI played politics and abrogated the ordinance in 1461, restored it later, and eventually in 1472 reached an agreement with Pope Sixtus IV (r. 1471–84) in the concordat of Amboise. It was finally abrogated by the concordat of BOLOGNA in 1516. Its effect was always to replace papal power over the French church with that of the monarchy. It has been considered the foundational charter of a Gallican church independent of the Holy See.

See also PROVISIONS, ECCLESIASTICAL.

Further reading: Paul Murray Kendall, *Louis XI: The Universal Spider* (New York: W. W. Norton, 1970); P. S. Lewis, *Later Medieval France: The Polity* (London: Melbourne, 1968); Malcolm G. Vale, *Charles VII* (Berkeley: University of California Press, 1974).

Prague (Praha)   Prague, the capital of BOHEMIA and the present capital of the Czech Republic, is situated in the Prague basin over both banks of the river Vltava. Slavs settled there toward the end of the sixth century and in the course of the next two centuries erected there numerous fortresses. On the site of one of these forts, a PREMYSLID prince, Bohvoj I (r. 870–895), built a CASTLE and made it the political center of his duchy. In the ninth century churches were built, including the church of the Holy

Virgin in about 885, the basilica of Saint George between 915 and 921, the church of Saint Guy shortly before 935, and a BENEDICTINE monastery in 970. The bishopric of Prague was established in 973. Another residence of the Premyslid princes was built in the 10th century at Vysehrad further south on the right bank of the river Vltava. Between these two castles there developed a network of roads and houses. In the late 11th century, commercial activities moved from the left to the right bank and from the mid-12th century, a more sophisticated urban settlement developed, complete with dressed stone buildings, impressive houses, and workshops of artisans. At the start of the 13th century, the town was still small with maybe 3,500 inhabitants, but it was encircled by a fortified wall from 1231. King Premysl Ottokar II (r. 1253–78) in 1257 undertook to build a planned town at the foot of Prague castle.

In the 13th and 14th centuries, Prague's political and economic importance grew. CHARLES IV in 1348 created another planned an urban center called the new town (Nove Mesto). This enlarged city formed by the four urban cells, founded at different times, soon numbered perhaps some 50,000 inhabitants, rivaling PARIS or BRUGES. In the reign of Charles, 1346 to 1378, the Gothic cathedral of Saint Guy and a new stone bridge were built. Charles University or the University of Prague, the first in central Europe, was founded in 1348. The city was at the center of the Hussite Wars with the Germans in the 15th century as it declined in wealth and importance.

Further reading: Albert Kutal, *Gothic Art in Bohemia and Moravia,* trans. Till Gottheiner (London: Hamlyn, 1972); Karel Neubert, *Portrait of Prague,* trans. John Eisler (New York: Hamlyn, 1969); Karel Stejskal, *European Art in the Fourteenth Century,* trans. Till Gottheinerová (London: Octopus Books, 1978); Lisa Wolverton, *Hastening toward Prague: Power and Society in the Medieval Czech Lands* (Philadelphia: University of Pennsylvania Press, 2001).

prayer and prayers (Arabic, *salat;* Hebrew, *tefillah*) Prayer held a fundamental place in religious life in the Middle Ages, when it was believed that the order of things and the destiny of each person depended on a providence influenced by his or her requests or prayers. In both Christianity and JUDAISM, one could influence the course of events by asking GOD for help, or at least divine mercy. Along with FASTING and almsgiving, prayer reconciled the sinner with God. It could foster spiritual solidarity with one's fellow Christians, the heavenly spirits, and the saints and even help the dead. It had to be sincere and well intended.

Common or public prayer was offered to God in the name of the people by the clerical ministers of the church, an intermediary way to God. It consisted of external acts of worship, the divine OFFICE, PROCESSIONS, and PILGRIMAGES. Private prayer could be vocal or interior, performed by an individual.

The earliest collections of prayers were Celtic or Anglo-Saxon. They consisted of invocations and supplications addressed to the Trinity, Christ, the Virgin MARY, the ANGELS, and the saints. Litanies solicited the protection of HEAVEN against spiritual or temporal dangers. The Carolingians favored the spread on the Continent of the PSALTER. Later Saint ANSELM tried to facilitate more sustained personal meditation by favoring simple adoration, praise, and prayer celebrating God's greatness, goodness, and mercy. This would produce humility and trust within the person who prayed. Group prayer was promoted for religious and clerics, lay brothers, penitents, members of CONFRATERNITIES, and LAITY of all conditions. For the more educated, in the later Middle Ages, BOOKS OF HOURS appeared. Theologians at the same time speculated on the structure, forms, and degrees of prayer. Programs were devised that if followed would lead the praying Christian to a better relationship with Christ and to SALVATION itself. In the later Middle Ages movements such as the Modern Devotion or *DEVOTIO MODERNA* promoted these programs of prayers.

PRAYER IN ISLAM

Prayer, or *salat,* was derived from the HADITH and was regarded as the second of the five major duties of the Muslim, ranking only after the declaration of FAITH. ISLAM required direct communication with God, so that no priest or intermediate performed this function. Prayer was to be performed five times a day, each with particular qualities of performance. The prayers could be done with a group or alone. All must be accompanied by a ritual purification, declared a prayer, and be done in the direction of MECCA, with prostrations and formulaic recitations. These rituals were to create a sense of community and group solidarity.

See also FRIDAY PRAYER.

Further reading: Richard C. Trexler, *The Christian at Prayer: An Illustrated Prayer Manual Attributed to Peter the Chanter (d. 1197)* (Binghamton: Medieval & Renaissance Texts & Studies, 1987); Megan McLaughlin, *Consorting with Saints: Prayer for the Dead in Early Medieval France* (Ithaca, N.Y.: Cornell University Press, 1994); Sergius Wroblewski, *Bonaventurian Theology of Prayer* (Pulaski, Wisc.: Franciscan Publishers, 1967).

Preachers, Order of *See* DOMINICAN ORDER.

preaching and preachers (homiletics) Medieval preaching might be defined as explicating in the VERNACULAR the texts of the liturgy of the day. According to a CAROLINGIAN council in 813, bishops and their CLERGY were to preach at least on Sundays and on feast days. Collections of sermons by AUGUSTINE, Caesarius of

Arles (469/470–542), and Pope GREGORY I THE GREAT were compiled and recopied from Christian late antiquity. One model for this was a homiliary written by the LOMBARD monk PAUL the Deacon. He collected patristic texts meant for particular feasts for a lectionary to use in the liturgy and in preaching to the people. Preaching was, however, secondary to the liturgy and the sacraments in pastoral care.

In the 13th century, with the rise of the MENDICANT orders and an increased awareness of HERESY, the PAPACY began to promote more preaching activity to assist people in understanding and practicing a true Christian life. An increased emphasis was placed on clerical education to enable priests to preach more effectively, to combat evangelization by heretical groups, and to avoid unknowingly spreading unacceptable doctrine.

The DOMINICANS and the FRANCISCANS adopted the technique of the so-called modern SERMON. In form the preacher began with a verse from the liturgy of the day, or the theme, and explained it point by point. Collections of model sermons were compiled for general use according to the CALENDAR of the church, for the feasts of saints, for occasions such as funerals and for certain social classes of people. Aids for the preacher soon followed. These were treatises on the art of preaching, or ARS PRAEDICANDI, concordances of Scripture, summaries of the lives of the saints, the writings of more or less contemporary Scholastic theologians and the FATHERS OF THE CHURCH, and lists of exemplary stories for the edification of the hearer. Some of the friars became famous for their effective and entertaining preaching. They drew huge open-air crowds, especially for their sermons during the seasons of ADVENT and LENT. The parish clergy also began to preach much more frequently, backing up the friars in the towns and particularly in rural parishes, where the mendicants rarely appeared. The 15th century was the great age of mendicant preachers.

See also ANTHONY OF PADUA, SAINT; ANTONINUS, SAINT; BERNARDINO OF SIENA, SAINT; BERTHOLD OF REGENSBURG OR RATISBON; EXEMPLUM; RHETORIC; SAVONAROLA, GIROLAMO; VITTORINO DA FELTRE.

Further reading: Jonathan Porter Berkey, *Popular Preaching and Religious Authority in the Medieval Islamic Near East* (Seattle: University of Washington Press, 2001); Marianne G. Briscoe, *Artes praedicandi* (Turnhout: Brepols, 1992); David L. D'Avray, *The Preaching of the Friars: Sermons Diffused from Paris before 1300* (Oxford: Clarendon Press, 1985); David L. D'Avray, *Death and the Prince: Memorial Preaching before 1350* (Oxford: Clarendon Press, 1994); Carolyn Muessig, ed., *Medieval Monastic Preaching* (Leiden: Brill, 1998); James J. Murphy, ed., *Three Medieval Rhetorical Arts* (Berkeley: University of California Press, 1971); John W. O'Malley, *Praise and Blame in Renaissance Rome: Rhetoric, Doctrine, and Reform in the Sacred Orators of the Papal Court, c. 1450–1521*

(Durham, N.C.: Duke University Press, 1979); Marc Saperstein, ed., *Jewish Preaching, 1200–1800: An Anthology* (New Haven, Conn.: Yale University Press, 1989); P. S. Wilson, *A Concise History of Preaching* (Nashville: Abingdon Press, 1992).

predestination   Predestination in the Middle Ages was the idea that some people, the elect, were gratuitously already destined for and were infallibly guided to SALVATION. It was considered a HERESY in the Middle Ages, but it and its implications were a part of much theological discussion and dispute. It could abrogate or at least question the doctrine of free will: that people can chose to do good or evil and then suffer the consequences, either salvation or damnation. GOD could also let people fall short of what was destined for them by their own actions or reprobation.

Predestination was a profound problem for medieval THEOLOGY and became an even greater issue in the 16th-century Reformation. It raised questions about the nature of GRACE, the universal saving will of GOD, divine gratuity, human merit and the value of good actions, future contingency, and, most important, human freedom and divine prescience. For the medieval church grace was a prerequisite for salvation, but it was not arbitrarily bestowed and could be earned.

See also AUGUSTINE OF HIPPO, SAINT; HUS, JOHN; JOHN SCOTTUS ERIUGENA; PELAGIANISM; WILLIAM OF OCKHAM; WYCLIFFE, JOHN.

Further reading: John Scottus Eriugena, *Treatise on Divine Predestination,* trans. Mary Brennan (Notre Dame, Ind.: University of Notre Dame Press, 1998); William, of Ockham, *Predestination, God's Foreknowledge, and Future Contingents,* trans. Marilyn McCord Adams and Norman Kretzmann, 2d ed. (Indianapolis: Hackett, 1983); Harm J. M. J. Goris, *Free Creatures of an Eternal God: Thomas Aquinas on God's Infallible Foreknowledge and Irresistible Will* (Louvain: Peeters, 1996); James L. Halverson, *Peter Aureol on Predestination: A Challenge to Late Medieval Thought* (Leiden: Brill, 1998).

Premonstratensians (Norbertines, White Canons)   The Order of Canons Regular of Prémontré in the Middle Ages was an order of regular canons living together in autonomous abbeys under the AUGUSTINIAN Rule. The foundation of the order was part of the great 12th-century reforming movement known as the GREGORIAN REFORM. When NORBERT OF XANTEN and his first disciples, all clerics and canons, made a profession in the solitude of Prémontré, near the town of LAON, on Christmas night 1121, the order was born. They aimed to establish a community based on the common ownership of goods, hospitality to the poor and pilgrims, solemn liturgical worship, and PREACHING. Their influence soon spread, producing a network of abbeys in FRANCE, GERMANY, ENGLAND, HUNGARY,

SPAIN and PORTUGAL, the NETHERLANDS, Scandinavia, POLAND, ITALY, PALESTINE, GREECE, and CYPRUS.

Norbert was made archbishop of Magdeburg and chancellor of the empire in 1126. In 1128 he entrusted the abbey of Prémontré to a successor, Hugh de Fosses (d. 1164). Hugh governed the order until his death in 1164. Under his leadership, it acquired a stable structure and set of practices consisting of an annual general chapter under the presidency of the abbot of Prémontré, a liturgical unity, and a convent life inspired by the CISTER-CIAN customs of Cîteaux. It had great success because it fulfilled the need for more pastoral care in the church, which the well-educated members of this order were equipped to provide.

LAY BROTHERS AND A FEMALE COMMUNITY

The order also included *fratres conversi,* or "lay brothers," who were by far the most numerous in the 12th century but whose number declined thereafter. They were present at a part of the divine OFFICE and dedicated their day to manual labor, playing a decisive role in the economic foundations of the abbeys. After Norbert settled at Prémontré, he welcomed women, whom he allowed a place complementary to his ideal of the male apostolic life, that is, nearby but in the background. The female community lived in a building of the abbey, making it a double monastery. The sisters spent their time in PRAYER and domestic duties, under the prioress and the abbot. In about 1140 the general chapter suppressed double monasteries. This measure marked the disappearance of all but a few of the Premonstratensian women's monasteries. A few survived in BOHEMIA and Poland. In the mid-12th century, the LAITY was allowed to participate in the spiritual life of the order, which changed over the Middle Ages into more withdrawn and contemplative life than active in pastoral care.

Further reading: David N. Bell, ed., *The Libraries of the Cistercians, Gilbertines, and Premonstratensians* (London: British Library in Association with the British Academy, 1992); James Bulloch, *Adam of Dryburgh* (London: S.P.C.K., 1958); Howard Montagu Colvin, *The White Canons in England* (Oxford: Clarendon Press, 1951); Cornelius James Kirkfleet, *History of Saint Norbert: Founder of the Norbertine (Premonstratensian) Order, Apostle of the Blessed Sacrament, Archbishop of Magdeburg* (St. Louis: B. Herder, 1916).

Premyslid dynasty (Pfemyslids, Przemsl) This dynasty held power in BOHEMIA from its beginnings in about 870 until 1306. The family name is from a legendary farmer, Premysl (Pfimizl). Libusč, a mythical prophetess appeared at an assembly for consultation on governance. She ordered that Premysl become prince and marry her. He then united the tribes of Bohemia, founded the first part of the city of PRAGUE, and established a principality.

The first documented member of this family at the end of the ninth century, was Bofivoj, who was baptized. Bofivoj's wife, Ludmilla, and his grandson, Prince Wenceslas the Saint, who reigned in the years 921/922–929, became the country's patron saints. The reigns of Boleslav I (r. 929–967) and Boleslav II (r. 967–999) consolidated the realm into the kingdom of Bohemia but subordinated it to the HOLY ROMAN EMPIRE. In the 11th and 12th centuries, Bohemia declined in importance, though princes such as Bretislav I (r. 1034– 55) and Vratislav II (r. 1061–92) succeeded in maintaining and promoting the interests of the state.

In the 13th century, Premysl Ottokar I (r. 1197–1230) unified the country and established the principle of hereditary succession for the dynasty. He also received recognition from the emperors as the prince of Bohemia. His grandson, Premysl Ottokar II the Great (r. 1253–78), journeyed to the shores of the Baltic, supporting troops of the TEUTONIC KNIGHTS. He occupied AUSTRIA and what are now Slovenia, Carinthia, and Carniola. RUDOLF of Habsburg was elected king of Germany in 1273 and halted this Czech expansion southward. Ottokar II's son, Wenceslas II (r. 1278–1305), turned his attention northward and obtained in 1300 the title of king of POLAND. After the extinction of the ÁRPÁD dynasty in HUNGARY in 1301, Wenceslas II's son, called Wenceslas III (r. 1305–06), was crowned as king of Hungary. For a short time, in 1305–06, the Premyslids united three Central European monarchies under their rule. The assassination of Wenceslas III in 1305/06, however, put a dramatic end to rule of the Premyslid dynasty.

See also PIAST DYNASTY.

Further reading: Francis Dvornik, *The Slavs in European History and Civilization* (New Brunswick, N.J.: Rutgers University Press, 1962); Francis Dvornik, *The Making of Central and Eastern Europe,* 2d ed. (Gulf Breeze, Fla.: Academic International Press, 1974); Mikulás Teich, ed., *Bohemia in History* (Cambridge: Cambridge University Press, 1998).

Prester John (Presbyter John) Prester John was a legendary wealthy ruler somewhere in the East. During the CRUSADES, stories circulated about a priest-king from the East, practicing a form of NESTORIANISM, who was thought to have marched to help liberate JERUSALEM from the Muslims. OTTO of Freising mentioned such a possibility. In 1160/65 a famous letter from him supposedly circulated among the rulers of Christendom. It described the power of a sovereign who reigned over a fabulously rich and exotic country earlier converted by the apostle Saint Thomas, perhaps India. The letter also showed the value of a realm where the church and the secular power worked well together. Even Hebrew versions referred to the lost tribes of Israel as living there. In 1177, Pope ALEXANDER III received a message from a certain "John,

King of the Indies," which might have been from ABYSSINIA or Ethiopia.

After an invasion of Persia by the MONGOLS in 1221, additional information reached the West through the intermediary of the Christians migrating from the East. They attributed these conquests to a "King David," the son of Prester John, but they seem to have confused him with JENGHIZ KHAN. Throughout the 13th century, travelers sought to identify this Christian "king of the Indies." He was a Christian king, sometimes defeated by the Mongols, sometimes holding out against them. His kingdom was at times identified with the land of the three kings of the Nativity of Christ and was situated either near China or in India. This was probably connected to the dying Nestorian Christian principalities in central Asia being swept aside by the Mongols. There were references to him and his kingdom on maps and in literary references.

In about 1321 a certain Jordan of Sévérac sought him in AFRICA and identified his realm with Ethiopia or Abyssinia, which was then regarded as one of the "Indies." The Ethiopians had encountered Europeans in Jerusalem. It was hoped that any Christian king from there could help the Christians in their struggle with the Muslims of EGYPT. Travelers in the 13th century continued to try to reach Prester John's kingdom in India or Africa. When the church, however, finally did make contact with the Ethiopians in the middle of the 15th century, Prester John was only a vague memory.

See also JOHN OF PLANO CARPINI; MANDEVILLE, JOHN, AND *MANDEVILLE'S TRAVELS*; MARCO POLO; WILLIAM OF RUBRUCK.

Further reading: L. N. Gumilev, *Searches for an Imaginary Kingdom: The Legend of the Kingdom of Prester John*, trans. R. E. F. Smith (Cambridge: Cambridge University Press, 1987); Charles F. Beckingham and Bernard Hamilton, eds., *Prester John, the Mongols, and the Ten Lost Tribes* (Aldershot, England: Variorum, 1996); Vsevolod Slessarev, *Prester John: The Letter and the Legend* (Minneapolis: University of Minnesota Press, 1959).

priests and priesthood (presbyter) Christianity was constructed as an alternative to Jewish ritualism and priestly tradition. That tradition attributed to the priesthood the management of the sacred. In the Christian New Testament, there was little allusion to a priesthood. In the early third century, the CLERGY gradually emerged and separated from the LAITY. Until then there was evidence that all Christians were deemed priests.

Eventually Christianity fixed on several traits of the concept of priest, which it then marshaled to clarify the role of the priest in the Christian religion. Jesus became the one mediator and model for the clergy. There was a vague concept of the priesthood of the whole church. Priesthood could be accorded by the GRACE of baptism. They further promoted the idea of a ministerial priest-hood with a necessary role in the administration and validity of the sacraments. These ideas were worked out through numerous conflicts lasting centuries. The specialized function of the priest was capped by a fundamental demand for a vow of CELIBACY, reception of the sacrament of Holy Orders, and a system of economic support. Many Christians questioned the necessity of all of this during the Middle Ages, especially the idea of a priest as a link between GOD and humankind, the privileged place of the priest in the world, and the relationship between the clerical and papal church and the rest of CHRISTENDOM.

See also ANTICLERICALISM; BENEFICE; CLERGY AND CLERICAL ORDERS; GREGORIAN REFORM; INVESTITURE CONTROVERSY OR DISPUTES; HUS, JOHN; LOLLARDS; SEVEN SACRAMENTS, WYCLIFFE, JOHN.

Further reading: Robert B. Ekelund, *Sacred Trust: The Medieval Church as an Economic Firm* (New York: Oxford University Press, 1996); Richard W. Southern, *Western Society and the Church in the Middle Ages* (Harmondsworth: Penguin Books, 1970); Robert N. Swanson, *Religion and Devotion in Europe, c. 1215–c. 1515* (Cambridge: Cambridge University Press, 1995).

primacy of pope *See* PAPACY.

printing, origins of Printing emerged in the 15th century. It was already known in China but probably developed independently in the West. The mechanical problems of producing printed matter were resolved into a workable method by the Mainz goldsmith Johann GUTENBERG. In 1455–56 he published his first printed book, the Gutenberg Bible, on paper and vellum. His lead type font was cut by hand in the German Gothic script of contemporary writing. This technique spread rapidly. By 1500 presses in Germany numbered about 60. Outside GERMANY Gothic type persisted for religious and law books for another century or far longer in some cases, but elsewhere it was replaced by a Roman type based on a 15th-century Italian humanist script similar to Caroline minuscule. The first press in ENGLAND was established in 1476 by William CAXTON, and the first dated English printed book appeared in 1477. The early printers were artists, craftsmen, publishers, and booksellers, who favored commercial centers, such as VENICE. The effect of printing and the shift from handwritten script to print on the distribution and communication of culture was obviously important, but the exact trends and the implications of this change are complex and much debated.

See also PARCHMENT; PUNCTUATION.

Further reading: Elizabeth L. Eisenstein, *The Printing Press as an Agent of Change: Communications and Cultural Transformations in Early Modern Europe*, 2 vols. (Cambridge: Cambridge University Press, 1979); Lucien P. Febvre and Henri-Jean Martin, *The Coming of the Book:*

The Impact of Printing 1450–1800, trans. David Gerard and ed. Geoffrey Nowell-Smith and David Wootton (London: N.L.B., 1976); Martin Lowry, *The World of Aldus Manutius: Business and Scholarship in Renaissance Venice* (Ithaca, N.Y.: Cornell University Press, 1979); David McKitterick, "The Beginning of Printing," in *The New Cambridge Medieval History*. Vol. 7, *c. 1415–c. 1500*, ed. Christopher Allmand (Cambridge: Cambridge University Press, 1998), 287–298; James Moran, *Printing Presses: History and Development from the Fifteenth Century to Modern Times* (Berkeley: University of California Press, 1973).

prisons In the Middle Ages *prison* could refer to an arrest and subsequent temporary confinement until the accused was obliged to appear before a judge on a fixed day. The prisons ensured that appearance and were not considered a punishment in themselves. Only rarely were they used as permanent or even temporary places to confine those being punished for a crime, or considered a threat to the safety of society for various reasons determined locally. This category comprised closed prisons in buildings intended for that purpose and under the surveillance of a jailer. Confinement in them was reserved for those who could not meet financial or human pledges guaranteeing their appearance for justice. If one could not pay the fine imposed by a court, one would have to remain in these houses of detention until the fine was paid. Ecclesiastical courts sometimes considered such sojourns an opportunity for reform. Since

The imprisoned Saint Columba of Sens is saved by a bear from an attack on her person (ca. 1350, Giovanni Baronzio), Pinacoteca di Brera, Milan, Italy *(Erich Lessing / Art Resource)*

ecclesiastical authorities did not practice the death penalty, they replaced it with perpetual confinement. Nonetheless, prisons in the late Middle Ages had bad or dangerous reputations. The inmates were poorly supported in this system. Conditions were particularly unpleasant and dangerous because of the bad and unhealthy state of the places themselves. Moreover, prisoners were obligated to pay for their own keep, whether they had the resources to do so or not. Security was never very strict or competent, however, and there were frequent prison escapes and breaks. There were benevolent organizations, such as certain CONFRATERNITIES, whose charitable mission was to help those in prison.

See also CRIME, PUNISHMENT, AND THE COURTS; JUSTICE; OUTLAWRY.

Further reading: John G. Bellamy, *Crime and Public Order in England in the Later Middle Ages* (London: Routledge and Kegan Paul, 1973); Christopher Harding, *Imprisonment in England and Wales: A Concise History* (London: Croom Helm, 1985); Norvall Morris and David J. Rothman, eds., *The Oxford History of the Prison: The Practice of Punishment in Western Society* (New York: Oxford University Press, 1995); Ralph B. Pugh, *Imprisonment in Medieval England* (London: Cambridge University Press, 1968).

processions, liturgical When ritual required positional changes within the church during liturgy—for example, at an entrance, the offering, or moving forward for communion—these changes were done to the accompaniment of music and followed an organized ritual of movement. "Procession" was reserved for important movements, distinguished by their function or by their occurrence often answering a special event or necessity. Other motion within a church service was "ordinary," or usually occurring regularly. Medieval processions occurred daily, such as at vespers; weekly, such as during Sunday blessings or Wednesday and Friday penitential processions; or annually, such as at Candlemas or Easter eve. During pilgrimage visits to prestigious sanctuaries, there were often festive processions to Roman sacred places. The Palm Sunday procession commemorated Jesus's entry into JERUSALEM. All these processions became associated with the notion of PILGRIMAGE. The music of all these processions might vary from a penitential psalm, with ANTIPHONS that served as refrains, to a festive or joyous HYMN for a happy commemoration.

Religious processions were more numerous at CONSTANTINOPLE than elsewhere, lent the capital a particular festive dignity, and provided a good example of Christianity's dominating the urban milieu. The system of processions seems to have developed in the fifth and sixth centuries as Constantinople built more churches. Processions could be organized on the occasion of a rare event such as earthquakes, invasions, translations of RELICS, and demonstrations of obedience to the emperor. Other occasions for processions were feasts of Christ, the Virgin MARY, the saints; the anniversary of the dedication of Constantinople on May 21; deliverance from siege; or commemoration of a victory. There were, moreover, some 68 annual processions filling out the calendar at Constantinople.

Further reading: Terence Bailey, *The Processions of Sarum and the Western Church* (Toronto: Pontifical Institute of Mediaeval Studies, 1971); Colin Dunlop, *Processions: A Dissertation, Together with Practical Suggestions* (London: Oxford University Press, 1932); Michael McCormick, *Eternal Victory: Triumphal Rulership in Late Antiquity, Byzantium, and the Early Medieval West* (Cambridge: Cambridge University Press, 1986); Edward Muir, *Ritual in Early Modern Europe* (Cambridge: Cambridge University Press, 1997).

Procopius of Caesarea (ca. 500–ca. 560/565) *historian*
Procopius was born in Caesarea in PALESTINE. After a classical education and practicing as a lawyer or advocate and rhetorician, he became secretary to the general BELIS-ARIUS in 527. He took part in his wars against the Persians, the VANDALS, and the OSTROGOTHS. Disillusioned with Belisarius, he probably had returned to CON-STANTINOPLE by 542; there besides witnessing the great PLAGUE, he wrote a history of Belisarius's wars and an account of the public buildings, including HAGIA SOPHIA, constructed during the reign of JUSTINIAN. His notorious, but remarkable *Secret History* from about 550 recorded the scandals of the court of Justinian and his wife, THEODORA, including, if not highlighting, their personal failings. Some have claimed that he could not have intended that it ever be circulated or published. He died sometime after 560.

Further reading: Procopius, *Procopius,* trans. H. B. Dewing, 7 vols. (Cambridge, Mass.: Harvard University Press, 1953–1962); Averil Cameron, *Procopius and the Sixth Century* (Berkeley: University of California Press, 1985); J. A. S. Evans, *Procopius* (New York: Twayne Publishers, 1972).

prohibited degrees   *See* FAMILY AND KINSHIP; MARRIAGE.

prophecy   Prophets were the inspired deliverers of God's message in Christianity, JUDAISM, and ISLAM. Prophecy in the Hebrew Bible and the Christian Old Testament was uttered by the prophets of Israel who were chosen by God and were sent as a guiding spirit. Among their roles were announcing the coming of a Messiah by explaining signs and reminding kings of their fidelity to an alliance between God and his chosen people. Jesus was considered by some the culmination of this prophetic tradition; with him revelation was

now complete. For Muslims, Moses and Jesus were prophets of God but had an incomplete message fully conveyed later by Muhammad, who was the last true prophet of God.

For medieval Christianity prophecy and the status of the prophet changed. It was no longer necessary to decode obscure passages from the past, particularly those linked to the time when the Messiah would return. The belief evolved that prophetic abilities or at least interpretation of the intentions of God was now reserved to the pope, bishops, and clergy, who were charged with guiding CHRISTENDOM. As the sole interpreters of Scripture, they considered themselves to have the power and responsibility for distinguishing true and false prophets. All prophecy outside Christendom including the message of Muhammad, was considered inauthentic.

The writings of HILDEGARD of Bingen in the late 12th century made warnings of dire punishments by several popes and the emperor FREDERICK I Barbarossa because of their political and religious conflicts. Medieval prophecy about the ages of the world and its end was made more complicated around 1200 by the work of JOACHIM of Fiore.

The first half of the 14th century was distinguished by numerous odd prophetic groups in Languedoc, such as those around Peter John OLIVI; Arnold of Villanova (ca. 1240–1311), a doctor for the king of Aragon; and the Franciscan Angelo Clareno (ca. 1255–1337) in Italy. They stressed the possible eschatological role for the laity. The papacy reacted quickly and brutally to what was perceived as a threat to its spiritual hegemony, often killing inopportune prophets. Still other prophets linked the crises of plague, military defeats, and all kinds of other problems with the arrival of an ANTICHRIST. He was already born and would soon cause the end of the world. The prophets' roles had changed to interpreting contemporary events and to identifying an Antichrist or a messianic king among the princes of his time. Prophecy had become a political genre especially interested in the worldly fate of Christendom, its kingdoms, or even down to the level of the Italian cities. The ecclesiastical chaos and the consequent discrediting of the clergy during the GREAT SCHISM between 1378 and 1417 increased this kind of activity. For the rest of the 15th century prophets cast doubt on the magisterium or the teaching authority of the papacy and of learned university professors and on the role of the clergy as the exclusive intermediary between God and humans.

See also BIRGITTA OF SWEDEN, SAINT; CATHERINE OF SIENA, SAINT; ESCHATOLOGY; GERSON, JOHN; JOAN OF ARC, SAINT.

Further reading: Lesley A. Coote, *Prophecy and Public Affairs in Later Medieval England* (Woodbridge: Boydell Press, 2000); Yohanan Friedmann, *Prophecy Continuous: Aspects of Ahmadi Religious Thought and Its Medieval Background* (Berkeley: University of California Press,

1989); Abraham Joshua Heschel, *Prophetic Inspiration after the Prophets: Maimonides and Other Medieval Authorities,* ed. Morris M. Faierstein (Hoboken, N.J.: Ktav, 1996); Theodore L. Steinberg, *Piers Plowman and Prophecy: An Approach to the C-Text* (New York: Garland, 1991).

prostitution (*zina*) Medieval prostitution was the selling of one's body for the pleasure of others in exchange for financial or other forms of profit. There were several levels or kinds of prostitution in the Middle Ages and RENAISSANCE. Some prostitutes worked in rural communities and some in cities at a variety of social levels, accessibility, and exploitation. Some of the medieval public considered them to be a social necessity and guarantee of matrimonial order.

Prostitution was justified as a necessary sexual outlet for the young until they could marry and for the relief it afforded to the tense and restrictive systems of marriage. Prostitutes could turn people away from more sinful unions that led to concubinage and grave adultery, thus threatening social organization and elite status or succession. They could function out of regular houses well known for this activity or else find their work on streets at certain locations, sometimes even approved by the government. Those who sold their body were usually driven to this by poverty and a lack of alternatives for survival. For women this could include being victims of rape, which, if known, severely limited their prospects for marriage. Sometimes they wore distinctive clothing to demonstrate their status. Selling one's body might have felt empowering to some, given the alternatives of complete poverty. Prostitution was considered reflective of the fallen state of humankind. There was little concern for the people forced to work as prostitutes. On the other hand, there were examples of municipal governments, or even ecclesiastical authorities, who actually profited from prostitutes' activities. In Islam, prostitution, or *zina,* was any unlawful intercourse and was punishable by stoning, whipping, or exile.

See also CHARITY AND POVERTY; CONTRACEPTION AND ABORTION; MARRIAGE; SEXUALITY AND SEXUAL ATTITUDES.

Further reading: Ruth Mazo Karras, *Common Women: Prostitution and Sexuality in Medieval England* (New York: Oxford University Press, 1996); Leah Lydia Otis, *Prostitution in Medieval Society: The History of an Urban Institution in Languedoc* (1980; reprint, Chicago: University of Chicago Press, 1985); Jacques Rossiaud, *Medieval Prostitution,* trans. Lydia G. Cochrane (1984; reprint, Oxford: Basil Blackwell, 1988).

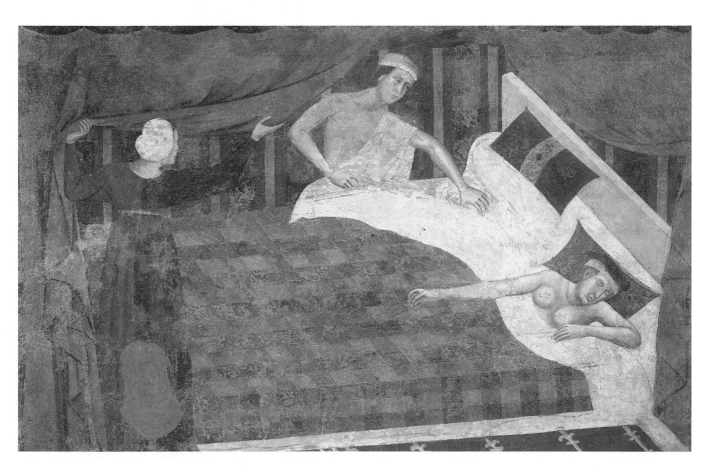

Bathhouse romance from the story of the dissolute young man. Fresco, ca. 1303–05, attributed to Memmo di Filippuccio (fl. 1294–1326), Museo Civico, San Gimignano, Italy *(Scala / Art Resource)*

Provence The name of the region of Provence developed from the Latin *provincial*. That geographical area had formed the Roman province of Cisalpina, later Narbonensis, and initially had covered the whole of southern Gaul. During the Middle Ages, it referred to a larger area than the French region does today, including CATALONIA in Spain and eastward to Liguria in Italy.

EARLY MIDDLE AGES

In the early Middle Ages, the BURGUNDIANS, the VISIGOTHS, the OSTROGOTHS, and the FRANKS all periodically controlled this region, which included the towns of Marseille, Arles, Aix, Fréjus, Riez, and Cimiez. There was considerable continuity of settlement and habitation between the fifth and the eighth centuries and trade continued with North Africa and the East until the late sixth century. This began to change after 739 and the Battle of POITIERS, when CHARLES Martel took control of this region at the margins of the Frankish kingdom. From 855, the progressive disintegration of the Carolingian Empire led to the creation of the Burgundian kingdom, or the kingdom of Arles. With the weakening of that government, Muslim raiders even set up a century-long settlement at Fraxinetum or La Garde-Freinet from 883.

ECONOMIC REVIVAL AND CULTURE

There was a revival of economic activity in the 11th century, and ecclesiastical activity fostered by the GREGORIAN REFORM movement and the foundation or expansion of monastic institutions. The second half of the 12th century was marked by a flowering of Provençal ROMANESQUE art and architecture and by development of the language and poetry of the TROUBADOURS.

A divided succession led in 1125 to a partition of Provence with the house of TOULOUSE, which acquired the land north of the Durance; the rest settled on the counts of BARCELONA. Provence would not have native or genuinely local rulers until modern times but did preserve a local assembly that had to be consulted on many matters. At the beginning of the 13th century, Raymond Berenguer V (d. 1246) established his rule and made Aix-en-Provence the seat of his government and court. In 1246, a representative of the northern French Crown. CHARLES I OF ANJOU, took control. Provence embarked on an era of economic growth and prosperity, supplemented by the settlement of the popes and their court at AVIGNON in the early 14th century. Most of the towns grew in prosperity and size, benefiting more than suffering from the provisioning and troop movements necessary for Crusades and other warfare, now almost constant. The MENDICANT ORDERS entered the cities, built churches, and tried to improve pastoral care of growing populations.

LATER MIDDLE AGES

Despite the presence of the papacy in Avignon, the 14th century was more difficult. There were sporadic famines from the 1310s to the 1330s. The Black Death entered Europe and Provence through the port of Marseille in 1348. Outbreaks of this disease became endemic, and it killed at least a third of the population. The warfare associated with the Hundred Years' War sent bands of mercenaries into the region, when they destroyed property, killed civilians, and demanded huge bribes to leave. Not until the peace treaties of the middle of the 15th century did a renewal of peaceful prosperity in the countryside and a revival or urban activity occur. The region was able to do well even under the harshly exploitative circumstances of the reign of King René of Anjou (1409–80). Though famous as a patron of the arts, he chose to wage expensive wars in northern France and in Italy to protect and regain his property and rights on NAPLES. In 1474, René left the region to his nephew, Charles of Maine, who in 1481 bequeathed Provence to another of René's nephews, King LOUIS XI of France. It then became formally part of the kingdom of France.

See also LANGUEDOC.

Further reading: John H. Pryor, *Business Contracts of Medieval Provence: Selected Notulae from the Cartulary of Giraud Amalric of Marseilles, 1248* (Toronto: Pontifical Institute of Mediaeval Studies, 1981); Kathryn Reyerson and John Drendel, eds., *Urban and Rural Communities in Medieval France: Provence and Languedoc, 1000–1500* (Leiden: Brill, 1998); Daniel Lord Smail, *Imaginary Cartography: Possession and Identity in Late Medieval Marseilles* (Ithaca, N.Y.: Cornell University Press, 2000).

provisions, ecclesiastical Ecclesiastical provisions were appointments by the pope to an ecclesiastical BENEFICE for which the pontiff received a fee. The new practice of ecclesiastical provision in the 12th century replaced elections for major benefices, self-appointment, and presentation by a patron for minor benefices. Beginning as a recommendation in ecclesiastical reform movements, it had become mandatory and was the usual practice by the 13th century. Very financially lucrative for the Holy See, it grew ceaselessly from then until the Great SCHISM in the late 14th century, when it was reduced by concordats between the papacy and the nationalistic governments of the 15th century. Such appointments could even take the form of expectative placements or promises for the possession of benefices not yet even vacant. The ability to do this was given to papal legates for the regions to which they had been sent. It was an important part of the expansion of papal power and papal taxation in the 14th century, all done for the needy popes in AVIGNON.

See also GREGORIAN REFORM; INVESTITURE CONTROVERSY OR DISPUTES; PAPACY; PRAEMUNIRE; PRAGMATIC SANCTION OF BOURGES; SIMONY.

Further reading: Guillaume Mollat, *The Popes at Avignon, 1305–1378*, trans. Janet Love (1949; reprint, New

York: T. Nelson, 1963); Yves Renouard, *Avignon Papacy, 1305–1403,* trans. Denis Bethell (London: Faber, 1970).

Prudentius (Aurelius Prudentius Clemens) (ca. 348–ca. 410) *Christian Latin poet*

Almost all knowledge of Prudentius's life has to be based on his own writings. He was born a Christian in Spain about 348 and as an adult practiced law. After a successful career as a civil administrator, in which he rose to a position at the imperial court, he decided to devote himself to composing didactic Christian poetry and to writing about other ecclesiastical and theological matters. He published most of this poetry in a collection in 405. It showed a close acquaintance with classical Latin poetry.

OTHER WORKS

His work consisted of treatises in several genres. One was his lyrical *Hymns for Every Day,* made up of 12 poems, six for use at particular hours of the day and six for occasional use. His didactic *The Divinity of Christ* treated the nature of Christ, while *The Origin of Sin* was aimed at the Gnostic errors and the teachings of the the second-century heretic Marcion (d. ca. 154). The *Spiritual Combat* (Pyscomachia) was his most popular work in the Middle Ages. It was allegorical, describing combat between the personified VIRTUES and the vices. His tract *Against Symmachus* concerned the controversy over the removal of the altar of Victory, a great symbol of paganism, from the Roman senate house in 382. His arguments were similar to those of AMBROSE of Milan, especially in their ideas that the empire might now incorporate everyone as one people. It ended with an appeal to the emperor Honorius (r. 395–423) to end the gladiatorial games that still occurred. He also wrote hymns about Spanish and Italian martyrs and sets of verses linked to specific scenes from Scripture. He died about 410.

See also BREVIARY; HYMNS, HYMNALS, AND HYMNOLOGY.

Further reading: Prudentius, *The Poems of Prudentius,* trans. M. Clement Eagan, 2 vols. (Washington, D.C.: Catholic University of America Press, 1962); Martha A. Malamud, *A Poetics of Transformation: Prudentius and Classical Mythology* (Ithaca, N.Y.: Cornell University Press, 1989); Anne-Marie Palmer, *Prudentius on the Martyrs* (Oxford: Clarendon Press, 1989).

Prussia

Medieval Prussia was a region on the southern coast of the Baltic Sea, between the Vistula and Niemen Rivers and inhabited from the sixth century by the Prussian tribes, related to the Lithuanians. Despite their contacts with Christian POLAND from the 11th and 12th centuries, they preserved their tribal structure and remained pagan. In 1220, the emperor FREDERICK II, urged the TEUTONIC KNIGHTS and their grand master, Hermann of Salza (d. 1239), to invade, conquer, and Christianize Prussia. Consequently the Prussians were forcibly converted. Those who resisted were killed. In their desire to control the region, the Teutonic Order introduced German settlers into Prussia. The Teutonic Knights expanded their control during the 13th century, both along the Baltic coast toward LIVONIA and Pomerania and to the south. This expansionary process of Germanization and the economic activity of the HANSEATIC LEAGUE yielded prosperity and led to the establishment of cities. These urban centers in the 14th century sought communal privileges. Conflict between the cities and the order weakened the power of the knights, and in the early 15th century Polish kings intervened. In 1410 King Ladislas II (r. 1399–1434) defeated the knights at Tannenberg. Prussia after that was tied to the emergence of Brandenbury and the HOHENZOLLERN dynasty.

See also LITHUANIA.

Further reading: Michael Burleigh, *Prussian Society and the German Order: An Aristocratic Corporation in Crisis c. 1410–1466* (Cambridge: Cambridge University Press, 1984); F. L. Carsten, *The Origins of Prussia* (Oxford: Clarendon Press, 1954); Andrzej Nowakowski, *Arms and Armour in the Medieval Teutonic Order's State in Prussia,* trans, Maria Abramowicz (Lódz: Oficyna Naukowa MS, 1994); William L. Urban, *The Prussian Crusade* (Lanham, Md.: University of America, 1980); Stanislaw Zajaczkowski, *Rise and Fall of the Teutonic Order in Prussia* (London: J. S. Bergson, 1935).

Psalter

The traditional medieval Psalter was a collection of 150 lyric poems from the BIBLE, probably composed between the 10th and third centuries B.C.E. Although originally written in Hebrew, the contents were translated into Latin using the Greek Septuagint version of the texts. These poems were well adapted to encourage meditation. The Psalter became a liturgical book used by monks to be read or heard as part of the daily OFFICE, as had been defined by the Rule of Saint BENEDICT. In the Middle Ages, monastic life involved an almost continual reading of the Psalter.

BIBLICAL AND LITURGICAL PSALTERS

From the early Middle Ages, a distinction developed between the biblical Psalter and the liturgical Psalter. The former retained the biblical version of the Psalter, the liturgical Psalter had seven subdivisions that corresponded to each day of the week. During the Carolingian period, the liturgical Psalter was enriched with HYMNS, ANTIPHONS, canticles, and prayers, all forming the core of the BREVIARY. From 1100, new collections were made and became more specialized, created for night offices, morning hours, or daytime hours.

ILLUSTRATION AND DECORATION

Throughout the Middle Ages, Psalters were also viewed as luxurious books and were decorated. In both the East

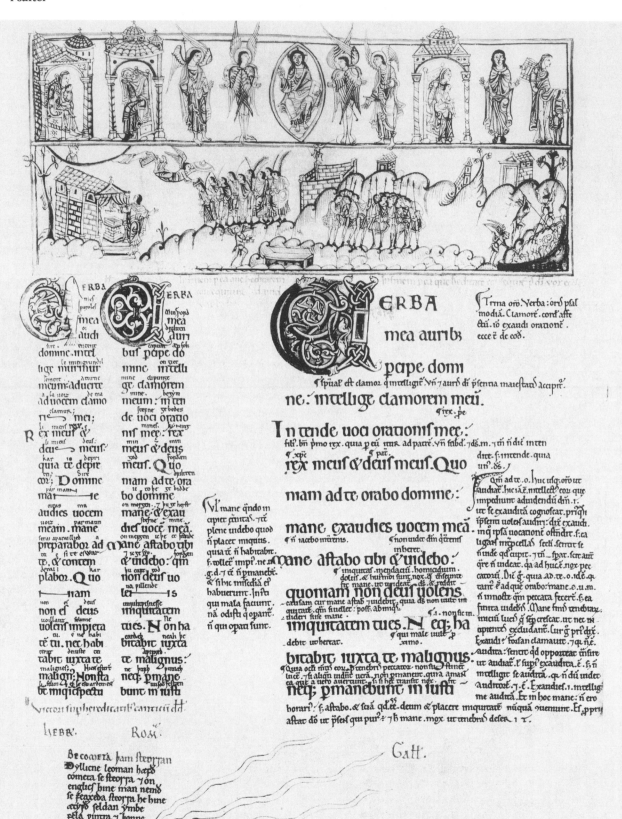

The Canterbury Psalter, an illuminated manuscript with an illustration thought to be of Halley's comet (12th century) *(Courtesy Library of Congress)*

and the West, illustrated Psalters had full-page paintings, decorated with ornate initials, glosses, and marginal illustrations. These Psalter illustrations in the Middle Ages were intended to transform the text of the psalms into literal and didactic images that reflected the content, meaning, and sentiment of the psalms.

See also ILLUMINATION; PRAYER.

Further reading: Janet Backhouse, *Medieval Rural Life in the Luttrell Psalter* (Toronto: University of Toronto Press, 2000); Anthony Cutler, *The Aristocratic Psalters of Byzantium* (Paris: Picard, 1984); Michael Camille, *Mirror in Parchment: The Luttrell Psalter and the Making of Medieval England* (Chicago: University of Chicago Press, 1998); Adam Cleghorn Welch, *The Psalter in Life, Worship and History* (Oxford: Clarendon Press, 1926).

Psellos, Michael (Constantine) (1018–ca. 1078) *Byzantine writer, statesman*

Constantine Psellos or Psellus was born at CONSTANTINOPLE or Nicomedia in 1018, in a noble but not rich family. He later as a monk took the name Michael. He was raised by his mother, for whom he expressed great admiration in her funeral eulogy. He received a broad education in the law, rhetoric, and PHILOSOPHY. After beginning a legal career and service as a judge's clerk in ANATOLIA, he entered the administration of the central government in Constantinople in about 1042, being favored as a counselor of the intellectual emperor Constantine IX Monomachos (r. 1042–55). Appointed to the prestigious office of chief of philosophers, Psellos taught philosophy at the new University of Constantinople. He had wide interests and wrote treatises on RHETORIC, the law, philosophy (including NEOPLATONISM), MEDICINE, history, and ALCHEMY.

This interest in the pagan philosophers and occult sciences made him suspicious to some of the clergy of the Orthodox Church. After accusations of being a pagan, he had to make an explicit profession of the Orthodox faith in 1054. In the meantime he had fallen into disgrace for political reasons. Psellos had to move with his friend, the patriarch of Constantinople, John VIII Xiphilinos (r. 1064–75), to a remote monastery on Mount Olympus. He was recalled to court and once more played a political role by helping secure the accession of Michael VII Doukas (r. 1071–78) in 1071, after unscrupulously helping in the deposing of the emperor Romanos IV Diogenes (r. 1067–71), who had lost the catastrophic Battle of MANZIKERT that same year. However, another turn of events and fortunes led to his retirement from the world again in 1074. He died as a monk in about 1078 at the monastery of Narsou.

BREADTH OF WRITING

Besides being known for his personal vanity and dubiously ethical political activities, Psellos left a wide variety of written work, including an encyclopedic manual on the origin of numerous aspects of the fields of THEOLOGY, PHILOSOPHY, and the natural sciences. In addition, he wrote a legal treatise, important historical works on the Byzantine Empire in the 10th and 11th centuries, funeral eulogies, grammatical treatises, letters, several smaller philosophical essays, his lecture notes, and a collection of answers to miscellaneous philosophical and cultural questions posed by students. He always strenuously denied any belief in the pagan doctrines he discussed and studied, asserting that he explored them better to serve the Orthodox faith, though he continued to be attacked throughout his life for his alleged pagan ideas.

See also MACEDONIAN DYNASTY.

Further reading: Michael Psellus, *The Chronographia of Michael Psellus*, trans. E. R. A. Sewter (London: Routledge & Kegan Paul, 1953); Michael Psellus, *Fourteen Byzantine Rulers: The Chronographia*, trans. E. R. A. Sewter (Baltimore: Penguin Books, 1966); Anitra Gadolin, *A Theory of History and Society with Special Reference to the Chronographia of Michael Psellus: Eleventh Century Byzantium and a Related Section on Islamic Ethics* (Amsterdam: Adolf M. Hakkert, 1987); Joan Hussey, *Church & Learning in the Byzantine Empire, 867–1185* (London: Oxford University Press, 1937); Anthony Kaldellis, *The Argument of Psellos' Chronographia* (Leiden: Brill, 1999); Jaroslav L. Pelikan, *The Christian Tradition: A History of the Development of Doctrine.* Vol. 2, *The Spirit of Eastern Christendom (600–1700)* (Chicago: University of Chicago Press, 1974); Steven Runciman, *The Eastern Schism: A Study of the Papacy and the Eastern Churches during the XIth and the XIIth Centuries* (Oxford: Clarendon Press, 1955).

Pseudo-Dionysian writings See DIONYSIS THE AREOPAGITE.

Ptolemeic astronomy See ASTRONOMY.

Ptolemy of Lucca (Bartolommeo Fiadoni, Tolomeo) (ca. 1236–1327) *civic and ecclesiastical author*

Born into the Fiadoni family in LUCCA, Ptolemy joined the DOMINICANS as an adult. He became a close friend of Thomas AQUINAS, whose *On the Regime of Princes* he supposedly finished, in the early 1270s. Prior of convents at Lucca and FLORENCE, Ptolemy spent a decade at AVIGNON, between 1309 and 1319. As the bishop of Torcello from 1318, he was imprisoned by the patriarch of Grado, but he was freed on orders from Pope JOHN XXII in 1323. He was a supporter of communal theory of government and a strong promoter of the hierocratic theory of papal power. He also wrote a respected history of the church. He died at Torcello in 1327.

Further reading: Ptolemy of Lucca, *On the Government of Rulers*, De regimine principum, trans. James M.

Blythe (Philadelphia: University of Pennsylvania Press, 1997); James M. Blythe, *Ideal Government and the Mixed Constitution in the Middle Ages* (Princeton, N.J.: Princeton University Press, 1992).

Pucelle, Jean (ca. 1295–ca. 1334) *French illuminator of manuscripts*
We know little about Jean's place of birth or the training of this manuscript illuminator. Between 1319 and 1327, he directed an important studio for decorating manuscripts at PARIS. Two of his known and signed works were accomplished in collaboration, the *Belleville Breviary* (1323–26) and the *Bible of Robert de Billyng*. On the other hand, his masterpiece, the *Hours of Jeanne d' Évreux* (1325–28), was probably created entirely by him alone. He drew it in grisaille, a Flemish style in shades of gray. This work was commissioned by King Charles IV the Fair (r. 1322–28) for his third wife, Queen Jeanne d'Évreux. It is now in the Cloisters at the Metropolitan Museum in New York. According to stylistic similarities, other manuscripts have been attributed to Jean Pucelle and his studio: the *Breviary of Blanche of France*, the *Hours of Jeanne of Savoy*, the *Hours of Yolande of Flanders*, the *Hours of Jeanne II Navarre*, and the *Psalter of Queen Bonne of Luxembourg*.

Known for his complex programs of uneven quality, he usually surrounded the text with grotesque figures. His taste for pictorial space and naturalistic PAINTING probably derived from a trip to ITALY, where he visited PISA, FLORENCE, and SIENA. He created somewhat awkward perspective and foreshortening. Pucelle was an early participant in the development of the international GOTHIC style and dominated Parisian art in the first half of the 14th century. He died in Paris sometime after 1334.

See also ILLUMINATION.

Further reading: François Avril, *Manuscript Painting at the Court of France: The Fourteenth Century, 1310–1380*, trans. Ursule Molinaro with the assistance of Bruce Benderson (New York: G. Braziller, 1978); Barbara Drake Boehm, Abigail Quandt, and William D. Wixom, *The Hours of Jeanne d'Évreux: Acc. No. 54.I.2, The Metropolitan Museum of Art, The Cloisters Collection, New York* (New York: Metropolitan Museum of Art, 2000); Kathleen Morand, *Jean Pucelle* (Oxford: Clarendon Press, 1962).

Puglia   *See* APULIA.

punctuation (pointing)   The use of punctuation in medieval texts and writing was a way of clarifying visually the elements of meaning or the grammatical structure of a written text as they might be clearly enunciated and distinguished in speech. Punctuation was also useful in reading aloud, according a clear rhythm. Conventions of punctuation developed over time according to a number of variables and needs, including the language used and the purpose of reading. A result of the growth in literacy, punctuation developed to make writing readable by a wider audience, who might not be completely familiar with a text. Its development showed clear growth and changes in the number, range, and meaning of its signs over time, as texts were read silently more often and dissociated from oral performance. In addition to marks of punctuation, there were changes in the conventions of textual layout such as the use of capital or majuscule letters, spacing between words, lineation, and division into chapters, books, or sections. All of this was ultimately intended to contribute to clarifying the meaning of written texts.

Separation between words was not consistently practiced until the Carolingian period. Ancient grammarians had employed three signs for marking divisions of speech, the point low down, or comma, for a brief pause; the point halfway up, or the colon, for medial-length pauses; and the point at the top, or the period, for the end of sentences. This simple classical system became the basis for medieval punctuation. It was further modified by the introduction of new signs such as the semicolon and the two-point colon for medial pauses and the question mark during the Carolingian era. Other marks of punctuation were added in the later Middle Ages to divide texts according to content, such as the paragraph sign (¶ and the section mark (§). The use of all of these conventions varied with time and place. Modern punctuation was derived from these medieval conventions.

See also CASSIODORUS, SENATOR; PALEOGRAPHY; PRINTING, ORIGINS OF.

Further reading: Bernhard Bischoff, *Latin Paleography: Antiquity and the Middle Ages,* trans. Dáibhí óCróinín and David Ganz (Cambridge: Cambridge University Press, 1990); Peter Clemoes, *Liturgical Influence on Punctuation in Late Old English and Early Middle English Manuscripts* (Binghamton: CEMERS, 1980); Malcolm B. Parkes, *Pause and Effect: An Introduction to the History of Punctuation in the West* (Berkeley: University of California Press, 1993).

punishment   *See* CRIME, PUNISHMENT AND THE COURTS; LAST JUDGMENT.

purgatory   Purgatory designated the place where the SOUL of those who had not yet expiated their venial sins went after DEATH. This idea gradually took shape from a slow development of ideas, beliefs, and practices concerning the destiny of the soul immediately after death. Purgatory did not have a scriptural basis. It was tied essentially to the custom and practice of praying for the dead, which in turn was linked to the belief that the condition of life beyond the grave could be alleviated by

Christ in Purgatory and Descent into Hell, engraving by Andrea Mantegna *(Courtesy Library of Congress)*

efforts among the living. Some of the FATHERS OF THE CHURCH thought that between the particular judgment of a soul at death and the LAST JUDGMENT there could be sinners who might still attain salvation through a purification and could be helped by the prayers of the living.

Purgatory was a sort of midpoint for those who had committed sins that did not condemn one to hell yet barred one from PARADISE or HEAVEN. These were pardonable or venial, but not mortal sins. Purgatory was a place of expiation or punishment carried out beyond the grave. Punishment there was dual: the pain of postponement from the BEATIFIC VISION and the pain of cleansing fire. The intensity and duration of the pain were to be proportional to the fault and could be alleviated by the prayers of the church in this world. This doctrine was defined in the early 12th century and elaborated in the 13th century by Scholastics such as Thomas AQUINAS. Papal and conciliar approval followed in the 13th through 15th centuries. It was a comforting thought to Christians that the deceased, though not perfect in this world, might still have a chance for salvation when assisted by the actions of those still alive. An economy of salvation that quantified ways of assistance, such as paying for clerical prayers and gaining or buying INDULGENCES for the deceased, developed. Such ideas did not exist in JUDAISM or ISLAM. Their assumption was that only the mercy and JUSTICE of GOD were involved in one's fate after death.

See also ALIGHIERI, DANTE; HARROWING OF HELL; INDULGENCES; LIMBO; REDEMPTION.

Further reading: Michael Haren and Yolande de Pontfarcy, ed., *The Medieval Pilgrimage to St. Patrick's Purgatory: Lough Derg and the European Tradition* (Enniskillen: Clogher Historical Society, 1988); Jacques Le Goff, *The Birth of Purgatory,* trans. Arthur Goldhammer (Chicago: University of Chicago Press, 1986); Takami Matsuda, *Death and Purgatory in Middle English Didactic Poetry* (Woodbridge: D.S. Brewer, 1997); Alison Morgan, *Dante and the Medieval Other World* (Cambridge: Cambridge University Press, 1990).

pyx and pyxis (boxwood vessel)   The pyx is a generally small object, usually a cylindrical box of IVORY, silver, GOLD, or other metal. Such boxes or containers had been used in antiquity to store jewels or incense. In the Middle Ages there were two main uses for such boxes, as a reliquary or as a receptacle to store consecrated hosts from one eucharistic to another eucharistic service. Such a reliquary was designed by the term *capsa* and contained the consecrated host. It too was called *pyxis* or *pyx* and was used for taking communion to the ill or dying.

See also METALSMITHS AND METAL WORK, METALLURGY.

Further reading: "Pyx," in *The Oxford Dictionary of the Christian Church,* 1353.

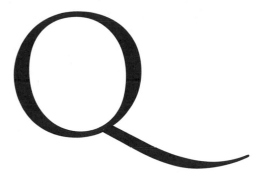

Qaba *See* KABA.

qadi (*cadi*) In Islamic society, the *qadi,* or "judge," was a salaried official responsible for interpreting details and rendering judgments in legal cases. The first qadis were appointed by the CALIPHS in MEDINA in the 630s. During the UMAYYAD Caliphate between 661 and 750 C.E. most qadis were appointed by local governors. Qadis represented and personified the judicial authority of the caliph, who of course could not be everywhere. With no hierarchy of courts or judges, there could be little appeal actions on his own. He heard cases in MOSQUES or in his own home. The role of the qadi grew in Umayyad provincial administration, in which local governors had much autonomy. Over time the duties of the qadi grew to encompass a range of administrative as well as judicial duties.

Until more than a century after the life of MUHAMMAD, there was no written or as yet commonly accepted corpus of Islamic legal doctrine on which to base judicial decisions. So qadis had to be learned in the QURAN themselves and knowledgeable about the ideas and practices of Muhammad. When the core of a case was not directly addressed in the Quran, they relied on local customary law, local consensus (*ijma*), and their own personal reasoning. Not all qadis were known for their piety or religious learning—some had received their positions because of political connections. Toward the end of the Umayyad period, they were more often in conflict with governors as their decisions became more specifically identified with enforcing and defining religious law, the nascent sharia.

ABBASIDS from 750 tried to implement more explicitly the Islamic religious law, or the sharia, which was not clearly defined until the 11th century. Beginning with reign of HARUN AL-RASHID, his central government and established appointed of local judges a chief judge in BAGHDAD. From then on qadis confined to cases explicitly involving Islamic law. The Abbasid government tried to assume more responsibility for administrative and criminal cases in private, civil, and public matters.

Pious men were reluctant to accept the role of *qadi* because of fear of divine punishment for wrongful or mistaken verdicts or of reprisals by vengeful governors.

Further reading: Antony J. Black, *The History of Islamic Political Thought: From the Prophet to the Present* (New York: Routledge, 2001); Joseph H. Escovitz, *The Office of Qadi al-Qudat in Cairo under the Bahri Mamluks* (Berlin: Klaus Schwarz, 1984); Ignaz Goldziher, *Introduction to Islamic Theology and Law,* trans. Andras and Ruth Hamori (1910; reprint, Princeton, N.J.: Princeton University Press, 1981); Joseph Schacht, *The Origins of Muhammadan Jurisprudence* (Oxford: Clarendon Press, 1950).

al-Qayrawan (**al-Kairouan, Kairwan, Qairouan**) Medieval al-Qayrawan was a city in present-day TUNISIA, now called Kairouan. It was founded in 670 by Uqbah ibn Nafi (d. 682), the Arab general who conquered Ifriqiya. It started as a military camp, because the early Muslim armies were quartered apart from the newly subjected populations. The principal monument in al-Qayrawan is the Great Mosque, also known as the MOSQUE of Sidi Uqba. It was built in 724–43. The present MINARET was added in 836. It was modified and rebuilt several times between then and 1294. There were three satellite cities, impressive cisterns, and a town wall from 1052. Until the

11th century, it was the administrative, religious, and commercial capital of Islamic North Africa.

See also AFRICA; AGHLABIDS; BERBERS; FATIMIDS.

Further reading: William Dallam Armes, *The African Mecca: The Holy City of Kairouan* (Berkeley: University of California Press, 1915); Markus Hattstein and Peter Delius, eds., *Islam: Art and Architecture,* trans. George Ansell et al. (Cologne: Könemann, 2000); Graham Petrie, *Tunis, Kairouan and Carthage: Described and Illustrated with Forty-Eight Paintings* (London: Darf, 1985).

Qipchaqs   *See* CUMANS.

quadrivium   *See* SEVEN LIBERAL ARTS.

Qubilai   *See* KUBLAI KHAN.

quodlibet (whatever you please)   This was a special kind of disputed question in medieval universities. The discussion was not on a prearranged subject, but a master had to answer spontaneous questions posed by the audience. As a literary genre it had origins in PARIS in the first quarter of the 13th century and was further developed by Thomas AQUINAS. At the end of the century and the start of the 14th, it became one of the preferred modes of teaching. Giles of Rome (1247–1316), Richard of Middleton (d. 1305), Godfrey of Fontaines (d. 1302), and especially HENRY OF GHENT often worked in this format. During the 14th century it gradually fell out of use in Paris for THEOLOGY, but it remained alive in other faculties within universities there and elsewhere.

See also PHILOSOPHY AND THEOLOGY; SCHOLASTICISM AND SCHOLASTIC METHOD; UNIVERSITIES AND SCHOOLS.

Further reading: Thomas, Aquinas, *Quodlibetal Questions 1 and 2,* trans. Sandra Edwards (Toronto: Pontifical Institute of Mediaeval Studies, 1983); Louis Jacques Bataillon, "Quodlibet," *EMA* 2.1,207.

Quran (Koran, al-Kuran, Recitation, Proclamation)   The Quran was and has remained the Islamic Scripture. It contained the revelations from GOD to MUHAMMAD, who recited it to his followers over a period of about 20 years, up to his death in 632 C.E. During his lifetime and for some time afterward, most of the 114 units of the revelation, later to be called suras, did not have an agreed-upon form but were constantly revised and expanded to be as he was believed to have recited them.

CONTENT

One distinctive characteristic of the Quran was that its content followed the circumstances of Muhammad's life. So its content offered encouragement in moments of persecution and doubt; while at other moments, they refuted accusations that he was a magician, soothsayer, or poet inspired by an evil spirit. Muhammad sometimes also responded to specific questions raised by his followers. God was always the the "speaker" throughout the Quran, and Muhammad was frequently the person addressed. Certain passages were addressed to contemporaries of Muhammad, his opponents in MECCA, Jews in MEDINA, hesitant followers, and wives. All of it was taken to be normative and didactic.

Much of the Meccan portions were of narratives similar to stories in the BIBLE. However their details were sometimes only found in Jewish and Christian apocryphal writings and oral traditions. There were stories about Adam, Noah, Abraham or Ibrahim, Moses or Musa, and Jesus or Isa ibn Maryam (Jesus, son of Mary). These biblical characters promoted submission to the one true God, the core of ISLAM. In later Islamic teaching God through the angel Gabriel had given portions of his truth to these earlier prophets. The Jews and Christians then distorted it further. Only the Quran was an exact copy of the heavenly book of revelation and instruction. Previous Scripture was only valid when it conformed to the Quran.

Some parts of the Quran were from the last 10 years of Muhammad's life, when he was organizing a new religious community in Medina, one that was independent of and consciously trying to be different from those of the Jews or the Christians. It was then that he instituted fundamental Islamic practices, such as the daily PRAYER ritual called the *salat,* fasting during the month of RAMADAN, and an obligatory pilgrimage to Mecca. Other Quranic statements made clear the required belief in one God, his ANGELS, his Scriptures, his prophet Muhammad, and the future last day of judgment.

EVOLUTION OF THE TEXT

A complete and official text was compiled and edited about 20 years after the death of Muhammad, during the reign of the third caliph, UTHMAN IBN AFAN. This text contained 114 *suras.* Early manuscripts of the Quran were written in a script that consisted only of consonants, without any diacritical marks to help with understanding and reading. Such diacritics were later used to indicate vowels and distinguish two or more consonantal sounds sharing the same written form. The Quran continued to be interpreted and recited in a variety of ways. The powerful governor of Iraq, al-Hajjaj (694–714), tried to stabilize this text and establish a standard system of signs for indicating vowels and dots for marking consonantal sounds. This way of writing was accepted very slowly, and even then it did not prevent the text from continuing to be read in sundry and diverse ways. Three centuries after the death of Muhammad, however, Ibn Mujahid (d. 936) established a uniform text of the Quran by asserting that only a Uthmanic consonantal text was authentic, rejecting so-called companion texts or codices. Eventually a version of these readings was accepted throughout the Muslim world. For Muslims the Quran was more than an equivalent to the sacred Scriptures of other religious communities.

RELIGIOUS SIGNIFICANCE

The Quran was explicitly and preeminently the word of God. A vast majority of Muslims experienced the Quran only in an oral form. After memorizing and reciting it, they then often encountered its words in a visual form written in Arabic calligraphy, which was a major decorative and didactic motif in Islamic architecture and art. The words must be approached within the context of a ritual piety, since they were divine signs and proofs of God. It should only be read and understood in the Arabic language, whatever the language of a believer. It was a guide for everything in life.

During the formative years of Islam, the Quran was the primary source of Islamic theology and law, the Sharia. The belief that the Quran was the eternal speech of God was one of the most important cornerstones of Islam. This produced a belief that it was the highest form of Arabic expression; its language came to influence and dominate standard Arabic grammar and lexicography. Christian reactions to the Quran were critical and tried to show that its message was at best derivative. However, Christian commentators did show a clear awareness of its importance for Islam.

See also ART AND ARCHITECTURE, ISLAMIC; LAST JUDGMENT.

Further reading: *The Koran,* trans. N. J. Dawood (1959; reprint, New York: Penguin, 1999); Muhammad Abu-Hamdiyyah, *The Qur'an: An Introduction* (New York: Routledge, 2000); M. A. Cook, *The Koran: A Very Short Introduction* (Oxford: Oxford University Press, 2000).

Quraysh The Quraysh were the dominant tribe in MECCA in the time of MUHAMMAD, who was a member of the Hashemite clan within it. The Quraysh seemed to have been named after an aquatic mammal, perhaps a shark or a dugong, of the Red Sea. This etymology suggested a trading group based on the sea. Later members of this tribe were eligible to serve in the office of CALIPH according to SUNNI ISLAM.

Further reading: Patricia Crone, *Meccan Trade and the Rise of Islam* (Princeton, N.J.: Princeton University Press, 1987); Wilfred Madelung, *The Succession to Muhammad: A Study of the Early Caliphate* (Cambridge: Cambridge University Press, 1997); Róbert Simon, *Meccan Trade and Islam: Problems of Origin and Structure,* trans. Feodora Sós (Budapest: Akadémiai Kiadó, 1989); W. Montgomery Watt, *Muhammad at Mecca* (1953; reprint, New York: Oxford University Press; 1979); W. Montgomery Watt, *Muhammad at Medina* (Oxford: Clarendon Press, 1956).

R

Rabanus Maurus *See* HRABANUS MAURUS.

Rabat (al-Ribat al-Fath) The medieval city of Rabat, the capital of present-day MOROCCO, was located on the southern side of the mouth of the Bou Regreg River as it entered the Atlantic Ocean. There were a twin city on the northern bank, Salé. There may have been a Roman town earlier; the present city was founded in the 12th century by the ALMOHAD ruler Abd al-Mumin (r. 1130–63) as a base for his invasion of the Iberian Peninsula. The walls and two gates that he built still stand. The MOSQUE of Hasan, the most famous monument in the city, was meant to be the largest in the Islamic world. Building was started in 1196 after an Almohad victory over Alfonso VIII the Noble (r. 1158–1214) at Alarcos in SPAIN. At the death of Abu Yaqub al-Mansur (r. 1184–99) in 1199, construction was stopped, but significant remains are extant, including the MINARET of Hasan.

The Marinids built the principal mosque in the city in the 13th century. An important MADRASA was founded in 1341 across the river in Salé. Rabat, however, was always a secondary city for the various dynasties who subsequently controlled Morocco.

Further reading: Markus Hattstein and Peter Delius, eds., *Islam: Art and Architecture,* trans. George Ansell et al. (Cologne: Könemann, 2000); E. Levi-Provençal and J. F. Troin, "Ribat al-Fath," *Encyclopedia of Islam* 8:506–508.

Radegund, Saint (Radegunda) (ca. 520–587) *founder of several monastic and charitable institutions*
An important participant in the establishment of female MONASTICISM in the early Middle Ages, Saint Radegund, was well represented by contemporary sources: in the letters of her friend Venantius Fortunatus (ca. 535–ca. 610), a life written by one of her followers, and a description of her by her protector, GREGORY OF TOURS. She was born in Thuringia, the king's daughter. On the conquest of her kingdom by the FRANKS in 531, Radegund at age 12 and her brother, were imprisoned and taken by King Clothar (r. 511–561), the king of Soissons and later a Merovingian king of the Franks, to his palace of Athies. He was an evil man, was completely unfaithful, and had debased tastes.

At Athies Radegund received an education in Christianity by studying the Scriptures and their patristic commentaries. From then on she grew more devoted to PRAYER and the care of the poor. Clothar decided to marry her because of her beauty and the political advantages of her royal background. After an unsuccessful attempt at escape, Radegund was forced into marriage; she became queen at Soissons in about 540. She continued her pious foundations and gave herself over to long hours of prayer and penance, deserting the conjugal bed to pray. Clothar unhappily nicknamed her the "queen-nun." His murder of her brother about 555 and his taunting about their childlessness drove her to desert him, this time successfully, and retreat to Noyon, where she became a nun, was consecrated a deaconess, and went on a PILGRIMAGE.

RADEGUND AS A NUN

Radegund then moved to Saix, where she founded a house for the poor and sick and started living a life in common with the companions who had followed her. She was soon threatened by Clothar's efforts to take her back as a wife. Avoiding him in about 561 she founded a monastery, Saint Mary's, at Poitiers, where she lived as a simple nun in her own cell. She gathered RELICS for the monastery, including a fragment of the True Cross in 569. As the renamed Monastery of the Holy Cross, it adopted the monastic rule of Caesarius of Arles (469/470–542) to guide the life of the 200 nuns who eventually joined. After her death there on August 13, 587, MIRACLES began to occur, and the monastery became an important place of pilgrimage.

Further reading: Venantius Fortunatus, *Venantius Fortunatus: Personal and Political Poems,* trans. Judith George (Liverpool: Liverpool University Press, 1995); Gregory of Tours, *History of the Franks,* trans. Ernest Brehaut (1916; reprint, New York, Octagon Books, 1965); Jo Ann McNamara, John E. Halborg, and E. Gordon Whatley, eds. and trans., *Sainted Women of the Dark Ages* (Durham, N.C.: Duke University Press, 1992), 70–105; Yitzhak Hen, *Culture and Religion in Merovingian Gaul,* A.D. *481–751* (Leiden: E. J. Brill, 1995); Raymond Van Dam, *Saints and Their Miracles in Late Antique Gaul* (Princeton, N.J.: Princeton University Press, 1993); Ian N. Wood, *The Merovingian Kingdoms, 450–751* (London: Longman, 1994).

Ragusa *See* DUBROVNIK.

Ramadan (Sawm, Siyam) Ramadan is the ninth month of the Muslim lunar calendar and occurs at different times of the Western calendar year. It was to be a period of FASTING, the fourth pillar of ISLAM. All eating, drinking, and sexual activity were forbidden from sunrise to sunset. All who had reached puberty and were in full possession of their senses were bound to observe it. The sick, elderly, travelers, and women who were breast-feeding, were menstruating, or had just given birth were excused. They were to compensate for not fasting by performing an equal number of days of fasting later. The ensuing sense of bodily deprivation was to make Muslims aware of their dependence on God for life. After sunset, there were traditionally joyful festivals and feasting. The QURAN was supposedly first revealed in this month.

Further reading: K. Wagtendonk, *Fasting in the Koran* (Leiden: E. J. Brill, 1968); Gustave von Grunebaum, *Muhammadan Festivals* (New York: Schuman, 1951); M. Plessner, "Ramadan," *Encyclopedia of Islam,* 8:417–418.

Rambam *See* MAIMONIDES, MOSES; NACHMANIDES, MOSES.

Ranulf de Glanville (d. 1190) *English author, judicial official, adviser to King Henry II*
The Anglo-Norman Ranulf was born in Stratford in Suffolk. He entered royal government, rising to the rank of sheriff. He demonstrated his loyalty and his competence to King HENRY II by his defense of the north during the rebellion of 1173–74. He even captured King WILLIAM I the LION of SCOTLAND near Alnwick in Northumberland.

When Henry went to FRANCE, he so trusted Ranulf that he appointed him as justiciar to act in his place in ENGLAND. In this capacity Ranulf succeeded Richard de Lucy (d. 1179) in 1179; he held the post until 1189, when RICHARD I LIONHEART removed him from office and imprisoned him. He was released on the payment of a ransom of 15,000 pounds and went with Richard on the Third CRUSADE, dying on the way at ACRE in 1190.

Ranulf's fame rests on the work traditionally attributed to him, *Treatise Concerning the Laws and Customs of England,* published in about 1188. There is some speculation that it was written by his nephew and secretary Hubert Walter (d. 1205). Based on his experience and knowledge of statutes, it was a manual and description in commentary format for the practice, procedures, and principles of the royal courts. It broadened and clarified common law by distinguishing it from canon and feudal law by means of specific examples. He further distinguished between criminal and civil cases and explained the function of royal writs. His goal was effective law enforcement by means of specific, impartial royal orders to overcome conflicting jurisdictions and to ensure the efficient maintenance of the king's peace. Ranulf's *Treatise* consolidated the position of common law for trials as against feudal, canon, and Roman legal systems and courts.

Further reading: Ranulf de Glanville, *The Treatise on the Laws and Customs of the Realm of England, Commonly Called Glanvill,* ed. and trans. G. D. G. Hall (1965; reprint, Oxford: Clarendon Press, 1998); John H. Baker, *An Introduction to English Legal History,* 3d ed. (London: Butterworth's, 1990); S. F. C. Milsom, *Historical Foundations of the Common Law,* 2d ed. (London: Butterworth's, 1981); W. L. Warren, *Henry II* (Berkeley: University of California Press, 1973).

Raoul Glaber (Rodulphus Glaber, the Bald) (ca. 985–ca. 1047) *French monk, historian*
Born about 985, Raoul was probably of Burgundian origin. In his youth he entered the monastery of Saint-Germain at Auxerre, where he was educated in the traditions of the CAROLINGIAN RENAISSANCE. Somewhat unstable, he moved frequently from monastic house to monastic house. He was attached to William of Volpiano (962–1031) at Dijon and became a disciple of Saint Maiolus (ca. 909–994) and Saint ODILO, abbots of CLUNY. At Cluny, he began a *Universal History,* which he finished shortly before his death at Saint-Germain d'Auxerre in 1047. It was an account of events and legends that happened around the millennium or, between 1000 and 1033. Although he was not very critical of his sources, it was a valuable and rare source for the early 11th century. It was accompanied by a meditation on the order of the world, reflecting the ideas of AMBROSE OF MILAN and Maximus Confessor (580–662).

Further reading: Raoul Glaber, *Rodulfi Glabri Historiarum libri quinque—The Five Books of the Histories/Rodulfus Glaber,* ed. and trans. John France; *Eiusdem auctoris Vita Domni Willelmi Abbatis—The Life of St. William,* ed. Neithard Bulst and trans. John France and Paul Reynolds (Oxford: Clarendon Press, 1989).

Rashi (Rabbi Solomon ben Isaac, Rabbi Shelomo Yitshaki) (ca. 1040–1105) *Jewish biblical scholar, commentator*
Solomon ben Isaac, called Rashi, was born at Troyes in BURGUNDY about 1040. He received his education from his learned father and maternal uncle. In about 1060, he went to Mainz, where he was a student of the person he would consider his master, Jacob ben Yaqar (d. 1064). He continued his training at Mainz, with Isaac ben Judah, then at Worms with Isaac ben Asher Halevi (d. 1133). It was at Mainz and Worms that Rashi began to consult manuscripts of the TALMUD and tried to establish a correct text. He also worked on a commentary, deploying and amending a method used in the Rhine cities by GERSHOM BEN JUDAH.

His method of commentary was simple and precedent-setting, a philological and grammatical explanation of words linked with an exegesis of themes and contents. The words and grammar were in Aramaic, Hebrew, and French. He led readers through the arguments systematically, pointing out the sometimes obscure breaks in the unpunctuated text and clarifying questions and answers in dialectic or dialogue format. He located the propositions of the masters in their historical period. He offered a plain meaning, then, if necessary, looked for a deeper meaning. He also analyzed the various techniques used by the previous masters of the Talmud. This form of exegesis was influential to later Christian and Jewish commentators and scholars. He identified his approach as combining a literal and a figurative reading that drew on midrashic and the philological methods. Rashi also wrote important responses to legal and religious questions. He lived to see the massacres of the Jews accompanying the First CRUSADE and died at Troyes in 1105.

See also BIBLE.

Further reading: Scot A. Berman, *Learning Talmud: A Guide to Talmud Terminology and Rashi Commentary* (Northvale, N.J.: J. Aronson, 1997); Pinchas Doron, *Rashi's Torah Commentary: Religious, Philosophical, Ethical, and Educational Insights* (Northvale, N.J.: Jason Aronson, 2000); Sampson A. Isseroff, *An Introduction to Rashi's Grammatical Explanations in the Book of Deuteronomy-Shaar le-Dikduke Rashi, Sefer Devarim* (New York: M. P. Press, 1993); Esra Shereshevsky, *Rashi: The Man and His World* (New York: Sepher-Hermon Press, 1982).

rauda See GARDENS.

Ravenna Medieval Ravenna was a city in northern Italy near the convergence of the Po River and the Adriatic Sea. The town of Ravenna, and the military port of Classis attached to it, had their origins as an important center when the Western Roman emperor Honorius (r. 395–423) established his official residence there in 402. Surrounded by mosquitoes and marshes, Ravenna offered him security from the barbarian raids and greater ease of contact by sea with the Eastern Empire.

A SUCCESSION OF RULERS
Ravenna remained a political capital throughout the fifth and sixth centuries under ODOACER, THEODORIC, and the Byzantine reconquest by JUSTINIAN in 540. It benefited during this time from large building projects. Two palaces were built, along with the churches of Saint John the Baptist, Santa Croce, San Vitale, Sant' Apollinare in Classe, and Sant' Apollinare Nuovo, as well as the mausoleums of GALLA PLACIDIA and Theodoric.

GRADUAL DOWNTURN
The Lombard invasion did little damage to the town but diminished its role as the political capital. However, it became the Italian seat by Byzantine power and until 751 was also the home of an exarch whose office gave its name to the region, the Exarchate. The Carolingian conquest in the mid- to late eighth century expelled the Lombards, but pillaged the palaces and churches for CHARLEMAGNE's palace at AACHEN. For years thereafter Ravenna was a place of contention between the Frankish monarchy and the PAPACY. The archbishops of Ravenna established their authority based on their rich temporal rural possessions, taxing commerce on the Po, and income from saltpans. The emperor OTTO I promised to restore the Exarchate to the papacy but never did. The archbishops of Ravenna, fearing papal ambition, invariably gave active support to the imperial party against the Holy See.

Ravenna's spiritual and temporal importance and powers were further curtailed in the 12th century despite the formation of a COMMUNE in 1218. The silting of its port prevented the city from competing with VENICE. FREDERICK II took control of the town in 1240. In 1270 the emperor RUDOLF OF HABSBURG ceded the town to the pope in exchange for recognition of his imperial position. After a period of independent lordship exercised by the Da Polenta family, there was an era of direct political control by the Venetian republic between 1449 and 1509.

See also ALARIC I, KING OF THE VISIGOTHS; ART AND ARCHITECTURE, BYZANTINE; BELISARIUS; LOMBARDY AND THE KINGDOM OF THE LOMBRADS; MOSAICS; PÉPIN III THE SHORT; STILICHO; TOTILA.

Further reading: Giuseppe Bovini, *Ravenna,* trans. Robert Erich Wolf (1971); reprint, New York: Abrams, 1973); Edward Hutton, *Ravenna* (London: J. M. Dent and

Sons, 1913); Spiro Kostof, *The Orthodox Baptistery of Ravenna* (New Haven, Conn.: Yale University Press, 1965); Otto Georg Simson, *Sacred Fortress: Byzantine Art and Statecraft in Ravenna* (1948; reprint, Chicago: University of Chicago Press, 1965); Annabel Jane Wharton, *Refiguring the Post Classical City: Dura Europos, Jerash, Jerusalem, and Ravenna* (Cambridge: Cambridge University Press, 1995).

Raymond IV of Saint Giles of Toulouse (ca. 1041–1105) *one of the leaders of the First Crusade*

Born about 1041, Raymond was the second son of Pons of Toulouse and the thrice married Almodis of La Marche. The marquis of PROVENCE from 1063, on the death of his brother, he became count of TOULOUSE in 1093. He was the first prince to respond to Pope URBAN II's call for a CRUSADE, and he left for the East in 1096. After refusing to pay homage to the BYZANTINE emperor ALEXIOS I, he eventually worked out an agreement with the Greeks to organize a joint crusade. After the siege and capture of ANTIOCH in 1098, he tried to restore that city to the Byzantines but failed, losing it to BOHEMOND I. From then on he played a more successful role in the leadership of the First Crusade, which captured JERUSALEM in 1099. He refused the offer to become king and protector of the holy places. Instead he founded the county of TRIPOLI, after campaigning in ANATOLIA. Settling in the East, he died in his CASTLE near Tripoli on February 28, 1105.

See also LATIN STATES IN GREECE.

Further reading: Edward Peters, ed., *The First Crusade: The Chronicle of Fulcher of Chartres and Other Source Materials,* 2d ed. (1971; reprint, Philadelphia: University of Pennsylvania Press, 1998); John Hugh Hill, *Raymond IV, Count of Toulouse* (Syracuse, N.Y.: Syracuse University Press, 1962); Jonathan Riley-Smith, *The First Crusade and the Idea of Crusading* (Philadelphia: University of Pennsylvania Press, 1986); Jonathan Riley-Smith, *The First Crusaders, 1095–1131* (Cambridge: Cambridge University Press, 1997); Steven Runciman, *A History of the Crusades.* Vol. 2, *The Kingdom of Jerusalem and the Frankish East, 1100–1187* (Cambridge: Cambridge University Press, 1952).

Raymond of Peñafort, Saint (ca. 1175/85–1275) *Catalan Dominican friar, canonist*

Raymond was born at Villafranca del Penedes near BARCELONA between 1175 and 1185. He studied there in 1204, then at BOLOGNA from 1210 and became a doctor of LAW in 1216. After teaching in Bologna for some years, he returned to Barcelona in 1220 or 1222 and entered the DOMINICAN ORDER in 1222. From 1228 he traveled with a papal LEGATE applying and enforcing the reforms of the Fourth Lateran Council of 1215. His fellow canonist, Pope GREGORY IX, called him to his court in 1229 as a

confessor and to assemble and order the papal and canonical documents from 1140 and GRATIAN's *Decretum.* This new collection called the *Decretals* was promulgated by Gregory IX on September 5, 1234.

Raymond returned to live in CATALONIA from 1236 to 1238. The meeting of the general chapter of the order at Bologna in 1238 chose him as master general. In that capacity he drew up the order's constitutions. In 1240 he resigned from his position and returned to Barcelona, where he intervened in the affairs of the kingdom of ARAGON and encouraged the conversion of JEWS and Muslims. He died on January 6, 1275, at Barcelona, perhaps 100 years old. His canonization process began at a council of Tarragona in 1279 but ended successfully only in 1601.

WORKS AND THOUGHT

He also wrote several other important canonical and ethical works, a summa on canon law after 1216, another summa on penance in 1220/21, a third one after 1234, and a treatise on matrimony between 1210 and 1214. The treatise on penance was a manual for Dominican confessors to deal with sins against GOD such as SIMONY, HERESY, apostasy, perjury, sorcery, sacrilege, and the withholding of tithes. Other topics were SINS against one's neighbor, including homicides, tournaments, duels, thefts, arson, and usury.

The penitential thought of Raymond of Peñafort tried to clarify the actual responsibility of the individual Christian. Priestly confessors were exhorted to judge an exterior act in terms of the person, his or her intention, and his or her circumstances, and to determine whether a SIN was actually committed and if so, to assess its magnitude and the appropriate response by the penitent.

See also PENITENTIALS.

Further reading: Stehan Kuttner, "Raymond of Peñafort as Editor: The Decretals and Constituitiones of Gregory IX," *Bulletin of Medieval Canon Law* 12 (1982): 65–80; Thomas M. Schwertner, *Saint Raymond of Penafort,* ed. G. M. Woodcock (Milwaukee: Bruce, 1935).

al-Razi, Abu Bakr Muhammad ibn Zakariyya (Rhazes) (ca. 854–925/935) *Persian philosopher, alchemist, scientist, physician*

Born at Rayy in Persia about 854, al-Razi wrote in Arabic. Although his philosophical thought was not known to the medieval West, his medical and pharmacological works were the object of Latin translations by GERARD of Cremona. There were other translations into the VERNACULAR languages. Al-Razi was a practicing clinician, who headed hospitals at Rayy and BAGHDAD. His *Treatise on Small-pox and Measles* contained the first accurate description of those deadly diseases. Al-Razi was aware of psychotherapy and opposed to metaphysical explanations and the idea of the natural predisposition. For him, the curing process required understanding the intelligible order of the world and acting on it to attain a determined end. Al-Razi's name is connected with experimentation and surgical procedures. He denounced charlatans, listing their fallacious procedures. In his *Proof of the Doctor,* he suggested norms and possible content for medical treatment, and in his *Treatise on Drugs,* he applied his alchemical or chemical knowledge to medicine. He died in 925/935 at Baghdad.

See also MEDICINE.

Further reading: Al-Razi, *A Treatise on Small-Pox and Measles,* trans. William A. Greenhill (1847; reprint, Baltimore: Williams & Williams, 1939); al-Razi, *The Spiritual Physick of Rhazes,* trans. Arthur J. Arberry (London: Murray, 1950); Donald E. H. Campbell, *Arabian Medicine and Its Influence on the Middle Ages* (London: K. Paul, Trench, Trubner, 1926); L. E. Goodman, "Al-Razi, Abu Bakr Muhammad ibn Zakariyya," *Encyclopedia of Islam* 8:474–477; Sarah Stroumsa, *Freethinkers of Medieval Islam: Ibn al-Rawandi, Abu Bakr al-Razi and Their Impact on Islamic Thought* (Leiden: Brill, 1999); Dominique Urvoy, "Rhazes," *EMA* 2.1,233–1,234.

realism For the question of universals, realism was any doctrine, generally Platonic, that held that the universal existed in things or even as a thing. For the philosophy of knowledge, realism was any doctrine that asserted the reality of a world external to thought and the ability of that thought to obtain authentic knowledge of it. Medieval Christianity claimed to be realistic. It was wary of speculation and tried to root itself in fact. Abstract concepts or universals did have a real existence apart from individuals for many medieval thinkers.

See also ABÉLARD, PETER; ADELARD OF BATH; AUGUSTINE OF HIPPO, SAINT; JOHN SCOTTUS ERIUGENA; MARTIANUS CAPELLA; NOMINALISM; PLATO AND PLATONISM.

Further reading: Frederick C. Copleston, *Medieval Philosophy* (1952; reprint, New York: Harper & Row, 1961); Robert Heinaman, ed., *Aristotle and Moral Realism* (Boulder, Colo.: Westview Press, 1995); Norman Kretzmann, Anthony Kenny, Jan Pinborg, and Eleonore Stump, eds., *The Cambridge History of Later Medieval Philosophy: From the Rediscovery of Aristotle to the Disintegration of Scholasticism, 1100–1600* (Cambridge: Cambridge University Press, 1982); Gordon Leff, *Medieval Thought: St. Augustine to Ockham* (Harmondsworth: Penguin Books, 1958); Charles B. Schmitt, Quentin Skinner, and Jill Kraye, eds., *The Cambridge History of Renaissance Philosophy* (Cambridge: Cambridge University Press, 1988).

Recared I (560–601) *king of the Visigoths*
Born about 560, Recared was the second son of Leovigild (r. 568–586). His reign unified the Iberian Peninsula under his royal authority. He continued his father's project of religious unification by converting the VISIGOTHS to Christianity. In the spring of 587, on the advice of Leander of Seville (540–599) and working with Pope GREGORY I THE GREAT, Recared deserted ARIANISM. This course was soon followed by the bishops, the nobility, and the whole of the Visigoths. There were minor centers of unsuccessful resistance at Merida and within the court of TOLEDO.

On May 8, 589, at the third council of Toledo, Recared declared his adherence to the anti-Arian dogma defined by the first four ecumenical orthodox councils. This conversion began the fusion of the Visigothic and Roman populations. By doing so he strengthened the ties between the church and the Crown, but he persecuted JEWS and uncooperative Arians. Besides suppressing several uprisings, he pushed the BYZANTINES back into an enclave around Cartagena. He died at about 601, the time of his deposition from the throne by the nobility.

See also BASQUES.

Further reading: E. A. Thompson, *The Goths in Spain* (Oxford: Clarendon Press, 1969); Alberto Ferreiro, *The Visigoths in Gaul and Spain, A.D. 418–711: A Bibliography* (Leiden: E. J. Brill, 1988).

Reconquest (Reconquista) One of the formative and the major events of medieval Spanish history the Reconquest of the peninsula by the Christians began in the mid-11th century and was fulfilled with the surrender of GRANADA in 1492. The ARABS had controlled much of the Iberian Peninsula from the early eighth century. The Reconquest a military and economic crusade, constituted close to a permanent state of war for both sides. Monarchs took the excuse to extend their powers, levy extraordinary taxes, and control the church. Christian CASTILE and ARAGON became societies organized for war. Knightly and military prowess was highly valued and social mobility was high, as Christians availed themselves of the frequent opportunities to move to newly controlled territories.

TOLEDO was taken in 1085. LISBON was captured in 1147. The Christian victory at the Battle of La Navas de Tolosa in 1212 led to the taking of SEVILLE and CÓRDOBA, leaving only the kingdom of GRANADA in Muslim hands. FERDINAND II and ISABEL I managed the surrender of the last stronghold the town of Granada in 1492. Despite all this conflict, there was cultural interaction, though continually declining, among the Christians, Muslims, and JEWS until after the fall of Granada.

See also ALMOHADS; ALMORAVIDS; ASTURIAS-LÉON, KINGDOM OF; BARCELONA; CRUSADES; RODRIGO DÍAZ DE VIVAR, HISTORY AND LEGENDS OF.

Further reading: Simon Barton and Richard Fletcher, trans., *The World of El Cid: Chronicles of the Spanish Reconquest* (Manchester: Manchester University Press, 2000); Health Dillard, *Daughters of the Reconquest: Women*

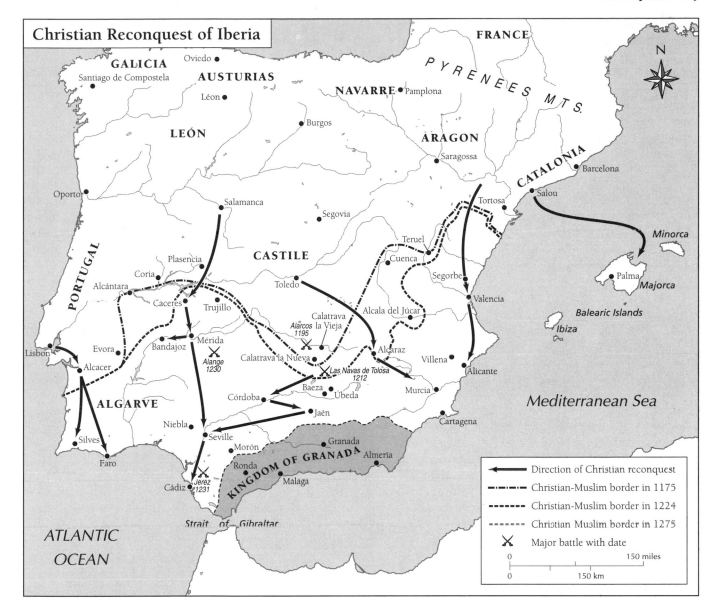

Christian Reconquest of Iberia

in *Castilian Town Society, 1100–1300* (Cambridge: Cambridge University Press, 1984); L. P. Harvey, *Islamic Spain, 1250 to 1500* (Chicago: University of Chicago Press, 1990); Derek W. Lomax, *The Reconquest of Spain* (London: Longman, 1978); Joseph F. O'Callaghan, *Reconquest and Crusade in Medieval Spain* (Philadelphia: University of Pennsylvania Press, 2003); Bernard F. Reilly, *The Contest of Christian and Muslim Spain: 1031–1157* (Cambridge: Blackwell, 1992).

Redemption In the Middle Ages, the concept of salvation departed from the patristic conception of exchange and moved toward a theory of Redemption that interpreted it in terms of ransom. Salvation could be part of creation and require Redemption. The Middle Ages approached this idea through the problem of the Incarnation of Christ.

The councils of Quierzy in 853 and Valence in 855 used the biblical terms *ransom* and Christ's *sacrifice*, ending a controversy over PREDESTINATION. ANSELM of Laon justified the Incarnation of Christ in his *Why God Became Man*, asserting that it was the only possible way of paying GOD for the debt by humankind owed for sin. Without paying a ransom for the acquittal of this debt, SIN could not be left punished and no sinner could attain salvation. Sinners could not pay for the remission of their sins by their own strength; thus the necessity of the compensatory Incarnation. Christ died for sinners and was the Redeemer. Through his divine and human natures, Christ alone could give God the price of this ransom, through his Passion, death, and Resurrection. God simply by means of his mercy supposedly was not able to remit sin. There had to be a just reparation, and no created being could restore wounded human nature and thus have eternal life or the BEATIFIC VISION. According to Thomas AQUINAS, sacrificial Redemption could only be carried out by the blood of God, who had created and recreated human nature. This notion depended on the concept of the Trinity and the sacrifice was commemorated in the Eucharist, one of the SEVEN SACRAMENTS. Medieval Christians believed that salvation occurred in and through the mediation of Jesus Christ, the second person of the Trinity, who shared completely in God's divinity. Whether this Redemption might lead all or only some people to salvation and the role of GRACE in this were problems.

See also BERNARD OF CLAIRVAUX, SAINT; BONAVENTURE, SAINT; CHRISTOLOGY AND CHRISTOLOGICAL CONTROVERSY; JOHN SCOTTUS ERIUGENA; TRINITARIAN DOCTRINE.

Further reading: Caroline Walker Bynum, *Fragmentation and Redemption: Essays on Gender and the Human Body in Medieval Religion* (New York: Zone Books, 1991); C. William Marx, *The Devil's Rights and the Redemption in the Literature of Medieval England* (Cambridge: D. S. Brewer, 1995); Brian Murdoch, *Adam's Grace: Fall and Redemption in Medieval Literature* (Cambridge: D. S. Brewer, 2000); Marie-Anne Vannier, "Redemption," *EMA*, 2.128–1,1219.

reform, idea of   In the Middle Ages, any concept or even the term *reform* was used only for religious matters. There was little concept of reform or change in the feudal, the political, and the secular legal systems or in the economic or social structure. Reform was a restoration or resumption of forgotten practices or institutions, now rediscovered or discerned. Some reform movements, such as that of the GREGORIAN REFORM, introduced new ideas about the relationship of the church and the state to restore its proper functioning. In the monastic world, there were "reforms" regularly all through the medieval period to set monks back on the right path. This could involve a general reform or reform of a particular convent or monastery. Other innovations included dispatching MENDICANT ORDERS out into the world to reform and help with pastoral care, to adapt to the needs of society and CHRISTENDOM. ISLAM, as did Christianity, underwent changes in religious practice and belief, all classified as reform and attempting to resume the original correct practice. For both religions these reform movements sometimes led to general changes and the secession of heretical groups.

See also HERESY AND HERESIES; MONASTICISM.

Further reading: Gerhart B. Ladner, *The Idea of Reform: Its Impact on Christian Thought and Action in the Age of the Fathers* (Cambridge, Mass.: Harvard University Press, 1959); Guy Fitch Lytle, *Reform and Authority in the Medieval and Reformation Church* (Washington, D.C. Catholic University of American Press, 1981); Herbert E. J. Cowdrey, *The Cluniacs and the Gregorian Reform* (Oxford: Clarendon Press, 1970); Steven E. Ozment, *The Age of Reform (1250–1550): An Intellectual and Religious History of Late Medieval and Reformation Europe* (New Haven, Conn.: Yale University Press, 1980); Gerd Tellenbach, *The Church in Western Europe from the Tenth to the Early Twelfth Century,* trans. Timothy Reuter (1988; reprint, Cambridge: Cambridge University Press, 1993).

relics   In the Middle Ages Christian relics were either the actual physical remains of men or women venerated as saints or objects sanctified by any contact or even vague association with them. The expectation of a physical resurrection lent value to the proximity of the remains of the Saints. From early Christian times this veneration of martyrs and, later, other selected holy persons at their tombs diverged from Hellenistic and Jewish traditions, which avoided polluting contact with corpses.

With their nearby bodies as signs of a pledge to help their communities, dead saints continued to be part of that local community of the faithful. They were expected to provide support through MIRACLES. The miracles of the saints, not done on their own but were believed to be the work of GOD, who was prompted by the saints and their relics. Veneration of the saints was absolutely secondary to the adoration reserved for God only. This distinction was not always clear to the faithful. Ecclesiastical authorities, recognized their value and tried to control these cults to their own benefit, even financial gain.

COMMERCIALIZATION

By the mid-fourth century bodies and body parts were being moved about or translated from east and west. In the west the dismemberment or translation, sale, or theft of saints did not become common until the eighth century. There was always some concern about authenticity, so superficial steps were taken to verify it. Doubts also arose about their efficacy throughout the Middle Ages, among both heretical groups and the skeptical orthodox. Relics tied to Jesus and his mother, the Blessed Virgin MARY, grew in importance in the later Middle Ages.

MATERIAL DESCRIPTIONS

In the Byzantine world, relics were primarily the bodies or pieces of the bodies of saints. Relics of Jesus were objects that supposedly had been in contact with him or his Passion. There were pieces of the cross in CONSTANTINOPLE and in JERUSALEM and many fragments were soon scattered all over Europe. The body of the Blessed Virgin had been assumed into heaven, so her relics were necessarily secondary, such as her girdle, cloak, or breast milk. The veneration of bodies of the saints and martyrs and of tombs was well established in Byzantine Christianity. The Iconoclasts, especially in the eighth century, sought to suppress the cult of relics, considering them idolatrous. When the crusaders sacked Constantinople in 1204, many relics were taken back to western Europe.

Relics in the East and the West were also owned by private individuals, who honored them at home or wore them as CHARMS. The reliquaries to hold relics multiplied, along with rings, bracelets, and necklaces containing holy fragments. When others were found in the central Middle Ages, their spiritual and economic value was recognized by the ecclesiastical and secular authorities. They could be related to both the Old and the New Testament. These included the rim of the Samaritans' well, the trumpets used to knock down the walls of Jericho, Christ's swaddling clothes, fragments of the cross, nails from the Crucifixion, the crown of thorns, baskets from the multiplication of loaves, Noah's ax, the crosses of the two thieves crucified with Christ, Mary Magdalene's vase of perfume, Moses' rod, and Saint Stephen's right hand.

See also RELIQUARY.

Further reading: John R. Butler, *The Quest for Becket's Bones: The Mystery of the Relics of St. Thomas Becket of Canterbury* (New Haven, Conn.: Yale University Press, 1995); Bernard Flusin, "Relics: Byzantium," *EMA* 2.1,224; Marie-Madeleine Gauthier, *Medieval Enamels: Masterpieces from the Keir Collection,* ed. and trans. Neil Stratford (London: British Museum Publications, 1981); Patrick J. Geary, *Furta sacra: Thefts of Relics in the Central Middle Ages* (Princeton, N.J.: Princeton University Press, 1978); D. W. Rollason, *Saints and Relics in Anglo-Saxon England* (Oxford: B. Blackwell, 1989); G. J. C. Snoek, *Medieval Piety from Relics to the Eucharist: A Process of Mutual Interaction* (Leiden: E. J. Brill, 1995); H. W. van Os, *The Way to Heaven: Relic Veneration in the Middle Ages* (Baarn: de Prom, 2000).

religious instruction *See* EXEMPLUM; PREACHING; SERMONS AND HOMILIES; SEVEN DEADLY OR CAPITAL SINS; SEVEN SACRAMENTS.

reliquary Reliquaries were containers that held RELICS. The earliest were the tomb or shrine containing a holy body of a martyr. Altars enclosed relics. The function of reliquaries was to promote, by the beauty of their artistic work, the potency of the relics they contained. No particular form was fixed for them: They could be decorated by an iconographical statement about their contents. They could be caskets decorated with ENAMELS or statues or could have the form of what they contained, such as an arm. The tendency to divide up the bodies of the saints and the spread of relics from the crusading expeditions to the East and the Holy Land led from the early Middle Ages to the creation of movable reliquaries for transport or ritual procession. Buildings such as the SAINTE-CHAPELLE OF PARIS built by LOUIS IX to house relics including the Crown of Thorns can be seen as similar to reliquaries. The smaller variety were kept in church treasuries, exposed to the faithful, or borne in PROCESSIONS.

See also IVORY.

Further reading: Marie-Madeleine Gauthier, *Highways of the Faith: Relics and Reliquaries from Jerusalem to Compostela,* trans. J. A. Underwood. (Secaucus, N.J.: Wellfleet, 1986); Raghnall Ó Floinn, *Irish Shrines and Reliquaries of the Middle Ages* (Dublin: Country House, in association with the National Museum of Ireland, 1994).

renaissance and revivals in art and culture The concept of a renaissance or rebirth is essentially a modern idea devised to describe and understand the objectives and driving forces for reform or change in various cultures in the past. Particular periods were designated as eras of renaissance and given such a label. They were deemed as being highly concerned about integrating the ideas, art, styles, practices, traditions, and literature of the classical Greek and Roman worlds into the culture of their own time. Intellectuals around 1400 in Italy were highly concerned with doing just that. The term was applied to several periods in European history from the ninth to the 15th century in particular. The 19th-century historians Jules Michelet and Jacob Burckhardt were especially instrumental in the introduction and evolution of that word and concept; they considered renaissances progressive evolutions toward better, more rational, and more modern ideas and practices, especially in intellectual and artistic matters.

Over the next century and a half, scholars discerned them in the ninth century (known as the CAROLINGIAN RENAISSANCE), in the 12th century, and archetypically in Italy in the late 14th and 15th centuries. The emergence of the individual and the state were considered the hallmarks of the most recent era, the classic Renaissance of the 15th and 16th centuries. Other periods were added by scholars of the Middle Ages to combat the stereotype of the "Dark Ages" sometimes applied to that period and to minimize the uniqueness and originality associated so strongly with the Italian and later northern Renaissances.

There were clear changes in educational ideals and styles of art, at the very least, during several periods before 1500. Certainly some intellectuals, in the midst of this change or in the effort to promote it, were highly aware of their actions and were consciously promoting a rebirth of culture and religion. This way of conceptualizing cultural changes and explaining creativity in certain periods can lead to oversimplification, to overemphasis on particular individuals, and to misunderstandings about the originality, roots, and context of change. The renaissance as a concept has not been much applied by scholars to creative eras in Jewish or Islamic history, perhaps because of preconceptions about the lack of change in those cultures and religious beliefs and practices.

See also MIDDLE AGES, CONCEPT OF; PETRARCH, FRANCESCO; REFORM, IDEA OF.

Further reading: Robert Benson and Giles Constable with Carol D. Lanham, eds. *Renaissance and Renewal in the Twelfth Century* (Cambridge, Mass.: Harvard University

Press, 1982); Jacob Burckhardt, *The Civilization of the Renaissance in Italy,* 2 vols., trans. S. G. C. Middlemore, introduction by Benjamin Nelson and Charles Trinkaus (New York: Harper, 1958); Peter Burke, *The Renaissance,* 2d ed. (New York: St. Martin's Press, 1997); Charles Burnett and Anna Contadini, eds., *Islam and the Italian Renaissance* (London: The Warburg Institute, University of London, 1999); Deno Geanakoplos, *Byzantine East and Latin West: Two Worlds of Christendom in Middle Ages and Renaissance* (New York: Barnes & Noble, 1966); Charles Homer Haskins, *The Renaissance of the Twelfth Century* (1927; reprint, New York: Meridian, 1957).

Renard the Fox *See* BEAST EPICS OR FABLES; FABLES AND FABLIAUX OR COMIC TALES.

representative assemblies and institutions Medieval representatives assemblies first appeared in the late 12th and 13th centuries and spread throughout Western Christendom in the 14th and 15th centuries. They were most common in towns and cities. Their members were in theory chosen to represent the people but usually actually represented the interests of the small ruling elite who elected them. At the same time regional or countrywide representative bodies composed initially of the feudal nobility, were established for communication with a king or prince and addressing subjects such as policy and taxation. In the 13th century, these feudal assemblies were enlarged to accept citizens who were elected to represent their towns, especially in fiscal matters. Elected representatives of the clergy and the knights then sat alongside prelates and barons, so that now the representative assemblies featured the three estates of society, the clergy, the nobility, and the middle class. In ENGLAND the word *Parliament* first appeared in 1236; in FRANCE the word *Parlement,* first used in 1250, was reserved for courts of justice. The HOLY ROMAN EMPIRE continued to use the term Diet.

Assemblies appeared earliest in southern Europe, for instance, in PROVENCE in the late 12th century and shortly thereafter in LEÓN and CASTILE. They spread throughout England and France in the 13th century and the Holy Roman Empire in the 14th century; but they did not gain real influence until the second half of the 14th century, when wars required extensive taxation. It was then also that they called and met more frequently and acquired the power to deal with princes.

These representative assemblies appealed to certain concepts and principles derived from Roman LAW and canon law, especially the principle that what concerns all must be approved by all, a basis for taxation by consent. The principle of the greater and wiser part of the members assembled evolved to the practice of discerning the majority by counting voices. The idea that another could represent one evolved to the idea that these representatives received a mandate from their electors to act in their name.

The decline of representative assemblies coincided with the end of CONCILIARISM in the mid-15th century. By then WARFARE was less frequent and monarchs had other resources that established regular systems of taxation and income that did not require the constant approval of subjects.

See also CORTES; CONCILIARISM AND CONCILIAR THEORY; PARLEMENT OF PARIS OR FRANCE; TAXATION, TAXES, AND TRIBUTE.

Further reading: Thomas N. Bisson, *Medieval Representative Institutions, Their Origins and Nature* (Hinsdale, Ill.: Dryden Press, 1973); Bertie Wilkinson, *The Creation of Medieval Parliaments* (New York: Wiley, 1972).

***Responsum* literature, Jewish** *See* GERSHOM BEN JUDAH; JACOB BEN MEIR; JEWS AND JUDAISM; MAIMONIDES, MOSES; TALMUD.

Resurrection, Christian *See* APOCALYPSE AND APOCALYPTIC LITERATURE; LAST JUDGMENT; REDEMPTION.

resurrection, Islamic (Bath) In pre-Islamic Arabia, there was a belief that the SOULS of the dead lived on in some shadowy way, but there was no concept of resurrection of the body. The QURAN suggested that there would be a resurrection of both the body and the soul, but in the Middle Ages, some Muslims believed only in the resurrection of the soul. The Quran described the day of resurrection, *Yawm al-Qiyam* or *Yawm al-Din,* with details about its cataclysmic terrors and judgments. One had to account for the way one had led his or her life.

See also HEAVEN; LAST JUDGMENT.

Further reading: al-Ghazali, *The Remembrance of Death and the Afterlife,* trans. T. J. Winter (1989; reprint, Cambridge: Islamic Texts Society, 1995); Jane I. Smith and Yvonne Yazbeck Haddad, *The Islamic Understanding of Death and Resurrection* (Albany: State University of New York Press, 1981).

Reynard the Fox *See* BEAST EPICS OR FABLES; FABLES AND FABLIAUX OR COMIC TALES.

Rheims and Rheims Cathedral (Reims) Rheims was initially the capital of the ancient Gallo-Roman province of Belgica Secunda. It had a bishop by the mid-third century. CLOVIS was baptized there on Christmas 498/499, the founding of a Christian kingdom. Its saintly Bishop Remigius (ca. 438–ca. 533) became one of the patrons of FRANCE. His successors claimed the privilege of consecrating the kings of France and conferring magic powers to cure kings' diseases. Its cathedral of Notre Dame became one of the best examples of 13th-century GOTHIC architecture with its façade decorated with a gallery of the kings of France. The town became well known for the quality of its schools until it was eclipsed by PARIS in the 12th century. The archbishop maintained tight control over Rheims which was populated with numerous clerics.

See also HINCMAR OF RHEIMS; STAINED GLASS; SYLVESTER II, POPE.

Further reading: Hans, Jantzen, *High Gothic: The Classic Cathedrals of Chartres, Reims, Amiens,* trans. James Palmes (New York: Pantheon Books, 1962).

rhetoric In ancient Rome rhetoric was taught to the elite to prepare them to deliver speeches. In the Middle Ages it was considered second among the SEVEN LIBERAL ARTS. It was taught with commentaries on ancient poets and prose writers, especially Cicero, and manuals and exercises created in imitation of the masters of antiquity. It was deemed especially important for diplomacy, chancery letter writing, and PREACHING. With the rediscovery of ARISTOTELIAN thought and the advent of SCHOLASTICISM, rhetoric began to be considered as more of a scientific system valuable in dialectical exposition. The notarial culture of 13th-century ITALY used rhetorical texts in its educational system, preparing students for notarial legal business and the conduct of communal government.

Rhetoric always had an important role in Byzantine culture and education. There it was considered an aristocratic art, the province of an elite who cultivated eloquence as a distinguishing and refined ability.

See also ARS PRAEDICANDI; BRUNETTO LATINI; GREGORY OF NAZIANZUS, SAINT; NOTARIES AND THE NOTARIATE; PSELLOS, MICHAEL; UNIVERSITIES AND SCHOOLS.

Further reading: Martin Camargo, "Rhetoric," in *The Seven Liberal Arts in the Middle Ages,* ed. David L. Wagner (Bloomington: Indiana University Press, 1983), 96–124; George A. Kennedy, *Classical Rhetoric and Its Christian and Secular Tradition from Ancient to Modern Times,* 2d ed. (Chapel Hill: University of North Carolina Press, 1999); Jerrold E. Seigel, *Rhetoric and Philosophy in Renaissance Humanism: The Union of Eloquence and Wisdom, Petrarch to Valla* (Princeton, N.J.: Princeton University Press, 1968); Jody Enders, *Rhetoric and the Origins of Medieval Drama* (Ithaca, N.Y.: Cornell University Press, 1992); Douglas Kelly, *Medieval Imagination: Rhetoric and the Poetry of Courtly Love* (Madison: University of Wisconsin Press, 1978); Joseph M. Miller, ed., *Readings in Medieval Rhetoric* (Bloomington: Indiana University Press, 1973); James J. Murphy, *Medieval Rhetoric: A Select Bibliography,* 2d ed. (Toronto: University of Toronto Press, 1989); Scott D. Troyan, *Textual Decorum: A Rhetoric of Attitudes in Medieval Literature* (New York: Garland, 1994).

Rhodes Medieval Rhodes was the principal island of the Dodecanese in the Aegean Sea. It was strategically situated at a crossroads in the eastern Mediterranean, at the juncture of the north-south route between CONSTANTINOPLE and ALEXANDRIA and the west-east route between ROME and PALESTINE and the Levant. It was captured in 654 by the Arabs and pillaged several times in the eighth century, especially between 751 and 753. It was soon reintegrated in the BYZANTINE Empire's system of naval defense, serving as an important base blocking the route to Constantinople from the south and east. Regaining prosperity in the 11th century, with the recovery of maritime commerce then, it became a staging area and port of passage for the CRUSADES. From 1204 to 1234, it was a principality temporarily held by Leo Gabalas (fl. 1190–1234), a former Byzantine governor who took possession of its during the chaos after the capture of Constantinople during the Fourth Crusade. From 1234 it was ruled by the Byzantines from the Empire of NICAEA, the Venetians, and then the Genoese. In 1309, it passed into the hands of the HOSPITALLERS, who made it their home base after their departure from SYRIA. The knights survived several attempts to conquer it by the OTTOMAN Turks in the 15th century, especially the famous siege in 1480, but in the end they were forced to surrender and abandon it in 1522 when they moved their headquarters west to MALTA.

See also ANATOLIA; VENICE.

Further reading: Marc Angel, *The Jews of Rhodes: The History of a Sephardic Community* (New York: Sepher-Hermon Press, 1978); Elias Kollias, *The Knights of Rhodes: The Palace and the City* (Athens: Ekdotike Athenon, 1991); Jonathan Riley-Smith, *Hospitallers: The History of the Order of St. John* (London: Hambledon Press, 1999); H. J. A. Sire, *The Knights of Malta* (New Haven, Conn.: Yale University Press, 1994)

Rhodes, Knights of *See* HOSPITALLERS; RHODES.

rib *See* GOTHIC.

Richard I Lionheart (Coeur de Lion) (1157–1199) *king of England, warrior, crusader*
Richard was born on September 8, 1157, the third son of HENRY II and ELEANOR of AQUITAINE. Richard was not expected to inherit the English Crown, but the premature death in 1183 of his older surviving brother, Henry, changed that. He was always more interested in AQUITAINE, his mother's duchy, which he obtained in 1172 as duke. He rebelled against his father with his brothers in 1173–74 but was defeated and pardoned by his father. Apart from a few months in 1189–90, when he was preparing for CRUSADE, and again in 1194, when he quelled a rebellion by his brother, JOHN LACKLAND, he was on crusade between 1190 and 1194 in the East or protecting his continental possessions from 1194 to 1199. The administrative institutions and competence of his father's government allowed him to leave his kingdom for long periods.

He was betrothed to Princess Alais of FRANCE but married Berengaria of NAVARRE in 1191. However, he showed little interest in women and produced no successor. Wounded during a siege by riding within the striking range or bow shot of the walls, he was hit by an arrow and suffered for several days, before he died at Chaluz in the Limousin in France on April 6, 1199. He was buried near his father at Fontevraud Abbey in France and was succeeded in his numerous realms by his brother John.

RICHARD AS CRUSADER

Richard was very successful as a crusader, taking Messina and the island of CYPRUS on the way, capturing ACRE, and defeating SALADIN in the Battle of Arsuf in 1191. Recognizing his genius in WARFARE, Saladin avoided battle with Richard thereafter. Disputes and quarrels with PHILIP II AUGUSTUS of France and Duke Leopold V of AUSTRIA (c. 1177–94) hampered efforts to capture JERUSALEM and ended the crusade. Philip abandoned the coalition in 1191, returned to France, and took advantage of Richard's absence to try to capture NORMANDY. Richard struck a truce with Saladin that give the Christians access to the holy places in peace. On his way back in disguise, Richard was captured by followers of Duke Leopold in VIENNA in December 1192. Richard was held until an enormous ransom of 150,000 marks was collected by some of the heaviest taxation ever imposed in England. Richard was also forced to pay homage for England to the emperor HENRY VI (r. 1190–97). On his return in March 1194, he remained in England only to effect the submission of his rebellious brother John. He then left the administration of the realm to Hubert Walter (d. 1205), archbishop of CANTERBURY. He returned to the Continent, defeated a French army at Fréteval in 1194, recaptured Normandy, and built the great defensive CASTLE of Château Gaillard to guard the Seine River and block the approaches to Normandy. All this reinforced his authority throughout his French dominions, but resistance to his rule required the constant warfare that led to his DEATH.

See also RANULF DE GLANVILLE.

Further reading: Ambroise, fl. ca. 1196, *The Crusade of Richard Lion-Heart,* trans. Merton Jerome Hubert (New York: Columbia University Press, 1941); John T. Appleby, *England without Richard, 1189–1199* (London: G. Bell, 1965); James A. Brundage, *Richard Lion Heart* (New York: Scribner, 1974); John Gillingham, *Richard I* (New Haven, Conn.: Yale University Press, 1999); Ralph V. Turner and Richard R. Heiser, *The Reign of Richard Lionheart: Ruler of the Angevin Empire, 1189–99* (Manchester: Manchester University Press, 2000).

Richard II (1367–1400) *king of England*
Richard was born on January 6, 1367, at the Abbey of Saint André in Bordeaux in FRANCE, the son of EDWARD THE BLACK PRINCE, and Joan of Kent (1328–85). Richard succeeded his grandfather, EDWARD III, as king of ENGLAND in 1377, when he was a boy of 10, with his uncle, JOHN OF GAUNT, the duke of Lancaster, as regent. In 1381 his regime was threatened by the Peasants' Revolt, in which he played a key but duplicitous role.

He married Anne of Bohemia (1366–94) in 1382. His dependence on unpopular favorites caused discontent; and in 1386, while John of Gaunt was in SPAIN, he was deprived of power by a council of nobles and ministers, the Lords Appellant. In 1388 a number of his close associates, such as Michael de la Pole (ca. 1330–89), were charged with treason by the Merciless PARLIAMENT. In 1389 he regained his right to rule. During the next few years, a peace was negotiated with France and Richard married his second wife, Isabel (1389–1409), the daughter of Charles VI of France (1368–1422). From 1397 he began to take revenge, punishing those who had been involved in opposition to him. His cousin, Henry Bolingbroke of Lancaster, the son of John of Gaunt, whom Richard had deprived of inheritance and then sent into exile, mounted an armed invasion in 1399. This royal confiscation in March 1399 from Henry caused Richard to be perceived as a threat to everyone's property rights in the realm. Henry easily took Richard prisoner, when he stupidly surrendered his person from the safety of a castle. Richard abdicated, and Henry seized the throne as Henry IV (r. 1399–1413). Richard died, probably starved to death, in Pontefract Castle in Yorkshire in February 1400. He was buried in WESTMINSTER ABBEY in 1413.

See also PARLIAMENT, ENGLISH; TYLER, WAT.

Further reading: Chris Given-Wilson, ed. and trans., *Chronicles of the Revolution, 1397–1400: The Reign of Richard II* (Manchester: Manchester University Press, 1993); Anthony Goodman and James L. Gillespie, eds.,

Richard II at the death of Wat Tyler in the Peasants Rebellion of 1381, *Chroniques de France et d'Angleterre,* British Library, London *(Art Resource)*

Richard II: The Art of Kingship (Oxford: Clarendon Press, 1999); Richard H. Jones, *The Royal Policy of Richard II: Absolutism in the Later Middle Ages* (New York: Barnes & Noble, 1968); Nigel Saul, *Richard II* (New Haven, Conn.: Yale University Press, 1997).

Richard III (1452–1485) *last Yorkist king of England*
Richard was born October 2, 1452, in Fortheringay Castle in Northamptonshire, the youngest son of Richard (1411–60), the duke of York, and Cecily of York. He was the youngest brother of EDWARD IV, during whose reign he became the duke of York and the powerful royal representative in the north of ENGLAND. He was a good soldier and an important commander in his brother's victories in the WARS OF THE ROSES. In the north he gained a reputation as a competent and fair administrator and ruler over one of the most lawless parts of England. In 1483 he was appointed guardian to his nephew, the boy-king Edward V (r. 1483). However, on the death of his brother on April 9, 1483, he seized the throne for himself, deposing the 13-year-old, and destroyed the family of his mother, Elizabeth Woodville (ca. 1437–92). She was the second wife of his brother, Edward IV, whose family Richard considered far too influential. He was endorsed on June 25 by an assembly of lords and commoners, who had been told that Edward IV's marriage to Elizabeth was not valid and her sons were illegitimate. Edward and his younger brother disappeared while in confinement in the Tower of London later that summer. Because Richard had much to gain from their disappearance, an accusation that he had them murdered resulted. Skeletons of two boys were later found hidden away in the tower presenting the opportunity for others to claim the throne. Richard's only son, Edward (1473–84), died in April 1484, and his wife, Anne Neville soon afterward on March 16, 1485. The duke of Buckingham failed in an attempt to gain the throne in 1483, but Henry Tudor, a distant Lancastrian claimant to the throne and later King Henry VII (r. 1485–1509), defeated Richard in the Battle of BOSWORTH FIELD in 1485. Deserted by allies and constrained by the terrain, Richard was killed in the battle on August 22, 1485. Tudor historians and playwrights later deliberately tried to destroy his reputation. No evidence supports the tradition, popularized by Shakespeare, that he was a hunchback.

See also TUDOR, HOUSE OF.

Further reading: Dominicus Mancinus, *The Usurpation of Richard the Third: Dominicus Mancinus ad Angelum Catonem de occupatione Regni Anglie per Ricardum Tercium libellus,* trans. C. A. J. Armstrong, 2d ed. (Oxford: Clarendon Press, 1969); Anne F. Sutton and P. W. Hammond, eds., *The Coronation of Richard III: The Extant Documents* (New York: St. Martin's Press, 1984); Alison Hanham, *Richard III and His Early Historians, 1483–1535* (Oxford: Clarendon Press, 1975); Michael Hicks, *Richard III,* rev. ed. (Stroud: Tempus, 2000); Rose-

mary Horrox, *Richard III: A Study of Service* (Cambridge: Cambridge University Press, 1989); Paul Murray Kendall, *Richard the Third* (New York: W. W. Norton, 1956); Jeremy Potter, *Good King Richard?: An Account of Richard III and His Reputation, 1483–1983* (London: Constable, 1983); Charles Ross, *Richard III* (Berkeley: University of California Press, 1981); Charles T. Wood, *Joan of Arc and Richard III: Sex, Saints, and Government in the Middle Ages* (New York: Oxford University Press, 1988).

Richard Rolle of Hampole (ca. 1295/1300–1349) *English hermit, mystic, author*
Richard Rolle was born about 1295/1300 at Thornton Dale in Yorkshire. After studying at Oxford, he returned to his family, but he soon left them again in about 1328 to become a hermit on the property of a friend. His PREACHING and denunciation of vice were not especially popular. After wandering around, he settled at Hampole near Doncaster. Toward the end of his life, he directed the NUNS of a small Cistercian community. Eventually popular in ENGLAND and on the Continent, he was venerated as a saint soon after his death.

Richard wrote numerous prose exegetical treatises, spiritual commentaries, and letters in LATIN and English as well as lyric poems. He made TRANSLATIONS of parts of the BIBLE, denounced the excesses and abstractions of Scholastic thought, and wrote a meditation on Christ's suffering. He liked to talk of how he was set on fire by a divine love that was physical and spiritual, painful and soothing. Rolle mistrusted all theological speculation. He died in 1349.

See also MYSTICISM, CHRISTIAN.

Further reading: Richard Rolle, *Richard Rolle, the English Writings,* trans. Rosamund S. Allen (New York: Paulist Press, 1988); Nicholas Watson, *Richard Rolle and the Invention of Authority* (Cambridge: Cambridge University Press, 1991).

Riga *See* HANSEATIC LEAGUE; LIVONIA.

ring *See* MARRIAGE.

ritual *See* DEATH AND THE DEAD; KINGS AND KINGSHIP, RITUALS OF; MASS, LITURGY OF; PROCESSIONS, LITURGICAL.

ritual murder Ritual murder, the alleged murder and cannibalism during their ceremony of the Eucharist, was an accusation initially formulated by pagans against Christians in the second and third centuries C.E. From the 12th century, the accusation was aimed at JEWS. At Norwich in ENGLAND in 1144, some Jews were accused of killing a Christian child, William (d. 1144) whose body was found in a nearby forest. According to a story in

1169 by Thomas of Monmouth, the Jews each year decided which community would be instructed to mimic and mock Christ's Passion on the body of a Christian child. At Blois in 1171, after a similar accusation but no corpse, a whole community was burned. This accusation surfaced periodically in several parts of Europe in incidents involving the deaths of Richard of Pontoise in 1179, Hugh of Lincoln in 1255, Werner of Bachrach in 1287, and others at Gloucester in 1168, Fulda in 1236, and Saragossa in 1250. There were further notorious incidents in the late Middle Ages, such as the murder of Simon of Trent in 1475, which led to the persecution of Jewish communities in ITALY.

These accusations and ensuing events followed a common pattern. The discovery of a corpse, usually of a child, was followed by suspicions of a conspiracy among a local Jewish community. Torture was alleged to have been inflicted on the victim. There was a quick condemnation of that community or individual members of it. Stories circulated that the victim's blood was used for making unleavened bread and then ritually consumed in derision of Christ and Christianity. MIRACLES soon followed at the tomb and a cult of the victim arose.

Some of these victims were even beatified. These cult figures were then memorialized in didactic Christian art. Church authorities only too feebly tried to stop these events, without much success. The emperor FREDERICK II gathered experts to denounce these hysterical claims, which were completely opposite to the tenets of JUDAISM. They continued long after the Middle Ages and became part of the stock in trade of vicious adherents of modern anti-Semitism.

See also ANTI-JUDAISM AND ANTI-SEMITISM; HOST DESECRATION LIBEL.

Further reading: Mary Désirée Anderson, *A Saint at Stake: The Strange Death of William of Norwich, 1144* (London: Faber and Faber, 1964); R. Po-chia Hsia, *Trent 1475: Stories of a Ritual Murder Trial* (New Haven, Conn.: Yale University Press, 1992); Gavin I. Langmuir, *Toward a Definition of Antisemitism* (Berkeley: University of California Press, 1990); Miri Rubin, *Gentile Tales: The Narrative Assault on Late Medieval Jews* (New Haven, Conn.: Yale University Press, 1999).

Riurik　*See* RURIK.

Riurikid dynasty (Rurikids)　*See* RURIK.

roads and bridges　The huge and strategic Roman road system was maintained in many parts of the empire until the fifth century. It followed ridges and was straight wherever possible. Most were not made of the dressed stone familiar from the Appian Way near ROME, but rather, usually of gravel or packed sand. They could favor

The medieval road between Siena and Massa Marittima (*Courtesy Edward English*)

the movement of invaders as well as the Roman army. They led between the major towns and cities and converged on Rome or CONSTANTINOPLE. By the early Middle Ages, there were definite signs of neglect and decay as communication and transport on them became much more difficult. However, many remained in use throughout the Middle Ages and beyond, at least as rights of way.

In the 12th and 13th centuries, there was an effort to improve the roads and bridges near the towns of LOMBARDY, the CHAMPAGNE FAIRS, and FLANDERS as the growth of commerce and urban development demanded better and faster transport and movement. Passages through mountains, especially over the Alps, were improved. Bridges were built or rebuilt and maintained through tolls. In the later Middle Ages and RENAISSANCE, kings and princes began to pay much more attention to roads and bridges, recognizing their value for promoting and taxing commerce and for maintaining political control.

Royal roads in England were legally required in theory to be wide enough for two wagons to pass or 16 KNIGHTS to ride abreast. In reality they were well-trodden paths surrounded by high grass or weeds on each side. Villages and towns, too, took more interest in the local situation by clearing and maintaining pathways to and from rural areas. Causeways through swamps were constructed. In the towns the main streets were paved and town squares for markets were created, paved, and maintained. The responsibility for all this was constantly disputed, but roads could be financed by tolls, as bridges were. Most travel would be done by foot, but certainly, some were able to travel by horse or donkey. Carriages and wagons were uncomfortable since they were not yet very well sprung, so they carried luggage and whatever was being transported. On a horse one could travel 20 to 30 miles a day under the right conditions. Guides or locals were often necessary to find one's way safely or expeditiously. Travel by water was slower but often more comfortable. Conditions in the Byzantine and Islamic worlds were similar.

See also MAPS; TRADE AND COMMERCE.

Further reading: Brian Paul Hindle, *Medieval Roads and Tracks,* 3d ed. (Princes Risborough: Shire, 1998); Albert C. Leighton, *Transport and Communication in Early Medieval Europe,* A.D. *500–1100* (New York: Barnes & Noble, 1972).

Robert I the Bruce (1274–1329) *king of Scotland*
Born on July 11, 1274, Robert was the son of Robert Bruce of Annandale (d. 1295) of the Anglo-Norman Bruce family of Scotland. His family was among the claimants to the throne on the death of King Alexander III (r. 1249–86) in 1286. EDWARD I of ENGLAND intervened and began the wars of Scottish independence. After wavering between some acceptance of JOHN Balliol, whom Edward had placed on the throne, and assisting the rebellions of William WALLACE, he claimed the Scottish Crown for himself against the wishes of Edward I. He was supported by most of the Scottish nobles, except for the Comyns family, as the champion of national independence. He killed a rival, John Comyns (d. 1306), and was hastily acknowledged as king at SCONE (without the presence of the stone of Scone) on March 25, 1306. He then lost two battles to the English and retreated into guerrilla warfare. His brothers were killed and his sisters were confined to cages by the enraged Edward I, who felt deeply betrayed by a man to whom he had shown favor.

After Edward I's death in 1307, Robert revolted against English rule and controlled most of Scotland from 1309. In 1314 he took EDINBURGH and defeated the inept EDWARD II at the Battle of BANNOCKBURN on June 24, 1314, then captured Berwick in 1318. He then allied Scotland with FRANCE and sought its support against England. Adopting English practices, Robert based his government on cooperation within a community of the realm. He was recognized as king by the treaty of Northampton in 1328 and sealed that with the marriage of Joan (1321–62), the sister of the English king, EDWARD III, to his son and successor, David (1329–71). He died on June 7, 1329, and his body was buried in Dunfermline Abbey.

Further reading: G. W. S. Barrow, *Robert Bruce and the Community of the Realm of Scotland,* 3d ed. (Edinburgh: Edinburgh University Press, 1988); Seán Duffy, ed., *Robert the Bruce's Irish Wars: The Invasions of Ireland 1306–1329* (Charleston, S.C.: Tempus, 2002); James A. Mackay, *Robert Bruce: King of Scots* (London: Hale, 1974); Ronald McNair Scott, *Robert the Bruce, King of Scots* (London: Hutchinson, 1982); Alan Young and Michael J. Stead, *In the Footsteps of Robert Bruce* (Stroud: Sutton, 1999).

Robert Grosseteste *See* GROSSETESTE, ROBERT.

Robert Guiscard *See* GUISCARD, ROBERT.

Robert of Arbrissel, Saint (ca. 1047–1116) *hermit, preacher, founder of the Order of Fontevrault*
Robert was born about 1047 at Arbrissel, in the diocese of Rennes in FRANCE. Not a good student, he nonetheless, succeeded his father as the village priest. In 1076 after he supported an election to the bishopric of Rennes of a cleric who was soon deposed, Robert had to leave for PARIS to resume his studies. In 1089 the deposed bishop, Sylvester of La Guerche (d. 1093), returned to his see and became a supporter of the GREGORIAN REFORM movement. He recalled Robert, by then a priest, to Rennes to assist him in reforming the CLERGY of BRITTANY. Robert battled SIMONY and NICOLAITISM. In 1093, on the death of Sylvester, Robert was so hated by the local clergy that he had to flee to Angers.

A few years later he moved to the wilderness to lead the ascetic life of a HERMIT and was described as resembling a wild lunatic. He gathered and founded an abbey at La Roë. In 1096 he preached before Pope URBAN II, but by 1098, he had resumed his wandering life. As a skillful preacher he drew a large number of penitents of both sexes who were soon camping unsupervised in the woods together. Robert was rebuked for allowing this potential sinful practice. He then chose in 1101 to settle his followers in the valley of Fontevrault, not far from Saumur. After further criticism, Robert, who refused to be called an abbot, though his deeds and leadership practices were autocratic, reordered his foundation more strictly and divided it among convents for men and women, both under a prior. He returned to preaching and attracted to Fontevrault lepers, the sick, nobles, the poor, wealthy matrons, and prostitutes.

In 1115 he entrusted his by now rich double order to an abbess. On February 18, 1116, he fell ill and died on February 25 in the priory of Orsan in Berry. There was a violent struggle over his body, but it was returned to Fontevrault by March 7, 1116. He had asked to be buried among the lepers and poor at Fontevrault but instead was interned in a place of high honor by the high altar. Robert of Arbrissel did not have much of a cult and has been the object of varied interpretations by historians. He has been portrayed as a defender of the exploited by some and a promoter of religious opportunity for women by others.

Further reading: Henrietta Leyser, *Hermits and the New Monasticism: A Study of Religious Communities in Western Europe, 1000–1150* (London: Macmillan, 1984).

Robin of Courson *See* COURSON, ROBERT.

Robin Hood Robin Hood has been the most famous of all medieval legendary outlaws. The obscure origins, appeal, and identity of Robin Hood have remained controversial. As a composite figure, he probably did have some historical basis, however. There are hints of someone with a similar name now and again in the 13th century, but there is little beyond a name. The first known reference to a popular enthusiasm for stories about a Robin Hood appeared in 1377 in one of the texts of William LANGLAND's *PIERS PLOWMAN*. During the 15th century, the Robin Hood ballads, such as *Robin Hood and the Monk* in 1450, established enduring themes. By 1500 he, as a yeoman, was inseparably associated with his skill as an archer and believed to have been a master of disguise and the leader of a band of "merry men." He had become a courteous and benign outlaw who treated the rich in ways they deserved. A class hero, he nonetheless respected the Crown, except in his indulgence in deer poaching. He fought against abuses of power while yet showing little concern for the real conditions of the PEASANTRY. He was religious but had little respect for corrupt clergy. Other plays and works provided the other characters of the fully developed legend, such as Friar Tuck and Maid Marion.

See also OUTLAWRY.

Further reading: R. B. Dobson and J. Taylor, eds., *Rymes of Robyn Hood: An Introduction to the English Outlaw* (London: Heinemann, 1976); John C. Bellamy, *Robin Hood: An Historical Enquiry* (Beckenham, Kent: Croom Helm, 1985); John C. Holt, *Robin Hood* (London: Thames and Hudson, 1982); Maurice Keen, *The Outlaws of Medieval Legend,* 3d ed. (London: Routledge, 2000); Stephen Thomas Knight, *Robin Hood: A Complete Study of the English Outlaw* (Cambridge: Blackwell, 1994); John Matthews, *Robin Hood: Green Lord of the Wildwood* (Glastonbury: Gothic Images, 1993).

Rodrigo Díaz de Vivar (El Cid Campeador, al-Sid, the Lord), **history and legends of** (ca. 1043–1099) *mercenary soldier, hero of a Spanish epic story*
Rodrigo Díaz was born into a family of the lower nobility in the village of Bivar near Burgos. He was raised at the court of Ferdinand I of CASTILE and LEÓN (r. 1038–65) and educated with Sancho II of Castile (ca. 1065–72), the future king of Castile, who made him a leader of his army. In January 1072, at Golpejera, he defeated Sancho's brother, Alfonso VI of León (r. 1065–1109). A few months later, however, Sancho was assassinated or died during a siege at Zamora. Alfonso VI was suspected of ordering the death but inherited the Crown anyway, becoming the king of Castile and León (r. 1072–1109). Despite resenting a humiliating OATH of purgation imposed on him by Rodrigo Díaz, Alfonso still needed Díaz de Vivar's military ability and sent him to collect a protective tribute from the emir of SEVILLE and then to conduct a campaign against GRANADA.

SERVING GOD AND MAMMON

On his return to Castile, Rodrigo fell completely out of favor because of his feuds with other court nobles.

Alfonso VI exiled him in 1081, and he entered the service of the Muslim ruler of Saragossa. In 1082 he took prisoner Ramón Berenguer II (r. 1076–82), the count of BARCELONA, on the first of two occasions. Two years later, he defeated Sancho I Ramírez (r. 1063–94), the king of ARAGON. In 1097 Alfonso VI, whose kingdom was threatened by the ALMORAVIDS, recalled him. But a second banishment soon forced Rodrigo, whose lands had been expropriated by the king, to consider moving on VALENCIA. He captured fortresses leading to the city and defeated an army sent by the count of Barcelona in 1090. He then defended the emir of Valencia from an Almoravid attack. But in 1093, after his Muslim ally or employer was assassinated during a revolt in Valencia, Rodrigo laid siege and captured the town the next year. With the help of Peter I of Aragon (r. 1094–1104), he stopped Muslim advances at the Battles of Cuarte in 1094 and Bairén in 1097. After suppressing rebellions by Muslims in Valencia, he championed the Christians there and turned the major MOSQUE of the city into a CATHEDRAL.

Reconciled yet again with Alfonso VI, he ruled Valencia in his name. Rodrigo did not promote toleration among Christians and Muslims, who had once been allies. He had married a woman named Jimena or Ximena; their only son was killed in a battle in 1097. In 1098 he married his daughters to the king of NAVARRE and the count of Barcelona. Their descendants became the kings of Castile and León in the 12th century and even entered the royal line in ENGLAND through a 13th-century marriage. He died on July 10, 1099, in Valencia. The city was back under Almoravid rule by 1102.

Rodrigo was a skilled mercenary soldier who worked for whoever paid most. He was considered a cruel oppressor by the Muslims but a saint by some Christians. His name Cid, given to him by the Muslims, means "lord." The *Poem of the Cid* was written about 1207. In it he was presented unrealistically as a brave, loyal, resourceful, wise, courageous ruler and ideal KNIGHT.

Further reading: *The Poem of the Cid,* trans. W. S. Merwin (London: Dent, 1959); Simon Barton and Richard Fletcher, eds., *The World of El Cid: Chronicles of the Spanish Reconquest* (Manchester: Manchester University Press, 2000), especially 90–147; Richard Fletcher, *The Quest for El Cid* (New York: Oxford University Press, 1989); Richard Hitchcock, "Al-Sid," *Encyclopedia of Islam* 9:533–535; Colin Smith, "The Cid in Epic and Ballad," in *European Writers: The Middle Ages and the Renaissance.* Vol. 1, *Prudentius to Medieval Drama,* ed. William T. H. Jackson and George Stade (New York: Charles Scribner's Sons, 1983), 113–136.

Roger I (1031–1101) *count of Sicily and Calabria*
Roger was born in 1031, the youngest son of Tancred of Hauteville (fl. 1000–35). He joined his relative in Calabria, ROBERT GUISCARD, in 1057 and was especially

helpful in capturing Reggio in 1060. He was installed as Roger I of SICILY, called the Great Count, in 1061. He exploited disputes among the Muslim rulers of Sicily and successfully completed its conquest between 1060 and 1072. Supported by the Christians of the northeastern side of the island and the Pisan fleet, he captured Nolo, the last Muslim stronghold, in 1091. He established a strong government on the island and relied on an administrative and fiscal regime run by Greek and Muslim personnel. On Guiscard's death in 1085, he assumed the rule of both Sicily and Calabria. He obtained from Pope URBAN II the privilege of an apostolic legateship for Sicily in 1099. A tolerant ruler, he granted religious freedom to JEWS and Muslims, evidence that he exercised effective control of the CLERGY of Sicily and Calabria. He died on June 22, 1101, leaving behind his third wife Adelasia (d. 1118) as regent for his son ROGER II.

See also NORMANS IN ITALY.

Further reading: Edmund Curtis, *Roger of Sicily and the Normans in Lower Italy, 1016–1154* (New York: G. P. Putnam's Sons, 1912); D. A. Loud, *Conquerors and Churchmen in Norman Italy* (Aldershot: Variorum, 1999); Donald Matthew, *The Norman Kingdom of Sicily* (Cambridge: Cambridge University Press, 1992).

Roger II (1095–1154) *count, king of Sicily*

The son of ROGER I of SICILY and Adelasia (d. 1118), Roger II was born in 1095. He succeeded his brother, Simon (d. 1105, as count of Sicily at age nine in 1105 and assumed full control in 1112. As an initial act, he transferred the seat of power to PALERMO. Roger gained control over the other Norman possessions on the mainland, the duchy of APULIA and the principality of Capua. He was crowned at Christmas 1130, with the consent of the antipope Anacletus (r. 1130–38). Pope Innocent II (r. 1130–43) later reluctantly recognized his coronation in 1138 after being captured. Roger entrusted the reorganization of his kingdom to an authoritarian and bureaucratic regime to the Syrian Christian George of Antioch (ca. 1085–ca. 1150), exploiting as further support Norman traditional feudal ties. His ships, mostly Greek, captured Corfu, raided up to the walls of CONSTANTINOPLE, and set up a temporary base in Tunisia. His court was an important center of cultural and intellectual patronage in the 12th century, in which Jewish, Islamic, and Christian ideas met. He died on February 26 or 27, 1154, either of a fever or, in the mind of some, of an excess of sexual activity.

See also NORMANS IN ITALY.

Further reading: D. C. Douglas, *The Norman Fate, 1100–1154* (London: Eyre Methuen, 1976); Hubert Houben, *Roger II of Sicily: A Ruler between East and West*, trans. Graham A. Loud and Diane Milburn (Cambridge: Cambridge University Press, 2002); Jeremy Johns, *Arabic Administration in Norman Sicily: The Royal Dīwān* (Cambridge: Cambridge University Press, 2002); Donald Matthew, *The Norman Kingdom of Sicily* (Cambridge:

Coronation of King Roger II of Sicily, Byzantine mosaic, La Martorana, Palermo, Italy *(Scala / Art Resource)*

Cambridge University Press, 1992); John Julius Norwich, *The Kingdom in the Sun, 1130–1194* (Harlow: Longmans, 1970); William Tronzo, *The Cultures of His Kingdom: Roger II and the Cappella Palatina in Palermo* (Princeton, N.J.: Princeton University Press, 1997); Kenneth Baxter Wolf, *Making History, The Normans and Their Historians in Eleventh-Century Italy* (Philadelphia: University of Pennsylvania Press, 1995).

Roger Bacon *See* BACON, ROGER.

Rolle, Richard *See* RICHARD ROLLE.

Rollo (Hrolfr) (ca. 860–ca. 932) *Viking chief*

Born about 860, Rollo was perhaps of Norwegian origin but called a Dane in Norman sources. In 911 he received from King Charles III the Simple (r. 893–923, d. 929) grants of territory around ROUEN and Évreux in modern NORMANDY, on the condition that he protect the approaches to PARIS from raids. Considered the first "duke of Normandy," he has remained a mysterious figure even with uncertain dates. Under the name of

Göngu-Hrólfr, or Hrolf the Ganger, he became a legendary figure to whom a saga was dedicated in the 14th century. Some texts said that he had been banned by the king of NORWAY. He certainly had stayed in the north of the British Isles on the Orkney and Hebrides Islands, before he entered the Seine Valley, where Viking raids had been endemic since 820.

Frankish sources were unclear as to the circumstances of Rollo's arrival on the Seine, but he was in control of ROUEN early in the 10th century. In 911 his army was defeated close to CHARTRES. In 912 Rollo was baptized and allowed the Christian clergy into Rouen. About then the agreement was struck with Charles the Simple whereby he also married Charles's daughter, Gisla. A later royal CHARTER of 918 referred to a concession to the NORMANS of an area situated on both sides of the Seine. Supposedly in control of a dependent FIEF, in 924 Rollo acted quite autonomously, in 924 adding territory to the original grant. He kept order in his county asserting his authority over its Scandinavian colonists. Rollo died in about 930/932. He was succeeded by his son, William Longsword (d. 942).

Further reading: David Bates, *Normandy before 1066* (London: Longman, 1982); Charles Homer Haskins, *The Normans in European History* (Boston: Houghton Mifflin, 1915); Eleanor Searle, *Predatory Kinship and the Creation of Norman Power, 840–1066* (Berkeley: University of California Press, 1988).

Romagna   The medieval Romagna was a region in north central Italy bordering the Adriatic Sea, south of the Po River and northeast of the Apennine Mountains, now part of the modern province of Emilia-Romagna. The use of the name first occurred in the sixth century in a political division, when its western part was occupied by the LOMBARDS and its eastern region remained part of the BYZANTINE EMPIRE, with a strong Greek presence. The borders of Romagna varied over the Middle Ages, but the towns of RAVENNA, Imola, Forlì, Cesena, and Rimini were always considered part of its core. Other cities were frequently considered to be within its boundaries, such as BOLOGNA, Modena, Parma, and FERRARA. From the eighth century, the popes claimed sovereignty over the Romagna, arguing from an alleged restitution made by PÉPIN III the Short to Pope Stephen II (III) (r. 752–757) in 754. It supposedly was merely restoring papal control initially gained in the DONATION OF CONSTANTINE. Nonetheless, the region was long controlled by the German emperors and a shadowy count of the Romagna. In the 13th century the Romagna was used as a base of operations by FREDERICK II in his struggle against the towns of northern Italy of the second Lombard League.

The defeat of Frederick II and RUDOLF of Habsburg's formal renunciation of sovereignty over Romagna in 1278 still did not make papal control over the region much easier. Diplomatic and military activities by the papal legates, such as Bertold Orsini, Bertrand du Poujet (ca. 1280–1352), Cardinal ALBORNOZ, and others in the 14th and 15th centuries, ultimately resulted only in a strengthening of the autonomy of rival towns, some of which were ruled by tough lords such as those of the Da Polenta at Ravenna and Malatesta at Rimini. Romagna also became a cockpit of control of northern Italy among MILAN, FLORENCE, VENICE, and the papacy in the later Middle Ages and Renaissance. Despite this warfare and violence, Romagna remained a region famous for producing horses, grain, and wine. It was rich in mercenaries much esteemed by the great Italian powers, and finally a land of art inspired by the Byzantine tradition in Ravenna and the new style fostered by GIOTTO in Rimini. It lost its political designation and was at last fully integrated into the PAPAL STATES in 1503 by Pope Julius II (r. 1503–13).

Further reading: John Larner, *The Lords of the Romagna: Romagnol Society and the Origins of the Signorie* (London: Macmillan, 1965); Peter Partner, *The Lands of St. Peter: The Papal States in the Middle Ages and the Early Renaissance* (London: Eyre Methuen, 1972); Daniel P. Waley, *The Papal State in the Thirteenth Century* (London: Macmillan, 1961).

Romance of the Rose   *See* ROMAN DE LA ROSE.

romances   The word *romance,* which first appeared in the 12th century, originally referred to a poem written in French, itself a "Romance" language derived from the popular or rustic LATIN spoken by some of the inhabitants of what became France. French was also spoken in ENGLAND, the Low Countries, and Lorraine. Romances constituted a diverse genre of literature: prose narratives or poems telling stories and tales based on legends, chivalric love, adventure, religious or secular allegories, and the supernatural. They included narratives from the ancient world (Alexander the Great and Troy in particular), the court of CHARLEMAGNE, and the Celtic tradition concerning ARTHUR, a legendary ruler of the Britons.

Lavish in detail, romances often focused on the exotic, the remote, and the miraculous, almost anything except real local situations. Their love stories usually ended happily, but not always. They had their origins in the aristocratic courts of the 12th century, such as that of ELEANOR OF AQUITAINE. Later, when they were written in English, they encompassed stories about legendary and historical English heroes, such as HAVELOCK THE DANE and RICHARD I LIONHEART. They emphasized courtesy, quests taken on as challenges, tests of honor, and the acquisition of wisdom through trials. All were set and accomplished within chivalric codes of behavior. They contained details about feasts, dancing, tournaments, hunting, and sparkling conversations. When romances were set in the ancient world, the details of clothing, conduct, and activity remained contemporary. They were read and enjoyed not only by the knightly aristocracy, but by the literate mercantile class.

See also ALEXANDER ROMANCES; CHANSONS DE GESTE; CHRÉTIEN DE TROYES; EPIC LITERATURE; GAWAIN AND THE GAWAIN ROMANCES; HARTMANN VON ANE; *ROMAN DE LA ROSE*; WACE.

Further reading: W. R. J. Barron, *English Medieval Romance* (London: Longman, 1987); Douglas Kelly, *The Art of Medieval French Romance* (Madison, University of Wisconsin Press, 1992); Roberta L. Krueger, ed., *The Cambridge Companion to Medieval Romance* (Cambridge: Cambridge University Press, 2000); Eugène Vinaver, *Form and Meaning in Medieval Romance* (Cambridge: Modern Humanities Research Association, 1966).

Roman de la Rose (**Romance of the Rose**) The *Romance of the Rose* has been regarded as the greatest of the Old French medieval romances. This poem, 23,000 lines long, was written by William de Lorris (d. 1240) and JEAN de Meun, both from near Orléans. William was the author of the earlier and much shorter section of the *Roman de la Rose;* almost nothing has been discovered about him except that he lived in the region of the Loiret. He wrote the first 4,500 lines, which were characterized by a vivid allegorical story and beautiful language. His technique of allegorical presentation was an innovation and became a model for later writers. The whole first part was rich in allegory and the main ideas of COURTLY love. In it love was attainable while the VIRTUES AND VICES were portrayed in the context of life and love. There were numerous disapproving observations about idleness, pleasure, danger, shame, the evils of clerical CELIBACY, the abuse of power, and jealousy. The second very popular and much more ironical and satirical part by Meun, was written as a continuation of the first between 1275 and 1280. It told the tale of a youth who dreamed about a rose or maiden enclosed in a GARDEN. He struggled to reach her and encountered and overcame numerous problems and confrontations along the way. Immensely popular in France and England, especially for the long digressive speeches, the poem had references to real contemporary characters and problems.

Further reading: Guillaume de Lorris and Jean de Meun, *The Romance of the Rose,* trans. Charles Dahlberg (Princeton, N.J.: Princeton University Press, 1971); Kevin Brownlee and Sylvia Huot, *Rethinking the Romance of the Rose: Text, Image, Reception* (Philadelphia: University of Pennsylvania Press, 1992); John V. Fleming, *The Roman de la Rose: A Study in Allegory and Iconography* (Princeton, N.J.: Princeton University Press, 1969).

Romanesque art and architecture The term *Romanesque* was first used pejoratively by a French archaeologist in the 19th century to describe a style supposedly derived from Roman art and paralleling the development of Romance languages. It was formerly considered meager and impoverished in comparison with the glorious GOTHIC style that followed. The term Romanesque now describes the art of Western Europe from the 10th to the 13th century. It varied over time and according to local influences and circumstances. The sources of Romanesque art were not only Roman, but also Byzantine, Islamic, Germanic or Nordic, and Celtic.

RANGE AND FEATURES OF STYLE

Romanesque art began to evolve in the 11th century and became dominant in the 12th century. Its origins were closely linked with the reform of religious life and ritual in the 10th and 11th centuries. This artistic style was predominantly the result of monastic patronage and was often produced by monastic workmanship. The development of GREGORIAN CHANT suggested a need for the good acoustic space that was provided by its new system of vaulting. The early copying of liturgical and other texts for worship and reading in this style was done in the monasteries, although the decoration of books with miniatures soon passed to secular or lay artisans.

Some of the standard Romanesque characteristics were simplicity, sequences in spaces and spacing, a love of decorative pattern, and grandeur in size, scale, and desired effect. Stylistic similarities existed in book ILLUMINATION, MOSAIC, intricate GOLD work, IVORY carving, TEXTILES, and sculpture in wood and stone. The craftsmen and artisans were experienced and highly trained to work in several media. Each region under Romanesque influence developed a particular artistic tradition and style, all now classified as Romanesque.

ARCHITECTURAL INNOVATIONS

Besides vaulting large spans to improve acoustics and help protect a building from fire, Romanesque MASONS and architects introduced several innovations, including a choir with ambulatory and radiating chapels enclosing an eastern apse. This was ideal for the display of shrines with RELICS and for the easy circulation of large crowds of pilgrims. The interiors of these Romanesque buildings were divided into bays through the use of shafts, columns, and other devices. Rib vaulting prefigured the Gothic style of vaulting. Romanesque churches still required thick walls to carry the great weight of this stone vaulting. Only later pointed arches enabled buildings to have spans over bays of various shapes and of larger sizes. Windows were small, since the walls had to bear considerable weight. Interiors were thus dark. Sculptural decoration using stiff and formal figures became common, in particular by doorways and later in pulpits. Mural painting also was regularly employed for interior decoration, though more abstract than earlier work.

Eve as temptress, carved by Gislebertus in the 12th century at the Musée Rolin, Autun *(Courtesy Edward English)*

See also CRYPTS; OTTONIAN ART; PILGRIMAGE AND PILGRIMAGE SITES; SUGER OF SAINT DENIS, ABBOT; SANTIAGO DE COMPOSTELA; VÉZELAY, CHURCH OF LA MADELEINE.

Further reading: Walter Cahn, *Romanesque Bible Illumination* (Ithaca, N.Y.: Cornell University Press, 1982); Kenneth John Conant, *Carolingian and Romanesque Architecture, 800–1200,* 4th ed. (New Haven, Conn.: Yale University Press, 1978); Otto Demus, *Romanesque Mural Painting* trans. Mary Whittall (1968; reprint, New York: H. N. Abrams, 1970); Lawrence Nees, *Early Medieval Art* (Oxford: Oxford University Press, 2002); Andreas Petzold, *Romanesque Art* (New York: Harry N. Abrams, 1995); Meyer Schapiro, *Romanesque Art* (New York: G. Braziller, 1977); Rolf Toman, ed., *Romanesque: Architecture, Sculpture, Painting,* trans. Fiona Hulse and Ian Macmillan (Cologne: Könemann, 1997).

Rome   The city of Rome was important throughout the Middle Ages and early RENAISSANCE, though compared to those of its long period as the capital of the Roman Empire its population, size, and vitality, were diminished considerably. The population might still have been 500,000 in the mid-fifth century, down from the figure of one million 200 years before. Rome's importance at this point centered on the PAPACY and its court. After the establishment of CONSTANTINOPLE and various sacks, in 410 by ALARIC and in 455 by GAISERIC Rome's history can be divided into two periods. The first period included a slow recovery and irregular growth from the depths of its decay and destruction during Justinian's Gothic wars in the sixth century to the 13th century and the great jubilee or HOLY YEAR of 1300. Soon after that the papacy moved to AVIGNON and later a long era of schism produced two or three claimants to the papal throne. When the schism ended in the early 15th century, another period of growth for the city began and lasted into the 16th century and beyond.

EARLY MIDDLE AGES

From the mid-sixth to the mid-eighth century, Rome underwent one of the darkest periods of its history. The population fell to a few tens of thousands, yet it was still one of the most populous cities in Europe. In the second half of the eighth and in the ninth century, public building was resumed, both religious and secular. The population for this period cannot even be estimated. The Vatican region underwent remarkable growth at this time with the development of accommodations for pilgrims, and a new palace near Old Saint Peter's built by CHARLEMAGNE. This area was sacked in 846 by Arab raiders, who pillaged the basilica. The quarter was enclosed by a wall under Pope Leo IV (847–855), forming the Leonine City, a new religious and political center. This affirmation of the city as a religious capital did not support much economic or population growth in the rest of the city. By then the city had broken down into scattered villages within the Aurelian walls. The largest ones were in the forum, on the Campus Martius, in the Leonine City, and in Trastevere, the area across the Tiber. There were also numerous scattered monasteries and churches with large holdings of land throughout the area of the classical city.

CYCLICAL REBIRTH

The population had started to grow again by the 11th century, but the sack of the city by the NORMANS under Robert GUISCARD in 1085 did tremendous damage. In the meantime the GREGORIAN REFORM movement tied the government of the popes more closely to the prestigious city of Rome and its surrounding territory. The Holy See also sought to impose its will much more thoroughly on the city and its people. The city recovered again as the PAPACY gained more income and prestige. The population may have risen to some 30,000 in the 13th century. This growth probably lasted until about 1300, peaking during the jubilee of 1300 proclaimed by Pope BONIFACE VIII. After the disasters of the end of Boniface's pontificate, the popes departed for AVIGNON, to the great detriment of the city.

In the meantime a COMMUNE had arisen in the mid-12th century. Strongly opposed by the Holy See, it had few moments of independence from the temporal rule of the popes, though the popes did not always live in the city in the 12th and 13th centuries. They frequently moved around central Italy, usually trying to assert control over the Patrimony of Saint Peter and opposing the ambitions of FREDERICK II and CHARLES I OF ANJOU to control central Italy and Rome. When they returned to Rome in the 15th century, the popes had much more control over the city than ever before. That control led to a new era of growth, population expansion, building, and prosperity.

See also ALBORNOZ, GIL, CARDINAL; ALEXANDER VI, POPE; BELISARIO; CARDINALS, COLLEGE OF; CLEMENT V, POPE; GREGORY I THE GREAT, POPE; GREGORY VII, POPE; HOLY YEAR; INNOCENT III, POPE; PAPAL STATES; *LIBER PONTIFICALIS*; PETRARCH, FRANCESCO; PILGRIMAGE; URBAN VI, POPE.

Further reading: Debra J. Birch, *Pilgrimage to Rome in the Middle Ages: Continuity and Change* (Woodbridge, England: Boydell Press, 1998; Robert Brentano, *Rome before Avignon: A Social History of Thirteenth-Century Rome* (New York: Basic Books, 1974); Ferdinand A. Gregorovius, *History of the City of Rome in the Middle Ages,* trans. Annie Hamilton, 8 vols. (London: G. Bell, 1894–1902); Richard Krautheimer, *Rome, Profile of a City, 312–1308* (Princeton, N.J.: Princeton University Press, 1980); Peter Llewellyn, *Rome in the Dark Ages* (London: Faber, 1971).

Roncevaux, Battle of (Roncesvalles) Roncevaux was a historic battle immortalized but somewhat altered in the epic *La Chanson de Roland*. In it the hero Roland, the prefect or warden of the Breton march for the emperor CHARLEMAGNE, was killed in a titanic fight with Muslims, which historically was actually a battle with BASQUES. In charge of the rear guard of a retreating army led by Charlemagne, Roland was trapped in 778 in a valley between FRANCE and SPAIN. He and his great army fought gloriously until he and many of them were killed. In the epic, much bravery was demonstrated. In the real battle numerous Carolingian dignitaries were actually killed. This extremely popular epic poem, some 4,000 lines, was written in the 11th century. It drew on elements of the real battle to tell a story highlighting feudal values of loyalty among lords, vassals, and knights.

See also EPIC LITERATURE.

Further reading: Frances F. Beer, trans., *The Chanson de Roland* (Cambridge, Mass.: Harvard University Press, 1969); Robert Francis Cook, *The Sense of the Song of Roland* (Ithaca, N.Y.: Cornell University Press, 1987); Barton Sholod, *Charlemagne in Spain: The Cultural Legacy of Roncesvalles* (Geneva: Droz, 1966).

rosary The term *rosary* was attached in the 15th century to an exercise of PRAYER previously known as the "psalter of the Virgin," which had consisted of reciting either the Ave Maria, as many as 150 times or the same number of psalms. This "psalter of the Virgin" had originated in the eighth century, when those who could not recite psalms from memory instead said a series of prayers. The development of the cult of MARY from the 12th and 13th centuries introduced specific prayers addressed to her, other than the old Ave Maria. The regular recitation was begun by the CISTERCIANS, well known for their devotion to the Blessed Virgin. The Carthusians suggested that Mary would collect these prayers as if gathering roses, and the name *rosary* thus evolved.

The rosary was much practiced in the Rhineland, COLOGNE, and eventually ITALY. It was particularly cultivated by the DOMINICANS, who turned it into meditations on the five joyful mysteries of the life of the Virgin, such as the ANNUNCIATION and Nativity of Christ, and the five sorrowful mysteries, such as the agony in the garden and the CRUCIFIXION. Suggested also was contemplation of the five glorious mysteries, including the Resurrection. Each set of five formed decades or sets of repeated prayers. It became the usual practice to recite five decades and their surrounding prayers while contemplating a mystery of the faith. Fifteen decades comprised all of the 15 mysteries.

Further reading: Franz Michel Willam, *The Rosary: Its History and Meaning,* trans. Edwin Kaiser (New York: Benziger, 1953); John Desmond Miller, *Beads and Prayers: The Rosary in History and Devotion* (Tunbridge Wells: Burns and Oates, 2002); Catherine Vincent, "Rosary." *EMA* 2.1,261; Anne Winston-Allen, *Stories of the Rose: The Making of the Rosary in the Middle Ages* (University Park: Pennsylvania State University Press, 1997).

rose window   A medieval rose window was a circular window shaped with ribs to resemble a rose. It was designed to draw light into the interior. It could be in the façade, the transepts, or the choirs. This usually exquisite form was developed in ROMANESQUE and especially GOTHIC architecture. It had a technical and symbolic aspect all set within other STAINED GLASS in a church. It developed a clear wheel-with-spokes shape, eventually with delicate tracery added.

Further reading: Painton Cowen, *Rose Windows* (San Francisco: Chronicle Books, 1979).

rota   The term *rota* denoted a specialized judicial body formed by the papacy in the Middle Ages. It had its origins in the pontificate of the prominent jurist Pope ALEXANDER III, when the number of cases brought to papal arbitration increased. This increase caused reorganization within the judicial procedures of the Roman Curia

A rose window from the transept of the cathedral of Notre-Dame in Paris, with its original glass *(Courtesy Edward English)*

or court. Its areas of jurisdiction and competence were originally almost unlimited, since it was soon intended to be the court of last appeal and could involve the pope himself. Only criminal cases were outside its purview.

The term *rota* was first used for this court about 1360 and probably designated a desk mounted on wheels in the deliberation room at the Papal Palace at AVIGNON, on which the registers of cases were laid out. Equally likely, however, was that the term referred to a porphyry table in the Vatican Palace around which popes, cardinals, and their advisers assembled to judge major cases. From the early 13th century, papal chaplains began to replace cardinals in this system of administration of justice. This centralization of the administration was part of the attempt of the Holy See to control more closely the affairs of the church. The secular powers, bishops, and local churches opposed its jurisdictional interference.

Further reading: Guillaume Mollat, *The Popes at Avignon, 1305–1378,* trans. Janet Love (1949; reprint, New York: T. Nelsons 1963); Walter Ullman, *The Growth of Papal Government in the Middle Ages: A Study in the Ideological Relation of Clerical to Lay Power,* 3d ed. (1955; reprint, London: Methuen, 1970).

Rouen   Medieval Rouen was positioned on an alluvial bank of a loop in the Seine River in FRANCE. The first town wall of this originally Gallo-Roman town was hastily built in the late third or early fourth century. There was a mint from the ninth century, an era dominated by the Scandinavian invasions. In 841 a VIKING fleet attacked and burned the town. With the concession to ROLLO in 911 of the districts of the lower Seine, the town became the main center of his county and then of the duchy of NORMANDY. A ducal tower was built in the 10th century in the southeast of the town. The Norman Conquest of ENGLAND in 1066 linked Rouen with England.

In the next century King HENRY II gave the town a communal CHARTER. After capturing it in 1204, King PHILIP II AUGUSTUS built a new fortress within the city. During the 13th century, a new city wall was built. The insecurity of the HUNDRED YEARS' WAR led in the mid-14th century to an eastward expansion and repair of the town's walls. Through the 13th and 14th centuries, there were internal conflicts and uprisings against power being monopolized by a few families and the imposition of heavy financial burdens arising from war. In 1419 King HENRY V took the town. It remained in English hands for the next 30 years, despite several attempts by the French to retake it. JOAN OF ARC was executed there. After 1449 it was returned to the control of the French kingdom.

See also HENRY I; JOHN LACKLAND; WILLIAM I THE CONQUEROR.

Further reading: David C. Douglas, *William the Conqueror: The Norman Impact on England* (Berkeley: University of California Press, 1964); Jonathan Sumption, *The*

Hundred Years' War: Trial by Fire (1990; reprint, Philadelphia: University of Pennsylvania Press, 1999); Jenny Stratford, ed., *Medieval Art, Architecture, and Archaeology at Rouen* (London: British Archaeological Association, 1993).

Round Table   The Round Table was first mentioned by the WACE in his romance, *Brut,* taking the idea from GEOFFREY of Monmouth's *History of the Kings of Britain.* The Round Table represented the idea of a brilliant collection of KNIGHTS under the authority of King ARTHUR. The form of the table ensured meant that there were to be no quarrels over prestige. Its destruction meant the loss of the Arthurian idealistic kingdom. Robert de Boron (fl. 1200) in his book *Merlin* said that it was made by Merlin for Arthur's father. It was meant to be reminiscent of the table for the Last Supper and another where the GRAIL rested. One seat was to be vacant until the coming of a chosen knight, who only by means of his perfect virtue would be able to sit at the real table of the Grail. Developing the idea further CHRÉTIEN DE TROYES listed the Knights of the Round Table. The valor and prowess of these knights were the pillars of the Arthurian court but also ultimately the sources of the end of the dream of Camelot.

See also GALAHAD; GAWAIN AND THE GAWAIN ROMANCES; GUINEVERE; LANCELOT; MALORY, THOMAS; PERCEVAL; TRISTAN AND ISEULT.

Further reading: Anne Berthelot, *King Arthur and the Knights of the Round Table* (New York: Harry N. Abrams, 1997); Christopher Dean, *Arthur of England: English Attitudes to King Arthur and Knights of the Round Table in the Middle Ages and the Renaissance* (Toronto: University of Toronto Press, 1987); James A. Schultz, *The Shape of the Round Table: Structures of Middle High German Arthurian Romance* (Toronto: University of Toronto Press, 1983).

Rudel, Jaufré   *See* JAUFRÉ RUDEL.

Rudolf of Habsburg (1218–1291) *king of Germany, emperor*
Rudolf, the count of HABSBURG, was born in 1218 in a family with property and substance in upper Alsace and near Zurich. He was elected king of the Romans in September 1273 after a long interregnum. He did not maintain the Italian policies of the HOHENSTAUFEN dynasty and refused an imperial coronation in ROME, being crowned instead at AACHEN. At the Diet of Nuremburg in 1274, he began a policy of claiming all the imperial rights once held by FREDERICK II. He defeated and killed Premysl Ottokar II (r. 1253–78), the king of BOHEMIA, his rival for the imperial office, in 1278 at the Battle of Drünkrut or Marchfeld. He tried systematically then to increase his power by taking possession of the duchies of AUSTRIA, Carinthia, and Styria which became the bases of Habsburg power for centuries. He was a capable and fair administrator, created peaceful conditions in the empire, and gained the support of the magnates and many of the princes of GERMANY. He was moderate in his dealings with the PAPACY, even surrendering claims to SICILY and parts of the PAPAL STATES. Nonetheless, at his death July 15, 1291, he was unable to pass on the imperial and royal titles to his son Albert I (r. 1298–1308).

See also SWABIA.

Further reading: Benjamin Arnold, *Medieval Germany 500–1300: A Political Interpretation* (Basingstoke, England: Macmillan, 1997); F. R. H. Du Boulay, *Germany in the Later Middle Ages* (New York: St. Martin's Press, 1983); Joseph P. Huffman, *The Social Politics of Medieval Diplomacy: Anglo-German Relations (1066–1307)* (Ann Arbor: University of Michigan Press, 2000); Joachim Leuschner, *Germany in the Late Middle Ages,* trans. Sabine MacCormack (Amsterdam: North-Holland 1980).

Ruiz, Juan (Archpriest of Hita) (ca. 1283–ca. 1350) *Spanish poet, cleric*
Juan was born about 1283 and was educated at TOLEDO. Little is known of his life. While he was the archpriest in the village of Hita near Alcalá, he wrote in about 1330 *The Book of Good Love.* There were later versions, including one from 1343 which consisted of 12 narrative poems describing different love affairs in a morally ambiguous way. The author distinguished between good LOVE, that of GOD, and carnal love. He praised spiritual love but described in great detail a male hero's unsuccessful attempts at seductions of women. It contained high-spirited descriptions of amorous adventures and satirical pictures of life. He drew on FABLES, FABLIAUX, mock heroic allegory, and parodies. Ruiz employed lower-class characters, mostly comical, and used popular speech and proverbs drawn from a variety of sources, including the BIBLE and ancient and Arabic authors. He died about 1350.

Further reading: Juan Ruiz, *The Book of Good Love,* trans. Elizabeth Drayson MacDonald (London: Dent, 1999); John Dagenais, *The Ethics of Reading in Manuscript Culture: Glossing the Libro de buen amor* (Princeton, N.J.: Princeton University Press, 1994); Laurence De Looze, *Pseudo-Autobiography in the Fourteenth Century: Juan Ruiz, Guillaume de Machaut, Jean Froissart, and Geoffrey Chaucer* (Gainesville: University Press of Florida, 1997) Henry Ansgar Kelly, *Canon Law and the Archpriest of Hita* (Binghamton: Medieval & Renaissance Texts & Studies, 1984); Rigo Mignani, ed., *A Concordance to Juan Ruiz, Libro de buen amor* (Albany: State University of New York Press, 1977).

Rumi (Jalal al-Din, Mawlana, Our Lord, Djelaleddin, Jelalod-din) (1207–1273) *Persian mystic, poet*
Rumi was born perhaps on September 30, 1207, at Balkh in Khurasan, modern-day Afghanistan. Jalal al-Din Rumi

was called *Mawlana,* "Our Master," in Persian. He was the founder of the confraternity of the *Mevlevis,* known as the dancing or whirling dervishes in the West. With his family, he left his homeland because of the devastations of the MONGOL invasions in the 1220s and after a period of wandering settled at Konya in ANATOLIA in 1228, then the capital of the SELJUKS of Rum and the place where his father had taught theology. There he soon began to teach and to play an important role in intellectual and religious life. His most influential and didactic work was the mystical poem the *Mathnawi,* of some 25,000 verses. Rumi also wrote *Rubaiyat* and a lyrical and metaphorical poem, the *Diwan-e Shams,* in honor of his teacher, Shams al-Din of Tabriz (d. 1247). Rumi had been so obsessed with this wandering mystic that his students supposedly murdered Shams in order to refocus Rumi's attention on them. His ideas and visions were based on an intense desire for union with GOD through LOVE and the spiritual dance or *sama* to the sound of a reed flute. His work remained popular throughout the Islamic world until this day. He died at Konya in Anatolia on December 17, 1273.

See also SUFISM.

Further reading: Jalal al-Din Rumi, *The Mathnawi of Jalaluddin Rumi,* ed. Reynold A. Nicholson, 3 vols. (London: Printed for the Trustees of the E. J. W. Gibb Memorial, 1977); Jalal al-Din Rumi, *The Mystical Poems of Rumi,* trans. Arthur J. Arberry (Chicago: University of Chicago Press, 1968); Afzal Iqbal, *The Life and Work of Jalal-ud-din Rumi* (London: Octagon Press, 1983); Fatemeh Keshavarz, *Reading Mystical Lyric: The Case of Jalal al-Din Rumi* (Columbia: University of South Carolina Press, 1998); Annemarie Schimmel, *I Am Wind, You Are Fire: The Life and Work of Rumi* (Boston: Shambhala, 1992).

runes, runic script, and inscriptions   The name *runic* has been applied to the script that the early Germans used from the third century C.E. It became almost an exclusively Scandinavian art after the conversion of most of the Germans to Christianity and their adoption of the Latin script. The runic alphabet first comprised 24 signs, in three groups of eight runes each. These were reduced to 16 around the year 800 for the business requirements of VIKING MERCHANTS. The 24 runes initially corresponded to the phonetic needs of a language, early Norse. The 16 new runes could be thought of as similar to modern shorthand. Runes at the same time were thought to be magic signs, a more or less esoteric means of communication, even in a secular sense or for religious purposes. The word *rune* can also be read as a "mystery," a "secret," or a "whispered message." Runes were usually engraved with a stylus or a punch on a hard surface such as stone, wood, bone, IVORY, metal, or, leather and did not lend themselves to the writing of long texts.

Further reading: Elmer H. Antonsen, *A Concise Grammar of the Older Runic Inscriptions* (Tübingen: M.

Niemeyer, 1975); Ralph W. V. Elliott, *Runes: An Introduction* (New York: Philosophical Library, 1959); R. I. Page, *Runes* (Berkeley: University of California Press, 1987).

Rupert of Deutz   (1075–1129/30) *reactionary monastic theologian, conservative reformer*
Rupert was born in 1075 in the region of Liège and there entered Saint Lawrence's monastery in Liège for his education. Rupert followed his abbot into exile between 1092 and 1095. The abbot had been expelled in favor of an appointment bought by SIMONY. He fought with the bishop of Liège and was not reconciled with him until 1108. At about the same time, he experienced a spiritual change marked by visions encouraging him to write. Between 1111 and 1117, he wrote *On the Trinity,* which analyzed the historical books of the BIBLE. He also wrote a commentary on the gospel of John. In another, *On the Will of God,* he began to try to refute early Scholastic ideas and practices.

From 1116 he found a safer and calmer refuge with the abbot of Siegburg, and later the archbishop of COLOGNE, who allowed, in 1120, his election as the abbot of Deutz. After his earlier writings had been approved by the pope, he went on to compose a *Commentary on the Song of Songs,* the *Glorification of the Trinity,* and a dialogue between a Jew and a Christian. The dialogue was intended to demonstrate the superiority of the Christian New Testament over the Jewish Bible. He then went on to write polemics against the German emperor; pre-Scholastics such as ANSELM of Laon; the CISTERCIAN ORDER; and regular canons, such as those linked with NORBERT of Xanten. He unfailingly rejected the new dialectic method and nascent Scholastic intellectual speculations. He emphasized the value of PRAYER and celebrated the Virgin MARY, whom he proposed as an ideal model for the church. He died in 1129/30.

Further reading: Jean Leclercq, *The Love of Learning and the Desire for God: A Study of Monastic Culture,* trans. Catharine Misrahi (New York: Fordham University Press, 1961); John Van Engen, *Rupert of Deutz* (Berkeley: University of California Press, 1983).

Rurik   (Rlurik Ryurik, Roerck) (d. 879) *Viking leader, founder of the first principality at Novgorod*
Rurik is known basically only as a legendary Scandinavian chieftain of the VARANGIANS. With his brothers Rurik took power at NOVGOROD in the ninth century. IGOR, perhaps his son, was the first historically attested member of the family. Igor reigned at Kiev in the first half of the 10th century and was the real founder of the dynasty. After him, the throne of Kiev passed to his son, Svatyslav (r. 945–972); his grandson, VLADIMIR I THE GREAT; and then YAROSLAV THE WISE, whose direct descendants reigned over the principality until the Mongol invasion. Rurik died in 879 probably near Novgorod.

The Rurikid dynasty ruled RUSSIA AND RUŚ from the ninth century until 1598 or 1614.

See also KIEV AND KIEVAN RUŚ; MONGOLS AND THE MONGOL EMPIRE.

Further reading: Samuel H. Cross and Olgerd P. Sherbowitz-Wetzor, trans., *The Russian Primary Chronicle: Laurentian Text* (Cambridge, Mass.: Mediaeval Academy of America, 1953); Nora K. Chadwick, *The Beginnings of Russian History: An Enquiry into Sources* (Cambridge: Cambridge University Press, 1946); H. R. Ellis Davidson, *The Viking Road to Byzantium* (London: Allen and Unwin, 1976); Simon Franklin and Jonathan Shepard, *The Emergence of Ruś, 750–1200* (New York: Longman, 1996).

Rushd, Ibn See IBN RUSHD.

Russia and Ruś Modern Russia had its origins in Kievan Ruś, which was formed during the ninth century under the leadership of a merchant and military elite of Scandinavian origin. That principality had its own origins from the late eighth century in the region between Lake Ladoga and NOVGOROD. These armed bands traded with the lands of the ARABS and the MERCHANTS of CONSTANTINOPLE. They lived in settlements along the river journey to the BLACK SEA. They had to subdue the Slavic tribes who lived along that route from the Baltic and North Seas. Kiev was the principal river port on this route and soon became the residence of the leading merchants and entrepreneurs.

THE PRINCES OF KIEV

In 860, these aggressive merchant-raiders even besieged Constantinople itself. The first princes of Kiev, OLEG and IGOR, attacked the Byzantine capital and obtained peace treaties and commercial privileges in 911 and 944. Later in the 10th century, Igor's son, Svatyslav (r. 945–972), tried to extend his power eastward into the KHAZAR kingdom that controlled the route from the Volga River to the Caspian Sea. He then attacked BULGARIA but was countered by opposition from the Byzantines. The Kievan princes continued to try to control the Slav and Finnish subject tribes. During the 10th and 11th centuries, the old tribal regions were replaced by administrative centers controlled by strongholds and fortified towns. From the early 11th century, the term Ruś designated the territories subjected to the princes of Kiev or from the shores of the Baltic to the course of the Dniepr River, and from the Dvina River to the upper course of the Volga.

CHRISTIANIZATION

The official adoption of Christianity by VLADIMIR I THE GREAT in 988 was the next step in a process of cultural unification of these territories. The Orthodox Church in Constantinople sent priests and helped in establishing a diocesan organization. Kiev was elevated to rank of metropolitan for the area in about 990 and retained this ecclesiastical preeminence until the 14th century. The allegiance of the Kievan church to the Greek Orthodox Church in Constantinople played a decisive role in the development of Russian culture, literature, intellectual models, and the arts.

MONGOL INVASIONS AND THE FORMATION OF A NEW CENTER

By the late 12th century, Ruś had been transformed into a federation of principalities, independent but seemingly allied against the new Mongol threat. With the capture of Kiev by the Mongol Khan Batu in 1240, a new center of government had to be established in the "grand principalities" of northeast Russia, a hitherto marginal region for Kievan Ruś, between the courses of the Volga and Oka Rivers. This area became the cradle of the later Russian nation. Populated by Finno-Ugrian tribes it was covered with forests but was crossed by commerce linking the Baltic to the Caspian Sea. It was called the land of Rostov or Suzdal from the name of its major towns. In the 11th century, it was already under the control of the princes of Kiev and now presented itself as the sole heir to Kievan Ruś. Agriculture there was then progressively dominated by great landowners, princes, and BOYARS. With a social and economic system that soon led to the establishment of an oppressive serfdom, it suffered periodically from Mongol incursions and the paying of a large tribute. From 1243 to 1480 North-East Ruś was a province of a part of the Mongol Empire, the western march of the Golden Horde. It has remained unclear how much economic and social damage this new state suffered from the Mongols.

THE PRINCES OF MOSCOW

From this the grand duchy of Moscow emerged, and the son of Alexander NEVSKY, David (r. 1280–1303), became the first to be called the prince of MOSCOW. The prestige of the grand principality of Vladimir or Moscow was assisted when a metropolitan, Maximus, fleeing Kiev, settled there in 1299. These princes of Moscow, especially IVAN III THE GREAT, began to break Mongol control. At Kulikovo, DIMITRI of the Don had already won a great victory over the Mongols, which led to the virtual independence of Moscow. Russia was dominated by Moscow from then on.

See also KIEV AND KIEVAN RUŚ; MONGOLS AND THE MONGOL EMPIRE.

Further reading: Robert Auty and Dimitri Obolensky, eds., *An Introduction to Russian Language and Literature* (Cambridge: Cambridge University Press, 1977); Pavel Markovich Dolukhanov, *The Early Slavs: Eastern Europe from the Initial Settlement to the Kievan Ruś* (London: Longman, 1996); Simon Franklin and Jonathan Shepard, *The Emergence of Ruś, 750–1200* (New York:

Longman, 1996); Thomas S. Noonan, "European Russia, c. 900–1016," in *The New Cambridge Medieval History. Vol. 3, c. 900–c. 1024,* ed. Timothy Reuter (Cambridge: Cambridge University Press, 1999), 487–513; P. B. Golden, "Ruś," *Encyclopedia of Islam,* 8:618–629.

Ruysbroeck, Jan van, Blessed (Ruusbroec, Rusbrochius) (1293–1381) *Flemish mystic, participant in the movement of Free Spirit*

Jan van Ruysbroeck was born in 1293 at Ruusbroec, a small town near Brussels in BRABANT. In 1304 he moved to Brussels, where he was educated at the school of the collegiate church. Intended for the priesthood, he was ordained in 1317. For 25 years, he was the vicar of the collegiate church of Saint Gudule but in close contact with BEGUINES of Brussels. Through them he was probably exposed to the writings of HADEWIJCH OF ANTWERP, Beatrice of Nazareth (ca. 1200–68), and MARGARET PORETTE. This led him to the ideas of the FREE SPIRIT. Under the influence of Meister ECKHART, and trying to promote a more orthodox spirituality, yet at the same time one critical of the institutional church, he wrote spiritual and mystical treatises in the VERNACULAR, Flemish or Middle Dutch. His great work, among several others, was *Adornment of Spiritual Marriage.* Some of these were later translated into LATIN.

Around Easter of 1343, Ruysbroeck moved with some friends to Groenendaal in the forest of Soignes, where they lived for seven years in a community without rule. In 1350 they adopted the AUGUSTINIAN RULE becoming a community of regular canons. There he was perhaps visited by JOHN Tauler and undoubtedly by his disciple, Gerhard GROOTE. He died at Groenendaal on December 2, 1381. In 1908 he was beatified by the pope, and his feast is commemorated in dioceses in Flanders on December 2.

See also DEVOTIO MODERNA; KEMPIS, THOMAS À; MYSTICISM, CHRISTIAN.

Further reading: Louis K. Dupré, *The Common Life: The Origins of Trinitarian Mysticism and Its Development by Jan Ruusbroec* (New York: Crossroad, 1984); Paul Mommaers, *The Land Within: The Process of Possessing and Being Possessed by God According to the Mystic Jan van Ruysbroeck,* trans. David N. Smith (Chicago: Franciscan Herald Press, 1975); Paul Verdeyen, *Ruusbroec and His Mysticism,* trans. André Lefevere (Collegeville, Minn.: Liturgical Press, 1994).

S

Saba *See* SAVA NEMANJA OF SERBIA, SAINT.

sabbath and witches' sabbath The sabbath had two meanings in the Middle Ages and RENAISSANCE. It was the seventh day of the week for JEWS and Christians, Saturday. It initially did and in some denominations still does prohibit work. It was to be a day limited to rest and the worship of GOD, for God himself had rested on the seventh day during his creation of the world. Christians transferred this custom to Sunday during the Middle Ages, presumably because they believed that Christ's Resurrection and the descent of the Holy Spirit on Pentecost both occurred on this first day of the week. For the Jews the sabbath retained its initial character and there was considerable discussion about what they were and were not allowed to do on that day of the week.

In very different terms, the witches' sabbath occupied an important place in the definition of the crime of WITCHCRAFT, as described in the theoretical treatises and trial confessions from at least the 15th century. If someone was found, or perceived, to have participated in its celebration or practice, he or she was assumed to be a witch and was thus liable to execution. The witches' sabbath was thought to be the central ritual of a cult antithetical to Christian worship. Its fundamental aspects allegedly included nocturnal flights, sometimes on a stick rubbed with an unguent, sometimes on an animal, to the place where dreamlike, yet voluntary and "sabbatical" acts were performed. These acts might include carnal unions with demons or and cannibalism of newborn children. No proof exists that these events actually took place. In witchcraft trials, they could have emerged from the imaginations and the cultural and religious superstitions of the accusers and melded into the confessions of the accused.

See also VISIONS AND DREAMS.

Further reading: Montague Summers, trans., *The Malleus Maleficarum of Heinrich Kramer and James Sprenger* (1928; reprint, New York: Dover, 1971); Alan C. Kors and Edward Peters, eds., *Witchcraft in Europe, 1100–1700: A Documentary History* (Philadelphia: University of Pennsylvania Press, 1972); Jeffrey Burton Russell, *Witchcraft in the Middle Ages* (Ithaca, N.Y.: Cornell University Press, 1972); E. P. Sanders, *Jewish Law from Jesus to the Mishnah: Five Studies* (London: SCM Press, 1990).

Sachsenspiegel **(the Mirror of Saxon Law)** The *Sachsenspiegel* was a collection of customary on feudal laws mainly from SAXONY which was compiled first in Latin then in the German vernacular about 1225 by Eike von Repgow (ca. 1180–ca. 1235) with a final version appearing in 1270. It synthesized German law in reaction and opposition to the centralizing efforts of the ambitious HOHENSTAUFEN dynasty, who were trying to increase their control over the German states by imposing a centralized, standard, and imperial code of law. The *Sachsenspiegel* was heavily influenced by Roman law, which favored imperial authority. The *Sachsenspiegel* was divided into two parts, the law of the land and the law of fiefs or feudal law. It assumed a duality of law between the secular and the ecclesiastical but gave the papacy no role in the Law of Germany. GREGORY XI condemned 14 articles in it in 1374. The HOLY ROMAN EMPIRE was in theory to be based on a common and unifying law within a collection of interacting polities or states. The *Sachsenspiegel* later became one of the bases for an electoral system for the Holy Roman Empire by defining who were the seven electors. It consisted of two parts. The first covered customary law on inheritance, the family, legal procedure, criminal law, and laws to maintain public peace. The second part concerned feudal obligations, especially those of Saxony.

See also FEUDALISM AND THE FEUDAL SYSTEM; FREDERICK II, EMPEROR AND KING OF SICILY.

Further reading: Maria Dobozy, trans., *The Saxon Mirror: A Sachsenspiegel of the Fourteenth Century* (Philadelphia: University of Pennsylvania Press, 1999); Guido Kisch, *Sachsenspiegel and Bible: Researches in the Source History of the Sachsenspiegel and the Influence of the Bible on Mediaeval German Law* (1941; reprint, Notre Dame, Ind.: University of Notre Dame Press, 1960); Guillermo F. Margadant, *The Illustrations of the Sachsenspiegel: A Medieval German Law Book* (Austin: Joseph D. Jamail Center for Legal Research, The University of Texas School of Law, 2000); Theodore John Rivers, "Sachsenspiegel" *DMA* 10.602–604.

sacramentary During the Middle Ages, the sacramentary was principal book used for the celebration of MASS. In it nearly all the PRAYERS of the Christian Church were preserved. It was also among the most illustrated liturgical books of the early Middle Ages. It contained all the prayers for the celebrant, whether pope, bishop, or priest, for each day of the liturgical year. It also contained the canon of the Mass or eucharistic prayer. The sacramentary contained the formularies, usually three orations and a preface for the temporal and the sanctoral. These were usually supplemented by a CALENDAR, ritual prayers, and blessings for baptism, EXORCISM, funerals, penitential services, and various votive masses. Many of these were made and decorated simply or lavishly. They are recorded from the time of Pope LEO I in the fifth century. The most common model for them was associated with Pope GREGORY I THE GREAT, whose prestige enhanced its authority. During the CAROLINGIAN RENAISSANCE and reform, these books were standardized for a common liturgy throughout the empire. In the 12th century, the contents of the sacramentary were included in the MISSAL.

See also ILLUMINATION; LITURGICAL BOOKS.

Further reading: Yitzhak Hen, ed., *The Sacramentary of Echternach (Paris, Bibliothèque nationale, MS. lat. 9433)* (London: Henry Bradshaw Society, 1997); Richard W. Pfaff, *Medieval Latin Liturgy: A Select Bibliography* (Toronto: University of Toronto Press, 1982), 72–79; Cyrille Vogel, *Medieval Liturgy: An Introduction to the Sources,* trans. William G. Storey and Niels Krogh Rasmussen (Washington, D.C.: Pastoral Press, 1986).

sacraments *See* SEVEN SACRAMENTS.

Sacred College *See* CARDINALS, COLLEGE OF.

sacristy The sacristy or *sacrarium* in LATIN was the place where sacred and valuable objects, such as RELICS, liturgical vessels, and VESTMENTS, were kept. It was the place where the priest and the ministers put on those vestments. Most of these areas or rooms in medieval churches have not survived or have been heavily redone. Only a few CATHEDRALS from the late middle Ages and RENAISSANCE have kept their original sacristies.

See also AMIENS CATHEDRAL; CHARTRES, CATHEDRAL OF.

Further reading: Reinhard Bentmann, *Churches of the Middle Ages,* trans. Anthony Lloyd (London: Cassell, 1979); Paul Hetherington, *Byzantine and Medieval Greece: Churches, Castles, and Art of the Mainland and Peloponnese* (London: J. Murray, 1991); H. W. van Os, *Vecchietta and the Sacristy of the Siena Hospital Church: A Study in Renaissance Religious Symbolism,* trans. Eva Biesta (New York: A. Schram, 1974); Colin Platt, *The Parish Churches of Medieval England* (London: Secker and Warburg, 1981).

Saffarids (Safawids) The Saffarids were a ruling Muslim dynasty from Sistan in eastern Persia or IRAN between 873 and 900. The dynasty founded in Khorasan by Yaqub ibn al-Layth (al-Saffar, the coppersmith) (r. 867–79), a former MERCHANT who organized a local militia of merchants and craftsmen to defend their trades. By 873 the Saffarids had conquered the major part of Khorasan, most of Persia, and territory well east into Afghanistan and even India. Yaqub died in 879 and was succeeded as emir by his brother, Amr (r. 879–900). The dynasty reigned until 900, when Emir Amr was captured and dethroned by the SAMANIDS. The empire quickly fell apart, but the family remained a local power in Sistan for several centuries, even surviving the invasion of the MONGOLS.

Further reading: Clifford Edmund Bosworth, *The Islamic Dynasties* (Edinburgh: Edinburgh University Press, 1967), 103–106; Clifford Edmund Bosworth, *The History of the Saffarids of Sistan and the Maliks of Nimruz: (247/861 to 949/1542–3)* (Costa Mesa, Calif.: Mazda Publishers in Association with Bibliotheca Persica, 1994); R. M. Savory et al., "Safawids," *Encyclopedia of Islam* 8.765–793; Roger Savory, *Iran under the Safavids* (Cambridge: Cambridge University Press, 1980); Colin Turner, *Islam without Allah?: The Rise of Religious Externalism in Safavid Iran* (Richmond, England: Curzon, 2000).

saffron Saffron in the Middle Ages was an expensive and important spice used primarily as flavoring for food, particularly in Mediterranean foods, especially those using fish or rice. It also served as a dyestuff for yellow to bright orange and as a medicinal drink. Saffron consisted of the whole or powdered dried stigmas of the flowers of the plant *Crocus sativus*. That somewhat rare plant usually only annually bloomed for a two-week period in late autumn. The word *saffron* was derived from the Arabic word *zaaran* or "yellow." It could require perhaps 70,000 flowers to yield a single pound of saffron.

The taste for and use of saffron were probably introduced to ITALY, FRANCE, Iberia, and GERMANY by returning crusaders during the 13th and 14th centuries. Saffron from VALENCIA and CATALONIA initially dominated the market in Western Europe, while saffron from Tuscany did so in the eastern Mediterranean market. Certain towns, such as MONTPELLIER and San Gimignano in TUSCANY soon specialized in its production, and made fortunes from its production.

See also FOOD, DRINK, AND NUTRITION; SPICES AND THE SPICE TRADE.

Further reading: John W. Parry, *Spices: Their Morphology, Histology and Chemistry* (New York: Chemical, 1962); Frederick Rosengarten, *The Book of Spices* (Wynnewood, Pa.: Livingston, 1969).

sagas Medieval sagas were prose narratives, sometimes including skaldic strophes or even long poems, composed in ICELAND from the 12th to the 14th century. Some followed classical and hagiographical Latin models. The word itself derived from the verb *segja*, "to say" or "to recount." They were not intended as history but often reflected considerable historical reality. Most were written by literate lay or clerical authors, much under the influence of oral traditions. There were pagan elements running through them, but they were influenced by Christian ethical ideas.

GENRES

Dating from the early 13th century, the historical sagas tried to trace the lives of the kings of NORWAY or DENMARK, such as in SNORRI STURLUSON'S HEIMSKRINGLA from about 1225. The Icelandic sagas or family sagas were tales about the great colonizers of Iceland or their immediate descendants, such as *Saga of Burnt Njal* and the *Saga of Egill Son of Grimr the Bald*. Those later-named contemporary sagas were chronicles of events contemporary with their anonymous authors, such as the *Sturlunga Saga*. There were the knights' sagas (*riddarasogur*), adaptations of courtly texts from the romantic and Germanic courtly world. Last there were sagas set in ancient times, basically legendary, archaic, and more generally Germanic, such as the *Volsunga Saga*.

See also ICELAND AND ICELANDIC LITERATURE.

Further reading: Jesse L. Byock, *Medieval Iceland: Society, Sagas, and Power* (Berkeley: University of California Press, 1988); Carol J. Clover, *The Medieval Saga* (Ithaca, N.Y.: Cornell University Press, 1982); Paul Schach, "Norse Sagas" in *European Writers: The Middle Ages and the Renaissance*. Vol. 1, *Prudentius to Medieval Drama*, eds. William T. H. Jackson and George Stade (New York: Charles Scribner's Sons, 1983), 377–404.

Saint-Denis, abbey and church of Around 475 Saint Geneviève (d. 500) had an oratory built on the tomb and in memory of Denis or Dionysius (d. ca. 250), a Christian missionary, patron saint of France, and the bishop of Paris who was martyred in the midthird century on a road north of Paris. He was buried there by a pious woman. The Merovingian dynasty soon took an interest in the sanctuary because of its powerful RELICS. Around 550 Childebert I (r. 511–58) enlarged the monastery and made it the religious heart of his kingdom. He also made it the royal necropolis. By the late sixth century, many members of royal family were buried there. The abbey became very rich. The Carolingians built a new church and also used it as a burial site for their kings, CHARLES Martel and CHARLES THE BALD, among others. The Capetians, as lay abbots of Saint Denis, enriched the abbey's position still further and allied it even more closely with the Crown. To show this the royal battle insignia from the 12th century, the oriflamme, became the banner of the abbey.

A new church built by SUGER between 1130 and 1144 housed the tombs of all the Capetian kings except Philip I (r. 1060–1108), who was at Fleury; Louis VII (r. 1137–80), who was at Barbeau, and Louis IX who was at Cléry. The abbey fared poorly during the HUNDRED YEARS' WAR and thereafter never regained its prominence and links with the new VALOIS dynasty.

See also CRYPTS; DEATH AND THE DEAD; GOTHIC.

Further reading: Pamela Z. Blum, *Early Gothic Saint-Denis: Restorations and Survivals* (Berkeley: University of California Press, 1992); Paula Lieber Gerson, ed., *Abbot Suger and Saint-Denis: A Symposium* (New York: Metropolitan Museum of Art, 1986); Sumner M. Crosby, *The Royal Abbey of Saint-Denis: From Its Beginnings to the Death of Suger, 475–1151*, ed. Pamela Z. Blum (New Haven, Conn.: Yale University Press, 1987); Anne F. Rockwell, *Glass, Stones and Crown: The Abbé Suger and the Building of St. Denis* (New York: Atheneum, 1968); Suger, Abbot of Saint Denis, *Abbot Suger on the Abbey Church of St.-Denis and Its Art Treasures*, ed. and trans. Erwin Panofsky (Princeton, N.J.: Princeton University Press, 1946).

Sainte-Chapelle of Paris The Sainte-Chapelle of PARIS was built for King LOUIS IX, in a courtyard of the Palace of the Cité, to house the RELICS of the Passion taken by Baldwin II the Latin emperor, from Byzantium and the Near East between 1239 and 1247. It was modeled on a palace of the Byzantine emperors, Bucoleon, on the edge of CONSTANTINOPLE. This treasure house was enriched later by gifts, and exchanges of relics and, in 1306, by a RELIQUARY of Saint Louis IX, who had been canonized in 1297. They were placed behind the high ALTAR of the upper chapel and displayed to the people of Paris during HOLY WEEK and to important visitors. Some relics, such as a cross of victory or a crown of thorns, were carried in the great Parisian processions.

Designed and built in a very short time by an unknown architect, the Sainte-Chapelle was consecrated on April 26, 1248, just before Louis's departure on a Crusade the following June. It was a reliquary church on two levels, the upper level having immense and dazzling STAINED glass windows, including a ROSE WINDOW. The windows included biblical themes and the history of the relics of the Passion. Considered a prime GOTHIC example of the mid-13th-century court style, the Sainte-Chapelle was frequently imitated. A major and heavy-handed restoration was accomplished in the 19th century. Some of its medieval contents are known today, especially IVORY work, jeweled book covers, and small reliquaries. An abundant staff of canons and court officials were commissioned by Louis to serve as caretakers of the Sainte-Chapelle.

Further reading: Yves Bottineau, *Notre-Dame de Paris and the Sainte-Chapelle,* trans. Lovett F. Edwards (London: Allen, 1967); Robert Branner, *The Painted Medallions*

The Gothic exterior of the Sainte-Chapelle rising in the center of Paris *(Courtesy Edward English)*

in the Sainte-Chapelle in Paris (Philadelphia: American Philosophical Society, 1968); Alyce A. Jordan, *Visualizing Kingship in the Windows of the Sainte-Chapelle* (Turnhout: Brepols, 2002).

Saint Patrick's Purgatory *Saint Patrick's Purgatory* was a visionary text written by an English Cistercian monk about 1190. In it a knight, Owein, entered a particular well God had revealed to Saint PATRICK, in order to cleanse himself of his sins and attain HEAVEN. This well or Saint Patrick's purgatory was situated on an island in IRELAND. Inside it the knight passed through several regions where souls suffered infernal tortures in order to fulfill the penance earned by their terrestrial SIN. The qualities and length of their passage were proportional to the gravity of their sins but could be lessened or cut short by the PRAYERS of those still living. After enduring such purgation, souls emerged to an earthly and then a heavenly PARADISE. Owein escaped the torments due him by invoking the name of Jesus Christ and becoming a monk. This was a popular tale and was translated into several languages including one by MARIE DE FRANCE. A well on Station Island in county Donegal in Ireland became identified with Saint Patrick's Purgatory and was reputed to be this entrance to penance and salvation. It became a great site of PILGRIMAGE from the 12th century.

See also PURGATORY; VISIONS AND DREAMS.

Further reading: Jean-Michel Picard, trans., *Saint Patrick's Purgatory: A Twelfth Century Tale of a Journey to the Other World* (Dublin: Four Courts Press, 1985); Howard R. Patch, *The Other World, According to Descriptions in Medieval Literature* (Cambridge, Mass.: Harvard University Press, 1950); Shane Leslie, *Saint Patrick's Purgatory* (Dublin: Colm O Lochlainn, at the Sign of the Three Candles, 1961).

Saladin (Salah al-Din Yusuf ibn Ayyub, al-Malik al-Nasir Abu l-Muzaffar) (1137/38–1193) *Kurdish sultan of Egypt, founder of the Ayyubid dynasty*
The son of al-Ayyub, a minister of Zengi and NUR AL-DIN, Saladin was born at Tikrit in IRAQ about 1137 or 1138. Of Kurdish origin, he was at first in the service of Prince Nur al-Din, who was trying to reunify the Muslim world to oppose the crusading Europeans. Once they achieved Syrian unity in 1154, Nur al-Din sent Saladin with his uncle, Shirkuh (d. 1171), to conquer EGYPT. It was there that his military career began to flourish. Shirkuh held the post of vizier of CAIRO by 1169. After his death, Saladin succeeded him, and in 1171 he restored Sunni rule, ending two centuries of Shiite FATIMID rule in Egypt. He subsequently seized power in Egypt, risking the enmity of Nur al-Din in DAMASCUS, who was preparing to attack him when he died in 1174.

Saladin immediately sought to succeed him. Branded as a usurper by the partisans of Nur al-Din's young son, another Nur al-Din (d. 1181), Saladin claimed that he was the only prince capable of leading a successful war or JIHAD against the Franks in the Levant. Saladin controlled Damascus and central SYRIA by 1174 and then eventually upper Mesopotamia, or IRAQ, and northern Syria by 1183. He then attacked the Christians. Profiting from a crisis of succession in the kingdom of JERUSALEM, in 1187 Saladin won a resounding victory over the Kingdom of Jerusalem at the Horns at HATTIN near Tiberias. The kingdom of Jerusalem was suddenly defenseless and fell into his hands. Jerusalem was taken on October 2, 1187, without much bloodshed, and in the following months many fortresses capitulated in northern Syria. Only TYRE, TRIPOLI, ANTIOCH, and a few CASTLES remained in Frankish hands. The West soon organized a Third CRUSADE, in which FREDERICK I BARBAROSSA, PHILIP II AUGUSTUS, and RICHARD I LIONHEART took part. They failed to retake Jerusalem on this crusade but did capture ACRE and some coastal strongholds. Saladin skillfully avoided a decisive battle, especially with Richard I. The treaty of Jaffa in 1192 allowed the reestablishment of a second kingdom of Jerusalem, or the kingdom of Acre, much reduced from the first but easier to defend. Saladin died of a fever following year, March 4, 1193, in Damascus.

IDEALIZED LEGACY

Saladin's success rested on the support given him by powerful religious leaders including Kurdish and Turkish emirs. He sought to restore economic support for Sunnite ISLAM by granting important landed incomes. He restored the Egyptian fleet and sought good relations with the Italian towns to ensure that they would supply him with the wood and iron necessary for his armaments. He concluded alliances with the SELJUKS of ANATOLIA in 1180 and the BYZANTINES in 1185. The unity of his state collapsed soon after his death, in part because of financial difficulties and in part because of its division among his sons. Known for his toleration of non-Muslim subjects, he has remained a hero for many Muslims to this day.

See also ALEPPO; MOSUL.

Further reading: Ibn Shaddad, *The Rare and Excellent History of Saladin—or, al-Nawadir al-Sultaniyya wal-Mahasin al-Yusufiyya,* trans. D. S. Richards (Aldershot: Ashgate, 2002); Andrew S. Ehrenkreutz, *Saladin* (Albany: State University of New York Press, 1972); H. A. R. Gibb, *The Life of Saladin: From the Works of Imad ad-Din and Baha ad-Din* (Oxford: Clarendon Press, 1973); Geoffrey Hindley, *Saladin* (London: Constable, 1976); R. Stephen Humphreys, *From Saladin to the Mongols: The Ayyubids of Damascus, 1193–1260* (Albany: State University of New York Press, 1977); Margaret A. Jubb, *The Legend of Saladin in Western Literature and Historiography* (Lewiston, Maine: Edwin Mellen Press, 2000); Malcolm Cameron Lyons and D. E. P. Jackson, *Saladin: The Politics of War* (Cambridge: Cambridge University Press, 1997; P. H. Newby, *Saladin in His Time* (London: Faber and Faber,

1983); D. S. Richards, "Salaln al-Dīn," *Encyclopedia of Islam* 8.910–914.

salat See PRAYER AND PRAYERS.

Salerno See MEDICINE; UNIVERSITIES AND SCHOOLS; TROTA.

Salian dynasty (Salier dynasty) The Salians were the imperial family who reigned from 1024 to 1125 over the HOLY ROMAN EMPIRE. Named for the Salian FRANKS, they were originally from the Middle Rhine region. The dynasty began when the duke of Lotharingia, Conrad the Red (r. 944–953), married Liudgard (d. 953), a daughter of the emperor OTTO I. Conrad's great-grandson, Conrad II (r. 1024–39), was proclaimed king in 1024. Conrad II and his three successors, all called Henry, ruled the empire for a century. One, Henry IV, reigned for 50 years, from 1056 to 1106.

The Salians based their power and patrimony on lands and fiefs in FRANCONIA and the Rhineland. They rebuilt and enlarged the CATHEDRAL of Speyer for a family necropolis. Heirs to the policies of the Ottonians and Henry II the Saint (r. 1002–24), they continued to foster an imperial dominated church, as did Conrad II. HENRY III (r. 1039–56) was unsympathetic to SIMONY, nonetheless used his authority over the church to appoint three successive popes and preside over a council with one of them, Leo IX (r. 1049–54). Henry IV battled but failed both in taking control of SAXONY and in gaining influence with Pope GREGORY VII. His sons finally rose against and deposed him in 1105. Henry V (r. 1105–25) fought with popes but also reached an accord with the church in the Concordat of Worms in 1122. The last Salian, Lothair III, ruled from 1125 to 1137. At his death the HOHENSTAUFEN dynasty took over.

See also CANOSSA; GREGORIAN REFORM; PASCHAL II, POPE.

Further reading: Karl Hampe, *Germany under the Salian and Hohenstaufen Emperors,* trans. Ralph Bennett (1968; reprinted Oxford: Blackwell, 1973); Stefan Weinfurter, *The Salian Century: Main Currents in an Age of Transition,* trans. Barbara M. Bowlus (1991, reprint, Philadelphia: University of Pennsylvania Press, 1999); James Westfall Thompson, *Feudal Germany* (Chicago: University of Chicago Press, 1928).

Salimbene de Adam (Ognibene) (1221–after 1288) *Italian Franciscan friar, traveler, chronicler*
Salimbene was born at Parma in 1221, the son of Guido de Adamo and Iumelda de Cassio, who were related to Pope INNOCENT IV. The sources for his life are found almost completely in his *Chronicle.* On February 4, 1238, at Parma, he was admitted into the FRANCISCAN ORDER by

Saxon and Salian Emperors (919–1125)

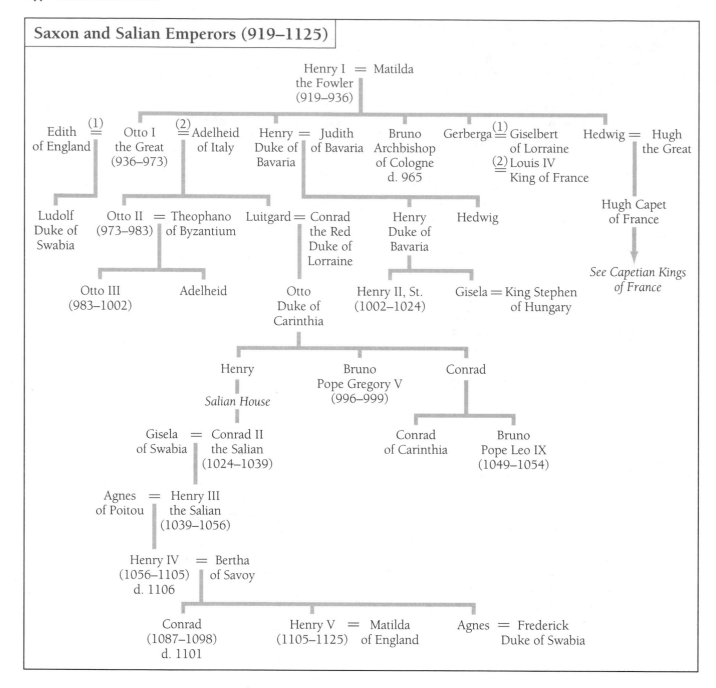

the minister general, Friar Elias of Cortona (d. 1253), much against the advice of his father. He studied and led the itinerant life of a Franciscan friar, perhaps spying on what he saw in his travels for the PAPACY. From 1239 to 1241, he studied Scripture, THEOLOGY, and singing at Lucca. It was there that he met the emperor FREDERICK II. In 1241 he was at SIENA, where he encountered the ideas of JOACHIM OF FIORE. In November of 1247, he was in Parma while the town was besieged by Frederick II. He was sent by the city to the pope at LYON to beg for help.

Thereafter he continued his travels from town to town and carefully wrote about what and whom he saw in his *Chronicle*. At Tarascon he met the Franciscan min-

ister general John of Parma (d. 1288) and received authorization to preach in public but was ordered to live at GENOA. After he arrived there early in December 1248, he was ordained a priest but left almost immediately for FRANCE in February 1249. He traveled to AVIGNON and Lyon, where he again joined John of Parma and returned to ITALY through SAVOY, GENOA, Parma, and FERRARA, where he settled for seven years between 1249 and 1256 and began to write full time. In 1260, when the prophecies of Joachim of Fiore were not fulfilled, he abandoned his Joachite convictions and resumed his travels across northern and central Italy from 1261 to 1287, and finally settled at Reggio Emilia.

Salimbene's *Chronicle* is known from a single incomplete but autographed manuscript. An original work of history and autobiography, it is loaded with sharp and insightful anecdotes along with legal, literary, and historical knowledge. A unique work, it is an important source for historians of the tumultuous 13th century. He died sometime after 1288.

Further reading: Salimbene, da Parma, *The Chronicle of Salimbene de Adam,* trans. Joseph L. Baird, Guiseppe Baglivi, and John Robert Kane (Binghamton: Medieval & Renaissance Texts & Studies, 1986); Robert Brentano, *Two Churches: England and Italy in the Thirteenth Century* (1968; reprint, Berkeley: University of California Press, 1988); Rosalind B. Brooke, *Early Franciscan Government: Elias to Bonaventure* (Cambridge: Cambridge University Press, 1959); John Moorman, *A History of the Franciscan Order from Its Origins to the Year 1517* (Oxford: Clarendon Press, 1968).

Salisbury, cathedral of

The CATHEDRAL of Salisbury in Wiltshire, ENGLAND, was in its organizational practices and liturgy was one of the most influential of English cathedrals in the Middle Ages. The diocese of Salisbury was established as an episcopal see in 1075. The first cathedral of Salisbury was at Old Sarum, north of the present city, and within the walls of a Norman CASTLE. That church was dedicated in 1092 by Bishop and Saint Osmund (1078–99), the nephew of WILLIAM I.

By the end of the 12th century, the location of Old Sarum was be considered inappropriate for a cathedral. In 1218 its chapter decided to move to the planned town of New Salisbury. In 1220 Bishop Richard Poor (d. 1237) laid the foundation stone of the new cathedral which was consecrated in 1258; with roof completed in 1266. The cloisters, chapter house, and spire, the highest in England, were added over the course of the 13th century. This cathedral was remarkable for its architectural unity, a version of the GOTHIC style known as Early English or decorative style.

The statutes and administrative practices of the cathedral chapter and the conduct of services were recorded in the late 12th and early 13th centuries. They formed a guide to what became known as the *Use of Sarum.* It exercised enormous influence on constitutional and liturgical practice in English cathedrals in the later Middle Ages. By the mid-15th century it was used throughout England, WALES, and IRELAND. The cathedral community became famous for its learning and liturgy. Its surviving manuscript books from the late 11th and early 12th centuries have lent support to the assertion of the chronicler WILLIAM of Malmesbury that the Salisbury chapter was the most learned community of canons in England. In the 13th century Salisbury reached the height of its fame as a center of learning.

Further reading: G. L. Cochrane, *Salisbury Cathedral: The West Front with a Description of the Statues* (Salisbury: Friends of Salisbury Cathedral, 1971); Thomas Cocke and Peter Kidson, *Salisbury Cathedral: Perspectives on the Architectural History* (London: H.M.S.O., 1993); Laurence Keen and Thomas Cocke, eds., *Medieval Art and Architecture at Salisbury Cathedral* (London: British Archaeological Association, 1996); R. O. C. Spring, *The Stained Glass of Salisbury Cathedral,* 2d ed. (Salisbury: Friends of Salisbury Cathedral, 1979); Teresa Webber, *Scribes and Scholars at Salisbury Cathedral, c. 1075–c. 1125* (Oxford: Clarendon Press, 1992).

salt and salt trade

Salt is generally considered essential to the well-being of human beings and animals. It gives savor to foods and plays an important physiological role in digestion, cellular health, and the transmission of nerve impulses. It has been used for centuries to desiccate and preserve fish, meat, and vegetable by preventing the growth of bacteria.

In medieval Europe the main sources of salt were along the seashore and from mining inland. In the early Middle Ages, sea salt was gathered from salt marshes. Away from the coasts, rock salt was mined from deposits underground. A new technique was added in the 12th century in which water was poured to dissolve rock salt, thereby producing a brine that was then carried by channels to a saltworks, where it was boiled in pans to remove the remaining water to produce a granulated salt. Transport costs were always high since salt is heavy and bulky. The salt trade was considered essential to the public good and from the 13th century was organized by states and cities as monopolies to facilitate taxation and guarantee supplies.

See also FOOD, DRINK, AND NUTRITION; RAVENNA; SARDINIA; TRANSYLVANIA; VENICE.

Further reading: Samuel Adrian M. Adshead, *Salt and Civilization* (New York: St. Martin's Press, 1992); Mark Kurlansky, *Salt: A World History* (New York: Walker, 2002); Robert P. Multhauf, *Neptune's Gift: A History of Common Salt* (Baltimore: Johns Hopkins University Press, 1978).

Salutati, Coluccio (1331–1406) *Florentine humanist scholar, bureaucrat, chancellor*

Born at Stignano in Valdinievole in 1331, Coluccio, studied the notarial art at BOLOGNA under the patronage of the powerful Pepoli family. From 1350 he was a professional NOTARY in many Italian cities while following his literary studies. He maintained a close correspondence with BOCCACCIO and especially with PETRARCH. He worked for the town bureaucracies of Todi, LUCCA, and the PAPACY. In 1374 he moved to FLORENCE, hired first as notary of the *Tratte* or the electoral system and eventually chancellor of the COMMUNE in 1375. In this office, which he held until his death, he was renowned for his powerful diplomatic correspondence. He found ways to apply an ideology of civic HUMANISM to engage in an impassioned and intense defense of republican institutions and Florentine freedom. The immediate historical and most productive setting for this were the difficult years of the War of the Eight Saints (1375–78) against both the PAPACY and the expansionist policies of the VISCONTI of MILAN.

Coluccio's humanist ideal assigned to people, intellectuals in particular, the duty to defend the dignity and necessity of political intervention by scholars and citizens in the affairs of this world. One should read the classics to learn how to accomplish this most effectively. One should not withdraw into an intellectual exile. Classical culture thus influenced if not permeated the writings from his Florentine chancery further enriched the style of Florence's embassies, adding a solemnity and competence enhancing the civil and political prestige of the city. He encouraged the study of Greek and Hellenic culture in the educational system and welcomed the Byzantine humanist Manuel CHRYSOLORAS to the city in 1397.

In his philological and rhetorical studies Salutati transcribed and studied Cicero's letters and was the first to attribute to Julius Caesar the *Gallic Wars*. Coluccio wrote treatises on many of the themes important to humanist culture, from the defense of poetry and classical studies to the philosophical contrasts between an active life and a contemplative or monastic life, educational reform, and a comparison between fate and free will. Like PETRARCH, he demonstrated how the classical pagan myths and allegories could be useful and instructive to Christians. He collected a great library and made it available to young scholars. He died on May 4, 1406.

See also BRACCIOLINI, POGGIO; BRUNI, LEONARDO; TRAVERSARI, AMBROGIO.

Further reading: Ephraim Emerton, *Humanism and Tyranny: Studies in the Italian Trecento* (Cambridge, Mass.: Harvard University Press, 1925); Stephanie H. Jed, *Chaste Thinking: The Rape of Lucretia and the Birth of Humanism* (Bloomington: Indiana University Press, 1989); Berthold L. Ullman, *The Humanism of Coluccio Salutati* (Padova: Antenore, 1963); Ronald G. Witt, *Hercules at the Crossroads: The Life, Works, and Thought of Coluccio Salutati* (Durham, N.C.: Duke University Press, 1983).

salvation (soteriology) *See* REDEMPTION.

Samanids They were a dynasty of emirs who were autonomous from, but loyal to, the ABBASID caliphs in BAGHDAD. They began their dynasty in Transoxiana from 875 but soon took over the region around Khurasan in eastern IRAN from 900. They were the descendants of a local landowner from the Balkh region in northern Afghanistan, Saman-Khuda (819–864), who was a recent convert to Islam. Basing their power on an aristocratic class, they organized a complex state system. They benefited from the slave trade and the general economic prosperity of Transoxiana, which they protected from the predations of TURKS from Central Asia. Their capital BUKHARA became a great intellectual center of Persian literature. The Samanids were supported by Turkish mercenary units. However, after a series of palace revolutions, they would be deposed in the late 10th century by two dynasties of Turkish origin. The GHAZNAWIDS took over around Khurasan in eastern Iran and the Qarakhanids seized power in Transoxiana. The last fugitive Samanid pretender to the throne was killed in 1005.

See also BUYIDS; SAFFARIDS; SAMARKAND.

Further reading: Iraj Bashiri, ed. and trans., *The Samanids and the Revival of the Civilization of Iranian Peoples: Collected Research Materials* (Dushanbe: Irfon, 1998); Clifford Edward Bosworth and Yolande Crowe, "Samanids," *Encyclopedia of Islam* 8.1,025–1,031; Clifford Edward Bosworth, *The Islamic Dynasties* (Edinburgh: Edinburgh University Press, 1967), 101–102; Richard Frye, *The Golden Age of Persia: The Arabs in the East* (New York: Barnes & Noble, 1975).

Samarkand (Marakanda, Mawaraal-Nahr) Medieval Samarkand was a city in central Asia or Uzbekistan on the Zeravshan River about 120 miles from BUKHARA. Called Afrasiyab, it was the main town of Sogdiana, and under Turkish rule from the fifth century. It retained its Sogdian language and culture until the 10th century, and Buddhism, Manichaeism, and Christianity all coexisted there. The Arab conquest of 712 and 713 did not eliminate the Christian community. It became something of a NESTORIAN metropolis between 712 and 728 and propagated that version of Christianity in central Asia. In the eighth through 10th centuries, Samarkand developed into an important commercial and industrial center famous for its steel, PAPER, and rug industries. Under the rule of the SAMANIDS in the ninth and 10th centuries, the city became a brilliant cultural and artistic center. In 1220 it was destroyed by JENGHIZ Khan, but during the 13th century the inhabitants who survived rebuilt it. An important Christian community still existed into the late 13th century. A Latin bishopric was created at Samarkand for a DOMINICAN friar in 1329.

Christianity was later persecuted when TAMERLANE and the TIMURIDS made Samarkand their capital from 1369 and promoted the building of still extant and impressive MOSQUES such as the Bibi Khanum Mosque. They also left impressive tombs, a MADRASA, and an observatory from the 15th century.

See also KHWARIZMSHAHS; MONGOLS AND THE MONGOL EMPIRE.

Further reading: Wilfrid Blunt, *The Golden Road to Samarkand* (New York: Viking Press, 1973); René Grousset, *The Empire of the Steppe: A History of Central Asia*, trans. Naomi Walford (New Brunswick, N.J.: Rutgers University Press, 1970); Vadim Evgenevich Gippenreiter,

Fabled Cities of Central Asia: Samarkand, Bukhara, Khiva (New York: Abbeville Press, 1989); Luc Kwanten, *Imperial Nomads: A History of Central Asia, 500–1500* (Philadelphia: University of Pennsylvania Press, 1979); J. Lawton and F. Venturi, *Samarkand and Bukhara* (London: Tauris Parke Books, 1991); H. H. Schaeder, C. E. Bosworth, and Yolande Crowe, "Samarkand," *Encyclopedia of Islam* 8:1,031–1,039.

Samuel, czar of Bulgaria (Samuil of Bulgaria) (ca. 980–1014) *king of the Bulgarians*

The son of a provincial governor, Shishman, in MACEDONIA Samuel restored the Bulgarian empire, which had been destroyed by the Byzantine emperor John Tzimiskes (r. 969–976). Samuel established his capital at Preslav and then OCHRIDA. After successful military campaigns and overrunning Macedonia and SERBIA, his rule extended over most of the Balkans and Thessaly in GREECE. From 1005 Samuel was attacked by Emperor BASIL II, who systematically campaigned and defeated the Bulgarians twice and in 1014 destroying most of the Bulgar army. Tradition has it that Basil blinded 15,000 prisoners and sent them, led by a few men who were left with one eye, back to Samuel. He supposedly died of an apoplectic fit or stroke when he saw such treatment. This ended any semblance of Bulgarian independence from the BYZANTINE EMPIRE.

Further reading: John V. A. Fine, *The Early Medieval Balkans: A Critical Survey from the Sixth to the Late Twelfth Century* (Ann Arbor: University of Michigan Press, 1991); Steven Runciman, *A History of the First Bulgarian Empire* (London: G. Bell and Sons, 1930).

Santiago de Compostela

Santiago de Compostela is a city in northwestern SPAIN in the province of GALICIA. Local traditions from the 10th and 11th centuries claimed that Compostela was the burial site of Saint James the Great (d. 44), the apostle and "brother of Christ." The body of James was supposedly spirited away from JERUSALEM after his martyrdom by his followers. It was taken west and eventually buried in Compostela (the original place-name) at the western end of the Roman Empire. He was to become the patron saint of the RECONQUEST. From the end of the 10th century his grave was promoted as a shrine and attracted great numbers of pilgrims from all over Western Europe. Santiago de Compostela became a major pilgrimage site, behind only Jerusalem and ROME.

In the 11th and 12th centuries, hospices and Cluniac abbeys were built along the roads to Santiago de Compostela. The city revived in prosperity. The popularity of this cult and pilgrimage in the 11th and 12th centuries was helpful in recruiting pious knights from FRANCE for the wars against the Muslims in Spain. The see was elevated to that of an archbishop and a great new cathedral was begun in 1128 and consecrated in 1211. The name of the city was officially changed to Santiago de Compostela. A military order, the Knights of Santiago, was founded there in 1170 to protect pilgrims.

See also ASTURIAS-LEÓN, KINGDOM OF; CALATRAVA, ORDER OF; PILGRIMAGES AND PILGRIMAGE SITES; ROMANESQUE ART AND ARCHITECTURE.

Further reading: Maryjane Dunn and Linda Kay Davidson, *The Pilgrimage to Santiago de Compostela: A Comprehensive, Annotated Bibliography* (New York: Garland, 1994); Paula Gerson, ed., *The Pilgrim's Guide to Santiago de Compostela: The Pilgrim's Guide: A Critical Edition*, 2 vols. (London: Harvey Miller Publishers, 1998); William Melczer, *The Pilgrim's Guide to Santiago de Compostela* (New York: Italica Press, 1993); Edwin B. Mullins, *The Pilgrimage to Santiago* (London: Secker and Warburg, 1974); Marilyn Jane Stokstad, *Santiago de Compostela in the Age of the Great Pilgrimages* (Norman: University of Oklahoma Press, 1978).

Saracens

Sarakenoi in Greek, Saraceni in Latin was the term commonly used in the Christian West for Arabs and Muslims. The term Sarakenoi initially appeared in classical authors as a name for a nomadic Arab tribe living between the Sinai Peninsula and the Dead Sea. This suggested another Greek word, *skénitai,* or "those who live under tents." Some ecclesiastical authors in the early Middle Ages, such as ISIDORE OF SEVILLE, gave this word another origin, linking it with Sarah, the wife of Abraham. According to the odd, but clearly hostile version of Isidore, some Muslims were trying to claim their origins from the legitimate son of Abraham by Sarah, Isaac, instead of the illegitimate son, Ishmael, by Abraham's servant girl, Hagar. Both the biblical and Quranic traditions said that Sarah was the mother of Isaac, the ancestor of the Jewish tribes, and Abraham's servant-girl Hagar was the mother of Ishmael, who was considered by Muslims to be the ancestor of the Arab tribes.

From the eighth century, Latin authors such as BEDE began to call the new invaders who raided into Gaul, ITALY, and PROVENCE Saracens. Other such names were used, such as Moors, Agarenes, Ishmaelites, pagans, infidels, and Mahometans. The slanderous word Saracen stereotypically meant an idolatrous pagan warrior, a treacherous and debauched destroyer and pillager, or even a servant of the devil. This representation was based on a misunderstanding of Islam and hostility to a perceived and real threat. It had little if any relation to Muslims or Islamic civilization. By the time of the CRUSADES, chronicles and *chansons de geste* used this term. The word continued to be used throughout the Middle Ages and far longer in polemics and in propaganda promoting crusading or colonization efforts. Other Christians who had more direct experience with Islam sometimes did have a more accurate appreciation of Muslims, but continued to use the term.

See also ISLAM; LULL, RAMÓN, AND LULLISM; RECONQUEST.

Further reading: Clifford Edward Bosworth, "Saracens," *Encyclopedia of Islam*, 9.27–28; Norman Daniel, *Islam and the West: The Making of an Image* (Edinburgh: Edinburgh University Press, 1960); Richard Fletcher, *The Cross and the Crescent: Christianity and Islam from Muhammad to the Reformation* (New York: Viking, 2004); Richard Southern, *Western Views of Islam in the Middle Ages* (Cambridge, Mass.: Harvard University Press, 1962); John V. Tolan, *Saracens: Islam in the Medieval European Imagination* (New York: Columbia University Press, 2002).

Sardinia (Sardegna) Sardinia is the largest island in the Mediterranean and is about 145 miles west of Italy. Western Sardinia is made of plains and hills and is richer, more populated, and more Romanized than the other regions. Eastern and central Sardinia are mountainous, wooded, and isolated with a smaller population who struggled to survive on sparser resources. It was conquered by ROME in 238 B.C.E. Held by the VANDALS from the mid-fifth to the mid-sixth century, Sardinia underwent only a partial Christianization.

Retaken by the Byzantines under JUSTINIAN in 533, Sardinia remained under Greek control until the 10th century. Greek culture and religion had significant influence on language and religious practice. By the 10th century the island was essentially independent of CONSTANTINOPLE and had to face almost constant attacks from Muslim raiders, some of whom settled on the island. The PAPACY claimed Sardinia as part of the Patrimony of Saint Peter and in 1015 encouraged the Genoese and Pisans to try to expel the Muslims; they succeeded, but papal control never really took effect and the island became disputed between GENOA and PISA. The papacy did reform and reshape the church on Sardinia into a more Western form, partially by sponsoring numerous settlements of Benedictine monks. The influence of Pisans continued to grow, and during the late 12th century, they took control, but a smaller colony from Genoa also established itself on the island.

Sardinia then became closely tied to the mainland and attained considerable prosperity through its production of cheese, grain, SALT, wool, metals, and hides. The largest town, Cagliari, became an important trading center in the western Mediterranean. The emperor FREDERICK II made Sardinia into a kingdom for his son, Enzo (1220–72), in 1239. In 1284 Genoa wrested control of it from the Pisans. In 1325 the Aragonese, with papal sponsorship, began to take over, and with the completion of their conquest in 1348, Sardinia remained under Aragonese, Catalan, and Spanish control until 1713. There were periodic successful rebellions, especially under Queen Eleanora of Arborea (d. 1421), but at her death, ALFONSO V regained control of the island.

Further reading: Marco Tangheroni, "Sardinia and Corsica from the Mid-Twelfth to the Early Fourteenth Century," in *The New Cambridge Medieval History*. Vol. 5, *c. 1198–c. 1300*, ed. David Abulafia (Cambridge: Cambridge University Press, 1999), 447–457; Robert Rowland, *The Periphery in the Center: Sardinia in the Ancient and Medieval Worlds* (Oxford: Archaeopress, 2001).

Sassanians (Sasanids) The Sassanians were a Persian dynasty founded about 224 by Ardashir I (r. 224–40), replacing the Parthian dynasty. From Fars in IRAN they might have been distant relatives of the former Persian Achaemenid dynasty. They replaced Parthian rule in Iran and made their capital in Ctesiphon in IRAQ. Their government consisted of a centralized bureaucracy and legal system. It used Pahlavi as the official language and sponsored ZOROASTRIANISM as the state religion. Zoroastrianism especially regarded the king or *shahanshah,* as chosen by GOD. He possessed a divine right to rule as protector and as an impartial judge of his subjects. The Sassanians fought frequent and devastating wars with the Roman Empire but were conquered by Arabic Islamic armies after the major Battles of Qadisiyya in 636 and Nihavand in 642. Yazdegird III (r. 632–651), was the dynasty's last ruler.

See also BYZANTINE EMPIRE AND BYZANTIUM; HERAKLEIOS I, BYZANTINE EMPIRE; ISLAM; LAKHMIDS.

Further reading: Nina G. Garsoïan, *Armenia between Byzantium and the Sasanians* (London: Variorum Reprints, 1985); Roman Ghirshman, *Iran: Parthians and Sassanians,* trans. Stuart Gilbert and James Emmons (London: Thames and Hudson, 1962); M. Moray, "Sasanids," *Encyclopedia of Islam* 9.70–83; Ahmad Tafazzoli, *Sasanian Society* (New York: Bibliotheca Persica Press, 2000).

Sassetta (Stefano di Giovanni di Consolo) (ca. 1390/ 1400–1450) *Sienese painter*
Stefano de Giovanni di Consolo, called il Sassetta, was born in SIENA between 1390 and 1400. He introduced a new and original figurative language to painting, paralleling contemporary Florentine PAINTING. Among his first works was the polyptych for the chapel of the wool GUILD of Siena (1423–26) now dismembered and scattered in various museums. In the figures of the saints and prophets or in the episodes of the predella, he was influenced by SIMONE MARTINI, the LORENZETTI, Masolino (ca. 1383/4–1447?), and MASACCIO. He created a highly original synthesis of elegant late Gothic linearism and the spatial depth of RENAISSANCE perspective. Sassetta painted ALTARPIECES between 1430 and 1432 for San Domenico in Cortona and an important polyptych for the church of San Francesco at Borgo Sansepolcro between 1437 and 1444. His very personal style was derived from various past experiences, and he used light and elegant images to produce a medieval courtly world, even while portraying religious scenes. His colors were delicate, and

his landscapes and spaces have been called ethereal. His last work was a FRESCO of the *Coronation of the Virgin,* once at the Porta Romana in Siena in 1450. He had numerous Sienese followers. He died in 1450.

See also ANGELICO, FRA; GENTILE DA FABRIANO; GOTHIC.

Further reading: Bruce Cole, *Sienese Painting in the Age of the Renaissance* Bloomington: Indiana University Press, 1985); John Wyndham Pope-Hennessy, *Sassetta* (London: Chatto & Windus, 1939).

Satan   *See* DEVIL.

Sava Nemanja of Serbia, Saint (Rastko Nemanyic, Saba) (1175–1235) *patron of the arts, theologian, founder of the Serbian Church, statesman*

Sava of SERBIA, or Rastko, was born about 1170/75, the third son of Stefan Nemanja (r. ca. 1167/68–96), grand Zupan or king of Serbia, and his wife, Anne. He became a monk on MOUNT ATHOS in 1192. Sava and his father, who had joined him in the monastic life, later founded the Serbian monastery of Chilandar in about 1196. He established the cult of Saint Symeon near Chilandar and then at Studenitsa, where the RELICS of this first Serbian saint were transferred in 1206 or 1207. At Studenitsa or Studentica between 1207 and 1217, Sava sponsored FRESCOES and the building of two monasteries in 1208–09. Highly educated and a connoisseur of the arts, he influenced numerous artistic projects at Studenitsa and elsewhere, reproducing the styles of the artists of CONSTANTINOPLE, thus linking Serbian religious art and culture to the great artistic centers of Byzantium.

In 1219, having the confidence of the patriarch and emperor of NICAEA because of his consistent Orthodoxy, Sava was consecrated an archbishop. The Serbian Church soon became independent under his leadership. In 1220 Sava organized Serbian bishoprics, consecrated bishops, and drew up dioceses. He founded monasteries in Serbia, on Mount Athos, and at JERUSALEM, overseeing the drawing of their foundation charters endowments. As the leader of the Serbian Church, he was carried out important diplomatic ecclesiastical missions to CONSTANTINOPLE, Nicaea, PALESTINE, Sinai, ALEXANDRIA, EGYPT, and ANTIOCH. Sava died at Turnovo in 1235. In 1236/7 his relics were transferred to Mileseva. In 1594/5 the OTTOMAN TURKS exhumed and publicly burned them at Belgrade in an attempt to suppress his nationalistic cult.

Further reading: Nicholas Velimirovič, *The Life of St. Sava* (Libertyville, Ill.: Serbian Eastern Orthodox Diocese for United States of America and Canada, 1951); Alain Ducellier, "Albania, Serbia and Bulgaria," in *The New Cambridge Medieval History.* Vol. 5, *c. 1198–c. 1300,* ed. David Abulafia (Cambridge: Cambridge University Press, 1999), 779–795; Mateja Matejic, *Biography of Saint Sava* (Columbus: Kosovo, 1976).

Savonarola, Girolamo (Socrates of Ferrara) (1452–1498) *Italian Dominican friar, reformer*

He was born at FERRARA in northern ITALY on September 21, 1452. He received a good education through the efforts of his grandfather, a Paduan physician at the court of the ESTE. Perceiving that he had a vocation to the priesthood, in 1475 he entered the DOMINICAN ORDER at BOLOGNA. In 1479 he was sent back to Ferrara as a novice master and in 1482 he moved to Florence and the Convent of Saint Mark. There he taught biblical exegesis and began to preach ineffectively at first. At San Gimignano, in 1485, he felt himself to be inspired with a prophetic mission for the reform of the church through preaching. After trips to Bologna and other towns, he returned to Florence in 1490. There he began preaching on the theme of living a true Christian life and predicting that a catastrophe that would soon bring about a new life for the church.

REFORMING IDEAS

On April 6, 1491, he publicly denounced the tyrannical government of the first citizen of Florence, Lorenzo de' Medici, the Magnificent (1449–92). After being elected as prior of Saint Mark's, he continued to preach along the same lines. After the death of Lorenzo on May 8, 1492, he predicted the imminent arrival of a divine punishment for the city. Savonarola in the meantime published a series of treatises on his own spiritual life as guides for others. Assuming that the reform of the whole church must begin with the one at Florence, he obtained an order on August 13, 1493 from Pope ALEXANDER VI removing Saint Mark's Convent from the Dominican province of LOMBARDY. This autonomy allowed him to work more ardently for beginning reform from Saint Mark's.

In August 1494, King Charles VIII (r. 1483–98) of France invaded Italy. On September 21 Savonarola preached in the cathedral to a terrified congregation that a real retribution for the many sins of the city was on its way. Piero de' Medici (1471–1503), Lorenzo's son and successor, fled the city. Savonarola met the king of France and persuaded him to go around the city on his way to NAPLES to claim his Angevin inheritance of that kingdom of Naples. Given more prestige by this, Savonarola preached and sought to persuade Florence to effect internal peace and a moral reform that would make it a model for institutional and personal reform. As part of this, he preached against gambling, carnival festivities, and worldly adornment and display. Great bonfires of the vanities soon followed. Such preaching and officially mandated austerity, however, was only temporarily popular.

FLORENTINE AND PAPAL POLITICS

The flight of the Medici at the same time led to the establishment of a new republic of Florence in late December 1494. Nonetheless internal discord remained strong in the city and led to the formation of two parties, the

"Weepers" for Savonarola and the "Enraged," supporters of the Medici. Soon afterward Savonarola opposed Florence's participation in a league established among cities against Charles VIII's expedition. In the meantime his enemies gained the support of the pope, Alexander VI, who in September and October 1495 accused Savonarola of heresy, false prophecy, and disobedience. On October 16 the pope forbade him even to preach. On February 7, 1496, invited by a somewhat sympathetic Florentine regime, he began to preach again. On August 15, he publicly refused the pope's odd offer of a cardinalate, saying he desired only reform and martyrdom.

LOSS OF SUPPORT IN FLORENCE AND DEATH

After anti-Savonarola changes in the membership of the councils governing Florence left the friar deprived of his protective support, Alexander VI approved the excommunication of Savonarola on May 12, 1497. Over the next few months he wrote new tracts on prophecy as still having a proper and useful status within the life of the church, while proclaiming the legitimacy of his own actions and continuing to attack the pope. In February 1498 he started to preach again, and on April 8, the regime in control of Florence decided to arrest him. He was tortured in prison with two of his Dominican followers. Between May 19 and May 22 civil and ecclesiastical trials were held that condemned all three to death as heretics and schismatics. Savonarola and his two companions were hanged and burned on May 23, 1498, on the piazza in front of the town hall of Florence.

Further reading: Lorenzo Polizzotto, *The Elect Nation: The Savonarolan Movement in Florence, 1494–1545* (Oxford: Clarendon Press, 1994); Roberto Ridolfi, *The Life of Girolamo Savonarola,* trans. Cecil Grayson (London: Routledge and Paul, 1959); Ronald M. Steinberg, *Fra Girolamo Savonarola, Florentine Art, and Renaissance Historiography* (Athens: Ohio University Press, 1977); Pasquale Villari, *Life and Times of Girolamo Savonarola,* trans. by Linda Villari, 2d ed. (London: T. F. Unwin, 1889); Donald Weinstein, *Savonarola and Florence: Prophecy and Patriotism in the Renaissance* (Princeton, N.J.: Princeton University Press, 1970).

Savoy, county and duchy of (Piedmont-Savoy, Savoia, Savoie) Now an Alpine French province on the Italian border, Savoy from the 11th century onward was tied to the history of the house of Savoy. They were a family who borrowed their name from the province. Throughout the early Middle Ages, Savoy had no autonomous political existence. In 443 it was occupied by the BURGUNDIANS, and in 532 it became part of the Merovingian and later Carolingian Kingdom and Empire. From 888 Savoy was integrated into the short-lived kingdom of BURGUNDY. It rejoined the HOLY ROMAN EMPIRE in 1032, when the first documented count

appeared, Humbert I "Whitehands" (r. ca. 1003–1046/7). Because one of his sons was the bishop of Aosta, then the archbishop of LYON, and another was the bishop of Sion, Humbert benefited from the territorial rights and incomes that accrued. Later another of his sons, Odo I (ca. 1051–57), acquired by a marriage several possessions in Piedmont, extending their property into present-day ITALY. The dynasty flourished in its remarkably strategic position on major passes over the Alps.

WARS AND CONSOLIDATION

From the 11th century, the counts of Savoy worked to overcome this difficult mountainous terrain and to unite these dispersed possessions. The Savoyards fought long and frequent wars until the mid-14th century with their neighbors, the rulers of Geneva and the Viennois. The Savoyard state took a decisive turn in the 13th century when Count Thomas I (r. 1189–1233) took over Valais and the *pays de Vaud,* part of the Piedmontese, and finally in 1223 acquired the town of Chambéry, their new capital. The family married into the royal family in ENGLAND through Eleanor of Provence (1223–91), the wife of HENRY III. Count Peter II (r. 1263–68) introduced the efficient methods of English administration into his judicial and legal systems. He ordered the building of numerous CASTLES to maintain his states. At the same time, the princes of Savoy acquired an important position in the church, accumulating numerous incomes and prestigious bishoprics. Amadeus V (r. 1285–1322) became count in 1285 and, by his marriage, united Bresse to Savoy. Although his sons were provided with their own parts of the state at his death, these soon returned to the control of the main line of the family. The power of the county of Savoy was reinforced still further in the 14th century as they acquired more land and gained access to the sea at Nice. Counts such as Amadeus VI, the "Green Count" (r. 1343–83), acquired international importance as military leaders and arbitrators of disputes. Amadeus VIII (r. 1416–40) was even elected pope (Felix V [r. 1439–49]), in an effort to end the Great Schism.

DECLINE AND DIVISION

Their successors were not as successful at maintaining control. Internal conflict weakened the duchy. The king of France, LOUIS XI, profiting from this internal discord, acquired great influence in Savoy. The confederate Swiss cantons also seized the opportunity to expand their territories. The decline of Savoy continued until its division in 1536 between France and SWITZERLAND.

See also BASEL, COUNCIL OF; EUGENIUS IV, POPE.

Further reading: Eugene L. Cox, *The Green Count of Savoy, Amadeus VI and Transalpine Savoy in the Fourteenth Century* (Princeton, N.J.: Princeton University Press, 1967); Eugene L. Cox, *The Eagles of Savoy: The House of Savoy in Thirteenth-Century Europe* (Princeton, N.J.:

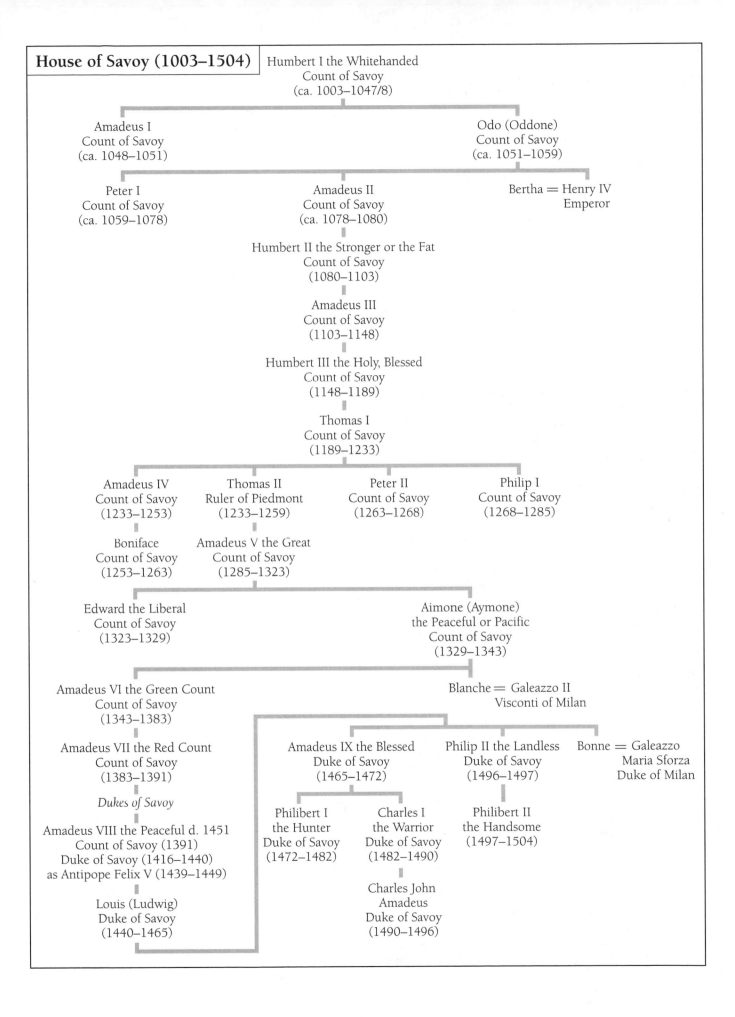

House of Savoy (1003–1504)

Humbert I the Whitehanded
Count of Savoy
(ca. 1003–1047/8)

Amadeus I
Count of Savoy
(ca. 1048–1051)

Odo (Oddone)
Count of Savoy
(ca. 1051–1059)

Peter I
Count of Savoy
(ca. 1059–1078)

Amadeus II
Count of Savoy
(ca. 1078–1080)

Bertha = Henry IV
Emperor

Humbert II the Stronger or the Fat
Count of Savoy
(1080–1103)

Amadeus III
Count of Savoy
(1103–1148)

Humbert III the Holy, Blessed
Count of Savoy
(1148–1189)

Thomas I
Count of Savoy
(1189–1233)

Amadeus IV
Count of Savoy
(1233–1253)

Thomas II
Ruler of Piedmont
(1233–1259)

Peter II
Count of Savoy
(1263–1268)

Philip I
Count of Savoy
(1268–1285)

Boniface
Count of Savoy
(1253–1263)

Amadeus V the Great
Count of Savoy
(1285–1323)

Edward the Liberal
Count of Savoy
(1323–1329)

Aimone (Aymone)
the Peaceful or Pacific
Count of Savoy
(1329–1343)

Amadeus VI the Green Count
Count of Savoy
(1343–1383)

Blanche = Galeazzo II
Visconti of Milan

Amadeus VII the Red Count
Count of Savoy
(1383–1391)

Amadeus IX the Blessed
Duke of Savoy
(1465–1472)

Philip II the Landless
Duke of Savoy
(1496–1497)

Bonne = Galeazzo
Maria Sforza
Duke of Milan

Dukes of Savoy

Amadeus VIII the Peaceful d. 1451
Count of Savoy (1391)
Duke of Savoy (1416–1440)
as Antipope Felix V (1439–1449)

Philibert I
the Hunter
Duke of Savoy
(1472–1482)

Charles I
the Warrior
Duke of Savoy
(1482–1490)

Philibert II
the Handsome
(1497–1504)

Louis (Ludwig)
Duke of Savoy
(1440–1465)

Charles John
Amadeus
Duke of Savoy
(1490–1496)

Princeton University Press, 1974); Eugene L. Cox, "The Kingdom of Burgundy, the Lands of the House of Savoy and Adjacent Territories," in *The New Cambridge Medieval History*. Vol. 5, *c. 1198–c. 1300*, ed. David Abulafia (Cambridge: Cambridge University Press, 1999), 358–374; Charles W. Previté-Orton, *The Early History of the House of Savoy (1000–1233)* (Cambridge: Cambridge University Press, 1912).

Saxo Grammaticus (ca. 1150–1220) *Danish cleric, writer*

Saxo Grammaticus, an assumed name, was born probably at Zealand in DENMARK about 1150. A Danish cleric, perhaps a scribe and monk, he wrote at the order of his archbishop, with the help of Latin models and inspired by sources such as ADAM of Bremen, a history. His *Deeds of the Danes* in 16 books related a mythical history and then a factual history of Denmark. His ornate style and skill as a writer earned him his nickname *Grammaticus* or "fine stylist." With a rare talent as a storyteller and historian, Saxo described a number of traditions that compare with those of the Icelander SNORRI STURLUSON in his prose *Edda*. They included sagas, lays, and tales of Hamlet and WILLIAM TELL. He died in 1220.

See also CANUTE II THE GREAT; WALDEMAR I THE GREAT; WALDEMAR II THE CONQUEROR.

Further reading: Saxo Grammaticus, *The History of the Danes*, trans. Peter Fisher and ed. Hilda Ellis Davidson (Cambridge: D. S. Brewer, 1979–1980); Eric Christiansen, *The Northern Crusades,* 2d ed. (London: Penguin, 1997); Karsten Friis-Jensen, ed., *Saxo Grammaticus: A Medieval Author between Norse and Latin Culture* (Copenhagen: Museum Tusculanum Press, 1981).

Saxons and Saxony (Sachsen)   The Saxons were a German people who appeared first in the first century C.E. in the region north of the mouth of the Elbe, neighboring the Jutes and Angles. Around 200, some of them left their original home for the northwestern coasts of FRANCE and later for ENGLAND. Fighting frequently with the Thuringians and the FRANKS, the remaining population gradually occupied the territory extending from the Ems to the Elbe and Saale Rivers, from the Harz Mountains north to the sea.

The Saxons seem to have comprised four kinds of people: dominant nobles; free men, essentially small farmers; freed men from conquered ethnic groups; and slaves. They settled into four districts: Westphalia, Angaria, Eastphalia, and Nordalbingia. Lacking a king, they held annual general assemblies of tribal groups.

In the eighth century and early in the reign of CHARLEMAGNE, the Franks carried out a military conquest and forced conversion to Christianity. Begun in 772, this took almost 30 years of frequent war and was marked by violent outbreaks of rebellions in 777–785

by the famous WIDUKIND and a more general one in 794–799. By the ninth century, Saxony had become a still somewhat marginal part of the Frankish Empire. Christianization had taken hold and a rich group of monasteries was founded, including the famous abbey of Corvey in 822. Its aristocratic class became linked to the Frankish nobility. By the end of the ninth century, the Liudolfid family from Eastphalia had begun to dominate the country.

SAXON DYNASTY AND THE LATER MIDDLE AGES

In 919 the duke of Saxony, Henry I or Henry the Fowler (d. 936), became king of GERMANY. His son, OTTO I, was a great warrior, restoring and assuming the imperial title in 962. In 50 years Saxony had risen high in the Christian world. But the duties and success of the Ottonians distracted them from Saxony, and hence its northern section was entrusted as the duchy of Saxony to the Billung family. By the 11th century, Saxony was just another state in the mosaic of German principalities and HOLY ROMAN EMPIRE. Its duke became one of the electors. It was divided into small FIEFS in 1180 and its ducal title was given to Bernhard of Anhalt (d. 1212), the son of Albert the Bear (d. 1170). The name became attached to various other areas during the later Middle Ages. In 1423 Frederick I the Warlike (1369–1428) was granted Saxony by the emperor SIGISMUND of Luxembourg. It was partitioned again in 1485. By then its principal towns had become Dresden and Leipzig.

See also HROSWITHAS OF GANDERSHEIM; HUS, JOHN; OTTO III.

Further reading: Gerd Althoff "Saxony and the Elbe Slavs in the Tenth Century," in *The New Cambridge Medieval History*. Vol. 3, *c. 900–c. 1024,* ed. Timothy Reuter (Cambridge: Cambridge University Press, 1999), 267–292; Karl J. Leyser, *Rule and Conflict in an Early Medieval Society: Ottonian Saxony* (London: Edward Arnold, 1979).

Scanderberg   *See* SKANDERBEG.

Scandinavia   *See* DENMARK; ICELAND AND ICELANDIC LITERATURE; NORWAY; SWEDEN; VIKINGS.

Schism, Great (1054)   This willful and conscious separation of the Western and Eastern Churches the mid-11th century was based on a mutual consensus, the outcome of a dispute between the pope and the Western clergy with the ecclesiastical establishment and patriarch of CONSTANTINOPLE. The ordination of priests, the installation of bishops, and the validity of the sacraments were not initially questioned. The main controversy centered on recognition of the pope's ultimate authority.

Negotiations begun by legates from the West failed, and the sides excommunicated each other in 1054, though the validity of either EXCOMMUNICATION was not clear, even at the time. The schism lasted throughout the Middle Ages and RENAISSANCE, only temporarily suspended to support mutual efforts against the OTTOMAN TURKS in the 15th century. The actual anathemas or condemnations were not lifted until 1965.

See also CHURCH, EASTERN ORTHODOX; FERRARA-FLORENCE, COUNCIL OF; HUMBERT OF SILVA CANDIDA, CARDINAL; PHOTIOS I THE GREAT.

Further reading: Francis Dvornik, *Photian and Byzantine Ecclesiastical Studies* (London: Variorum Reprints, 1974); J. M. Hussey, *The Orthodox Church in the Byzantine Empire* (Oxford: Clarendon Press, 1986); Steven Runciman, *The Eastern Schism: A Study of the Papacy and the Eastern Churches during the XIth and the XIIth Centuries* (Oxford: Clarendon Press, 1955).

Schism, Great (1378–1417) This division occurred within the Western Church over the question of who was the rightful pope and lasted from 1378 to 1417. It began with the death of Pope Gregory XI (r. 1371–78) in 1378 and the dubious election of the arrogant and strange Italian pope, URBAN VI (r. 1378–89). Some of the cardinals withdrew from ROME and elected the tough warrior and cardinal Robert of Geneva, as Clement VII (r. 1378–94), and he promptly returned to AVIGNON in southern FRANCE. The popes had only returned from there, an era called the "Babylonian Captivity," in Avignon, to Rome a few years before. The governments of Europe took sides backing a particular papal claimant and the division intensified and persisted as successors were elected to the various two lines of popes.

A general council met at PISA in 1409 to try to end the schism. It elected yet another pope (Alexander V, 1409–10), but the two other reigning popes refused to resign. CHRISTENDOM now had three popes and three sets of allegiances and appointments to offices. Alexander's successor, the onetime mercenary soldier now pope John XXIII (r. 1411–15), convened the Council of CONSTANCE (1414–18). It ended the schism by electing Martin V (r. 1417–31), accepting the resignation of one pope, and deposing John XXIII and Benedict XIII (r. 1394–1417). This scandal weakened papal authority for decades and sparked the growth of the conciliar movement, while limiting discussion of obviously needed reform of the clergy.

See also AILLY, PIERRE D'; GERSON, JOHN; HUS, JOHN; WYCLIFFE, JOHN.

Further reading: Margaret Harvey, *Solutions to the Schism: A Study of Some English Attitudes 1378 to 1409* (St. Ottilien: EOS Verlag, 1983); Howard Kaminsky, "The Great Schism," in *The New Cambridge Medieval History*. Vol. 6, *c. 1300–c. 1415*, ed. Michael Jones (Cambridge:

Cambridge University Press, 2000), 674–696; J. Holland Smith, *The Great Schism, 1378* (London: Hamilton, 1970); Robert W. Swanson, *Universities, Academics and the Great Schism* (Cambridge: Cambridge University Press, 1979); Walter Ullman, *The Origins of the Great Schism: A Study in Fourteenth-Century Ecclesiastical History* (London: Burns, Oates & Washbourne, 1948).

Schism, Photian   *See* PHOTIOS I, THE GREAT.

Scholasticism and Scholastic method   Medieval Scholasticism was a form of rationalist thought, a methodology, and an intellectual approach that was not limited to one historical period. The word Scholasticism was coined as a pejorative way to describe the discourse followed in the university system. The Scholastic way of thinking is not only found in the Middle Ages; nor is it limited to theological speculation. In the Middle Ages it was applied in every discipline and many methodologies. It developed in the 12th century under the impetus of a variety of rationalism and developed further with the introduction of the works of ARISTOTLE in the 13th century.

At its core were readings and analysis of texts. For example a reading of the BIBLE was succeeded by a structured exposition of theological themes in the manner of a structured academic analytical manual. The most famous of these standard texts was the *Sentences* of PETER Lombard. Scholasticism and academic teaching started with texts, but proceeded to questions about internal consistency in texts and thought and comparisons involving conflicting ideas. In the 14th century, the same old texts generated wider and more practical questions. The literary genres of Scholastic studies were the lecture, commentaries, questions, and structured compilations collected into *summae*.

The *quaestio* or question was specific and one of the primary methods of Scholasticism. For a single question, arguments for as well as against were advanced and answered. Such confrontations, especially over the consistency of thought behind opinions elucidated the richness and pertinence of various points of view. This in turn improved with the study of logic and led to even more detailed analysis of texts. Thousands of commentaries on a few standard texts were produced.

Scholasticism can also be seen as an attempt to reconcile reason, revelation, FAITH, and authority. It could also be viewed as a search for a SCIENCE and unity of thought and even a way to integrate some of the ideas of the Muslims and the ancient pagan Greeks into Christian thought.

See also ABÉLARD, PETER; ALBERTUS MAGNUS; ARISTOTLE AND ARISTOTELIANISM; AQUINAS, THOMAS, SAINT; DUNS SCOTUS; JOHN, BLESSED; PARIS AND THE UNIVERSITY OF PARIS; PHILOSOPHY AND THEOLOGY; *QUODLIBET;* SENTENCES; UNIVERSITIES AND SCHOOLS; WILLIAM OF OCKHAM.

Further reading: John W. Baldwin, *The Scholastic Culture of the Middle Ages, 1000–1300* (Lexington, Mass.: Heath, 1971); Étienne Gilson, *History of Christian Philosophy in the Middle Ages* (New York: Random House, 1955); George Makdisi, *The Rise of Humanism in Classical Islam and the Christian West: With Special Reference to Scholasticism* (Edinburgh: Edinburgh University Press, 1990); James H. Overfield, *Humanism and Scholasticism in Late Medieval Germany* (Princeton, N.J.: Princeton University Press, 1984); Josef Pieper, *Scholasticism: Personalities and Problems of Medieval Philosophy,* trans. Richard and Clara Winston (New York: Pantheon Books, 1960); Erika Rummel, *The Humanist-Scholastic Debate in the Renaissance & Reformation* (Cambridge, Mass.: Harvard University Press, 1995); Jacques Verger, "The Universities and Scholasticism," in *The New Cambridge Medieval History.* Vol. 5, *c. 119–c. 1300,* ed. David Abulafia (Cambridge: Cambridge University Press, 1999), 256–276.

schools *See* UNIVERSITIES AND SCHOOLS.

science Science in the Middle Ages in Europe and ISLAM involved the search for truth in many branches of knowledge. The roots of modern science were planted in the Middle Ages. THEOLOGY, regarded as the queen of sciences, had a considerable impact on the free exercise of the intellect. Moreover, irrational superstition, religious assumptions, and strong beliefs in MAGIC inhibited scientific investigation into natural phenomena. Real advances nonetheless occurred in mathematics, OPTICS, ALCHEMY or chemistry, natural history, and MEDICINE. The scientific culture and knowledge of the classical world, especially Aristotle's natural philosophy, were also transmitted in the Middle Ages, often through Arabic texts and scholars. The development of UNIVERSITIES furthered scientific study and speculation and provided opportunities for advanced research.

Christianity accommodated secular learning, but within limits. Attitudes toward science could vary enormously in both Islam and Christianity in that both religions were obliged to reconcile it with revelation from divinely inspired texts. Various individuals and ideas were condemned at specific moments. However, both religions often cautiously accepted and justified the pursuit of scientific knowledge as possibly useful for religious understanding. Both perceived that positive technological advances could also be derived from scientific enterprise.

See also BACON, ROGER; AL-BIRUNI, ABU RAYHAN MUHAMMAD; FIBONACCI, LEONARDO; IBN AL-HAYTHAM, ABU ALI AL-HASAN IBN AL-HASAN, AL-BASRA; IBN SINA, ABU ALI AL-HUSAYN; ORESME, NICHOLAS; SEVEN LIBERAL ARTS; SYLVESTER II, POPE.

Further reading: A. C. Crombie, *Medieval and Early Modern Science,* 2d ed., 2 vols. (Cambridge, Mass.: Harvard University Press, 1961); Edward Grant, ed., *A Source Book in Medieval Science* (Cambridge, Mass.: Harvard University Press, 1974); Claudia Kren, *Medieval Science and Technology: A Selected, Annotated Bibliography* (New York: Garland, 1985); Y. Tzvi Langermann, "Science, Jewish," *DMA,* 11.89–94; A. I. Sabra, "Science, Islamic," *DMA* 11.81–89; Howard R. Turner, *Science in Medieval Islam: An Illustrated Introduction* (Austin: University of Texas Press, 1997); Ziauddin Sardar, *Explorations in Islamic Science* (London: Mansell, 1989).

Scone, Stone of The Stone of Scone, or Stone of Destiny, was taken to Scone by Kenneth MACALPIN, who took possession of the throne of the PICTS in 843. He placed a royal stone in a church built on the hill of Scone. For the next 500 years, each new king of SCOTLAND traveled there "to be raised on the stone." The stone was an important part of medieval Scottish coronation rites until 1296, when it was either hidden to prevent it from falling into the hands of EDWARD I, or, according to legend, taken to WESTMINSTER ABBEY in LONDON to be controlled and used by the kings of ENGLAND. What was once in London was only recently returned to Scotland.

See also ROBERT I THE BRUCE.

Further reading: A. D. M. Barrell, *Medieval Scotland* (Cambridge: Cambridge University Press, 2000); G. W. S. Barrow, *Kingship and Unity: Scotland, 1000–1306* (London: Edward Arnold, 1981).

Scotland Scotland became a kingdom in the northern part of the British Isles in the ninth century. In the fifth century, it had been inhabited by the PICTS, Scots, Britons, and Angles. These peoples eventually formed the Scottish kingdom. The Picts occupied the region north of the Forth River. From northern IRELAND, the Scots in the late fifth century took over the Argyll region. The somewhat Romanized Britons lost southern Scotland to the Angles in the early seventh century; but they did retain a kingdom of Strathclyde in the southwest. The Angles from across the North Sea began migrating to Scotland from the fifth century and created in the seventh century the kingdom of Northumbria between the Humber River and the Forth.

Irish monks settled in Scotland and introduced Christianity. The most famous of them was Saint COLUMBA, who traveled to Iona in 563 and converted the northern Scots. In the eighth century these four ethnic elements began to coalesce into a political organization but still retained in a tribal basis. Clans with chieftains remained the organization of the mountainous Highlands. The VIKING raids in the ninth century, mainly from NORWAY, forced these tribal units to defend themselves better. In 844 Kenneth MACALPIN, the king of the Scots, assumed leadership over the Picts, uniting the two groups into Scotland. In the 10th century, this kingdom

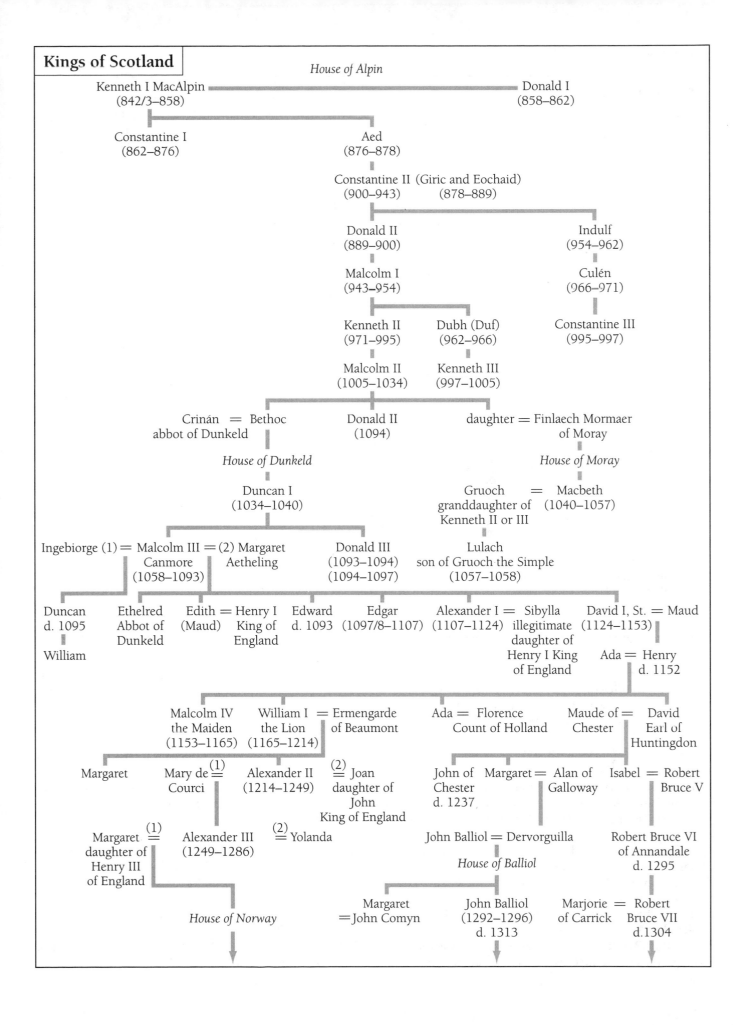

Kings of Scotland

House of Alpin

Kenneth I MacAlpin ——————————————————————— Donald I
(842/3–858)   (858–862)

Constantine I   Aed
(862–876)   (876–878)

Constantine II (Giric and Eochaid)
(900–943)   (878–889)

Donald II   Indulf
(889–900)   (954–962)

Malcolm I   Culén
(943–954)   (966–971)

Kenneth II   Dubh (Duf)   Constantine III
(971–995)   (962–966)   (995–997)

Malcolm II   Kenneth III
(1005–1034)   (997–1005)

Crinán = Bethoc   Donald II   daughter = Finlaech Mormaer
abbot of Dunkeld   (1094)   of Moray

House of Dunkeld   *House of Moray*

Duncan I   Gruoch   =   Macbeth
(1034–1040)   granddaughter of   (1040–1057)
                        Kenneth II or III

Ingebiorge (1) = Malcolm III = (2) Margaret   Donald III   Lulach
               Canmore   Aetheling   (1093–1094)   son of Gruoch the Simple
               (1058–1093)   (1094–1097)   (1057–1058)

Duncan   Ethelred   Edith = Henry I   Edward   Edgar   Alexander I = Sibylla   David I, St. = Maud
d. 1095   Abbot of   (Maud) King of   d. 1093 (1097/8–1107) (1107–1124) illegitimate (1124–1153)
          Dunkeld   England   daughter of
William   Henry I King   Ada = Henry
                                                                            of England   d. 1152

         Malcolm IV   William I = Ermengarde   Ada = Florence   Maude of = David
         the Maiden   the Lion   of Beaumont   Count of Holland   Chester   Earl of
         (1153–1165)   (1165–1214)   Huntingdon

Margaret   Mary de =(1) Alexander II =(2) Joan   John of   Margaret = Alan of   Isabel = Robert
            Courci   (1214–1249)   daughter of Chester   Galloway   Bruce V
                                        John   d. 1237
                                        King of England

Margaret =(1) Alexander III =(2) Yolanda   John Balliol = Dervorguilla   Robert Bruce VI
daughter of   (1249–1286)   of Annandale
Henry III   *House of Balliol*   d. 1295
of England

                                             Margaret   John Balliol   Marjorie = Robert
         House of Norway   =John Comyn   (1292–1296)   of Carrick Bruce VII
                                                           d. 1313   d.1304

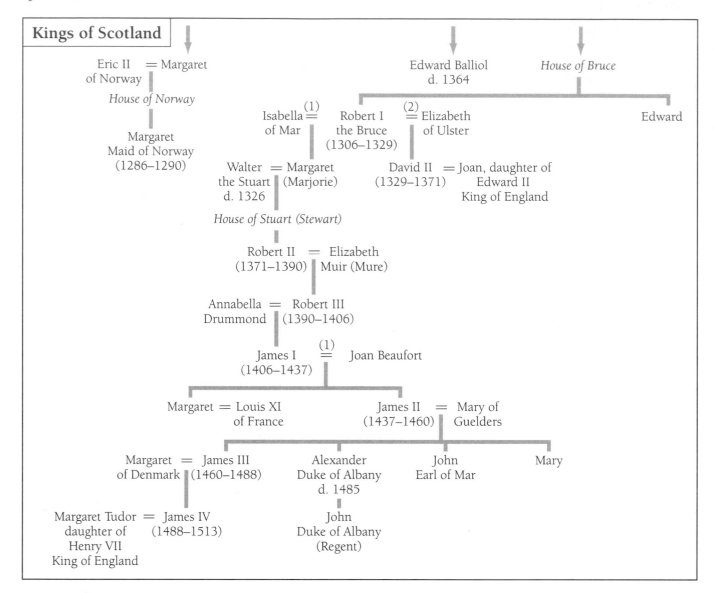

expanded southward into the Lothian region and EDINBURGH. Around 940 the old kingdom of Strathclyde was ceded to the future king, Malcolm I (r. 943–54).

ANGLO-SAXON INCURSION

In the second half of the 11th century Anglo-Saxon culture entered to the kingdom, brought by the Saxon wife of King Malcolm III (ca. 1031–93), Saint Margaret (ca. 1045–93). During the reign of DAVID I in the mid-12th century, Anglo-Norman families to Scotland were attracted by offers of estates and positions in government. The almost continuous generally unsuccessful wars with ENGLAND in the 12th century expedited an Anglicization process, such as when in 1167 the English king, HENRY II, forced his prisoner, WILLIAM I THE LION, the king of Scotland, to become his vassal.

In the 13th century the Hebrides were ceded by the Norwegians and became part of the kingdom under the terms of the Treaty of Perth in 1266. King Alexander III (r. 1249–86) died in 1286 with no direct heir leading to a dynastic crisis. The ambitious EDWARD I started to try to absorb it into his realm. JOHN BALLIOL gained the support of Edward who arbitrated among the claimants. Balliol agreed to pay homage to Edward for the kingdom of Scotland, but instead the Scottish nobility compelled Balliol to declare war on England in 1295. Edward took control of much of Scotland and installed an English puppet government. Scottish resistance, however, continued under the leadership of William WALLACE. Edward eventually captured Wallace and had him executed in 1305, but only after suffering several defeats and the devastation of northern England.

SCOTTISH INDEPENDENCE

ROBERT I THE BRUCE led the resistance to English control after Wallace's execution. Allying himself with FRANCE, he inflicted a defeat on the incompetent EDWARD II at the Battle of BANNOCKBURN in 1314. This victory secured Scottish independence for some time. In the 15th century the Orkney and Shetland Islands were ceded to Scotland and Saint Andrews University was created in 1401. A second Scottish university was founded by Pope Nicholas V (r. 1447–55) at Glasgow in 1451, and a third at Aberdeen in 1495.

A new dynasty, the Stuarts, or Stewarts, was faced in the 15th century with the almost insurmountable problem of dealing with the local power of the feudal nobility and clan chieftains. The country's PARLIAMENT was modeled on that of England but was of small consequence most of the time. Frequent conflicts between the kings and the nobility weakened the realm in the second half of the 15th century. There was growing penetration by English cultural influences, but local culture survived and developed. The church generally maintained its independence from England, but rivalries between local episcopal sees did not contribute to national unity.

See also DAVID I; DAVID II THE BRUCE; MACBETH; PICTS.

Further reading: A. D. M. Barrell, *Medieval Scotland* (Cambridge: Cambridge University Press, 2000); Ian Borthwick Cowan, *The Medieval Church in Scotland,* ed. James Kirk (Edinburgh: Scottish Academic Press, 1995); R. James Goldstein, *The Matter of Scotland: Historical Narrative in Medieval Scotland* (Lincoln: University of Nebraska Press, 1993); Jenny Wormald, "Scotland: 1406–1513," in *The New Cambridge Medieval History.* Vol. 7, *c. 1415–c. 1500,* ed. Christopher Allmand (Cambridge: Cambridge University Press, 1998), 514–531.

scriptorium In the early Middle Ages, monasteries maintained rooms, scriptoria, dedicated to writing and listening to texts. The church at this time and later had a great need for books, including biblical and patristic texts, liturgical books, and pedagogical texts for the CLERGY and the LAITY. Books had to be copied and libraries were needed so classical and patristic Christian literature were preserved and circulated at CATHEDRALS or in monasteries. Two great religious establishments in Italy, VIVARIUM and the Benedictine monastery MONTE CASSINO, laid the foundations for the preservation and compilation of books. Following the Rule of Saint BENEDICT, Benedictine monks kept alive most of what we have of the literature of the classical world and late Christian antiquity by borrowing, sharing, and copying texts among themselves.

Certain *scriptoria* became famous for the skill and style of their scribes, such as those at Iona, Durrow, LINDISFARNE, Luxeuill, Bobbio, Corbie, Jarrow, and FULDA. These were workshops for copying texts and producing edifying ILLUMINATION. The CAROLINGIAN RENAISSANCE encouraged this even more, since aspects of its program were the standardization of texts, the reform of handwriting, and the encouragement of clerical and monastic learning. Cathedral schools, such as those at RHEIMS and CHARTRES in the 10th century joined in the copying, production, and dissemination of the texts. We knew little of the actual organization and working practices of these institutions. With the development of UNIVERSITIES, another system of text reproduction evolved in response to a greater demand. Some of these were clerical operations, but more often they were established by the laity and overseen by universities.

See also PALEOGRAPHY; PECIA; SALISBURY; SCRIPTS.

Further reading: Elizabeth P. McLachlan, *The Scriptorium of Bury St. Edmunds in the Twelfth Century* (New York: Garland, 1986); Aliza Cohen-Mushlin, *A Medieval Scriptorium: Sancta Maria Magdalena de Frankendal* (Wiesbaden: Otto Harrassowitz, 1990); Francis Newton, *The Scriptorium and Library at Monte Cassino, 1058–1105* (Cambridge: Cambridge University Press, 1999); Vera Trost, *Scriptorium: Book Production in the Middle Ages,* trans. Christopher Reinish and Theodore Kwasman (Heidelberg: Universität Heidelberg, 1986?); Teresa Webber, *Scribes and Scholars at Salisbury Cathedral, c. 1075– c. 1125* (Oxford: Clarendon Press, 1992).

scripts Medieval handwriting or script style was a direct heir of the style of Latin script used throughout the territory of the Roman Empire. By the end of the fifth century, Latin script had evolved into two families, a formal capital script that was clear, dignified, and deliberate, and a common or cursive script for much faster writing. From the third century, the capital script became uncial, an artificial and elegant display script used in luxury books and also for the initials, titles, and rubrics of medieval manuscripts. Common cursive script passed from a left-inclining oblique position to a vertical position with an abundance of ligatures. Varieties of this style were used by the VISIGOTHS and the ANGLO-SAXONS.

CAROLINGIAN SCRIPT

In the early Middle Ages, the great monasteries on the Continent founded by Irish missionary monks became flourishing centers of intellectual life and writing. Their script, had to be simpler, and more harmonious. This style resulted from the perfecting and harmonization of preexisting forms into a unified, clear, and readable alphabet that was soon favored and followed by CHARLEMAGNE and his court creating some partial graphic unity in the West once more. This Carolingian script had no joining strokes or other ligature save that of the letters *et, ct,* and *st.* It evolved slowly at first into round, detached forms and then, during the 11th century, into more oval forms written closer to each other. From the 12th century onward, it was embellished with fleeing strokes, serifs, or bends on the writing line. This era also saw the first appearance of the script called Gothic which led   once more to two distinct styles: a formal book script, and a more cursive hand used in CHARTERS and documents.

EVOLUTION OF GOTHIC SCRIPT

During the 12th century, because of the rise of schools and UNIVERSITIES, and the consequent increased demand for schoolbooks, the writing style for these books evolved toward the new Gothic script. It was not necessarily convenient for practical use but was more economical. Its graphic forms were simplified, rapidly drawn and huddled up. It used many abbreviations. It can be exemplified by the university or "Scholastic" scripts, including regional variations in BOLOGNA, PARIS, and OXFORD. These Gothic variations were more or less derived from notarial scripts and from actual and practical usage. From the 13th century, Latin script was written in three styles: book script, university script, and documentary script.

AWAY FROM GOTHIC SCRIPT

There was radical reaction against the Scholastic or "Gothic" hand by the early humanists. They promoted, initially for their private use, a clear chancery script. The humanists were the great discoverers of antiquities and "antique" manuscripts and promoted a style of writing done for clarity and legibility. It was derived from the script fostered by the Carolingian reform movement.

In the 14th century PETRARCH denounced Gothic script as artificial and too hard for easy reading. This criticism was seconded by Coluccio SALUTATI (1331–1406), the chancellor of the Florentine Republic, and Niccolò Niccoli (1364–1437). Another promoter was Poggio BRACCIOLINI (1380–1459) later chancellor of the Florentine Republic and one of the greatest discoverers of classical manuscripts. From about 1402 he had perfected a copy of Carolingian hand for his transcriptions of the manuscripts of Cicero's works. His writing was the foundational style for the humanist reform of writing. These forms of letters were soon noticed and used by the first printers and eventually became a standard type form, of which the modern roman type is a direct descendant.

See also PALEOGRAPHY: SCRIPTORIUM.

Further reading: Rutherford Aris, *Explicatio formarum litterarum—The Unfolding of Letterforms: From the First Century to the Fifteenth* (St. Paul: Calligraphy Connection, 1990); Michelle P. Brown, *A Guide to Western Historical Scripts from Antiquity to 1600* (Toronto: University of Toronto Press, 1990); Michelle P. Brown and Patricia Lovett, *The Historical Source Book for Scribes* (London: The British Library, 1999); Stan Knight, *Historical Scripts: A Handbook for Calligraphers* (London: A. & C. Black, 1984); John Lancaster, *Writing Medieval Scripts* (London: Dryad Press, 1988).

Scriptures   *See* BIBLE.

Scrovegni Family   *See* GIOTTO DI BONDONE.

Scutage (Latin, *scutum;* French, *écuage;* shield)   Scutage was a tax imposed on KNIGHTS instead of personal military service. In the Carolingian era, it was a fine paid by those who reneged on or could not fulfill their military duty. In the 12th century the tax was considered another source of fiscal revenue for the Crown. HENRY II of ENGLAND imposed scutage to pay his mercenary armies on the continent and to make the Crown less dependent on feudal service.

See also FEUDALISM AND THE FEUDAL SYSTEM; FIEF; KNIGHTS AND KNIGHTHOOD; TAXATION, TAXES, AND TRIBUTE.

Further reading: James F. Baldwin, *The Scutage and Knight Service in England* (Chicago: University of Chicago Press, 1897); Robert Bartlett, *England under the Norman and Angevin Kings, 1075–1225* (Oxford: Clarendon Press, 2000).

Scythia and Scythians   In ancient and medieval geography, Scythia was a vague region to the northeast of the known world, north of the BLACK SEA and stretching east into the steppe of Eurasia or Inner Asia, the homeland of nomadic horse people. Known to the classical Mediterranean world, the Scythians were a nomadic people who spoke an Iranian language. The last Scythian stronghold, in the CRIMEA, survived until about 275 C.E., when it was destroyed by the GOTHS.

In the literature of the Middle Ages, the name Scythians was applied to ethnically unrelated nomadic federations, such as the Hungarians and MONGOLS. The Scythians, though called "barbarians," were known to the medieval West as an ancient and prestigious people to whom some Europeans tried to establish genealogical links. The Byzantines used the name Scythians as a generic term for any barbarian peoples north of the empire, including Turks and the RUś. Scandinavian geographers claimed Scythia as the mythical homeland of the Scandinavians.

See also GEOGRAPHY AND CARTOGRAPHY.

Further reading: C. Scott Littleton, *From Scythia to Camelot: A Radical Reassessment of the Legends of King Arthur, the Knights of the Round Table, and the Holy Grail* (New York: Garland, 1994); William Montgomery McGovern, *The Early Empires of Central Asia: A Study of the Scythians and the Huns and the Part They Played in World History, with Special Reference to the Chinese Sources* (Chapel Hill, University of North Carolina Press, 1939); Tamara Talbot Rice, *The Scythians,* 2d ed. (London: Thames and Hudson, 1958); Renate Rolle, *The World of the Scythians,* trans. Gayna Walls (London: B. T. Batsford, 1989); Ellen D. Reeder, ed., *Scythian Gold: Treasures from Ancient Ukraine* (New York: Harry Abrams, 1999).

seals and sigillography The wax seal was commonly used from the ninth to the 15th century as a means of validating documents in northwestern Europe. Use of metal BULLS, bullae or seals, usually of lead but sometimes of GOLD, became confined to BYZANTIUM and the PAPACY as well as Italian MERCHANT COMMUNES for especially important and prestigious documents. Seals in wax were still emblems of the privileges of the ruler, as a sign of validation and a symbol of power, between the 10th and 12th centuries. Images in wax, which became individualized and recognizable, if not unique, validated a document as if it were signed by the participants. It was a testimony that they were there either actors in or witnesses to a document.

Some seals can tell us about the people to whom they belonged. They usually gave the name of the person, his or her dignity or status, as well as some justification for the authority to act. Seal images could reflect power and connection, even linking a person with an institution or suggesting some kind of divine approval. They were used privately to seal confidential correspondence and offer various kinds of guarantee, including the quality and quantity of merchandise or the authenticity of RELICS. Various types of material, including gold, silver, lead, wax, and clay, could be employed. Those in wax were fragile and those in metal always ran the risk of being melted down and used again in other ways.

See also ARCHIVES AND ARCHIVAL INSTITUTIONS; CHARTERS; HERALDRY AND HERALDS.

Further reading: Brigitte Bedos Rezak, "Seals and Sigillography, Western European," *DMA,* 11.123–131; Brigitte Bedos Rezak, *Form and Order in Medieval France: Studies in Social and Quantitative Sigillography* (Aldershot: Variorum, 1993); Daniel M. Friedenberg, *Medieval Jewish Seals from Europe* (Detroit: Wayne State University Press, 1987); P. D. A. Harvey and Andrew McGuinness, *A Guide to British Medieval Seals* (Toronto: University of Toronto Press, 1996); Ludvik Kalus, *Catalogue of Islamic Seals and Talismans* (Oxford: Clarendon Press, 1996); Ludvik Kalus, *Catalogue of Islamic Seals and Talismans* (Oxford: Clarendon Press, 1986); Nicolas Oikonomides, ed., *Studies in Byzantine Sigillography,* 2 vols. (Washington, D.C.: Dumbarton Oaks Research Library and Collection, 1987–1990).

sea routes *See* NAVIGATION.

sects *See* HERESY AND HERESIES; ISMAILIS; KHARIJITES; SHIA; SHITISM AND SHIITES.

Seljuk Turks of Rum (Saljuqs, Saldjukids) The Seljuks were TURKS of the Oghuz tribe who converted to ISLAM in the late 10th century. They then conquered IRAN from the GHAZNAWIDS in the first half of the 11th century.

In 1055 TUGHRUL BEG entered BAGHDAD, where he was well received by the ABBASID puppet caliph then freed from the BUYIDS. In 1058 he acquired the title of sultan. His nephew, ALP ARSLAN, extended Seljuk territory toward ARMENIA and Georgia. In 1071 he defeated the Byzantine emperor Romanos IV Diogenes (r. 1067–71) at the BATTLE OF MANZIKERT and opened the way to the Seljuks into ANATOLIA. This expansion was facilitated by Byzantine internal divisions and the discontent of Monophysite Christians within Anatolia. The Seljuks also undertook the conquest of SYRIA and PALESTINE between 1071 and 1086. The Seljuks now ruled autonomously, challenged in Anatolia only by another Turkish family, the Danishmenddids. In Syria, Palestine, IRAQ, and Iran, the Seljuks promptly contended among themselves for power. These divisions partially explain Christians in the First CRUSADE established themselves in the East from 1098.

Within their loosely connected states, the Seljuks showed themselves defenders of the Sunni version of Islam. At Baghdad they restored the prestige of the Sunni CALIPH, and in Syria and Palestine they took possession of a great number of territories that were under the control of the SHIITE FATIMIDS of EGYPT. To promote Sunni religious practices and ideas, they favored the construction of schools for teaching Sunni LAW and religious science. Such a religious policy, however, did not lead to a persecution of non-Muslim communities, the DHIMMI.

In institutional matters, the Seljuks maintain administrative traditions system already in and introduced only a few Turkish customs. The local power of certain leaders in the army was strengthened by the development of a system of rewards permitting him to collect the taxes of his district for his own coffers. None of this promoted much unity among the various Seljuk states. In the 12th century, Syria and Palestine broke free of the Seljuks; in Iran and Iraq, they were eliminated in the last years of the century by another Turkish dynasty, the KHWARIZMSHAHS. An Anatolian branch survived and continued to oppose the passage of the crusaders across their territory. After losing a Battle at Kosedagh on June 26, 1243, they accepted MONGOL domination, which deprived them of autonomy. Seljuks disappeared as a ruling dynasty in 1307.

See also ALEXIOS I KOMNENOS.

Further reading: John Andrew Boyle, ed., *The Cambridge History of Iran.* Vol. 5, *The Saljuk and Mongol Periods* (Cambridge: Cambridge University Press, 1968); Claude Cahen, *The Formation of Turkey: The Seljukid Sultanate of Rūm, Eleventh to Fourteenth Century,* trans. P. M. Holt (1988; reprint, New York: Longman, 2001); Mehmet Fuat Köprülü, *The Seljuks of Anatolia: Their History and Culture according to Local Muslim Sources,* trans. and ed. Gary Leiser (Salt Lake City: University of Utah Press, 1992); Tamara Talbot Rice, *The Seljuks in Asia Minor* (New York: Praeger, 1961); Alexes G. K. Savvides,

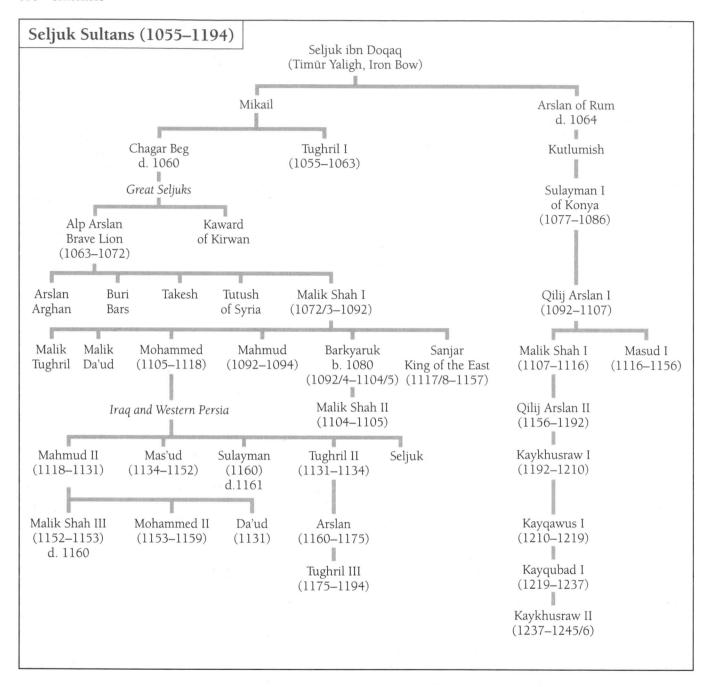

Seljuk Sultans (1055–1194)

Seljuk ibn Doqaq
(Timür Yaligh, Iron Bow)

Mikail — Arslan of Rum d. 1064

Chagar Beg d. 1060 — Tughril I (1055–1063)

Kutlumish

Great Seljuks

Sulayman I of Konya (1077–1086)

Alp Arslan Brave Lion (1063–1072) — Kaward of Kirwan

Qilij Arslan I (1092–1107)

Arslan Arghan — Buri Bars — Takesh — Tutush of Syria — Malik Shah I (1072/3–1092)

Malik Tughril — Malik Da'ud — Mohammed (1105–1118) — Mahmud (1092–1094) — Barkyaruk b. 1080 (1092/4–1104/5) — Sanjar King of the East (1117/8–1157)

Malik Shah I (1107–1116) — Masud I (1116–1156)

Iraq and Western Persia

Malik Shah II (1104–1105)

Qilij Arslan II (1156–1192)

Mahmud II (1118–1131) — Mas'ud (1134–1152) — Sulayman (1160) d.1161 — Tughril II (1131–1134) — Seljuk

Kaykhusraw I (1192–1210)

Malik Shah III (1152–1153) d. 1160 — Mohammed II (1153–1159) — Da'ud (1131) — Arslan (1160–1175)

Kayqawus I (1210–1219)

Tughril III (1175–1194)

Kayqubad I (1219–1237)

Kaykhusraw II (1237–1245/6)

Byzantium in the Near East: Its Relations with the Seljuk Sultanate of Rum in Asia Minor, the Armenians of Cilicia and the Mongols, A.D. *c. 1192–1237* (Thessaloniki: Kentpon Byzantinon Epeynon, 1981); Speros Vryonis, Jr., *The Decline of Medieval Hellenism in Asia Minor and the Process of Islamization from the Eleventh through the Fifteenth Century* (Berkeley: University of California Press, 1971).

sentences   The classical meaning of the Latin *sententia* derives from the verb *sentio,* "to feel about" or "to have a thought or judgment on." From about 1120, sentences were made up of collections of theological texts, citations of the FATHERS OF THE CHURCH, and explanations of other theologians. This term eventually especially referred to the *Liber sententiarum* of PETER LOMBARD.

In 1155–57, Peter Lombard collected together the materials taught in the schools and separated theological thought and problems into four books divided into distinctions. The idea of ST. AUGUSTINE that all knowledge concerned either things or their signs provided him with a guiding framework. His *Book of Sentences* was superior to any previous and was moderate in its principles and ideas. It became a standard textbook of theology. From this starting point each master now had to write a commentary displaying his personal way of reading the *Book of Sentences* then writing solutions to a common set of problems based on Lombard's work and unresolved doubts about answers presented by others.

See also PHILOSOPHY AND THEOLOGY; SCHOLASTICISM AND SCHOLASTIC METHOD.

Further reading: G. R. Evans, ed., *Mediaeval Commentaries on the Sentences of Peter Lombard: Current Research* (Leiden: Brill, 2002).

Sephardim They were Jewish communities in Muslim and Christian Spain who followed a particular religious culture within Judaism in terms of liturgy, legal traditions, and customs. The word was first widely used in the eighth century in AL-ANDALUS. The term was applied to communities outside Iberia, if they were linked somehow with the Sephardic practices or way of life. The Sephardi spread far outside Spain after the expulsions of 1492, especially into the Ottoman Empire and North Africa. They were known for their active participation in the culture in which they lived and for their cultivation of literature in Hebrew and the vernacular, philosophy, the natural sciences, the HALAKHAH, commentary and interpretation of the TALMUD, biblical exegesis, and Hebrew grammar. During the Middle Ages they were well known for their philosophical interest in the heritage of the ancient world.

See also ASHKENAZ AND ASHKENAZIM; JEWS AND JUDAISM; JUDAH BEN SAMUEL HALEVI; MAIMONIDES, MOSES; NACHMANIDES, MOSES.

Further reading: Yitzhak F. Baer, *A History of the Jews in Christian Spain,* 2 vols., trans. Louis Schoffman (Philadelphia: Jewish Publication Society of America, 1961–1966); Paloma Díaz Más, *Sephardim: The Jews from Spain,* trans. George K. Zucker (Chicago: University of Chicago Press, 1992); Cecil Roth, *The World of the Sephardim* (Tel Aviv: WIZO, 1954).

Sepulcher, Holy *See* HOLY SEPULCHER.

Serbia and Serbs Serb tribes migrated down from the Carpathian Mountains into the Balkans. They settled from the ninth century in Raška and BOSNIA. They had contact with Croatians in the northwest, the inhabitants of PANNONIA and eventually the Hungarians in the northeast, and the BULGARS and BYZANTINES in the south. They accepted Orthodox Christianity through the disciples of Saints CYRIL AND METHODIOS. From the ninth to the 11th century, CONSTANTINOPLE vainly sought to impose control over the Serbs, who gained real independence from the Byzantines during the 12th century. Stefan I the First Crowned (r. 1196–ca. 1228) declared himself king in 1217 and was recognized by the pope. His brother, SAVA, became the independent archbishop of Serbia in 1219. This Serbian kingdom attained its greatest power in the reigns of Stephen Milutin (r. 1282–1321) and STEPHEN DUŠAN (r. 1331–55). The OTTOMAN TURKS destroyed the Serb army at the BATTLE OF KOSOVO in 1389 and took over the country for 500 years.

See also BAYAZID I; BULGARIA AND BULGARS; HUNGARY; HUNYADI, JOHN CORVINUS MATTHIAS; MURAD I; MURAD II.

Further reading: Alain Ducellier, "Albania, Serbia and Bulgaria," in *The New Cambridge Medieval History,* Vol. 5, *c. 1198–c. 1300,* ed. David Abulafia (Cambridge: Cambridge University Press, 1999), 779–795; John V. A. Fine, *The Early Medieval Balkans: A Critical Survey from the Sixth to the Late Twelfth Century* (Ann Arbor: University of Michigan Press, 1991); John V. A. Fine, *The Late Medieval Balkans: A Critical Survey from the Late Twelfth Century to the Ottoman Conquest* (Ann Arbor: University of Michigan Press, 1994); Harold William V. Temperley, *History of Serbia* (1919; reprint, New York: H. Fertig, 1969); Georgios C. Soules, *The Serbs and Byzantium during the Reign of Tsar Stephen Dusan (1331–1355) and His Successors* (Athenai: Hetaireia ton Philon tou Laou, 1995).

serfs and serfdom The serfs were at the bottom rung of the agricultural laboring population or PEASANTRY, having little freedom from arbitrary demands, or at least heavy impositions of payments and work by their lords. Not all peasants were serfs. Some were their lords' men and women, practically their physical property. Not quite slaves, they had to be very subservient to the people who owned rights over them. They could not own land; all their property actually belonged to their lords. They could not move from place to place nor pass property to their descendants. This status was inheritable. They usually had to pay a fine to marry and often their lords' approval of a spouse was a further requirement. The church condoned their servitude but did not approve of overt cruelty.

The work involved in agrarian or farming/pastoral practices, the demographic conditions of rural populations, the availability of employment alternatives, and opportunities to run away all affected the real life of these oppressed peasants. They also suffered the stigma of negative stereotyping by their more fortunate contemporaries. By the end of the Middle Ages, genuine serfdom had mainly disappeared from Western Europe. That was not the case in Eastern Europe and in parts of the Islamic world until the 20th century. Even in Western Europe, there were attempts to reimpose arduous labor conditions during labor shortages. It is important to note also that serfdom was always limited to certain places and times.

See also AGRICULTURE; BAN; FEUDALISM AND THE FEUDAL SYSTEM; MANORS AND MANORIAL LORDSHIP; MORTMAIN; SOCIAL STATUS AND STRUCTURE; VILLEIN AND VILLEINAGE.

Further reading: Jerome Blum, *Lord and Peasant in Russia from the Ninth to the Nineteenth Century* (New York: Atheneum, 1961); Paul Freedman, *The Origins of*

Peasant Servitude in Medieval Catalonia (Cambridge: Cambridge University Press, 1991); Paul Freedman, *Images of the medieval Peasant* (Stanford, Calif.: Stanford University Press, 1999); Paul Hyams, *King, Lords, and Peasants in Medieval England: The Common Law of Villeinage in the Twelfth and Thirteenth Centuries* (Oxford: Clarendon Press, 1980); R. H. Hilton, *The English Peasantry in the Later Middle Ages* (Oxford: Clarendon Press, 1975); R. H. Hilton, *The Decline of Serfdom in Medieval England,* 2d ed. (London: Macmillan, 1983).

sermons and homilies   Technically a sermon is distinct from a homily. The homily was often on a biblical text, usually from the New Testament, perhaps a parable or miracle by Christ. The preached commentary that followed the text tried to resolve any difficulties in the message and to clarify its concrete moral and spiritual implications. In a sermon, the speaker did not comment on a scriptural text in detail. At the beginning he presented a single citation or quotation, generally biblical. Sermons were generally more diversified and often based in the Old Testament. Any real distinctions between a homily and a sermon were not so neat or clear. Homilies and sermons were preached on Sundays and feast days and were addressed to all of the faithful.

PREACHING sermons and homilies was the duty of bishops and became the duty of PRIESTS and friars by the 13th century. The MENDICANT ORDERS were also supposed to preach as one of their main duties on doctrines and ideas other than biblical material. Sermons were mainly preached in churches at certain services, but they could also be part of less formal occasions. They were supposed to reform the moral lives of their hearers, either lay or clerical.

See also ALAN OF LILLE; *ARS PRAEDICANDI*; JAMES OF VITRY.

Further reading: Nicole Bériou, ed., *Modern Questions about Medieval Sermons: Essays on Marriage, Death, History and Sanctity* (Spoleto: Centro italiano di studi sull'Alto medioevo, 1994); Jonathan Porter Berkey, *Popular Preaching and Religious Authority in the Medieval Islamic Near East* (Seattle: University of Washington Press, 2001); David L. D'Avray, *Medieval Marriage Sermons: Mass Communication in a Culture without Print* (Oxford: Oxford University Press, 2001); Daniel R. Lesnick, *Preaching in Medieval Florence: The Social World of Franciscan and Dominican Spirituality* (Athens: University of Georgia Press, 1989); Carolyn Muessig, ed., *Medieval Monastic Preaching* (Leiden: Brill, 1998).

Seuse, Heinrich   *See* SUSO, HENRY.

seven deadly or capital sins   The seven deadly sins for Christians (now and) in the Middle Ages (are) were envy, pride, anger, sloth (negligence or indifference), avarice, gluttony, and lust. This list existed since the time of Pope GREGORY I, from around 600. They were usually used in opposition to the VIRTUES, which were to be practiced to prevent descent into the sinful state arising from succumbing to these deficiencies of character. The seven deadly sins were often featured in all kinds of art, since artists enjoyed portraying them in varied guises, from amusing to terrifying. They were useful also to preachers as didactic and graphic images.

See also PENITENTIALS; PREACHING; SIN.

Further reading: Morton W. Bloomfield, *The Seven Deadly Sins: An Introduction to the History of a Religious Concept, with Special Reference to Medieval English Literature* (East Lansing: Michigan State College Press, 1952); Adolf Katzenellenbogen, *Allegories of the Virtues and Vices in Mediaeval Arts: From Early Christian Times to the Thirteenth Century,* trans. Alan J. P. Crick (New York: W. W. Norton, 1964).

seven liberal arts (*quadrivium, trivium*)   The teachers and educational theorists initially of antiquity and later of the Middle Ages understood the seven liberal arts to be the disciplines preparatory to the study of philosophy proper and the acquisition of wisdom. Philosophy was conceived as leading to wisdom. The liberal arts were to be pursued by free individuals, unlike the "mechanical" or manual arts, which were the province of slaves. The negative attitude toward the mechanical arts changed over the course of the Middle Ages, as culture and society began to value more highly the skilled crafts of artisans and the beneficial services of traders and merchants.

MARTIANUS Capella compiled one of the first lists of seven in his influential *Marriage of Mercury and Philology* in about 420. In that work he distinguished the arts of the *trivium,* or arts of the word, such as grammar, RHETORIC, LOGIC, or dialectic, from those of the *quadrivium,* or arts of the number, such as arithmetic, MUSIC, geometry, or astronomy. About the same time AUGUSTINE of Hippo in his *On Christian Doctrine* suggested what became an influential plan for a Christian education. After purging it of its dangerous pagan elements, classical literature could be safely be assimilated into Christian pedagogy and the disciplines useful for the fruitful study and explanation of Holy Scripture.

All of the seven liberal arts became the subjects of study in the faculty of arts within UNIVERSITIES, or what was essentially undergraduate higher education. Dialectic became especially important to Scholastic education after the 12th century. At the end of the Middle Ages, with the rise of humanism and a renewed interest in grammar, rhetoric, and the mathematical sciences, there was a renewed interest in the ideas and the teaching of the liberal arts.

See also PHILOSOPHY AND THEOLOGY; SCHOLASTICISM AND SBD SCHOLASTIC METHOD.

Further reading: David L. Wagner, ed. *The Seven Liberal Arts in the Middle Ages* (Bloomington: Indiana University Press, 1983).

seven sacraments For the Catholic Church in the Middle Ages, the seven sacraments were, as they are today, baptism; confession, or penance; the Eucharist, or communion; confirmation; matrimony, or MARRIAGE; ordination to the priesthood, and the blessing at DEATH, or Extreme Unction. In the Middle Ages it was believed and taught by the church that Christ instituted baptism, the Eucharist, penance, and ordination, and his words could be interpreted as justifying the others. The Orthodox Church also accepted seven sacraments from 1267. They were believed to be actions or ceremonies that conveyed GRACE and provided access for Christians to Christ as their savior and salvation. They acted as signs composed of words and material elements for the saving actions of Christ, the ultimate minister of the sacraments. Their precise definitions were worked out in the 12th century by GRATIAN, HUGH OF ST. VICTOR, and PETER LOMBARD.

See also AUGUSTINE OF HIPPO, SAINT; CLERGY AND CLERICAL ORDERS; MASS; REDEMPTION; SIN.

A baptismal font from about 1400 in the Cathedral of Orvieto in central Italy *(Courtesy Edward English)*

Further reading: J. M. Gallagher, *Significando causant: A Study of Sacramental Efficacy* (Fribourg: University Press, 1965); Jaroslav Pelikan, *The Christian Tradition: A History of the Development of Doctrine. 2, The Spirit of Eastern Christendom (600–1700)* (Chicago: University of Chicago Press, 1974); Elizabeth F. Rogers, *Peter Lombard and the Sacramental System* (1917; reprinted Merrick, N.Y.: Richwood, 1976); Edward Schillebeeckx, *Christ the Sacrament of the Encounter with God* (New York: Sheed & Ward, 1963); Thomas N. Tentler, *Sin and Confession on the Eve of the Reformation* (Princeton: Princeton University Press, 1977).

Seville, city and kingdom of (Ishbiliyya) Medieval Seville was a city in southern SPAIN on the Guadalquivir River, and the principal city and capital of Muslim AL-ANDALUS. The Roman and BYZANTINE city was occupied first by VANDALS and then the VISIGOTHS until the Arab conquest in 711. Seville was the capital of a branch of the Abbasid dynasty from 1023 to 1091. It became famous for its beautiful MOSQUES, walls, markets, prosperous population, and GARDENS. It was also tolerant of its minority Mozarab Christians and JEWS. It fell in the RECONQUEST to King Ferdinand III (r. 1217–52) of LEÓN and CASTILE in 1248. Most of the Muslim population was deported. King ALFONSO X, Ferdinand's eldest son, resided there and was a strong patron of cultural activity, building, translation projects, and learning. After the mid-14th century, the economy of the city benefited especially from its rich TRADE in olive oil. In the 15th century, it became an area of great activity for the INQUISITION, especially in its persecution of the Jews.

See also ALMOHADS; ALMORAVIDS; IBN RUSHD, ABU L-WALID MUHAMMAD; ISIDORE OF SEVILLE, SAINT; UMAYYADS OF CÓRDOBA.

Further reading: Richard A. Fletcher, *Moorish Spain* (Berkeley: University of California Press, 1993); Enrique Sordo, *Moorish Spain: Córdoba, Seville and Granada,* trans. Ian Michael (New York: Crown, 1963).

sexuality and sexual attitudes Sexuality is the set of meanings put on sexual activity by a culture. In Medieval Christianity sex was permitted primarily for purposes of procreation. Such activity used for pleasure was dubiously ethical although physicians recognized it as a healthy activity. Christians were allowed no carnal relations except within marriage. Married couples were to be abstinent during all periods when conception of a child was impossible or inopportune, such as during pregnancy, menstrual periods, the time of impurity after childbirth, and the years of nursing. Once a couple had produced successors, they were encouraged to be abstinent. Marriage was considered one of the SEVEN SACRAMENTS, but a state of CELIBACY was always considered a higher vocation. Sexuality within marriage was for those who were too weak to avoid it. It was a consequence of original sin placed on all human beings after the fall of Adam and Eve. This extreme doctrine lasted throughout the Middle Ages and Renaissance but was probably not well observed by the LAITY or the supposedly celibate CLERGY.

HOMOSEXUALITY and masturbation were prohibited as unnatural and not conducive to the conception of children. There was plenty of evidence that people had sex and many were not much troubled by feelings of guilt. There were numerous illegitimate births and many clerics maintained relationships with women and men. Periodic prosecutions were accompanied by unpleasant punishments during the later Middle Ages, as the state showed special concern about problems of succession caused by childbirth outside marriages.

Contraceptive practices were banned. Noble families were especially concerned that women of their kinship networks were kept chaste. PROSTITUTION was tolerated, and assaults by upper-class males on lower-class women were frequently overlooked. The Orthodox Church had essentially the same ideas about marriage and the exaltation of sexual renunciation but did permit priests to be married, though bishops were supposed to be celibate.

See also ASCETISM; CELIBACY; CONCUPISCENCE; CONTRACEPTION AND ABORTION; COURTLY LOVE; FORNICATION; GREGORIAN REFORM; VIRGINITY; VIRTUES AND VICES; WIDOWS AND WIDOWHOOD; WOMEN, STATUS OF.

Further reading: James A. Brundage, *Law, Sex, and Christian Society in Medieval Europe* (Chicago: University of Chicago Press, 1987); A. Lynn Martin, *Alcohol, Sex, and Gender in Late Medieval and Early Modern Europe* (New York: Palgrave, 2001); Pierre J. Payer, *The Bridling of Desire: Views of Sex in the Later Middle Ages* (Toronto: University of Toronto Press, 1993); Jeffrey Richards, *Sex, Dissidence, and Damnation: Minority Groups in the Middle Ages* (London: Routledge, 1990); Guido Ruggiero, *The Boundaries of Eros: Sex Crime and Sexuality in Renaissance Venice* (New York: Oxford University Press, 1985); Joyce E. Salisbury, ed., *Sex in the Middle Ages: A Book of Essays* (New York: Garland, 1991).

Sforza family The Sforza family were originally from ROMAGNA and TUSCANY. They gained the duchy of MILAN in 1450, when the mercenary captain Francesco Sforza (1400–60) entered Milan on February 25, 1450, ending a chaotic republican interlude after the death of Filippo Maria VISCONTI in 1447. They were to maintain control of duchy until the end of the 15th century. Francesco died in 1466 and was succeeded by his son, the vicious and despotic Galeazzo Maria (r. 1466–76), who tried to solidify his princely power by acting as a barely veiled absolute ruler. This led to a rebellion of part of the Milanese aristocracy on December 26, 1476, when Galeazzo Maria was assassinated and succeeded by Gian Galeazzo II Maria (r. 1476–94). At he was under the

tutelage first of his mother, Bona of Savoy then from 1480 his uncle, Lodovico, called il Moro (r. 1494–99, 1500). It supposedly was Lodovico's appeal to the king of France, Charles VIII (r. 1483–98), that led to a French invasion to secure control of NAPLES. This led to the end of Milanese and Italian independence from outside forces.

The policy of the Sforza toward the church followed that of the Visconti family, as both sought to control the religious institutions in and around Milan. Francesco obtained a privilege from the pope in 1450 to present candidates for the benefices until then under the control of the papacy. This privilege ended at his death, but the Sforza dynasty maintained important influence over all ecclesiastical appointments within their state. Members of the family also built several important HOSPITALS and funded other charitable institutions as concrete symbols of their prestige and power. They were also ardent supporters of monastic and mendicant foundations sympathetic to their rule. Their patronage of artists, such as Leonardo Da Vinci (1452–1519), and the impressive building projects were also intended to confirm the value and worthiness of their rule in the eyes of God and to their usually reluctant subjects. Lodovico was deposed, reinstated, and deposed again in 1499 and 1500. He was the last independent Sforza duke and died in a French prison in 1508.

Further reading: Cecilia M. Ady, *A History of Milan under the Sforza*, ed. Edward Armstrong (London: Methuen, 1907); Gregory Lubkin, *A Renaissance Court: Milan under Galeazzo Maria Sforza* (Berkeley: University of California Press, 1994); Evelyn S. Welch, *Art and Authority in Renaissance Milan* (New Haven, Conn.: Yale University Press, 1995).

Shana *See* HADITH; LAW, CANON AND ECCLESIASTICAL; QURAN; SUNNA.

sheep *See* AGRICULTURE; ANIMALS AND ANIMAL HUSBANDRY; FOOD, DRINK, AND NUTRITION.

Shia, Shiism, and Shiites (party, sect) From the Arabic, Shia means "partisans," of ALI IBN ABU TALIB and his descendants by his wife, Fatima (605–633) the daughter of MUHAMMAD, who considered the true IMAMS, guides, or leaders of ISLAM after the death of the prophet. The most distinctive heterodox trait of Shiism was its concept of the personal and sacred function of the imam. Ali was supposed to be the first CALIPH, since he was the rightful imam, appointed by Muhammad himself. The election of ABU BAKR by almost a general consensus at first caliph was perceived by Shiism as a usurpation of the rights of Ali, who had been designated by Muhammad as his successor. The Shiites saw this as treason against the will of the Messenger of GOD. Those who eventually were

Sunni believed that this authority rested more widely on all of the companions of the Prophet. Ali also refused to follow the precedents set by Abu Bakr and UMAR I, when he was offered the caliphate at Umar's death. The "martyrdom" of the next imam, Husayn, in 680 marked the beginning of an independent Shia course.

All this provided evidence for the importance Shia places on the office of imam, who embodies divine spiritual authority and the temporal power to rule: The imam held the *wa laya* or guardianship; that is that as the imam, in his universal dimension as a perfect man, he is a manifestation of God. Shiism was always a theory of imamate, from which other disciplines such as THEOLOGY, LAW, MYSTICISM, ethics, and PHILOSOPHY were formed and derived. Shiism constituted a party of opposition and religion, the most important "variant" of Islam, as opposed to the majority tendency considered to represent a Muslim "orthodoxy," commonly called SUNNA or SUNNISM.

Shiism has included several branches. There were four periods of imamism. The DEATH of each imam gave rise to one or more schisms, which, in nearly every case, had only an ephemeral existence. The main branches of the Shia have been the majority Twelvers (Ithan Asharis), the ISMAILI, the Nizaris, the Mutazila (Seceders), the Zaydis, and the Alawis or Nusayris. There also evolved further differences with the Sunni over rituals, MARRIAGE, and inheritance.

See also ABBASIDS; ASSASSINS; FATIMIDS; al-HUSAYN IBN ALI IBN ABI TALIB.

Further reading: Syed Husain M. Jafri, *The Origins and Early Development of Shia Islam* (Oxford: Oxford University Press, 2000); Moojan Momen, *An Introduction to Shii Islam: The History and Doctrines of Twelver Shiism* (London: G. Ronald, 1985).

ships and shipbuilding There were great advances in the shipbuilding arts in the Middle Ages. Transport by water, across the seas and along the rivers, then was the simplest, most efficient, and often the safest means of communication and transport. The classical Roman legacy was transmitted intact to the BYZANTINE EMPIRE. Their ships and weapons, such as GREEK FIRE, were important to the survival of CONSTANTINOPLE. The ARABS introduced their own traditions to Mediterranean waters from the Red Sea and Persian Gulf. They also took over the shipbuilding yards and expertise of ALEXANDRIA and Carthage. The great successes of the VIKINGS in the ninth and 10th centuries were founded on their abilities to sail on the open sea and to move up rivers for raiding or trade. At nearly the same time, the cog evolved for moving bulky material.

Galleys were common for WARFARE in the Mediterranean and ships propelled by sails became more sophisticated in the Middle Ages, especially in the Atlantic. Sailing ships with or without oars were more efficient in the rougher waters of the Atlantic. Rigging, masts, sail shapes, hull shapes, crew skills, and rudders all became more efficient as late medieval ships in the north reached 200 to 300 tons.

See also COMPASS; CRUSADES; GENOA; GOKSTAD SHIP; GREENLAND; HANSEATIC LEAGUE; HENRY "THE NAVIGATOR," PRINCE; NAVIGATION; PISA; PORTUGAL; TRADE AND COMMERCE; VENICE; WARFARE.

Further reading: Aly Mohammed Fahmy, *Muslim Sea-Power in the Eastern Mediterranean from the Seventh to the Tenth Century A.D.* (Cairo: National Publication & Printing House, 1966); Basil Greenhill, *The Evolution of the Sailing Ship, 1250–1580* (London: Conway Maritime Press, 1995); George F. Hourani, *Arab Seafaring in the Indian Ocean in Ancient and Early Medieval Times,* ed. John Carswell rev. and expanded ed. (Princeton, Princeton University Press, 1995); Gillian Hutchinson, *Medieval Ships and Shipping* (London: Leicester University Press, 1994); Frederic C. Lane, *Venetian Ships and Shipbuilders of the Renaissance* (Baltimore: Johns Hopkins Press, 1934); Richard W. Unger, *The Ship in the Medieval Economy, 600–1600* (London: Croom Helm, 1980).

Sicilian Vespers This was a popular rebellion or revolution that usurped control of the island of SICILY from the Angevins of NAPLES, essentially from the French control of CHARLES I OF ANJOU. It began at the hour of vespers on Easter Monday, March 30, 1282, at PALERMO. It started with an insult to a Sicilian woman; within a few hours thousands of French men, women, and children were killed. It began as an attempt to form the "commune of the island of Sicily" and quickly spread throughout the island. A parliament was called, and it proclaimed a republic. Some of the towns at the western end of the island placed themselves under papal rule, a decision that Martin IV (r. 1281–85), a Frenchman, refused to accept; instead, he excommunicated the rebels. The latter now turned to the Ghibellines and had to accept help from Peter III (r. 1239–85) of ARAGON, who was crowned king of Sicily in August 2, 1282. Peter promised to administer the island according to its own laws, treating it as separate country from Aragon. Its new leaders were the former HOHENSTAUFEN councilors of MANFRED, who had been defeated by Charles in 1266. Actual popular support for this was minimal until Charles provoked local resistance by his stern measures and then attacked the island to restore his authority. The conflict lasted for two decades and the Aragonese in the end triumphed. However, Sicily remained under foreign domination, albeit slightly less exploitative. Frederick III (r. 1272–1337) became its second Aragonese king in 1296.

Further reading: David Abulatia, *The Western Mediterranean Kingdoms, 1200–1500* (London: Longman, 1997); Jean Dunbabin, *Charles I of Anjou: Power, Kingship and State-Making in Thirteenth-Century Europe* (New York: Longman, 1998); Steven Runciman, *The Sicilian*

Vespers: A History of the Mediterranean World in the Later Thirteenth Century (Cambridge: Cambridge University Press, 1958); Helene Wieruszowski, *Politics and Culture in Medieval Spain and Italy* (Roma: Edizioni di storia e letteratura, 1971).

Sicily Medieval Sicily was a large island in the central Mediterranean, off the southern coast of ITALY. It was an important part of the BYZANTINE EMPIRE in the seventh century. During the revolt in 826, the Byzantine governor, who was rebelling against the emperor, asked the AGHLABIDS of North Africa for help. This paved the way for an army of volunteers, led by a Malikite scholar from AL-QAYRAWAN, to begin a slow and difficult conquest. He landed in 827 and finally took Palermo in 831; Syracuse fell in 878. Much of the Greek population fled and was replaced by Muslim settlers from North Africa; many inhabitants stayed and the population became genuinely mixed. There was considerable Arabization in terms of language and culture. In 909 Sicily fell under the control of the FATIMIDS and remained a frontier land, especially after a Byzantine counterattack failed in 965.

ARRIVAL OF THE NORMANS

The collapse of Muslim Sicily began with a religious crisis. In around 1030, religious differences intensified as questions about the legitimacy of the Fatimid imamate arose as the local Arab emirs fought among themselves. The Muslim Sicilians' appeal to the NORMANS of Calabria, ROGER I and ROBERT GUISCARD. This proved fatal to Muslim domination of the island. The Normans took Palermo in 1072 and Syracuse in 1086, establishing a competent administration on the island and carefully resettling Muslims in locations vulnerable to Norman forces. Roger I worked out an advantageous accord with Pope URBAN II that gave his dynasty effective control over the Sicilian church on the island. There was considerable religious toleration of Muslims, JEWS, and Greeks on the island, especially under ROGER II. A literary and geographical culture, elaborate court ceremonial, an impressive palace, and religious architecture borrowed from Byzantium and ISLAM made the island a cultural center that synthesized in many ways all the civilizations of the Mediterranean Sea. This balance was maintained until 1160, when WILLIAM I was forced by seditious activities to reduce the level of his tolerance toward the religions of those whom he employed in his administration. The HOHENSTAUFEN dynasty from the mainland took over in 1196, and with their rule much of the island's economy declined and was handed over to control by merchants from GENOA and PISA.

THE RETURN OF FEUDALISM

FREDERICK II was the heir to the Mediterranean ambitions of his grandfather, Roger II, but had to move the center of his kingdom to APULIA, in southeastern Italy. He and his successors were unable to finish a program of planning and developing settlements on the island. The insurrection of the SICILIAN VESPERS in 1282 provoked by French or Angevin oppression led to an appeal to MANFRED's son-in-law, Peter III of Aragon (r. 1276–85). This new regime tried to reconstitute a systematic FEUDALISM on the island. A huge fiscal, naval, and military effort allowed Frederick III to defeat the formidable coalition of Angevin NAPLES, Capetian FRANCE, the PAPACY, and even opposition within ARAGON. There followed nearly a century of periodic conflict, leading to the economic exhaustion of Naples as well as of the island, a long INTERDICT on Sicilian churches, and a stultifying refeudalization of the aristocracy over the towns. A later Catalan conquest of 1392–98 reestablished yet another feudal framework of exploitation. In 1412 the Aragonese Crown passed to the cadet branch of the Trastámara family of CASTILE attaching the island first to BARCELONA, then to Naples. From there it became part of the Mediterranean empire of ALFONSO V THE MAGNANIMOUS in the mid-15th century. New economic, demographic, and cultural changes occurred at the end of the 15th century with the resumption of the export of grain and the development of new products such as sugar and raw SILK. This enriched an urban patriciate but failed to benefit the rural feudal nobility. Sicily passed under the control of the Spanish Crown under FERDINAND II and ISABEL I in 1502. All of these governments after the Vespers were exploitative of Sicily and that led to political, social, and in the end economic decline.

See also PALERMO; SARDINIA.

Further reading: Graham A. Loud and Thomas Wiedemann, trans., *The History of the Tyrants of Sicily by "Hugo Falcandus," 1154–1569* (Manchester: Manchester University Press, 1998); David Abulaffia, *The Two Italies: Economic Relations between the Norman Kingdom of Sicily and the Northern Communes* (Cambridge: Cambridge University Press, 1977); Aziz Ahmad, *A History of Islamic Sicily* (Edinburgh: Edinburgh University Press, 1975); Clifford R. Backman, *The Decline and Fall of Medieval Sicily: Politics, Religion, and Economy in the Reign of Frederick III, 1296–1337* (Cambridge: Cambridge University Press, 1995); Stephan R. Epstein, *An Island for Itself: Economic Development and Social Change in Late Medieval Sicily* (Cambridge: Cambridge University Press, 1991); Jeremy Johns, *Arabic Administration in Norman Sicily: The Royal Diwan* (Cambridge: Cambridge University Press, 2002); Hugh Kennedy, "Sicily and al-Andalus under Muslim Rule," in *The New Cambridge Medieval History*, Vol. 3, *c. 900–c. 1024*, ed. Timothy Reuter (Cambridge: Cambridge University Press, 1999), 646–669; Denis Mack Smith, *A History of Sicily: Medieval Sicily, 800–1713* (London: Chatto & Windus, 1968); Donald Matthew, *The Norman Kingdom of Sicily* (Cambridge: Cambridge University Press, 1992).

sickness and disease In a medieval Christian context in the East and the West, sickness was a consequence of original sin, but sometimes had the ambivalent status of a metaphor of punishment for SIN or even HERESY. Physical suffering, on the other hand, was compared with the redemptive suffering of Christ. MEDICINE involved palliative care for the body and the SOUL as victims were being prepared to meet their maker. LEPROSY was closely linked with carnal sin, and the horrifying and implacable Black Death of 1348 was sometimes cast as punishment for sin. Medicine had few treatments for disease beyond occasionally alleviating the symptoms, still often blaming much on an imbalance of humors. This imbalance meant a rupture of the equilibrium of the complexion, the mixture of the primary qualities of hot, cold, dry, and wet, proper to a part of the body or to the whole of it.

The causes of most diseases were not understood at all through most of the Middle Ages. When remedies were effective, success was more attributable to chance than to any understanding of causes. Ancient classical Greek ideas became better known by the 15th century, but they were only partially helpful. The effects of certain drugs were known and were employed by skillful physicians and local folk practitioners to ease pain. Midwives had considerable skill in assisting in childbirth, and physicians and surgeons intervened to perform cesarean deliveries. Skin and intestinal diseases were almost universal; fever caused by many kinds of infection was common, since personal hygiene was primitive. Smallpox, malaria, typhoid, tuberculosis, measles, meningitis, and other infectious diseases regularly reached epidemic proportions. Cancer and diabetes doubtlessly were present but were masked by other problems. Mental illness and INSANITY were recognized and sometimes received protective care. Malnutrition and parasitic invasions lowered resistance to disease, when they did not themselves kill. The Arab–Islamic medical tradition understood better and earlier the ideas of classical medicine but was only marginally more successful in combating and treating disease.

See also CONTRACEPTION AND ABORTION; HOSPITALS; IBN SINA, ABU ALI AL-HUSAYN; MAIMONIDES, MOSES; PARASITES; PSELLOS, MICHAEL; TROTA.

Further reading: Saul Nathaniel Brody, *The Disease of the Soul: Leprosy in Medieval Literature* (Ithaca, N.Y.: Cornell University Press, 1974); Sheila Campbell, Bert Hall, and David Klausner, eds., *Health, Disease, and Healing in Medieval Culture* (New York: St. Martin's Press, 1992); Luis García-Ballester, ed., *Practical Medicine from Salerno to the Black Death* (Cambridge: Cambridge University Press, 1994); J. N. Hays, *The Burdens of Disease: Epidemics and Human Response in Western History* (New Brunswick, N.J.: Rutgers University Press, 1998); Donald R. Hopkins, *Princes and Peasants: Smallpox in History* (Chicago: University of Chicago Press, 1983); Vivian Nutton, "Medicine in Medieval Western Europe, 1000–1500," in *The Western Medical Tradition, 800 B.C. to A.D. 1800,* ed. Lawrence I. Conrad et al. (Cambridge: Cambridge University Press, 1995), 139–205, 500–502.

sieges and fortifications *See* CASTLES AND FORTIFICATIONS; WARFARE.

Siena Medieval Siena was a city in TUSCANY set on the intersection of three hills about 1,000 feet above sea level. In the Middle Ages, it was part of the kingdom of ITALY and part of the HOLY ROMAN EMPIRE. It was on a major PILGRIMAGE route to ROME, the Via Francigena or Via Romea. In the 12th century it became a COMMUNE and tried to protect its independence from the emperor, the pope, and other nearby cities, such as its great rival FLORENCE. Siena soon constructed a *contado,* or rural jurisdiction, beyond the limits of its diocese. In this *contado* it imposed its own LAW and taxation and obtained the submission of the rural lords, towns, and peasant communities. By the 14th century, Sienese territory included southern Tuscany and the Maremma and coast near the Mediterranean Sea.

In the 13th century, Siena's trading activities and particularly papal banking prospered. Sienese companies were among the largest in Europe, and its family companies conducted business with ROME, the FAIRS of Champagne, PARIS, LONDON, and elsewhere. Despite its papal banking connections, it led the Ghibelline cities that opposed Guelf Florence and the PAPACY. With the aid of German mercenaries sent by MANFRED in 1260, it inflicted a major defeat on Florence in 1260 at the Battle of Montaperti but was unable to take any long-term advantage of its temporary dominance of Tuscany. The Tuscan GUELFS regrouped and forced a Guelf regime on the city which became the regime of the Nine, which lasted until 1355. Around 1300 all of the Sienese banking companies failed and were usually replaced by new Florentine firms. The Sienese families and MERCHANTS who had run the companies managed to preserve much of their wealth but retreated to business and politics within the Sienese state. Without the water resources of its rival Florence, Siena did not develop much of a lucrative cloth industry: Its economy instead became even more closely tied to its rich agricultural region.

FOURTEENTH CENTURY AND LATER

In the early 14th century, the town's population reached about 50,000. During the second half of the 14th century, internal politics was characterized by almost constant conflict and included several barely suppressed magnate rebellions, especially after the Black Death killed as much as one-third of its population. The city was hugely burdened by mercenary bands demanding bribes in return for the safety of both the countryside and the city itself.

Siena, Piazza del Campo, town hall (Palazzo Pubblico) *(Courtesy Library of Congress)*

Siena remained independent, however, until the mid-16th century, when it was taken after a difficult and devastating siege by the Florentines and Spanish in 1555.

CULTURE

Siena also produced a fine artistic and architectural tradition as reflected in the artistic achievement of DUCCIO, Simone MARTINI, the LORENZETTI brothers, and SASSETTA. It was a great center of Italian civic and Gothic art. Its cathedral, begun in the 12th century, has maintained much of its 14th-century adornment. The 13th-century town hall and the paved piazza from the 14th century in front of it have long been among the most famous in Europe. Its rich religious culture also produced two of the most popular saints of the later Middle Ages, CATHERINE and BERNARDINO.

Further reading: William M. Bowsky, *A Medieval Italian Commune: Siena under the Nine, 1287–1355* (Berkeley: University of California Press, 1981); William Caferro, *Mercenary Companies and the Decline of Siena* (Baltimore: Johns Hopkins University Press, 1998); Bruce Cole, *Sienese Painting, from Its Origins to the Fifteenth Century* (New York: Harper & Row, 1980); Edward D. English, *Enterprise and Liability in Sienese Banking, 1230–1350*

(Cambridge: Medieval Academy of America, 1988); Diana Norman, *Siena and the Virgin: Art and Politics in a Late Medieval City State* (New Haven, Conn.: Yale University Press, 1999); Daniel Waley, *Siena and the Sienese in the Thirteenth Century* (Cambridge: Cambridge University Press, 1991).

Siger of Brabant (ca. 1235/40–1284) *philosopher who sparked conflict through his use of Aristotelian ideas*
Born in BRABANT between 1235 and 1240, Siger studied at the arts faculty of the University of PARIS just as the works of ARISTOTLE were becoming available. Not a cleric, he became a master there between 1260 and 1265. His first work set out a version of Aristotelian psychology that was inspired by IBN RUSHD (Averroës) and incompatible with Christian doctrine. It presented the SOUL as a separate substance, eternal as one intellect for the whole human race which completed the body but was not its substantial form. Siger's Averroism actually derived from the interpretations of Ibn Rushd by such theologians as Robert Kilwardby (d. 1279), BONAVENTURE, and Thomas AQUINAS. Despite this Siger was identified as the leader of a rational approach or of "Latin

Averroism." However, with the criticism he received from Aquinas and from Bishop Stephen Tempier's (r. 1268–79) first condemnation of 1270, Siger modified his ideas to resemble those of Aquinas. He continued to advocate the use of reason to compare and judge ideas, whatever their implications for Christian FAITH. While recognizing the superior certainty of revelation, he claimed for philosophy the right to proceed independently of both theologians and Aristotle. This view of the relationship between reason and faith aroused vehement opposition from many Parisian theologians.

By 1276 he seemed to have abandoned teaching but was cited by the inquisitor of France as a possible heretic. He was directly implicated in the second great condemnation promulgated on March 7, 1277, by Tempier. The rest of his life was obscure. He was perhaps imprisoned. Around February 1281, he was murdered at Orvieto by an insane secretary who was supposed to be caring for him. He was viewed with admiration by some of his contemporaries, such as Dante ALIGHERI, for promoting the autonomy of philosophical knowledge.

Further reading: Saint Thomas Aquinas, Siger of Brabant, and Saint Bonaventure, *On the Eternity of the World = De aeternitate mundi,* trans. Cyril Vollert, Lottie H. Kendzierski, and Paul M. Byrne, 2d ed. (Milwaukee: Marquette University Press, 1984); Étienne Gilson, *Dante and Philosophy,* trans. David Moore (1949; New York: Harper & Row, 1963); Armand Maurer, *Medieval Philosophy,* rev. ed. (Toronto: Pontifical Institute of Mediaeval Studies, 1982).

sigillography *See* SEALS AND SIGILLOGRAPHY.

Sigismund of Luxembourg (1368–1437) *Holy Roman Emperor*
He was the second son of the emperor CHARLES IV and younger brother of Wenceslas (1361–1419). He was elected king of HUNGARY in 1387 after his marriage to Mary of Hungary; king of BOHEMIA in 1420, when his brother, the incompetent Wenceslas the Drunkard, king of the Romans, resigned in 1410; he was consecrated emperor at ROME on May 31, 1433. He could not maintain his position as prospective ruler of POLAND against the JAGIELLONIANS. He led the disastrous CRUSADE of NICOPOLIS in 1396 and barely escaped capture in the battle.

Once elected king of the Romans and then expected to succeed as Holy Roman Emperor, he was faced with serious problems and expectations, realizing that the empire needed reform, as did the church, with an end to the GREAT SCHISM (1378–1417). There was also the problem of the HERESY of John HUS in BOHEMIA. Sigismund, however, lacked the political and economic resources to intervene in any of these areas. He gamely called a council at CONSTANCE (1414–18), in which he helped to end the

schism caused by three popes' claiming the office. This was also the council that deceived, with Sigismund's help; condemned; and burned John Hus on July 6, 1415, enraging his followers, the Hussites, in Bohemia. The resulting long and vicious war lasted for decades. Sigismund's reforms of the empire accomplished little in gaining control over the prince-electors, who wanted to perpetuate the usual weakness of the office. The council of BASEL failed to accomplish much reform near the end of his reign. Sigismund was perceived by many as having attempted much and accomplished little. He died in 1437.

See also HOLY ROMAN EMPIRE; MORAVIA.

Further reading: Aziz Suryal Atiya, *The Crusade of Nicopolis* (London: Methuen, 1934); Frederick G. Heymann, *George of Bohemia, King of Heretics* (Princeton, N.J.: Princeton University Press, 1965).

silk and silk roads Far Eastern silk, used for the liturgy and in princely courts, was highly sought after in Europe from antiquity. It entered the Mediterranean from China, which gave its name to one of the routes that joined that country to the Near East, SYRIA, and IRAN through Ecbatana, Ctesiphon, Dura Europos, and ANTIOCH or TYRE. In Persia, a transit thoroughfare for silk, silkworms were cultivated after the route was established. This was an industry kept secret until two Greek monks smuggled the procedures of sericulture clandestinely to the BYZANTINE EMPIRE. From the sixth century, Byzantine silk production prospered in Syria at Antioch, BEIRUT, and Tyre, and later at CONSTANTINOPLE itself after the loss of the Eastern provinces. It was also practiced in GREECE from the 11th century in the Peloponnese, including Corinth, Thebes, Patras, and the island of Andros.

The Byzantines enforced an imperial monopoly on the most precious silks, in particular those dyed with murex or imperial purple. The emperor used silk gifts in diplomatic transactions. In the West in the 11th century a silk industry developed in Byzantine or southern ITALY. Under the NORMANS it spread to SICILY, around Messina, PALERMO, and Cefalù. Silkworm rearing houses reached northern Italy as a result of the demands and needs of great and rich cities such as FLORENCE, VENICE, MILAN, and GENOA. In the 12th century, LUCCA became a great center of silk cloth weaving. In 1466 King LOUIS XI introduced the raising of silkworms into FRANCE but the project had little success. In SPAIN silkworm culture was imported into AL-ANDALUS by Syrian refugees in the eighth century.

Silk had long been used for liturgical vestments such as chasubles, veils, or altar frontals and at courts for prestigious garments. From the 13th century silk became a much more common material for the tailored clothes of both the court and business elites.

Further reading: Michel Balard, "Silk," *EMA* 2.1,355; Irene M. Frank and David M. Brownstone, *The Silk-Road:*

A History (New York: Facts On File, 1986); Luca Molà, *The Silk Industry of Renaissance Venice* (Baltimore: Johns Hopkins University Press, 2000); John H. Munro, "Silk," *DMA* 11.293–296; Anna Muthesius, *Studies in Byzantine and Islamic Silk Weaving* (London: Pindar Press, 1995); Anna Muthesius, *Byzantine Silk Weaving: A.D. 400 to A.D. 1200* (Vienna: Fassbaender, 1997).

silver and silversmiths   *See* METALSMITHS AND METAL WORK, METALLURGY.

Simeon I (Symeon) (r. 893–927) *prince, czar of the Bulgars*
Simeon was studying for a religious career in CONSTANTINOPLE, when he was recalled by his father, BORIS I, who had just blinded his eldest son and successor, Vladimir (r. 889–93), because he had given permission for, and actually restored, pagan practices. During Simeon's reign there was a series of victorious campaigns against Byzantium, which even reached the city of Constantinople in 913. His military successes in eastern Thrace against the Magyars and Petchenegs by 920 again took him to the Byzantine capital. He could not take the city and died suddenly in 927. In the meantime he had temporarily annexed SERBIA. Contemplating having himself crowned at Constantinople, Simeon, in imitation of the Eastern emperors, took the title of czar of the Bulgars and Romans. Deeply religious, he was a protector and patron of literature and the arts. His reign marked the cultural apex of medieval BULGARIA.
    Further reading: John V. A. Fine, *the Early Medieval Balkans: A Critical Survey from the Sixth to the Late Twelfth Century* (Ann Arbor: University of Michigan Press, 1991).

Simon IV de Montfort, the Elder (ca. 1160–1218) *one of the leaders of the Albigensian Crusade*
Born about 1160, Simon de Montfort was an important lord of the Yvelines, on the margins of the French royal domain. He was called the earl of Leicester, although he had long been dispossessed of that English county. In 1202, he became a crusader with many other barons of FRANCE, but he refused to go to CONSTANTINOPLE and set out with his own band of soldiers to wage war in SYRIA.
    In August 1209 he took the cross again against the ALBIGENSIAN heretics of southern France. He agreed to become the viscount of Béziers and Carcassonne in place of others who had already refused that honor. He clung tenuously to this power in the south with his companions and the bishop of TOULOUSE. In 1210 he was reinforced with new crusaders just in time to hold out longer. In 1211 he managed to capture several of the main strongholds of the HERETICS. In the late spring of 1211, he invaded the lands of the recently excommunicated Raymond VI of Toulouse (r. 1194–1222). In the late summer of 1211, he won a battle at Castelnaudary. During the next year he reduced the strongholds of heretics. He then had to delay further warfare, short of total victory, because of the start of the preaching of the Fifth CRUSADE and an order from INNOCENT III. Despite this, he skillfully won on September 13, 1213, the Battle of Muret, at which King Peter II of Aragon (r. 1196–1214), an ally of Raymond VI, was killed. In 1214 he completed his conquest and was joined by the future king, Louis VIII (1187–1226). In 1215, he was made count of Toulouse at the Fourth Lateran Council, which had disinherited Raymond VI. He was recognized as count by King PHILIP II AUGUSTUS. His luck then changed. He could not prevent the retaking of Beaucaire by Count Raymond VII (r. 1222–49) or the revolt in the city of Toulouse that expelled his friend the bishop and allowed the return to the city of Raymond VII and his son. The rest of PROVENCE then rose against him. He was killed besieging Toulouse by a catapult, operated perhaps by women, or in a skirmish with the enemy on June 25, 1218.
    Further reading: Joseph R. Strayer, *The Albigensian Crusades,* with a new epilogue by Carol Lansing (Ann Arbor: University of Michigan Press, 1992); Michael D. Costen, *The Cathars and the Albigensian Crusade* (Manchester: Manchester University Press, 1997).

Simon de Montfort, the Younger (ca. 1200–1265) *one of the leaders of the Barons' Revolt against the English Crown*
French by birth, Simon went to ENGLAND in 1230 to press the claim of his grandfather, SIMON DE MONTFORT, THE ELDER, to the earldom of Leicester. He secured his inheritance between 1231 and 1239 and so impressed King HENRY III that he rose quickly in royal favor. In 1238 he married Eleanor (d. 1275), the king's sister. More masterful and tenacious of his rights than other royal favorites, he soon quarreled with the king. Over the next two decades their relations were stormy, especially after Simon's controversial period as a brutal governor of Gascony between 1248 and 1252. However, he was away in France on a diplomatic mission and actually little involved in the movement that forced Henry to submit to baronial control in the Provisions of Oxford in 1258. These went much further than MAGNA CARTA in limiting royal prerogatives, in effect reviving the council that ruled while Henry was a minor. After the disintegration of the baronial government, Simon became a focal point of opposition to the king. Early in 1264 he rejected the Mise of Amiens, an attempt by LOUIS IX of France to arbitrate the dispute. He took Henry III and his son, the future EDWARD I, prisoners at the Battle of LEWES on May 14, 1264. A new scheme of government was then drawn up later that year, the Mise of Lewes, and Simon became a leading member of a triumvirate empowered to control

the king. He eagerly sought reconciliation with Henry. He even assembled the Great PARLIAMENT of 1265, which included, for the first time, representatives of the shires and boroughs, all in the hope of securing his position and obtaining a lasting peace. The king refused to compromise on royal rule and power. Simon quarreled with his leading ally, Gilbert de Clare the Red, earl of Gloucester (d. 1295). Edward escaped from custody May 28. Simon was defeated and killed at the Battle of Evesham on August 4, 1265. His tomb soon became a place of pilgrimage.

Further reading: R. F. Treharne and I. J. Sanders, eds., *Documents of the Baronial Movement of Reform and Rebellion, 1258–1267* (Oxford: Clarendon Press, 1973); Margaret W. Labarge, *Simon de Montfort* (New York: Norton, 1963); J. R. Maddicott, *Simon de Montfort* (Cambridge: Cambridge University Press, 1994); R. F. Treharne, *Simon de Montfort and Baronial Reform: Thirteenth-Century Essays*, ed. E. B. Fryde (London: Hambledon Press, 1986).

Simone Martini   *See* MARTINI, SIMONE.

simony   The idea of *simony* was taken from the New Testament (Acts 8:81–24). There the magician Simon Magus tried to buy priestly power. ISIDORE OF SEVILLE discussed a HERESY of the Simoniacs. The councils of Orléans in 533 and 549 and of Clermont in 535, deposed candidates who had bought their election. This practice was further denounced by GREGORY OF TOURS, Pope GREGORY I THE GREAT, and Pope GREGORY VII. In the 11th century, imperial interventions in the life of the church were denounced once again in 1049. Although simony doubtlessly was still practiced, this prohibition was maintained throughout the Middle Ages: One should not buy or sell an ecclesiastical benefice or its revenue.

See also BENEFICE; GREGORIAN REFORM; INVESTITURE CONTROVERSY OR DISPUTES; PATRONAGE.

Further reading: Joseph H. Lynch, *Simoniacal Entry into Religious Life from 1000 to 1260: A Social, Economic, and Legal Study* (Columbus: Ohio State University Press, 1976); Raymond A. Ryder, *Simony, an Historical Synopsis and Commentary* (Washington, D.C.: The Catholic University of America, 1931).

sin   Sin from the time of Saint AUGUSTINE of Hippo was considered to be "that which is willfully, freely, and voluntarily done, said, or willed against the law of GOD." It would have a legal, psychological, and theological dimension. One's intent became more paramount from the 12th century onward. Sin was a disorder, a human act, and a sign of a disharmony between human reason and the will of God and humankind. It was done against the good, including one's own good, a fault against God. One was supposed to know and seek only the best. All sin was

transgression of the LAW, but not all transgression against the law was sin. WILLIAM OF OCKHAM would say that sin was human will's transgressing God's will. Islamic ideas about sin were not much different. In Muslim legal practice, serious sins were associated with *hadd*, punishment under the legal system or *shariah*. A sinner was held accountable for his or her actions of omission and commission. Mortal sin was the most serious category of sin. It must be committed with full consent of the will and involve a grave matter. Venial sin disposed the SOUL to DEATH and was the greatest of all evils except mortal sin. But unlike mortal sin, it did not wholly deprive the soul of sanctifying GRACE and lead by itself to eternal damnation. Sincere repentance might mitigate some of the consequences of all kinds of sin. In ISLAM, polytheism, however, might not be forgiven, according to the QURAN.

See also PENITENTIALS; REDEMPTION; SEVEN DEADLY OR CAPITAL SINS; SEVEN SACRAMENTS; VIRTUES AND VICES.

Further reading: Étienne Gilson, *Moral Values and the Moral Life: The Ethical Theory of St. Thomas Aquinas*, trans. Leo Richard Ward (1931; reprint, Hamden, Conn.: Shoe String Press, 1961); Ralph M. McInerny, *Ethica Thomistica: The Moral Philosophy of Thomas Aquinas* (Washington, D.C.: Catholic University of America Press, 1997); Richard Newhauser, *The Early History of Greed: The Sin of Avarice in Early Medieval Thought and Literature* (Cambridge: Cambridge University Press, 2000); Siegfried Wenzel, *The Sin of Sloth: Acedia in Medieval Thought and Literature* (Chapel Hill. University of North Carolina Press, 1967).

Sina, Ibn   *See* IBN SINA, ABU ALI AL-HUSAYN.

Sinai   The Medieval Sinai was the mountainous and arid peninsula between the modern states of Israel and Egypt. Mount Sinai was in this region. It was sacred in Christian and Islamic traditions from its associations with Moses. There he met the burning bush that told him to return to EGYPT, where he received the commandments or the Law. The body of Saint Catherine of Alexandria (4th century), according to legend, was carried there by ANGELS where it was maintained by HERMITS and monks from at least the fourth century. A fortified monastery, Saint Catherine's, was built there under the emperor JUSTINIAN in 530. Its sixth-century MOSAIC of the TRANSFIGURATION survives in the main church. This monastery has an important collection of rare ICONS from the period before ICONOCLASM. It also possessed an extremely important collection of similarly ancient manuscripts.

Further reading: C. Bailey, "Sīnā," *Encyclopedia of Islam* 9.625; James Bentley, *Secrets of Mount Sinai: The Story of the Codex Sinaiticus* (London: Orbis, 1985); John Galey, *Sinai and the Monastery of St. Catherine* (Garden City, N.Y.: Doubleday, 1980).

skaldic poetry *See* ICELAND AND ICELANDIC LITERATURE.

Skanderbeg (George Castriota, Iskander Bey) (1404–1468) *Albanian national hero*
George Castriota, later called Skanderbeg, was born in 1404 in the clan of the Castriotes, from the high valleys of Drin and Mat near the Adriatic. In 1423 he was taken as hostage to the court of Sultan MURAD II. There he acquired an excellent education and the surname Skanderbeg, in Turkish Iskander Bey or Lord Alexander. As a JANISSARY he rose to become a general in the Turkish army. He won numerous battles but reverted to Christianity and returned to ALBANIA in 1443. There he organized the struggle against the OTTOMAN TURKS. He won numerous, as many as 13, victories against an enemy far superior in number and arms. With little help from the outside except minor assistance from the PAPACY, he held back the advance of the Turkish army in the Balkans between 1444 and 1468. He died undefeated at Lezhe January 17, 1468. With his death there ended any effective resistance to the Turks by the Albanians.

Further reading: John V. A. Fine, *The Late Medieval Balkans: A Critical Survey from the Late Twelfth Century to the Ottoman Conquest* (Ann Arbor: University of Michigan Press, 1994).

slave trade and slavery Throughout the medieval world, serfdom had the humiliating and exploitative elements of ancient slavery, including the loss of personal freedom and real or bodily dependence on the lord. True slavery never totally disappeared. Some authors defended the universal right to personal freedom; however, slavery was fully recognized as a necessity in the early Middle Ages. Based by divine punishment from the curse of Cain, slavery depended on the violent appropriation of human beings, as in the classical world. ISLAM forbade the enslavement of Muslims and non-Muslims living under Muslim rule. The only legal slaves were to be non-Muslims or their children imprisoned or taken beyond the borders of Islam. Islam was regularly supplied with domestic slaves by Saharan dealers, and the first organized states of West AFRICA were heavily dependent on slavery. Some Islamic armies were made up of slaves.

In the BYZANTINE EMPIRE before the 10th century, large-scale slave labor was used in AGRICULTURE and in industry within the city of CONSTANTINOPLE. By the 11th century slave labor had ended in those activities, but slaves still passed through its markets to Western Europe, and particularly into the Islamic world. In the West Christians were not supposed to be enslaved, but pagans were fair game. By the later Middle Ages and the RENAISSANCE, slavery in Europe was limited to domestic servitude in ITALY, with some agricultural labor in Iberia and its new Atlantic and Mediterranean colonies. These slaves were from the region around the BLACK SEA and the eastern Mediterranean and were then being supplemented by others captured by Portuguese expeditions along the West African coast in the 15th century. In the 16th century, the conquest of the Americas involved massive enslavement of the local populations and soon thereafter large transport of Africans. There was some opposition to slavery in the early 14th century from the followers of Ramón LULL; however, economic incentives proved stronger than moral qualms, so that the practice was not limited but instead ultimately spread.

See also JANISARRIES AND JANISSARY CORPS; MAMLUKS; SERFS AND SERFDOM; SLAVS; VILLEINS AND VILLEINAGE.

Further reading: David Ayalon, *Islam and the Abode of War: Military Slaves and Islamic Adversaries* (Aldershot: Variorum, 1994); Robert Brunshvig, "'Abd," *Encyclopedia of Islam,* 1.24–34; Pierre Dockès, *Medieval Slavery and Liberation,* trans. Arthur Goldhammer (Chicago: University of Chicago Press, 1982); Steven A. Epstein, *Speaking of Slavery: Color, Ethnicity, and Human Bondage in Italy* (Ithaca, N.Y.: Cornell University Press, 2001); Carl I. Hammer, *A Large-Scale Slave Society of the Early Middle Ages: Slaves and their Families in Early Medieval Bavaria* (Aldershot: Ashgate, 2002); Bernard Lewis, *Race and Slavery in the Middle East: An Historical Enquiry* (New York: Oxford University Press, 1990); Iris Origo, "The Domestic Enemy: The Eastern Slaves in Tuscany in the Fourteenth and Fifteenth Centuries," *Speculum* 30 (1955): 321–366; William D. Phillips Jr., *Slavery from Roman Times to the Early Transatlantic Trade* (Minneapolis: University of Minnesota Press, 1985); Susan Stuard, "Ancillary Evidence for the Decline of Medieval Slavery," *Past and Present* 149 (1995): 3–28.

Slavs The word Slav might be derived from two roots. One referred to those who lived in swampy places, and the other was linked with a word for "glory" or those who had an "intelligible language." As a people they first appear in the sixth century as Sclaveni or Sclavi. By the central Middle Ages, the name had become linked with SLAVERY in places such as VENICE that traded in human beings for slave labor and could obtain people from the Slavic population in the Balkans and from around the BLACK SEA.

Slav society was united by a common Indo-European language and was organized into a tribal structure, under the leadership of military chiefs. Its economy was based on AGRICULTURE and ANIMAL HUSBANDRY. Early in the fifth century, bursting with large populations, the Slav tribes invaded the Byzantine Empire; by the end of the sixth century they had settled throughout the Balkan Peninsula and as far south as the Peloponnese. Other Slavs moved into what became MORAVIA and BOHEMIA. They eventually settled in the former ILLYRICUM on the Dalmatian coast, the valleys of the Elbe, Vistula, Bug, and the Oder Rivers; and finally in the valleys of the Dniepr and Volga and along Lakes Peipus and Ladoga, displacing Balt and Finnish tribes. Between the sixth and the ninth centuries, three linguistic groups had evolved: the Western, Eastern, and Southern Slavs. In the ninth century, CYRIL AND METHODIUS were able to use in their missionary and liturgical activities the language spoken around THESSALONIKI. This became Slavonic, which was used for translating Scripture and the liturgy and written in GLAGOLITIC. The Slavs of the east and southeast used a script wrongly called CYRILLIC.

The various Slavic peoples eventually followed either the Roman Church or the Orthodox Church. This choice depended on who converted them and had fostered links with the local ruling families. From the ninth century, the history of the Slavs became tied to the individual national and regional groups they had established. The differences among many of these groups actually remained fairly fluid and only became clearly defined by nationalistic historians, folklorists, and philologists in the 19th century.

See also BARBARIANS AND BARBARIAN MIGRATIONS; BULGARIA; CROATIA; DALMATIA; POLAND; RUSSIA AND RUŚ; SERBIA; SLAVE TRADE AND SLAVERY.

Further reading: Francis Dvornik, *The Slavs in European History and Civilization* (New Brunswick, N.J.: Rutgers University Press, 1962); Marija Alseikaité Gimbutas, *The Slavs* (London: Thames & Hudson, 1971); Dimitri Obolensky, *The Byzantine Commonwealth: Eastern Europe, 500–1453* (London: Weidenfeld and Nicolson, 1971); Zdeněk Váňa, *The World of the Ancient Slavs*, trans. Till Gottheiner (London: Orbis, 1983).

Snorri Sturluson (1178/79–1241) *Norwegian and Icelandic author*
Snorri Sturluson was born in 1178 or 1179 either in Hvamm in ICELAND or in NORWAY. He lived in Iceland, a descendent of Egill Skallagrímsson, in the household of Jón Loptsson, one of the most influential chiefs in Iceland. From him Snorri learned much about Icelandic traditions and the wider world. In 1199 he married an heiress and gained considerable property and land. From 1206 he lived in Reykjaholt, where he did most of his writing. He became famous for his adaptations of the Norse sagas. His main achievement, the HEIMSKRINGLA, was a set of poetic biographies of legendary and genuine Norse chieftains and heroes. These histories were widely read in the 13th century. The *Prose Edda* was a handbook of poetics and a telling of some of the major Norse myths that preserved the world of pagan northern Europe. Known as the richest man in Iceland, Snorri served as a chief in the Icelandic high court from 1215 to 1218 and from 1222 to 1232. Involved in politics, he became Haakon IV's (1204–63) vassal. He eventually fell out of favor and was assassinated on Haakon's order on September 22, 1241.

Further reading: Snorri Sturluson, *The Prose Edda of Snorri Sturluson: Tales from Norse Mythology*, trans. Jean I. Young (Berkeley: University of California Press, 1964); Snorri Sturluson, *Heimskringla: History of the Kings of Norway*, trans. Lee M. Hollander (Austin: Published for the American-Scandinavian Foundation by the University of Texas Press, 1964); Sverre Bagge, *Society and Politics in Snorri Sturluson's Heimskringla* (Berkeley: University of California Press, 1991); Stefán Einarsson, *A History of Icelandic Literature* (New York: Johns Hopkins Press for the American-Scandinavian Foundation, 1957); Marlene Ciklamini, *Snorri Sturluson* (Boston: Twayne, 1978).

social status and structure The Middle Ages knew social stratification, but the social structure rested on a division into orders, not classes. These were believed to be willed by GOD and considered immutable by some. Legal status was important. People were either free or unfree. The free could bear arms, could pay taxes for protection, could appeal to the LAW, could move about, could marry, and could testify in a court of law. The unfree were slaves with no rights, though better treated than in ancient times, or SERFS liable to stringent obligations and limitations. Others, more fortunate, were born into aristocratic families and therefore were often judged superior from birth. They commanded because they were lords, whether armed or not. Some were warriors, ordained clerics, public and private officials, artisans, MERCHANTS, or peasants.

From the 12th century, wealth divided people into groups. For some in the Middle Ages, social order reflected a world order willed by God with a hierarchy resting on the functions of social groups, and natural inequality. This had been perceived by historians in an oversimplified scheme of those who pray, those who fight, and those who work, with the king overseeing all. In all the religions of the medieval world, the weak were to be protected and JUSTICE was to be observed in social and economic exchange.

See also CHARITY AND POVERTY; CHIVALRY; NOBILITY AND NOBLES; SLAVE TRADE AND SLAVERY; WIDOWS AND WIDOWHOOD.

Further reading: David Herlihy, *Medieval Culture and Society* (New York: Walker, 1968); Christopher N. L. Brooke, *The Structure of Medieval Society* (London: Thames and Hudson, 1971); S. H. Rigby, *English Society in the Later Middle Ages: Class, Status and Gender* (London: Macmillan Press, 1995); Tsugitaka Sato, *State and Rural Society in Medieval Islam: Sultans, Muqtas, and Fallahun* (Leiden: E. J. Brill, 1997); R. N. Swanson, *Church and Society in Late Medieval England* (Oxford: Blackwell, 1989).

Sofia (Serdica, Sofya) Medieval Sofia became the capital of modern-day BULGARIA. Sofia's predecessor, the classical city of Serdica, fell into decline during the early Middle Ages. It was sacked by the HUNS in 447 and rebuilt by JUSTINIAN I in the sixth century. Its name and ethnic character changed in the seventh century, when it became the Slavic and Bulgarian town of Sofia. Captured by the BULGARS in 809, the town became subordinate to the new centers of the medieval Bulgarian Empire, such as Tirnovo and OCHRIDA. The Byzantines retook control of the town in the 11th and 12th centuries. By 1385 the OTTOMAN TURKS, commanded by Sultan MURAD I, had conquered Sofia and it had become the Turkish capital of western Bulgaria.

Further reading: Svetlana Ivanova, "Sofya," *Encyclopedia of Islam,* 9.702–706; Stoiko Kozhukharov, *Sofia,* trans. Donka Minkova (Sofia: Foreign Languages Press, 1967).

Songhai (Songhay, Sonraï, Sonrhai) From as early as the seventh century, Songhai was an empire in North AFRICA on the northern bend of the Niger River. It became part of the empire of MALI in the 13th century. In 1135 the Songhai people freed themselves from Mali and started to conquer the surrounding area where the capital was Gao. The Songhai people deployed a skillful and sophisticated army that included cavalry. They remained mostly pagan. Their empire was to reach its greatest extent and power in the early 16th century under the Muslim Muhammad I Askia (1493–1528). Its wealth was derived from the TRADE in salt and GOLD and probably the slave trade with the north.

Further reading: Daniel Chu and Elliott Skinner, *A Glorious Age in Africa: The Story of Three Great African Empires* (Trenton, N.J.: Africa World Press, 1990); Patricia and Fredrick McKissack, *The Royal Kingdoms of Ghana, Mali, and Songhay: Life in Medieval Africa* (New York: H. Holt, 1994); Djibril Tamsir Niane, ed., *General History of Africa. IV, Africa from the Twelfth to the Sixteenth Century* (Berkeley: University of California Press for UNESCO, 1984); abridged ed., ed. Jospeh Ki-Zerbo and Djibril Tamsir Niane (Berkeley: James Currey, 1997); Roland Oliver and Anthony Atmore, *Medieval Africa, 1250–1800,* 2d ed. (Cambridge: Cambridge University Press, 2001).

Song of Songs One of the Wisdom Books of the BIBLE, the Song of Songs had only a spiritual interpretation in both Jewish and Christian exegesis. This dialogue of a lover and the beloved was understood in JUDAISM as between Israel and its GOD. Christian exegetes saw a dialogue between the church and Christ or between the converted SOUL and the divine Word. ORIGEN's commentaries had great influence during the Middle Ages. The Song of Songs was one of the books of the Bible most commented upon in the medieval period. It furnished a repertoire of images for religious poetry as well as secular love poetry in the VERNACULAR. In the vernacular it was a favorite text for mystics.

See also BERNARD OF CLAIRVAUX, SAINT; MYSTICISM, CHRISTIAN; RICHARD ROLLE OF HAMPOLE.

Further reading: Michael Casey, ed., *A thirst for God: Spiritual Desire in Bernard of Clairvaux's Sermons on the Song of Songs* (Kalamazoo, Mich.: Cistercian, 1988); E. Ann Matter, *The Voice of My Beloved: The Song of Songs in Western Medieval Christianity* (Philadelphia: University of Pennsylvania Press, 1990); Ann W. Astell, *The Song of Songs in the Middle Ages* (Ithaca, N.Y.: Cornell University Press, 1990).

sorcery *See* MAGIC AND FOLKLORE.

soul (nafs) The soul in Christianity, Judaism, and Islam can mean "the spirit," "the person," "the life breath," "the self," or "the mind of the individual." In medieval religious terms, *soul* usually meant "the spiritual part of the human being" and designated the principal and immortal aspect necessary for vital animation or life in any animate being, either beast or human. In the Middle Ages, the human soul had two main properties: a trinitarian image and immortality. There were medieval debates about the dual or singular nature of human beings, about the soul as a separate and separable substance from the body, and about the timing and source of animation, either through human action or directly from GOD. The soul carried the personal identity of the individual. There were also discussions about whether both the body and the soul would rise at the LAST JUDGMENT, or the soul only.

See also AUGUSTINE OF HIPPO, SAINT; ETERNITY OF THE WORLD AND OF THE SOUL; IBN SINA, ABU ALI AL-HUSAYN; REDEMPTION.

Further reading: Muhammad Naquib Syed Al-Attas, *The Nature of Man and the Psychology of the Human Soul: A Brief Outline and a Framework for an Islamic Psychology and Epistemology* (Kuala Lumpur: International Institute of Islamic Thought and Civilization, 1990); Piero Boitani and Anna Torti, eds., *The Body and the Soul in Medieval Literature: The J. A. W. Bennett Memorial Lectures, Tenth Series, Perugia, 1998* (Suffolk: D. S. Brewer, 1999); Philip David Bookstaber, *The Idea of Development of the Soul in Medieval Jewish Philosophy* (Philadelphia: M. Jacobs, 1950); A. C. Pegis, *St. Thomas and the Problem of the Soul in the Thirteenth Century* (Toronto: Pontifical Institute of Mediaeval Studies, 1934).

Spain Spain was divided into several provinces under the Roman Empire. After the VANDALS passed through, the VISIGOTHS took control of it in the fifth century. With the conversion to Catholicism of the Visigothic king, RECARED I, in 589, the Iberian Peninsula became a mostly Christian kingdom. In the Middle Ages it lost its political significance and became only a geographical area. The Muslim conquest of 711–18 put the greater part of the peninsula under Muslim rule, AL-ANDALUS, with only a few weak and divided Christian enclaves or kingdoms in the north. From then the history and culture of the peninsula followed several courses of development. Running through its history from about 1031 was the struggle between the Christians and the Muslims for control or the RECONQUEST. This reunification was not not won by the Christians until 1492 with the conquest of GRANADA by the Catholic Monarchs, FERDINAND II and ISABEL I, who also finally united all the petty Christian kingdoms into one state, or Spain. Its amalgamation of Christianity, ISLAM, and JUDAISM had lasted in various forms throughout the Middle Ages. All these religious cultures developed impressive and mutually influenced forms of art, architecture, literature, learning, and thought.

See also ALMOHADS; ALMORAVIDS; AL-ANDALUS; ARAGON; ASTURIAS-LEÓN; BARCELONA; BASQUES; CASTILE, KINGDOM OF; CATALONIA; CÓRDOBA; LEÓN; NASRIDS; NAVARRE, KINGDOM OF; PORTUGAL; SANTIAGO DE COMPOSTELA; SEVILLE, CITY AND KINGDOM OF; TOLEDO; UMAYYADS OF CÓRDOBA; VALLADOLID; INDIVIDUAL NAMES OF KINGS, MONUMENTS, PEOPLE, AND CALIPHS.

Further reading: Yitzhak Baer, *A History of the Jews in Christian Spain,* 2 vols. (Philadelphia: Jewish Publication Society of America, 1961–1966); Roger Collins, *Early Medieval Spain: Unity in Diversity, 400–1000* (London: Macmillan, 1983); Thomas F. Glick, *Islamic and Christian Spain in the Early Middle Ages* (Princeton, N.J.: Princeton University Press, 1979); Gabriel Jackson, *The Making of Medieval Spain* (London: Thames and Hudson, 1972); Angus MacKay, *Spain in the Middle Ages: From Frontier to Empire, 1000–1500* (New York: St. Martin's Press, 1977); Joseph O'Callaghan, *A History of Medieval Spain* (Ithaca, N.Y.: Cornell University Press, 1975); John P. O'Neill, ed., *The Art of Medieval Spain, A.D. 500–1200* (New York: The Metropolitan Museum of Art, 1993).

spices and spice trade The word *spice* had a much wider meaning in the Middle Ages than today encompassing condiments, drugs used in the medieval pharmacopoeia, perfumes, colorants, exotic fruits, sugar, honey, and even the ingredients and materials of craftsmanship, such as cotton, wax, PAPER, or pitch. Many spices were products commonly used in the medieval pharmacopoeia and were derived from the three natural kingdoms, animal, vegetable, and mineral. Others were industrial products for dyeing such as alum, yellow arsenic, or Brazil wood. The most familiar to us are pepper, cinnamon, ginger, and cloves, among others. They were the objects of a great long-distant TRADE system from China, India, the Indian Ocean, and Indonesia to the Mediterranean, through the commercial activities of Hindu, Arab, and then Western MERCHANTS. Many were also produced in IRAN, Central Asia, the Near East, EGYPT, AFRICA, and the coastal regions of the Mediterranean.

The spice trade was a lucrative part of the commercial renaissance of the 12th century centered in the Mediterranean and dominated by GENOA, PISA, and VENICE. Ginger, SAFFRON, and sugar became commodities traded in the later Middle Ages. The search for spices was one of the motivations for the European expansion carried out by Prince HENRY THE NAVIGATOR, Christopher COLUMBUS, and VASCO DA GAMA that began in the 15th century.

Further reading: K. N. Chaudhuri, *Trade and Civilization in the Indian Ocean* (Cambridge: Cambridge University Press, 1985); Robert S. Lopez and Irving W. Raymond, eds., *Medieval Trade in the Mediterranean World: Illustrative Documents with Introductions and Notes* (New York: Columbia University Press, 1995); Robert S. Lopez, *The Commercial Revolution of the Middle Ages, 950–1350* (Englewood Cliffs, N.J.: Prentice-Hall, 1971).

Spiritual Franciscans (Spirituals) They were a group of FRANCISCANS who advocated a life of absolute VOLUNTARY POVERTY. They were particularly strong in three different regions, the March of Ancona, TUSCANY, and southern FRANCE. They were particularly influenced by three friars: Angelo Clareno (d. 1337), UBERTINO DA CASALE, and Peter John OLIVI. They espoused several themes: the attachment to absolute poverty for the order itself, the inviolability of a rule and the *Testament* of FRANCIS, criticism of the worldliness of the church and of the MENDICANT ORDERS, and a vague belief in a special role to be played by certain friars in the days leading up to the LAST JUDGMENT. After the Second Council of Lyon, the Spirituals were persecuted and some were expelled from Europe. A papal decree in 1312 by CLEMENT V ordered them to obey their superiors. Michael of Cesena (ca. 1270–1342) tried to control them, but several left the order to form a splinter group, the FRATICELLI. Their ideas about poverty in the church were deemed highly dangerous by the ecclesiastical authorities, who perceived the necessity of wealth for the church so that it might carry out its mission in the world.

See also BONIFACE VIII, POPE; CELESTINE V, POPE AND THE CELESTINES; JOACHIM, ABBOT OF FIORE; JOHN XXII, POPE.

Further reading: David Burr, *The Spiritual Franciscans: From Protest to Persecution in the Century after Saint Francis* (University Park: Pennsylvania State University Press, 2001); Malcolm D. Lambert, *Franciscan Poverty: The Doctrine of the Absolute Poverty of Christ and the Apostles in the Franciscan Order, 1210–1323* (London: S.P.C.K., 1961); John R. H. Moorman, *A History of the Franciscan Order from Its Origins to the Year 1517* (Oxford: Clarendon Press, 1968).

Split (Spalato) Medieval Split was a city in DALMATIA, founded in 615 on the ruins of the ancient palace of DIOCLETIAN at Salona, which became a Byzantine stronghold in Dalmatia and on the Adriatic Sea. In the ninth century

Croatian princes established an independent principality there and it was annexed by Tomislav I to the kingdom of Croatia. It was conquered by Hungary in 1133. It remained Hungarian until 1420, when it was annexed to Venice. It had, however, fallen under Venetian colonial domination and been a colony long before that annexation.

Further reading: John V. A. Fine, *The Early Medieval Balkans: A Critical Survey from the Sixth to the Late Twelfth Century* (Ann Arbor: University of Michigan Press, 1991); John V. A. Fine, *The Late Medieval Balkans: A Critical Survey from the Late Twelfth Century to the Ottoman Conquest* (Ann Arbor: University of Michigan Press, 1994).

spolia **and right of spoil** The right of spoil in the Middle Ages was the ability or right of anyone who had or claimed to have a right over a church to claim the movable goods of the deceased cleric who had served that church. The goods assigned to churches were originally considered the property of the whole Christian community. So bishops were merely administrators and could not dispose of them. Soon the relatives of the patrons of churches began to claim rights of inheritance even on clerical property and of a church's revenues. Clerics were considered as employees of their bishop and even sought to seize episcopal property. Pope Gregory I the Great ruled that any acquisition of church goods by a clerical officeholder made after elevation to an episcopal see must be returned to the church, but any goods possessed beforehand could be freely bequeathed by testament.

The property of parishes began to be considered as part of the patrimony of the church. This idea deprived the cleric and his family of any possibility of keeping or disposing of them. At the same time kings and great lay owners of rights over a church simply appropriated property. In the 11th and 12th centuries, the church's effort at reform to escape from this loss of wealth resorted to transforming formally this kind of private property only into rights of patronage or appointment. The laity would renounce the right of spoil in exchange for compensatory rents, or influence of the choice of appointee. Nevertheless, kings, princes, patrons, popes, and clerics continued to seize the movable goods of benefice holders who had depended in some way on them. Some distinction was established at that time between personal movable goods and landed property tied to a supporting benefice. The latter was to remain untouchable.

The landed property of a benefice holder himself, however, could be bequeathed by testament by the 19th century. Pope John XXII, by the constitution *Ex debito* in 1316, retained the right of spoil over any benefice whose collation or appointment he had managed to reserve. This was understood to be liturgical objects, manuscripts, cash, vestments, provisions, rentals to be collected, and debts due. Pope Clement VI, listening to the complaints of the clergy, excluded from the right of spoil books and liturgical objects acquired by the deceased cleric. This included also implements, and animals for agriculture. At the same time Clement also charged papal collectors of spoils with paying the debts of the deceased, covering the expenses of funerals, satisfying the salaries of servants, and fulfilling the pious testamentary legacies of the deceased. This right generated the papacy for important profits in the 14th century. The Council of Constance obliged Pope Martin V (r. 1417–31) to limit the application of the papal right of spoil to the benefices of members of the papal Curia.

See also Mortmain; wills and testaments.

Further reading: Bernard Guillemain, "Spoil, Right of," *EMA* 2.1,377–1,378; Daniel Williman, *Records of the Papal Right, Spoil, 1316–1412* (Paris: Éditions du Centre national de la recherche scientifique, 1974); Daniel Williman, *The Right of Spoil of the Popes of Avignon, 1316–1415* (Philadelphia: American Philosophical Society, 1988).

stained glass In the Middle Ages and Renaissance, stained glass was a translucent material intended to fill in and decorate a window bay. It was made of pieces of glass, colored or plain, perhaps painted, and all set in a framework usually of lead. The origins of this art have remained little known. The earliest evidence of such window glass was in Ravenna in the sixth century, Jarrow in the ninth century, and Rouen in the midninth century. Any early history of extant stained glass must begin at Neuwiller from the late 11th century, Augsburg from about 1100, and Le Mans from about 1125. In the 12th century, stained glass windows began to become larger to allow more light into churches. They were usually brightly colored, however, the Cistercians used only plain or clear glass. In the Gothic art and architecture of the 13th century, stained glass became walls of buildings yet full of light with many colors. Designs of programs became much more complex such as at Sainte-Chapelle in Paris, but still to demonstrate the good effects of the light of God on the soul. From the 14th century, stained glass became clearer, and more three-dimensional. The iconography of stained glass remained conservative throughout the Middle Ages, using illustrations from the Bible, the Gospels, and the lives of saints.

See also Gothic art and architecture; rose windows.

Further reading: Madeline H. Caviness, *Stained Glass before 1540: An Annotated Bibliography* (Boston: G. K. Hall, 1983); Madeline Caviness, *Stained Glass Windows* (Turnhout: Brepols, 1996); Louis Grodecki, *Gothic Stained Glass, 1200–1300* (Ithaca, N.Y.: Cornell University Press, 1985); Richard Marks, *Stained Glass in England during the Middle Ages* (Toronto: University of Toronto Press, 1993).

states of the church *See* Albornoz, Gil, cardinal; *Donation of Constantine*; papacy; Papal States.

statutes Beside collections of ecclesiastical laws, in the Middle Ages this term referred to collections of laws made by urban and rural COMMUNES of north central ITALY. They approved them through the deliberation of their own assemblies, especially after the Peace of Constance in 1183, which gave them more independence from the HOLY ROMAN EMPIRE. Italian communes joined together in these collections of customary and local LAW that originated in an earlier period; the compacts and oaths of the consuls or government officials on first entering their offices; and most of the laws recently approved by communal legislative organs or the consuls. The term *statutum* from the verb *statuere*, "to establish, fix, decide," was chosen for its implication that these were the norms of the law for the commune.

These were expanded into books of statutes. Over time they became more organized by type or intent of law. They had to be updated regularly as changes or additions were constantly made to the law by the government of the commune.

With the growth of knowledge and expertise in Roman law from the 12th century, jurists and university teachers became more involved in their drafting and compilation. The statutes also became more available to the citizenry, now written on paper instead of parchment. In the 14th century, some were translated from LATIN into the VERNACULAR to widen the circle of those able to read, understand, and discuss them. Outside Italy towns began to follow the Italian example, as did regional governments and states. Statutes remained primarily urban phenomena, however.

ECCLESIASTICAL

In the 12th century, ecclesiastical meetings such as local synods or councils began to keep more careful track of their prescriptions on clerical conduct, the rules for the administration of the SEVEN SACRAMENTS, pastoral care, and parish or diocesan government. Older local decisions and legislation were updated and new material, often from the PAPACY or councils such as those of the Lateran, was gathered and made more accessible to regional clergy. Not very organized or systematic, these could even include admonitory tracts and treatises on particular problems of procedure, marriage regulations, testamentary or liturgical rules, and confessors' manuals. These collections were usually kept up to date throughout the rest of Middle Ages and well beyond 1500.

Further reading: C. R. Cheney, *English Synodalia of the Thirteenth Century* (Oxford: Oxford University Press, 1941); C. R. Cheney, *Councils and Synods with Other Documents Relating to the English Church,* 2 vols. (Oxford: Clarendon Press, 1964–1981); Daniel Waley, *The Italian City-Republics,* 3d ed. (1969; London: Longman, 1988); Walter Ullman, *Law and Politics in the Middle Ages: An Introduction to the Sources of Medieval Political Ideas* (Ithaca; N.Y. Cornell University Press, 1975).

Staufen dynasty *See* HOHENSTAUFEN.

Stephen I of Hungary, Saint (Vajk) (ca. 975–1038)
king of Hungary
Stephen was born in 975 at Esztergom in HUNGARY, the son of the ruler of the Magyars, Géza I (r. 970?-97). He adopted the Christian Faith and made it the official religion of the kingdom in 1000. He suppressed pagan uprisings and converted by force any refusing to give up PAGANISM. In the following year Pope SYLVESTER II, in acknowledgment of his conversion, sent him a royal crown, which was later named the "Crown of Saint Stephen." It grew to symbolize Hungary's independence

Madonna and Child in stained glass (1300–10), Germanisches Nationalmuseum, Nuremberg Germany *(Scala / Art Resource)*

from the HOLY ROMAN EMPIRE. Stephen also organized his realm, established an army, promoted agricultural development and settlement, and established the kingdom's legal institutions. He died on August 15, 1038, at Royal Alba in Hungary.

See also ÁRPÁDS DYNASTY.

Further reading: Pál Engle, *The Realm of St. Stephen: A History of Medieval Hungary, 895–1526*, trans. Tamás Pálosfalvi and ed. Andrew Ayton (London: I. B. Tauris, 2001); György Györffy, *King Saint Stephen of Hungary* (Boulder: Social Science Monographs, 1994); Attila Zsoldos, ed., *Saint Stephen and His Country: A Newborn Kingdom in Central Europe, Hungary* (Budapest: Lucidus, 2001).

Stephen Dušan (Stefan Uroš IV Dušan, Dušan the Mighty, Stephen Dushan) (1308–1355) *king and later czar of the Serbs and Greeks*

Stephen was born in 1308, the son of Stephen III Dečanski (r. 1321–31), in central SERBIA. He grew up in exile with his father in CONSTANTINOPLE between 1314 and 1320. After campaigning successfully against the Bosnians and BULGARS, he deposed his father with the support of aristocrats and assumed the Crown in 1331. He enlarged the Serbian state far into GREECE, ALBANIA, around DURAZZO, MACEDONIA, and Mount ATHOS. On April 16, 1346, he was crowned czar at Skopje by the patriarch of the Serbian Church with the participation of the archbishop of OCHRIDA and the patriarch of Trnovo. This led to a break from Constantinople and a condemnation of Stephen and the patriarch of Serbia in 1350. Dušan convened diets in 1349 and 1354 that drew up a code of laws. He founded the monastery of the Holy Archangels in 1348. He remained on good terms with the PAPACY but was never made the leader of a CRUSADE against the OTTOMAN TURKS in the Balkans. He died on December 20, 1355, near Prizen in Serbia.

Further reading: John V. A. Fine, *The Late Medieval Balkans: A Critical Survey from the Late Twelfth Century to the Ottoman Conquest* (Ann Arbor: University of Michigan Press, 1994); George C. Soulis, *The Serbs and Byzantium during the Reign of Tsar Stephen Dusan (1331–1355) and his Successors* (Washington, D.C.: Dumbarton Oaks Library and Collection, 1984)

Stephen Langton (ca. 1155–1228) *teacher, preacher, scholar, archbishop of Canterbury*

Stephen Langton was born about 1155, the son of a Lincolnshire Knight. He was educated at PARIS as a pupil of Peter Cantor (d. 1197). From about 1180 he was a master of THEOLOGY at the University of Paris. His method of dividing the book of the BIBLE formed the basis for the present system. He also wrote significant theological studies, glosses, commentaries, and collections of SERMONS. At Paris he met Lothario di Segni, the later Pope INNOCENT III. Innocent later made him the cardinal-priest of San Crisogono on June 22, 1206. He was archbishop of CANTERBURY from December 1206 (with consecration on June 17, 1207) until his death on July 9, 1228. He was a compromise papal choice for Canterbury because of a dispute over the election between King JOHN LACKLAND and the monks of Canterbury. John rejected Stephen, and ENGLAND then suffered an INTERDICT from 1207 onward. John was excommunicated from 1209 until he agreed to accept Stephen.

Stephen arrived in England at the moment when a baronial revolt that led to the MAGNA CARTA was beginning in 1213. Cooperating with the barons, he was present at Runnymede in June 1215, and his name was affixed to the Magna Carta. He associated himself with the rebels to limit John's arbitrary behavior. His continued support of the barons, even after the king had made his peace with Innocent III, earned him the pope's displeasure because of his lack of support for a papal ally. Innocent then suspended him. Both John and Innocent died in 1216. So Stephen was restored to his archbishopric in 1218 and became influential in the regency of the young HENRY III. Stephen attended the Fourth Lateran Council in Rome in 1215 and promulgated its important reforming decrees at a provincial council at OXFORD in 1222. He was also a supporter of his martyred predecessor, Thomas BECKET. Becket's martyrdom was depicted on Stephen's seal and he presided in 1220 at the translation of Becket's bones to a specially constructed chapel in Canterbury Cathedral. He died July 9, 1228.

Further reading: Frederick M. Powicke, *Stephen Langton, Being the Ford Lectures Delivered in the University of Oxford in Hilary Term 1927* (Oxford: Clarendon Press, 1928); Phyllis Roberts, *Studies in the Sermons of Stephen Langton* (Toronto: Pontifical Institute of Mediaeval Studies, 1968).

Stilicho (Flavius) (ca. 365–408) *barbarian general for the late Roman Empire*

Born half Vandal and half Roman, Stilicho was the military commander of the Western Roman Empire between 395 and 408. As regent for the young Honorius (r. 395–423), he defeated a Visigothic invasion of ITALY led by ALARIC in 401–2. He later destroyed other gangs of Gothic invaders, in 405 and 406. On December 31, 406, however, more tribes flooded in as the VANDALS, ALANS, and Suevi crossed the Rhine River. Stilicho's subsequent attempt to extend imperial control over ILLYRICUM, in 407 failed, and he was forced to pay Alaric, then an ally in the campaign, 5,000 pounds of GOLD. After he lost the favor of Honorius, in 408 a palace revolution led to his acceptance of defeat, imprisonment, and execution.

Further reading: Alan Cameron, *Claudian: Poetry and Propaganda at the Court of Honorius* (Oxford: Clarendon Press, 1970); John Matthews, *Western Aristocracies and Imperial Court, A.D. 364–425* (Oxford: Clarendon Press, 1975).

stirrup   See CAVALRY.

Studium Generale   See UNIVERSITIES AND SCHOOLS.

Sturluson, Snorri   See SNORRI STURLUSON.

Sufism (*Tasawwuf*)   The exact meaning of Sufi or who is a Sufi is disputed. Sufism can designate Muslim MYSTI-CISM and ASCETICISM. Whether in Arabic, Persian, Turkish, or any other Asian or African language, it must be based on the QURAN. It can be seen as a reaction to the excessive worldliness at any one moment of the Islamic world. It is not a sectarian term and cannot be used in opposition to SUNNA or SHIA. Sufi orders, or *tariqahs*, are expressions of personal piety and social organization. The English term has been constructed from an Arabic word referring to one who wears a woolen robe. Muslim mysticism was not at all connected with Islam's tribal and Arabic origins. There were mystics in BAGHDAD in the late ninth century who collectively received the name of Sufis. This term had been applied individually to people whose elaborate mortifications caused shock. Their model was probably the practices of Christian eremitism. The execution of the Sufi al-Hallaj at Baghdad in 922 caused a migration of practitioners toward eastern IRAN. They were considered heterodox and persecuted for a time. They returned to have great influence on the CALIPHATE in the 11th century and in SYRIA, EGYPT, and AL-ANDALUS in the 12th century. With this the integration of Sufism into ISLAM became irreversible.

From the late 12th century, mystical CONFRATERNITIES were established and supported by networks of charitable institutions financed by public donations or official authority. These institutions had different names at different times and places such as *ribat, khanqdh, zawiya, tarl-gat,* or *tekkeh/takkiya*. This kind of organization has survived up to the present time.

Especially important in the later spread of Islam, Sufism gained prominence in all the Muslim territories from the 13th and 14th centuries. Outside this organized movement, Sufism has known great spiritual masters. The most notable of them was Ibn Arabi from AL-ANDALUS, who died at DAMASCUS in 1240. Some were great poets, such as JALAL AD-DIN RUMI, the founder of the Mevlevi order of whirling dervishes.

See also AL-GHAZALI; HAFIZ; OMAR KHAYYAM.

Further reading: "Tasawwuf," *Encyclopedia of Islam,* 4.681–685 (1929); J. J. Spencer Trimingham, *The Sufi Orders in Islam* (New York: Oxford University Press, 1998); A. M. Schimmel; Titus Burckhardt, *An Introduction to Sufism,* trans. D. M. Matheson (London: Thorsons, 1995); Leonard Lewisohn, ed., *Classical Persian Sufism: From Its Origins to Rumi* (London: Khaniqahi Nimatullahi Publications, 1993).

Suger of Saint Denis, Abbot (1081–1151) *adviser to the king of France, historian, talented abbot of Saint Denis*
Suger was born into a peasant family near PARIS and was given to the abbey of Saint Denis as an oblate at the age of about 10. He professed and took his vows at the age of 20. As a church archivist, he distinguished himself in 1107 by documenting the abbey's privileges before Pope PASCHAL II. He was later appointed the provost of Berneval-en-Caux in NORMANDY, and then in 1109 of Toury in Beauce. There he took part in King Louis VI the Fat's (1081–1137) war against the lord of Le Puiset in 1111 and 1112. Elected abbot of Saint Denis in March of 1122, he soon began to give aid and counsel to the king, traveling to RHEIMS during a military campaign against the emperor Henry V (r. 1106–25) in 1124 and in 1125 to Mainz for the election of the emperor Lothair III (r. 1125–37). He used that occasion to assert rights over abbeys in Lorraine. When he subsequently reformed the practices of the Abbey of Saint Denis in 1127, he received much praise from BERNARD OF CLAIRVAUX.

From then on, he tried to exploit the incomes of the properties of the abbey to allow him to rebuild the abbey church in the new GOTHIC style. He accompanied the young King Louis VII (r. 1137–80) to Bordeaux for his marriage with ELEANOR of Aquitaine in 1137. He soon retired to his abbey to write the *Deeds of Louis the Fat* and to oversee the rebuilding of the church in the early 1140s. He was asked to assist in the regency during Louis VII's absence on the Second CRUSADE in 1147. He quelled a revolt by nobles and earned the nickname "father of his country" during Louis's absence. On the king's return in 1149, his influence in the church of France continued; his opinion was considered in the appointment of all bishops. After reforming and adding to the finances of the abbey, he used the new funds to design and build the new abbey church, an early model of the Gothic style. He dreamed of going to the East himself to rectify the failed Second Crusade but fell ill and died on January 13, 1151, at Saint Denis at age 70.

Further reading: Suger, Abbot of Saint Denis, *The Deeds of Louis the Fat,* trans. Richard Cusimano and John Moorhead (Washington, D.C.: Catholic University of America Press, 1992); Suger, Abbot of Saint Denis, *Abbot Suger on the Abbey Church of St.-Denis and Its Art Treasures,* ed. and trans., Erwin Panofsky, 2d ed. (1948; reprint, Princeton, N.J.: Princeton University Press, 1979); Sumner McKnight Crosby, *The Royal Abbey of Saint-Denis: From Its Beginnings to the Death of Suger, 475–1151,* ed. Pamela Z. Blum (New Haven, Conn.: Yale University Press, 1987); Lindy Grant, *Abbot Suger of St.-Denis: Church and State in Early Twelfth-Century France* (London: Longman, 1998); Conrad Rudolph, *Artistic Change at St.-Denis: Abbot Suger's Program and the Early Twelfth-Century Controversy over Art* (Princeton, N.J.: Princeton University Press, 1990).

suicide Suicide was seemingly rare in the Middle Ages. Sources are reticent, but it is evident that suicides occurred among all social classes. The basic motives and natural methods were comparable to those of later centuries. The motives were physical and mental illness, chronic or sudden poverty, arrest, disgrace, heartbreak in love, and depression. The law in some Italian COMMUNES following Roman law considered suicide as an intrinsically innocent act. However, most legal systems condemned self-slaughter which was to be punished by the denial of church burial. Theologians corroborated general condemnations of suicide as a mortal sin with promises of hell and damnation. There is evidence that individual priests and religious orders sympathetically sought to soften the penalties and even prayed for the soul of suicides.

Further reading: Georges Minois, *History of Suicide: Voluntary Death in Western Culture,* trans. Lydia G. Cochrane (Baltimore: Johns Hopkins University Press, 1999); Alexander Murray, *Suicide in the Middle Ages.* Vol. 1, *The Violent against Themselves;* Vol. 2, *The Curse on Self-Murder* (Oxford: Oxford University Press, 1998–2000).

summa The philosophical and theological genre summa, developed in the 12th century, was supposed to be an exposition of a totality that is, a compilation or a summary and systematic presentation of knowledge in a given field. Summae were written for advancement in every field of medieval scholarship and knowledge in universities, including MEDICINE, the liberal arts, LOGIC, PHILOSOPHY, RHETORIC, SERMONS, liturgy, biblical exegesis, penitential guidance, but especially in LAW and THEOLOGY. They were intended as an overall view of an author's original thought and as a verification of his learning in a subject.

See also SCHOLASTICISM AND SCHOLASTIC METHOD; UNIVERSITIES AND SCHOOLS.

Further reading: John W. Baldwin, *The Scholastic Culture of the Middle Ages, 1000–1300* (Lexington, Mass.: Heath, 1971); Gordon Leff, *Paris and Oxford Universities in the Thirteenth and Fourteenth Centuries: An Institutional History* (New York: Wiley, 1968); Lynn Thorndike, ed., *University Records and Life in the Middle Ages* (New York: Columbia University Press, 1944).

sumptuary laws *See* CLOTHING AND COSTUME.

Sunna, Sunnis, Sunnites, and Sunnism The term Sunna designates a "usage sanctioned by tradition" or the "well-marked way." In ISLAM *sunna* designates the exemplary practice of the Prophet, or the facts, deeds, words, and silent approvals. Custom, normative precedent, conduct, and traditions are therefore based on the actions and example of MUHAMMAD and collected in the HADITH;

these actions and sayings complement the divinely revealed message of the QURAN. This orthodox knowledge, which became the *sunnah,* was passed down through generations. Sunnis stress the importance of this tradition, seeking consensus and in this process calling themselves *Ahl al-Sunnah wal-Ijma* or "the People of Custom and Community."

The Sunna movement arose out of the conflict of the midseventh century and was meant to be a middle way to help reconcile believers who had a variety of ideas. Sunni life was guided during the period up to 1500 by four schools of legal thought or *madhhabs* the Hanafi, Maliki, Shafi, and Hanbali. It was further divided by historical setting, locale, and broader culture of different groups of Muslims. Sunni Muslims were united by a belief in the legitimacy of the first four CALIPHS and agreed also that other sects had introduced dubious innovations that departed from majority belief. They considered themselves to be the orthodox Muslims and rejected excessive rationalism and intellectualism.

See also SHIA, SHIISM, AND SHIITES.

Further reading: Binyamin Abrahamov, *Islamic Theology: Traditionalism and Rationalism* Edinburgh: Edinburgh University Press, 1998); Mohamed Mohamed Yunis Ali, *Medieval Islamic Pragmatics: Sunni Legal Theorists' Models of Textual Communication* (Richmond: Curzon, 2000); Daphna Ephrat, *A Learned Society in a Period of Transition: The Sunni "ulama" of Elevent Century Baghdad* (Albany: State University of New York Press, 2000); Wael B. Hallaq, *A History of Islamic Legal Theories: An Introduction to Sunni Usul al-fiqh* (Cambridge: Cambridge University Press, 1997); G. H. A. Juynboll, "Sunna," *Encyclopedia of Islam,* 9.878–881; Christopher Melchert, *The Formation of the Sunni Schools of Law, 9th–10th Centuries* C.E. (Leiden: E. J. Brill, 1997).

Suso, Henry *See* HENRY SUSO.

Sutton Hoo Sutton Hoo was a sixth- to eighth-century Anglo-Saxon barrow grave field in Suffolk, claimed as a burial ground of the kings of East Anglia. Most of the finds were from the seventh century. It consisted of 15 to 20 circular burial visible mounds. It was best known for an extraordinary ship burial in which the impression of an 80-foot-long open boat was discovered in the sand beneath a mound. The various other burials contained rich and diverse grave goods, including a decorated helmet with face mask, a pattern welded sword, spears, a shield, gold jewelry with cloisonné garnets, glass, bits and a harness, a saddle, and fragments of a maple wood lyre. Some of these items were from the Continent and the Mediterranean. There were inhumations of three children, a woman, and a young man, some with coffins, some showing ritual trauma and evidence of cremation, along with a horse and other domestic animals. It was a place of execution during the Middle Ages and was looted many times before the 19th century.

See also BURIAL RULES AND PRACTICES; GOKSTAD SHIP; OSEBERG FIND OR SHIP.

Further reading: Rupert Bruce-Mitford, ed., *The Sutton Hoo Ship-Burial: A Handbook*, 3d ed. (London: Published for the Trustees of the British Museum by British Museum Publications Limited, 1979); M. O. H. Carver, ed., *The Age of Sutton Hoo: The Seventh Century in North-Western Europe* (Woodbridge: Boydell Press, 1992); Angela Care Evans, *The Sutton Hoo Ship Burial*, rev. ed. (London: Published for the Trustees of the British Museum by British Museum Press, 1994); Charles Green, *Sutton Hoo: The Excavation of a Royal Ship-Burial* (London: Merlin, 1988).

Swabia (Alamannia, Schwaben) Medieval Swabia, a duchy from the 10th century, took its name from the Suevi, a people who had once lived there. It became the Roman province of Rhaetia and was occupied by the Alamanni from the third century. The region had little geographical unity but included people who spoke Alemannic dialects and became modern-day SWITZERLAND, Alsace, southern Baden-Württemberg, and part of BAVARIA.

Swabia as a state was founded in the early 10th century when a comitial family appointed by the Carolingians, made their nascent state independent. Burchard I (r. 917–926) was recognized as duke, and, with his victory at Winterthur in 919, ensured control of his western frontiers with BURGUNDY. He then became the founder of the duchy of Swabia. At his death in 926 without an heir, King Henry I the Fowler of Germany (ca. 876–936) gave the title and the duchy to a Frankish noble who became Hermann I (r. 926–949). The emperor OTTO I placed his own son, Luidolf (r. 949–954), in charge of the duchy. In the second half of the 10th century, the duchy enjoyed its most success and prosperity under Duke Bouchard III (r. 954–973). Its main centers were in that area north of Lake Constance near Zurich and the Breisgau.

In the 11th century, the emperor Henry IV (r. 1050–1106) gave the duchy to his son-in-law, FREDERICK I BARBAROSSA, of the HOHENSTAUFEN family, who retained the title under their disappearance with the death of Conrad V (1252–68) or Conradin in 1268. RUDOLF of HABSBURG unsuccessfully tried to revive the duchy in the late 13th century. The title died out in 1290 and from then on Swabia was only a geographical region. The true heirs to this dukedom were the counts of Württemberg. In the early 14th century, an independent league of local towns dominated the area until the counts defeated it in battle in the late 14th century.

See also FREDERICK II, EMPEROR AND KING OF SICILY.

Further reading: Benjamin Arnold, *Medieval Germany, 500–1300: A Political Interpretation* (Toronto: University of Toronto Press, 1997); Alfred Haverkamp, *Medieval Germany, 1056–1273*, 2d ed., trans. Helga Braun and Richard Mortimer (1984; reprint, Oxford: Oxford University Press, 1988); Boyd H. Hill, *Medieval Monarchy in Action: The German Empire from Henry I to Henry IV* (New York: Barnes & Noble, 1972).

Sweden Medieval Sweden was a kingdom in eastern Scandinavia. At various times it was united with NORWAY and DENMARK. At the time of the great migrations from at least the fourth and fifth centuries, there were important population emigrations. It has been viewed contemporarily and traditionally as the area of origin for several Germanic peoples such as the Danes, the GOTHS, and the LOMBARDS.

In the very early Middle Ages, Sweden became a federation of provinces that recognized the nominal supremacy of a king designated by the Sviar or the inhabitants of Svealand. Shortly before the year 1000, the Yngling dynasty from Norway managed to unify the kingdom. Baptized early in the 11th century, Olaf Skötkonung (r. 995–1022) was the first Christian king of Sweden. Christianization was accomplished by English and German MISSIONS, and the region was put under the authority of the archbishop of Hamburg. A new episcopal see was created in about 1060 at Sigtuna near the old pagan sanctuary at Uppsala while other districts became dependent on Lund. The church in Sweden was generally to be free of much lay control.

POLITICAL CONFLICT AND A NEW CAPITAL

From the 1120s and for more than a century, Sweden was torn apart by internal struggles between two dynasties. During this period, five kings perished by violent deaths, that of Sverker I the Elder in 1155/56, Saint Erik IX Jedvardsson in 1160, Magnus Eriksson in 1161, Charles Sverkersson in 1167, and Sverker II the Younger in 1210. Canute Ericsson (r. 1173–95/96) sought the support of the towns of the HANSEATIC LEAGUE, especially LÜBECK, whose merchants were already installed at the major trading center at Visby. They developed commerce in local crafts and iron production. Erik X Canutesson (r. 1208–16) was the first Swedish king whose actual coronation was recorded in 1210. With the death of John I Sverkersson (r. 1216–22), the descendants of King Sverker I the Elder (r. 1131–55/56) died out in the male line. His successor Erik XI Ericsson (r. 1234–50) later left no direct heir at his death. A new dynasty, the Folkung, began when Waldemar (r. 1250–75) was elected as king in 1250 with Birger Jarl as regent until 1266. This monarchy was weak, exercised little if any judicial authority, and was dependent on supporting elements it could not control, such as the Thing, a sovereign assembly.

A new capital, however, was founded at Stockholm. In 1275, King Waldemar was forced off the throne by his brother, Magnus I Barnlock (r. 1275–90). In about 1280, to strengthen his military resources, Magnus granted fiscal privileges to all those who performed mounted military service for him, attaching this new aristocracy to the Crown. Taxation measures were established to provide for territorial defense. After the death of Magnus I, a struggle broke out between King Birger Magnusson (r. 1290–1318) and his brothers, Dukes Erik and Waldemar. The conflict was promoted and made possible by the restless and ambitious nobility. A civil war ended with Birger's murder of his brothers in 1317. Duke Erik's son, Magnus II Ericsson (r. 1319–63/64), ascended the throne under a regency in 1319. This young Magnus II was already king of NORWAY through his mother's family. In 1332, he added to his realm the Danish provinces of Scania and Blekinge. In about 1350, he tried to enforce a common code of law throughout the whole of this large kingdom.

UNION WITH OTHER SCANDINAVIAN KINGDOMS

In the middle of the 14th century, the Black Death created a great drop in population. The king had to face opposition from the Norwegian nobility from 1343 and then from the Swedish nobility between 1356 and 1359. He soon lost possession of Scania, Blekinge, and GOTLAND by 1361. After these disasters, the Swedish aristocracy deposed Magnus II and placed Albert of Mecklenburg (r. 1364–89) on the throne, but he was never able to establish authority over this swollen country. Albert of Mecklenburg in 1389 had to appeal for help in governing to Queen MARGARET of Denmark, who had already become the ruler of Norway and Denmark.

Striving to carry out a permanent dynastic union of Scandinavia in 1397, she called an assembly of its nobility and bishops to Kalmar in order to establish a legal basis for this Union of Kalmar, with her nephew, Erik of Pomerania (r. 1396–1439), as heir to all three thrones. By the time of her death in 1412, Margaret, however, had failed to make this union permanent and each country retained its own laws with no central governing administration. Throughout the rest of the 15th century there were numerous temporary kingships and regencies.

Engelbrekt Engelbrektsson, a noble from the Swedish mining districts of Dalecarlia, started a revolt that rapidly spread over the whole kingdom between 1434 and 1436. Erik of Pomerania was forced to recognize Engelbrekt as the regent of Sweden in 1435. Despite Engelbrekt's assassination in 1436, Erik of Pomerania never succeeded in restoring his authority over Sweden. At the death of his successor, Christopher of Bavaria (r. 1440/41–48), the Swedes refused to accept the king designated by the Danes, Christian I of Oldenburg (r. 1457–64, 1465–67). In 1448, they chose as ruler Charles Canutesson Bonde (1448–57, 1465, 1467–70). Nevertheless, Christian I was able to assume the Crown of Sweden in 1457. At his

death in 1470, he left the regency to his nephew, Sten Sture the Elder (regent 1470/71–97, 1501–03). In reality Sweden was being governed by an oligarchic regime dominated by a few powerful families, the Tott, Oxenstierna, and Vasa. Sten Sture the Elder had to recognize the sovereignty of King John of Denmark (r. 1497–1501).

See also ADAM OF BREMEN; VIKINGS.

Further reading: Ingvar Andersson, *A History of Sweden,* trans. Carolyn Hannay and Alan Blair, 2d ed. (New York: Praeger, 1970); Anna Götlind, *Technology and Religion in Medieval Sweden* (Göteborg: Distribution, Department of History, University of Göteborg, 1993); Henrik Roelvink, *Franciscans in Sweden: Medieval Remnants of Franciscan Activities* (Assen: Van Gorcum, 1998); Birgit and Peter Sawyer, *Medieval Scandinavia: From Conversion to Reformation, circa 800–1500* (Minneapolis: University of Minnesota Press, 1993); Franklin Scott, *Sweden: The Nation's History* (Minneapolis: University of Minnesota Press, 1977).

swine *See* AGRICULTURE; ANIMALS AND ANIMAL HUSBANDRY; FOOD, DRINK, AND NUTRITION.

Switzerland (Schwyz, Helvetia) The name Switzerland derives from a community of free peasants and shepherds from the valley of Schwyz, the first canton of the Swiss Confederation, which was formed in 1291. The territories that converged in the late Middle Ages to from present-day Switzerland were situated between the Jura Mountains and the Alps. They extended from Lake Leman to Lake Constance, as well as into northern LOMBARDY. They were initially peopled by Celts, Rhaetians, and Ligurians. Christianity arrived in the early fourth century. Between the early sixth century and the eighth century, all these territories passed under the control of the FRANKS when they conquered the kingdom of the BURGUNDIANS. They were subsequently divided among several rulers in the late Carolingian Empire and within the Carolingian kingdoms that followed.

They all belonged to the HOLY ROMAN EMPIRE from 1032, when HENRY III (1017–56) became king of BURGUNDY. The episcopal towns and the main abbeys became the centers of small ecclesiastical principalities that maintained themselves up to the Reformation of the 16th century and later. The Confederation formed in 1291 of numerous alliances between communities in the Alpine region connected all these free communities, both rural and urban. It was rapidly reinforced by eight new members in 1353 struggling against the HABSBURGS, the main lords of the region. In the second half of the 14th century, this *confederation* designated the territory formed by members, no longer just an alliance. The existence of this region as a sovereign country was confirmed between 1315 and 1386 in victorious battles against the Hapsburgs.

The survival of Switzerland was therefore based on political alliances and military successes against lay and ecclesiastical lords. A national identity was formed in the 15th century based on revolts against unworthy and unacceptable authorities. Switzerland, invoking divine protection soon distanced itself from any ecclesiastical hierarchy, including the PAPACY. So the COUNCILS of CONSTANCE and BASEL were held there in the 15th century. Switzerland maintained a strong military force based on its famous pikemen in the 15th century to protect its independence from the French, the dukes of Burgundy, the Habsburgs, the house of SAVOY, and the duchy of MILAN.

See also WILLIAM TELL.

Further reading: Roger Sablonier, "The Swiss Confederation," in *The New Cambridge Medieval History.* Vol. 7, *c. 1415–c. 1500,* ed. Christopher Allmand (Cambridge: Cambridge University Press, 1998), 645–670; Edgar Bonjour, H. S. Offler, and G. R. Potter, *A Short History of Switzerland* (Oxford: Clarendon Press, 1952); Jonathan Steinberg, *Why Switzerland?* 2d ed. (Cambridge: Cambridge University Press, 1996).

swords and daggers   *See* WEAPONS AND WEAPONRY.

Sylvester II, Pope (Gerbert of Aurillac) (ca. 945–1003) *scholar*
Gerbert, later Sylvester II, was born about 945 perhaps in Aurillac in the Auvergne or in Aquitaine. Of humble birth, he was educated at the BENEDICTINE monastery of Aurillac and sent to BARCELONA to study. After meeting the emperor OTTO I in ROME in 970, Gerbert spent much of the rest of his life within the orbit of the German empire. About 972 he went to RHEIMS to study and lectured there for many years. In 997 he left FRANCE for the court of OTTO III, whom he had met in Rome in 996. The emperor welcomed him as an old supporter of the imperial family and obtained his appointment as the archbishop of RAVENNA in 998. A year later Otto secured his elevation to the PAPACY. He was the first Frenchman to hold this office, taking the name Pope Sylvester II.

Sylvester II is usually credited with encouraging Otto's ambitious and universalistic visions of a restored Roman Empire with perhaps a major role for the papacy. Besides trying to encourage the spread of Christianity in Eastern Europe, he worked against SIMONY and promoted clerical CELIBACY. An accomplished scholar who devised influential teaching methods, he promoted and contributed to the study of astronomy, LOGIC, and dialectic; assisted with the introduction of Arabic numerals into mathematics; and collected ancient manuscripts. He had a reputation for dabbling in MAGIC. Leaving behind some 220 letters, he died in Rome on May 12, 1003, and was buried in Saint John Lateran.

See also HUGH CAPET, KING OF FRANCE; STEPHEN I OF HUNGARY, SAINT.

Further reading: Harriet Pratt Lattin, trans., *The Letters of Gerbert, with His Papal Privileges as Sylvester II* (New York: Columbia University Press, 1961); Eleanor Shipley Duckett, *Death and Life in the Tenth Century* (Ann Arbor: University of Michigan Press, 1967); Richard W. Southern, *The Making of the Middle Ages* (New Haven, Conn.: Yale University Press, 1953).

Symeon of Bulgaria   *See* SIMEON I.

synagogue (assembly house) A concept inherited from the ancient world in Greek *synagogue* meant "a place of assembly" as did the Hebrew, *Beth-Knesset.* In Latin it referred to the *schola judeorum* or "school of the Jews" or "*synagoga.*" This was identified with the community. In the Middle Ages the term, referred to Judaism as a whole, as opposed to the Christian Church, and was used as a widely diffused iconographical theme that intended to teach contempt for Israel.

Interior view of the Synagogue El Tránsito (Sefardi Museum) in Toledo, Spain (1366) *(Vanni / Art Resource)*

Within CHRISTENDOM lay and ecclesiastical administration usually tolerated the synagogue. Jews could use and repair synagogues but not embellish or enlarge them, nor build new ones. Jews obliged to build synagogues for public worship made them smaller or often installed them in private dwellings. The scope of activity at the synagogue included worship, education, community administration, a court of justice, and a meeting place for CONFRATERNITIES and community assemblies—it was the center of Jewish life.

There has survived little information on the origins of synagogues in Europe. They were mostly mentioned in descriptions of destruction or attack. Surviving medieval synagogues are rare. There are examples at CÓRDOBA, TOLEDO, Worms, PRAGUE, Sopron in HUNGARY, and ROUEN. Some had the external appearance of private houses. Synagogue architecture could be Moorish in SPAIN and Romanesque or Gothic in northern Europe. The interiors shared single or double naves, the *hekhal* or an ark that housed the Torah in the eastern wall, and in the center the *teba* or rostrum with a lectern for the reading of the Torah. There were benches along the sides for listeners and galleries for women. Their decoration was usually symbolic and geometrical, but sometimes figures were represented. There were frequently ritual baths.

See also ANTI-JUDAISM AND ANTI-SEMITISM; JEWS AND JUDAISM.

Further reading: Joseph Gutmann, *The Synagogue: Studies in Origins, Archaeology, and Architecture* (New York: Ktav, 1975); Lee I. Levine, *The Ancient Synagogue: The First Thousand Years* (New Haven, Conn.: Yale University Press, 2000); Anders Runesson, *The Origins of the Synagogue: A Socio-Historical Study* (Stockholm: Almqvist & Wiksell, 2001); Wolfgang S. Seiferth, *Synagogue and Church in the Middle Ages: Two Symbols in Art and Literature,* trans. Lee Chadeayne and Paul Gottwald. (New York: Ungar, 1970); Rachel Wischnitzer, *The Architecture of the European Synagogue* (Philadelphia: Jewish Publication Society of America, 1964).

Syria　Syria is the geographical area extending from the Mediterranean to the Tigris River. It is bordered to the north by the Taurus Mountains and Kurdistan and to the south by desert regions, the traditional grazing grounds of Arab nomads. It has rarely been politically unified but notably was between 660 and 1248 under the authority of the CALIPHATES of DAMASCUS and then BAGHDAD. Until the arrival of the Islamized ARABS between 634 and 636, it had been divided between, and fought over extensively by the Roman-Byzantine and Persian-Sassanid Empires. Its borders were always vague and disputed.

ONE CONQUEST AFTER THE OTHER

The conquest of Damascus in 634 and the Battle of Yarmuk in 636 led to Arab rule over Syria. From the time of the emperor JUSTINIAN it was part of the patriarchate of ANTIOCH. Authority was disputed and diffused by the creation of national churches that had rejected formulations of the Christian confession promulgated as imperial laws after the COUNCILS of EPHESUS in 431 and CHALCEDON in 451. These disagreements were anti-Byzantine reactions based on an attachment to the Aramaic language and culture as much as any doctrine. There developed a Malikite church, MONOPHYSITE versions of Christianity, the Jacobite Church, and various forms of NESTORIANISM.

The UMAYYAD dynasty, with its capital in Damascus, brought prosperity and prestige to Syria. Christians and Jews had the status of DHIMMI and were allowed to maintain their customs and law, although they had to pay a poll tax. The ABBASIDS moved their capital to Baghdad in 750 and the SELJUK TURKS in the 11th century divided the region into smaller states based around Damascus, Homs, Hamah, and ALEPPO. The FATIMIDS of EGYPT took over the eastern and coastal part of Syria in the 10th century.

During the CRUSADES in the 12th and 13th centuries, the region was the scene of much WARFARE and destruction, as the Christians and Muslims fought for control. That ended with the fall of ACRE in 1291. During that era, however, trading links were developed between Syria and the Italian MERCHANT republics of GENOA and PISA. Egyptian influence was strong and the AYYUBID dynasty of SALADIN took control of the region in the late 12th century. The MONGOLS reached Syria in 1258. The capture of Baghdad by TAMERLANE in 1401 finally ended prosperity. Syria began a long decline that lasted beyond its incorporation into the OTTOMAN EMPIRE by Selim I the Grim (r. 1512–20) in 1516.

See also AYN JALUT, BATTLE OF; BAYBARS I, SULTAN; DRUZES; JIHAD; MAMLUKS; MOSUL; NUR AL-DIN MUHAMMAD IBN ZANGI.

Further reading: Erica Dodd, *The Frescoes of Mar Musa al-Habashi: A Study in Medieval Painting in Syria* (Toronto: Pontifical Institute of Mediaeval Studies, 2001); Fred M. Donner, *The Early Islamic Conquests* (Princeton, N.J.: Princeton University Press, 1981); Josef W. Meri, *The Cult of Saints among Muslims and Jews in Medieval Syria* (Oxford: Oxford University Press, 2002); Kamal S. Salibi, *Syria under Islam: Empire on Trial, 634–1097* (Delmar: Caravan Books, 1977); Maya Shatzmiller, ed., *Crusaders and Muslims in Twelfth-Century Syria* (Leiden: E. J. Brill, 1993); Suhayl Zakkar, *The Emirate of Aleppo, 1004–1094* (Beirut: Dar al-Amanah, 1971); Nicola A. Ziadeh, *Urban Life in Syria under the Early Mamluks* (Beirut: American Press, 1953).

T

al-Tabari, Abu Jafar Muhammad ibn Jarir (839–923) *Persian historian, legal scholar, commentator on the Quran*

Born about 839 at Tabaristan in northern IRAN, al-Tabari traveled to the great centers of ISLAM. His exegesis or *Commentary* on the QURAN was among the most influential among those extant. In it he collected the philological, grammatical, legal, and theological material of earlier scholars using the orthodox SUNNI approach developed during the classical period and still used today. He inspired a school of LAW, the Jaririyya, named after him in which he sought a more exact system than the one employed until then. Besides writing a biographical dictionary, he authored a *History of the Prophets and Rulers* that ran from the creation of the world to his own time. In that he concentrated on the personal decisions of individual Muslims rather than only those of the CALIPHS or rulers. He included different perspectives and interpretations of events and motivations in Islamic and world history. As his *Commentary* was, his *History* was interpreted and compiled from traditional material. In it he gave a Muslim and universal representation of salvation history. He died in 923 at BAGHDAD.

See also IBN AL-ATHIR, IZZ AL-DIN; IBN KHALDUN, WALI AL-DIN ABD AL-RAHMAN IBN MUHAMMAD.

Further reading: al-Tabari, *The Abbasid Caliphate in Equilibrium*, trans. C. E. Bosworth (Albany: State University of New York Press, 1989), one of many volumes of translations of his history in the State University of New York series in Near Eastern Studies, Bibliotheca Persica, *The History of al-Tabari—Tarikh al-rusul wal-muluk*; Alfred J. Butler, *The Treaty of Misr in Tabari: An Essay in Criticism* (Oxford: Clarendon Press, 1913); Joseph Dahmus, *Seven Medieval Historians* (Chicago: Nelson-Hall, 1982).

Taborites   They were among the radical wings of the Czech reform movement in the years between 1419 and 1452. The first Taborites secretly met for forbidden Hussite rituals and prayers. That they celebrated at a place in southern BOHEMIA called by the biblical name of Mount Tábor, the site of Jesus' TRANSFIGURATION. One of its ideas, also discussed by John HUS, was the reception by the LAITY of communion under the form or species of both bread and wine or utraquism. The church permitted only the CLERGY to partake in both the bread and the wine. Its mission was largely nonviolent but based on far more radical ideas than those held by most other followers of Hus. There were persecutions of the Hussites' ideals after the death of King Wenceslas IV (r. 1378–1419) in August 1419 accompanied by a wave of eschatological visions about the end of the world, which they saw as imminent within a few months.

A second Tábor movement arose in March 1420, when the more radical Hussites while vainly awaiting Christ's arrival, founded a community of brothers and sisters on a biblical model and installed on a strategically important site. It, too, was given the name Tábor. These Taborites scorned reasoned THEOLOGY and dispensed with institutional churches and feast days. They sought the abolition of OATHS, courts of JUSTICE, and all worldly honors. Meanwhile, Emperor Sigismund of Luxembourg (r. 1410–37), the orthodox claimant to the throne of Bohemia from PRAGUE, launched a CRUSADE against the Hussites in July 1420. Led by Jan Žižka of Trocnov, the Taborite "soldiers of God," repelled the crusaders. But the Taborites soon succumbed to internal discord and expelled and even executed dissidents within their movement. After Žižka's death they split into two parties. Some joined the Catholic Bohemian nationalists after the Compactata of Prague in

1433 and others, the Adamites, led by Prokop Holy (d. 1434) retreated into exaggerated spiritualism and sexual excesses in an autonomous military republic in eastern Bohemia between 1425 and 1433. Initially successful, the Adamites took control of the greater part of Bohemia and MORAVIA but lost the Battle of Lipany in 1434 to the more moderate Hussites. After years of resistance, the Adamites finally gave up their religious independence and submitted to the regent of the kingdom, George of Podebrady (r. 1458–71), in September 1452.

See also BOHEMIAN BRETHREN; UTRAQUISTS AND UTRAQUISM.

Further reading: Norman Cohn, *The Pursuit of the Millennium: Revolutionary Millenarians and Mystical Anarchists of the Middle Ages* (London: Seeker & Warburg, 1957); Howard Kaminsky, *A History of the Hussite Revolution* (Berkeley: University of California Press, 1967).

Talmud   After the Hebrew Bible, the Talmud was the most important book for Medieval Judaism. Compiled over centuries by many scholars, the Talmud, was a redaction of the Jewish oral law, intended to be a complete written law or the Hebrew BIBLE. It started with a largely legislative collection, the *Mishna* completed in the early third century, that included two redactions, the Jerusalem Talmud (*Yerushalmi*) completed in Palestine in the early fifth century and the Babylonian Talmud (*Bavli*) completed early in the sixth century. Only the Babylonian Talmud was known in the West until the 12th century. A series of treatises classified into six orders, it was the traditional object of numerous commentaries the most important of which were by RASHI (Rabbi Solomon ben Isaac) and his school. Deemed essential to understanding of the Bible by Jews, the Talmud was little known to Christians before the mid-13th century except through the work of the converted Jew Petrus Alfonsi (1062–ca. 1130) and by PETER THE VENERABLE in his *Treatise against the Inveterate Obstinacy of the Jews*. During a disputation in 1240, Christian scholars discovered a Talmud, which was subsequently burned at PARIS in 1242 or 1244. As a book it was formally condemned by Pope INNOCENT IV in 1248. It was mined for polemical material and condemned by Christian authorities throughout the rest of the Middle Ages.

See also ANTI-JUDAISM AND ANTI-SEMITISM; BIBLE; JEWS AND JUDAISM; PENTATEUCH; TAM, JACOB BEN MEIR.

Further reading: Jeremy Cohen, *Living Letters of the Law: Ideas of the Jew in Medieval Christianity* (Berkeley: University of California Press, 1999); Hyam Maccoby, *The Philosophy of the Talmud* (London: Routledge Curzon, 2002); Jacob Neusner, *The Emergence of Judaism: Jewish Religion in Response to the Critical Issues of the First Six Centuries* (Lanham, Md.: University Press of America, 2000); Jacob Neusner, *The Reader's Guide to the Talmud* (Leiden: E. J. Brill, 2001); David Menahem Shohet, *The Jewish Court in the Middle Ages: Studies in Jewish Jurisprudence according to the Talmud, Geonic, and Medieval German Responsa* (1931; reprint, New York: Hermon Press, 1974).

Tam, Jacob ben Meir (Rabbenu Tam) (1100–1171) *Jewish scholar*
Born about 1100, Jacob was educated at the school of RASHI, his grandfather, at Troyes. After his formative years, he settled in the small town of Ramerupt in Champagne, where he prepared and sold wine and was also active in moneylending. His business associations gave him close contact with county authorities, and he mingled as well with large portions of the population, developing his skills for bargaining and negotiating. Jacob had become a wealthy man by the time he left Ramerupt in 1146 to settle at Troyes, where he became a leader of the Jewish community and was able devote time to scholarly work. He wrote a series of commentaries on the TALMUD, mainly concerned with demonstrating the agreement among authorities. He became well known and was consulted by the greatest of his contemporary rabbis on concerning daily life of Jews within their own communities and their relations with their Christian neighbors. His *Responsa*, which became authoritative, were scholarly treatises offering answers based on earlier interpretations. From 1160 until his death, Jacob presided over gatherings of delegations from numerous Jewish communities, from Champagne but then from all of northern FRANCE. Jacob's decisions were considered binding and were recognized as valid by communities throughout northwestern Europe. With his almost unique standing, he issued decrees and insisted that other rabbis approve them by countersigning. At the same time he wrote Tosafist biblical commentaries and hymns. He died in 1171.

Further reading: Louis Finkelstein, *Jewish Self-Government in the Middle Ages* (New York: Jewish Theological Seminary of America, 1924); Israel Moses Ta-Shama and Nissan Netzer, "Tam, Jacob ben Meir," *Encyclopedia Judaica* 15.779–781; Kenneth R. Stow, *Alienated Minority: The Jews of Medieval Latin Europe* (Cambridge, Mass.: Harvard University Press, 1992).

Tamerlane (Timur Lang, Timur Lank, Timur Leng) (1336–1405) *Mongol conqueror*
Tamerlane was born at Kesh or Kish (Shahr-I Sabz) in 1336 in Transoxiana, south of SAMARKAND. He was a member of a family of Turkish princes attached to MONGOL khans but claiming descent from JENGHIZ Khan. He was handicapped by deformities on his right side, probably from an old wound. He set himself the task of reconstructing the empire of Jenghiz Khan and of becoming the greatest conqueror of all time. After years of war, in 1364–65 he freed Transoxiana from the rule of a Mongol khan, and he became the king of that province five years later. He maintained the fiction of Mongol power but

substituted the rule of the Turks for that of the Mongols. He was supported by local Muslim elites and Sufis and employed religious leaders of the Naqshbandi Tariqah, a Sufi order from BUKHARA, in his administration.

CONQUEST AND PLUNDER

From 1370 he began the first of many expeditions, often ill coordinated and aborted but backed by a strong military force in a purposefully intimidating climate of terror. He captured Khwarizm and pushed farther east. In India he destroyed Delhi in 1398. He invaded and conquered AFGHANISTAN and IRAN with frightful massacres in 1387. He entered conflict with the khan of the Golden Horde and ravaged southern RUSSIA. He then entered IRAQ, pillaged BAGHDAD, and marched on to ravage ALEPPO and DAMASCUS. He forced the MAMLUKS to recognize his hegemony. In 1400 the princes of eastern ANATOLIA, worried about the progress of the OTTOMANS, called Timerlane to help them. He defeated the forces of Sultan BAYAZID in a decisive battle at Ankara on July 28, 1402. The sultan was taken prisoner and died the following year, murdered in a cage in prison. In 1403 he left Anatolia and was preparing to undertake a great expedition against China when he divided his empire among his sons. He died at Otrar in 1405. His empire soon fell apart; the Timurid dynasty survived only as the Moghuls of Delhi in India and local rulers in Khurasan and Transoxania.

LEGACY

Tamerlane failed to establish a lasting state. His expeditions were only massively devastating raids rather than anything leading to lasting conquests. He was considered by CHRISTENDOM as an ally against the Ottoman Turks. He reduced Ottoman power and prolonged the survival of the BYZANTINE EMPIRE for another 50 years. His capital, Samarkand, was a great commercial center which he embellished with numerous MOSQUES and MADRASAS. His RELICS in Samarkand are still visited by pilgrims.

Further reading: Ahmad ibn Muhammad ibn Arabshah, *Tamerlane: or Timur, the Great Amir,* trans. J. H. Sanders (Lahore: Progressive Books, 1976); Ruy González de Clavijo, *Embassy to Tamerlane, 1403–1406,* trans. Guy Le Strange (New York: Harper & Row, 1928); Beatice Forbes Manz, *The Rise and Rule of Tamerlane* (Cambridge: Cambridge University Press, 1989); Thomas W. Lentz and Glen D. Lowry, *Timur and the Princely Vision: Persian Art and Culture in the Fifteenth Century* (Washington, D.C.: Arthur M. Sackler, Gallery, 1989).

Tancred of Hauteville (1075/76–1112) *Norman crusader, prince of Antioch*

Tancred was the cousin or nephew of BOHEMOND of Taranto. His mother was Emma, the wife of Odo of Montferrat and the sister of ROBERT Guiscard. He was born in 1075/76, a younger son in the Hauteville family. He was ambitious, violent, unscrupulous, landless, and poor. In the fall of 1096 he set out with Bohemond on the First CRUSADE. He fought well against mercenaries sent to the Balkan Peninsula by the Byzantine emperor ALEXIOS I to block the Norman advance. After crossing into ANATOLIA, Tancred was present at the conquest of the town of Nicaea in 1097. Along with Baldwin of Boulogne, he separated from the rest of the army and with the assistance of some Armenian Christians took possession of several cities in Cilicia in southeastern Anatolia. Unable to get along with Baldwin, Tancred rejoined the crusading army besieging ANTIOCH. After that city's fall in June 1098, Tancred joined the Crusading armies in the capture of JERUSALEM in 1099.

With GODFREY de Bouillon, Tancred took part in the founding of the Kingdom of Jerusalem, becoming the vassal prince of Galilee. After Bohemond had been captured by Muslims in 1100, Tancred gave the principality of Galilee to Baldwin of Boulogne, now King BALDWIN I of Jerusalem, who had recently been his rival for the Crown, and moved north to act as regent for the captive Bohemond for the rich principalities of Antioch and EDESSA. This arrangement became permanent when Bohemond had to return to Europe in 1111 for money and armed aid. Arriving in his new principality, Tancred embarked on a policy of expansion against the Muslims and Byzantines, as he tried to establish a defensible state in SYRIA and Cilicia and along the upper Euphrates River. In 1112 as he was about to attack Armenians in Cilicia, he died, perhaps of typhus, on December 12, 1112. He left his principalities to his nephew, Roger of Salerno (r. 1112–19).

See also LATIN STATES IN GREECE; NORMANS IN ITALY.

The siege and surrender of Tarsus to Tancred of Hauteville, from the *Roman de Godefroi de Bouillon,* Ms. fr. 22495, fol. 32v (1337), Bibliothèque Nationale, Paris *(Giraudon / Art Resource)*

Further reading: Raimundus de Agiles, *Historia Francorum qui ceperunt Iherusalem,* trans. John Hugh Hill and Laurita L. Hill (Philadelphia: American Philosophical Society, 1968); Michael Foss, *People of the First Crusade* (New York: Arcade, 1997); John France, *Victory in the East: A Military History of the First Crusade* (Cambridge: Cambridge University Press, 1994); Robert L. Nicholson, *Tancred: A Study of His Career and Work in Their Relation to the First Crusade and the Establishment of the Latin States in Syria and Palestine* (1940; reprint, New York: AMS Press, 1978).

tapestry　This textile is created by sewing patterns with different colored threads of wool or needlework to create a desired iconographical representation, design, or motif across a cloth canvas stretched on a loom, a technique that resembles carpet making.

The art or craft of tapestry originated in the East, probably in central Asia. The oldest surviving example in Europe dates from the 11th century. Its real development began in the 14th century, when tapestry was seen not just as a fabric but as a way to preserve stories, as in mural painting. Tapestry was portable and was warmer than other media used for painting, especially when it could cover large, drafty wall surfaces in chambers in castles or churches.

The rooms of the wealthy in Europe soon became covered with tapestries made in FLANDERS and BRABANT, in such towns as Arras, Tournai, and Brussels. The tapestry market was brokered by MERCHANTS who took orders. Painters worked out models to be placed behind the loom as models or patterns for weavers. Several weavers and workshops were then needed to accomplish the labor needed for any single hanging. A single weaver could create square yard or meter in a year. The threads were of wool, silk for light colors, silver, and gold, all within a restricted range of natural colors. In the later Middle Ages and Renaissance, tapestry began merely to reproduce already known paintings; thus weavers lost their autonomy as designers and tapestry lost much of its individuality and originality.

Further reading: Anna G. Bennett, ed., *Five Centuries of Tapestry from the Fine Arts Museums of San Francisco* (San Francisco: Fine Arts Museums of San Francisco, 1992); Metropolitan Museum of Art, New York, *Medieval Tapestries in the Metropolitan Museum of Art,* ed. Adolfo Salvatore Cavallo (New York: H. N. Abrams, 1993); Victoria and Albert Museum, *The Tapestry Collection: Medieval and Renaissance,* ed. George Wingfield Digby and Wendy Hefford (London: H.M.S.O., 1980).

Tatars (Tartars)　*See* MONGOLS AND MONGOL EMPIRE.

Tauler, John　*See* JOHN TAULER.

taverns　*See* INNS AND TAVERNS.

taxation, taxes, and tribute　Medieval taxation, or sometimes tribute, were required payments in kind or coin to a public authority for protection or other services. It was not repayable. Taxation was fundamental to the development of the national state, the rise of parliamentary institutions, the consequent limiting of royal power, economic development, innovation in commercial and banking techniques, and demands for reform of the church. Taxes could be direct on wealth or indirect on consumption.

The history of taxation in the barbarian kingdoms of the early Middle Ages involved the disappearance many of the fiscal practices of the Roman Empire, by the time of CHARLEMAGNE, all that remained were tolls and taxes on goods transported by land and water. At the same time, the armed service required from freemen was giving way to or being traded for the payment of a replacement tax, such as SCUTAGE. The collapse of the central Carolingian government from the second half of the ninth century led to the weakened of the collection system of the tax structure and fiscal authority. Until the 13th century, feudal rights and seigniorial rents continued to make up the greater part of the revenues of the royal treasuries. The papacy tried to help or manipulate and motivate princes financially by organizing proposed Crusades in the 12th century and offering to tax the clergy. During the 13th century, as the revenues of princes became insufficient, states and bureaucracies were to seek new sources of income in various forms of direct and indirect taxes on property and commerce. New taxation systems of states were established, but they sometimes then had to be legitimized and eventually approved by the subjects of the Crown or state. PARLIAMENT and the representation of social estates became necessary involved and tended to set conditions and limits of taxation, either direct or indirect taxes. In cities, representative bodies became similarly involved. There were disagreements about sources of revenue, methods of evaluation, and means of collection. Their consent, although not always needed, was clearly crucial to tax collection.

BYZANTINE TAXATION

The Byzantine fiscal system rested on a land tax that was in turn based on an assessment, on a variety of customs taxes, and on municipal sales taxes. The most essential role was played by a cadastral land tax linked with defined pieces of property. This tax was calculated in cash but sometimes paid in kind. In the middle Byzantine period, these land taxes of peasants were calculated in terms of surface area of their holding according to a fiscal value established by periodic surveys. In about 1300, livestock began to be taxed.

ECCLESIASTICAL TAXATION

The church's first financial system rested on its landed property or patrimony, as well as gifts, alms, and legacies. All these forms continued throughout the Middle Ages. Bishops administered the goods and incomes of their churches. However, clerical families, lay donors or founders, and their descendants considered their church and its fabric and fiscal rights as a private property. This was an issue of lay control and was one of the principal concerns of the GREGORIAN REFORM. TITHES on incomes of all types were to be paid by the laity and were used mainly to support pastoral care, local churches, and parishes. Bishops and dioceses taxed these parishes and collected money in other ways such as the right of SPOIL on deceased clerics. Clerics began to charge for specific services. The popes, especially those residing at AVIGNON, sought every opportunity to tax the clergy, developed an elaborate fiscal bureaucracy, and needed strong links with Italian bankers to move their monies around. The costly Crusades demanded large taxes and elaborate machinery to collect funds, move the wealth around Europe, and send it to the eastern Mediterranean. The church as a result became more and more identified with this sort of fund-raising. The avarice of the church and its clergy became a topic of satire and a cause of demands for reform in the later Middle Ages and Renaissance, but little was done to control even abuses.

TAXATION IN ISLAM

Payment of taxes is considered a religious duty by Muslims. The most important tax was the *zakah*. It was based on wealth at a standard rate of 2.5 percent of what was considered to be surplus income. It was to be paid to the poor and needy. The *jizyah* or poll tax was paid by non-Muslim but protected members of an Islamic state, the DHIMMI, in exchange for protection and toleration. The land tax or *kharaj* was applied to Muslims and non-Muslims according to the amount of land they owned and its potential output.

Further reading: J. B. Henneman, *Royal Taxation in Fourteenth Century France: The Development of War Financing, 1322–1356* (Princeton, N.J.: Princeton University Press, 1971); A. H. M. Jones, *The Later Roman Empire, 284–602: A Social, Economic and Administrative Survey* (Oxford: Blackwell, 1964); Walter Goffart, *Caput and Colonate: Towards a History of Late Roman Taxation* (Toronto: University of Toronto Press, 1974); Frede Løkkegaard, *Islamic Taxation in the Classic Period, with Special Reference to Circumstances in Iraq* (Copenhagen: Branner & Korch, 1950); Sydney Knox Mitchell, *Taxation in Medieval England,* ed. Sidney Painter (New Haven, Conn.: Yale University Press, 1951).

technology   There was little systematic or theoretical thought about work and technology in the Middle Ages, although people were constantly and rationally finding technological assistance for what they had to do. There were numerous technological advances during the period. In the 12th century HUGH OF SAINT-VICTOR was attentive to the reality of work and eager to associate a certain intellectual dignity with the production of objects. He included in his universal classification of knowledge the seven mechanical arts as complementary to the SEVEN LIBERAL ARTS. The mechanical arts comprised the manufacture of woolen cloth, the production of armaments, and the practices of NAVIGATION, AGRICULTURE, HUNTING, MEDICINE, and the THEATER. Iconography, archaeological sources, manorial documents, accounts, commercial correspondence, and travel literature reflect considerable technological change and innovation, in mining, metalworking, water and wind MILLS, agriculture, cloth production, shipbuilding, methods of work, record keeping on accounting, and business technique and organization.

See also ALCHEMY; METALSMITHS AND METAL WORKING, METALLURGY; SHIPS AND SHIPBUILDING; TEXTILES.

Further reading: Grenville Astill and John Langdon, eds., *Medieval Farming and Technology: The Impact of Agricultural Change in Northwest Europe* (Leiden: E. J. Brill, 1997); Kelly DeVries, *A Cumulative Bibliography of Medieval Military History and Technology* (Leiden: E. J. Brill, 2002); Ahmad Yusuf Hasan, *Islamic Technology: An Illustrated History* (Cambridge: Cambridge University Press, 1986); Claudia Kren, *Medieval Science and Technology: A Selected, Annotated Bibliography* (New York: Garland, 1985); Pamela O. Long, ed., *Science and Technology in Medieval Society* (New York: New York Academy of Sciences, 1985).

Templars (Knights of the Temple Pauperes commilitones Christi templi Solomonici)   They were a military and religious order founded to protect pilgrims and the Christian states founded on Palestine and the Lerant. After the capture of JERUSALEM in July 1099, some KNIGHTS decided to stay there to protect and serve the canons of the church of the HOLY SEPULCHER. A small group under Hugh de Payens (ca. 1070–1136) determined to live according to a religious rule, which was approved by the king of Jerusalem and the patriarch in 1120. This first military order, called the Order of the Chivalry of the Poor Knights or Soldiers of Christ, was better known by the name of their house, the Temple of Solomon. They were approved again in January 1128 at the Council of Troyes. Their rule was written by BERNARD OF CLAIRVAUX. The Templars' main mission then was the armed protection of pilgrims. A papal bull in 1139 made them responsible only to the PAPACY.

The Templars wore a white cloak or mantle with a red cross with a half-white, half-black banner. Their constitution provided for an elected grand master, provinces, districts, and individual preceptories, some

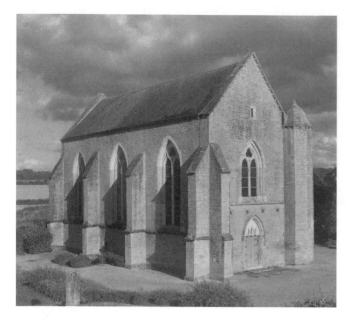

A 13th-century Templar chapel on one of their former estates near Vézelay in central France (*Courtesy Edward English*)

with distinctive round churches. The Templars took the vows of obedience, CHASTITY, and POVERTY. They were fanatically and singularly dedicated to war, especially against Muslims, and soon were engaged in battles for the defense of the LATIN STATES in the East, making up a veritable standing defense force. They were disciplined and efficient fighters and became essential to the survival of those states.

The number of fighting knights, never more than 300 or 400, was supplemented by light CAVALRY, archers, and foot soldiers. They built powerful fortresses at Baghras, Tortosa, Le Fève, and Safed which acquired importance in the 13th century when the Latins were limited to the defensive. They also fought in SPAIN in the RECONQUEST. Empowered by copious donations, they became rich and sent men, war material, provisions, and money to PALESTINE. Their wealth and privileges provoked jealously, especially after the disastrous collapse of the crusading states with the fall of ACRE in 1291. Their link with the papacy positioned them between the popes and the kingdom of FRANCE under PHILIP IV THE FAIR, who accused the Templars of many crimes, including HERESY and WITCHCRAFT, and had them arrested in his realm in October of 1307. This ultimately led to the suppression of the order at the Council of Vienne in 1312 and the execution of the last master, JAMES of Molay, in 1314. Their property was confiscated by the Crown and parts of it were distributed to other orders, especially the HOSPITALLERS.

See also CHIVALRY; CLEMENT V, POPE; CRUSADES; HATTIN, BATTLE OF HORNS OF; MILITARY ORDERS.

Further reading: J. M. Upton-Ward, trans., *The Rule of the Templars: The French Text of the Rule of the Order of the Knights Templar* (Woodbridge, England: Boydell Press,

2001); Malcolm Barber, *The Trial of the Templars* (Cambridge: Cambridge University Press, 1978); Malcolm Barber, *The New Knighthood: A History of the Order of the Temple* (Cambridge: Cambridge University Press, 1994); Alan Forey, *The Military Orders: From the Twelfth to the Early Fourteenth Century* (Toronto: University of Toronto Press, 1992); Peter Partner, *The Murdered Magicians: The Templars and Their Myth* (Oxford: Oxford University Press, 1982).

testaments   *See* WILLS AND TESTAMENTS.

Teutonic Knights, Order of (*Ordo domus sanctae Mariae Teutonicorum*)   The military order of the Teutonic Knights was similar to the other orders but less concerned with the Holy Land and the CRUSADES in the Levant. It originated at a hospital at Saint John of ACRE established by German crusaders. This hospice, reserved for German pilgrims, was founded by MERCHANTS from LÜBECK and Bremen and linked to the German army of the duke of SWABIA in 1191. With military intent of the TEMPLARS and the charitable ones of the HOSPITALLERS, the hospital of the Germans at Acre led to an order that was approve by Pope Celestine III (r. 1191–98) in 1196 and confirmed in 1198. Its members and support were almost exclusively from Germany.

GROWTH OF POWER

At the end of the 12th century, however, the Teutonic Knights had little opportunity to do much in the Holy Land. The orders of the Templars and Hospitallers had been established much longer and dominated its defense. The Germans built the CASTLE of Montfort, where the grand master had his residence until 1271, did participate in the last wars of the crusaders. The father of Saint ELIZABETH of Hungary called them to help defend central Europe. Between 1211 and 1225, they moved to TRANSYLVANIA to defend against the CUMANS. Elizabeth founded a hospital at Marburg and gave it to the knights, who made it their center in Europe. About 1225, they were asked for assistance against the pagan Prussians living along the Baltic Sea. The order's early years were dominated by the grand master Hermann of Salza (r. 1209–39). After Hermann alone supported the excommunicated emperor FREDERICK II during his successful crusade, in JERUSALEM, the order gained many advantages, rights, donations, and privileges. After Frederick's death, however, the order followed a policy independent of subsequent emperors.

The order initially followed the Rule of the Temple or Templars and that of the Hospitallers. By 1215 it had detailed internal regulations. Members were to be nobles without other obligations older than 14 years of age, without a wife, debts, or physical handicap. They wore a white cloak with a black cross. Their daily life consisted of brief prayers, MASS, military duties, and, for monks, FASTING, personal poverty, and vows of obedience. The head of the order was an elected grand master, who was assisted by a grand commander and a general chapter. Any WARFARE was entrusted to a marshal. The grateful Frederick II in 1226 by the Golden Bull of Rimini had granted them seigniorial rights, including taxation of customs, a mint, a market, and the BAN to enforce peasant labor. This allowed the Teutonic Order, as did the bishoprics and abbeys of the empire, to form territorial states, as in East Prussia from the 13th century, and to become a regional political, economic, and religious power.

COLONIZATION AND DECLINE

From then on the knights' history was basically confined to PRUSSIA. They were instrumental in great planned colonization movements that settled perhaps 400,000 people in their newly carved out domain. In the course of their progress east, the Teutonic Knights were stopped in the penetration of Russia in 1242 or 1243 at Lake Pevipus by the troops of Prince Alexander NEVSKY. The grand master then established himself in Marienburg from 1309. After the knights took Pomerania, their progress eastward was halted by a crushing defeat at the Battle of Tannenberg or Grünwald in 1411 in a confrontation with Ladislas II Jagiello of LITHUANIA and POLAND. By 1466 their power was reduced to East Prussia as vassals to the king of Poland.

See also CHIVALRY; HANSEATIC LEAGUE; LIVONIA; LÜBECK; MILITARY ORDERS.

Further reading: William L. Urban, *The Baltic Crusade,* 2d ed. (1975; reprint, Chicago: Lithuanian Research and Studies Center, 1994); William L. Urban, *The Prussian Crusade* (Lanham, Md.: University Press of America, 1980); Michael Burleigh, *Prussian Society and the German Order: An Aristocratic Corporation in Crisis c. 1410–1466* (Cambridge: Cambridge University Press, 1984); Eric Christiansen, *The Northern Crusades: The Baltic and the Catholic Frontier, 1100–1525* (1980; reprint, New York: Penguin Books, 1997); Alan Forey, *The Military Orders: From the Twelfth to the Early Fourteenth Century* (Toronto: University of Toronto Press, 1992); Helen Nicholson, *Love, War and the Grail* (Leiden: Brill, 2001).

textiles   Textiles in the Middle Ages were made from vegetable and animal materials. Flax was produced in the humid regions of northwestern Europe and was much prized for the production of high-quality linen cloth. Cotton was grown and was an object of commerce in Mediterranean regions. Hemp was used to make up household linen of mediocre quality and was commercially produced for ropes and sails. Wool from the 12th century was the object of long- and mid-distance commerce. English wool and Mediterranean merino were considered to be the best. Luxury fabrics. Flemish textiles were initially produced in the LOW COUNTRIES and BRABANT, but NORMANDY, ENGLAND, the LANGUEDOC, Roussillon, CATALONIA, and ITALY were also centers of production of increasingly better-quality fabrics. Cloth manufacture and the weaving industry were major activities in many towns in the later Middle Ages, with some production done in the countryside.

Flourishing first in the Sassanian and Byzantine East, the rearing of silkworms and the preparation of SILK thread reached the West through the Muslim world, in SPAIN and SICILY. From there it spread to towns all over Europe, but especially in Spain, northern Italy, and AVIGNON, many of which became well known for its production.

See also CLOTHING AND COSTUME; FLORENCE; LUCCA; SILK AND SILK ROADS; TAPESTRY.

Further reading: Elisabeth Crowfoot, *Textiles and Clothing: c. 1150–c. 1450* (London: H.M.S.O., 1992); Désirée G. Koslin and Janet E. Snyder, eds., *Encountering Medieval Textiles and Dress: Objects, Texts, Images* (New York: Palgrave Macmillan, 2002); John H. A. Munro, *Textiles, Towns and Trade: Essays in the Economic History of Late-Medieval England and the Low Countries* (Aldershot: Variorum, 1994); Annemarie Stauffer, *Textiles of Late Antiquity* (New York: Metropolitan Museum of Art, 1995); Thelma K. Thomas, *Textiles from Medieval Egypt, A.D. 300–1300* (Pittsburgh: Carnegie Museum of Natural History, 1990).

theater   Theater in the Middle Ages began with simple forms usually in LATIN sponsored by the church. This eventually led to a wide variety of VERNACULAR and secular productions in the later Middle Ages which included real characters. The plays were performed out of doors, not necessarily next to a church, and were sponsored by lay organizations such as CONFRATERNITIES and craft GUILDS. They often included popular and courtly entertainment such as dancing, games, festivals, and folk rituals, with performances of professional minstrels, dancers, jugglers, and acrobats, singly or in roving bands.

Most theatrical activity was not approved by the CLERGY since their control of the content was allegedly minimal, although many clerics actually participated in their production, particularly as writers. The medieval theater remained, however, heavily didactic. Even the more secular productions were full of the dramatic problems of the human condition and the relation of humankind to GOD. The tales depicted in medieval theater reinforced moral teachings rather than dealing with doctrinal problems or the discussion of the issues found in SERMONS and other forms of religious instruction. They were especially concerned with the consequences of SIN and the value to the individual of the VIRTUES.

See also DRAMA; FABLES AND FABLIAUX OR COMIC TALES; HROTSWITHA OF GANDERSHEIM; MORALITY PLAYS; MYSTERY AND MIRACLE PLAYS; YORK PLAYS.

Further reading: Richard Beadle, ed., *The Cambridge Companion to Medieval English Theatre* (Cambridge: Cambridge University Press, 1994); Jody Enders, *The Medieval Theater of Cruelty: Rhetoric, Memory, Violence* (Ithaca, N.Y.: Cornell University Press, 1999); Shmuel Moreh, *Live Theatre and Dramatic Literature in the Medieval Arab World* (Edinburgh: Edinburgh University Press, 1992); Eckehard Simon, ed., *The Theatre of Medieval Europe: New Research in Early Drama* (Cambridge: Cambridge University Press, 1991); Charlotte Stern, *The Medieval Theater in Castile* (Binghamton: Medieval & Renaissance Texts & Studies, 1996); Ronald W. Vince, ed., *A Companion to the Medieval Theatre* (New York: Greenwood Press, 1989).

Theodora I (495/500–548) *Byzantine empress, wife of Justinian I*

Theodora's life has been related to us primarily through the writings of PROCOPIUS OF CAESAREA. In his *Secret History* he was particularly revealing about her notorious and scandalous life. She supposedly grew up amid the disreputable carnival atmosphere of the circus factions in CONSTANTINOPLE. She was said to have been an actress and a prostitute. Justinian persuaded his uncle, the emperor Justin I (ca. 450–527), to abrogate the laws that prevented members of the senatorial class from marrying actresses in 525. It would appear that Justinian, who became emperor in 527, was devoted to her and that her influence was substantial. She particularly helped fortify his resolve in quelling the "Nika revolt" in 532.

Though despised by the aristocracy, Theodora became well known and loved for her charitable works, palace, intrigues, and ruthless political maneuvers. She and Justinian never produced children, although she had had children by other men before her marriage. In matters of ecclesiastical policy, she took a particularly independent line, remaining a convinced and supportive MONOPHYSITE in opposition to her husband. However, she did not in the end much influence Justinian's religious policies. She died of cancer in Constantinople on June 28, 548.

See also BELISARIUS; BYZANTINE EMPIRE AND BYZANTIUM; CONSTANTINOPLE; HAGIA SOPHIA.

Further reading: Procopius, *Secret History of Procopius*, trans. Richard Atwater (Ann Arbor: University of Michigan Press, 1963); Antony C. Bridge, *Theodora: Portrait in a Byzantine Landscape* (London: Cassell, 1978); Robert Browning, *Justinian and Theodora* (London: Weidenfeld and Nicolson, 1971); Averil Cameron, *Procopius and the Sixth Century* (Berkeley: University of California

The court of Empress Theodora, Byzantine mosaic, sixth century, San Vitale, Ravenna, Italy *(Scala / Art Resource)*

Press, 1985); Charles Diehl, *Byzantine Empresses,* trans. Harold Bell and Theresa de Kerpely (New York: Knopf, 1963); J. A. S. Evans, *The Age of Justinian: The Circumstances of Imperial Power* (New York: Routledge, 1996).

Theodoric the Great, the Ostrogoth (Theoderic, Theodoric the Amal, Dietrich of Bern in the *Nibelungenlied*) (ca. 454/455–526) *Ostrogothic king of northern Italy*

The son of Theodemir of the ruling Ostrogothic Amal dynasty, Theodoric was born around 454 or 455 in PANNONIA. At the time his tribe, the OSTROGOTHS, were federates or allies of the Roman Empire, Theodoric was sent in 462 as a hostage to the imperial court at CONSTANTINOPLE, where he received a classical education. He returned home in 472 to defeat, and kill the king of the Sarmatians and then captured Singidunum or Belgrade claiming it for himself, even though he was in the service and pay of the Eastern Empire. In 484 his dying father named him leader of the Ostrogoths.

Theodoric eventually was made a patrician and military official for the Eastern Empire. He persuaded the emperor Zeno (r. 474–491) to allow him go to ITALY to free it from the domination of another barbarian general, ODOACER. Through diplomatic maneuvering and military successes, he had defeated Odoacer by 493. In the meantime other BARBARIAN tribes entered Italy and caused considerable damage. He worked out a deal with Odoacer, who had fled to RAVENNA, to divide power in Italy. But he soon accused Odoacer of plotting against him and supposedly executed him with his own hands in 493/494. As a result, he became king of the Germanic or Gothic barbarians in Italy and a representative of the Eastern Empire.

THEODORIC'S POWER EXPANDS

At Ravenna Theodoric assumed the title of lord and began to wear purple clothing confirming his imperial ambitions. He fought successful wars against the kings in the north such as CLOVIS, even annexing PROVENCE to Italy and linking himself with the VISIGOTHS in SPAIN and southern FRANCE. From then on his rule in Italy was generally moderate and peaceful; he never claimed to be an emperor but behaved as if he were. He employed Romans such as BOETHIUS and CASSIODORUS. In about 500 he issued an important edict setting out civil and criminal law and legal procedures for both the GOTHS and the Romans but recognizing their traditional and national laws in other matters. Although he remained an ARIAN, he was initially impartial in his dealings with the church of Rome, helping to settle administrative questions but avoiding doctrinal matters to prevent offending the Eastern Church in Constantinople. This policy was effective for a while, but the Byzantines were not ready to abandon their meddling in the ecclesiastical affairs of the West. For a while his government was influential over SICILY, PROVENCE, BAVARIA, and southern AUSTRIA.

THE TROUBLED END OF HIS REIGN

In the later years of his life, Theodoric became suspicious, almost paranoid, about the loyalty of those around him. He also responded to the Byzantine emperor's opposition to Arians in the empire by imposing stricter constraints on the Catholics in Italy. He had Boethius executed for treason on little evidence, except his alleged involvement in a vague senatorial conspiracy. He became less moderate in his religious policies and intervened directly in ecclesiastical affairs to install his own candidate in office as pope. He died suddenly of dysentery on August 30, 526 and was buried in Ravenna. At the time he was planning stronger measures against the Catholics but urging reconciliation and recommending Athalaric (r. 526–534), the son of his daughter, Amalasuntha (498–535), as his heir. However, the succession was disputed and the Byzantines intervened militarily. The long and destructive Gothic Wars resulted.

See also JUSTINIAN I, BYZANTINE EMPEROR; NIBELUNGENLIED.

Further reading: Patrick Amory, *People and Identity in Ostrogothic Italy, 489–554* (Cambridge: Cambridge University Press, 1997); Thomas S. Burns, *A History of the Ostrogoths* (Bloomington: Indiana University Press, 1984); Peter Heather, *The Goths* (Oxford: Blackwell Publishers, 1996); Thomas Hodgkin, *Theodoric the Goth: the Barbarian Champion of Civilization* (New York: G. P. Putnam's Sons, 1891); John Moorhead, *Theoderic in Italy* (Oxford: Clarendon Press, 1992).

Theodosian Code

The Theodosian Code was a collection of imperial constitutions running from Constantine's proclamation of Christianity in 312 up until 437. Divided into 16 books, it was compiled in six to eight years by a commission established by the emperor Theodosios II (r. 401–450) in 429. Theodosios promulgated the code in CONSTANTINOPLE, shortly after he gave his daughter, Eudokia, in marriage to the Western emperor, Valentinian III (r. 425–455), on October 29, 437. He then proclaimed that after January 1, 438, no law from the era of Constantine and issued before the end of 437 could have legal force unless it was repeated in the new code, which superseded all earlier collections. A copy of the code was taken to ROME and officially received in December 438. It is from this copy that all surviving manuscripts, extracts in Latin, or quotations in Latin of the Theodosian Code have been derived. Though compiled in Constantinople, most of its contents involve western material.

The Theodosian Code was designed for practical use by magistrates in deciding court cases and as a supplement to existing law and the writings of the pre-Constantinian jurists. Because the compilers did not seek to impose internal consistency, contradictory rulings were allowed to stand. There was probably no central archival source, and much therefore had to be assembled and discovered in dispersed regional and personal archives. Indexes were planned, and wording was only amended for the sake of textual clarity. Modern research has exposed an error rate as high as 35 percent in transcription; the dating necessary for the validity of the laws and applied to many entries is unreliable, and not all of the texts originally collected have survived except in other collections.

Further reading: Clyde Pharr, trans., *The Theodosian Code and Novels and the Sirmondian Constitutions* (Princeton, N.J.: Princeton University Press, 1952); this translation, unreliable in tenor and meaning, it must be used with care; Jill Harries and Ian Wood, eds., *The Theodosian Code* (Ithaca, N.Y.: Cornell University Press, 1993); John Matthews, *Laying Down the Law: A Study of the Theodosian Code* (New Haven, Conn.: Yale University Press, 2000).

Theodulf of Orléans (ca. 750–821) *bishop of Orléans, abbot of Fleury*

Originally a Visigoth from Spain, Theodulf moved to the court of CHARLEMAGNE in 788 and soon became highly respected for his theological and learning. He was a legate in FRANCE in 798 and took part in the council examining the false charges made against Pope LEO III (r. 795–816) in ROME in 800. A skilled poet, he was interested in educational and diocesan reforms. He wrote theological treatises on the HOLY SPIRIT and on Baptism. Charlemagne appointed him bishop of Orléans, where he founded what was to become a famous school. He also constructed and restored churches, was active in promoting pastoral care, and is now considered to be the author of the *LIBRI CAROLINI*, whose focus was the ICONOCLASM dispute then dividing East and West. Implicated in the revolt of Bernard of Italy in 817, Theodulf was deposed by LOUIS THE PIOUS and sent into exile. He died in 821.

See also CAROLINGIAN RENAISSANCE.

Further reading: Carl I. Hammer, *Charlemagne's Months and Their Bavarian Labours: The Politics of the Seasons in the Carolingian Empire* (Oxford: Archeopress, 1997); Lawrence Nees, *A Tainted Mantle: Hercules and the Classical Tradition at the Carolingian Court* (Philadelphia: University of Pennsylvania Press, 1991); Lawrence Nees, *Early Medieval Art* (Oxford: Oxford University Press, 2002); Luitpold Wallach, *Diplomatic Studies in Latin and Greek Documents from the Carolingian Age* (Ithaca, N.Y.: Cornell University Press, 1977).

theology, schools of

Theology is a Greek concept of study taken over by Christian thinkers to provide an intellectual framework for the correct knowledge and understanding of GOD. From at least the fourth century theology encompassed almost constant conflicts over many and varied issues. In the fourth century, many of these concerned the question whether MARY was the mother of Christ, or God, and the relationship between the human and divine natures of Christ. By the 11th century, with the application of principles from grammar and dialectic to Christian doctrine, theological questions had evolved into discussions about the presence of the body and blood of Christ in the Eucharist, why humankind needed to be redeemed by Christ, the union of God with human nature, the reconciliation of faith and reason, the Trinity, the conflict between belief and understanding, and the exercise of free will.

The 13th century was marked by the profound and questioned influence of the newly translated writings of ARISTOTLE. This led to questions about causation, form, matter, essence, existence or being, potency, and act. All this was compounded by a new knowledge of other non-Christian writers such as IBN SINA (Avicenna), IBN RUSHD (Averroës), and MAIMONIDES. In the university environment of the 14th and 15th centuries, theology was shaped by the rival influences of AUGUSTINE of Hippo and Aristotle, as well as by the standard practice of commenting on the *Sentences* of PETER LOMBARD. There were debates about whether theology was a science or simply a consideration of the given truths of FAITH. Greater attention to logic and language provoked discussion about whether human beings could define God or his power in any way.

ISLAM

In ISLAM dogma was sometimes the object of intense speculation and controversy in KALAM. In the Middle Ages, the fundamental opposition was between SUNNIS and Mutazilites on two points, the nature of God and the relations between God and human beings. They both assumed that their theologians could be rationalist and believed that most of the truths of faith could be established by reasoning, without recourse to revelation, which would merely confirm them. Both schools generally admitted one and the same world system, based on the theory of atomism and the distinction between substance and accident. They differed over the attributes of God; the nature of the QURAN—whether it was created or eternal; and ideas about God's JUSTICE, the GRACE of God, and rewards and punishments in the afterlife.

See also ABÉLARD, PETER; ALBERTUS MAGNUS; ANSELM OF LAON; AQUINAS, THOMAS, SAINT; ARIANISM; BASIL THE GREAT; BERNARD OF CLAIRVAUX, SAINT; BOETHIUS, ANICIUS MANLUS TORQUATUS SEVERINUS; DIONYSIUS THE AREOPAGITE; GILBERT OF POITIERS; GREGORY OF NAZIANZUS, SAINT; GREGORY OF NYSSA, SAINT; HUGH OF SAINT VICTOR; JEWS AND JUDAISM; JOHN SCOTTUS ERIUGENA; MONOPHYSITISM; MYSTICISM; NESTORIANISM; NOMINALISM; PALAMAS, GREGORY; REALISM; SCHOLASTICISM AND SCHOLASTIC METHOD.

Further reading: David N. Bell, *Many Mansions: An Introduction to the Development and Diversity of Medieval*

Theology West and East (Kalamazoo, Mich.: Cistercian, 1996); Peter Biller and A. J. Minnis, eds., *Medieval Theology and the Natural Body* (Rochester: York Medieval Press, 1997); George Englert McCracken, ed., *Early Medieval Theology* (Philadelphia: Westminster Press, 1957); John Meyendorff, *Byzantine Theology: Historical Trends and Doctrinal Themes*, 2d ed. (New York: Fordham University Press, 1979); Emmanuel Sivan, *Radical Islam: Medieval Theology and Modern Politics* (New Haven, Conn.: Yale University Press, 1985).

Theophano (Theophanu) (942–991) *empress of the Holy Roman Empire, wife of Emperor Otto II*
While her parents are not really known, Theophano was perhaps the daughter of the emperor Romanos II (r. 959–63) and his wife, the scandalous and alleged poisoner Theophano (d. 969), perhaps the niece of the emperor John Tzimiskes (r. 969–76). The younger Theophano married Otto II (955–83) on Easter Sunday 972, according to an agreement between the emperors OTTO I and John Tzimiskes. This agreement implied recognition by the Byzantines of the Western emperor. She made of her husband's Saxon court an important cultural center, supporting theologians, scholars, and artists. Court ceremonies became distinctly more Byzantine and elaborate. She had three daughters before she had a son. After Otto II's death in 983, she assumed joint regency with her mother-in-law, ADELAIDE, for her son, the minor OTTO III. This lasted until her death in 991.

Further reading: Adlebert Davids, ed., *The Empress Theophano: Byzantium and the West at the Turn of the First Millennium* (Cambridge: Cambridge University Press, 1995); Romilly Jenkins, *Byzantium: The Imperial Centuries, A.D. 610–1071* (New York: Random House, 1995).

Thessaloniki (Thessalonike, Thessalonica, Salonika)
A port city at the head of the Thermaic Gulf, Thessaloniki was an important stop on the Via Egnatia, between DURAZZO on the Adriatic Sea and CONSTANTINOPLE. The barbarian attacks of the third century increased Thessaloniki's strategic importance. During DIOCLETIAN's reorganization of the empire it became the residence for the emperor Galerius (r. 293–305). There survive some remains of his palace, a triumphal arch, and a rotunda that was probably his intended tomb. Theodosios I (r. 379–395) made Thessaloniki his official capital for the prefecture of ILLYRICUM and a base for his wars with the VISIGOTHS. In the city he issued in 380 his decrees that established Orthodox Christianity as the Roman Empire's official state religion. Ten years later, after the populace of the town rioted against his Gothic mercenaries, Theodosios ordered the massacre of thousands in its HIPPODROME.

Thessaloniki enjoyed relative tranquility and prosperity for the next few centuries and became the second city of the BYZANTINE EMPIRE. It had impressive churches and strong walls, which, with the help of Saint Demetrius (d. 231/232), the city's patron saint, warded off barbarians on several occasions. During the eighth century the archbishopric of Thessaloniki, previously under the jurisdiction of Rome, was transferred to the see of Constantinople. By the ninth century, Thessaloniki was the capital of one of the new European imperial themes or the military and administrative provinces of the Byzantine Empire. Thessaloniki was captured and sacked in 904 by Muslim pirates led by Leo of TRIPOLI, but the city revived and remained the second city. It was temporarily taken by the Western crusaders but soon passed back into Greek hands in the early 13th century. It fell to the KOMNENOI despots of EPIRUS from 1224 to 1239. In 1239 the emperor John III Vatatzes (r. 1221–54) of Nicaea captured the town as part of his plan to retake Constantinople. From then on the city declined in wealth and prestige until the OTTOMAN TURKS captured it in the 15th century.

Further reading: Eustathius, Archbishop of Thessalonica, *Eustathios of Thessaloniki: The Capture of Thessaloniki*, trans. John R. Melville Jones (Canberra: Australian Association for Byzantine Studies, 1988); Georgios G. Gounares, *The Walls of Thessaloniki* (Thessaloniki: Institute for Balkan Studies, 1982); James Constantine Skedros, *Saint Demetrios of Thessaloniki: Civic Patron and Divine Protector, 4th–7th Centuries C.E.* (Harrisburg, Pa.: Trinity Press International, 1999); Kalliopi Theoharidou, *The Architecture of Hagia Sophia, Thessaloniki: From Its Erection up to the Turkish Conquest* (Oxford: B.A.R., 1988).

Thierry of Chartres (Thierry the Breton) (ca. 1100–1151) *theologian, teacher, philosopher*
Thierry was the brother of Bernard of Chartres (d. 1130), another famous intellectual of the school of CHARTRES. Thierry became one of the best known teachers of that school. He specialized in the teaching of the SEVEN LIBERAL ARTS. After teaching in PARIS and surrounding area in the 1130s, he became chancellor at Chartres in 1142, a position he held until his death in 1151. One of his works, the *Heptateuchon*, became a standard textbook for the teaching of the seven liberal arts in the 12th century. He also wrote commentaries on Cicero, the book of Genesis, and BOETHIUS and a book on cosmology. He was influential in transmitting the ideas of PLATO into the West. He was at the Council of RHEIMS that condemned GILBERT OF POITIERS in 1148.

Further reading: Thierry of Chartres, *The Latin Rhetorical Commentaries by Thierry of Chartres*, ed. Karin Margareta Fredborg (Toronto: Pontifical Institute of Mediaeval Studies, 1988); Richard W. Southern, *Scholastic Humanism and the Unification of Europe*. Vol. 1, Foundations (Oxford: Blackwell, 1995); Richard W. Southern, *Scholastic Humanism and the Unification of Europe*. Vol. 2,

The Heroic Age, with notes and additions by Lesley Smith and Benedicta Ward (Oxford: Blackwell, 2001).

Third Orders *See* DOMINICAN ORDER; FRANCISCAN ORDER.

Thomas à Becket *See* BECKET, THOMAS.

Thomas à Kempis (Thomas Hemerken) (1379/80– 1471) *canon near Cologne, writer*

Born Thomas Hemerken at Kempen in the Rhineland in 1379, he studied after 1392 at the school of Deventer, which was greatly influenced by the DEVOTIO MODERNA. In 1406 he entered and took his vows at the convent of Saint Agnietenberg near Zwolle. He became procurator, subprior twice, novice master, chronicler, and official scribe of the convent. He wrote ascetic works and traditionally composed the *Imitation of Christ,* for which he was at least one of the final reviewers. That famous work, which began to circulate in 1418, promoted an essentially christologically centered spirituality. He has also been considered one of the most representative figures of the movement of the *Devotio moderna.* He also wrote sermons, devotional tracts, and saints' lives. He died in the monastery of Saint Agnietenberg on August 8, 1471.

Further reading: Thomas à Kempis, *The Imitation of Christ,* trans. Ronald Knox and Michael Oakley (New York: Sheed & Ward, 1960); Albert Hyma, *The Christian Renaissance: A History of the "Devotio Moderna,"* 2d ed. (Hamden, Conn.: Archon Books, 1965); J. E. G. de Montmorency, *Thomas à Kempis: His Age and Book* (1906; reprint, Port Washington, N.Y.: Kennikat Press, 1970); R. R. Post, *The Modern Devotion: Confrontation with Reformation and Humanism* (Leiden: E. J. Brill, 1968).

Thomas Aquinas *See* AQUINAS, THOMAS.

Thousand and One Nights (The Arabic entertainment, *Alf layla wa-layala*)

The *Thousand and One Nights* was a collection of Arabic popular narrative tales that encompasses adventure, war, trickery, love, animal fables, travel stories, folktales, and historical anecdotes. Animals speak and normal humans deal with demons. Scheherazade or Shahrazad, the daughter of a king's minister, was its storyteller who supposedly spontaneously tells tales to delay her execution. She tells them to King Shahryar, who loathed women because an earlier wife was unfaithful. He thus married and killed a new wife every day. In an effort to induce him to cease this evil practice, Scheherazade married him and told a story without an ending every night that must be finished the following night.

The *Thousand and One Nights,* then, was a narrative about storytelling with an important lesson. Storytelling functioned here, and in the stories themselves, to prevent killing and even to obtain mercy and pardons. In some versions, it included stories about the seven voyages of Sindbad and the adventures of Ali Baba and Aladdin. It was only "discovered" by Western readers in the 18th and 19th centuries, but the tales were known in many and various ways in Europe earlier. Scheherazade eventually persuaded the king to abandon his cruel practice.

Further reading: *The Arabian Nights,* trans. Husain Haddawy (New York: W. W. Norton, 1990); Ferial Ghazoul, *The Arabian Nights: A Structural Analysis* (Cairo: Cairo Associated Institution for the Study and Presentation of Arab Cultural Values, 1980); Richard C. Hovannisian and Georges Sabagh, eds., *The Thousand and One Nights in Arabic Literature and Society* (Cambridge: Cambridge University Press, 1997); Robert Irwin, *The Arabian Nights: A Companion* (London: Allen Lane, 1994); Eva Sallis, *Sheherazade through the Looking Glass: The Metamorphosis of the Thousand and One Nights* (Richmond: Curzon, 1999).

tidjara *See* TRADE AND COMMERCE.

Timbuktu (Tombouctou, Timbuctoo)

A city in West AFRICA, Timbuktu is located on the Niger River in present-day MALI. It was always important because of its location on the trade routes between north and south, especially those for GOLD. It started out as a seasonal camp for nomadic Tuaregs, who used the area around it for grazing. Named after one of the slaves who worked there, it quickly became a trading center for SALT, gold, and TEXTILES. It became Muslim under the Mali Empire around 1240. The king of Mali, Mansa Musa (r. 1307–37), built the town's great MOSQUE on his return from his pilgrimage to MECCA. He also made it the center of Muslim culture in West Africa. The SONGHAI made it part of their empire in 1468 and the city continued to flourish. Muslim and Christian visitors remarked on its schools, palaces, mosques, markets, and sophisticated court life. Timbuktu remained prosperous until the late 16th century, when it fell to invaders from MOROCCO.

Further reading: Abd al-Rahman ibn Abd Allah Sadi, *Timbuktu and the Songhay Empire: Al-Sadi's Ta'rikh al-Sudan down to 1613, and Other Contemporary Documents,* trans. and ed. John O. Hunwick (Leiden: E. J. Brill, 1999); Brian Gardner, *The Quest for Timbuctoo* (London: Cassell, 1968); Elias N. Saad, *Social History of Timbuktu: The Role of Muslim Scholars and Notables, 1400–1900* (Cambridge: Cambridge University Press, 1983).

time and its practical application

In the early Middle Ages time was considered an ordered reality that monks devised and to which they submitted their life to introduce order into daily regimens. These canonical hours designated precise moments in days and nights to which were assigned particular devotions or activities. There were difficulties in using instruments measuring and keeping track of time. The *horologium* evaluated an interval, or clepsydra, of time; other instruments expressed a moment in a scale of time such as sundials, and from the late 13th century, mechanical clocks. The computation of time and the establishment of a commonly known calendar had taken place by the 1340s. These public CLOCKS rang or sounded to establish the time and particular hours within the town where they were installed. Work was more regimented and tied to a fairly obvious schedule as it was announced by bells and on publicly visible clocks. Time in Islam was also publicly proclaimed so Muslims could order and fulfill their prayer obligations.

See also CALENDARS AND THE RECKONING OF DATES; ESCHATOLOGY; LABOR; OFFICES, MONASTIC AND CANONICAL.

Further reading: Muhammad Taqi Amini, *Time Changes and Islamic Law*, trans. Ghulam Ahmed Khan (Delhi: Idarah-i Adabiyat-i Delli, 1988); Pierre Duhem, *Medieval Cosmology: Theories of Infinity, Place, Time, Void, and the Plurality of Worlds*, ed. and trans. Roger Ariew (Chicago: University of Chicago Press, 1985); Richard Lock, *Aspects of Time in Medieval Literature* (New York: Garland, 1985); Reginald Lane Poole, *Medieval Reckonings of Time* (London: Society for Promoting Christian Knowledge, 1918); Pasquale Porro, ed., *The Medieval Concept of Time: Studies on the Scholastic Debate and Its Reception in Early Modern Philosophy* (Leiden: Brill, 2001); Tamar Rudavsky, *Time Matters: Time, Creation, and Cosmology in Medieval Jewish Philosophy* (Albany: State University of New York Press, 2000).

Timurids The Timurids were a Mongol-Turkish dynasty founded in central Asia, India, and Persia by the descendants of TAMERLANE in the 15th century. Just before his death, Tamerlane divided his territories among his sons and grandsons. Constant disputes over parts of the empire led to their eventual fall. Among the Timurids, the most important group was the dynasty who ruled Persia between 1405 and 1517. However, their rule created civil war, POVERTY, and ruin. On the other hand, they promoted achievements in architecture, in Persian, Turkish literature, and in PAINTING and book production. They were the last Islamic dynasty of steppe origin.

See also IRAN; SAMARKAND.

Further reading: Khvurshah ibn Qubad al-Husayni, "From Timur to Akbar," in *Tarikh-i-Qutbi: Also Known as Tarikh-i-elchi-i-Nizam Shah of Khwurshah bin Qubad al-Husaini: A Work of the History of the Timurids*, ed. Mujahid Husain Zaidi (New Delhi: Jamia Millia Islamia, 1965); Bernard O'Kane, *Timurid Architecture in Khurasan* (Costa Mesa, Calif.: Mazdâ Publishers in association with Undena Publications, 1987); Syed Jamaluddin, *The State*

under Timur: A Study in Empire Building (New Delhi: Har-Anand, 1995); W. M. Thackston, ed. and trans., *A Century of Princes: Sources on Timurid History and Art* (Cambridge: Aga Khan Program for Islamic Architecture, 1989); John E. Woods, *The Timurid Dynasty* (Bloomington: Indiana University, Research Institute for Inner Asian Studies, 1990).

tithes Based on a biblical injunction to give a tenth part of the harvest to a priestly tribe, tithes evolved into a medieval tax on agrarian produce, fruits, and profits to be paid to the church. The New Testament put greater emphasis on voluntary giving. From the fourth century, the church promoted the collection of tithes which were due to the local bishop and canonically divided among the bishop, the clergy, the fabric of the church, and poor relief. As church communal structures evolved and advanced, the rector of a parish supported himself by receiving a tenth part of the agricultural produce of his parishioners. In a wealthy parish this could prove to be a valuable form of endowment. For the care of souls, a vicar would take what came to be known as the lesser tithes, which included milk, calves, eggs, and young animals. The greater tithes were taken by the monastery as a corporate right of income. From the ninth to the 11th century, the ownership of tithes was purchased or usurped by lay lords and families. In certain cases the tithes were donated by their lay owners to abbeys. There was much resistance to paying the tithe at various times during the Middle Ages.

See also ANTICLERICALISM.

Further reading: Catherine E. Boyd, *Tithes and Parishes in Medieval Italy: The Historical Roots of a Modern Problem* (Ithaca, N.Y.: Cornell University Press, 1952); Giles Constable, *Monastic Tithes: From Their Origins to the Twelfth Century* (Cambridge: Cambridge University Press, 1964); Piotr Górecki, *Parishes, Tithes, and Society in Earlier Medieval Poland, c. 1100–c. 1250* (Philadelphia: American Philosophical Society, 1993).

Toledo A city in central SPAIN on the Tago River, Toledo has been attested from the time of the Roman conquest. The VISIGOTHS chose Toledo as their capital from 520. After the conversion to Catholicism by the Visigothic king RECARED I, important general COUNCILS of the Spanish church were held in Toledo in the sixth and seventh centuries. Its canons involved the bishops in secular as well as ecclesiastical affairs. The town was controlled by Muslims between 711 and 1085 with its governors dependent on caliphs in DAMASCUS, BAGHDAD, CÓRDOBA, and later in the kingdoms of the Taifas or local emirs. The population became more and more Islamized during this period.

The two centuries following the capture of Toledo by Alfonso VI (r. 1065–1109), king of CASTILE and LEÓN, in 1085 began what has been called the Mozarabic stage of the town's history. Up to about 1300 Arabic was the language of written expression in Toledo and probably oral communication as well. It was a center for translation of Arabic texts, often with the assistance of Jewish intermediaries. There was also a strong Jewish presence in the city during this period, and it was a center of Sephradic culture.

Until the Battle of Las Navas de Tolosa in 1212 when the wars of the RECONQUEST moved on to GRANADA, Toledo was a frontier town where the Reconquests attempted by the ALMORAVIDS and ALMOHADS were stopped and from which military expeditions into the Muslim south were organized and launched. The town became more Christian and integrated with the north during the 13th century. In the 14th century, the city was hit by the PLAGUES of the midcentury and damaged by the wars of succession of Peter I the Cruel (r. 1350–69). These were followed by a monetary crisis in 1391 and bloody anti-Jewish pogroms at the end of the century. The INQUISITION against false converts to Christianity was very active in the city by the late 15th century. There was considerable economic prosperity in the 15th century, although Toledo lost its political and intellectual importance to VALLADOLID with its university and royal residence.

See also AL-ANDALUS; MOZARABS; SEPHARDIM.

Further reading: Yitzhak Baer, *A History of the Jews in Christian Spain,* 2 vols. (Philadelphia: Jewish Publication Society of America, 1961–1966); Roger Highfield, ed., *Spain in the Fifteenth Century, 1369–1516: Essays and Extracts by Historians of Spain* (London: Macmillan, 1972); Edward James, ed., *Visigothic Spain: New Approaches* (Oxford: Clarendon Press, 1980); Derek W. Lomax, *The Reconquest of Spain* (London: Longman, 1978); Bernard F. Reilly, *The Contest of Christian and Muslim Spain: 1031–1157* (Cambridge: Blackwell, 1992).

tombs   *See* BURIAL RULES AND PRACTICES; CEMETERIES; DEATH AND THE DEAD; GRAVEYARDS.

Tomislav (910–928) *founder of the kingdom of Croatia*
Probably the son of the ruler Mutimir (r. 892–ca. 900/910), Tomislav has been assumed to have succeeded him by 910. Victorious after a period of anarchy and tribal warfare, Tomislav was recognized as the leader of the Croats. He unified the northern regions and DALMATIA, thus becoming the true founder of the kingdom of CROATIA. Tomislav maintained ties with the PAPACY and prevented a possible religious dispute by uniting his kingdom with ROME and the Catholic Church. In 920 in return he was recognized as king by Pope John X (r. 914–928) and perhaps crowned by the same pope by 925. Though without a permanent capital, he established a chancellery and conducted friendly diplomatic relations

with the BYZANTINE EMPIRE. He soundly defeated Bulgarian invasions in the 920s. He died in 928, although according to one source, he lived until 940.

See also SIMEON I.

Further reading: John V. A. Fine, *The Early Medieval Balkans: A Critical Survey from the Sixth to the Late Twelfth Century* (Ann Arbor: University of Michigan Press, 1991); Stanko Guldescu, *History of Medieval Croatia* (The Hague: Mouton, 1964); Tajana Sekelj Ivancan, *Catalogue of Medieval Sites in Continental Croatia* (Oxford: Tempus Reparatum, 1995).

tonsure   Tonsure was the cutting or shearing of hair on the head in a style that reduced it to a crown. Even with a scriptural basis, it was an aspect of a rite of initiation into the world of the clergy, signaling the advancing the recipient from the status of minor orders. Its practice was recorded in Gaul from the sixth century and was mentioned by GREGORY of Tours. In itself it did not constitute ordination to the priesthood but was a sign of a higher ecclesiastical status and was created in a style distinguishing the clergy from mere penitents who had been obliged to wear temporarily short hair. This signification was officially recognized from the ninth century in several canonical collections. Wearing the tonsure was the mark of clerics and was valuable because it helped them escape the administration of secular JUSTICE in case of a crime. If a cleric stopped cutting his hair in this manner, he could be punished by the authorities of the church by the removal of his ecclesiastical BENEFICES or incomes.

See also CLARENDON, CONSTITUTIONS OF; CLERGY AND CLERICAL ORDERS.

Further reading: Roger E. Reynolds, *Clerical Orders in the Early Middle Ages: Duties and Ordination* (Aldershot: Ashgate, 1999); Roger E. Reynolds, *Clerics in the Early Middle Ages: Hierarchy and Image* (Aldershot: Ashgate, 1999).

Torah   *See* PENTATEUCH.

Torquemada, Tomás de (1420–1498) *Dominican Spanish inquisitor general*
Of Jewish descent, Tomás de Torquemada was born in 1420 at Torquemada or VALLADOLID in SPAIN, the nephew of a cardinal, Juan de Torquemada (1388–1468). He entered the DOMINICAN ORDER at Valladolid with his uncle's sponsorship and was trained in THEOLOGY. He was prior of the convent of the Holy Cross at Segovia when in about 1477 he became the confessor to Queen ISABEL I of CASTILE, then married to FERDINAND II of ARAGON. He enjoyed great influence in the religious policies of the two monarchs. He soon presented them with a memorandum on an allegedly serious problem caused by the numerous newly converted Jews, whom he accused of

practicing their old religion in secret, even when they had been baptized. He was involved in the creation of an INQUISITION in Spain in 1478 but did not personally become an inquisitor himself until 1483.

Eventually, with the support of the rulers, Torquemada, however, rapidly did take charge of the Inquisition. In 1485 he acquired the right to appoint its judges without referring them to a pope and from 1488 assumed the title of inquisitor-general. He also pursued the alleged practitioners of WITCHCRAFT and HERESY. To uncover these alleged crimes, he endorsed TORTURE. He made the Inquisition into an effective means for prosecuting and persecuting new converts by his personal interest in precise examinations and questioning techniques. He was probably behind the expulsion of the JEWS from Spain in 1492 soon after the conquest of GRANADA. Uncomfortable with the extent of his control of the Inquisition, the PAPACY added deputies in an attempt to limit his power. He retired to a convent in Avila and died there on September 16, 1498, still nominally in charge of the Inquisition. He was hated by many and acquired a justifiably sinister reputation for cruelty, although the documentation for this is unclear.

Further reading: Thomas Hope, *Torquemada, Scourge of the Jews: A Biography* (London: G. Allen & Unwin, 1939); John Edward Longhurst, *The Age of Torquemada* (Sandoval, N.M.: Coronado Press, 1962); Benito Perez Galdos, *Torquemada*, trans. M. López-Morillas (New York: Columbia University Press, 1986); Benzion Netanyahu, *The Origins of the Inquisition in Fifteenth Century Spain* (New York: Random House, 1995); Rafael Sabatini, *Torquemada and the Spanish Inquisition: A History*, 6th ed. (London: S. Paul, 1927).

torture The medieval rules for torture in criminal procedure had their origins in Roman law in the second century and are mentioned in the THEODOSIAN CODE of 438 and that of JUSTINIAN in 534. The "barbarian" tribes did not use it except on slaves. The Romans generally limited its use to slaves and noncitizens. During most of the earlier Middle Ages, the truth was sought by means of magical legal practices and rites such as the ORDEAL. In the 12th century the church began to question the magical properties of the ordeal and the resurgence of Roman legal procedures validated torture as a legal practice. The Italian towns were among the first to employ it in their criminal courts, although monarchs such as FREDERICK II soon allowed it. Torture was still not systematically employed and was limited to notorious crimes. However, the INQUISITION in 1233 saw its usefulness in eliciting truth, or at least what the inquisitor wanted to hear, so Pope INNOCENT IV gave it official approval in 1252. It became a way to force heretics to recognize their guilt and name their accomplices. However, mutilation, bloodshed, and death were forbidden in this process of examination.

At first administered in the absence of clerical inquisitors, torture was soon practiced in their presence and under their direction. Its use was not systematic and the manuals of inquisitors even began to doubt its effectiveness in eliciting truth from guilty parties. The influence of this ecclesiastical inquisitorial procedure on secular courts of JUSTICE and procedures was strong from the second half of the 13th century. From then torture was applied in royal courts throughout Europe, but much more rarely in ENGLAND.

Further reading: James Heath, *Torture and English Law: An Administrative and Legal History from the Plantagenets to the Stuarts* (Westport, Conn.: Greenwood Press, 1982); Michael Kerrigan, *The Instruments of Torture: A History* (Staplehurst: Spellmount, 2001); John H. Langbein, *Torture and the Law of Proof: Europe and England in the Ancien Régime* (Chicago: University of Chicago Press, 1977); H. C. Lea, *Superstition and Force: Essays on the Wager of Law, the Wager of Battle, the Ordeal, the Torture*, 3d ed. (Philadelphia: H. C. Lea, 1878); Edward Peters, *Torture*, expanded ed. (Philadelphia: University of Pennsylvania Press, 1996).

Totila (Baduila) (r. 541–552) *Ostrogothic king of Italy*
From his election to the throne by Gothic nobles, Totila had to fight against the Byzantine generals BELISARIUS on his second expedition and Narses (ca. 478–568), sent by JUSTINIAN to conquer ITALY. Recruiting slaves and peasants as soldiers, he skillfully recovered central and southern Italy from the BYZANTINE EMPIRE in 540, capturing NAPLES in 541 and ROME in 546 and even employing a Gothic navy. His lenient treatment of prisoners of war captured in the Byzantine war attracted many of these soldiers to serve him when their own commanders failed to pay them. Belisarius returned to Italy and recaptured Rome for the Byzantines; but at his recall in 549, Totila retook the city. Failing in his offers of peace with Justinian and defeated in 552 in a battle at Sena Gallica, Totila was killed, perhaps by an arrow, in the Battle of Busta Gallorum or Teginae in June or July of 552. When his successor was also defeated by Narses, the Ostrogothic kingdom ended.

See also OSTROGOTHS; PROCOPIUS OF CAESAREA.

Further reading: Thomas Burns, *A History of the Ostrogoths* (Bloomington: Indiana University Press, 1984); Peter Heather, *The Goths* (Oxford: Blackwell, 1996).

Toulouse A city in southern FRANCE in LANGUEDOC, Toulouse was a capital of the Visigothic kingdom in SPAIN and Gaul from 419 to 507. CLOVIS captured it in 508, and it became part of the kingdom of the FRANKS. In the ninth century it became the capital of a large principality that included much of AQUITAINE and Languedoc. When the counts of Toulouse failed to take control of more of

Aquitaine, they turned their attention south, moving on BARCELONA to seize in an attempt to enlarge their power over all of PROVENCE.

Toulouse prospered in the 11th century through its position on the north-south TRADE and PILGRIMAGE routes. The pilgrimage church of Saint-Semin was started there in 1075. Recognizing its sympathy to heretics, SIMON DE MONTFORT, THE ELDER, captured it during the Albigensian Crusade. Numerous religious houses were founded there to combat the heretical beliefs common in the city. The Dominicans introduced the INQUISITION to the town in 1234. Rule by counts ended in 1249 and the brother of King LOUIS IX, Alphonse of Poitiers (d. 1270), inherited the town and changed its government to resemble more closely those of northern French towns, more readily influenced by the Crown. Toulouse then acquired an estates-general and a provincial parliament. At Alphonse's death, Toulouse passed to the direct control of the Crown of France.

See also PILGRIMAGE AND PILGRIMAGE SITES.

Further reading: Kathryn Horste, *Cloister Design and Monastic Reform in Toulouse: The Romanesque Sculpture of La Daurade* (Oxford: Clarendon Press, 1992); John H. Mundy, *Liberty and Political Power in Toulouse, 1050–1230* (New York: Columbia University Press, 1954); John H. Mundy, *The Repression of Catharism at Toulouse: The Royal Diploma of 1279* (Toronto: Pontifical Institute of Mediaeval Studies, 1985); John H. Mundy, *Men and Women at Toulouse in the Age of Cathars* (Toronto: Pontifical Institute of Mediaeval Studies, 1990); John H. Mundy, *Society and Government at Toulouse in the Age of the Cathars* (Toronto: Pontifical Institute of Mediaeval Studies, 1997).

tournament   From its appearance in the mid-11th century in western France, the tournament initially took the form of a confrontation or *melée* between two groups of 40 to 50 mounted combatants over a large area away from inhabited places. It resembled a battle and was a training ground for KNIGHTS, an outlet for aggression and warlike attitudes, and a way to make a fortune and a career. Its objective was to capture an adversary, hold him to ransom, and take his arms and horse or HORSES. The participants had to develop signs to allow recognition on the battlefield, which led to the heraldic devices of the later Middle Ages. Opposed to such violent activities, the church forbade Christian burial to those killed in tournament fighting. Nor did monarchs like these assemblies of soldiers outside their control, among whom sedition might be plotted and armed forces mustered and assembled.

In the 13th century, the tournament changed, becoming more domesticated. The battlefields became smaller arenas solely for spectacles, including jousts or duels, between two knights and thus even more the most prestigious forms of noble entertainment and sport. Tour-

naments remained dangerous but were more artificial, regulated for safety, and ritualized according to literary and artificial ideals of form and style. In most of them two knights charged one another while separated by a barrier, carrying blunted lances, seeking to unhorse one another. Crowds of men and women watched these jousts. The English king, EDWARD III, was particularly fond of this style of tournament, recognizing its prestige value for English arms. In the 15th century the element of display and pageantry was cultivated to fanciful extremes at the court of BURGUNDY.

See also CHIVALRY; KNIGHTS AND KNIGHTHOOD; WILLIAM THE MARSHALL.

Further reading: Richard W. Barber, *Tournaments: Jousts, Chivalry and Pageants in the Middle Ages* (Woodbridge, England: Boydell, 1989); Richard W. Kaeuper, *Chivalry and Violence in Medieval Europe* (Oxford: Oxford University Press, 1999); Maurice Keen, *Chivalry* (New Haven, Conn.: Yale University Press, 1984).

towns   *See* NAMES OF INDIVIDUAL CITIES AND TOWNS.

trade and commerce   Trade and commerce in the Middle Ages revolved around the Baltic Sea in the north, the Mediterranean Sea in the south, and the overland routes from Asia and AFRICA. It could involve luxury items but also more common bulky material, often foodstuffs or manufactured goods. Increased population, better agricultural organization and productivity, improved techniques of capital formation, better and more efficient means of transport, and more innovative mercantile entrepreneurship led to a commercial revolution in the 13th century. The urban centers of the Low Countries, CHAMPAGNE in FRANCE, and ITALY were at the heart of this development, but it was not limited to them. The MONGOL conquests of the 13th century led to more stable conditions in the regions between Europe and Asia and produced an increase in trade. GOLD and later slaves promoted the trans-Saharan trade in Africa. Islamic merchants maintained commercial links in the Persian Gulf and the Red Sea and down the coast of Africa and across the Indian Ocean to India. The CRUSADES, though destructive, also promoted links between the eastern and western Mediterranean. Such expansion of trade led to the growth of cities and urban populations who consumed, distributed, and manufactured trade goods. WARFARE and disease in the 14th and 15th centuries certainly impaired international, local, and regional trade and commerce, though they continued everywhere.

See also BANKS AND BANKING; BRUGES; CAIRO; CONSTANTINOPLE; FAIRS AND MARKETS; FLORENCE; FOOD, DRINK, AND NUTRITION; GENOA; PISA; SHIPS AND SHIPBUILDING; SIENA; VENICE.

Further reading: Robert S. Lopez and Irving W. Raymond, eds. *Medieval Trade in the Mediterranean World:*

Illustrative Documents with Introductions and Notes (New York: Columbia University Press, 1955); K. N. Chaudhuri, *Trade and Civilisation in the Indian Ocean: An Economic History from the Rise of Islam to 1750* (Cambridge: Cambridge University Press, 1985); Philip D. Curtin, *Cross-Cultural Trade in World History* (Cambridge: Cambridge University Press, 1984); Richard Hodges, *Dark Age Economics: The Origins of Towns and Trade A.D. 500–1000*, 2d ed. (London: Duckworth, 1989); Robert S. Lopez, *The Commercial Revolution of the Middle Ages, 950–1350* (Englewood Cliffs, N.J.: Prentice-Hall, 1971).

Transfiguration   The Transfiguration was one of the major symbolic episodes of Christ's public life. Jesus took three of his disciples, Peter, James, and John, up a mountain, perhaps Mount Tabor in Galilee, where he was transfigured into GOD or something like a divine being before them. Moses and Elijah on either side spoke with him about his oncoming Passion at JERUSALEM. God the father announced that Jesus was his Son and he should be heard. It became one of the 12 great feasts of the church, commemorated on August 6. It also became a common image in Christian art to show Christ's glory and acceptance of mission, the eclipse of the LAW of the Old Testament, and the promise of a second coming.

See also CHRISTOLOGY AND CHRISTOLOGICAL CONTROVERSY.

Further reading: John Anthony McGuckin, *The Transfiguration of Christ in Scripture and Tradition* (Lewiston, N.Y.: Edwin Mellen Press, 1986); Barbara E. Reid, *The Transfiguration: A Source- and Redaction-Critical Study of Luke 9:28–36* (Paris: Gabalda, 1993).

Transylvania   Bounded within the Carpathian Mountains, medieval Transylvania was a region now forming part of modern-day HUNGARY and ROMANIA. It was initially populated by Romanians seeking refuge after the collapse of the Roman Empire from the numerous tribes who passed through the area, the Gepids, the AVARS, the BULGARS, the LOMBARDS, the HUNS, and the SLAVS. Doubtless some of these peoples remained behind or left evidence of their passing in the human population. From the 10th century the Hungarians entered the region and a Hungarian noble class headed by a duke was placed over a Hungarian and Romanian PEASANTRY. German and Jewish settlers entered the area in the 13th century, further diversifying the population.

Transylvania's rich deposits of SALT and precious metals drew people to the region. The population was converted to the Eastern or Byzantine form of Christianity, but Hungarian domination was linked with the Catholic or Western form of Christianity. Missions and the military orders were sent by the pope to further this conversion in the 13th century.

The MONGOLS passed through the country in 1240 and 1241, causing considerable devastation, but they withdrew in 1241 because of the death of their leader. For the rest of the century, Transylvania could not be effectively ruled by the Hungarians. A new dynasty from the Neapolitan branch of the Angevin family took over Hungary in 1308. Taking a renewed interest in Transylvania, they sought further reduction of the peasant population to burdensome SERFDOM. Threatened by the OTTOMANS, King Louis the Great of Anjou (r. 1342–82) tried to regain the loyalty to the Hungarian Crown of the Germans in Transylvania by granting trading privileges to the towns and ensuring them of a near-monopoly over commerce.

After the extinction of the Angevin dynasty, a new king, Sigismund of Luxembourg (1387–1437), commenced the crusade against the Ottomans. The resulting and oppressive high taxation caused a revolt of the Transylvanian peasants between 1437 and 1438. A coalition of nobles put down the revolt, but the situation of serfs there continued to deteriorate. From 1440 a Transylvanian noble of Romanian origin, John HUNYADI, provided the greatest resistance to the Ottomans. The long reign of his son Matthias CORVINUS, was taken up with wars and high taxes. Transylvania suffered rebellions and growing discontent because of the insecurity of its frontiers. The policies of Matthias Corvinus and his successors weakened the kingdom and the dominance of its aristocracy, who grew more incapable of defending Hungary or Transylvania against the Ottomans for the rest of the 15th century.

See also VLAD III THE IMPALER.

Further reading: Serban Papacostea, *Between the Crusade and the Mongol Empire: The Romanians in the 13th Century*, trans. Liviu Bleoca (Cluj-Napoca: Center for Transylvanian Studies, Romanian Cultural Foundation, 1998); László Péter, ed., *Historians and the History of Transylvania* (New York: Columbia University Press, 1992); Ioan Aurel Pop, *The Ethno-Confessional Structure of Medieval Transylvania and Hungary* (Cluj-Napoca: Romanian Cultural Foundation, 1994); Ioan Aurel Pop, *Romanians and Hungarians from the 9th to the 14th Century: The Genesis of the Transylvanian Medieval State* (Cluj-Napoca: Centrul de Studii Transilvane, Fundatia Cultrala Româna, 1996).

Traversari, Ambrogio (Ambrose of Camaldoli) (1386–1439) *Italian humanist, Camaldolese monk, translator*
Ambrogio was born at Portico di Romanna in September of 1386. At the age of 14, he went to FLORENCE to become a Camaldolese monk in the convent of Santa Maria degli Angeli. There he learned LATIN and GREEK and taught the sons of Cosimo de' MEDICI and other patrician children. He became a friend of Cosimo and a number of the other humanists in Florence at that time,

such as Niccolò Niccoli (1364–1437). He interceded for Cosimo on the latter's imprisonment in 1433. He translated into Latin works of some of the Greek fathers, especially BASIL THE GREAT, John CHRYSOSTOM, and DIONYSIUS THE AREOPAGITE.

From 1431 to 1434, Ambrogio led the reform of his own order as superior general. He was a papal legate at the Council of BASEL, where he made a speech against the ideas of CONCILIARISM on August 26, 1435. As an authority on Greek, he participated in a decree of union between the Eastern and Western Churches at the Council of Florence of July 5, 1439. He was one of the Florentine humanists who frequented the papal court at that time. He was a great patron of art at the Monastery of Santa Maria degli Angeli and sponsored an important SCRIPTORIUM for the new humanist script. He was important in introducing Byzantine and early Christian ideas in humanist philosophical and theological thought. On October 21, 1439, Traversari died suddenly at Florence. He was buried in the hermitage church at Camaldoli near Florence.

See also EUGENIUS IV, POPE.

Further reading: Deno John Geanakoplos, *Byzantine East and Latin West: Two Worlds of Christendom in Middle Ages and Renaissance* (New York: Barnes & Noble, 1966); Charles L. Stinger, *Humanism and the Church Fathers: Ambrogio Traversari (1386–1439) and Christian Antiquity in the Italian Renaissance* (Albany: State University of New York Press, 1977).

treason *See* IMPEACHMENT AND ATTAINDER.

Trebizond Empire Medieval Trebizond was a former classical Greek colony in northeastern ANATOLIA on the south shore of the Black Sea and later an outpost on the northeast frontiers of the Roman and Byzantine Empires. Important in the emperor JUSTINIAN's Armenian and Georgian foreign and military policies, it had been well fortified and thus had escaped Arab conquest. It then became an outlet on a commercial route to and from the Muslim world, for Persia or IRAN. SELJUK expansion in the 11th century increased its isolation, but it remained a Byzantine outpost. In the 13th century MERCHANTS of GENOA and VENICE were very active in its markets. It suffered periods of vassalage to the Seljuks and MONGOLS in the 13th century but maintained considerable commercial success by trading in cloth, WINE, silver, and iron. After the town had refused to acknowledge the political expulsion of the KOMNENOI dynasty from Constantinople in 1185, two family members later retreated to Trebizond and in 1204 made it the capital of the empire of the Great Komnenoi or Trebizond. That empire lasted until 1461, when the OTTOMAN TURKS took and essentially destroyed the city.

See also BESSARION, JOHN CARDINAL.

Further reading: Anthony A. M. Bryer, *The Empire of Trebizond and the Pontos* (London: Variorum, 1980); Raymond Mercier, *An Almanac for Trebizond for the Year 1336* (Louvain-la-Neuve: Academia, 1994); William Miller, *Trebizond, the Last Greek Empire* (New York: Macmillan, 1926).

Tribonian (d. ca. 542/545) *legal scholar*
Named quaestor by JUSTINIAN in 529, Tribonian acted as his legal adviser. He was one of eight members of a committee appointed to create a new collection of Roman LAW formulated since the reign of the second-century emperor Hadrian (r. 98–117). With 16 prominent lawyers from BEIRUT, Tribonian issued in 534 a revised version of the 529 compilation. He worked especially on the *Digest* in which he attempted to systematize the rulings of legal scholars based on 200 to 300 treatises of some 40 writers. He also produced a handbook for students, the *Institutes*. Justinian had to remove him from office because of his reputation for dubious legal chicanery, but the emperor soon restored Tribonian to office. He died between 542 and 545.

Further reading: Tony Honoré, *Tribonian* (Ithaca, N.Y.: Cornell University Press, 1978).

Trinitarian doctrine Trinitarian doctrine has been one of the central, but often disputed, mysteries and concepts of Christianity. The Trinity was not designated clearly in Scripture, but ultimately was defined in the first centuries after Christ by the FATHERS OF THE CHURCH, especially BASIL THE GREAT and AUGUSTINE of HIPPO. They definitively linked Christianity with a Trinitarian monotheism. In their scheme, GOD was one being and one substance made up of three persons, the Father, the Son or Christ, and the HOLY SPIRIT. God was revealed to humankind in three distinct equal modes of existence, yet God remained one through all eternity. This doctrine, difficult and disputed throughout the period before 1500, remains a dogma of the Catholic Church.

See also ANSELM OF LAON; AQUINAS, THOMAS, SAINT; ARIANISM; BOETHIUS, ANICIUS MANLIUS TORQUATUS SEVERINUS; CHRISTOLOGY AND CHRISTOLOGICAL CONTROVERSY; *FILIOQUE* CLAUSE, DISPUTE OVER; PERSON.

Further reading: Matthew Alfs, *Concepts of Father, Son, and Holy Spirit: A Classification and Description of the Trinitarian and Non-Trinitarian Theologies Existent within Christendom* (Minneapolis: Old Theology Book House, 1984); Michel R. Barnes and Daniel H. Williams, eds., *Arianism after Arius: Essays on the Development of the Fourth Century Trinitarian Conflicts* (Edinburgh: T. & T. Clark, 1993); Richard S. Haugh, *Photius and the Carolingians: The Trinitarian Controversy* (Belmont, Mass.: Nordland, 1975); Duncan Reid, *Energies of the Spirit: Trinitarian Models in Eastern Orthodox and Western Theology* (Atlanta: Scholars Press, 1997).

Tripoli (Tarabulus, Atrabulus, the western Tripoli) A city in North AFRICA in present-day LIBYA, Tripoli should not be confused with the TRIPOLI in LEBANON. Founded by the Phoenicians, it became a Roman city in the province of Tripoliltania. During the fifth and sixth centuries, the VANDALS and the BYZANTINES fought over it until BELISARIUS conquered it in 532. It was raided by local nomad tribes regularly throughout its history. In 643 it was captured by Muslim ARABS. The FATIMIDS ruled it, and remains of their building projects there, especially the Naqah MOSQUE, are extant. In 1150 ROGER II of SICILY captured the city and held it between 1146 and 1158; Norman and Sicilian rule there ended soon after his death.

Further reading: Edward Rae, *The Country of the Moors: A Journey from Tripoli in Barbary to the City of Kairwân* (London: Darf, 1985).

Tripoli (Tarabulus, Atrabulus, the eastern Tripoli) A city on the coast of LEBANON, this Tripoli should not be confused with TRIPOLI or western Tripoli in North Africa. The town was an important city and legal center of the BYZANTINE Empire until its conquest in 640 by the Arabs. Calip Muawiya ibn Abi Sufyan I (r. 661–80) settled Muslims in the city and a rapid process of Islamization was carried out. At the beginning of the 11th century Tripoli fell under the FATIMIDS of EGYPT and was governed by an emir, sent by their government in CAIRO. It became a flourishing seaport. In 1104 the crusader RAYMOND IV OF SAINT-GILLES began a siege of the city, after building the nearby castle of Mont Pèlerin, where he died in 1105. The crusaders did not actually take the city until 1109, under Bertram (r. 1109–12), Raymond's son. It then became the capital of an autonomous county and was ruled by a collateral branch of the dynasty of Toulouse until 1187, when it passed to the princes of ANTIOCH. It was one of the three principal crusader states located between the Kingdom of JERUSALEM in the south and the principality of Antioch in the north. The constitution of the county was modeled on southern French traditions. The main cities of the state besides Tripoli were Margat, Tortosa, and Jebeil. Within its boundaries was the famous crusader castle of KRAK des Chevaliers.

In the 13th century a commune was established in the city under the princes of Antioch. It was one of the last Christian strongholds to fall to the Muslims when the MAMLUKS destroyed it in 1289. They initiated an ambitious building and reconstruction program, but on a new more defensible site. This new planned city was established slightly inland from the location of the old town, which was still vulnerable to raids from Christian CYPRUS. A new principal mosque was built in 1294 incorporating a crusader tower. It became a prosperous county of the Mamluk Empire and maintained much of its commercial importance in the trade with Christian Europe until its capture by the OTTOMANS in the 16th century.

See also CRUSADES; LATIN STATES IN GREECE.

Further reading: Robert Irwin, *The Middle East in the Middle Ages: The Early Mamluk Sultanate, 1250–1382* (London: Croom Helm, 1986); Hayam Salam-Liebich, *The Architecture of the Mamluk City of Tripoli* (Cambridge: Harvard University Press, 1983); Kenneth M. Setton, ed., *A History of the Crusades,* 6 vols. (Madison: University of Wisconsin Press, 1969–1989).

Tristan and Iseult (Tristram, Yseult) This medieval story was a ROMANCE from a Celtic Ireland source, or one from "Viking Age" Ireland and Britain. It became one of the most popular love stories in Western Europe from the end of the 12th century. It is about the love between Tristan, a knight, and Iseult, the wife of King Mark of Cornwall. Their passion and fate were aroused and set in motion by a love potion that caused problems within the context of marital and knightly loyalty to a husband or lord. It was first written in French by Béroul in the 12th century and adapted into German by GOTTFRIED von Strassburg in the 13th. By the later 13th century there were Italian, English, and Old Norse versions. This tale of Tristan and Iseult formed a main part of the ARTHURIAN and chivalric tradition in the later Middle Ages.

See also COURTLY LOVE; MALORY, THOMAS.

Further reading: Béroul, *The Romance of Tristan,* trans. Alan S. Federick (London: Penguin Books, 1970); Sigmund Eisner, *The Tristan Legend: A Study in Sources* (Evanston, Ill.: Northwestern University Press, 1969); Joan M. Ferrante, *The Conflict of Love and Honor: The Medieval Tristan Legend in France, Germany and Italy* (The Hague: Mouton, 1973); Gertrude Schoepperle Loomis, *Tristan and Isolt: A Study of the Sources of the Romance,* 2d ed., 2 vols. (1913; reprint, New York: B. Franklin, 1963).

Trivium *See* SEVEN LIBERAL ARTS.

trobairitz *See* TROUBADOURS.

Trota (Trotula) The Trota was a highly influential treatise or compendium on women's MEDICINE. It may have been composed or compiled by a female professor, Trota, at the University of Salerno, a major medical center, in the 11th or 12th century. It consisted of three works probably by three different authors. It seemed to synthesize the local popular customs of the region around NAPLES with the ideas and practices entering Europe from the newly available texts on Arabic and Greek medicine. It was full of ideas about COSMETICS, human generation, gynecology, SEXUALITY, and the workings of the female body.

See also MEDICINE.

Further reading: Monica H. Green, ed. and trans., *The Trota: A Medieval Compendium of Women's Medicine* (Philadelphia: University of Pennsylvania Press, 2001); John F. Benton, "Trota, Women's Problems, and the Professionalization of Medicine in the Middle Ages," *Bulletin of the History of Medicine* 59 (1985); 30–53; Joan Cadden, *Meanings of Sexual Difference in the Middle Ages: Medicine, Science, and Culture* (Cambridge: Cambridge University Press, 1993).

troubadours (trouvères, trobairitz) From the beginning of the 12th century among aristocratic circles of southern France, a distinctive style of lyric poetry and songs in the Provençal or Occitan language was composed (or "invented") by the troubadours, a class of courtly poets. They were, mostly men but some women (the *trobairitz*), with an ideal of life based on courtesy, which to them meant "generosity, distinction of manners, and COURTLY LOVE." Some of their work was bawdy. They also wrote devotional poems about the Virgin MARY. The songs and poems of the troubadours were usually based on the veneration or ritual glorification of a particular woman. Among the first of these troubadours were William IX, duke of AQUITAINE (r. 1086–1127); JAUFRÉ RUDEL, a KNIGHT BERTRAN DE BORN, a knight and later a monk; and even a few clerics. The troubadours composed both the words and the melody for love poetry and poems on political, literary, and religious questions, all following strict poetic rules. By 1150 CHRÉTIEN DE TROYES, RICHARD I LIONHEART, the counts of Champagne, and a king of Navarre, among others, were attempting to compose in this genre.

The troubadours of northern France, now sometimes called minstrels, more reserved in their expressions of love, added satirical and narrative elements and anecdotal and personal material. By the 13th century, such poets were concentrated in the rich towns of the north and often tied to CONFRATERNITIES who even held regular competitions. Some 2,500 songs survive with 250 melodies from this genre.

Further reading: F. R. P. Akehurst and Judith M. Davis, eds., *A Handbook of the Troubadours* (Berkeley: University of California Press, 1995); Elizabeth Aubrey, *The Music of the Troubadours* (Bloomington: Indiana University Press, 1996); Magda Bogin, *The Women Troubadours* (New York: Paddington Press, 1976); William E. Burgwinkle, *Love for Sale: Materialist Readings of the Troubadour Razo Corpus* (New York: Garland, 1997); Fredric L. Cheyette, *Ermengard of Narbonne and the World of the Toubadours* (Ithaca, N.Y.: Cornell University Press, 2001); Simon Gaunt and Sarah Kay, eds., *The Troubadours: An Introduction* (Cambridge: Cambridge University Press, 1999); Linda M. Paterson, *The World of the Troubadours: Medieval Occitan Society, c. 1100–c. 1300* (Cambridge: Cambridge University Press, 1993); Leslie Topsfield, "Troubadours and Trouvères," in *European Writers: The Middle Ages and the Renaissance.* Vol. 1, *Prudentius to Medieval Drama,* ed. William T. H. Jackson and George Stade (New York: Charles Scribner's Sons, 1983), 161–185.

Truce of God *See* PEACE AND TRUCE OF GOD.

Tudor, house of The Tudors were the dynasty who took the English throne in 1485 and held it into the 17th century. After 1471, the last surviving member of the Lancastrian lineage was Margaret Beaufort (1443–1509). She first married Edmund Tudor (ca. 1430–56), the earl of Richmond, who was the son of Catherine de Valois (1401–37), the widow of HENRY V, when Henry died, she subsequently secretly married a Welsh soldier charged to guard her, Owen Tudor (d. 1461), in about 1432. Owen was Edmund's father. The Tudor family had been Welsh soldiers, often working for the English Crown. This marriage was kept secret essentially up to Margaret's death in 1437, when Owen was imprisoned for a short period. In 1439 he received a pension from his half brother, King Henry VI (r. 1422–61, 1470–71), and died fighting for him in 1461. Owen's two sons, Edmund and Jasper (ca. 1431–95), were knighted by Henry, who also granted them titles. Edmund married Margaret Beaufort in 1455, died of an illness the following year, but left a son, Henry, who was born in 1457 and with his mother fled to BRITTANY after the failure of the Lancastrian restoration of 1471. There he waited for an opportunity to return to ENGLAND and even claim the throne. Henry fulfilled that opportunity when he defeated RICHARD III (YORK) at the Battle of BOSWORTH FIELD on August 22, 1485. Henry, now Henry VII (r. 1457–1509), took the Crown and married Elizabeth of York (1465–1503), the daughter of EDWARD IV, giving his descendants ties to both the house of Lancaster and the house of York, the contending families in the WARS OF THE ROSES. The Tudors occupied the throne of England until 1603.

See also EDWARD IV, KING OF ENGLAND; WALES.

Further reading: Michael Van Cleave Alexander, *The First of the Tudors: A Study of Henry VII and His Reign* (London: Croom Helm, 1980); Alexander Grant, *Henry VII: The Importance of His Reign in English History* (London: Methuen, 1985); S. J. Gunn and P. G. Lindley, eds., *Cardinal Wolsey: Church, State, and Art* (Cambridge: Cambridge University Press, 1991); Roger Lockyer, *Henry VII,* 2d. ed. (London: Longman, 1983); Alison Plowden, *The House of Tudor* (London: Weidenfeld and Nicolson, 1976).

Tughrul Beg (Tughril, Toghril) (r. 1037–1063) *founder of the Seljuk Empire, sultan*
Tughrul first appeared in history when he imposed his authority on several Turkish tribes who had been auxiliary

troops and had recently converted to SUNNI ISLAM. In 1037 he began the conquest of Persia and the ABBASID caliphate. After defeating the GHAZNAWIDS, he captured Khorasan in 1040 and established his capital at Nishapur in eastern IRAN. In 1051 he conquered Isfahan and the western part of Iran and invaded IRAQ, where he defeated several Arab armies. In 1055 he took BAGHDAD. Tughrul now exercised military and political control but allowed a BUYID caliph to continue as an Islamic spiritual leader, albeit Shia, and the formal sovereign of the city. Tughrul emphasized Sunni orthodoxy. Tughrul's new status was eventually confirmed in 1058 proclaiming him the king of the East and West. His government was based on a Persian bureaucracy and a Turkish controlled military. It dominated the region for several decades but quickly was troubled by the formation of squabbling petty kingdoms. Tughrul himself died in 1063.

See also ALP ARSLAN; SELJUK TURKS OF RUM.

Further reading: Clifford Edmund Bosworth, *The Islamic Dynasties* (Edinburgh: University of Edinburgh Press, 1967); John Andrew Boyle, ed., *The Cambridge History of Iran.* Vol. 5, *The Saljuk and Mongol Periods* (Cambridge: Cambridge University Press, 1968); R. N. Frye, ed., *The Cambridge History of Iran.* Vol. 4, *The Period from the Arab Invasion to the Saljuks* (Cambridge: Cambridge University Press, 1975); Mehmet Fuat Koprulu, *The Seljuks of Anatolia: Their History and Culture According to Local Muslim Sources,* trans. and ed. Gary Leiser (Salt Lake City: University of Utah Press, 1992).

Tulunids   The Tulunids were a dynasty who ruled EGYPT and SYRIA between 868 and 905, founded by Ahmad ibn Tulun (r. 868–884), the governor of Egypt. Of Turkish origin and the son of a freed slave Ahmad served as a soldier the ABBASID CALIPH in BAGHDAD. In 868 he was appointed vice-governor for Egypt where he deposed the civil governor and seized power. Revolting against the caliphate, he moved to conquer parts of PALESTINE and Syria. He raised an excellent military force based on a slave army of Turks, Greeks, and Nubians. Though formally recognizing the caliph's sovereignty, he created an independent state in Egypt and in the coastal region of Palestine up to Syria. A successful ruler, he encouraged economic and fiscal reform, built markets, and repaired important harbors such as the one at ACRE. From this base he founded the short-lived dynasty of the Tulunids.

The Tulunids introduced local rule to Egypt and left important monuments behind, such as the MOSQUE of Ibn Tulun at AL-FUSTAT, near the future city of CAIRO. His son, Khumarawayh (r. 884–896), successful and hugely extravagant in his spending habits received recognition of his position from the caliph in return for a tribute of 300,000 dinars. They were replaced by direct Abbasid rule in 905.

Further reading: Clifford Edmund Bosworth, *The Islamic Dynasties* (Edinburgh: Edinburgh University Press, 1967), 43–44; K. A. C. Creswell, *Early Muslim Architecture,* 2 vols. (1932–1940; reprint, New York: Hacher Art Books, 1979); Oleg Grabar, *The Coinage of the Tulunids* (New York: American Numismatic Society, 1957).

Tunis (Tunus, Tunis)   A city in North AFRICA Tunis was founded by the ARABS near the site of Carthage and was dependent on the rulers of AL-QAYRAWAN from the eighth to the 12th century. It was an important harbor of the AGHLABIDS who built the Great Mosque, the Jami al-Zaituna, in the ninth century. In 1150 ROGER II, captured the city and the Norman Sicilian government dominated the town until the middle of the 13th century. In 1217–20 Tunis became the frequent scene of early missionary activities by the Franciscans. After his conquest of SICILY in the 1260s, CHARLES I OF ANJOU tried to restore Sicilian rule over Tunis. His brother, LOUIS IX of France, launched a CRUSADE against the city, but that project failed miserably at Louis's death there in 1270. The wars for control of southern ITALY and the western Mediterranean for the next several decades diverted Christian attention from Tunis. In the meantime the HAFSIDS had secured control of the city and much of the region. The MARINIDS dislodged them with grew difficulty in the mid-14th century.

Further reading: Markus Hattstein and Peter Delius, eds., *Islam: Art and Architecture,* trans. George Ansell et al. (Cologne: Könemann, 2000); Graham Petrie, *Tunis, Kairouan & Carthage. Described and Illustrated with Forty-Eight Paintings* (London: Darf, 1985).

Tunisia   *See* AGHLABIDS; ALMOHADS; ALMORAVIDS; FATIMIDS; HAFSIDS; AL-QAYRAWAN; TUNIS; ZIRIDS.

Turks and Turkomans   The Turks and Turkomans were a group of peoples and tribes, recognizable from the fourth century, who spoke dialects of the Ural-Altaic language called Turkic. Their probable original home was in the Altai Mountains in Central Asia, from which they spread all over Eurasia while practicing a shamanic religion. Between about 840 and 1240, they formed several kingdoms between Mongolia and eastern Turkistan, absorbing the culture and religion of their neighbors such as Buddhism from China or Manichaeism and NESTORIANISM from IRAN. By the ninth century many had converted to ISLAM and become a major source of military manpower, both slave and free, of the Muslim dynasties in IRAN and IRAQ. From the 11th century onward, they divided themselves into several independent dynasties and military aristocracies who dominated the Islamic world. Another group, the Uighurs, merged with the

MONGOLS in the 13th century. The Seljuks and the Ottomans eventually dominated the Middle East and absorbed the BYZANTINE EMPIRE.

See also ANATOLIA; AVARS; CUMANS; GHAZNAWIDS; HUNS; KHAZARS; MAMLUKS; OTTOMAN TURKS AND EMPIRE; SAMANIDS; SELJUK TURKS OF RUM; TAMERLANE; TUGHRUL BEG; TULUNIDS.

Further reading: Margaret Bainbridge, ed., *The Turkic Peoples of the World* (London: Kegan Paul International, 1993); Peter B. Golden, *An Introduction to the History of the Turkic Peoples: Ethnogenesis and State-Formation in Medieval and Early Modern Eurasia and the Middle East* (Wiesbaden: O. Harrassowitz, 1992); Peter B. Golden, *Nomads and Sedentary Societies in Medieval Eurasia* (Washington, D.C.: American Historical Association, 1998); Vladimir Minorsky, *The Turks, Iran and the Caucasus in the Middle* (London: Variorum Reprints, 1978).

Tuscany Medieval Tuscany was a region in central ITALY bounded by the sea to the west and the Apennine Mountains to the north and east, with a much less defined border to the south. It was a major part of a pre-Roman Etruscan network of kingships. The LOMBARDS and Carolingians established territorial states there in the early Middle Ages. After the year 1000, Tuscany was divided into many small territorial lordships only nominally controlled by any emperor, lord, or monarch. By the 12th century numerous towns had sprung up and were assuming autonomy from the rural lords. By the end of that century, the towns were beginning to dominate the local nobility and were functioning independently of the Holy Roman Emperor. The cities then proceed to fight among themselves, and the large ones tried to asset their control over the smaller adjacent towns.

A rich agricultural region, Tuscany was famous in the Middle Ages and RENAISSANCE for its wines, oils, and other agricultural products. From the 13th century, its merchants dominated European TRADE, commerce, and BANKING. Its history from 1200 to 1550 is best followed by studying its important cities, which established republican and signorial forms of government. The populations of these towns were among the highest in Europe, with FLORENCE at around 100,000 and SIENA at approximately 50,000. Devastated by PLAGUE, these figures, however, had fallen to half at best by the 15th century. By 1500 the city-state of Florence dominated the region and only Siena retained any semblance of autonomy. The region was also extremely important in the development of literature and of ROMANESQUE and GOTHIC art and architecture, producing such writers and artists as DANTE ALIGHIERI, BOCCACCIO, GIOTTO, DUCCIO DI BUONINSEGNA, SIMONE MARTINI, MASACCIO, and FRA ANGELICO. Its dialect of Italian later became a standard form for the Italian language in general.

See also COMMUNE; GUELFS AND GHIBELLINES; LUCCA; PISA; SAFFRON; WINE AND WINEMAKING.

Further reading: Thomas W. Blomquist and Maureen F. Mazzaoui, eds., *The "Other Tuscany": Essays in the History of Lucca, Pisa, and Siena during the Thirteenth, Fourteenth, and Fifteenth Centuries* (Kalamazoo, Mich.: Medieval Institute Publications, Western Michigan University, 1994); Anthony McIntyre, *Medieval Tuscany and Umbria* (San Francisco: Chronicle Books, 1992).

Tyler, Wat (Walter) (d. 1381) *one of the leaders of the Peasants' Revolt in England*
Probably influenced by the priest John BALL, Wat Tyler left his work in Kent and participated in the organization of the English Peasants' Revolt in Kent and Essex Counties against the king, the nobility, and the church establishments. He seems to have become a captain of the rebels around June 7, 1381, perhaps because he had some military experience. In the spring and summer of 1381, he led the revolt successfully if temporarily, seizing CANTERBURY, and even LONDON. Violence of the rebels in the city turned the towns people against them, so London adopted at best a neutral attitude toward the rebellion. Tyler and the rebels made progressively more radical demands for more social equality, livable working conditions, and lower taxes. RICHARD II promised concessions, but at a meeting on June 15, 1381, Tyler, perhaps considering an assassination of the king, was killed whether by a prearranged plan or by chance. Richard promptly made more promises and the rebels, essentially leaderless, rashly disbanded. The king soon reneged on his promises and had many rebels hunted down and executed, despite their pardons.

See also JACQUÉRIE; PEASANT REBELLIONS.

Further reading: R. B. Dobson, ed., *The Peasants' Revolt of 1381* (London: Macmillan, 1970); Rodney H. Hilton and T. H. Aston, eds., *The English of 1381* (Cambridge: Cambridge University Press, 1984); Steven Justice, *Writing and Rebellion: England in 1381* (Berkeley: University of California Press, 1994); Philip Lindsay and Reg Groves, *The Peasants' Revolt, 1381* (Westport, Conn.: Greenwood Press, 1974); Charles Oman, *The Great Revolt of 1381* (1906; reprint, New York: Greenwood Press, 1969).

Tyre Medieval Tyre was a city in LEBANON with a history extending back thousands of years. Under the Byzantines in late antiquity and the early Middle Ages, its harbor was among the most important industrial, trading, and shipping centers along the eastern coast of the Mediterranean. It continued to play that role until the 14th century. Tyre was also a major religious center and linked to ANTIOCH. After the Arab conquest of 638, the Greek population mostly left and the city declined in economic terms. In 1123 it was conquered by the crusaders after a siege of five months with the help of naval support from VENICE. Consequently, Venice was granted one-third of the city and control of its harbor, which was second only to that of ACRE in importance. In 1187, after the defeat at the Battle of the Horns of HATTIN and the collapse of the Latin Kingdom of JERUSALEM, Tyre became the only city of the kingdom that successfully resisted conquest by SALADIN. It was thus the most important base for the Third CRUSADE of RICHARD I LIONHEART and PHILIP II AUGUSTUS. In the 13th century a COMMUNE was established at Tyre, but it remained, dominated by Venice. It had a famous glass industry, but its reconquest by the Muslims forced many of its Christian artisans to move to Venice, onto the nearby island of Murano. It was conquered by the MAMLUKS in 1291, was neglected, and then declined in the later Middle Ages. The OTTOMAN TURKS took over the city in 1516.

Further reading: Wallace Bruce Fleming, *The History of Tyre* (1915; reprint, New York: AMS Press, 1966); Nina Jidejian, *Tyre through the Ages* (Beirut: Dar el-Mashreq Publishers, 1969).

U

Ubertino da Casale (ca. 1259–ca. 1329/30) *mystic, theologian*

Probably from near GENOA, Ubertino entered the FRANCISCAN ORDER in 1273 and was at the *studium* of Santa Croce at FLORENCE between 1285 and 1289 as a pupil of Peter John OLIVI. He then studied in PARIS between 1289 and 1298. Returning to ITALY, he joined circles around ANGELA OF FOLIGNO and began to preach widely in central Italy. Although protected for a while by important cardinals such as Giacomo Colonna (d. 1318), he was exiled to Alverna for criticism of the pope and the overly worldly concerns of the church in 1304. It was then that he wrote his famous work *The Tree of the Crucified life of Jesus* which dealt with the life of the Christ or the Word, from before the Incarnation, the infancy of Jesus, his public life, and his Passion, DEATH, Resurrection, and ascent into HEAVEN, including his meeting with his mother. His ideas were based on orthodox and traditional writings by BONAVENTURE, Thomas AQUINAS, and BERNARD OF CLAIRVAUX. However, the *Arbor vitae* also offers an apocalyptic reading of the history of the church, mimicking Olivi's writing on the APOCALYPSE. He followed Olivi's ideas about the seven ages of the world, the role of Saint FRANCIS, and an imminent age of peace. Ubertino identified the figure of the ANTICHRIST with Popes BONIFACE VIII and Benedict XI (r. 1303–04) and linked the church with the Babylon of the Apocalypse. With invective against the hierarchy of the church, he railed against the leadership of the Franciscan order, claiming the order had departed from its original vows of complete poverty espoused by its founder.

From 1309 to 1310 Ubertino lived at the papal court in AVIGNON, representing the spiritual faction of the Franciscans but failed to acquire recognition or sanction for their ideas. He wrote several short treatises at this time about POVERTY, the reform of the order, and the correctness of Olivi's ideas. He then joined a Benedictine monastery. Pope JOHN XXII officially consulted him in his efforts to deal with the poverty question. Eventually he was persecuted for his ideas and had to flee Avignon in 1325. It is unclear where he spent his last years in hiding. Living a vagabond existence because he was wanted by the PAPACY, he last appeared preaching against Pope John XXII in Como in northern Italy in 1329. He had apparently died and possibly met a violent end by 1330.

See also CELESTINE V, POPE AND THE CELESTINE ORDER; POVERTY, VOLUNTARY; SPIRITUAL FRANCISCANS.

Further reading: David Burr, *The Spiritual Franciscans: From Protest to Persecution in the Century after Saint Francis* (University Park: Pennsylvania State University Press, 2001); Decima L. Douie, *The Nature and the Effect of the Heresy of the Fraticelli* (Manchester: Manchester University Press, 1932); Malcolm D. Lambert, *Franciscan Poverty: The Doctrine of the Absolute Poverty of Christ and the Apostles in the Franciscan Order, 1210–1323* (London: S.P.C.K., 1961).

Uccello, Paolo (Paolo di Dono) (1397–1475) *Florentine painter*

Born about 1397, Paolo studied between 1407 and 1414 in the studio of Lorenzo GHIBERTI, working on the bronze doors for the baptistery at FLORENCE. He received training as a goldsmith at the same time. Between 1425 and 1430, he lived in VENICE, working perhaps on a MOSAIC in Saint Mark's cathedral, and became familiar with the styles of other artists such as GENTILE DA FABRIANO, Antonio PISANELLO, and Jacopo BELLINI. He began to combine naturalism with particular attention to realism and detail. He soon turned to ideas and practices of perspective in painting. Back in Florence he painted the equestrian FRESCO of the mercenary captain John HAWKWOOD in the cathedral of Florence in 1436 and a series of frescoes on Noah and the flood in the cloister of Santa Maria Novella in the same city in the 1440s. These both demonstrated his innovative use of perspective and foreshortening. He was also employed at Urbino and PADUA about the same time.

Around 1456, fulfilling a commission from the MEDICI family, Uccello produced three panels depicting the *Battle of San Romano*, now in Florence, PARIS, and LONDON. The two small, almost surreal panels of a *Saint George and the Dragon* and the *Night Hunt* are among his last documented works from about 1460. In a tax document of 1469, he claimed to be poor and ill and to have a sick wife. He died probably in poverty and isolation in Florence in 1475.

Further reading: Franco Borsi, *Paolo Uccello*, trans. Elfreda Powell (New York: H. N. Abrams, 1994); John Pope-Hennessy, *Paolo Uccello: Complete Edition*, 2d ed. (1950; reprint, London: Phaidon, 1969); Jean Louis Schefer, *The Deluge, the Plague—Paolo Uccello*, trans. Tom Conley (Ann Arbor: University of Michigan Press, 1995).

ulama (ulema) Among the SUNNI Muslims the *ulama* were (and are) men of knowledge trained in the religious sciences, who formed groups called *alim*. From the early years or the classical age of ISLAM, they were the formulators of the religion: the bearers of wisdom, leaders of the religious community, civil servants, and interpreters of Islam. This élite was required to have extensive knowledge of the QURAN and ability to apply it to Muslim society often as QADIS, muftis, IMAMS, and mullahs. The *ulama* were the teachers, preachers, authors, social critics, and promoters of the status quo. Some promoted Islamic change and revolution. They could not be considered CLERGY, though they did have considerable training and were all recognized for their religious knowledge and roles as the custodians of "orthodoxy."

Further reading: Daphna Ephrat, *A Learned Society in a Period of Transition: The Sunni "Ulama" of Eleventh Century Baghdad* (Albany: State University of New York Press, 2000); Ira M. Lapidus, *A History of Islamic Societies* (Cambridge: Cambridge University Press, 1988); W. Montgomery Watt, *The Formative Period of Islamic Thought* (Oxford: Oneworld Publications, 1998).

Ulphilas (Ulfilas, Wulfila Ulfila) (ca. 311–ca. 382) *apostle of the Goths, translator of the Bible into Gothic*
Ulphilas was born in ANATOLIA about 311, perhaps in Cappadocia or Romania, to a Christian family Captured by GOTHS, he was eventually sent to CONSTANTINOPLE, where he became fluent in LATIN, Greek, and Gothic. After a Christian education, he was in about 338 made bishop of the still-heathen VISIGOTHS by the Arian bishop of Constantinople. Working initially in the area north of the Danube but forced back into a safer area controlled by the Byzantines, he slowly and with great difficulty succeeded in converting them to an Arian form of Christianity which at the time had not been clearly branded as HERESY. This Arianism then spread to many of the other Germanic tribes. To accomplish this conversion, Ulphilas and his collaborators devised a Gothic alphabet and translated much of the BIBLE into Gothic. Active in ecclesiastical affairs throughout his life, he died in Constantinople while attending a synod in about 382.

See also ARIANISM.

Further reading: C. A. Anderson Scott, *Ulfilas, Apostle of the Goths Together with an Account of the Gothic Churches and Their Decline* (Cambridge: Macmillan and Bowes, 1885); M. J. Hunter, "The Gothic Bible" in *The Cambridge History of the Bible*, ed. G. W. H. Lampe (Cambridge: Cambridge University Press, 1969), 2.338–362; James Woodrow Marchand, *The Sounds and Phonemes of Wulfila's Gothic* (The Hague: Mouton, 1973); E. A. Thompson, *The Visigoths in the Time of Ulfila* (Oxford: Clarendon Press, 1966).

Umar I ibn al-Khattab, Caliph (Omar, Abu Hafsa ibn al-Khattab) (ca. 586–644) *second Sunni caliph, companion of Muhammad*
A member of a patrician family, the clan of the Adi ibn Kab of the tribe of the QURAYSH in MECCA, Umar I was among the first to convert to ISLAM in 618. He fought in the Battles of BADR and Uhud. He was a strong supporter of ABU BAKR both before and after his reign as caliph. There has been some dispute about whether he was appointed CALIPH by the dying Abu Bakr. As the second caliph from 634 to 644, Umar I promoted Arab unity, oversaw major territorial expansion, and was a great military leader who earned the name "Commander of the Faithful."

Enjoying universal support, Umar led the ARABS to the conquest of PALESTINE, SYRIA, EGYPT, and IRAQ. He transformed Arab conquerors into a separate military class who were to rule the newly conquered territories and could not engage in AGRICULTURE or commerce. They lived in tent cities. He permitted the conquered peoples to practice their own religious rather than insisting on conversion but required them to pay a poll tax for protection. He was instrumental in transmitting numerous HADITH. He instituted the method of selecting caliphs by means of a committee with election then accompanied by the clasping of hands and the exchange of OATHS of allegiance to the successor. He was assassinated for his tyranny in 644 in the MOSQUE at MEDINA by a Persian slave, Abu Luluah.

Further reading: Fred M. Donner, *The Early Islamic Conquests* (Princeton, N.J.: Princeton University Press, 1981); Francesco Gabrieli, *Muhammad and the Conquests of Islam,* trans. Virginia Luling and Rosamund Linell (New York: McGraw-Hill, 1968); Donald R. Hill, *The Termination of Hostilities in the Early Arab Conquests,* A.D. 634–656 (London: Luzac, 1971); Wilferd Madelung, "Umar: Commander of the Faithful, Islamic Meritocracy, Consultation and Arab Empire," in *The Succession to Muhammad: A Study of the Early Caliphate* (Cambridge: Cambridge University Press, 1997), 57–77.

Umayyads (Omayyads) This initially aristocratic and merchant Arab dynasty dominated the lands of ISLAM from 660 to 750, with its capital at DAMASCUS in SYRIA. It was founded by Muawiya ibn Abi Sufyan (r. 661–680), the son of a companion of MUHAMMAD who was the gifted governor of Syria at the time of the assassination of the third CALIPH, UTHMAN, in 656. It fell to Muawiya according to the prescriptions of the QURAN, to avenge his kinsman and oppose the fourth caliph, ALI IBN ABU TALIB. Ali was himself responsible for Uthman's murder, though Muawiya thought he was. Moreover, Ali had refused to hand over its perpetrators. After the Battle of Siffin on the Euphrates River, Muawiya was acknowledged as caliph at JERUSALEM in place of Ali, who was assassinated at Kufa in IRAQ later in 661. Muawiya introduced dynastic succession into Islam, since he was the first to designate his son as heir and have him so acknowledged in his lifetime. He moved the capital to Damascus and made the caliphate more secular. The Umayyads successfully continued conquest and organized the newly established empire. Under the caliphs from the Marinid branch of the family, ABD AL-MALIK and AL-WALID, the empire reached its greatest extent, with conquests from the Iberian Peninsula to AFGHANISTAN and India, and its forces almost captured CONSTANTINOPLE in the 670s. Under the Umayyads, Arabic was declared the official language of the empire, and ARABS took over governments from Greeks and Persians.

By the reign of the caliph Umar II (r. 717–720), who also furthered the Islamization of the empire, the state had serious religious, social, and financial problems. By Hisham's reign between 724 and 743, external expansion had halted, sometimes in defeat as at the Battle of POITIERS IN 732. Opposition continued to grow and the perceived secularization of the empire was strongly opposed by some. Partisans of Ali's descendants, the SHIITES, began to foment revolts. At MECCA an anticaliph, Ibn Zubayr, held the city for several years. In the mideighth century, the descendants of an uncle of the Prophet, the ABBASIDS, started insurrections in eastern IRAN at Khurasan that soon ended the Umayyad dynasty. The Abbasids defeated the last Umayyad caliph, Marwan II (r. 744–750), and his army at the Battle of the Great Zab River in 750. Marwan was subsequently killed while trying to escape in EGYPT, and the other members of the family were massacred. One survivor, ABD AL-RAHMAN, fled to SPAIN, where in 756, he founded the Umayyad caliphate at CÓRDOBA, which flourished in the ninth and 10th centuries.

See also ART AND ARCHITECTURE, ISLAMIC; CÓRDOBA; ISLAM; SHIA, SHIISM, AND SHIITES.

Further reading: Gerald R. Hawting, *The First Dynasty of Islam: The Umayyad Caliphate* A.D. 661–750, 2d ed. (London: Routledge, 2000); Naji Hasan, *The Role of the Arab Tribes in the East during the Period of the Umayyads (40/660–132/749)* (Baghdad: Al-Jamea's Press, 1978); Hugh Kennedy, *The Armies of the Caliphs: Military and Society in the Early Islamic State* (London: Routledge, 2001); Jirji Zaydan, *Umayyads and Abbasids: Being the Fourth Part of Jurjí Zaydan's History of Islamic Civilization,* trans. D. S. Margoliouth (London: Darf, 1987).

Umayyads of Córdoba *See* ABD AL-RAHMAN; AL-ANDALUS; UMAYYADS.

umma (ummah) Derived from the Arabic word for "mother," the word *umma* is borrowed from Hebrew or Aramaic. In the QURAN it means "people" or "community," designating the people to whom GOD has sent a prophet to make them the objects of a divine plan of salvation. At the beginnings of ISLAM, each political and religious group conceived of itself as an *umma* or the community most faithful to the teachings of MUHAMMAD. The term was applied to all Muslims as the best of communities willed by God and established by Muhammad to live under Islamic law. Despite dissent, this identification of all Muslims with this community, the proclaiming of its essential unity, and the assertion of the theoretical equality of Muslims, regardless of their diverse cultural and geographical settings, have always been strong elements of Islam.

Further reading: Antony J. Black, *The History of Islamic Political Thought: From the Prophet to the Present* (New York: Routledge, 2001); R. Stephen Humphreys, *Islamic History: A Framework for Inquiry,* rev. ed. (Princeton, N.J.: Princeton University Press, 1991).

unction of the sick *See* SEVEN SACRAMENTS.

unicorn The unicorn is a mythical beast, perhaps based on the rhinoceros. The story of the unicorn is often found in medieval BESTIARIES based on the *Physiologus* (The naturalist), a collection of stories composed in ALEXANDRIA between the second and fourth centuries. It is a fantastic animal resembling a small white goat, wild ass, or horse. It is extremely fierce, with a single horn in the middle of its head capable of killing elephants. With that horn it kills any hunter who tries to go near it. However, if a virgin approaches it, the animal meekly walks to her lap, the girl nourishes it, and then hunters can capture it. The girl must be chaste if this kind of hunt is to work. The unicorn has symbolic values and moral interpretations that were important in medieval imagery and iconography. It symbolized Christ's Incarnation and self-chosen Passion as well as the value of the chastity of the Blessed Virgin MARY. Its horn was also used as a symbol for the purifying cross on which Christ died. The horn of a unicorn also acquired therapeutic and erotic value and was a much sought after prize with supposed examples on display in cathedral and palace treasuries. The horn could magically protect against PLAGUE, LEPROSY, and poisonings.

Further reading: Gottfried Büttner, *The Lady and the Unicorn: The Development of the Human Soul as Pictured in the Cluny Tapestries,* trans. Roland Everett (Stroud: Hawthorn Press, 1995); Adolph S. Cavallo, *The Unicorn Tapestries at the Metropolitan Museum of Art* (New York: H. N. Abrams, 1998); Michael Green, *Unicornis: On the History and Truth of the Unicorn* (Philadelphia: Running Press, 1988); Paul A. Johnsgard, *Dragons and Unicorns: A Natural History* (New York: St. Martin's Press, 1992).

universals Universals can be defined as "signs common to several things." The term can also mean "natures signified by a common word." For the Middle Ages this ambiguity challenged the status and function of the universal at the intersection of metaphysical and semantic questions: whether the universal was really common to several things or was merely said of several things. In the former view, philosophers or theologians studied the form or the common nature or the universal in things. In the latter, they made the universal a name, a concept, or a sign. So the question became, especially in the 12th century, whether general names, genera, and species were merely words or really things. The reality of common natures was accepted more in the 13th century. In the late 14th and the early 15th centuries, new ideas of realism were promoted by JOHN WYCLIFFE, WILLIAM OF OCKHAM, and JOHN BURIDAN. In general, in their eyes, the universal could not exist in things because everything that existed was singular. So the universal was a sign, a concept, or a word and the universal existed singularly, as a quality or an act created by the mind. It was only universal because it signified a plurality. This discussion dominated speculative thought throughout the 15th century.

See also ABÉLARD, PETER; ALBERTUS MAGNUS; DUNS SCOTUS, JOHN; GILBERT OF POITIERS; IBN SINA, ABU ALI AL-HUSAYN.

Further reading: Marilyn McCord Adams, *William Ockham,* 2 vols. (Notre Dame, Ind.: University of Notre Dame Press, 1987); John Marenbon, *Later Medieval Philosophy (1150–1350): An Introduction* (London: Routledge & K. Paul, 1987); James A. Summers, *St. Thomas and the Universal* (Washington, D.C.: Catholic University of American Press, 1955); Martin M. Tweedale, *Scotus vs. Ockham: A Medieval Dispute over Universals,* 2 vols. (Lewiston, N.Y.: E. Mellen Press, 1999).

universities and schools Before 1500 education in schools and universities was a religious domain in both Christianity and ISLAM. Medieval schools in CHRISTENDOM continued much of the legacy of classical education and were based on the study of the SEVEN LIBERAL ARTS; professional training was acquired through apprenticeships.

EDUCATION IN BYZANTIUM

In BYZANTIUM urban schools in the classical format continued, offering more advanced study in history, THEOLOGY, and LAW at imperial academies in CONSTANTINOPLE. The teachers were state employees. This system, primarily designed to educate bureaucrats and clerics, was destroyed when Western Europeans took over Constantinople in the Fourth Crusade. Some remnants of it survived in Nicaea and then were revived again in Constantinople in the later Middle Ages, when Orthodox theological ideas in particular were retained.

ISLAMIC EDUCATION

Islamic education from the beginning was based on studies of the commentaries on the QURAN and of philology or the linguistic rules of Arabic. By the eighth century Greek and Persian philosophical and scientific ideas were incorporated into the Muslim schools. This educational system reached its peak of influence and prestige at the beginning of the ninth century with the founding of the Academy of BAGHDAD by the CALIPH AL-MAMUN. This curriculum now included theology, jurisprudence, Aristotelian PHILOSOPHY, and the sciences, including mathematics, physics, astronomy, and ASTROLOGY. Other centers followed this model at AL-QAYRAWAN, CAIRO, and CÓRDOBA. In the second half of the 12th century, the regime of NUR AL-DIN closed the traditional philosophical and scientific schools and created the system of the *MADRASA* whose goal was to produce proponents of SUNNI Islam and train competent and loyal government officials. This system as based primarily on an authoritative and normative study by rote of Muslim law and religion. The MONGOL invasions of the 13th century completed the destruction of the older system, but the madrasa system was maintained.

EDUCATION IN WESTERN EUROPE

In Western Europe in the early Middle Ages, the classical educational system based on urban schools had collapsed by the seventh century. The church, however, maintained a monopoly on education by supporting monastic schools according to the system proposed by CASSIODORUS at the

712 Urban II, Blessed

beginning of the sixth century. They spread throughout western Christian Europe over the next two centuries. The Carolingian Reform movement, led by ALCUIN OF YORK in the ninth century, was a product of these schools. The educational reforms of CHARLEMAGNE required the establishment of a school in every bishopric and monastery of his empire. In them the CLERGY would be trained to the new standards. Many of these monastic schools continued to educate the clergy and the LAITY throughout the period up to 1500. There was even some provision to educate talented men of poor families, whose skills could be put to work for the church and the developing institutions of government. There were also schools at the courts of monarchs such as Charlemagne. From the 12th century these palace and monastic schools sent some of their lay and clerical students to the new higher education system of the universities. From that same era the newly developed towns began sponsoring schools that educated the laity, which soon expanded into business, literacy and arithmetic, and the notarial arts. All of this had to done by memorization and at an oral level than later, since usually only teachers had books and students could only copy and learn what they were told.

JEWISH EDUCATION

Judaism had its own educational system in the Middle Ages. It was based on the great Talmudic academies that originated in Mesopotamia. They emphasized the study of the law and interpretation of Scriptures and the commentaries of earlier sages and scholars. From the 10th century, Spanish or Sephardic Jews influenced by Arab literature and thought concentrated more on philosophical, scientific, and linguistic studies. The Ashkenazi Jews of FRANCE and GERMANY emphasized legal and exegetic studies.

PROFESSIONALIZATION IN WESTERN EUROPE

From the 11th century a revival of learning in Europe led to growing professionalization of knowledge. New schools that developed at BOLOGNA and PARIS for the study of law and theology became the basis for the autonomous institutions called universities. They were to function initially as GUILDS of teachers or masters who granted degrees and admitted candidates to the professions. This wide autonomy was not to last very long, but the roles and powers of the masters endured within a more institutional framework. The Universities of CAMBRIDGE and OXFORD in ENGLAND originated in response to the same needs and with the same initial organization. The balance of power between the students and the teaching faculties could and did change, and the students became better organized and gained greater control of the finances or salaries of their teachers. The study of theology and philosophy played a considerable role in the early curricula along with the seven liberal arts, but subjects turned much more vocational as students progressed to a degree

through the system; not everyone attained a degree, however, since that was really only necessary for the profession of teaching.

Universities sprouted all over Europe in the period after 1200, with Paris as the model for the course of study based on lecturing and disputation and institutional organization. They played important roles in the intellectual, political, and social life of Europe and Christendom. The idea of a community of masters licensed to teach at the highest level, in other words, a university, is one that we owe entirely to the Middle Ages.

See also HUMANISM; LANFRANC OF BEC; NOTARIES AND THE NOTARIATE; SCHOLASTICISM AND THE SCHOLASTIC METHOD.

Further reading: Robert Black, *Humanism and Education in Medieval and Renaissance Italy: Tradition and Innovation in Latin Schools from the Twelfth to the Fifteenth Century* (Cambridge: Cambridge University Press, 2001); Paul F. Grendler, *The Universities of the Italian Renaissance* (Baltimore: Johns Hopkins University Press, 2002); Wilfred Madelung, *Religious Schools and Sects in Medieval Islam* (London: Variorum, 1985); Nicholas Orme, *English Schools in the Middle Ages* (London: Methuen, 1973); Nicholas Orme, *Education and Society in Medieval and Renaissance England* (London: Hambledon Press, 1989); Hastings Rashdall, *The Universities of Europe in the Middle Ages,* ed. F. M. Powicke and A. B. Emden, 3 vols. (Oxford: Clarendon Press, 1936); Jacques Verger, "The Universities," in *The New Cambridge Medieval History.* Vol. 6, *c. 1300–c. 1415,* ed. Michael Jones (Cambridge: Cambridge University Press, 2000), 82–101.

Urban II, Blessed (Odo of Châtillon, Oddone, Eudes, Otto or Odo of Lagery) (ca. 1039–1099) *French pope who launched the First Crusade*
Odo, later Urban was born about 1042 in Châtillon-sur-Marne in a noble family of Champagne. After studying with Saint BRUNO at RHEIMS, he entered the monastery of CLUNY between 1067 and 1070, soon serving as its grand prior between 1074 and 1079. He then became an ardent supporter of the GREGORIAN REFORM and was rewarded by promotion to the rank of cardinal-bishop of Ostia by Pope GREGORY VII.

At the death of Victor III (r. 1087), Gregory's successor, on September 6, 1087, ROME was under the control of an antipope. Six chaotic months elapsed before Odo was finally elected pope as Urban II. He was consecrated at Terracina, south of Rome, on March 12, 1088. Urban II was more moderate but still strongly reaffirmed the positions of Gregory VII on SIMONY, NICOLAITISM, and lay investiture. On the other hand, he was more conciliatory about questionable ordinations during the INVESTITURE CONTROVERSY. He did bring about legislation that forbade the clergy to take feudal OATHS binding them to any of the LAITY. Aided by various political changes of allegiance

Arrival of Pope Urban II at the Council of Clermont in France, miniature from *Roman de Godefroi de Bouillon* (1337), Ms. fr. 22495, fol. 15, Bibliothèque Nationale, Paris *(Giraudon / Art Resource)*

and the support of the NORMANS in ITALY, he was able to return to Rome in 1093.

The major event of Urban's reign was his call to CRUSADE launched at the Council of CLERMONT between November 18 and November 28 of 1095. Urban had earlier sponsored a Truce of God on CHRISTENDOM at the Council of Melfi in 1089, at Troia in 1093, and finally at Clermont. Violence could be legitimate when it was employed for the glory of GOD as in the RECONQUEST already under way in SPAIN and SICILY. Christendom was to unite with the BYZANTINE EMPIRE to free the Holy Land or PALESTINE from the Muslims. He succeeded beyond what he must have expected but died before the capture of JERUSALEM in 1099. In the meantime he had to deal with the marital problems of the king of France, Philip I (r. 1060–1108), and a dispute between the king of ENGLAND, WILLIAM II RUFUS, and the archbishop of CANTERBURY, ANSELM. He died at Rome on July 29, 1099, in the Palace of the Pierleone in Rome two weeks after the crusaders took Jerusalem. He was buried in Saint Peter's and was beatified in 1881.

See also PEACE AND TRUCE OF GOD.

Further reading: Francis J. Gossman, *Pope Urban II and Canon Law* (Washington, D.C.: Catholic University of America Press, 1960); Jonathan Riley-Smith, *The First Crusade and the Idea of Crusading* (Philadelphia: University of Pennsylvania Press, 1986); Robert Somerville and Stephan Kuttner, *Pope Urban II, the Collectio Britannica, and the Council of Melfi (1089)* (Oxford: Clarendon Press, 1996).

Urban VI (Bartolomeo Prignano) (1318–1389) *mentally disturbed and brutal pope*
Bartolomeo, later Urban VI, was descended from an influential Neapolitan family and was pontifical chancellor of Pope Gregory XI (r. 1371–78) and archbishop of BARI on his election in 1377. On the death in 1378 of Gregory XI,

who had moved the papacy back to Rome, the Roman populace was fearful that the election of a French pope would mean the transfer of the PAPACY back to the city of AVIGNON. Six cardinals remained in Avignon and did not even attend the conclave to elect a new pope. The Romans raised such a threatening riot that the CARDINALS meeting to elect the new pope were forced to elect an Italian rapidly. A mob had actually entered the meeting place to try to influence the election. On April 8, 1378, Bartolomeo was viewed as a competent administrator and seemed to be a well-known commodity to the cardinals who intimidated again by a crowd, elected him pope as Urban VI. He was the last noncardinal to be elected pope.

Urban's wild tirades and threats to appoint a majority of Italian cardinals soon scared the French cardinals, who withdrew to Anagni outside Rome during the summer of 1378. By August 9, 1378, they had called a new election and then designated Cardinal Robert of Geneva as Pope Clement VII (r. 1378–94). Robert was a tough and experienced soldier who had been involved in the slaughter of 4,000 rebels against papal rule in Cesena in 1377. Urban VI naturally persisted in considering himself as the sole legitimate pope. He quickly formed a new College of Cardinals, though he soon fell out even with them, condemning five of them to death a few years later. These dual questionable elections and events led to the Great SCHISM, which lasted until 1417.

Urban proved to be a very authoritarian and ineffective reformer of a now seriously divided church. Needing money and seeking to solidify his support in the tourist-based industry of Rome, he proclaimed a HOLY YEAR for 1390. To accomplish that, he had to change the interval between jubilee celebrations to 33 years, the length of Christ's life. He paid special attention during his reign to securing the throne of NAPLES for one of his nephews, Charles of Durazzo (1345–86), and very little indeed to settling the election question. Eventually he went to war with his own nephew. He seems to have actually led armies in the field. With the PAPAL STATES in chaos, he died, probably poisoned, on October 15, 1389.

See also CATHERINE OF SIENA, SAINT.

Further reading: Welbore St. Clair Baddeley, *Charles III of Naples and Urban VI: Also Cecco d'Ascoli, Poet, Astrologer, Physician, Two Historical Essays* (London: W. Heinemann, 1894); Guillaume Mollat, *The Popes at Avignon, 1305–1378*, trans. Janet Love (1949; reprint, New York: T. Nelson 1963); Yves Renouard, *Avignon Papacy, 1305–1403*, trans. Dennis Bethell (London: Faber, 1970).

Ursula, Saint, and her companions, legend of   The legend of Ursula and her companions originated in a single Latin inscription from about 400 in the church of Saint Ursula in COLOGNE that recorded the BURIAL of some local virgin-martyrs. By the ninth century this became a tale of a princess and her companions who were martyred in the persecutions of the emperors Maximian (r. 286–305) and DIOCLETIAN. There also occurred a misreading of a text specifying 11 virgin-martyrs which was probably corrupted into 11,000 virgins. In this form the story became part of the *GOLDEN LEGEND,* one of the most popular collections of stories about the saints of the Middle Ages.

According to the *Golden Legend,* Ursula was the daughter of a British Christian king, betrothed for political reasons to a pagan English prince, but obtained a delay of three years during which she and her betrothed went on a PILGRIMAGE. The couple sailed down the Rhine River and then on to ROME, where they were received by the pope and the prince was baptized. On their way home, they arrived at Cologne, where the pilgrims were all martyred by the HUNS. The Huns could have been in Cologne in the midfifth century, but a pope mentioned in the text is not recorded elsewhere.

CULT

In 1155 a large number of bones from a forgotten cemetery were discovered at Cologne. These were interpreted as RELICS of the princess and her companions. A cult evolved in the Rhineland, the Low Countries, and VENICE. Ursula became a patron saint of educational institutions for girls. She and her martyrdom became the subject of numerous paintings in Northern Europe and the famous series created about 1490 by Vittore Carpaccio (ca. 1460–ca. 1525) in Venice. Her feast day, October 21, was suppressed in 1969.

Further reading: C. M. Kauffmann, *The Legend of Saint Ursula* (London: H.M.S.O., 1964).

usury   Usury initially referred to the charging of any interest at all for any sort of loan. It did not have to be excessive. The prohibition of usury was based on Scripture, which forbade the exploitation of those in desperate need. Its prohibition was common to Christians, Muslims, and JEWS. The prohibition was linked then with the principles of JUSTICE and CHARITY. With the commercial and business development of the 12th century, the legitimacy of loan contracts began to be based on and determined by what was given and what was received in exchange. One could not licitly receive more. Usury could occur when nothing was actually produced, added, or transformed for example, in the process of investing in enterprises. One was not to charge for the use of money or of time, which actually belonged to GOD. Money was not fruitful or fungible and was thus incapable of producing anything. It was at best only a medium of exchange. One perhaps could collect it from enemies or maybe even foreigners, the sin then would be avarice, that is, an offense against justice, rather like theft.

Usurers were certainly endangering their salvation and REDEMPTION while risking graphic and unpleasant punishments in the afterlife unless they returned any gains to those from whom they had collected them. Excommunicated and banned from Christian BURIAL usurers could lose their ill-gotten gains to confiscations by the state. The WILLS of the LAITY were scrutinized for repayments for usury in the later Middle Ages. Various commercial devices and legalistic and moral arguments were developed to handle covert charging of interest and to justify certain ways of collecting interest. However, the prohibition of usury remained a staple subject of sermons throughout this period. In time the definitions and penalties became more flexible. In the context of economic and moral realities, profit, even certain gain, from business activity was permitted or deemed marginally licit, especially if joint risk could be suggested. Nevertheless, one could be called to the attention of the ecclesiastical and secular authorities if perceived as too rapacious and exploitative of other people or of those in genuine need.

THE BYZANTINE EMPIRE, MUSLIMS, AND JEWS

In the BYZANTINE EMPIRE usury was handled in much the same way. JEWS were sometimes allowed to practice it,

Usurers suffer in hell, from Jean Gerson, *Le Trésor de Sapience,* Ms. 146 (15th century), Musée Condé, Chantilly, France *(Giraudon / Art Resource)*

disguising it in ways similar to those devised by Christians. Such actually rare activity, by then surfaced in the popular rationale of anti-Jewish riots and pogroms. For Muslims usury, or *riba,* was also defined as "the charging of interest on a loan," which was forbidden in the QURAN in very clear terms. Its prohibition was only partially enforced and various devices or *hiyal* were employed to give it some kind of cover. The argument of equality of risk and profit of the partners to a transaction was used to justify investment and banking activities. For ISLAM MONEY also had no time value.

See also BANKS AND BANKING; ECONOMIC THOUGHT AND JUSTICE; MERCHANTS.

Further reading: John W. Baldwin, *Masters, Princes and Merchants: The Social Views of Peter the Chanter and His Circle,* 2 vols. (Princeton, N.J.: Princeton University Press, 1970); John T. Gilchrist, *The Church and Economic Activity in the Middle Ages* (New York: St. Martin's Press, 1969); Benjamin Nelson, *The Idea of Usury: From Tribal Brotherhood to Universal Otherhood,* 2d ed. (Chicago: University of Chicago Press, 1969); John T. Noonan Jr., *The Scholastic Analysis of Usury* (Cambridge, Mass.: Harvard University Press, 1957); Abraham L. Udovitch, *Partnership and Profit in Medieval Islam* (Princeton, N.J.: Princeton University Press, 1970).

Uthman ibn Affan (Othman) (r. 644–656) *companion of the Prophet, third caliph*

Uthman was a member of the Umayyad clan, a family who initially opposed MUHAMMAD. A wealthy MERCHANT, Uthman, among the first converts to ISLAM, married two daughters of Muhammad, Ruqayya (d. 624) and then Umm Kulthum (d. 630). He played a minor role in the growth of Islam while Muhammad was still alive and did not take part in the battles, being famously wary of bloodshed then and during his reign. Despite his lack of experience, he was elected caliph by a committee appointed by his predecessor, UMAR I, on his deathbed in 644. He was perhaps the only alternative to ALI IBN ABU TALIB.

Muslim historians have tended to view Uthman's 12-year reign as six years of good rule and six years of bad rule. Not much of an administrator, he had a religious vision and made the first efforts to standardize the sacred text of the QURAN and attempted to have all the variant collections destroyed. His name remained on that version of the text. He was accused of ruling ineptly, making illegal and arbitrary grants of lands, and practicing nepotism by appointing many relatives to high positions. Uthman was then faced with strong popular discontent that led to a military mutiny. He was assassinated in MEDINA in 656. The nomination of Ali as his successor led to the first civil war in Islam.

Further reading: "Wilfred Madelung, Uthmān: The Vicegerent of God and the Reign of Abd Shams," in *The Succession to Muhammad: A Study of the Early Caliphate* (Cambridge: Cambridge University Press, 1997), 78–140; W. Montgomery Watt, *The Formative Period of Islamic Thought* (Oxford: Oneworld, 1998).

utraquists and utraquism

Utraquism in the Middle Ages was the belief that it was permissible and preferable to receive communion or the Eucharist in both kinds or under both species. In other words, the LAITY could, and should, receive at communion both the consecrated bread and the wine, or the body and the blood of Christ. This concept was one of the few common points among the different sects of Hussites in BOHEMIA and MORAVIA. It was the main difference that they had with the rest of the church under the leadership of the pope. The Catholic Church of the time allowed only the bread to be given to the lay communicant. Only the priest partook of both species a tradition called subunism.

The Councils of CONSTANCE in 1415 and BASEL in 1432 both condemned utraquism. To the Hussites, utraquism confirmed the equality of all Christians before GOD. It was also justifiable to them as a practice of the early church. The first distribution of communion in both kinds to Czech lay people took place in the autumn of 1414. Taking the chalice became one of the essential points of the Hussite program in the *Four Articles of Prague* of 1420.

The utraquists did not consider themselves to be in heresy from the Roman church, but only more perfect Catholics. A more moderate group was called the Calixtines, referring to the Latin word for the "chalice." The success of utraquism became tied to the course of the Hussite wars in Bohemia. After the defeat of the most radical wing of the utraquists at the Battle of Lipany in 1435, a pact worked out in 1436 limited utraquist practice to Bohemia and Moravia. Pope PIUS II later cancelled this permission in 1462; but it was maintained by the Bohemian Diet until 1567. The idea lived on among the Moravian Brethren and resurfaced in various reform movements of the 16th century.

See also HUS, JOHN; SEVEN SACRAMENTS; TABORITES.

Further reading: Frantisek Michálek Bartoš, *The Hussite Revolution, 1424–1437,* trans. John M. Klassen (New York: Columbia University Press, 1986); Howard Kaminsky, *A History of the Hussite Revolution* (Berkeley: University of California Press, 1967); Josef Macek, *The Hussite Movement in Bohemia* (New York: AMS Press, 1980); David V. Zdeněk, *Finding the Middle Way: the Utraquists' Liberal Challenge to Rome and Luther* (Baltimore: Johns Hopkins University Press, 2003).

V

Valdemar I the Great   *See* WALDEMAR I THE GREAT.

Valdemar II the Conqueror   *See* WALDEMAR II THE CONQUEROR.

Valencia   Medieval Valencia was the capital of the agriculturally rich Valencia region in eastern SPAIN on the Mediterranean. The VISIGOTHS conquered this Roman colony in 413. The Muslims captured it in 714 and made it the capital of a Muslim kingdom on the eastern coast of the Iberian Peninsula. It was attacked by the Christians in 1065 and taken by RODRIGO DÍAZ DE VIVAR, the Cid, in 1094 but was lost to the ALMORAVIDS in 1102. It fell permanently into the hands of the Aragonese in 1238 under JAMES I the Conqueror and became the center of a new Christian kingdom of Valencia. The city and region were incorporated into the state of CASTILE and ARAGON in 1479.

Muslims remained numerous in the city there, though their number slowly shrank over the centuries. They maintained links with other Muslims on the coast of North AFRICA and the kingdom of GRANADA. Jewish communities in the city and region were weakened by the riots of 1391 and the conversions of 1412–13. King FERDINAND II was more tolerant of both minorities, but as his kingdom became more integrated with that of ISABEL I OF CASTILE, conditions for these minorities deteriorated markedly and ended in expulsion on March 31, 1492. Assisted by the lingering presence of the commercial links of the expelled JEWS and Muslims, the economy of Valencia prospered in the period before 1500, especially in commerce, trade in foodstuffs, shipbuilding, and paper making.

The first printing press in Spain was established in Valencia in 1474. MERCHANTS dominated the local government and put heavy restrictions on the local craft GUILDS and artisans, generating considerable class and social tension. The tax burden increased greatly over the last years of the 15th century to pay for the conquest of Granada in 1492.

See also IRRIGATION.

Further reading: Robert Ignatius Burns, *The Crusader Kingdom of Valencia: Reconstruction on a Thirteenth-Century Frontier,* 2 vols. (Cambridge, Mass.: Harvard University Press, 1967); Robert Ignatius Burns, *Islam under the Crusaders, Colonial Survival in the Thirteenth-Century Kingdom of Valencia* (Princeton, N.J.: Princeton University Press 1973); Robert Ignatius Burns, *Medieval Colonialism: Postcrusade Exploitation of Islamic Valencia* (Princeton, N.J.: Princeton University Press, 1975); Robert Ignatius Burns, *Muslims, Christians, and Jews in the Crusader Kingdom of Valencia: Societies in Symbiosis* (Cambridge: Cambridge University Press, 1984); Thomas F. Glick, *Irrigation and Society in Medieval Valencia* (Cambridge, Mass.: The Belknap Press of Harvard University Press, 1970); Mark D. Meyerson, *The Muslims of Valencia in the Age of Fernando and Isabel: Between Coexistence and Crusade* (Berkeley: University of California Press, 1991).

Valhalla (Valhöll, the Hall of the Slain, Carrion Hall)   The mythical Valhalla was the great hall of the high god Odin in Asgard, the citadel of gods, and the home to the souls of brave warriors killed in battle. Chosen by Odin and led to Valhalla by the VALKYRIES, they were welcomed by Bragi, the Norse god of poetry. Valhalla's roof was made of spears, and the interior of the hall itself was covered with shields and coats of mail. There were 640 doors through which the warriors would pour out to do battle with one another every day. If they were killed, they were restored to life in order to spend the night feasting on the flesh of a boar and drinking mead with Odin, while still served by the valkyries. This daily ever-lasting battle was to end only at Ragnarok or "the Doom or Twilight of the Gods," when the human warriors would join the gods to do battle with giants, actually a cataclysmic battle between good and evil. In pagan times Valhalla may have originated as a symbol of a grave due a great warrior rather than a kind of Paradise. Nearby was the hall for the righteous, Gimli.

Further reading: H. R. Ellis Davidson, *Gods and Myths of Northern Europe* (Baltimore: Penguin Books, 1964).

Valkyrie (Walkyrie, Chooser of the Slain) They were the mythical maiden warriors who lived with the high god Odin in VALHALLA. Odin decided the outcome of battles and who was to fall and who survive. The souls of the braves were chosen by him to join him in Valhalla. The valkyries hovered over these battles and carried the chosen warriors to Valhalla, giving them cups of mead on their arrival and thereafter. Odin could give valkyries as brides to warrior kings who had merited it and had worshiped him as their protector god. Present in many Scandinavian legends valkyries could appear as both fearsome supernatural beings and humans. Valkyries were sometimes called shield maidens or *skjaldmcer,* a term that was also used in legendary literature for human female warriors.

See also ICELAND AND ICELANDIC LITERATURE.

Further reading: Theodore Murdock Anderson, *The Legend of Brynhild* (Ithaca, N.Y.: Cornell University Press, 1980); Helen Damico, *Beowulf's Wealhtheow and the Valkyrie Tradition* (Madison: University of Wisconsin Press, 1984).

Valla, Lorenzo (1407–1457) *humanist*
Born to a family of jurists at ROME in 1407, Lorenzo Villa was ordained a priest in 1431. Even when he was only 20 years old, his critical humanist studies were provocative. His first work, a comparison of Cicero and Quintilian, earned him the lasting enmity of Poggio BRACCIOLINI who prevented him from obtaining his long-desired papal curial post.

Lorenzo left Rome and became a professor of rhetoric at the University of Pavia but had to leave that town in March 1433 because he attacked the legal scholarship of BARTOLO of Sassoferrato. He then became a secretary to King ALFONSO V in NAPLES and later a scribe in the papal court. Both Alfonso and Pope Nicholas V (r. 1447–55) later had to defend him against charges of HERESY. Despite these problems, from 1455 he was supported by the revenues of numerous BENEFICES, including a canonry of Saint John Lateran in Rome.

LITERARY ACCOMPLISHMENTS

The INQUISITION had attacked Lorenzo's philosophical opinions and his view on the origin at the first council of NICAEA of the Apostle's Creed. His treatise on the eloquence of the Latin language was the first work to describe the history of Latin. This attention to philology led him to denounce the authenticity of the DONATION of Constantine in 1440 at the request of Alfonso V. He showed that the donation was a much later creation, probably done for the benefit of papal temporal power. He also corrected Saint Jerome's Latin translation of the New Testament in 1442, criticized SCHOLATICISM and its methods, and completed philosophical and theological works on will, historical biography of Alfonso, and translations of the Greek authors Homer, Xenophon, Aesop, Thucydides, and Herodotus. He died in Rome on August 1, 1457.

See also BRUNI, LEONARDO; FILELFO, FRANCESCO; VULGATE.

Further reading: Lorenzo Valla, *The Treatise of Lorenzo Valla on the Donation of Constantine,* trans. Christopher B. Coleman (Toronto: University of Toronto Press in Association with the Renaissance Society of America, 1993); Maristella di Panizza Lorch, *A Defense of Life: Lorenzo Valla's Theory of Pleasure* (Munich: W. Fink Verlag, 1985); Charles Edward Trinkaus, *In Our Image and Likeness: Humanity and Divinity in Italian Humanist Thought,* 2 vols. (Chicago: University of Chicago Press, 1970); Charles Edward Trinkaus, *Adversity's Noblemen: The Italian Humanists on Happiness* (1940; reprint, New York: Octagon Books, 1965).

Valladolid This city in northwestern SPAIN, called Belad Ulid by the Muslims, was founded anew in the second half of the 11th century as part of the program of repopulating Christians into the Duero Valley. Set in a region rich in corn, wines, and pasture, it became a principal town of the royal domain and remained loyal to the Crown of CASTILE, becoming the royal residence. Laws imposed by the Crown in 1265 strengthened the alliance with the royal government and confirmed the power of a small patriciate, who then organized themselves into two groups of factions to share government jobs.

In the late 13th century, Valladolid obtained a larger administrative region and built a wall that enclosed 13 parishes and numerous convents. ALFONSO X created a university that received papal recognition in 1346. Between 1258 and 1506, there were 19 meetings of the Castilian CORTES and Valladolid (as the capital of the realm) usually served as a royal residence, a site for the royal courts of justice, and the location of the chancery. The Jewish community, once large, gradually declined as synagogues were destroyed in 1367 and later when Jews were attacked by the sermons of Vincent FERRER. Their persecution by the INQUISITION continued even after many converted to Christianity. Valladolid remained an important administrative center until the Spanish capital was moved to MADRID in the 16th century.

See also RECONQUEST.

Further reading: Albert Frederick Calvert, *Valladolid, Oviedo, Segovia, Zamora, Avila, and Zaragoza: An Historical and Descriptive Account* (London: J. Lane, 1908).

Vallombrosa The Vallombrosan order of monks was established in the 11th century by John Gualbert (ca. 995–1073) as part of the GREGORIAN REFORM, under the influence of CLUNY, and as part of the reform of eremetical MONASTICISM. The Vallombrosans started out as a community of hermits who, grouping together from 1036, committed themselves to communal or coenobic living. The congregation began with the donation of the mountainous territory of Vallombrosa in the Tuscan Apennines about 20 miles east of FLORENCE at an altitude of 3,000 feet. John Gualbert became prior in about 1040. Its rule and organization were approved by Pope URBAN II in 1090. Life at Vallombrosa was that of a community who alternated stays in the monastery and in individual hermitages. The Vallombrosans observed the Benedictine Rule but did no work outside the enclosure and remained extreme centralized under a single abbot who was elected for life. They employed lay brothers as workers, who also fielded outside affairs. The order spread into the rest of ITALY and into FRANCE. By the mid-13th century, the congregation had 79 abbeys, 29 priories, and nine monasteries of NUNS.

Further reading: George W. Dameron, *Episcopal Power and Florentine Society, 1000–1320* (Cambridge, Mass.: Harvard University Press, 1991).

Valois dynasty The Valois, named after the county of Valois near PARIS, were the reigning dynasty in FRANCE from 1328 to 1589, eventually divided into three lines in 1498. The first Valois, Philip VI (r. 1328–50), was the closest male relation of the last direct CAPETIAN, Charles IV (r. 1322–28). The English king, EDWARD III, was a more direct descendant, but through the female line; he was therefore excluded in succession by the Salic Law, which did not allow succession through the female line. This dynastic dispute became a main factor in the first phase of the HUNDRED YEARS' WAR. CHARLES V and CHARLES VII were successful Valois kings who presided over French recoveries during the Hundred Years' War. LOUIS XI in the second half of the 15th century contributed to the growth and consolidation of the French state.

Despite temporary reverses and setbacks, the Valois enlarged the royal domain by adding the great fiefs of BRITTANY and the Bourbonnais in the 16th century as well as principalities from the HOLY ROMAN EMPIRE such a

Dauphiné and PROVENCE. Their meddling in Italian affairs led to the introduction of many of the ideas associated with the Italian RENAISSANCE to France. They were the patrons of important artists such as Jean FOUQUET and the LIMBOURG BROTHERS.

Further reading: Keith Cameron, ed., *From Valois to Bourbon: Dynasty, State and Society in Early Modern France* (Exeter: University of Exeter, 1989); Kenneth Alan Fowler, *The Age of Plantagenet and Valois: The Struggle for Supremacy, 1328–1498* (New York: Putnam, 1967); P. S. Lewis, *Later Medieval France: The Polity* (New York: St. Martin's Press, 1968).

Vandals The Vandals were a notoriously ruthless Germanic tribe who founded a kingdom in northern AFRICA. They seem to have originated in Scandinavia, probably DENMARK, then moved to Silesia and modern eastern POLAND. Driven toward the Western Empire by the HUNS, they crossed through FRANCE and entered SPAIN between 406 and 409. There one branch, the Silingis, were attacked and almost totally wiped out in fighting with the VISIGOTHS between 415 and 418. The remnants of the Silings united with another branch, the Hasdings.

CONQUEST OF NORTH AFRICA

Their king GAISERIC led them, perhaps as many as 80,000, to North Africa in about 428. There they were reluctantly accepted by the local Romans as allies. In 439 Gaiseric overthrew the Roman regime and established a Vandal state with Carthage as its capital. This was recognized by the Romans in a treaty in 442. The Vandals expropriated land around Carthage but retained Roman institutions in the rest of the country. They did not, however, mix with the local Catholic population and preserved their zealous ARIAN beliefs.

Gaiseric constructed a strong centralized state and established an unquestioned succession for his son. The Vandals developed a powerful fleet and controlled much of the western Mediterranean Sea. From North Africa they conquered the BALEARIC ISLANDS, SARDINIA, CORSICA, and parts of SICILY. They even sacked ROME in 455, linking their name with wanton destruction.

FALL OF THE VANDALS

After Gaiseric's death in 477, the Vandals abandoned wars and piracy, which had been substantial sources of income. Fierce persecutions of Catholics followed in around 484. Their later kings were unable to control the Berber tribes, who grew more and more aggressive in their raiding. King Hilderic (r. 523–530) established peaceful relations with the BYZANTINE EMPIRE and increased toleration for Roman and Greek Christianity. His overthrow by Gelimer (r. 530–533/534) in 530 became the pretext for a Byzantine invasion of Africa in 533 by BELISARIUS who easily defeated the Vandal army and made most of the males

Valois Dynasty

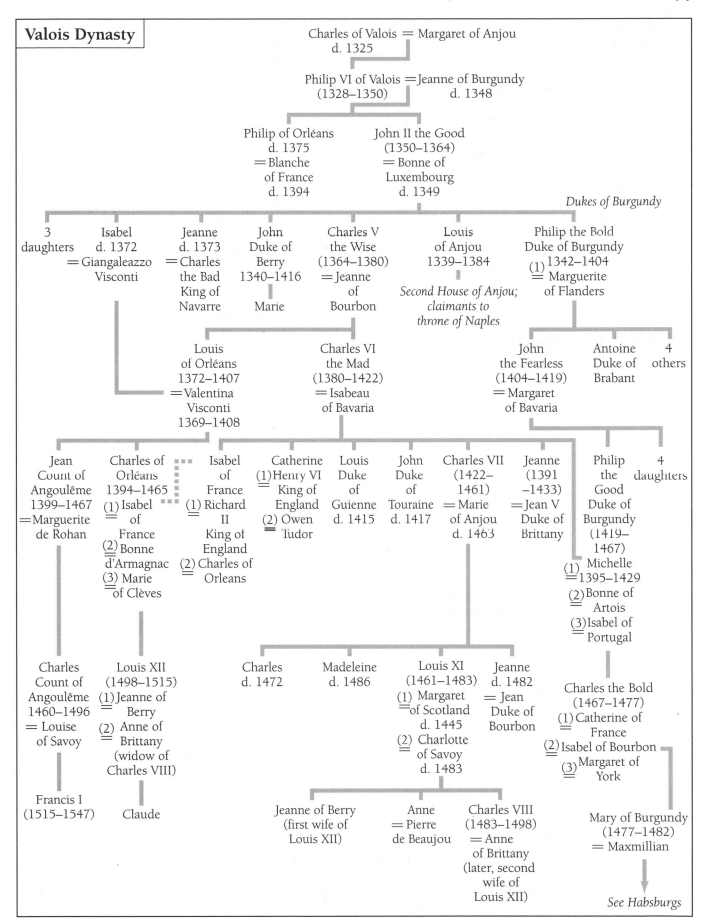

slaves or soldiers for the wars against the Persians thus ending the Vandal kingdom.

See also GOTHS; OSTROGOTHS.

Further reading: Averil Cameron, "Vandal and Byzantine Africa," in *The Cambridge Ancient History*. Vol. 14, *Late Antiquity: Empire and Successors,* A.D. *425–600,* ed. Averil Cameron, Bryan Ward-Perkins, and Michael Whitby (Cambridge: Cambridge University Press, 2000), 552–569; F. M. Clover, *The Late Roman West and the Vandals* (London: Ashgate, 1993); Malcolm Todd, *The Early Germans* (Oxford: Blackwell, 1992); Malcolm Todd, *The Northern Barbarians, 100* BC–AD *300,* rev. ed. (New York: B. Blackwell, 1987); J. M. Wallace-Hadrill, *The Barbarian West, 400–1000,* rev. ed. (Oxford: B. Blackwell, 1996); Lucien Musset, *The Germanic Invasions: The Making of Europe,* AD *400–600,* trans. Edward and Columba James (1969; reprint, University Park: Pennsylvania State University Press, 1975).

Van der Weyden, Rogier *See* WEYDEN, ROGIER VAN DER.

Van Eyck *See* EYCK, HUBERT VAN, AND EYCK, JAN VAN.

Varangians and Varangian Guard (the Sworn Men)
The Varangians were initially in Scandinavian sources designated as trusted MERCHANTS or trusted soldiers who were affiliated by an OATH to some kind of traveling group. The Varangians at first seem mainly to have been traders moving by boat who were forced by their dangerous business expeditions to arm themselves. They were soon defined and employed as mercenary soldiers, who became famous for their reliability and valor. At CONSTANTINOPLE they formed a particular, fierce, and elite regiment detailed to guard personally the emperor. For the BYZANTINE EMPIRE the Varangians were associated with Russians, but by the 11th century they also included NORMANS. At various times they were also enlisted to overthrow emperors.

Russian princes had also frequently employed Varangian mercenaries in their conflicts with each another or on distant expeditions. The name was also associated in general ways with the founders of the new Russian or Ruś kingdom.

See also KIEV AND KIEVAN RUŚ; NOVGOROD; RURIK; VIKINGS.

Further reading: Sigfús Blöndal, *The Varangians of Byzantium: an Aspect of Byzantine Military History,* trans., rev., and rewritten by Benedikt S. Benedikz (Cambridge: Cambridge University Press, 1978).

Vasco da Gama (ca. 1469–December 25, 1524) *Portuguese navigator*
Vasco da Gama was born in Sines in southwest PORTUGAL in about 1469. The king of Portugal, Manuel I (r. 1495–1521), commissioned him to lead an expedition to follow the route found by Bartholomew DIAZ around AFRICA to India. A nobleman, he was an experienced soldier and trained navigator who proved to be a tough, arrogant, intelligent, and compassionate commander. He left LISBON on July 8, 1497, with four ships manned by 170 sailors and equipped with translators and trinkets for trade. Sailing far out into the Atlantic to take best advantage of the prevailing winds, he rounded the Cape on November 18, 1497, and sailed up the coast of eastern Africa. Hiring a pilot from a local sultan, he sailed across the Indian Ocean and made landfall near Calicut, or present-day Kozhikode in Kerala in India, on May 18, 1498. He spent three months there and, having lost his pilot, was barely able to cross back over the Indian Ocean, with little actually to show from his time in India. He reached Portugal in early September 1499 with only 54 of his original crew left. He had reached India, however.

In 1502 he returned to India to establish colonies en route and there. He managed to establish Portuguese dominance in the Indian Ocean by winning several battles and showing no mercy to those who opposed him. After returning to Portugal, he retired with much honor. Called out of retirement 20 years later, he was made viceroy of India. He died in Goa on December 25, 1524, soon after his return.

Further reading: Vasco da Gama, *A Journal of the First Voyage,* ed. E. G. Ravenstein (London: Hakluyt Society, 1898); G. R. Crone, *The Discovery of the East* (London: Hamish Hamilton, 1972), especially "Vasco da Gama Reaches Calicut," 27–39; Sanjay Subrahmanyam, *The Career and Legend of Vasco da Gama* (Cambridge: Cambridge University Press, 1997).

vassalage *See* FEUDALISM AND THE FEUDAL SYSTEM.

vaults *See* GOTHIC.

vellum *See* PARCHMENT.

Venerable Bede *See* BEDE THE VENERABLE, SAINT.

venial sin *See* SIN.

Venice A city in northeastern ITALY, Venice was first established on some 118 small islands in the middle of a lagoon in the sixth century as a refuge from invaders. People from the coastal area between RAVENNA and Aquileia fled there to avoid dominance first by the HUNS and then by the OSTROGOTHS. These early settlements, living off fishing and the production of SALT, were much expanded during the Lombard invasions of the later sixth century as more people fled out to them. The Venetian

Venice, Italy, Saint Mark's Square *(Courtesy Library of Congress)*

villages maintained their links with the BYZANTINES in Ravenna, although by the eighth century this tie had become theoretical since the locals had begun electing their own leader, the doge, in 697.

GROWTH IN TRADE AND COMMERCE

Between the eighth and 11th centuries, the core of Venice was fixed around the islands around the Rialto which dominated the rest of the island settlements. Venetian MERCHANTS stole the RELICS or body of the evangelist Saint Mark from ALEXANDRIA in 828 and Mark became the patron saint of the town. His relics were kept in the chapel of the doge's fortress, which became the basilica of Saint Mark. The institutions of the government with the doge as the chief executive became more elaborate during these centuries. A merchant elite grew and elected the doge and

many members of the administration. Although this elite had some possessions on the mainland, their real wealth arose from the growing commerce and shipping industries of the town. They benefited greatly from their position as the trading link between East and West, especially in terms of slaves, wood, SPICES, SILKS, salt, and fish. They developed a strong fleet to protect their interests in the Adriatic Sea and eastern Mediterranean. They cooperated with the Byzantines in controlling the Adriatic and its coasts, battling SLAVS, Croatians, and Dalmatians. At the same time the town remained autonomous from outside authority.

Early in the 12th century, with the success of the First CRUSADE, the Venetians acquired the ports and privileges in the Latin East essential for transport and trade there. Merchants developed extensive ties all over the eastern Mediterranean and devised new ways of organizing their capital and their businesses. They at least equaled the economic success of their rivals in PISA and GENOA. In the Fourth Crusade, with the terrible sack of CONSTANTINOPLE in April 1204, which they manipulated to their advantage, they acquired a large section of the BYZANTINE EMPIRE in GREECE itself and around the whole Aegean Sea.

DOMINATING TRADE WITH THE EAST

Venice reached the height of its prosperity in the following centuries as its fleet and merchants dominated the TRADE with the East. The area around the island of the Rialto became the core of the city as of remains, with a population between 80,000 and 100,000 living along a complex system of canals. By the later Middle Ages, Venice had developed a complex electoral system that rotated political offices among its 200 elite or oligarchic families. This system produced a remarkably stable government and set of commercial policies, though this point has been overemphasized by historians. The state consistently participated in actual business and protected commerce. The Venetian church was notoriously independent of outside influences, including the PAPACY.

In the 15th century, the city turned to acquiring towns and land on the mainland or *terrafirma* of Italy. This trend led to endless wars with the city-states of the region such as PADUA and VERONA, and with the dukes of MILAN such as the VISCONTI and SFORZA. The Venetians intended to secure foodstuffs to feed the city and to protect their overland trade route to northern Europe. With the rise of the OTTOMAN TURKS in the 15th century, they had to protect their colonies in the Balkans and eastern Mediterranean. The fall of Constantinople in 1453 to the Turks deprived them of another market and set of trading concessions. They then made many arrangements with the Turks and preserved many of their colonies in Greece, CYPRUS, and CRETE almost until the 16th century.

WARFARE, NEW INDUSTRY, AND ART

From the 1450s to the 1490s, Italy benefited from a few decades of diminished WARFARE. This changed in the 1490s, as French invasions led to major wars after 1500 that required Venice to work hard to maintain its independence. At home the Venetians developed local industries such as glass, wool, cloth, tourism, PRINTING, and leather making in the years leading up to 1500. The great wealth of the city produced a distinctive art, sculpture, and architecture. In the simplest terms they were mixtures of BYZANTINE and even Islamic styles, combined with the developing ROMANESQUE and GOTHIC of the rest of Western Europe. Venetian PAINTING became famous for its use of light and color and its portrayal of space.

See also BARI; BELLINI FAMILY; BLACK SEA; DALMATIA; DANDOLO, ENRICO, DOGE OF VENICE; DUBROVNIK; FOSCARI, FRANCESCO; GLASSWARE; LATIN EMPIRE OF CONSTANTINOPLE; LATIN STATES IN GREECE; MARCO POLO; SHIPS AND SHIPBUILDING.

Further reading: Patricia Fortini Brown, *Art and Life in Renaissance Venice* (New York: H. N. Abrams, 1997); Richard G. Goy, *Venice, the City and Its Architecture* (London: Phaidon, 1997); Christopher Hibbert, *Venice: The Biography of a City* (New York: W. W. Norton, 1989); Frederic C. Lane, *Venice: A Maritime Republic* (Baltimore: Johns Hopkins University Press, 1973); Edward Muir, *Civic Ritual in Renaissance Venice* (Princeton, N.J.: Princeton University Press, 1981); Garry Wills, *Venice: Lion City, The Religion of Empire* (New York: Simon & Schuster, 2001); Alvise Zorzi, *Venice: The Golden Age, 697–1797,* trans. Nicoletta Simborowski and Simon Mackenzie (New York: Abbeville, 1980).

Verdun, Treaty of The Treaty of Verdun was drawn up in 843 to settle a devastating dynastic civil war among the grandsons of CHARLEMAGNE. It was written in two languages, which resembled medieval French and German. It divided the empire into three kingdoms. CHARLES I THE BALD was granted the kingdom of the West FRANKS, NEUSTRIA, AQUITAINE, and the Spanish March. Its eastern frontier was along the Schildt, Saône, and Rhone Rivers. This region, primarily speaking languages related to Latin, became the historic kingdom of FRANCE. Louis the German (r. 840–855) was to rule the eastern Frankish kingdom, which consisted of the four duchies of FRANCONIA, SAXONY, BAVARIA, and SWABIA, the future kingdom of GERMANY. Lothair (r. 840–855) the eldest, inherited the imperial title and the territory known as the Middle Kingdom or Francia Media, a long, incoherent stretch of land running from the North Sea to south of Rome, which included Lorraine, BURGUNDY, SWITZERLAND, and most of ITALY. Although even for the ninth century it was somewhat contrived, the Treaty of Verdun established a precedent for future political patterns. It also produced a permanent fragmentation of Europe. It did not end the dynastic wars.

See also CAROLINGIAN FAMILY AND DYNASTY; FONTENAY, BATTLE OF; LOUIS I THE PIOUS.

Further reading: Rosamond McKitterick, *The Frankish Kingdoms under the Carolingians, 751–987* (London: Longman, 1983).

vernacular For the period up to 1500 and beyond, the vernacular languages were the popular spoken languages of the Latin West. In Western Europe up to 1300, these languages were distinct from LATIN, subordinate to it for literature and learning, and were mostly confined to speech or rare documentary needs. Latin was the language of the élite culture of CHRISTENDOM and the church. The application of such a classification rests on an overly neat binary opposition involving dominant and dominated, standardized and disordered, grammatical and without grammar, and unity and plurality.

Among the other languages of the medieval world, there were a learned and religious language such as

Arabic or Greek and other regional languages with various histories spoken by the majority of the population. Many people always had to speak Latin, Greek, or Arabic in their daily life. Everywhere there were local dialects with some similarities to one another but often mutually incomprehensible. Urban dialects differed from rural ones, and other variations were attributable to social class and degree of literacy in any particular region.

In Anglo-Saxon ENGLAND and the Scandinavian countries, Germanic vernaculars early on produced rich literatures. In Western Europe after 1300, literature in languages other than Latin became more respected and acceptable. Latin, Greek, and Arabic retained their importance as languages of culture and religion. In Slavic and Germanic regions, languages evolved out of spoken forms for specialized use in religion, culture, and governmental administration. All became more standardized in vocabulary, syntax, and grammar.

See also ALIGHIERI, DANTE; ANGLO-SAXONS; ICELAND AND ICELANDIC LITERATURE; LATIN LANGUAGE AND LITERATURE.

Further reading: Renate Blumenfeld-Kosinski, Duncan Robertson, and Nancy Bradley Warren, eds., *The Vernacular Spirit: Essays on Medieval Religious Literature* (New York: Palgrave, 2002); Nicholas Brooks, ed., *Latin and the Vernacular Languages in Early Medieval Britain* (Leicester: Leicester University Press, 1982); A. J. Minnis, ed., *Latin and Vernacular: Studies in Late-Medieval Texts and Manuscripts* (Cambridge: D. S. Brewer, 1989); Colin C. Smith, "The Vernacular," in *The New Cambridge Medieval History.* Vol. 5, *c. 1198–c. 1300,* ed. David Abulafia (Cambridge: Cambridge University Press, 1999), 71–83; Philippe Wolff, *Western Languages,* A.D. *100–1500,* trans. Frances Partridge (New York: McGraw-Hill, 1971).

Verona A city on the Adige River in northern ITALY, medieval Verona was at the crossroads of routes between the Po Valley, the Alps, and Eastern Europe. It was an important town under the Roman Empire and for the OSTROGOTHS. In the Lombard era between 569 and 774, the ARIANISM of the town was suppressed, and under the Carolingians the Benedictine monasteries of San Zeno and Santa Maria in Organo were established. Verona became a center of power for the German emperors and remained a supporter of imperial policies. By the end of the 11th century, the economy and population continued to benefit from the town's strategic commercial location and the growth of the textile industry. Its population grew to around 35,000 to 40,000 in the early 14th century.

A COMMUNE was formed in 1136. Though opposed to FREDERICK I BARBAROSSA it was supportive of FREDERICK II. By the 13th century, the city was dominated by tyrants such as Ezzelino III da Romano (1194–1259). A Ghi-

belline and antipapal policy prevailed under the lordship of the Della Scala and the Scaligeri between 1277 and 1387. After the fall of the Della Scala, who had built impressive monuments to themselves, Verona was dominated by the VISCONTI of MILAN between 1387 and 1404. It finally was taken over by the republic of VENICE in 1405.

Further reading: Rather of Verona, *The Complete Works of Rather of Verona,* trans. and ed. Peter L. D. Reid (Binghamton, N.Y.: Medieval and Renaissance Texts and Studies, 1991); Rolandino Potavino, *The Chronicles of the Trevisan March,* trans. Joseph R. Berrigan (Lawrence, Kan. Coronado, 1980); A. M. Allen, *A History of Verona,* ed. Edward Armstrong (London: Methuen, 1910); Maureen C. Miller, *The Formation of a Medieval Church: Ecclesiastical Change in Verona, 950–1150* (Ithaca, N.Y.: Cornell University Press, 1993); Alethea Wiel, *The Story of Verona* (1902; reprint, Nendeln: Kraus Reprint, 1971).

vespers Vespers was an evening service at sundown performed by both the Eastern and Western Churches. It was one of the oldest and most important parts of the DIVINE OFFICE. The name was derived from the Latin word for the last hours of the day. It began as a Jewish and early Christian blessing of the lamps lighted as evening began. In earlier terms, it referred to the sacrifice of the burning of incense every evening in the temple. Christianity changed this evening sacrifice into a hymn of praise in memory of the Passion of Christ and the Last Supper. A distinctly Christian form of evening prayer evolved in the third century. In the Middle Ages it consisted of an introduction, five psalms, a short reading from Scripture, a hymn, the end of the Magnificat, prayers for various purposes, a homily, and concluding verses. By the sixth century, from the inception of the Benedictine Rule, vespers had acquired a customary and basic form, which was followed during the rest of the Middle Ages.

Further reading: Paul F. Bradshaw, *Daily Prayer in the Early Church: A Study of the Origin and Early Development of the Divine Office* (London: Published for the Alcuin Club by SPCK, 1981); Robert F. Taft, *The Liturgy of the Hours in East and West: The Origins of the Divine Office and Its Meaning for Today* (Collegeville, Minn.: Liturgical Press, 1986).

Vespers, Sicilian *See* SICILIAN VESPERS.

vestments, liturgical In the Middle Ages liturgical vestments were the distinctive dress worn by the CLERGY when performing the services of the church. This dress derived from the ordinary secular costume of the world of the late Roman Empire. Between the fourth and the ninth centuries, a specific priestly costume for sacred functions evolved. At the same time, the LAITY abandoned long tunics and cloaks, but their use continued in the services of the church. By the 10th century, the principal liturgical vestments and their use had become established in the Western Church, and there were only minor changes in these costumes from the 13th century. Surplices, loose white garments with wide sleeves, were introduced as a substitute for albs or longer, tight-fitting gowns, for many occasions. The chasuble, similar to a cloak, were mainly reserved for the celebration of MASS. The tunicle, similar to an overcoat, became the distinctive vestment of the subdeaconate, a lower clerical order on the way to the priesthood. During the same period, bishops, demonstrating an enhanced importance, began to wear additional and more prestigious vestments such as luxurious sandals, miters, and gloves. The vestments of the Eastern Church were similar to those of the Western, but a few differed: the dalmatic, worn over a tunic, was not used in the East, and the epigonation, a stiff lozenge-shaped vestment, was not worn in the West.

See also CLOTHING AND COSTUME.

Further reading: Robert Lesage, *Vestments and Church Furniture,* trans. Fergus Murphy (New York: Hawthorn Books, 1960); Janet Mayo, *A History of Ecclesiastical Dress* (New York: Holmes & Meier, 1984); Cyril Edward Pocknee, *Liturgical Vesture: Its Origins and Development* (London: Mowbray, 1960); Roger E. Reynolds, *Law and Liturgy in the Latin Church, Fifth–Twelfth Centuries* (Aldershot: Variorum, 1994).

Vézelay, Church of La Madeleine Founded about 860 by the legendary Girard de Roussillon, this church had its beginnings as a Benedictine monastery in northern BURGUNDY. Girard had supposedly placed it under the direct protection of the pope in ROME. After the first monastery and church were devastated in a VIKING raid, it was moved to the top of Mount Scorpion and was transferred to the jurisdiction of CLUNY, which promoted its development as a PILGRIMAGE site devoted to Mary Magdalene in the mid-11th century.

As the starting point of one of the four routes to SANTIAGO DE COMPOSTELA, Vézelay earned great prosperity but also envy among the nearby bishop of Autun and the counts of Nevers. Actual battles were fought and an abbot was assassinated in 1106. Despite these problems, in 1146 BERNARD OF CLAIRVAUX preached the Second CRUSADE there. The link to Cluny was abolished in 1159. RICHARD I LIONHEART and PHILIP II AUGUSTUS met there to set out for the Third CRUSADE. Thomas BECKET antagonized HENRY II by preaching against the king there shortly before his murder in 1170. King LOUIS IX stopped there several times to pray and mediate local conflicts. He was in attendance in 1267 for a solemn recognition of the RELICS of Mary Magdalene, long certified as authentic by a papal bull in 1058. These conflicts, however, did not diminish the church's attraction for pilgrims during the later Middle Ages.

REMNANTS AND BUILDING HISTORY

Of the Benedictine monastery, there has remained only the abbey church, which was restored by Prosper Mérimée and Viollet-le-Duc in the 19th century. There were fires in 1120 in the NAVE and in 1165 in the CRYPT. Its three aisles had to be rebuilt between 1120 and 1140, and high windows and groined vaults were also constructed. In the 12th century there were also built in the Gothic style a NARTHEX, a chapel to Saint Michael on the upper story, and the celebrated tympanum showing Christ judging souls. The crypt and nave were rebuilt between 1170 and 1220, and the heavy Romanesque buttresses were reinforced by flying buttresses. Its rich collection of sculptures of biblical subjects, lives of the saints, and odd pagan themes inside has not been much restored.

See also ROMANESQUE ART AND ARCHITECTURE.

Further reading: Hugh of Poitiers, *The Vézelay Chronicle and Other Documents from MS. Auxerre 227 and Elsewhere,* trans. John Scott and John O. Ward (Binghamton: Medieval & Renaissance Texts & Studies, 1992); Robert Branner, BURGUNDIAN GOTHIC ARCHITECTURE (London: A. Zwemmer, 1985); Kevin D. Murphy, *Memory and Modernity: Viollet-le-Duc at Vézelay* (University Park: Pennsylvania State University Press, 2000); Véronique Rouchon-Mouilleron, *Vézelay: The Great Romanesque Church,* trans. Laurel Hirsch (New York: Harry N. Abrams, 1999).

vicar During the Middle Ages vicars were the replacements for clerics who wished to be absent from their appointments. Vicars were provided with powers that were extensive but revocable at the will of the holder of the office of BENEFICE. For parishes this meant the PRIEST covering for the nonresident parish priest, with whom he had agreed to a contract for one or two years, subject to approval by the local bishop. The vicar collected all the revenues, took on the care of souls or sacramental responsibilities for the parish, lived on the site, and paid rent. Bishops also sometimes had vicars to cover their sacramental and administrative duties. The popes sent out vicars-general to look after their affairs in particular places, attend councils and synods, and oversee the local clergy.

These situations did not always produce good or even adequate pastoral care. There was considerable concern for abuses in reform legislation, but vicars were a valuable way of freeing the clergy for other duties while providing their substitutes and themselves with reliable incomes at the same time.

Further reading: F. Donald Logan, *A History of the Church in the Middle Ages* (London: Routledge, 2002); Joseph H. Lynch, *The Medieval Church: A Brief History* (New York: Longman, 1992).

vices   *See* VIRTUES AND VICES.

Vienna   Vienna is the present capital of AUSTRIA. In the Middle Ages, it owed its late prosperity to the HABSBURGS, who made this town the center of their territorial and dynastic possessions around the Alps, BAVARIA, and BOHEMIA. It was always a center of transit and exchange between the West and the Byzantine East through the Balkans. During the Roman Empire it was called Vindobona and was a strategic town of the Danubian line of fortification. By 395 it was apparently destroyed and mostly abandoned.

The town disappeared from history, except for a possible visit by CHARLEMAGNE, until 881. By the ninth century there were apparently a church and a market there. In 1156 it was made the capital of the Eastern March; the church and future cathedral of Saint Stephen were documented from 1147. In 1221 the duke of Austria, Leopold VI the Glorious (r. 1198–1230), granted the town its first privileges and a right to hold a market. From the control of the Babenberg family, the town passed in 1251 to the domain of the king of Bohemia, Ottokar II (r. 1251–76). In 1278 the Habsburgs took over, Vienna then lost its status as a free imperial city because of opposition to their rule. The dynasty embarked on a policy determined to make Vienna their political, intellectual, and monumental center, supporting Habsburg imperial and dynastic plans. They founded a university, the famous ducal college, in 1384.

From 1438 Vienna became a regular residence for the Holy Roman Emperor. In 1469 the town obtained from Pope Paul II (r. 1464–71) a bishopric, for its cathedral, the church of Saint Stephen. Surrounded by extensive walls, Vienna at its height had a population of 50,000 to 60,000 in the later Middle Ages with a strong Jewish presence.

Further reading: Gerhard Milchram, ed., *Museum Judenplatz for Medieval Jewish Life in Vienna*, trans. David Gogarty and Nick Somers (Vienna: Pichler Verlag, 2000); Michael H. Shank, *Unless You Believe, You Shall Not Understand: Logic, University, and Society in Late Medieval Vienna* (Princeton, N.J.: Princeton University Press, 1988).

Vikings (Northmen)   The Vikings were Scandinavian sailors, warriors, pirates, raiders, and traders who conducted expeditions of TRADE and plunder all over Europe and even into the Mediterranean between the ninth and 11th centuries. They could be the bloodthirsty raiders of tradition, but they were also skillful traders, artisans, explorers, and settlers who produced a rich vernacular

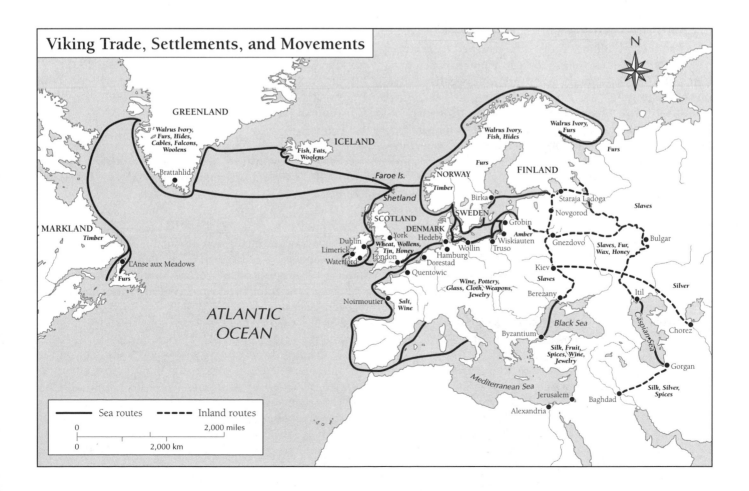

Viking Trade, Settlements, and Movements

literature. Their era is said to have begun on June 8, 793, with the sack of Lindisfarne Abbey in Northumbria in northern ENGLAND and to have ended in the mid-11th century with the conquest of England by their descendents the NORMANS. The motivations for this expansion could have been demographic pressure, climate, food needs, and political problems.

The Vikings initially raided near defenseless and wealthy places such as abbeys, nunneries, churches, and cathedrals. They were not always completely destructive and sometimes accomplished commercial exchanges that benefited the other parties. Entrepreneurial Vikings who habitually traveled from place to place were only too ready to turn to looting, however, especially in the ninth century. They moved freely through the Baltic Sea, through modern-day RUSSIA to the BLACK Sea and CONSTANTINOPLE; through the Atlantic to the British Isles, ICELAND, GREENLAND, and even North America; and down the eastern coast of the mainland of Europe and all the way into the Mediterranean.

The Vikings became known and feared almost everywhere along these coasts. On all these travels they mixed adventure, conquest, war, looting, and TRADE. Initially these expeditions were spontaneous, but with the recognition of the possible riches to be collected they became in the ninth century carefully planned military operations.

The Vikings were famous for their navigational abilities and accomplishments and their fast oared and sailing SHIPS and shipbuilding skills. They traded in amber, skins, FURS, precious woods, looted or purchased luxury items, and slaves. In the 10th century, they began to settle down and colonize areas, often expecting and receiving bribes to do so. From 1000 many became Christian by choice or by the force of kings or rulers. The monarchies of the Scandinavian countries were their descendants. The HANSEATIC LEAGUE eventually took over their trading routes and practices in the north.

See also ANGLO-SAXONS; CANUTE II THE GREAT; DENMARK; GOKSTAD SHIP; ICELAND AND ICELANDIC LITERATURE; IRELAND; NORMANDY AND THE NORMANS; NORWAY; OSEBERG FIND OR SHIP; ROLLO; RUSSIA AND RUŚ; SEVILLE, CITY AND KINGDOM OF; SLAVE TRADE AND SLAVERY; SWEDEN; VALHALLA; VARANGIANS AND VARANGIAN GUARD; VINLAND AND VINLAND SAGAS; WILLIAM I THE CONQUEROR.

Further reading: Yvest Cohat, *The Vikings: Lords of the Sea*, trans. Ruth Daniel (1987; reprint, New York: Harry N. Abrams, 1992); Gwyn Jones, *A History of the Vikings*, rev. ed. (1968; Oxford: Oxford University Press, 1984); R. I. Page, *Chronicles of the Vikings: Records, Memorials, and Myths* (Toronto: University of Toronto Press, 1995); Else Roesdahl, *The Vikings*, 2d ed., trans. Susan M. Margeson and Kirsten Williams (1987; London: Penguin Books, 1998); see "VIII. Vikings and Northern Europe" in the Bibliography.

village communities and settlements Early medieval villages were often small, mobile, and short lived in most of Europe, but less so in the lands of Byzantium in Anatolia and the Near East. From the 11th century such European villages were characterized more by the existence of a settled rural community having legal recognition and an organized agrarian territory with known boundaries. In them a number of functions were carried out such as activities in a religious center or church, funerary rituals and burials in a cemetery, courts for communal and manorial administrative regulation, facilities for the storage of foodstuffs and seeds, centers for artisan production for trade and local use, some defensive capabilities, and locations for economic markets for exchange and for peasant labor. Between 1000 and 1500 they became more elaborate, organized, and settled, in the spots that many have occupied to this day. They had various levels of independence from a lord or an institution, usually a religious one. Their social organization varied, and a village might contain people of several levels of economic and social status from rich peasants to mere serfs.

See also AGRICULTURE; FEUDALISM AND THE FEUDAL SYSTEM; MANORS AND MANORIAL LORDSHIP; PEASANTRY; SERFS AND SERFDOM; VILLEIN AND VILLEINAGE.

Further reading: Warren O. Ault, *Open-Field Farming in Medieval England: A Study of Village By-Laws* (London: Allen and Unwin, 1972); Jean Chapelot and Robert Fossier, *The Village and House in the Middle Ages*, trans. Henry Cleere (London: B. T. Batsford, 1985); George C. Homans, *English Villagers of the Thirteenth Century* (Cambridge, Mass.: Harvard University Press, 1941); J. Ambrose Raftis, *The Estates of Ramsey Abbey: A Study in Economic Growth and Organization* (Toronto: Pontifical Institute of Mediaeval Studies, 1957).

Villani, Giovanni (ca. 1275–1348) **and Matteo** (d. 1363) *Florentine politicians, bankers, historians, chroniclers*

GIOVANNI

Giovanni was born the son of Villano de Stoldo in FLORENCE about 1275. He worked at BRUGES between 1302 and 1307 as agent of the Peruzzi Companies. He was an official of the mint in 1316; served as a prior in the city government in 1316–17, 1321–22, and 1328; was an officer of the walls in 1324, sat as a superintendent of gold and silver coinage in 1327–28; and participated in the committee of the COMMUNE for provisioning food in the famine years of 1329–30. He was the superintendent for the construction of baptistery doors between 1330 and 1331. Beyond that, he served in many other capacities during the period 1320–30, obviously extremely familiar with the government of the commune. Giovanni fell political and financial victim to the collapse of the Peruzzi companies in the 1340s, which forced him out of government and even into a short stay in debtors' prison in February 1346. He died in the Black Death in the summer of 1348.

He claimed he began his *Chronicle* in 1300 after a visit to ROME for the HOLY YEAR and wrote it over an almost 50-year time span in chronological order and using the VERNACULAR. Over time he became more sophisticated as a historian, for instance, including the political and economic role of Florence throughout Europe to provide a context for his discussions of local politics and institutions. He knew his great near-contemporary and politician, the poet Dante ALIGHIERI, and was familiar with the work of BRUNETTO Latini.

MATTEO

Matteo was a member, as was his brother, Giovanni, of the companies of the Peruzzi and Buonaccorsi and worked for them in NAPLES. His life was equally eventful, but he performed much less government service. He, too, was caught up in the failures of the great banking family companies in the 1340, and his wife, Lisa Buondelmonti, suffered a period of incarceration because of his flight from creditors. In 1362 he was prosecuted on suspicion of Ghibelline sympathies and plots and was forbidden to hold public office. He continued his brother's *Chronicle* from 1348 until his own death in 1363 in a more gloomy and pessimistic style. He also wrote more rhetorical introductions to his chapters, celebrating the virtues he emphasized in them. He died in the second great visitation of the PLAGUE in 1363. His son, Filippo (1325–ca. 1405), added a few more chapters to the *Chronicle* after his father's death.

See also CHRONICLES AND ANNALS; GIANO DELLA BELLA; GUELFS AND GHIBELLINES.

Further reading: Giovanni Villani, *Selections from the First Nine Books of the Croniche florentine of Giovanni Villani: Tr. for the Use of Students of Dante and Others,* ed. P. H. Wicksteed (Westminster: A. Constable, 1897); Louis Green, *Chronicle into History: An Essay on the Interpretation of History in Florentine Fourteenth-Century Chronicles* (Cambridge: Cambridge University Press, 1972); Ferdinand Schevill, *History of Florence, from the Founding of the City through the Renaissance* (New York: Harcourt, Brace & Company, 1936).

Villehardouin, Geoffroi de (Geoffroy) (ca. 1150–ca. 1213) *a leader of the Fourth Crusade, historian*

Geoffroi was probably born near Bar-sur-Aube near Troyes in about 1150 and became a KNIGHT and an official of the count of Champagne. According to his own chronicles he played a prominent role in the organization of the Fourth Crusade and in the diplomatic maneuvering that followed the sack of CONSTANTINOPLE in 1204. Recognized for administrative and military talent, he became the marshal of the Balkan mainland or Romania. From there he led a few expeditions into BULGARIA. His *Conquest of Constantinople* was a firsthand account by a participant in its decision-making process and the first medieval historical work in Europe written in the VERNACULAR. It is the main, but biased, source for the study of the Fourth Crusade. His attitudes in the history reflect those of French aristocracy of the period. He died about 1213 perhaps in GREECE; his relatives governed a state until the late 13th century.

See also LATIN STATES IN GREECE.

Further reading: M. R. B Shaw, trans., *Joinville and Villehardouin: Chronicles of the Crusades* (Baltimore: Penguin Books, 1963), 29–160; Jeanette M. A. Beer, *Villehardouin: Epic Historian* (Geneva: Droz, 1968); Donald E. Queller and Thomas F. Madden, eds., *The Fourth Crusade: The Conquest of Constantinople,* 2d ed. (Philadelphia: University of Pennsylvania Press, 1997).

villein and villeinage This was a technical and legal tenure involving the personal status of certain "unfree" peasants, primarily in ENGLAND, who owed demeaning, onerous, and uncertain services to their lords as part of their tenure for land. The word existed in France, but French *vileins* were regarded as free in public law. In a complex system of rural property holdings, one might hold one piece of property on terms of villeinage and others for more free or certain terms of payments or services. So a peasant might be villein in some circumstances and not in others. The origins of English villeinage were in the Anglo-Saxon period in England. Then peasants had greater dependence on their lord for land, housing, and protection, accepting from him an uncertain or undefined amount of heavy labor services. This often meant that they worked on the lord's own land for several days a week technically at the will of the lord. In the 12th century, the king's justices determined that this liability to perform labor service at the discretion of the lord was one of the legal signs of status as villeins. Such a tenant who owed so much work per week for the lord on his demesne was a villein. Those who did not owe such services were considered free peasants and accorded more personal legal rights. By the 13th century villeinage was accepted as a hereditary condition of a personal character viewed much as slavery was, thus placing definite limitations on one's freedom. These limitations included the inability to leave one's village, certain undefined labor services, and fiscal liability for such payments of fees for MARRIAGE and even succession to the tenure involved. If one was born a villein, one and one's children would always be villeins. With the demographic collapse of the PLAGUES in the mid-14th century, conditions for their labor and the tenure of workable property had to be improved as supply and demand set better terms of rural work, thus softening villeins' obligations for labor on the estates or demesnes of lords.

See also MANORS AND THE MANORIAL SYSTEM; PEASANTRY; PEASANT REBELLIONS; SERFS AND SERFDOM.

Further reading: Rodney H. Hilton, *The English Peasantry in the Later Middle Ages* (Oxford: Clarendon Press, 1975); George C. Homans, *English Villagers of the Thirteenth Century* (Cambridge, Mass.: Harvard University Press, 1941); S. H. Rigby, *English Society in the Later Middle Ages: Class, Status and Gender* (London: Macmillan Press, 1995).

Villon, François (ca. 1431–after 1463) *Parisian lyric poet*
François was born, perhaps, as François de Montcorbier or François des Loges at PARIS in 1431. In March of 1449 he received a bachelor's degree from the University of Paris and was made a master by that institution in 1452. While drinking with some friends in 1455, he fought with a member of the CLERGY, whom he stabbed to death. This led to a temporary banishment, but he received a pardon in January of 1456. He was implicated in a theft at the Collège of NAVARRE that forced him to leave Paris. He was condemned to hang in 1463 and finally banished from Paris.

François disappeared from the historical record after 1463. Despite all this reputation for dissolute friends, crime, and debauchery, he at the same time wrote memorable and personal poetry famous for its compassion for the suffering of humanity and regret for a wasted life. The *Testament* (1461–62) explored DEATH. Villon dealt with his failed love affairs, deception by women, his bungled existence, POVERTY decrepit old age, and dying. This all parodied a typical written testament or last will.

Further reading: François Villon, *Complete Works,* trans. Anthony Bonner (New York: D. McKay, 1960); John H. Fox, *The Poetry of Villon* (London: T. Nelson, 1962); Stephen G. Nichols, "François Villon" in *European Writers: The Middle Ages and the Renaissance.* Vol. 1, *Prudentius to Medieval Drama,* ed. William T. H. Jackson and George Stade (New York: Charles Scribner's Sons, 1983), 535–570; Evelyn Birge Vitz, *The Crossroad of Intentions: A Study of Symbolic Expression in the Poetry of François Villon* (The Hague: Mouton, 1974).

Vincent of Beauvais (ca. 1190–1264) *French Dominican, writer*
Vincent was born about 1190 in Beauvais in FRANCE. As a Dominican friar from 1220, Vincent of Beauvais was the subprior of the convent of Beauvais founded in 1225 and a visitor at the nearby Cistercian abbey of Royaumont. There he became a close friend of its founder, the king and Saint, LOUIS IX. Under the patronage of the king and his court, he wrote a treatise on the education of noble children between 1247 and 1250, a letter of consolation on the death of the king's eldest son in 1260, and a treatise on the proper conduct of a prince between 1260 and 1262.

Vincent's most important work was the *Speculum maius* (the great mirror), an encyclopedic collection in three parts, *Naturale, Doctrinale,* and *Historiale.* He wrote it in the 1240s and 1250s while moving between Paris and Beauvais. A fourth section by another author on moral questions was added later in the century. In it Vincent tried to present in an organized manner the totality of knowledge up to the time of his contemporary Louis IX. He drew on all the written sources accessible to him from antiquity to the present. This work was intended to promote the study and understanding of dogmatic teachings, assist in the instruction of morals, and foster appropriate interpretations of the BIBLE. In other words it was to direct the reader toward REDEMPTION. Vincent incorporated much of the new study of Aristotelian and Jewish-Arabic natural PHILOSOPHY and the teaching of the Dominican and Franciscan masters such as ALBERTUS MAGNUS, Thomas AQUINAS, RAYMOND OF PEÑAFORT, and Alexander of Hales (1170–1245). It amounted to an intellectual tool and a collection and summary of mid-13th-century knowledge and thought a compendium of HAGIOGRAPHY, history, economics, ALCHEMY, and scientific knowledge in some 80 books. It survived in a large number of manuscripts and was translated into French and Flemish. Vincent died in Beauvais in 1264.

Further reading: W. J. Aerts, E. R. Smits, and J. B. Voorbij, eds., *Vincent of Beauvais and Alexander the Great: Studies on the Speculum maius and Its Translations into Medieval Vernaculars* (Groningen: E. Forsten, 1986); Astrik L. Gabriel, *The Educational Ideas of Vincent of Beauvais* (Notre Dame, Ind.: University of Notre Dame Press, 1962); Joseph M. McCarthy, *Humanistic Emphasis in the Educational Thought of Vincent of Beauvais* (Leiden: E. J. Brill, 1976); Rosemary Barton Tobin, *Vincent of Beauvais' "De eruditione filiorum nobelium": The Education of Women* (New York: P. Lang, 1984).

vines and vineyards   In the ancient world viticulture had attained a high degree of production and quality. During the Middle Ages, WINE was drunk widely in Western Europe, especially in the south. In Christian worship in the MASS, wine was used and consumed by the celebrant to represent symbolically, and controversially, the actual substance of the blood of Christ. Since it was not easy to transport and very perishable, wherever the climate permitted the cultivation of the grape was extensive, from the 12th and 13th centuries, even in northern countries such as England and in mountainous regions. These marginal vineyards tended to be abandoned in the 14th century as the climate grew colder and population and demand fell.

Viticulture in the Middle Ages did not require large investments of time or financial resources. Peasants and town dwellers cultivated and drank their own production, as in the present. Certain regions such as TUSCANY produced wine in bulk for sale outside the immediate region because of its reputed high quality. Other regions produced large amounts because their climate was adequate and they had easy access to transport by water.

The significance of the cultivation of grapes in the Middle Ages can also be confirmed by its prominent place in medieval art. The iconography of grapes and vines was employed in decorative motifs and was prominent in activities portrayed in calendars and landscapes. Such biblical episodes as the wedding feast at Cana and the drunkenness of Noah were often portrayed as symbolic of Christ's bounty and didactically represented the dangers of drunkenness.

ATTITUDES OF JUDAISM AND ISLAM

Wine also played a prominent role in Jewish ritual and religious usage, though some sects completely prohibited its consumption. Prominent Jewish sages were sometimes vintners, and wine produced by non-Jews was generally not to be consumed or to be used in the common rituals of CIRCUMCISION and MARRIAGE or the PASSOVER seder. Drinking wine or *khamr* made primarily from dates, raisins, barley, or honey was prohibited in the QURAN; but that prohibition was not always honored by all Muslims, especially the adherents of the Hanafi School of Islamic law.

See also AGRICULTURE; FOOD, DRINK AND NUTRITION.

Further reading: Edward Hyams, *Dionysus: A Social History of the Wine Vine* (London: Thames and Hudson, 1965); Margery Kirkbride James, *Studies in the Medieval Wine Trade,* ed. Elspeth M. Veale (Oxford: Clarendon Press, 1971); Patrick E. McGovern, Stuart J. Fleming and Solomon H. Katz, eds., *The Origins and Ancient History of Wine* (Philadelphia: Gordon and Breach Publishers, 1995); P. T. H. Unwin, *Wine and the Vine: An Historical Geography of Viticulture and the Wine Trade* (London: Routledge, 1991).

Vinland and Vinland sagas Two 13th-century Icelandic sagas describe in slightly different ways the discovery by sailors from ICELAND and GREENLAND the land called Vinland. Around 1000 Erik the Red's (d. ca. 1002) son, Leif Eriksson the Lucky (fl. early 11th century), sailed west, where he found land and disembarked for a short period. After Ericksson's landing, there were supposedly four colonizing expeditions to Vinland in vain attempts to stay for more than a short period. The settlers never seem to have reached any accommodation with the native peoples they encountered there, and the trip from Greenland was too difficult to justify any possible material gains.

The meaning of the name Vinland may refer to grapevines or natural grassland they found there. An actual Viking settlement, perhaps Vinland, was discovered near L'Anse aux Meadows on the bleak northernmost tip of the Great Northern Peninsula of Newfoundland, Canada, by the archaeologists Helge Ingstad and Anne Stine Ingstad. The site was excavated from 1961 to 1976 and buildings and artifacts dated securely from about 1000 were found. It seems to have been a typical Icelandic- or Greenlandic-style settlement for about 100 people. The settlement appears to have been used for 20 or 25 years as a base camp for exploration of the eastern North American coastline and the Gulf of Saint Lawrence. No graves or livestock pens were found.

See also SAGAS.

Further reading: Magnus Magnusson and Herman Pálson, trans., *The Vinland Sagas: The Norse Discovery of America* (London: Penguin, 1965); Herman Pálson and Paul Edwards, trans., *The Book of Settlements [Landnámabók]* (Winnipeg: University of Manitoba Press, 1972); Anne Stine Ingstad, *The Norse Discovery of America,* trans. Elizabeth S. Seeberg , 2 vols. (Oxford: Oxford University Press, 1985).

virginity The basic medieval concept and ideal of virginity were initially formed in liturgy of the early Christian religion and in the ideas of the early Christian fathers, especially ORIGEN and AUGUSTINE. Throughout the medieval period virginity was viewed as corporeal integrity for men and women but also was considered as embodying a spiritual condition that reflected a fundamental state of being. It could be institutionally organized and almost sacramentally consecrated. It could be, and was, blessed and acknowledged by a promise to God. It could be practiced by those married, theoretically also accepted by the spouse, and those not married and living in secular society.

From the 11th century and the GREGORIAN REFORM, virginity was considered the chief of the moral virtues and absolutely proper and necessary for a clerical state of life. However, it had to be practiced in a humble manner. It meant carnal integrity or the absence of carnal or sexual enjoyment, and the will to abstain forever from such pleasures. In virtue it now surpassed marital chastity and was another sign of the higher value of the clerical state. It was a common attribute in saints' lives and a major, if not essential, factor in canonization. In the secular world of the elite in Christendom, it was expected of a bride and reflected the honor of her family. The perpetual virginity of MARY, the Mother of God, was a major aspect of her state of life. She had an absolute purity of spiritual life and thus a total union with Christ, whom she had borne. In Islam and Judaism, virginity was expected for women at first marriage but was not much valued as a spiritual state for human beings. Both religions had severe laws to enforce this premarital condition, on women in particular.

See also CELIBACY; SEXUALITY AND SEXUAL ATTITUDES; SONG OF SONGS; VIRTUES AND VICES.

Further reading: Peter R. L. Brown, *The Body and Society: Men, Women, and Sexual Renunciation in Early Christianity* (New York: Columbia University Press, 1988); John Bugge, *Virginitas: An Essay in the History of a Medieval Idea* (The Hague: Martinus Hijhoff, 1975); Kate Cooper, *The Virgin and the Bride: Idealized Womanhood in Late Antiquity* (Cambridge, Mass.: Harvard University Press, 1996); Dyan Elliott, *Spiritual Marriage: Sexual Abstinence in Medieval Wedlock* (Princeton, N.J.: Princeton University Press, 1993); Susanna Elm, *"Virgins of God": The Making of Asceticism in Late Antiquity* (Oxford: Clarendon Press, 1996).

Virgin Mary, cult of   *See* MARY, CULT OF.

virtues and vices   A virtue in the Middle Ages was an excellence practiced habitually in a particular aspect of one's moral life that was at the same time evaluated and promoted by a set of religious and philosophical ideas. A vice was defined as exactly the opposite habitual practice. The definition, acquisition, and cultivation of virtue and the eschewing of vice were much considered by Greek and Roman philosophers and were fundamental aspects of the Christian and Hebrew Bibles, and the QURAN and HADITH.

MEDIEVAL CHRISTENDOM

ARISTOTELIANISM, when it entered Christendom in full force in the 13th century, strengthened these concepts as central elements in its systematic discourses on the right practice of human life. Aristotelian virtue or *habitus* was defined more explicitly as the fostered or cultivated capacity to act for good or for ill. Such a quality in humans grew or was enforced with each act. Any decision was to be based on good reason, while each accompanying movement of the will strengthened a person's habitual capacity to act in moral and virtuous ways. So in that way, human beings could became what they did, whether good or evil. AUGUSTINE had earlier added to this equation the gratuitous, gracious character of virtue as a gift from GOD. Thomas AQUINAS said that he considered virtue the capacity to act and to act well with a free will. In an attempt to make this a perpetual state, one had to practice a virtue continuously; otherwise, one would cease to act virtuously and relinquish REDEMPTION or Salvation.

The Scholastics classified virtue as the three theological virtues of FAITH, HOPE, and charity and the four moral virtues of prudence, JUSTICE, temperance, and fortitude. The struggle against vices and for the acquisition of virtues structured Christian ethics. The list of vices, that is, capital or deadly sins, might include gluttony, luxury or sexual indulgence, avarice, anger, sadness or sloth,

envy, and vainglory or pride. These vices all fed on one another and were interconnected. Vices and virtues were contrary to each other and in sermons and iconography were portrayed by using a literary and iconographic tradition derived from antiquity that personified the vices and virtues, making them fight against each other.

See also CARDINAL VIRTUES; PENITENTIALS; SERMONS AND HOMILIES; SEVEN DEADLY OR CAPITAL SINS.

Further reading: Morton W. Bloomfield, *The Seven Deadly Sins: An Introduction to the History of a Religious Concept, with Special Reference to Medieval English Literature* (East Lansing: Michigan State College Press, 1952); Colum Hourihane, ed., *Virtue and Vice: The Personifications in the Index of Christian Art* (Princeton, N.J.: Princeton University Press, 2000); Adolf Katzenellenbogen, *Allegories of the Virtues and Vices and Mediaeval Art: From Early Christian Times to the Thirteenth Century,* trans. Alan J. P. Crick (New York: W. W. Norton, 1964); Ruth Ellis Messenger, *Ethical Teachings in the Latin Hymns of Medieval England, with Special Reference to the Seven Deadly Sins and the Seven Principal Virtues* (New York: AMS Press, 1967).

Visconti family   The Visconti were a noble Lombard family, who can be traced back to the 10th century, but from the late 13th century held the lordship of MILAN and other cities, with the title of duke from 1395. They obtained the lordship of Milan in 1277 after the Ghibelline or proimperial archbishop, Ottone Visconti (d. 1295), was victorious over a Guelf faction led by the rival della Torre family. The regimes of Ottone (r. 1277–95) and his nephew, Matteo (r. 1287–1302 and 1317–22, d. 1322), were marked by conflicts with political rivals. In fact they were temporarily expelled from the city in 1302. Their power was recovered in 1311 by Matteo and expanded and consolidated under his successors, Galeazzo I (r. 1322–27), Azzone (r. 1328–39), Giovanni (1349–54), also the archbishop of Milan from 1342), Luchino (r. 1339–49), Matteo II (r. 1354–55), Galeazzo II (r. 1354–78), and Bernarbò (r. 1354–85).

During this period the Visconti had expanded their control over a large part of the Po Valley and LOMBARDY. They were careful to control the ecclesiastical wealth and institutions of the city even when they did not occupy the bishopric themselves. They also carried out impressive building projects to demonstrate the prestige and power of the family. Milan became one the major states of the Italian Peninsula. In 1395 the emperor Wenceslas (r. 1378–1400) granted for a payment of 100,000 florins a ducal title to Gian Galeazzo (r. 1385–1402). This and marriages into the royal families of FRANCE and ENGLAND sanctioned the family's success by transforming it into a princely dynasty. But the premature death of Gian Galeazzo as he was about to attack FLORENCE itself marked the start of a decade of crises under the weak

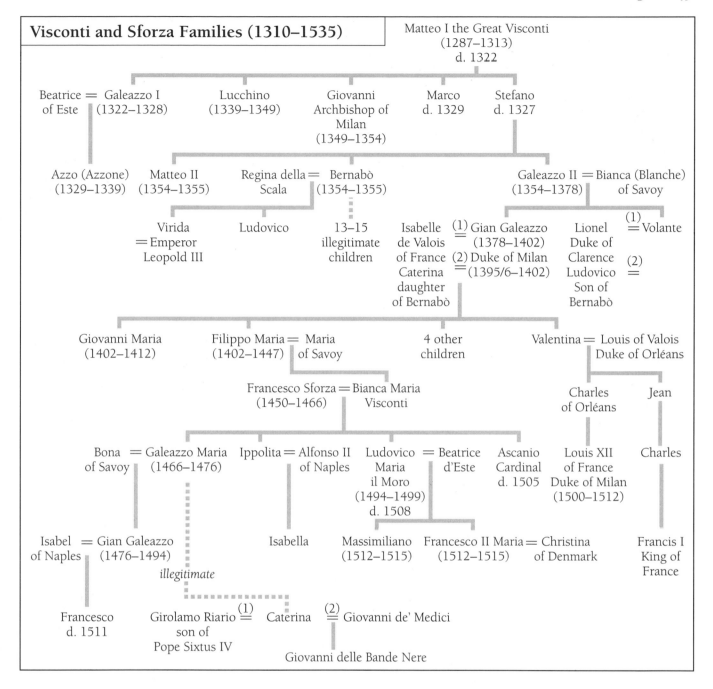

Visconti and Sforza Families (1310–1535)

government of the vicious Giovanni Maria (1402–12), who was eventually assassinated by conspirators. His brother and ruthless successor, Filippo Maria (1412–47), then undertook the reconstruction of the state, fighting almost constantly against Florence and VENICE. He died without legitimate heirs, ending the dynasty. A short-lived republic followed, and then Francesco Sforza (1401–66), who had married a Visconti, seized control of Milan and its subject territory.

See also GUELFS AND GHIBELLINES; SFORZA FAMILY.

Further reading: Hans Baron, *The Crisis of the Early Italian Renaissance: Civic Humanism and Republican Liberty in an Age of Classicism and Tyranny* (Princeton, N.J.:

Princeton University Press, 1955); Edward Burman, *Italian Dynasties: The Great Families of Italy from the Renaissance to the Present Day* (Wellingborough: Equation, 1989); E. R. Chamberlin, *The Count of Virtue: Giangaleazzo Visconti, Duke of Milan* (New York: Scribner, 1965); Dorothy Muir, *A History of Milan under the Visconti* (London: Methuen, 1924).

Visigoths (West Goths) The Visigoths were a branch of the GOTHS who arrived as allies in AQUITAINE in Gaul in 412, invited there to attack the VANDALS. They had earlier defeated the Romans at the Battle of ADRIANOPLE in 378 and had sacked ROME in 410 under the kingship of ALARIC I. After absorbing other tribal groups, they created a kingdom that extended under King Euric (r. 466–84), from the Loire and the Rhône into the Iberian Peninsula. They played an important role in stopping the advance of the HUNS into Gaul in 451. Alaric's successor, Alaric II (r. 484–507), was defeated at the Battle of Vouille in 507 by the king of the FRANKS, CLOVIS, and the kingdom was obliged to retreat into SPAIN, retaining north of the Pyrenees of only parts of southeastern FRANCE.

This Visigothic kingdom had a problematic existence because of a stable rule of uncontested succession, so no early dynasty managed to impose itself permanently. Kingship became and remained a objective in factional rivalries. King Leovigild (r. 568–86) tried to unify the peninsula, made his capital at TOLEDO, struck gold coins, and wore a royal crown. The ARIANISM of the Visigoths did not promote unity within their state. RECARED I converted to Catholicism at the Council of Toledo in May 589. This conversion gave the dynasty more legitimacy by a religious ceremony of consecration and gained the backing of the powerful local episcopacy. The final decades of the seventh century began a period of decline with economic and social troubles, including famines in 680–87 and plagues in 687–702. There was increasing fiscal pressure and after the conversion to Catholicism there were harsh policies against the Jews, who had once supported the kingdom. Aristocratic rivalries over succession grew more intense. All this made it easy for a quick Muslim conquest, which swept into the peninsula in April of 711. In a few years the Muslims controlled nearly the whole peninsula and the Visigothic people were absorbed into its population. Their kingdom, the only barbarian kingdom favorable to intellectual life, vanished but left a heritage in canon law, art, and culture.

See also ATTILA, KING OF THE HUNS; ISIDORE OF SEVILLE; JUSTINIAN I, BYZANTINE EMPEROR; SEVILLE, CITY AND KINGDOM OF; STILICHO; ULPHILAS.

Further reading: P. D. King, *Law and Society in the Visigothic Kingdom* (Cambridge: Cambridge University Press, 1972); E. A. Thompson, *The Visigoths in the Time of Ulfila* (Oxford: The Clarendon Press, 1966); E. A. Thompson, *The Goths in Spain* (Oxford: The Clarendon Press, 1969); Joyce E. Salisbury, *Iberian Popular Religion, 600 B.C. to 700 A.D.: Celts, Romans, and Visigoths* (New York: E. Mellen Press, 1985); Norman Roth, *Jews, Visigoths, and Muslims in Medieval Spain: Cooperation and Conflict* (Leiden: E. J. Brill, 1994).

visions and dreams Visions and dreams in the Middle Ages were considered to be real and even divinely inspired, but just as likely chimeras or foolish or malevolent fantasies. Dreams and visions were plentiful in the Hebrew Bible and less so in the Christian Bible. Yet biblical Judaism was distrustful of deriving meaningful interpretations of reality or divinely inspired readings of God's intent from visions or dreams. The classical late antique world was somewhat more favorably disposed to their meaningfulness, partially because of the possible direct roles of the gods in the lives of humans and their places in religious culture such as at oracles, but Cicero considered interpreting them as meaningful to be mere superstition. Christianity was more skeptical, even suspicious they could be diabolical. Part of this distrust was based on their possible experience and interpretation as being outside the control of the clergy, contrary to reason, and possibly violative of the traditions and dogmas of the church. Pope GREGORY I THE GREAT distinguished five causes of dreams, which became the common modes of viewing them and their interpretation for the rest of the Middle Ages. Dreams could be caused by excessive eating, by the promptings of the devil, by mere reflection on or obsession with the concerns of daily life, by divine inspiration, or by a more specific obsession or preoccupation of the sleeper or visionary. These skeptical concepts overflowed into a distrust of the visions experienced or perceived by saints, mystics, or any Christians.

LITERARY VISIONS

With the passage of time visions in the Middle Ages were defined as a literary genre and as a form of perception and contact with another world. As literary modes of expression they resembled allegory. Individuals visited HELL, LIMBO, PARADISE, and PURGATORY in an ecstasy, dream, or journey to the other world. Visions could be deemed flashes of intuition and representations of a symbolic universe, echoing personal spiritual experiences. Remaining problematic in the eyes of the church, they could sometimes now be seen as morally valuable, promoting access to the contemplation of scenes from Christ's life and Passion or to episodes from the life of the Virgin MARY. They were tamed as these literary and explicitly imaginary devices or entertaining and didactic stories. Preachers in the later Middle Ages were not reluctant to use them as good yarns in sermons to set the stage for warnings about the consequences of an immoral life.

See also ALIGHIERI, DANTE; ANGELA OF FOLIGNO; BIRGITTA OF SWEDEN, SAINT; CATHERINE OF SIENA, SAINT; GERSON, JOHN; MYSTICISM, CHRISTIAN; PREACHING AND PREACHERS.

Further reading: Paul Edward Dutton, *The Politics of Dreaming in the Carolingian Empire* (Lincoln: University of Nebraska Press, 1994); S. F. Kruger, *Dreaming in the Middle Ages* (Cambridge: Cambridge University Press, 1992); Isabel Moreira, *Dreams, Visions, and Spiritual Authority in Merovingian* (Ithaca, N.Y.: Cornell University Press, 2000); Eileen Gardiner, *Medieval Visions of Heaven and Hell: A Sourcebook* (New York: Garland, 1993); Forrest S. Smith, *Secular and Sacred Visionaries in the Late Middle Ages* (New York: Garland, 1986);

Kathryn L. Lynch, *The High Medieval Dream Vision: Poetry, Philosophy, and Literary Form* (Stanford, Calif.: Stanford University Press, 1988).

viticulture   *See* VINES AND VINEYARDS.

Vitry, Jacques   *See* JAMES OF VITRY.

Vittorino da Feltre (1378–1446) *teacher, educational theorist*

Born at Feltre near VENICE about 1378 Vittorino studied at the University of Padua with GUARINO DA VERONA and Pietro Paolo Vergerio (1370–1444), absorbing their ideas about the moral qualities of Greek and Roman literature in combination with polite customs. In 1423 he moved to Mantua at the invitation of the Gonzaga family to establish a school for the children of the family. Vittorino opened this school to the sons of the poor. He taught grammar and classical authors such as Cicero and Virgil to Lorenzo VALLA and the translator of Greek texts Antonio Beccaria (ca. 1400–74). He thought the rote study of RHETORIC and dialectic would produce eloquent and virtuous people. He also insisted his students practice physical activity and learn languages, mathematics, and PHILOSOPHY to give them a broad foundation for further study. He also made his students read a great deal of Christian devotional literature. He died in 1446, and with him his school.

See also UNIVERSITIES AND SCHOOLS.

Further reading: Paul F. Grendler, *Schooling in Renaissance Italy: Literacy and Learning, 1300–1600* (Baltimore: Johns Hopkins University Press, 1989); William Harrison Woodward, *Vittorino da Feltre and Other Humanist Educators* (1921; reprint, New York: Bureau of Publications, Teachers College, Columbia University, 1963); William Harrison Woodward, *Studies in Education during the Age of the Renaissance, 1400–1600* (1906; reprint, New York: Teachers College Press, 1967).

Vivarium   Vivarium was a monastery founded in about 555 by CASSIODORUS on his lands in Calabria. Its monastic buildings were probably located at San Martino de Copanello in the center of the Gulf of Squillace. This foundation was not regulated by any particular rule. Cassiodorus was not a cleric and entrusted its rule to abbots. Its main objectives were to copy, correct, and translate ancient texts as promoted by the manual of *Institutions* drawn up by Cassiodorus for the monks of Vivarium. He equipped the monastery with a large library and a SCRIPTORIUM. Although the number of manuscripts actually copied there that survive to this day is minimal, this monastery probably did preserve the manuscripts that were used for the later copying of many important works. Vivarium showed the way that monastic culture could

preserve classical culture for the study of Scripture and Christian literature throughout the rest of the Middle Ages and RENAISSANCE. After the sixth century, however, such activities there ceased and the monastery soon passed into ruin.

Further reading: Cassiodorus, *An Introduction to Divine and Human Readings,* trans. Leslie Webber Jones (1946; reprint, New York: W. W. Norton, 1969); L. D. Reynolds and N. G. Wilson, *Scribes and Scholars: A Guide to the Transmission of Greek and Latin Literature,* 3d ed. (Oxford: Oxford University Press, 1991).

Vlachs   This was the name usually given by the Byzantines and SLAVS to the Romanians. They have been the subject of heated nationalistic controversies. Romanian historians thought that they were descendants of the Roman colonists who had settled in the second century in ILLYRICUM. Some Hungarian historians said they were nomadic shepherds from south of the Danube River. Whatever their origin, the Vlachs played important roles in a number of transitory states from the 12th century. There was a Bulgarian and Vlach empire north of the Danube between 1185 and 1257. They were also part of Great Vlachin in the mountains of Thessaly from the second half of the 11th century to 1393 and of the principality of WALLACHIA between the southern Carpathians and MOLDAVIA in the 15th century.

See also HUNGARY; TRANSYLVANIA.

Further reading: André Du Nay, *The Origins of the Rumanians: The Early History of the Rumanian Language* (Toronto: Matthias Corvinus Publishing, 1996); John V. A. Fine Jr., *The Late Medieval Balkans: A Critical Survey from the Late Twelfth Century to the Ottoman Conquest* (Ann Arbor: University of Michigan Press, 1994); Robert W. Seton-Watson, *A History of the Roumanians: From Roman Times to the Completion of Unity* (Cambridge: Cambridge University Press, 1934); Tom J. Winnifrith, *The Vlachs: The History of a Balkan People* (New York: St. Martin's Press, 1987).

Vlad III the Impaler (Vlad Tepeş, Dracul [the Dragon]) (ca. 1431–76) *legendary ferocious prince of Wallachia*

Born about 1431 and educated in WALLACHIA, he inherited his nickname "Dracul" from his father, who had been a member the imperial Order of the Dragon. In 1448 he returned from exile to claim the throne after his father, Vlad II Dracul (r. 1443–47/8), the prince of Wallachia, had been overthrown and executed by John HUNYADI. The younger Vlad failed in this first attempt to take the throne, fled to MOLDAVIA, and had to wait until 1456 to become prince with the help of the king of HUNGARY, Ladislas V Posthumous (r. 1444/45–57), but he remained permanently caught between the ambitions of the Ottomans and the Hungarians to control Wallachia. He

Vlad Tepes, also known as Vlad the Impaler or Dracula
(Courtesy Library of Congress)

Vladimir I the Great, Saint (ca. 955/958–1015)
grand prince of Kiev

Vladimir was born between 955 and 958 in KIEV in the modern Ukraine, the son of Sviatoslav (r. 962–971/972) of Kiev. His education was influenced by his Christian grandmother, Saint Olga (ca. 890–969), who had been baptized in 955. He was placed on the throne of NOVGOROD with help from his Scandinavian relatives in 970. From about 979/980 Vladimir took over all of Kievan Ruś, enlarging the borders of the state and strengthening its defenses against the attacks of the Pechenegs. Agreeing to a treaty in 987 with the BYZANTINE EMPIRE, he helped the future emperor, BASIL II, win a civil war. As a reward he became Basil's brother-in-law after promising to make Christianity the state religion. On January 6, 988, he was baptized, and at the following

The baptism of Vladimir I, prince of Kiev, in Cherson in 988, from the *Radziwill Chronicle*, p. 62v. (late fifteenth century), Academy of Science, Saint Petersburg, Russia *(Erich Lessing / Art Resource)*

spent the next six years periodically fighting the OTTOMAN Turks, and the Bulgarians and establishing his own rule by controlling his own people. He was brutal in his methods and became famous for his method of killing his enemies—impaling on a sharpened post. He was deposed in 1462 but returned to power again in 1476. Perhaps assassinated by false allies, he was likely killed in battle, the details of which have been much disputed by historians, in 1476 while trying to maintain Wallachian independence from foreign domination. The Turks took control of the region shortly after his death. In his famous 1897 novel, Bram Stoker based his character of Dracula on some of the legends of Vlad that had been circulated widely in the 15th and 16th centuries.

Further reading: Radu Florescu and Raymond T. McNally, *Dracula: A Biography of Vlad the Impaler, 1431–1476* (New York: Hawthorn Books, 1973); Douglas Myles, *Prince Dracula: Son of the Devil* (New York: McGraw-Hill, 1988); Nicolae Stoicescu, *Vlad Tepes, Prince of Walachia,* trans. Cristina Krikorian (Bucharest: Editura Academiei Republicii Socialiste Romănia, 1978); Kurt W. Treptow, ed., *Dracula: Essays on the Life and Times of Vlad Tepes* (Boulder, Colo.: East European Monographs, 1991).

PENTECOST Sunday a few months later, he ordered the mass baptism of his subjects. During the same summer he married a Byzantine princess, Anne (963–1011). He ordered the building of many wooden churches at Kiev as well as a palace church of stone by 996. He moved in Kiev more clerics and church furnishings from Cherson on the BLACK SEA, which he conquered in 989 after it had revolted against Basil II. By 988 the metropolitanate of Ruś as well as four or five bishoprics had formed the 60th ecclesiastical province of the patriarchate of CONSTANTINOPLE. This process of Christianization was thorough and permanent, giving rise to his later canonization and his nickname as the "New Constantine." He died on July 15, 1015, in Berestova near Kiev and was soon venerated as a saint in the teeth of the violence and chaos among his sons, all fighting to succeed him.

Further reading: Samuel Hazzard Cross and Olgerd P. Sherbowitz-Wetzor, trans., *The Russian Primary Chronicle: Laurentian Text* (Cambridge, Mass.: Mediaeval Academy of America, 1973); John Fennell, *A History of the Russian Church to 1448* (London: Longman, 1995); Yves Hamant, ed., *The Christianization of Ancient Russia: A Millennium, 988–1988* (Paris: UNESCO, 1992); Andrzej Poppe, *The Rise of Christian Russia* (London: Variorum Reprints, 1982); Vladimir Volkoff, *Vladimir the Russian Viking* (London: Honeyglen, 1984).

Voyage of Saint Brendan *See* BRENDAN, SAINT.

Vulgate The Vulgate is the medieval and modern name of the Latin translation of the BIBLE commonly used in the Middle Ages in Western Europe and officially recognized as the only authentic version by the Council of Trent in 1546. In the fifth century JEROME was dissatisfied with earlier translations based on the Greek Septuagint version. So commissioned he translated much of the Old Testament from the Hebrew and revised the texts of the New Testament. From the sixth century and overcoming the considerable opposition of those accustomed to the traditional texts, this translation, except Jerome's version of the Psalms, was the most commonly used and accepted. As the texts were transmitted by manuscripts over centuries, the texts became corrupted over time and various revisions were attempted by scholars such as ALCUIN. It was first printed by GUTENBERG in 1456. However, the Vulgate remained the accepted Latin text until it was reedited in the mid-16th century after the Protestant Reformation. From then on its text was better preserved since it could be printed and thus more carefully maintained as the standard Catholic version for study and the liturgy.

Further reading: Hans H. Glunz, *History of the Vulgate in England from Alcuin to Roger Bacon: Being an Inquiry into the Text of Some English Manuscripts of the Vulgate Gospels* (Cambridge: Cambridge University Press, 1933); G. W. H. Lampe, ed., *The Cambridge History of the Bible. Vol. 2, The West from the Fathers to the Reformation* (Cambridge: Cambridge University Press, 1969); Beryl Smalley, *The Study of the Bible in the Middle Ages,* 3d ed. (Oxford: B. Blackwell, 1983).

W

Wace (Robert or William?) (ca. 1100–ca. 1175) *Anglo-Norman author*
Born in Jersey in the Channel Islands to a noble family in about 1100. Wace was educated for an ecclesiastical career and studied at Caen and PARIS. After he returned to Caen in about 1130, he was employed by King HENRY I. He eventually became a canon in about 1160 when he was patronized by King HENRY II, for Bayeux in 1169. He died about 1175.

He wrote devotional lives of the saints Margaret and Nicholas and two metrical chronicles in Norman French. The *Roman de Brut* was completed in 1155 and dedicated to ELEANOR OF AQUITAINE, the mother of Henry II. It was an imaginative translation of the Latin *History of the Kings of Britain* by GEOFFREY OF MONMOUTH, which traced the history of Britain from its founding by the legendary Brutus the Trojan, including many aspects of the Arthurian legends. His *Roman du Rou* was a chronicle of the dukes of NORMANDY from the time of ROLLO to that of Wace's contemporary, Robert II Curthose (d. 1124). It was written in 1160–62 but never finished. It had been dedicated to Henry II, but Henry withdrew his patronage before Wace could complete it.

See also ANGLO-NORMAN LANGUAGE AND LITERATURE; ARTHUR, KING, AND ARTHURIAN LITERATURE; BRUT; ROUND TABLE.

Further reading: Wace, *Arthurian Chronicles,* trans. Eugene Mason. Toronto: University of Toronto Press, 1996); Wace, *Wace's Roman de Brut: A History of the English: Text and Translation,* trans. Judith Weiss (Exeter: University of Exeter Press, 1999); Margaret Evah Houck, *Sources of the Roman de Brut of Wace* (Berkeley: University of California Press, 1941); J. H.

Philpot, *Maistre Wace: A Pioneer in Two Literatures* (London: Methuen, 1925).

Walahfrid Strabo (ca. 808–849) *German Benedictine abbot, poet, theologian*
Born in SWABIA, Walafrid (Strabo means "squinter") was raised at the monastery of Reichenau and then at FULDA, where he was a pupil of HRABANUS Maurus. He became abbot of Reichenau after having been a teacher of CHARLES I THE BALD, with whom he retained a tenuous relationship. He had to flee Reichenau for supporting an opponent of Charles in 839, only to return in 842. He died while on mission for Charles on August 8, 849. He composed poetic works, biblical commentaries, homilies, and saints' lives. He was also known for his poetry which dealt with several subjects, including a polemic against the erection of a statue of the Ostrogothic king THEODORIC at AACHEN and a treatise on the medicinal plants and flowers of Reichenau's monastic GARDEN. Besides his revision of the biography of CHARLEMAGNE by EINHARD, his most important work was a commentary on the Scriptures, which remained a standard text for the rest of the Middle Ages.

See also CAROLINGIAN RENAISSANCE.

Further reading: Walahfrid Strabo, *The Life of St. Gall,* trans. Maud Joynt (Toronto: Macmillan, 1927); Walahfrid Strabo, *Walahfrid Strabo's Visio Wettini: Text, Translation and Commentary,* ed. David A. Traill (Bern: H. Lang, 1974); Eleanor Shipley Duckett, *Carolingian Portraits: A Study in the Ninth Century* (Ann Arbor: University of Michigan Press, 1962), 121–160; M. L. W. Laistner, *Thought and Letters in Western Europe,* A.D. *500 to 900*

(Ithaca, N.Y.: Cornell University Press, 1931); Janet L. Nelson, *Charles the Bald* (New York: Longman, 1992).

Waldemar I the Great (Valdemar) (1131–1182) *warrior, king of Denmark*

Heir to an ancient royal line in DENMARK, Waldemar was the son of the duke of Schleswig, Canute III Lavard (d. 1131). Born about 1131, perhaps on January 14, 1131, he became a contender to the throne on the death of King Erik the Lamb in 1156/7. By 1157 he had defeated his rivals and become the undisputed ruler and quickly consolidated his rule. In 1169 he captured an island stronghold of the Wendish pirates destroyed their idols, and forcibly Christianized them. Waldemar acknowledged the suzerainty of Emperor FREDERICK I BARBAROSSA in 1162, since he was dependent on Frederick's help against his aggressive German neighbors such as HENRY THE LION. After Henry's death in 1180, Waldemar and Frederick met in 1182 and arranged a double marriage between their children significantly improving the links of Denmark with the German emperor. Shortly before his death, one of his officials suppressed a serious uprising of some provinces opposing his heavy taxation. Waldemar died about May 9–12, 1182.

Further reading: John H. S. Birch, *Denmark in History* (London: J. Murray, 1938); Niels Skyum-Nielsen and Niels Lund, *Danish Medieval History: New Currents* (Copenhagen: Museum Tusculanum Press, 1981).

Waldemar II the Conqueror (Valdemar) (1170–1241) *king of Denmark*

Born May 9, 1170, he was the second son of WALDEMAR I and became the duke of Schleswig in 1188. He succeeded his brother, Canute IV (VI) (r. 1182–1202), in 1202 after having already captured the county of Holstein. In exchange for Waldemar's support of his holding the imperial title, the emperor Otto IV (d. 1218) acknowledged his rule over German lands north of the Elbe River, including important trading cities such as LÜBECK. In return, Waldemar then temporarily recognized Otto as the German emperor, only to switch his allegiance to FREDERICK II later. Waldemar also gained the support of Pope INNOCENT III, after he led a Crusade against the pagan Estonians and the Pomeranians in 1206 and 1210. However, at the height of his power and the greatest extent of his realm in 1223, he and his sons were kidnapped by a guest, a certain Count Henry of Schwerin. He was released only after paying a crippling heavy ransom and surrendering Northalbingia and most of his Wendish conquests in 1225, when his vassals and the Danish nobility had refused to go to his aid. He was later defeated by Henry at the Battle of Bornhöved in 1227 but was able to keep control of most of LIVONIA or Estonia by the Compact of Stensby made with the Knights of the Sword in 1238. Among the domestic reforms carried out toward the end of his reign was the great codification of Danish laws called the Jutland Code in 1241. He died on March 28, 1241, in Vordingborg in Denmark.

Further reading: J. H. S. Birch, *Denmark in History* (London: J. Murray, 1938); Palle Lauring, *A History of Denmark,* trans. David Hohnen, 5th ed. (Copenhagen: Høst & Søn, 1981); William L. Urban, *The Baltic Crusade,* 2d (Chicago: Lithuanian Research and Studies Center, 1994).

Waldensians (Waldenses, Poor of Lyon)

The Waldensians comprised a diverse sect that developed out of the followers of Peter Waldo (d. 1217) and were initially called the Poor of LYON but themselves never used the name Waldensians. Over the centuries this term referred to diverse religious sects with many different and changing ideas that fluidly diverged in many aspects from mainstream medieval Catholicism—especially among later groups called by this name in GERMANY and ITALY. The term was convenient for inquisitors who were trying to label and correct dissenters.

Peter Waldo, traditionally credited with the original initiative for the Waldensian movement was a rich merchant of Lyon, who converted to a religious life in the early 1170s. He gave away his wealth for Christ and at the same time became a preacher of the GOSPELS, gathering around himself LAITY and clerics. He wanted to remain there and reform the church but was expelled from the city. Not a dualist, unlike many contemporary dissidents he seems to have tried to preach the gospel outside the authority of the church and was critical of the worldliness of the CLERGY. Not all of his followers were so eager to remain orthodox. The movement was critical of the SEVEN SACRAMENTS, of the holiness and necessity of the priesthood, of the destiny of souls after death, and of the cult of the saints and RELICS.

By 1200 the Waldensian movement already encompassed a diversity of orientations about the meaning of POVERTY to the church and to good Christians. They were condemned and banned at the Third Lateran Council of 1181–85 and Pope INNOCENT III launched a CRUSADE against them in 1209. They meanwhile developed a clerical organization and grew and survived persecutions in isolated areas, such as in the Alps and BOHEMIA, where they later ultimately merged with the followers of John HUS. They were deemed among the most dangerous of heretical groups because they lived piously and believed in much of the orthodox and loudly attacked creed the institutional church, its rituals, and its clergy.

See also ALEXANDER III, POPE.

Further reading: Euan Cameron, *The Reformation of the Heretics: The Waldenses of the Alps, 1480–1580* (Oxford: Clarendon Press, 1984); Euan Cameron,

Waldenses: Rejections of Holy Church in Medieval Europe (Oxford: Blackwell, 2000); Walter L. Wakefield and Austin Evans, eds., *Heresies of the High Middle Ages* (1969; reprint, New York: Columbia University Press, 1969), 200–242, 278–289, 346–351.

Wales (Cymru)

Wales (Cymru) Medieval Wales was a mountainous country in the western peninsula of Britain. Strongly Celtic, it had its foundation as a distinct political, linguistic, and cultural unit with the building by the English king Offa of Mercia (r. 757–796) of an earthwork wall, called Offa's Dike, that divided Wales from Anglo-Saxon England. Wales grew to consist of a number of petty kingdoms, each ruled by its own ruling dynasty. The principal ones were at Gwynedd in the north, at Powys in the center, at Dyfed in the southwest, and at Morgannwg or Glamorgan in the southeast. There were temporary unifications of these kingdoms under individual rulers such as Rhodri Mawr the Great of Gwynedd (r. 844–878) or Hywel Dda the Good of Dyfed (r. 942–950). At their deaths these kingdoms went their separate ways, a trend that continued even during the VIKING invasions. At last Gruffydd ap Llywelyn (r. 1039–63), who attained power in Gwynedd in 1039, aggressively managed to extend his rule over most of Wales. The English responded to this by invading, as they were to do many times in the future. Resisting these invasions led by HAROLD with some success, Gruffydd ap Llywelyn was eventually killed by his own men, and the Welsh princes temporarily became the clients of EDWARD THE CONFESSOR.

NORMAN EXPANSION AND EQUILIBRIUM

After the Norman Conquest of England in 1066, there was an effort to establish stability on the borders of the two regions. This led to the founding of the earldoms on the border with Wales of Chester, Shrewsbury, and Hereford by WILLIAM I THE CONQUEROR. Nonetheless, ambitious Norman adventurers independently moved to carve lordships or kingdoms out of Wales for themselves. By these intrusions they made themselves local rulers and soon received royal recognition as Marcher lords or as Anglo-Norman lords ruling in parts of Wales by right of conquest, but they were not actually part of the Norman kingdom. These Anglo-Norman magnate families exercised control of most of eastern Wales with the western part left under the control of native but usually peaceful rulers. By the mid-12th century, balance, peace, and equilibrium was the usual situation along the border and with the English, as cultural interaction and intermarriage took place. This was an era rich in poetic accomplishment and reform of the Welsh church and law.

CONFLICT AND WARFARE WITH ENGLAND

In the late 12th century, under LLEWELYN Fawr ab Iorwerth, this tense but generally peaceful coexistence changed as he tried to establish a principality encompassing all of Wales. He accomplished this by 1200 during the reign of King JOHN with the help of the French king, PHILIP II Augustus. He even married the illegitimate daughter of the hard-pressed King John. Forced to compromise with Llewelyn's participation in the barons' rebellion and in the temporary reconciliation of MAGNA CARTA, John recognized Llewelyn's rights and control, in exchange for which Llewelyn paid homage to the English Crown on behalf of himself and all the Welsh lords.

John's successor, Henry III, was not willing to accept a permanent united Wales on his western border and the relationship was much more confrontational until the Treaty of Montgomery in 1267, when Wales was recognized as essentially a sovereign principality. LLEWELLYN AP GRUFFYDD, by then the prince of Wales, tried to put his principality on a sounder military, financial, and administrative footing. This project was halted, however, when the new king of England, EDWARD I, decided on the conquest of Wales. Llewellyn was forced to seek terms in the Treaty of Aberconwy of 1277, which left him with only his ancestral lands at Gwynedd. After a period of tense peace, war began again; the prince was killed on December 11, 1282, and his brother was captured and executed a few months later, marking the end of Welsh independence.

INTEGRATION INTO THE KINGDOM OF ENGLAND

The Statute of Wales of 1284 established a new administrative regime for the principality now tied to the English Crown. The title of prince of Wales was granted in 1301 to the king's eldest surviving son, in this case the future EDWARD II. There were scattered revolts throughout the 14th century, but in general terms accommodation with England yielded prosperity for the first half of the century. This was also the era of the great poetic accomplishments of DAFYDD AP GWILYM. Wales was affected by the plagues and the social, economic, and severe population declines of the mid-14th century. There were a growing discontent among the Welsh lords and a definite rise in ethnic tension between them and the mostly urban English colonists. In 1400, the Welsh, led by OWAIN GLYN DWR, a descendant of the Powys and Deheubarth dynasties, revolted. The rising lasted 10 years, but the resources and determination of the English Crown were strong and its was suppressed. The leaders of the native ruling community nonetheless continued to exercise considerable power and control because of their loyalty to the English Crown. The victors of the WARS OF THE ROSES, the Lancastrian House of TUDOR had strong roots in Wales, which superficially mitigated many of the tensions between the two peoples, as the king of England, Henry VII Tudor (r. 1485–1509), was seen by many to be Welsh. In 1536, Wales officially became part of the English kingdom.

See also GERALD OF WALES; HENRY V, KING OF ENGLAND; MABINOGI.

Further reading: Gerald of Wales, *The Journey through Wales/The Description of Wales,* trans. Lewis Thorpe (New York: Penguin Books, 1978); Antony D. Carr, "Wales," in *The New Cambridge Medieval History.* Vol. 6, *c. 1300–c. 1415,* ed. Michael Jones (Cambridge: Cambridge University Press, 2000), 334–344; Antony D. Carr, "Wales," in *The New Cambridge Medieval History.* Vol. 7, *c. 1415–c. 1500,* ed. Christopher Allmand (Cambridge: Cambridge University Press, 1998), 532–546; R. Ian Jack, *Medieval Wales* (Ithaca, N.Y.: Cornell University Press, 1972); David Walker, *Medieval Wales* (Cambridge: Cambridge University Press, 1990); Glanmor Williams, *The Welsh Church from Conquest to Reformation,* rev. ed. (Cardiff: University of Wales Press, 1976).

al-Walid, Abd al-Malik (r. 705–715) *Umayyad caliph*
Ruling from 705, al-Walid became known for his religious fervor, cultural patronage, and building activities. Although it had hitherto been shared by Christians and Muslims, he confiscated and razed the Basilica of Saint John the Baptist in his capital, Damascus, against the wishes of the local Christians. He turned it into the present magnificent Grand Mosque between 706 and 715. He intended it to be the most sumptuous mosque yet built and summoned workers and craftsmen, both Christian and Muslim, from all over the world to build and decorate it. Heavily damaged in a fire in 1893 and having suffered considerable rebuilding, it had long been a model for the architecture of such buildings and remained one of the most important mosques in Islam. He also built schools, HOSPITALS, and orphanages in the city. Under his rule the administration of the caliphate was taken out of the hands of the Syrian Christians, who were replaced by Muslim officials, further Islamizing the caliphate. He started the construction of the new great mosques in MEDINA and MECCA. Under his rule the Arab empire, continuously expanded through conquest approaching its greatest extent, reaching from Transoxiana to Spain. He died in 715.

See also ISLAMIC CONQUESTS AND EARLY EMPIRE; UMAYYADS.

Further reading: al-Tabari, *The Zenith of the Marwanid House: The Last Years of Abd al-Malik and the Caliphate of al-Walid,* trans. Martin Hinds (Albany: State University of New York Press, 1988); Sulayman Bashir, *Arabs and Others in Early Islam* (Princeton, N.J.: Darwin Press, 1997); G. R. Hawting, *The First Dynasty of Islam: The Umayyad Caliphate* A.D. *661–750* (Kent: Croom Helm, 1986).

Wallace, William, Sir (ca. 1270–1305) *a leader of Scots resistance*
Of noble descent, William was born in about 1270 in Ellerslie or Elderslie near Paisley in Ayrshire in SCOTLAND, the son of Sir Malcolm Wallace. He killed an Englishman who insulted him and was declared an outlaw in May 1297. He started a guerrilla war and was joined by patriotic nobles and began to enlarge the scope of his operations and ambitions. After being elected guardian of the kingdom in 1297 for the imprisoned JOHN BALLIOL, he destroyed an English army at Stirling Bridge near Abbey Craig in September 1297 and drove the English out of Scotland. In 1298 a new invading army led by King EDWARD I himself met and defeated Wallace's forces at the Battle of Falkirk on July 22, 1298. He then resigned his office of guardian to ROBERT I THE BRUCE and John Comyn the Younger (d. 1306). After the submission of the Scottish nobles in about 1303, he unsuccessfully sought help from Pope Boniface VIII and PHILIP IV of France. Wallace returned to Scotland and continued to conduct a guerrilla war but was captured by treachery and taken to LONDON. He was tried as a traitor, although he had never taken an oath of allegiance to England, and executed on August 23/24, 1305. The quarters of his body were publicly exhibited at Newcastle-on-Tyne, Berwick, Stirling, and Perth.

Further reading: G. W. S. Barrow, *Kingship and Unity: Scotland 1000–1306* (London: Edward Arnold, 1981); Andrew Fisher, *William Wallace* (Atlantic Highlands, N.J.: Humanities Press, 1986); Graeme Morton, *William Wallace: Man and Myth* (Stroud: Sutton, 2001); Alan Young and Michael J. Stead, *In the Footsteps of William Wallace* (Stroud: Sutton, 2002).

Wallachia Medieval Wallachia was a region between the Carpathian Mountains and the Danube and is now part of modern-day Romania. There had once been an earlier region called Wallachia in the Bulgarian province of Thessaly. Both seem to have been inhabited by people called VLACHS. In the 10th century, the majority of the population of Wallachia was Romanian and Christian but used Slavonic as the language of its liturgy and culture. After the fall of the first Bulgar state to the Byzantine Empire in the 10th and 11th centuries, Byzantine control was reestablished over the whole lower Danube as far as its mouth and the shores of the BLACK SEA. The Turkish Petchenegs and CUMANS raided and then moved into the eastern plains of Wallachia in the 11th and 12th centuries. The Cumans were slowly destroyed by the combined efforts of the Hungarians, the Latin Empire of CONSTANTINOPLE, and the MONGOLS.

Around 1300 several small principalities appeared in western and central Wallachia. By the early 14th century the principality of Arges in the center of the country united Wallachia under a Romanian dynasty, the Basarab. From then on the country would be called Land of the Romanians, but other sources continued to refer to it as Wallachia. Wallachian princes paid tribute to HUNGARY but tried to distance themselves from it by obtaining from Constantinople the title of autocrats and the creation of their own orthodox archbishopric at Arges in 1359. The king of Hungary, Louis I of Anjou (r. 1342–82), however, was able to impose Catholic bishops on Arges and Severin in 1370. The OTTOMAN TURKS conquered BULGARIA and SERBIA in the early 15th century and obliged the Wallachian prince, Mircea the Old (1386–1418), to pay them tribute. Wallachia was then caught between the Hungarians and the Ottomans. An attempt by VLAD III THE IMPALER to oppose Sultan MEHMED II in 1462 failed. Wallachia and MOLDAVIA, however, did manage to avoid complete conquest, complete integration, and Islamization by the Turks. Together they eventually became the modern state of Romania.

See also EPIROS AND THE DESPOTATE OF.

Further reading: Nicolae Iorga, *Byzantium after Byzantium* (Portland: Center for Romanian Studies, 2000).

wall painting   *See* PAINTING.

Walsingham, Thomas (ca. 1355–ca. 1422) *English chronicler, monk*

He was a scriptor, historian, and monk in the monastery of Saint Albans, with a term as prior of its subordinate house at Wymondham. After writing a list of benefactors for the abbey in 1380, between then and 1394 he wrote his *Major Chronicle* (Chronica majora), actually a continuation from 1259 of MATTHEW Paris's *Great Chronicle,* and *The Deeds of the Abbots,* a history of the abbots of Saint Albans. At Wymondham he wrote a condensed version of the *Major Chronicle.* After returning to Saint Albans, he completed his greatest and most famous work, the *Saint Albans Chronicle.* His work has been of fundamental importance for the study of Anglo-Norman and ecclesiastical history up to 1419 and particularly important for the reigns of his contemporaries, Kings RICHARD II, and Henry IV (r. 1399–1413), and HENRY V. He had a strong distaste for John WYCLIFFE, whom he denounced in no uncertain terms. He died at Saint Albans in about 1422.

Further reading: Thomas Walsingham, *The Saint Albans Chronicle, 1406–1420: Edited from Bodley Ms. 462,* ed. V. H. Galbraith (Oxford: Clarendon Press, 1937); Antonia Gransden, *Historical Writing in England. II, c. 1307 to the Early Sixteenth Century* (Ithaca, N.Y.: Cornell University Press, 1982); Ernest Fraser Jacob, *The Fifteenth Century, 1399–1485* (Oxford: Clarendon Press, 1961).

Walter of Châtillon (fl. 1135–ca. 1190) *French poet*

Born in Lille in about 1135, Walter of Châtillon studied at PARIS and then at RHEIMS. He taught at the school of Châtillon and later studied LAW at BOLOGNA. He was employed by King HENRY II of ENGLAND. Returning to FRANCE, he was appointed secretary to the archbishop of Rheims and later a canon of Amiens. He is the author of a Latin poem written in 1184 on Alexander the Great. His moralistic and satirical lyrical works were enjoyed by the LAITY for their attacks on the higher CLERGY. He also wrote an anti-Jewish tract and another on the Trinity. His *Alexandreis* (1171–81), the epic about Alexander the Great, was a very popular book about the East and world geography. His Alexander was a moralistic model for crusaders, such as PHILIP II AUGUSTUS. He died in about 1190.

Further reading: Walter of Châtillon, *Alexandreis,* trans. David Townsend (Philadelphia: University of Pennsylvania Press, 1997); Ernst Robert Curtius, *European Literature and the Latin Middle Ages,* trans. Walter Trask (1948; reprint, Princeton, N.J.: Princeton University Press, 1953); Dennis Kratz, *Mocking Epic: Waltharius, Alexandries, and the Problems of Christian Heroism* (Madrid: José Porrúa Turanzas, 1980).

Walter of Henley (d. 1250) *English friar*

Walter wrote a treatise called *Housebondrie,* a manual of estate management. It included detailed descriptions of the agrarian practices of his age. The work was used as an agricultural handbook in the later Middle Ages and was considered by many the best of its kind in the 13th and 14th centuries. It had abundant information on successful agricultural practices, fertilizing techniques, prices, comparative productivity of domestic animals, and information on farming equipment and tools. Among his interesting ideas was his belief that agricultural land must yield three times what was sown to be worth the effort. He died about 1250.

Further reading: Dorothea Oschinsky, *Walter of Henley and Other Treatises on Estate Management and Accounting* (Oxford: Clarendon Press, 1971).

Walter Sansavoir of Poissy the Penniless (d. 1096) *French knight, a leader of the People's Crusade*

Born near PARIS Walter Sansavoir, along with four other members of his family, embarked on CRUSADE initially as a collaborator with PETER THE HERMIT. Unwilling to wait for the arrival of most of the crusading army, Walter, his uncle, and his three brothers set out on May 1, 1095, from COLOGNE with a few thousand compatriots, mostly peasants. Entering HUNGARY on May 21, 1095, and passing into Byzantine territory at Belgrade, his followers pillaged the countryside to survive. In doing so some of his men were killed, burned alive in a church. Pushing on to a Byzantine provincial capital, the crusaders were well received and fed. They were then sent under Greek escort to CONSTANTINOPLE, where they arrived on August 1. They were joined in a week or so by a group led by Peter the Hermit. After crossing the Bosphorus on August 6 and 7 with an army of 25,000 infantry and 500 cavalry. Walter, though advocating more caution, was killed along with most of the rest of his army on October 21, 1096, in a Turkish ambush or the Battle of Civetot.

Further reading: Jonathan Riley-Smith, *The First Crusade and the Idea of Crusading* (Philadelphia: University of Pennsylvania Press, 1986); Jonathan Riley-Smith, *The First Crusaders, 1095–1131* (Cambridge: Cambridge University Press, 1997).

Walther von der Vogelweide (ca. 1170–ca. 1230)
German lyric, poet, knight

Born about 1170, probably in lower AUSTRIA or the Tyrol Walter began his poetic career at the court of VIENNA, where he met and was taught by Reinmar van Hagen the Elder (d. ca. 1205), famous poet-musician. Walther became a roving minstrel, whose verse was loaded with sarcastic political comments. Leopold VI the Glorious (1176–1230) and Frederick I the Catholic (1194–98) patronized him for a while, but the hostility of a later archduke obliged him to travel to the other German courts. At Mainz he composed a magnificent poem for the coronation of Philip of SWABIA (1178–1208). In 1204 he was a guest of the landgrave Hermann I of Thuringia (d. 1217) where he met WOLFRAM VON ESCHENBACH. In the struggle between the candidate of Brunswick to the imperial throne, Otto IV (d. 1218), and Pope INNOCENT III, Walther supported the imperial party. In doing so he opposed the temporal power of popes and was critical of the institutional church. Along the same political lines, when the emperor FREDERICK II set out on Crusade in the 1220s, Walther composed songs in support of the venture and was granted a fief in the diocese of Würzburg in about 1224. Although he sang about German politics, imperial ideas, and knightly values, he wrote and sang best about COURTLY LOVE. He produced religious lyric and moral-didactic poetry and composed HYMNS to the Virgin MARY and the Trinity. He died near Würzburg in BAVARIA in about 1230.

Further reading: Walther von der Vogelweide, *Selected Poems*, ed. Margaret Fitzgerald Richey, 3d ed. by Hugh Sacker (Oxford: Blackwell, 1965); Franz Bäuml, ed., *From Symbol to Mimesis: The Generation of Walther von der Vogelweide* (Göppingen: Kümmerle Verlag, 1984); George F. Jones, *Walther von der Vogelweide* (New York: Twayne, 1968); Kenneth J. Northcott, "Walther von der Vogelweide" in *European Writers: The Middle Ages and the Renaissance*. Vol. 1, *Prudentius to Medieval Drama*, ed. William T. H. Jackson and George Stade (New York: Charles Scribner's Sons, 1983), 287–308.

Wandering Jew, legend of

The 13th-century Christian legend of the Wandering Jew was about a character who was doomed to live until the end of time. He had taunted or struck Jesus when he was on his way to the Crucifixion, though he had converted to Christianity and was living piously. The story was based on the New Testament (John 18:20–22) and on parallel narratives the Wandering Jew was identified as perhaps the high priest's guard or Pontius Pilate's doorkeeper, who was condemned to live and wander perpetually. The story first appeared in 1228 in a Cistercian chronicle, in which some pilgrims and a bishop in ARMENIA encountered a Jew who was present at the Passion. The English monastic historians Roger of Wendover (d. 1236) and MATTHEW PARIS told it. There was little attention to this story until the 17th century. There continued to be sightings this person in the 19th century, until the last one in Salt Lake City supposedly in 1868.

Further reading: G. K. Anderson, *The Legend of the Wandering Jew* (Providence, R.I.: Brown University Press, 1965); G. Hasan-Rokem and Alan Dundes, eds., *The Wandering Jew: Essays in the Interpretation of a Christian Legend* (Bloomington: Indiana University Press, 1986).

waqf (awqaf, hubs, habuus)

In Muslim legal terminology *waqf* was the prohibition of a third party's claiming property rights over any object, such state lands from the time of a conquest or to a later pious or family foundation. The object in question must be lasting and tangibly productive. The owner had limited access to the proceeds of the principle but no access to the principle, whatever it might be. The *waqf* or foundation had always to be irrevocable, pleasing to GOD, and conducive to the spread of ISLAM. Such objectives had to be specified in the document establishing it and explicitly used for religious foundations such as MOSQUES, HOSPITALS, schools, libraries, town walls, and public fountains. They could involve family foundations involving children, grandchildren, or other relatives and be a means to prevent the fragmentation of estates. They were controlled by a paid administrator and were subject to review by a QADI.

See also MORTMAIN.

Further reading: Claude Gilliot, "Waqf," *EMA*, 2.1,536; R. Stephen Humphreys, *Islamic History: A Framework for Inquiry*, rev. ed. (Princeton, N.J.: Princeton University Press, 1991).

warfare

Warfare was important to the economic, social, and political history of the period from 300 to 1500. Its organization, practice, and methods underwent many changes on land and sea. There were many technical innovations in WEAPONS and fortifications. In late antiquity and the Middle Ages, many peoples moved around the medieval world as invading armies or hordes trying to invade and settle in the Roman Empire, Byzantium, and Islam. These states in turn made massive efforts to control them militarily or incorporate them into its system of government. This conflict tempered by assimilation continued in the early Middle Ages and lasted through the incursions by the VIKINGS into Carolingian Europe in the 10th century. Internal and external warfare and violence remained common throughout the Middle Ages.

The CRUSADES were military invasions of the Islamic world from about 1100. The period 1350 to 1450 was characterized by many wars between national states and city-states all trying to control more territory. The church tried to control these violent tendencies but more often tried to exploit them for its own ends. Lay society turned to the ideas of CHIVALRY to pacify or domesticate the drive toward military aggression. ISLAM initially expanded through the use of force and maintained the idea of JIHAD throughout its history. The MONGOLS destroyed much of Islamic civilization but did open links between Islam and Europe and central Asia and the Far East. By 1500 European society was structured around militarism and eager for internal and external conquest. It was, moreover, now armed with impressive and effective gunpowder weapons and the naval and land technologies to deploy them.

See also CASTLES AND FORTIFICATIONS; CAVALRY; CONDOTTIERI, COMPANIES, AND MERCENARIES; FEUDALISM AND THE FEUDAL SYSTEM; FIREARMS; HUNDRED YEARS' WAR; JUST WAR; KNIGHTS AND KNIGHTHOOD; MAMLUKS; NOBILITY AND NOBLES; PEACE AND TRUCE OF GOD; RECONQUEST; TOURNAMENTS; WEAPONS AND WEAPONRY.

Further reading: John Beeler, *Warfare in Feudal Europe, 730–1200* (Ithaca, N.Y.: Cornell University Press, 1971); Philippe Contamine, *War in the Middle Ages,* trans. Michael Jones (1980; reprint, Oxford: Basil Blackwell, 1984); Kelly DeVries, *A Cumulative Bibliography of Medieval Military History and Technology* (Leiden: E. J. Brill, 2002); Bert S. Hall, *Weapons and Warfare in Renaissance Europe: Gunpowder, Technology, and Tactics* (Baltimore: Johns Hopkins University Press, 1997); Maurice Keen, ed., *Medieval War: A History* (Oxford: Oxford University Press, 1999); Hugh Kennedy, *The Armies of the Caliphs: Military and Society in the Early Islamic State* (London: Routledge, 2001); J. F. Verbruggen, *The Art of Warfare in Western Europe during the Middle Ages: From the Eighth Century to 1340,* trans. Sumner Willard and R. W. Southern, 2d ed. (Woodbridge: Boydell Press, 1997).

Wars of the Roses The Wars of the Roses was the name given to the English civil, factional, and dynastic wars between 1455 and 1485. The Roses referred to the badges worn by the two sides. The Lancastrians wore red roses and the Yorkists wore white. This took place in the context of a declining prosperity for the landed classes, who had become tied to a few major families in a system called bastard FEUDALISM. The richest families contested for control over the weak King Henry VI (r. 1422–61, 1470–71) and then for the throne itself. Succession to that throne had been questionable since the end of the reign and deposition of RICHARD II. Besides reflecting the general lawlessness of society, these wars reflected the problem of exercising a central authority in the 15th century, when local ambitious magnate families had ready access to military resources and the Crown had financial difficulties.

The Wars of the Roses began in the 1450s when Richard, the duke of York (d. 1460), with the backing of Richard Neville, the duke of Warwick (1428–71), the Kingmaker, tried to control the royal government and person of Henry VI. They failed and had to flee abroad in 1459. The Lancastrian line and its forces regrouped and won two major victories, in 1460 at Sandal, where York lost his life, and in 1461 at Saint Albans. However, the Lancastrians and Henry's queen, Margaret of Anjou (1430–82), failed to gain the support of LONDON. They were forced to retreat to the north. The duke of York's son, the future EDWARD IV, won a victory over another Lancastrian army at Mortimer's Cross on February 2, 1461, and marched on London to proclaim and install himself as king again with the backing of the duke of Warwick. At Towton on March 29, 1461, Edward IV's forces won a major victory in the largest battle of the war. Edward ruled during the 1460s but had a falling out with Warwick, who, with French help, put Henry back on the throne in 1470. Edward then left the country but returned in 1471 and defeated the Lancastrians and his former supporters again at the Battles of Barnet on April 14, 1471, and decisively at Tewkesbury on May 4, 1471. Warwick was killed; the captured Henry VI soon died in the Tower of London under mysterious circumstances; and Queen Margaret was imprisoned and then exiled. With Henry dead, the Lancastrian line was no longer a factor in the closing years of the conflict in the 1480s.

Edward was secure on the throne. After his death in 1483, he was succeeded by his son, Edward V (1470–83). Edward IV's brother, the future RICHARD III, acted as regent but soon usurped the throne for himself. Edward V and his brother might have been murdered in the Tower of London to secure Richard's kingship. In 1485 Henry TUDOR, a distant Lancastrian, profited from the problems and discontents of Richard III's reign and invaded England. He defeated Richard at the BATTLE OF BOSWORTH FIELD in 1485 and took the throne for himself, ending the Wars of the Roses.

See also LOUIS XI, KING OF FRANCE.

Further reading: Edward Powell, "Lancastrian England," in *The New Cambridge Medieval History.* Vol. 7, *c. 1415–c. 1500,* ed. Christopher Allmand (Cambridge: Cambridge University Press, 1998), 457–476; Rosemary Horrox, "Yorkist and Early Tudor England," in *The New Cambridge Medieval History.* Vol. 7, *c. 1415–c. 1500,* ed. Christopher Allmand (Cambridge: Cambridge University Press, 1998), 477–495; John A. Wagner, ed., *Encyclopedia of the Wars of the Roses* (Santa Barbara, Calif.: ABC-CLIO, 2001); J. R. Lander, *The Wars of the Roses* (New York: St. Martin's Press, 1990); Charles Derek Ross, *The Wars of the Roses: A Concise History* (London: Thames and Hudson, 1976).

water *See* IRRIGATION; MILLS, WIND AND WATER.

England During the Wars of the Roses, 1455–85

Lancastrian areas
Yorkist areas
Neutral areas
X Major battles

0   50 miles
0   50 km

SCOTLAND

IRELAND

North
Sea

Hedgely Moor
1464 X

Hexham X
1464

Isle
of
Man

Irish
Sea

Lancaster ●

York ●
Towton X
1461

Wakefield X
1460

ENGLAND
Lincoln ●

Chester ●
Stoke X
1487

Lose-coat Field
1470 X

PRINCIPALITY

Bloreheath X
1459
Shrewsbury ●

Bosworth X
1485

OF

Ludford Bridge X
1459

Northampton X
1460

WALES

Mortimer's Cross X
1461

Edgecote X
1469

St. Albans X
1455 and 1461

Tewkesbury X
1471

Barnet X
1471

London ●

Canterbury ●

Bristol Channel

Hastings ●

English Channel

water mills *See* MILLS, WIND AND WATER.

weapons and weaponry The weapons available to soldiers in the period from 300 to 1500 varied according to individuals' ability to purchase them themselves or to obtain them from a central authority. There were different styles for fighting as CAVALRY and for using HORSES over the course of the Middle Ages. In some eras one fought mounted with lances and in others dismounted with swords or other hand weapons. Mounted combat also reflected higher social status and the possession of sufficient wealth to maintain a horse and groom. The weapons of the infantry evolved to enable them to fight the mounted noble, who could, and frequently did, hold a distinct advantage. Armor, always expensive, developed in response to the type of weapon it was supposed to protect against.

ARCHERY AND FIREARMS

By 1100, archery became much more of a threat to everyone with the development of the crossbow. The crossbow was not quick to reload or cheap to produce but was not difficult to learn to use by the inexperienced. Less than noble archers were now able to kill mounted nobles at safe ranges. After 1300 the English longbow, or a very large self-bow, was even more deadly and far easier to launch quickly against an enemy. Crude firearms began to be used in the 14th century, and they, too, were effective within a fairly short range. Backed up by the older system of chain mail, armor plate grew thicker and expensive but only marginally more effective against all these threats.

SWORDS AND LANCES

Swords of one form or another were used throughout the period by all combatants. They could be expensive, and high-quality versions were difficult to produce. The quality swords available to foot soldiers therefore varied. They were double-edged in the central Middle Ages to be effective in slashing attacks. In the later Middle Ages and Renaissance, swords acquired sharp points for stabbing into the small vulnerable areas left exposed by even the best armor. Swords were used in and evolved in HUNTING. They began to have magical or mystical qualities in literature and legend. Lances were used in cavalry charges but usually had to be abandoned in the melées of actual combat. Halberds with axe-shaped heads and bill hooks for pulling people off horses were prominent in the battles of the later period. The Swiss became famous and deadly effective in the use of massed pike men from the 14th century. The pike could be 18 feet long and when deployed by close-order blocks of infantry was decisive in combat until the 16th century.

CANNONRY

Cannons were used in combination with various instruments using torsion energy or the power of a sprung seesaw, the trebuchet. All were able to hurl stones or objects a few hundred yards. As cannons using gunpowder became more reliable, powerful, and accurate in the mid-15th century, they forced a complete change in fortifications. The defenses of towns could be battered down and overcome in days rather than months. On the battlefield itself, cannons and firearms were slower to affect tactics and decisively influence the outcome of battles between mobile forces.

See also CASTLES AND FORTIFICATION; FIREARMS; GREEK FIRE; HORSES; WARFARE.

Further reading: Bért S. Hall, *Weapons and Warfare in Renaissance Europe: Gunpowder, Technology, and Tactics* (Baltimore: Johns Hopkins University Press, 1997); Jim Bradbury, *The Medieval Archer* (Woodbridge: St. Martin's Press, 1985); Anne Curry and Michael Hughes, eds., *Arms, Armies and Fortifications in the Hundred Years' War* (Woodbridge, England: Boydell Press, 1994); Anne Curry and Michael Hughes, eds., *Arms, Armies and Fortifications in the Hundred Years' War* (Woodbridge, England: Boydell Press, 1994); Arthur Norris Kennard, *Gunfounding and Gunfounders: A Directory of Cannon Founders from Earliest Times to 1850* (London: Arms and Armour Press, 1986); J. R. Partington, *A History of Greek Fire and Gunpowder* (Baltimore: Johns Hopkins University Press, 1999).

wedding *See* MARRIAGE.

Wenceslas, Saint (Wenzel, Václav) (r. 921/922– 929/ 935) *Czech prince, duke of Bohemia*
Wenceslas was the son of Vratislav I, a Premyslid prince (r. 915–921), and his pagan mother Drahomíra of the Stodorans. The principality of the Premyslids was then situated around what became the city of PRAGUE; it was preeminent and the most successful among the lordships of BOHEMIA because of its effectiveness in collecting taxes. In the late ninth century under rule of Bofhvoj I (r. 850–894) and under the influence of his grandmother Saint Ludmilla, Wenceslas was baptized by Saint Methodios, the archbishop of Great Moravia, and later he strongly supported MISSIONS and the efforts of missionaries to convert his people. He became duke in 921 or 922.

REIGN AND MURDER

After the invasions of the Hungarians in the early ninth century, the German Holy Roman Empire was reestablished under Henry I the Fowler (ca. 876–936) who considered Bohemia a fief of BAVARIA or part of his own domain. After invading Bohemia, he made Wenceslas pay an annual tribute in 929. Throughout his reign, Wenceslas had concentrated on consolidating his lordship over many surrounding principalities in order to make Bohemia a unified Premyslid state able to oppose the Germans. This political plan of refusal to submit to German domination was also the attitude of Wenceslas's younger brother and successor, Boleslav I the Cruel (r. 929/935–967/972). They quarreled over strategy to attain this end. Within the context of this fraternal animosity and lingering pagan sentiments of the Bohemian nobles. Wenceslas was murdered near his brother's castle on his way to church, traditionally on September 28 sometime between 929 and 935, a political martyr not a religious one. Wenceslas was quickly perceived to be a victim of fratricide and a martyr and gained a reputation as a just prince and a saint. Even his brother, Boleslav, who had been implicated in the assassination, skillfully exploited this for himself and his dynasty and exploited the murder to obtain from the pope a bishopric of PRAGUE. Wenceslas became a very popular saint, considered the perpetual prince of Bohemia.

Further reading: Marvin Kantor, *The Origins of Christianity in Bohemia: Sources and Commentary* (Evanston, Ill.: Northwestern University Press, 1990), 59–110, 143–244; Frantisek Dvorník, *The Life of Saint Wenceslas* (Prague: State Printing Office, 1929); Karel Stloukal, *Saint Wenceslas in the History and the Traditions of the Czechoslovak People* (Prague: National Democrat Political Club, 1929).

Wends Wends were initially a German collective designation used from the sixth century for SLAVS. It continued to have that meaning for those Slavs living in the German part of the HOLY ROMAN EMPIRE. It was also applied to the peoples the Germans encountered in their armed colonization and missionary efforts along the Baltic Sea. As late as the 15th century the term was still applied to towns situated in that region, such as LÜBECK, Hamburg, Luneburg, Rostock, Wismar, and Stralsund. The name had its specific origins in a tribal confederation that migrated into the region between the Oder and the Elbe-Saale Rivers, during the second half of the sixth century and the early seventh century. These Wendish tribes actually had little in common. They originated in various regions; had different religious, cultural, and economic traditions, and spoke different dialects. They evolved from the ninth century into numerous other Slav and Baltic peoples. They were converted to Christianity with considerable difficulty in several waves and Crusades from the 10th to the 13th century.

See also TEUTONIC KNIGHTS, ORDER OF; WALDEMAR I THE GREAT.

Further reading: A. P. Vlasto, *The Entry of the Slavs into Christendom: An Introduction to the Medieval History of the Slavs* (Cambridge: Cambridge University Press, 1970).

wergild (wergeld) *Wergild* was literally the "price of a man" or "man payment." It was an initially optional composition paid by the offender to the victim or to the family of the victim under the direction of public or tribal authorities. It was designed to replace, or at least offer an alternative to, the right of private vengeance, at that time a generally accepted recourse for damaged parties. It could furthermore be seen as an effort by nascent public authorities to assert their power over subjects. The traditional right of vengeance was related to the principle of family solidarity and joint liability, since the actions of one member of a group could produce consequences for the whole group. While offering protection to members, it could also cause severe problems to everyone in a group because of the irresponsible actions of one member. At the same time the early medieval state offered little as a source of justice.

Law codes minutely fixed tariffs according to the social quality, age, or gender of the offended person and the gravity of the offense committed. Initially established for the handling of serious offenses, it expanded in scope to include all kinds of damages. Even compensation for a broken tooth was covered, still tied to the eminence or social status of the victim. Such compositions were at first optional. The MEROVINGIAN kings were among the first to try to enforce this procedure to replace private vengeance, with such procedure related to their authority. They even began enforcing the death penalty when it was deemed appropriate. The CAROLINGIANS continued the practice. By the 11th century, private vengeance had usually been eliminated as an acceptable judicial alternative. The concept of the payment of wergild for satisfying public or private justice, based at first on a subjective scale of remedies, was on its way to becoming more objective and impersonal in theory and practice, taking into consideration the personal qualities of the parties involved in applying or arbitrating justice in legal disputes.

Further reading: B. S. Phillpotts, *Kindred and Clan in the Middle Ages and After: A Study in the Sociology of the Teutonic Races* (Cambridge: Cambridge University Press, 1913); Marc Bloch, *Feudal Society*, 2 vols., trans. L. A. Manyon (Chicago: University of Chicago Press, 1961 [1939]); Alexander Callander Murray, *Germanic Kingship Structure: Studies in Law and Society in Antiquity and the Early Middle Ages* (Toronto: Pontifical Institute of Mediaeval Studies, 1983), 135–155.

Wessex Wessex was a kingdom in Anglo-Saxon Britain. Its origins were in the convergence of two groups of West Saxons. Their migration west was opposed by the Britons of Devon in a series of battles from the early sixth century to the Battle of Durham in 577. In that battle the Saxons gained possession of the old Roman cities of Cirencester, Gloucester, and Bath. The Saxons then controlled the coast and cutting off the Britons of Cornwall from those of WALES. After pausing in the early seventh century, Wessex resumed expansion from about 650. This group of Saxons accepted Christianity in 635, but it was not universally accepted for another 50 years. It took more than 40 years to defeat the inhabitants of Somerset and Devon, who were driven to cross the channel to BRITTANY.

By 700, most of Devonshire and all of Somerset and Dorset were under the control of the kings of Wessex. In the ninth century Wessex began to expand again, engulfing eastward the modern countries of Sussex, Surrey, Kent, and Essex. The Wessex king, ALFRED THE GREAT, defeated a great Danish invasion in 878. By 886, with the extinction of the line of the Mercian kings, Alfred's authority was recognized in all parts of ENGLAND not under Danish rule, which he had limited to the DANELAW. Alfred had become the king of an Anglo-Saxon England, and the history of Wessex become the history of England and its ruling dynasties.

Further reading: J. H. Bettey, *Wessex from A.D. 1000* (London: Longman, 1986); D. N. Dumville, *Wessex and England from Alfred to Edgar: Six Essays on Political, Cultural, and Ecclesiastical Revival* (Woodbridge: Boydell

Press, 1992); David Alban Hinton, *Alfred's Kingdom: Wessex and the South 800–1500* (London: Dent, 1977); Barbara Yorke, *Wessex in the Early Middle Ages* (London: Leicester University Press, 1995).

Westminster Abbey Westminster Abbey was originally founded in the seventh century but reendowed by Saint DUNSTAN in about 960. Originally a Benedictine monastery, it was expanded and endowed much more richly by King EDWARD THE CONFESSOR in the 11th century. It became the royal monastery and continued to be enriched by many English kings before 1500. Among the richest English monasteries of the Middle Ages, it possessed properties all over ENGLAND.

The present church was built by the master MASONS Henry of Reyns, John of Gloucester, and Robert of Beverley for King HENRY III between 1245 and 1260. It employed a GOTHIC style much influenced by contemporary cathedrals in northern FRANCE. The NAVE was finally completed in the 15th century. The spectacular late Gothic chapel of King Henry VII (r. 1485–1509), was added in the early 16th century.

Westminster Abbey has been the scene of nearly every coronation of an English monarch since WILLIAM I the Conqueror in 1066. From 1272 to 1760 it was also the accustomed royal burial place. There were numerous royal tombs around the shrine of Edward the Confessor, which still contains the saint's body. There were also examples of fine sculpture and a beautiful 13th-century flooring before the high altar. The surviving monastic buildings include a CLOISTER, built over the 13th and 14th centuries, an 11th-century vaulted undercroft, a hall and chamber built in the 1370s, and an octagonal chapter house built between 1250 and 1257. There also survive several manuscripts from the monastic library and a large archive of the administration of the medieval monastery. Westminster Abbey was frequently the center of financial and legal operations of the royal government during the Middle Ages and an important center for English learning in the 12th century.

Further reading: H. M. Colvin, ed., *Building Accounts of King Henry III* (Oxford: Clarendon Press, 1971); Paul Binski, *Westminster Abbey and the Plantagenets: Kingship and the Representation of Power, 1200–1400* (New Haven, Conn.: Yale University Press, 1995); Edward Carpenter, *A House of Kings: The Official History of Westminster Abbey* (New York: John Day, 1966); Barbara F. Harvey, *Westminster Abbey and Its Estates in the Middle Ages* (Oxford: Clarendon Press, 1977); Emma Mason, *Westminster Abbey and Its People, c. 1050–1216* (Rochester: Boydell Press, 1996).

Weyden, Rogier van der (Roger de la Pasture) (ca. 1399–1464) *Flemish painter*
Rogier was born to a well-off artisan family and probably was a pupil between 1427 and 1432 of the master painter Robert Campin (ca. 1378–1444) in Tournai, where he

Choir at Westminster Abbey, 1893 etching *(Courtesy Library of Congress)*

had been born about 1399. After meeting Jan van EYCK in 1427, he moved permanently to Brussels around 1435; married a local woman, Elizabeth Goffaert, in 1426; and became the official city painter with a comfortable income. He traveled to Italy and was probably there for the HOLY YEAR of 1450 while working for the ESTE and MEDICI families. He never held a royal appointment but worked for several members of the Burgundian court, for whom he produced dramatic and severe portraits. In 1446, he painted his most celebrated painting, the Last Judgment, still in the city of Beaune in Burgundy. He died on June 18, 1464.

See also MEMLING, HANS.

Further reading: Loren Campbell, *Van der Weyden* (New York: Harper & Row, 1980); Dirk de Vos, *Rogier van der Weyden: The Complete Works* (New York: Harry N. Abrams, 1999).

wheat *See* GRAIN CROPS.

wheel of fortune The wheel of fortune in medieval art was an expression of the variability of luck or fortune. One could be great or well off today, but in dire circumstances tomorrow. Everything about life would change. It was used in literature and linked to variations in fortune in literary figures and as an iconographic device. In art it usually involved a wheel turning with people either going up or going down, climbing or descending. Sometimes these wheels were wheels of avarice with gluttonous animals lurking in the spokes. Such iconography was portrayed in ROSE WINDOWS, since their shape naturally led to ideas about wheels. Another visualization of this wheel involved a woman who was turning a wheel device with human representations riding up and down.

Fortune had been a formidable and protective goddess in classical culture. This goddess was somewhat Christianized and introduced into medieval literature in *The Consolation of Philosophy* by BOETHIUS. As Fortuna she could regulate only the distribution of property and wealth and had no hold over the free will, body, and soul of Christians. Under the watchful eye of God, she was blind or arbitrary or an instrument for the punishment of sins. Such a concept did not suggest much of a belief in any real chance for lasting social and economic promotion. In the ideology held by some in the Middle Ages, one should stay in one's place and concentrate on gaining salvation.

See also ECONOMIC THOUGHT AND JUSTICE; SOCIAL STATUS AND STRUCTURE; VIRTUES AND VICES.

Further reading: John B. Friedman and Jessica M. Wegmann, *Medieval Iconography: A Research Guide* (New York: Garland, 1998); Émile Mâle, *Religious Art in France: The Late Middle Ages: A Study of Medieval Iconography and Its Sources,* ed. Harry Bober, trans. Marthiel Mathews (Princeton, N.J.: Princeton University Press, 1986).

The Wheel of Fortune, illumination by Chrétien Legouais in *Ovid Moralise,* Ms. 1044, fol. 74 (14th century), Bibliothèque Municipale, Rouen, France *(Giraudon / Art Resource)*

Whitby, Abbey and Monastery and Synod of Situated on a headland in East Yorkshire, Whitby was a double monastery known to BEDE. It was founded in about 657 on estates donated by King Oswiu (d. 670). Its first abbess, Hilda (d. 680), made Whitby into training ground for clergy and the burial place of the kings of Northumbria. It was the site of the important synod of 664. At this meeting the English church decided to conform to the Roman way, sponsored by Saint WILFRID, rather than the Irish method of calculating the movable feasts of EASTER, style of TONSURE, and the rituals used at baptism, among other issues. In the eighth century the monastery was a center of learning. The illiterate poet and saint CAEDMON produced his vernacular religious poems there. In the ninth century the monastery was abandoned, but it was reestablished in a nearly site in the late 11th century by monks from Evesham, though it never attained the cultural and religious importance it had around 700.

Further reading: Alfred William Clapham, *Whitby Abbey, Yorkshire* (London: H. M. Stationery Office, 1952); Henry Mayr-Harting, *The Coming of Christianity to Anglo-Saxon England,* 3d ed. (University Park: Pennsylvania State University Press, 1991).

widows and widowhood As a result of the demographic conditions of the Middle Ages many women survived their husbands. Women were usually considerably younger than their husbands, and the high mortality rate of childbirth did not equalize the survival rate. The regulation of widows was the object of particular attention in medieval LAW, religious regulation, and society. The DEATH of a husband produced anxiety about the posthumous disposition of his resources, wife, and children. Males, their female close relatives, and families wanted to know and control resources, keep control of surviving children, and oversee the management of property open to inheritance. These objectives often led to concern about whether widows should remarry.

There were also questions in the later Middle Ages about the disposition of dowries and the continuation and prosperity of lineages. The church promoted CELIBACY and discouraged remarriage, unless one was incapable of chastity. It was probably best to enter a nunnery, especially if there were no children. Widows who lived alone were suspicious characters, at best only too open to temptation and passing or squandering of wealth outside their late husband's family. In theory widows could control their resources, but the realities of surviving in medieval society and economic matters encouraged remarriage, even if it meant the loss of control of one's children, dowry, or personal property. All of this depended, of course, on the social and economic condition of the couple involved. Peasants and artisans had more immediate concerns and had to act accordingly to manage immediate and serious survival issues. Jewish and Islamic law protected the rights of widows to financial support and housing after the death of the husband. The social status and capabilities of female widows varied over the course of the Middle Ages and early Renaissance.

See also MARRIAGE.

Further reading: Caroline M. Barron and Anne F. Sutton, eds., *Medieval London Widows, 1300–1500* (London: Hambledon Press, 1994); Sandra Cavallo and Lyndan Warner, eds., *Widowhood in Medieval and Early Modern Europe* (New York: Longman, 1999); Louise Mirrer, ed., *Upon My Husband's Death: Widows in the Literature and Histories of Medieval Europe* (Ann Arbor: University of Michigan Press, 1992); Sue Sheridan Walker, ed., *Wife and Widow in Medieval England* (Ann Arbor: University of Michigan Press, 1993).

Widukind (d. 807) *leader of Saxon resistance*

Widukind was a member of the noble Saxon family of Angaria in Westphalia. He was first mentioned in 777 at the time of the first uprising of the Saxons. After its failure, he had to take refuge with the Danes but resumed the revolt and won a clear victory at the Süntelgebirge in 782. However, a major Carolingian offensive and severe defeats soon forced him to submit. He accepted baptism with CHARLEMAGNE as his godfather at Attigny in 785 and took no part in later rebellions. His descendants, the Immedings, formed an influential clan in ninth- and 10th-century SAXONY. His life became the basis of numerous medieval legends and Saxon nationalistic tales that were often political in character and antagonistic to the Carolingian tradition. He died in 807.

Further reading: Donald Bullough, *The Age of Charlemagne* (London: Eleck Books, 1965); Friedrich Heer, *Charlemagne and His World* (New York: Macmillan, 1975); Rosamond McKitterick, *The Frankish Kingdoms under the Carolingians, 751–987* (London: Longman, 1983).

Wilfrid, Saint (634–709) *abbot, bishop of York, ecclesiastical politician*

Wilfrid was born into a noble family in Northumbria and educated at the monastery of LINDISFARNE. In the 650s he spent time at LYON and ROME, where he learned the ritual practices of the Roman church. Later as the abbot of Ripon, he played a major role in introducing and promoting Roman Catholic ideas and practices into northern ENGLAND in 664, replacing the Irish or Celtic traditions especially at the Synod of WHITBY in 663 and 644. As bishop of YORK in 669, he sent the first English appeal to Rome, in a dispute with the archbishop of CANTERBURY. The papal decision in his favor generated the disfavor of secular authorities and he had to take refuge in Sussex in the south. From there he tried to Christianize the local heathen SAXONS. He was recalled to the north in 686 to direct the see of Hexham. An ardent missionary, he never managed to get along with the secular authorities, thereby undoing much of his work. He died at Oundle, probably on April 24, 709.

See also MISSIONS AND MISSIONARIES, CHRISTIAN.

Further reading: Eddius Stephanus, *The Life of Bishop Wilfrid*, trans. Bertram Colgrave (Cambridge: Cambridge University Press, 1985); D. P. Kirby, ed., *Saint Wilfrid at Hexham* (Newcastle upon Tyne: Oriel Press, 1974); Wilhelm Levison, *England and the Continent in the Eighth Century* (Oxford: Clarendon Press, 1946); Henry Mayr-Harting, *The Coming of Christianity to Anglo-Saxon England*, 3d ed. (University Park: Pennsylvania State University Press, 1991).

William I the Bad (1120–1166) *Norman king of Sicily*

William was the younger son of Roger II of SICILY, born about 1120, and after the deaths of three older brothers, he was crowned as coruler in 1151 and ruled under the factional aegis of the hated Maio of Bari (d. 1160). William had to be allied to the Muslim PALACE eunuchs and was detested by the Norman nobility, who tried to ally themselves with FREDERICK I BARBAROSSA and the BYZANTINES. William gained papal approval for his rule on June 18, 1156, at the Concordat of Benevento. Though he defeated a Byzantine invasion in 1155, he lost the Crown's African possessions in 1160 to the ALMOHADS. Maio's assassination on November 10, 1160, unleashed a crisis. The king was arrested. His son and heir, Roger, was murdered, and Muslims were massacred at PALERMO and all over Sicily. William regained control and punished the rebellious counts of the Italian mainland and the towns of Sicily that had supported the massacres. Until his death William stayed in his palace and entrusted the exercise of power to others. Their harsh regime earned William his nickname "the Bad," which, however, was only applied to him from the 14th century. He was a patron of cultural activities and drew Muslim scholars to his court. He died suddenly on May 7, 1166.

See also AL-IDRISI.

Further reading: Ugo Falcando, *The History of the Tyrants of Sicily by "Hugo Falcandus," 1154–69*, trans. Graham A. Loud and Thomas Wiedemann (Manchester: Manchester University Press, 1998); Donald Matthew, *The Norman Kingdom of Sicily* (Cambridge: Cambridge University Press, 1992); John Julius Norwich, *The Kingdom in the Sun, 1130–1194* (New York: Harper & Row, 1970).

William I the Conqueror (ca. 1028–1087) *duke of Normandy, king of England*

William was born about 1028 in Falaise in NORMANDY as the illegitimate son of Duke Robert I (r. 1027–35) and Herleva or Arlette, the daughter of an undertaker. In 1035, at the age of seven or eight, he survived a disputed succession and succeeded his father, eventually fully establishing his authority as duke by defeating rebels at Val-ès-Dunes in 1047 and at Arques in 1053. He later defeated his overlord, King Henry I (r. 1031–60) of FRANCE, in the Battles of Mortemer in 1054 and Varaville in 1057, despite Henry's help in the succession crisis. In 1063 he added Maine and other regions to the duchy of Normandy. In

1050 or 1051 he had married Matilda (d. 1083), the daughter of Count Baldwin V of FLANDERS (d. 1167). They had five daughters and four sons, including Robert Curthose (d. 1134), the later duke of Normany, and the English monarchs WILLIAM II RUFUS and HENRY I.

With his duchy secure, William turned his attention to ENGLAND at the death of EDWARD THE CONFESSOR in 1066. Duke William disputed the coronation HAROLD II GOD-WINESON as the new king since he claimed that in 1051 King Edward had promised the throne of England to him. Harold had admitted this during a strange visit to Normandy in 1064. William invaded England; won the Battle of HASTINGS, where Harold was killed, and was crowned king in WESTMINSTER ABBEY on Christmas Day 1066.

After years of warfare, William finally crushed the resistance of the Anglo-Saxon nobility in 1075. To control the resources necessary to rule his new highly centralized kingdom, he had an inventory of property carried out, the DOMESDAY BOOK of the 1080s. To intimate the ANGLO-SAXONS, he had harshly suppressed any rebellions that broke out and built impressive CASTLES all over England. With the help of ANSELM, the archbishop of CANTERBURY, he reformed the church in England, making it more amenable to royal control and replacing the Anglo-Saxon hierarchy with Normans. Injured in a riding accident, William died at Rouen on September 9, 1087. His eldest son, Robert, succeeded him in Normandy, while William II Rufus became king of England.

See also BAYEUX TAPESTRY; ODO; LANFRANC OF BEC.

Further reading: Wido, Bishop of Amiens, *The Carmen de Hastingae Proelio of Guy, Bishop of Amiens,* ed. and trans. Frank Barlow, 2d ed. (Oxford: Clarendon Press, 1999); David Bates, *Normandy before 1066* (London: Longman, 1982); David Bates, *William the Conqueror* (London: G. Philip. 1989); David C. Douglas, *William the Conqueror: The Norman Impact upon England* (Berkeley: University of California Press, 1964).

William I the Lion (1143–1214) *king of Scotland*
Born in 1143, William became king in 1165 on the death of his elder brother, Malcolm IV (r. 1153–65). To an attempt remain independent of ENGLAND, he entered into an alliance with Louis VII (ca. 1120–80) of FRANCE in 1168 and interfered in a filial revolt against HENRY II of England in 1173. He was taken prisoner near Alnwick in 1174, but he gained his release by consenting to the Treaty of Falaise in which he accepted English sovereignty over SCOTLAND and the Scottish church. In 1198 the needy RICHARD I LIONHEART surrendered his claims over Scotland in exchange for a payment of 10,000 marks. After the accession of King JOHN, the English sought control of Scotland, and war almost occurred in 1199 and again in 1209. However, both times peace was preserved by negotiations and the acceptance of a limited English suzerainty. In 1188 a papal bull secured from Celestine III (r. 1191–98) freed the Scottish church from the claims of an English archbishop. William had to assert his authority over the independent chieftains of outlying regions of his kingdom frequently. He died on December 4, 1214, at Stirling in Scotland.

Further reading: A. A. M. Duncan, *Scotland: The Making of the Kingdom* (Edinburgh: Oliver & Boyd, 1975); D. D. R. Owen, *William the Lion, 1143–1214: Kingship and Culture* (East Linton, Scotland: Tuckwell, 1997).

William II Rufus (ca. 1057–1100) *duke of Normandy, Norman king of England*
William was born about 1057 as a younger son of WILLIAM I the Conqueror and Matilda of Flanders (d. 1083). He was called Rufus because of his ruddy complexion. In 1087 at the death of William I, the eldest son, Robert Curthose (d. 1134), succeeded to the duchy of NORMANDY and then seized the kingdom of ENGLAND. In 1096, Robert pawned the duchy to William for 10,000 marks in order to join the First Crusade. William's reign was marred by his conflict with ANSELM of Bec of Canterbury, whom he had rashly, when Anselm was on his presumed deathbed, appointed the archbishop of CANTERBURY in 1093 and quickly sought to depose in 1095. He was a competent and successful soldier in SCOTLAND in defense of his domains in France, but was viewed in England as a grim and brutal monarch and was frequently assailed by baronial rebellions. William was, however, a generally effective ruler, whose unsavory reputation was probably inflated in the sources because of his taxation of clerical property; the history of his reign was written by disgruntled clerics. He was killed, struck by an arrow, while hunting in New Forest on August 2, 1100, with the issues of control of Normandy and Anselm's tenure at Canterbury still unresolved. There were strong rumors that this was a murder arranged by William's younger brother and successor, HENRY I. William was unceremoniously buried under a tower at Winchester without the benefit of a Christian burial. The tower's later collapse was taken as a sign of God's disapproval of the clerical taxation policies of William.

See also ODO, BISHOP OF BAYEAUX.

Further reading: Eadmer, *Eadmer's History of Recent Events in England: Historia novorum in Anglia,* trans. Geoffrey Bosanquet, with a foreword by R. W. Southern (London: Cresset Press, 1964); Frank Barlow, *William Rufus* (Berkeley: University of California Press, 1983); E. A. Freeman, *The Reign of William Rufus and the Accession of Henry the First,* 2 vols. (Oxford: Clarendon Press, 1882); Duncan William Grinnell-Milne, *The Killing of William Rufus: An Investigation in the New Forest* (New York: A. M. Kelley, 1968).

William II the Good (1154–1189) *the last Norman king of Sicily*
Born the son of WILLIAM I of SICILY, William II ascended the throne in 1166 at about age 12, under the regency of his mother, Margaret of NAVARRE. His chief minister, a

eunuch, was hated and threatened by the nobility and deserted to the service of the ALMOHADS. Marguerite continued to govern with Stephen of Perche as chancellor and archbishop of PALERMO. Stephen was, however, expelled in 1168 with his French entourage. Governing power then was exercised by his household, bishops, eunuchs, and the grand chancellor, Matthew of Ajello (d. 1193), of the Norman aristocracy.

William himself took control in 1171. Perceiving that the threat of intervention by FREDERICK I BARBAROSSA has lessened, William made a German alliance by marrying his aunt, CONSTANCE OF HAUTEVILLE, to the future HENRY VI (1165–97). He married Joan (1165–99), the daughter of HENRY II of ENGLAND. With the help of his strong fleet, he tried to invade AFRICA but was defeated near ALEXANDRIA in 1174. He also sought a way to carry out an expedition against the BYZANTINE EMPIRE and ISLAM. He had some success, capturing Thessaloniki, and invaded only to be defeated near CONSTANTINOPLE in 1185. While planning his participation in the Third CRUSADE, he suddenly died childless on November 18, 1189, at Palermo. This opened the way to a HOHENSTAUFEN monarchy over Sicily and southern ITALY.

See also MONREALE.

Further reading: Ugo Falcando, *The History of the Tyrants of Sicily by "Hugo Falcandus," 1154–69,* trans. Graham A. Loud and Thomas Wiedemann (Manchester: Manchester University Press, 1998); Donald Matthew, *The Norman Kingdom of Sicily* (Cambridge: Cambridge University Press, 1992); John Julius Norwich, *The Kingdom in the Sun, 1130–1194* (New York: Harper & Row, 1970).

William IX (Guilhem) (1071–1127) *duke of Aquitaine, literary patron, soldier, poet*

William IX was born on October 22, 1071, the son of William VIII (r. 1058–86). Spending most of his life in WARFARE, he twice attempted to annex the city of TOULOUSE, in 1098 and in 1119. As the duke of AQUITAINE, he managed to take that city but was never able to maintain authority there. He took part in an unsuccessful CRUSADE to the Holy Land in 1101 and 1102. He also participated in a Crusade in SPAIN in 1120–23. He had a love affair with the wife of the viscount of Châtellerault, leading to a papal EXCOMMUNICATION. All the while William continued to write, recite, and sing his boisterous, humorous, and sometimes coarse love poems. William was known as "the first troubadour" and assembled poets and troubadours at his court at Poitiers, making it a center of secular culture and concepts of CHIVALRY. He died on February 10, 1127.

See also COURTLY LOVE.

Further reading: William IX, Duke of Aquitaine, *The Poetry of William VII, Count of Poitiers, IX Duke of Aquitaine,* ed. and trans. Gerald A. Bond (New York: Garland, 1982); Frede Jensen, *Provençal Philology and the Poetry of Guillaume of Poitiers* (Odense: Odense University Press, 1983); Linda M. Paterson, *The World of the Troubadours: Medieval Occitan Society, c. 1100–c. 1300* (Cambridge: Cambridge University Press, 1993).

William of Auvergne (ca. 1180/90–1249) *French theologian, philosopher, bishop of Paris*

William was born at Aurillac near Auvergne between 1180 and 1190. He studied at PARIS, became a teacher, gained an appointment as a canon from about 1223, and became a master of THEOLOGY by 1225. As part of the group who opposed an election to the bishopric of Paris in 1227, he went to ROME. Pope GREGORY IX annulled the election and instead chose William as the bishop of Paris on April 10, 1228. However, he always remained more interested in scholarly work than ecclesiastical administration.

As bishop he presided over a university strike between 1229 and 1231, a conflict with the Crown in 1238, and the condemnation of the TALMUD in 1244. Various popes and King LOUIS IX employed him on several diplomatic missions. Besides trying to refute heretical movements, he tried to reform monasteries and favored the new mendicant orders. Along with his administrative duties, William wrote extensive scriptural commentaries, philosophical and theological works, SERMONS, and treatises on spirituality and pastoral care. William also attempted to limit the impact of the new ARISTOTELIANISM and especially the material added by Arabic commentators in the effort to assimilate ancient PHILOSOPHY into Christianity. He died in Paris on March 30, 1249.

See also WILLIAM OF AUXERRE.

Further reading: William of Auvergne, *The Immortality of the Soul,* trans. Roland J. Teske and Francis C. Wade (Milwaukee: Marquette University Press, 1991); William of Auvergne, *The Trinity or First Principles,* trans. Roland J. Teske and Francis C. Wade (Milwaukee: Marquette University Press, 1989); Steven P. Marrone, *William of Auvergne and Robert Grosseteste: New Ideas of Truth in the Early Thirteenth Century* (Princeton, N.J.: Princeton University Press, 1983); E. A. Moody, *Platonism and Aristotelianism in the Psychology of William of Auvergne* (New York: Columbia University Press, 1933), 1–109.

William of Auxerre (ca. 1150–1231) *French Scholastic philosopher, theologian*

William was born about 1150 in Auxerre, and became the archdeacon of Beauvais. He eventually taught at PARIS and made two journeys to ROME, where he was involved in a conflict in 1229 about the teaching of ARISTOTELIANISM, which had been forbidden by a council of Paris in 1210. He issued a bull (*Parens scientiarum*) that has been called a foundational document for the University of Paris. He was again part of a three-person commission appointed by GREGORY IX on April 23, 1231, to examine and clarify the position of the thought of Aristotle in university teaching. He was also to prepare a new edition of the scientific and metaphysical works of Aristotle. His *Golden Summa,* which followed the form of PETER LOMBARD's *Sentences,* was one of the first to incorporate into and reconcile a limited Aristotelianism with Christian theology. He died in Rome on November 3, 1231.

See also WILLIAM OF AUVERGNE.

Further reading: Walter H. Principe, *The Theology of the Hypostatic Union in the Early Thirteenth Century.* Vol. 1, *William of Auxerre's Theology of the Hypostatic Union* (Toronto: Pontifical Institute of Mediaeval Studies, 1963).

William of Malmesbury (ca. 1085–ca. 1142) *English Benedictine monk, historian*

William was born in Wiltshire about 1085, the son of a Norman and Saxon family. After receiving some primary education, he entered as an adolescent at the Benedictine monastery of Malmesbury, where he remained for the rest of his life. William became precentor of that abbey in about 1137 and was much involved with its library. In 1139 he represented the monastery at the Council of Winchester but always refused election as abbot. William died about 1142.

William of Malmesbury was among the best historians of his time. Between 1119 and 1125, he compiled a version of the history of the popes. After this he was commissioned by Queen Matilda (1102–67) to write a *History of the Deeds of the Kings of England.* He spent the next 15 years writing these histories. Just before his death he wrote the unfinished *New History* about the events of the civil war in ENGLAND between Matilda and Stephen (ca. 1097–1154). He did research in LIBRARIES and paid attention to documents. He also composed lives of local saints, a treatise on the MIRACLES of the Virgin MARY, a history of GLASTONBURY Abbey, and biblical commentaries. He wrote in a fine Latin style but included some dubious but interesting stories and anecdotes.

Further reading: William of Malmesbury, *The Historian Novella,* trans. K. R. Potter (New York: Thomas Nelson, 1955); William of Malmesbury, *Chronicles of the Kings of England: From the Earliest Period to the Reign of King Stephen,* trans. J. A. Giles (London: Bell and Dalchy, 1866); John Scott, *The Early History of Glastonbury: An Edition, Translation, and Study of William of Malmesbury's De antiquitate Glastonie ecclesie* (Woodbridge, England: Boydell Press, 1981); R. M. Thomson, *William of Malmesbury* (Woodbridge, England: Boydell Press, 1987).

William of Moerbeke (ca. 1215–ca. 1286) *Flemish Dominican friar, translator*

William was born in Moerbeke near GHENT in FLANDERS in about 1215. He probably studied at PARIS and COLOGNE with ALBERTUS MAGNUS and THOMAS AQUINAS, who probably asked him to produce translations into LATIN of the works of ARISTOTLE, which he began about 1260. He was a chaplain, apostolic penitentiary, and confessor to Popes Clement IV (1265–68) and Gregory X (1271–76). Well known for his knowledge of Greek, he was present at the Second Council of LYON in 1274 and was appointed the bishop of Corinth in Greece on April 9, 1278. He died at Corinth or at the papal court sometimes before October 26, 1286. He translated works of Aristotle, Proclus, Alexander of Aphrodisias, Ptolemy, Galen, and Archimedes, among other ancient Greek authors. His translations were important in the introduction of this body of PHILOSOPHY and science into the West.

See also NEOPLATONISM AND PLATONISM IN THE MIDDLE AGES.

Further reading: Aristotle, *De anima, in the Version of William of Moerbeke; and The Commentary of St. Thomas Aquinas,* trans. Kenelm Foster and Silvester Humphries (New Haven, Conn.: Yale University Press, 1951).

William of Ockham (William of Occam, Doctor Invincibiulis) (ca. 1285–1347) *Franciscan, nominalist philosopher*

William of Ockham was born in Ockham in Surrey in ENGLAND about 1285. He became a FRANCISCAN friar and a student of THEOLOGY at the University of OXFORD. He was ordained subdeacon of Southwark in 1306. While at Oxford as a young student and teacher, he lectured on PETER Lombard's *Sentence* between 1317 and 1319. In 1320 he moved a Franciscan convent at LONDON or Reading to study and write to be accepted as a master. He lost the position as a regent master to others, probably because the chancellor of the University of Oxford, John Lutterell (d. 1335), strongly opposed his appointment. A little later, in 1323, Lutterell collected 56 extracts from Ockham's lectures and sent them to the pope hoping for condemnation. A papal commission in 1324 brought Ockham to AVIGNON on charges of HERESY. He spent the next four years there, and eventually 51 of his ideas were said to be open to censure but never formally condemned.

William then left Avignon with Michael of Cesena (ca. 1280–1342), the head of the FRANCISCAN ORDER who was linked with ideas about POVERTY of the CLERGY also condemned by Pope JOHN XXII. They fled to PISA and then Munich, where the excommunicated Emperor Louis of BAVARIA (r. 1314–47) gave them protection. Ockham then took part in the controversy about poverty and wrote polemics against the pretensions to temporal power of JOHN XXII and later popes. After the death of Louis of Bavaria in 1347, Ockham, perhaps on his deathbed, tried to achieve reconciliation with the pope by renouncing all but his early work. However, he died soon afterward in a Franciscan convent in Munich on April 10, 1347/48.

WORK AND IDEAS

From his large and varied body of work, William of Ockham was important for his ideas on metaphysical, theological, and political questions. The first of these was the principle of Ockham's razor, which stressed that the simplest explanation for any problem was the best explanation. He did not see the need to reconcile God's power with human reason; this meant that much of the work attempting that by the scholastics was fruitless. As a nominalist, he believed that abstract terms were merely names that did not exist in reality. Contrary to much of Scholastic thought and Thomas AQUINAS in particular, Ockham believed that only revelation and personal experience led to GOD. Reason was of little use. He also questioned the concept of transubstantiation in the Eucharist, believing that the matter of the bread and wine was not changed into the body and blood of Christ. William argued against papal supremacy and the assumption that secular governments could tax ecclesiastical property. All these ideas and questions were of great importance in the intellectual world of the later Middle Ages and RENAISSANCE.

See also LOGIC; MARSILIUS OF PADUA; NOMINALISM; REALISM; SPIRITUAL FRANCISCANS.

Further reading: William of Ockham, *A Letter to the Friars Minor and Writings,* ed. Arthur Stephen McGrade and John Kilcullen (Cambridge: Cambridge University Press, 1995); William of Ockham, *Ockham: Philosophical Writings,* ed. and trans. Philotheus Boehner (London: Nelson, 1957); Marilyn McCord Adams, *William Ockham,*. 2 vols. (Notre Dame, Ind.: University of Notre Dame Press, 1987); Katherine H. Tachau, *Vision and Certitude in the Age of Ockham: Optics, Epistemology, and the Foundations of Semantics, 1250–1345* (Leiden: E. J. Brill, 1988).

William of Rubruck (Rubruquis, Willem van Ruysbroeck) (ca. 1215–ca. 1270/95) *Franciscan, traveler*
William was probably born between 1210 and 1215 in Rubruck near Cassel in FLANDERS. In addition to his native fluency in Flemish, he was fluent in French and had a passable knowledge of LATIN. he apparently did not have had much education but proved himself an excellent observer. In 1253 he was sent by King LOUIS IX to seekout the Mongol khan and explore the possibilities for converting the MONGOLS to Christianity. He traveled through CONSTANTINOPLE and left ACRE in April of 1253. Encountering the Mongols first near the Volga River, he proceeded to Karakorum, their capital, to see the khan Möngke. He stayed there until May 1254. He began the journey back by passing the Caspian Sea, then south through ARMENIA into southern ANATOLIA; he arrived at CYPRUS to track down Louis IX, whom he was not able to see until 1257.

William was disappointed because he failed to convert many Mongols and was not optimistic about the future chances for their conversion. Perceiving that Mongol westward expansion was not imminent, he concentrated in his description of his travel on Buddhism, geography, shamanic religions, and culture. The extent of influence of his original report of his travels was not clear. He died sometime after 1270.

See also CUMANS; JOHN OF PLANO CARPINI; MARCO POLO.

Further reading: Willem van Ruysbroeck, *The Mission of Friar William of Rubruck: His Journey to the Court of the Great Khan Möngke, 1253–1255,* trans. Peter Jackson (London: Hakluyt Society, 1990); Christopher Dawson, *The Mongol Mission: Narratives and Letters of the Franciscan Missionaries in Mongolia and China in the Thirteenth and Fourteenth Centuries* (New York: Sheed and Ward, 1966).

William of Tyre (ca. 1130–1185/90) *archbishop, historian of the crusaders*
William was probably the son of a noble French or Italian family and was born about 1130 in SYRIA or PALESTINE. He studied in Europe at PARIS between 1145 and 1161 and at BOLOGNA between 1161 and 1165. He returned home to be appointed as archdeacon of TYRE in 1167 with the condition that he write a history of the current king of Jerusalem, Amalric I (r. 1162–73/74). In 1170 he became a tutor to the young future king, BALDWIN IV. After the Baldwin's accession in 1173/74, William was made chancellor of the Kingdom of JERUSALEM on 1174 and then archbishop of Tyre in 1175. William traveled to CONSTANTINOPLE and Europe on several occasions to seek military help for the kingdom, now under attack by a revived and better organized onslaught by the local Muslim rulers, and to attend the Third Lateran Council in 1178/79. He was employed by Pope ALEXANDER III as a papal representative. At the council he managed to gain marginally greater control over the MILITARY ORDERS for the local authorities. He was known for his abilities in Greek, Latin, and Arabic.

HISTORIES

In the 1170s William had turned more to writing and had become the chief authority for the history of the eastern Mediterranean and the Latin kingdom between 614 and 1184, especially from 1147. His *General History of the Crusades and the Kingdom of Jerusalem* was written between 1169 and 1173. Later translated into French and widely circulated, it consisted of 23 volumes and was carefully based on earlier sources, documents, and William's personal experiences in the politics and government of the church and the kingdom. He also wrote an account of the Third Lateran Council of 1179 and a *History of the Eastern Kings,* which survived only in fragments. He failed in his attempt to be made the patriarch of Jerusalem in 1183 and retired to Rome, where he finished his histories and died between 1185 and 1190.

See also FULCHER OF CHARTRES; LATIN STATES IN GREECE.

Further reading: William of Tyre, *A History of Deeds Done beyond the Sea,* trans. Emily A. Babcock and A. C. Krey, 2 vols. (New York: Columbia University Press, 1943); P. W. Edbury, *William of Tyre, Historian of the Latin East* (Cambridge: Cambridge University Press, 1988); Margaret Ruth Morgan, *The Chronicle of Ernoul and the Continuations of William of Tyre* (Oxford: Oxford University Press, 1973).

William of Wyckham (Wykeham) (1324–1404) *bishop of Winchester, royal official*
From a poor family, he was educated at Winchester and became the secretary to the constable of Winchester Castle in about 1349. There he drew the attention of King EDWARD III and in 1356 became one of the king's clerks and a surveyor of the works at Windsor Castle and elsewhere. In the following years he accumulated numerous benefices and was keeper of several royal castles and manors, which he rebuilt. Further recognized for his abilities, William was made keeper of the privy seal in 1364, bishop of Winchester in 1366, and royal chancellor in 1367. Making an enemy of JOHN OF GAUNT, he was forced out of office for incompetence and lost many of his benefices and was a useful scapegoat for the losses in a bad period for the English in the HUNDRED YEARS' WAR with France in 1371. He was cleared and pardoned of the charges and restored to office at the accession of RICHARD II in 1377, serving again as a moderating influence as chancellor between 1389 and 1391. He founded and richly endowed New College at OXFORD and Saint Mary's Grammar School at Winchester, including scholarships for poor boys. He died in 1404.

Further reading: G. H. Moberley, *Life of William Wyckham, Sometime Bishop of Winchester* (Winchester: Warren, 1887); Nicholas Orme, *English Schools in the Middle Ages* (London: Methuen, 1973).

William Tell *legendary hero*
According to the legend for which there have not been found any corroborating documents, as a leader, though a peasant, of the canton of Uri, William refused to obey an order issued by Gessler, a tyrannical Austrian official. The locals were supposed to make a payment of homage to a symbolic cap hung in the town square of Altdorf. As punishment for his refusal to pay, Gessler forced William to endanger the life of his son by shooting an arrow at an apple placed on the boy's head. William succeeded but was arrested anyway for insulting Gessler. He escaped while he and his guards were crossing Lake Lucerne. Later in an ambush at a narrow pass, William killed Gessler and became a leader of the Swiss military struggle against AUSTRIA. William was first mentioned in legends in the 1470s and his story emerged as fully developed in the 16th century.

See also HABSBURG DYNASTY; SWITZERLAND.

Further reading: Walter Dettwiler, *William Tell, Portrait of a Legend* (Zurich: Swiss National Museum, 1991).

William the Marshal (1146–1219) *soldier, first earl of Pembroke and Striguil*
Born in 1146, William was the landless younger son of John FitzGilbert the Marshal (d. 1165). A frequent and rich winner of tournaments, he was made a tutor in CHIVALRY to Henry II's eldest son, Henry the Young King (1155–83). In 1189 William married Isabel, daughter and heiress of Richard de Clare (d. 1176), the earl of Pembroke and lord of Striguil. In this manner he inherited the rich and huge estates of the Clare family and the lordship of Leinster in IRELAND. He was soon able to buy half the lands of the earls of Giffard. He then became known as one of the foremost KNIGHTS of his time and one of the most powerful barons in ENGLAND.

Loyal to RICHARD I LIONHEART, until that king's death, William helped JOHN LACKLAND succeed to the throne. John rewarded him with recognition of his title earl of Pembroke. In 1205 he probably swore allegiance to PHILIP II AUGUSTUS of FRANCE for his estates in NORMANDY. To escape John's wrath though he might have given permission for that oath, William went to Ireland between 1207 and 1213. Remaining loyal to the Crown, he helped govern England in John's absence on the Continent in 1214. As John's chief adviser, he was prominent in his support for the prerogatives of the Crown in the negotiations that led to the issue of the MAGNA CARTA in June 1215 and supported John in the ensuing civil war. At John's death in October 1216, William became executor of his will and regent for the young HENRY III. William's efforts were instrumental in defeating a French invasion and in gaining peace for England by 1217. After turning over the regency to the pope and perhaps taking the habit of a Templar, he died peacefully after an illness of a few months on May 14, 1219.

Further reading: David Crouch, *William Marshal: Court, Career and Chivalry in the Angevin Empire, 1147–1219* (New York: Longman, 1990); George S. Duby, *William Marshal: The Flower of Chivalry,* trans. Richard Howard (1984; reprint, New York: Pantheon Books, 1985); Sidney Painter, *William Marshal: Knight-Errant, Baron, and Regent of England* (Baltimore: Johns Hopkins Press, 1933).

wills and testaments In the Middle Ages wills and testaments were revocable acts in which persons enjoying legal capacity declared their last wishes about the disposition of their property after their death. Men and women could compose and have wills written if they were considered to be of sound mind and body, had the money to pay the scribe or notary, and met all the other legal requirements. It could be done orally or more formally with witnesses. There were many different procedures in Europe according to the many varieties of legal systems.

LEGAL CONTEXT

Of classical Roman origin, the testament reappeared in the 12th century with the revival of Roman LAW and elaboration of the notarial system. The document had to be written by a proper authority and had to follow certain forms and contain appropriate clauses in order to be valid. It was a popular device for controlling one's religious and secular bequests and inheritable property. In Roman law it had been used primarily to name an heir. Germanic traditions and later written laws in the early Middle Ages gave people less freedom to dispose of their material life, mostly by stipulating that most donations could only be made in life. At death certain limiting procedures were defined to protect and clarify male succession.

The church saw the will and last testament as an opportunity to offer the faithful a way of ensuring their salvation and remitting guilt for past sins. It supported the use of wills, and by the 13th century friars and other clerics were notorious for attending the deathbed of the sick and dying to promote pious bequests to the institutions of the church.

In civic law and familial terms the will was a device to try to enforce one's posthumous desires about primarily movable property in the context of the web of regulation established by customary law, Roman law, and interpretations of these in the context of many legal regimes and systems.

ISLAM

In ISLAM there was diversity in concept and procedure according to various schools of law and between the SUNNI and SHIA systems. The QURAN provided the legal doctrines behind the rules for treatment of heirs and donations after death. Muslim women had clear rights of inheritance, but they were more limited under Sunni Islam. A WAQF or foundation was often used for estate control and pious objectives.

See also NOTARIES AND THE NOTARIAL SYSTEM.

Further reading: Dorothy Whitelock, ed. and trans., *Anglo-Saxon Wills* (Cambridge: Cambridge University Press, 1930); Steven Epstein, *Wills and Wealth in Medieval Genoa, 1150–1250* (Cambridge, Mass.: Harvard University Press, 1984); Michael M. Sheehan, *The Will in Medieval England, from the Conversion of the Anglo-Saxons to the End of the Thirteenth Century* (Toronto: Pontifical Institute of Mediaeval Studies, 1963).

windmills   *See* MILLS, WIND AND WATER.

wine and winemaking   In the Middle Ages as now wine was the fermented juice made primarily from grapes. In the early Middle Ages its cultivation and production expanded from the regions around the Mediterranean into northern Europe. Often it even supplanted other beverages such as barley beer, and its use rivaled

Gathering grapes and pressing them for wine, the harvest in the month of October (15th century), Castello del Buonconsiglio, Trent, Italy *(Scala / Art Resource)*

the consumption of hop beer except in Germanic regions. Christianization and the spread of monasticism promoted the growing of grapes and the drinking and appreciation of the consumption of wine, since it was necessary for the MASS and highly symbolic in the Eucharist.

The consumption of wine was determined by economic class and availability. Wine was preferred and appreciated as an alternative to unhealthy water. Its alcoholic content was often lower than that of modern wine, and it was drunk in fairly large amounts on a daily basis. It was also used in cooking as vinegar and as a medicinal remedy. It was an important trading commodity but bulky and fragile to ship and move about. Some regions such as TUSCANY, PORTUGAL, Gascony, and the upper Rhineland specialized in its production in the later Middle Ages. The quality and variety of medieval wines were diversified and depended on local usages and production. There can be little doubt, however, that wine was drunk regularly by those able to afford it and was seen as a major aspect of social conviviality. In Judaism wine was treated much as in Christianity, but drunkenness was strongly condemned. In ISLAM the QURAN forbade the drinking of wine as part of its strict prohibition of alcohol.

See also FOOD, DRINK, AND NUTRITION; EUCHARISTIC CONTROVERSIES; UTRAQUISTS AND UTRAQUISM; VINES AND VINEYARDS.

Further reading: Jean-Louis Flandrin and Massimo Montanari, eds., *Food: A Culinary History from Antiquity to the Present,* trans. Clarissa Botsford, Arthur Goldhammer, et al. (1996; reprint, New York: Columbia University Press, 1999), especially 165–346; I. W. Raymond, *The Teaching of the Early Church on the Use of Wine and Strong Drink* (New York: Columbia University Press, 1927); Desmond Stewart, *Monks and Wine* (New York: Crown, 1979).

witchcraft During the Middle Ages witchcraft was considered an inappropriate form of MAGIC and condemned as a pagan practice and a superstitious SIN prompted by the DEVIL. It was seen to be used for evil ends and was condemned and prosecuted as a sin throughout the period 300 to 1500. The concern that authorities showed for its repression varied over time but had reached a fevered pitch by 1500, leading to the great and deadly witch hunts of the 16th and 17th centuries. By then it was deemed an alternative system of practice and belief to Christianity. There is little evidence that it was a continuation and survival of an ancient system of belief, however.

The sources for any belief in it and its actual practice are not very clear, since they were compiled by those in charge of its suppression, who believed they knew what they were looking for among its alleged practitioners. Over the course of centuries, all kinds of magical practices gradually became associated with it. Most of the time witchcraft was not of much concern, and witches were considered a marginal group of heretics. If it was perceived as bargaining with the devil to benefit one's life or do evil in the real world, however, it was taken seriously. There were many executions for witchcraft before the 15th century but rare systematic hunts or persecutions.

By the 1480s a complete system had been worked out for what had been perceived about its beliefs and practices and methods to detect them during legal examinations. The *Hammer of Witches,* written by two Dominican inquisitors, became the authoritative source. This book laid the groundwork for the stereotypes deployed in the great persecutions, especially of women, of the following centuries.

See also INQUISITION; MAGIC AND FOLKLORE; SABBATH AND WITCHES' SABBATH.

Further reading: Richard Kieckhefer, *European Witch Trials: Their Foundations in Popular and Learned Culture, 1300–1500* (Berkeley: University of California Press, 1976); Charles Kors and Edward Peters, eds., *Witchcraft in Europe, 400–1700: A Documentary History,* 2d ed. (Philadelphia: University of Pennsylvania Press, 2001); Edward Peters, *The Magician, the Witch, and the Law* (Philadelphia: University of Pennsylvania Press, 1978); Jeffrey Burton Russell, *Witchcraft in the Middle Ages* (Ithaca, N.Y.: Cornell University Press, 1972).

Wittelsbach family The Wittelsbach family was the Bavarian noble dynasty who produced the dukes of BAVARIA from 1180 and of the Rhenish palatine from 1214 until 1918. They were probably a branch of the family of the Liutpoldings and split into two branches during the reign of the emperor Louis IV the Bavarian (r. 1314–47). They had been made dukes by FREDERICK I BARBAROSSA. They skillfully held the duchy by building CASTLES, refusing to restore defeated rival families to their estates, and establishing new towns. They also took advantage of the problems of the HOHENSTAUFEN family to protect and extend their authority. Although they tried to become more than a regional power, they were always overshined by the HABSBURGS.

Further reading: Peter Oluf Krückmann, *The Wittelsbach Palaces: From Landshut and Höchstadt to Munich* (Munich: Prestel Verlag, 2001).

Wolfram von Eschenbach (ca. 1170–ca. 1220) *German courtly poet*
A native of BAVARIA or FRANCONIA, Wolfram was born about 1170 to a family of the minor nobility. He was a member of the court of Herman I the landgrave of Thuringia (d. 1217), in which he knew WALTHER VON DER VOGELWEIDE. He wrote eight lyric poems, parts of two religious epics, and *Parzival.* Wolfram adapted CHRÉTIEN DE TROYES's *Conte du Graal* to the German language and achieved a unity of the romance of PERCEVAL and that of GAWAIN. It was a powerful allegory about a quest

for spiritual growth. He tolerantly joined Arthurian and Oriental concepts of CHIVALRY, urging toleration between the Christian and Muslim worlds. Wolfram wrote about aristocratic and chivalrous ideals and chaste MARRIAGE and fulfillment of duty. *Parzival* was a religious poem about Perceval and was quite different from most courtly romance. He died about 1220.

See also GRAIL, LEGEND OF, AND GRAIL ROMANCES.

Further reading: Wolfram von Eschenbach, *Parzival*, trans. A. T. Hatto (London: Penguin Books, 1980); Wolfram von Eschenbach, *Willehalm* trans. Mario E. Gibbs and Sidney M. Johnson (London: Penguin Books, 1984); Wolfram von Eschenbach, *Titurel; and the Songs*, ed. Marion E. Gibbs and Sidney M. Johnson (New York: Garland, 1988); D. H. Green, "Wolfram von Eschenbach," in *European Writers: The Middle Ages and the Renaissance*, Vol. 1, *Prudentius to Medieval Drama*, ed. William T. H. Jackson and George Stade (New York: Charles Scribner's Sons, 1983), 263–286; James F. Poag, *Wolfram von Eschenbach* (New York: Twayne, 1972); Hermann J. Weigand, ed., *Wolfram's Parzival: Five Essays with an Introduction* (Ithaca, N.Y.: Cornell University Press, 1969).

women, status of The status of women during the period 300 to 1500 varied according to class and many other factors, some permanent and some transitory. The Christian church in the East and the West had an ambivalent but generally misogynist attitude, but it did accept women as having different, perhaps imperfect, natures; souls like those of men; and capacity for REDEMPTION. Their role in producing other Christians was appreciated, but their SEXUALITY was deemed always dangerous to the celibate clergy, if not to males in general. Their legal status varied according to class and constantly evolving laws and legal systems. Their freedom of action or agency also varied over time and space. They were generally and in various degrees under the authority of a male relative or husband. In terms of succession, they were usually in line after males. Both ecclesiastical and civil law granted women certain rights and often did try to protect them from male exploitation and abuse. Some women did exercise power and authority over property at the dynastic, estate, and, more commonly, household levels. The status and rights of Jewish women paralleled those of Christian women; CELIBACY after MARRIAGE or as a vocation was not an ideal option. Marriage and reproduction were expected. They were learned from the study of TORAH and segregated in SYNAGOGUES.

MARRIAGE AND RELIGIOUS PURSUITS

In theory marriage was a contract in which women had certain rights and obligations. Monogamy in marriage was the rule and divorce impossible, though separations were available to some. Women's obligations included obedience and acquiescence to their husband's procreative access to their body. Their rights included some idea

of support even after the death of the husband. Although at the upper level of society women were viewed almost as commodities valued for their prospective fertility, dowries, and inheritances or family connections with other males, the reality of married life could work out to be more equitable than one might expect. For the unmarried LAITY, celibacy was the only acceptable way of life. In Christianity NUNS had an honorable religious status as celibates dedicated to GOD but were never considered to be eligible for the priesthood or real clerical status. The access to learning and scholarship of all women was limited, but numerous religious and lay women did produce written and artistic material. Women could attain sainthood but did so far less often than males. Women had clear cultural impact as patrons of authors and artists.

All these contradictory capabilities and disabilities, attitudes, and practices did not remain the same throughout the Middle Ages. Working-class women spent their life, as did the men of that class, continuously striving to eke out a living at rural agricultural tasks or endless toil in artisan trades such as brewing or cloth making. Such economic status could lead to more equitable relationships as the partners needed one another for survival.

WOMEN IN ISLAM

In ISLAM the QURAN granted women a legal personality, confirmed rights in their marriage, and made divorce possible under certain circumstances. Early Islam forbade female infanticide and recognized women's full personhood. They had the same religious obligations as Muslims as men. Both sexes were completely equal before God, but the differences in their nature required different roles in society. Other disadvantages compared to male prerogatives were more clear; for example, men were allowed to marry someone of another religion, who was not required to convert to Islam. Males were favored in inheritance. Their testimony in court had more weight. Men could have up to four wives.

See also BEGUINES AND BEGHARDS; CHIVALRY; CONCUPISCENCE; COURTLY LOVE; FAMILY AND KINSHIP; HERESY AND HERESIES; IRENE; MARY, CULT OF; MYSTICISM, CHRISTIAN; THEODORA I; TROUBADOURS; WIDOWS AND WIDOWHOOD; WILLS AND TESTAMENTS.

Further reading: "X: Women in the Medieval World" in the Bibliography; Gillian Clark, *Women in Late Antiquity: Pagan and Christian Life Styles* (Oxford: Clarendon Press, 1993); Lynda Garland, *Byzantine Empresses: Women and Power in Byzantium, A.D. 527–1204* (London: Routledge, 1999); Margaret L. King, *Women of the Renaissance* (Chicago: University of Chicago Press, 1991); Denise Spellberg, *Politics, Gender, and the Islamic Past: The Legacy of A'isha bint Abi Bakr* (New York: Columbia University Press, 1994); Barbara Freyer Stowasser, *Women in the Qur'an, Traditions, and Interpretation* (New York: Oxford University Press, 1994); Merry E. Weisner, *Women and Gender in Early Modern Europe*, 2d ed. (New York: Cambridge University Press, 2000).

women's religious orders   *See* NUNS AND NUNNERIES.

wool   *See* ANIMALS AND ANIMAL HUSBANDRY.

works of mercy   The works of mercy were demonstrations of love for neighbors and were done as a consequence of love for GOD. The theologians of the Scholastic period in the 13th century defined seven corporeal and seven spiritual works of mercy. They were based on traditional Orthodox and Western concepts of practicing and cultivating the VIRTUES. The seven corporeal works of mercy were to feed the hungry, to give drink to the thirsty, to clothe the naked, to visit the sick, to visit prisoners, to harbor strangers, and to bury the dead. They were all based on the words of Christ in the GOSPELS. The seven spiritual works of mercy were to convert the sinner, to teach the ignorant, to counsel the doubtful, to comfort the sorrowing, to bear wrongs patiently, to forgive injuries, and to pray for the living and the dead. To help another in these ways was to see Christ in that person and act as Christ himself would act. Christians were to practice the works of mercy at every opportunity. They were much demonstrated as practiced by the saints in hagiographical literature and in didactic art. Their practice would assist in gaining salvation; and those who were helped would later intercede for the practitioner.

Over the course of the period 300 to 1500, the church established institutions to carry out these works. To help these activities was to help the recipients of the largesse or kindness.

See also BURIAL RULES AND PRACTICES, CHARITY AND POVERTY; DEATH AND THE DEAD; HAGIOGRAPHY; HOSPITALS; PREACHING AND PREACHERS; SERMONS AND HOMILIES; WILLS AND TESTAMENTS.

Further reading: Michel Mollat, *The Poor in the Middle Ages: An Essay in Social History,* trans. Arthur Goldhammer (New Haven, Conn.: Yale University Press, 1986); Fritz Eichenberg, *Works of Mercy,* ed. Robert Ellsberg (Maryknoll, N.Y.: Orbis Books, 1992).

Wulfila   *See* ULPHILAS.

Wulfstan of Worcester, Saint   (ca. 1008–1095) *Anglo-Saxon monk, bishop*
Born about 1008 to a family closely connected with the church of Worcester, Wulfstan became a priest before 1038, then a monk in the cathedral priory there and successively novice master, precentor, sacrist, and prior of that house. He was elected bishop of Worcester in 1062 and was in that office until his death on January 20, 1095. In the meantime he became famous for his private PRAYER, HOMILIES, PREACHING, and labors opposing the slave trade. After the Norman Conquest of ENGLAND in 1066, he submitted to WILLIAM I, though he had supported HAROLD, and played a leading role in maintaining and transmitting English monastic values as the spiritual leader of the surviving English church. He aided in the compilation of the DOMESDAY BOOK. Trying to preserve writing in Old English, he maintained a SCRIPTORIUM that was an important means for the preservation and transmission of texts in Old English. He also sponsored the writing of the *Chronicle of John of Worcester* and the compilation of *Hemming's Chartulary* to protect the documents containing the history of the property of the cathedral of Worcester. He was canonized by Pope INNOCENT III on April 21, 1203.

Further reading: J. E. Cross and Andrew Hamer, eds., *Wulfstan's Canon Law Collection* (Cambridge: D. S. Brewer, 1999); Emma Mason, *Saint Wulfstan of Worcester, c. 1008–1095* (Oxford: B. Blackwell, 1990).

Wycliffe, John   (Wyclif) (ca. 1329–1384) *academic philosopher and reformer*
John Wycliffe was born about 1329 in Wiclif-on-Tees in Yorkshire. Between 1356 and 1381 he lived mainly in OXFORD, supporting himself as a nonresident holder of several ecclesiastical BENEFICES. He became a fellow of Meron College and then regent or master of Balliol College but resigned to be vicar of Fillingham. In the 1360s his university reputation was based on his work in LOGIC and PHILOSOPHY; he was well noted for his opposition as a realist to the NOMINALISM of the followers of WILLIAM OF OCKHAM. From 1371 he lectured on THEOLOGY. During the 1370s he played a role as a polemicist against ecclesiastical privileges and as a preacher to the LAITY.

Already involved in JOHN of Gaunt's anticlerical movement, from 1379, Wycliffe began to express more radical views on the Eucharist and from 1380 to attack the friars, calling them mere marginal sects within Christianity. About the Eucharist he thought that after consecration of the bread and wine the accidents of shape and color but also their substance remained as they were seen. He thus denied the doctrine of transubstantiation. This was a product of his philosophical REALISM and belief in the indestructibility of substance. He also used historical arguments based on his reading of Scripture and the father of the church. Furthermore, he did not see the need for the almost magical intervention of priests with GOD. He was readily condemned by the Pope Gregory XI (r. 1370–78) in 1377. A university commission in Oxford in 1380 declared his views on the Eucharist heretical. In 1382 a mendicant commission at Blackfriars, "the Earthquake Council," in LONDON condemned 24 heresies in his writings. He was even associated in the mind of some with the breakdown of public order in the Peasants' Revolt in 1381.

In 1381 Wycliffe had retired from Oxford to Lutterworth, still under the protection of John of Gaunt. John HUS and his followers in BOHEMIA assimilated many of Wycliffe's ideas, which became part of their program of reform. These had a later life in England and were associated with the LOLLARDS and their heretical notions and the suspicious movement to translate the BIBLE into English. Wycliffe was linked, too, with the questioning of unworthy ecclesiastical authority and the practices of images, PILGRIMAGES, INDULGENCES, and prayers for the dead. He spent the last years of his life attacking his enemies. He was left alone and died peacefully at Lutterworth in Leicestershire on December 31, 1384. The Council of CONSTANCE (1414–18) ordered his writing burned and his remains removed from consecrated ground.

See also ANTICLERICALISM; SIMONY; WALDENSIANS.

Further reading: John Wycliffe, *On Simony,* trans. Terrence A. McVeigh (New York: Fordham University Press, 1992); John Wycliffe, *Select English Works of John Wyclif* (Oxford: Clarendon Press, 1869–1871); Anne Hudson, ed., *English Wycliffite Sermons,* 5 vols. (Oxford: Clarendon Press, 1983–1996); Jeremy Catto, "Wycliff and Wyclifism at Oxford, 1356–1430," in *History of the University of Oxford,* Vol. 2 (Oxford: Oxford University Press, 1992), 175–261; Joseph H. Dahmus, *The Prosecution of John Wyclyf* (New Haven, Conn.: Yale University Press, 1952); Anthony Kenny, *Wyclif* (Oxford: Oxford University Press, 1985); K. B. McFarlane, *John Wycliffe and the Beginnings of English Nonconformity* (New York: Macmillan, 1953); John Robon, *Wyclif and the Oxford Schools: The Relation of the "Summa de ente" to Scholastic Debates at Oxford in the Later Fourteenth Century* (Cambridge: Cambridge University Press, 1961).

Y

Yaroslav the Wise (980–1054) *grand prince of Kievan Rus'*

The son of VLADIMIR I THE GREAT, Yaroslav had to deal with a long struggle with his brother, Sviatoslav I the Damned (r. 1015–19), and his elder brother, Mstislav (d. 1035), before finally becoming the great prince of KIEV in 1019. Lame since childhood, he was nevertheless a good soldier. It was not until 1035 or 1036 with the childless death of Mstislav, that he won real control of all of his father's dominions and assumed the title *kagan*. This began a prosperous period for Kievan Rus'.

Despite an unsuccessful war with the BYZANTINE EMPIRE between 1043 and 1046, trading and religious connections between the two states grew. Christianity solidified its position and KIEV was recognized by the patriarch of Constantinople as the seat of a metropolitan. Yaroslav made Kiev his capital, where he started a building program which culminated in the CATHEDRAL of Saint Sophia in 1037. He established schools in Kiev and NOVGOROD. Laws were clarified and codified in the *Ruskasis Pravada*. Religious texts were translated into Slavic. Yaroslav extended and consolidated the frontiers of Kievan Rus', especially in the Baltic region and maintained and solidified peaceful relations with the West through dynastic marriages. After Yaroslav's death in 1054, authority was again distributed among various members of his family. This fragmentation began a decline in fortunes of Kievan Rus'.

Further reading: Samuel H. Cross and Olgerd P. Sherbowitz-Wetzor, trans., *The Russian Primary Chronicle: Laurentian Text,* (Cambridge, Mass.: Mediaeval Academy of America, 1973); Boris D. Grekov, *Kiev Rus'*, trans. Y. Sdobnikov, ed. Dennis Ogden (Moscow: Foreign Languages Publishing House, 1959); Boris A. Rybakov, *Early Centuries of Russian History,* trans. John Weir (Moscow: Progress, 1965).

Yazid I bin Muawiya (r. 680–683) *second Umayyad caliph*

Yazid was an experienced soldier and the son of Muawiya (r. 661–680). After succeeding his father despite opposition, he was the UMAYYAD caliph who sent forces against AL-HUSAYN and his followers at Karbala in IRAQ in 680, resulting in their massacres and martyrdom. Through this act he began to personify evil for the SHIA. He also had to put down a rebellion in MECCA, which his troops pillaged and burned at the moment of his death. He was an able general, though unsuccessful in besieging the city of CONSTANTINOPLE. A good administrator, he reformed the caliphate's financial system and improved AGRICULTURE. He died in 683 and was succeeded by a minor.

See also ALI IBN ABU TALIB; SCHIA, SHIISM, AND SHIITES.

Further reading: Syed Husain M. Jafri, *The Origins and Early Development of Shia Islam* (Oxford: Oxford University Press, 2000); W. Montgomery Watt, *The Formative Period of Islamic Thought* (Oxford: Oneworld, 1998).

year 1000 The year 1000 was associated with apocalyptic expectations linked with the end of the millennium or 1,000 years after the Incarnation and birth of Christ. The perception of this fear seems mostly to have been a creation of later historians. Although the overwhelming majority of people then were not very conscious of what year it was, there was some concern and anticipation among more learned contemporaries such as ABBO OF FLEURY and Raoul Glaber (d. 1047). The anticipation of this ominous date of the supposed end of the world did lead to more sophisticated efforts to calculate the year and when Christ was born and died. This was an attempt to clarify the CALENDAR. Some also thought that the real date for the end of the world might actually be 1033 or 1,000 years after the Crucifixion. There was a genuine impulse to reform many aspects of society and the church about this time. For example, this was the era of the beginning of the PEACE AND TRUCE OF GOD movement to reduce violence in society, especially against the property of the church. The practice of PILGRIMAGE became much more popular. Around 1000 emperor OTTO III had linked a secular and religious crisis with his program of imperial reform and renewal. Perhaps the year 1000 might be better linked with religious, social, and political revival than with supposed terror of Christians who expected the imminent end of the world.

See also ANTICHRIST; APOCALYPSE AND APOCALYPTIC LITERATURE; SYLVESTER II, POPE.

Further reading: Henri Focillon, *The Year 1000*, trans. Fred D. Wieck (New York: F. Ungar, 1969); Michael Frassetto, ed., *The Year 1000: Religious and Social Response to the Turning of the First Millennium* (New York: Palgrave Macmillan, 2002); John Man, *Atlas of the Year 1000* (Cambridge, Mass.: Harvard University Press, 1999).

Yiddish (Yidish-daytsh, Judeo-German)

Yiddish was the VERNACULAR language written in the Hebrew alphabet of the ASHKENAZI JEWS and called *taytsh, ivritaytsh*. It was close to German but consciously different from the Christian ways of speaking. Scholars date the origin of Yiddish to the ninth and 10th centuries, when Jews from northern FRANCE and ITALY settled in Lorraine and central Germany at Mainz, Worms, and Speyer. Yiddish gradually developed out of interaction among elements of Romance speech, Hebrew, Aramaean, and dialects of Middle High German. It became better defined after the crises of the massacres and migrations around the beginning of the First CRUSADE in 1096. Slavic elements were added in the 16th century as some Jews moved into Eastern Europe. This vernacular was used in parallel with Hebrew in official documents, PRAYERS, translations of literary texts, complex Talmudic arguments, medical treatises, and glosses on biblical texts in the later Middle Ages.

Further reading: Solomon Liptzin, *A History of Yiddish Literature* (Middle Village, N.Y.: Jonathan David, 1985); Max Weinreich, *History of the Yiddish Language*, trans. Shlomo Noble (Chicago: University of Chicago Press, 1980).

Yolanda of Brienne (Isabel, Isabella II) (ca. 1212–1228) *heiress to the Kingdom of Jerusalem, wife of Emperor Frederick II*

Given the name Isabella, but more usually known as Yolanda, she was heiress to the Kingdom of JERUSALEM through her mother, Maria of Montferrat (d. 1212). Her father, John of Brienne (ca. 1148–1237), acted as regent during her minority. In August 1225 she was married by proxy to the widower emperor FREDERICK II. Promoted by Pope Honorius III (r. 1216–27), this match offered the prospect of a revived Kingdom of Jerusalem to Frederick so that he would much more quickly to go on CRUSADE. After being crowned queen of Jerusalem and married in ACRE, the 12- or 13-year-old Yolanda or Isabella traveled to Brindisi, where the marriage was solemnized on November 9, 1225. It was perceived as confirming Frederick's pledge to undertake a crusade.

Frederick immediately offended and dispossessed her father and guardian, John of Brienne, by assuming the rights and title of king consort. Frederick may or may not have neglected her for her older cousin, but in April 1228 Yolanda bore a son, Conrad (1228–54). She died a few days later on May 1, leaving her infant as the enfant king of Jerusalem. Frederick was probably unfairly blamed for her death. Their son as Conrad IV of HOHENSTAUFEN became the king of GERMANY and of Jerusalem at his birth but never visited PALESTINE to be crowned as king of Jerusalem; nor was his son, Conradin (1252–68), ever crowned. With Conradin's death fighting CHARLES I OF ANJOU in 1268, the line of descent through Yolanda ended.

Further reading: David Abulafia, *Frederick II: A Medieval Emperor* (London: Allen Lane The Penguin Press, 1988); Georgina Masson, *Frederick II of Hohenstaufen: A Life* (London: Secker & Warburg, 1957).

York (Eboracum, Eoforwic, Jórvík)

The medieval city of York had been founded by the Romans in about 71 C.E. and became the principal Roman military center in northern Britain and the capital of the Roman province of Britannia Inferior. In the fifth and sixth centuries, after disappearing from the historical record, York or Eoforwic emerged as the most important town in northern ENGLAND. King Edwin of Northumbria's (d. 632) conversion to Christianity took place in the city in 627, and the first cathedral or Minister of York was built soon afterward. In 735 York became the seat of one of the only two archbishoprics in medieval England, supposedly second only to CANTERBURY.

At the end of the eighth century, the prosperity and intellectual accomplishments of York were shattered by Viking invasions. From 866 York or *Jórvík* was the capital of Danish and Norwegian kings. Viking York remained a dynamic commercial center throughout this period of prolonged political turbulence. After the Norman Conquest in 1066, York rebelled, was damaged, and then controlled by two new Norman CASTLES. It became the center of the largest county in the country. By the early 13th century, the citizenry of York had succeeded in establishing considerable self-government with a mayor from 1213. It had also become an active manufacturing town with a prominent Jewish community. The JEWS, however, became the victims of a murderous pogrom in 1190 and were finally expelled in 1290.

During the wars between SCOTLAND and EDWARD I and in the 14th century, York again became a major military stronghold. The Scots never succeeded in capturing York itself. By the late 14th century, conditions had settled and York was prosperous again. Despite the ravages of PLAGUES of the mid-14th century, York was probably the largest provincial town, with perhaps 15,000 inhabitants in England. In the 15th century, the town was dominated by GUILDS of MERCHANTS who paid for the impressive buildings still standing today, such as a Guildhall from about 1449 to 1459, a Tailors' Hall from about 1405, and some 40 rebuilt or refurbished parish churches. By 1450 York had become famous for its walls and cathedral with its STAINED GLASS, and the annual performances of its Corpus Christi MYSTERY plays. By the end of the 15th century, however, the local merchants were lamenting the city's economic decline.

Further reading: R. Barry Dobson, *The Jews of Medieval York and the Massacre of March 1190* (York: St. Anthony's Press, 1974); P. J. P. Goldberg, *Women, Work, and Life Cycle in a Medieval Economy: Women in York and Yorkshire c. 1300–1520* (Oxford: Clarendon Press, 1992); S. R. Jones, ed., *The Government of Medieval York: Essays in Commemoration of the 1396 Royal Charter* (York: Borthwick Institute of Historical Research, University of York, 1997); Jennifer Kermode, *Medieval Merchants: York, Beverley, and Hull in the Later Middle Ages* (Cambridge: Cambridge University Press, 1998); Heather Swanson, *Medieval Artisans: An Urban Class in Late Medieval England* (Oxford: Basil Blackwell, 1989).

York dynasty   *See* EDWARD IV; RICHARD III; WARS OF THE ROSES.

York Plays   The York Plays were a cycle of plays of unknown authorship that were enacted at YORK from the late 14th century to the third quarter of the 16th century. They were a cycle of 48 or 50 plays or pageants that contained more than 300 speaking parts and more than 14,000 lines of Middle English stanzaic verse. The cycle dramatically covered all of sacred history from the fall of the Angels, through creation, the temptation of Adam and Eve by the DEVIL, the expulsion from Eden, the flood, the story of Moses, the Incarnation, the life of Christ, his temptations by the devil, his trial and Crucifixion, the Resurrection, and the LAST JUDGMENT. They were performed by the craft GUILDS of the city on the movable summer feast day of Corpus Christi. They were all performed on one day on pageant wagons.

See also DRAMA; MYSTERY PLAYS.

Further reading: Richard Beadle and Pamela M. King, eds., *York Mystery Plays: A Selection in Modern Spelling* (Oxford: Clarendon Press, 1984); Richard Beadle, "The York Cycle," in *The Cambridge Companion to Medieval English Theatre,* ed. Richard Beadle (Cambridge: Cambridge University Press, 1994), 85–108; Richard J. Collier, *Poetry and Drama in the York Corpus Christi Play* (Hamden, Conn.: Archon Books, 1978); Clifford Davidson, *From Creation to Doom: The York Cycle of Mystery Plays* (New York: AMS Press, 1984).

youth, concept of   Any concept of "youth" in the Middle Ages and Renaissance was not actually a clearly defined age group of all members of society but a temporary limited social status one characteristically passed through while growing up as a noble. The idea of youth meant little to the majority of society, whose members were locked into labor or service as soon as they were able to perform it. In the development of the young, primarily male, noble it was a status beyond that of childhood or adolescent yet with limited rights and certainly not the privileges of a fully free and independent adult.

The term was primarily applied to a grown man who had been educated and become a knight. However, but not yet in control of his property or recognized as the head of a family or lineage. He was dependent on his father, who was the holder of patrimony and had authority over him and the rest of the family and household. It did not end at a particular age. The younger sons or cadets in this status might have little hope or prospect of ever succeeding their father or attaining economic independence. Males, excluded from much autonomy by this nebulous and perhaps irresponsible state, were thus often drawn to violence, the abduction of women, and predatory behavior as they sought to make their way in the world. TOURNAMENTS provided other opportunities for advancement, as in the case of WILLIAM THE MARSHAL. The younger sons of monarchs often participated in rebellions against their father as RICHARD I Lionheart did against HENRY II. Historians are only recently beginning to study what being a youth meant to women and other classes and groups in the societies of the Medieval world, if it meant anything at all.

See also AGING; CHILDHOOD; CHIVALRY; FAMILY AND KINSHIP.

Further reading: Georges Duby, *The Chivalrous Society* (Berkeley: University of California Press, 1977); Konrad Eisenbichler, ed., *The Premodern Teenager: Youth in Society, 1150–1650* (Toronto: Centre for Reformation and Renaissance Studies, 2002); Giovanni Levi and Jean-Claude Schmitt, eds., *A History of Young People,* Vol. 1, *Ancient and Medieval Rites of Passage,* trans. Camille Nash (1994; reprint, Cambridge, Mass.: Harvard University Press, 1997); Shulamith Shahar,

Childhood in the Middle Ages (London: Routledge, 1990); Hasan A. Shuraydi, *The Medieval Muslim Attitude toward Youth* (thesis, Yale University, 1970); Kaykavus ibn Iskandar ibn Qabus, Unsur al-Maali, *A Mirror for Princes: "The Qabus nama,"* trans. Reuben Levy (London: Cresset Press, 1951); Fiona Harris Stoertz, *Adolescence in Medieval Culture: The High Medieval Transformation* (Ph.D. thesis, University of California, Santa Barbara, 1999).

Ysengrimus   *See* BEAST EPICS OR FABLES.

Yuan dynasty   *See* MONGOLS AND MONGOL EMPIRE.

Z

Zabarella, Francesco (Zabarellis) (1360–1417) *Italian jurist, canonist*
Francesco was born at PADUA about 1360 and studied canon law there and then at BOLOGNA, where he obtained a licentiate in 1383. He taught at Bologna, FLORENCE, and Padua. The antipope, John XXIII (r. 1410–15), appointed him the archbishop of Florence in 1410 and the next year appointed him a cardinal-deacon. John sent him to the emperor SIGISMUND OF LUXEMBOURG to promote the calling of a council, which finally opened at CONSTANCE in 1414. Francesco was a supporter of a moderate CONCILIARISM and promoted the restoration of peace and reform of the church. His treatise on ending the Great SCHISM, an important conciliarist document, was critical of papal power and thus later condemned by the PAPACY. Though Francesco had been charged by John XXIII to preside over the council as his legate, he became one of the important sponsors of that pope's deposition. He died at Constance on September 26, 1417.

Further reading: Walter Ullman, *The Origins of the Great Schism: A Study in Fourteenth-Century Ecclesiastical History* (London: Burns, Oates & Washbourne, 1948); Brian Tierney, *Foundations of the Conciliar Theory: The Contribution of the Medieval Canonists from Gratian to the Great Schism* (Cambridge: Cambridge University Press, 1955).

Zagwa *See* ABYSSINIA.

Zirids (Banū Zīrī) The Zirids were a Berber dynasty who ruled in North AFRICA and al-MAGHRIB between 972 and 1125. The founder of the dynasty, Yusuf Buluggin I ibn Ziri (r. 972–84), was a governor in Ifriqiyya for the FATIMID caliphs in EGYPT. He moved to take over all of the al-Maghrib. When this region proved too extensive to control, it was divided around 990 between the two branches of the family, the Zirids and the Hammadids, who received the western part of north Africa. The Zirids made their capital at AL-QAYRAWAN. In 1041 they renounced their allegiance to the Fatimids, who promptly incited Bedouin tribes against them, and these nearly destroyed the territory of the Zirids. The Zirids, now confined to the coast, built up a fleet. The NORMANS under ROGER II eventually extracted tribute from them. The last Zirid ruler, al-Hasan (1121–48), lost their remaining territory to the ALMOHADS in 1148.

Further reading: Clifford Edward Bosworth, *The Islamic Dynasties* (Edinburgh: Edinburgh University Press, 1967); Michael Brett and Werner Forman, *The Moors: Islam in the West* (London: Orbis, 1980).

Žižka, Jan (ca. 1360–October 11, 1424) *military leader*
Born into a noble family about 1360 in Trocnov in BOHEMIA, Jan became a mercenary and fought for POLAND. He was later to lose an eye in the Bohemian civil wars during the reign of King Wenceslas IV (1361–1419), at whose court he had grown up. He became a zealous follower of John HUS and led those who threw the city councilors of PRAGUE out of the windows of the town hall in 1419.

Žižka then joined the TABORITES and helped them organize a fanatical army. In 1420 he defeated the German army of the emperor and German king of BOHEMIA, SIGISMUND (r. 1419–37), at Vitkov. He continued to fight the subsequent invasion forces of 1421 and 1422. While fighting against the Bohemian partisans of Sigismund and the Catholics, he lost his other eye in battle. Despite internal conflicts among the Taborites, he continued to lead them against the more conservative but heretical forces of Prague in 1423. In the summer of that year, Žižka undertook an unsuccessful invasion of HUNGARY. After beating the more conservative Hussite nobles and the forces of Prague again in 1424, he died of the PLAGUE on October 11, 1424, while preparing an attack on MORAVIA. His military tactic of using CAVALRY, infantry, and cannons together was innovative for the time and produced dramatic victories.

Further reading: Frantisek Michálek Bartos, *The Hussite Revolution, 1424–1437* (New York: Columbia University Press, 1986); F. G. Heymann, *John Zizka and the Hussite Revolution* (Princeton, N.J.: Princeton University Press, 1955); Norman Housley, *The Later Crusades: From Lyons to Alcazar, 1274–1580* (Oxford: Oxford University Press, 1992); Howard Kaminsky, *A History of the Hussite Revolution* (Berkeley: University of California Press, 1967).

Zoroastrianism (Mazdaism) Late antique and medieval Zoroastrianism was the system of religious doctrines ascribed to Zoroaster or Zarathustra. It was a dominant religion in IRAN where under the SASSANIAN dynasty between 226 and 651 it was the official state religion. After the conversion of Iran to ISLAM, many Zoroastrians moved to India, where they were called Parsis (Persians).

Of Zoroaster (ca. 658–ca. 551 B.C.E. or perhaps 1,000 years earlier) the person, little or nothing with much certainty has been found. He probably was active in northeastern Iran, western Afghanistan, and the Turkmen Republic of the former Soviet Union in the early sixth century B.C.E. The *Gathas*, hymns ascribed to him, have always been among the most sacred writings or Scriptures (Avesta) of the Zoroastrians.

BELIEFS

Essentially monotheistic, Zoroastrianism was probably less dualistic in its cosmology at its beginning than it would later become. According to that later rigid doctrinal system, the world was made by one "Wise Lord," or Ahura Mazda, the creator and the source of light and darkness, who had the help of a spirit and six immortals. This lord was not all-powerful and was opposed by an uncreated "Evil Spirit" or Ahriman who was in turn assisted by other evil spirits. The created world was then an arena of combat between good and evil represented in these two beings. Human beings created to help Ahura Mazda in his struggle with evil did have free will but at the same time had the absolute duty to choose the good. In fact all human effort was to be directed toward attaining salvation. At death each individual soul was judged according to his or her words and deeds. Those who failed this judgment were cast into a HELL or a LIMBO to be purified of the consequences of their transgressions. There was to be a return of a savior who would arrive for a final battle between good and evil at the end of the world. Later there was even an idea of resurrection of the dead. Much of this was based on earlier Iranian religious beliefs. Fire was regarded as a life force for the whole of creation and was at the center of Zoroastrian initiations and rituals in temples. This religion influenced Judaism, Christianity, and Islam in ways that have remained unclear. There are still some Zoroastrians in present-day IRAQ and Iran.

See also DUALISM; ESCHATOLOGY; MANICHAEISM AND MANI.

Further reading: Mary Boyce, *Zoroastrians: Their Religious Beliefs and Practices* (London: Routledge & Kegan Paul, 1984); Mary Boyce, *A History of Zoroastrianism,* 3 vols. (Leiden: E. J. Brill, 1989–1991); Jamsheed Choksy, *Conflict and Cooperation: Zoroastrian Subalterns and Muslim Elites in Medieval Iranian Society* (New York: Columbia University Press, 1997); Robert C. Zaehner, *The Dawn and Twilight of Zoroastrianism* (New York: Putnam, 1961).

APPENDIX I
MONARCHS AND RULERS OF THE MEDIEVAL WORLD

WESTERN EUROPE

Name	Period	Status
	Denmark	
	Gorm or Jelling Dynasty	
Gorm the Old, king of Jutland	ca. 936–958	
Harald Bluetooth (Harald Gormsson)	958–986/987	
Svein Forkbeard (Svein Haraldsson)	986/987–1014	
Harald II	1014–1018	
Canute the Great	1018–1035	
Harthcanute (Harde Knud)	1035–1042	
Magnus I the Good, king of Norway	1042–1046/7	
	Estrith (Estitd) Dynasty	
Svein Estrithson	1042–1074	
Harald III Hén	1074–1080	
Canute II (IV)	1080 1086	
Olaf I Hunger	1086–1095	
Eric I the Evergood	1095–1103	
Niels	1104–1134	
Eric II the Memorable	1134–1137	
Eric III the Lamb	1137/38–1146	
Canute III (V) Lavard, Bread Giver	1146–1157	
Waldemar I the Great	1157–1182	
Canute IV (VI)	1182–1202	
Waldemar II the Conqueror or Victorious	1202–1241	
Waldemar the Younger	1215–1231	co-regent
Eric IV Plovpennig or Plough penny	1241–1250	co-regent, 1232
Abel	1250–1252	
Christopher I	1252–1259	
Eric V Klipping	1259–1286	
Eric VI Menved	1286–1319	
Christopher II	1320–1326, 1330–1332	deposed, restored
Waldemar III	1326–1330	
Eric	1330–1332	
Interregnum	1332–1340	
	Holstein Counts (Norway, Pomerania)	
Waldemar IV Atterdag	1340–1375	
Olaf II, son of Margaret and Haakon	1375/76–1387	
Margaret I of Norway	1387–1412	
Eric VII of Pomerania	1412–1439	deposed, d. 1459

Name	Period	Status
	Palatinate	
Christopher III of Bavaria	1440–1448	
	Oldenburg Dynasty	
Christian I Oldenburg	1448–1481	
John I	1481–1513	

England

Name	Period	Status
	Wessex	
Cerdic or Cedric	519–534	
Cynric	534–560	
Ceawlin	560–592	deposed, d. 593
Ceol	592–597	
Ceolwulf	597–611	
Cynegils	611–642	
Cenwealh	642–672	
Æscwine	673–676	
Centwine	676–685/686	
Cædwalla	685/686–688	abdicated, d. 689
Ine	688–726	abdicated
Æthelheard	726–740	
Cuthred	740–756	
Sigeberht	756–757	
Cynewulf	757–786	
Berhtric	786–802	
Egbert	802–839	
Æthelwold (Æthelwulf)	839–858	
Æthelbald	858–860	
Æthelbert	860–866	
Æthelred I	866–871	
Alfred the Great	871–899	
	Northumbria	
Æthelfrith	592/593–616	
Edwin	616–633	
Oswald, Saint	633/634–641	
Oswy (Oswiu)	640/641–670	
Ecgfrith	670–685	
Aldfrith	685–705	
Eadwulf I	705–706	joint
Osred I	705–716	
Cenred	716–718	
Osric	718–729	
Ceolwulf	729–737	abdicated, d. 760
	Saxons	
Edward the Elder	899–924	
Æthelstan the Glorious	924–939/940	
Edmund I the Magnificent	939/940–946	
Eadred	946–955	
Edwig the Fair	955–959	Wessex only, 957–959
Edgar the Peaceable	957–975	Mercia and Northumbria, 957–959
Edward the Martyr, Saint	975–978	
Æthelred II the Unready (Unræd)	978–1016	
Swein Forkbeard	1013–1014	
Edmund II Ironside	1016	
	House of Denmark	
Canute the Great	1016–1035	
Harold I Harefoot	1035–1040	regent 1035–1037
Hardacanute	1040–1042	

Name	Period	Status
	House of Wessex	
Edward the Confessor, Saint	1042–1066	
Harold II Godewineson	1066	
	Norman Dynasty	
William I the Conqueror	1066–1087	
William II Rufus	1087–1100	
Henry I Beauclerc	1100–1135	
	House of Blois	
Stephen of Blois	1135–1154	
	Angevin (Plantagenet) Dynasty	
Henry II Fitzemperess or Plantagenet	1154–1189	
Henry	1170–1183	co-regent, d. 1183
Richard I Lionheart	1189–1199	
John Lackland	1199–1216	
	Plantagenet Dynasty	
Henry III	1216–1272	
Edward I Longshanks	1272–1307	
Edward II	1307–1327	deposed, d. 1327
Edward III	1327–1377	
Richard II	1377–1399	deposed, d. 1400
	Lancastrian Dynasty	
Henry IV	1399–1413	
Henry V	1413–1422	
Henry VI	1422–1471	deposed, restored, deposed
	Yorkist Dynasty	
Edward IV	1461–1483	
Edward V	1483	deposed, d.? 1483
Richard III	1483–1485	
	Tudor Dynasty	
Henry VII	1485–1509	

France

Merovingian Dynasty (some are only regional)

Name	Period	Status
Merovech	d. 458	
Childeric I	458–481/482	
Clovis	481/482–511	
Clothair I	511–558, 558–561	
Thierry I, king of Austrasia	511–543	
Clodomir I, king of Orléans	511–524	
Childebert I, king of Paris	511–558	
Charibert, king of Paris	561–567	
Guntram, king of Burgundy and Orléans	561–592	
Sigebert I, king of Austrasia	561–575	
Chilperic I, king of Soissons and Orléans	561–584	
Childebert II, king of Austrasia	575	
king of Burgundy and Orléans	593–596	
Thierry II (Theuderic), king of Burgundy	596–613	
Théodebert II, king of Austrasia	595–612	
Clothar II	584–629	sole king 613–629
Charibert, duke of Burgundy	628–631/632	
Dagobert I, sole king	629–639	
Clovis II, king of Neustria and Burgundy	637/638–656	king of France 656/7
Sigebert II, king of Austrasia, Saint	634–659	
Dagobert II, king of Austrasia, Saint	674–679	
Childeric II, king of Austrasia	656–670	king of France 670–673

Name	Period	Status
Clotaire III, king of Neustria and Burgundy	656–670	
Thierry III (Theuderic), king of Neustria and Burgundy	673	king of France 679–691
Clovis III	675–676	
Clovis IV	691–695	
Childebert III	694/695–711	
Dagobert III	711–715	
Chilperic III	715–720	
Thierry IV (Theuderic), king of Neustria and Burgundy	720/721–737	
Interregnum	737–742	
Childeric III	742–751/752	deposed

Pepinid Dynasty

Name	Period	Status
Pépin I of Landen	d. 640	mayor of the Palace
Pépin II of Héristal	d. 714	mayor of the Palace
Charles Martel	ca. 714–741	
Pépin III the Short	751–768	

Carolingian Dynasty (some are only regional, some outside present-day France, and some disputed)

Name	Period	Status
Charlemagne	768–814	
Carloman	768–771	joint
Louis I the Pious	814–840	
Charles, king of Neustria and Aquitaine	d. 811	
Pépin, king of Italy	d. 810	
Bernard, son of Pépin, king of Italy	810–818	
Charles I the Bald	843–877	
Lothair, emperor	840–855	
Pépin, king of Aquitaine	d. 838	
Louis the German, king of Germany	840–876	
Louis II the Stammerer	877–879	
Louis III	879–882	
Carloman	879–884	
Charles III the Simple	893–923	deposed
Charles II the Fat, emperor of Germany	876	king of France 884–887
Louis IV of Outremer	936–954	
Lothair	954–986	
Louis V the Sluggard	986–987	

Capetian Dynasty

Name	Period	Status
Hugh Capet	987–996	
Robert II the Pious	996–1031	
Henry I	1031–1060	
Philip I	1060–1108	
Louis VI the Fat	1108/09–1137	
Louis VII the Young	1137–1180	
Philip II Augustus	1180–1223	
Louis VIII the Lion	1223–1226	
Louis IX, Saint	1226–1270	
Philip III the Bold	1270–1285	
Philip IV the Fair	1285–1314	
Louis X the Quarrelsome	1314–1316	
Philip V the Tall	1316–1322	
Charles IV the Fair	1322–1328	

Valois Dynasty

Name	Period	Status
Philip VI of Valois	1328–1350	
John II the Good	1350–1364	
Charles V the Wise	1364–1380	
Charles VI the Well-Beloved (or the Mad)	1380–1422	
Charles VII the Victorious	1422–1461	
Louis XI	1461–1483	
Charles VIII	1483–1498	
Louis XII	1498–1515	

Name	Period	Status

Germanic Kingdoms

Vandals

Gaiseric	ca. 427/429–477	
Hunneric	477–484	
Gunthamund	484–496	
Thrasamund	496–523	
Hilderic	523–530	deposed
Gelimir	530–533/534	

Ostrogoths

Theodoric	493–526	
Athalric	526–534	
Theodahat	534–536	
Witigis	536–540	
Hildibad	540–541	
Eraric	541	
Totila (Baduila)	541–552	
Teia	552–553	

Visigoths

Alaric I	395–410	
Athaulf I	410–415	
Sigeric	415	
Wallia	415–418	
Theodoric I	418–451	
Thorismund	451–453	
Theodoric II	453–466	
Euric	466–483	
Alaric II	483–506/507	
Theodoric and Amalric	506–522	
Amalric	511–531	
Theudis	531–548	
Theudigisel	548–549	
Agila I	549–554	
Athanagild	554–567	
Leova I (Liuva)	567–572	Septimania
Leovigild	568/570–586	Spain, sole ruler
Recared I	586–601	
Leova II (Liuva)	601–603	
Witteric	603–610	
Gundimar	610–612	
Sisibut	612–620/621	
Recared II	620–621	
Swinthila	620–631	deposed
Sisinand	631–636	
Chintila	636–639/640	
Tulga	640–641/642	deposed
Chindaswinth	641/642–652/653	
Recceswinth	652–672	
Wamba	672–680	deposed
Erwig	680–687	
Egica	687–701/702	
Witiza	701/702–710	
Roderic	710–711	
Agila II	711–714	

Lombard Kings of Italy

House of Alboin

Alboin	568/569–572	
Cleph	572–573/574	

Name	Period	Status
Autheri	583/584–590	
Agilulf	590–615/616	
Adaloald	615–625/626	
Arioald	625/626–636	
Rothari	636–652	not of the House of Alboin
Aribert I	653–661/662	
Rodoald	652–653	not of the House of Alboin
Godebert	661–662	
Grimoald	662–671/672	
Perctarit	672–688	
Cunipert	688–700	
Liutbert	700–701	
Aribert II	701–711	
Ansprand	712	
Liutprand	712–743	
Hildebrand	743–744	
Ratchis	744–749, 756–757	deposed, restored
Aistulf	749–756	
Desiderius	756–774	

Holy Roman Empire after the Carolingians

Saxon Dynasty

Henry I the Fowler	919–936	
Otto I the Great	936–973	
Otto II	973–983	
Otto III	983–1002	
Henry II	1002–1024	

Salian or Franconian Dynasty

Conrad II the Salian	1024–1039	
Henry III the Salian	1039–1056	
Henry IV	1056–1105/06	deposed
Henry V	1105/06–1125	
Lothair III of Supplinburg, duke of Saxony	1125–1137	

Hohenstaufen Dynasty

Conrad III	1138–1152	
Frederick I Barbarossa	1152–1190	
Henry VI	1190–1196/97	
Philip of Swabia	1197–1208	
Otto IV of Brunswick	antiking 1198	deposed 1215
Frederick II	1215–1250	
Conrad IV	1250–1254	
William, count of Holland	antiking 1247–1256	
Conradin	1252–1268	
Interregnum	1254–1273	
Rudolf I of Habsburg	1273–1291	
Adolph of Nassau	1292–1298	deposed
Albert I of Austria	1298–1308	
Henry VII of Luxembourg	1308–1313	
Louis IV of Bavaria	1314–1346	
Charles IV	1346–1378	
Wenceslas	1378–1400	
Rupert of the Palatine	1400–1410	
Sigismund	1410–1437	

Habsburg Dynasty

Albert II	1438–1439	
Frederick III	1440–1493	
Maximilian I	1493–1519	

Name	Period	Status

Iberian Peninsula

Aragon (broken succession and rule by other dynasties)

Name	Period	Status
Aznar I Galindo	ca. 809–839	
Galindo I Aznarez	ca. 844–867	
Aznar II Galindo	867–893	
Galindo II Aznarez	893–922	
Sancho II Garcés	970–994	
Garcia II Sanchez	994–1000	
Sancho III Garcés el Mayor	1000–1035	
Ramiro I	1035–1063	
Sancho I Ramírez	1063–1094	co-regent 1062, king of Navarre 1076
Peter I	1094–1104	co-regent 1085
Alfonso I the Battler	1104–1134	
Ramiro II the Monk	1134–1137	
Petronilla	1137–1164	abdicated, d. 1173
Alfonso II the Chaste	1162–1196	
Peter II the Catholic	1196–1213	
James I the Conqueror	1213–1276	
Peter III the Great	1276–1285	
Alfonso III the Liberal	1285–1291	
James II the Just	1291–1327	
Alfonso IV the Benign	1327–1336	
Peter IV the Ceremonious	1336–1387	
John I the Hunter	1387–1395	
Martin I the Humane	1395–1410	
Ferdinand I Trastámara	1412–1416	
Alfonso V the Magnanimous	1416–1458	
John II	1458–1479	
Ferdinand II the Catholic	1479–1516	
Union with Castile	1479–1504 and from 1516	

Asturias-León-Castile

Name	Period	Status
Pelayo	718–737	
Fáfila	737–739	
Alfonso I the Catholic	739–757	
Fruela I	757–768	
Aurelio	768–774	
Silo	774–783	
Mauregato	783–788	
Vermudo I	788–791	abdicated
Alfonso II the Chaste	791–842	
Ramiro I	842–850	
Ordoño I	850–866	
Alfonso III the Great	866–910	deposed

Kings of León

Name	Period	Status
Garcia	910–914	
Ordoño II	914–924	
Fruela II	924–925	
Alfonso IV the Monk	925–930	abdicated, d. 933
Ramíro II	930–951	
Ordoño III	951–956	
Sancho I the Fat	956–966	
Ramíro III	966–984/985	
Vermudo II the Gouty	984–999	
Alfonso V	999–1028	
Vermudo III	1028–1037	

House of Navarre

Name	Period	Status
Ferdinand I of Castile and León	1035–1065	
Castile: Sancho II the Strong	1065–1072	

Name	Period	Status
León: Alfonso VI	1065–1109	Castile 1072–1109
Galicia: García	1065–1072	
Urraca and Raymond of Burgundy	1109–1126	
House of Burgundy		
Alfonso VII	1126–1157	
Castile: Sancho III the Desired	1157–1158	
León: Ferdinand II	1157–1188	
Castile: Alfonso VIII	1158–1214	
León: Alfonso IX	1188–1230	
Henry I	1214–1217	
Ferdinand III	1217–1252	León 1230–1252
Inigo Arista	ca. 810–851	
García Iniquez	851–870	
Fortun Garcés	870–905	
Sancho I Garcés	905–925/926	
Jimeno	925–931	
García I Sanchéz	931–970	
Sancho II Garcés	970–994	
García II Sanchéz the Tremulous	994–1000	
Sancho III Garcés the Great	1000–1035	
García III Sancéz of Nájera	1035–1054	
Sancho IV Garcés of Peñalén	1054–1076	
García IV Ramírez the Restorer	1134–1150	
Sancho VI the Wise	1150–1194	
Sancho VII the Strong	1194–1234	
House of Champagne		
Thibault I the Posthumous	1234–1253	
Thibault II	1253–1270	
Henry I the Fat	1270–1274	
House of France		
Joan I	1274–1305	
Louis X the Stubborn (Capetian)	1314–1316	union with France
Philip V	1316–1322	
Alfonso X	1252–1284	
Sancho IV	1284–1295	
Ferdinand IV	1295–1312	
Alfonso XI	1312–1350	
Peter I the Cruel	1350–1369	
House of Trastámara		
Henry II	1369–1379	
John I	1379–1390	
Henry III the Sickly	1390–1406	
John II	1406–1454	
Henry IV the Impotent	1454–1474	
Isabel I	1474–1504	and Ferdinand V 1474–1516
Catalonia and County of Barcelona		
Ramón Berenguer I the Elder	1035–1076	
Ramón Berenguer II the Towhead	1076–1082	
Berenguer Ramón II the Fratricide	1076–1097	
Ramón Berenguer III the Great	1097–1131	
Ramón Berenguer IV, Saint	1131–1162	
Alfonso	1162–1196, 1164	union with Aragon
Navarre		
Charles X (IV)	1322–1328	
Joan II	1328–1349	
Charles II the Bad	1349–1387	

Name	Period	Status
Charles III the Noble	1387–1425	

House of Aragon

Name	Period	Status
John II	1425–1479	king of Aragon 1458
Blanche	1425–1441	
Madeleine (Eleanor)	1479	
Francisco (Francis Fébus, Phoebus)	1479–1483	

Portugal

Name	Period	Status
Henry of Burgundy	1093–1112	
Afonso I Henriques	1112–1185	count, then king in 1139
Sancho I	1185–1211	
Afonso II the Fat	1211–1223	
Sancho II	1223–1248	
Afonso III	1248–1279	
Denis I the Farmer (Deniz)	1279–1325	
Afonso IV	1325–1357	
Peter I the Justicer	1357–1367	
Ferdinand I	1367–1383	

House of Avis

Name	Period	Status
John (João) I of Avis	1385–1433	
Duarte	1433–1438	
Afonso V	1438–1481	
John (João) II the Perfect Prince	1481–1495	
Manuel I the Fortunate	1495–1521	

Latin Kings of Jerusalem

Name	Period	Status
Godfrey of Bouillon, defender of the Holy Sepulcher	1099–1100	
Baldwin I	1100–1118	
Baldwin II of Bourg	1118–1131	
Fulk of Anjou	1131–1143	
Melisande, queen-regent	1143–1152	deposed, d. 1161
Baldwin III	1143–1162/63	
Amalric I	1162/63–1173/74	
Baldwin IV the Leper	1173/74–1185	
Baldwin V	1185–1186	
Sybil	1186–1190	
Guy de Lusignan	1186–1192	deposed, d. 1194

Norway

Yngling Dynasty

Name	Period	Status
Hafldan the Black	d. a. 880	
Harald I Fairhair	860/880–930/940	
Eric I Bloodaxe	930–934	deposed, d. 954
Haakon I the Good	933/934–959/961	
Harald II Graycloak	954/961–968	
Haakon II of Lade the Great	968–995	
Olaf I Tryggvason	994/995–999/1000	
Earls Eric and Sven	1000–1015/16	
Olaf II Haraldsson, Saint	1015/16–1030	
Canute II the Great and Sven Alfivason	1028–1035	
Magnus I the Good	1035–1046/47	
Harald III Hardraade the Pitiless	1047–1066	
Magnus II	1066–1069	
Olaf III Kyrri the Peaceful or Gentle	1066–1093	
Magnus III Barelegs	1093–1103	
Olaf IV	1103–1115/16	
Eystein I	1103–1122/23	
Sigurd I the Crusader	1103–1130	

Name	Period	Status
Magnus IV the Blind	1130–1135	deposed, d. 1139
Harald IV Gilchrist (Gille)	1130–1136	
Sigurd II the Mouth	1136–1139	
Inge I the Hunchback	1136–1161	
Eystein II	1142–1157	
Haakon II the Broadshouldered	1157–1162	
Magnus V Erlingsson	1161/62–1184	
Sverre Sigurdsson	1177–1202	
Haakon III	1202–1204	
Guttorm	1204	
Inge II Bardson	1204–1217	
Haakon IV the Old	1217–1263	
Haakon the Younger	1240–1257	co-regent 1240–1257, joint from 1257
Magnus VI the Lawmender	1263–1280	
Eric II the Priesthater	1280–1299	
Haakon V Longlegs	1299–1319	

Folkung Dynasty or House of Sweden

Name	Period	Status
Magnus VII Eriksson	1319–1355	(Magnus II Eriksson of Sweden, d. 1374)
Haakon VI	1355–1380	co-regent from 1343
Olaf IV	1380–1387	
Margaret of Denmark	1387/8–1405	
Erik of Pomerania	1389–1442	
Christopher of Bavaria	1442–1448	
Charles VIII Canutesson and Christian of Oldenburg, rival	1448–1457, 1464–1465, 1467–1470	deposed, restored, deposed restored
Christian I	1457–1481	
Interregnum	1481–1483	
John II	1483–1513	

Scotland

Alpin, Dunkeld, Moray, and Canmore Dynasties

Name	Period	Status
House of Alpin		
Kenneth I MacAlpin	843–858	
Donald I	858–862	
Constantine I	862–876/877	
Aed	876/877–878	
Eochaid and Giric	878–889	
Donald II	889–900	
Constantine II	900–943	
Malcolm I	943–954	
Indulf	954–962	
Dubh (Duf)	962–966	
Culén	966–971	
Kenneth II	971–995	
Constantine III	995–997	
Kenneth III and Giric (son)	997–1005	
House of Dunkeld		
Malcolm II	1005–1034	
Duncan I	1034–1040	
House of Moray		
Macbeth	1040–1057/58	
Lulach	1057/58	
House of Dunkeld		
Malcolm III Canmore	1058–1093	
Donald III Bán	1093–1097	
Duncan II	1094	

Name	Period	Status
Edgar	1097–1107	
Alexander I	1107 1124	
David I, Saint	1124–1153	
Malcolm IV the Maiden	1153–1165	
William I the Lion	1165–1214	
Alexander II	1214–1249	
Alexander III	1249–1286	

House of Norway

Margaret of Norway	1286–1290	

Balliol, Bruce, and Stuart (Stewart) Dynasties

John Balliol (Toom Tabard)	1291/92–1296	
Robert I the Bruce	1306–1329	
David II	1329–1371	
Robert II	1371–1390	
Robert III	1390–1406	
James I	1406–1437	
James II	1437–1460	
James III	1460–1488	
James IV	1488–1513	

Rulers of Sicily (dukes, counts, kings) Title and possession were disputed but claimed by two dynasties after 1282

Roger I the Great Count	1061–1101	
Simon, Count	1101–1105	
Roger II the Great	1105–1154, king from 1130	
William I the Bad	1154–1166	
William II the Good	1166–1189	
Tancred of Lecce	1189–1194	
William III	1194	deposed, d. 1198?
Henry VI	1194–1197/98	
Frederick II (I)	1197/98–1250	
Conrad IV	1250–1254	
Interregnum	1254–1258	
Manfred	1258–1266	

House of Anjou and Kings of Naples

Charles I of Anjou	1266–1285	lost Sicily from 1282
Charles II the Lame	1289–1309	
Robert the Wise	1309–1343	
Joan I	1343–1381	deposed, d. 1382
Louis of Taranto	1352–1362	
Charles III of Durazzo	1382–1386	
Louis of Anjou	1383–1384	
Ladislas III of Durazzo	1390–1414	
Louis (Ladislas) II of Anjou	1384/86–1414/17	
Joan II	1414–1435	
Jacques de la Marche	1415–1419	
Louis III of Anjou	1417–1434	
René of Anjou (the Good)	1434–1442/43	deposed, d. 1480
Alfonso I the Magnanimous of Aragon	1443–1458	
Ferdinand I	1458–1494	
Ferdinand II	1495–1496	
Frederick	1496–1501	deposed, d. 1504

House of Aragon from 1282

Peter I the Great	1282–1285	
James the Just	1285–1295	abdicated, d. 1327
Frederick II	1296–1337	
Peter II	1337–1342	
Louis	1342–1355	

Name	Period	Status
Frederick III the Simple	1355–1377	
Mary	1377–1401	and Martin I the Younger 1390–1409
Martin II the Humane	1409–1410	

Sweden

Early Rulers

Eric	ca. 800	
Anund and Björn	ca. 825	
Olaf	ca. 850	
Ring	ca. 930	
Eric and Edmund	ca. 935	
Emund Ericsson	ca. 970	

Yngling House

Eric the Victorious	980–995	
Olaf Skötkonung	995–1022	
Anund Jacob	1022–1056	
Edmund the Old	1056–1060	

Stenkil House

Stenkil Ragnvaldsson	ca. 1060–1066	
Halsten and Inge the Elder	ca. 1080–1110/11, ca. 1111–1112	deposed, restored
Philip	1110–1118	
Inge II the Younger	1118–1130	

Sverker and Eric Dynasties

Sverker I the Elder	1131–1155/56	
Eric IX, Saint	ca. 1155/56–1160	
Magnus Henriksson	1160–1161	
Charles VII Sverkersson	1161–1167	
Kol Jonsson	1167–1173	
Canute Eriksson	1167–1196	
Sverker II Charlesson	1196–1208	deposed, d. 1210
Eric X Canutesson	1208–1216	
John I Sverkersson	1216–1222	
Eric XI Ericsson	1222–1229, 1234–1250	deposed, restored
Canute II the Tall	1229–1234	

Folkung Dynasty

Birger Jarl	1250–1266	regent
Waldemar	1250–1275	deposed, d. 1302
Magnus I Barnlock	1275–1290	
Birger	1290–1318, regent 1298	deposed, 1321
Magnus II Eriksson	regent, 1319–1332, 1319–1363	also king of Norway, deposed, d. 1374
Eric XII Magnusson	1357–1359	co-regent from 1344
Hagon Magnusson	1362–1365	deposed

House of Mecklenburg

Albert of Mecklenburg	1364–1389	
Margaret of Denmark	regent, 1389–1412	
Eric XIII of Pomerania	regent, 1396–1400, 1396–1439	
Engelbrekt	regent, 1435–1436	
Charles Canutesson	1436–1440	regent
Christopher of Bavaria	1440–1448	
Charles VIII Canutesson	1448–1457, 1465, 1467–1470	deposed, restored, deposed
Christian I of Oldenburg	1457–1464, 1465–1467	deposed, restored, deposed
Sten Sture the Elder	1470–1497, 1501–1503	regent
John II	1497–1501	king of Denmark 1483–1513 deposed

CHRISTIAN RELIGIOUS LEADERS

Name	Period	Status
Patriarchs of Constantinople, 582–1464		
John IV Mesteues the Faster	582–595	
Kyriacus	595–606	
Thomas I	607–610	
Sergios I	610–638	
Pyrrhos	638–641	
Paul II	641–653	
Pyrrhos (second tenure)	654	
Peter	654–666	
Thomas II	667–669	
John V	669–675	
Constantine I	675–677	
Theodore I	677–679	
George I	679–686	
Theodore I (second tenure)	686–687	
Paul III	688–694	
Kallinicos I	694–706	
Kyros	706–712	
John VI	712–715	
Germanos I	715–730	
Anastasios	730–754	
Constantine II	754–766	
Niketas I	766–780	
Paul IV	780–784	
Tarasios	784–806	
Nikephoros I	806–815	
Theodotos Kassiteras	815–821	
Anthony I Kassimatas	821–ca. 837	
John VII Grammatikos	ca. 837–843	
Methodios I	843–847	
Ignatios	847–858	
Photios	858–867	
Ignatios (second tenure)	867–877	
Photios (second tenure)	877–886	
Stephen I	886–893	
Anthony II Kauleas	893–901	
Nicholas I Mysticos	901–907	
Euthymios I	907–912	
Nicholas I Mysticus (second tenure)	912–925	
Stephen II	925–927	
Tryphon	927–931	
Theophylaktos	933–956	
Polyeuktus	956–970	
Basil I Skamandrenos	970–974	
Anthony III Stoudites	974–979	
Nicholas II Chrysoberges	979–991/992	
Vacancy	992–996	
Sisinnios II	996–998	
Sergios II	1001–1019	
Eustathios	1019–1025	
Alexios of Stoudites	1025–1043	
Michael I Kerularios	1043–1058	
Constantine III Leichoudes	1059–1063	
John VIII Xiphilinos	1064–1075	
Kosmas I	1075–1081	
Eustratios Garidas	1081–1084	
Nicholas III Grammatikos	1084–1111	

Name	Period	Status
John IX Agepetos	1111–1134	
Leo Styppeiotes	1134–1143	
Michael II Kourkouas	1143–1146	
Kosmas II Attikos	1146–1147	
Nicholas IV Mouzalon	1147–1151	
Theodotos II	1151–1153	
Neophytos I	1153/54	
Constantine IV Chliarenos	1154–1157	
Luke Chrysoberges	1157–1169/70	
Michael III	1170–1178	
Chariton Eugeniotes	1178–1179	
Theodosios Boradiotes	1179–1183	
Basil II Kamateros	1183–1186	
Niketas II Mountanes	1186–1189	
Dositheus of Jerusalem	February 1189	
Leontios Theotokites	1189	
Dositheus of Jerusalem (second tenure)	1189–1191	
George II Xiphilinos	1191–1198	
John X Kamateros	1198–1206	
Michael IV Autorianos	1208–1214	
Theodore II Eirenikos	1214–1216	
Maximos II	1216	
Manuel I Sarantenos	1217–1222	
Germanos II	1222–1240	
Methodios II	1240	
Manuel II	1243/44–1255	
Arsenios Autorianos	1255–1259	
Nikephorus II	1260–1261	
Arsenios Autorianos (second tenure)	1261–1265	
Germanos III	1265–1266/67	
Joseph I	1266–1275	
John XI Bekkos	1275–1282	
Joseph I (second tenure)	1282–1283	
Gregory II of Cyprus	1283–1289	
Athanasios I	1289–1293	
John XII Kosmas	1294–1303	
Athanasios I (second tenure)	1303–1309	
Niphon I	1310–1314	
John XIII Glykys	1315–1319	
Gerasimos I	1320–1321	
Isaias	1323–1332	
John XIV Kalecas	1334–1347	
Isidore I Boucheiras	1347–1350	
Kallistos I	1350–1353	
Philotheos Kokkinos	1353–1354	
Kallistos I (second tenure)	1355–1363	
Philotheos Kokkinos (second tenure)	1364–1376	
Makarios	1376–1379	
Neilos Kerameus	1379–1388	
Anthony IV	1389–1390	
Makarios (second tenure)	1390–1391	
Antony IV (second tenure)	1391–1397	
Kallistus II Xanthopoulos	1397	
Matthew I	1397–1402, 1403–1410	
Euthymios II	1410–1416	
Joseph II	1416–1439	
Metrophanes II	1440–1443	
Gregory III Mammas	1443–1450?	
Athanasios II	1450	
Gennadios II Scholarios	1454–1456, 1463, 1464–1465	

Name	Period	Status
Popes, 440–1503		
Leo I the Great, Saint	440–461	
Hilary, Saint	461–468	
Simplicius, Saint	468–483	
Felix III (II), Saint	483–492	
Gelasius I, Saint	492–496	
Anastasius II	496–498	
Symmachus, Saint	498–514	
Hormisdas, Saint	514–523	
John I, Saint	523–526	
Felix IV (III), Saint	526–530	
Boniface II	530–532	
John II	533–535	
Agapitus I, Saint	535–536	
Silverius, Saint	536–537	
Vigilius	537–555	
Pelagius I	556–561	
John III	561–574	
Benedict I	575–579	
Pelagius II	579–590	
Gregory I the Great, Saint	590–604	
Sabinian	604–606	
Boniface III	607	
Boniface IV, Saint	608–615	
Deusdedit (Adeodatus), Saint	615–618	
Boniface V	619–625	
Honorius I	625–638	
Severinus	640	
John IV	640–642	
Theodore I	642–649	
Martin I, Saint	649–655	
Eugenius (Eugene) I, Saint	654–657	
Vitalian, Saint	657–672	
Adeodatus II	672–676	
Donus	676–678	
Agatho, Saint	678–681	
Leo II, Saint	682–683	
Benedict II, Saint	684–685	
John V	685–686	
Conon	686–687	
Sergius I, Saint	687–701	
John VI	701–705	
John VII	705–707	
Sisinnius	708	
Constantine	708–715	
Gregory II, Saint	715–731	
George III, Saint	731–741	
Zacharias (Zachary), Saint	741–752	
Stephen II (III)	752–757	
Paul I, Saint	757–767	
Stephen III (IV)	768–772	
Hadrian (Adrian) I	772–795	
Leo III, Saint	795–816	
Stephen IV (V)	816–817	
Paschal I, Saint	817–824	
Eugenius (Eugene) II	824–827	
Valentine	827	
Gregory IV	827–844	
Sergius II	844–847	
Leo IV, Saint	847–855	
Benedict III	855–858	
Nicholas I the Great, Saint	858–867	

Name	Period	Status
Hadrian (Adrian) II	867–872	
John VIII	872–882	
Marinus I	882–884	
Adrian (Hadrian) III	884–885	
Stephen V (VI)	885–891	
Formosus	891–896	
Boniface VI	896	
Stephen VI (VII)	896–897	
Romanus	897	
Theodore II	897	
John IX	898–900	
Benedict IV	900–903	
Leo V	903	
Sergius III	904–911	
Anastasius III	911–913	
Lando (Landus)	913–914	
John X	914–928	
Leo VI	928	
Stephen VII (VIII)	928–931	
John XI	931–935/936	
Leo VII	936–939	
Stephen VIII (IX)	939–942	
Marinus II	942–946	
Agapitus II	946–955	
John XII	955–964	
Leo VIII	963–965	
Benedict V	964	
John XIII	965–972	
Benedict VI	973–974	
Benedict VII	974–983	
John XIV	983–984	
John XV	985–996	
Gregory V	996–999	
Sylvester II	999–1003	
John XVII	1003	
John XVIII	1003/04–1009	
Sergius IV	1009–1012	
Benedict VIII	1012–1024	
John XIX	1024–1032	
Benedict IX	1032–1044	
Sylvester III	1045	
Benedict IX	second reign, 1045	
Gregory VI	1045–1046	
Clement II	1046–1047	
Benedict IX	third reign, 1047–1048	
Damasus II	1048	
Leo IX, Saint	1049–1054	
Victor II	1055–1057	
Stephen IX (X)	1057–1058	
Nicholas II	1058–1061	
Alexander II	1061–1073	
Gregory VII, Saint	1073–1085	
Victor III, Blessed	1087	
Urban II, Blessed	1088–1099	
Paschal II	1099–1118	
Gelasius II	1118–1119	
Calixtus (Callistus) II	1119–1124	
Honorius II	1124–1130	
Innocent II	1130–1143	
Celestine II	1143–1144	
Lucius II	1144–1145	
Eugenius (Eugene) III, Blessed	1145–1153	

Name	Period	Status
Anastasius IV	1153–1154	
Hadrian (Adrian) IV	1154–1159	
Alexander III	1159–1181	
Lucius III	1181–1185	
Urban III	1185–1187	
Gregory VIII	1187	
Clement III	1187–1191	
Celestine III	1191–1198	
Innocent III	1198–1216	
Honorius III	1216–1227	
Gregory IX	1227–1241	
Celestine IV	1241	
Innocent IV	1243–1254	
Alexander IV	1254–1261	
Urban IV	1261–1264	
Clement IV	1265–1268	
Gregory X, Blessed	1271–1276	
Innocent V, Blessed	1276	
Hadrian (Hadrian) V	1276	
John XXI	1276–1277	
Nicholas III	1277–1280	
Martin IV	1281–1285	
Honorius IV	1285–1287	
Nicholas IV	1288–1292	
Celestine V, Saint	1293–1294	
Boniface VIII	1294–1303	
Benedict XI, Blessed	1303–1304	
Clement V	1305–1314	
John XXII	1316–1334	
Benedict XII	1335–1342	
Clement VI	1342–1352	
Innocent VI	1352–1362	
Urban V, Blessed	1362–1370	
Gregory XI	1371–1378	
Urban VI	1378–1389	
Boniface IX	1389–1404	
Innocent VII	1404–1406	
Gregory XII	1406–1415	
Martin V	1417–1431	
Eugenius (Eugene) IV	1431–1447	
Nicholas V	1447–1455	
Callixtus (Calistus) III	1455–1458	
Pius II	1458–1464	
Paul II	1464–1471	
Sixtus IV	1471–1484	
Innocent VIII	1484–1492	
Alexander VI	1492–1503	

EASTERN AND CENTRAL EUROPE

Name	Period	Status

Bohemia

Dukes

Name	Period	Status
Bohvoj I	ca. 850–894	
Spitigniev I	ca. 895–ca. 905/915	
Vratislav I	ca. 905/915–921	
Wenceslas (Václav), Saint	921–929/935	
Boleslav I the Cruel	929/935–967/972	

Name	Period	Status
Boleslav II the Pious	967/973–999	
Boleslav III the Red	999–1003	deposed
Vladivoj	1002–1003	deposed
Jaromír	1003, 1004–1112, 1033–1034	deposed, restored, deposed, restored, deposed, d. 1035
Boleslav (I) the Brave, duke of Poland	1003–1004	deposed
Oldřich (Udalrich)	1012–1033, 1034	deposed, d. 1034
Bretislav I	1034–1055	
Spitigniev II	1055–1061	
Vratislav II	1061–1092, crowned king 1085	
Conrad I Otto	1092	
Bretislav II	1092–1100	
Bohvoj II	1100–1107, 1117–1121	deposed, d. 1124
Svatopluk	1107–1109	
Vladislav I	1109–1117, 1121–1125	abdicated
Sobieslav I Oldřich	1125–1140	
Vladislav II	1140–1172, king 1158	abdicated, d. 1174
Frederick	1172–1173, 1178	deposed, restored
Sobieslav II	1173–1178	
Conrad II Otto	1189–1191	
Wenceslas II	1191–1192	deposed
Premysl Ottokar I	1192–1193, 1197, king 1198–1230	deposed, restored, crowned 1198
Henry Bretislav, bishop of Prague	1193–1197	
Vladislav III Henry	1197	abdicated, d. 1222

Kings

Premysl Ottokar I	1198–1230	crowned 1198
Wenceslas I (Vaclav)	1230–1253	
Premysl Ottokar II the Great	1253–1278	
Wenceslas II (Vaclav)	1278–1305	
Wenceslas III	1305–1306	
Rudolf of Habsburg	1306–1307	
Henry of Carinthia	1307–1310	deposed, d. 1335

House of Luxembourg

John the Blind of Luxembourg	1310–1346	
Charles I (IV)	1346–1378, emperor 1355	
Wenceslas IV	1378–1419, king of the Romans 1378–1400	
Sigismund	1419–1437, emperor 1433	
Albert II of Habsburg	1437–1439	
Interregnum	1439–1453	
Ladislas Posthumous	1453–1457	
George of Podebrady	1458–1471	
Ladislas II (Vladislav)	1471–1516	

Bulgaria

First Bulgarian Empire

Asparuch (Asparukh)	680–701	
Tervel	700/701–718	
Kormisos	721–738	
Sevar	724–739	
Vinech	736–760/762	
Teletz	762–764	
Sabin	764–766	deposed
Umar (Omar)	767	deposed
Toktu	766–772	
Pagan	772	
Telerig	ca. 772–777	deposed
Kardam	777–ca. 803	
Krum	803–814	
Omurtag	814–831	
Malamir	831–836	

Name	Period	Status
Presiam (possibly Malomir)	836–852	
Boris I (Michael)	852–889	abdicated, d. 907
Vladimir	889–893	deposed
Symeon I	893–927	
Peter	927–969	abdicated, d. 969
Boris II	969–971/972	deposed, d. 976

Macedonian Empire

Samuel	980–1014	crowned 997
Gabriel Radomir	1014–1015	
John (Ivan) Vladislav	1015–1018	

Second Bulgarian Empire

Peter II	1185–1187, 1196–1197	deposed, restored
Asen I	1187–1196	
Kalojan (Kaloyan)	1197–1207	
Boril	1207–1218	deposed
John (Ivan) Asen II	1218–1241	
Koloman I Asen	1241–1246	
Michael II Asen	1246–1256	
Koloman II	1256–1257	
Constantine Tich	1257–1277	
Ivaljo	1278–1279	deposed, d. 1280
John (Ivan) Asen III	1279–1280	deposed

House of Terter

George I Terter	1280–1292	deposed
Smiletz (Smilets)	1292–1298	
Interregnum	ca. 1298–1300	
Caka	1300	deposed
Theodore Svetoslav	1300–1322	
George II Terter	1322–1323	

House of Sisman

Michael III Sisman	1323–1330	
John (Ivan) Stephen	1330–1331	
John (Ivan) Alexander	1331–1371	
John (Ivan) Sisman	1371–1393	
John (Ivan) Stracimir	1365–1396	

Byzantine and Roman Empires

Late Roman Empire

Dynasty of Constantine

Constantine I the Great	324–337	
Constantius	337–361	
Constantine II	337–340	
Constans I	337–350	
Constantine II	337–361	
Magnentius	350–353	
Julian the Apostate	361–363	
Jovian	363–364	

Dynasty of Valentinian

Valentinian I	364–375	
Valens	364–378	
Gratian	375–383	co-regent 376
Valentinian II	375–392	

The Roman Empire splits into the Eastern and the Western Empires under Theodosios I the Great

Western Empire

Honorius	395–423	
Constantius III	421	

Name	Period	Status
John	423–425	
Valentinian III	425–455	
Petronius Maximus	455	
Avitus	455–456	
Majorian	457–461	
Libius Severus	461–465	
Anthemius	467–472	
Olybrius	472	
Glycerius	473–474	deposed
Julius Nepos	474–475	
Romanus (Romulus) Augustus	475–476	deposed

Eastern Empire

Dynasty of Theodosios

Theodosios (Theodosius) I the Great	379–395	
Arkadios	395–408	co-regent 383
Theodosius II	408–450	co-regent 402
Marcian	450–457	

Dynasty of Leo

Leo I the Thracian	457–474	
Leo II	473/474	co-regent 473
Zeno the Isaurian	474–475, 476–491	deposed, restored
Basiliskos	475–476	
Anastasios I	491–518	

Dynasty of Justin

Justin I	518–527	
Justinian I the Great	527–565	co-regent 527
Justin II	565–578	
Tiberios I (II) Constantine	578–582	co-regent 578
Maurice	582–602	co-regent 582
Phokas	602–610	

Dynasty of Herakleios

Herakleios (Heraclios)	610–641	
Herakleios Constantine III	641	co-regent 613
Heraklonas	641	co-regent 638, deposed
Constans II Pogonatos	641–668	co-regent 641
Constantine IV	668–685	co-regent 776, deposed
Justinian II	685–695, 705–711	deposed, restored
Leontios	695–698	deposed, d. 706?
Tiberios II (III)	698–705	deposed, d. 706
Philippikos	711–713	deposed
Anastasios II	713–715	deposed d. 719
Theodosius III	715–717	deposed

Isaurian or Syrian Dynasty

Leo III the Syrian	717–741	
Constantine V Kopronymos	741–775	co-regent 720, deposed
Artavasdus	741–743	deposed
Leo IV the Khazar	775–780	co-regent 751
Constantine VI	780–797	co-regent, deposed
Irene	797–802	co-regent 780–790, 793–797, deposed, d. 803
Nikephoros I	802–811	
Staurakios	811	co-regent 803, deposed, d. 812
Michael I Rangabè	811–813	deposed, d. 844
Leo V the Armenian	813–820	

Amorian Dynasty

Michael II the Amorian	820–829	
Theophilos	829–842	co-regent 821
Michael III the Drunkard	842–867	co-regent 840

Name	Period	Status
Macedonian Dynasty		
Basil I the Macedonian	867–886	co-regent 866
Leo VI the Wise	886–912	co-regent 870
Alexander	912–913	co-regent 879
Regency for Constantine VII Porphyrogenitus	913–920	
Romanos I Lekapenos	920–944	deposed, d. 948
Christopher Lekapenos		921–931
Stephen and Constantine Lekapenos	944–945	
Constantine VII Porphyrogenitus	913–959	
Romanos II	959–963	
Nikephoros II Phokas	963–969	
John I Tzimiskes	969–976	
Basil II the Bulgar Slayer	976–1025	
Constantine VIII	1025–1028	co-regent 962
Romanos III Argyros	1028–1034	
Michael IV the Paphlagonian	1034–1041	
Michael V Kalaphates (The Caulker)	1041–1042	deposed
Zoë and Theodora	1042	co-regent 1028–1050
Constantine IX Monomachos	1042–1055	
Theodora	1055–1056	
Michael VI Straitiokos	1056–1057	deposed
Isaac I Komnenos	1057–1059	abdicated, d. 1060
Doukas Dynasty		
Constantine X Doukas	1059–1067	
Eudocia	1067–1068, 1071	deposed
Romanos IV Diogenes	1067–1071	deposed, d. 1072
Michael VII Doukas Parapinaces	1071–1078	co-regent, deposed
Nikephorus III Botaneiates	1078–1081	deposed
Komnenian Dynasty		
Alexios I Komnenos	1081–1118	
John II Komnenos	1118–1143	co-regent 1092
Manuel I Komnenos	1143–1180	
Alexios II Komnenos	1180–1183	
Andronikos I Komnenos	1183–1185	co-regent 1183
Angelos Dynasty		
Isaac II Angelos	1185–1195, 1203–1204	deposed, restored
Alexios III Angelos	1195–1203	deposed
Alexios IV Angelos	1203–1204	deposed, d. 1204
Alexios V Doukas	1204	
Lascarid Dynasty		
Theodore I Laskaris	1205–1221/22	
John III Vatatzes	1222–1254	
Theodore II Laskaris	1254–1258	
John IV Laskaris	1258–1261	deposed, d. 1305?
Palaiologos Dynasty		
Michael VIII Palaiologos	1258/59–1282	co-regent 1259
Andronikos II Palaiologos	1282–1328	co-regent 1272, deposed, d. 1332
Michael IX Palaiologos	1294/95–1320	
Andronikos III Palaiologos	1328–1341	co-regent 1325
John V Palaiologos	1341–1376, 1379–1390, 1390–1391	deposed, restored, deposed, restored
John VI Kantakouzenos	1347–1354	deposed, d. 1383
Matthew I Kantakouzenos	1353–1357	deposed, d. 1383
Andronikos IV Palaiologos	1376–1379	deposed, d. 1385
John VII Palaiologos	1390, 1399–1408	deposed, restored
Manuel II Palaiologos	1391–1425	co-regent 1373
John VIII Palaiologos	1425–1448	co-regent, 1421
Constantine XI Deragases	1449–1453	

Name	Period	Status

Latin Empire of Constantinople and States in Greece
House of Flanders

Baldwin I of Flanders	1204–1205	deposed, d. 1206?
Henry I of Hainault	1206–1216	regent 1205–1206

House of Courtenay

Peter I of Courtenay	1217	deposed, d. 1218/9
Yolanda (Isabel)	1217–1219	
Robert I of Courtenay	1221–1228	
John of Brienne, co-emperor	1231–1237	
Baldwin II	1240–1261	deposed, d. 1273

Despotate of Epiros

Michael I Komnenos Doukas	1204–ca. 1215
Theodore Komnenos Doukas	ca. 1215–1230
Manuel Angelos	1230–ca. 1240
John	1240–1244
Demetrios Angelos Doukas	1244–1246

Despots of Epiros

Michael II Komnenos Doukas	ca. 1227–1267/68
Nikephorus I Komnenos Doukas	1267–1296/98
Thomas Doukas	1296–1318
Nicholas Orsini	1318–1323
John Orsini	1323–1355
Nikephoros II	1335–1340

Hungary
Arpád Dynasty

Géza	972–997	
Stephen I, Saint	997–1038	
Peter Urseolo or Orseolo	1038–1041, 1044–1046	deposed, restored
Samuel Aba	1041–1044	
Andrew I	1047–1061	
Béla I	1061–1063	
Solomon (Salamon)	1063–1074	
Géza I	1074–1077	
Ladislas I, Saint	1077–1095	
Coloman I	1095–1114	
Stephen II	1114–1131	
Béla II the Blind	1131–1141	
Géza II	1141–1161/62	
Stephen III	1161/62–1172/73	
Béla III	1172/73–1196	
Emeric I	1196–1204	
Ladislas III	1204–1205	
Andrew II	1205–1235	
Béla IV	1235–1270	
Stephen V	1270–1272	
Ladislas IV the Cumanian	1272–1290	
Andrew III	1290–1301	
Interregnum	1301–1307/08	
Wenceslas III Premysl of Bohemia	1305–1306	
Charles Robert I of Anjou	1307/08–1342	
Louis I the Great of Anjou	1342–1382	
Mary of Anjou	1382–1385	
Charles II of Durazzo	1385–1386	
Sigismund of Luxembourg	1387–1437	
Albert II of Habsburg	1437–1439	
Ladislas (Vladislav, Wladysav) I (III) of Poland	1441–1444	

Name	Period	Status
Ladislas V Posthumous	1444/45–1457	
Matthias I Corvinus	1458–1490	

Poland

Piast Dynasty

Piast		
Siemowit (Ziemowit)		
Leszek (Lestko)		
Siemomysl (Ziemomysl)		
Mieszko I	ca. 963–992	
Boleslav I the Brave	992–1025	
Mieszko II Lambert	1025–1034	
Interregnum	1034–1039	
Casimir I the Restorer	1039–1058	
Boleslav II the Bold	1058–1079	exiled in 1079
Ladislav I Herman	1079–1102	
Zbigniev	1102–1108	deposed
Boleslav III the Wrymouthed	1102–1138	

Seniors and Dukes of Cracow

Wladyslav II the Exile	1138–1146	deposed, d. 1159
Boleslav IV the Curly	1146–1173	

Silesian Piasts

Mieszko III the Old	1173–1177, 1199–1202	deposed, restored
Casimir II the Just	1177–1194	
Leszik I the White	1194–1199, 1202–1227	
Konrad of Mazovia	1229–1232, 1241–1243	deposed, restored, deposed, d. 1247
Henry I the Bearded	1228–1229, 1232–1238	deposed, restored
Henry II the Pious	1238–1241	
Boleslav V the Chaste	1243–1279	
Leszek II the Black	1279–1288	
Henry III Probus	1288–1290	
Vaclav II, king of Bohemia	1289–1292	
Premysl II, duke of Greater Poland	1295–1296	

House of Bohemia

Wenceslas (Vaclav) II of Bohemia	1290/01–1305	

House of Piast

Ladislas I the Short	1305–1333	
Casimir III the Great	1333–1370	

House of Anjou

Louis I the Great of Hungary	1370–1382	

Jagiello Dynasty and House of Lithuania

Jadwiga (Hedwig) and Ladislas II Jagiello	1382–1399	
Ladislas II (sole ruler)	1399–1434	
Ladislas III	1434–1444	
Interregnum	1444–1446/47	
Casimir IV Jagiellonczyk	1446/47–1492	
John I Albert	1492–1501	

Russia

Rurik Dynasty (some are only regional)

Princes of Kiev

Rurik	862–879	
Oleg	879–912	
Igor I	913–945	

Name	Period	Status
Olga	945–969	
Sviatoslav	962–971/972	
Yaropolk I	973–980	
Vladimir I the Great, Saint	978/80–1015	
Sviatoslav the Damned	1015–1019	
Yaroslav I the Wise	1019–1054	
Izyaslav I	1054–1068, 1069–1073, 1077–1078	deposed, restored, deposed, restored
Vseslav	1068–1069	deposed
Sviatoslav	1073–1076	
Vsevolod I	1076–1077, 1078–1093	deposed, restored
Svatapolk II	1093–1113	
Vladimir II Monomakh	1113–1125	
Mstislav	1125–1132	
Yaropolk II	1132–1139	
Vsevold II	1139–1146	
Igor II	1146	deposed, d. 1147
Izyaslav (Volyn) II	1146–1154	
Izyaslav III	1154–1155, 1157–1158	deposed, restored
Yurii I Dolgorukii (Suzdal)	1154/55–1157	
Mstislav II	1157–1158, 1167–1169	deposed, restored, deposed, d. 1170
Rostislav I	1159–1161, 1161–1167	deposed, restored
Gleb	1169–1171	

Princes of Vladimir

Name	Period	Status
Andrei I Bogolyubskii	1157–1174	
Roman	1172–1205	
Michael	1174–1176	
Vsevolod III Big Nest	1176–1212	
Constantine	1212–1218/19	
Yurii II	1212–1238, 1218–1238	deposed, restored
Daniel	1230–1264	
Vasilko	1230–1269	
Yaroslav II	1236/8–1246	
Yaroslav (Tver)	1236–1273	
Sviatoslav	1246–1248	deposed, d. 1253
Andrew II (Suzdal)	1246–1252	deposed, d. 1264
Alexander I Nevsky, Saint	1252–1263	
Yaroslav III	1264–1271	
Vasilii	1272–1277	
Dimitri I	1277–1282, 1283–1294	
Daniel Nevsky	1263–1304	prince of Moscow from 1263
Andrei III	1282–1283, 1294–1304	deposed, restored
Michael II, Saint	1304/05–1319/20	
Yurii III	1318/19–1325	prince of Moscow 1303–1325, deposed
Alexander III	1326–1328	

Grand Princes of Moscow

Name	Period	Status
Ivan I Kalita	1328–1340/41	prince of Moscow from 1325
Simeon (Semyon) the Proud	1340/41–1353	
Ivan II the Red or the Meek	1353–1359	
Dimitri II	1359–1362	
Dimitri III Donskoi	1362–1389	
Basil (Vasily) Dimitrievitch I	1389–1425	
Basil (Vasily) Dimitrievitch II the Blind	1425–1462	
Ivan III the Great	1462–1505	

Serbia

Name	Period	Status
John Vlastimir	mid-ninth century	
Mutimir	ca. 891	

Name	Period	Status
Proslav	891–892	
Peter Gojnikovic	892–917	
Paul (Pavel) Branovic	917–920	
Zacharias (Zaharije) Prvoslavljevic	920–ca. 924	
Caslav Klonimirovic	927–after 950	

Zeta Dynasty

Name	Period	Status
John Vladimir, Saint	d. 1018	
Stephen Vojislav	ca. 1040–ca. 1052	
Michael	ca. 1052–ca. 1081/82	
Constantine Bodin	ca. 1081–ca. 1101	

Rascia and Nemanjíci Dynasties

Name	Period	Status
Vukan	ca. 1083–1114	
Uroš	1125	
Various rulers	ca. 1114–1167	
Stephen Nemanja	ca. 1167–1196	abdicated, d. 1200
Stephen I the First Crowned, Saint	1196–ca. 1228	crowned 1217
Stephen Radoslav	ca. 1228–1233/34	
Stephen Vladislav	ca. 1233/34–1242/44	
Stephen Uroš I	1242/43–1276	
Stephen Dragutin	1276–1282	
Stephen Uroš II Milutin	1282–1321	
Stephen Uroš III Dečanski	1321–1331	
Stephen Dušan	1322–1355	czar from 1345
Stephen Uroš V czar	1355–1371	
Vukašin king,	1366–1371	
Prince Lazar (Stefan)	1371–1389	
Stephen Lazarević	1389–1427	
George (Djuradi) Branković	1427–1456	
Lazar Branković	1456–1458	

Islam

The First Caliphs

Name	Period	Status
Abu Bakr	632–634	
Umar ibn Abd al-Khattab	634–644	
Uthman ibn Affan	644–656	
Ali ibn Abi Talib	656–661	

Umayyad Caliphate

Name	Period	Status
Muawiya I Ibn Abi-Sufyan I	661–680	
Yazid I	680–683	
Muawiya II	683–684	
Marwan I ibn al-Hakam	684–685	
Abd al-Malik	685–705	
al-Walid, Abd al-Malik	705–715	
Sulaiman	715–717	
Umar II ibn Abd al-Aziz	717–720	
Yazid II	720–724	
Hisham	724–743	
al-Walid II	743–744	
Yazid III	744	
Ibrahim	744	deposed, d. 750
Marwan II al-Himar	744–749/750	

Abbasid Caliphate

Name	Period	Status
Abul-Abbas al-Saffah	749/750–754	
al-Mansur	754–775	
al-Mahdi	775—785	
al-Hadi	785–786	
Harun al-Rashid	786–809	
al-Amin	809–813	

Name	Period	Status
al-Mamun	813–833	
al-Mutasim	833–842	
al-Wathiq	842–847	
al-Mutawakkil	847–861	
al-Muntasir	861–862	
al-Mustain	862–866	deposed
al-Mutazz	866–869	
al-Muhtadi	869–870	
al-Mutamid	870–892	
al-Mutadid	892–902	
al-Muktafi	902–908	
al-Mugtadir	908–932	
al-Qahir	932–934	deposed, d. 950
al-Radi	934–940	
al-Muttaqi	940–944	deposed, d. 968
al-Mustakfi	944–946	deposed, d. 949
al-Muti	946–974	deposed
at-Tai	974–991	deposed, d. 1003
al-Qadir	991–1031	
al-Qaim	1031–1075	
al-Mugtadi	1075–1094	
al-Mustansir	1094–1118	
al-Mustarshid	1118–1135	
al-Rashid	1135–1136	deposed, d. 1138
al-Muqtafi	1136–1160	
al-Mustanjid	1160–1170	
al-Mustadi	1170–1180	
al-Nasir	1180–1225	
al-Zahir	1225–1226	
al-Mustansir	1226–1242	
al-Muztasim	1242–1258	deposed

The Twelve Imams

Name	Period
Ali	d. 661
al-Hasan	d. 669
al-Husayn	d. 680
Ali Zayn al-Abidin	d. 714
Muhammad al-Bagir	d. 731
Jafar al-Sadiq	d. 765
Musa al-Kazim	d. 799
Ali al-Rida	d. 818
Muhammad al-Jawad	d. 835
Ali al-Hadi	d. 868
Hasan al-Askari	d. 874
Muhammad al-Muntazar	d. ca. 873

The Seven Imams

Name	Period
al-Hasan	d. 669
al-Husayn	d. 680
Ali Zayn al-Abidin	d. 714
Muhammad al-Bagir	d. 731
Jafar al-Sadiq	d. 765
Ismail	d. 760
Muhammad al-Mahdi	

Fatimid Caliphate

Name	Period
Ubayd Allah al-Mahdi	909–934
al-Qaim	934–945
al-Mansur	945–952
al-Muizz	952–975
al-Aziz	975–996
al-Hakim	996–1021
al-Zahir	1021–1036

Name	Period	Status
al-Mustansir	1036–1094	
al-Mustali	1094–1101	
al-Amir	1101–1130	
al-Hafiz	1132–1149	
al-Zafir	1149–1154	
al-Faiz	1154–1160	
al-Adid	1160–1171	
Nominal Abbasid rule	1171–1175	

Aghlabids

Name	Period	Status
Ibrahim ibn al-Aghlab	800–812	
Abdallah I	812–817	
Ziyadat Allah I	817–838	
Abu Zikal	838–841	
Muhammad I	841–856	
Ahmad	856–863	
Ziyadat Allah II	863–864	
Muhammad II	864–875	
Ibrahim II	875–902	
Abdallah II	902–903	
Ziyadat Allah III	903–909	

Hafsids

Name	Period	Status
Yahya I	1229–1249	
Muhammad I	1249–1277	
Yahya II	1277–1279	deposed, d. 1280
Ibrahim I	1279–1283	deposed, d. 1283
Abd al-Aziz I	1283	
Ahmad b. Marzuq	1283–1284	
Umar I	1284–1295	
Muhammad II	1295–1309	
Abu Bakr I	1309	
Khalid I	1309–1311	deposed, d. 1313
Zakariya I	1311–1317	deposed, d. 1326
Muhammad III	1317–1318	deposed
Abu Bakr II	1318–1346	
Ahmad I	1346–1347	
Umar II	1347	
Marinid rule	1347–1350	
al-Fadl	1350	
Ibrahim II	1350–1369	
Khalid II	1369–1370	deposed, d. 1370
Ahmad II	1370–1394	
Abd al Aziz II	1394–1434	
Muhammad IV	1434–1435	
Uthman	1435–1488	
Yahya III	1488–1489	
Abd al-Mumin	1489–1490	deposed
Zakariya II	1490–1494	
Muhammad V	1494–1526	

Mamluks of Egypt
Bahri Mamluks

Name	Period	Status
al-Muizz Aybak	1250–1257	
al-Manzur Ali I	1257–1259	deposed
al-Muzaffir Qutuz	1259–1260	
al-Zahir Baybars I	1260–1277	
al-Said Baraka Khan	1277–1279	deposed
al-Adil Salamish	1279	deposed
al-Mansur Qala'un	1279–1290	
al-Ashraf Khalil	1290–1293	
al-Nasir Muhammad I	1293–1294, 1299–1309, 1310–1340/41	deposed, restored, abdicated, restored

Name	Period	Status
al-Adil Kitbugha	1294–1296	deposed, d. 1303
al-Mansur Lajin	1296–1299	
al-Nasir Muhammad I	1299–1309, 1310–1341	restored; abdicated
al-Muzaffar Baybars II	1309–1310	
al-Mansur Abu Bakr	1341	
al-Ashraf Kujkuk	1341–1342	deposed
al-Nasir Ahmad I	1342	deposed, d. 1344
al-Salih Ismail	1342–1345	
al-Kamil Shaban I	1345–1346	
al-Muzaffar Hajji I	1346–1347	
al-Nasir al-Hasan	1347–1351, 1354–1361	deposed, restored
al-Salih Salih	1351–1354	deposed
al-Mansur Muhammad II	1361–1363	deposed
al-Ashraf Shaban II	1363–1377	
al-Mansur Ali II	1377–1381	
al-Salih Hajji II	1381–1382	deposed
al-Zahir Barquq [Burji]	1382–1389, 1390–1399	deposed, restored, first Burji 1390–1399
al-Muzaffar Hajji II	1389–1390	deposed, d. 1412

Burji Mamluks

Name	Period	Status
al-Nasir Faraj	1399–1405, 1405–1412	deposed, restored
al-Mansur Abd al-Aziz	1405	deposed, d. 1406
al Adil al-Mustain	1412	Abbasid caliph in Cairo, deposed, d. 1430
al Muayyad Shaykh	1412–1421	
al-Muzaffar Ahmad II	1421	deposed, d. 1430
al-Zahir Tatar	1421	
al-Salih Muhammad III	1421–1422	deposed, d. 1430
al-Ashraf Barsbay	1422–1438	
al-Aziz Yusuf	1438	deposed
al-Zahir Jaqmaq	1438–1453	
al-Mansur Uthman	1453	deposed
al-Ashraf Inal	1453–1461	
al-Muayyad Ahmad III	1461	deposed
al-Zahir Khushqadam	1461–1467	
al-Zahir Bilbay	1467	deposed, d. 1468
al-Zahir Timuburgha	1467–1468	deposed, d. 1475
al-Ashraf Qaitbay	1468–1496	
al-Nasir Muhammad IV	1469–1498	
al-Zahir Qansuh	1498–1500	deposed
al-Ashraf Janbalat	1500–1501	deposed

Nasrids (Banu-l-Ahmar), Kingdom of Granada

Name	Period	Status
Muhammad I al-Ghalib	1232–1272/73	
Muhammad II	1272–1302	
Muhammad III	1302–1309	deposed, d. 1314
Nasr	1309–1314	deposed, d. 1322
Ismail	1341–1325	
Muhammad IV	1325–1333	
Yusuf I	1333–1354	
Muhammad V	1354–1359, 1362–1391	deposed, restored
Ismail II	1359–1360	
Muhammad VI	1360–1362	deposed, d. 1362
Yusuf II	1391–1392	
Muhammad VII	1392–1408	
Yusuf III	1408–1417	
Muhammad VIII	1417–1418, 1427–1429	deposed, restored, deposed, d. 1431
Muhammad IX	1419–1427, 1429–1445, 1447–1453	deposed, restored, deposed, restored, deposed
Yusuf IV	1430–1432	deposed

Name	Period	Status
Yusuf V	1445–1446, 1450, 1462–1463	deposed, restored, deposed, d. 1463
Muhammad X	1445–1447	deposed, restored, deposed
Muhammad XI	1448–1454	
Sad	1455–1462, 1462–1464	deposed, restored, deposed, d. 1465
Abu Hasan Ali	1464–1482, 1483–1485	deposed, restored, deposed
Muhammad XII (Bobadilla, Boabdil)	1482–1483, 1487–1492	deposed, restored, d. 1534
Muhammad XIII	1485–1487	deposed, d. 1494

Ottomans

Name	Period	Status
Uthman I (Osman)	1280–1324/26	
Orhan	1326–1362	
Murad I	1362–1389	
Bayazid I the Thunderbolt	1389–1402	deposed, d. 1403
Isa	1402–1403	
Mehmed I	1402–1421	sole ruler from 1413
Sulayman	1402–1410/11	
Musa	1409–1413	
Murad II	1421–1444, 1446–1451	abdicated, restored
Mehmed II the Conqueror	1444–1446, 1451–1481	abdicated, restored
Bayazid II	1481–1512	deposed

Samanids

Name	Period	Status
Saman Khuda		
Ahmad I ibn Asad	819–864	
Nasr (Nesr) I	864–92	
Ismail I	892–907	
Ahmad II	907–914	
Nasr II	914–943	
Nuh I	943–954	
Abd al-Malik I	954–961	
Mansur I	961–976	
Nuh II	976–997	
Mansur II	997–999	deposed
Abd al-Malik II	999–1000	deposed
Ismail II	1000–1005	

Seljuk Dynasties

Great Seljuks

Name	Period	Status
Tughril Beg, Duqaq Seljuk Mikhail	1038–1063	
Alp Arslan	1063–1072	
Malik Shah	1072/73–1092	
Berkyaruk	1092/94–1104/05	
Malik Shah II	1104	deposed
Muhammad Tapar	1105–1118	
Sanjar	1117/18–1157	

Seljuks of Iraq

Name	Period	Status
Muhammad Tapar	1105–1118	
Mahmud II	1118–1131	
Daud	1131–1132	
Tughril I	1131/32–1134/35	
Masud	1134–1152	
Malik Shah III	1152–1153	deposed, d. 1161
Muhammad II	1153–1159	
Sulayman Shah	1159–1161	
Arslan Shah	1161–1177	
Tughril II	1177–1194	

Seljuks of Syria

Name	Period	Status
Taj-ad-Dawla	1078–1094	
Ridwan	1095–1113	

Name	Period	Status
Duqaq	1098–1113	
Alp Arslan	1113–1114	
Sultan Shah	1114–1117	
Seljuks of Anatolia (Rum)		
Sulayman I Shah, of Konya	1077–1186	
Qilich (Kilij) Arslan I	1092–1107	
Malik Shah	ca. 1107–1116	
Masud I	1116–1156	
Qilich Arslan II	1155/56–1192	
Malik II Shah	1192	
Kaykhusraw I	1192–1196, 1204–1210	deposed, restored
Sulayman Shah II	1196–1203	
Qilich (Kilij) Arsland III	1203–1204	
Kaykawus I	1210–1219	
Kayqubadh I	1219–1236/37	
Kaykhusraw II	1236/37–1246	
Kayku'us II	1246–1259	
Qilich (Qilij) Arslan IV	1248–1264	
Kayqubad II	1249–1257	
Kaykhusraw III	1264–1283	
Masud II	1283–1298	
Kayqbad III	1284–1307	
Masud II	1303–1308	
Masud III	1307–1307/08	
Umayyads and Hammudids of Spain		
Abd al-Rahman I	756–788	
Hisham I	788–796	
al-Hakam I	796–822	
Abd al-Rahman II	822–852	
Muhammad I	852–886	
al-Mundhir	886–888	
Abd Allah	888–912	
Abd al-Rahman III	912–961	
al-Hakim (Hakam) II	961–976	
Hisham II	976–1009, 1010–1013	deposed, restored
Muhammad II	1009–1010	deposed, restored
Sulayman	1009–1010, 1013–1016	deposed, restored
Ali ibn Hammud al-Nasir	1016–1018	
Abd al-Rahman IV	1018	
al-Qaim	1018–1021, 1023	deposed, restored, deposed
Yahya al-Mutali	1021–1023, 1025–1027	deposed, restored, d. 1035
Abd al-Rahman V	1023–1024	
Muhammad III	1024–1025	
Hisham III	1027–1031	deposed, d. 1036

APPENDIX II
GENEALOGIES

ENGLAND, DYNASTIES AND RULERS OF (802–1500)

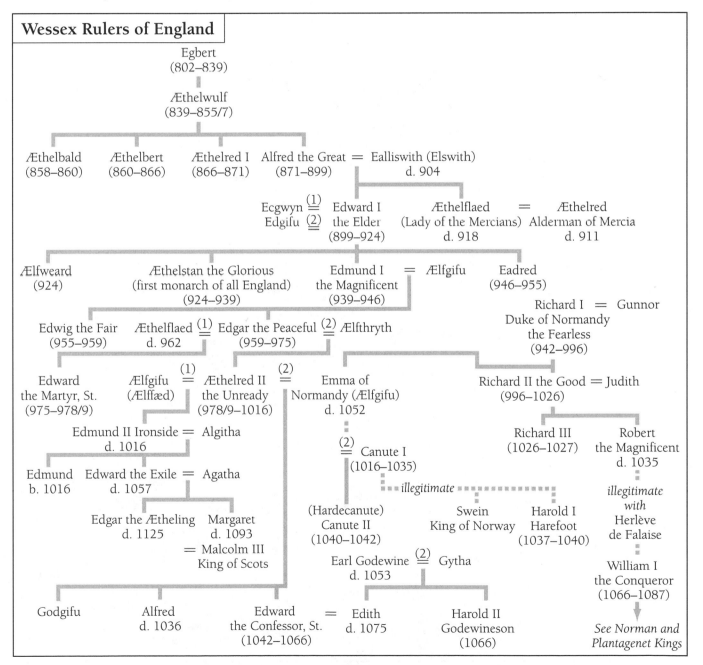

Wessex Rulers of England

Egbert
(802–839)

Æthelwulf
(839–855/7)

Æthelbald (858–860) Æthelbert (860–866) Æthelred I (866–871) Alfred the Great (871–899) = Ealliswith (Elswith) d. 904

Ecgwyn (1) = / Edgifu (2) = Edward I the Elder (899–924)

Æthelflaed (Lady of the Mercians) d. 918 = Æthelred Alderman of Mercia d. 911

Ælfweard (924)

Æthelstan the Glorious (first monarch of all England) (924–939)

Edmund I the Magnificent (939–946) = Ælfgifu

Eadred (946–955)

Richard I = Gunnor Duke of Normandy the Fearless (942–996)

Edwig the Fair (955–959)

Æthelflaed (1) d. 962 = Edgar the Peaceful (959–975) (2) = Ælfthryth

Edward the Martyr, St. (975–978/9)

Ælfgifu (Ælffæd) (1) = Æthelred II the Unready (978/9–1016) (2) = Emma of Normandy (Ælfgifu) d. 1052

Richard II the Good (996–1026) = Judith

Edmund II Ironside = Algitha d. 1016

(2) = Canute I (1016–1035)

Richard III (1026–1027)

Robert the Magnificent d. 1035

Edmund b. 1016

Edward the Exile = Agatha d. 1057

illegitimate

(Hardecanute) Canute II (1040–1042)

Swein King of Norway

Harold I Harefoot (1037–1040)

illegitimate with Herlève de Falaise

Edgar the Ætheling d. 1125

Margaret d. 1093 = Malcolm III King of Scots

Earl Godewine (2) = Gytha d. 1053

William I the Conqueror (1066–1087)

Godgifu

Alfred d. 1036

Edward the Confessor, St. (1042–1066) = Edith d. 1075

Harold II Godewineson (1066)

See Norman and Plantagenet Kings

795

England: The Norman and Plantagenet Kings (1066–1377)

See Wessex Rulers of England

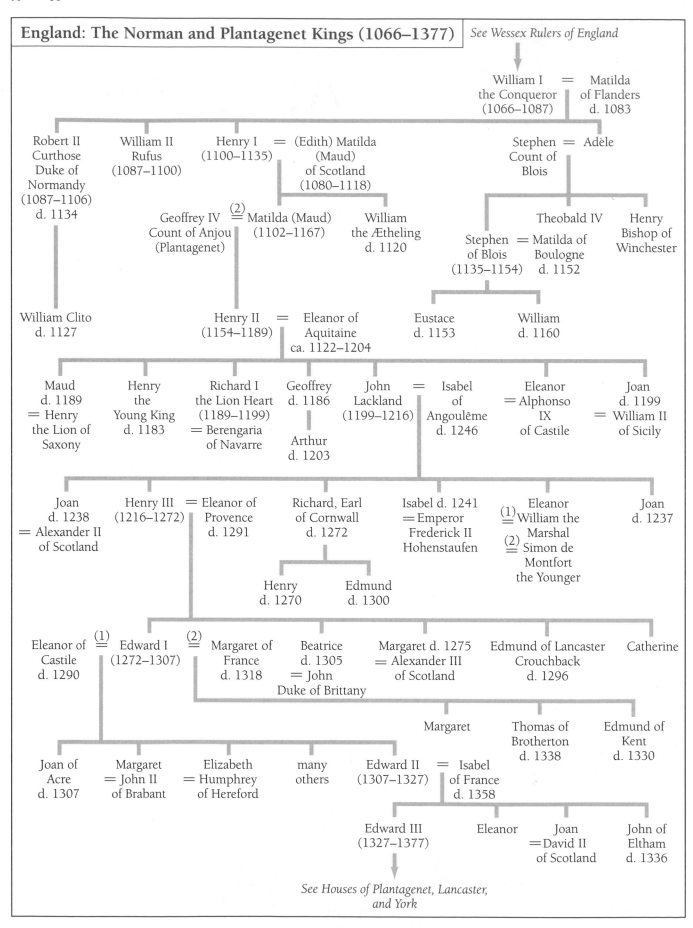

See Houses of Plantagenet, Lancaster, and York

Houses of Plantagenet, Lancaster, and York (1377–1485)

See Norman and Plantagenet Kings

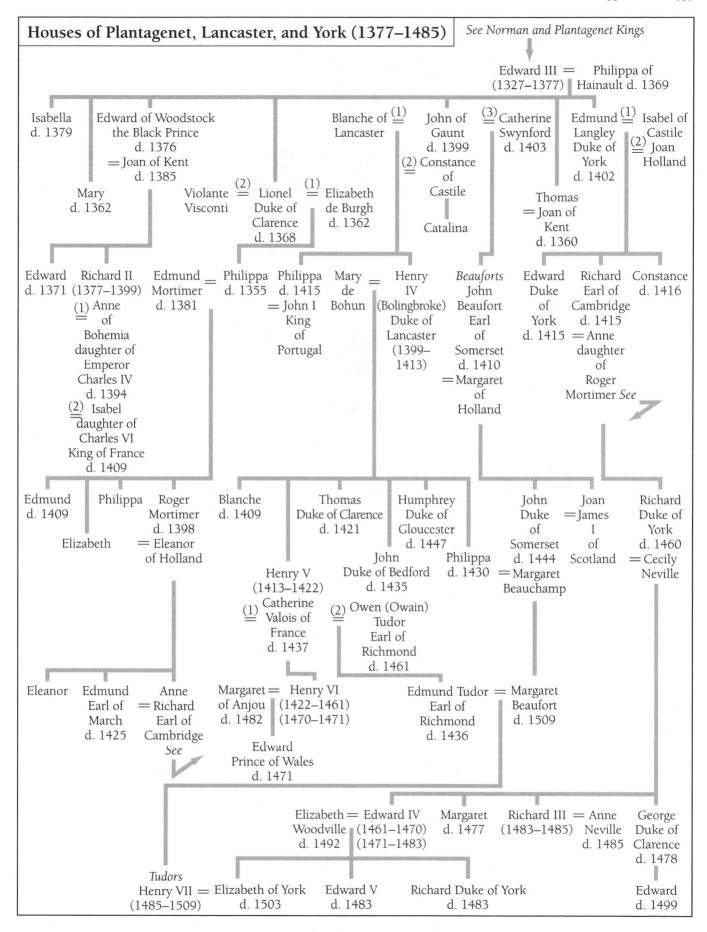

ROMAN AND BYZANTINE DYNASTIES (300-1453)

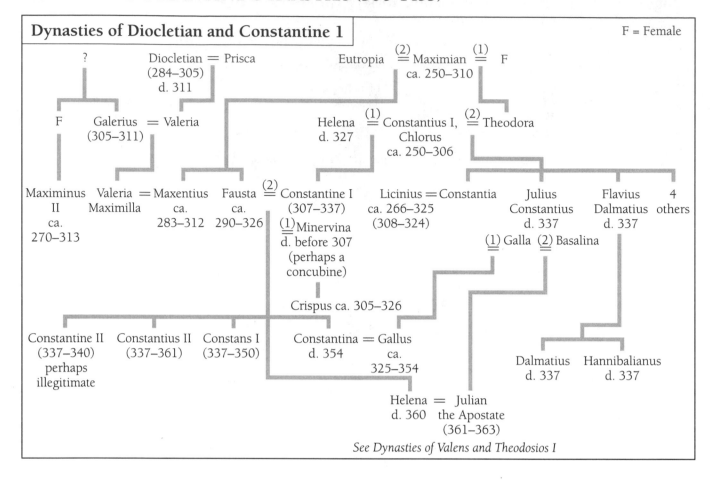

Dynasties of Diocletian and Constantine 1

F = Female

See Dynasties of Valens and Theodosios I

Dynasties of Valens and Theodosios 1

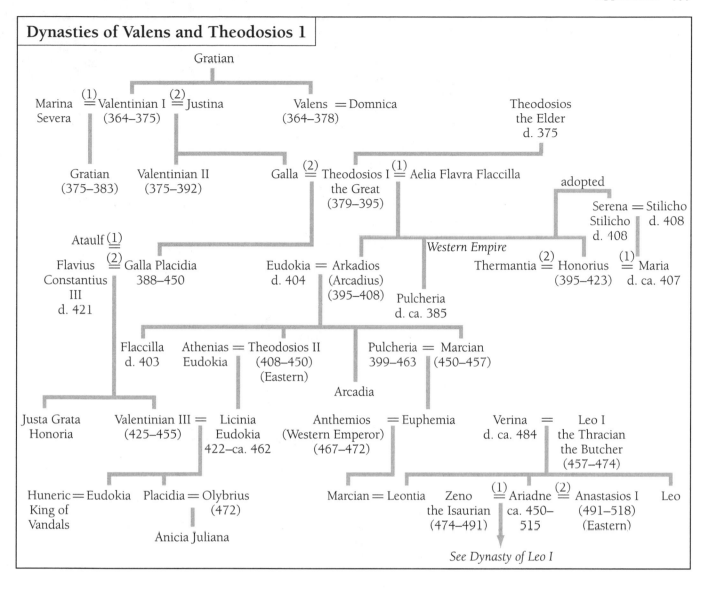

Dynasty of Leo I

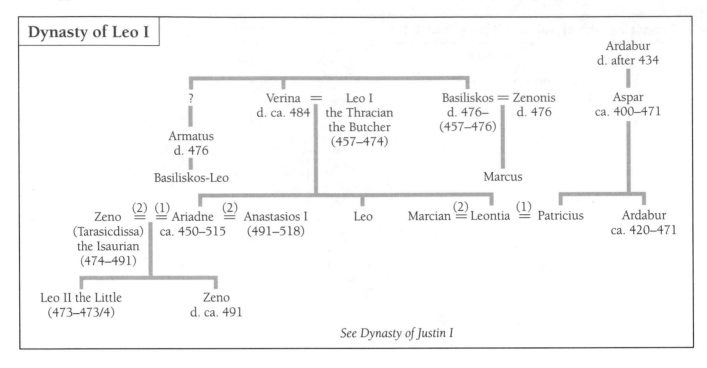

Ardabur
d. after 434

?   Verina = Leo I   Basiliskos = Zenonis   Aspar
d. ca. 484   the Thracian   d. 476–   d. 476   ca. 400–471
the Butcher   (457–476)
(457–474)

Armatus
d. 476

Basiliskos-Leo   Marcus

Zeno $\overset{(2)}{=}$ $\overset{(1)}{=}$ Ariadne $\overset{(2)}{=}$ Anastasios I   Leo   Marcian $\overset{(2)}{=}$ Leontia $\overset{(1)}{=}$ Patricius   Ardabur
(Tarasicdissa)   ca. 450–515   (491–518)   ca. 420–471
the Isaurian
(474–491)

Leo II the Little   Zeno
(473–473/4)   d. ca. 491

See Dynasty of Justin I

Dynasty of Justin I

F = Female

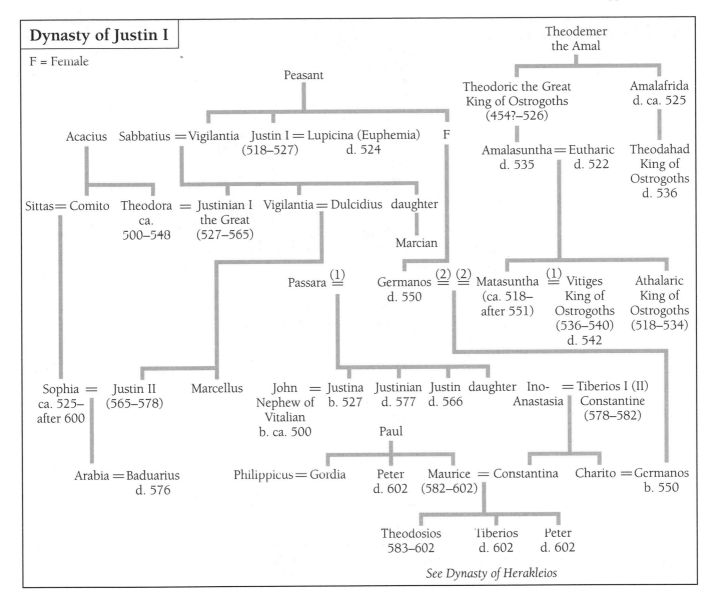

See Dynasty of Herakleios

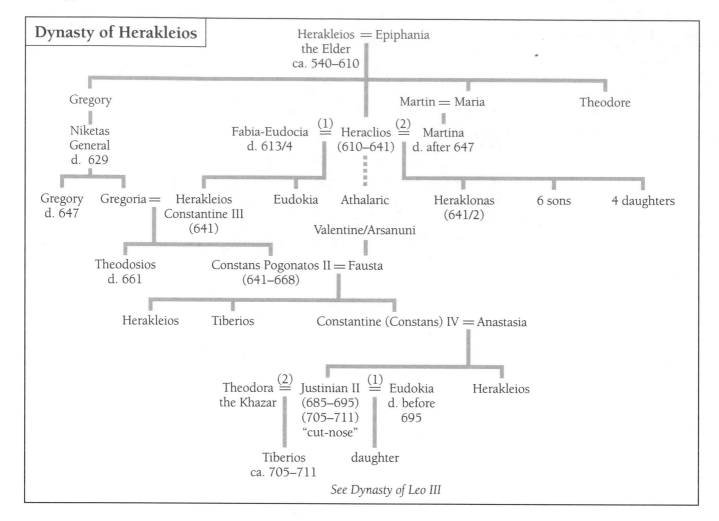

Dynasty of Herakleios

Herakleios = Epiphania
the Elder
ca. 540–610

Gregory   Martin = Maria   Theodore

Niketas   Fabia-Eudocia (1)= Heraclios (2)= Martina
General   d. 613/4   (610–641)   d. after 647
d. 629

Gregory   Gregoria = Herakleios   Eudokia   Athalaric   Heraklonas   6 sons   4 daughters
d. 647   Constantine III   (641/2)
                    (641)

                                        Valentine/Arsanuni

Theodosios   Constans Pogonatos II = Fausta
d. 661   (641–668)

Herakleios   Tiberios   Constantine (Constans) IV = Anastasia

Theodora (2)= Justinian II (1)= Eudokia   Herakleios
the Khazar   (685–695)   d. before
               (705–711)   695
               "cut-nose"

            Tiberios   daughter
            ca. 705–711

See Dynasty of Leo III

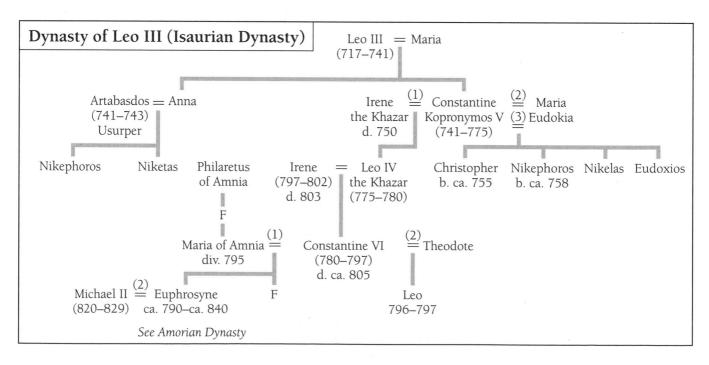

Dynasty of Leo III (Isaurian Dynasty)

Leo III = Maria
(717–741)

Artabasdos = Anna   Irene (1)= Constantine (2)= Maria
(741–743)   the Khazar Kopronymos V (3)= Eudokia
Usurper   d. 750   (741–775)

Nikephoros   Niketas   Philaretus   Irene   = Leo IV   Christopher   Nikephoros   Nikelas   Eudoxios
                         of Amnia   (797–802)   the Khazar b. ca. 755   b. ca. 758
                                     d. 803   (775–780)

                              F

                    Maria of Amnia (1)= Constantine VI   (2)= Theodote
                    div. 795   (780–797)
                                       d. ca. 805

Michael II (2)= Euphrosyne   F   Leo
(820–829)   ca. 790–ca. 840   796–797

See Amorian Dynasty

Amorian Dynasty

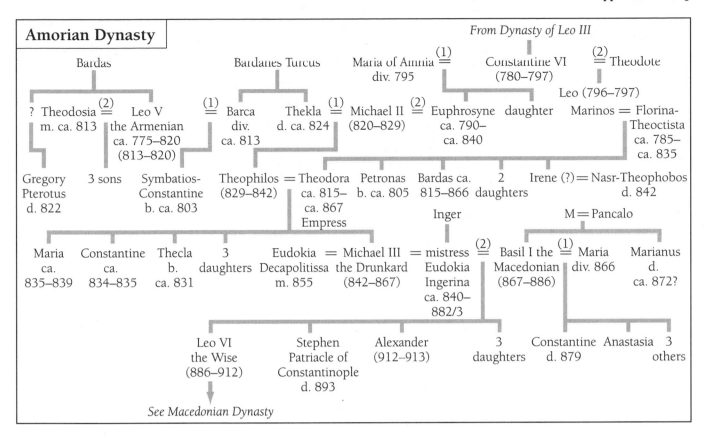

See Macedonian Dynasty

Macedonian Dynasty

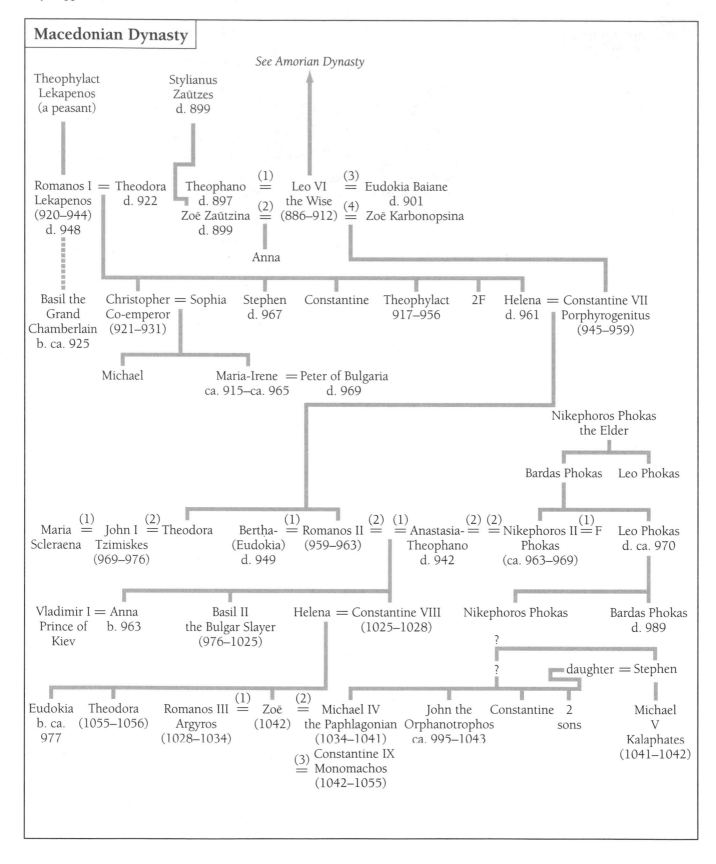

Komnenian and Doukas Dynasties (1)

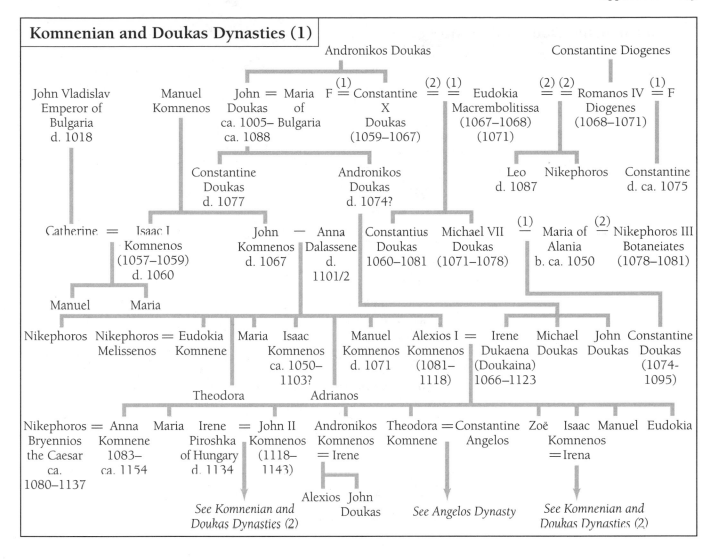

Komnenian and Doukas Dynasties (2)

See Komnenian and Doukas Dynasties (1)

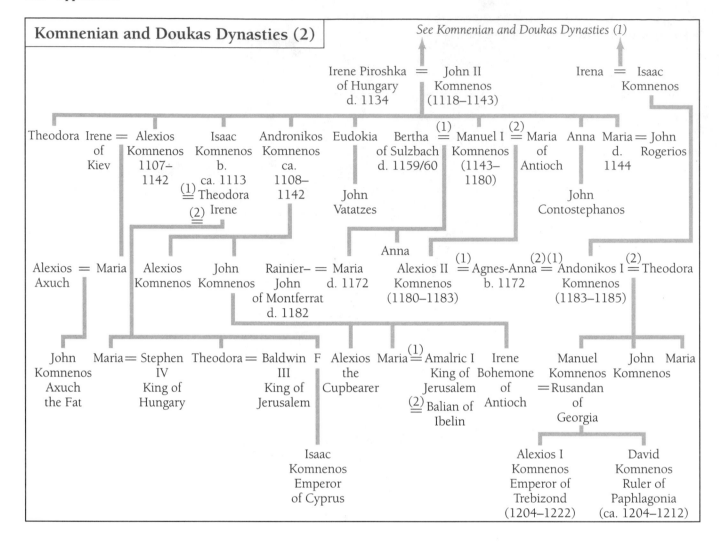

Angelos Dynasty

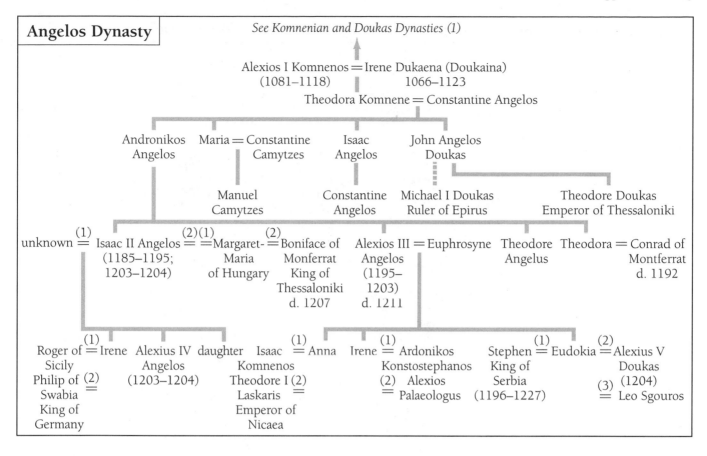

See Komnenian and Doukas Dynasties (1)

Alexios I Komnenos ═ Irene Dukaena (Doukaina)
(1081–1118)   1066–1123

Theodora Komnene ═ Constantine Angelos

Andronikos Angelos

Maria ═ Constantine Camytzes

Isaac Angelos

John Angelos Doukas

Manuel Camytzes

Constantine Angelos

Michael I Doukas Ruler of Epirus

Theodore Doukas Emperor of Thessaloniki

unknown ═(1) Isaac II Angelos (1185–1195; 1203–1204)

(2)(1)═Margaret-Maria of Hungary

(2)═Boniface of Monferrat King of Thessaloniki d. 1207

Alexios III Angelos (1195–1203) d. 1211 ═ Euphrosyne

Theodore Angelus

Theodora ═ Conrad of Montferrat d. 1192

Roger of Sicily ═(1) Irene
Philip of Swabia (2)═ King of Germany

Alexius IV Angelos (1203–1204)

daughter

Isaac Komnenos (1)═ Anna
Theodore I (2)═ Laskaris Emperor of Nicaea

Irene ═(1) Ardonikos Konstostephanos
(2)═ Alexios Palaeologus

Stephen ═(1) Eudokia ═(2) Alexius V Doukas
King of Serbia (1196–1227)   (3)═ (1204) Leo Sgouros

Laskarid Dynasty and Thessalonian and Latin Emperors of Constantinople

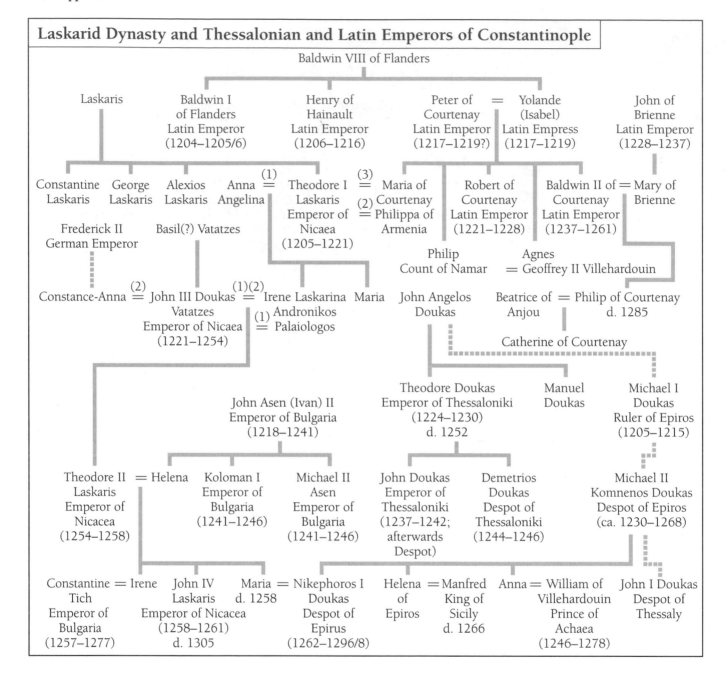

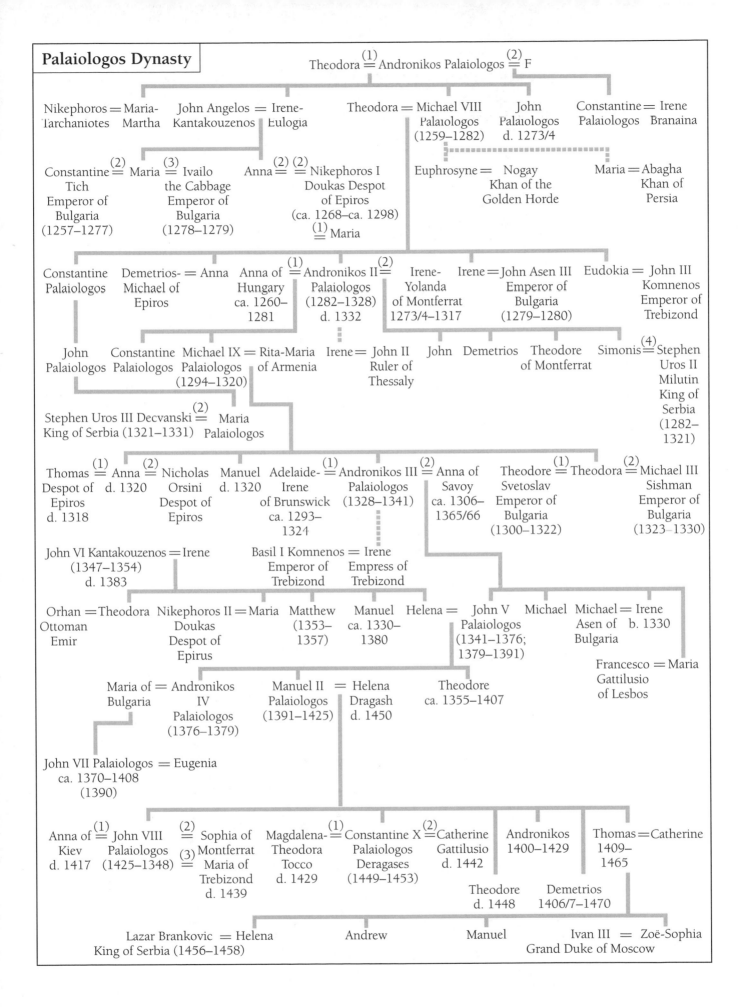

Palaiologos Dynasty

Theodora $\stackrel{(1)}{=}$ Andronikos Palaiologos $\stackrel{(2)}{=}$ F

Nikephoros = Maria-   John Angelos = Irene-   Theodora = Michael VIII   John   Constantine = Irene
Tarchaniotes Martha   Kantakouzenos Eulogia   Palaiologos   Palaiologos   Palaiologos   Branaina
                                                                (1259–1282)   d. 1273/4

Constantine $\stackrel{(2)}{=}$ Maria $\stackrel{(3)}{=}$ Ivailo   Anna $\stackrel{(2)}{=}$ $\stackrel{(2)}{=}$ Nikephoros I   Euphrosyne = Nogay   Maria = Abagha
Tich   the Cabbage   Doukas Despot   Khan of the   Khan of
Emperor of   Emperor of   of Epiros   Golden Horde   Persia
Bulgaria   Bulgaria   (ca. 1268–ca. 1298)
(1257–1277)   (1278–1279) $\stackrel{(1)}{=}$ Maria

Constantine   Demetrios- = Anna   Anna of $\stackrel{(1)}{=}$ Andronikos II $\stackrel{(2)}{=}$ Irene-   Irene = John Asen III   Eudokia = John III
Palaiologos   Michael of   Hungary   Palaiologos   Yolanda   Emperor of   Komnenos
              Epiros   ca. 1260–   (1282–1328)   of Montferrat   Bulgaria   Emperor of
                                    1281   d. 1332   1273/4–1317   (1279–1280)   Trebizond

John   Constantine Michael IX = Rita-Maria   Irene = John II   John Demetrios Theodore   Simonis $\stackrel{(4)}{=}$ Stephen
Palaiologos Palaiologos Palaiologos   of Armenia   Ruler of   of Montferrat   Uros II
                         (1294–1320)   Thessaly   Milutin
                                                                                                              King of
                                                                                                              Serbia
Stephen Uros III Decvanski $\stackrel{(2)}{=}$ Maria   (1282–
King of Serbia (1321–1331)   Palaiologos   1321)

Thomas $\stackrel{(1)}{=}$ Anna $\stackrel{(2)}{=}$ Nicholas   Manuel Adelaide- $\stackrel{(1)}{=}$ Andronikos III $\stackrel{(2)}{=}$ Anna of   Theodore $\stackrel{(1)}{=}$ Theodora $\stackrel{(2)}{=}$ Michael III
Despot of   d. 1320   Orsini   d. 1320   Irene   Palaiologos   Savoy   Svetoslav   Sishman
Epiros   Despot of   of Brunswick   (1328–1341)   ca. 1306–   Emperor of   Emperor of
d. 1318   Epiros   ca. 1293–   1365/66   Bulgaria   Bulgaria
                                             1324   (1300–1322)   (1323–1330)

John VI Kantakouzenos = Irene   Basil I Komnenos = Irene
   (1347–1354)   Emperor of   Empress of
   d. 1383   Trebizond   Trebizond

Orhan = Theodora Nikephoros II = Maria Matthew   Manuel   Helena =   John V   Michael   Michael = Irene
Ottoman   Doukas   (1353–   ca. 1330–   Palaiologos Asen of   b. 1330
Emir   Despot of   1357)   1380   (1341–1376; Bulgaria
                  Epirus   1379–1391)
                                                                                  Francesco = Maria
                                                                                  Gattilusio
Maria of = Andronikos   Manuel II = Helena   Theodore   of Lesbos
Bulgaria   IV   Palaiologos Dragash   ca. 1355–1407
             Palaiologos   (1391–1425) d. 1450
             (1376–1379)

John VII Palaiologos = Eugenia
   ca. 1370–1408
   (1390)

Anna of $\stackrel{(1)}{=}$ John VIII $\stackrel{(2)}{=}$ Sophia of   Magdalena- $\stackrel{(1)}{=}$ Constantine X $\stackrel{(2)}{=}$ Catherine   Andronikos   Thomas = Catherine
Kiev   Palaiologos   Montferrat   Theodora   Palaiologos   Gattilusio   1400–1429   1409–
d. 1417   (1425–1348) $\stackrel{(3)}{=}$ Maria of   Tocco   Deragases   d. 1442   1465
                              Trebizond   d. 1429   (1449–1453)
                              d. 1439   Theodore   Demetrios
                                                                                  d. 1448   1406/7–1470

Lazar Brankovic = Helena   Andrew   Manuel   Ivan III = Zoë-Sophia
King of Serbia (1456–1458)   Grand Duke of Moscow

RULING DYNASTIES OF HUNGARY, POLAND, AND LITHUANIA (1205–1492)

Rulers of Hungary, Poland, and Lithuania (1205–1492)

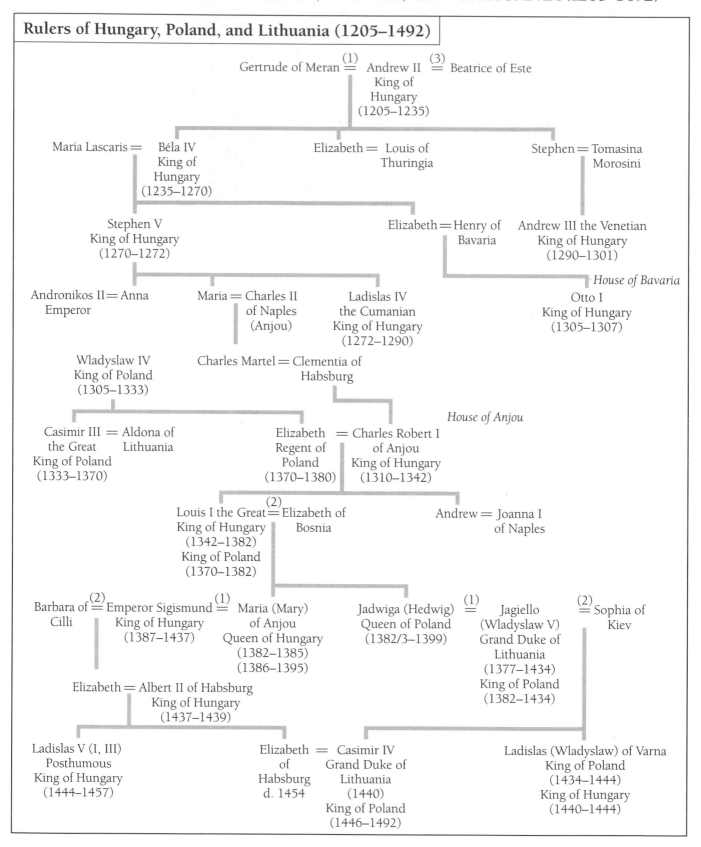

RULING DYNASTIES OF THE CHRISTIAN IBERIAN KINGDOMS FROM 970 TO THE LATE THIRTEENTH CENTURY

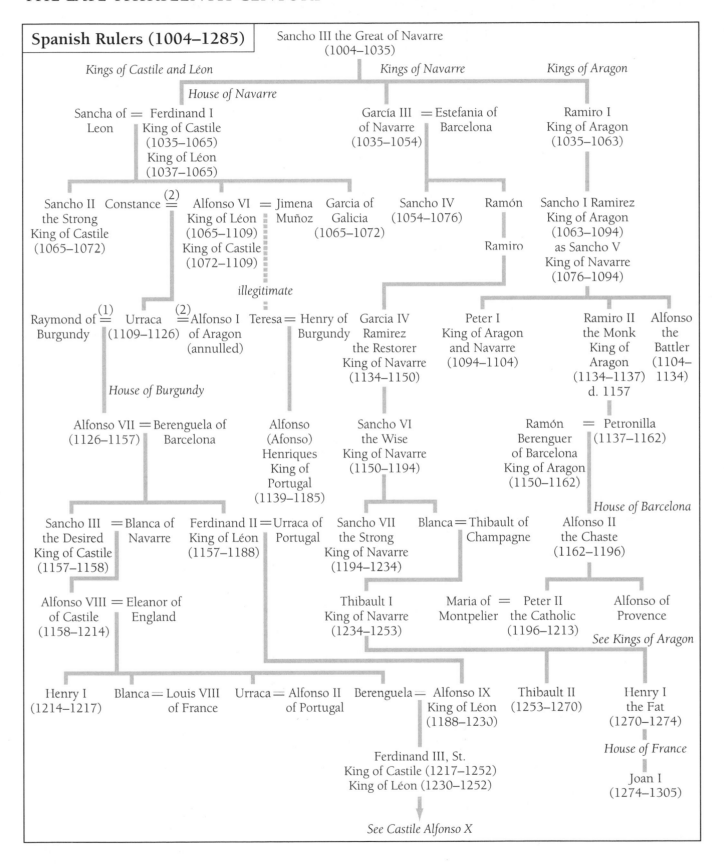

Spanish Rulers (1004–1285)

Sancho III the Great of Navarre
(1004–1035)

Kings of Castile and Léon   *Kings of Navarre*   *Kings of Aragon*

House of Navarre

Sancha of = Ferdinand I
Leon   King of Castile
(1035–1065)
King of Léon
(1037–1065)

García III = Estefania of
of Navarre   Barcelona
(1035–1054)

Ramiro I
King of Aragon
(1035–1063)

Sancho II   Constance $\overset{(2)}{=}$ Alfonso VI = Jimena   Garcia of
the Strong   King of Léon   Muñoz   Galicia
King of Castile   (1065–1109)   (1065–1072)
(1065–1072)   King of Castile
     (1072–1109)

Sancho IV   Ramón
(1054–1076)

     Ramiro

Sancho I Ramirez
King of Aragon
(1063–1094)
as Sancho V
King of Navarre
(1076–1094)

illegitimate

Raymond of $\overset{(1)}{=}$ Urraca $\overset{(2)}{=}$ Alfonso I   Teresa = Henry of   Garcia IV
Burgundy   (1109–1126)   of Aragon   Burgundy   Ramirez
       (annulled)   the Restorer
                       King of Navarre
                       (1134–1150)

Peter I
King of Aragon
and Navarre
(1094–1104)

Ramiro II   Alfonso
the Monk   the
King of   Battler
Aragon   (1104–
(1134–1137)   1134)
d. 1157

House of Burgundy

Alfonso VII = Berenguela of
(1126–1157)   Barcelona

Alfonso
(Afonso)
Henriques
King of
Portugal
(1139–1185)

Sancho VI
the Wise
King of Navarre
(1150–1194)

Ramón = Petronilla
Berenguer   (1137–1162)
of Barcelona
King of Aragon
(1150–1162)

House of Barcelona

Sancho III = Blanca of   Ferdinand II = Urraca of   Sancho VII   Blanca = Thibault of   Alfonso II
the Desired   Navarre   King of Léon   Portugal   the Strong   Champagne   the Chaste
King of Castile   (1157–1188)   King of Navarre   (1162–1196)
(1157–1158)   (1194–1234)

Alfonso VIII = Eleanor of
of Castile   England
(1158–1214)

Thibault I
King of Navarre
(1234–1253)

Maria of = Peter II   Alfonso of
Montpelier   the Catholic   Provence
        (1196–1213)
               See Kings of Aragon

Henry I   Blanca = Louis VIII   Urraca = Alfonso II   Berenguela = Alfonso IX   Thibault II   Henry I
(1214–1217)   of France   of Portugal   King of Léon   (1253–1270)   the Fat
                                      (1188–1230)   (1270–1274)

House of France

Ferdinand III, St.
King of Castile (1217–1252)
King of Léon (1230–1252)

Joan I
(1274–1305)

See Castile Alfonso X

RULERS AND DYNASTIES OF KIEVAN RUŚ, MOSCOW, AND RUSSIA

Grand Princes of Kiev and Vladimir (862–1212)

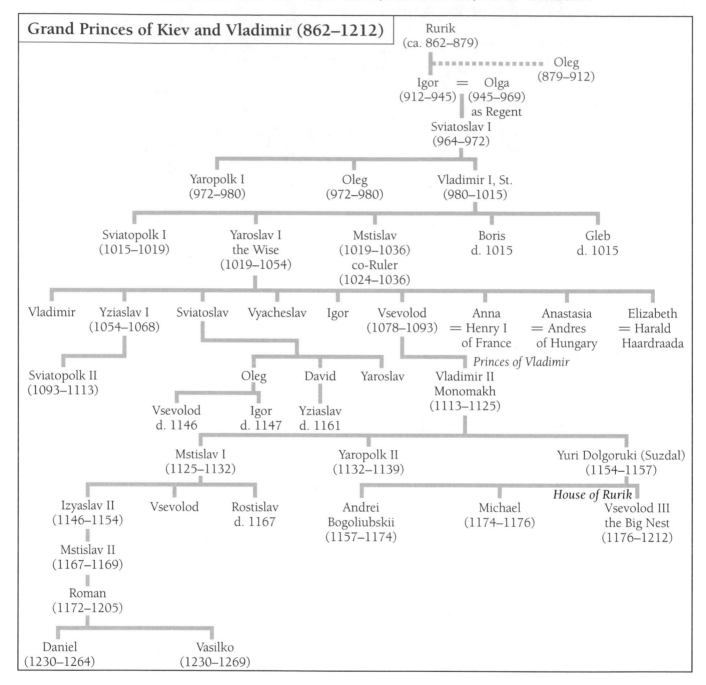

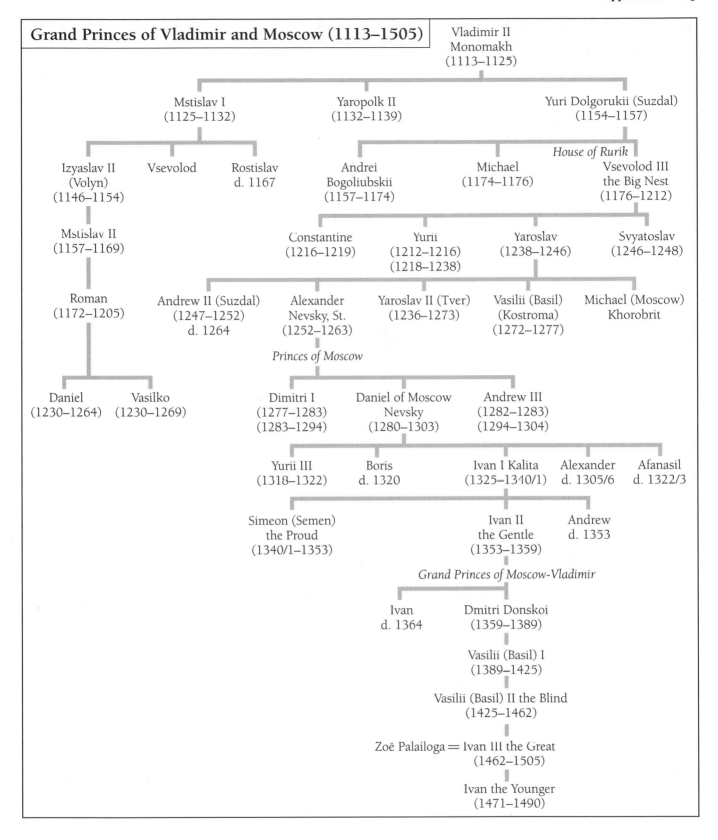

Grand Princes of Vladimir and Moscow (1113–1505)

Vladimir II
Monomakh
(1113–1125)

Mstislav I
(1125–1132)

Yaropolk II
(1132–1139)

Yuri Dolgorukii (Suzdal)
(1154–1157)

House of Rurik

Izyaslav II
(Volyn)
(1146–1154)

Vsevolod

Rostislav
d. 1167

Andrei
Bogoliubskii
(1157–1174)

Michael
(1174–1176)

Vsevolod III
the Big Nest
(1176–1212)

Mstislav II
(1157–1169)

Constantine
(1216–1219)

Yurii
(1212–1216)
(1218–1238)

Yaroslav
(1238–1246)

Svyatoslav
(1246–1248)

Roman
(1172–1205)

Andrew II (Suzdal)
(1247–1252)
d. 1264

Alexander
Nevsky, St.
(1252–1263)

Yaroslav II (Tver)
(1236–1273)

Vasilii (Basil)
(Kostroma)
(1272–1277)

Michael (Moscow)
Khorobrit

Princes of Moscow

Daniel
(1230–1264)

Vasilko
(1230–1269)

Dimitri I
(1277–1283)
(1283–1294)

Daniel of Moscow
Nevsky
(1280–1303)

Andrew III
(1282–1283)
(1294–1304)

Yurii III
(1318–1322)

Boris
d. 1320

Ivan I Kalita
(1325–1340/1)

Alexander
d. 1305/6

Afanasil
d. 1322/3

Simeon (Semen)
the Proud
(1340/1–1353)

Ivan II
the Gentle
(1353–1359)

Andrew
d. 1353

Grand Princes of Moscow-Vladimir

Ivan
d. 1364

Dmitri Donskoi
(1359–1389)

Vasilii (Basil) I
(1389–1425)

Vasilii (Basil) II the Blind
(1425–1462)

Zoë Palailoga = Ivan III the Great
(1462–1505)

Ivan the Younger
(1471–1490)

RULERS AND DYNASTIES OF SCANDINAVIA IN THE LATER MIDDLE AGES FOR DENMARK, NORWAY, AND SWEDEN

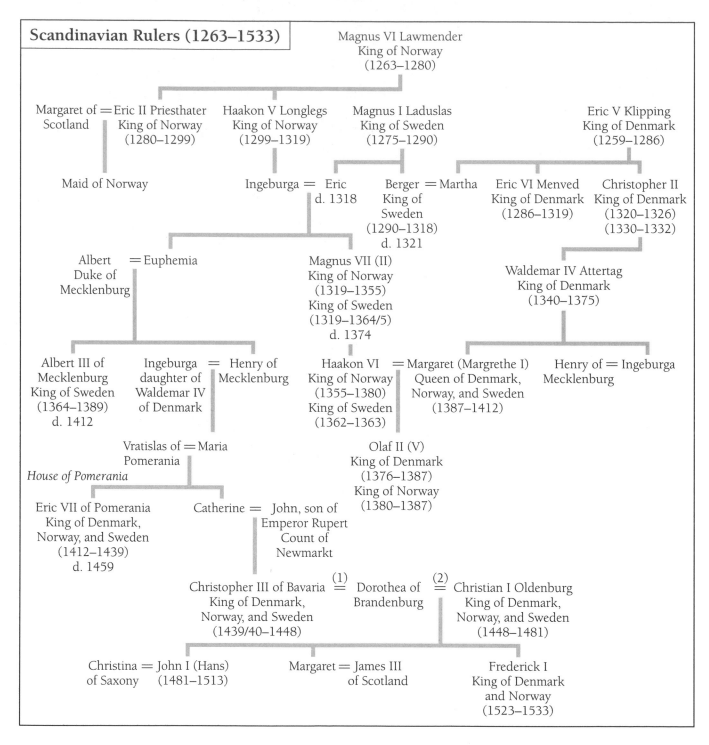

Scandinavian Rulers (1263–1533)

BIBLIOGRAPHY

I. ENCYCLOPEDIAS, HANDBOOKS, AND DICTIONARIES

Appiah, Kwame Anthony, and Henry Louis Gates, Jr., eds. *The Dictionary of Global Culture.* New York: Vintage Books, 1996.

Avery, Catherine B. *The New Century Italian Renaissance Encyclopedia.* New York: Appleton-Century-Crofts, 1972.

Barnavi, Eli, ed. *A Historical Atlas of the Jewish People.* New York: Schocken Books, 1992.

Beinart, Haim. *Atlas of Medieval Jewish History.* New York: Simon & Schuster, 1992.

Bennett, Matthew, ed. *The Hutchinson Dictionary of Ancient and Medieval Warfare.* Oxford: Helicon, 1998.

Bergin, Thomas G., and Jennifer Speake, eds. *Encyclopedia of the Renaissance.* New York: Facts On File, 1987.

Bowersock, G. W., Peter Brown, and Oleg Grabar, eds. "The Alphabetical Guide." In *Late Antiquity: A Guide to the Postclassical World.* Cambridge, Mass.: The Belknap Press of Harvard University Press, 1999.

Boyd, Kelly, ed. *Encyclopedia of Historians and Historical Writing.* 2 vols. Chicago: Fitzroy Dearborn, 1999.

Broughton, Bradford B. *Dictionary of Medieval Knighthood and Chivalry: Concepts and Terms.* New York: Greenwood Press, 1986.

Brown, Mary Ellen, and Bruce A. Rosenberg, eds. *Encyclopedia of Folklore and Literature.* Santa Barbara: ABC-CLIO, 1998.

Brumble, H. David. *Classical Myths and Legends in the Middle Ages and Renaissance: A Dictionary of Allegorical Meanings.* Westport, Conn.: Greenwood Press, 1998.

Bunson, Matthew E. *Encyclopedia of the Middle Ages.* New York: Facts On File, 1995.

Cannon, John, ed. *The Oxford Companion to British History.* Oxford: Oxford University Press, 1997.

Cantor, Norman F., ed. *The Encyclopedia of the Middle Ages.* New York: Viking, 1999.

Chadwick, Henry, and G. R. Evans. *Atlas of the Christian Church.* 1987. Reprint, Oxford: Phaidon, 1990.

Chilvers, Ian, and Harold Osborne, eds. *The Oxford Dictionary of Art.* New edition. Oxford: Oxford University Press, 1997.

Cohn-Sherbok, Dan, ed. *The Blackwell Dictionary of Judaica.* Oxford: Blackwell, 1992.

Cosman, Madeleine Pelner. *Medieval Wordbook.* New York: Checkmark Books, 1996.

Crabtree, Pam J., ed. *Medieval Archaeology: An Encyclopedia.* New York: Garland, 2001.

Cross, F. L., and E. A. Livingstone, eds. *The Oxford Dictionary of the Christian Church.* 3d ed. Oxford: Oxford University Press, 1997.

Dahmus, Joseph. *Dictionary of Medieval Civilization.* New York: Macmillan, 1984.

Di Bernardino, Angelo, ed. *Encyclopedia of the Early Church.* Trans. Adrian Walford. 2 vol. New York: Oxford University Press, 1992.

Drees, Clayton J., ed. *The Late Medieval Age of Crisis and Renewal, 1300–1500: A Biographical Dictionary.* Westport, Conn.: Greenwood Press, 2001.

Echols, Anne, and Mary Williams, eds. *An Annotated Index of Medieval Women.* New York: Wiener, 1992.

The Encyclopaedia of Islam. New ed. 9 vols. Leiden: E. J. Brill, 1960.

Encyclopaedia Judaica. 16 vols. New York: Macmillan, 1971–1972.

Evans, G. R. *Fifty Key Medieval Thinkers.* New York: Routledge, 2002.

Fahlbusch, Erwin, et al., eds. *The Encyclopedia of Christianity.* 2 vols. Leiden: Brill, 1999.

Farmer, David Hugh, ed. *The Oxford Dictionary of Saints.* 4th ed. Oxford: Oxford University Press, 1997.

Ferguson, Everett, ed. *The Encyclopedia of Early Christianity.* 2d ed. 2 vols. New York: Garland, 1997.

Fines, John. *Who's Who in the Middle Ages: From the Collapse of the Roman Empire to the Renaissance.* 1970. Reprint, New York: Barnes & Noble, 1995.

Fletcher, Richard. *Who's Who in Roman Britain and Anglo-Saxon England.* London: Shepheard-Walwyn, 1989.

Fletcher, Stella. *The Longman Companion to Renaissance Europe, 1390–1530.* London: Longman, 2000.

Freeman-Greenville, G. S. P. *Oxford Atlas of the Middle East.* New York: Simon & Schuster, 1993.

Friedman, John Block, and Kristen Mossler Figg, eds. *Trade, Travel, and Exploration in the Middle Ages: An Encyclopedia.* New York: Garland, 2000.

Gerli, E. Michael, ed. *Medieval Iberia: An Encyclopedia.* New York: Garland, 2003.

Gentry, Francis G. et al., eds. *The Nibelungen Tradition: An Encyclopedia.* New York: Routledge, 2002.

Gerritsen, Willem P., and Anthony G. Van Melle, eds. *A Dictionary of Medieval Heroes: Characters in Medieval Narrative Traditions and Their Afterlife in Literature, Theatre and the Visual Arts.* 1993. Reprint, Rochester, N.Y.: The Boydell Press, 1998.

Gillispie, Charles Cordston, ed. *Dictionary of Scientific Biography.* 18 vols. New York: Charles Scribner's Sons, 1970–1980.

Glassé, Cyril. *The Concise Dictionary of Islam.* London: Stacey International, 1989.

Grabois, Aryeh. *The Illustrated Encyclopedia of Medieval Civilization.* London: Octopus Books, 1980.

Grendler. Paul, ed. *Encyclopedia of the Renaissance.* 6 vols. New York: Charles Scribner's Sons, 1999.

Haigh, Christopher, ed. *The Cambridge Historical Encyclopedia of Great Britain and Ireland.* Cambridge: Cambridge University Press, 1985.

Hale, J. R., ed. *A Concise Encyclopedia of the Italian Renaissance.* New York: Oxford University Press, 1981.

Hardin, James, and Max Reinhart, eds. *Dictionary of Literary Biography.* Vol. 179. *German Writers of the Renaissance and Reformation, 1280–1580.* Detroit: Gale Research, 1997.

Hardin, James, and Will Hasty, eds. *Dictionary of Literary Biography.* Vol. 138. *German Writers and Works of the High Middle Ages, 1170–1280.* Detroit: Gale Research, 1994.

Harty, Kevin J. *The Reel Middle Ages: American, Western and Eastern European, Middle Eastern, and Asian Films about Medieval Europe.* Jefferson, N.C.: McFarland, 1999.

Harvey, John Hooper. *English Mediaeval Architects: A Biographical Dictionary Down to 1550, Including Master Masons, Carpenters, Carvers, Building Contractors and Others Responsible for Design.* Rev. edition. Gloucester: A. Sutton, 1987.

Hastings, Adrian, Alistair Mason, and Hugh Pyper, eds. *The Oxford Companion to Christian Thought.* Oxford: Oxford University Press, 2000.

Hasty, Will, and James Hardin, eds. *Dictionary of Literary Biography.* Vol. 148. *German Writers and Works of the Early Middle Ages, 800–1170.* Detroit: Gale Research, 1997.

Haywood, John. *The Penguin Historical Atlas of the Vikings.* New York: Penguin Books, 1995.

Haywood, John. *Historical Atlas of the Medieval World,* A.D. *600–1492.* New York: Barnes & Noble, 2001.

Helterman, Jeffrey, and Jerome Mitchell, eds. *Dictionary of Literary Biography.* Vol. 146. *Old and Middle English Literature.* Detroit: Gale Research, 1994.

Hicks, Michael A. *Who's Who in Late Medieval England, 1272–1485.* London: Shepheard-Walwyn, 1991.

Hooper, Nicholas, and Matthew Bennett. *Cambridge Illustrated Atlas of Warfare: The Middle Ages, 768–1487.* Cambridge: Cambridge University Press, 1996.

Hornblower, Simon, and Anthony Spawforth, eds. *The Oxford Companion to Classical Civilization.* Oxford: Oxford University Press, 1998.

Hughes, Thomas Patrick, ed. *A Dictionary of Islam: A Cyclopedia of the Doctrines, Rites, Ceremonies, and Customs, Together with the Technical and Theological Terms, of the Muhammadan Religion.* 1885. Reprint, Clifton, N.J.: Reference Book Publishers, 1965.

Huyghe, René, ed. *Larousse Encyclopedia of Byzantine and Medieval Art.* Rev. ed. London: Hamlyn, 1968.

Jackson, William T. H., and George Stade, eds. *European Writers: The Middle Ages and the Renaissance.* Vol. 1. *Prudentius to Medieval Drama.* New York: Charles Scribner's Sons, 1983.

Jackson, William T. H., and George Stade, eds. *European Writers: The Middle Ages and the Renaissance.* Vol. 2. *Petrarch to Renaissance Short Fiction.* New York: Charles Scribner's Sons, 1983.

Jeep, John M., ed. *Medieval Germany: An Encyclopedia.* New York: Garland, 2001.

Johnston, William M., ed. *Encyclopedia of Monasticism.* 2 vols. Chicago: Fitzroy Dearborn, 2000.

Jordan, William Chester, ed. *Dictionary of the Middle Ages,* Supplement 1. New York: Charles Scribner's Sons, 2004.

Kazhdan, Alexander P., ed. *The Oxford Dictionary of Byzantium.* 3 vols. New York: Oxford University Press, 1991.

Kibler, William W., and Grover A. Zinn, eds. *Medieval France: An Encyclopedia.* New York: Garland, 1995.

Kleinhenz, Christopher, ed. *Medieval Italy: An Encyclopedia.* New York: Garland, 2004.

Konstam, Angus. *Atlas of Medieval Europe.* New York: Checkmark Books, 2000.

Konstam, Angus. *Historical Atlas of the Celtic World.* New York: Checkmark Books, 2001.

Konstam, Angus. *Historical Atlas of the Crusades.* New York: Checkmark Books, 2002.

Lacy, Norris J., ed. *The New Arthurian Encyclopedia.* New York: Garland, 1996.

Lambdin, Robert Thomas, and Laura Cooner Lambdin, eds. *Encyclopedia of Medieval Literature.* Westport, Conn.: Greenwood Press, 2000.

Lansing, Richard, ed. *The Dante Encyclopedia.* New York: Garland, 2000.

Lapidge, Michael, Simon Keyes, and Donald Scragg, eds. *The Blackwell Encyclopedia of Anglo-Saxon England.* Oxford: Blackwell, 1999.

Lawler, Jennifer. *Encyclopedia of Women in the Middle Ages.* Jefferson, N.C.: McFarland, 2001.

Lever, Jill. *Illustrated Dictionary of Architecture, 800–1914.* 2d ed. London: Faber and Faber, 1993.

Lindahl, Carl, John McNamara, and John Lindow, eds. *Medieval Folklore: An Encyclopedia of Myths, Legends, Tales, Beliefs, and Customs.* 2000. Reprint, Oxford: Oxford University Press, 2002.

Lindow, John, ed. *Scandinavian Mythology: An Annotated Bibliography.* New York: Garland, 1988.

Lindow, John ed., *Norse Mythology: A Guide to the Gods, Heroes, Rituals, and Beliefs.* 2001. Reprint, Oxford: Oxford University Press, 2002.

Loyn, H. R., ed. *The Middle Ages: A Concise Encyclopedia.* London: Thames and Hudson, 1989.

MacKay, Angus, with David Ditchburn, eds. *Atlas of Medieval Europe.* New York: Routledge, 1997.

McEvedy, Colin. *The Penguin Atlas of Medieval History.* Maps drawn by John Woodcock. Harmondsworth: Penguin Books, 1961.

McEvedy, Colin. *The Penguin Atlas of African History.* New ed. New York: Penguin Books, 1995.

Magill, Frank N., ed. *Dictionary of World Biography.* Vol. 2. *The Middle Ages.* Chicago: Fitzroy Dearborn, 1998.

Magill, Frank N., ed. *Dictionary of World Biography.* Vol. 3. *The Renaissance.* Chicago: Fitzroy Dearborn, 1999.

Magocsi, Paul R. *Historical Atlas of East Central Europe.* Seattle: University of Washington Press, 1993.

Man, John. *Atlas of the Year 1000.* Cambridge, Mass.: Harvard University Press, 1999.

Marwick, Arthur, ed. *The Illustrated Dictionary of British History.* London: Thames and Hudson, 1980.

McAuliffe, Jane Dammen, ed. *Encyclopedia of the Quran.* Vol. 1, *A–D.* Leiden: Brill, 2001.

McGurk, John James Noel. *A Dictionary of Medieval Terms for the Use of History Students.* Reigate: Reigate Press, 1970.

Murray, Peter, and Linda Murray, eds. *The Oxford Companion to Christian Art and Architecture.* Oxford: Oxford University Press, 1996.

Murray, Peter, and Linda Murray, eds. *A Dictionary of Christian Art.* Oxford: Oxford University Press, 1996.

Netton, Ian Richard. *A Popular Dictionary of Islam.* London: Curzon Press, 1992.

Neusner, Jacob, Alan J. Avery-Peck, and William Scott Green, eds. *The Encyclopedia of Judaism.* 3 vols. New York: Continuum, 1999.

Newby, Gordon S., ed. *A Concise Encyclopedia of Islam.* Oxford: One World, 2002.

New Catholic Encyclopedia. 15 vols. New York: McGraw-Hill, 1967.

Nicol, Donald. *A Biographical Dictionary of the Byzantine Empire.* London: Seaby, 1991.

Nordstrom, Byron J., ed. *Dictionary of Scandinavian History.* London: Greenwood Press, 1986.

Pallattino, Massimo, ed. *Encyclopedia of World Art.* 17 vols. New York: McGraw-Hill, 1959–1987.

Parry, Ken et al., eds. *The Blackwell Dictionary of Eastern Christianity.* Oxford: Blackwell, 1999.

Paxton, John, ed. *Encyclopedia of Russian History: From the Christianization of Kiev to the Break-Up of the U.S.S.R.* Santa Barbara, Calif.: ABC-CLIO, 1993.

Pulsiano, Phillip, ed. *Medieval Scandinavia: An Encyclopedia.* New York: Garland, 1993.

Riley-Smith, Jonathan. *The Atlas of the Crusades.* London: Times Books, 1991.

Ross, Leslie, ed. *Medieval Art: A Topical Dictionary.* London: Greenwood Press, 1996.

Rosser, John H., ed. *Historical Dictionary of Byzantium.* London: Scarecrow Press, 2001.

Roth, Norman, ed. *Medieval Jewish Civilization: An Encyclopedia.* New York: Garland, 2003.

Royal Geographical Society. *Oxford Atlas of Exploration.* Oxford: Oxford University Press, 1997.

Rundle, David, ed. *The Hutchinson Encyclopedia of the Renaissance.* Oxford: Helicon, 1999.

Sadie, Stanley, ed. *The New Grove Dictionary of Music and Musicians.* 2d ed. 29 vols. New York: Grove's Dictionary, 2001.

Saul, Nigel. *The Batsford Companion to Medieval England.* London: Batsford Academic and Educational, 1983; reprinted as *A Companion to Medieval England, 1066–1485.* Charleston, S.C.: Tempus, 2001.

Schulman, Jana K., ed. *The Rise of the Medieval World, 500–1300: A Biographical Dictionary.* Westport, Conn.: Greenwood Press, 2002.

Sheehan, Michael M., and Jacqueline Murray, eds. *Domestic Society in Medieval Europe: A Select Bibliography.* Toronto: Pontifical Institute of Mediaeval Studies, 1990.

Sinnreich-Levi, Deborah, and Ian S. Laurie, eds. *Dictionary of Literary Biography.* Vol. 208. *Literature of the French and Occitan Middle Ages: Eleventh to Fifteenth Centuries.* Detroit: The Gale Group, 1999.

Sitwell, Gerard. ed. *Spiritual Writers of the Middle Ages.* New York: Hawthorn Books, 1961.

Snodgrass, Mary Ellen. *Who's Who in the Middle Ages.* Jefferson, N.C.: McFarland, 2001.

Stearns, Peter N., ed. *The Encyclopedia of World History: Ancient, Medieval, and Modern, Chronologically Arranged.* 6th ed. Boston: Houghton Mifflin, 2001.

Steib, Murray, ed. *Reader's Guide to Music History, Theory, Criticism.* Chicago: Fitzroy Dearborn, 1999.

Storey, R. L. *Chronology of the Medieval World: 800 to 1491.* Oxford: Helicon, 1994.

Strayer, Joseph, ed. *The Dictionary of the Middle Ages.* 13 vols. New York: Charles Scribner's Sons, 1982–1989.

Szarmach, Paul E., M. Teresa Tavormina, and Joel T. Rosenthal, eds. *Medieval England: An Encyclopedia.* New York: Garland, 1998.

Tasker, Edward G., ed. *Encyclopedia of Medieval Church Art.* London: B. T. Batsford, 1993.

Terry, Michael, ed. *Reader's Guide to Judaism.* Chicago: Fitzroy Dearborn, 2000.

Thomas, Anabel. *An Illustrated Dictionary of Narrative Painting.* London: John Murray in association with National Gallery Publications, 1994.

Turner, Jane, ed. *The Dictionary of Art.* 34 vols. New York: Macmillan, 1996.

Turner, Jane, ed. *Encyclopedia of Italian Renaissance and Mannerist Art.* 2 vols. in *Grove Encyclopedia of Art.* London: Macmillan Reference, 2000.

Uden, Grant. *A Dictionary of Chivalry.* New York: T. Y. Crowell, 1968.

Vauchez, André, with Barrie Dobson and Michael Lapidge, eds. *Encyclopedia of the Middle Ages.* 2 vols. Trans. Adrian Walford. Chicago: Fitzroy Dearborn, 2001.

Vogel, Joseph, and Jean Vogel. *Encyclopedia of Precolonial Africa: Archaeology, History, Languages, Cultures, and Environments.* London: Altamura Press, 1997.

Wigoder, Geoffrey, ed. *The New Standard Jewish Encyclopedia.* 7th ed. New York: Facts On File, 1992.

Williams, Ann, ed., *A Biographical Dictionary of Dark Age Britain: England, Scotland, and Wales, c. 500–c. 1050.* London: Seaby, 1991.

Woolf, D. R., ed. *A Global Encyclopedia of Historical Writing.* 2 vols. New York: Garland, 1998.

II. THE MEDIEVAL WORLD IN GENERAL

Aberth, John. *From the Brink of the Apocalypse: Confronting War Famine, War, Plague, and Death in the Later Middle Ages.* New York: Routledge, 2000.

Abou-El-Haj, Barbara. *The Medieval Cult of Saints: Formations and Transformations.* Cambridge: Cambridge University Press, 1994.

Abu-Lughod, Janet L. *Before European Hegemony: The World System A.D. 1250–1350.* Oxford: Oxford University Press, 1989.

Abulafia, David. *The Two Italies: Economic Relations between the Norman Kingdom of Sicily and the Northern Communes.* Cambridge: Cambridge University Press, 1977.

Abulafia, David. *The Western Mediterranean Kingdoms, 1200–1500: The Struggle for Dominion.* London: Longman, 1997.

Abulafia, David, ed. *The French Descent into Renaissance Italy, 1494–95: Antecedents and Effects.* Aldershot: Variorum, 1995.

Abulafia, David, ed. *The New Cambridge Medieval History.* Vol. 5. *c. 1198–c. 1300.* Cambridge: Cambridge University Press, 1999.

Adelson, Howard L., ed. *Medieval Commerce.* New York: Van Nostrand, 1962.

Allmand, Christopher T. *Society at War: The Experience of England and France during the Hundred Years War.* New York: Barnes & Noble, 1973.

Allmand, Christopher T., ed. *The New Cambridge Medieval History.* Vol. 7. *c. 1415–c. 1500.* Cambridge: Cambridge University Press, 1998.

Amundsen, Darrel W. *Medicine, Society, and Faith in the Ancient and Medieval Worlds.* Baltimore: Johns Hopkins University Press, 1996.

Ariès, Philip, and Georges Duby, eds. *A History of Private Life.* Vol. 2. *Revelations of the Medieval World.* Cambridge, Mass.: Harvard University Press, 1988.

Arnold, Benjamin. *Princes and Territories in Medieval Germany.* Cambridge: Cambridge University Press, 1991.

Arnold, Benjamin. *Count and Bishop in Medieval Germany: A Study of Regional Power, 1100–1350.* Philadelphia: University of Pennsylvania Press, 1991.

Arnold, Benjamin. *Medieval Germany, 500–1300: A Political Interpretation.* Toronto: University of Toronto Press, 1997.

Aston, T. H., and C. H. E. Philpin, eds. *The Brenner Debate: Agrarian Class Structure and Economic Development in Pre-Industrial Europe.* Cambridge: Cambridge University Press, 1985.

Bachrach, Bernard S., ed. *The Medieval Church: Success or Failure?* New York: Holt, Rinehart & Winston, 1972.

Bachrach, Bernard S., ed. *Merovingian Military Organization, 481–751.* Minneapolis, University of Minnesota Press, 1972.

Bachrach, Bernard S., ed. *Armies and Politics in the Early Medieval West.* Aldershot: Variorum, 1993.

Bachrach, Bernard S., ed. *State-Building in Medieval France: Studies in Early Angevin History.* Aldershot: Variorum, 1995.

Bachrach, Bernard S., ed. *Early Carolingian Warfare: Prelude to Empire.* Philadelphia: University of Pennsylvania Press, 2001.

Bak, János M. *Medieval Narrative Sources: A Chronological Guide, with a List of Major Letter Collections.* New York: Garland, 1987.

Bak, János M., ed. *Coronations: Medieval and Early Modern Monarchic Ritual.* Berkeley: University of California Press, 1990.

al-Bakhit, M. A., L. Bazin, S. M. Cissoko, eds. *History of Humanity, Scientific and Cultural Development.* Vol. 4. *From the Seventh to the Sixteenth Century.* New York: Routledge for UNESCO, 2000.

Baldwin, John W. *Masters, Princes, and Merchants: The Social Views of Peter the Chanter and His Circle.* 2 vols. Princeton, N.J.: Princeton University Press, 1970.

Baldwin, John W. *The Scholastic Culture of the Middle Ages, 1000–1300.* Lexington, Mass.: Heath, 1971.

Baldwin, John W. *The Government of Philip Augustus: Foundations of French Royal Power in the Middle Ages.* Berkeley: University of California Press, 1986.

Baldwin, John W. *The Language of Sex: Five Voices from Northern France around 1200.* Chicago: University of Chicago Press, 1994.

Ball, Warwick. *Rome in the East: The Transformation of an Empire.* London: Routledge, 2000.

Barber, Malcolm. *The Two Cities: Medieval Europe, 1050–1320.* New York: Routledge, 1992.

Barber, Richard. *The Knight and Chivalry.* Rev. ed. Woodbridge, England: Boydell Press, 1995.

Baron, Hans. *The Crisis of the Early Italian Renaissance Civic Humanism and Republican Liberty in an Age of Classicism and Tyranny.* Princeton, N.J.: Princeton University Press, 1955.

Baron, Hans. *In Search of Florentine Civic Humanism: Essays on the Transition from Medieval to Modern Thought.* 2 vols. Princeton, N.J.: Princeton University Press, 1988.

Barraclough, Geoffrey. *Medieval Germany, 911–1250.* 2 vols. Oxford: Blackwell, 1938.

Barraclough, Geoffrey. *The Medieval Empire: Idea and Reality.* London: The Historical Association, 1950. Reprinted in *History in a Changing World.* Oxford: Blackwell, 1956, 105–130.

Barraclough, Geoffrey. *The Origins of Modern Germany.* Oxford: Blackwell, 1957.

Barraclough, Geoffrey. *The Medieval Papacy.* London: Thames and Hudson, 1968.

Barraclough, Geoffrey, ed. *Eastern and Western Europe in the Middle Ages.* London: Thames and Hudson, 1970.

Barraclough, Geoffrey. *The Crucible of Europe: The Ninth and Tenth Centuries in European History.* Berkeley: University of California Press, 1976.

Bartlett, Robert. *Trial by Fire and Water: The Medieval Judicial Ordeal.* Oxford: Oxford University Press, 1986.

Bartlett, Robert. *The Making of Europe: Conquest, Colonization and Cultural Change, 950–1350.* Princeton, N.J.: Princeton University Press, 1993.

Bartlett, Robert, ed. *Medieval Panorama.* Los Angeles: J. Paul Getty Museum, 2001.

Bartlett, Robert, and Angus MacKay, eds. *Medieval Frontier Societies.* Oxford: Clarendon Press, 1989.

Becker, Marvin B. *Florence in Transition.* 2 vols. Baltimore: Johns Hopkins University Press, 1967–1968.

Becker, Marvin B. *Medieval Italy: Constraints and Creativity.* Bloomington: Indiana University Press, 1981.

Becker, Marvin B. *Florentine Essays: Selected Writings of Marvin B. Becker.* Ann Arbor: University of Michigan Press, 2002.

Beckwith, Sarah. *Christ's Body: Identity, Culture and Society in Late Medieval Writings.* New York: Routledge, 1993.

Beeler, John. *Warfare in Feudal Europe, 730–1200.* Ithaca, N.Y.: Cornell University Press, 1971.

Bell, Rudolph M. *Holy Anorexia.* Chicago: University of Chicago Press, 1985.

Bell, Rudolph M. *How to Do It: Guide to Good Living for Renaissance Italians.* Chicago: University of Chicago Press, 1999.

Bell-Fialkoff, Andrew, ed. *The Role of Migration in the History of the Eurasian Steppe: Sedentary Civilization vs.*

"Barbarian" and Nomad. New York: St. Martin's Press, 2000.

Bellomo, Manlio. *The Common Legal Past of Europe, 1000–1800.* Trans. Lydia G. Cochrane. Washington, D.C.: Catholic University of America Press, 1995.

Benson, Robert, and Giles Constable with Carol D. Lanham, eds. *Renaissance and Renewal in the Twelfth Century.* Cambridge, Mass.: Harvard University Press, 1982.

Berman, Harold J. *Law and Revolution: The Formation of the Western Legal Tradition.* Cambridge, Mass.: Harvard University Press, 1983.

Bernhardt, John W. *Itinerant Kingship and Royal Monasteries in Early Medieval Germany, c. 936–1075.* Cambridge: Cambridge University Press, 1993.

Berschin, Walter. *Greek Letters and the Latin Middle Ages: From Jerome to Nicholas of Cusa.* Trans. Jerold C. Frakes. Washington, D.C.: Catholic University of America Press, 1988.

Bertelli, Sergio. *The Courts of the Italian Renaissance.* New York: Facts On File, 1986.

Biller, Peter, and A. J. Minnis, eds. *Medieval Theology and the Natural Body.* Rochester: York Medieval Press, 1997.

Biller, Peter, and A. J. Minnis, eds. *Handling Sin: Confession in the Middle Ages.* Woodbridge: York Medieval Press, 1998.

Bisson, Thomas N. *Medieval France and Her Neighbours: Essays in Early Intsitutional History.* London: Hambledon Press, 1989.

Bisson, Thomas N., ed. *Cultures of Power: Lordship, Status, and Process in Twelfth-Century Europe.* Philadelphia: University of Pennsylvania Press, 1995.

Biow, Douglas. *Doctors, Ambassadors, Secretaries: Humanism and Professions in Renaissance Italy.* Chicago: University of Chicago Press, 2002.

Black, Antony. *Political Thought in Europe, 1250–1450.* Cambridge: Cambridge University Press, 1992.

Bloch, Marc. *Feudal Society.* 2 vols. Trans. L. A. Manyon, 1939. Reprint, Chicago: University of Chicago Press, 1961.

Bloch, R. Howard. *Medieval Misogyny and the Invention of Western Romantic Love.* Chicago: University of Chicago Press, 1991.

Blumenthal, Uta-Renate. *The Investiture Controversy: Church and Monarchy from the Ninth to the Twelfth Century.* Philadelphia: University of Pennsylvania Press, 1988.

Bois, Guy. *The Crisis of Feudalism: Economy and Society in Eastern Normandy c. 1300–1550.* Cambridge: Cambridge University Press, 1984.

Bolgar, R. R. *The Classical Heritage and Its Beneficiaries: From the Carolingian Age to the End of the Renaissance.* Cambridge: Cambridge University Press, 1954.

Bolton, Brenda. *The Medieval Reformation.* London: Edward Arnold, 1983.

Bonnassie, Pierre. *From Slavery to Feudalism in South-Western Europe.* Trans. Jean Birrell. Cambridge: Cambridge University Press, 1991.

Bossy, John. *Christianity in the West, 1400–1700.* Oxford: Oxford University Press, 1985.

Boswell, John. *Christianity, Social Tolerance, and Homosexuality: Gay People in Western Europe from the Beginning of the Christian Era to the Fourteenth Century.* Chicago: University of Chicago Press, 1980.

Boswell, John. *The Kindness of Strangers: The Abandonment of Children in Western Europe from Late Antiquity to the Renaissance.* New York: Pantheon Books, 1988.

Boswell, John. *Same-Sex Unions in Premodern Europe.* New York: Villard Books, 1994.

Bouchard, Constance Brittain. *Strong of Body, Brave and Noble: Chivalry and Society in Medieval France.* Ithaca, N.Y.: Cornell University Press, 1998.

Bouchard, Constance Brittain. *"Those of My Blood": Constructing Noble Families in Medieval Francia.* Philadelphia: University of Pennsylvania Press, 2001.

Bowsky, William M. *The Black Death: A Turning Point in History?* New York: Holt, Rinehart & Winston, 1971.

Brentano, Robert. *Rome before Avignon: A Social History of Thirteenth-Century Rome.* New York: Basic Books, 1974.

Brentano, Robert. *Two Churches: England and Italy in the Thirteenth Century.* 1968. Reprint, Berkeley: University of California Press, 1988.

Brentano, Robert. *A New World in a Small Place: Church and Religion in the Diocese of Rieti, 1188–1378.* Berkeley: University of California Press, 1994.

Brooke, Christopher N. L. *The Twelfth Century Renaissance.* London: Thames and Hudson, 1969.

Brooke, Christopher N. L. *The Medieval Idea of Marriage.* Oxford: Oxford University Press, 1989.

Brooke, Christopher N. L. *Europe in the Central Middle Ages, 962–1154.* 3d ed. Harlow: Longman, 2000.

Brooke, Rosalind B., ed. *The Coming of the Friars.* London: George Allen and Unwin, 1975.

Brooke, Rosalind B., and Christopher N. L. Brooke. *Popular Religion in the Middle Ages: Western Europe, 1000–1300.* London: Thames and Hudson, 1984.

Brown, Elizabeth A. R. *The Monarchy of Capetian France and Royal Ceremonial.* London: Variorum, 1991.

Brown, Judith C., and Robert C. Davis, eds. *Gender and Society in Renaissance Italy.* London: Longman, 1998.

Brown, Peter Robert Lamont. *The Making of Late Antiquity.* Cambridge, Mass.: Harvard University Press, 1978.

Brown, Peter Robert Lamont. *The Cult of the Saints: Its Rise and Function in Latin Christianity.* Chicago: University of Chicago Press, 1981.

Brown, Peter Robert Lamont. *Society and the Holy in Late Antiquity.* Berkeley: University of California Press, 1982.

Brown, Peter Robert Lamont. *The Body and Society: Men, Women, and Sexual Renunciation in Early Christianity.* New York: Columbia University Press, 1988.

Brown, Peter Robert Lamont. *Power and Persuasion in Late Antiquity: Towards a Christian Empire.* Madison: University of Wisconsin Press, 1992.

Brown, Peter Robert Lamont. *Authority and the Sacred: Aspects of the Christianisation of the Roman World.* Cambridge: Cambridge University Press, 1995.

Brown, Peter Robert Lamont. *The Rise of Western Christendom: Triumph and Diversity,* A.D. *200–1000.* Cambridge, Mass.: Blackwell, 1996.

Brown, Peter Robert Lamont. *Poverty and Leadership in the Later Roman Empire.* London: Brandeis University Press, 2002.

Brucker, Gene A. *Florentine Politics and Society, 1343–1378.* Princeton, N.J.: Princeton University Press, 1962.

Brucker, Gene A., ed. *Two Memoirs of Renaissance Florence: The Diaries of Buonaccorso Pitti and Gregorio Dati.* New York: Harper & Row, 1967.

Brucker, Gene A., ed. *The Society of Renaissance Florence: A Documentary Study.* New York: Harper & Row, 1971.

Brucker, Gene A. *The Civic World of Early Renaissance Florence.* Princeton, N.J.: Princeton University Press, 1977.

Brucker, Gene A. *Florence, the Golden Age, 1138–1737.* New York: Abbeville Press, 1984.

Brucker, Gene A. *Giovanni and Lusanna: Love and Marriage in Renaissance Florence.* Berkeley: University of California Press, 1986.

Brundage, James A. *The Crusades: Motives and Achievements.* Boston: D. C. Heath, 1964.

Brundage, James A. *Medieval Canon Law and the Crusader.* Madison: University of Wisconsin Press, 1969.

Brundage, James A. *Law, Sex and Christian Society in Medieval Europe.* Chicago: University of Chicago Press, 1987.

Brundage, James A. *Medieval Canon Law.* New York: Longman, 1995.

Bullough, Donald. *The Age of Charlemagne.* London: Eleck Books, 1965.

Burckhardt, Jacob. *The Civilization of the Renaissance in Italy.* 2 vols. Trans. S. G. C. Middlemore. Introduction by Benjamin Nelson and Charles Trinkaus. New York: Harper, 1958.

Burke, Peter. *The Italian Renaissance: Culture and Society in Italy.* 1972. Reprint, Princeton, N.J.: Princeton University Press, 1986.

Burke, Peter. *The Historical Anthropology of Early Modern Italy: Essays on Perception and Communication.* Cambridge: Cambridge University Press, 1987.

Burke, Peter. *The Renaissance.* 2d ed. New York: St. Martin's Press, 1997.

Burke, Peter. *The European Renaissance: Centres and Peripheries.* Oxford: Blackwell, 1998.

Burns, J. H., ed. *The Cambridge History of Medieval Political Thought, c. 350–c. 1450.* Cambridge: Cambridge University Press, 1988.

Burns, J. H. ed. *The Cambridge History of Political Thought, 1450–1700.* Cambridge: Cambridge University Press, 1991.

Burns, J. H. and Thomas M. Izbicki, eds. *Conciliarism and Papalism.* Cambridge: Cambridge University Press, 1997.

Burns, Robert Ignatius. *The Crusader Kingdom of Valencia: Reconstruction on a Thirteenth-Century Frontier.* 2 vols. Cambridge, Mass.: Harvard University Press, 1967.

Burns, Robert Ignatius. *Medieval Colonialism: Postcrusade Exploitation of Islamic Valencia.* Princeton, N.J.: Princeton University Press, 1975.

Burns, Robert Ignatius. *Muslims, Christians, and Jews in the Crusader Kingdom of Valencia: Societies in Symbiosis.* Cambridge: Cambridge University Press, 1984.

Bynum, Carolyn Walker. *Jesus as Mother: Studies in the Spirituality of the High Middle Ages.* Berkeley: University of California Press, 1982.

Bynum, Carolyn Walker. *Holy Feast and Holy Fast: The Religious Significance of Food to Medieval Women.* Berkeley: University of California Press, 1987.

Bynum, Carolyn Walker. *Fragmentation and Redemption: Essays on Gender and the Human Body in Medieval Religion.* New York: Zone Books, 1991.

Bynum, Carolyn Walker. *The Resurrection of the Body in Western Christianity, 200–1336.* New York: Columbia University Press, 1995.

Bynum, Carolyn Walker, and Paul Freedman, eds. *Last Things: Death and the Apocalypse in the Middle Ages.* Philadelphia: University of Pennsylvania Press, 2000.

Cadden, Joan. *Meanings of Sex Difference in the Middle Ages: Medicine, Science, and Culture.* Cambridge: Cambridge University Press, 1993.

Caenegem, R. C. van. *Guide to the Sources of Medieval History.* New York: North-Holland, 1978.

Cameron, Averil. *The Mediterranean World in Late Antiquity,* A.D. *395–600.* London: Routledge, 1993.

Cameron, Averil, and Peter Garnsey, eds. *The Cambridge Ancient History.* Vol. 13. *The Late Empire,* A.D. *337–425.* Cambridge: Cambridge University Press, 1998.

Canning, Joseph. *A History of Medieval Political Thought, 300–1450.* New York: Routledge, 1996.

Cantor, Norman F. *In the Wake of the Plague: The Black Death and the World It Made.* New York: Free Press, 2001.

Carmichael, Ann G. *Plague and the Poor in Renaissance Florence.* Cambridge: Cambridge University Press, 1986.

Carruthers, Mary. *The Book of Memory: A Study of Memory in Medieval Culture.* Cambridge: Cambridge University Press, 1990.

Carruthers, Mary. *The Craft of Thought: Mediation, Rhetoric, and the Making of Images, 400–1200.* New York: Cambridge University Press, 1998.

Cattin, Giulio. *Music of the Middle Ages.* 2 vols. Trans. Steven Botterill. Cambridge: Cambridge University Press, 1984–1985.

Chambers, David, and Trevor Dean. *Clean Hands and Rough Justice: An Investigating Magistrate in Renaissance Italy.* Ann Arbor: University of Michigan Press, 1997.

Chaunu, Pierre. *European Expansion in the Later Middle Ages.* Trans. Katharine Bertram. Amsterdam: North Holland, 1979.

Chenu, Marie-Dominique. *Toward Understanding Saint Thomas.* Trans. A. M. Landry and D. Hughes. Chicago: H. Regnery, 1964.

Chenu, Marie-Dominique. *Nature, Man, and Society in the Twelfth Century: Essays on New Theological Perspectives in the Latin West.* Trans. Jerome Taylor and Lester K. Little. 1957. Reprint, Chicago: University of Chicago Press, 1968.

Cheyette, Fredric L. *Ermengard of Narbonne and the World of the Troubadours.* Ithaca, N.Y.: Cornell University Press, 2001.

Chibnall, Marjorie. *The Normans.* Oxford: Blackwell, 2000.

Christiansen, Eric. *The Northern Crusades: The Baltic and the Catholic Frontier, 1100–1525.* New York: Penguin Books, 1997.

Christie, Neil. *The Lombards.* Oxford: Blackwell, 1995.

Ciappelli, Giovanni, and Patricia Lee Rubin, eds. *Art, Memory, and Family in Renaissance Florence.* Cambridge: Cambridge University Press, 2000.

Cipolla, Carlo M. *Before the Industrial Revolution: European Society and Economy, 1000–1700.* 3d ed. New York: Norton, 1993.

Cobban, Alan B. *The Medieval Universities: Their Development and Organization.* London: Methuen, 1975.

Cobban, Alan B. *Universities in the Middle Ages.* Liverpool: Liverpool University Press, 1990.

Cohn, Samuel Kline, Jr., *The Laboring Classes in Renaissance Florence.* New York: Academic Press, 1980.

Cohn, Samuel Kline, Jr. *Death and Property in Siena, 1205–1800: Strategies for the Afterlife.* Baltimore: Johns Hopkins University Press, 1988.

Cohn, Samuel Kline, Jr. *The Cult of Remembrance and the Black Death: Six Renaissance Cities in Central Italy.* Baltimore: Johns Hopkins University Press, 1992.

Cohn, Samuel Kline, Jr. *Creating the Florentine State: Peasants and Rebellion, 1348–1434.* Cambridge: Cambridge University Press, 1999.

Colish, Marcia. *Medieval Foundations of the Western Tradition, 400–1400.* New Haven, Conn.: Yale University Press, 1997.

Collins, Roger. *Early Medieval Spain: Unity in Diversity, 400–1000.* London: Macmillan, 1983.

Collins, Roger. *Early Medieval Europe, 300–1000.* Rev. ed. New York: St. Martin's Press, 1995.

Collins, Roger. *Spain: An Oxford Archaeological Guide.* Oxford: Oxford University Press, 1998.

Connell, William J., and Andrea Zorzi, eds. *Florentine Tuscany: Structures and Practices of Power.* Cambridge: Cambridge University Press, 2000.

Connell, William J., ed. *Society and Individual in Renaissance Florence.* Berkeley: University of California Press, 2002.

Constable, Giles. *Monastic Tithes: From Their Origins to the Twelfth Century.* Cambridge: Cambridge University Press, 1964.

Constable, Giles, ed. *Medieval Monasticism: A Select Bibliography.* Toronto: University of Toronto Press, 1976.

Constable, Giles. *Three Studies in Medieval Religious and Social Thought.* Cambridge: Cambridge University Press, 1995.

Constable, Giles. *The Reformation of the Twelfth Century.* Cambridge: Cambridge University Press, 1996.

Constable, Olivia Remie, ed. *Medieval Iberia: Readings from Christian, Muslim, and Jewish Sources.* Philadelphia: University of Pennsylvania Press, 1997.

Contamine, Philippe. *War in the Middle Ages.* Trans. Michael Jones. 1980. Reprint, Oxford: Blackwell, 1984.

Crane, Susan. *The Performance of Self: Ritual, Clothing and Identity during the Hundred Years War.* Philadelphia: University of Pennsylvania Press, 2002.

Crocker, Richard. *The Early Medieval Sequence.* Berkeley: University of California Press, 1977.

Crocker, Richard. *An Introduction to Gregorian Chant.* New Haven, Conn.: Yale University Press, 2000.

Crocker, Richard, and David Hiley, eds. *New Oxford History of Music.* Vol. 2. *The Early Middle Ages to 1300.* 2d ed. Oxford: Oxford University Press, 1990.

Curtius, Ernst Robert. *European Literature and the Latin Middle Ages.* Trans. Walter Trask. 1948. Reprint, Princeton, N.J.: Princeton University Press, 1953.

Davies, Norman. *God's Playground: A History of Poland.* Vol. 1. New York: Columbia University Press, 1984.

Davies, Wendy, and Paul Fouracre, eds. *Property and Power in the Early Middle Ages.* Cambridge: Cambridge University Press, 1995.

Davies, Wendy, and Paul Fouracre, eds. *The Settlement of Disputes in Early Medieval Europe.* Cambridge: Cambridge University Press, 1986.

d'Avray, David L. *The Preaching of the Friars: Sermons Diffused from Paris before 1300.* Oxford: Clarendon Press, 1985.

d'Avray, David L. *Death and the Prince: Memorial Preaching before 1350.* Oxford: Clarendon Press, 1994.

Dean, Trevor, ed. *The Towns of Italy in the Later Middle Ages.* Manchester: Manchester University Press, 2000.

Dean, Trevor, ed. *Marriage in Italy, 1300–1650.* Cambridge: Cambridge University Press, 1998.

Dean, Trevor. *Crime in Medieval Europe, 1200–1550.* New York: Longman, 2001.

Dean, Trevor, and K. J. P. Lowe, eds. *Crime, Society, and the Law in Renaissance Italy.* Cambridge: Cambridge University Press, 1994.

Deaux, George. *The Black Death 1347.* London: Hamish Hamilton, 1969.

Debby, Nirit Ben-Aryeh. *Renaissance Florence in the Rhetoric of Two Popular Preachers: Giovanni Dominici (1356–1419) and Bernardino da Siena (1380–1444).* Turnhout: Brepols, 2001.

Delumeau, Jean. *Sin and Fear: The Emergence of a Western Guilt Culture 13th–18th Centuries.* Trans. Eric Nicholson. 1983. Reprint, New York: St. Martin's Press, 1990.

DeVries, Kelly. *Medieval Military Technology.* Peterborough, Canada: Broadview Press, 1992.

DeVries, Kelly. *A Cumulative Bibliography of Medieval Military History and Technology.* Leiden: Brill, 2002.

Duffy, Eamon. *Saints and Sinners: A History of the Popes.* New Haven, Conn.: Yale University Press, 1997.

Dunbabin, Jean. *France in the Making, 843–1180.* Oxford: Oxford University Press, 1985.

Du Boulay, F. R. H. *Germany in the Later Middle Ages.* New York: St. Martin's Press, 1983.

Duby, Georges. *Rural Economy and Country Life in the Medieval West.* Trans. Cynthia Postan. 1962. Reprint, Columbia: University of South Carolina Press, 1968.

Duby, Georges. *The Early Growth of the European Economy; Warriors and Peasants from the Seventh to the Twelfth*

Century. Trans. Howard B. Clarke. Ithaca, N.Y.: Cornell University Press, 1974.

Duby, Georges. *The Chivalrous Society.* Berkeley: University of California Press, 1977.

Duby, Georges. *Medieval Marriage: Two Models from Twelfth-Century France.* Trans. Elborg Foster. Baltimore: Johns Hopkins University Press, 1978.

Duby, Georges. *The Three Orders: Feudal Society Imagined.* Trans. Arthur Goldhammer. 1978. Reprint, Chicago: University of Chicago Press, 1980.

Duby, Georges. *The Knight, the Lady and the Priest: The Making of Modern Marriage in Medieval France.* Trans. Barbara Bray. New York: Pantheon, 1983.

Duby, Georges. *Love and Marriage in the Middle Ages.* Trans. Jane Dunnett. Chicago: University of Chicago Press, 1994.

Duckett, Eleanor Shipley. *Carolingian Portraits: A Study in the Ninth Century.* Ann Arbor: University of Michigan Press, 1962.

Duckett, Eleanor Shipley. *Death and Life in the Tenth Century.* Ann Arbor: University of Michigan Press, 1967.

Eamon, William. *Science and the Secrets of Nature: Books of Secrets in Medieval and Early Modern Culture.* Princeton, N.J.: Princeton University Press, 1994.

Edgerton, Samuel Y., Jr. *Pictures and Punishment: Art and Criminal Prosecution during the Florentine Renaissance.* Ithaca, N.Y.: Cornell University Press, 1985.

Edwards, Robert R., and Stephen Spector, eds. *The Olde Daunce: Love, Friendship, Sex and Marriage in the Medieval World.* Albany: State University of New York Press, 1991.

Elliott, Dyan. *Spiritual Marriage: Sexual Abstinence in Medieval Wedlock.* Princeton, N.J.: Princeton University Press, 1993.

Elliott, Dyan. *Fallen Bodies: Pollution, Sexuality, and Demonology in the Middle Ages.* Philadelphia: University of Pennsylvania Press, 1999.

Ekelund, Robert B. *Sacred Trust: The Medieval Church as an Economic Firm.* New York: Oxford University Press, 1996.

Emery, Kent, Jr. *Monastic, Scholastic, and Mystical Theologies from the Later Middle Ages.* Aldershot: Variorum, 1996.

Emery, Kent, Jr., and Joseph Wawrykow, eds. *Christ among the Medieval Dominicans: Representations of Christ in the Texts and Images of the Order of Preachers.* Notre Dame, Ind.: University of Notre Dame Press, 1998.

Ennen, Edith. *The Medieval Town.* Trans. Natalie Fryde. Amsterdam: North Holland, 1979.

Erdmann, Carl. *The Origin of the Idea of Crusade.* Trans. Marshall W. Baldwin and Walter Goffart. 1935. Reprint, Princeton, N.J.: Princeton University Press, 1977.

Evans, Gillian, ed. *The Medieval Theologians: An Introduction to Theology in the Medieval Period.* Oxford: Blackwell, 2001.

Evergates, Theodore, ed. *Feudal Society in Medieval France: Documents from the County of Champagne.* Philadelphia: University of Pennsylvania Press, 1993.

Febvre, Lucien Paul Victor, and Henri-Jean Martin. *The Coming of the Book: The Impact of Printing 1450–1800.*

Trans. David Gerard and ed. Geoffrey Nowell-Smith and David Wootton. London: N.L.B., 1976.

Fenster, Thelma, and Clare A. Lees, eds. *Gender in Debate from the Early Middle Ages to the Renaissance.* New York: Palgrave, 2002.

Ferreiro, Alberto, ed. *The Visigoths: Studies in Culture and Society.* Leiden: Brill, 1999.

Ferruolo, Stephen C. *The Origins of the University: The Schools of Paris and Their Critics, 1100–1215.* Stanford, Calif.: Stanford University Press, 1985.

Fichtenau, Heinrich. *Living in the Tenth Century: Mentalities and Social Orders.* Trans. Patrick J. Geary. Chicago: University of Chicago Press, 1991.

Findlen, Paula, ed. *The Italian Renaissance: The Essential Readings.* New York: Blackwell, 2002.

Finucane, Ronald C. *Miracles and Pilgrims: Popular Beliefs in Medieval England.* London: J. M. Dent, 1977.

Finucane, Ronald C. *Soldiers of the Faith: Crusaders and Moslems at War.* London: J. M. Dent, 1983.

Finucane, Ronald C. *Appearances of the Dead: A Cultural History of Ghosts.* Buffalo, N.Y.: Prometheus Books, 1984.

Finucane, Ronald C. *The Rescue of the Innocents: Endangered Children in Medieval Miracles.* New York: St. Martin's Press, 1997.

Fletcher, Richard. *The Barbarian Conversion from Paganism to Christianity.* New York: Henry Holt, 1997.

Folz, Robert. *The Concept of Empire in Western Europe from the Fifth to the Fourteenth Century.* 1953. Reprint, New York: Harper & Row, 1969.

Fortin, Ernest L., ed. "Political Philosophy in Christianity." In *Medieval Political Philosophy* ed. Ralph Lerner and Muhsin Mahdi. Ithaca, N.Y.: Cornell University Press, 1963, 271–526.

Fossier, Robert, ed. *The Cambridge Illustrated History of the Middle Ages.* Vol. 1, *350–950.* Trans. Janet Sondheimer. Cambridge: Cambridge University Press, 1989.

Fossier, Robert, ed. *The Cambridge Illustrated History of the Middle Ages.* Vol. 2, *950–1250.* Trans. Stuart Airlie and Robyn Marsack. Cambridge: Cambridge University Press, 1997.

Fossier, Robert, ed. *The Cambridge Illustrated History of the Middle Ages.* Vol. 3, *1250–1520.* Trans. Sarah Hanbury Tenison. Cambridge: Cambridge University Press, 1986.

France, John. *Victory in the East: A Military History of the First Crusade.* Cambridge: Cambridge University Press, 1994.

France, John. *Western Warfare in the Age of the Crusades, 1000–1300.* Ithaca, N.Y.: Cornell University Press, 1999.

Freedman, Paul. *The Origins of Peasant Servitude in Medieval Catalonia.* Cambridge: Cambridge University Press, 1991.

Freedman, Paul. *Images of the Medieval Peasant.* Stanford, Calif.: Stanford University Press, 1999.

Frend, W. H. C. *The Rise of Christianity.* Philadelphia: Fortress Press, 1984.

Fuhrmann, Horst. *Germany in the High Middle Ages, c. 1050–1200.* Cambridge: Cambridge University Press, 1986.

Gallo, F. Alberto. *Music of the Middle Ages.* Vol. 2, Trans. Karen Ellis. 1977. Reprint, Cambridge: Cambridge University Press, 1985.

Gallo, F. Alberto. *Music in the Castle: Troubadours, Books, and Orators in Italian Courts of the Thirteenth, Fourteenth, and Fifteenth Centuries.* Trans. Anna Herklotz and Kathryn Krug. Chicago: University of Chicago Press, 1995.

Ganshof, François Louis. *Frankish Institutions under Charlemagne.* Trans. Bryce and Mary Lyon. Providence, R.I.: Brown University Press, 1968.

Ganshof, François Louis. *The Carolingians and the Frankish Monarchy: Studies in Carolingian History.* Trans. Janet Sondheimer. Ithaca, N.Y.: Cornell University Press, 1971.

Ganshof, François Louis. *Feudalism.* Trans. Philip Grierson. 1964. Reprint, Toronto: University of Toronto Press, 1996.

Garin, Eugenio. *Italian Humanism: Philosophy and Civic Life in the Renaissance.* Trans. Peter Munz. Oxford: Blackwell, 1965.

Garin, Eugenio. *Science and Civic Life in the Italian Renaissance.* Trans. Peter Munz. 1966. Reprint, Garden City, N.Y.: Anchor Books, 1969.

Garin, Eugenio, ed. *Renaissance Characters.* Trans. Lydia G. Cochrane. 1988. Reprint, Chicago: University of Chicago Press, 1991.

Gavitt, Philip. *Charity and Children in Renaissance Florence: The Ospedale degli Innocenti, 1410–1536.* Ann Arbor: University of Michigan Press, 1990.

Geary, Patrick J. *Furta Sacra: Thefts of Relics in the Central Middle Ages.* Princeton, N.J.: Princeton University Press, 1978.

Geary, Patrick J. *Phantoms of Remembrance: Memory and Oblivion at the End of the First Millennium.* Princeton, N.J.: Princeton University Press, 1994.

Geary, Patrick J. *Living with the Dead in the Middle Ages.* Ithaca, N.Y.: Cornell University Press, 1994.

Gellrich, Jesse M. *The Idea of the Book in the Middle Ages: Language Theory, Mythology, and Fiction.* Ithaca, N.Y.: Cornell University Press, 1985.

Genicot, Léopold. *Rural Communities in the Medieval West.* Baltimore: Johns Hopkins University Press, 1990.

Geremek, Bronislaw. *The Margins of Society in Late Medieval Paris.* Trans. Jean Birrell. Cambridge: Cambridge University Press, 1987.

Gies, Frances, and Joseph Gies. *Life in a Medieval City.* New York: Crowell, 1969.

Gies, Frances, and Joseph Gies. *Merchants and Moneymen: The Commercial Revolution, 1000–1500.* New York: Crowell, 1972.

Gies, Frances, and Joseph Gies. *Marriage and the Family in the Middle Ages.* New York: Harper & Row, 1987.

Gies, Frances, and Joseph Gies. *Life in a Medieval Village.* New York: Harper & Row, 1990.

Gieysztor, Alexander, "Medieval Poland." In *History of Poland,* ed. Alexander Gieysztor et al. Warsaw: Polish Scientific Publishers, 1968, 31–165.

Gillingham, J. B. *The Kingdom of Germany in the High Middle Ages.* London: Historical Association, 1971.

Gilson, Étienne. *Reason and Revelation in the Middle Ages.* New York: Charles Scribners's Sons, 1938.

Gilson, Étienne. *History of Christian Philosophy in the Middle Ages.* New York: Random House, 1955.

Gilson, Étienne. *The Spirit of Medieval Philosophy.* Trans. A. H. C. Downes. London: Sheed and Ward, 1936.

Gimpel, Jean. *The Medieval Machine: The Industrial Revolution of the Middle Ages.* New York: Holt, Rinehart & Winston, 1976.

Given, James. *State and Society in Medieval Europe: Gwynedd and Languedoc under Outside Rule.* Ithaca, N.Y.: Cornell University Press, 1990.

Glick, Thomas F. *Irrigation and Society in Medieval Valencia.* Cambridge, Mass.: Belknap Press of Harvard University Press, 1970.

Glick, Thomas F. *Islamic and Christian Spain in the Early Middle Ages.* Princeton, N.J.: Princeton University Press, 1979.

Glick, Thomas F. *From Muslim Fortress to Christian Castle: Social and Cultural Change in Medieval Spain.* Manchester: Manchester University Press, 1995.

Goetz, Hans-Werner. *Life in the Middle Ages from the Seventh to the Thirteenth Century.* Trans. Albert Wimmer and ed. Steven Rowan. 1986. Reprint, Notre Dame, Ind.: University of Notre Dame Press, 1993.

Goffart, Walter A. *Barbarians and Romans, A.D. 418–584: The Techniques of Accommodation.* Princeton, N.J.: Princeton University Press, 1980.

Goffart, Walter A. *The Narrators of Barbarian History (A.D. 550–800): Jordanes, Gregory of Tours, Bede, and Paul the Deacon.* Princeton, N.J.: Princeton University Press, 1988.

Gold, Penny Schine. *The Lady and the Virgin: Image, Attitude, and Experience in Twelfth-Century France.* Chicago: University of Chicago Press, 1985.

Goldberg, Jonathan. *Sodometries: Renaissance Texts, Modern Sexualities.* Stanford, Calif.: Stanford University Press, 1992.

Goldthwaite, Richard A. *Private Wealth in Renaissance Florence: A Study of Four Families.* Princeton, N.J.: Princeton University Press, 1968.

Goodich, Michael E. *From Birth to Old Age: The Human Life Cycle in Medieval Thought, 1250–1350.* London: University Press of American, 1989.

Goodich, Michael E. *Violence and Miracle in the Fourteenth Century: Private Grief and Public Salvation.* Chicago: University of Chicago Press, 1995.

Goodich, Michael E., ed. *Other Middle Ages: Witnesses at the Margins of Medieval Society.* Philadelphia: University of Pennsylvania Press, 1998.

Goodman, Anthony, and Angus MacKay, eds. *The Impact of Humanism on Western Europe.* New York: Longman, 1990.

Goody, Jack. *The Development of the Family and Marriage in Europe.* Cambridge: Cambridge University Press, 1983.

Gottfried, Robert S. *The Black Death: Natural and Human Disaster in Medieval Europe.* New York: Free Press, 1983.

Grant, Edward, ed. *A Source Book in Medieval Science.* Cambridge, Mass.: Harvard University Press, 1974.

Grant, Edward. *Planets, Stars, and Orbs: The Medieval Cosmos, 1200–1687.* Cambridge: Cambridge University Press, 1994.

Grant, Edward. *The Foundations of Modern Science in the Middle Ages: Their Religious, Institutional and Intellectual Contexts.* Cambridge: Cambridge University Press, 1996.

Grendler, Paul F. *Schooling in Renaissance Italy: Literacy and Learning, 1300–1600.* Baltimore: Johns Hopkins University Press, 1989.

Grendler, Paul F. *Books and Schools in the Italian Renaissance.* Aldershot: Variorum, 1995.

Grendler, Paul F. *The Universities of the Italian Renaissance:* Baltimore: John Hopkins University, 2002.

Grubb, James S. *Firstborn of Venice: Vicenza in the Early Renaissance.* Baltimore: Johns Hopkins University Press, 1988.

Grubb, James S. *Provincial Families of the Renaissance: Private and Public Life in the Veneto.* Baltimore: Johns Hopkins University Press, 1996.

Grundmann, Herbert. *Religious Movements in the Middle Ages: The Historical Links between Heresy, the Mendicant Orders, and the Women's Religious Movement in the Twelfth and Thirteenth Century, with the Historical Foundation of German Mysticism.* Trans. Steven Rowan. 2d. ed. Reprint, Notre Dame, Ind.: University of Notre Dame Press, 1995.

Gurevich, Aaron J. *Categories of Medieval Culture.* Trans. G. L. Campbell. London: Routledge and Kegan Paul, 1985.

Gurevich, Aaron J. *Medieval Popular Culture: Problems of Belief and Perception.* Trans. János M. Bak and Paul A. Hollingsworth. Cambridge: Cambridge University Press, 1988.

Gurevich, Aaron J. *Historical Anthropology of the Middle Ages.* Ed. Jana Howlett. Chicago: University of Chicago Press, 1992.

Gurevich, Aaron J. *The Origins of European Individualism.* Trans. Katherine Judelson. Oxford: Blackwell, 1995.

Hale, John R. *Florence and the Medici: The Pattern of Control.* London: Thames and Hudson, 1977.

Hale, John R. *War and Society in Renaissance Europe, 1450–1620.* London: Fontana, 1985.

Hale, John R. *Artists and Warfare in the Renaissance.* New Haven, Conn.: Yale University Press, 1990.

Hale, John R. *The Civilization of Europe in the Renaissance.* New York: Maxwell Macmillan International, 1994.

Hale, John R., Roger Highfield, and Beryl Smalley, eds., *Europe in the Late Middle Ages.* London: Faber and Faber, 1965.

Hall, Bert S. *Weapons and Warfare in Renaissance Europe: Gunpowder, Technology, and Tactics.* Baltimore: Johns Hopkins University Press, 1997.

Hallam, Elizabeth M., ed. *Chronicles of the Crusades: Nine Crusades and Two Hundred Years of Bitter Conflict for the Holy Land Brought to Life through the Words of Those Who Were Actually There.* New York: Weidenfeld and Nicolson, 1989.

Hallam, Elizabeth M., and Judith Everard. *Capetian France, 987–1328.* 2d ed. New York: Longman, 2001.

Hamilton, Bernard. *The Medieval Inquisition.* London: Edward Arnold, 1981.

Hamilton, Bernard. *Religion in the Medieval West.* London: Edward Arnold, 1986.

Hamilton, Bernard. *The Leper King and His Heirs: Baldwin IV and the Crusader Kingdom of Jerusalem.* Cambridge: Cambridge University Press, 2000.

Hampe, Karl. *Germany under the Salian and Hohenstaufen Emperors.* Trans. Ralph Bennett. 1968. Reprint, Oxford: Blackwell, 1973.

Hankins, James, ed. *Renaissance Civic Humanism: Reappraisals and Reflections.* Cambridge: Cambridge University Press, 2000.

Haren, Michael. *Medieval Thought: The Western Intellectual Tradition from Antiquity to the 13th Century.* London: Macmillan, 1985.

Harley, J. B., and David Woodward, eds. *The History of Cartography.* Vol. 1, *Cartography in Prehistoric, Ancient, and Medieval Europe and the Mediterranean.* Chicago: University of Chicago Press, 1987.

Harvey, P. D. A. *Medieval Maps.* Toronto: University of Toronto Press, 1991.

Haskins, Charles Homer. *The Renaissance of the Twelfth Century.* 1927. Reprint, New York: Meridian, 1957.

Haverkamp, Alfred. *Medieval Germany, 1056–1273.* 2d ed. Trans. Helga Braun and Richard Mortimer. 1984. Reprint, Oxford: Oxford University Press, 1988.

Hay, Denys. *Europe: The Emergence of an Idea.* Edinburgh: Edinburgh University Press, 1968.

Hay, Denys. *The Church in Italy in the Fifteenth Century.* Cambridge: Cambridge University Press, 1977.

Hay, Denys. *The Italian Renaissance in Its Historical Background.* 2d ed. Cambridge: Cambridge University Press, 1977.

Hay, Denys. *Europe in the Fourteenth and Fifteenth Centuries.* 2d ed. London: Longman, 1989.

Hay, Denys, and John Law. *Italy in the Age of the Renaissance, 1380–1530.* New York: Longman, 1989.

Head, Thomas, and Richard Landes, eds. *The Peace of God: Social Violence and Religious Response in France around the Year 1000.* Ithaca, N.Y.: Cornell University Press, 1992.

Heers, Jacques. *Family Clans in the Middle Ages: A Study of Political and Social Structures in Urban Areas.* Trans. Barry Herbert. Amsterdam: North-Holland, 1977.

Heers, Jacques. *Parties and Political Life in the Medieval West.* Trans. David Nicholas. Amsterdam: North-Holland, 1977.

Henneman, John Bell. *Royal Taxation in Fourteenth Century France: The Development of War Financing, 1322–1356.* Princeton, N.J.: Princeton University Press, 1971.

Henneman, John Bell. *The Medieval French Monarchy.* Hinsdale, Ill.: Dryden Press, 1973.

Herlihy, David. *The Social History of Italy and Western Europe, 700–1500.* London: Variorum, 1978.

Herlihy, David. *Cities and Society in Medieval Italy.* London: Variorum, 1980.

Herlihy, David. *Medieval Households.* Cambridge, Mass.: Harvard University Press, 1985.

Herlihy, David. *The Black Death and the Transformation of the West.* Edited with an introduction by Samuel K. Cohn, Jr. Cambridge, Mass.: Harvard University Press, 1997.

Herlihy, David, and Christiane Klapisch-Zuber. *Tuscans and Their Families: A Study of the Florentine Catasto of 1427.* New Haven, Conn.: Yale University Press, 1985.

Herrin, Judith. *The Formation of Christendom.* Princeton, N.J.: Princeton University Press, 1987.

Herrin, Judith, ed. *A Medieval Miscellany.* London: Weidenfeld and Nicolson Illustrated Books, 1999.

Herrmann, Joachim, and Erik Zürcher, eds. *History of Humanity, Scientific and Cultural Development.* Vol. 3, *From the Seventh Century* B.C. *to the Seventh Century* A.D. New York: Routledge for UNESCO, 1996.

Herztein, Robert E., ed. *The Holy Roman Empire in the Middle Ages: Universal State or German Catastrophe?* Lexington, Mass.: D.C. Heath, 1966.

Highfield, Roger, ed. *Spain in the Fifteenth Century, 1369–1516: Essays and Extracts by Historians of Spain.* London: Macmillan, 1972.

Hill, Bennett D., ed. *Church and State in the Middle Ages.* New York: Wiley, 1970.

Hill, Boyd H., ed. *The Rise of the First Reich: Germany in the Tenth Century.* New York: Wiley, 1969.

Hill, Boyd H. *Medieval Monarchy in Action: The German Empire from Henry I to Henry IV.* New York: Barnes & Noble, 1972.

Hillgarth, J. N., ed. *The Conversion of Western Europe, 350–750.* 1969. Reprint, Philadelphia: University of Pennsylvania Press, 1985.

Hillgarth, J. N. *The Spanish Kingdoms 1250–1516.* Vol. 1, *Precarious Balance, 1250–1410.* Oxford: Oxford University Press, 1976.

Hillgarth, J. N. *The Spanish Kingdoms 1250–1516.* Vol. 2, *Castilian Hegemony, 1410–1516.* Oxford: Oxford University Press, 1978.

Hodges, Richard. *The Anglo-Saxon Achievement: Archaeology and the Beginnings of English Society.* London: Duckworth, 1989.

Hodges, Richard. *Dark Age Economics: The Origins of Towns and Trade* A.D. *500–1000.* 2d ed. London: Duckworth, 1989.

Hodges, Richard. *Light in the Dark Ages: The Rise and Fall of San Vincenzo al Volturno.* Ithaca, N.Y.: Cornell University Press, 1997.

Hodges, Richard. *Towns and Trade in the Age of Charlemagne.* London: Duckworth, 2000.

Hodges, Richard, and David Whitehouse. *Mohammed, Charlemagne and the Origins of Europe: Archaeology and the Pirenne Thesis.* Ithaca, N.Y.: Cornell University Press, 1983.

Hodges, Richard, and Brian Hobley, eds. *The Rebirth of Towns in the West* A.D. *700–1050: A Review of Current Research into How, When, and Why There was a Rebirth of Towns between 700 and 1050.* London: Council for British Archaeology, 1988.

Holmes, George. *The Florentine Enlightenment, 1400–50.* London: Weidenfeld and Nicolson, 1969.

Holmes, George. *Florence, Rome, and the Origins of the Renaissance.* Oxford: Clarendon Press, 1986.

Holmes, George, ed. *The Oxford Illustrated History of Medieval Europe.* Oxford: Oxford University Press, 1988.

Holmes, George. *Renaissance.* New York: St. Martin's Press, 1996.

Holmes, George. *Europe, Hierarchy and Revolt, 1320–1450.* 1975 2d ed. Oxford: Blackwell, 2000.

Hooper, Nicholas. *Cambridge Illustrated Atlas, Warfare: The Middle Ages, 768–1487.* Cambridge: Cambridge University Press, 1996.

Hopkins, Keith. *A World Full of Gods: The Strange Triumph of Christianity.* New York: Penguin Putnam, 1999.

Hoppin, Richard H. *Medieval Music.* New York: W. W. Norton, 1978.

Horrox, Rosemary, ed. and trans. *The Black Death.* Manchester: Manchester University Press, 1994.

Housley, Norman. *The Italian Crusades: The Papal–Angevin Alliance and the Crusades against Christian Lay Powers, 1254–1343.* Oxford: Clarendon Press, 1982.

Housley, Norman. *The Avignon Papacy and the Crusades, 1305–1378.* Oxford: Clarendon Press, 1986.

Housley, Norman. *The Later Crusades: From Lyons to Alcazar, 1274–1580.* Oxford: Oxford University Press, 1992.

Housley, Norman. ed. and trans. *Documents on the Later Crusades, 1274–1580.* New York: St. Martin's Press, 1996.

Howell, Martha C. *Women, Production, and Patriarchy in Late Medieval Cities.* Chicago: University of Chicago Press, 1986.

Howell, Martha C. *The Marriage Exchange: Property, Social Place, and Gender in Cities of the Low Countries, 1300–1550.* Chicago: University of Chicago Press, 1998.

Howell, Martha C. and Walter Prevenier. *From Reliable Sources: An Introduction to Historical Methods.* Ithaca, N.Y.: Cornell University Press, 2001.

Hughes, Andrew. *Medieval Music: The Sixth Liberal Art.* Revised ed. Toronto: University of Toronto Press, 1980.

Hughes, Anselm, ed. *New Oxford History of Music.* Vol. 2, *Early Medieval Music up to 1300.* London: Oxford University Press, 1954.

Hughes, Anselm, and Gerald Abraham, eds. *New Oxford History of Music.* Vol. 3, *Ars Nova and the Renaissance, 1300–1540.* 1960. Reprint, London: Oxford University Press, 1969.

Huizinga, Johan. *The Autumn of the Middle Ages.* Trans. Rodney J. Payton and Ulrich Mammitzsch. 1921. Reprint, Chicago: University of Chicago Press, 1996.

Hyde, J. K. *Padua in the Ages of Dante: A Social History of an Italian City State.* Manchester: Manchester University Press, 1966.

Hyde, J. K. *Society and Politics in Medieval Italy: The Evolution of the Civil Life, 1000–1350.* London: Macmillan, 1973.

Hyde, J. K. *Literacy and Its Uses: Studies on Late Medieval Italy.* Ed. Daniel Waley. Manchester: Manchester University Press, 1993.

Itnyre, Cathy Jorgenson, ed. *Medieval Family Roles: A Book of Essays.* New York: Garland, 1996.

Jackson, Gabriel. *The Making of Medieval Spain.* London: Thames and Hudson, 1972.

Jacquart, Danielle, and Claude Thomasset. *Sexuality and Medicine in the Middle Ages.* Princeton, N.J.: Princeton University Press, 1988.

Jaeger, C. Stephen. *The Origins of Courtliness: Civilizing Trends and the Formation of Courtly Ideals, 939–1210.* Philadelphia: University of Pennsylvania Press, 1985.

Jaeger, C. Stephen. *The Envy of Angels: Cathedral Schools and Social Ideals in Medieval Europe, 950–1200.* Philadelphia: University of Pennsylvania Press, 1994.

Jaeger, C. Stephen. *Ennobling Love: In Search of a Lost Sensibility.* Philadelphia: University of Pennsylvania Press, 1999.

James, Edward, ed. *Visigothic Spain: New Approaches.* Oxford: Clarendon Press, 1980.

James, Edward. *The Origins of France: From Clovis to the Capetians, 500–1000.* New York: St. Martin's Press, 1982.

Jantzen, Grace M. *Power, Gender and Christian Mysticism.* Cambridge: Cambridge University Press, 1995.

Jardine, Lisa. *Worldly Goods: A New History of the Renaissance.* New York: Doubleday, 1996.

Jardine, Lisa. *Global Interests: Renaissance Art between East and West.* Ithaca, N.Y.: Cornell University Press, 2000.

Jones, A. H. M. *The Later Roman Empire, 284–602: A Social, Economic, and Administrative Survey.* 2 vols. Baltimore: Johns Hopkins University Press, 1986.

Jones, Philip J. *The Italian City-State: From Commune to Signoria.* Oxford: Clarendon Press, 1997.

Jordan, William Chester. *From Servitude to Freedom: Manumission in the Sénonais in the Thirteenth Century.* Philadelphia: University of Pennsylvania Press, 1986.

Jordan, William Chester. *The Great Famine: Northern Europe in the Early Fourteenth Century.* Princeton, N.J.: Princeton University Press, 1996.

Jordan, William Chester. *Europe in the High Middle Ages.* London: Allen Lane, 2001.

Kaeuper, Richard W. *Chivalry and Violence in Medieval Europe.* Oxford: Oxford University Press, 1999.

Kantorowicz, Ernst H. *The King's Two Bodies: A Study in Medieval Political Theology.* Princeton, N.J.: Princeton University Press, 1957.

Kay, Sarah, and Miri Rubin, eds. *Framing Medieval Bodies.* Manchester: Manchester University Press, 1994.

Kedar, Benjamin Z. *Crusade and Mission: European Approaches toward the Muslims.* Princeton, N.J.: Princeton University press, 1984.

Keen, Maurice. *The Outlaws of Medieval Legend.* 3d ed. London: Routledge, 2000.

Keen, Maurice. *The Laws of War in the Late Middle Ages.* London: Routledge and K. Paul, 1965.

Keen, Maurice. *Chivalry.* New Haven, Conn.: Yale University Press, 1984.

Keen, Maurice. ed. *Medieval War: A History.* Oxford: Oxford University Press, 1999.

Kelley, Donald R. *Renaissance Humanism.* Boston: Twayne Publishers, 1991.

Kent, Francis William. *Household and Lineage in Renaissance Florence: The Family Life of the Capponi, Ginori, and Rucellai.* Princeton, N.J.: Princeton University Press, 1977.

Kieckhefer, Richard. *European Witch Trials: Their Foundations in Popular and Learned Culture, 1300–1500.* Berkeley: University of California Press, 1976.

Kieckhefer, Richard. *Repression of Heresy in Medieval Germany.* Philadelphia: University of Pennsylvania Press, 1979.

Kieckhefer, Richard. *Unquiet Souls: Fourteenth-Century Saints and Their Religious Milieu.* Chicago: University of Chicago Press, 1984.

Kieckhefer, Richard. *Magic in the Middle Ages.* Cambridge: Cambridge University Press, 1990.

King, Margaret L. *Venetian Humanism in an Age of Patrician Dominance.* Princeton, N.J.: Princeton University Press, 1986.

King, P. D. *Charlemagne.* London: Methuen, 1986.

Kirshner, Julius, ed. *The Origins of the State in Italy.* Chicago: University of Chicago Press, 1995.

Kleinberg, Aviad M. *Prophets in Their Own Country: Living Saints and the Making of Sainthood in the Later Middle Ages.* Chicago: University of Chicago Press, 1992.

Knighton, Tess, and David Fallows, eds. *Companion to Medieval and Renaissance Music.* London: Dent, 1992.

Knoll, Paul W. *The Rise of the Polish Monarchy: Piast Poland in East-Central Europe, 1320–1370.* Chicago: University of Chicago Press, 1972.

Knowles, David. *From Pachomius to Ignatius: A Study in the Constitutional History of the Religious Orders.* Oxford: Oxford University Press, 1966.

Knowles, David. *Christian Monasticism.* New York: McGraw-Hill, 1969.

Knowles, David. *The Evolution of Medieval Thought.* 2d ed. Ed. D. E. Luscombe and C. N. L. Brooke. London: Longman, 1988.

Kohl, Benjamin G. and Ronald G. Witt. *The Earthly Republic: Italian Humanists on Government and Society.* Philadelphia: University of Pennsylvania Press, 1978.

Kors, Alan C. and Edward Peters, eds. *Witchcraft in Europe, 1100–1700: A Documentary History.* 2d ed. Philadelphia: University of Pennsylvania Press, 1972.

Kosto, Adam J. *Making Agreements in Medieval Catalonia: Power, Order, and the Written Word, 1000–1200.* Cambridge: Cambridge University Press, 2001.

Krautheimer, Richard. *Three Christian Capitals: Topography and Politics.* Berkeley: University of California Press, 1983.

Kraye, Jill, ed. *The Cambridge Companion to Renaissance Humanism.* Cambridge: Cambridge University Press, 1996.

Kretzmann, Norman, Anthony Kenny, Jan Pinborg, and Eleonore Stump, eds. *The Cambridge History of Later Medieval Philosophy: From the Rediscovery of Aristotle to the Disintegration of Scholasticism, 1100–1600.* Cambridge: Cambridge University Press, 1982.

Kretzmann, Norman, and Eleonore Stump, eds. *The Cambridge Companion to Augustine*. Cambridge: Cambridge University Press, 2001.

Kristeller, Paul Oskar. *Renaissance Thought: The Classic, Scholastic, and Humanistic Strains*. New York: Harper, 1961.

Kristeller, Paul Oskar. *Eight Philosophers of the Italian Renaissance*. Stanford, Calif.: Stanford University Press, 1964.

Kristeller, Paul Oskar. *Renaissance Concepts of Man, and Other Essays*. New York: Harper & Row, 1972.

Kristeller, Paul Oskar. *Medieval Aspects of Renaissance Learning: Three Essays*. Ed. Edward P. Mahoney. Durham, N.C.: Duke University Press, 1974.

Kristeller, Paul Oskar. *Renaissance Thought and Its Sources*. Ed. Michael Mooney. New York: Columbia University Press, 1979.

Kuehn, Thomas. *Emancipation in Late Medieval Florence*. New Brunswick, N.J.: Rutgers University Press, 1982.

Kuehn, Thomas. *Law, Family, and Women: Toward a Legal Anthropology of Renaissance Italy*. Chicago: University of Chicago Press, 1991.

Kuehn, Thomas. *Illegitimacy in Renaissance Florence*. Ann Arbor: University of Michigan Press, 2002.

Kuttner, Stephan. *Harmony from Dissonance: An Interpretation of Medieval Canon Law*. Latrobe, Penn.: Archabbey Press, 1960.

Laiou, Angeliki E. ed. *Consent and Coercion to Sex and Marriage in Ancient and Medieval Societies*. Washington, D.C.: Dumbarton Oaks Research Library and Collection, 1993.

Lambert, Malcolm. *Franciscan Poverty: The Doctrine of the Absolute Poverty of Christ and the Apostles in the Franciscan Order, 1210–1323*. London: S. P. C. K. 1961.

Lambert, Malcolm. *The Cathars*. Oxford: Blackwell, 1998.

Lambert, Malcolm. *Medieval Heresy: Popular Movements from Bogomil to Hus*. 3d ed. Oxford: Blackwell, 2002.

Lane, Frederic C. *Venice and History: The Collected Papers of Frederic C. Lane*. Baltimore: Johns Hopkins University Press, 1966.

Lane, Frederic C. *Venice: A Maritime Republic*. Baltimore: Johns Hopkins University Press, 1973.

Lane Fox, Robin. *Pagans and Christians*. New York: Alfred A. Knopf, 1987.

Langholm, Odd. *Economics in the Schools: Wealth, Exchange, Valeu, Money and Usury According to the Paris Theological Tradition, 1200–1350*. Leiden: E. J. Brill, 1992.

Lansing, Carol. *The Florentine Magnates: Lineage and Faction in a Medieval Commune*. Princeton, N.J.: Princeton University Press, 1991.

Larner, John. *Culture and Society in Italy, 1290–1420*. London: B. T. Batsford, 1971.

Larner, John. *Italy in the Age of Dante and Petrarch, 1216–1380*. London: Longman, 1980.

Latouche, Robert. *The Birth of the Western Economy: Economic Aspects of the Dark Ages*. Trans. E. M. Wilkinson. 1956. Reprint, London: Methuen, 1967.

Law, John E. *The Lords of Renaissance Italy: The Signori, 1250–1500*. London: Historical Association, 1981.

Lawrence, C. H. *Medieval Monasticism: Forms of Religious Life in Western Europe in the Middle Ages*. New York: Longman, 1989.

Lawrence, C. H. *The Friars: The Impact of the Early Mendicant Movement on Western Society*. New York: Longman, 1994.

Leclercq, Jean. *The Love of Learning and the Desire for God: A Study of Monastic Culture*. Trans. Catherine Misrahi. New York: Fordham University Press, 1961.

Leclercq, Jean. *Love and Marriage in Twelfth-Century Europe*. University of Tasmania Occasional Papers, 13. Hobart: University of Tasmania, 1978.

Less, Clare A. ed. *Medieval Masculinities: Regarding Men in the Middle Ages*. Minneapolis: University of Minnesota Press, 1994.

Leff, Gordon. *Medieval Thought: St. Augustine to Ockham*. Harmondsworth: Penguin Books, 1958.

Leff, Gordon. *Heresy in the Later Middle Ages: The Relation of Heterodoxy to Dissent, c. 1250–1450*. 2 vols. Manchester: Manchester University Press, 1967.

Leff, Gordon. *Paris and Oxford Universities in the Thirteenth and Fourteenth Centuries: An Institutional and Intellectual History*. New York: Wiley, 1968.

Leff, Gordon. *The Dissolution of the Medieval Outlook: An Essay on Intellectual and Spiritual Change in the Fourteenth Century*. New York: New York University Press, 1976.

Le Goff, Jacques. *Time, Work and Culture in the Middle Ages*. Trans. Arthur Goldhammer. 1977. Reprint, Chicago: University of Chicago Press, 1980.

Le Goff, Jacques. *Your Money or Your Life: Economy and Religion in the Middle Ages*. Trans. Patricia Ranum. 1986. Reprint, New York: Zone Books, 1988.

Le Goff, Jacques. *Medieval Civilization, 400–1500*. Trans. Julia Barrow. 1964. Reprint, Oxford: Blackwell, 1988.

Le Goff, Jacques. *The Medieval Imagination*. Trans. Arthur Goldhammer. 1985. Reprint, Chicago: University of Chicago Press, 1988.

Le Goff, Jacques. ed. *Medieval Callings*. Trans. Lydia G. Cochrane. 1987. Reprint, Chicago: University of Chicago Press, 1990.

Le Goff, Jacques. *Intellectuals in the Middle Ages*. Trans. Teresa Lavender Fagan. 1957. Reprint, New York: Blackwell, 1993.

Lerner, Robert E. *The Age of Adversity: The Fourteenth Century*. Ithaca, N.Y.: Cornell University Press, 1968.

Lerner, Robert E. *The Heresy of the Free Spirit in the Later Middle Ages*. Berkeley: University of California Press, 1972.

Le Roy Ladurie, Emmanuel. *Montaillou: The Promised Land of Error*. Trans. Barbara Bray. 1975. Reprint, New York: George Braziller, 1978.

Leuschner, Joachim. *Germany in the Late Middle Ages*. Amsterdam: North-Holland, 1980.

Leyser, Henrietta. *Hermits and the New Monasticism: A Study of Religious Communities in Western Europe, 1000–1150*. London: Macmillan 1984.

Leyser, Karl J. *Rule and Conflict in an Early Medieval Society: Ottonian Saxony.* London: Edward Arnold, 1979.

Leyser, Karl J. *Medieval Germany and Its Neighbours, 900–1250.* London: Hambledon Press, 1982.

Leyser, Karl J. *Communications and Power in Medieval Europe: The Carolingian and Ottonian Centuries.* Ed. Timothy Reuter. London: Hambledon Press, 1994.

Lilley, Keith D. *Urban Life in the Middle Ages, 1000–1450.* New York: Palgrave, 2002.

Lindberg, David C. *The Beginnings of Western Science: The European Scientific Tradition in Philosophical, Religious, and Institutional Context, 600 B.C. to A.D. 1450.* Chicago: University of Chicago Press, 1992.

Linehan, Peter. *History and the Historians of Medieval Spain.* Oxford: Clarendon Press, 1993.

Linehan, Peter, and Janet L. Nelson, eds. *The Medieval World.* New York: Routledge, 2001.

Little, Lester K. *Religious Poverty and the Profit Economy in Medieval Europe.* Ithaca, N.Y.: Cornell University Press, 1978.

Lochrie, Karma, Peggy McCracken, and James A. Schultz, eds. *Constructing Medieval Sexuality.* Minneapolis: University of Minnesota Press, 1997.

Lock, Peter. *The Franks in the Aegean, 1204–1500.* New York: Longman, 1995.

Logan, F. Donald. *A History of the Church in the Middle Ages.* London: Routledge, 2002.

Lomax, Derek W. *The Reconquest of Spain.* London: Longman, 1978.

Lopez, Robert S., and Irving W. Raymond, eds. *Medieval Trade in the Mediterranean World: Illustrative Documents with Introductions and Notes.* New York: Columbia University Press, 1955.

Lopez, Robert S., and Irving W. Raymond, eds. *The Birth of Europe.* New York: Lippincott, 1967.

Lopez, Robert S., and Irving W. Raymond, eds. *The Three Ages of the Italian Renaissance.* Boston: Little, Brown, 1970.

Lopez, Robert S. *The Commercial Revolution of the Middle Ages 950–1350.* Englewood Cliffs, N.J.: Prentice-Hall, 1971.

Lynch, Joseph H. *Godparents and Kinship in Early Medieval Europe.* Princeton, N.J.: Princeton University Press, 1986.

Lynch, Joseph H. *The Medieval Church: A Brief History.* New York: Longman, 1992.

MacKay, Angus. *Spain in the Middle Ages: From Frontier to Empire, 1000–1500.* New York: St. Martin's Press, 1977.

MacMullen, Ramsay. *Christianizing the Roman Empire, A.D. 100–400.* New Haven, Conn.: Yale University Press, 1984.

MacMullen, Ramsay. *Christianity and Paganism in the Fourth to Eighth Centuries.* New Haven, Conn.: Yale University Press, 1997.

Madden, Thomas F. *A Concise History of the Crusades.* New York: Rowman & Littlefield, 1999.

Madden, Thomas F. ed. *The Concise History of the Crusades.* Oxford: Blackwell, 2002.

Maier, Christoph T. *Preaching the Crusades: Mendicant Friars and the Cross in the Thirteenth Century.* Cambridge: Cambridge University Press, 1994.

Maier, Christoph T. *Crusade Propaganda and Ideology: Model Sermons for the Preaching of the Cross.* Cambridge: Cambridge University Press, 2000.

Markus, Robert A. *The End of Ancient Christianity.* Cambridge: Cambridge University Press, 1990.

Marenbon, John. *From the Circle of Alcuin to the School of Auxerre: Logic, Theology, and Philosophy in the Early Middle Ages.* Cambridge: Cambridge University Press, 1981.

Marenbon, John. *Early Medieval Philosophy (480–1150): An Introduction.* London: Routledge and K. Paul, 1983.

Marenbon, John. *Later Medieval Philosophy (1150–1350): An Introduction.* London: Routledge and K. Paul, 1987.

Marenbon, John. *Medieval Philosophy.* London: New York: Routledge, 1998.

Martines, Lauro. *The Social World of the Florentine Humanists, 1390–1460.* London: Routledge and Kegan Paul, 1963.

Martines, Lauro, ed. *Violence and Civil Disorder in Italian Cities, 1200–1500.* Los Angeles: University of California Press, 1972.

Martines, Lauro. *Power and Imagination: City-States in Renaissance Italy.* New York: Alfred A. Knopf, 1979.

Matthew, Donald. *The Norman Kingdom of Sicily.* Cambridge: Cambridge University Press, 1992.

Mayer, Hans E. *The Crusades.* 2d ed. Trans. John Gillingham. Oxford: Oxford University Press, 1988.

McCormick, Michael. *Eternal Victory: Triumphal Rulership in Late Antiquity, Byzantium, and the Early Medieval West.* Cambridge: Cambridge University Press, 1986.

McCormick, Michael. *Origins of the European Economy: Communications and Commerce, A.D. 300–900.* Cambridge: Cambridge University Press, 2001.

McGrath, Alister E. *Historical Theology: An Introduction to the History of Christian Thought.* New York: Blackwell, 1998.

McKitterick, Rosamond. *The Frankish Church and the Carolingian Reforms, 789–895.* London: Royal Historical Society, 1977.

McKitterick, Rosamond. *The Frankish Kingdoms under the Carolingians, 751–987.* London: Longman, 1983.

McKitterick, Rosamond, *The Carolingians and the Written Word.* Cambridge: Cambridge University Press, 1989.

McKitterick, Rosamond, ed. *The Uses of Literacy in Early Mediaeval Europe.* Cambridge: Cambridge University Press, 1990.

McKitterick, Rosamond. *Carolingian Culture: Emulation and Innovation.* Cambridge: Cambridge University Press, 1994.

McKitterick, Rosamond, ed. *The New Cambridge Medieval History.* Vol. 2. *c. 700–900.* Cambridge: Cambridge University Press, 1995.

McKitterick, Rosamond, ed. *The Early Middle Ages: Europe 400–1000.* Oxford: Oxford University Press, 2001.

McNeil, John T., and Helena M. Gamer *Medieval Handbooks of Penance: A Translation of the Principal "Libri poenitentiales" and Selections from Related Documents*. 1938. Reprint, New York: Columbia University Press, 1990.

McNeil, William H. *Plagues and Peoples*. Garden City, N.Y.: Anchor Books, 1977.

McNeil, William H. *The Pursuit of Power: Technology, Armed Force, and Society since A.D. 1000*. Oxford: B. Blackwell, 1983.

Miskimin, Harry A. *The Economy of Early Renaissance Europe, 1300–1460*. Englewood Cliffs, N.J.: Prentice-Hall, 1969.

Miskimin, Harry A. *The Economy of Later Renaissance Europe, 1460–1600*. Cambridge: Cambridge University Press, 1977.

Mitteis, Heinrich, *The State in the Middle Ages: A Comparative Constitutional History of Feudal Europe*. Trans. H. F. Orton. Amsterdam: North-Holland, 1975.

Molho, Anthony, ed. *Social and Economic Foundations of the Italian Renaissance*. New York: Wiley, 1969.

Molho, Anthony. *Marriage Alliance in Late Medieval Florence*. Cambridge, Mass.: Harvard University Press, 1994.

Mollat, Guillaume, *The Popes at Avignon, 1305–1378*. Trans. Janet Love. 1949. Reprint, New York: T. Nelson 1963.

Mollat, Michael, and Philippe Wolff. *The Popular Revolutions of the Late Middle Ages*. Trans. A. L. Lytton-Sells. London: Allen and Unwin, 1973.

Mollat, Michel, and Philippe Wolff. *The Poor in the Middle Ages: An Essay in Social History*. Trans. Arthur Goldhammer. New Haven, Conn.: Yale University Press, 1986.

Moore, Robert I. *The Origins of European Dissent*. Oxford: Blackwell, 1977.

Moore, Robert I, ed. *The Birth of Popular Heresy*. London: Edward Arnold, 1975.

Moore, Robert I. *The Formation of a Persecuting Society: Power and Deviance in Western Europe, 950–1250*. New York: Basil Blackwell, 1987.

Moore, Robert I. *The First European Revolution, c. 970–1215*. Oxford: Blackwell, 2000.

Moorhead, John. *Theoderic in Italy*. Oxford: Clarendon Press: 1992.

Moorhead, John. *Justinian*. London: Longman, 1994.

Moorhead, John. *Ambrose: Church and Society in the Late Roman World*. New York: Longman, 1999.

Moorhead, John. *The Roman Empire Divided, 400–700*. New York: Longman, 2001.

Morrall, John B. *Political Thought in Medieval Times*. 3d ed. London: Hutchinson University Library, 1971.

Morris, Colin. *The Discovery of the Individual, 1050–1200*. London: S.P.C.K., 1972.

Morris, Colin. *The Papal Monarchy: The Western Church from 1050 to 1250*. Oxford: Clarendon Press, 1989.

Muir, Edward. *Civic Ritual in Renaissance Venice*. Princeton, N.J.: Princeton University Press, 1981.

Muir, Edward. *Mad Blood Stirring: Vendetta and Factions in Friuli during the Renaissance*. Baltimore: Johns Hopkins University Press, 1993.

Muir, Lynette R. *Literature and Society in Medieval France: The Mirror and the Image, 1100–1500*. London: Macmillan, 1985.

Mundy, John H. *Europe in the High Middle Ages, 1150–1300*. 3d ed. New York: Longman, 2000.

Mundy, John H., and Peter Riesenberg, eds. *The Medieval Town*. Princeton, N.J.: Van Nostrand, 1958.

Munro, John H. A. *Wool, Cloth, and Gold: The Struggle for Bullion in Anglo-Burgundian Trade, 1340–1478*. Toronto: University of Toronto Press, 1972.

Murray, Alexander. *Reason and Society in the Middle Ages*. Oxford: Clarendon Press, 1978.

Murray, Alexander. *Suicide in the Middle Ages*. Vol. 1. *The Violent against Themselves;* Vol. 2. *The Curse on Self-Murder.* Oxford: Oxford University Press, 1998–2000.

Murray, Alexander C. *Germanic Kinship Structure: Studies in Law and Society in Antiquity and the Early Middle Ages*. Toronto: Pontifical Institute of Mediaeval Studies, 1983.

Murray, Alexander C., ed. *From Roman to Merovingian Gaul: A Reader*. Peterborough, Canada: Broadview Press, 2000.

Murray, Jacqueline, ed. *Love, Marriage, and Family in the Middle Ages*. Peterborough, Canada: Broadview Press, 2001.

Musset, Lucien. *The Germanic Invasions: The Making of Europe, A.D. 400–600*. Trans. Edward and Columba James. University Park: The Pennsylvania State University Press, 1975.

Nauert, Charles G., ed. *Humanism and the Culture of Renaissance Europe*. Cambridge: Cambridge University Press, 1995.

Nederman, Cary J., and Kate Langdon Forhan, eds. *Medieval Political Theory—a Reader: The Quest for the Body Politic, 1100–1400*. New York: Routledge, 1993.

Neillands, Robin. *The Hundred Years War*. New York: Routledge, 1990.

Nicholas, David. *The Evolution of the Medieval World: Society, Government and Thought in Europe, 312–1500*. New York: Longman, 1992.

Nicholas, David. *The Growth of the Medieval City: From Late Antiquity to the Fourteenth Century*. New York: Longman, 1997.

Nicholas, David. *The Later Medieval City, 1300–1500*. New York: Longman, 1997.

Nirenberg, David. *Communities of Violence: Persecution of Minorities in the Middle Ages*. Princeton, N.J.: Princeton University Press, 1996.

Nohl, Johannes. *The Black Death: A Chronicle of the Plague Compiled from Contemporary Sources*. Trans. C. H. Clarke. London: Unwin Books, 1926.

Noonan, John T., Jr. *The Scholastic Analysis of Usury*. Cambridge, Mass.: Harvard University Press, 1957.

O'Callaghan, Joseph. *A History of Medieval Spain*. Ithaca, N.Y.: Cornell University Press, 1975.

O'Callaghan, Joseph. *The Cortes of Castile-León, 1188–1350*. Philadelphia: University of Pennsylvania Press, 1989.

O'Callaghan, Joseph F. *The Learned King: The Reign of Alfonso X of Castile*. Philadelphia: University of Pennsylvania Press, 1993.

Oakley, Francis. *The Western Church in the Later Middle Ages*. Ithaca, N.Y.: Cornell University Press, 1979.

Ohly, Friedrich. *The Damned and the Elect: Guilt in Western Culture*. Trans. Linda Archibald. 1976. Reprint, Cambridge: Cambridge University Press, 1992.

Olson, Glending. *Literature as Recreation in the Later Middle Ages*. Ithaca, N.Y.: Cornell University Press, 1982.

Oman, C. W. C. *The Art of War in the Middle Ages, A.D. 378–1515*. 1885. Reprint, Ithaca, N.Y.: Cornell University Press, 1953.

Orme, Nicholas. *From Childhood to Chivalry: The Education of the English Kings and Aristocracy, 1066–1530*. London: Methuen, 1984.

Orme, Nicholas. *Medieval Children*. New Haven, Conn.: Yale University Press, 2001.

Ozment, Steven E. *The Age of Reform (1250–1550): An Intellectual and Religious History of Late Medieval and Reformation Europe*. New Haven, Conn.: Yale University Press, 1980.

Ozment, Steven E. *Ancestors: The Loving Family in Old Europe*. Cambridge, Mass.: Harvard University Press, 2001.

Painter, Sidney. *French Chivalry: Chivalric Ideas and Practice in Medieval France*. 1940. Reprint, Ithaca, N.Y.: Cornell University Press, 1967.

Paravicini Bagliani, Agostino. *The Pope's Body*. Trans. David S. Peterson. 1994 Reprint, Chicago: University of Chicago Press, 2000.

Park, Katharine. *Doctors and Medicine in Early Renaissance Florence*. Princeton, N.J.: Princeton University Press, 1985.

Park, Katharine. *Wonders and the Order of Nature, 1150–1750*. New York: Zone Books, 1998.

Parry, J. H. *The Establishment of the European Hegemony, 1415–1715: Trade and Exploration in the Age of the Renaissance*. New York: Harper & Row, 1961.

Parry, J. H. *The Discovery of the Sea*. Berkeley: University of California Press, 1981.

Partner, Peter. *The Lands of St. Peter: The Papal State in the Middle Ages and the Early Renaissance*. London: Eyre Methuen, 1972.

Pearsall, Derek. *Gothic Europe, 1200–1450*. London: Longman, 2001.

Pelikan, Jaroslav. *The Christian Tradition: A History of the Development of Doctrine*. Vol. 1. *The Emergence of the Catholic Tradition (100–600)*; Vol. 2. *The Spirit of Eastern Christendom (600–700)*; Vol. 3. *The Growth of Medieval Theology (600–1300)*; Vol. 4. *Reformation of Church and Dogma (1300–1700)*. Chicago: University of Chicago Press, 1971–1984.

Peters, Edward. *The Magician, the Witch, and the Law*. Philadelphia: University of Pennsylvania Press, 1978.

Peters, Edward. *Inquisition*. New York: Free Press, 1988.

Petrucci, Armando. *Public Lettering: Script, Power, and Culture*. Trans. Linda Lappin. Chicago: University of Chicago Press, 1993.

Petrucci, Armando. *Writers and Readers in Medieval Italy: Studies in the History of Written Culture*. Ed. and trans. Charles M. Radding. New Haven, Conn.: Yale University Press, 1995.

Petrucci, Armando. *Writing the Dead: Death and Writing Strategies in the Western Tradition*. Trans. Michael Sullivan. Stanford, Calif.: Stanford University Press, 1998.

Pfaff, Richard W. *Medieval Latin Liturgy: A Select Bibliography*. Toronto: University of Toronto Press, 1982.

Phillips, Jonathan. *Defenders of the Holy Land: Relations between the Latin East and the West, 1119–1187*. Oxford: Clarendon Press, 1996.

Phillips, Jonathan, ed. *The First Crusade: Origins and Impact*. Manchester: Manchester University Press, 1997.

Phillips, Jonathan, and Martin Hoch, eds. *The Second Crusade: Scope and Consequences*. Manchester: Manchester University Press, 2001.

Phillips, Jonathan. *The Crusades, 1095–1197*. New York: Longman, 2002.

Piltz, Anders. *The World of Medieval Learning*. Trans. David Jones. Oxford: Blackwell, 1981.

Pirenne, Henri. *Medieval Cities: Their Origins and the Revival of Trade*. Trans. Frank D. Halsey. Princeton, N.J.: Princeton University Press, 1925.

Pirenne, Henri. *Economic and Social History of Medieval Europe*. New York: Harcourt, Brace, 1937.

Pirenne, Henri. *Mohammed and Charlemagne*. New York: Norton, 1939.

Pohl, Walter, ed. *Kingdoms of the Empire: The Integration of Barbarians in Late Antiquity*. Leiden: Brill, 1997.

Pohl, Walter, and Helmut Reimitz, eds. *Strategies of Distinction: The Construction of Ethnic Communities, 300–800*. Leiden: Brill, 1998.

Pohl, Walter, Ian Wood, and Helmut Reimitz, eds. *The Transformation of Frontiers from Late Antiquity to the Carolingians*. Leiden: Brill, 2001.

Poly, Jean-Piere, and Eric Bournazel. *The Feudal Transformation, 900–1200*. Trans. Caroline Higgitt. New York: Holmes & Meier, 1991.

Poschmann, Bernhard. *Penance and the Anointing of the Sick*. Trans. Francis Courtney. Freiburg: Herder and Herder, 1964.

Postan, Michael M., ed. *The Cambridge Economic History of Europe*. Vol. 1 The Agrarian Life of the Middle Ages. 2d ed. Cambridge: Cambridge University Press, 1966.

Postan, Michael M., and Edward Miller, eds. *The Cambridge Economic History of Europe*. Vol. 2. Trade and Industry in the Middle Ages. 2d ed. Cambridge: Cambridge University Press, 1987.

Postan, Michael M., E. E. Rich, and Edward Miller, eds. *The Cambridge Economic History of Europe*. Vol. 3. Economic Organization and Policies in the Middle Ages. Cambridge: Cambridge University Press, 1965.

Pounds, N. J. G. *An Historical Geography of Europe, 450 B.C.–A.D. 1330*. Cambridge: Cambridge University Press, 1973.

Pounds, N. J. G. *An Economic History of Medieval Europe*. London: Longman, 1974.

Powell, James M. *Anatomy of a Crusade, 1213–1221*. Philadelphia: University of Pennsylvania Press, 1986.

Powell, James M., ed. *Medieval Studies: An Introduction.* 2d ed. Syracuse, N.Y.: Syracuse University Press, 1992.

Prawer, Joshua. *The Latin Kingdom of Jerusalem: European Colonialism in the Middle Ages.* London: Weidenfeld and Nicolson, 1972.

Price, B. B. *Medieval Thought: An Introduction.* Oxford: Blackwell, 1992.

Pryor, John H. *Business Contracts of Medieval Provence: Selected Notulae from the Cartulary of Giraud Amalric of Marseilles, 1248.* Toronto: Pontifical Institute of Mediaeval Studies, 1981.

Pryor, John H. *Geography, Technology, and War: Studies in the Maritime History of the Mediterranean, 649–1571.* Cambridge: Cambridge University Press, 1988.

Pullan, Brian. *A History of Early Renaissance Italy from the Mid-Thirteenth to the Mid-Fifteenth Century.* London: Allen Lane, 1973.

Queller, Donald E. *The Venetian Patriciate: Reality versus Myth.* Urbana: University of Illinois Press, 1986.

Queller, Donald E., and Thomas Madden, eds. *The Fourth Crusade: The Conquest of Constantinople.* 2d ed. Philadelphia: University of Pennsylvania Press, 1997.

Rabil, Albert, ed. *Renaissance Humanism: Foundations, Forms, and Legacy.* 3 vols. Philadelphia: University of Pennsylvania Press, 1988.

Radding, Charles M. *A World Made by Men: Cognition and Society, 400–1200.* Chapel Hill: University of North Carolina Press, 1985.

Rashdall, Hastings. *The Universities of Europe in the Middle Ages.* 3 vols. Ed. F. M. Powicke and A. B. Emden. 1895. Reprint, Oxford: Clarendon Press, 1936.

Reddaway, W. F., ed. *The Cambridge History of Poland.* Cambridge: Cambridge University Press, 1941.

Reilly, Bernard F. *The Kingdom of León-Castilla under Queen Urraca, 1109–1126.* Princeton; N.J.: Princeton University Press, 1982.

Reilly, Bernard F. *The Kingdom of León-Castilla under King Alfonso VI, 1065–1109.* Princeton: N.J.: Princeton University Press, 1988.

Reilly, Bernard F. *The Contest of Christian and Muslim Spain: 1031–1157.* Cambridge: Blackwell, 1992.

Reilly, Bernard F. *The Medieval Spains.* Cambridge: Cambridge University Press, 1993.

Reilly, Bernard F. *The Kingdom of León-Castilla under King Alfonso VII, 1126–1157.* Philadelphia: University of Pennsylvania Press, 1998.

Renouard, Yves. *Avignon Papacy, 1305–1403.* Trans. Denis Bethell. London: Faber, 1970.

Reuter, Timothy, ed. *The Medieval Nobility: Studies on the Ruling Classes of France and Germany from the Sixth to the Twelfth Century.* New York: North-Holland, 1979.

Reuter, Timothy. *Germany in the Early Middle Ages, c. 800–1056.* London: Longman, 1991.

Reyerson, Kathryn. *Business, Banking, and Finance in Medieval Montpellier.* Toronto: Pontifical Institute of Mediaeval Studies, 1985.

Reyerson, Kathryn. *The Art of the Deal: Intermediaries of Trade in Medieval Montpellier.* Leiden: Brill, 2002.

Reyerson, Kathryn, and Faye Powe, eds. *The Medieval Castle: Romance and Reality.* Dubuque, Iowa: Kendall/Hunt, 1984.

Reyerson, Kathryn, and John Drendel, eds. *Urban and Rural Communities in Medieval France: Provence and Languedoc, 1000–1500.* Leiden: Brill, 1998.

Reynolds, L. D., and N. G. Wilson. *Scribes and Scholars: A Guide to the Transmission of Greek and Latin Literature.* 3d ed. Oxford: Oxford University Press, 1991.

Reynolds, Susan. *An Introduction to the History of English Medieval Towns.* Oxford: Clarendon Press, 1978.

Reynolds, Susan. *Kingdoms and Communities in Western Europe, 900–1300.* Oxford: Oxford University Press, 1984.

Reynolds, Susan. *Fiefs and Vassals: The Medieval Evidence Reinterpreted.* Oxford: Oxford University Press, 1994.

Rich, John, ed. *The City in Late Antiquity.* London: Routledge, 1996.

Rich, John, and Andrew Wallace-Hadrill, eds. *City and Country in the Ancient World.* London: Routledge, 1991.

Richard, Jean. *The Latin Kingdom of Jerusalem.* 2 vols. Trans. Janet Shirley. Amsterdam: North-Holland, 1979.

Richard, Jean. *The Crusades, c. 1071–c. 1291.* Trans. Jean Birrell. Cambridge: Cambridge University Press, 1999.

Richards, Jeffrey. *Sex, Dissidence and Damnation: Minority Groups in the Middle Ages.* New York: Routledge, 1991.

Riché, Pierre. *Education and Culture in the Barbarian West: From the Sixth through the Eighth Century.* Trans. John J. Contreni. Columbia: University of South Carolina Press, 1976.

Riley-Smith, Jonathan. *The First Crusade and the Idea of Crusading.* Philadelphia: University of Pennsylvania Press, 1986.

Riley-Smith, Jonathan. *The Crusades: A Short History.* New Haven, Conn.: Yale University Press, 1987.

Riley-Smith, Jonathan. *The First Crusaders, 1095–1131.* Cambridge: Cambridge University Press, 1997.

Riley-Smith, Jonathan, ed. *The Oxford Illustrated History of the Crusades.* Oxford: Oxford University Press, 1995.

Riley-Smith, Jonathan, and Louise Riley-Smith. *The Crusades, Idea and Reality, 1095–1274.* London: Edward Arnold, 1981.

Robinson, I. S. *The Papacy, 1073–1198: Continuity and Innovation.* Cambridge: Cambridge University Press, 1990.

Roover, Raymond de. *Money, Banking and Credit in Medieval Bruges, Italian Merchant-Bankers, Lombards and Money-Changers: A Study in the Origins of Banking.* Cambridge: The Medieval Academy of America, 1948.

Roover, Raymond de. *The Rise and Decline of the Medici Bank, 1397–1494.* Cambridge, Mass.: Harvard University Press, 1963.

Roover, Raymond de. *Business, Banking and Economic Thought in Late Medieval and Early Modern Europe: Selected Studies of Raymond de Roover.* Ed. Julius Kirshner. Chicago: University of Chicago Press, 1974.

Rörig, Fritz. *The Medieval Town.* Berkeley: University of California Press, 1971.

Rose, Susan. *Medieval Naval Warfare, 1000–1500*. New York: Routledge, 2002.

Rösener, Werner. *The Peasantry of Europe*. Trans. Thomas M. Barer. 1993. Reprint, Oxford: Blackwell, 1994.

Rousseau, Philip. *The Early Christian Centuries*. New York: Longman, 2002.

Rubin, Miri. *Corpus Christi: The Eucharist in Late Medieval Culture*. Cambridge: Cambridge University Press, 1991.

Rubinstein, Nicolai. *The Government of Florence under the Medici (1434 to 1494)*. Oxford: Clarendon Press, 1966.

Ruggiero, Guido. *Violence in Early Renaissance Venice*. New Brunswick, N.J.: Rutgers University Press, 1980.

Ruggiero, Guido. *The Boundaries of Eros: Sex Crime and Sexuality in Renaissance Venice*. New York: Oxford University Press, 1985.

Ruggiero, Guido, ed. *A Companion to the Worlds of the Renaissance*. New York: Blackwell, 2002.

Runciman, Steven. *A History of the Crusades*. Vol. 1. *The First Crusade and the Foundation of the Kingdom of Jerusalem*; Vol. 2. *The Kingdom of Jerusalem and the Frankish East, 1100–1187*; Vol. 3. *The Kingdom of Acre and the Later Crusades*. Cambridge: Cambridge University Press, 1951–1954.

Russell, Frederick H. *The Just War in the Middle Ages*. Cambridge: Cambridge University Press, 1975.

Russell, James C. *The Germanization of Early Medieval Christianity. A Sociohistorical Approach to Religious Transformation*. New York: Oxford University Press, 1994.

Russell, Jeffrey Burton. *Dissent and Reform in the Early Middle Ages*. Berkeley: University of California Press, 1965.

Russell, Jeffrey Burton. *A History of Medieval Christianity: Prophecy and Order*. New York: Thomas Y. Crowell, 1968.

Russell, Jeffrey Burton, ed. *Religious Dissent in the Middle Ages*. New York: Wiley, 1971.

Russell, Jeffrey Burton. *Witchcraft in the Middle Ages*. Ithaca, N.Y.: Cornell University Press, 1972.

Russell, Jeffrey Burton. *Lucifer: The Devil in the Middle Ages*. Ithaca, N.Y.: Cornell University Press, 1984.

Russell, Jeffrey Burton. *Dissent and Order in the Middle Ages: The Search for Legitimate Authority*. New York: Twayne Publishers, 1992.

Saalman, Howard. *Medieval Cities*. New York: Braziller, 1968.

Salisbury, Joyce E., ed. *Sex in the Middle Ages: A Book of Essays*. New York: Garland, 1991.

Sapori, Armando. *The Italian Merchant in the Middle Ages*. Trans. Patricia Ann Kennen. New York: Norton, 1970.

Sawyer, P. H., ed. *Medieval Settlement: Continuity and Change*. London: Edward Arnold, 1976.

Scammell, Geoffrey Vaughn. *The World Encompassed: The First European Maritime Empires, c. 800–1650*. Berkeley: University of California Press, 1981.

Scammell, Geoffrey Vaughn. *The First Imperial Age: European Overseas Expansion, c. 1400–1715*. London: Unwin Hymnan, 1989.

Schimmelpfennig, Bernhard. *The Papacy*. Trans. James Sievert. New York: Columbia University Press, 1992.

Schmitt, Jean-Claude. *The Holy Greyhound: Guinefort, Healer of Children since the Thirteenth Century*. Trans. Martin Thom. 1979. Reprint, Cambridge: Cambridge University Press, 1983.

Setton, Kenneth M. *Catalan Domination of Athens, 1311–1388*. Cambridge, Mass.: Medieval Academy of America, 1948.

Setton, Kenneth M., ed. *A History of the Crusades*. 6 vols. Madison: University of Wisconsin Press, 1969–1989.

Setton, Kenneth M. *The Papacy and the Levant, 1204–1571*. 4 vols. Philadelphia: American Philosophical Society, 1976–1984.

Shinners, John, ed. *Medieval Popular Religion, 1000–1500: A Reader*. Peterborough, Canada: Broadview Press, 1997.

Siberry, Elizabeth. *Criticism of Crusading, 1095–1274*. Oxford: Oxford University Press, 1985.

Skinner, Quentin. *The Foundations of Modern Political Thought*. Vol. 1. *The Renaissance*. Cambridge: Cambridge University Press, 1978.

Skinner, Quentin, and Eckhard Kessler, eds. *The Cambridge History of Renaissance Philosophy*. Cambrige: Cambridge University Press, 1989.

Smail, R. C. *Crusading Warfare, 1097–1193*. 2d ed. 1956. Reprint, Cambridge: Cambridge University Press, 1995.

Smalley, Beryl. *The Study of the Bible in the Middle Ages*. 3d ed. Oxford: B. Blackwell, 1983.

Smalley, Beryl. *The Gospels in the Schools, c. 1100–c. 1280*. London: Hambledon Press, 1985.

Smyth, Alfred P., ed. *Medieval Europeans: Studies in Ethnic Identity and National Perspectives in Medieval Europe*. New York: St. Martin's Press, 1998.

Southern, Richard W. *The Making of the Middle Ages*. New Haven, Conn.: Yale University Press, 1953.

Southern, Richard W. *Medieval Humanism and Other Studies*. New York: Harper & Row, 1970.

Southern, Richard W. *Western Society and the Church in the Middle Ages*. Harmondsworth: Penguin, 1970.

Southern, Richard W. *Scholastic Humanism and the Unification of Europe*. Vol. 1. *Foundations*. Oxford: Blackwell, 1995.

Southern, Richard W. *Scholastic Humanism and the Unification of Europe*. Vol. 2. *The Heroic Age*. With notes and additions by Lesley Smith and Benedicta Ward. Oxford: Blackwell, 2001.

Spufford, Peter. *Money and Its Use in the Middle Ages*. Cambridge: Cambridge University Press, 1988.

Spufford, Peter, with Wendy Wilkinson and Sarah Tolley. *Handbook of Medieval Exchange*. London: Royal Historical Society, 1986.

Ste. Croix, G. E. M. de. *The Class Struggle in the Classical World from the Archaic Age to the Arab Conquests*. London: Duckworth, 1981.

Stabel, Peter. *Dwarfs among Giants: The Flemish Urban Network in the Late Middle Ages*. Louvain: Garant, 1997.

Stephens, John. *The Italian Renaissance: The Origins of Intellectual and Artistic Change before the Renaissance*. New York: Longman, 1990.

Sternfeld, Frederick William, ed. *Music from the Middle Ages to the Renaissance.* New York: Praeger, 1973.

Sterns, Indrikis. *The Greater Medieval Historians: An Interpretation and a Bibliography.* Lanham, Md.: University Press of America, 1980.

Stock, Brian. *The Implications of Literacy: Written Language and Models of Interpretation in the Eleventh and Twelfth Centuries.* Princeton, N.J.: Princeton University Press, 1983.

Strayer, Joseph R. *On the Medieval Origins of the Modern State.* Princeton, N.J.: Princeton University Press, 1970.

Swanson, Robert N. *Religion and Devotion in Europe, c. 1215–c. 1515.* Cambridge: Cambridge University Press, 1995.

Swanson, Robert N. *The Twelfth-Century Renaissance.* Manchester: Manchester University Press, 1999.

Tabacco, Giovanni. *The Struggle for Power in Medieval Italy: Structures of Political Rule.* Trans. Rosalind Brown Jensen. Cambridge: Cambridge University Press, 1989.

Tanner, Norman P., ed. *Decrees of the Ecumenical Councils.* 2 vols. London: Sheed and Ward, 1990.

Tellenbach, Gerd. *Church, State and Christian Society at the Time of the Investiture Contest.* Trans. R. F. Bennett. New York: Harper & Row, 1959.

Tellenbach, Gerd. *The Church in Western Europe from the Tenth to the Early Twelfth Century.* Trans. Timothy Reuter. 1988. Reprint, Cambridge: Cambridge University Press, 1993.

Tentler, Thomas N. *Sin and Confession on the Eve of the Reformation.* Princeton, N.J.: Princeton University Press, 1977.

Thomson, John A. F. *Popes and Princes, 1417–1517: Politics and Polity in the Late Medieval Church.* London: George Allen and Unwin, 1980.

Thorndike, Lynn, ed. *University Records and Life in the Middle Ages.* New York: Columbia University Press, 1944.

Tierney, Brian. *Foundation of the Conciliar Theory: The Contribution of the Medieval Canonists from Gratian to the Great Schism.* Cambridge: Cambridge University Press, 1955.

Tierney, Brian, ed. *The Crisis of Church and State, 1050–1300.* Englewood Cliffs, N.J.: Prentice-Hall, 1964.

Tierney, Brian. *Origins of Papal Infallibility, 1150–1350: A Study on the Concepts of Infallibility, Sovereignty and Tradition in the Middle Ages.* Leiden: Brill, 1972.

Todd, Malcolm. *The Northern Barbarians, 100 BC–AD 300.* Rev. ed. New York: B. Blackwell, 1987.

Todd, Malcolm. *The Early Germans.* Oxford: Blackwell, 1992.

Tomasello, Andrew. *Music and Ritual at Papal Avignon, 1309–1403.* Ann Arbor, Mich.: UMI Research Press, 1983.

Trachtenberg, Marvin. *Dominion of the Eye: Urbanism, Art, and Power in Early Modern Florence.* Cambridge: Cambridge University Press, 1997.

Trexler, Richard C. *Public Life in Renaissance Florence.* New York: Academic Press, 1980.

Tyerman, Christopher. *The Invention of the Crusades.* Toronto: University of Toronto Press, 1998.

Ullmann, Walter. *Principles of Government and Politics in the Middle Ages.* London: Methuen, 1961.

Ullmann, Walter. *A History of Political Thought: The Middle Ages.* Baltimore: Penguin, 1965.

Ullmann, Walter. *A Short History of the Papacy in the Middle Ages.* London: Methuen, 1972.

Vale, Malcolm G. A. *War and Chivalry: Warfare and Aristocratic Culture in England, France, and Burgundy at the End of the Middle Ages.* London: Duckworth, 1981.

Van Dam, Raymond. *Saints and Their Miracles in Late Antique Gaul.* Princeton, N.J.: Princeton University Press, 1993.

Vaughan, Richard. *Valois Burgundy.* Hamden, Conn.: Archon Books, 1975.

Vauchez, André. *The Spirituality of the Medieval West: The Eighth to the Twelfth Century.* Trans. Colette Friedlander. 1975. Reprint, Kalamazoo, Mich.: Cistercian, 1993.

Vauchez, André. *The Laity in the Middle Ages: Religious Beliefs and Devotional Practices.* Ed. Daniel Bornstein. Trans. Margery J. Schneider. 1987. Reprint, Notre Dame, Ind.: University of Notre Dame Press, 1993.

Vauchez, André. *Sainthood in the Later Middle Ages.* Trans. Jean Birrell. 1988. Reprint, Cambridge: Cambridge University Press, 1997.

Verbruggen, J. F. *The Art of Warfare in Western Europe during the Middle Ages: From the Eighth Century to 1340.* 2d ed. Trans. Sumner Willard and R. W. Southern. 1954. Reprint, Woodbridge, England: Boydell and Brewer, 1997.

Verger, Jacques. *Men of Learning in Europe at the End of the Middle Ages.* Trans. Lisa Neal and Steven Rendall. Notre Dame, Ind.: University of Notre Dame Press, 2000.

Verhulst, Adriaan. *The Rise of Cities in North-West Europe.* Cambridge: Cambridge University Press, 1999.

Verhulst, Adriaan. *The Carolingian Economy.* Cambridge: Cambridge University Press, 2002.

Waddell, Helen. *The Wandering Scholars.* 7th ed. London: Collins, 1968.

Wakefield, Walter L., and Austin P. Evans, eds. *Heresies of the High Middle Ages.* 1969. Reprint, New York: Columbia University Press, 1991.

Waley, Daniel. *The Italian City-Republics.* 3d ed. 1969. Reprint, London: Longman, 1988.

Wallace-Hadrill, J. M. *The Long-Haired Kings and Other Studies in Frankish History.* London: Methuen, 1962.

Wallace-Hadrill, J. M. *Early Germanic Kingship in England and on the Continent.* Oxford: Clarendon Press, 1971.

Wallace-Hadrill, J. M. *The Frankish Church.* Oxford: Clarendon Press, 1983.

Wallace-Hadrill, J. M., ed. *Bede's Ecclesiastical History of the English People: A Historical Commentary.* Oxford: Clarendon Press, 1988.

Wallace-Hadrill, J. M. *The Barbarian West, 400–1000.* Rev. ed. Oxford: B. Blackwell, 1996.

Ward, Benedicta. *Miracles and the Medieval Mind: Theory, Record and Event, 1000–1215.* Rev. ed. Philadelphia: University of Pennsylvania Press, 1987.

Ward-Perkins, Bryan. *From Classical Antiquity to the Middle Ages: Urban Public Building in Northern and Central Italy, A.D. 300–850.* Oxford: Oxford University Press, 1984.

Ward-Perkins, Bryan, and G. P. Brogiolo, eds. *The Idea and Ideal of the Town between Late Antiquity and the Early Middle Ages.* Leiden: Brill, 1999.

Weinfurter, Stefan. *The Salian Century: Main Currents in an Age of Transition.* Trans. Barbara M. Bowlus. 1991. Reprint, Philadelphia: University of Pennsylvania Press, 1999.

Weinstein, Donald, and Rudolph M. Bell. *Saints and Society: The Two Worlds of Western Christendom, 1000–1700.* Chicago: University of Chicago Press, 1982.

Weiss, Roberto. *The Renaissance Discovery of Classical Antiquity.* Oxford: Blackwell, 1969.

White, Lynn, Jr. *Medieval Technology and Social Change.* Oxford: Oxford University Press, 1962.

White, Stephen D. *Custom, Kinship, and Gifts to Saints: The "Laudatio parentum" in Western France, 1050–1150.* Chapel Hill: University of North Carolina Press, 1988.

Wickham, Chris. *Early Medieval Italy: Central Power and Local Society, 400–1000.* London: Macmillan, 1981.

Wickham, Chris. *The Mountains and the City: The Tuscan Appennines in the Early Middle Ages.* Oxford: Clarendon Press, 1988.

Wickham, Chris. *Land and Power: Studies in Italian and European Social History, 400–1200.* London: British School at Rome, 1994.

Wickham, Chris. *Community and Clientele in Twelfth-Century Tuscany: The Origins of the Rural Commune in the Plain of Lucca.* Oxford: Clarendon Press, 1998.

Wieruszowski, Helene, ed. *The Medieval University.* Princeton, N.J.: Van Nostrand, 1966.

Witt, Ronald G. *Hercules at the Crossroads: The Life, Works, and Thought of Coluccio Salutati.* Durham, N.C.: Duke University Press, 1983.

Witt, Ronald G. *In the Footsteps of the Ancients: The Origins of Humanism from Lovato to Bruni.* Leiden: Brill, 2000.

Witt, Ronald G., and Benjamin G. Kohl with Elizabeth B. Welles, eds. *The Earthly Republic: Italian Humanists on Government and Society.* Manchester: Manchester University Press, 1978.

Wolf, Philippe. *The Pelican History of European Thought.* Vol. 1. *The Awaking of Europe.* Trans. Anne Carter. Middlesex: Penguin, 1968.

Wolff, Philippe. *Western Languages, AD 100–1500.* Trans. Frances Partridge. New York: McGraw-Hill, 1971.

Wood, Charles T. *The Quest for Eternity: Medieval Manners and Morals.* Garden City, N.Y.: Anchor Books, 1971.

Wood, Diana. *Medieval Economic Thought.* Cambridge: Cambridge University Press, 2002.

Wood, Ian N. *The Merovingian Kingdoms, 450–751.* New York: Longman, 1994.

Wood, Ian, ed. *Franks and Alamanni in the Merovingian Period: An Ethnographic Perspective.* San Marino, Calif.: Center for Interdisciplinary Research on Social Stress, 1998.

Wright, Craig M. *Music at the Court of Burgundy, 1364–1419: A Documentary History.* Henryville, Pa.: Institute of Medieval Music, 1979.

Wright, Craig M. *Music and Ceremony at Notre Dame of Paris, 500–1550.* Cambridge: Cambridge University Press, 1989.

Wright, Craig M. *The Maze and the Warrior: Symbols in Architecture, Theology, and Music.* Cambridge, Mass.: Harvard University Press, 2001.

Young, Charles R., ed. *The Twelfth-Century Renaissance.* New York: Holt, Rinehart & Winston, 1969.

Ziegler, Philip. *The Black Death.* Middlesex: Penguin Books, 1969.

III. ART, ARCHITECTURE, AND MANUSCRIPT STUDIES

Alexander, J. J. G. *English Illuminated Manuscripts 700–1500.* Brussels: Bibliothèque Royale Albert Ier, 1973.

Alexander, J. J. G. *Italian Renaissance Illuminations.* New York: Braziller, 1977.

Alexander, J. J. G. *Medieval Illuminators and Their Methods of Work.* New Haven, Conn.: Yale University Press, 1992.

Alexander, J. J. G., and Paul Binski, eds. *Age of Chivalry: Art in Plantagenet England, 1200–1400.* London: Royal Academy of Arts in Association with Weidenfeld and Nicolson, 1987.

Ames-Lewis, Francis. *The Intellectual Life of the Early Renaissance Artist.* New Haven, Conn.: Yale University Press, 2000.

Ames-Lewis, Francis. *Drawing in Early Renaissance Italy.* New Haven, Conn.: Yale University Press, 2000.

Ames-Lewis, Francis, and Mary Rogers, eds. *Concepts of Beauty in Renaissance Art.* Aldershot: Ashgate, 1998.

Antal, Frederick. *Florentine Painting and Its Social Background. The Bourgeois Republic before Cosimo de'Medici's Advent to Power: XIV and Early XV Centuries.* New York: Routledge & K. Paul, 1948.

Arnould, Alain. *Splendours of Flanders.* Cambridge: Cambridge University Press, 1993.

Avril, François. *Manuscript Painting at the Court of France: The Fourteenth Century, 1310–1380.* Trans. Ursule Molinaro, with the Assistance of Bruce Benderson. New York: G. Braziller, 1978.

Backhouse, Janet. *The Illuminated Manuscript.* Oxford: Phaidon, 1979.

Backhouse, Janet. *The Illuminated Page: Ten Centuries of Manuscript Painting in the British Library.* Toronto: University of Toronto Press, 1997.

Backhouse, Janet, D. H. Turner, and Leslie Webster, eds. *The Golden Age of Anglo-Saxon Art, 966–1066.* London: British Museum, 1984.

Barasch, Moshe. *Gestures of Despair in Medieval and Early Renaissance Art.* New York: New York University Press, 1976.

Barasch, Moshe. *Light and Color in the Italian Renaissance Theory of Art.* New York: New York University Press, 1978.

Barasch, Moshe. *Giotto and the Language of Gesture.* Cambridge: Cambridge University Press, 1987.

Barkan, Leonard. *The Gods Made Flesh: Metamorphosis and the Pursuit of Paganism*. New Haven, Conn.: Yale University Press, 1986.

Barkan, Leonard. *Transuming Passion: Ganymede and the Erotics of Humanism*. Stanford, Calif.: Stanford University Press, 1991.

Barkan, Leonard. *Unearthing the Past: Archaeology and Aesthetics in the Making of Renaissance Culture*. New Haven, Conn.: Yale University Press, 1999.

Baxandall, Michael. *Giotto and the Orators: Humanist Observers of Painting in Italy and the Discovery of Pictorial Composition, 1350–1450*. Oxford: Clarendon Press, 1971.

Baxandall, Michael. *Painting and Experience in Fifteenth Century Italy: A Primer in the Social History of Pictorial Style*. Oxford: Oxford University Press, 1972.

Baxandall, Michael. *The Limewood Sculptors of Renaissance Germany*. New Haven, Conn.: Yale University Press, 1980.

Beckwith, John. *Early Medieval Art: Carolingian, Ottonian, Romanesque*. London: Thames and Hudson, 1964.

Beckwith, John. *Early Christian and Byzantine Art*. 2d ed. Harmondsworth: Penguin, 1979.

Belting, Hans. *The Image and Its Public in the Middle Ages: Form and Function of Early Paintings of the Passion*. Trans. Mark Bartusis and Raymond Meyer. 1981. Reprint, New Rochelle, N.Y.: A. D. Caratzas, 1990.

Belting, Hans. *Likeness and Presence: A History of the Image before the Era of Art*. Trans. Edmund Jephcott. 1990. Reprint, Chicago: University of Chicago Press, 1994.

Benton, Janetta Rebold. *Art of the Middle Ages*. New York: Thames & Hudson, 2002.

Bischoff, Bernhard. *Manuscripts and Libraries in the Age of Charlemagne*. Trans. and ed. Michael Gorman. Cambridge: Cambridge University Press, 1994.

Bony, Jean. *The English Decorated Style: Gothic Architecture Transformed, 1250–1350*. Ithaca, N.Y.: Cornell University Press, 1979.

Bony, Jean. *French Gothic Architecture of the 12th and 13th Centuries*. Berkeley: University of California Press, 1983.

Boyle, Leonard E. *A Survey of the Vatican Archives and Its Medieval Holdings*. Toronto: Pontifical Institute of Mediaeval Studies, 1972.

Boyle, Leonard E. *Medieval Latin Palaeography: A Bibliographical Introduction*. Toronto: University of Toronto Press, 1984.

Branner, Robert. *St. Louis and the Court Style in Gothic Architecture*. 1965. Reprint, London: A. Zwemmer, 1965.

Branner, Robert. *Manuscripts Painting in Paris during the Reign of Saint Louis: A Study of Styles*. Berkeley: University of California Press, 1977.

Branner, Robert. *Burgundian Gothic Architecture*. London: A. Zwemmer, 1985.

Branner, Robert. *The Cathedral of Bourges and Its Place in Gothic Architecture*. Cambridge, Mass.: MIT Press, 1989.

Brown, Michelle P. *A Guide to Western Historical Scripts from Antiquity to 1600*. Toronto: University of Toronto Press, 1990.

Brown, Michelle P., and Patricia Lovett. *The Historical Source Book for Scribes*. London: British Library, 1999.

Cahn, Walter. *Romanesque Bible Illumination*. Ithaca, N.Y.: Cornell University Press, 1982.

Cahn, Walter. *Romanesque Manuscripts: The Twelfth Century*. 2 vols. London: H. Miller, 1996.

Calkins, Robert G. *Monuments of Medieval Art*. Ithaca, N.Y.: Cornell University Press, 1979.

Calkins, Robert G. *Illuminated Books of the Middle Ages*. Ithaca, N.Y.: Cornell University Press, 1983.

Calkins, Robert G. *Medieval Architecture in Western Europe: From A.D. 300 to 1500*. New York: Oxford University Press, 1998.

Camille, Michael. *The Gothic Idol: Ideology and Image-Making in Medieval Art*. Cambridge: Cambridge University Press, 1989.

Camille, Michael. *Image on the Edge: The Margins of Medieval Art*. Cambridge, Mass.: Harvard University Press, 1992.

Camille, Michael. *Gothic Art: Glorious Visions*. New York: Harry N. Abrams, 1996.

Camille, Michael. *Master of Death: The Lifeless Art of Pierre Remiet, Illuminator*. New Haven, Conn.: Yale University Press, 1996.

Camille, Michael. *The Medieval Art of Love: Objects and Subjects of Desire*. New York: Harry Abrams, 1998.

Chambers, D. S., ed. *Patrons and Artists in the Italian Renaissance*. London: Macmillan, 1970.

Chambers, D. S. *Individuals and Institutions in Renaissance Italy*. Aldershot: Ashgate/Variorum, 1998.

Coldstream, Nicola. *Masons and Sculptors*. Toronto: University of Toronto Press, 1991.

Coldstream, Nicola. *The Decorated Style: Architecture and Ornament 1240–1360*. Toronto: University of Toronto Press, 1994.

Coldstream, Nicola. *Medieval Architecture*. Oxford: Oxford University Press, 2002.

Cole, Alison. *Virtue and Magnificence: Art of the Italian Renaissance Courts*. New York: Harry Abrams, 1995.

Cole, Bruce. *Sienese Painting, from Its Origins to the Fifteenth Century*. New York: Harper & Row, 1980.

Cole, Bruce. *The Renaissance Artist at Work: From Pisano to Titian*. London: Jonh Murray, 1983.

Cole Bruce, *Sienese Painting in the Age of the Renaissance*. Bloomington: Indiana University Press, 1985.

Cole, Bruce. *Italian Art, 1250–1550: The Relation of Renaissance Art to Life and Society*. New York: Harper & Row, 1987.

Conant, Kenneth John. *Carolingian and Romanesque Architecture, 800–1200*. 4th ed. New Haven, Conn.: Yale University Press, 1978.

Davis-Weyer, Caecilia. *Early Medieval Art, 300–1150: Sources and Documents*. Toronto: University of Toronto Press in Association with the Medieval Academy of America, 1986.

De Hamel, Christopher. *Scribes and Illuminators*. Toronto: University of Toronto Press, 1992.

De Hamel, Christopher. *A History of Illuminated Manuscripts*. 2d ed. London: Phaidon Press, 1994.

Demus, Otto. *Romanesque Mural Painting*. Trans. Mary Whittall. 1968. Reprint, New York: Harry N. Abrams, 1970.

Deshman, Robert. *Anglo-Saxon and Anglo-Scandinavian Art: An Annotated Bibliography.* Boston: G. K. Hall, 1984.

Dodds, Jerrilynn D. *Architecture and Ideology in Early Medieval Spain.* University Park: Pennsylvania State University Press, 1990.

Dodwell, C. R. *Anglo-Saxon Art: A New Perspective.* Ithaca, N.Y.: Cornell University Press, 1982.

Dodwell, C. R. *The Pictorial Arts of the West, 800–1200.* New Haven, Conn.: Yale University Press, 1993.

Dodwell, C. R. *Aspects of Art of the Eleventh and Twelfth Centuries.* London: Pindar Press, 1996.

Duby, Georges. *The Age of the Cathedrals: Art and Society, 980–1420.* Trans. Eleanor Levieux and Barbara Thompson. Chicago: University of Chicago Press, 1981.

Eco, Umberto. *Art and Beauty in the Middle Ages.* 1959. Reprint, New Haven, Conn.: Yale University Press, 1986.

Erlande-Brandenburg, Alain. *The Cathedral: The Social and Architectural Dynamics of Construction.* Trans. Martin Thom. Cambridge: Cambridge University Press, 1994.

Fernie, Eric. C. *The Architecture of the Anglo-Saxons.* New York: Holmes & Meier, 1983.

Fernie, Eric C. *Romanesque Architecture: Design, Meaning and Metrology.* London: Pindar Press, 1995.

Fernie, Eric C. *The Architecture of Norman England.* Oxford: Oxford University Press, 2000.

Fleming, John V. *From Bonaventure to Bellini: An Essay in Franciscan Exegesis.* Princeton, N.J.: Princeton University Press, 1982.

Folda, Jaroslav. *Crusader Manuscript Illumination at Saint-Jean d'Acre, 1275–1291.* Princeton, N.J.: Princeton University Press, 1976.

Folda, Jaroslav. *The Art of the Crusaders in the Holy Land, 1098–1187.* Cambridge: Cambridge University Press, 1995.

Frankl, Paul. *The Gothic: Literary Sources and Interpretations through Eight Centuries.* Princeton, N.J.: Princeton University Press, 1960.

Frankl, Paul. *Gothic Architecture.* Revised by Paul Crossley. 1962. Reprint, New Haven, Conn.: Yale University Press, 2000.

Freedberg, David. *The Power of Images: Studies in the History and Theory of Response.* Chicago: University of Chicago Press, 1989.

Friedman, John Block. *The Monstrous in Medieval Art and Thought.* Cambridge, Mass.: Harvard University Press, 1981.

Friedman, John B., and Jessica M. Wegmann. *Medieval Iconography: A Research Guide.* New York: Garland, 1998.

Frisch, Teresa Grace. *Gothic Art 1140–c. 1450: Sources and Documents.* Englewood Cliffs, N.J.: Prentice-Hall, 1971.

Frugoni, Chiara. *A Distant City: Images of Urban Experience in the Medieval World.* Trans. William McCuaig. Princeton, N.J.: Princeton University Press, 1991.

Gameson, Richard. *The Manuscripts of Early Norman England (c. 1066–1130).* Oxford: Oxford University Press, 1999.

Gilbert, Creighton E. *History of Renaissance Art: Painting, Sculpture, Architecture throughout Europe.* New York: Harry Abrams, 1973.

Gilbert, Creighton E. *Italian Art 1400–1500. Sources and Documents.* Englewood Cliffs, N.J.: Prentice-Hall, 1980.

Gimpel, Jean. *The Cathedral Builders.* Trans. Teresa Waugh. 1980. Reprint, London: Cresset Library, 1983.

Goldthwaite, Richard A. *The Building of Renaissance Florence: An Economic and Social History.* Baltimore: Johns Hopkins University Press, 1980.

Goldthwaite, Richard A. *Wealth and Demand for Art in Italy, 1300–1600.* Baltimore: Johns Hopkins University Press, 1993.

Gombrich, E. H. *Norm and Form.* London: Phaidon, 1966.

Gombrich, E. H. *Meditations on a Hobby Horse and Other Essays on the Theory of Art.* 2d ed. London: Phaidon, 1971.

Gombrich, E. H. *Symbolic Images.* London: Phaidon, 1972.

Gombrich, E. H. *The Heritage of Apelles: Studies in the Art of the Renaissance.* Ithaca, N.Y.: Cornell University Press, 1976.

Gombrich, E. H. *Means and Ends: Reflections on the History of Fresco Painting.* London: Thames and Hudson, 1976.

Goy, Richard J. *Venetian Vernacular Architecture: Traditional Housing in the Venetian Lagoon.* Cambridge: Cambridge University Press, 1989.

Goy, Richard J. *The House of Gold: Building a Palace in Medieval Venice.* Cambridge: Cambridge University Press, 1992.

Gough, Michael. *The Origins of Christian Art.* London: Thames and Hudson, 1973.

Grabar, André, ed. *The Golden Age of Justinian: From the Death of Theodosius to the Rise of Islam.* Trans. Stuart Gilbert and James Emmons. New York: Odyssey Press, 1967.

Grodecki, Louis. *Gothic Architecture.* Trans. I. Mark Paris. 1978. Reprint, New York: Electa/Rizzoli, 1985.

Grössinger, Christa. *Picturing Women in Late Medieval and Renaissance Art.* Manchester: Manchester University Press, 1997.

Hamburger, Jeffrey F. *The Rothschild Canticles: Art and Mysticism in Flanders and the Rhineland circa 1300.* New Haven, Conn.: Yale University Press, 1990.

Hamburger, Jeffrey F. *Nuns as Artists: The Visual Culture of a Medieval Convent.* Berkeley: University of California Press, 1997.

Hamburger, Jeffrey F. *The Visual and the Visionary: Art and Female Spirituality in Late Medieval Germany.* New York: Zone Books, 1998.

Harthan, John P. *Books of Hours and Their Owners.* New York: Crowell, 1977.

Henderson, George. *Early Medieval.* Harmondsworth: Penguin, 1972.

Henderson, George. *From Durrow to Kells: The Insular Gospel-Books, 650–800.* London: Thames and Hudson, 1987.

Henderson, George. *Vision and Image in Early Christian England.* Cambridge: Cambridge University Press, 1999.

Hills, Paul. *The Light of Early Italian Painting*. New Haven, Conn.: Yale University Press, 1987.

Hollingsworth, Mary. *Patronage in Renaissance Italy: From 1400 to the Early Sixteenth Century*. London: John Murray, 1994.

Horn, Walter William. *The Plan of St. Gall: A Study of the Architecture and Economy and Life in a Paradigmatic Carolingian Monastery*. 3 vols. Berkeley: University of California Press, 1979.

Howard, Deborah. *The Architectural History of Venice*. New York: Holmes & Meier, 1981.

Howard, Deborah. *Venice and the East: The Impact of the Islamic World on Venetian Architecture, 1100–1500*. New Haven, Conn.: Yale University Press, 2000.

Humfrey, Peter. *Painting in Renaissance Venice*. New Haven, Conn.: Yale University Press, 1995.

Humfrey, Peter, and Martin Kemp, eds. *The Altarpiece in the Renaissance*. Cambridge: Cambridge University Press, 1990.

Hunt, Lucy-Anne. *Byzantium, Eastern Christendom and Islam: Art at the Crossroads of the Medieval Mediterranean*. 2 vols. London: Pindar Press, 1998.

Jensen, Robin Margaret. *Understanding Early Christian Art*. New York: Routledge, 2000.

Johnson, Geraldine A., and Sara F. Mathews Grieco, eds. *Picturing Women in Renaissance and Baroque Italy*. Cambridge: Cambridge University Press, 1997.

Katzenellenbogen, Adolf. *Allegories of the Virtues and Vices in Medieval Art*. 1939. Reprint, Toronto: Medieval Academy of America, 1989.

Kempers, Bram. *Painting, Power and Patronage: The Rise of the Professional Artist in Renaissance Italy*. Trans. Beverley Jackson. 1987. Reprint, London: Allen Lane the Penguin Press, 1992.

Kendrick, Laura. *Animating the Letter: The Figurative Embodiment of Writing from Late Antiquity to the Renaissance*. Columbus: Ohio State University Press, 1999.

Kennedy, Hugh. *Crusader Castles*. Cambridge: Cambridge University Press, 1994.

Kent, Francis William, and Patricia Simons, eds. *Patronage, Art and Society in Renaissance Italy*. Oxford: Oxford University Press, 1987.

Kidson, Peter. *The Medieval World*. New York: McGraw-Hill, 1967.

King, Catherine E. *Renaissance Women Patrons: Wives and Widows in Italy, c. 1300–1550*. Manchester: Manchester University Press, 1998.

Krautheimer, Richard. *Early Christian and Byzantine Architecture*. 3d ed. Baltimore: Penguin Books, 1975.

Krautheimer, Richard. *Rome, Profile of a City, 312–1308*. Princeton, N.J.: Princeton University Press, 1980.

Larner, John. *Culture and Society in Italy, 1290–1420*. New York: Scribner, 1971.

Lasko, Peter. *Ars Sacra, 800–1200*. 2d ed. New Haven, Conn.: Yale University Press, 1994.

Lasko, Peter. *Studies on Metalwork, Ivories and Stone*. London: Pindar Press, 1994.

Levey, Michael. *Early Renaissance*. New York: Penguin, 1967.

Lipton, Sara. *Images of Intolerance: The Representation of Jews and Judaism in the Bible Moralisée*. Berkeley: University of California Press, 1999.

Marks, Richard, and Nigel Morgan. *The Golden Age of English Manuscript Painting, 1200–1500*. New York: G. Braziller, 1981.

Martindale, Andrew. *Gothic Art from the Twelfth to the Fifteenth Century*. New York: Frederick A. Praeger, 1967.

Martindale, Andrew. *The Rise of the Artist in the Middle Ages and Early Renaissance*. New York: McGraw-Hill, 1972.

Martindale, Andrew. *Painting the Palace: Studies in the History of Medieval Secular Painting*. London: Pindar Press, 1995.

Mathews, Thomas F. *The Clash of Gods: A Reinterpretation of Early Christian Art*. Princeton, N.J.: Princeton University Press, 1993.

Mayr-Harting, Henry. *Ottonian Book Illumination: An Historical Study*. 2 vols. 2d ed. London: Harvey Miller, 1999.

Meiss, Millard. *Painting in Florence and Siena after the Black Death: The Arts, Religion and Society in the Mid-Fourteenth Century*. New York: Harper & Row, 1964.

Meiss, Millard. *The Great Age of Fresco: Discoveries, Recoveries, and Survivals*. New York: G. Braziller in Association with the Metropolitan Museum of Art, 1970.

Meiss, Millard. *French Painting in the Time of Jean de Berry: The Limbourgs and Their Contemporaries*. New York: G. Braziller, 1974.

Meiss, Millard. *The Painter's Choice: Problems in the Interpretation of Renaissance Art*. New York: Harper & Row, 1976.

Morgan, Nigel J. *Early Gothic Manuscripts*. 2 vols. Oxford: Oxford University Press, 1982–1988.

Moritz, Bernhard, ed. *Arabic Palaeography: A Collection of Arabic Texts from the First Century of the Hidjra till the Year 1000*. Osnabrück: Biblio, 1986.

Murray, Peter. *The Architecture of the Italian Renaissance*. New York: Schocken, 1963.

Murray, Peter, and Linda Murray. *The Art of the Renaissance*. New York: Oxford University Press, 1963.

Nees, Lawrence. *From Justinian to Charlemagne: European Art, 565–787: An Annotated Bibliography*. Boston: G. K. Hall, 1985.

Nees, Lawrence. *Early Medieval Art*. Oxford: Oxford University Press, 2002.

Norman, Diana, ed. *Siena, Florence and Padua: Art, Society and Religion, 1280–1400*. 2 vols. New Haven, Conn.: Yale University Press, 1995.

Nussbaum, Norbert. *German Gothic Church Architecture*. Trans. Scott Kleager. New Haven, Conn.: Yale University Press, 2000.

O'Meadhra, Uaininn. *Early Christian, Viking and Romanesque Art: Motif-Pieces from Ireland*. Stockholm: Almqvist and Wiksell International, 1979.

O'Neill, John P., ed. *The Art of Medieval Spain, A.D. 500–1200*. New York: The Metropolitan Museum of Art, 1993.

Os, H. W. van. *Studies in Early Tuscan Painting*. London: Pindar, 1992.

Os, H. W. van. *The Art of Devotion in the Late Middle Ages in Europe, 1300–1500*. Trans. Michael Hoyle. Princeton, N.J.: Princeton University Press, 1994.

Pächt, Otto. *The Rise of Pictorial Narrative in Twelfth-Century England*. Oxford: Clarendon Press, 1962.

Pächt, Otto. *Book Illumination in the Middle Ages: An Introduction*. Trans. Kay Davenport. Oxford: Oxford University Press, 1986.

Pächt, Otto. *Van Eyck and the Founders of Early Netherlandish Painting*. Ed. Maria Schmidt-Dengler. Trans. David Britt. London: H. Miller, 1994.

Pächt, Otto. *Early Netherlandish Painting: From Rogier van der Weyden to Gerard David*. Ed. Monika Rosenauer. Trans. David Britt. London: Harvey Miller, 1997.

Panofsky, Erwin. *Gothic Architecture and Scholasticism*. New York: New American Library, 1957.

Panofsky, Erwin. *Renaissance and Renascences in Western Art*. London: Paladin, 1965.

Panofsky, Erwin. *Early Netherlandish Painting: Its Origins and Character*. 1953. Reprint, New York: Harper & Row, 1971.

Panofsky, Erwin. *Studies in Iconology: Humanistic Themes in the Art of the Renaissance*. New York: Harper & Row, 1972.

Petzold, Andreas. *Romanesque Art*. New York: Harry N. Abrams, 1995.

Price, Lorna, ed. *The Plan of St. Gall in Brief: An Overview Based on the Three-Volume Work by Walter Horn and Ernest Born*. Berkeley: University of California Press, 1982.

Radding, Charles, and William W. Clark. *Medieval Architecture, Medieval Learning: Builders and Masters in the Age of Romanesque and Gothic*. New Haven, Conn.: Yale University Press, 1992.

Randall, Lillian M. C. *Images in the Margins of Gothic Manuscripts*. Berkeley: University of California Press, 1966.

Rosenberg, Charles M., ed. *Art and Politics in Late Medieval and Early Renaissance Italy, 1250–1500*. Notre Dame, Ind.: University of Notre Dame Press, 1990.

Saalman, Howard. *Medieval Architecture: European Architecture, 600–1200*. New York: Braziller, 1962.

Sandler, Lucy Freeman. *Gothic Manuscripts, 1285–1385*. 2 vols. New York: Oxford University Press, 1986.

Sauerländer, Willibald. *Gothic Sculpture in France, 1140–1270*. Trans. Janet Sondheimer. New York: Harry Abrams, 1972.

Saul, Nigel E., ed. *The Age of Chivalry: Art and Society in the Late Medieval England*. New York: St. Martin's Press, 1992.

Schapiro, Meyer. *Romanesque Art*. New York: G. Braziller, 1977.

Schapiro, Meyer. *Late Antique, Early Christian and Mediaeval Art*. New York: G. Braziller, 1979.

Schapiro, Meyer. *The Romanesque Sculpture of Moissac*. New York: G. Braziller, 1985.

Scheller, Robert Walter Hans Peter. *Exemplum: Model-Book Drawings and the Practice of Artistic Transmission in the Middle Ages (ca. 900–ca. 1470)*. Trans. Michael Hoyle. Amsterdam: Amsterdam University Press, 1995.

Scott, Kathleen L. *Later Gothic Manuscripts, 1390–1490*. 2 vols. London: H. Miller, 1996.

Seidel, Linda. *Songs of Glory: The Romanesque Façades of Aquitaine*. Chicago: University of Chicago Press, 1981.

Seidel, Linda. *Jan Van Eyck's Arnolfini Portrait: Stories of an Icon*. Cambridge: Cambridge University Press, 1993.

Sekules, Veronica. *Medieval Art*. Oxford: Oxford University Press, 2001.

Shailor, Barbara, A. *The Medieval Book: Illustrated from the Beinecke Rare Book and Manuscript Library*. 1988. Reprint, Toronto: University of Toronto Press, 1991.

Simson, Otto von. *The Gothic Cathedral: Origins of Gothic Architecture and the Medieval Concept of Order*. 2d ed. New York: Harper & Row, 1962.

Smart, Alastair. *The Assisi Problem and the Art of Giotto: A Study of the Legend of St. Francis in the Upper Church of San Francesco, Assisi*. Oxford: Clarendon Press, 1971.

Smart, Alastair. *The Dawn of Italian Painting, 1250–1400*. Ithaca, N.Y.: Cornell University Press, 1978.

Snyder, James. *Medieval Art*. New York: Harry Abrams, 1989.

Stalley, Roger. *Early Medieval Architecture*. Oxford: Oxford University Press, 1999.

Starn, Randolph, and Loren Partridge. *Arts of Power: Three Halls of State in Italy, 1300–1600*. Berkeley: University of California Press, 1992.

Swaan, Wim. *The Late Middle Ages: Art and Architecture from 1350 to the Advent of the Renaissance*. Ithaca, N.Y.: Cornell University Press, 1977.

Taylor, Harold McCarter, and Joan Taylor. *Anglo-Saxon Architecture*. 3 vols. Cambridge: Cambridge University Press, 1965–1978.

Thomas, Anabel. *The Painter's Practice in Renaissance Tuscany*. Cambridge: Cambridge University Press, 1995.

Thompson, M. W. *The Decline of the Castle*. Cambridge: Cambridge University Press, 1987.

Thompson, M. W. *The Medieval Hall: The Basis of Secular Domestic Life, 600–1600 A.D.* Aldershot, England: Scolar Press, 1995.

Tinagli, Paola. *Women in Italian Renaissance Art: Gender, Representation, Identity*. Manchester: Manchester University Press, 1997.

Wackernagel, Martin. *The World of the Florentine Renaissance Artist: Projects and Patrons, Workshop and Art Market*. 1938. Reprint, Princeton, N.J.: Princeton University Press, 1981.

Webster, Leslie, and Janet Backhouse, eds. *The Making of England: Anglo-Saxon Art and Culture, A.D. 600–900*. Toronto: University of Toronto Press, 1991.

Webster, Leslie, and Michelle Brown, eds. *The Transformation of the Roman World*. Berkeley: University of California Press, 1997.

Welch, Evelyn S. *Art and Authority in Renaissance Milan*. New Haven, Conn.: Yale University Press, 1995.

White, John. *The Birth and Rebirth of Pictorial Space.* New York: Harper & Row, 1967.

White, John. *Art and Architecture in Italy, 1250–1400.* 2d ed. New York: Viking Penguin, 1987.

Williamson, Paul. *Gothic Sculpture, 1140–1300.* New Haven, Conn.: Yale University Press, 1995.

Wilson, Christopher. *The Gothic Cathedral: The Architecture of the Great Church, 1130–1530.* New York: Thames & Hudson, 1990.

Wilson, David M. *Anglo-Saxon Art: From the Seventh Century to the Norman Conquest.* Woodstock, N.Y.: Overlook Press, 1984.

Wolfthal, Diane. *The Beginnings of Netherlandish Canvas Painting, 1400–1530.* Cambridge: Cambridge University Press, 1989.

Wolfthal, Diane. *Images of Rape: The "Heroic" Tradition and Its Alternatives.* Cambridge: Cambridge University Press, 1999.

Zarnecki, George. *Romanesque Art.* New York: Universe Books, 1971.

Zarnecki, George. *Art of the Medieval World, Architecture, Sculpture, Painting, and Sacred Arts.* New York: Harry Abrams, 1975.

IV. BRITISH ISLES

Aers, David. *Community, Gender, and Individual Identity: English Writing, 1360–1430.* London: Routledge, 1988.

Alexander, J. J. G. *English Illuminated Manuscripts 700–1500.* Brussels: Bibliothèque Royale Albert Ier, 1973.

Alexander, J. J. G. and Paul Binski, eds. *Age of Chivalry: Art in Plantagenet England, 1200–1400.* London: Royal Academy of Arts in association with Weidenfeld and Nicolson, 1987.

Anderson, Alan Orr. *Early Sources of Scottish History, A.D. 500 to 1286.* 2 vols. Edinburgh: Oliver and Boyd, 1922.

Backhouse, Janet, D. H. Turner, and Leslie Webster, eds. *The Golden Age of Anglo-Saxon Art, 966–1066.* London: British Museum, 1984.

Baker, John H. *An Introduction to English Legal History.* 3d ed. London: Butterworth's, 1990.

Barlow, Frank. *The English Church, 1000–1066: A History of the Later Anglo-Saxon Church.* 2d ed. New York: Longman, 1979.

Barlow, Frank. *The English Church, 1066–1154: A History of the Anglo-Norman Church.* New York: Longman, 1979.

Barlow, Frank. *Edward the Confessor.* London: Eyre Methuen, 1979.

Barlow, Frank. *Thomas Becket.* Berkeley: University of California Press, 1986.

Barlow, Frank. *The Feudal Kingdom of England, 1042–1216.* 5th ed. Harlow, Essex: Addison Wesley Longman, 1999.

Barrell, A. D. M. *Medieval Scotland.* Cambridge: Cambridge University Press, 2000.

Barrow, G. W. S. *Kingship and Unity: Scotland, 1000–1306.* London: Edward Arnold, 1981.

Bassett, Steven, ed. *The Origins of Anglo-Saxon Kingdoms.* London: Leicester University Press, 1989.

Bassett, Steven, ed. *Death in Towns: Urban Responses to the Dying and the Dead, 100–1600.* Leicester: Leicester University Press, 1992.

Bean, J. M. W. *From Lord to Patron: Lordship in Late Medieval England.* Philadelphia: University of Pennsylvania Press, 1989.

Blair, Peter Hunter. *An Introduction to Anglo-Saxon England.* Cambridge: Cambridge University Press, 1962.

Blair, Peter Hunter. *The World of Bede.* Cambridge: Cambridge University Press, 1990.

Bolton, J. L. *The Medieval English Economy, 1150–1500.* London: J. M. Dent, 1980.

Bony, Jean. *The English Decorated Style: Gothic Architecture Transformed, 1250–1350.* Ithaca, N.Y.: Cornell University Press, 1979.

Brentano, Robert. *Two Churches: England and Italy in the Thirteenth Century.* Princeton, N.J.: Princeton University Press, 1968.

Bridbury, A. R. *Economic Growth: England in the Later Middle Ages.* 1962. Reprint, New York: Barnes & Noble, 1975.

Britnell, Richard H. *The Commercialisation of English Society, 1000–1500.* Manchester: Manchester University Press, 1996.

Brown, R. Allen. *Origins of English Feudalism.* New York: Barnes & Noble, 1973.

Brown, R. Allen. *English Castles.* 3d ed. London: Batsford, 1976.

Brown, R. Allen. *The Normans.* Woodbridge, Suffolk: Boydell Press, 1984.

Brown, R. Allen. *The Normans and the Norman Conquest.* 2d ed. Dover, N. H.: Boydell Press, 1985.

Burton, Janet E. *Monastic and Religious Orders in Britain, 1000–1300.* Cambridge: Cambridge University Press, 1994.

Caenegem, Raoul C. Van. *The Birth of the English Common Law.* 2d ed. Cambridge: Cambridge University Press, 1988.

Charles-Edwards, T. M. *Early Christian Ireland.* Cambridge: Cambridge University Press, 2000.

Chibnall, Marjorie. *Anglo-Norman England, 1066–1166.* Oxford: Blackwell, 1986.

Chibnall, Marjorie. *The Empress Matilda: Queen Consort, Queen Mother, and Lady of the English.* Oxford: Blackwell, 1992.

Chibnall, Marjorie. *The Debate on the Norman Conquest.* Manchester: Manchester University Press, 1999.

Chibnall, Marjorie. *Piety, Power, and History in Medieval England and Normandy.* Aldershot: Ashgate, 2000.

Clanchy, Michael T. *From Memory and Written Record: England, 1066–1307.* 2d ed. Oxford: Blackwell, 1993.

Cobban, Alan B. *The Medieval English Universities: Oxford and Cambridge to c. 1500.* Berkeley: University of California Press, 1988.

Cobban, Alan B. *English University Life in the Middle Ages.* London: UCL Press, 1999.

Cosgrove, Art. *Late Medieval Ireland, 1370–1541.* Dublin: Helicon, 1981.

Davies, R. R. *Lordship and Society in the March of Wales, 1282–1400.* Oxford: Clarendon Press, 1978.

Davies, R. R. *Conquest, Coexistence and Change, Wales 1063–1415.* Oxford: Oxford University Press, 1987.

Davies, R. R. *Domination and Conquest: The Experience of Ireland, Scotland and Wales, 1100–1300.* Cambridge: Cambridge University Press, 1990.

Davies, R. R. *The Revolt of Owain Glyn Dwr.* Oxford: Oxford University Press, 1995.

Davies, Wendy. *Wales in the Early Middle Ages.* Leicester: Leicester University Press, 1982.

Davies, Wendy. *Small Worlds: The Village Community in Early Medieval Brittany.* Berkeley: University of California Press, 1988.

Deshman, Robert. *Anglo-Saxon and Anglo-Scandinavian Art: An Annotated Bibliography.* Boston: G. K. Hall, 1984.

Dodwell, C. R. *Anglo-Saxon Art: A New Perspective.* Ithaca, N.Y.: Cornell University Press, 1982.

Douglas, David C. *William the Conqueror: The Norman Impact on England.* Berkeley: University of California Press, 1964.

Dixon, Philip. "Part II: Roman Britain and Early Medieval Britain," In *The National Trust Historical Atlas of Britain: Prehistoric and Medieval.* Ed. Nigel Saul. London: Alan Sutton, 1994, 53–112.

Du Boulay, F. R. H. *An Age of Ambition: English Society in the Late Middle Ages.* London: Thomas Nelson, 1970.

Duffy, Eamon. *The Stripping of the Altars: Traditional Religion in England, c. 1400–c. 1580.* New Haven, Conn.: Yale University Press, 1992.

Duffy, Seán. *Ireland in the Middle Ages.* New York: St. Martin's Press, 1997.

Duncan, A. A. M. *Scotland: The Making of the Kingdom.* Edinburgh: Oliver and Boyd, 1975.

Dyer, Christopher. *Standards of Living in the Later Middle Ages: Social Change in England c. 1200–1520.* Cambridge: Cambridge University Press, 1989.

Fernie, Eric C. *The Architecture of the Anglo-Saxons.* New York: Holmes & Meier, 1983.

Finberg, H. P. R. *The Formation of England, 550–1042.* St. Albans: Paladin, 1976.

Finberg, H. P. R. ed., *An Agrarian History of England.* Vol. 3. *1350–1500* Cambridge: Cambridge University Press, 1991.

Finucane, Ronald C. *Miracles and Pilgrims: Popular Beliefs in Medieval England.* Totowa, N.J.: Rowman & Littlefield, 1977.

Fleming, Robin. *Kings and Lords and Conquest England.* Cambridge: Cambridge University Press, 1991.

Ford, Boris ed. *The Cambridge Guide to the Arts in Britain: The Middle Ages.* Cambridge: Cambridge University Press, 1988.

Frame, Robin. *The Political Development of the British Isles, 1100–1400.* Oxford: Oxford University Press, 1990.

Frantzen, Allen J. *The Literature of Penance in Anglo-Saxon England.* New Brunswick, N.J.: Rutgers University Press, 1983.

Gameson, Richard. *The Manuscripts of Early Norman England (c. 1066–1130).* Oxford: Oxford University Press, 1999.

Given-Wilson, Chris. *The Royal Household and the King's Affinity: Service, Politics, and Finance in England, 1360–1413.* New Haven, Conn.: Yale University Press, 1986.

Given-Wilson, Chris. *The English Nobility in the Late Middle Ages: The Fourteenth-Century Political Community.* London: Routledge and Kegan Paul, 1987.

Given-Wilson, Chris, ed. *An Illustrated History of Late Medieval England.* Manchester: Manchester University Press, 1996.

Goodman, Anthony. *The Wars of the Roses: Military Activity and English Society, 1452–97.* London: Routledge and Kegan Paul, 1981.

Grant, Alexander. *Independence and Nationhood: Scotland, 1306–1469.* London: Edward Arnold, 1984.

Green, Judith A. *The Aristocracy of Norman England* Cambridge: Cambridge University Press, 1997.

Hale, John R. *England and the Italian Renaissance: The Growth of Interest in Its History and Art.* London: Faber and Faber, 1954.

Hallam, H. E. *Rural England, 1066–1348.* Glasgow: Fontana, 1981.

Hallam, H. E., ed. *An Agrarian History of England.* Vol. 2. *1042–1350,* Cambridge: Cambridge University Press, 1989.

Hanawalt, Barbara A. *The Ties That Bound: Peasant Families in Medieval England.* Oxford: Oxford University Press, 1986.

Hanawalt, Barbara A. *Growing Up in Medieval London: The Experience of Childhood in History.* Oxford: Oxford University Press, 1993.

Harvey, Barbara. *Living and Dying in England, 1100–1540: The Monastic Experience.* Oxford: Clarendon Press, 1993.

Harvey, Barbara, ed. *The Twelfth and Thirteenth Centuries.* Oxford: Oxford University Press, 2001

Hatcher, John. *Plague, Population and the English Economy, 1348–1530.* London: Macmillan, 1977.

Hatcher, John, and Mark Bailey. *Modeling the Middle Ages: The History and Theory of England's Economic Development.* Oxford: Oxford University Press, 2001.

Heath, Peter. *Church and Realm, 1272–1461: Conflict and Collaboration in an Age of Crises.* London: Fontana, 1988.

Hellinga, Lotte, and J. B. Trapp, eds. *The Cambridge History of the Book in Britain.* Cambridge: Cambridge University Press, 1998.

Helmholz, R. H. *Marriage Litigation in Medieval England.* London: Cambridge University Press, 1974.

Henderson, George. *From Durrow to Kells: The Insular Gospel-Books, 650–800.* New York: Thames and Hudson, 1987.

Henderson, George. *Vision and Image in Early Christian England.* Cambridge: Cambridge University Press, 1999.

Hicks, Michael. *Bastard Feudalism.* New York: Longman, 1995.

Hicks, Michael, ed. *Revolution and Consumption in Late Medieval England.* Woodbridge: Boydell Press, 2001.

Hicks, Michael. *English Political Culture in the Fifteenth Century.* New York: Routledge, 2002.

Hilton, Rodney H. *A Medieval Society: The West Midlands at the End of the Thirteenth Century.* London: Weidenfeld and Nicolson, 1966.

Hilton, Rodney H. *Bond Men Made Free: Medieval Peasant Movements and the English Rising of 1381.* London: Temple Smith, 1973.

Hilton, Rodney H. *The English Peasantry in the Later Middle Ages.* Oxford: Clarendon Press, 1975.

Hilton, Rodney H. and T. H. Aston, eds. *The English Rising of 1381.* Cambridge: Cambridge University Press, 1984.

Holt, J. C. "Feudal Society and the Family in Early Medieval England." *Transactions of the Royal Historical Society,* 5th Ser., 32–35 (1982–1985); 193–212, 193–220, 1–25, 1–29.

Holt, Richard, and Gervase Rosser, eds. *The English Medieval Town: A Reader in English Urban History, 1200–1540.* New York: Longman, 1990.

Homans, George C. *English Villagers of the Thirteenth Century.* Cambridge, Mass.: Harvard University Press, 1941.

Horrox, Rosemary, ed. *Fifteenth-Century Attitudes: Perceptions of Society in Late Medieval England.* Cambridge: Cambridge University Press, 1994.

Hoskins, W. G. *The Making of the English Landscape.* 1955, Reprint, Baltimore: Penguin, 1970.

Houlbrooke, Ralph A. *The English Family, 1450–1700.* New York: Longman, 1984.

Hudson, John. *Land, Law, and Lordship in Anglo-Norman England.* Oxford: Clarendon Press, 1994.

Hudson, John. *The Formation of the English Common Law: Law and Society in England from the Norman Conquest to Magna Carta.* New York: Longman, 1996.

Jack, R. Ian. *Medieval Wales.* Ithaca, N.Y.: Cornell University Press, 1972.

Jacob, E. F. *The Fifteenth Century.* Oxford: Clarendon Press, 1961.

John, Eric. *Land Tenure in Early England: A Discussion of Some Problems.* Leicester: Leicester University Press, 1960.

John, Eric. *Reassessing Anglo-Saxon England.* Manchester: Manchester University Press, 1996.

Justice, Steven. *Writing and Rebellion: England in 1381.* Berkeley: University of California Press, 1994.

Keen, Maurice H. *England in the Later Middle Ages: A Political History.* London: Methuen, 1973.

Keen, Maurice H. *English Society in the Later Middle Ages, 1348–1500.* London: Penguin, 1990.

Kelly, Henry Ansgar. *Love and Marriage in the Age of Chaucer.* Ithaca, N.Y.: Cornell University Press, 1975.

Knowles, David. *The Religious Orders in England.* Vol. 1. *The Old Orders, 1216–1340; The Friars, 1216–1340; The Monasteries and Their World;* Vol. 2. *The End of the Middle Ages.* Cambridge: Cambridge University Press, 1948–1959.

Knowles, David. *The Monastic Order in England: A History of Its Development from the Times of St. Dunstan to the Fourth Lateran Council, 943–1216.* 2d ed. Cambridge: Cambridge University Press, 1963.

Lawson, M. K. *Cnut: The Danes in England in the Early Eleventh Century.* New York: Longman, 1993.

Lloyd, Simon. *English Society and the Crusade, 1216–1307.* Oxford: Clarendon Press, 1988.

Loyn, H. R. *Anglo-Saxon England and the Norman Conquest.* London: Longman, 1962.

Loyn, H. R. *The Governance of Anglo-Saxon England, 500–1087.* Stanford, Calif.: Stanford University Press, 1984.

Lydon, James F. *The Lordship of Ireland in the Middle Ages.* Toronto: University of Toronto Press, 1972.

Lydon, James F. *The Making of Ireland: From Ancient Times to the Present.* London: Routledge, 1998.

Maitland, Frederic William. *Domesday and Beyond: Three Essays in the Early History of England.* 1897. Reprint, New York: Norton, 1966.

Marks, Richard, and Nigel Morgan. *The Golden Age of English Manuscript Painting, 1200–1500.* New York: G. Braziller, 1981.

Martin, John E. *Feudalism to Capitalism: Peasant and Landlord in English Agrarian Development.* London: Macmillan, 1983.

Macfarlane, Alan. *The Origins of English Individualism: The Family, Property and Social Transition.* Oxford: Blackwell, 1978.

Macfarlane, Alan. *Marriage and Love in England: Modes of Reproduction, 1300–1840.* Oxford: Blackwell, 1986.

Maund, K. L. *Ireland, Wales, and England in the Eleventh Century.* Woodbridge: Boydell Press, 1991.

Mayr-Harting, Henry. *The Coming of Christianity to Anglo-Saxon England.* 3d ed. University Park: Pennsylvania State University Press, 1991.

McFarlane, K. B. *Lancastrian Kings and Lollard Knights.* Oxford: Clarendon Press, 1972.

McFarlane, K. B. *The Nobility of Later Medieval England: The Ford Lectures for 1953 and Related Studies.* Oxford: Clarendon Press, 1973.

McKisack, May. *The Fourteenth Century, 1307–1399.* Oxford: Clarendon Press, 1959.

McKisack, May. *Medieval History in the Tudor Age.* Oxford: Clarendon Press, 1971.

Mertes, Kate. *The English Noble Household, 1250–1600: Good Governance and Political Rule.* Oxford: Blackwell, 1988.

Miller, Edward, and John Hatcher. *Medieval England: Rural Society and Economic Change, 1086–1348.* London: Longman, 1978.

Miller, Edward, and John Hatcher. *Medieval England: Towns, Commerce, and Crafts, 1086–1348.* London: Longman, 1995.

Milsom, S. F. C. *Historical Foundations of the Common Law.* 2d ed. London: Butterworth's, 1981.

Milsom, S. F. C. *Sources of English Legal History: Private Law to 1750.* London: Butterworth's, 1986.

Nicholls, K. W. *Gaelic and Gaelicised Ireland in the Middle Ages.* Dublin: Gill and Macmillan, 1972.

Nicholson, Ranald. *Edward III and the Scot: The Formative Years of a Military Career, 1327–1335.* Oxford: Oxford University Press, 1965.

Nicholson, Ranald. *Scotland: The Later Middle Ages.* Edinburgh: Oliver and Boyd, 1974.

Nightingale, Pamela. *A Medieval Mercantile Community: The Grocers' Company and Trade of London, 1000–1485.* New Haven, Conn.: Yale University Press, 1995.

Ó Cróinín, Dáibhí. *Early Medieval Ireland, 400–1200.* New York: Longman, 1995.

Orme, Nicholas. *English Schools in the Middle Ages.* London: Methuen, 1973.

Orme, Nicholas. *From Childhood to Chivalry: The Education of the English Kings and Aristocracy, 1066–1530.* London: Methuen, 1984.

Otway-Ruthven, Annette Jocelyn. *The Native Irish and English Law in Medieval Ireland.* Dublin: Hodges, Figgis, 1951.

Otway-Ruthven, Annette Jocelyn. *A History of Medieval Ireland.* 2d ed. London: E. Benn, 1980.

Palmer, Robert C. *The County Courts of Medieval England, 1150–1350.* Princeton, N.J.: Princeton University Press, 1982.

Palmer, Robert C. *The Whilton Dispute, 1264–1380: A Social–Legal Study of Dispute Settlement in Medieval England.* Princeton, N.J.: Princeton University Press, 1984.

Palmer, Robert C. *English Law in the Age of the Black Death, 1348–1381: A Transformation of Governance and Law.* Chapel Hill: University of North Carolina Press, 1993.

Pantin, W. A. *The English Church in the Fourteenth Century.* 1955. Reprint, Notre Dame, Ind.: University of Notre Dame Press, 1963.

Parsons, John Carmi. *Eleanor of Castile: Queen and Society in Thirteenth-Century England.* New York: St. Martin's Press, 1995.

Platt, Colin. *The English Medieval Town.* London: Secker and Warburg, 1976.

Platt, Colin. *Medieval England: A Social History and Archaeology from the Conquest to A.D. 1600.* London: Routledge and Kegan Paul, 1978.

Platt, Colin. *The Abbeys and Priories of Medieval England.* London: Secker and Warburg, 1984.

Platt, Colin. *The National Trust Guide to Late Medieval and Renaissance Britain: From the Black Death to the Civil War.* London: G. Philip, 1986.

Platt, Colin. *The Architecture of Medieval Britain: A Social History.* New Haven, Conn.: Yale University Press, 1990.

Platt, Colin. *King Death: The Black Death and Its Aftermath in Late-Medieval England.* Toronto: University of Toronto Press, 1996.

Pollard, A. J. *The Wars of the Roses.* 2d ed. Basingstoke, England: Palgrave, 2001.

Pollock, Frederick, and Frederic William Maitland. *The History of English Law before the Time of Edward I.* 2d ed. 2 vols. Cambridge: Cambridge University Press, 1968.

Poole, Austin Lane. *From Domesday Book to Magna Carta, 1087–1216.* 2d ed. Oxford: Clarendon Press, 1955.

Postan, Michael M. *The Medieval Economy and Society: An Economic History of Britain, 1100–1500.* London: Weidenfeld and Nicolson, 1972.

Postan, Michael M. *Essays on Medieval Agriculture and General Problems of the Medieval Economy.* Cambridge: Cambridge University Press, 1973.

Pounds, N. J. G. *The Medieval Castle in England and Wales: A Social and Political History.* Cambridge: Cambridge University Press, 1990.

Powicke, Maurice. *The Thirteenth Century, 1216–1307.* 2d ed. Oxford: Clarendon Press, 1962.

Prestwich, Michael. *War, Politics and Finance under Edward I.* London: Faber, 1972.

Prestwich, Michael. *The Three Edwards: War and State in England, 1272–1377.* London: Methuen, 1980.

Prestwich, Michael. *English Politics in the Thirteenth Century.* Houndmills, England: Macmillan, 1990.

Prestwich, Michael. *Armies and Warfare in the Middle Ages: The English Experience.* New Haven, Conn.: Yale University Press, 1996.

Raban, Sandra. *England under Edward I and Edward II, 1259–1327.* Oxford: Blackwell Publishers, 2000.

Raftis, J. Ambrose. *The Estates of Ramsey Abbey: A Study in Economic Growth and Organization.* Toronto: Pontifical Institute of Mediaeval Studies, 1957.

Raftis, J. Ambrose. *Tenure and Mobility: Studies in the Social History of the Mediaeval English Village.* Toronto: Pontifical Institute of Mediaeval Studies, 1964.

Raftis, J. Ambrose. *Peasant Economic Development within the English Manorial System.* Montreal: McGill-Queen's University Press, 1996.

Razi, Zvi. *Life, Marriage and Death in a Medieval English Parish: Economy, Society and Demography in Halesowen, 1270–1400.* Cambridge: Cambridge University Press, 1980.

Razi, Zvi, and Richard Smith, eds. *Medieval Society and the Manor Court.* Oxford: Clarendon Press, 1996.

Reynolds, Susan. *An Introduction to the History of English Medieval Towns.* Oxford: Clarendon Press, 1977.

Richardson, H. G., and G. O. Sayles, *The Governance of Mediaeval England from the Conquest to Magna Carta.* Edinburgh: University Press, 1964.

Rigby, S. H. *Chaucer in Context: Society, Allegory, and Gender.* Manchester: Manchester University Press, 1996.

Rigby, S. H. *English Society in the Later Middle Ages: Class, Status and Gender.* London: Macmillan, 1995.

Roffe, David. *Domesday: The Inquest and the Book.* Oxford: Oxford University Press, 2000.

Rosenthal, Joel T. *The Purchase of Paradise.* Toronto: University of Toronto Press, 1972.

Rosenthal, Joel T. *Nobles and the Noble Life, 1295–1500.* London: George Allen and Unwin, 1976.

Rosenthal, Joel T. *Patriarchy and Families of Privilege in Fifteenth-Century England.* Philadelphia: University of Pennsylvania Press, 1991.

Rowley, Trevor. *The High Middle Ages, 1200–1550.* London: Routledge and Kegan Paul, 1986.

Saul, Nigel. *Scenes from Provincial Life: Knightly Families in Sussex, 1280–1400.* Oxford: Clarendon Press, 1986.

Saul, Nigel, ed. *Age of Chivalry.* New York: St. Martin's Press, 1992.

Saul, Nigel. "Part III: Medieval Britain." In *The National Trust Historical Atlas of Britain: Prehistoric and Medieval.* Ed. Nigel Saul. London: Alan Sutton, 1994, 113–204.

Saul, Nigel, ed. *The Oxford Illustrated History of England.* Oxford: Oxford University Press, 1997.

Simms, Katharine. *From Kings to Warlords: The Changing Political Structure of Gaelic Ireland in the Later Middle Ages.* Woodbridge: Boydell Press, 1987.

Smith, Brendan, ed. *Britain and Ireland, 900–1300: Insular Responses to Medieval European Change.* Cambridge: Cambridge University Press, 1999.

Smith, Richard M., ed. *Land, Kinship and Life-Cycle.* Cambridge: Cambridge University Press, 1984.

Smyth, Alfred P. *Scandinavian Kings in the British Isles, 850–880.* Oxford: Oxford University Press, 1977.

Smyth, Alfred P. *Warlords and Holy Men: Scotland AD 80–1000.* London: Edward Arnold, 1984.

Stafford, Pauline. *Unification and Conquest: A Political and Social History of England in the Tenth and Eleventh Centuries.* London: Edward Arnold, 1989.

Stafford, Pauline. *Queen Emma and Queen Edith: Queenship and Women's Power in Eleventh-Century England.* Oxford: Blackwell, 1997.

Stenton, F. M. *Anglo-Saxon England.* 3d ed. Oxford: Clarendon Press, 1971.

Strohm, Paul. *England's Empty Throne: Usurpation and the Language of Legitimation, 1399–1422.* New Haven, Conn.: Yale University Press, 1998.

Swanson, Heather. *Medieval Artisans: An Urban Class in Late Medieval England.* Oxford: Blackwell, 1989.

Swanson, R. N. *Catholic England: Faith, Religion and Observance before the Reformation.* New York: Manchester University Press, 1993.

Taylor, Harold McCarter, and Joan Taylor. *Anglo-Saxon Architecture.* 3 vols. Cambridge: Cambridge University Press, 1965–1978.

Thomson, John A. F. *The Transformation of Medieval England, 1370–1529.* London: Longman, 1983.

Thrupp, Sylvia L. *The Merchant Class of Medieval London.* Ann Arbor: University of Michigan Press, 1948.

Titow, J. Z. *English Rural Society, 1200–1350.* London: George Allen and Unwin, 1969.

Tout, Thomas Frederick. *Chapters in the Administrative History of Medieval England: The Wardrobe, the Chamber and the Small Seals.* 6 vols. Manchester: Manchester University Press, 1920–33.

Tuck, Anthony. *Crown and Nobility, 1272–1461: Political Conflict in Late Medieval England.* 2d ed. Oxford: Blackwell, 1999.

Tyerman, Christopher. *England and the Crusades, 1095–1588.* Chicago: University of Chicago Press, 1988.

Virgoe, Roger, ed. *Private Life in the Fifteenth Century: Illustrated Letters of the Paston Family.* New York: Weidenfeld and Nicolson, 1989.

Walker, David. *Medieval Wales.* Cambridge: Cambridge University Press, 1990.

Ward, Jennifer C. *English Noblewomen in the Later Middle Ages.* London: Longman, 1992.

Warren, Michelle R. *History on the Edge: Excalibur and the Borders of Britain, 1100–1300.* Minneapolis: University of Minnesota Press, 2000.

Warren, W. L. *Henry II.* Berkeley: University of California Press, 1973.

Warren, W. L. *The Governance of Norman and Angevin England, 1086–1272.* Stanford, Calif.: Stanford University Press, 1987.

Watt, John A. *The Church and the Two Nations in Medieval Ireland.* Cambridge: Cambridge University Press, 1970.

Watt, John A. *The Church in Medieval Ireland.* 2d ed. Dublin: University College Dublin Press, 1998.

Waugh, Scott L. *The Lordship of England: Royal Wardships and Marriages in English Society and Politics, 1217–1327.* Princeton, N.J.: Princeton University Press, 1988.

Waugh, Scott L. *England in the Reign of Edward III.* Cambridge: Cambridge University Press, 1991.

Webster, Bruce. *Medieval Scotland: The Making of an Identity.* New York: St. Martin's Press, 1997.

Webster, Leslie, and Janet Backhouse, eds. *The Making of England: Anglo-Saxon Art and Culture, AD 600–900.* Toronto: University of Toronto Press, 1991.

Weiss, Roberto. *Humanism in England during the Fifteenth Century.* 3d ed. Oxford: Blackwell, 1967.

Williams, Gwyn A. *Medieval London: From Commune to Capital.* London: University of London Press, The Athlone Press, 1963.

Wilson, David M. *The Anglo-Saxons.* Rev. ed. Harmondsworth: Penguin, 1971.

Wilson, David M., ed. *The Archaeology of Anglo-Saxon England.* London: Methuen, 1976.

Wilson, David M. *Anglo-Saxon Art: From the Seventh Century to the Norman Conquest.* Woodstock, N.Y.: Overlook Press, 1984.

Charles T. Wood. *Joan of Arc and Richard III: Sex, Saints, and Government in the Middle Ages.* Oxford: Oxford University Press, 1988.

V. BYZANTINE EMPIRE AND EASTERN EUROPE

Allen, Jelisaveta S., ed. *Literature on Byzantine Art, 1892–1967.* 2 vols. London: Mansell for the Dumbarton Oaks Center for Byzantine Studies, 1973–1976.

Angold, Michael J. *Church and Society in Byzantium under the Comneni, 1081–1261.* Cambridge: Cambridge University Press, 1995.

Angold, Michael J, ed. *The Byzantine Aristocracy, IX to XIII Centuries.* Oxford: B.A.R., 1984.

Angold, Michael J. *The Byzantine Empire, 1025–1204: A Political History.* 1984. 2d. ed. New York: Longman, 1997.

Arbel, Benjamin, Bernard Hamilton, and David Jacoby, eds. *Latins and Greeks in the Eastern Mediterranean after 1204.* London: Frank Cass, 1989.

Barker, Ernest. *Social and Political Thought in Byzantium from Justinian I to the Last Palaeologus.* Oxford: Clarendon Press, 1957.

Barker, John W. *Justinian and the Later Roman Empire.* Madison: University of Wisconsin Press, 1966.

Bartusis, Mark C. *The Late Byzantine Army: Arms and Society, 1204–1453.* Philadelphia: University of Pennsylvania Press, 1992.

Baynes, Norman Hepburn. *The Byzantine Empire.* London: Williams and Norgate, 1925.

Beckwith, John. *The Art of Constantinople: An Introduction to Byzantine Art 330–1453.* London: Phaidon, 1961.

Beckwith, John. *Early Christian and Byzantine Art.* 2d ed. New York: Penguin, 1970.

Blöndel, Sigfús. *The Varangians of Byzantium: An Aspect of Byzantine Military History.* Translated, revised, and rewritten by Benedikt S. Benedikz. Cambridge: Cambridge University Press, 1978.

Blum, Jerome. *Lord and Peasant in Russia: From the Ninth to the Nineteenth Century.* Princeton, N.J.: Princeton University Press, 1961.

Boba, Imre. *Nomads, Northmen and Slavs: Eastern Europe in the Ninth Century.* The Hague: Mouton, 1967.

Brand, Charles M. *Byzantium Confronts the West, 1180–1204.* Cambridge, Mass.: Harvard University Press, 1968.

Browning, Robert. *Justinian and Theodora.* London: Weidenfeld and Nicolson, 1971.

Browning, Robert. *Byzantium and Bulgaria: A Comparative Study across the Early Medieval Frontier.* Berkeley: University of California Press, 1975.

Brubaker, Leslie. *Vision and Meaning in Ninth-Century Byzantium: Image as Exegesis in the Homilies of Gregory of Nazianzus.* Cambridge: Cambridge University Press, 1999.

Brubaker, Leslie, and Robert Ousterhout, eds, *The Sacred Image East and West.* Urbana: University of Illinois Press, 1995.

Brumfield, William Craft. *A History of Russian Architecture.* Cambridge: Cambridge University Press, 1993.

Bury, J. B. *A History of the Eastern Roman Empire from the Fall of Irene to the Accession of Basil I.* New York: Russell & Russell, 1965.

Cameron, Alan. *Circus Factions: Blues and Greens at Rome and Byzantium.* Oxford: Clarendon Press, 1976.

Cameron, Alan. *Literature and Society in the Early Byzantine World.* Berkeley: University of California Press, 1991.

Cameron, Alan, and L. L. Conrad. *The Byzantine and Early Islamic Near East.* 3 vols. Princeton, N.J.: Darwin Press, 1992–1995.

Carter, Francis W., ed. *An Historical Geography of the Balkans.* London: Academic Press, 1977.

Carter, Francis W., and David Turnock, eds. *The States of Eastern Europe.* 2 vols. Aldershot: Ashgate, 1999.

Cavallo, Guglielmo, ed. *The Byzantines.* Trans. Thomas Dunlap, Teresa Lavender Fagan, and Charles Lambert. 1992. Reprint, Chicago: University of Chicago Press, 1997.

Chadwick, Nora K., ed. *Russian Heroic Poetry.* New York: Russell & Russell, 1964.

Charanis, Peter. *Studies on the Demography of the Byzantine Empire.* London: Variorum, 1972.

Cheetham, Nicolas. *Mediaeval Greece.* New Haven, Conn.: Yale University Press, 1981.

Cormack, Robin. *Writing in Gold: Byzantine Society and Its Icons.* London: George Philip, 1985.

Cormack, Robin. *Byzantine Art.* Oxford: Oxford University Press, 2000.

Cross, Samuel Hazard, and O. P. Sherbowitz-Wetzor, trans. *The Russian Primary Chronicle.* Cambridge: Medieval Academy of America, 1953.

Crummey, Robert O. *The Formation of Muscovy, 1304–1613.* New York: Longman, 1987.

Curcic, Slobodan. *Art and Architecture in the Balkans: An Annotated Bibliography.* Boston: G. K. Hall, 1984.

Demus, Otto. *Byzantine Art and the West.* New York: New York University Press, 1970.

Demus, Otto. *Byzantine Mosaic Decoration: Aspects of Monumental Art in Byzantium.* 1953. Reprint, New Rochelle, N.Y.: Caratzas Bros., 1976.

Dennis, George, trans. *Maurice's Strategikon: Handbook of Byzantine Military Strategy.* Philadelphia: University of Pennsylvania Press, 1984.

Dennis, George, trans. *Three Byzantine Military Treatises.* Washington, D.C.: Dumbarton Oaks, Research Library and Collection, 1985.

Dmytryshyn, Basil, ed. *Medieval Russia: A Source Book, 900–1700.* 3d ed. Fort Worth: Holt, Rinehart & Winston, 1991.

Doukas, Michael. *Decline and Fall of Byzantium to the Ottoman Turks: An Annotated Translation of "Historia Turco-Byzantina."* Trans. Harry J. Magoulias. Detroit: Wayne State University Press, 1975.

Durand, Jannic. *Byzantine Art.* London: Hi Marketing, 1999.

Dvornik, Francis. *The Photian Schism, History and Legend.* 1948. Reprint, Cambridge: Cambridge University Press, 1970.

Dvornik, Francis. *The Slavs in European History and Civilization.* New Brunswick, N.J.: Rutgers University Press, 1962.

Dvornik, Francis. *Byzantium and the Roman Primacy.* New York: Fordham University Press, 1966.

Dvornik, Francis. *The Making of Central and Eastern Europe.* 2d ed. Gulf Breeze, Fla.: Academic International Press, 1974.

Dvornik, Francis. *Origins of Intelligence Services: The Ancient Near East, Persia, Greece, Rome, Byzantium, the Arab Muslim Empires, the Mongol Empire, China, Muscovy.* New Brunswick, N.J.: Rutgers University Press, 1974.

Evans, Helen C., and William D. Wixom, eds. *The Glory of Byzantium: Art and Culture of the Middle Byzantine Era, A.D. 843–1261.* New York: Metropolitan Museum of Art, 1997.

Evans, J. A. S. *The Age of Justinian: The Circumstances of Imperial Power.* London: Routledge, 1996.

Fedotov, G. P. *The Russian Religious Mind.* 2 vols. Cambridge, Mass.: Harvard University Press, 1946–1966.

Fennell, John L. I. *The Emergence of Moscow, 1304–1359.* Berkeley: University of California Press, 1968.

Fennell, John L. I. *Early Russian Literature.* Berkeley: University of California Press, 1974.

Fennell, John L. I. *The Crisis of Medieval Russia, 1200–1304.* New York: Longman, 1983.

Fennell, John L. I. *A History of the Russian Church to 1448*. London: Longman, 1995.

Fine, John V. A. *The Early Medieval Balkans: A Critical Survey from the Sixth to the Late Twelfth Century*. Ann Arbor: University of Michigan Press, 1991.

Fine, John V. A. *The Late Medieval Balkans: A Critical Survey from the Late Twelfth Century to the Ottoman Conquest*. Ann Arbor: University of Michigan Press, 1994.

Foss, Clive, and Paul Magdalino, eds. *Rome and Byzantium*. Oxford: Elsevier-Phaidon, 1977.

Franklin, Simon, and Jonathan Shepard. *The Emergence of Rus, 750–1200*. New York: Longman, 1996.

Fryde, Edmund. *The Early Palaeologan Renaissance (1261–c. 1360)*. New York: Brill, 2000.

Garland, Lynda. *Byzantine Empresses: Women and Power in Byzantium, AD 527–1204*. London: Routledge, 1999.

Geanakoplos, Deno John. *Emperor Michael Palaeologus and the West, 1258–1282: A Study in Byzantine-Latin Relations*. Cambridge, Mass.: Harvard University Press, 1959.

Geanakoplos, Deno John. *Byzantine East and Latin West: Two Worlds of Christendom in Middle Ages and Renaissance*. New York: Barnes & Noble, 1966.

Gill, Joseph. *Byzantium and the Papacy, 1198–1400*. New Brunswick, N.J.: Rutgers University Press, 1979.

Gimbutas, Marija Alseikaité. *The Slavs*. London: Thames and Hudson, 1971.

Gjuzelev, Vasil. *The Proto-Bulgarians: Pre-History of Asparouhian Bulgaria*. Sofia: Sofia Press, 1979.

Gjuzelev, Vasil. *Medieval Bulgaria: Byzantine Empire, Black Sea Venice, Genoa*. Villach: Verlag Baier, 1988.

Haldon, John F. *Byzantium in the Seventh Century: The Transformation of a Culture*. Cambridge: Cambridge University Press, 1990.

Haldon, John F. *Warfare, State, and Society in the Byzantine World, 565–1204*. London: UCL Press, 1999.

Halperin, Charles J. *Russia and the Golden Horde: The Mongol Impact on Medieval Russian History*. Bloomington: Indiana University Press, 1985.

Halperin, Charles J. *The Tatar Yoke*. Columbus, Ohio: SLavica, 1986.

Hamm, Michael F., ed. *The City in Russian History*. Lexington: University Press of Kentucky, 1976.

Harvey, Alan. *Economic Expansion in the Byzantine Empire, 900–1200*. Cambridge: Cambridge University Press, 1989.

Head, Constance. *Justinian II of Byzantium*. Madison: University of Wisconsin Press, 1972.

Head, Constance. *Imperial Twilight: The Palaiologos Dynasty and the Decline of Byzantium*. Chicago: Nelson-Hall, 1977.

Hendy, M. F. *Studies in the Byzantine Monetary Economy, c. 300–1450*. Cambridge: Cambridge University Press, 1985.

Herrin, Judith. *Woman in Purple: Rulers of Medieval Byzantium*. London: Weidenfeld and Nicolson, 2001.

Hill, Barbara. *Imperial Women in Byzantium, 1025–1204: Power, Patronage and Ideology*. New York: Longman, 1999.

Hunt, Lucy-Anne. *Byzantium, Eastern Christendom and Islam: Art at the Crossroads of the Medieval Mediterranean*. 2 vols. London: Pindar Press, 1998.

Hussey, Joan M. *The Byzantine World*. London: Hutchinson, 1961.

Hussey, Joan M., ed. *The Cambridge Medieval History*. Vol. 4. *The Byzantine Empire*. Cambridge: Cambridge University Press, 1966.

Hussey, Joan M. *The Orthodox Church in the Byzantine Empire*. Oxford: Clarendon Press, 1986.

James, Liz. *Light and Colour in Byzantine Art*. Oxford: Clarendon Press, 1996.

James, Liz, ed. *Desire and Denial in Byzantium*. Aldershot: Ashgate, 1999.

Jenkins, Romilly. *Byzantium: The Imperial Centuries, AD 610–1071*. New York: Random House, 1966.

Kaegi, Walter. *Byzantium and the Early Islamic Conquests*. Cambridge: Cambridge University Press, 1992.

Kaiser, Daniel H. *The Growth of the Law in Medieval Russia*. Princeton, N.J.: Princeton University Press, 1980.

Karger, M. *Novgorod the Great*. Moscow: Progress Publishers, 1973.

Kartsonis, Anna D. *Anastasis: The Making of an Image*. Princeton, N.J.: Princeton University Press, 1986.

Kazhdan, A. P., and Ann Wharton Epstein. *Change in Byzantine Culture in the Eleventh and Twelfth Centuries*. Berkeley: University of California Press, 1985.

Kazhdan, A. P., and Giles Constable, eds. *People and Power in Byzantium: An Introduction to Modern Byzantine Studies*. Washington, D.C.: Dumbarton Oaks Center for Byzantine Studies, 1982.

Kazhdan, A. P., and Simon Franklin. *Studies on Byzantine Literature of the Eleventh and Twelfth Centuries*. Cambridge: Cambridge University Press, 1984.

Kennedy, George Alexander. *Greek Rhetoric under Christian Emperors*. Princeton, N.J.: Princeton University Press, 1983.

Kitzinger, Ernest. *Byzantine Art in the Making: Main Lines of Stylistic Development in Mediterranean Art, 3rd–7th Century*. Cambridge, Mass.: Harvard University Press, 1977.

Kitzinger, Ernest. *Byzantine Art*. Oxford: E. Kitzinger, 1994.

Kochan, Lionel, and Richard Abraham. *The Making of Modern Russia*. 2d ed. New York: St. Martin's Press, 1983.

Kollmann, Nancy Shields. *Kinship and Politics: The Making of the Muscovite Political System, 1345–1547*. Stanford, Calif.: Stanford University Press, 1987.

Krautheimer, Richard. *Early Christian and Byzantine Architecture*. 3d ed. Harmondsworth: Penguin, 1979.

Laiou, Angeliki E. *Constantinople and the Latins: The Foreign Policy of Andronicus II, 1282–1328*. Cambridge, Mass.: Harvard University Press, 1972.

Laiou, Angeliki E. *Peasant Society in the Late Byzantine Period: A Social and Demographic Study*. Princeton, N.J.: Princeton University Press, 1977.

Laiou, Angeliki E., and Henry Maguire, eds. *Byzantium: A World Civilization*. Washington, D.C.: Dumbarton Oaks Research Library and Collection, 1992.

Lilie, Ralph-Johannes. *Byzantium and the Crusader States, 1096–1204*. Trans. J. C. Morris and Jean E. Ridings. 1981. Oxford: Clarendon Press, 1988.

Lock, Peter. *The Franks in the Aegean, 1204–1500*. New York: Longman, 1995.

Lowden, John. *Early Christian and Byzantine Art*. London: Phaidon, 1997.

Lurier, Harold E., ed. and trans. *Crusaders as Conquerors: The Chronicle of Morea*. New York: Columbia University Press, 1964.

Magdalino, Paul. *The Empire of Manuel I Komnenos, 1143–1180*. Cambridge: Cambridge University Press, 1993.

Maguire, Henry, ed. *Byzantine Court Culture from 829 to 1204*. Washington, D.C.: Dumbarton Oaks Research Library and Collection, 1997.

Mango, Cyril, ed. *Art of the Byzantine Empire, 312–1453: Sources and Documents*. 1972. Reprint, Toronto: University of Toronto Press, 1986.

Mango, Cyril. *Byzantium: The Empire of New Rome*. New York: Charles Scribner's Sons, 1980.

Mango, Cyril. *Byzantine Architecture*. 1976. Reprint, London: Faber and Faber, 1986.

Mango, Cyril, ed. *The Oxford History of Byzantium*. Oxford: Oxford University Press, 2002.

Martin, Janet. *Medieval Russia, 980–1584*. Cambridge: Cambridge University Press, 1995.

Mathew, Gervase. *Byzantine Aesthetics*. New York: Viking, 1964.

Mathews, Thomas J. *Byzantine Churches of Istanbul: A Photographic Survey*. University Park: Pennsylvania State University Press, 1976.

Mathews, Thomas J. *Byzantium: From Antiquity to the Renaissance*. New York: Harry Abrams, 1998.

McGeer, Eric. *Sowing the Dragon's Teeth: Byzantine Warfare in the Tenth Century*. Washington, D.C.: Dumbarton Oaks Research Library and Collection, 1995.

Meyendorff, John. *Byzantine Theology: Historical Trends and Doctrinal Matters*. London: Mowbrays, 1974.

Meyendorff, John. *Byzantium and the Rise of Russia: A Study of Byzantino-Russian Relations in the Fourteenth Century*. Cambridge: Cambridge University Press, 1981.

Meyer, Peter. *Byzantine Mosaics: Torcello, Venice, Monreale, Palermo, Cafalù*. New York: Oxford University Press, 1952.

Miller, Dean A. *Imperial Constantinople*. New York: Wiley, 1969.

Miller, T. S. *The Birth of the Hospital in the Byzantine Empire*. Baltimore: Johns Hopkins University Press, 1985.

Milner-Gulland, Robin. *The Russians*. Oxford: Blackwell, 1997.

Moorhead, John. *Justinian*. New York: Longman, 1994.

Morris, R. *Monks and Laymen in Byzantium, 843–1118*. Cambridge: Cambridge University Press, 1995.

Nicol, Donald M. *The Last Centuries of Byzantium, 1261–1453*. London: Rupert Hart-Davis, 1972.

Nicol, Donald M. *The End of the Byzantine Empire*. London: Edward Arnold, 1979.

Nicol, Donald M. *The Despotate of Epiros, 1267–1479: A Contribution to the History of Greece in the Middle Ages*. Cambridge: Cambridge University Press, 1984.

Nicol, Donald M. *Byzantium and Venice: A Study in Diplomatic and Cultural Relations*. Cambridge: Cambridge University Press, 1988.

Nicol, Donald M. *The Immortal Emperor: The Life and Legend of Constantine Palaiologos, Last Emperor of the Romans*. Cambridge: Cambridge University Press, 1992.

Nicol, Donald M. *The Byzantine Lady: Ten Portraits, 1250–1500*. Cambridge: Cambridge University Press, 1994.

Nicol, Donald M. *The Reluctant Emperor: A Biography of John Cantacuzene, Byzantine Emperor and Monk, c. 1295–1383*. Cambridge: Cambridge University Press, 1996.

Noonan, Thomas S. *The Islamic World, Russia and the Vikings, 750–900: THe Numismatic Evidence*. Aldershot, Hampshire: Ashgate, 1998.

Nordhagen, Per Jonas. *Studies in Byzantine and Early Medieval Painting*. London: Pindar, 1990.

Norwich, John Julius. *Byzantium*. Vol. 1. *Byzantium: The Early Centuries*; Vol. 2. *Byzantium: The Aposee*; Vol. 3. *Byzantium: The Decline and Fall*. New York: Knopf, 1988–1996.

Obolensky, Dimitri. *The Byzantine Commonwealth: Eastern Europe, 500–1453*. London: Weidenfeld and Nicolson, 1971.

Obolensky, Dimitri. *Byzantium and the Slavs*. Crestwood, N.Y.: St. Vladimir's Seminary Press, 1994.

Ostrogorsky, George. *History of the Byzantine State*. Trans. Joan Hussey. Oxford: Blackwell, 1956.

Ostrowski, Donald. *Muscovy and the Mongols: Cross-Cultural Influences on the Steppe Frontier, 1304–1589*. Cambridge: Cambridge University Press, 1998.

Petravich, M. B. *History of Serbia*. 2 vols. New York: Harcourt, Brace & Jovanovich, 1976.

Pelikan, Jaroslav. *The Christian Tradition, A History of the Development of Doctrine*. Vol. 2. *The Spirit of Eastern Christendom (600–1700)*. Chicago: University of Chicago Press, 1974.

Portal, Roger. *The Slavs: A Cultural and Historical Survey of the Slavonic Peoples*. Trans. Patrick Evans. 1965. Reprint, London: Weidenfeld and Nicholson, 1969.

Pritsak, Omeljan. *The Origin of Rus'*. Vol. 1. *Old Scandinavian Sources Other than the Sagas*. Cambridge, Mass.: Harvard University Press, 1981.

Pritsak, Omeljan. *Studies in Medieval Eurasian History*. London: Variorum, 1981.

Rice, Tamara Talbot. *A Concise History of Russian Art*. New York: Praeger, 1963.

Rodley, Lyn. *Byzantine Art and Architecture: An Introduction*. Cambridge: Cambridge University Press, 1994.

Rowell, S. C. *Lithuania Ascending: A Pagan Empire within East-Central Europe, 1295–1345*. Cambridge: Cambridge University Press, 1994.

Runciman, Steven. *A History of the First Bulgarian Empire*. London: G. Bell, 1930.

Runciman, Steven. *Byzantine Civilization*. London: St. Martin's Press, 1933.

Runciman, Steven. *The Eastern Schism: A Study of the Papacy and the Eastern Churches during the 11th and 12th Centuries.* Oxford: Clarendon Press, 1955.

Runciman, Steven. *The Sicilian Vespers: A History of the Mediterranean World in the Later Thirteenth Century.* Cambridge: Cambridge University Press, 1958.

Runciman, Steven. *The Fall of Constantinople 1453.* Cambridge: Cambridge University Press, 1969.

Runciman, Steven. *The Last Byzantine Renaissance.* Cambridge: Cambridge University Press, 1970.

Runciman, Steven. *Mistra: Byzantine Capital of the Peloponnese.* London: Thames and Hudson, 1980.

Runciman, Steven. *The Emperor Romanus Lecapenus and His Reign: A Study of 10th-Century Byzantium.* 1929. Reprint, Cambridge: Cambridge University Press, 1988.

Safran, Linda, ed. *Heaven on Earth: Art and the Church in Byzantium.* University Park: Pennsylvania State University Press, 1998.

Sahas, Daniel, ed. *Icon and Logos: Sources in Eighth Century Iconoclasm.* Toronto: University of Toronto Press, 1986.

Shchapov, Iaroslav Nikolaevich. *State and Church in Early Russia, 10th–13th Centuries.* Trans. Vic Shneierson. New Rochelle, N.Y.: A. D. Caratzas, 1993.

Sedlar, Jean W. *East Central Europe in the Middle Ages, 1000–1500.* Seattle: University of Washington Press, 1994.

Shahîd, Irfan. *Byzantium and the Arabs in the Fourth Century.* Washington, D.C.: Dumbarton Oaks Research Library and Collection, 1984.

Shahîd, Irfan. *Byzantium and the Arabs in the Fifth Century.* Washington, D.C.: Dumbarton Oaks Research Library and Collection, 1989.

Shahîd, Irfan. *Byzantium and the Arabs in the Sixth Century.* Washington, D.C.: Dumbarton Oaks Research Library and Collection, 1995.

Simeonova, Liliana. *Diplomacy of the Letter and the Cross: Photios, Bulgaria and the Papacy, 860s–880s.* Amsterdam: A. M. Hakkert, 1998.

Stephenson, Paul. *Byzantium's Balkan Frontier: A Political Study of the Northern Balkans, 900–1204.* Cambridge: Cambridge University Press, 2000.

Stratos, Andreas N. *Byzantium in the Seventh Century.* Vol. 1. *602–634.* Trans. Marc Ogilvie-Grant. Amsterdam: Hakkert, 1968.

Subotic, Gojko. *Art of Kosovo: The Sacred Land.* New York: Monacelli Press, 1998.

Taft, Robert F. *The Byzantine Rite: A Short History.* Collegeville, Minn.: Liturgical Press, 1992.

Talbot Rice, David. *The Art of Byzantium.* New York: Harry Abrams, 1959.

Talbot Rice, David. *The Art of Byzantium: Text and Notes.* New York: Harry Abrams, 1959.

Talbot Rice, David. *The Byzantines.* New York: Praeger, 1962.

Talbot Rice, David. *Art of the Byzantine Era.* London: Thames and Hudson, 1963.

Talbot Rice, David. *Byzantine Art.* Harmondsworth, Penguin, 1968.

Talbot Rice, David. *Byzantine Painting: The Last Phase.* New York: Dial Press, 1968.

Talbot Rice, David. *The Appreciation of Byzantine Art.* London: Oxford University Press, 1972.

Teteriatnikov, Natalia. *Russian Icons of the Golden Age, 1400–1700.* Huntingdon, Pa.: Juniata College, 1988.

Tougher, Shaun. *The Reign of Leo VI (886–912): Politics and People.* Leiden: Brill, 1997.

Toynbee, Arnold. *Constantine Porhyrogenitus and His World.* Oxford: Oxford University Press, 1973.

Treadgold, Warren. *The Byzantine Revival, 780–842.* Stanford, Calif.: Stanford University Press, 1988.

Treadgold, Warren. *Byzantium and Its Army, 284–1081.* Stanford, Calif.: Stanford University Press, 1995.

Treadgold, Warren. *A History of the Byzantine State and Society.* Stanford, Calif.: Stanford University Press, 1997.

Urbanczyk, Przemyslaw, ed. *Early Christianity in Central and East Europe.* Warsaw: Semper, 1997.

Váňa, Zdeněk. *The World of the Ancient Slavs.* Trans. Till Gottheiner. London: Orbis, 1983.

Vasiliev, A. A. *History of the Byzantine Empire, 324–1453.* 2 vols. Madison: University of Wisconsin Press, 1952.

Vernadsky, George A. *The Mongols and Russia.* New Haven, Conn. and London: Yale University Press, 1953.

Vernadsky, George A. *Kievan Russia.* New Haven, Conn.: Yale University Press, 1959.

Vernadsky, George A. *Ancient Russia.* 1943. Reprint, New Haven, Conn.: Yale University Press, 1964.

Vernadsky, George A., ed. *Medieval Russian Laws,* 1947. Reprint, New York: Octagon Books, 1965.

Vernadsky, George A. *The Origins of Russia.* Oxford: Clarendon Press, 1959.

Vlasto, A. P. *The Entry of the Slavs into Christendom: An Introduction to the Medieval History of the Slavs.* Cambridge: Cambridge University Press, 1970.

Vryonis, Speros, Jr. *Byzantium and Europe.* London: Thames and Hudson, 1967.

Vryonis, Speros, Jr. *The Decline of Medieval Hellenism in Asia Minor and the Process of Islamization from the Eleventh through the Fifteenth Century.* Berkeley: University of California Press, 1971.

Walter, Christopher. *Art and Ritual of the Byzantine Church.* London: Variorum, 1982.

Weitzmann, Kurt. *The Place of Book Illumination in Byzantine Art.* Princeton, N.J.: Princeton University Press, 1975.

Weitzmann, Kurt. *Classical Heritage in Byzantine and Near Eastern Art.* London: Variorum, 1981.

Weitzmann, Kurt. *Art in the Medieval West and Its Contacts with Byzantium.* London: Variorum, 1982.

Wellesz, Egon. *A History of Byzantine Music and Hymnography.* 3d ed. Oxford: Oxford University Press, 1963.

Wharton, Annabel Jane. *Art of Empire: Painting and Architecture of the Byzantine Periphery, a Comparative Study of Four Provinces.* University Park: Pennsylvania State University Press, 1988.

Whitting, Philip D., ed. *Byzantium: An Introduction.* Oxford: Blackwell, 1972.

Whittow, Mark. *The Making of Byzantium, 600–1025.* Berkeley: University of California Press, 1996.

Wilson, N. G., ed. *An Anthology of Byzantine Prose*. Berlin: De Gruyter, 1971.

Wilson, N. G. *Mediaeval Greek Bookhands: Examples Selected from Greek Manuscripts in Oxford Libraries*. Cambridge, Mass.: Mediaeval Academy of America, 1973.

Wilson, N. G. *Scholars of Byzantium*. Baltimore: Johns Hopkins University Press, 1983.

Wilson, N. G. *From Byzantium to Italy: Greek Studies in the Italian Renaissance*. Baltimore: Johns Hopkins University Press, 1992.

Wilson, N. G., and L. D. Reynolds. *Scribes and Scholars: A Guide to the Transmission of Greek and Latin Literature*. 3d ed. Oxford: Oxford University Press, 1991.

Winnifrith, Tom J. *The Vlachs: The History of a Balkan People*. New York: St. Martin's Press, 1987.

Woodhouse, C. M. *George Gemistos Plethon: The Last of the Hellenes*. Oxford: Clarendon Press, 1986.

Zenkovsky, Serge A., ed. and trans. *Medieval Russia's Epics, Chronicles, and Tales*. 2d ed. New York: Dutton, 1974.

VI. JEWS IN THE MIDDLE AGES

Abulafia, Anna Sapir. *Christians and Jews in the Twelfth-Century Renaissance*. London: Routledge, 1995.

Abulafia, Anna Sapir, ed. *Religious Violence between Christians and Jews: Medieval Roots, Modern Perspectives*. New York: Palgrave, 2002.

Agus, Irving A. *Urban Civilization in Pre-Crusade Europe: A Study of Organized Town-Life in Northwestern Europe during the Tenth and Eleventh Centuries Based on the Responsa Literature*. Leiden: Brill, 1965.

Agus, Irving A. *The Heroic Age of Franco-German Jewry: The Jews of Germany and France of the Tenth and Eleventh Centuries, the Pioneers and Builders of Town-Life, Town-Government, and Institutions*. New York: Yeshiva University Press, 1969.

Agus, Irving A. *Rabbi Meir of Rothenberg: His Life and Works as Sources for the Religious, Legal and Social History of the Jews of Germany in the Thirteenth Century*. 2 vols. New York: Ktav, 1970.

Avi-Yonah, Michael. *The Jews of Palestine: A Political History from the Bar Kokhba War to the Arab Conquest*. Oxford: Blackwell, 1976.

Bachrach, Bernard S. *Early Medieval Jewish Policy in Western Europe*. Minneapolis: University of Minnesota Press, 1977.

Bachrach, Bernard S. *Jews in Barbarian Europe*. Lawrence, Kans.: Coronado Press, 1977.

Baer, Yitzhak F. *A History of the Jews in Christian Spain*. 2 vols. Trans. Louis Schoffman. Philadelphia: Jewish Publication Society, 1961–1966.

Berger, David. *The Jewish-Christian Debate in the High Middle Ages: A Critical Edition of the Nizzahon Vetus with an Introduction, Translation, and Commentary*. Philadelphia: Jewish Publication Society, 1979.

Berger, David. *History and Hate: The Dimensions of Anti-Semitism*. Philadelphia: Jewish Publication Society, 1986.

Berger, David. "Mission to the Jews and Jewish-Christian Contacts in the Polemical Literature of the High Middle Ages"; Jeremy Cohen, "Scholarship and Intolerance in the Medieval Academy: The Study and Evaluation of Judaism in European Christendom"; Gavin Langmuir, "Comment." *The American Historical Review* 91 (June 1986): 576–591, 592–613, 614–624.

Bonfil, Robert. *Rabbis and Jewish Communities in Renaissance Italy*. Trans. Jonathan Chipman. London: Littman Library of Jewish Civilization, 1993.

Bonfil, Robert. *Jewish Life in Renaissance Italy*. Trans. Anthony Oldcorn. 1991. Reprint, Berkeley: University of California Press, 1994.

Bosworth, C. E. "The *Protected Peoples* (Christians and Jews) in Medieval Egypt." *Bulletin of the John Rylands University Library* 62 (Autumn, 1979): 11–36.

Bowman, S. B. *The Jews of Byzantium, 1204–1453*. Tuscaloosa: University of Alabama Press, 1985.

Boyarin, Daniel. *Carnal Israel: Reading Sex in Talmudic Culture*. Berkeley: University of California Press, 1993.

Boyarin, Daniel. *Dying for God: Martyrdom and the Making of Christianity and Judaism*. Stanford, Calif.: Stanford University Press, 1999.

Brann, Ross. *The Compunctious Poet: Cultural Ambiguity and Hebrew Poetry in Muslim Spain*. Baltimore: Johns Hopkins University Press, 1991.

Brann, Ross, ed. *Languages of Power in Islamic Spain*. Bethesda, Md.: CDL Press, 1997.

Brann, Ross. *Power in the Portrayal: Representations of Jews and Muslims in Eleventh- and Twelfth-Century Islamic Spain*. Princeton, N.J.: Princeton University Press, 2002.

Burns, Robert I. *Muslims, Christians, and Jews in the Crusader Kingdom of Valencia: Societies in Symbiosis*. Cambridge: Cambridge University Press, 1984.

Burns, Robert I. *Jews in the Notarial Culture: Latinate Wills in Mediterranean Spain, 1250–1350*. Berkeley: University of California Press, 1996.

Carmichael, Joel. *The Satanizing of the Jews: Origin and Development of Mystical Anti-Semitism*. New York: Fromm International, 1992.

Carpenter, Dwayne E., ed. *Alfonso X and the Jews: An Edition of and Commentary on Siete partidas 7.24 "De los judíos."* Berkeley: University of California Press, 1986.

Carroll, James. *Constantine's Sword: The Church and the Jews, a History*. Boston: Houghton Mifflin, 2001.

Chazan, Robert. *Medieval Jewry in Northern France: A Political and Social History*. Baltimore: Johns Hopkins University Press, 1973.

Chazan, Robert. *Church, State, and Jew in the Middle Ages*. New York: Behrman House, 1980.

Chazan, Robert. *European Jewry and the First Crusade*. Berkeley: University of California Press, 1987.

Chazan, Robert. *Daggers of Faith: Thirteenth-Century Christian Missionizing and Jewish Response*. Berkeley: University of California Press, 1989.

Chazan, Robert. *Barcelona and Beyond: The Disputation of 1263 and Its Aftermath*. Berkeley: University of California Press, 1992.

Chazan, Robert. *In the Year 1096: The First Crusade and the Jews*. Philadelphia: Jewish Publication Society, 1996.

Chazan, Robert. *Medieval Stereotypes and Modern Anti-Semiticism.* Berkeley: University of California Press, 1997.

Chazan, Robert. *God, Humanity and History: The Hebrew First Crusade Chronicles.* Berkeley: University of California Press, 2000.

Cohen, Jeremy. *The Friars and the Jews: The Evolution of Medieval Anti-Judaism.* Ithaca, N.Y.: Cornell University Press, 1982.

Cohen, Jeremy. *Be Fertile and Increase, Fill the Earth and Master It: The Ancient and Medieval Career of a Biblical Text.* Ithaca, N.Y.: Cornell University Press, 1989.

Cohen, Jeremy, ed. *Essential Papers on Judaism and Christianity in Conflict: From Late Antiquity to the Reformation.* New York: New York University Press, 1991.

Cohen, Jeremy. *Living Letters of the Law: Ideas of the Jew in Medieval Christianity.* Berkeley: University of California Press, 1999.

Cohen, Mark R. *Jewish Self-Government in Medieval Egypt: The Origins of the Office of Head of the Jews, ca. 1065–1126.* Princeton, N.J.: Princeton University Press, 1980.

Cohen, Mark R. *Under Crescent and Cross: The Jews in the Middle Ages.* Princeton, N.J.: Princeton University Press, 1994.

Constable, Olivia Remie, ed. *Medieval Iberia: Readings from Christian, Muslim, and Jewish Sources.* Philadelphia: University of Pennsylvania Press, 1997.

Dobson, R. B. *The Jews of Medieval York and the Massacre of March 1190.* York: St. Anthony's Press, 1974.

Dundes, Alan, ed. *The Blood Libel Legend: A Casebook in Anti-Semitic Folklore.* Madison: University of Wisconsin Press, 1991.

Eidelberg, Shlomo. *Jewish Life in Austria in the XVth Century: As Reflected in the Legal Writings of Rabbi Israel Isserlein and His Contemporaries.* Philadelphia: Dropsie College for Hebrew and Cognate Learning, 1962.

Eidelberg, Shlomo, trans. *The Jews and the Crusaders: The Hebrew Chronicles of the First and Second Crusades.* Madison: University of Wisconsin Press, 1977.

Goitein, S. D. *A Mediterranean Society: The Jewish Communities of the Arab World as Portrayed in the Documents of the Cairo Geniza.* 6 vols. Berkeley: University of California Press, 1967–1993.

Goitein, S. D., ed. *Letters of Medieval Jewish Traders.* Princeton, N.J.: Princeton University Press, 1973.

Grayzel, Solomon. *The Church and the Jews in the XIII Century.* New York: Jewish Theological Seminary, 1989.

Holtz, Barry W., ed. *Back to the Sources: Reading the Classic Jewish Texts.* New York: Simon & Schuster, 1984.

Hood, John Y. B. *Aquinas and the Jews.* Philadelphia: University of Pennsylvania Press, 1995.

Hsia, R. Po-Chia. *The Myth of Ritual Murder: Jews and Magic in Reformation Germany.* New Haven, Conn.: Yale University Press, 1988.

Hsia, R. Po-Chia. *Trent 1475: Stories of a Ritual Murder.* New Haven, Conn.: Yale University Press, 1992.

Jordan, William C. *The French Monarchy and Jews: From Philip Augustus to the Last Capetians.* Philadelphia: University of Pennsylvania Press, 1989.

Kanarfogel, Ephraim. *Jewish Education and Society in the High Middle Ages.* Detroit: Wayne State University Press, 1992.

Kisch, Guido. *The Jews in Medieval Germany: A Study of Their Legal and Social Status.* 2d ed. New York: Ktav, 1970.

Langmuir, Gavin I. *History, Religion, and Antisemitism.* Berkeley: University of California Press, 1990.

Langmuir, Gavin I. *Toward a Definition of Antisemitism.* Berkeley: University of California Press, 1990.

Lassner, Jacob. *Demonizing the Queen of Sheba: Boundaries of Gender and Culture in Postbiblical Judaism and Medieval Islam.* Chicago: University of Chicago Press, 1993.

Lerner, Ralph, ed. "Political Philosophy in Judaism." In *Medieval Political Philosophy.* Ed. Ralph Lerner and Muhsin Mahdi. Ithaca, N.Y.: Cornell University Press, 1963, 188–270.

Lerner, Robert E. *The Feast of Saint Abraham: Medieval Millenarians and the Jews.* Philadelphia: University of Pennsylvania Press, 2001.

Lewis, Bernard. *The Jews of Islam.* Princeton, N.J.: Princeton University Press, 1984.

Linder, Amnon, ed. *The Jews in the Legal Sources of the Early Middle Ages.* Detroit: Wayne State University Press, 1997.

Mann, Vivian B., Thomas F. Glick, and Jerrilynn D. Dodds, eds., *Convivencia: Jews, Muslims, and Christians in Medieval Spain.* New York: George Braziller, 1992.

Marcus, Ivan G. *Piety and Society: The Jewish Pietists of Medieval Germany.* Leiden: Brill, 1981.

Marcus, Ivan G. *Rituals of Childhood: Jewish Acculturation in Medieval Europe.* New Haven, Conn.: Yale University Press, 1996.

Marcus, Jacob R. *The Jew in the Medieval World, A Source Book: 315–1791.* New York: Meridian, 1938.

Melammed, Renée Levine. *Heretics or Daughters of Israel?: The Crypto-Jewish Women of Castile.* Oxford: Oxford University Press, 1999.

Moore, Rebecca. *Jews and Christians in the Life and Thought of Hugh of St. Victor.* Atlanta: Scholars Press, 1998.

Mundill, Robin. *England's Jewish Solution: Experiment and Expulsion, 1262–1290.* London: Cambridge University Press, 1998.

Nirenberg, David. *Communities of Violence: Persecution of Minorities in the Middle Ages.* Princeton, N.J.: Princeton University Press, 1996.

Poliakov, Léon. *The History of Anti-Semitism.* Trans. Richard Howard. 1956. Reprint, New York: Vanguard Press, 1965.

Poliakov, Léon. *Jewish Bankers and the Holy See from the Thirteenth to the Seventeenth Century.* Trans. Miriam Kocham. London: Routledge and K. Paul, 1977.

Prawer, Joshua. *Crusader Institutions.* Oxford: Clarendon Press, 1980.

Prawer, Joshua. *The History of the Jews in the Latin Kingdom of Jerusalem.* Oxford: Clarendon Press, 1988.

Rabinowitz, Louis I. *The Social Life of the Jews of Northern France in the XII–XIV Centuries as Reflected in the Rabbinical Literature of the Period.* London: Edward Goldston, 1938.

Richardson, H. G. *The English Jewry under Angevin Kings.* London: Methuen, 1960.

Rosenthal, E. I. J. *Judaism and Islam.* New York: T. Yoseloff, 1961.

Roth, Norman. *Jews, Visigoths, and Muslims in Medieval Spain: Cooperation and Conflict.* Leiden: Brill, 1994.

Roth, Norman. *Conversos, Inquisition, and the Expulsion of the Jews from Spain.* Madison: University of Wisconsin Press, 1995.

Rubin, Miri. *Gentile Tales: The Narrative Assault on Late Medieval Jews.* New Haven, Conn.: Yale University Press, 1999.

Saperstein, Marc, ed. *Jewish Preaching, 1200–1800: An Anthology.* New Haven, Conn.: Yale University Press, 1989.

Shatzmiller, Joseph. *Shylock Reconsidered: Jews, Moneylending, and Medieval Society.* Berkeley: University of California Press, 1990.

Shatzmiller, Joseph. *Jews, Medicine, and Medieval Society.* Berkeley: University of California Press, 1994.

Simonsohn, Shlomo. *The Apostolic See and the Jews, Documents.* Vol. 1. *492–1401;* Vol. 2. *1394–1464;* Vol. 3. *1464–1521.* Toronto: Pontifical Institute of Mediaeval Studies, 1988–1990.

Simonsohn, Shlomo, ed. *The Jews in Sicily.* Leiden: Brill, 1997.

Stow, Kenneth R. *The "1007 Anonymous" and Papal Sovereignty: Jewish Perceptions of the Papacy and Papal Policy in the High Middle Ages.* Cincinnati: Hebrew Union College-Jewish Institute of Religion, 1984.

Stow, Kenneth R. *Alienated Minority: The Jews of Medieval Latin Europe.* Cambridge, Mass.: Harvard University Press, 1992.

Stow, Kenneth R. "The Jewish Family in the Rhineland in the High Middle Ages: Form and Function." *The American Historical Review* 92 (1987): 1085–1110.

Taitz, Emily. *The Jews of Medieval France: The Community of Champagne.* Westport, Conn.: Greenwood Press, 1994.

Trachtenberg, Joshua. *The Devil and the Jews: The Medieval Conception of the Jew and Its Relation to Modern Anti-Semitism.* Philadelphia: Jewish Publication Society, 1943.

Wood, Diana, ed. *Christianity and Judaism.* Studies in Church History, 29. Oxford: Blackwell, 1992.

VII. LITERATURE IN THE MIDDLE AGES

Aers, David. *Community, Gender, and Individual Identity: English Writing, 1360–1430.* London: Routledge, 1988.

Aers, David, ed. *Culture and History, 1350–1600: Essays on English Communities, Identities and Writing.* Detroit: Wayne State University Press, 1992.

Aetsen, Henk, and Alasdair A. MacDonald, eds. *Companion to Middle English Romance.* Amsterdam: VU University Press, 1990.

Aitken, Adam J., Matthew P. McDiarmid, and Derick S. Thomson, eds. *Bards and Makars: Scottish Language and Literature, Medieval and Renaissance.* Glasgow: University of Glasgow Press, 1977.

Akehurst, F. R. P., and Judith M. Davis, eds. *A Handbook of the Troubadours.* Berkeley: University of California Press, 1995.

Ashtiany, Julia, et al., ed. *'Abbasid Belles-Lettres.* Cambridge: Cambridge Unversity Press, 1990.

Auerbach, Eric. *Mimesis: The Representation of Reality in Western Literature.* Trans. Willard R. Trask. Princeton, N.J.: Princeton University Press, 1953.

Barron, W. R. J. *English Medieval Romance.* London: Longman, 1987.

Baldwin, John W. *Aristocratic Life in Medieval France: The Romances of Jean Renart and Gerbert de Montreuil, 1190–1230.* Baltimore: Johns Hopkins University Press, 2000.

Bayless, Martha. *Parody in the Middle Ages: The Latin Tradition.* Ann Arbor: University of Michigan Press, 1996.

Beadle, Richard, ed. *The Cambridge Companion to Medieval English Theatre.* Cambridge: Cambridge University Press, 1994.

Beeston, A. F. L. *Samples of Arabic Prose in Its Historical Development: A Manual for English-Speaking Students.* Oxford: Oxford University Press, 1977.

Beeston, A. F. L., ed. *Arabic Literature to the End of the Umayyad Period.* Cambridge: Cambridge University Press, 1983.

Bennett, J. A. W. *Middle English Literature.* Ed. Douglas Gray. Oxford: Oxford University Press, 1986.

Bevington, David, ed. *Medieval Drama.* Boston: Houghton Mifflin, 1975.

Birnbaum, Henrik. *On Medieval and Renaissance Slavic Writing: Selected Essays.* The Hague: Mouton, 1974.

Bloch, R. Howard. *Medieval French Literature and the Law.* Berkeley: University of California Press, 1977.

Bloch, R. Howard. *Etymologies and Genealogies: A Literary Anthropology of the French Middle Ages.* Chicago: University of Chicago Press, 1983.

Bloch, R. Howard. *Medieval Misogyny and the Invention of Western Romantic Love.* Chicago: University of Chicago Press, 1991.

Boase, Roger. *The Troubadour Revival: A Study of Social Change and Traditionalism Late Medieval Spain.* London: Routledge and Kegan Paul, 1978.

Bogin, Magda. *The Women Troubadours.* New York: Paddington, 1976.

Boitani, Piero. *English Medieval Narrative in the 13th and 14th Centuries.* Cambridge: Cambridge University Press, 1982.

Boitani, Piero, and Torti, Anna, eds., *Poetics: Theory and Practice in Medieval English Literature. The J. A. W. Bennett Memorial Lectures.* Cambridge: D. S. Brewer, 1991.

Bolton, W. F. *A History of Anglo-Latin Literature, 597–1066.* Princeton, N.J.: Princeton University Press, 1967.

Bolton, W. F., ed. *The Middle Ages*. Rev. ed. London: Sphere Reference, 1986.

Bond, Gerald A. *The Loving Subject: Desire, Eloquence, and Power in Romanesque France*. Philadelphia: University of Pennsylvania Press, 1995.

Brand, Peter, and Lino Pertile, eds. *The Cambridge History of Italian Literature*. Cambridge: Cambridge University Press, 1996.

Brewer, Derek, ed. *Studies in Medieval English Romances*. Cambridge: Cambridge University Press, 1988.

Brown, Peter. *A Companion to Chaucer*. Malden, Mass.: Blackwell, 2000.

Bumke, Joachim. *Courtly Culture: Literature and Society in the High Middle Ages*. Trans. Thomas Dunlap. 1986. Reprint, New York: Overlook Press, 2000.

Burns, E. Jane. *Bodytalk: When Women Speak in Old French Literature*. Philadelphia: University of Pennsylvania Press, 1993.

Burrow, J. A. *Medieval Writers and Their Work: Middle English Literature and Its Background, 1100–1500*. Oxford: Oxford University Press, 1982.

Burrow, J. A. *Essays on Medieval Literature*. Oxford: Oxford University Press, 1984.

Carruthers, Mary. *The Book of Memory: A Study of Memory in Medieval Culture*. Cambridge: Cambridge University Press, 1990.

Carruthers, Mary. *The Craft of Thought: Meditation, Rhetoric, and the Making of Images, 400–1200*. New York: Cambridge University Press, 1998.

Cazelles, Brigitte. *The Lady as Saint: A Collection of French Hagiographic Romances of the Thirteenth Century*. Philadelphia: University of Pennsylvania Press, 1991.

Chambers, E. K. *The Medieval Stage*. 2 vols. Oxford: Clarendon Press, 1903.

Coleman, Janet. *English Literature in History, 1350–1400: Medieval Readers and Writers*. London: Hutchinson, 1981.

Copeland, Rita. *Rhetoric, Hermeneutics, and Translation in the Middle Ages: Academic Traditions and Vernacular Texts*. Cambridge: Cambridge University Press, 1991.

Crane, Susan. *Insular Romance: Politics, Faith and Culture in Anglo-Norman and Middle English Romance*. Berkeley: University of California Press, 1986.

Dinshaw, Carolyn. *Chaucer's Sexual Poetics*. Madison: University of Wisconsin Press, 1989.

Dronke, Peter. *Medieval Latin and the Rise of European Love-Lyric*. 2d ed. 2 vols. Oxford: Clarendon Press, 1968.

Dronke, Peter. *Poetic Individuality in the Middle Ages: New Departures in Poetry, 1000–1150*. Oxford: Clarendon Press, 1970.

Dronke, Peter. *Fabula: Explorations into the Uses of Myth in Medieval Platonism*. Leiden: Brill, 1974.

Dronke, Peter, ed. *A History of Twelfth-Century Western Philosophy*. Cambridge: Cambridge University Press, 1988.

Dronke, Peter. *The Medieval Lyric*. 3d ed. Woodbridge, England: D. S. Brewer, 1996.

Edwards, A. S. G., ed. *Middle English Prose: Essays on Bibliographical Problems*. New York: Garland, 1981.

Edwards, A. S. G., ed. *Middle English Prose: A Critical Guide to Major Authors and Genres*. New Brunswick, N.J.: Rutgers University Press, 1984.

Ellis, Roger, assisted by Jocelyn Price, Stephen Medcalf, and Peter Meredith, eds. *The Medieval Translator: The Theory and Practice of Translation in the Middle Ages*. Woodbridge, England: D. S. Brewer, 1989.

Famiglietti, R. C. *Tales of the Marriage Bed from France (1300–1500)*. Providence, R.I.: Picardy Press, 1992.

Fennell, John Lister Illingworth. *Early Russian Literature*. Berkeley: University of California Press, 1974.

Fenster, Thelma S., ed. *Arthurian Women: A Casebook*. New York: Garland, 1996.

Ferrante, Joan M. *The Conflict of Lover and Honor: The Medieval Tristan Legend in France, Germany and Italy*. The Hague: Mouton, 1973.

Ferrante, Joan M. *In Pursuit of Perfection: Courtly Love in Medieval Literature*. Port Washington, N.Y.: Kennikat Press, 1975.

Ford, Boris, ed. *Medieval Literature: Chaucer and the Alliterative Tradition*. The New Pelican Guide to English Literature, Vol. I, part I. Harmondsworth: Penguin, 1982.

Garbáty, Thomas J. ed. *Medieval English Literature*. Lexington, Mass.: D. C. Heath, 1984.

Gaunt, Simon. *Gender and Genre in Medieval French Literature*. Cambridge: Cambridge University Press, 1995.

Gaunt, Simon, and Sarah Kay, eds. *The Troubadours: An Introduction*. Cambridge: Cambridge University Press, 1999.

Gellrich, Jesse M. *Discourse and Dominion in the Fourteenth Century: Oral Contexts of Writing in Philosophy, Politics, and Poetry*. Princeton, N.J.: Princeton University Press, 1995.

Gibbs, Marion E., and Sidney M. Johnson. *Medieval German Literature: A Companion*. New York: Garland, 1997.

Godden, Malcolm, and Michael Lapidge, ed. *The Cambridge Companion to Old English Literature*. Cambridge: Cambridge University Press, 1991.

Godman, Peter, ed. *Poetry of the Carolingian Renaissance*. London: Duckworth, 1985.

Godman, Peter. *The Silent Masters: Latin Literature and Its Censors in the High Middle Ages*. Princeton, N.J.: Princeton University Press, 2000.

Gold, Barbara K., Paul Allen Miller, and Charles Platter, eds. *Sex and Gender in Medieval and Renaissance Texts: The Latin Tradition*. Albany: State University Press of New York, 1997.

Gradon, Pamela. *From and Style in Early English Literature*. London: Methuen, 1971.

Gravdal, Kathryn. *Ravishing Maidens: Writing Rape in Medieval French Literature and Law*. Philadelphia: University of Pennsylvania Press, 1991.

Green, Dennis H. *Medieval Listening and Reading: The Primary Reception of German Literature, 800–1300*. Cambridge: Cambridge University Press, 1994.

Green, Richard Firth. *Poets and Princepleasers: Literature and the English Court in the Late Middle Ages*. Toronto: University of Toronto Press, 1980.

Green, Richard Firth. *A Crisis of Truth: Literature and Law in Ricardian England.* Philadelphia: University of Pennsylvania Press, 1999.

Griffiths, Jeremy, and Derek Pearsall, eds. *Book Production and Publishing in Britain 1375–1475.* Cambridge: Cambridge University Press, 1989.

Hanning, Robert W. *The Individual in Twelfth-Century Romance.* New Haven, Conn.: Yale University Press, 1977.

Hansen, Elaine Tuttle. *Chaucer and the Fictions of Gender.* Berkeley: University of California Press, 1992.

Havely, Nick. "Literature in Italian, French and English: Uses and Muses of the Vernacular." In *The New Cambridge Medieval History.* Vol. 6. *c. 1300–c. 1415.* Ed. Michael Jones. Cambridge: Cambridge University Press, 2000, 257–70.

Huot, Sylvia. *From Song to Book: The Poetics of Writing in Old French Lyric and Lyrical Narrative Poetry.* Ithaca, N.Y.: Cornell University Press, 1987.

Irwin, Robert, ed. *Night and Horses and the Desert: An Anthology of Classical Arabic Literature.* New York: Anchor Books, 1999.

Jack, R. D. S., and P. A. T. Rozendaal, eds. *The Mercat Anthology of Early Scottish Literature, 1375–1707.* Edinburgh: Mercat Press, 1997.

Jackson, W. T. H. *The Literature of the Middle Ages.* New York: Columbia University Press, 1960.

Jackson, W. T. H. *Medieval Literature: A History and a Guide.* New York: Collier Books, 1966.

Jackson, W. T. H., ed. *The Interpretation of Medieval Lyric Poetry.* New York: Columbia University Press, 1980.

Kahrl, Stanley J. *Traditions of Medieval English Drama.* London: Hutchinson, 1974.

Kay, Sarah. *Subjectivity in Troubadour Poetry.* Cambridge: Cambridge University Press, 1990.

Kelly, Douglas. *The Art of Medieval French Romance.* Madison: University of Wisconsin Press, 1992.

Kelly, Douglas. *Medieval French Romance.* New York: Twayne, 1993.

Krueger, Roberta L. *Women Readers and the Ideology of Gender in Old French Verse Romance.* Cambridge: Cambridge University Press, 1993.

Lapidge, Michael, and Malcolm Godden, eds. *The Cambridge Companion to Old English Literature.* Cambridge: Cambridge University Press, 1991.

Leupin, Alexandre. *Barbarolexis: Medieval Writing and Sexuality.* Cambridge, Mass.: Harvard University Press, 1989.

Lewis, C. S. *The Allegory of Love: A Study in Medieval Tradition.* Oxford: Oxford University Press, 1936.

Lewis, C. S. *The Discarded Image. An Introduction to Medieval and Renaissance Literature.* Cambridge: Cambridge University Press, 1964.

Lomperis, Linda, and Sarah Stanbury, eds. *Feminist Approaches to the Body in Medieval Literature.* Philadelphia: University of Pennsylvania Press, 1993.

Loomis, Roger Sherman, ed. *Arthurian Literature in the Middle Ages: A Collaborative History.* Oxford: Clarendon Press, 1959.

Loomis, Roger Sherman. *The Development of Arthurian Romance.* London: Hutchinson, 1963.

Machan, Tim William. *Textual Criticism and Middle English Texts.* Charlottesville: University of Virginia Press, 1994.

McCracken, Peggy. *The Romance of Adultery: Queenship and Sexual Transgression in Old French Literature.* Philadelphia: University of Pennsylvania Press, 1998.

Meale, Carol M., ed. *Women and Literature in Britain, 1150–1500.* Cambridge: Cambridge University Press, 1993.

Mehl, Dieter. *English Literature in the Age of Chaucer.* New York: Longman, 2001.

Menocal, Maria Rosa. *The Arabic Role in Medieval Literary History: A Forgotten Heritage.* Philadelphia: University of Pennsylvania Press, 1987.

Menocal, Maria Rosa, Raymond P. Scheindlin, and Michael Sells, eds. *The Literature of Al-Andalus.* Cambridge: Cambridge University Press, 2000.

Minnis, A. J. *Medieval Theory of Authorship: Scholastic Literary Attitudes in the Later Middle Ages.* 2d ed. Philadelphia: University of Pennsylvania Press, 1988.

Minnis, A. J., and Charlotte Brewer, eds. *Crux and Controversy in Middle English Textual Criticism.* Cambridge: Cambridge University Press, 1992.

Minnis, A. J., and A. B. Scott, eds. *Medieval Literary Theory and Criticism c. 1100–c. 1375: The Commentary Tradition.* Rev. ed. Oxford: Oxford University Press, 1991.

Moore, John C. *Love in Twelfth-Century France.* Philadelphia: University of Pennsylvania Press, 1972.

Moser, Charles A., ed. *The Cambridge History of Russian Literature.* Rev. ed. Cambridge: Cambridge University Press, 1992.

Muir, Lynette R. *Literature and Society in Medieval France: The Mirror and the Image, 1100–1500.* London: Macmillan, 1985.

Newman, F. X., ed. *The Meaning of Courtly Love.* Albany: State University of New York Press, 1969.

Oakden, J. P. *Alliterative Poetry in Middle English.* 2 vols. Manchester: Manchester University Press, 1930–1935.

Olson, Glending. *Literature as Recreation in the Later Middle Ages.* Ithaca, N.Y.: Cornell University Press, 1982.

Owst, G. R. *Literature and Pulpit in Medieval England: A Neglected Chapter in the History of English Letters and of the English People.* 2d ed. Oxford: Oxford University Press, 1961.

Paden, William D., ed. *The Voice of the Trobairitz: Perspectives on the Women Troubadours.* Philadelphia: University of Pennsylvania Press, 1989.

Patterson, Lee. *Negotiating the Past: The Historical Understanding of Medieval Literature.* Madison: University of Wisconsin Press, 1987.

Pearsall, Derek. *Old English and Middle English Poetry.* London: Routledge and K. Paul, 1977.

Scaglione, Aldo. *Knights at Court: Courtliness, Chivalry and Courtesy from Ottonian Germany to the Italian Renaissance.* Berkeley: University of California Press, 1991.

Schultz, James A. *The Shape of the Round Table: Structures of Middle High German Arthurian Romance.* Toronto: University of Toronto Press, 1983.

Simon, Eckehard, ed. *The Theatre of Medieval Europe: New Research in Early Drama.* Cambridge: Cambridge University Press, 1991.

Solterer, Helen. *The Master and the Minerva: Disputing Women in French Medieval Culture.* Berkeley: University of California Press, 1995.

Strohm, Paul. *Social Chaucer.* Cambridge, Mass.: Harvard University Press, 1989.

Strohm, Paul. *Hochon's Arrow: The Social Imagination of Fourteenth-Century Texts.* Princeton, N.J.: Princeton University Press, 1992.

Swanton, Michael James. *English Literature before Chaucer.* London: Longman, 1987.

Szittya, Penn R. *The Antifraternal Tradition in Medieval Literature.* Princeton, N.J.: Princeton University Press, 1986.

Taylor, John. *English Historical Literature in the Fourteenth Century.* Oxford: Clarendon Press, 1987.

Trapp, J. B., Douglas Gray, and Julia Boffey, eds. *Medieval English Literature.* 2d ed. New York: Oxford University Press, 2002.

Tydeman, William. *The Theatre in the Middle Ages: Western European Stage Conditions, c. 800–1576.* Cambridge: Cambridge University Press, 1978.

Tydeman, William. *Medieval English Drama.* London: Routledge and K. Paul, 1986.

Vance, Eugene. *Mervelous Signals: Poetics and Sign Theory in the Middle Ages.* Lincoln: University of Nebraska Press, 1986.

Vinaver, Eugène. *The Rise of Romance.* Oxford: Oxford University Press, 1971.

Vitz, Evelyn Birge. *Medieval Narrative and Modern Narratology: Subjects and Objects of Desire.* New York: New York University Press, 1989.

Wack, Mary Francis. *Lovesickness in the Middle Ages: The "Viaticum" and Its Commentaries.* Philadelphia: University of Pennsylvania Press, 1990.

Wallace, David, ed. *The Cambridge History of Medieval English Literature.* Cambridge: Cambridge University Press, 1999.

Walshe, Maurice O'C. *Medieval German Literature: A Survey.* Cambridge, Mass.: Harvard University Press, 1962.

Wright, Roger. *Late Latin and Early Romance in Spain and Carolingian France.* Liverpool: F. Cairns, 1982.

Young, Karl. *The Drama of the Medieval Church.* 2 vols. Oxford: Clarendon Press, 1933.

Young, M. J. L., J. D. Latham, and R. B. Serjeant, eds. *Religion, Learning, and Science in the 'Abbasid Period.* Cambridge: Cambridge University Press, 1990.

VIII. VIKINGS AND NORTHERN EUROPE

Aðalsteinsson, Jón Hnefill. *Under the Cloak: The Acceptance of Christianity in Iceland with Particular Reference to the Religious Attitudes Prevailing at the Time.* Uppsala: Almqvist and Wiksell, 1978.

Almgren, Bertil, et al., eds., *The Viking.* Gothenburg: Tre Tryckare, 1967.

Benedictow, Ole Jørgen. *Plague in the Late Medieval Nordic Countries: Epidemiological Studies.* 2d ed. Oslo: Middelalderforlaget, 1993.

Brønsted, Johannes. *The Vikings.* Baltimore: Penguin Books, 1960.

Byock, Jesse L. *Feud in the Icelandic Saga.* Berkeley: University of California Press, 1982.

Byock, Jesse L. *Medieval Iceland: Society, Sagas, and Power.* Berkeley: University of California Press, 1988.

Byock, Jesse L. *Viking Age Iceland.* London: Penguin Books, 2001.

Byock, Jesse L. "Saga Form, Oral Prehistory, and the Icelandic Social Context." *New Literary History* 16 (1984): 153–173.

Christiansen, Eric. *The Norsemen in the Viking Age.* Malden, Mass.: Blackwell, 2002.

Clover, Carol J. *The Medieval Saga.* Ithaca, N.Y.: Cornell University Press, 1982.

Clover, Carol J. "Family Sagas, Icelandic." In *Dictionary of the Middle Ages.* New York: Charles Scribner's Sons, 1984, 4.612–619.

Clover, Carol J. "Regardless of Sex: Men, Women, and Power in Early Northern Europe." *Speculum* 68 (1993): 363–382.

Clover, Carol J., and John Lindow, eds. *Old Norse-Icelandic Literature: A Critical Guide.* Ithaca, N.Y.: Cornell University Press, 1985.

Ellis Davidson, H. R. *Gods and Myths of Northern Europe.* Baltimore: Penguin, 1964.

Fitzhugh, William W., and Elisabeth Ward, eds. *Vikings: The North Atlantic Saga.* Washington, D.C.: Smithsonian Institution Press, 2000.

Foote, Peter G., and David M. Wilson. *The Viking Achievement: The Society and Culture of Early Medieval Scandinavia.* London: Sidgwick and Jackson, 1970.

Frank, Roberta. "Marriage in Twelfth- and Thirteenth-Century Iceland," *Viator* 4 (1973): 473–484.

Gelsinger, Bruce E. *Icelandic Enterprise: Commerce and Economy in the Middle Ages.* Columbia: University of South Carolina Press, 1981.

Glubok, Shirley. *The Art of the Vikings.* New York: Macmillan, 1978.

Graham-Campbell, James, and Dafydd Kidd, eds. *The Vikings.* New York: W. Morrow, 1980.

Graham-Campbell, James et al., *The Viking World.* New Haven, Conn.: Ticknor and Fields, 1980.

Hastrup, Kirsten. *Culture and History in Medieval Iceland: An Anthropological Assessment of Structure and Change.* Oxford: Clarendon Press, 1985.

Ingstad, Anne Stine. *The Norse Discovery of America.* 2 vols. Trans. Elizabeth S. Seeberg. Oxford: Oxford University Press, 1985.

Jesch, Judith. *Women in the Viking Age.* Woodbridge: Boydell Press, 1991.

Jochens, Jenny M. *Women in Old Norse Society.* Ithaca, N.Y.: Cornell University Press, 1995.

Jochens, Jenny M. "The Church and Sexuality in Medieval Iceland." *Journal of Medieval History* 6 (1980): 377–392.

Jochens, Jenny M. "The Medieval Icelandic Heroine: Fact or Fiction?" *Viator* 17 (1986): 35–50.

Jochens, Jenny M. "Marching to a Different Drummer: New Trends in Medieval Icelandic Scholarship: A Review

Article." *Comparative Studies in Society and History* 35 (1993): 197–207.

Jochens, Jenny M. *Old Norse Images of Women*. Philadelphia: University of Pennsylvania Press, 1996.

Jóhannesson, Jón. *A History of the Old Icelandic Commonwealth: Íslendinga Saga*. Trans. Haraldur Bessason. Winnipeg: University of Manitoba Press, 1974.

Jones, Gwyn. *A History of the Vikings*. Rev. ed. Oxford: Oxford University Press, 1984.

Logan, F. Donald. *The Vikings in History*. 2d ed. London: Routledge, 1992.

Loyn, H. R. *The Vikings in Britain*. London: B. T. Batsford, 1977.

Melnikova, E. A. *The Eastern World of the Vikings: Eight Essays about Scandinavia and Eastern Europe in the Early Middle Ages*. Gothenburg: Litteraturvetenskapliga Institutionen, Göteborgs Universitet, 1996.

Miller, William Ian. *Bloodtaking and Peacemaking: Feud, Law, and Society in Saga Iceland*. Chicago: University of Chicago Press, 1990.

Miller, William Ian. "Choosing the Avenger: Some Aspects of the Bloodfeud in Medieval Iceland and England." *Law and History Review* 1 (1983): 159–204.

Miller, William Ian. "Some Aspects of Householding in the Medieval Icelandic Commonwealth." *Continuity and Change* 3 (1988): 321–355.

Nordal, Sigurður. *Icelandic Culture*. Trans. Vilhjalmur T. Bjarnar. Ithaca, N.Y.: Cornell University Press, 1990.

O'Meadhra, Uaininn. *Early Christian, Viking and Romanesque Art: Motif-Pieces from Ireland*. Stockholm: Almqvist and Wiksell International, 1979.

Page, R. I. *Chronicles of the Vikings: Records, Memorials, and Myths*. Toronto: University of Toronto Press, 1995.

Roesdahl, Else. *The Vikings*. 2d ed. Trans. Susan M. Margeson and Kirsten Williams. London: Penguin, 1998.

Roesdahl, Else, and David M. Wilson, eds. *From Viking to Crusader: The Scandinavians and Europe, 800–1200*. New York: Rizzoli, 1992.

Sawyer, Brigit, and Peter Sawyer. *Medieval Scandinavia: From Conversion to Reformation, circa 800–1500*. Minneapolis: University of Minnesota Press, 1993.

Sawyer, Peter H. *The Age of the Vikings*. 2d ed. London: Edward Arnold, 1971.

Sawyer, Peter H. *Kings and Vikings: Scandinavia and Europe, A.D. 700–1100*. London: Methuen, 1982.

Sawyer, Peter H., ed. *The Oxford Illustrated History of the Vikings*. Oxford: Oxford University Press, 1997.

Smyth, Alfred P. *Scandinavian Kings in the British Isles, 850–880*. Oxford: Oxford University Press, 1977.

Sørensen, Preben Meulengracht. *Saga and Society: An Introduction to Old Norse Literature*. Trans. John Tucker. Odense: Odense University Press, 1993.

Strömbäck, Dag. *The Conversion of Iceland*. Trans. Peter Foote. London: Viking Society for Northern Research, 1975.

Wilson, David M. *The Vikings and Their Origins: Scandinavia in the First Millennium*. London: Thames and Hudson, 1970.

Wilson, David M., ed. *The Northern World: The History and Heritage of Northern Europe, AD 400–1100*. London: Thames and Hudson, 1980.

IX. AFRICA, ISLAM, AND ASIA

Ahmed, Sheikh. *Muslim Architecture: From the Advent of Islam in Arabia to the Rise of the Great Ummayad Khilafat in Spain*. Karachi: Pakistan Institute of Arts and Design of Book Production, 1974.

Ali, Wijdan. *The Arab Contribution to Islamic Art: From the Seventh to the Fifteenth Centuries*. Cairo: American University in Cairo Press, 1999.

Allsen, Thomas T. *Mongol Imperialism: The Policies of the Grand Qan Möngke in China, Russia, and the Islamic Lands, 1251–1259*. Berkeley: University of California Press, 1987.

Allsen, Thomas T. *Culture and Conquest in Mongol Eurasia*. Cambridge: Cambridge University Press, 2001.

Amitai-Preiss, Reuven. *Mongols and Mamluks: The Mamluk-Īlkhānid War, 1260–1281*. Cambridge: Cambridge University Press, 1995.

Anderson, Margaret. *Arabic Materials in English Translation: A Bibliography of Works from the Pre-Islamic Period to 1977*. Boston: G. K. Hall, 1980.

Arnold, Thomas Walker. *Painting in Islam: A Study of the Place of Pictorial Art in Muslim Culture*. Oxford: Clarendon Press, 1928.

Ashtiany, Julia et al., ed. *'Abbasid Belles-Lettres*. Cambridge: Cambridge University Press, 1990.

Ashtor, Eliyahu L. *A Social and Economic History of the Near East in the Middle Ages*. London: Collier's, 1976.

Ashtor, Eliyahu L. *Levant Trade in the Later Middle Ages*. Princeton, N.J.: Princeton University Press, 1983.

Aslanapa, Oktay. *Turkish Art and Architecture*. London: Faber, 1971.

Atil, Esin. *Art of the Arab World*. Washington, D.C.: Smithsonian Institution Press, 1975.

Atil, Esin, ed. *Turkish Art*. Washington, D.C.: Smithsonian Institution Press, 1980.

Atil, Esin, ed. *Renaissance of Islam: Art of the Mamluks*. Washington, D.C.: Smithsonian Institution Press, 1981.

Axelson, Eric. *Congo to Cape: Early Portuguese Explorers*. Ed. John Woodcock. London: Faber and Faber, 1973.

Babinger, Franz. *Mehmed the Conqueror and His Time*. Trans. Ralph Manheim. Princeton, N.J.: Princeton University Press, 1978.

Bahnassi, Afif. Jami' al-Umawi al-Kabir. *The Great Omayyad Mosque of Damascus: The First Masterpieces of Islamic Art*. Trans. Batrechia McDonel and Samir Tower. Damascus: Tlass, 1989.

Beckingham, C. F. *Between Islam and Christendom: Travelers, Facts, and Legends in the Middle Ages and the Renaissance*. London: Variorum, 1983.

Beeston, A. F. L. *Samples of Arabic Prose in Its Historical Development: A Manual for English-Speaking Students*. Oxford: Oxford University Press, 1977.

Beeston, A. F. L., ed. *Arabic Literature to the End of the Umayyad Period*. Cambridge: Cambridge University Press, 1983.

Bentley, Jerry H. *Old World Encounters: Cross-Cultural Contacts and Exchanges in Pre-Modern Times.* New York: Oxford University Press, 1993.

Berkey, Jonathan P. *The Formation of Islam: Religion and Society in the Near East, 600–1800.* Cambridge: Cambridge University Press, 2003.

Birashk, Ahmad. *A Comparative Calendar of the Iranian, Muslim Lunar, and Christian Eras for Three Thousand Years: 1260 B.H.–2000 A.H./639 B.C.–2621 A.D.* Costa Mesa, Calif.: Mazda Publishers, in Association with Bibliotheca Persica, 1993.

Black, Antony J. *The History of Islamic Political Thought: From the Prophet to the Present.* New York: Routledge, 2001.

Blair, Sheila, and Jonathan M. Bloom. *The Art and Architecture of Islam, 1250–1800.* New Haven, Conn.: Yale University Press, 1995.

Bloom, Jonathan. *Minaret, Symbol of Islam.* Oxford: Board of the Faculty of Oriental Studies, University of Oxford, 1989.

Boswell, John. *The Royal Treasure: Muslim Communities under the Crown of Aragon in the Fourteenth Century.* New Haven, Conn.: Yale University Press, 1977.

Bosworth, Clifford Edmund. *The Islamic Dynasties.* Edinburgh: Edinburgh University Press, 1967.

Bosworth, Clifford Edmund. *The Mediaeval Islamic Underworld: The Banu Sasan in Arabic Society and Literature.* 2 vols. Leiden: Brill, 1976.

Bovil, E. W. *The Golden Trade of the Moors: West African Kingdoms in the Fourteen the Century.* 2d ed. Oxford: Oxford University Press, 1970.

Boyle, John Andrew. ed. *The Cambridge History of Iran.* Vol. 5. *The Saljuk and Mongol Periods.* Cambridge: Cambridge University Press, 1968.

Boyle, John Andrew. *The Mongol World Empire, 1206–1370.* London: Variorum, 1977.

Brann, Ross. *The Compunctious Poet: Cultural Ambiguity and Hebrew Poetry in Muslim Spain.* Baltimore: Johns Hopkins University Press, 1991.

Brann, Ross, ed. *Languages of Power in Islamic Spain.* Bethesda, Md.: CDL Press, 1997.

Brann, Ross. *Power in the Portrayal: Representations of Jews and Muslims in Eleventh- and Twelfth-Century Islamic Spain.* Princeton, N.J.: Princeton University Press, 2002.

Brend, Barbara. *Islamic Art.* Cambridge, Mass.: Harvard University Press, 1991.

Brent, Peter. *The Mongol Empire.* London: Weidenfeld and Nicholson, 1976.

Brett, Michael, and Elizabeth Fentress. *The Berbers.* Oxford: Blackwell, 1996.

Brett, Michael, and Werner Forman. *The Moors: Islam in the West.* London: Orbis, 1980.

Bulliet, Richard W. *The Patricians of Nishapur: A Study in Medieval Islam.* Cambridge, Mass.: Harvard University Press, 1972.

Bulliet, Richard W. *Conversion to Islam in the Medieval Period: An Essay in Quantitative History.* Cambridge, Mass.: Harvard University Press, 1979.

Bulliet, Richard W. *The Camel and the Wheel.* New York: Columbia University Press, 1990.

Cahen, Claude. *The Formation of Turkey: The Seljukid Sultanate of Rūum, Eleventh to Fourteenth Century.* Trans. P. M. Holt. New York: Longman, 2001.

Campbell, Mary B. *The Witness and the Other World: Exotic European Travel Writing, 400–1600.* Ithaca, N.Y.: Cornell University Press, 1988.

Cardini, Franco. *Europe and Islam.* Trans. Caroline Beamish. Oxford: Blackwell, 2001.

Chamberlain, Michael. *Knowledge and Social Practice in Medieval Damascus, 1190–1350.* Cambridge: Cambridge University Press, 1994.

Chambers, James. *The Devil's Horsemen.* Rev. ed. London: Cassell, 1988.

Chaudhuri, K. N. *Trade and Civilisation in the Indian Ocean: An Economic History from the Rise of Islam to 1750.* Cambridge: Cambridge University Press, 1985.

Chaudhuri, K. N. *Asia before Europe: Economy and Civilisation of the Indian Ocean from the Rise of Islam to 1750.* Cambridge: Cambridge University Press, 1990.

Christopher, John B. *The Islamic Tradition.* New York: Harper & Row, 1972.

Chiappelli, Fredi, ed. *First Images of America: The Impact of the New World on the Old.* 2 vols. Berkeley: University of California Press, 1976.

Cipolla, Carlo M. *Guns and Sails in the Early Phase of European Expansion, 1400–1700: European Culture and Overseas Expansion.* Baltimore: Penguin, 1970.

Collins, Roger. *The Arab Conquest of Spain, 710–797.* Oxford: Blackwell, 1989.

Constable, Olivia Remie. *Trade and Traders in Muslim Spain: The Commercial Realignment of the Iberian Peninsula, 900–1500.* Cambridge: Cambridge University Press, 1994.

Constable, Olivia Remie, ed. *Medieval Iberia: Readings from Christian, Muslim, and Jewish Sources.* Philadelphia: University of Pennsylvania Press, 1997.

Corbin, Henry. *History of Islamic Philosophy.* Trans. Liadain Sherrard. London: Kegan Paul International, 1993.

Creswell, K. A. C. *A Bibliography of Painting in Islam.* Cairo: Impr. de l'Institut français d'archéologie orientale, 1953.

Creswell, K. A. C. *Early Muslim Architecture.* 2d ed. 2 vols. Oxford: Clarendon Press, 1979.

Creswell, K. A. C. *The Muslim Architecture of Egypt.* 2 vols. *1952–1959.* Reprint, New York: Hacker Art Books, 1979.

Creswell, K. A. C. *A Short Account of Early Muslim Architecture.* Rev. ed. Aldershot: Scolar Press, 1989.

Crone, G. R. *The Discovery of the East.* London: Hamish Hamilton, 1972.

Crone, Patricia. *Hagarism: The Making of the Islamic World.* Cambridge: Cambridge University Press, 1977.

Crone, Patricia. *Slaves on Horses: The Evolution of the Islamic Polity.* Cambridge: Cambridge University Press, 1980.

Crone, Patricia. *Meccan Trade and the Rise of Islam.* Princeton, N.J.: Princeton University Press, 1987.

Crone, Patricia, and Martin Hinds. *God's Caliph: Religious Authority in the First Centuries of Islam.* Cambridge: Cambridge University Press, 1986.

Curtin, Philip D. *Cross-Cultural Trade in World History.* Cambridge: Cambridge University Press, 1984.

Daftary, Farhad. *The Isma'ilis: Their History and Doctrines.* Cambridge: Cambridge University Press, 1990.

Daftary, Farhad, ed. *Mediaeval Isma'ili History and Thought.* Cambridge: Cambridge University Press, 1996.

Daniel, Norman. *Islam and the West: The Making of an Image.* Edinburgh: Edinburgh University Press, 1960.

Daniel, Norman. *Islam, Europe and Empire.* Edinburgh: Edinburgh University Press, 1966.

Daniel, Norman. *The Arabs and Mediaeval Europe.* 2d ed. London: Longman, 1979.

Daniel, Norman. *Heroes and Saracens: An Interpretation of the Chansons de Geste.* Edinburgh: Edinburgh University Press, 1984.

Davidson, Basil. *A History of West Africa 1000–1800.* London, Longmans, 1967.

Dols, Michael W. *The Black Death in the Middle East.* Princeton, N.J.: Princeton University Press, 1977.

Donner, Fred M. *The Early Islamic Conquests.* Princeton, N.J.: Princeton University Press, 1981.

Donner, Fred M. *Narratives of Islamic Origins: The Beginnings of Islamic Historical Writing.* Princeton, N.J.: Darwin Press, 1998.

Echevarria, Ana. *The Fortress of Faith: The Attitude towards Muslims in Fifteenth Century Spain.* Leiden: Brill, 1999.

El Fasi, Muhammad, ed. *General History of Africa.* Vol. 3. *Africa from the Seventh to the Eleventh Century.* Berkeley: University of California Press for UNESCO, 1988.

Endress, Gerhard. *Islam: An Historical Introduction.* 2d ed. Trans. Carole Hillenbrand. New York: Columbia University Press, 2002.

Esposito, John L. *Islam and Politics.* Syracuse, N.Y.: Syracuse University Press, 1984.

Esposito, John L., ed. *The Oxford History of Islam.* Oxford: Oxford University Press, 1999.

Ettinghausen, Richard. *Treasures of Asia: Arab Painting.* Lausanne: Skira, 1962.

Ettinghausen, Richard. *From Byzantium to Sasanian Iran and the Islamic World: Three Modes of Artistic Influence.* Leiden: Brill, 1972.

Ettinghausen, Richard, and Oleg Grabar. *The Art and Architecture of Islam, 650–1250.* Harmondsworth: Penguin, 1987.

Fage, J. D. ed. *The Cambridge History of Africa.* Vol. 2. *From c. 500 BC to AD 1050.* Cambridge: Cambridge University Press, 1978.

Fernández-Armesto, Felipe. *Before Columbus: Exploration and Colonization from the Mediterranean to the Atlantic, 1229–1492.* Philadelphia: University of Pennsylvania Press, 1987.

Fletcher, Richard A. *Moorish Spain.* Berkeley: University of California Press, 1992.

Frishman, Martin, and Hasan-Uddin Khan, eds. *The Mosque: History, Architectural Development and Regional Diversity.* London: Thames and Hudson, 2002.

Frye, R. N., ed. *The Cambridge History of Iran.* Vol. 4. *The Period from the Arab Invasion to the Saljuks.* Cambridge: Cambridge University Press, 1975.

Gabrieli, Francesco. *Muhammad and the Conquests of Islam.* Trans. Virginia Luling and Rosamund Linell. New York: McGraw-Hill, 1968.

Gibb, H. A. R. *Islamic Society and the West: A Study of the Impact of Western Civilization on Moslem Culture in the Near East.* Oxford: Oxford University Press, 1950.

Gibb, H. A. R. *Mohammedanism: An Historical Survey.* Oxford: Oxford University Press, 1962.

Gibb, H. A. R. *Arabic Literature: An Introduction.* 2d ed. Oxford: Clarendon Press, 1963.

Gibson, M. *Genghis Khan and the Mongols.* London: Wayland, 1973.

Goldziher, Ignaz. *Introduction to Islamic Theology and Law.* Trans. Andras and Ruth Hamori. Princeton, N.J.: Princeton University Press, 1981.

Goodwin, Jason. *Lords of the Horizons: A History of the Ottoman Empire.* New York: H. Holt, 1999.

Grabar, Oleg. *City in the Desert.* 2 vols. Cambridge, Mass.: Harvard University Press, 1978.

Grabar, Oleg. *The Foundation of Islamic Art.* Rev. ed. New Haven, Conn.: Yale University Press, 1987.

Grube, E. J. *Islamic Pottery.* London: Faber and Faber, 1976.

Guillaume, Alfred. *Islam.* Baltimore: Penguin, 1954.

Guthrie, Shirley. *Arab Social Life in the Middle Ages: An Illustrated Study.* London: Saqui Books, 1995.

Hale, John R. *Age of Exploration.* New York: Time, 1966.

Handler, Andrew. *The Zirids of Granada.* Coral Cables, Fla.: University of Miami Press, 1974.

Harvey, L. P. *Islamic Spain, 1250 to 1500.* Chicago: University of Chicago Press, 1990.

al-Hassan, Ahmad Yusuf. *Islamic Technology: An Illustrated History.* Cambridge: Cambridge University Press, 1986.

Hattstein, Markus, and Peter Delius, eds. *Islam: Art and Architecture.* Trans. George Ansell et al. Cologne: Könemann, 2000.

Hayes, J. R. *The Genius of Arab Civilization.* London: Phaidon, 1978.

Hill, Derek. *Islamic Architecture and Its Decoration A.D. 800–1500: A Photographic Survey.* 2d ed. London: Faber, 1967.

Hillenbrand, Carole. *The Crusades: Islamic Perspectives.* New York: Routledge, 1999.

Hillenbrand, Robert. *Islamic Art and Architecture.* New York: Thames & Hudson, 1999.

Hitti, Philip K. *History of the Arabs from the Earliest Times to the Present.* 9th ed. London: Macmillan, 1966.

Hitti, Philip K. *Capital Cities of Arab Islam.* Minneapolis: University of Minnesota Press, 1973.

Hoag, John D. *Western Islamic Architecture.* New York: G. Braziller, 1963.

Hoag, John D. *Islamic Architecture.* 1975. Reprint, New York: Harry Abrams, 1977.

Hodgson, Marshall G. S. *The Venture of Islam, Conscience and History in a World Civilization.* Vol. 1. *The Classical Age of Islam.* Chicago: University of Chicago Press, 1974.

Hodgson, Marshall G. S. *The Venture of Islam, Conscience and History in a World Civilization.* Vol. 2. *The Expansion of Islam in the Middle Periods.* Chicago: University of Chicago Press, 1974.

Holt, P. M., Ann K. S. Lambton, and Bernard Lewis, eds. *The Cambridge History of Islam.* Vol. 1. *The Central Islamic Lands.* Cambridge: Cambridge University Press, 1970.

Holt, P. M., ed. *The Eastern Mediterranean Lands in the Period of the Crusades.* Warminster: Aris and Phillips, 1977.

Holt, P. M. *The Age of the Crusades: The Near East from the Eleventh Century to 1517.* New York: Longman, 1986.

Hourani, Albert H., and S. M. Stern, eds. *The Islamic City: A Colloquium.* Philadelphia: University of Pennsylvania Press, 1970.

Hourani, Albert H. *A History of the Arab Peoples.* Cambridge, Mass.: Harvard University Press, 1991.

Hourani, George Fadlo, ed. *Essays on Islamic Philosophy and Science.* Albany: State University of New York Press, 1975.

Hoyland, Robert G. *Seeing Islam as Others Saw It: A Survey and Evaluation of Christian, Jewish, and Zoroastrian Writings on Early Islam.* Princeton, N.J.: Darwin Press, 1997.

Humble, Richard. *Marco Polo.* London: Weidenfeld and Nicholson, 1975.

Humphreys, R. Stephen. *From Saladin to the Mongols: The Ayyubids of Damascus, 1193–1260.* Albany: State University of New York Press, 1977.

Humphreys, R. Stephen. *Islamic History: A Framework for Inquiry.* Rev. ed. Princeton, N.J.: Princeton University Press, 1991.

Hunt, Lucy-Anne. *Byzantium, Eastern Christendom and Islam: Art at the Crossroads of the Medieval Mediterranean.* 2 vols. London: Pindar Press, 1998.

Inalcik, Halil. *The Ottoman Empire: The Classical Age.* Trans. Norman Itzkowitz and Colin Imber. London: Phoenix Press, 1973.

Inalcik, Halil. *An Economic and Social History of the Ottoman Empire.* Vol. 1. *1300–1600.* Cambridge: Cambridge University Press, 1994.

Ipsiroglu, M. S. *Painting and Culture of the Mongols.* Trans. E. D. Phillips. London: Thames and Hudson, 1967.

Irwin, Robert. *The Middle East in the Middle Ages: The Early Mamluk Sultanate, 1250–1382.* London: Croom Helm, 1986.

Irwin, Robert. *The Arabian Nights: A Companion.* London: Allen Lane, 1994.

Irwin, Robert. *Islamic Art in Context: Art, Architecture, and the Literary World.* New York: Harry N. Abrams, 1997.

Jackson, Peter, and Laurence Lockhart, eds. *The Cambridge History of Iran.* Vol. 6. *The Timurid and Safavid Periods.* Cambridge: Cambridge University Press, 1986.

Julien, Charles-André. *History of North Africa: Tunisia, Algeria, Morocco.* Trans. John Petrie and ed. C. C. Stewart. London: Routledge and Kegan Paul, 1970.

Kafadar, Cemal. *Between Two Worlds: The Construction of the Ottoman State.* Berkeley: University of California Press, 1995.

Kennedy, Edward S. *Studies in the Islamic Exact Sciences.* Beirut: American University of Beirut, 1983.

Kennedy, Hugh. *The Prophet and the Age of the Caliphates: The Islamic Near East from the Sixth to the Eleventh Century.* New York: Longman, 1986.

Kennedy, Hugh. *Muslim Spain and Portugal: A Political History of al-Andalus.* New York: Longman, 1996.

Kennedy, Hugh. *The Armies of the Caliphs: Military and Society in the Early Islamic State.* London: Routledge, 2001.

Kennedy, Hugh. *Mongols, Huns and Vikings: Nomads at War.* London: Cassell, 2002.

Kennedy, Hugh. *The Early Abbasid Caliphate.* London: Croom Helm, 1981.

Khalidi, Tarif. *Classical Arab Islam: The Culture and Heritage of the Golden Age.* Princeton, N.J.: Darwin Press, 1985.

Khalidi, Tarif. *Arabic Historical Thought in the Classical Period.* Cambridge: Cambridge University Press, 1994.

Khan, Gabriel Mandel. *Arabic Script: Styles, Variants, and Calligraphic Adaptions.* Trans. Rosanna M. Giammanco Frongia. New York: Abbeville Press, 2001.

Kobishchanov, Yuri M. *Axum.* Ed. Joseph W. Michaels and trans. Lorraine T. Kapitanoff. University Park: Pennsylvania State University Press, 1979.

Kühnel, Ernst. *Islamic Art and Architecture.* Trans. Katherine Watson. London: Bell 1966.

Kühnel, Ernst. *The Minor Arts of Islam.* Trans. Katherine Watson. Ithaca, N.Y.: Cornell University Press, 1971.

Lapidus, Ira M. *A History of Islamic Societies.* Cambridge: Cambridge University Press, 1988.

Lapidus, Ira M. *Muslim Cities in the Later Middle Ages.* Student ed. Cambridge: Cambridge University Press, 1984.

Lev, Yaacov. *State and Society in Fatimid Egypt.* Leiden: Brill, 1991.

Lev, Yaacov, ed. *War and Society in the Eastern Mediterranean, 7th–15th Centuries.* Leiden: Brill, 1997.

Levtzion, Nehemia. *Conversion to Islam.* New York: Holmes & Meier, 1979.

Levtzion, Nehemia, and J. F. Hopkins, eds. *Corpus of Early Arabic Sources for West African History.* Trans. J. F. P. Hopkins. Cambridge: Cambridge University Press, 1981.

Lewis, Archibald, ed. *The Islamic World and the West, A.D. 622–1492.* New York: Wiley, 1970.

Lewis, Archibald. *Nomads and Crusaders, A.D. 1000–1368.* Bloomington: Indiana University Press, 1988.

Lewis, Bernard. *The Middle East and the West.* Bloomington, Ind.: Indiana University Press, 1964.

Lewis, Bernard. *The Assassins: A Radical Sect in Islam.* Oxford: Oxford University Press, 1967.

Lewis, Bernard, ed. *Islam: From the Prophet Muhammad to the Capture of Constantinople.* 2 vols. New York: Harper & Row, 1974.

Lewis, Bernard, ed. *The World of Islam: Faith, People, Culture.* London: Thames and Hudson, 1976.

Lewis, Bernard. *The Muslim Discovery of Europe.* New York: Norton, 1982.

Lewis, Bernard. *The Political Language of Islam.* Chicago: University of Chicago Press, 1988.

Lewis, Bernard. *Race and Slavery in the Middle East: An Historical Enquiry.* Oxford: Oxford University Press, 1990.

Lewis, Bernard. *The Arabs in History.* 6th ed. Oxford: Oxford University Press, 1993.

Lewis, Bernard. *Islam and the West.* Oxford: Oxford University Press, 1993.

Lewis, Bernard. *Cultures in Conflict: Christians, Muslims, and Jews in the Age of Discovery.* Oxford: Oxford University Press, 1995.

Lindholm, Charles. *The Islamic Middle East: An Historical Anthropology.* Oxford: Blackwell, 1996.

Lunenfeld, Marvin, ed. *1492—Discovery, Invasion, Encounter: Sources and Interpretations.* Lexington, Mass.: D.C. Heath, 1991.

Madelung, Wilferd. *The Succession to Muhammad: A Study of the Early Caliphate.* Cambridge: Cambridge University Press, 1997.

Mahdi, Muhsin, ed. "Political Philosophy in Islam." In *Medieval Political Philosophy.* Ed. Ralph Lerner and Muhsin Mahdi. Ithaca, N.Y.: Cornell University Press, 1963, 21–186.

Makdisi, George. *The Rise of Humanism in Classical Islam and the Christian West with Special Reference to Scholasticism.* Edinburgh: Edinburgh University Press, 1990.

Mann, Vivian B., Thomas F. Glick, and Jerrilynn D. Dodds, eds. *Convivencia: Jews, Muslims, and Christians in Medieval Spain.* New York: George Braziller, 1992.

Marshall, Robert. *Storm from the East: From Ghenghis Khan to Khubilai Khan.* Berkeley: University of California Press, 1993.

Masalouf, Amin. *The Crusades through Arab Eyes.* Trans. Jon Rothschild. New York: Schoken Books, 1984.

Menocal, Maria Rosa. *The Ornament of the World: How Muslims, Jews, and Christians Created a Culture of Tolerance in Medieval Spain.* Boston: Little, Brown, 2002.

Menocal, Maria Rosa, Raymond P. Scheindlin, and Michael Sells, eds. *The Literature of Al-Andalus.* Cambridge: Cambridge University Press, 2000.

Meyerson, Mark D., and Edward D. English, eds. *Christians, Muslims, and Jews in Medieval and Early Modern Spain.* Notre Dame, Ind.: University of Notre Dame Press, 1999.

Morgan, David. *The Mongols.* New York: Blackwell, 1986.

Morgan, David. *Medieval Persia, 1040–1797.* London: Longman, 1988.

Muldoon, James. *The Expansion of Europe: The First Phase.* Philadelphia: University of Pennsylvania Press, 1977.

Muldoon, James. *Popes, Lawyers and Infidels: The Church and the Non-Christian World, 1250–1550.* Philadelphia: University of Pennsylvania Press, 1979.

Nasr, Seyyed Hossein. *Islamic Science: An Illustrated Study.* [s.1.]: World of Islam Festival Publishing, 1976.

Nasr, Seyyed Hossein, ed. *Islamic Spirituality.* 2 vols. New York: Crossroad, 1987–1991.

Nasr, Seyyed Hossein, and Oliver Leaman, eds. *History of Islamic Philosophy.* 2 vols. New York: Routledge, 1996.

Niane, Djibril Tamsir, ed. *General History of Africa.* Vol. 4. *Africa from the Twelfth to the Sixteenth Century.* Berkeley: University of California Press for UNESCO, 1984.

Nicholson, Reynold A. *A Literary History of the Arabs.* Cambridge: Cambridge University Press, 1966.

Oliver, Roland, ed. *The Cambridge History of Africa.* Vol. 3. *From c. 1050 to c. 1600.* Cambridge: Cambridge University Press, 1977.

Oliver, Roland, and Anthony Atmore. *Medieval Africa, 1250–1800.* 2d ed. Cambridge: Cambridge University Press, 2001.

Pagden, Anthony. *Peoples and Empires: A Short History of European Migration, Exploration, and Conquest, from Greece to the Present.* New York: Modern Library, 2001.

Pereira, José. *Islamic Sacred Architecture: A Stylistic History.* New Delhi: Books and Books, 1994.

Petry, Carl F. *The Civilian Elite of Cairo in the Later Middle Ages.* Princeton, N.J.: Princeton University Press, 1981.

Phillips, E. D. *The Mongols.* London: Thames and Hudson, 1969.

Phillips, J. R. S. *The Medieval Expansion of Europe.* 1988. 2d ed. Oxford: Oxford University Press, 1998.

Powell, James, M., ed. *Muslims under Latin Rule, 1100–1300.* Princeton, N.J.: Princeton University Press, 1990.

Quinn, David B., ed. *North American Discovery, circa 1000–1612.* Columbia: University of South Carolina Press, 1971.

Quinn, David B. *European Approaches to North America, 1450–1640.* Aldershot, England: Ashgate/Variorum, 1998.

Raby, Julian. *The Art of Syria and the Jazira, 1100–1250.* Oxford: Oxford University Press for the Board of the Faculty of Oriental Studies, University of Oxford, 1985.

Raymond, André. *Cairo.* Trans. Willard Wood. Cambridge, Mass.: Harvard University Press, 2000.

Rahman, Habib Ur. *A Chronology of Islamic History, 570–1000 CE.* Boston: G. K. Hall, 1989.

Reilly, Bernard F. *The Context of Christian and Muslim Spain, 1031–1157.* Oxford: Blackwell, 1992.

Rey, Louis, ed. *Unveiling the Arctic.* Fairbanks: University of Alaska Press, 1984.

Rice, David Talbot. *Islamic Painting: A Survey.* Edinburgh: Edinburgh University Press, 1971.

Rice, David Talbot. *Islamic Art.* London: Thames and Hudson, 1975.

Robinson, Neal. *Christ in Islam and Christianity: The Representation of Jesus in the Qur'an and the Classical Muslim Commentaries.* Basingstoke: Macmillan, 1991.

Robinson, Chase F. *Islamic Historiography.* Cambridge: Cambridge University Press, 2003.

Robinson, Francis, ed. *The Cambridge Illustrated History of the Islamic World.* Cambridge: Cambridge University Press, 1996.

Rodenbeck, Max. *Cairo: The City Victorious.* New York: Vintage, 1998.

Rodinson, Maxime. *Muhammad.* 1971. Trans. Anne Carter. 1971. Reprint, New York: Pantheon Books, 1980.

Rogers, Michael. *The Spread of Islam.* Oxford: Elsevier-Phaidon, 1976.

Russell, P. E. *Portugal, Spain, and the African Atlantic, 1343–1490: Chivalry and Crusade from John of Gaunt to*

Henry the Navigator. Aldershot, England: Variorum, 1995.

Said, Edward W. *Orientalism.* New York: Pantheon, 1978.

Salibi, Kamal S. *A History of Arabia.* Delmar, N.Y.: Caravan Books, 1980.

Saunders, J. J. *A History of Medieval Islam.* London: Routledge and Kegan Paul, 1965.

Saunders, J. J., ed. *The Muslim World on the Eve of Europe's Expansion.* Englewood Cliffs, N.J.: Prentice-Hall, 1966.

Saunders, J. J. *The History of the Mongol Conquests.* London: Routledge and Kegan Paul, 1971.

Schacht, Joseph, and C. E. Bosworth, eds. *The Legacy of Islam,* 2d ed. Oxford: Clarendon Press, 1974.

Schafer, Edward. *The Golden Peaches of Samarkand.* Berkeley: University of California Press, 1985.

Schimmel, Annemarie. *Islamic Names.* Edinburgh: Edinburgh University Press, 1989.

Schwoebel, Robert. *The Shadow of the Crescent: The Renaissance Image of the Turk, 1453–1517.* New York: St. Martin's Press, 1967.

Semann, Khalil I., ed. *Islam and the Medieval West: Aspects of Intercultural Relations.* Albany: State University of New York Press, 1980.

Shahid, Irfan. *Byzantium and the Arabs in the Fourth Century.* Washington, D.C.: Dumbarton Oaks Research Library and Collection, 1984.

Shahid, Irfan. *Byzantium and the Arabs in the Fifth Century.* Washington, D.C.: Dumbarton Oaks Research Library and Collection, 1989.

Shahid, Irfan. *Byzantium and the Arabs in the Sixth Century.* Washington, D.C.: Dumbarton Oaks Research Library and Collection, 1995.

Shatzmiller, Maya, ed. *Crusaders and Muslims in Twelfth-Century Syria.* Leiden: Brill, 1993.

Shaw, Stanford J. *History of the Ottoman Empire and Modern Turkey.* 2 vols. Cambridge: Cambridge University Press, 1976–1977.

Sicker, Martin. *The Islamic World in Ascendancy: From the Arab Conquests to the Siege of Vienna.* London: Praeger, 2000.

Sinor, Denis. *Inner Asia and Its Contacts with Medieval Europe.* London: Variorum, 1977.

Sinor, Denis, ed. *The Cambridge History of Early Inner Asia.* Cambridge: Cambridge University Press, 1990.

Soucek, Svat. *A History of Inner Asia.* Cambridge: Cambridge University Press, 2000.

Southern, Richard W. *Western Views of Islam in the Middle Ages.* Cambridge, Mass.: Harvard University Press, 1962.

Spuler, Bertold. *History of the Mongols: Based on Eastern and Western Accounts of the Thirteenth and Fourteenth Centuries.* Trans. Helga Drummond and Stuart Drummond. New York: Dorset Press, 1968.

Stanton, Charles Michael. *Higher Learning in Islam: The Classical Period,* A.D. *700–1300.* Savage, Md.: Rowman & Littlefield, 1990.

al-Tabarī. *The Early 'Abbāsī Empire.* Vol. 1. *The Reign of Abū Ja'far al-Mansūr* A.D. *754–775.* Trans. John Alden Williams. Cambridge: Cambridge University Press, 1988.

al-Tabarī. *The Early 'Abbāsī Empire.* Vol. 2. *The Son and Grandsons of al-Mansūr: The Reigns of al-Mahdī, al-Hādī and Hārāū al-Rashī.* Trans. John Alden Williams. Cambridge: Cambridge University Press, 1989.

Taha, 'Abd al-Wahid Dhannun. *The Muslim Conquest and Settlement of North Africa and Spain.* London: Routledge, 1989.

Talbot Rice, Tamara. *The Seljuks in Asia Minor.* New York: Praeger, 1961.

Thornton, John Kelly. *Africa and Africans in the Making of the Atlantic World, 1400–1800.* 2d ed. Cambridge: Cambridge University Press, 1998.

Tolan, John V., ed. *Medieval Christian Perceptions of Islam: A Book of Essays.* New York: Garland, 1995.

Tolan, John V. *Saracens: Islams in the Medieval European Imagination.* New York: Columbia University Press, 2002.

Tracy, James D., ed. *The Rise of Merchant Empires: Long-Distance Trade in the Early Modern World, 1350–1750.* Cambridge: Cambridge University Press, 1990.

Trimingham, J. Spencer. *Christianity among the Arabs in Pre-Islamic Times.* London: Longman, 1979.

Udovitch, Abraham L. *Partnership and Profit in Medieval Islam.* Princeton, N.J.: Princeton University Press, 1970.

Verlinden, Charles. *The Beginnings of Modern Colonization: Eleven Essays with an Introduction.* Trans. Yvonne Freccero. Ithaca, N.Y.: Cornell University Press, 1970.

Von Grunebaum, Gustave E. *Medieval Islam: A Study in Cultural Orientation.* 1946. 2d ed. Chicago: University of Chicago Press, 1961.

Von Grunebaum, Gustave E. *Classical Islam: A History, 600–1258.* Trans. Katherine Watson. Chicago: Aldine, 1970.

Vryonis, Speros. *The Decline of Medieval Hellenism in Asia Minor and the Process of Islamization from the Eleventh through the Fifteenth Century.* Berkeley: University of California Press, 1971.

Wasserstein, David. *The Rise and Fall of the Party-Kings: Politics and Society in Islamic Spain 1002–1086.* Princeton, N.J.: Princeton University Press, 1985.

Wasserstein, David. *The Caliphate in the West: An Islamic Political Institution in the Iberian Peninsula.* Oxford: Clarendon Press, 1993.

Watt, W. Montgomery. *The Influence of Islam on Medieval Europe.* Edinburgh: Edinburgh University Press, 1972.

Watt, W. Montgomery. *Islamic Philosophy and Theology: An Extended Survey.* 2d ed. Edinburgh: Edinburgh University Press, 1985.

Watt, W. Montgomery. *Muslim-Christian Encounters: Perceptions and Misperceptions.* New York: Routledge, 1991.

Watt, W. Montgomery. trans. *Islamic Creeds: A Selection.* Edinburgh: Edinburgh University Press, 1994.

Watt, W. Montgomery. *A Short History of Islam.* Oxford: Oneworld, 1996.

Watt, W. Montgomery. *The Formative Period of Islamic Thought.* Oxford: Oneworld Publications, 1998.

Westrem, Scott D., ed. *Discovering New Worlds: Essays on Medieval Exploration and Imagination.* New York: Garland, 1991.

Whitfield, Susan. *Life along the Silk Road.* Berkeley: University of California Press, 1999.

Young, M. J. L., J. D. Latham, and R. B. Serjeant, eds. *Religion, Learning, and Science in the 'Abbasid Period.* Cambridge: Cambridge University Press, 1990.

Ziadeh, Nicola A. *Urban Life in Syria under the Early Mamluks.* Beirut: American Press, 1953.

X. WOMEN IN THE MEDIEVAL WORLD

Anderson, Sarah M., with Karen Swenson, eds. *Cold Counsel: Women in Old Norse Literature and Mythology: A Collection of Essays.* New York: Routledge, 2002.

Arjava, Antti. *Women and Law in Late Antiquity.* Oxford: Clarendon Press, 1996.

Atkinson, Clarissa W. *The Oldest Vocation: Christian Motherhood in the Middle Ages.* Ithaca, N.Y.: Cornell University Press, 1991.

Baker, Derek, ed. *Medieval Women.* Studies in Church History, Subsidia, 1. Oxford: Blackwell, 1978.

Bell, Rudolph M. *Holy Anorexia.* Chicago: University of Chicago Press, 1985.

Bennett, Judith M. *Women in the Medieval English Countryside: Gender and Household in Brigstock before the Plague.* Oxford: Oxford University Press, 1987.

Bennett, Judith M. *A Medieval Life: Cecilia Penifader of Brigstock, c. 1295–1344.* New York: McGraw-Hill, 2002.

Bennett, Judith M. et al., eds. *Sisters and Workers in the Middle Ages.* Chicago: University of Chicago Press, 1989.

Bitel, Lisa M. *Women in Early Medieval Europe, 400–1100.* Cambridge: Cambridge University Press, 2002.

Blamires, Alcuin, ed. *Woman Defamed and Woman Defended: An Anthology of Medieval Texts.* Oxford: Oxford University Press, 1992.

Blamires, Alcuin. *The Case for Women in Medieval Culture.* Oxford: Clarendon Press, 1997.

Bloch, R. Howard. *Medieval Misogyny and the Invention of Western Romantic Love.* Chicago: University of Chicago Press, 1991.

Bogin, Magda. *The Women Troubadours.* New York: Paddington, 1976.

Brooten, Bernadette J. *Love between Women: Early Christian Responses to Female Homoeroticism.* Chicago: University of Chicago Press, 1996.

Bornstein, Daniel, and Roberto Rusconi, eds. *Women and Religion in Medieval and Renaissance Italy.* Trans. Margery J. Schneider. Chicago: University of Chicago Press, 1996.

Brown, Judith C. *Immodest Acts: The Life of a Lesbian Nun in Renaissance Italy.* Oxford: Oxford University Press, 1986.

Burns, E. Jane, ed. *Bodytalk: When Women Speak in Old French Literature.* Philadelphia: University of Pennsylvania Press, 1993.

Bynum, Caroline Walker. *Holy Feast and Holy Fast: The Religious Significance of Food to Medieval Women.* Berkeley: University of California Press, 1987.

Clark, Gillian. *Women in Late Antiquity: Pagan and Christian Life Styles.* Oxford: Clarendon Press, 1993.

Cohn, Samuel K., Jr. *Women in the Streets: Essays on Sex and Power in Renaissance Italy.* Baltimore: Johns Hopkins University Press, 1996.

Dillard, Heath. *Daughters of the Reconquest: Women in Castilian Town Society, 1100–1300.* Cambridge: Cambridge University Press, 1984.

Dronke, Peter. *Women Writers of the Middle Ages: A Critical Study of Texts from Perpetua (†203) to Marguerite Porete (†1310).* Cambridge: Cambridge University Press, 1984.

Duby, Georges. *Women of the Twelfth Century.* 3 vols. Trans. Jean Birrell. Chicago: University of Chicago Press, 1997–1998.

Edwards, Robert, and Vickie Ziegler, eds. *Matrons and Marginal Women in Medieval Society.* Woodbridge, England: Boydell Press, 1995.

Elm, Susanna. *"Virgins of God": The Making of Asceticism in Late Antiquity.* Oxford: Clarendon Press, 1994.

Ennen, Edith. *The Medieval Woman.* Trans. Edmund Jephcott. Oxford: Blackwell, 1989.

Erler, Mary, and Maryanne Kowaleski, eds. *Women and Power in the Middle Ages.* Athens: University of Georgia Press, 1988.

Ferrante, Joan. *Woman as Image in Medieval Literature: From the Twelfth Century to Dante.* New York: Columbia University Press, 1975.

Ferrante, Joan. *To the Glory of Her Sex: Women's Roles in the Composition of Medieval Texts.* Bloomington: Indiana University Press, 1997.

Fiero, Gloria K., Wendy Pfeffer, and Mathé Allain, ed. and trans. *Three Medieval Views of Women: "La contenance des fames," "Le bien des fames," "Le blasme des fames."* New Haven, Conn.: Yale University Press, 1989.

Gilchrist, Roberta. *Gender and Material Culture: The Archaeology of Religious Women.* New York: Routledge, 1994.

Gold, Penny Schine. *The Lady and the Virgin: Image, Attitude, and Experience in Twelfth-Century France.* Chicago: University of Chicago Press, 1985.

Goldberg P. J. P. *Women, Work, and Life Cycle in a Medieval Economy: Women in York and Yorkshire, c. 1300–1520.* Oxford: Clarendon Press, 1992.

Gravdal, Kathryn. *Ravishing Maidens: Writing Rape in Medieval French Literature and Law.* Philadelphia: University of Pennsylvania Press, 1991.

Grubbs, Judith Evans. *Law and Family in Late Antiquity: The Emperor Constantine's Marriage Legislation.* Oxford: Clarendon Press, 1995.

Hanawalt, Barbara A. *Women and Work in Preindustrial Europe.* Bloomington: Indiana University Press, 1986.

Herlihy, David. *Opera Muliebria: Women and Work in Medieval Europe.* New York: McGraw-Hill, 1990.

Howell, Martha C. *Women, Production, and Patriarchy in Late Medieval Cities.* Chicago: University of Chicago Press, 1968.

Jochens, Jenny M. *Women in Old Norse Society.* Ithaca, N.Y.: Cornell University Press, 1995.

Jochens, Jenny M. *Old Norse Images of Women.* Philadelphia: University of Pennsylvania Press, 1996.

Johnson, Penelope D. *Equal in Monastic Profession: Religious Women in Medieval France.* Chicago: University of Chicago Press, 1991.

Jordan, William C. *Women and Credit in Pre-Industrial and Developing Societies.* Philadelphia: University of Pennsylvania Press, 1993.

Kaplan, Marion A. *The Marriage Bargain: Women and Dowries in European History.* New York: Harrington Park Press, 1985.

Kelly, Joan. "Did Women Have a Renaissance?" In *Women, History, and Theory: The Essays of Joan Kelly.* Chicago: University of Chicago Press, 1984, 19–50.

King, Margaret L. *Women of the Renaissance.* Chicago: University of Chicago Press, 1991.

Kirshner, Julius, and Suzanne F. Wemple, eds. *Women of the Medieval World: Essays in Honor of John H. Mundy.* Oxford: Blackwell, 1985.

Klapisch-Zuber, Christiane. *Women, Family, and Ritual in Renaissance Italy.* Chicago: University of Chicago Press, 1985.

Klapisch-Zuber, Christiane, ed. *A History of Women.* Vol. 2. *Silences of the Middle Ages.* 1990. Reprint, Cambridge, Mass.: Belknap Press, 1992.

Krueger, Roberta L. *Women Readers and the Ideology of Gender in Old French Verse Romance.* Cambridge: Cambridge University Press, 1993.

Kuehn, Thomas. *Law, Family, and Women: Toward a Legal Anthropology of Renaissance Italy.* Chicago: University of Chicago Press, 1991.

Labalme, Patricia H. *Beyond Their Sex: Learned Women of the European Past.* New York: New York University Press, 1980.

Larrington, Carolyne, ed. *Women and Writing in Medieval Europe: A Sourcebook.* New York: Routledge, 1995.

Lewis, Gertrud Jaron. *By Women, for Women, about Women: The Sister-Books of Fourteenth-Century Germany.* Toronto: Pontifical Institute of Mediaeval Studies, 1996.

Lomperis, Linda, and Sarah Stanbury, eds. *Feminist Approaches to the Body in Medieval Literature.* Philadelphia: University of Pennsylvania Press, 1993.

Maclean, Ian. *The Renaissance Notion of Woman: A Study in the Fortunes of Scholasticism and Medical Science in European Intellectual Life.* Cambridge: Cambridge University Press, 1980.

McCash, June Hall, ed. *The Cultural Patronage of Medieval Women.* Athens: University of Georgia Press, 1996.

Mate, Mavis E. *Women in Medieval English Society.* Cambridge: Cambridge University Press, 1999.

Migiel, Marilyn, and Juliana Schiesari, eds. *Refiguring Woman: Perspectives on Gender and the Italian Renaissance.* Ithaca, N.Y.: Cornell University Press, 1991.

Mirrer, Louise, ed. *Upon My Husband's Death: Widows in the Literature and Histories of Medieval Europe.* Ann Arbor: University of Michigan Press, 1992.

Newman, Barbara. *From Virile Woman to WomanChrist: Studies in Medieval Religion and Literature.* Philadelphia: University of Pennsylvania Press, 1995.

Nicholas, David. *The Domestic Life of a Medieval City: Women, Children, and the Family in Fourteenth-Century Ghent.* Lincoln: University of Nebraska Press, 1985.

O'Faolain, Julia, and Lauro Martines, eds. *Not in God's Image: Women in History from the Greeks to the Victorians.* New York: Harper & Row, 1973.

Paden, William D. *The Voice of the Trobairitz: Perspectives on Women Troubadours.* Philadelphia: University of Pennsylvania Press, 1989.

Panizza, Letizia, ed. *Women in Italian Renaissance Culture and Society.* Oxford: European Humanities Research Centre, 2000.

Parsons, John Carmi, ed. *Medieval Queenship.* New York: St. Martin's Press, 1993.

Petroff, Elizabeth Alvilda, ed. *Medieval Women's Visionary Literature.* Oxford: Oxford University Press, 1986.

Petroff, Elizabeth Alvilda. *Body and Soul: Essays on Medieval Women and Mysticism.* New York: Oxford University Press, 1994.

Power, Eileen. *Medieval Women.* Ed. Michael Postan. Cambridge: Cambridge University Press, 1975.

Rasmussen, Ann Marie. *Mothers and Daughters in Medieval German Literature.* Syracuse, N.Y.: Syracuse University Press, 1997.

Rosenthal, Joel T., ed. *Medieval Women and the Sources of Medieval History.* Athens: University of Georgia Press, 1990.

Salisbury, Joyce E. *Church Fathers, Independent Virgins.* New York: Verso, 1991.

Sautman, Francesca Canadé, and Pamela Sheingorn, eds. *Same Sex Love and Desire among Women in the Middle Ages.* New York: Palgrave, 2001.

Schulenberg, Jane. *Forgetful of Their Sex: Female Sanctity and Society, ca. 500–1100.* Chicago: University of Chicago Press, 1995.

Shahar, Shulamith. *The Fourth Estate: A History of Women in the Middle Ages.* Trans. Chaya Galai. London: Methuen, 1983.

Stafford, Pauline. *Queens, Concubines, and Dowagers: The King's Wife in the Early Middle Ages.* Athens: University of Georgia Press, 1983.

Stuard, Susan Mosher, ed. *Women in Medieval Society.* Philadelphia: University of Pennsylvania Press, 1976.

Thiébaux, Marcelle, ed. *The Writings of Medieval Women: An Anthology.* 2d ed. New York: Garland, 1994.

van Houts, Elisabeth. *Memory and Gender in Medieval Europe, 900–1200.* Toronto: University of Toronto Press, 1999.

Vernade, Bruce. *Women's Monasticism and Medieval Society: Nunneries in France and England, 890–1215.* Ithaca, N.Y.: Cornell University Press, 1997.

Ward, Jennifer, ed. *Women of the English Nobility and Gentry, 1066–1500.* Manchester: Manchester University Press, 1995.

Wemple, Suzanne Fonay. *Women in Frankish Society: Marriage and the Cloister, 500–900.* Philadelphia: University of Pennsylvania Press, 1985.

Wilson, Katharina M., ed. *Medieval Women Writers.* Athens: University of Georgia Press, 1984.

INDEX